T0189292

Communications
in Computer and Information Science   **735**

Commenced Publication in 2007
Founding and Former Series Editors:
Alfredo Cuzzocrea, Orhun Kara, Dominik Ślęzak, and Xiaokang Yang

More information about this series at http://www.springer.com/series/7899

Andrés Solano · Hugo Ordoñez (Eds.)

Advances in Computing

12th Colombian Conference, CCC 2017
Cali, Colombia, September 19–22, 2017
Proceedings

 Springer

Editors
Andrés Solano
Universidad Autónoma de Occidente
Cali
Colombia

Hugo Ordoñez
Universidad de San Buenaventura
Cali
Colombia

ISSN 1865-0929   ISSN 1865-0937   (electronic)
Communications in Computer and Information Science
ISBN 978-3-319-66561-0   ISBN 978-3-319-66562-7   (eBook)
DOI 10.1007/978-3-319-66562-7

Library of Congress Control Number: 2017950045

This Springer imprint is published by Springer Nature
The registered company is Springer International Publishing AG
The registered company address is: Gewerbestrasse 11, 6330 Cham, Switzerland

Preface

The Colombian Conference on Computing is an annual gathering organized by the Colombian Computer Society (www.sco2.org). It aims to promote and strengthen the Colombian community in computer science, bringing together researchers, students and practitioners, both national and international. The contributions were received in English and Spanish. Contributions written and accepted in English as full papers are published in this volume of the Communications in Computer and Information Science (CCIS) series of Springer.

The Colombian Computer Society first organized this conference in 2005 in Cali, and successive events have been held in Bogotá (2007), Medellín (2008), Bucaramanga 2010), Manizales (2011), Medellín (2012), Armenia (2013), Pereira (2014), Bogotá (2015) and Popayán (2016).

The 12th Colombian Conference on Computing (12CCC) was held in Cali again, the city of its birth, from September 19 to 22, 2017. The conference was attended by national and international researchers. This year the conference was organized by the Colombian Computer Society, the Universidad Autónoma de Occidente and the Universidad de San Buenaventura. This conference was an opportunity to discuss and exchange ideas about computing (techniques, methodologies, tools, among others) with a multidisciplinary approach, strengthening the synergies between researchers, professionals and companies related to the topics of interest of the conference.

The conference covers the following areas:

- Information and knowledge management
- Software engineering and IT architectures
- Educational informatics
- Intelligent systems and robotics
- Human-Computer Interaction
- Distributed systems and large-scale architectures
- Image processing, computer vision and multimedia
- Security of information
- Formal methods, computational logic and theory of computation

The conference allowed the presentation of research papers with (i) a significant contribution to knowledge or (ii) innovative experiences in the different areas of computing. This conference included plenary lectures, discussion forums, tutorials and a symposium for master's and doctoral students.

All paper submissions were reviewed by three experts. Authors removed personal details, the acknowledgements section and any references that may disclose the authors' identity. Papers not satisfying these conditions were rejected without reviews. All contributions were written following the Springer template and the first anonymous version was submitted in PDF format.

The conference received 186 submissions, of which 56 were accepted as full papers, 12 were accepted as full papers in Spanish, 12 were accepted as short papers in Spanish and 11 were accepted as short papers in English. Reviewing was performed by national and international reviewers. Moreover, the Easychair system was used for the management and review of submissions.

We are grateful to all authors, especially the ones who presented their papers at the conference, and to the 12CCC conference organizers and Springer.

September 2017   Andrés Solano
                                                                                 Hugo Ordoñez

Organization

Program Committee

Alexander Gelbukh	Instituto Politécnico Nacional, Mexico
Alejandro Fernández	Universidad Nacional de La Plata, Argentina
Alexandra Pomares	Pontificia Universidad Javeriana, Colombia
Alexandre Pinheiro	Centro de Ciências Exatas e Tecnologia, Brazil
Alfonso Infante Moro	Universidad de Huelva, Spain
Alicia Mon	Universidad Nacional de La Matanza, Argentina
Ana Isabel Molina Díaz	University of Castilla-La Mancha, Spain
Ana Paula Kuhn	Universidad Federal de Mato Grosso, Brazil
Andrea Rueda	Pontificia Universidad Javeriana, Colombia
Andreia Libório	Universidade Federal do Ceará, Brazil
Andrés Adolfo Navarro Newball	Pontificia Universidad Javeriana, Colombia
Andres Felipe Barco	Universidad San Buenaventura, Colombia
Andrés Moreno	Universidad de los Andes, Colombia
Andres Paolo Castaño	Universidad de Caldas, Colombia
Andrés Rosso-Mateus	Universidad Nacional de Colombia, Colombia
Andrés Sicard Ramírez	Universidad EAFIT, Colombia
Angel Alfonso Cruz Roa	Universidad Nacional de Colombia, Colombia
Ángela Carrillo	Pontificia Universidad Javeriana, Colombia
Ángela Villarreal	Universidad del Cauca, Colombia
Antoni Granollers	Universidad de Lleida, Spain
Artur Boronat	University of Leicester, UK
Carina González	Universidad de La Laguna, Spain
Carlos Mario Zapata Jaramillo	Universidad Nacional de Colombia, Colombia
Carlos Peláez	Universidad Autónoma de Occidente, Colombia
Carlos Varela	Rensselaer Polytecnic Institute, USA
Christian Fernando Ariza Porras	Universidad de los Andes, Colombia
Claudia Roncancio	Grenoble University, France
Cristian Rusu	Pontificia Universidad Católica de Valparaíso, Chile
Cristiano Maciel	Universidade Federal de Mato Grosso, Brazil
Cristina Manresa Yee	University of the Balearic Islands, Spain
Daniel Muñoz	Universidad de Brasilia, Brazil
Daniel Saad	Universidade de Brasilia, Brazil
Daniela Quiñones	Pontificia Universidad Católica de Valparaíso, Chile
David Naranjo	Universidad de los Andes, Colombia
Diana Parra	Universidad Autónoma de Bucaramanga, Colombia

Diego Torres	Universidad Nacional de La Plata, Argentina
Edwin Puertas	Universidad Tecnológica de Bolívar, Colombia
Elizabeth Suescun Monsalve	Universidad EAFIT, Colombia
Emilcy Juliana Hernández Leal	Universidad Nacional de Colombia, Colombia
Enrique Herrera-Viedma	Universidad de Granada, Spain
Esperanza Espitia	Universidad del Quindio, Colombia
Eunice Nunes	Universidad Federal de Mato Grosso, Brazil
Faber Giraldo	Universidad del Quindio, Colombia
Fabio González	Universidad Nacional de Colombia, Colombia
Fabio Martínez Carrillo	Universidad Nacional de Colombia, Colombia
Federico Barber	Technical University of Valencia, Spain
Federico Botella	Universidad Miguel Hernández, Spain
Fernando Barraza	Universidad de San Buenaventura, Colombia
Fernando De La Rosa	Universidad de los Andes, Colombia
Francisco Álvarez Rodríguez	Universidad Autónoma de Aguascalientes, Mexico
Francisco Garijo	Telefónica I+D
Francisco José Correa Zabala	Universidad EAFIT, Colombia
Francisco Luis Gutiérrez Vela	Universidad de Granada, Spain
Gerardo Sarria	Pontificia Universidad Javeriana, Colombia
German Bravo	Universidad de los Andes, Colombia
Germán Osorio	Universidad Nacional de Colombia, Colombia
Germán Regis	Universidad Nacional de Río Cuarto, Argentina
Gisela T. de Clunie	Universidad Tecnológica de Panamá, Panama
Gloria Inés Álvarez	Pontificia Universidad Javeriana, Colombia
Grigori Sidorov	Instituto Politécnico Nacional, Mexico
Grissa Maturana	Universidad Nacional de Colombia, Colombia
Gustavo Isaza	Universidad de Caldas, Colombia
Harold Castro	Universidad de Los Andes, Colombia
Héctor Flórez	Universidad de los Andes, Colombia
Helga Duarte	Universidad Nacional de Colombia, Colombia
Henry Arguello	Universidad Industrial de Santander, Colombia
Hugo Armando Ordóñez	Universidad de San Buenaventura, Colombia
Hugo Arnoldo Mitre Hernández	Centro de Investigación en Matemáticas, Mexico
Hugo Jair Escalante	INAOE, Mexico
Iris Jiménez	Universidad de la Guajira, Colombia
Iván Claros	Universidad Autónoma de Madrid, Spain
Ivette Kafure	Universidade de Brasília, Brazil
Jaime Bohórquez	CIMAT, Mexico
Jaime Chavarriaga	Vrije Universiteit Brussel, Belgium
Jaime Muñoz Arteaga	Universidad Autónoma de Aguascalientes, Mexico

Jaime Pavlich Mariscal	Pontificia Universidad Javeriana, Colombia
Jairo Aponte	Universidad Nacional de Colombia, Colombia
Jairo Iván Vélez- Bedoya	Universidad de Caldas, Colombia
Jairo Serrano	Universidad Tecnológica de Bolívar, Colombia
Jesse Padilla	Universidad de los Andes, Colombia
Jesús Alberto Verduzco	Instituto Tecnológico de Colima, Mexico
Jesús Andrés Hincapié Londoño	Universidad de Medellín, Colombia
Jesús Antonio Hernández	Universidad Nacional de Colombia, Colombia
Jesús Insuasti	Universidad Nacional de Colombia, Colombia
Jhon Edisson Villareal	Universidad Piloto de Colombia, Colombia
Johany Armando Carreño Gamboa	Politécnico Grancolombiano, Colombia
John Arévalo	Universidad Nacional de Colombia, Colombia
John Osorio	Universidad Tecnológica de Pereira, Colombia
Jorge Alberto Jaramillo Garzón	Universidad de Caldas, Colombia
Jorge Camargo	Universidad Antonio Nariño, Colombia
Jorge Iván Ríos	Universidad Tecnológica de Pereira, Colombia
José A. Sánchez	Universidad de Oviedo, Spain
José Antonio Macías Iglesias	Universidad Autónoma de Madrid, Spain
José Antonio Pow Sang	Pontificia Universidad Católica del Perú, Peru
José Luis Arciniegas	Universidad del Cauca, Colombia
José Luis Soncco-Álvarez	Universidad de Brasilia, Brazil
José Luis Villa	Universidad Tecnológica de Bolívar, Colombia
José Palazzo Moreira de Oliveira	Universidade Federal do Rio Grande do Sul, Brazil
José Torres Jiménez	Cinvestav, Mexico
Josefina Guerrero	BUAP, Mexico
Juan Carlos Martínez	Universidad Tecnológica de Bolívar, Colombia
Juan Pavón	Universidad Complutense de Madrid, Spain
Juan Vicente Pradilla	Universidad Autónoma de Occidente, Colombia
Julio Abascal	Universidad del País Vasco, Spain
Julio Ariel Hurtado	Universidad del Cauca, Colombia
Julio Chavarro	Universidad Tecnológica de Pereira, Colombia
Kyungmin Bae	Carnegie Mellon University, USA
Laura Pozueco	Universidad de Oviedo, Spain
Leandro Krug	Universidade Federal do Rio Grande do Sul, Brazil
Leonardo Arturo Bautista Gómez	Argonne National Laboratory, USA
Luciana Nedel	Universidade Federal do Rio Grande do Sul, Brazil
Lucineia Heloisa Thom	Federal University of Rio Grande do Sul, Brazil
Luis Fernando Castillo	Universidad de Caldas, Colombia

Pere Ponsa   Technical University of Catalonia, Spain
Philippe Palanque   University of Toulouse, France
Ralf Sasse   ETH, Switzerland
Renzo Degiovanni   Universidad Nacional de Río Cuarto, Argentina
Ricardo Azambuja Silveira   Universidade Federal de Santa Catarina, Brazil
Roberto García   Universidad de Lleida, Spain
Robinson Ramírez   Universidad Industrial de Santander, Colombia
Rodrigo Cardoso   Universidad de los Andes, Colombia
Rosa Gil   Universidad de Lleida, Spain
Rosa Vicari   Universidade Federal do Rio Grande do Sul, Brazil
Ruby Casallas   Universidad de los Andes, Colombia
Sandra Cano   Universidad de San Buenaventura, Colombia
Sandra Macia   Barcelona Supercomputing Center, Spain
Sandra Victoria Hurtado-Gil   Universidad de Caldas, Colombia
Sebastián Monsalve   Universidad de Medellín, Colombia
Sergio Cardona   Universidad del Quindio, Colombia
Sergio Rojas   Universidad Distrital, Colombia
Silvana Aciar   Universidad Nacional de San Juan, Argentina
Simone Balocco   Universitat de Barcelona, Spain
Sonia Contreras Ortiz   Universidad Tecnológica de Bolívar, Colombia
Tiago Primo   Samsung Research Institute, Brazil
Vanessa Agredo   Universidad del Cauca, Colombia
Vicenç Beltran   Barcelona Supercomputing Center, Spain
Víctor Andrés Bucheli   Universidad del Valle, Colombia
Víctor Corcoba Magaña   Universidad de Oviedo, Spain
Víctor Manuel González   Instituto Tecnológico Autónomo de México, Mexico
Víctor Manuel Ruiz   Castilla-La Mancha University, Spain
  Penichet
Víctor Martínez   Universidade Federal do Rio Grande do Sul, Brazil
Virginica Rusu   Universidad de Playa Ancha, Chile
William Caicedo   Universidad Tecnológica de Bolívar, Colombia
Wilmar Campo   Universidad del Quindio, Colombia
Wilson Javier Sarmiento   Universidad Militar Nueva Granada, Colombia
Xabiel Garcia Pañeda   Universidad de Oviedo, Spain
Xavier Ferre   Universidad Politécnica de Madrid, Spain
Yannis Dimitriadis   University of Valladolid, Spain
Yenny Mendez   Universidad Nacional Abierta y a Distancia, Colombia
Yensy Helena Gómez   Universidad Tecnológica de Pereira, Colombia
Yezid Donoso   Universidad de los Andes, Colombia
Zeida Solarte   Universidad Autónoma de Occidente, Colombia

Steering Committee

General Chairs

Andrés Solano   Universidad Autónoma de Occidente, Colombia
Víctor Peñeñory   Universidad de San Buenaventura, Colombia

Technical Committee

Software Engineering and IT Architectures

Mauricio Alba   Universidad Autónoma de Manizales, Colombia
Luis Fernando Castro   Universidad del Quindio, Colombia

Human-Computer Interaction

William Giraldo   Universidad del Quindio, Colombia
César Collazos   Universidad del Cauca, Colombia
Toni Granollers   Universidad de Lleida, Spain

Security of the Information

Juan Carlos Martínez Santos Universidad Tecnológica de Bolívar, Colombia
Andrés Velázquez   Mattica, Mexico

Image Processing, Computer Vision and Multimedia

Leonardo Flórez   Pontificia Universidad Javeriana de Bogotá, Colombia
María Patricia Trujillo   Universidad del Valle, Colombia

Intelligent Systems and Robotics

Néstor Duque   Universidad Nacional de Colombia, Colombia
Iván Cabezas   Universidad de San Buenaventura, Colombia

Educational Informatics

Johany Armando Carreño   Universitaria de Investigación y Desarrollo, Colombia
María Clara Gómez   Universidad de Medellín, Colombia
Marta Mena   Universidad Tecnológica Nacional, Argentina

Information and Knowledge Management

Carlos Hernán Gómez   Universidad de Caldas, Colombia
Claudia Jímenez Guarín   Universidad de los Andes, Colombia

Distributed Systems and Large-Scale Architectures

Harold Castro   Universidad de los Andes, Colombia
Carlos Barrios   Universidad Industrial de Santander, Colombia

Formal Methods

Camilo Rocha   Escuela Colombiana de Ingeniería, Colombia

Logistics Committee

David Castro   Universidad Autónoma de Occidente, Colombia
Andrés Solano   Universidad Autónoma de Occidente, Colombia

Financial Committee

Lyda Peña   Universidad Autónoma de Occidente, Colombia

Marketing and Advertising Committee

Víctor Peñeñory   Universidad de San Buenaventura, Colombia
Sandra Mosquera   Universidad de San Buenaventura, Colombia
Beatriz Grass   Universidad de San Buenaventura, Colombia

Editorial Committee

Andrés Solano   Universidad Autónoma de Occidente, Colombia
Hugo Ordoñez   Universidad de San Buenaventura, Colombia

UNIVERSIDAD DE
SAN BUENAVENTURA

Institución vigilada por **MinEducación**

Contents

Educational Informatics

Distributed Systems and Large-Scale Architectures

Image Processing, Computer Vision and Multimedia

Information and Knowledge Management

Exploring the Use of Linked Open Data
for User Research Interest Modeling

Rubén Manrique, Omar Herazo, and Olga Mariño(⊠)

Systems and Computing Engineering Department, School of Engineering,
Universidad de los Andes, Bogotá, Colombia
{rf.manrique,oa.herazo3009,olmarino}@uniandes.edu.co

Abstract. In the context of the Social Web, user' profiles reflecting
an individual's interests are being modeled using semantic techniques
that consider the users posts' and take advantage of the rich background
knowledge in a Linked Open Dataset (LOD). To enrich the user profile, expansion strategies are applied. While these strategies are useful in
Social Network posts, their suitability for modeling users' interests with
larger documents as input has not yet been validated. Thus, we built
a profile of user's research interests to recommend academic documents
of possible interest. Contrary to the results obtained in the Social Web,
the expansion techniques are inadequate for the academic texts scenario
when all of text in the documents are used as input. Our results show a
new filtering strategy performs better in such a scenario. An additional
contribution was our creation of a DBpedia annotated dataset for academic document recommendation, which was built from a corpus of open
access papers available through Core and Arxiv. Findings suggest the
need to further explore new strategies to construct semantic models that
are able to operate in different domains.

Keywords: User modeling · Linked Open Data · Semantic web

1 Introduction

With the advent of the Semantic Web and the Linked Open Data (LOD) cloud,
new ways of semantically representing users have been proposed [1,8,14,16]. In
these new modeling approaches, the user profile is created using a set of entities
in the LOD cloud that are discovered from information collected about the user.
The advantage of using such representations is the additional knowledge that
can be gathered about the entities and the relationships between them (i.e.
background knowledge). Using this information, it is possible to extend the user
profile and to infer previously unknown interests. Additionally, the LOD cloud
provides a set of comprehensive datasets with domain-independent capabilities
like DBPedia, which support user modeling in different contexts.

Although considerable research has been devoted to evaluating different LOD
user modeling strategies from Twitter and Facebook content [2,14,17], this Social
Web based approach has some limitations. On one hand, it is difficult to access

© Springer International Publishing AG 2017
A. Solano and H. Ordoñez (Eds.): CCC 2017, CCIS 735, pp. 3–16, 2017.
DOI: 10.1007/978-3-319-66562-7_1

the information produced by users in social networks, either because the accounts are no longer active or the user refuses to give access to their accounts. On the other hand, since most Social Web contents produced by a user express interests associated with short term events like news, natural disasters, sports matches, political debates, etc., user profiles based on this information may only reflect short-term or fleeting interests, thus overlooking more lasting interests such as research and work.

This paper addresses the problem of building an accurate LOD user profile nurtured by the user's consumption and production of digital documents, namely academic documents. This document-based approach presents a major challenge due to increased length and complexity compared with social networks. On the Social Networks, published content is limited in the number of words or characters per post, so it is more likely that the user will express only information of interest [5]. That is to say, due to concision of the message and the need for it to be self-contained, it is more likely that entities discovered in posts are of interest to the user. Thus, it is expected that extending the profile using the rich knowledge of LOD datasets will enhance the user profile without creating significant drift from the user's interests. However, in longer documents like academic texts, it is likely that not all the entities found will represent the real interests of the user. Extending the profile through entities in less succinct documents could generate important noise.

In this paper, we are interested in creating LOD research interests profiles based on a set of academic documents, and we present a more reliable strategy for building these user profiles. This began by constructing the base semantic user profile starting with concepts identified in the publication list of each user. Building on this, strategies that have been successfully used in Social Networks to expand the profile by using the background knowledge found in a linked dataset were applied. We evaluated these strategies in recommending relevant academic documents of potential interest to the user. Recommender systems have the ability to predict whether a user would prefer an item or not based on a user profile. In order to evaluate the effectiveness of different user profiles at predicting users' research interests, we built an academic document recommendation engine. Our evaluation suggests that expansion strategies do not necessarily improve the user profile; indeed, some of them degrade the user profile quality. Hence, instead of an expansion strategy, a filtering strategy that prunes the resources and leaves only those that are related to each other in the KB was proposed. This strategy proved to be better suited than expansion for modeling the user's lasting interests in the context of academic research.

In the process of arriving to this final filtering strategy, we also made the following contributions to the work on this topic. These began with creating a DBpedia annotated dataset for academic document recommendation, which was built from a corpus of open access papers available through Core[1] and Arxiv[2] services. To the best of our knowledge, no other academic recommendation dataset

---

[1] https://core.ac.uk/.
[2] https://arxiv.org/.

with these characteristics exists. The second contribution is the evaluation of semantic modeling techniques in a non Social Web scenario. Other discourse communities would likely benefit from the filtering strategy provided.

The paper is organized as follows: In Sect. 2, we review related work in user interest modeling and recent research in content based academic paper recommendation. In Sect. 3, we present the semantic profiling process and the diverse expansion and filtering strategies. In Sect. 4, we describe the protocol used to build the dataset and the evaluation framework. Results and conclusions are discussed in Sects. 5 and 6 respectively.

2   Related Work

A user model or profile[3] is a representation of information about an individual [9] used to personalize applications. Different kinds of information about the individual could be part of the profile; however, most user profiles in retrieval and recommendation systems are based on the user's interests [18]. The most common representation of the user's interests is the keyword-based representation [18]. In this type of profile, users are represented as a weighted vector of words. The weights signify the importance of the term for the user, and they are implicitly calculated from the input content (i.e. documents or posts from which it is possible to infer the user's interest). Weighting schemas such as the word frequency and the TF-IDF (term frequency/inverse document frequency) have been extensively used [4,10,19]. The disadvantage of this representation is that it cannot provide additional information about the semantic relationships of the entities or concepts present in the text.

More recent approaches [2,16,17] have focused on representing the user as a bag of concepts where a concept is any kind of entity that has an explicit representation in a Knowledge Base (KB). In this context, LOD can be used as KB. Indeed, the current web of data offers a large set of linked semantic datasets encoded in machine-understandable RDF standard. They provide excellent modeling capabilities thanks to their cross-domain vocabularies. DBpedia, one of the main datasets in the LOD initiative, for example, currently describes 6 million entities, 1.7 million categories and close to 5 billion facts in its English version alone.

Different research has been evaluated in the context of the Social Web. Abel et al. [2] explore the use of LOD to build user profiles that improve link recommendation on Twitter. They also explore expansion strategies, which they call "indirect mentions", that take advantage of the rich background knowledge in DBpedia. Expansion strategies are better at recommendation. Orlandi et al. [14] follow a similar approach and compute user profiles by harvesting the user's posts in Twitter and Facebook. They propose two representation models based on DBpedia: one based on the entities found in the text, and the other on these

---

[3] Although some authors distinguish between a user model and a user profile [12], we will use both terms interchangeably.

entities and their categorical information. No significant differences between the two were reported.

Recent work by Piao and Breslin [16,17], compare diverse semantic modeling and expansion strategies for Twitter link recommendation. First, they show the superior behaviour of the Inverse Document Frequency (IDF) strategy as a weighting scheme for concept-based profiles. Second, they compare three strategies for user profile expansion using DBpedia: class-based, category-based and property-based. Class and category-based strategies incorporate the DBpedia classes and categories of the initial entities found in the user's Tweets into the profiles. Property expansion includes other entities connected to primitive interests through properties in DBpedia Ontology. According to the results obtained, categorical and property expansion have superior expansion capabilities.

We did not find any studies evaluating LOD user profiling techniques outside of the Social Web even though these profiles are frequently used in LOD recommender systems. Our literature review reveals that recent contributions to LOD recommender systems are more focused on the recommendation algorithm than on the user profile [7,8,13]. Moreover, the current LOD recommenders work almost exclusively on domains where there is already a direct map between the recommendation object and a concept in the KB. For example, the ESWC 2014 Challenge [6] worked on books that were mapped to their corresponding DBpedia resource. Similarly, DiNoia et al. [8] reduce the MoviLens dataset to those movies that have a corresponding DBpedia resource. Our recommendation approach is different from those because we are not limited to a candidate set in which each item has a direct resource that represents it in the LOD. Instead, we address the problem by taking the textual information of documents as input and identifying the set of concepts present.

3   Semantic Profiling Process

This section presents the process for building the different semantic user profiles, and takes into account semantic information recovered from a KB in the Linked Open Data Cloud. The process involves four different modules (Fig. 1). The first one, called the Semantic Document Annotator, receives a document and identifies entities of the KB in the text. We will use the word annotations to refer to these entities. The set of annotations found constitutes a initial semantic user profile ($ISUP$). Then, the Expansion Module receives the initial profile and expands it through the rich number of relationships in the KB. In this module, new expanded concepts that are not found in the text, but are related with the annotation, are incorporated into the user profile. In the Filtering Module, we apply our proposed filtering technique to select concepts that are highly connected. The strategy looks for connection paths between annotations as it uses these to select and assign the concept's initial weight in the user profile representation. Finally, the Weighting Module checks the importance of each concept in the interest profile and assigns a weight accordingly. We use an IDF approach to assign the annotation weights [17], and different discount strategies to assign the weights to the expanded concepts.

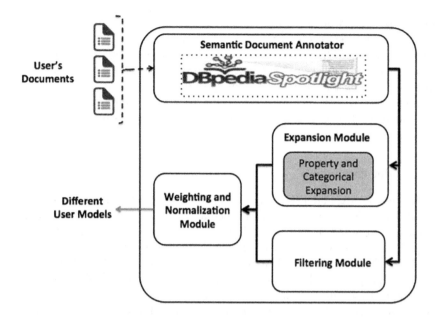

Fig. 1. Semantic profiling process

To implement the aforementioned semantic profiling process, we rely on DBpedia as the KB. Its comprehensive vocabularies, extensive relationships between concepts and continuous updating enable cross-domain modeling capabilities. DBpedia consists of a set of resources R (i.e. we will use the word "resources" to refer to DBpedia entities such as "http://dbpedia.org/resouce/Colombia" and categories such as "http://dbpedia.org/resource/Category:Republics") and literals L interrelated through a set of properties P, which are used to denote specific relationships. Under a RDF model, the DBpedia data consist of a set of statements $E \subset R \times P \times (R \setminus L)$. Each $e \in E$ is a triplet composed of a subject, a predicate and an object/literal. We define a user profile as the set of pairs (r_i, w_i), where r_i is a DBpedia resource and w_i is the associated weight that represents the resource importance in the user profile:

$$UP = \{(r_1, w_1), (r_2, w_2) \ldots (r_i, w_i) \mid r_j \in R\} \qquad (1)$$

Since there are multiple users, this process is repeated multiple times, and for each user we obtain multiple profiles according to the different strategies. English and Spanish versions of DBpedia 2016 are used in a instance in Virtuoso. In the following sub-sections, each step in the process is described in detail.

3.1 Semantic Document Annotator

In this step, we were interested in finding annotations of DBpedia resources in the text. In order to find these annotations, DBpedia Spotlight service with a

JAVA heap memory of 16 GB was employed. The outcome of this step is an initial semantic user interest profile $ISUP_{u_i} = \{(r_1, w_{ini_1}), (r_2, w_{ini_2}) \ldots (r_i, w_{ini_i}) | r_j \in R\}$ for the user u_i. The initial resource weight w_{ini_i} is calculated as the number of occurrences in the user document collection (i.e. users publications). It is important to mention that we do not perform any additional verification on the annotations discovered. As was mentioned by [22], there is no guarantee of a correct identification of annotations, so a manual cleaning is suggested. However, in a realistic scenario, a manual correction process is not feasible.

3.2   Model Expansion

In this step, we expand ISUP by relating its resources to new ones employing the rich background knowledge in DBpedia. We follow two different expansion approaches proposed by [2,14] which were later expanded upon in [16,17]:

Categorical expansion (CE): We add the DBpedia categories of each resource in $ISUP$. Then, we find such categorical resources through the Dublin Core dct:subject property and calculate their initial weight as the number of resources belonging to that category in the user document collection.

Property expansion (PE): The $ISUP$ is enriched with the set of resources recovered by following the set of properties $p : p \in DBpediaOntology$ of all the resources $r \in ISUP$.

3.3   Weighting and Normalization Module

Annotations Weighting. The final weight of each resource is calculated taking into account its presence in the total set of user profiles. Thus, the final weight of a resource r_i is calculated as the initial weight multiplied by its IDF as follows [17]:

$$w_{idf_i} = w_{ini_i} \times log\frac{M}{m_{r_i}} \tag{2}$$

where M is the total number of users and m_{r_i} is the number of users interested in a resource r_i. The IDF strategy penalizes annotations that appear in multiple user profiles. We will refer to the user profile without the extension, but with IDF weighting strategy as follows:

$$SUP = \{(r_1, w_1), (r_2, w_2) \ldots (r_i, w_i) \mid r_j \in R\} \tag{3}$$

Expanded Resource Weighting. The weights of the expanded resources incorporated through CE and PE follow the discount formulas proposed in [14,17]. For an CE extended resource cat_{e_i} and an PE extended resource pro_{e_i} obtained from the resource $r_i \in SUP$, the weights with which they are incorporated into the user profile are calculated as:

$$w_{cat_{e_i}} = w_{idf_{cat_{e_i}}} \times \frac{1}{log(SP)} \times \frac{1}{log(SC)} \tag{4}$$

$$w_{pro_{e_i}} = w_{idf_{pro_{e_i}}} \times \frac{1}{log(P)} \tag{5}$$

where SP is the set of resources belonging to the category, SC is the set of sub-categories in the DBpedia categorical hierarchical and P is the number of occurrences of a property in the whole DBpedia graph. Only categories in the hierarchical structure processed by [11] were used to avoid disconnected categories and cycles. Finally, $w_{idf_{pro_{e_i}}}$ and $w_{idf_{cat_{e_i}}}$ are calculated in the same way as the weights for the annotations were.

3.4   Model Filtering

We argue that the weighting strategies explained above may not be enough to avoid the drift from the real user interests given that many resources found in a long document may be unrelated to the main topic. In academic papers, for example, multiple concepts could be found in the references sections that are not necessary related with the academic research interests of the user (universities, people, years, etc.). Actually, noise could increase if these two conditions occur: the same reference appears in multiple publications of the same user profile and it does not appear in other users' profiles. In this case, the IDF raises the noise for this user. The hypothesis is that the expansion strategies explained before could actually make the situation worse given that they could reinforce the noise in the user profile through the incorporation of other irrelevant resources. Consider the following subset of resources of a user profiles built from academic publications as an example:

SUP={ (Self-esteem,3.71), (Education,1.96), (Université du Québec, 4.11), (Undergraduate education, 2.72), (Higher education, 3.3), (Aquaculture, 3.12)}

Université du Québec and Aquaculture are two resources identified in the text, but they drift from the real user interests. Université du Québec appears in the reference section in multiple publications by the same author. Aquaculture appears in the middle of the results section as part of an example that shows some of the author's findings. Université du Québec has a high IDF because it does not appear in any other user profiles, yet neither of these reflect the main interests of the user. Consequently, these resources lead to a poor representation of the real user interests. In order to address this problem, it is possible to analyze how connected the resources are by taking advantage of the graph representation of LOD datasets as DBpedia. Analyzing connecting paths[4] of length 1 (i.e. a direct relationship between two resources through a DBpedia property) for each possible pair of resources, it is possible to find the following connections:

(Self-esteem, Education), (Education, Undergraduate education), (Education, Undergraduate education), (Education, Higher education), (Education, Higher education), (Undergraduate education, Higher education), (Undergraduate education, Higher education), (Higher education, Undergraduate education)

In some cases there are multiple connections for the same pair of annotations; for example, there are two connections between Education and Undergraduate

---

[4] https://www.w3.org/TR/sparql11-property-paths/.

education through properties seeAlso and wikiPageLink. In contrast, no connections were found for Université du Québec and Aquaculture resources. Based on these findings, we think that analyzing the connections between annotations could be a useful approach to reducing noisy resources in SUP. Additionally, the number of times that a resource appears in connection paths can be used as an indicator of the importance of the resource in the interest profile, so we use this frequency as the basis for the weighting strategy.

We also take advantage of the analysis of connection path lengths greater than one. For those paths, there is the possibility of finding new resources that are related to two annotations in the connection path, but are not part of SUP. Additionally, we evaluate the incorporation of such resources into the user representation. The intuition behind this expansion is that resources that connect two annotations are more likely to reinforce the real user interests than those that are incorporated from the annotation properties or categories.

Our filtering strategy follows four steps:

– Step 1: Build a connection set with the highest w_{idf_i} in SUP. For all our experiments we select the top 100 resources in SUP.
– Step 2: Find all paths of length l ($1 <= l <= l_{maxpath}$) for each possible pair of resources r_i,r_j in the connection set. Following previous experimental suggestions [15], we only consider outgoing edges from r_i and r_j in order to avoid the noise produced by highly indegree resources in DBpedia.
– Step 3: Build a filtered user profile incorporating all the resources found in the paths, and associating an initial weight representing the number of distinct paths in which the resource appears.
– Step 4: Apply the IDF weighting scheme explained in Sect. 3.3.1, but using as w_{ini_i} the connection frequency of the above step.

For the rest of the document, we will refer to the filter user semantic model as $FSUP$.

4   Evaluation

We conducted our experimental setup to determine if: (i) semantic representations of the user perform better than classical user TF-IDF vector representation; (ii) expansion techniques improve the quality of the semantic user profile build from non-Social Web content; and (iii) our filter strategy outperforms expansion strategies in such cases.

Academic document recommendation is an appropriate scenario to address the above issues since academic documents are usually long; thus, it is possible to find many more annotations than those found in a Tweet or a Facebook post. Academic papers often use formal language and involve concepts that have complex relationships. Additionally, the task of recommending academic documents is a good scenario to evaluate content-based profiling techniques since textual data is the main (and sometimes the only) reliable source of information upon which to base recommendations [19]. The full text of some of the user's publications will be used as input for the process based on the hypothesis that the user's academic interests are reflected in the documents they produce. This hypothesis is logical and has already been used in recent content-based recommendation systems [19–21].

4.1 Data Set

One of the main contributions of this work is the construction of a complete, semantically annotated dataset for academic document recommendation. We built our own dataset given that the Semantic Document Annotator process requires the text of the publication in order to correctly identify the annotations. Datasets used in previous research published the feature vector of the users and documents instead of the texts themselves (in a bag of words approach) mainly because they use sources that do not allow them to share the full text [19, 20].

Our dataset contains the user profiles of 11 professors in the area of computer science. It was built from some of the most recent publications found on their Google Scholar web pages. At least a minimum of twelve of each professor's most recent publications were used as input for the semantic profiling process. The candidate set is a starting set of papers from which the recommended set of papers for the user is produced. In our case, it is a subset of Core and Arvix open corpora that was retrieved using different topic keywords in computer science as queries. After identifying and eliminating duplicate publications and unreadable pdf files, the final candidate set totaled 5710 different academic documents. The ground truth of papers is a subset of the candidate set in which the user expresses an explicit interest. Users interacted with a web-based search system to build this set. In order to reduce the possibility of selecting a paper unrelated to the main content, the web-based search system does not show the source of the academic document (journal or conference title). In the data set, we have at least 10 academic documents for which each user shows an explicit interest. The full dataset is available in https://github.com/Ruframapi. It contains the annotations found in the publications list of each user and the complete candidate set. The corresponding Arxiv and Core identifications are also shared in order to allow the access to the full text of the candidate set documents. It is important to signal that the process of building a ground truth for academic documents recommendation based on content is a challenging task, for it requires a time expensive participation of the users in order to analyze the text and explicitly assert its relevance. Hence, we also rely on a limited number of users as do previous studies.

The whole candidate set is annotated under the same representation as the user profile. However, the calculation of the IDF is made taking all the documents in the corpus into account. When the evaluation involved an expansion strategy, the corpora documents were also expanded.

4.2   Recommendation Algorithm

We follow a offline comparative framework that measures the quality of the recommendations for the different user profiles. Since the objective is to measure
the influence of the user profile on the recommendation task, we must use a
common, content-based recommendation algorithm. In other words, we want to
measure the effects of the different user profiles as input for a common recommendation algorithm. For the purpose of this research, we select the documents
with the highest cosine similarity with a given user profile.

4.3   Evaluation Metrics

We use the following typical metrics for the evaluation of Top-N recommender
tasks [21]: MRR (Mean Reciprocal Rank), MAP@10 (Mean Average Precision),
and NDCG@10 (Normalized Discounted Cumulative Gain). We select $N = 10$
as the recommendation objective since it is a common rank used in multiple
applications [16,19] and it is not common to recommend a larger set of items. In
our data set, the relevance measures are binaries (i.e. the recommended documents are relevant to the user or are not), so we use a binary relevance scale for
the calculation of NDCG. The final NDCG for each user strategy is calculated
averaging the results for each user.

5   Results

In this section, experimental results of different semantic user profiles are shown.
Our first question was related to the performance of a classical TF-IDF vector
space model representation in comparison to a semantic user profile (SUP). In
order to answer this question, we built a representation of the user and corpus
documents with a TF-IDF scheme. According to [3] TF-IDF is the most frequent
weighting scheme in research paper recommender systems. We carried out typical
text processing operations including tokenizer, stop word removal and stemming.
For all the experiments, we used the entire text of the publications as input.
Table 1 shows the results obtained using the evaluation metrics explain above.
Based on these results, the semantic approach performed better than TF-IDF.
We noticed that the classical TF-IDF approach has the problem of retrieving
documents that are too similar to the final top 10 recommendations list. In
order to solve the problem of retrieving too similar documents, diversification
strategies could be implemented [3]. We do not use them as these strategies
operate to improve the recommendation not the user model.

   In our second experiment, the different expansion strategies were evaluated.
We compared the semantic user profile with categorical expansion ($SUP + CE$),
the semantic user profile with property expansion ($SUP + PE$), the semantic user
profile with categorical and property expansion ($SUP + CE + PE$) and the profile
filtering strategy for different path lengths ($FSUP_{l_{maxpath}=1}$, $FSUP_{l_{maxpath}=2}$,
$FSUP_{l_{maxpath}=3}$). The average number of resources for each type of user profile

Table 1. Semantic User Profile (vs) TF-IDF vector space model

	MRR	MAP	NDCG
SUP	**0.4015**	**0.3429**	**0.4731**
TF-IDF	0.3720	0.2718	0.3961

Table 2. Average number of resources for each type of user profile

SUP	1911
SUP+CE	9889
SUP+PE	2024
SUP+CE+PE	10001
$FSUP_{l_{maxpath}=1}$	71
$FSUP_{l_{maxpath}=2}$	1369
$FSUP_{l_{maxpath}=3}$	>8000

is shown in Table 2. As was expected, the $SUP + CE$ and $SUP + CE + PE$ have a higher number of resources, which is five times the number of resources found in the profile without expansion. On the contrary, our filtering strategy for $l_{maxpath}$ of 1 and 2 reduced the number of resources in SUP. It is worth noting that the exact number for $FSUP_{l_{maxpath}=3}$ might be a bit higher than shown as restrictions on the infrastructure configuration SPARQL queries took a maximum of 700 seconds for the result; queries taking more time were discarded.

The results using the evaluation measures described in Sect. 4.3 are summarized in Fig. 2. Only for categorical expansion $(SUP + CE)$ is there a slight increase in the quality of the recommendation in comparison with the profile without expansion (SUP). In contrast, the other expansion strategies $(SUP + PE, SUP + CE + PRO)$ lead to a deterioration of the semantic profile. These results differ from those obtained in the Twitter link recommendation [17] where property-based expansion obtained similar results as categorical expansion.

The recommendation accuracy obtained using our proposed filtering approach outperformed the expansion strategies. Interestingly, the best performance was achieved with the filtering strategy containing paths of length 1 $(FSUP_{l_{maxpath}=1})$. This result validates our initial hypothesis about the need to filter the annotations found in the text to build the user profile. For paths of length 3 $(FSUP_{l_{maxpath}=3})$, the filtering strategy includes more resources than those in the original SUP representation, yet the filtering strategy with length of 3 performs better in comparison with expansion strategies. We argue that longer paths could lead to negative effects since resources in DBpedia tend to be highly connected if the full set of ontology properties are taken into account[5]. So, instead of a filter, we could add additional noise to the user profile.

---

[5] http://konect.uni-koblenz.de/networks/dbpedia-all.

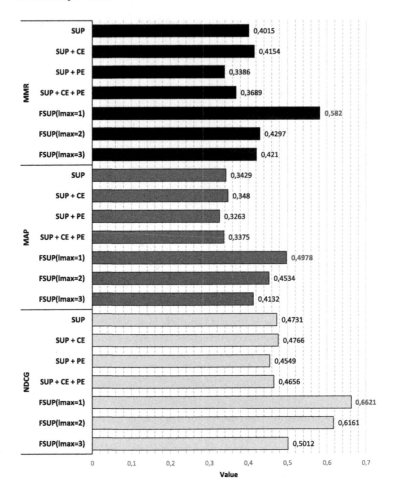

Fig. 2. Evaluation of expansion and filtering strategies.

In summary, our results suggest that: (i) there is a need for filtering tech-niques to refine the user profile and reduce the noise produced by the annota-tion process; (ii) expansion strategies applied directly to the annotations are not adequate in scenarios where the content input is not short texts; and (iii) it is possible to build better user interest profiles than those produced by the clas-sical TF-IDF approach in the context of academic documents recommendation through a LOD knowledge base like DBpedia.

6   Conclusions and Future Work

In this paper, we presented the evaluation of different semantic user model-ing strategies in an academic paper recommendation scenario. We showed that expansion strategies useful in the Social Web could increase the noise in the user representation when dealing with longer documents. Because of this, in scenarios where the input content is a long document, filtering strategies outperform expansion strategies as this type of document involves multiple concepts that do not necessarily express the real interests of the user. Although our filtering strategy displayed superior performance than all the other models, further experimentation is needed to explore better ways to remove noise resources in the user representation. Reducing the set of possible properties in the paths or employing semantic similarity measures between resources are future routes to explore. Since the focus of our research was on the comparison of different user profile strategies and not on the recommendation itself, issues related to the recommendation process itself such as the temporality of the interests, which was addressed as a key issue in profile research interests [3], was not addressed. Future experimentation should be conducted in order to determine the ideal temporal frame to include the user's papers, and the weighting strategies to incorporate them in the user profile. Finally, we will continue working on increasing the size of the dataset to validate these findings with a larger number of examples. The objective is to build a common scenario to measure and compare future semantic user profile strategies.

Acknowledgment. This work was partially supported by COLCIENCIAS PhD scholarship (Call 647-2014).

References

1. Abel, F., Gao, Q., Houben, G.-J., Tao, K.: Analyzing user modeling on Twitter for personalized news recommendations. In: Konstan, J.A., Conejo, R., Marzo, J.L., Oliver, N. (eds.) UMAP 2011. LNCS, vol. 6787, pp. 1–12. Springer, Heidelberg (2011). doi:10.1007/978-3-642-22362-4_1
2. Abel, F., Hauff, C., Houben, G.-J., Tao, K.: Leveraging user modeling on the social web with linked data. In: Brambilla, M., Tokuda, T., Tolksdorf, R. (eds.) ICWE 2012. LNCS, vol. 7387, pp. 378–385. Springer, Heidelberg (2012). doi:10.1007/978-3-642-31753-8_31
3. Beel, J., Gipp, B., Langer, S., Breitinger, C.: Research-paper recommender systems: a literature survey. Int. J. Digit. Libr. **17**(4), 305–338 (2016)
4. Beel, J., Langer, S., Gipp, B.: TF-IDuF: a novel term-weighting scheme for user modeling based on users' personal document collections. In: Proceedings of the iConference 2017 (2017)
5. Berrizbeita, F., Vidal, M.E.: Traversing the linking open data cloud to create news from Tweets. In: Meersman, R., et al. (eds.) On the Move to Meaningful Internet Systems: OTM 2014 Workshops. LNCS, vol. 8842, pp. 479–488. Springer, Heidelberg (2014). doi:10.1007/978-3-662-45550-0_48
6. Di Noia, T., Cantador, I., Ostuni, V.C.: Linked open data-enabled recommender systems: ESWC 2014 challenge on book recommendation. In: Presutti, V., Stankovic, M., Cambria, E., Cantador, I., Di Iorio, A., Di Noia, T., Lange, C., Recupero, D.R., Tordai, A. (eds.) Semantic Web Evaluation Challenge. Communications in Computer and Information Science, pp. 129–143. Springer International Publishing, Cham (2014)

7. Di Noia, T., Mirizzi, R., Ostuni, V.C., Romito, D.: Exploiting the web of data in model-based recommender systems. In: Proceedings of the Sixth ACM Conference on Recommender Systems, RecSys 2012, pp. 253–256. ACM, New York (2012)
8. Di Noia, T., Mirizzi, R., Ostuni, V.C., Romito, D., Zanker, M.: Linked open data to support content-based recommender systems. In: Proceedings of the 8th International Conference on Semantic Systems, I-SEMANTICS 2012, pp. 1–8. ACM, New York (2012)
9. Froschl, C.: User Modeling and User Profiling in Adaptive E-learning Systems. Master's thesis, Graz University of Technology (2005)
10. Godoy, D., Amandi, A.: A conceptual clustering approach for user profiling in personal information agents. AI Commun. **19**, 207–227 (2006)
11. Kapanipathi, P., Jain, P., Venkataramani, C.: Hierarchical interest graph. Technical report (2015)
12. Koch, N.: Software Engineering for Adaptive Hypermedia Systems: Reference Model, Modeling Techniques and Development Process. Ph.D. thesis, Ludwig-Maximilians-University (2000)
13. Meymandpour, R., Davis, J.: Enhancing recommender systems using linked open data-based semantic analysis of items. In: Davis, J.G., Bozzon, A. (eds.) 3rd Australasian Web Conference (AWC 2015). CRPIT, vol. 166, pp. 11–17. ACS, Sydney, Australia (2015)
14. Orlandi, F., Breslin, J., Passant, A.: Aggregated, interoperable and multi-domain user profiles for the social web. In: Proceedings of the 8th International Conference on Semantic Systems, I-SEMANTICS 2012, pp. 41–48. ACM, New York (2012)
15. Paul, C., Rettinger, A., Mogadala, A., Knoblock, C.A., Szekely, P.: Efficient graph-based document similarity. In: Sack, H., Blomqvist, E., d'Aquin, M., Ghidini, C., Ponzetto, S.P., Lange, C. (eds.) ESWC 2016. LNCS, vol. 9678, pp. 334–349. Springer, Cham (2016). doi:10.1007/978-3-319-34129-3_21
16. Piao, G., Breslin, J.G.: Analyzing aggregated semantics-enabled user modeling on Google+ and Twitter for personalized link recommendations. In: Proceedings of the 2016 Conference on User Modeling Adaptation and Personalization, UMAP 2016, pp. 105–109. ACM, New York (2016)
17. Piao, G., Breslin, J.G.: Exploring dynamics and semantics of user interests for user modeling on Twitter for link recommendations. In: Proceedings of the 12th International Conference on Semantic Systems, SEMANTiCS 2016, pp. 81–88. ACM, New York (2016)
18. Schiaffino, S., Amandi, A.: Intelligent user profiling. In: Bramer, M. (ed.) Artificial Intelligence An International Perspective. LNCS, vol. 5640, pp. 193–216. Springer, Heidelberg (2009). doi:10.1007/978-3-642-03226-4_11
19. Sugiyama, K., Kan, M.Y.: Scholarly paper recommendation via user's recent research interests. In: Proceedings of the 10th Annual Joint Conference on Digital Libraries, JCDL 2010, pp. 29–38. ACM, New York (2010). http://doi.acm.org/10.1145/1816123.1816129
20. Sugiyama, K., Kan, M.Y.: Exploiting potential citation papers in scholarly paper recommendation. In: Proceedings of the 13th ACM/IEEE-CS Joint Conference on Digital Libraries, JCDL 2013, pp. 153–162. ACM, New York (2013)
21. Sugiyama, K., Kan, M.Y.: A comprehensive evaluation of scholarly paper recommendation using potential citation papers. Int. J. Digit. Libr. **16**(2), 91–109 (2015)
22. Waitelonis, J., Exeler, C., Sack, H.: Linked data enabled generalized vector space model to improve document retrieval. In: Proceedings of 3rd International Workshop on NLP & DBpedia 2015 (2015)

BiDArch: BigData Architect, Generator of Big Data Solution Architectures

Julio Sosa⬤ and Claudia Jiménez-Guarín$^{(\boxtimes)}$⬤

Systems and Computing Engineering Department, School of Engineering,
Universidad de los Andes, Colombia Carrera 1 Este M°19A-40 Oficina ML772,
111711 Bogotá, Colombia
{jm.sosa,cjimenez}@uniandes.edu.co

Abstract. The design of highly scalable architectures based on the Hadoop ecosystem is highly complex due to the wide and dynamic portfolio of available tools. The feasible solution generator for big data problems, BiDArch, allows to automatically establish a feasible architecture from the characterization of a problem in terms of tools features. This process enriches the solution proposed from semantic knowledge allowing the architect to not require a thorough knowledge of the ecosystem, getting him to focus mainly on the characterization of his problem or design goal.

Keywords: Big Data solutions · Hadoop ecosystem · Feasible architecture generator

1 Introduction

In the scenario in which man generates heterogeneous information that can be structured or not, transmitted massively at high speed; new challenges and problems related to the discovery, storage, processing, and analysis of such information arise. A new technological and scientific boom emerges around a concept called *big data* and is interested transversely in this problematic [1, p. 3]. However, in treatable space of these problems, a set of requirements has been identified in terms of scalability, consistency and availability in information flows.

There is not only a high complexity around the problems, but also the functional and non-functional requirements impact on the elaboration of complex solution strategies that orchestrate some technology components and tools from an overwhelming set of potential candidates—with several possible configurations—to obtain a feasible solution architecture to the problem.

Hadoop represents the core of a vast tools ecosystem to build *big data* solutions. This ecosystem, which initially was limited to a base of no more than a dozen tools, today is made up of more than 60 tools [2] and *plugins* such as distributed file systems, multi-facet distributed frameworks, NoSQL repositories with different data models and specialized tools for activities like *machine learning*, deployment of distributed systems, service programming and *workflows*.

© Springer International Publishing AG 2017
A. Solano and H. Ordoñez (Eds.): CCC 2017, CCIS 735, pp. 17–31, 2017.
DOI: 10.1007/978-3-319-66562-7_2

The existing difficulty in establishing a connection that bridges the gap between the complex domain of *big data* problems and the related knowledge to achieve an adequate tools selection to solve them, is the main motivator for developing an artifact that provides feasible solution architectures for problems using Hadoop ecosystem tools.

This problem is of great interest to any organization that intends to obtain built-in *big data* solutions, in order to provide additional value in its business processes. This problematic worries software architects who are directly faced with deciding what tools should be used and how they should be deployed, and finally, software developers who build these solutions.

The main contribution of this work is the construction of a feasible solution architecture automatic generator for problems in the domain of *big data* using Hadoop ecosystem tools. The requirements demanded by these problems are defined in terms of the functionalities offered by the tools. Another significant contribution is the development of an ontology that provides a description of a set of ecosystem tools.

2   The Complexity of Dealing with *Big Data* Problems and the Hadoop Ecosystem

Within the domain of *big data*, there are many use cases such as data exploration, business operations analysis, real-time predictive analysis, datawarehousing operations, fraud detection and risk management among many others [1, p. 1]; They focus on different sectors of industry such as financial services, health care, telecommunications and cybersecurity, among many others.

Naturally, each one of these use cases demands a high and dynamic amount of functional requirements that are aligned with the particular interests of a particular business sector, and unfortunately, are completely heterogeneous. For this reason, the complexity of performing the characterization of all problem instances achieving the functional requirements integration for all business processes is intractable. However, this whole heterogeneous set of functional requirements needs to rely on some combination of information life cycle activities in the *big data*. The above mentioned indicates that solutions will always need to discover, collect, process, analyze and visualize information flows that have enormous magnitude in dimensions of volume, speed, variety and veracity [3].

Considering that the implementation of these activities is effectively achieved with a combination of ecosystem tools, there is an immediate need to describe the tools ecosystem in terms of features that are useful to support the activities demanded directly by the functional requirements of every use case.

The problem characterization is not the only one complex stuff. The ecosystem itself also shows a high complexity, due to its constant and continuous evolution [4]. This complexity hinders the process of selecting and characterizing an initial subset of tools. This ecosystem is made up of a wide range of software projects in two licensing flavors (free and open source) [2]. Because of this main characteristic, the elements of this ecosystem mutate with ease incubating new tools, they present wide differences in the level of maturity of the same, they produce frequent updates that impact both as an accelerated growth of the wealth of offered functionalities as in compatibility issues with other tools. In addition, the construction of specialized tools is enabled in a particular domain (scientific or commercial), such as MLlib [5] and Mahout [6] in the context of *machine learning*.

Furthermore, the identification and representation of the functionalities offered by tools is also complex, in a way that they can be abstracted to represent requirements that describe traditional problem instances.

To achieve the implementation of an effective solution, an in-depth analysis of the factors and variables is required to allow that a large variety of problems be represented and the tools selection process be measured. It is also necessary to represent explicitly the useful and relevant knowledge for designing solution architectures to these problems. These solution architectures must be built based on requirements, factors and variables considered in the characterization of a given problem and the benefits offered by the tools in the ecosystem.

BiDArch, the architecture generator presented in this work provides an important support for software architects in small and medium-sized companies that are interested in building *in-house* solutions, allowing them to characterize problem instances and providing a feasible solution architecture that is justified and enriched with a list of configuration recommendations and a knowledge related to the set of available interfaces for solution integration.

3   BiDArch: Automatic Generator of Feasible Architectures from *Big Data* Problem Specifications

The wide variety of problem instances with different processes and business interests generates a huge and complex set of requirements related to the nature of the activities carried out by each business sector that experiences these challenges. For instance, the functional requirements of an application to perform fraud detection in the financial sector do not match the requirements of a platform that wishes to integrate several data sources to provide a 360° view of a company and eliminate information silos.

However, there is a set of common requirements that are related to the features of a component or tool in a big data system and serve as input to support the requirements of each challenge in a particular business sector. Within these requirements, there are some aspects that are common to all tools such as scalability, ease of use, cost of development, cost of maintenance and feature richness, among many others. Also, there are specific requirements related to the activities that are managed by tools and contribute to orchestrate a solution to the problem or challenge of interest. In this group, there are needs around the tasks of storage, ingestion, extraction, processing and analysis of large datasets.

The purpose of BiDArch is to match the requirements of a problem instance with the features supported by the selected tools that appear in Table 1 to construct a feasible architecture with the more related tools.

Table 1. Hadoop ecosystem selected tools.

Context	Tool
Data storage	Apache Hadoop HDFS
	Apache HBase
Data ingestion	Apache Flume
	Apache Kafka
	Apache Sqoop
Data processing	Apache Hadoop MapReduce
	Apache Spark
	Apache Pig
	Apache Crunch
	Apache Cascading
	Apache Hive
	Apache Impala
Orchestration	Apache Oozie

The selection of these tools is performed considering aspects such as a high degree of maturity, stability, coverage, verifiable effectiveness in cases of success and integration with the ecosystem itself.

To achieve the goal, a phase-segmented solution strategy is planned as shown in Fig. 1.

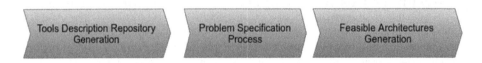

Fig. 1. BiDarch solution strategy phases.

The phases of the proposed strategy are based on the interaction of a series of macro processes that are supported on several models. Each one of the strategy phases is detailed below.

3.1   Phase 1: Tools Description Repository Generation

After a deep study and analysis of the official documentation of the list of tools presented in Table 1, the process of generating an ontology that encapsulates the tool description repository is supported by a **tool model** designed with the aim of representing a set of features that defines properly every single tool contained into the repository.

The selection of these tools is not intended to be extensive in relation with the huge and growing number of existing free software tools around the Hadoop ecosystem, but prioritizes the depth in the study of more relevant tools. It is important to note that all of these tools are projects of the ASF (Apache Software Foundation) community.

3.2   Phase 2: Problem Instances Specification

The main objective of this phase is to describe any problem that a BiDArch user can define in terms of the features supported by the tools. In this phase, the **problem specification process** uses the **problem model** (which is based on the **generic requirement model**) and the tools description repository generated in the previous phase, to build a problem instance.

The main elements on this phase are set out below.

Generic Requirement Model: A generic requirement is modeled as a triple composed of: a feature r_f, a value to satisfy r_v and a weight r_w that allows to establish an order relationship between the problem requirements relevance. This can be represented as follows.

$$r = (r_f, r_v, r_w) \tag{1}$$

The required feature r_f belongs to the set of tool features contained in the description repository. The domain of r_v can be **boolean** or **categorical** and it is in function of a particular *feature* r_f. On the other hand, the value of r_w satisfies the constraint $r_w \in \{1, 2, 3...10\}$ and allows to set up the relevance of a requirement with respect to others during the tools selection process.

For instance, considering for a problem p, the need to highlight *richness of functionalities* and *high scalability* features in contrast to *encryption support* and *support level* features for the selected tools; this scenario can be modeled as presented in Table 2.

Problem Model: Let P be the space of treatable problems with the Hadoop ecosystem tools, AG a set of generic attributes of the problem, RG a set of general requirements and AR a set of the required activities. A problem instance is modeled as follows:

$$P = \{p|p = (AG, RG, AR)\} \tag{2}$$

Table 2. Problem requirements example.

r_i	r_f	r_v	r_w
r_1	Scalability	High	8
r_2	Support level	Medium	3
r_3	Feature richness	High	9
r_4	Encryption support	True	4

$$AG = \{ag_1, ag_2, ag_3, ..., ag_{l-1}, ag_l\} \tag{3}$$

$$RG = \{rg_1, rg_2, rg_3, ..., rg_{m-1}, rg_m\} \tag{4}$$

$$AR = \{ar_1, ar_2, ar_3, ..., ar_{n-1}, ar_n\} \tag{5}$$

The collection of generic attributes, AG, is nothing more than a set of descriptors that contains *metadata* and relevant information of the problem. This information facilitates the problems identification and quering.

The set of general requirements, RG, contains the requirements rg_i that are common and independent of the particularity of a specific problem. These types of requirements are built on needs that are transversal to all problem instances and are finally based on features of any tool in the repository.

The problem required activities suggest special and specific requirements. These are framed within the tasks that are normally managed by ecosystem tools such as storage, movement (ingestion and extraction) and scalable processing — in its several facets— of large datasets.

Any required activity ar_i from the collection of activities AR can be represented as an ordered pair composed of an activity a_i directly related to the traditional tasks managed by the Hadoop ecosystem tools and a set of special requirements RE_i related to a particular activity a_i as shown below:

$$ar_i = (a_i, RE_i) \tag{6}$$

$$RE_i = \{re_j\} \tag{7}$$

Problem Specification Process: This process consists of a sequence of stages developed under the problem model previously raised. These stages seek to characterize the problem in terms of generic attributes, a series of general requirements, and a list of required activities that are subject to particular requirements. Figure 2 illustrates the various stages of this process.

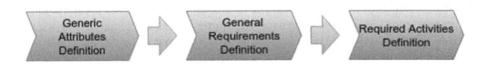

Fig. 2. Stages of the problem specification process.

3.3   Phase 3: Feasible Architectures Generation

The phase of feasible architectures generation corresponds to the final stage of the strategy and its purpose is to instantiate a feasible solution architecture diagram. To reach that goal, the previously described tool description repository and a proposed **reference architecture model** are used as inputs.

The most important components of this phase of the strategy are detailed below:

Reference Architecture Model: Any feasible architecture can be modeled as a non-empty set of tools that intercommunicate or share services through interfaces. In addition, a set of configuration recommendations are added that generate an important contribution in the solution implementation, as well as in solution effectiveness and efficiency.

A feasible architecture is modeled as a graph AF which has the Hadoop ecosystem tools as nodes and the connections between the compatible interfaces of such tools as edges. Formally a feasible architecture is be modeled as follows.

Let ECO be the set of tools described in the tools description repository, $C = \{c|c \in ECO\}$ the subset of tools required by a feasible architecture, and $I = \{(c_i, c_j)|c_i, cj \in C\}$ the set of interfaces that connect the required tools. The feasible architecture AF is defined as:

$$AF = (C, I) \tag{8}$$

subject to:

$$\forall (c_i, c_j) \in I : c_i \neq c_j \tag{9}$$
$$\forall u, v \in C : \exists \mu = \langle u, v \rangle \tag{10}$$

The constraint in Formula (9) denotes the non-existence of loops or interfaces that connect a tool to itself. For its part, Formula (10) specifies that the graph AF is connected.

Notion of Affinity Between the Hadoop Ecosystem Tools and Problem Instances: Let $p \in P$ be a problem instance and $h \in ECO$ be a tool described in the tools description repository, where $P = \{p|p = (AG, RG, AR)\}$, RG is the set of general requirements of a problem p, $AR = \{ar_i\}$ the set of required activities by p. And $RE = \bigcup RE_i$ the union of every special requirement for each required activity ar_i.

Let $R* = RG \cup RE$ be the set of all requirements of a problem instance, $r = (r_f, r_v, r_w)$ with $r \in R*$ be any requirement.

Let $H = \{(h_f, h_v)\}$ be the set of ordered pairs made up with a tool feature h_f and its respective value h_v.

The measure of affinity between a problem instance requirement r and a tool h described in the repository is defined as the function $f : R * \times ECO \rightarrow \mathbb{Z}$, as follows:

$$f(r, h) = \begin{cases} r_w * \left[(h_v - r_v) + 1 \right] & \text{si } h_v \geq r_v \wedge r_f = h_f \\ r_w * \left[h_v - r_v \right] & \text{si } h_v < r_v \wedge r_f = h_f \end{cases} \tag{11}$$

Based on the definition given in Formula 11, a measure of affinity between a problem p—in terms of its requirements $R*$—and a given tool h such as the function $F : P \times ECO \rightarrow \mathbb{Z}$ presented below:

$$F(p, h) = \sum_{r \in R*} f(r, h) \tag{12}$$

Feasible Architecture Generation Process: The process of generating feasible architectures aims to identify and interconnect a set of tools described in the repository that meet the requirements of a given problem with the highest possible affinity value.

Below are developed each one of the most relevant stages of this process:

Required Layers Identification: This first stage of the process aims to determine which layers are required to build a feasible architecture. This identification is done in function of the required activities that are described in the set $AR = \{ar_i\}$ defined in Formula (5) of the previously presented **problem model**. Formally, the set of required layers L is defined as:

$$L = \bigcup_{ar_i \in AR} \lambda(ar_i) \tag{13}$$

where $\lambda(ar_i) = \{l_i\}$ and l_i is a required layer by the required activity ar_i.

Tools Base Initialization for a Layer: In this phase, a base set of tools belonging to a layer is determined and the existence of at least one connection interface with the tools in the previously instantiated lower layers is validated. Formally, this set is defined as $H_{l_j} = \{h\}$ and it is subject to the following constraints:

Let H_{l_i} be the set of tools in the previously instantiated low level layer l_i, it is satisfied that:

$$\forall h \exists h' | h \in H_{l_j}, h' \in H_{l_i} : \exists \langle h, h' \rangle \tag{14}$$

Tools Weighting and Selection: For each one of the elements h inside the candidate tool base H_{l_i}, the measure of affinity with the requirements of the related problem $F(p, H)$ is computed. Then a selection of these tools that maximize the measure of affinity with the problem is performed, generating the subset of tools $H* \subseteq H$ with an optimal affinity value. Formally, this set is defined as follows:

$$H* = \left\{ h_i | h_i = \arg \max_{h \in H_{l_i}} F(p, h) \right\} \tag{15}$$

Feasible Architecture Instance Deployment and Evaluation: After determining the set of tools $H*$ for each required architectural layer, the following sequence of actions is performed:

1. Necessary connections are established between required interfaces.
2. Tools are enriched with the configuration recommendations and the related knowledge around its usage and implementation.
3. The affinity of the feasible architecture with the problem instance is evaluated. This evaluation is computed based on the affinities of the selected tools with the problem instance.

4 BiDArch: Design and Implementation

4.1 BiDArch Ontologies

BiDArch relies on a pair of ontologies to describe two domains of knowledge. In the first one, the Hadoop ecosystem toolkit repository is defined in terms of the features offered by tools. In the second one, the related knowledge to build a solution architecture is represented.

Figures 3 and 4 present the two ontologies previously mentioned. A high level abstraction model is shown with main classes and relationships for each of them.

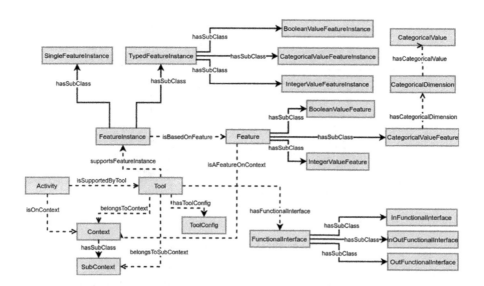

Fig. 3. Hadoop ecosystem toolkit repository ontology fragment.

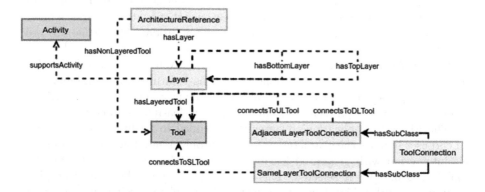

Fig. 4. Proposed reference model architecture ontology fragment.

4.2 BiDArch Architecture

The BiDArch Web application has a *client/server* architecture based on a three-layer model (data, process and presentation) as shown in Fig. 5. This application publishes a set of microservices that provides decoupled functionality and integrates information from various sources.

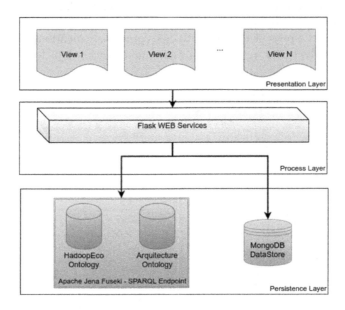

Fig. 5. BiDArch architecture.

BiDArch's user-defined problems instances are stored in a document-oriented database server instance, MongoDB [7]. Apache Jena Fuseki [8], a well-known SPARQL [9] *endpoint* stores the two application ontologies. Additionally, this server allows to set an inference engine or reasoner that is attached to the ontology, and in this way, triples that represent the additional knowledge are produced.

The application's business logic is deployed in Web services using the Web *microframework, Flask* [10]. It's done conceiving a future interoperability with external applications. In this Web application, many requests are received and attended to define a problem and build a solution feasible architecture.

The BiDArch application's frontend is intended to facilitate explicitly how an end user handles the characterization of a problem and dynamically supports his interaction with generated feasible solution architectures. To do this, the tool ExtJS 6.2 [11] is selected. This tool offers a large collection of graphics components with a high level of maturity. The problem specification process is supported by a wizard using a reversible sequence of steps. The visualization of the automatic built architectures is done using the open-source library, JointJS [12], taking advantage of the ease of use that it offers to model them as a graph.

5   Results

To show the obtained results in this paper, the following use case is presented:

The company NayroMan S.A.S, dedicated to the online marketing of bikes and spare parts, is interested in a software solution that allows to analyze its visitors' behavior while they are navigating on its concurrent website to browse product catalogs, compare bike parts and hopefully make a purchase. To do this, the company needs to ingest the web log activity during a long time, and then process and analyze the huge dataset obtained. Finally, the results need to be extracted to a traditional relational database management system to be used in its website.

This use case is based on the need for any architect to ingest and process data in a cluster and then extract the results to a relational database as Oracle. It was selected because it provides a composition of several required activities and represents a traditional scenario that can be associated with many problem instances.

BiDArch allowed to specify and build a feasible solution architecture for a real complete use case fully decomposed into several subproblems [13, pp. 74–84]. Each one of these five summarized problem instances are referenced below:

1. Data ingestion in a cluster [13, p. 75].
2. Batch processing after a previous data ingestion [13, p. 77].
3. Processed data extraction [13, p. 79].
4. ETL operations in a large dataset [13, p. 81].
5. Real time data querying in a large dataset [13, p. 83].

Tables 3 and 4 summarize the general requirements and specific required activities for a problem instance related to the presented use case respectively.

Table 3. General requirements for this problem instance.

Requirement	Weight	Value
Multilanguage	6	True
Fault tolerant	6	True
Security	7	True
Disk I/O usage	7	Low
Feature richness	7	High
Support level	5	High
Usability	7	Medium

BiDArch simplifies the definition of the problem model. The user is guided to select the main activities required to set a problem instance and the dependent related tasks are added automatically until Column 1 on Table 4 is complete.

Table 4. Requirements per activity for this problem instance.

Activity	Requirement	Weight	Value
Persistence	Data compression	5	True
	Strictly consistent writes	3	True
Ingestion	Filtering data to import	7	True
	Timeliness of data ingestion	5	Micro-batch
Batch processing	Job submission	5	True
	Automatic task execution optimization	7	True
	Resource manager independence	5	True
	Shared variables	3	True
Data extraction	Support for Oracle JDBC specific connectors	7	True
	Exporting with All-or-Nothing semantics	7	True
	Data copy validation	5	True
	Support for insertion and updates	5	True

Then, for each required activity, BiDArch suggests an indexed list of features that can be required, allowing to complete the requirements listed on Column 2. For each one of these requirements, the user is able to set up the importance updating the related requirement weight according to its particular problem's knowledge. Finally, a value of satisfaction for every feature is suggested and can be changed from a list of possible values in a specific domain.

Naturally, the richer a problem model is, the more effective the resulting selection of tools is. Therefore, the problem must be sufficiently well-defined regarding the general requirements and specific required activities to produce optimal feasible architectures. On the other hand, the definition of enough conditions to determine if every problem instance is well defined, is a very difficult task that can be done as future work.

BiDArch selects the tools highlighted on Table 5 that have the maximum value of affinity with the requirements of this problem instance.

Table 5. Selected tools with maximum affinity.

Layer	Activity	Tool	Affinity (units)
Persistence layer	Data storage	**HDFS**	**45**
		Apache HBase	18
Data movement layer	Data ingestion	**Apache Flume**	**57**
		Apache Kafka	15
		Apache Sqoop	35
Processing layer	Batch processing	**Apache Spark**	**58**
		Apache Hadoop MapReduce	5
Data movement layer	Data extraction	**Apache Sqoop**	**35**

The affinity calculations—presented on Table 5—are made using the notion of affinity expressed in Formula 11 and consuming the knowledge stored into the Hadoop ecosystem ontology. Additionally, the definition of more complex heuristics and processes to compute the affinity between tools and a problem instance can be very interesting. For example, a heuristic that considers the global impact of a group of features supplied by a particular tool, instead of the benefit obtained by individual features, can extremely reduce the complexity of generated feasible architectures.

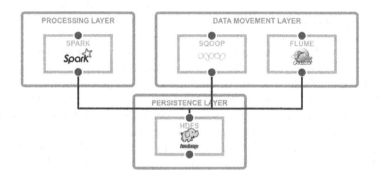

Fig. 6. Generated feasible solution architecture.

BiDArch automatically builds the feasible solution architecture shown in Fig. 6. Additionally, it provides an explanation to the question of why these tools were selected and evidences the notion of affinity they hold with the problem definition. It also enriches the architect's knowledge related to tools, showing him some parameters configuration suggestions and the available interfaces for integration with external tools.

6   Related Work

Big data players represent a set of large companies with the ability to overcome all the drawbacks and challenges facing many organizations interested in resolving big data problems. Among these companies are: Amazon AWS[1], IBM[2], HortonWorks[3], Cloudera[4], MapR[5]. The solutions provided by these companies focus in various use cases such as real-time analysis of security, risk detection and management in financial services, information flow processing, large datasets storage optimization, among many others. To do this, they use many ecosystem

---

[1] Amazon AWS, Inc. - Website: https://aws.amazon.com/.

[2] IBM, Inc. - Website: http://www.ibm.com/.

[3] Hortonworks, Inc. - Website: http://hortonworks.com/.

[4] Cloudera, Inc. - Website: https://www.cloudera.com/.

[5] MapR, Inc. - Website: https://www.mapr.com/.

tools such as Apache HBase [14], Apache Storm [15], Apache Hive [16], Apache Kafka [17] and obviously Apache Spark [18] among many others.

Some of these companies have their own Hadoop distributions with a range of additional features that represent differentiating values to their customers. Within these distributions of Hadoop stand out: HDP (Hortonworks Data Platform) [19], CDH (Cloudera Data Hub) [20] and MapR Data Platform [21].

Some experts on this area have made important publications to transmit their experience in the use of these tools and the lessons learned related to scenarios in which they are useful, as well as the way of how they should be used. For instance, the work [22] made by a group of Cloudera's members serves as a recommendation guide for the design Hadoop applications architectures and shows the implementation of some real use cases.

The project [2] presents an extensive list of tools that have some relationship with Hadoop ecosystem. The tools included in this repository are classified in several categories such as distributed file systems, multi-purpose distributed and scalable processing frameworks, NoSQL repositories and NewSQL repositories that aim to provide the same scalable performance of NoSQL systems for traditional relational database systems, among others.

As for reference architecture models, the Lambda architecture repository [23] consolidates a large number of electronic resources related to Lambda architecture real applications. This architecture was designed by Nathan Marz as a scalable and fault tolerant model for *big data* applications design. On the other hand, J. Kreps questions the Lambda architecture model in his article [24], exposing the weaknesses around the previous model and creating a new one that focuses on the possibility of offering the ability to develop, test, debug and operate solutions built on top of a simple processing framework.

7   Conclusions

This work presents the design and implementation of BiDArch, a feasible solution architectures generator for problem instances in *big data* domain. Based on a study and analysis of the documentation related to Hadoop ecosystem tools, we developed an ontology that describes the knowledge related to the tools' features.

The architectural requirements description process is performed according to the tools' features set on the previous ontology. This process is implemented using a three-step wizard that allows to represent three elements: a list of generic attributes, a set of general requirements that are related to transversal tools features and a set of requested activities. The particular requirements for any requested activity are defined in function of a specific set of features provided by a sub set of Hadoop ecosystem tools. This process is defined on top of two abstraction models: the **general requirement model** and the **problem model**. The first model encapsulates the definition of any requirement using the tool features and sets an order relationship between problem requirements. On the other hand, the problem model abstracts the three elements used to describe a problem instance.

With the tool presented in this work, we build feasible solution architectures for *big data* problems that require some traditional activities. These activities include: storage, ingestion, extraction, *batch* processing, ETL operations and querying on huge *datasets*. However, there are some specialized activities that need to be added, such as scalable processing on graphs and *machine learning*, which comprise an important domain of problem instances and enable high value solutions for some business targets.

References

1. Achari, S.: Hadoop Essentials - Tackling the Challenges of Big Data with Hadoop. Packt Publishing (2015)
2. Roman, J.: The Hadoop ecosystem table. https://hadoopecosystemtable.github. io/
3. IBM, Inc.: The four V's of big data. http://www.ibmbigdatahub.com/infographic/ four-vs-big-data
4. Scott, J.: 7 key technologies in the evolving hadoop ecosystem. http:// www.dbta.com/BigDataQuarterly/Articles/7-Key-Technologies-in-the-Evolving- Hadoop-Ecosystem-111505.aspx
5. Apache Spark MLlib. http://spark.apache.org/mllib/
6. Apache Mahout. https://mahout.apache.org/
7. MongoDB for giant ideas. https://www.mongodb.com/
8. Apache Jena Fuseki. https://jena.apache.org/documentation/fuseki2/index.html
9. W3C. SPARQL Query Language for RDF. https://www.w3.org/TR/ rdf-sparql-query/
10. Flask (A Python Microframework). http://flask.pocoo.org/
11. Ext JS 6.2.0. http://docs.sencha.com/extjs/6.2.0/
12. JointJS: Visualize and interact with diagrams and graphs. https://www.jointjs. com/opensource
13. Sosa, J.: Generador de arquitecturas de solución sobre el ecosistema Hadoop para problemas de Big Data. https://webcat.uniandes.edu.co/uhtbin/webcat
14. Apache HBase. http://hbase.apache.org/
15. Apache Storm. http://storm.apache.org/
16. Apache Hive. https://hive.apache.org/
17. Apache Kafka. https://kafka.apache.org/
18. Apache Spark. https://spark.apache.org/
19. Hortonworks, Inc.: Hortonworks data platform. https://hortonworks.com/ products/data-center/hdp/
20. Cloudera, Inc.: CDH is Cloudera's 100% open source platform distri- bution. https://www.cloudera.com/products/open-source/apache-hadoop/ key-cdh-components.html
21. MapR, Inc.: The MapR converged data platorm. https://mapr.com/products/ mapr-converged-data-platform/
22. Grover, M., Malaska, T., Seidman, J., Saphira, G.: Hadoop Application Architec- tures, 1st edn. O'Reilly Media Inc., Sebastopol (2015)
23. Bijnens, N., Hausenblas, M.: Lambda Architecture. A repository dedicated to the Lambda Architecture (LA). http://lambda-architecture.net/
24. Kreps, J.: Questioning the Lambda Architecture. https://www.oreilly.com/ideas/ questioning-the-lambda-architecture

Automatic Acquisition of Controlled Vocabularies from Wikipedia Using Wikilinks, Word Ranking, and a Dependency Parser

Ruben Dorado[1(✉)], Audrey Bramy[1], Camilo Mejía-Moncayo[2], and Alix E. Rojas[2]

[1] École de technologie supérieure, Université du Québec, Montreal, Canada
ruben.dorados@gmail.com, audrey.bramy@gmail.com
[2] Universidad EAN, Bogotá, Colombia
{cmejiam,aerojash}@universidadean.edu.co

Abstract. Controlled vocabularies are important resources used in several tasks such as machine translation, text summarization, and text analysis. However, the development of such resources is expensive and time-consuming. On the other hand, the Wikipedia, a free collaborative encyclopedia, contains plenty of semi-structured information that can be used by an automatic process to create new resources. This paper proposes a method to extract semantic information from the Wikipedia in the form of a controlled vocabulary. The method combines keywords obtained for a specific Wikipedia article with three different strategies: using Wikipedia annotations called wikilinks, a ranking measure to obtain keywords from text, and a dependency parser. To evaluate the model, we performed an analysis in terms of coverage and performance of the acquired vocabulary using WordNet as a gold standard.

1 Introduction

Wikipedia is a free-access encyclopedia, written by all people over the world. Wikipedia is targeted to a general public that can collaborate by improving its content through a web interface. Users of Wikipedia edit the content by adding new text that includes annotations with information such as links between articles and categories. These annotations turn a Wikipedia article into a complex semantic network of inter-related terms.

Wikipedia's articles contain different sort of metadata annotations: content tables, categories, inter-language links, and Wikipedia markup annotations in the text such as links to internal pages, called freelinks. That information has been used previously for knowledge discovery using the Wikipedia. Some examples include mining information from content tables or Wiki infoboxes [8], taxonomy deriving from Wiki categories [18], and topic hierarchies from Wiki categories [4].

In this study, we analyze the use of a Wikipedia to obtain a set of keywords given a specific article. We explore three different methods to acquire semantic related words. Such set of keywords can be seen as an entry in a semantic

© Springer International Publishing AG 2017
A. Solano and H. Ordoñez (Eds.): CCC 2017, CCIS 735, pp. 32–43, 2017.
DOI: 10.1007/978-3-319-66562-7_3

dictionary or a controlled vocabulary, where the title of the Wikipedia article is the concept and the terms related to the concept are the keywords. We argue that such set of semantically related keywords can be useful in many scenarios, such as text classification where they can be used as the features for a classifier to reduce the dimensionality. We propose to acquire a set of words is, in fact, a controlled vocabulary, where the name of the article is the main term and text and annotations on the article contain the edges to other nodes. For example, given a set of terms such as *Christianity*, *Bible*, *Computer*, and *Operating system*, it is possible to acquire a set of related terms for each of those articles. This controlled vocabulary can be used for different tasks like text classification, where each of the terms is related to one of the following categories: *Religion* or *Computers*. Then, the categorized vocabulary can be used as feature reduction method to classify the documents, reducing the time an usual method need to analyze a document since the possible set of features is being reduced.

In this study, we focus on using three different methods to obtain keywords from a specific Wikipedia article. The first one is using annotations or links to other articles in a Wikipedia article called wikilinks. The second one is extracting keywords from the text taking into account the frequency of the term in the article. The third one consists in extracting terms from syntactic relations in the sentences of the text. Finally, we propose a method to combine them all, improving the precision of the quality set of keywords.

We experimented with the information provided by a set of specific articles and compared the results with the well know resource called WordNet. WordNet organizes terms as a group of synonyms called synset, similar to a thesaurus. We used WordNet to measure the quality of the acquired set of words for each article by comparing it with the terms found on the WordNet synset.

The rest of this article is explained as follows. Section 2 provides information about the related work in information extraction using the Wikipedia. Section 3 contains an explanation of the three methods used to extract keywords. Empirical results are presented and discussed in Sect. 4, while Sect. 5 presents the conclusions.

2   Related Works

Recently, Wikipedia has been used as a source of information. To give some examples, [10] describes a method to obtain semantic information for word sense disambiguation. [9] presents a system that trains himself with data from Wikipedia to perform text annotation and add semantic information to plan texts. [2] extracts taxonomies from Wikipedia. Other works have proved that information such as hyperlink relations between a set of documents [1] can be used to obtain a set of interrelated terms. Another kind of studies have used hyperlinks in the Wikipedia provides more information than in a common website [11].

Dependency parsing has proven to be a method to acquire semantic patterns because they are capable of representing relations between elements of a sentence. For example, a dependency parser has been used to infer rules for automatic question answering [7] and paraphrase identification [15]. Generally, these systems have been focused on relation extraction, the identification of particular relations between items in the text. The relations used and the method to acquire them vary across studies. For example, [17] used an [s,v,o] (subject, verb, direct object) tuples as patterns while [14] allow any analysis to be a possible pattern. Machine learning algorithms are also used to learn and identify instances of relations such as iterative semi-supervised algorithms [3] where usually the algorithm is provided with an initial set of patterns and attempts to increase the number of patterns and relations between items. This work, however, is more related to the work of [13,14], in the sense it uses different sources to rank terms obtained by a dependency parser. [14] used tf-idf method to rank patterns according to where they tended to occur in documents which were known to contain information of interest while [13] proposed a ranking term measure to give a value to terms obtained by patterns obtained from the result of a dependency parser.

3   Acquiring a Controlled Vocabulary from Wikipedia

This section describes the proposed process to acquire a controlled vocabulary from the Wikipedia. First, we describe the general process to acquire a set of keywords related to a specific article using three approaches and then mixing them. Then, we explain each one of the three approaches: wikilinks, word ranking, and dependency parsing.

We define a controlled vocabulary as a list of concepts, also called entries, where each of them has selected list of words semantically related to such concept. A controlled vocabulary provides a method to organize knowledge. It is used in subject indexing schemes, subject headings, thesauri, taxonomies and other forms of knowledge organization systems. A controlled vocabulary specifies the use of terms and phrases related to a concept, similar to a dictionary, where each of the entries has a set related terms. In this case, we are interested in acquiring only the terms related to a concept. For example, given the concept 'cat', the task is to acquire a set of words that are related such as 'animal', 'eat', or 'kitty'.

We propose to acquire a controlled vocabulary for specific terms using articles from the Wikipedia. Figure 1 depicts the extraction process. Having an article from Wikipedia, two different extraction processes are performed: extraction of terms using wikilinks (1) and text extraction (2) Extraction of terms using wikilinks is explained in detail in Sect. 3.1, while text extraction consists in extracting the text of the article. Extraction of terms using term frequency (3) and a dependency parser (4) is performed on the extracted text. Both processes are explained in Sects. 3.2 and 3.3 respectively. Finally, the three set of keywords is combined to finally obtain one set of keywords (5) The combination process is explained in Sect. 3.4.

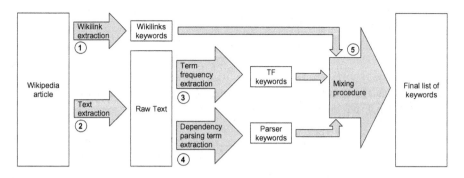

Fig. 1. Pipeline of the proposed method to extract the controlled vocabulary.

3.1   Extraction of Terms Using Wikilinks

The structure of Wikipedia can be exploited in several ways. In particular, we are interested in using the so-called *wikilinks*. A wikilink is a reference to different Wikipedia article. For example, the following wikitext has been extracted from the article *Operating system*:

> Examples of popular desktop operating systems include [[Apple Inc.|Apple]] [[OS X]], [[Linux]] and its variants, and [[Microsoft Windows]]. So-called [[mobile operating system]]s include [[Android (operating system)|Android]] and [[iOS]].

It can be seen in the above example that it is possible to extract valuable keywords such as *Linux, Microsoft Windows,* and *Android,* represented by wikilinks. Furthermore, this information can be easily extracted since wikilinks maintain a regular pattern in the source of the article. One of the questions addressed in this article is how much of this information provided by all the wikilinks of a specific article is closely related to the semantic meaning of the article.

3.2   Term Acquisition Using Frequency Ranking

Frequency word ranking has been used to distinguish important terms in texts under the assumption that the importance of a term that occurs in a document is proportional to its term frequency. In other words, a term that frequently appears in the text is supposed to be important. The frequency of a term t in a document a, in this case, a Wikipedia article, is calculated as follows:

$$f(t, a) = f_{t,a} = count(t, a),$$

where the $count(t, a)$ is number of times the term t occurs in the document a.

However, in cases where the length of documents vary adjustments and normalizations are often made. We use the following measures to evaluate the usefulness of a term t_i:

– Term Frequency score (TF):

$$\frac{f_{t,a}}{\max\{f_{t',a} : t' \in a\}},$$

where $f_{t,a}$ is the number of times the term t appears on the article a.

– Scaled Term Frequency score (STF):

$$(1-k) + k\frac{f_{t,a}}{\max\{f_{t',a} : t' \in a\}},$$

where $f_{t,a}$ is the number of times the term t appears on the article a and $k \in R^{+}, 0 < k \le 1$.

– Log-scaled Term Frequency score (LTF):

$$\frac{\log(f_{t,a})}{\log(\max\{f_{t',a} : t' \in a\})}$$

The term frequency score is the normalized count of the terms, where the value of term that occurs the most is 1 and a non important term in the document is close to 0. The scaled term frequency score provides a method to change the minimum weight of the frequency score using the k parameter. In other words, the STF score transforms any given value of the TF score from the range $[0,1]$ to $[k,1]$. The scale is k equal to 0.5. Finally, the log-scaled term frequency score allows to normalize a given value penalizing low occurrences. The logarithm is applied in both the numerator and denominator so that the value is a number between 0 and 1. It worth mentioning that the normalized and scaled scores only work when combining the scores with other functions or to compare ranked works in different documents. If the purpose is to extract words in a document, the transformations will not help since they are all monotonic functions.

3.3   Dependency Parsing

A dependency parser is a computational tool that takes a sentence as input and returns a tree, called a parse tree, that contains connections between words according to their relationships. In the tree, each node represents a word, child nodes are words that are dependent on the parent, and edges are labeled according to the relationship between the parent an the child. The set of relationships depends on the grammar. For example, The Universal Dependencies (UD) project defines a set of relations that by developing cross-linguistically treebank annotation for several languages [12]. Under such grammar, there is a relation called *nsubj* between two words $w1 \rightarrow w2$ that represents the case when $w2$ is a noun that is the syntactic subject of the clause. As an example, in the phrase 'Colombia won the tournament', the word Colombia' is related to the verb 'won' through the relation *nsubj*. Figure 2 shows the result of the parse tree of such sentence.

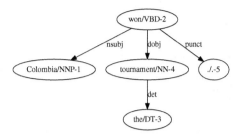

Fig. 2. An example of the dependency tree for the sentence 'Colombia won the tournament'.

We propose the use of three relations to consider possible terms as candidates:

– Any word that is the dominant of a nominal subject (nsubj) and is a verb and is related to the target concept. In Fig. 2 the word 'won' would be selected. The objective of this relation is to find verbs.
– Any word that is a noun, has a dominant relation of any type with another node m, and m is the target concept. In Fig. 2 the word 'tournament' would be selected. The objective of this relation is to find nouns.
– Any word that is a noun and also has dominant relation of any type with any node. The objective of this relation is also to find nouns.

3.4 Mixing Sets of Terms

The last part of the proposed method consists of combining the three previous methods to obtain keywords into one. We propose such combination by transforming each of the three previous methods into a normalized score and using a set of mixing coefficients, one for each of the scores. In the case of keywords extracted using the wikilink approachx, we propose the usage of an indicator function $WL(t, a)$ that returns 1 if the article a contains a wikilink with the term t and 0 if it does not. For the term frequency score for a particular document $WF(t, a)$, we propose the use one of the scores defined in Subsect. 3.2. For the third one, the dependency parser usage, we also propose to use an indicator function $DP(t, a)$ that returns 1 if any of the relations listed in Sect. 3.3 regarding the term t is found in the article a and 0 if it does not. Finally, a set of mixing coefficients α, β, and γ are used to control the importance of each score. The formal mathematical definition is stated as follows:

$$rank(t, a) = \alpha WL(t, a) + \beta WF(t, a) + \gamma DP(t, a),$$

where $\alpha \in R^+$, $\beta \in R^+$, and $\gamma \in R^+$, $\alpha + \beta + \gamma = 1$, are the mixing coefficients, $WL(t, a)$ is wikilinks indicator score, $WF(t, a)$ is a word frequency score, and $DP(t, a)$ is the dependency score.

3.5   Evaluation Measures

In order to test the performance of our method, we propose the use of *precision* and *recall* measures. More specifically, given this set of target terms for a specific article $S = \{s_1, s_2, ..., s_K\}$, the precision of a set of terms $T_a = \{t_1, t_2, ..., t_N\}$ obtained for an article a related to S is calculated as:

$$precision(T_a) = \frac{count(\{t' \in S\})}{N},$$

the recall as:

$$recall(T_a) = \frac{count(\{t' \in S\})}{K},$$

and F1 score as:

$$F1score(T_a) = 2 * \frac{precision * recall}{precision + recall}$$

4   Experimentation and Results

We used the Wikipedia dump, which is a file containing all the information stored in the Wikipedia in a specific time. To test our method, we used the also publicly available and well-known resource WordNet. WordNet organizes terms as a group of synonyms called synset. Each entry is called a synset and can be acquired using its surface word similar to a thesaurus. We used WordNet to measure the quality of the acquired set of words. For each selected article, we searched for all the possible terms that belong to the synset and that also are in the article. For example, given the article 'Sport', we included the term 'champion' if it is found in the Wikipedia article and also in the WordNet synset for 'sport'.

There are different measures to obtain synsets in the Wikipedia. We selected its the top terms using Wu-Palmer Similarity (WUP) [16] and Leacock-Chodorow Similarity (LCS) [6] with a threshold of 0.7. Finally, we used precision, recall, and F1 scores to evaluate the performance of the different strategies, as described in Subsect. 3.5.

For experimentation, we selected a set of articles related to four topics: entertainment, religion, countries, and computers. We made a list of concepts related to the four topics and verified their existence in the WordNet. After such selection, we end up with 18 articles to analyze the quality of keywords obtained by the different methods. The list of articles can be seen on Table 1. Each article was pre-processed to extract all the information described previously: the set of wikilinks and text from a set of preselected articles. We used the publicly available library *wikitools* to extract the text and wikilinks from a set of articles[1]. With the text, we removed stopwords, punctuation, and transformed the text to lower case. Then, we selected two set keywords for each article using term frequency and a dependency parser. We used the Stanford Dependency Parser [5]

---

[1] The library can be found the in the git repository: https://github.com/rdorado79/wikitools.

Table 1. Results of the experimentation in counts

Concept	Count	Wikilinks			TF-score			Parser		
		Prec	Rec	F1	Prec	Rec	F1	Prec	Rec	F1
Sport	177	0.083	0.107	0.094	0.155	**0.232**	**0.186**	**0.313**	0.028	0.052
Religion	128	0.076	**0.320**	0.123	0.120	0.180	**0.144**	**0.185**	0.094	0.124
Baseball	29	0.016	**0.276**	0.031	**0.093**	0.138	**0.111**	0.051	0.103	0.068
Soccer	9	0.025	**0.667**	0.049	0.308	0.444	**0.364**	**0.400**	0.222	0.286
CPU	34	0.009	0.059	0.016	**0.078**	**0.118**	**0.094**	0.068	0.088	0.077
Horse	95	0.070	**0.305**	0.114	0.056	0.084	0.068	**0.153**	0.095	**0.117**
Country	46	0.136	0.174	0.152	**0.159**	**0.239**	**0.191**	0.125	0.022	0.037
Computer	114	0.045	**0.158**	0.071	0.094	0.140	**0.112**	**0.109**	0.053	0.071
God	108	0.074	**0.278**	0.117	0.117	0.176	**0.141**	**0.189**	0.093	0.124
Dog	141	0.044	0.099	0.061	0.076	**0.113**	0.091	**0.164**	0.071	**0.099**
Planet	66	0.064	**0.379**	0.109	0.172	0.258	**0.206**	**0.200**	0.167	0.182
Jehovah	31	0.032	**0.226**	0.055	**0.065**	0.097	**0.078**	0.036	0.032	0.034
Music	269	0.093	**0.294**	0.141	0.141	0.212	**0.170**	**0.261**	0.112	0.156
Canada	35	0.013	**0.257**	0.024	**0.038**	0.057	0.046	0.036	0.086	**0.050**
Animal	171	**0.132**	0.234	**0.169**	0.070	0.105	0.084	0.000	0.000	NaN
Colombia	29	0.016	**0.448**	0.030	0.070	0.103	0.083	**0.111**	0.207	**0.145**
Cat	106	0.051	**0.198**	**0.082**	0.038	0.057	0.045	**0.060**	0.028	0.038
Japan	61	0.016	**0.180**	0.029	0.055	0.082	0.066	**0.059**	0.082	**0.068**
Average	91.61	0.055	**0.259**	0.081	0.106	0.157	**0.127**	**0.140**	0.088	0.096

as dependency parser in our experimentation. Finally, we measured how many of these terms are in the selected subset of terms from its WordNet synset.

Table 1 shows the results obtained. The first column shows the name of the article. The second column shows the number of targeted words for the specific article. Columns 3 to 5 show the results for wikilinks, 6 to 8 for term frequency, and columns 9 to 11 for the dependency parser. It can be concluded that Wikilink term extraction gives the best recall between the three methods. This suggests that the keywords obtained using the wikilinks contain similar semantic information to Wordnet. In terms of precision, the keywords obtained by the dependency parser strategy seem to correlate WordNet slightly better. However, the best F1-score on average is obtained by the keywords obtained using the term frequency measure.

Despite the relatively low values, a thorough analysis of the extracted word shows encouraging results. Table 2 depicts examples of the extracted words for each one of the three methods. It can be seen the nature of the words extracted by each method. Terms extracted from wikilinks tend to be concepts that complement the Wikipedia article since wikilinks are links to other articles. Examples of these are 'tie-breaking' for the article 'Sport', or 'equus ferus' for 'Horse'. Terms extracted using the frequency are generally those that are used to explain important concepts in the document and appear frequently. Examples of these

Table 2. Random examples of the words extracted for some articles

Concept	Wikilinks	TF score	Dependency
Sport	Competitive, physical activity, game, entertainment, tie-breaking methods, tournament, champion, playoffs	Participants, physical, participation, used, including, competition, increase, football, international, games	Charter, technology, participation, venue, popularity, definition, set, noun, running, spectator, football
Religion	Cultural system, behaviors, world view, sacred texts, societal organisation, human, existence, divine	World, one, people, law, study, faith, belief, beliefs, include, sacred, god, defined, science, countries	View, essence, king, edition, violence, absence, excess, influence, part, role, affects, morality, deals, science
CPU	Electronic circuit, computer, instruction, computer program, input/output, control unit, main memory, design	Instruction, cpus, clock, instructions, program, memory, data, performance, operation, processors, execution	Dissipation, cycle, context, perform, hardware, performance, designs, design, parallelism, operation, execute
Horse	Extant, subspecies, equus ferus, mammal, equidae, evolved, eohippus, domesticate, anatomy, colors	Breeds, developed, wild, domesticated, bones, four, animals, well, human, age, world	Tibia, blood, movement, appears, style, control, rider, breed, pedigree, domestication, remains, zebra, animal
Country	Political geography, sovereign state, political division, people, league of nations, united nations, states	Country, sovereign, state, word, political, independent, associated, territory, english, govpubs, gov, derived	Version, coal, part, sense, name, resident, sovereign state, region

are 'faith' in the article 'Religion' and 'territory' in 'Country'. Finally, terms extracted with the dependency parser are generally functional words related to the concept. For example, the word 'movement' for 'Horse' or the word 'affect' for religion. It worths mentioning that the patterns used were very simple and are susceptible to improvement in many ways. This is left for future work.

The last part of the method consist in combining all the previous scores. We combined all the three previous strategies using the method proposed in Sect. 3.5. We performed an exhaustive search to find the optimal values for α, β, and γ and found that appropriate values for the model are a high β and a γ value slightly higher than α. This is possible due that the TF score is lower than the other two and tend to be ruled out if it is not properly scaled and weighted.

Table 3. Results of mixing method with $\alpha = 0.08$, $\beta = 0.8$, and $\gamma = 0.12$ and $k = 0.8$ for the scaled TF score.

Concept	TF score			Scaled TF score			Log TF score		
	Prec	Rec	F1	Prec	Rec	F1	Prec	Rec	F1
Sport	0.121	0.215	0.155	0.137	0.243	0.175	**0.153**	**0.271**	**0.196**
Religion	**0.158**	**0.227**	**0.186**	**0.158**	**0.227**	**0.186**	0.119	0.180	0.143
Baseball	0.059	0.103	0.075	**0.136**	**0.207**	**0.164**	0.133	**0.207**	0.162
Soccer	0.182	0.222	0.200	**0.364**	**0.444**	**0.400**	**0.364**	**0.444**	**0.400**
CPU	0.078	0.118	0.094	**0.096**	**0.147**	**0.116**	0.077	0.118	0.093
Horse	**0.117**	**0.179**	**0.142**	0.117	0.179	0.142	0.106	0.168	0.130
Country	0.169	0.283	0.211	**0.182**	**0.304**	**0.228**	0.141	0.239	0.177
Computer	0.081	0.123	0.098	0.089	0.140	0.109	**0.108**	**0.175**	**0.134**
God	**0.170**	**0.241**	**0.199**	0.170	0.241	0.199	0.168	0.241	0.198
Dog	0.086	0.142	0.107	**0.091**	**0.149**	**0.113**	0.082	0.135	0.102
Planet	**0.212**	**0.273**	**0.238**	0.202	**0.273**	0.232	0.196	**0.273**	0.228
Jehovah	0.053	0.065	0.058	0.053	0.065	0.058	**0.077**	**0.097**	**0.086**
Music	**0.170**	0.227	0.194	**0.170**	0.227	0.194	0.169	**0.230**	**0.195**
Canada	0.063	**0.086**	0.072	**0.068**	**0.086**	**0.076**	0.037	0.057	0.045
Animal	**0.116**	**0.187**	**0.143**	0.083	0.135	0.103	0.080	0.129	0.098
Colombia	0.167	**0.207**	0.185	**0.188**	**0.207**	**0.197**	0.150	**0.207**	0.174
Cat	**0.045**	**0.075**	**0.057**	0.045	0.075	0.057	0.033	0.057	0.042
Japan	**0.074**	**0.115**	**0.090**	0.074	0.115	0.090	0.072	**0.115**	0.089
Average	0.118	0.171	0.139	**0.135**	**0.192**	**0.158**	0.126	0.185	0.149

Also, a higher γ allows preference from the dependency parser, since they have a high precision.

Table 3 shows the results with $\alpha = 0.12$, $\beta = 0.8$, and $\gamma = 0.1$ for the mixing model. We also set $k = 0.08$ for the k parameter of the scaled TF score. As stated previously, we obtained such values by performing an exhaustive search. It can be seen in the table that we successfully combined all the three strategies, wikilinks, term frequency, and the dependency parser, into one method obtaining an increment in the F1-score. It is also difficult to say which of the TF score used is better than other. Numerically, the scaled TF score outperforms the other two but log scaled TF score gives close values to the best found. An improvement of the proposed method in terms of the F1 score can be observed by comparing the best averaged the F1 score of a single method (term frequency score: 0.127) and the average of the best combined F1 score: 0.158, with an improvement of 0.031.

5   Conclusions

We presented a method to obtain a set of keywords, called a controlled vocabulary, from Wikipedia articles. The method consists in the combination of other three different methods to obtain keywords: wikilinks, term frequency, and a dependency parser. The presented method successfully combine all the three strategies, wikilinks, term frequency, and the dependency parser, into one achieving an increment in the F1-score.

In relation with the words extracted from each one of the methods, we can say that they differ substantially. As discussed in the results section, terms extracted from wikilinks tend to be additional concepts that complement the article. Terms extracted using the frequency are keywords that are used to explain important concepts in the document. Finally, terms extracted with the dependency parser are generally functional words related to the concept.

With respect to the dependency parser, we used three different relations: direct object of the term (dobj) to obtain verbs and two based on nominal subjects (nsubj) to obtain nouns. The method showed to be very promising in terms of precision and it worth improve the patterns in the future.

We expect to extend this work in many ways. First, we expect to perform a deeper analysis that involves a much higher number of articles. Second, we would like to explore the idea of acquiring automatically grammatical rules for dependency parsing based term acquisition. Third, we would want to perform a deeper analysis on the extraction of keywords using wikilinks. We used a binary function that does not allow to rank and compare words using such method. It would be interesting to propose a rank method for extraction of keywords using wikilinks.

Finally, the main contribution of this paper is to provide a method to improve the semantic acquisition of keywords from documents. Such set of keywords can be used for several tasks such as document classification, where the keywords can be used as features according to the categories. This is one of the main motivations of this study. The method can also be used to acquire more complex resources such as thesauri or semantic networks from resources such as the Wikipedia. For example, it can be used to create a semantic structure similar to WordNet, where each article is used as a concept and the list of keywords provides a semantic description of the concept. Then, a distance between two concepts can be calculated by several means such as counting the number of terms that are shared by the two concepts.

References

1. Davison, B.D.: Topical locality in the web. In: Proceedings of the 23rd Annual International Conference on Research and Development in Information Retrieval (SIGIR 2000), pp. 272–279 (2000)
2. Garcia, R.D., Rensing, C., Steinmetz, R.: Automatic acquisition of taxonomies in different languages from multiple wikipedia versions. In: Proceedings of the 11th International Conference on Knowledge Management and Knowledge Technologies (i-KNOW 2011) (2011)

3. Greenwood, M.A., Stevenson, M.: Improving semi-supervised acquisition of relation extraction patterns. In: Proceedings of the Workshop on Information Extraction Beyond The Document (IEBeyond Doc 2006), pp. 29–35 (2006)
4. Hu, L., Wang, X., Zhang, M., Li, J., Li, X., Shao, C., Tang, J., Liu, Y.: Learning topic hierarchies for wikipedia categories. In: Proceedings of the 53rd Annual Meeting of the Association for Computational Linguistics and the 7th International Joint Conference on Natural Language Processing (Volume 1: Long Papers) (2015)
5. Klein, D., Manning, C.D.: Accurate unlexicalized parsing. In: Proceedings of the 41st Annual Meeting on Association for Computational Linguistics (ACL 2003), vol. 1, pp. 423–430 (2003)
6. Leacock, C., Chodorow, M.: Combining Local Context and WordNet Similarity for Word Sense Identification. In: WordNet: An Electronic Lexical Database, pp. 265–283. MIT Press, Cambridge, MA (1998)
7. Lin, D., Pantel, P.: Discovery of inference rules for question-answering. J. Nat. Lang. Eng. **7**, 343–360 (2001)
8. Lin, W.P., Snover, M., Ji, H.: Unsupervised language-independent name translation mining from wikipedia infoboxes. In: Proceedings Conference on Empirical Methods in Natural Language Processing (EMNLP 2011), pp. 43–52 (2011)
9. Makris, C., Plegas, Y., Theodoridis, E.: Improved text annotation with wikipedia entities. In: Proceedings of the 28th Annual ACM Symposium on Applied Computing, pp. 288–295 (2013)
10. Mihalcea, R.: Using wikipedia for automatic word sense disambiguation. In: Proceedings of NAACL HLT 2007, pp. 196–203 (2007)
11. Nakayama, K., Hara, T., Nishio, S.: A thesaurus construction method from large scale web dictionaries. In: 21st International Conference on Advanced Information Networking and Applications, pp. 932–939 (2007)
12. Nivre, J., de Marneffe, M.C., Ginter, F., Goldberg, Y., Hajic, J., Manning, C.D., McDonald, R., Petrov, S., Pyysalo, S., Silveira, N., Tsarfaty, R., Zeman, D.: Universal dependencies v1: A multilingual treebank collection. In: LREC 2016 (2016)
13. Stevenson, M., Greenwood, M.A.: Dependency pattern models for information extraction. Depend. Pattern Model. Inf. Extract. **7**(13), 13–39 (2009)
14. Sudo, K., Sekine, S., Grishman, R.: Automatic pattern acquisition for Japanese information extraction. In: Proceedings of the Human Language Technology Conference (HLT 2001) (2001)
15. Szpektor, I., Tanev, H., Dagan, I., Coppola, B.: Scaling web-based acquisition of entailment relation. In: Proceedings of the 2009 Conference on Empirical Methods in Natural Language Processing, pp. 41–48 (2004)
16. Wu, Z., Palmer, M.: Verb semantics and lexical selection. In: Proceedings of the 32nd Annual Meeting of the Association for Computational Linguistics, pp. 133–138 (1994)
17. Yangarber, R.: Counter-training in discovery of semantic patterns. In: Proceedings of the 41st Annual Meeting on Association for Computational Linguistics, pp. 343–350 (2003)
18. Zesch, T., Gurevych, I.: Analysis of the wikipedia category graph for nlp applications. In: Proceedings of the TextGraphs-2 Workshop (NAACL HLT 2007), pp. 1–8 (2007)

Stochastic Traffic Analysis of Contemporary Internet High-Speed Links

Fabio G. Guerrero$^{(\boxtimes)}$

Universidad del Valle, Cali, Valle, Colombia
fabio.guerrero@correounivalle.edu.co

Abstract. The aim of this paper is to provide a better understanding of the stochastic properties of contemporary Internet traffic. Previous known studies on Internet Traffic are based on samples captured several years ago, where both Internet's applications and user behavior were quite different from today's world. In this paper, a stochastic traffic analysis of contemporary Internet traffic seen on high-speed backbone links, where the size of the analyzed samples amounts to the billions of packets, is presented. The probability distribution functions of packet inter-arrival time, number of packets per unit of time, and average packet length were both calculated and analyzed. A wide sense stationarity test for the observed traffic was performed on several time scales. In order to analyze the self-similarity properties of the process, the Hurst index, obtained through the wavelet transform method, was employed. Finally, decimation used a useful auxiliary technique in the process of scale invariance analysis is presented.

Keywords: Internet · Traffic · Stochastic process · Stationarity · Self-similar process

1 Introduction

Having a good understanding about the statistical nature of Internet traffic and its underlying processes is useful for many tasks on communication networks engineering. For example, suitable statistical models improve the ability of simulation tools to produce useful results. It also makes it easier translating traffic engineering results to the capacity planning of networking devices such as routers and switches. A better understanding of how the information is carried would allow planning better quality of service schemes. It can also be helpful to identify certain types of traffic anomalies. Traffic analysis results may also, within certain limits, be useful in similar problems such as vehicular network traffic and other types of networks with high traffic volumes, such as those expected, for instance, in the Smart Grid. There are several other reasons why it is important to analyze the nature of contemporary Internet traffic. The world's telecommunications capacity on the global information infrastructure has grown in recent years at a rate of 28% per year [5]. Core networks links nowadays can employ

© Springer International Publishing AG 2017
A. Solano and H. Ordoñez (Eds.): CCC 2017, CCIS 735, pp. 44–58, 2017.
DOI: 10.1007/978-3-319-66562-7_4

fiber optic links using DWDM (Dense Wavelength Division Multiplex), using 160 wavelengths, with rates of 40 Gbit/s, or more, per optical torrent or lambda. Beyond this increasing in data rates, the interaction between users, the information content being transported and the nature of the sources on the Internet have changed over the past decade [9]. For example, in recent years the use of social networks, applications peer-to-peer, commercial exploitation of multimedia content, content delivery networks, cloud-based applications, among others, are Internet usages solidly established. The ITU (International Telecommunication Union) has also identified a substantial change in the way the Internet is being used over the last five years [6]. Therefore it is important to study how these transformations are changing the statistical nature of Internet traffic and assess to what extent the findings of the initial studies on the subject are still valid.

However, there are several reasons why to analyze the statistical nature of Internet traffic can be a challenging task. For example, there can be reasons of security and confidentiality on the captured information which prevent network administrators making public the samples of the traffic seen on their networks. This is so because having access to the traffic would enable easily viewing the contents of the information carried by unencrypted protocols such as HTTP, POP3, DNS. It would also enable knowing the websites a user has browsed, identifying source and destination IP addresses to disclose geographic locations, etc. The very high data rates being used today at the interfaces of current networking devices, particularly at the network's core, also demand using specialized hardware to capture information with a minimum loss of packets or PDUs (Protocol Data Units) in terms of Rec. ITU-T X.200. For example, capturing traffic on a 10 Gbps link can quickly produce several dozens of millions of packets in just sixty seconds. Usually, traffic capturing is performed on packets flowing at the network layer level of the OSI (Open System Interconnection) model. Since the volume of captured data can be quite big, large amounts of storage resources would be required. Internet backbone links are being upgraded to 100 Gbps thus demanding even faster-capturing hardware. Once the traffic samples have been captured, the analysis and processing of such vast amounts of data could demand considerable computational resources and computation time. Other practical limitations could exist such as the ability for researchers located on the edge of the network to have access to traffic samples on links at the network core because Internet high-speed links are usually under the administrative authority of broadband providers. Also, there is a difficulty on controlling individual contributions on the total traffic to discriminate the effect of individual sources.

Despite having been published more than two decades ago, Leland's classic paper on scale invariance [7] is still a landmark on the self-similar nature of Internet traffic. Samples used in that work, such as *pAug*, are still employed in studies on the subject, see for example [12]. The most comprehensive modern study known by the author on the stochastic behavior of Internet traffic is [8], which employed samples from the year 2005. A work on identification of flows in Internet backbone traffic is presented in [13].

This paper presents an analysis of Internet traffic samples captured on the equinix-chicago data collection monitor and the equinix-sanjose monitor both maintained by the CAIDA project at University of California [3], San Diego, California. The equinix-chicago monitor, located at Chicago, IL, collects data on a high-speed link between Seattle and Chicago. The equinix-sanjose monitor, located at San Jose, CA, collects data on a high-speed link between San Jose and Los Angeles. The primary statistical analysis carried out in this work are on inter-arrival time, number of packets per time interval, packet length, scale invariance analysis, and wide sense stationarity. The rest of the paper is organized as follows: in Sect. 2 the methods and tools used in the work are presented. In Sect. 3 the main results of the work are presented. In Sect. 4 a discussion of the results is done, and in Sect. 5 the main conclusions of this work are summarized. All units employed are expressed in international system SI units. Aspects such as computational complexity, big data and similar are beyond the scope of this paper. For a good treatment on big data analysis the reader is referred to the work of Tsai [10].

2   Methodology

The samples employed in this work correspond to Internet traffic, IP packets, captured by the CAIDA project[1]. Both the equinix-chicago monitor and equinix-sanjose monitor collect data from high-speed Ethernet interfaces[2] associated to backbone links from a first-tier ISP. The Internet traffic information made available by the CAIDA project is provided essentially in two types of files: packet arrival time stamps, given to nanosecond precision, and packet headers in pcap format. A sixty-minute sample of anonymized traffic taken on 21 may 2015 (from 1300 UTC to 1359 UTC) equinix-chicago monitor is initially considered for detailed analysis, although traffic samples from other dates, including samples from 2016, are also discussed.

The sixty-minute sample of traffic observed on 21 may 2015 for direction A, for instance, totals 22.8 GB for time stamps files after decompression, and 68.2 GB for the pcap files. Similarly, for direction B totals 29.0 GB for time stamps, and 84.2 GB after decompression for the pcap files. For reducing memory requirements during processing, a pre-processing of the time stamps files using Linux commands was done. Similarly, the pcap files were preprocessed using the tshark command to extract the information of IP packets. All the data processing on this paper was done on a Linux Mint desktop PC with 6 GB of memory and a Intel Xeon X5670 @ 2.93 GHz processor.

2.1   Identification of Main Variables

Figure 1 shows the variables from the packet arrival process selected for analysis in this paper: packet inter-arrival time (IAT), number of packets per unit of

---

[1] All the traffic samples used in this work are available on request at CAIDA's project website.

[2] 10 Gbit/s data rate, later updated to 100 Gbit/s.

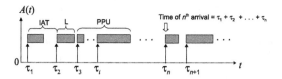

Fig. 1. Packet arrival process variables.

time (PPU), and packet length (L). For the PPU variable, the observation unit of time can be freely chosen (e.g. 1 ms, 20 ms, 1 s, etc.).

While additional variables could have also been identified such as, for instance, the number of bytes in a time interval[3] [1], these variables were chosen for considering them both the most relevant and used in the classical analysis of packet arrival processes.

2.2 Basic Statistics

Initially, we calculate the basic statistics for each variable during the observed sixty-minute period. However, calculating the mean and variance of such a large amount of data in a direct way would demand high computational resources. We use, to obtain the mean, the law of iterated expectations given by

$$m = E[X] = E[E[X|Y]] = \frac{1}{n} \sum_{s=1}^{k} n_s m_s \qquad (1)$$

where k is the number of sections, n_s is the number of elements in section s, m_s is the mean of section s, and n is the total number of elements. For example, if we obtain first the mean of each individual minute of traffic, the total mean over a period of sixty minutes would be $\frac{1}{n} \sum_{s=1}^{60} n_s m_s$.

Similarly, for the variance we can use the extended law of total variance given by

$$var[X] = E[var(X|Y)] + var(E[X|Y]) \qquad (2)$$

Table 1 shows the basic statistics for the traffic sample captured on 21 may 2015 on the equinix-chicago monitor. Direction A goes from Chicago to Seattle and direction B in the opposite way. For the variable PPU we choose the observation period $\Delta t = 10$ ms, that is, 3.6×10^5 bin counts over the entire sixty-minute period.

During the sixty-minute period, for direction A, 99.8985% of the packets found were IPv4 packets and the rest, 0.1015%, were IPv6 packets; for direction B, 99.8132% of the packets were IPv4 packets and the rest IPv6 packets. Since such a small number of IPv6 packets may lead to inconclusive results no further analysis was attempted for IPv6 packets.[4]

---

[3] Also called arrival work.

[4] The mean of the IPv6 payload length found in the sixty-minute samples was 182.018 bytes with standard deviation 372.498 bytes, for direction A. For direction B the mean of the payload length was 439.833 and the standard deviation 558.4 bytes.

Table 1. Traffic samples basic statistics (21 May 2015)

Variable	Direction A	Direction B
Number of packets	1 086 058 246	1 379 431 772
Mean (IAT)	3.31474×10^{-6}	2.60977×10^{-6}
Var (IAT)	1.05339×10^{-8}	8.29013×10^{-9}
Mean (PPU)	3016.83	3831.76
Var (PPU)	171430	183111
Mean (L_{IPv4})	777.717	846.405
Var (L_{IPv4})	470310	459008

2.3 Stationarity Analysis

To determine if the classical mathematical framework of stationary processes could be employed in the analysis, it is important to know whether the packet arrival process under study corresponds to a stationary process or not. As it is well known from stochastic process theory, the three properties a wide sense stationary (WSS) process must exhibit are: (1) the mean of the process is time invariant, (2) the variance of the process is time invariant, and (3) the correlation of the process does not depend on the origin of time but only on the difference of time observation $|i - j|$.

The first two conditions can be considered together by means of the $\frac{Var}{Mean}$ relation. Figure 2 shows a plot of $\frac{Var}{Mean}$ for the IAT variable using sixty sections of one minute each one. As shown in Fig. 2, the results are very similar in both directions, except for a slight proportion factor in direction B for small values of $\frac{Var}{Mean}$ due to smaller both mean and variance.

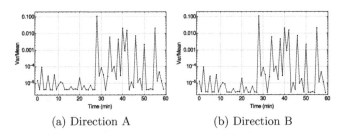

(a) Direction A   (b) Direction B

Fig. 2. IAT $\frac{Var}{Mean}$ relation (21 May 2015)

Figure 3 shows a plot of $\frac{Var}{Mean}$ for the PPU variable considering bins of 10 ms, that is $\Delta t = 10$ ms. As observed, the PPU variable has a somewhat similar profile than that of the IAT variable in the sixty-minute period. It can be also observed that the profile of $\frac{Var}{Mean}$ for PPU is quite similar in both directions.

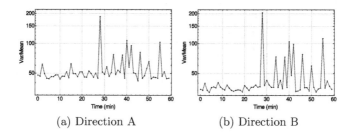

(a) Direction A   (b) Direction B

Fig. 3. PPU $\frac{Var}{Mean}$ relation (21 May 2015)

In both Figs. 2 and 3, we can observe that the first two stationarity conditions do not hold for the entire sixty minutes. This observation is in agreement with the well-known fact that Internet traffic varies considerably on large scales where some patterns can be identified (e.g. 24-hour traffic profiles).

In order to find a potential range of minutes where stationarity can hold we look for the largest range of adjacent minutes with the least values of the $\frac{Var}{Mean}$ relation. Applying this criteria, the range of minutes $t_{\{m51-m54\}}$ with values of $\frac{Var}{Mean}$ equal to $4.20861 \times 10^{-6}, 4.23225 \times 10^{-6}, 4.65925 \times 10^{-6}$, and 4.1806×10^{-6} for $t_{m51}, t_{m52}, t_{m53}$, and t_{m54} respectively, in direction A, is identified. We need to test next if the range $t_{\{m51-m54\}}$ satisfies the third condition of stationarity. In general, the autocorrelation function is a useful tool to estimate the degree of dependence (memory) of a time series. In the context of stochastic processes the autocorrelation function is equivalent to the normalized auto variance. The expression of the autocorrelation is

$$\rho(k) = \frac{\sum\limits_{i=1}^{n-k} (x_i - \mu)(x_{i+k} - \mu)}{\sum\limits_{i=1}^{n-k} (x_i - \mu)^2} \tag{3}$$

where $\mu = E[x]$.

To test if the autocorrelation function depends on the time difference but not on the particular time of observation, we calculate the autocorrelation function, using Eq. 3, for the traffic of the individual minutes $t_{m51}, t_{m52}, t_{m53}$, and t_{m54}. Figure 4 shows the autocorrelation curves for a lag k from 1 to 35000 using an exponential moving average with smoothing constant 2×10^{-3}. In Fig. 4 we can see that the autocorrelation curves are quite similar despite the fact that they correspond to different minutes of traffic, and therefore to different origins of time. The range of minutes $t_{\{m51-m54\}}$ thus satisfies the wide sense stationarity property in very reasonable terms.

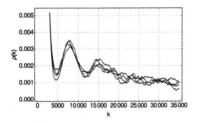

Fig. 4. IAT autocorrelation minutes t_{m51}, t_{m52}, t_{m53}, and t_{m54}.

3 Results

3.1 Packet Inter Arrival Time (IAT)

Figure 5 shows the probability density function (PDF) of IAT for the stationary range $t_{\{m51-m54\}}$ using a histogram with bins of width $0.15\,\mu s$, where for comparison purposes the probability of an exponential distribution function with the same λ has been overlaid (solid line). Figure 5 shows that the observed PDF of IAT does not fully follow the exponential distribution traditionally assumed for packet inter arrival time in communications networks queuing theory. As it will explained in Sect. 4, the shape of IAT's probability curve is related to the distribution of L (packet length).

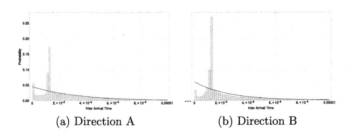

(a) Direction A   (b) Direction B

Fig. 5. Histogram of IAT probability

3.2 Number of Packets per Unit of Time (PPU)

Figure 6 shows the probability function distribution for the PPU variable during $t_{\{m51-m54\}}$, considering time intervals of 10 ms and 1 ms respectively. In Fig. 6 a Poisson probability distribution with $\mu = 3014.38$ packets/s (dir A) and $\mu = 301.438$ packets/s, and the same number of data in every case is overlaid for comparison purposes respectively. As observed in Fig. 6 there is also a discrepancy between the observed distribution and the Poisson distribution, the latter being both more concentrated around the mean and symmetrical.

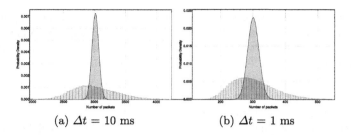

(a) $\Delta t = 10$ ms   (b) $\Delta t = 1$ ms

Fig. 6. Observed PPU pdf (histogram) versus Poisson distribution (continuous line). Direction A

3.3 Packet Length (L)

Figure 7 shows the probability distribution function for the length of IPv4 packets (variable L), over the range of minutes $t_{\{m51-m54\}}$. For direction A the mean was 755.343 bytes, and the standard deviation 687.304 bytes. For direction B, the mean was 856.057 bytes, and the standard deviation 213.895 bytes.

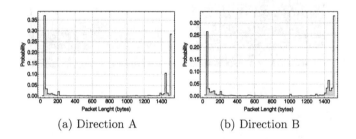

(a) Direction A   (b) Direction B

Fig. 7. IPv4 packet length distribution during $t_{\{m51-m54\}}$

As shown in Fig. 7, IP packets on average tend to be either very long or very short. As we will discuss in Sect. 4 this behavior is closely related to the way TCP/IP works. The observed distribution of L does not match a exponential distribution as commonly assumed in M/M/1 models, and hypothesis tests were also rejected.

A conjecture about the shape the PDF of L is related to the way TCP works. The TCP protocol is by far the most used transport layer protocol. In the analyzed samples, for example, TCP accounted for the 89.9% of the packets at the transport layer. In TCP a request made by the sender can be followed by a stream of packets of maximum length, whit the sender acknowledging them by short ACK packets [4].

3.4 Traffic Self-similarity

A traditional way to visually infer the existence of self-similarity in a process is seeing if the resulting process looks similar after m level aggregation [12]. The m

level aggregation technique consists in creating a new series averaging groups of m data. For example, the first value of the series $X^3(k)$ will be $\{X(1) + X(2) + X(3)\}/3$, and therefore, the length of the resulting series will be one third that of the original.

We prefer to use m *level decimation* instead, where a random choice is made out from every group of m data. For example, the first value of the series $X^3(k)$ will be a random choice from $\{X(1), X(2), X(3)\}$. While, in this example, two thirds of the data are also discarded, the surviving values still belong to the original series.

Figure 8 shows a plot for the decimation series $X(k), X^2(k), X^4(k)$, and $X^8(k)$ during $t_{\{m51-m54\}}$ in direction A for the PPU process, that is, the number of packets received during the time interval Δt. In Fig. 8, time intervals equal to $\Delta t \times df$ are used where df is the decimation factor, with $df = 1, 2, 4$, and 8 respectively. Although Fig. 8 suggests self-similarity or scale invariance of the PPU process under decimation, a more formal verification is required.

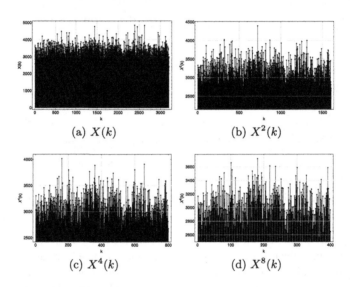

(a) $X(k)$ (b) $X^2(k)$

(c) $X^4(k)$ (d) $X^8(k)$

Fig. 8. Visual invariance behavior under decimation

There are several mathematical estimators for the analysis of scale invariance in stochastic processes, however some fail in the presence of non stationarity trends artifacts, such as, for instance, a deterministic frequency signal superimposed over the time series [8]. The solution to these kind of problems in the analysis of long range dependencies was given in [1], using the detail coefficients of the wavelet transform. Abry's method for estimating the Hurst index H, which was improved in [11], has also the nice property of being computationally efficient. In Abry's method the *logscale* diagram is essentially a plot of $log(var[dX(j, k)])$ versus j where the dX are the detail coefficients of the wavelet transform at octave j. A detailed explanation of Abry's method for long range dependency analysis is beyond the scope of this article. The interested reader is strongly advised to read the original article [11].

Figure 9 shows the logscale diagram of the PPU variable, $\Delta t = 1$ ms, using a discrete Daubechies wavelet transform of order four. In Fig. 9 several regimes of scale invariance can be identified, that is, the range of octaves where the logscale plot is linear. For example, the range of octaves from $j = 1$ to $j = 4$ where $H = 0.852261$; from $j = 6$ to $j = 8$ where $H = 0.804819$; and from $j = 8$ to $j = 11$ where $H = 0.756384$.[5]

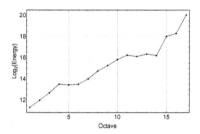

Fig. 9. PPU Logscale diagram $t_{\{m51-m54\}}$

Figure 10a shows the logscale diagram for the inter arrival time variable (IAT) for $t_{\{m51-m54\}}$ where, similarly, several regimes of invariance can be identified. For example, the range of octaves from $j = 5$ to $j = 11$ where $H = 0.764394$; and the range from $j = 14$ to $j = 20$ where $H = 0.779361$.

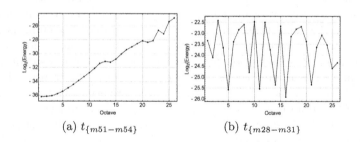

(a) $t_{\{m51-m54\}}$ (b) $t_{\{m28-m31\}}$

Fig. 10. IAT logscale diagram

However, when considering a non stationarity range, scale invariance is no longer identifiable. For instance, Fig. 10b shows the logscale diagram for IAT during the range of minutes $t_{\{m28-m31\}}$.

---

[5] For the range of octaves from $j = 4$ to $j = 6$, $H \approx 0.5$, indicating the process is essentially random with no memory at those scales.

3.5 Autocorrelation

Figure 11 shows the autocorrelation plot of PPU for the range $t_{\{m51-m54\}}$ for time units $\Delta t = 1\,\mathrm{ms}$ and $\Delta t = 10\,\mathrm{ms}$ respectively, using an exponential moving average with smoothing constant 0.1. As it can be observed in Fig. 11, the autocorrelation plots are very similar, providing thus another hint on the self similarity of the PPU process.

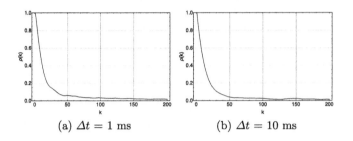

(a) $\Delta t = 1$ ms   (b) $\Delta t = 10$ ms

Fig. 11. Autocorrelation variable PPU, $t_{\{m51-m54\}}$

4 Discussion

4.1 Stationarity

Figure 12 shows a plot of the IAT $\frac{Var}{Mean}$ relation for samples acquired at two different dates on the Chicago monitor. Figure 12a corresponds to a date before an upgrading of the links capacity to 100 Gbit/s at the end of March 2015. As it is well known, statistical multiplexing, the principle used by packet switching, is very useful for bursty traffic sources so that transmission resources are not demanded at the same time, and if this condition occurs, queuing is allowed until the transmission resources become available. For example, in an average residential Internet subscription full transmission capacity is used only about 9.7% of time [5]. Increasing the transmission rate causes the transmission delay to be lowered so that the inter arrival time can experience much more variability. The plot of Fig. 12b (as well as that of Fig. 2) shows that after the link capacity update, on a scale of minutes, the traffic process was essentially not stationary, although some subranges holding the stationarity condition may be identified as it was explained in Subsect. 2.3. In simple words, for the analyzed samples after link upgrade, stationarity was the exception and not the rule on a scale of minutes. This in agreement with the fact that a fully loaded link will tend to produce a stationary process from the point of view of the IAT variable since there is much less variability on the inter-arrival process. Likewise, we attribute the similarity of the IAT plot in both directions, see Figs. 2 and 3 for instance, to the underlying TCP mechanism where usually every transmitted segment is answered by the receiver with an acknowledgment segment. This

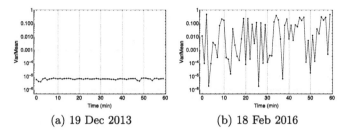

(a) 19 Dec 2013   (b) 18 Feb 2016

Fig. 12. IAT $\frac{Var}{Mean}$ relation $t_{\{m00-m59\}}$. Chicago monitor, direction A

observation suggests a correlation linking the PPU as well as the IAT variable in both directions.

Figure 13 shows a plot of the IAT $\frac{Var}{Mean}$ relation for samples acquired at two different dates on the San Jose monitor, between Los Angeles and San Jose, before link interface upgrading. The link load on 19 Dec 2013 was close to 47.1%, and on 19 Jun 2014, 46.4%.[6]

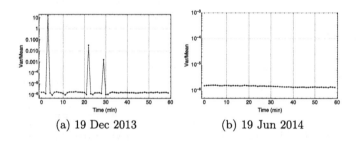

(a) 19 Dec 2013   (b) 19 Jun 2014

Fig. 13. IAT $\frac{Var}{Mean}$ relation $t_{\{m00-m59\}}$. San Jose monitor, direction A

4.2   Probability Distributions

The histogram of IAT probability density of Fig. 5a shows that the probability distribution does not fully follow an exponential probability distribution. The peaks observed in Fig. 5a are related to the most common packet lengths in the sample. In Fig. 7a, for example, the most common packet lengths seen during $t_{\{m51-m54\}}$ were 40, 1500 octets. This packet lengths means inter arrival times of at least $1.2\,\mu s$ and $32\,ns$ respectively, which are in agreement with the largest peaks observed in Fig. 5a. Figure 6 also shows that the probability distribution of the PPU variable does not match a Poisson distribution as traditionally has been considered[7].

---

[6] CAIDA's project reported that the San Jose monitor temporarily suspended providing captures after June 2014. At the time of this writing, no samples after that date were available.

[7] The main reason for using both the exponential and Poisson model, in many cases, is to make the analysis of the problem more tractable.

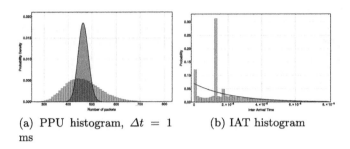

(a) PPU histogram, $\Delta t = 1$ ms   (b) IAT histogram

Fig. 14. May 17 2012, San Jose monitor, $t_{\{m00\}}$, direction A

The discrepancy for the PPU variable may be due to the process not being memoryless, as it is shown on the correlation plot of Fig. 11. These probability distributions were consistently observed when analyzing other traffic samples. For instance, Figs. 14 and 15 show a plot of PPU, $\Delta t = 10$ ms, and IAT, for the sixty seconds $t_{\{m00\}}$, from traffic taken on the San Jose monitor on May 17 2012 and Jun 19 2014 respectively.

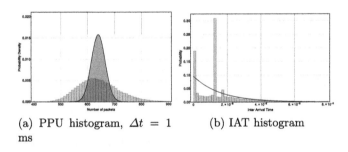

(a) PPU histogram, $\Delta t = 1$ ms   (b) IAT histogram

Fig. 15. June 19 2014, San Jose monitor, $t_{\{m00\}}$, direction A

4.3   Monofractality

It is known that for a stochastic process that exhibits monofractality the probability distribution of the detail coefficients of the wavelet transform when rescaled by a factor $2^{-j(\hat{H}-\frac{1}{2})}$ converge towards the same normal distribution [1]. Figure 16 shows the rescaled coefficients probability distributions of PPU during $t_{\{m51-m54\}}$ (Chicago monitor, 21 May 2015, direction A), for the range of octaves $j = 1, .., 4$, where $H = 0.852261$ with a almost constant curve slope. As expected, this coincidence does not hold for all ranks in the logscale diagram. The same is valid for the IAT variable, whose probability distribution function does not exactly match the probability distribution of an exponential random variable. This differs from the classical Poisson processes in which the arrival of each new package system is considered independent of past history [2]. The autocorrelation plot of Figs. 4 and 11 clearly show that both IAT and

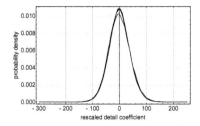

Fig. 16. PPU rescaled coefficients probability. Octaves $j = 1, ., 4$.

PPU processes have memory. However, this observation is only valid for those ranges that have the stationarity property. Unlike the traffic analyzed by Leland in his 1993 work [7], the PPU variable, Fig. 9, exhibits several scale invariance regimes in accordance with the much greater heterogeneity of the Internet traffic nowadays. However it should be noted that Leland's traffic was captured over a LAN (Local Area Network), instead of a WAN.

5   Conclusions

The Internet traffic samples analyzed in this work showed scale invariance by ranges on the logscale diagrams. This result suggests that the nature of Internet traffic has certainly changed in recent years, coinciding with the evolution experienced by the global information infrastructure protocols, usages, and behaviors. However, the self-similar behavior is observed only for those ranges of time where the wide sense stationarity condition is met. The probability distribution of both IAT and PPU variables found did not fully follow the standard exponential distributions and Poisson models respectively. The autocorrelation of the IAT and PPU processes similarly indicates that they both have memory. Likewise, the shape of the $\frac{var}{mean}$ relation plot for both the IAT and PPU variables on the studied samples were consistently similar in the both directions suggesting a correlation of these variables in both directions.

In general, the length of the IP packets is divided into rather long or short packets. Also, the probability distribution function of packet length L does not follow an exponential distribution. The traffic observed in the analyzed samples at the transport layer is mostly dominated by the TCP protocol. Thus the shape of L's distribution may be explained by the TCP transfer mechanism, where the download of a large object at the application layer triggers the transmission of a significant number of packets of maximum length with their corresponding short-length ACK segments in the opposite direction. The probability distribution of IAT supports this observation since its peaks of probability are in agreement with the most common packet lengths.

Before interface data rate upgrading, stationarity on a scale of minutes was easily found at both the Chicago, and San Jose monitors. After the link interface was upgraded, for the equinix-chicago monitor, determining ranges where stationarity holds on the analyzed samples on a time scales of minutes was more difficult due to the much more variability in inter-arrival times. Instead, it was easier to find regions where wide sense stationarity took place on a time scale of seconds. This clearly showed how strict the concept of stationarity is in practice. This work also showed how challenging it may be analyzing traffic behavior on a longer time scale using the traditional techniques. In this sense, decimation showed to be a useful tool helping to identify visual invariance.

References

1. Abry, P., Veitch, D.: Wavelet analysis of long-range-dependent traffic. IEEE Trans. Inf. Theory **44**(1), 2–15 (1998)
2. Bertsekas, D.P., Tsitsiklis, J.N.: Introduction to Probability, 2nd edn. Athena Scientific, Belmont (2008)
3. CAIDA: equinix-sanjose.dirA.20150521-130000.UTC.anon. The CAIDA UCSD Anonymized Internet Traces 2015 (2015). http://www.caida.org
4. Comer, D.E.: Internetworking with TCP/IP. Principles, Protocols, and Architecture, 6th edn. Pearson, Essex (2014)
5. Hilbert, M., López, P.: The world's technological capacity to store, communicate, and compute information. Science **332**(6025), 60–65 (2012)
6. ITU-D: Measuring the information society 2015. Technical report. International Telecommunictions Union (2015)
7. Leland, W.E., Wilson, D.V.: On the self-similar nature of ethernet traffic. Comput. Commun. Rev. **23**, 203–213 (1993)
8. Smith, R.D.: The dynamics of internet traffic: self-similarity, self-organization, and complex phenomena. Adv. Complex Syst. **14**(06), 905–949 (2011)
9. Sundaram, H., Xie, L., De Choudhury, M., Lin, Y.R., Natsev, A.: Multimedia semantics: interactions between content and community. Proc. IEEE **100**(9), 2737–2758 (2012)
10. Tsai, C.-W., Lai, C.-F., Chao, H.-C., Vasilakos, A.V.: Big data analytics: a survey. J. Big Data Springer Open J. (2015)
11. Veitch, D., Abry, P.: A wavelet-based joint estimator of the parameters of long-range dependence. IEEE Trans. Inf. Theory **45**(3), 878–897 (1999)
12. Veitch, D.: Scale invariance in computer network traffic. In: Scaling, Fractals and Wavelets, Chap. 12, pp. 413–436. Wiley, Hoboken (2009)
13. Zhang, Z., Wang, B., Lan, J.: Identifying elephant flows in internet backbone traffic with bloom filters and LRU. Comput. Commun. **61**, 70–78 (2015)

SEAbIRD: Sensor Activity Identification from Streams of Data

José Molano-Pulido ⑩ and Claudia Jiménez-Guarín (✉) ⑩

Computing and Systems Engineering Department, School of Engineering,
Universidad de los Andes, Bogotá, Colombia, Carrera 1 Este # 19A-40, 111711 Bogotá, Colombia
{jf.molano1587,cjimenez}@uniandes.edu.co

Abstract. Active Aging is a proposal that aims to improve life quality, as a person grows old. One of the main use cases of this concept is the application of products and services based on technology; this approach, known as Ambient Assisted Living (AAL). An important activity performed by AAL is the discovery of the user's activities of daily life (ADL) employing data retrieved from sensors set on an active home. Still, there is no much research on implementing a system for ADL discovery which contemplates factors as personalized configuration, sensor failure and user privacy. We identify the main requirements that an ADL discovery system must have. Then, we propose an ADL discovery schema that supports these necessities. Finally, we explore the application of adaptable and sensor-failure tolerant ADL discovery models over recorded data from a real user. This exploration evidences that our proposed models can adapt to the above-mentioned scenarios and still have an outstanding performance on activity discovery process.

Keywords: Ambient Assisted Living (AAL) · Sensor data analysis · Data stream mining

1 Introduction

Humankind has extended the average life expectative, this indicator has increased by one third over the last four decades. This can be regarded as an achievement, however concerns about the impact on quality of life standards arise from this phenomenon [1]. Beyond the global population growing, calculations show that 60 years old and beyond population will increase on a factor of 10 from 1950 to 2050 [2]. From this issue, World Health Organization (WHO) proposes Active Aging, defined as "the process of optimizing opportunities for health, participation and security in order to enhance quality of life as people age". Active Aging also intends to protect people autonomy and independency [3].

Many Active Aging approaches consist on technology based applications such as pervasive computing, they are known as Ambient Assisted Living (AAL) on this context [4]. An important task performed by AAL is the detection of Activities of Daily Living (ADL). This process is useful because it supports procedures as Noncommunicable diseases (NCD) detection by generating early alerts, reducing risk factors and

© Springer International Publishing AG 2017
A. Solano and H. Ordoñez (Eds.): CCC 2017, CCIS 735, pp. 59–71, 2017.
DOI: 10.1007/978-3-319-66562-7_5

diminishing caring costs [5]. However, current proposals for ADL discovery do not contemplate factors as personalized configuration, sensor failure and user privacy.

In this work, we present a model for ADL detection that process data flows from affordable home sensors in order to infer the inhabitant activities in a pervasive way. The target users are people living alone as we want to focus on independent elder adults. They represent a high risk for social security systems, and extend their safe life at home is a responsible and priority society choice. The model considers that each person has her own way of doing the daily routines and so it adapts to specific user patterns, behavioral changes over the time and sensor failures. The main contribution of this paper is the model proposal and experimentation about activity inference from stablished ADL datasets. Also, performance tests are done in order to validate the appliance of these models over different scenarios. This paper is organized as follows: Sect. 2 presents the main requirements and restrictions that an ADL discovery system must have, Sect. 3 introduce our proposed schema for ADL discovery, Sect. 4 summarizes the experimentation process, Sect. 5 recaps the main findings over the model application results, Sect. 6 gathers related work research and Sect. 7 presents the related conclusions and further work.

2 Activity Discovery from Sensor Data

The activity discovery from sensor data problem faces multiple issues associated with the hardware elements involved on a potential solution and the differences on user's behavior. Plus, the fact of applying a solution on an Active Aging context involves additional restrictions and requirements.

First, every application using sensors must consider that these devices are subject to functional errors that may lead to issues such as wrong or missing values. Chalmers [6] presents a list that collects the main sources of error and uncertainty when using sensors. Initially, he introduces the device error caused by a failure on sensor components, circuits or drivers. It can also be caused by low battery events. In addition, there is the deployment issue error, it may be caused by disconnections from the device and the object of interest. This can lead to distortion or even loses on the data measured. Another critical error source on the application of sensors is noise. Noise is defined as small oscillations on the recorded values caused mainly by electrical interference. Chalmers presents other known sources and describes some tactics and strategies to mitigate these error causes. Knowing about these error sources is useful to set the restrictions and requirements of any system which employs sensor data to discover user´s activities.

Also, sensors may have different sampling rates depending on the type of technology used. In practical terms, this means that data provided from these devices may arrive on different frequencies to a certain application. Therefore, it is necessary to propose methods that allow to represent data recorded in such way that temporal inconsistencies can be avoided.

Another issue that must be approached by a system for activities discovery is the variety of behavioral patterns that users may adopt. Lago et al. [7] proved that the application of a static model can negatively affect the performance of a system. In this study they showed that temporal, location and activity patterns differ notably between two test subjects. They also proved that even on the analysis of the same subject there are changes of behavior routines over the time. Finally, this study showed that the habits of a user also depend from the context. Variables such as the day of week or the season have an impact on a subject's activity pattern. This result is relevant because it states that a system for ADL discovery must be personalized and change-adaptable.

Finally, the Active Aging approach requires that the mechanism for activities discovery maintains the person's autonomy and independence [3]. This necessity is strongly tied with the privacy of the user, thus system implemented must guarantee that the recorded and processed data cannot be accessed by third parties.

3   Activity Discovery Model

The proposal of the current work follows the requirements from the stream data mining problem applied to an Active Aging context. As mentioned, a model which detects user's ADL must be able to fit personal patterns, behavioral changes over the time and sensor failures. From these premises, a general scheme for an Activity Discovery Model is proposed on Fig. 1.

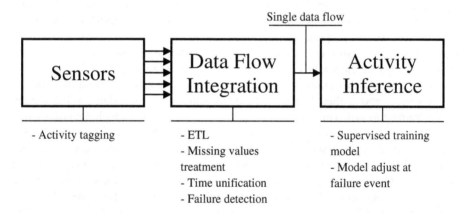

Fig. 1.   General schema for activity discovery model

A specific group of target activities must be defined prior to the process of device selection. ADL such as showering, sleeping and cooking may be candidates for this group. Then, for each particular activity discovery the appropriate set sensors must be defined. These devices must be able to measure the variables related with the ADL selection. For example, pressure sensors on beds may be necessary to detect sleeping activity. Also, this group of devices shall comply with the specifications from Active Aging context. In the context of this work, this requirement implies that devices must avoid possible privacy violations. Thereupon, a set of actions considered as potential privacy contraventions is defined. Particularly, this work includes on this category any actions related with video and sound recording. For these reasons, all the sensors related with video or photo cameras, as well as microphones acting further than noise level sensor, are discarded from this solution. Finally, the group of allowed sensors for the model includes any kind of device which does not interfere with user´s autonomy, independence and comfort. That is why sensors which require from ongoing maintenance or recurrent battery changing are also discarded. Some of the allowed devices on the solution model are: light, presence, noise, pressure, humidity, opening doors and household appliances sensors. Water-use sensors, mainly those installed in the toilet installation, are also included in the current work; however, from the definition of the privacy-friendly approach, it may be controversial and could be considered on the not allowed devices group as they could reveal user's intimate details.

The diagram on Fig. 1 presents the main elements of the proposed Activity Discovery Model. The sensors component of the solution is responsible of the data gathering. Another essential element that belongs to the sensors component of the solution is the device employed to tag the user current activity. This action is important because of the requirement of personalization. In this proposal, personalization is only possible if the activity inference component operates based on a supervised training model, otherwise, model could not adapt to patterns from different users. Then, the task of manually tagging the activities is needed, at least long enough to train the models properly. The tagging must be as friendly as possible, otherwise the adoption of the system is compromised. Lastly, the requirements of Active Aging shall drive the activity tagging component. That is why this element should interfere as little as possible in the user's routine. Some ideal devices for this purpose are smart watches or conversational interaction systems like Lark [8]. It is also important to perform this task strategically, manually activity tagging process should not be continuous on long time intervals.

The data flow integration component gathers the data recorded from the multiple sensor sources and applies the required transformations to consolidate a suitable input for the training model. This process of transformation consists on multiple task such as the binarization of data from sensors (necessary for the training of certain models), the unification of data from separate times (sensor reading can be continuous or event-oriented) and the treatment of missing values or sensor failures. The last task addressed must be capable of detecting any of the cases presented on [6] and take necessary actions to assure a proper activity identification. Possible actions may include the calculation of a variable recorded by a damaged sensor from redundant devices as proposed on [9]. If a value calculation from redundant sources is not possible, data flow integration module shall send a warning signal to the activity inference module in order to search for possible model modifications that allow a proper operation without the damaged sensor's variable. Alerts to the user can also been triggered.

Finally, the activity inference module is the component that deploys the supervised training model. This model shall be a classifier build from a set of tagged instances. The input of this component is a set of sensor values, the output is an activity prediction. The model selection should be in accordance with the sensor fault tolerance requirement. The present work employs decision trees as they are data structures that can be easily modified on the elimination process of a decision variable. Lastly, as classification on streams faces the issue of storage and processing over massive volumes of data, solutions as sliding windows are interesting as they allow to train the models online and on memory.

4   Experimentation

The first step on the model experimentation process was the test dataset exploration, using a dataset from the Amiqual4home Innovation Factory. This is an open research facility for innovation and experimentation with human-centered services based on the use of large-scale deployment of interconnected digital devices capable of perception, action, interaction and communication [10]. The data recorded from this facility is interesting because it contains information from multiple types of sensors such as, presence, water consumption, appliances use, doors and drawers state, bed pressure and music playing. This variety of devices is not available on other sources for ADL research like CASAS.

The dataset was recorded from a female, late-20's, who lived in the Amiqual4home in two periods of time, one in summer and the other in late autumn. The summer dataset records the activity of the user over seven days and the winter one records the activity over 22 days. The tagged activities on both datasets are toilet, cooking, eating, sleeping, shower, dishwashing, leaving home and working. Summer dataset has two additional activities: watching TV and relaxing. The sensors on the dataset include all those on the Amiqual4home Innovation Factory. Both datasets include two files; the first one contains the data recorded from each sensor when there is a change of state. The second one contains the data recorded from the activity tagging process. This process of tagging if done manually by the user using a mobile application. The dataset records the starting and ending time of each activity. A single record on the sensors file contains a time stamp, the sensor identification and the value recorded by the device. A single record on the activities file contains a time stamp, the sensor id (the activity tagging is considered a sensor itself) and a label which indicates either the starting or ending of the activity [11]. Figure 2 presents a sample of both file.

```
event_date,ms,sensor_id,sensor_value                    event_date,ms,sensor_id,sensor_value
2016-07-25 15:50:27,945,current_activity,Sortir_Stop     2016-11-14 17:45:39,079;Eau_Froide_Evier_Total;1487.0
2016-07-25 16:53:31,497,current_activity,Travail_Start    2016-11-14 17:45:39,438;Presence_Table;OFF
2016-07-25 16:56:18,815,current_activity,Musique_Start    2016-11-14 17:45:39,579;Eau_Froide_Lavabo_Total;175.0
2016-07-25 17:19:13,964,current_activity,Travail_End      2016-11-14 17:45:39.938:Eau Froide Douche Total:194.0
```

(a)   (b)

Fig. 2.   Activity (a) and sensor (b) dataset structure

This work proposes a data structure in order to create a supervised training model from the information provided from sensors and activities tagging. In this structure, there is one record per second. Each record contains the state of all the sensors and the current activity at a given second. This schema prevents errors caused by short time noise, as algorithms applied do not consider sequences. In order to build a dataset with the proposed structure, a transformation is applied. This process evaluates the state of all sensors and activities on each second by querying the time stamps from the original dataset. The transformation also stores the corresponding output on the resulting file.

The process of data transformation also includes a stage of binarization and data cleaning. The binarization process sets in '1' all sensor values different from 0 and seeks to simplify the classification model. The data cleaning removes the data from sensors whose state do not change in the analyzed time range as this can be a factor that introduce noise on the model generation process.

Then, the resulting set of records is transformed into Attribute-Relation File Format as it is the main format used by Waikato Environment for Knowledge Analysis (Weka). This work uses this software as it collects a considerable set of datamining algorithms, some oriented towards datamining on online streams. The resulting file from the transformation process is shown on Fig. 3. One instance on the dataset correspond to one second over the analyzed time span. The attribute labeled as the class for the supervised learning model is the activity performed. The remaining attributes correspond to the binary state of each sensor; these would be the decision variables of the classifier.

```
@relation 'sensorsActivityDormirDataset07_28_2016_12:00:00_to_07_29_2016_12:00:00_summer '

@attribute Agua_Caliente_Ducha_Instantaneo {0,1}
@attribute Agua_Caliente_Lavamanos_Instantaneo {0,1}
@attribute Agua_Caliente_Lavaplatos_Instantaneo {0,1}
@attribute Agua_Fria_Ducha_Instantaneo {0,1}
@attribute Agua_Fria_Inodoro_Instantaneo {0,1}
@attribute C10 {0,1}
@attribute C12 {0,1}

.|
.
.

@data

1,1,1,1,1,1,0,0,0,0,0,0,0,0,0,0,1,1,1,0,0,0,0,0,1,0,0,0 ... 0,0,0,0,1,0,0,0,1,1,1,1,1,1,1,0,No_Dormir,
1,1,1,1,1,1,0,0,0,0,0,0,0,0,0,0,1,1,1,0,0,0,0,0,1,0,0,0 ... 0,0,0,0,1,0,0,0,1,1,1,1,1,1,1,0,No_Dormir,
1,1,1,1,1,1,0,0,0,0,0,0,0,0,0,0,1,1,1,0,0,0,0,0,1,0,0,0 ... 0,0,0,0,1,0,0,0,1,1,1,1,1,1,1,0,No_Dormir,
1,1,1,1,1,1,0,0,0,0,0,0,0,0,0,0,1,1,1,0,0,0,0,0,1,0,0,0 ... 0,0,0,0,1,0,0,0,1,1,1,1,1,1,1,0,No_Dormir,
1,1,1,1,1,1,0,0,0,0,0,0,0,0,0,0,1,1,1,0,0,0,0,0,1,0,0,0 ... 0,0,0,0,1,0,0,0,1,1,1,1,1,1,1,0,No_Dormir,
1,1,1,1,1,1,0,0,0,0,0,0,0,0,0,0,1,1,1,0,0,0,0,0,1,0,0,0 ... 0,0,0,0,1,0,0,0,1,1,1,1,1,1,1,0,No_Dormir,
1,1,1,1,1,1,0,0,0,0,0,0,0,0,0,0,1,1,1,0,0,0,0,0,1,0,0,0 ... 0,0,0,0,1,0,0,0,1,1,1,1,1,1,1,0,No_Dormir,
```

Fig. 3. Resulting dataset on ARF Format

Using the described data transformation process, a file is created for each considered activity. The amount of records for each file is equal to the number of seconds of the corresponding period. The summer dataset has 529610 records and the winter dataset has 1815130 records. This file will be used both for training the classifier and for infer the target ADL. In each case, there are two possible classes to be analyzed by the classifier, either the occurrence or the no occurrence of the activity. Adopting such schema allows to decouple the identification process on single ADL models. This approach has several advantages as it allows to apply different algorithms on cases where it is more appropriate, as well as identifying concurrent activities.

Finally, the model generation process applies an algorithm over the dataset to build a classifier. SEAbIRD proposes the use of classification trees. These data structures allow to easily remove a decision value without the need of re-training, this would be the scenario of a failing sensor. In this case, the damaged device node on the decision tree is tagged as discarded and all the decision routes involved with this node return an unknown state response. Finally, using trees also allow to highlight the most discriminant sensors for each activity. Particularly, Hoeffding tree are used, an implementation of continuously-changing very fast decision tree (CVFDT). CVFDT is an algorithm intended to perform classification over high speed, concept-drifting data streams. This tree grows alternative subtrees online. When an old subtree become questionable when tested with new examples, the algorithm set a new tree if it is more precise. CVFDT tree also employs a time window of examples to keep the tree up-to-date and to apply the appropriate changes when a concept drift occurs. It is demonstrated that accuracy of CVFDT trees is comparable with the accuracy of a conventional model obtained from a retraining process [12].

Dataset was split on two subsets to train and test the model. The testing dataset is an arbitrary selection of a day when the activity has an occurrence. On both cases, this is equivalent to 86400 records. The training dataset is built from the records that

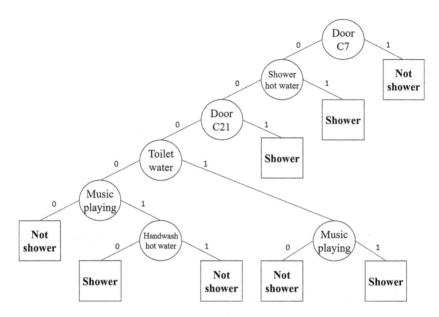

Fig. 4. Shower activity predicting tree model on summer

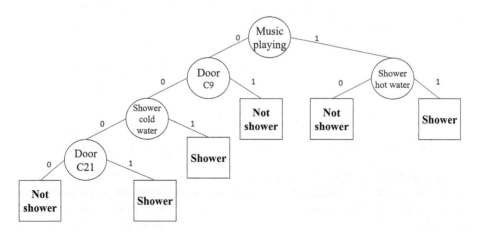

Fig. 5. Shower activity predicting tree model on winter

correspond to the remaining days when there are activities occurrence. This work presents the results of the shower activity discovery model it is one of the most relevant ADL to be detected. Initially, two trees are generated, one from the summer dataset and the other one from the autumn dataset. Results are shown on Figs. 4 and 5 respectively.

Lastly, this work proposes an alternative model on summer dataset. Based on the original summer tree, a failure-simulated model is done. The failure model is a tree, which returns an unknown state response when the decision is involved with the failing device. In this case, the damaged sensor is the music-playing indicator. Figure 6 presents the result.

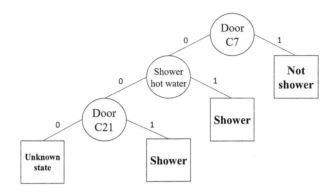

Fig. 6. Shower activity predicting tree model on summer with simulated failure

All the models are applied on the whole datasets in order to test the performance in each case.

5   Implementation and Discussion

The first test is the validation of the summer model applied over the whole dataset. Figures 7 and 8 show the results on different time scales.

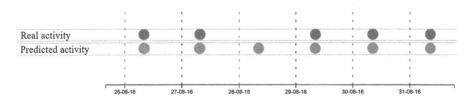

Fig. 7. Real activity tagging vs. predicted activity for summer dataset on all data

At first glance, model has an acceptable performance detecting the douche activity. Figure 7 shows the case of July 28th of 2016 when there is no douche activity recorded. However, this kind of seeming mistakes may be caused by tagging errors from the user. Particularly, the user of the datasets reported to have forgotten tagging some activities. On a more detailed view, it is evident that the predicted interval duration of the activity

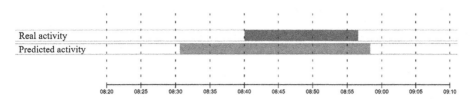

Fig. 8. Real activity tagging vs. predicted activity for summer dataset on activity detail

differs from the original one. This may be caused by differences between the tagging time of the activity and the real starting point. Statistics on Table 1 highlight a proper model operation. Recall, precision and F measure correspond to positive activity detection (shower). Kappa statistic shows the global performance. These results correspond to the application of the model over the days with reported activity.

Table 1. Summer classifier model performance statistics

Recall	0.9882
Precision	0.6507
F measure	0.7847
Kappa	0.7822

Statistics presented on Table 1 show a satisfactory performance in comparison with other approaches. Particularly, recall values are comparable with the results obtained by Urwyler et al. (recall = 0.9891) [13] and Toledo et al. (recall = 0.9619) [14]. The next test is the application of the model with sensor failure over the summer dataset; Fig. 9 presents the results of the model application over the time, Fig. 10 shows a performance statistics comparison of with-no-failure and with-failure models. The results from the failure simulation presents the statistics over the no-unknown state instances.

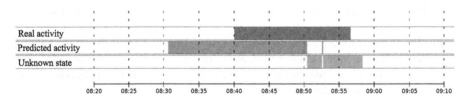

Fig. 9. Real activity tagging vs. predicted activity with sensor failure for summer dataset on activity detail

This test reveals that the model with sensor failure can detect an important proportion of the activity. 38.88% of the total activity instances are classified as unknown state, the remaining percentage (61.12%) are correctly classified. Statistics also show that the performance of both models is similar over the no-unknown state instances. This result is interesting as it proves that the proposed models have resiliency over sensor failures.

The last test is the validation of the winter model and the evaluation of the summer model applied over the winter dataset. The Fig. 11 presents the application of the winter

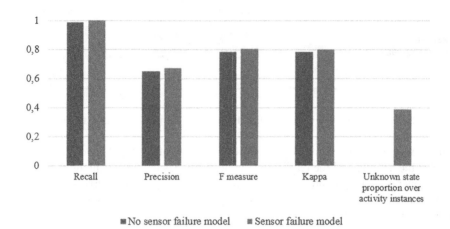

Fig. 10. Performance statistics of summer classifier over summer dataset with and without failure simulation

model over the winter dataset. This result reveals a similar behavior to the summer model over the summer dataset. An analysis over the real activity time line, particularly over the last week, reveals a case that highlights the possibility of the missing tags due to user oblivion.

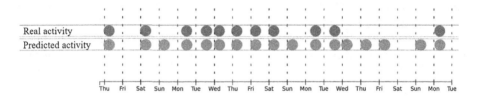

Fig. 11. Real activity tagging vs. predicted activity for winter dataset on all data

Finally, summer model is applied on the winter dataset in order to test the validity of a model behavior over a dataset from a different season. Figure 12 shows the time line of this test and Fig. 13 presents a performance statistic comparison between summer and winter test on the winter dataset.

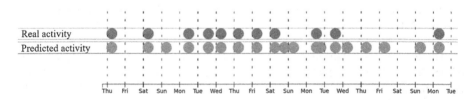

Fig. 12. Real activity tagging vs. predicted activity for winter dataset employing summer dataset on all data

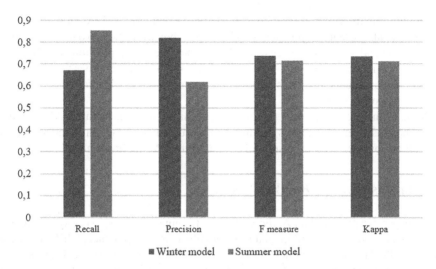

Fig. 13. Performance statistics of summer and winter classifiers over winter dataset

These statistics prove that summer model may have proper results over winter dataset, they are even similar to winter model in some cases as Kappa and F measure. This result is interesting as it raises the possibility of applying a pre-conceived model over a dataset without the necessity of a full training. As seen before, this pre-conceived model may have some adaptation process from new labeled examples, as it is structured over a CVFDT. Although winter classifier still has better performance statistics than summer classifier, this summer model has outstanding characteristics over the winter dataset.

Finally, an observation over the specific sensors from both models is interesting because the defining devices of a classification process are not necessarily related with the execution of the activity. The inclusion of decision nodes which evaluate the state of sensors such as the music playing indicator for the shower activity discovery is unexpected. This phenomenon raises the relevance of developing full-personalized models as not all users may behave similarly for certain activities.

6   Related Work

Several approaches have been suggested in order to detect ADL from an AAL perspective. Chen et al. proposes a knowledge-driven approach which performs activity detection by using modeling and semantic reasoning. They suggest a unified ontological modeling and representation for sensors and activities. Their mechanism also allows to perform the discovery on multiple levels of abstraction [15]. Dimitrievski et al. concentrates more on the sensor deployment but the propose a brief approach based on support vector machines and random forests [16].

There are video-based approaches. Amirjavid et al. suggest a video-based application which monitors the objects related with certain ADL and detect the current position.

Employing this information they infer the activity execution [17]. As in the previous case, Lun et al. present an approach based on video; however, they also include mobile smart phone and wearable devices in order to track the user's position and therefore define the current activity [18]. Negin et al. use employ video in order to record user and global movements, from this information the user's activity is inferred using unsupervised models [19].

None of the previous works presents sensor-failure tolerant features. Also, video-based approaches employ tactics that may be considered as privacy-unfriendly, so they may not be considered as valid solutions for an Active Aging implementations.

7 Conclusions and Further Work

In this paper, we proposed an Activity of Daily Living (ADL) discovery system which has resiliency over sensor failure and is eventually adaptable to concept drift. We were able to build classification models for activity discovery from a user's real sensor data. We also presented variations of these models by removing decision nodes on a sensor failure simulation context or applying models from different seasons on the testing datasets. Further work will explore the modeling of device failure over other algorithms in order to improve the detection on this specific circumstance. The performance measures on this testing scenarios proves that SEAbIRD operates properly in the cases of normal operation, sensor fault operation and no-initial-model operation. Finally, we were able to prove that sensors that indicate an activity occurrence may not be fully related with the execution of the activity itself.

Future work will focus on applying the methodologies of SEAbIRD on actual online data in order to further explore the adaptable feature of this system and develop a reliable product for ADL discovery on real time. Also, further work will explore ADL discovery over multi-inhabited environments.

Acknowledgments. This research was sponsored and supported by Alianza Caoba (Centro de Excelencia en Big Data y Data Analytics, Colombia). We thank our colleagues Claudia Roncancio, and Cyril Labbé from Universite Grenoble Alpes, LIG; and Paula Lago from Universidad de los Andes, who collaborate in our research project, provided expertise on the subjects under discussion and provided the datasets for the corresponding analysis.

References

1. Palacios, R.: The future of global ageing. Int. J. Epidemiol. **31**, 786–791 (2002)
2. Bloom, D.E., Boersch-Supan, A., McGee, P., Seike, A.: Population aging: facts, challenges, and responses. PGDA Work. Pap., no. 71 (2011)
3. Org, S.G., et al.: Envejecimiento activo: un marco político*, vol. 37, pp. 74–105 (2002)
4. Powell, J.L., Chen, S.: Technologies for Active Aging. Springer, London (2013)
5. World Health Organization, Noncommunicable diseases (2017). http://www.who.int/mediacentre/factsheets/fs355/en/. Accessed 19 May 2017
6. Chalmers, D.: Sensing and Systems in Pervasive Computing, 1st edn. Springer, London (2011)

7. Lago, P., Jiménez-Guarín, C., Roncancio, C.: A case study on the analysis of behavior patterns and pattern changes in smart environments. In: Pecchia, L., Chen, L.L., Nugent, C., Bravo, J. (eds.) IWAAL 2014. LNCS, vol. 8868, pp. 296–303. Springer, Cham (2014). doi: 10.1007/978-3-319-13105-4_43

8. Lark, Lark - About Us. http://www.web.lark.com/about/. Accessed 19 May 2017

9. Imai, S., Galli, A., Varela, C.A.: Dynamic data-driven avionics systems: inferring failure modes from data streams. Procedia Comput. Sci. **51**, 1665–1674 (2015)

10. INRIA, About - Amiqual4home. https://amiqual4home.inria.fr/home/. Accessed: 19 May 2017

11. Lago, P., Lang, F., Roncancio, C., Jiménez-Guarín, C., Mateescu, R., Bonnefond, N.: The ContextAct@A4H real-life dataset of daily-living activities. In: Brézillon, P., Turner, R., Penco, C. (eds.) CONTEXT 2017. LNCS, vol. 10257, pp. 175–188. Springer, Cham (2017). doi:10.1007/978-3-319-57837-8_14

12. Hulten, G., Spencer, L., Domingos, P.: Mining time-changing data streams. In: Proceedings of the Seventh ACM SIGKDD International Conference Knowledge Discovery and Data Mining, KDD 2001, vol. 18, pp. 97–106 (2001)

13. Urwyler, P., et al.: Recognition of activities of daily living in healthy subjects using two ad-hoc classifiers. Biomed. Eng. Online, 1–15 (2015)

14. Duque, A., Ordóñez, F.J., Toledo, P., Sanchis, A.: Offline and online activity recognition on mobile devices using accelerometer data. In: Bravo, J., Hervás, R., Rodríguez, M. (eds.) IWAAL 2012. LNCS, vol. 7657, pp. 208–215. Springer, Heidelberg (2012). doi: 10.1007/978-3-642-35395-6_29

15. Chen, L., Nugent, C., Wang, H.: A knowledge-driven approach to activity recognition in smart homes. IEEE Trans. Knowl. Data Eng. **24**(6), 961–974 (2012)

16. Dimitrievski, A., Zdravevski, E., Lameski, P., Trajkovik, V.: Towards application of non-invasive environmental sensors for risks and activity detection. In: Proceedings of the 2016 IEEE 12th International Conference on Intelligent Computer Communication and Processing, ICCP 2016, pp. 27–33 (2016)

17. Amirjavid, F., Spachos, P., Plataniotis, K.N.: 3-D object localization in smart homes: a distributed sensor and video mining approach, pp. 1–10 (2017)

18. Lun, R., Gordon, C., Zhao, W.: Tracking the activities of daily lives: an integrated approach. In: Proceedings of the Future Technologies Conference, FTC 2016, December 2017

19. Negin, F., Cosar, S., Koperski, M., Bremond, F.: Generating unsupervised models for online long-term activity recognition. In: 3rd IAPR Asian Conference on Pattern Recognition (2015)

Exploiting Context Information to Improve the Precision of Recommendation Systems in Retailing

Cristian Sánchez, Norha M. Villegas$^{(\boxtimes)}$, and Javier Díaz Cely

Universidad Icesi, Calle 18 No. 122-135, 760031 Cali, Colombia
{cesanchez,nvillega,jgdiaz}@icesi.edu.co

Abstract. In the retailing industry, recommendation systems analyze historical purchasing information with the purpose of predicting user product preferences. Nevertheless, despite the increasing use of these applications, their results still lack precision with respect to the real needs and preferences of customers. This is in part because the user's purchase history is insufficient to identify the products that a user would need to buy, given that user preferences are highly affected by changes in contextual situations (e.g., geographical location, special dates, activities of interest) over time. This paper presents a recommendation system that exploits context information to improve the precision of recommendations. Our system relies on the collaborative filtering approach, and the post-filtering paradigm as the mechanism to include context information into the recommendation algorithm. We tested our system using data provided by a Colombian retailing company finding that our recommendations are successful for a greater number of customers, compared to the baseline approach.

Keywords: Context-aware recommendation system · Contextual information · Recommendation process · Precision · Collaborative filtering · Post-filtering

1   Introduction

Currently, finance institutions, e-commerce, and retailing businesses, among other industries, rely on software systems to provide personalized products or services expected to satisfy costumer needs. In general, these solutions are known as recommendation systems (RS) and seek to predict the level of preference of a particular user for a product by taking into account information of past events and preferences from related users or the same user.

One important challenge for retailing businesses is to find smarter ways to exploit all the information collected from user profiles, historical purchasing records and product contents, in order to generate personalized offers that allow achieving customer satisfaction and fidelity, thus increasing sales. To tackle this challenge, RS are important to businesses because they exploit historical information to predict customer preferences, and recommend products that satisfy

© Springer International Publishing AG 2017
A. Solano and H. Ordoñez (Eds.): CCC 2017, CCIS 735, pp. 72–86, 2017.
DOI: 10.1007/978-3-319-66562-7_6

user expectations. Amazon.com, which recommends a variety of products such as books and clothing, and Netflix, which recommends movies, are examples of applications that consider customer preferences and product contents in their recommendations.

Despite the industrial application of RS, they still pose several open research challenges. One of these challenges is how to further improve their precision, since in many cases they still recommend products that are irrelevant to the user. The precision of recommendation systems, measured in terms of the relevance of recommendations with respect to user needs, is highly affected by two main aspects [16]: (i) the lack of context-awareness, and (ii) the static management of context information. The first one, addressed in this paper, refers to the capability of the system to integrate environmental information that affects user-system interaction. In RS, this information must be explicitly modeled in the recommendation process to be considered. The second one, not addressed in this paper, refers to the assumption of a static nature of this information. That is, assuming that context is immutable over time.

Context-aware recommendation systems (CARS) improve the relevance of recommendations by exploiting contextual information that influences user preferences, such as time, location, and user activity, to generate recommendations that are closer to the user real needs. For instance, in the case of news recommendations (or content of a Web site), it might not be enough to predict the content the user wants to read. It is equally important to understand when to deliver this content. A user may prefer to read local news on weekdays, and sport news on weekends. This example illustrates a close relation between purchasing behavior and context information that characterizes the situation of users. Indeed, under different context situations, a costumer may make different purchasing decisions for the same products or services [2].

In this paper we propose a context-aware recommendation system (CARS) based on the collaborative filtering approach, and the post-filtering paradigm as the mechanism to include contextual information. In this way, our approach combines data mining methods (i.e. analysis association) with statistical methods (i.e. naïve Bayes classifier) to compute the probability of occurrence of association rules under specific contextual factors related to the date at which the offer is made (i.e., the combination of contextual factors such as payment day and day of week). Following this, the rules with a high probability of occurrence will be used for the recommendation when the corresponding contextual situation arises.

We tested our CARS using real data provided by a Colombian retailer. Findings indicate that, on average, the percentage of recommendations that became purchases varies between 75% and 87%. Furthermore, recommendations were successful for a greater number of customers in our context-aware recommendation system, with respect to the baseline approach.

The remaining sections of this article are organized as follows. Section 2 briefly presents foundational concepts on recommendation systems, context information, and the exploitation of context in recommendation systems.

Section 3 explains our context-aware recommender system, the contribution of this paper. Section 4 presents the results of the validation of our approach. Section 5 discusses related work. Finally, Sect. 6 concludes the paper by presenting limitations of our approach and future work.

2   Theoretical Background

2.1   Recommendation Systems (RS)

According to Admonavicius and Tuzhilin [3], RS can be understood as strategies used to infer the preference of a costumer for items (e.g., products or services) that he or she has not consumed and/or rated before. That is, for products for which there is no information available about the preference of the customer. This inference is usually based on user profiles (e.g., preferences, likes, behavior patterns), content of items, and ratings given to items in the past. Formally, considering a set of users and a set of items, recommendation systems aim at finding the utility function f for the user-item pairs:

$$f : Users \times Items \rightarrow R$$

After inferring the preference of the customer for a set of items, the products with the highest ratings are recommended to the user. Recommendation systems use information from items, users, and preferences. It is worth mentioning that the number of items and users can be very large, coming near to the thousands or even millions, depending on the application domain. Preferences can be expressed directly by the user, for example in the form of ratings or likes, or can be inferred by interpreting user actions, such as time spent in a particular web site or the purchasing frequency of products.

Recommendation systems are usually classified into three approaches that are widely applied in industry [3]: *collaborative filtering* approaches, where recommendations are based on preferences of similar users; *content-based* approaches, where recommendations are based on past preferences of the user and the similarity of the recommended products; and *hybrid* approaches, a combination of collaborative and content-based methods.

2.2   Context Information and Its Integration into RS

The precision of recommendations is highly affected by factors that characterize user situations [7]. These factors are known as context, which can be defined as any information useful to characterize the situation of an entity (e.g., a user) that can affect user-system interactions [1].

Contextual information can be defined as static or dynamic [16]. In static context, recommender applications assume that this information is immutable over time. An example of static context is the birthday of a user. On the contrary, in dynamic context the user's situations change or evolve over time. Therefore, this type of context is closer to the current user's needs. Some instances of this type of context are location, time, and user activity. Based on this, RS require mechanisms to track and understand these changes and the way they may affect recommendations.

According to [4], there are three known paradigms to integrate contextual factors into recommendation systems: *contextual pre-filtering* (or reduction-based), where information about the current context is used for selecting or constructing the relevant set of data records that will be used in the recommendations; *contextual post-filtering*, where contextual information is initially ignored, the ratings of items to be recommended are predicted using any traditional technique, and the resulting set of recommendations is tailored according to each user using the contextual information; and *contextual modeling*, where contextual factors are directly integrated into the recommendation model as an explicit dimension that is used in the prediction of a user's rating for an item.

3   Our Approach

3.1   Overview

Our CARS relies on collaborative filtering as the recommendation approach and the post-filtering paradigm as the mechanism to exploit context information. Our system recommends items by taking into account user needs that may change under different context situations. For this, we combine data mining methods (i.e. association analysis) with statistical methods (i.e. naïve Bayes classifier) to compute the probability of occurrence of association rules under specific contextual factors associated with the date at which the offer is made (i.e., the combination of contextual factors such as payment day and day of week). In this way, the rules with a high probability of occurrence will be used to extract the relevant items to be recommended when the corresponding contextual situation arises.

The proposed recommendation system comprises four main elements. The first element is context-awareness. Given the characteristics of the data set, the only contextual factor we could extract from this data corresponds to time-context information. According to Campos et al. [6], time-context can be represented as a continuous or categorical variable. In our case, the former indicates that values of time are the specific times at which items are rated or consumed (e.g., January 1st, 2016 at 14:35:00). The latter corresponds to the "time periods of interest in the recommendation domain at hand". For instance, in a retailing school supply scenario, it may be convenient to consider the seasonal variable *seasonOfTheYear*, which can include the value *backToSchool*. In this way, we exploit time-context information using the timestamps of purchases to infer different time categories (i.e., day of the week and payment day). The second element is collaborative-filtering. We used collaborative filtering to identify items that may be relevant to a user, based on the preferences of similar users. The third element is association analysis to discover patterns, in the form of association rules, among purchase transactions. For instance, in the case of our data set, the rule *cheese, milk → toasts* suggests that there exists a relationship between

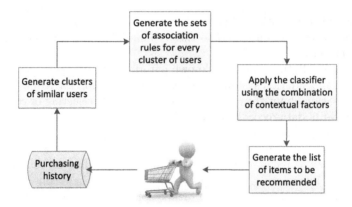

Fig. 1. The process followed by our system

the sale of cheese, milk and toast (i.e., costumers who buy cheese and milk also buy toasts). The last element is the naïve Bayes classifier, which allows us to compute the probability of occurrence of association rules under specific context situations, which constitutes the novelty of our approach.

Figure 1 depicts the process executed by our context-aware recommendation approach. Giving a data set of market basket transactions, our context-aware recommendation system: (i) generates clusters of similar users by considering similarities between user preferences, (ii) takes transactions from every group of users and generates association rules, (iii) applies the classifier for every customer to find the rules with their corresponding occurrence probability under a combination of contextual conditions, and (iv) selects the rules with at least 80% of occurrence probability and, based on these, generates the list of items to be recommended.

3.2   Data Set

This section characterizes the used data set, and how we prepared this data to make them suitable for the experiments conducted in this research.

The data set used in this research was provided by a Colombian retailing company, and is composed of 21,147,000 market basket transactions that include approximately 1,000,000 clients and 1,690,000 product references. These transactions correspond to six months of operations of five branches of the company. The data set was provided in the form of comma separated values (CSV) files. All sensible information was anonymized. Figure 2 illustrates the structure of each file provided with the data set.

Preprocessing. Not all the information provided with the data sate was relevant because of the existence of missing values, products infrequently purchased, and users who made only one single transaction. Therefore, we preprocessed the

(a) Transactions

	A	B	C	D
1	Date	Id_Branch	Id_Client	Product_Reference
2	01/01/2013	102	530	27
3	01/01/2013	102	530	52
4	01/01/2013	102	530	306
5	01/01/2013	102	530	404817
6	01/01/2013	102	530	745559
7	01/01/2013	102	530	2359228
8	01/01/2013	102	587	11
9	01/01/2013	102	587	111
10	01/01/2013	102	587	1693
11	01/01/2013	102	587	3003
12	01/01/2013	102	587	29113
13	01/01/2013	102	587	74091
14	01/01/2013	102	587	802745
15	01/01/2013	102	587	802746
16	01/01/2013	102	587	900108
17	01/01/2013	102	587	927994
18	01/01/2013	102	587	1234029
19	01/01/2013	102	587	2012134
20	01/01/2013	102	1508	53890
21	01/01/2013	102	1508	325165
22	01/01/2013	102	1508	2183052

(b) Products

	A	B	C	D
1	Product_Product_Name		Product_Brand	Category
2	922967 BUSO 5113242 10		OFF CORSS	CAMISETAS - BUSOS
3	74350 LOMO AHUMADO SUIZO x 1500 g		SIN MARCA	CARNES PROCESADAS AL VACIO
4	86144 ESMALTE SUPER FANTASTIC BATMAN		VOGUE	ESMALTES
5	14283 CUCHARON 33X14 R.2		SIN MARCA	CUCHARA-CUCHARONES
6	2879885 BATATA CHINA x 1000 g		SIN MARCA	VERDURAS RAIZ
7	1429920 PANTALON 4106676 2T		OFF CORSS	PANTALONES Y BLUE-JEAN
8	2120677 BLUSON ESTAMPADO M 3/4.		SIN MARCA	ROPA FORMAL
9	566786 OFTA PREPLANCHADO PISTOLA G/RPTO ALMIDON		SIN MARCA	CUIDADO DE LA ROPA
10	566784 CHICLE BOLON ACIDO x 20 g (1 und)		SIN MARCA	GOMAS DE MASCAR
11	1429928 PANTALON 4106681 3T		OFF CORSS	PANTALONES Y BLUE-JEAN
12	1612397 CAMISETA LISTADOR TIRITAS FREN		FACOL S.A.	ROPA FORMAL
13	86140 CUADERNO DURABOOK FERRARI 105-5-180-2		SIN MARCA	CUADERNOS
14	1716599 OFTA YOGURT ACTIVIA CUCHx100 P.5 LLEVE 6		ACTIVIA	YOGURT

(c) Clients

	A	B	C
1	Id_Client	Gender	Address
2	452287		CARRERA 67 # 40-06
3	452288		
4	452289		
5	452290		AV 3A #40N-187
6	452291		CRA 1C BIS # 67-41 APT 102 BLOQ 5D
7	452292		
8	452293		kra 42 #43-68
9	452294		CLIENTES GIROS
10	452295	M	CRA 29 # 26-14
11	452296		CLIENTES GIROS
12	452297		
13	452298		
14	452299		
15	452300	F	
16	452301	F	
17	958810		KRA 88 #4-20
18	958811		CR 24F NO.D70A-41
19	958812		
20	958813		KRA 7 D # 61-72
21	958814		
22	958815		CARRERA 47 # 11-88
23	958816		AV 3 NTE #8N-24

Fig. 2. Structure of files included in the data set

data set to clean and make the data more suitable for the recommendation process. This preprocessing comprised the following steps: (i) data cleaning and grouping, (ii) shopping frequency calculation, and (iii) variable transformation.

Data Cleaning and Grouping. To eliminate irrelevant elements that may affect the precision of recommendations, we selected only the transactions that belong to clients with at least twice purchases per month. Columns Gender and Address (cf. Fig. 2 (c)) were omitted due to the excessive number of records with missing values.

Products were not considered individually but grouped into categories. In this way, a set of items such as mango, apple, lettuce, and spinach was transformed into two elements: fruits and vegetables. In this way, we dealt with 2.051 categories instead of 1.690.000 products. By this way, precision is improved since working with categories decreases the sparsity of the matrix.

After grouping the products of transactions into categories, we computed the average of times that each category was purchased in every month. Based on these measures, and for every branch of the store, we selected the first 80 most purchased categories to be considered in the recommendations. This number was selected after testing with different sets of most-purchased categories: 50, 80, 100 and 400. After performing these tests we found that the 80 most purchased categories provided better results in terms of the precision of the recommendation.

Shopping Frequency Calculation. In general, recommendation systems rely on rankings that represent user preferences. However, the provided data set does not have rankings to represent user preferences, only purchasing transactions. Therefore, our data set was transformed into a user-item rating matrix that allows us to establish the utility of items for users.

We measured the utility of items for users through the shopping frequency. That is, how often a user u purchases each product that belongs to each category [12]. To calculate the shopping frequency of an item for a particular user, we computed, for the six months, the average number of times that a user bought every item. In this way, the utility is defined as the times that a user u purchase the product i per month.

Variable Transformation. Variable transformation refers to the transformation of all the values of a variable by means of a mathematical function. That is, each data point z_i of the data set is replaced with the transformed value $y_i = f(zi)$, where f is a function. For example, if x is a variable, it can be transformed with some functions such as x^k, $log(x)$, $sin(x)$ or $1/x$. In general, $log(x)$ is often applied to transform data that do not have a normal distribution into data that do. Thus, when there is evidence of substantial skew in the data, it is common to transform the data to a symmetric distribution using $log(x)$ [15].

We found some outliers that generate skew in our data set. After calculating purchasing frequencies, we found values ranging between 5 and 30. For instance, John and Lucy may buy fruits 30 times per month, but the rest of the users may buy fruits 5 times on average. In this case, the purchasing frequency distribution is asymmetric. To alleviate this problem, we transformed these values by applying the *log* function to deal with ranges between 0.69 and 1.48, to have a nearly symmetric distribution.

After transforming the values of purchasing frequencies, we generated the user-item rating matrix, where rows represent users, columns represent items (categories), and values represent user preferences. Table 1 presents the structure of the user-item rating matrix.

Table 1. Example of the user-item rating matrix

	Fruits	Wine	Coffee	...
Lucy	4	1	3	...
John	3	2	4	...
...	...	...	...	...

3.3   Clustering of Similar Users

This step consists in grouping users with a similar purchasing behavior. We used k-means as the clustering technique. K-means requires K initial centroids, where K is a user specified parameter and represents the number of desired clusters. Then, each user is assigned to the closest centroid, and the collection of users assigned to a centroid forms a cluster [9]. Finally, the algorithm recomputes centroids based on the elements assigned to the cluster. These steps are repeated until centroids do not change.

3.4   Generation of Association Rules

In this step, we obtained separately the transactions that belong to the users of each cluster obtained in the previous step.

Then, for the transactions associated with each cluster, we generated the set of association rules by applying the Top-K rules algorithm [8]. This algorithm receives two parameters: k and *minconf*. The first one corresponds to the number of rules that the user wants to discover, and the second one to the *confidence* value of the rules (i.e., the reliability of the inference made by the rule).

The strength of an association rule $X \rightarrow Y$ is measured in terms of their support and confidence. The first measure determines how often a rule is applicable to a giving data set, while the second one indicates how frequently items in Y appear in transactions that contain X. For instance, rule $milk, \; fruits \rightarrow cereal$ has 50% probability to be applicable to the set of transactions associated to cluster 1, while the probability of having *cereal* in the transactions that contain *milk* and *fruits* is 70%.

3.5   Naïve Bayes Classifier

The naïve Bayes classifier, based on Bayes' theorem, describes the probability of occurrence of a particular event (denoted as *class*), based on conditions related to that event. In our case, the idea is to calculate the probability that an association rule occurs under contextual conditions. This way, the classifier will allow us to generate personalized context-aware recommendations.

The idea consists in learning the class "the rule has high-occurrence/the rule has not high-occurrence" such that, for a particular cluster of users, we can check whether the products that compound the rule can be recommended under the combination of time-context factors (e.g., *weekend* and *payment day*). We denote contextual factors as $x = [x_1, x_2]$, and the class as C. Thus, C will depend on the factors x where $C = 1$ indicates a high confidence that the rule occurs, and $C = 0$ indicates a low confidence that the rule occurs. Thus if we know $P(C|x_1, x_2)$ when a user arrives at the store with conditions x_1 and x_2, we define our classifier as:

$$choose \begin{cases} C = 1 \text{ if } P(C = 1|x_1, x_2) > 0.8 \\ C = 0 \text{ Otherwise} \end{cases}$$

Then, the problem is to calculate $P(C|x)$. Using Bayes' theorem, it can be expressed as:

$$P(C|x) = \frac{P(x|C)P(C)}{P(x)} \tag{1}$$

where $P(C)$ is the prior probability of class C. In our example, $P(C = 1)$ corresponds to the probability that "the rule has high-occurrence", regardless the value of the contextual factor x. The value $P(x|C)$ is denoted as the likelihood and is the conditional probability that an event belonging to C has the associated value x. The value $P(x)$ is called the evidence and corresponds to the marginal probability that an x value is presented. Finally, $P(C|x)$ is denoted as the posterior probability, which is the combination of the prior and the likelihood of class C given a factor x [5].

In practice, the numerator is equivalent to the joint probability model.

$$P(C_k, x_1, ..., x_n) \tag{2}$$

Now, considering the naive conditional independence assumptions between features, the joint model can be expressed as follows:

$$\begin{aligned} P(C_k|x_1, ..., x_n) &\propto P(C_k|x_1, ..., x_n) \\ &\propto P(C_k)P(x_1|C_k)P(x_2|C_k)P(x_3|C_k)... \\ &\propto P(C_k)\prod_{i=1}^{n} P(x_i|C_k) \end{aligned} \tag{3}$$

Thus, under the independence assumptions, the conditional distribution over the class C is:

$$P(C_k|x_1, ..., x_n) = \frac{1}{Z}P(C_k)\prod_{i=1}^{n} P(x_i|C_k) \tag{4}$$

where $Z = P(x)$ is a constant if the values of the feature variables $(x_1, ..., x_n)$ are known. Thus, by considering the above assumptions we have to perform the following steps to build our classifier:

1. To define the time-context factors to be used (i.e., **x**): day type (weekend, weekdays), payment time (payment day, daily), and month of the year.
2. To generate the frequency table, that is, for every cluster and every time-context factor compute the frequency of occurrence of the rules. For this, we took into account the number of purchasing transactions performed by the client in a time slot. The result is the table with the frequency of occurrence of the rules. Examples of frequencies are presented in Fig. 3, for factors weekend and weekday. So, for the first one, we take the transactions performed in weekends, and compute the number of times rule r_i occurs, and the number of times that r_i does not occur. Similarly, for the second factor, we take the transactions performed in weekdays, and compute the number of times that the rule r_i occurs, and the number of times that r_i does not occur. We follow the same process for other contextual factors such as *payment time* (c.f. Fig. 4).

$P(x|C)=P(\text{Weekend}|\text{Yes})=5/7=0.71$ $P(x)=P(\text{Weekend})=7/10=0.70$

Frequency table		Is the rule r_i met?	
		Yes	No
Day Type	Weekend	5	2
	Weekdays	2	1

Likelihood table		Is the rule r_i met?		
		Yes	No	
Day Type	Weekend	5/7	2/3	7/10
	Weekdays	2/7	1/3	3/10
		7/10	3/10	

$P(C)=P(\text{Yes})=7/10=0.70$

Fig. 3. Transforming frequency to likelihood

Frequency table		Is the rule r_i met?	
		Yes	No
PaymentTime	Paymentday	6 6/7	1 1/3
	No_paymentday	1 1/7	2 2/3

Fig. 4. Payment day frequency

3. To compute the prior probability $P(C)$, the likelihood $P(x|C)$, the evidence $P(x)$, as illustrated in Fig. 3.
4. To compute the posterior probability $P(C|x)$.
5. To choose the rules with a posterior probability greater than a threshold. In our case, greater than 0.80.

Now, according to the information presented in Figs. 3 and 4, let's assume that we have rule $r_1 = wine, fruits \rightarrow cheese$ and the contextual factors:

- day type = weekend
- payment time = payment day

We need to determine which posterior probability is greater, "C_1: the rule has high-occurrence" or "C_2: the rule has not high-occurrence". Thus, the posterior probability is given by:

- Likelihood of C_1 = P(weekend|Yes) * P(payment day|Yes) * P(Yes) = 5/7 * 6/7 * 7/10 = 0.43
- Likelihood of C_2 = P(weekend|No) * P(payment day|No) * P(No) = 2/3 * 1/3 * 3/10 = 0.07
- Finally, we normalize and compute the posterior probability of C_1 given weekend & payment day : P(C_1|weekend, payment day) = 0.43/(0.43 + 0.07) = 0.86

As a result, P(C_1) indicates that the occurrence probability of rule r_1 under the presence of the contextual factors weekend and payment day is 86%. Given that this probability is greater than 0.8, we recommend the items associated with this rule.

4   Validation

This section presents how close the contextual recommendations generated by our approach are to the user real preferences. We validate our approach through two main tests: (i) precision, which indicates what percentage of recommended products were actually purchased by the corresponding customers of the retailing company; and (ii) the effectiveness of our approach with respect to the non-contextual recommender system used as a baseline.

4.1   Training Data and Test Data

Our data set is composed of transactions recording the daily sales of products in five branches of the retailing company. In order to find predictive relationships and evaluate whether these relationships hold, it is important to divide the information into training data and test data. In this case, 70% of the transactions, for every month, were selected as training data, and the rest as test data. In this way, we train the classifier using training data and we test its performance on test data.

4.2   Precision

In the first test, we validated the precision of our approach by determining the proportion of recommended items that were actually bought by the corresponding clients of the retailing company, under the defined context situations. In other words, we measured the fraction of recommended items that are relevant to the user [13]. The test consisted in separating the items recommended by our algorithm, under each context situation (i.e., for one or more contextual factors), into two classes: relevant or irrelevant. For this, we used a binary scale such that the set of recommended items that were purchased by the user are considered relevant and denoted as true-positive (tp), and those that were not purchased are considered irrelevant and denoted as false-positive (fp). Equation 5 indicates how this proportion is computed.

$$Precision = \frac{tp}{tp + fp} \tag{5}$$

The obtained results show that, on average, the percentage of recommendations that correspond to actual purchases varies between 75% and 87%. It is important to point out that the company must be careful when analyzing the resulting rules, since some of them may be too obvious, or may involve products that are not of their interest. These rules should not be taken into account. Table 2 presents the results of this validation for all store locations and clusters of users.

The results suggest an outstanding performance of our context-aware recommendation approach in terms of precision. For the company, this information may be useful to optimize the lift from promotion and advertisement. In marketing,

Table 2. Results of the precision tests

Groups of users	Store 102	Store 103	Store 107	Store 108	Store 110
1	86%	90%	87%	72%	60%
2	67%	91%	71%	82%	100%
3	96%	89%	69%	80%	100%
4	89%	81%	80%		
5	89%	64%	62%		
6	89%	71%	83%		
Total Average	**86%**	**81%**	**75%**	**78%**	**87%**

lift represents the improvement of sales in response to a promotion campaign. In particular, it can be seen that group 3 of branch store 102 has a precision of 96%, suggesting that the company could concentrate on this group of users to offer them special promotions based on the items recommended by our algorithm, which in this case shows a precision of 96%. This could mean that almost all of these offers may result in purchases.

4.3 Effectiveness

The second test performed in this experiment compared the effectiveness of our approach with respect to non-contextual recommendations generated by simply applying clustering and association rules, without exploiting context information as it is done in traditional approaches. For this, we computed the proportion of recommendations that resulted in purchases in both our approach and the non-contextual approach. Then, we calculated, from the results of each approach, the number of clients for whom the recommendations were effective. The results presented in of Table 3 suggest that the recommendations generated by our context-aware recommender system were effective, in most cases, for a greater number of users with respect to non-contextual recommendations. The exception is cluster 2 of store 107.

5 Related Work

As one of the first steps in our research, we conducted a systematic literature review (SLR) [11] to understand the way how context information is integrated into recommendation systems. We studied 55 papers that propose CARS by analyzing them through seven criteria: (i) *recommendation system approach*, whether it is content-based, collaborative filtering, or hybrid; (ii) *recommendation techniques*, the mechanisms used at the different stages of the recommendation process; (iii) *paradigm for incorporating context*, whether it is pre-filtering, post-filtering, or contextual modeling; (iv) *context types*, the context categories

Table 3. Results of the effectiveness tests

Cluster	Store 102	Store 103	Store 107	Store 108	Store 110
1	62%	100%	80%	100%	100%
2	100%	73%	0%	60%	100%
3	50%	29%	100%	100%	100%
4	85%	75%	100%		100%
5	100%	100%	85%		
6	92%	80%	100%		
Average	**82%**	**76%**	**78%**	**87%**	**100%**

that are exploited in the recommender system (based on the classification proposed by Villegas and Müller [17]); (v) *application domain* (if applicable), the specific area targeted by the proposed RS; (vi) *evaluation*, the methods and metrics used to validate the effectiveness of the proposed RS; and (vii) *data sets* (when reported), the data used to evaluate the proposed approach.

We found that only five out of the 55 CARS we surveyed rely on a collaborative filtering recommendation mechanism and have retailing, in particular e-retailing, as the application domain [10,12,14,18,19]. Surprisingly, we found no papers presenting CARS focused on traditional retailing. As in our approach, four of these systems exploit time context to improve the relevance of recommendations [10,12,18,19].

Regarding the means used to incorporate context into the recommendation system, the system proposed in [10] implements a pre-filtering strategy to filter information according to the current context. Then, it computes a rating for the given user and item, as an aggregation of the ratings of other similar users; the systems proposed in [14,18,19] rely on contextual modeling using tensor factorization, which considers the latent features of users and items, and the interaction of the user with an item under a given context. The latent feature of users, items and context types are stored in three matrices. Thus, the inference of preferences is computed as the inner product of the latent feature vectors of the matrices; the system proposed in [12] relies also on the contextual modeling paradigm by considering virtual users under different contexts and finding neighbors of contextually similar users to infer recommendations.

Concerning the evaluation of the proposed approaches, only two out of these five papers discuss the improvement obtained through the exploitation of context into the recommendation system [14,18]. Shi et al. [14] report to achieve a precision improvement that ranges between 8% and 100% for different sizes of datasets, whereas Zheng et al. [18] report a precision gain between 1.27% and 22.35% compared to other six approaches used as baselines.

6 Conclusion and Future Work

We proposed a solution that incorporates time context information into the recommendation system, in such a way that the precision of recommendations is improved with respect to the approach used as baseline. Our system is based on collaborative filtering and incorporates context using the post-filtering paradigm. In particular, our approach combines analysis association with the naïve Bayes classifier to compute the occurrence probability of association rules under specific contextual factors associated with the date at which the offer is made (i.e., the combination of contextual factors such as payment day or day of week). Following this, the rules with a high probability of occurrence will be used for the recommendation when the corresponding contextual situation arises.

Context information is a critical aspect to be considered in the precision of recommendations. In our solution, context is used by the classifier as a set of features that contributes to the probability of the occurrence of rules. Therefore, other context-factors such as the gender of users, the location where the user lives, and the age could have allowed the classifier to be more precise with respect to the calculation of the probability and produce better recommendations.

We are particularly interested in evaluating our approach with a data observation period of at least two years for the same company. This will allow us to include other context factors such as the season of the year, Christmas and holidays. In addition, we are interested in evaluating our system with data from different retailing companies. Finally, we want to validate our approach in other application domains.

References

1. Abowd, G.D., Dey, A.K., Brown, P.J., Davies, N., Smith, M., Steggles, P.: Towards a better understanding of context and context-awareness. In: Gellersen, H.-W. (ed.) HUC 1999. LNCS, vol. 1707, pp. 304–307. Springer, Heidelberg (1999). doi:10.1007/3-540-48157-5_29
2. Adomavicius, G., Sankaranarayanan, R., Sen, S., Tuzhilin, A.: Incorporating contextual information in recommender systems using a multidimensional approach. ACM Trans. Inf. Syst. (TOIS) **23**(1), 103–145 (2005)
3. Adomavicius, G., Tuzhilin, A.: Toward the next generation of recommender systems: a survey of the state-of-the-art and possible extensions. IEEE Trans. Knowl. Data Eng. **17**(6), 734–749 (2005)
4. Adomavicius, G., Tuzhilin, A.: Context-aware recommender systems. In: Ricci, F., Rokach, L., Shapira, B., Kantor, P. (eds.) Recommender Systems Handbook, pp. 217–253. Springer, Boston (2011). doi:10.1007/978-0-387-85820-3_7
5. Alpaydin, E.: Introduction to Machine Learning. MIT Press, Cambridge (2014)
6. Campos, P.G., Díez, F., Cantador, I.: Time-aware recommender systems: a comprehensive survey and analysis of existing evaluation protocols. User Model. User Adap. Inter. **24**(1–2), 67–119 (2014)
7. Ebrahimi, S., Villegas, N.M., Müller, H.A., Thomo, A.: SmarterDeals: a context-aware deal recommendation system based on the smartercontext engine. In: Proceedings of 2012 Conference of the Center for Advanced Studies on Collaborative Research, pp. 116–130. IBM Corporation (2012)

8. Fournier-Viger, P., Wu, C.W., Tseng, V.S.: Mining top-k association rules. In: Advances in Artificial Intelligence, pp. 61–73. Springer (2012)

9. Hartigan, J.A., Wong, M.A.: Algorithm as 136: a k-means clustering algorithm. J. R. Stat. Soc. Ser. C (Appl. Stat.) **28**(1), 100–108 (1979)

10. Hong, W., Li, L., Li, T.: Product recommendation with temporal dynamics. Expert Syst. Appl. **39**(16), 12398–12406 (2012)

11. Kitchenham, B., Charters, S.: Guidelines for performing systematic literature reviews in software engineering. Technical report, Keele University (2007)

12. Panniello, U., Gorgoglione, M.: Incorporating context into recommender systems: an empirical comparison of context-based approaches. Electron. Commer. Res. **12**(1), 1–30 (2012)

13. Shani, G., Gunawardana, A.: Evaluating recommendation systems. In: Ricci, F., Rokach, L., Shapira, B., Kantor, P.B. (eds.) Recommender Systems Handbook, pp. 257–297. Springer, Heidelberg (2011)

14. Shi, Y., Karatzoglou, A., Baltrunas, L., Larson, M., Hanjalic, A., Oliver, N.: TFMAP: optimizing map for top-n context-aware recommendation. In: Proceedings of 35th ACM SIGIR International Conference on Research and Development in Information Retrieval, pp. 155–164. ACM (2012)

15. Tan, P.N., Steinbach, M., Kumar, V., et al.: Introduction to Data Mining, vol. 1. Pearson Addison Wesley, Boston (2006)

16. Villegas, N.M.: Context Management and Self-Adaptivity for Situation-Aware Smart Software Systems. Ph.D. thesis, University of Victoria (2013)

17. Villegas, N.M., Müller, H.A.: Managing dynamic context to optimize smart interactions and services. In: Chignell, M., Cordy, J., Ng, J., Yesha, Y. (eds.) The Smart Internet. LNCS, vol. 6400, pp. 289–318. Springer, Heidelberg (2010). doi:10.1007/978-3-642-16599-3_18

18. Zheng, C., Haihong, E., Song, M., Song, J.: CMPTF: contextual modeling probabilistic tensor factorization for recommender systems. Neurocomputing **205**, 141–151 (2016)

19. Zou, B., Li, C., Tan, L., Chen, H.: GPUTENSOR: efficient tensor factorization for context-aware recommendations. Inf. Sci. **299**, 159–177 (2015)

CDCol: A Geoscience Data Cube that Meets Colombian Needs

Christian Ariza-Porras[1]([✉]), Germán Bravo[1], Mario Villamizar[1],
Andrés Moreno[1], Harold Castro[1], Gustavo Galindo[2], Edersson Cabera[2],
Saralux Valbuena[2], and Pilar Lozano[2]

[1] School of Engineering, Universidad de los Andes, Bogotá, Colombia
{cf.ariza975,gbravo,mj.villamizar24,dar-more,hcastro}@uniandes.edu.co
[2] Subdirección de Ecosistemas e Información Ambiental, Instituto de Hidrología
Meteorología y Estudios Ambientales (IDEAM), Bogotá, Colombia
plozano@ideam.gov.co

Abstract. Environmental analysts and researchers' time is an expensive and scarce resource that should be used efficiently. Creating analysis products from remote sensing images involves several steps that take time and can be either automatized or centralized. Among all these steps, product's lineage and reproducibility must be assured. We present CDCol, a geoscience data cube that addresses these concerns and fits the analysis needs of Colombian institutions, the forest and carbon monitoring system.

1 Introduction

Experts can analyze satellite imagery in, at least, four dimensions: latitude, longitude, time, and spectral. A geoscience data cube [12] is a solution that abstracts the satellite imagery as a multidimensional array of data that use, among others, these dimensions, allowing users to storage, query and process them.

Environmental analysts often work over a large set of images, selecting the best images from a larger data set that, often, must be downloaded to analysts? workstation. Once the suitable images are selected analysts process the images, limited by his machine storage and processing capabilities, using the proprietary or open software they have access to. Once the processing has been finished, analysts can use their expertise to analyze their results.

In a traditional case, each analyst must download, select, and process a large set of images. This download, selection and most of the pre-processing is common to a great share of the analysis. Thus, make it once and make it available to analysts can improve productivity, using effectively analysts time.

Results could be reused, often they can be used as part of other analysis, but this requires knowing the lineage of results and they must be replicable. This is not always possible. Algorithms can be not available or unknown, sometimes some parameters are not documented, and it is unknown if these results have

© Springer International Publishing AG 2017
A. Solano and H. Ordoñez (Eds.): CCC 2017, CCIS 735, pp. 87–99, 2017.
DOI: 10.1007/978-3-319-66562-7_7

been through further processing. A common interface with data and a common analytic platform, that considers lineage and reproducibility of results, can lead to results truthfulness making them reusable.

In Colombia, the hydrology, meteorology, and environmental studies institute (also known as IDEAM by its acronym in Spanish), provides environmental data, information, and knowledge to the Ministry of Environment, Housing and Territorial Development, and the governmental agencies that conforms the SINA, the national environmental information system. Among its tasks IDEAM is responsible of the forest and atmospheric carbon monitor system (SMBYC – Sistema de monitoreo de bosques y carbono) [10].

The SMBYC supports environmental policy making, implementation, and evaluation. It provides government agencies, both national and territorial, tools related to monitoring forest coverage, deforestation, forest carbon stocks, and carbon emissions from deforestation. To achieve this goal, the SMBYC need tools that provides timely, consistent, and cost-efficient results. Combination of tools and experts? knowledge have a global impact by helping to conserve forest ecosystems, which play and major role on the global carbon cycle [2,6].

For example, one of the products of the SMBYC is the annual deforestation report. To produce this report, it is necessary to process the available imagery of a given year for all the country. The first step is to produce an intermediate product, a statistical temporal compound that produce an image that represents the area in the given period and reduce the areas without information. Once these intermediate result is produced, it can be used to produce multiple coverage maps, for this report, the forest-no forest map.

Satellite image processing requires infrastructure with large storage and processing power. It also requires algorithms, and developers with imagery knowledge are a scarce resource. There are some intermediate products that can be reused, if they can be trusted. Analysts from IDEAM and other SINA agencies have similar standardized workflows, so they can benefit from use a common analytical platform. This is the main motivation behind this work.

Specific CDCol goals are described in Sect. 2, then we describe the most relevant related work and how they align with these goals in Sect. 3. We describe our solution strategy in Sect. 4 and the current implementation in Sect. 5. The current results and the future work is discussed on Sect. 6, and present our conclusions on Sect. 7.

2   CDCOL Goals

Along with expert analysts and developers of remote sensing analysis algorithms, we define the needs that must be covered by CDCol with the purpose of better alignment with the existing infrastructure, processes, policies, and roles existing in the creation of analysis from remote sensing imagery:

Data ownership. Historic analysis ready data should be available without dependency of an external service.

Extensibility. New sources and processing algorithms must be able to be easily added.

Lineage. The provenance of results must be identifiable by logging algorithms and parameters used.

Replicability. Results must be replicable.

Complexity abstraction. Developers must be able to create new algorithms without interact directly with the datacube query API. Developers should know how to work with multidimensional arrays.

Ease of use. The user interface should allow to analysts to execute algorithms without a long training. Developers should be able to create new algorithms using existent python knowledge with an small learning curve.

Parallelism. Available computational resources should be used effectively.

Fit to IDEAM Standards and work-flow. Most of IDEAM products are based on temporal medians' compounds. This should be taken into account in parallelization strategies. Each analysis process can be seen as a workflow. Although initially beyond development scope, CDCol design will allow us to implement a workflow management component in the near future.

3 Related Work

Due to the difficulties involved in creating analysis products from remote sensing images, several platforms have been developed to address the main issues present in remote sensing analysis at country scale. We would like to highlight the following platforms.

One of the main players in the remote sensing business is Planet Labs [16]. This company owns the RapidEye and PlanetScope satellite constellations, and recently has acquired Terra Bella [4,13] from Google. They offer two main services: Planet Explorer and Planet Platform. The first service allows users to easily download imagery products created from their collections and the latter offers an API to programmatically search and download analysis ready data for developers. For the moment, their products enable analysts to easily search and download analysis ready data from created from their imagery, but leaves the management and processing of the images to the analyst. This means that most of the complexity of managing the life cycle of the algorithm development, as well as the processing tools to efficiently execute these algorithms are outside the scope of the services.

Another important initiative is the Google Earth Engine API [7]. This engine allows users to efficiently execute user-specific algorithms using remote sensing imagery hosted on the Google infrastructure, users are allowed to upload their own imagery to be operated with public collections such as the Landsat catalogue. Although being a very efficient platform for hosting and processing remote sensing imagery, the platform by itself doesn't contemplate the life cycle of the algorithm development and the roles involved in an institution such as IDEAM, neither it allows to enforce the replicability and lineage of the resulting products.

Finally, the Australian Geoscience Data Cube (AGDC) initiative [11,12] has as its main objective the organization of the historical archive of Australian

LANDSAT imagery for convenient storage and processing. In its first version, that we will refer as v1, the data cube facilitated the process of ingestion and automated processing on a high performance computing infrastructure. The ingestion process guarantees that pixels among different scenes and different dates co-register; in order to do this, the ingestion process divides each Landsat scene in tiles, a predefined one degree by one degree (4000 × 4000 pixels) area, which are stored in GEOTIFF format. The ingestion process also indexes the images within a relational database (PostGIS) to help the data cube to determine which tiles should be accessed to answer the user queries. One of the limitations of this version is that the cube is only capable of ingesting preprocessed Landsat scenes in a process specific for Australian needs and policies and it is not publicly available. Users of the v1 data cube are able to efficiently query and process continental level analysis leveraged by the data-intensive computational infrastructure at the National Computational Infrastructure (NCI) High Performance Computer (HPC) at the Australian National University (ANU). Examples of works such as [14,15] were developed under this platform.

Since this first version heavily depended on proprietary preprocessing of scenes and on the NCI computational infrastructure, a new version, that we refer as v1.5, was made available to our team for evaluation that substituted the processing and parallelization scheme for an open source one based on the Celery Project[1] and is able to ingest data analysis ready files from the Landsat collection. One of the main limitations of this version was that it wasn't possible to ingest other data sources different from Landsat collections.

A further step in releasing the datacube in an open source project was the creation of the Open Data Cube [5], that we refer as AGDC v2. This is an open source development version whose main contribution implemented at the moment is the ability to ingest data analysis ready data sources and integrate them in order to create final analysis products.

In Table 1 we compare the current related works, drawing special attention to the criteria defined as the goals of the datacube.

Table 1. Comparison of evaluated alternatives

Feature/product	Planet	Earth engine	AGDC v1	AGDC V1.5	AGDC V2
Data ownership	No	No	Yes	Yes	Yes
Add new algorithms	Yes	Yes	Yes	Yes	Yes
Use new sources	No	No	Limited	Limited	Yes
Lineage	Yes	Yes	Yes	Yes	Yes
Enforced replicability	No	No	No	No	No
Complexity abstraction	No	No	No	No	Limited
Algorithms publication	No	Script sharing	No	No	No
Usability	Yes	Yes	No	Limited	No
Parallelization	N/A	N/A	Yes	Yes	In development
Fit to IDEAM's Standards	Yes	Yes	No	Yes	Yes

---

[1] http://www.celeryproject.org/.

3.1 CDCol Background

In 2015, we deployed a proof-of-concept based on AGDC v1.5. We ingested Colombian data for an area of interest, and implemented 4 algorithms additional to the one included in the first version (best pixel mosaic algorithm), the implemented algorithms were: Temporal medians compounds, NDVI, forest-no forest classification and change detection using PCA. With this experience, we designed a conceptual architecture of CDCol, that evolved in the current solution strategy [1].

4   Solution Strategy

In order to achieve the goals described in Sect. 2, CDCol solution strategy includes a bank of algorithms, roles and policies definition, web user interface, parallelism strategy, bulk ingestion mechanism and training workshops. The following sections describe this elements and how tackle the defined objectives.

4.1   Bank of Algorithms

A bank of algorithms allows analysts to find and execute algorithms, without coding skill required. Executions are repeatable and are logged, and results know their lineage. It also allows developers to publish their algorithms, manage their life cycle, and to receive feedback. Furthermore, the bank of algorithms hide complexity to developers through the generic algorithm.

Algorithms Life Cycle. In CDCol, algorithms are defined by a general description. The algorithm is implemented by a version. From publication to obsolescence, algorithms versions must be managed. Figure 1 shows the life-cycle of a version of an algorithm.

A new version is created with state in development. During the development process, versions are visible only to his developer owner and once they are finished, the developer owner can publish them. Published versions are listed in the bank of algorithms and are visible to analysts. Developers can withdraw publication of versions only if it hasn't been used by analysts. A published version can be marked as obsolete at the end of his life cycle. Only versions in development can be deleted.

Algorithm Version Configuration. For each new algorithm version, the developers can define the different parameters the analyst must enter during the execution process. For each parameter, the developer can define the name, the type (string, integer, time period, boolean, map area, among others), a description, a help text to include recommendations, if it is mandatory or optional, and the default value.

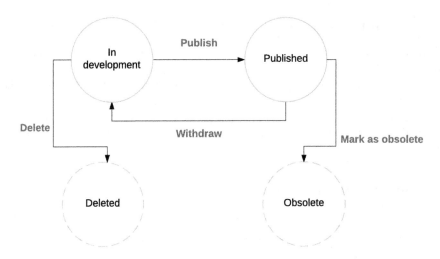

Fig. 1. Version life cycle

Generic Algorithm. A generic algorithm is defined in order to hide data cube internals and parallelization complexity to developers, and to add flexibility to the architecture making algorithms implementation independent of query API.

4.2   Roles

So far we have mentioned two of the roles that should be taken into account in CDCol: developers and analysts. Two more roles are introduced on CDCol: data and system administrators. With Roles, CDCol hides algorithms definition and implementation complexities to Analysts, and lead to a clear data ownership and quality responsibilities.

Analyst. Users with the analyst role can select an algorithm version and create an execution providing the required parameters, using available data.

Developer. Users with the developer role can define algorithms and create new versions of existing algorithms. Also, developers can manage the life-cycle of their algorithm versions.

Data Administrator. Users with the data administrator role can create new data set types and ingest new images.

System Administrator. Users with the system administrator role can edit system definitions and monitor system usage.

4.3   Web User Interface

A responsive web user interface gives the users the ability to work on a large set of satellite images from any device. The web user interface reduce the learning curve and access barriers to use the data cube. Each role has access to tasks they will perform. The web user interface hides the complexity of writing new algorithm' version to analysts, who can access to a set of published algorithms and execute them with the desired parameters. Developers can publish new algorithms without worry about parallelism strategy or data cube query API.

4.4   Parallelism Strategy

Most of the products of current users of CDCol are based on temporal compounds. For this reason, parallelization strategy should be along geographical axis, instead of time. It also must be automatic and hidden to algorithm developers.

4.5   Bulk Ingestion

Initial ingestion includes 15 years of satellite images from landsat 5, 7, and 8. There are around 14191 ingestable scenes, selected from 27070 downloaded images. A bulk ingestion mechanism is needed to perform this task.

4.6   Training Workshops

Training and diffusion workshops are essential to the success of the datacube. Train developers on multidimensional arrays manipulation on python, and analysts on datacube work-flow allows CDCol to have active users since its start.

5   Implementation

A high level view of CDCol components is depicted in Fig. 2. CDCol architecture is intended to have low coupling in order to minimize the impact of change on one component. In the following subsections we describe each of them, his responsibilities and current implementation.

Data Cube Core. Data Cube Core component is responsible of data sets types definition, data sets indexing and ingestion, persistence and query processing.

Implementation is based on AGDC v2. We created a stable fork from development branch on 2016-07-29. This version of AGDC provides dataset definition, ingestion mechanism and query API. We implemented bulk ingestion scripts, optimized for current infrastructure, used to both large initial and successive periodical ingestion. Configuration files were created to ingest data from Colombia, minimizing geometrical transformation error and using WGS84 coordinate reference system.

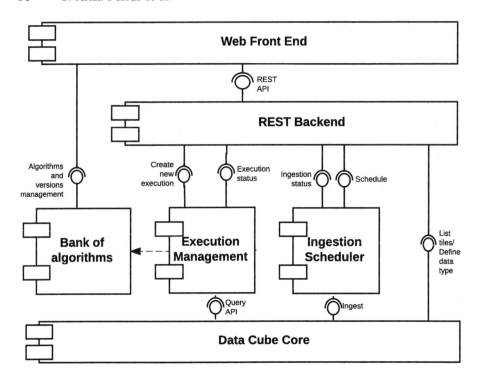

Fig. 2. CDCol high level components

Bank of Algorithms. The bank of algorithms is responsible of definition of algorithms and versions, and management of their life-cycle. Algorithm bank and web user interface were developed on python using DJango Framework.

Execution Management. Execution must be transparent to both analysts and algorithms developers. Execution management component implements a parallelization strategy and apply it to algorithms using the generic task definition. Generic task requires multidimensional arrays as parameters and accepts any additional parameter the algorithms require, and produces results in multidimensional arrays or text. Current parallelization strategy divides tasks by geographical tile. Execution manager is responsible of divide each task in subtasks and execute them. Celery was used as scheduler, using RabbitMQ as queue manager.

Ingestion Scheduler. Ingestion is a processing, memory and disk intensive task. For this reason it should be performed in bash and during times of low demand. Ingestion scheduler is implemented using a relational database management system, shared with rest back-end, and a posix crontab.

Web Front End. The CDCol web portal was designed with the goal of facilitating to the different roles (analysts, developers, data and system administrators) to easily manage and access the datacube through graphical user interfaces.

The Front-end of the web portal was implemented using cross-browser and cross-device technologies such as HTML5, CSS3 and Javascript (jQuery). Boostrap was used to provide responsive interfaces. The back of the web portal was developed in Python using the MVC (Model View Controller) Django framework.

The web portal was implemented using an agile methodology, involving all the project stakeholders. During the whole project, several meetings were planned with the IDEAM team to test and evaluate the different features that each role required and the user experience (UX) the web portal should provide.

For features related to data management and algorithm execution the web portal consumes the REST Back end services. Algorithm executions are processed in an asynchronous way. Analysts complete the execution form which is rendered dynamically including the set of parameters defined by the algorithm publisher; the web portal consume a REST Back end service, wait the confirmation the execution was received successfully, and the execution status is marked as "Pending to Execute". Once the execution is started, the Execution Management component change the status to "In Execution", and when the execution is finished its status is changed to "Finished" or "Finished with errors", in case of problems. During the whole execution cycle analysts can monitor their executions in a web interface that is updated every 30 s.

Ingest tasks are sent through the web portal by data administrators and they are also executed asynchronously. Data administrators select the storage unit to ingest, and the web portal register the task with the status "Pending to Execute". Once the ingestion scheduler process the task, the status task in changed to "Finished" or "Finished with errors", in case of problems.

All tasks related to algorithm management and system monitoring are processed synchronously and the users receive the final results of their actions in the web portal immediately without requiring the consumption of back-end services.

An example of the user interface used by analysts to send an algorithm execution is shown in Fig. 3.

REST Back-End. Rest back-end is implemented using Django REST framework to expose services that are consumed from the web portal.

The services exposed are mainly for actions related to algorithm execution and data management. The services published for algorithm execution receive the execution information from the web portal and send the execution to the Execution Management. The services published for data management receive the information from the web portal, execute the action on the local datacube file system and return the response.

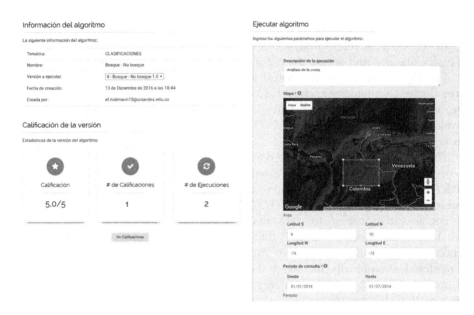

Fig. 3. Example CDCOL web user interface

6   Results and Discussion

After initial ingestion process, 15854 Landsat 5, 7, and 8 (T1 Surface Reflectance products from USGS) scenes, from 15 years, were ingested. That constitutes a centralized and controlled source of truth, and allows to analysts to use the time that used to be dedicated to download and selection of scenes, to processing and analysis.

At the bank of algorithms we implemented versions of algorithms that produces temporal medians compounds, NDVI maps, forest-no forest classification, and change detection using principal components analysis. Execution performance are comparable to our previous implementations presented on [1] with a lower development complexity, because of hiding to developer data cube internals and parallelization strategy. We also adapted an implementation of WOFS [14].

Developers training workshops were focused on python development and multidimensional data manipulations using xarray [8,9] and numpy [3]. At the end of the workshops developers were able to create their own algorithms for the datacube. Most of the assistants implemented coverture indexes and classification algorithms.

Analysts are able to use published algorithms in their analysis, giving them a set of tools, a large amount of curated data, and the necessary infrastructure to create products. These products are repeatable thanks to the executions historical on CDCol, and the history attribute in the resulting NetCDF files.

It is important to improve the quality of cloud masking process since the masks available with analysis ready data ingested into the data cube present some issues related to confusing water bodies and shadows and not identifying haze areas. This can be achieved at algorithms' layer, however, currently, it would need to be implemented in each algorithm. Once the work flow management is implemented, a masking algorithm can be created and used in the flows that require it.

6.1 Future Work

Some features were beyond this iteration, but are desired features on the data cube. The most visible features are horizontal scaling, algorithm dependent parallelization schemes, and workflows management.

Horizontal Scaling. Current implementation scale vertically, adding new storage and processing capability to existing infrastructure. This scaling strategy is limited to the expansion capabilities of the physical machine.

At short term, horizontal scaling can be achieved using shared storage and multiple processing nodes. Celery already allows to have multiple processing nodes and, even without this, our parallelization strategy allow us to map processing task across multiple nodes.

At medium-term, distributed storage can be used, allowing to scale on using multiple, less expensive, devices.

At long term, a geographically distributed architecture, with multiple data centers, can be used, joining storage and processing capabilities of multiple government institutions.

Algorithm Dependent Parallelization Schemes. Some algorithms, that works on time series (e.g. WOFS) rather than on temporal composites, does not fit well on the current parallelization scheme. These algorithms can have a better performance than actual if the scheduler split them by time. CDCol could allow the developer to select the parallelization strategy that best fits their implementation. Such strategy should be able to change without the need to change implementation.

Workflows Management. The generic task design is intended to be used in workflows. However, currently, each algorithm is implemented to be independent, starting from the data stored in the cube. This lead to code, and work, replication. A workflow management system would allow to reuse existing algorithms without re-implementing them.

7 Conclusions

We presented CDCol, a geoscience data cube addressed to Colombian environmental institutions' needs. With his implementation, we achieve a time of analysis reduction, a better use of experts' time, reproducibility of results, and extensibility both by integration of new types of images and by adding new algorithms or versions.

CDCol allows to developers to implement, with a low learning curve, new algorithms; to analysts to execute them over a large collection of images over time; and to data administrator to add new images to collection. The data cube helps analysts to produce information products such as temporal medians compounds for all the country in just 12 h. This kind of task used to take at least 72 h using a regular protocol.

As a first step of time series analysis, the data cube helps analyst to create NDVI maps, forest-no forest classification maps, or water-no water maps for a long-time period (15 years) using the image catalog ingested into the data cube.

Acknowledgments. We thank to Brian Killough from NASA, and Alfredo Delos Santos and Kayla Fox from AMA team, for their support and fruitfully discussions. We also thank to CEOS Australia group for its work and for share it with the world. We thank also to the Environmental Ministry for financial support.

CDCol uses NetCDF format UCAR/Unidata to storage ingested data and results (http://doi.org/10.5065/D6H70CW6).

References

1. Bravo, G., Castro, H., Moreno, A., Ariza-Porras, C., Galindo, G., Valbuena, S., Lozano, P.: Architecture for a Colombian data cube using satellite imagery for environmental applications. In: 2017 Proceedings of Advances in Computing, 12th Colombian Conference, CCC 2017, Cali, Colombia, 19–22 September, chap. 17. Springer International Publishing (2017, in press)
2. Clark, D.A.: Detecting tropical forests' responses to global climatic and atmospheric change: current challenges and a way forward. Biotropica **39**(1), 4–19 (2007)
3. Dubois, P.F., Hinsen, K., Hugunin, J.: Numerical python. Comput. Phys. **10**(3), 262–267 (1996)
4. Dyer, J.M., McClelland, J.: Paradigm change in earth observation-skybox imaging and SkySat-1. In: Hatton, S. (ed.) Proceedings of the 12th Reinventing Space Conference, pp. 69–89. Springer, Cham (2017). doi:10.1007/978-3-319-34024-1_5
5. Geoscience Australia, CSIRO, NCI: Open data cube core, December 2015. https://github.com/opendatacube/datacube-core
6. Gitay, H., Suárez, A., Watson, R.T., Dokken, D.J.: Climate change and biodiversity. IPCC Technical Paper V (2002)
7. Google Earth Engine: A planetary-scale geo-spatial analysis platform, December 2015. https://earthengine.google.com
8. Hoyer, S., Hamman, J.: xarray: N-D labeled arrays and datasets in Python. J. Open Res. Softw **5**(1), 10 (2017). http://doi.org/10.5334/jors.148
9. Hoyer, S., Fitzgerald, C., Hamman, J., et al.: xarray: v0.8.0, August 2010. http://dx.doi.org/10.5281/zenodo.59499
10. Instituto de Hidrología, M.Y.E.A.D.C.I.: Programa Nacional para el Monitoreo y Seguimiento a los Bosques y áreas de aptitud forestal (PMSB): Formulación y plan de implementación. IDEAM (2008). http://capacitacion.siac.ideam.gov.co/SIAC/Programa_nacional_monitoreo_bosques_PMSB_2008.pdf
11. Ip, A., Evans, B., Lymburner, L., Oliver, S.: The Australian geoscience data cube (AGDC)-a common analytical framework (2015). https://eresearchau.files.wordpress.com/2014/07/eresau2014_submission_85.pdf

12. Lewis, A., Oliver, S., Lymburner, L., Evans, B., Wyborn, L., Mueller, N., Raevksi, G., Hooke, J., Woodcock, R., Sixsmith, J., Wu, W., Tan, P., Li, F., Killough, B., Minchin, S., Roberts, D., Ayers, D., Bala, B., Dwyer, J., Dekker, A., Dhu, T., Hicks, A., Ip, A., Purss, M., Richards, C., Sagar, S., Trenham, C., Wang, P., Wang, L.W.: The Australian geoscience data cube–foundations and lessons learned. Remote Sens. Environ. (2017). http://www.sciencedirect.com/science/article/pii/S0034425717301086

13. MacLachlan, C.: Maneuverable microsatellites: the skybox case study. In: 14th International Conference on Space Operations, p. 2492 (2016) http://arc.aiaa.org/doi/pdf/10.2514/6.2016-2492

14. Mueller, N., Lewis, A., Roberts, D., Ring, S., Melrose, R., Sixsmith, J., Lymburner, L., McIntyre, A., Tan, P., Curnow, S., Ip, A.: Water observations from space: mapping surface water from 25 years of Landsat imagery across Australia. Remote Sens. Environ. **174**, 341–352 (2016). http://www.sciencedirect.com/science/article/pii/S0034425715301929

15. Ong, C., Caccetta, M., Lau, I., Malthus, T., Thapar, N.: The use of long term earth observation data archives to identify potential vicarious calibration targets in Australia. In: IEEE International Geoscience and Remote Sensing Symposium, Milan, Italy (2015)

16. Planet Team: Planet application program interface: in space for life on earth, San Francisco, CA, December 2017. https://api.planet.com

G-WordNet: Moving WordNet 3.0 and Its Resources to a Graph Database

Sergio Jimenez$^{(\boxtimes)}$ and George Dueñas

Instituto Caro y Cuervo, Bogotá, Colombia
{sergio.jimenez,george.duenas}@caroycuervo.gov.co
http://www.caroycuervo.gov.co

Abstract. In this paper, the convenience of storing a large lexical database (WordNet) in a graph database management system (Neo4j) is studied. The result is G-WordNet, which is a freely-available lexical database based on the Princeton WordNet 3.0 and all its sense-annotated corpora. We justify the need of this resource and the advantages of using a graph database in comparison with previous approaches. In addition, we present an application example of G-WordNet in the tasks of semantic lexical similarity using the declarative query language Cypher. Also, some possible usage scenarios of G-WordNet are discussed, particularly in the fields of lexicography, computational linguistics, natural language processing and NoSQL databases, for research, development, and teaching.

Keywords: WordNet · Lexical databases · Graph databases · Neo4j · Semantic lexical similarity

1 Introduction

WordNet is a large lexical-semantic graph composed of nodes, which represent lemmas, senses and synsets (i.e. set of synonym concepts), interconnected by edges representing semantic relationships (i.e. antonymy, hypernymy, meronymy, etc.) [15]. Also, WordNet is among the most-used resources in the field of Natural Language Processing. However, WordNet and its equivalents are onerous, time-consuming and difficult to build. Alternatively, collaborative lexicons such as Wiktionary are constructed by a significant number of authors who contribute to a more accurate view of current language use [14]. In this scenario, both WordNet and Wiktionary approaches have their pros and cons. On the one hand, WordNet has a very rich semantic representation of lexical units, but its content is geared primarily to machines, and its structure is difficult to update and consult by humans. On the other hand, Wiktionary is easy to use and update by humans, but its structure is not appropriate for computer applications and resembles a classic printed dictionary lacking many explicit semantic relationships.

In the last decade, the database research community has proposed the so-called graph databases with the idea of improving the modeling of large and

© Springer International Publishing AG 2017
A. Solano and H. Ordoñez (Eds.): CCC 2017, CCIS 735, pp. 100–114, 2017.
DOI: 10.1007/978-3-319-66562-7_8

highly interconnected data structures that cannot be properly stored and consulted with current technologies based on relational databases [2]. For example, the web social graph contains hundreds of millions of nodes representing people and billions of edges representing "friend", "like", and "follow" relationships. Querying such data structures requires specific graph operations that cannot be performed properly with classic query languages such as SQL. We believe that this technology can help in reconciling of the dilemma between WordNet and Wiktionary approaches.

For that, we moved WordNet 3.0 and all its sense-annotated corpora to a popular freely available graph-database engine, Neo4j. The proposed resource, G-WordNet, is searchable and updatable in a declarative language intended not only for technicians. It is specially designed for graph structures. In addition, the proposed approach is composed mainly of components available on the market that can be deployed with little cost and effort. This is a first step towards a long term goal of building a large collaboratively lexicographic resource with a rich semantic representation, while being usable and updatable either by either humans or computers.

In this paper we present the WordNet data model, its applications, storage issues and query methods (see Sect. 2). In Sect. 3, we briefly present some observations related to the relatively new paradigm of the graph databases. In Sect. 4, describes the the components of the proposed resource. Section 5 provides a brief guide for using G-WordNet and explains a example of usage. Finally, in Sect. 6 we discuss some research directions and usage scenarios, and Sect. 7 gives some concluding remarks.

2   WordNet

WordNet is a large lexical database for the English language [15]. Unlike the classical lexicographical approach of building dictionaries indexed alphabetically by words, WordNet is organized mainly in a graph of concepts (nodes) and semantic relations (edges). Since its inception, WordNet has been widely used by the Natural Language Processing research community and has had a major impact on the development of Artificial Intelligent applications. In addition, the WordNet data model has been used to develop similar databases in different languages [5] and inspired recent multilingual efforts like as ConceptNet [12] and BabelNet [20]. The effectiveness of WordNet in Artificial Intelligence may be related to the psycholinguistic theory that words (nouns in particular) are stored hierarchically in the human brain [25]. Therefore, it is possible that the WordNet data model is somehow related to the way humans store and retrieve words in their brains.

In lexicography, the WordNet data model contrasts with the classical approach of dictionary construction, in which information is stored alphabetically by words. Basically, each word entry contains a set of senses or meanings (optionally grouped by part-of-speech), each containing at least one textual definition and optionally a set of synonyms, antonyms, examples, and so on. Although the design of this model is inherently limited because it is more convenient that format for printing, most of the current on-line electronic dictionaries retain this structure (e.g. The Free Dictionary[1], Wiktionary[2], RAE[3], etc.). One of the problems of this data model is redundancy. For instance, in the English Wiktionary, the respective definitions of the first senses of the words "automobile", "car", "motorcar" are different paraphrased texts from each other describing the same concept. In addition, this model is prone to incompleteness since the list of synonyms for a set of synonym words rarely forms a coherent whole. For instance, also in the English Wiktionary, "smart" is not among the synonyms of "intelligent", "clever" is not synonymous with "smart" and "bright" is not synonymous with "clever". Clearly, classical dictionaries are designed to model polysemy (a word with many meanings) but fail to model synonymy (many words for lexicalizing a meaning). Moreover, other semantic relationships such as antonymy, hypernymy (*is-a*), meronymy (*is-part-of*), among others are subject to the same drawbacks in such model.

2.1   WordNet Data Model

The basic component of WordNet model is the *synset*, which represents a concept described by a single definition as a set of lemmas (i.e. words in their basic form, e.g. "sing" is the lemma of "singing"), which lexicalizes the concept. For instance, the lemmas "luck", "fortune", "chance", "hazard" are grouped into a synset sharing the following definition: "an unknown and unpredictable phenomenon that causes an event to result one way rather than another". For Miller [15], the lemmas in a synset are interchangeable in some contexts, precisely those that refer to the concept described by the synset. For example, in the sentence "we ran into each other by pure chance", the word "chance" can be replaced by "luck", and less naturally, but semantically equivalent by "fortune" and "hazard". Clearly, Miller said "some contexts", not "all", because lemmas like "fortune" have other meanings and can occur in other synsets.

Figure 1 shows a sample of the WordNet graph. In words, the lexicon of the English language is first modeled in WordNet by a set of lemmas. Then, each lemma is linked to one or more synsets, being each occurrence of a lemma in a synset, a sense (a meaning) for that lemma. Synsets and senses are interconnected semantically through by relations called *pointers*. These pointers can link pairs of synsets or pair of senses, but never a synset and a sense (in practice such a case can happen because synsets containing a single lemma-sense pair could be considered as lemmas).

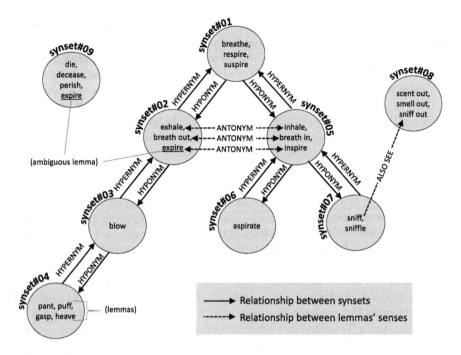

Fig. 1. Sample of the WordNet graph

2.2 Applications

WordNet is an essential resource for core tasks in natural language processing such as Word Sense Disambiguation (WSD) [18], semantic lexical similarity [21], semantic textual similarity [1] and textual entailment [10]. Among these, WSD is probably the best WordNet exploit. WSD aims to determine the correct meaning used for ambiguous words in a text. To do this, WordNet provides the inventory of senses and semantic structure necessary to determine the correct combination of senses.

WordNet is also used in an assortment or high level tasks, namely: question answering [16], sentiment analysis [3], named-entity recognition [13], information retrieval [8], text summarization [26], anaphora resolution [23], among others.

2.3 Issues of Storage Models

All versions of the Princeton WordNet have been distributed in a proprietary format using plain text files. The main lexical graph is stored in four "data" files (*data.noun*, *data.verb*, *data.adv* and *data.adj*) classified by part-of-speech. Each line in the "data" files describes a synset by listing its set of lemmas, definitions, examples, pointers to other synsets, and pointers to other lemmas (from lemmas in the line to lemmas in other synsets). The format is cryptic in some ways because it makes use of special characters to represent pointers (e.g. @ for hypernym,   for hyponym), mixes decimal and hexadecimal numbers, and uses other legacy practices because of many design and technology constraints of the 1980s. In most applications, this format is only used by a one-pass process, which reads the source files and builds a graph data structure in main memory; there are several tools for that purpose[4]. Once in main memory, standard programming is used to search for paths between lemmas, senses and synsets, and any other algorithmic processing of the graph.

However, if the application at hand requires data editing, integration with other lexical databases or multiuser interaction, the main memory-based approach is clearly inappropriate. These requirements have been effectively addressed through the use of relational database managements systems (RDBMS), since the WordNet data model can be straightforwardly expressed in a relational database schema. The common design approach involves three main tables (*lemmas, senses, synsets*) and a simple schema that expresses that a particular lemma has one or many senses, any sense is associated with a synset and that any synset has at least one sense. The pointers are modeled by *sense-sense* and *synset-synset* tables. Despite its consistency and simplicity, this model has an important limitation that constraints its convenience, which is the SQL query language. The problem lies in the fact that most of the natural language applications using WordNet involve finding a paths of pointers (edges) between two or more (nodes) synsets, senses or lemmas. In the typical relational model of WordNet, to establish the relationship between two nodes through an edge, a *join* operation is needed. In general, to reach any node at n edges of distance from any node, it would require $n - 1$ nested joins. For instance, let us assume that the *id* of the synset containing lemmas [*pant, puff, gasp, heave*] is known (i.e. "synset#4") and that its great-grand-parent synset [*breathe, respire, suspire*] in a hypernym chain is needed (use Fig. 1 as reference). The SQL query for obtaining that path in a single *synset-synset* table containing the pairwise relationships between synsets would be as follows:

```
SELECT source.synset1 as great_grand_child,
       grand_parent.synset2 as great_grand_parent
FROM (synset_synset AS source
      JOIN synset_synset AS parent
      ON source.synset2=parent.synset1)
         JOIN synset_synset as grand_parent
         ON parent.synset2=grand_parent.synset1
WHERE source.synset1="synset#4" AND
      source.rel_type="HYPERNYM" AND
      parent.rel_type="HYPERNYM" AND
      grand_parent.rel_type="HYPERNYM"
```

An example SQL query of two nesting JOINs to find the path, in a hypernym (*is-a*) hierarchy, between a synset and its great-grandparent synset

Since the *synset#4* and its great-grand-parent synset are connected by three edges, a two-nested JOINs query is required to bind them. In most scenarios,

---

[4] https://wordnet.princeton.edu/wordnet/related-projects/#local.

the number of edges connecting two nodes is unknown and usually large. In addition, in practice the use of a large number of nested joins is prohibited (even for relatively small databases) because of performance problems. Therefore, this example depicts the disadvantage of the SQL language for querying a graph in such conditions. Given such a limitation, the relational database is only useful for providing persistent storage, but any graph-oriented operation must be performed in main memory using the entire graph, or alternatively using sub-graphs if it does not fit into main memory.

The designers of BabelNet [20], a large multilingual lexical database similar to WordNet, addressed this problem using Apache Lucene[5] as storage platform and created a Java API to access the resource. Since the effort invested in such a development effort is enormous and the resources needed to keep the API available are considerable, replicating that solution is a difficult task. In this scenario, the most rational option is to access the resource through the API, but that alternative is restricted by usage limits and the read-only access constraint. In an effort to provide BabelNet in an standard and portable format, there is an alternative RDF-triple[6] repository hosted in a Virtuoso database server[7] that can be queried using SPARQL[8]. Although, the combination of RDF, SPARQL and Virtuoso provides a good framework, where the lexical graph can be queried without the limitations of SQL, the solution is limited by the SPARQL design constraint of being a read-only query language.

The goal of this work is to provide an alternative solution to the issues presented in this sub-section by providing a storage solution for lexical databases satisfying scalability, ease of deployment, updatability and the availability of a graph-oriented query language.

3   Graph Databases

A graph database is a data model for storing large data structures, which resembles a graph in the sense of topology [2], i.e. a set of nodes interconnected by edges or arcs. Contrasting with the classical relational model, the interconnection between data items in graph databases is as important, or even more, than the data itself [29]. Although, it is widely recognized that the relational model has limitations for modeling real-word entities, relational database management systems (RDBMS) and their query language SQL are, to this day, a de facto standard in the software industry.

Recently, RDBMS and SQL have been challenged by alternatives grouped under the blanket-term *NoSQL*, which refer to "non SQL" or "non relational" systems. These systems aim to provide better modeling, performance and scalability in the context of distributed systems. These improvements were generally

---

[5] http://lucene.apache.org.
[6] https://www.w3.org/RDF/.
[7] https://virtuoso.openlinksw.com/.
[8] https://www.w3.org/standards/techs/sparql.

produced as a trade-off of one or more of the popular principles of the relational model: *a*tomicity, *c*onsistency, *i*solation, and *d*urability, i.e. ACID databases [9].

The main gain of using a graph database is obtained when the data to be modeled are composed of elements highly interconnected by semantic or functional relationships. That is the case of social networks, geographical data, and as has been said, lexical data. It has been shown that for such data types, queries are executed considerably faster in a graph database than in an RDBMS [29]. Another advantage is that the declarative query language attached to a graph database system, generally includes a set of clauses for handling graph operations such as finding shortest paths, minimum spanning trees, neighborhoods, and so on. These operations are difficult to express using the SQL language and in some cases, the use of an auxiliary programming language is necessary.

Neo4j is a NoSQL graph database management system that relaxes the design constraint of using tables for data modeling, while preserving ACID principles [30]. Although, Neo4j is much less "mature" than the established SQL counterparts (e.g. MySQL, OracleDB, SQL Server, among others), it is being adopted by many on-line companies that deal with large social graphs (e.g. Stackoverflow, Glassdoor, etc.) These social graphs resemble lexical graphs on the number of nodes (millions) and edges (hundreds of millions). In addition, Neo4j is licensed under free a "Community Edition" license or alternatively by enterprise paid versions. The query language, *Cypher*, is on the way of becoming a standard with full open source access[9]. These are the reasons for selecting Neo4j as the storage back-end for WordNet. It is important to note that the Neo4j index engine is Lucene, making our choice somewhat similar to the decision made by the BabelNet designers. The main differences with their approach are that through the use of Neo4j, storage, indexing and querying is handled by a single tool, and that the graph is updatable using the Cypher query language.

4   G-WordNet

In this paper we introduce *G-WordNet*, ready-to-use lexical database for the English language based mainly on the Princeton WordNet version 3.0 [15] and the graph database environment Neo4j[10].

For convenience, G-WordNet is delivered in three sizes. G-WordNet-Small contains all the words and semantic relationships included in WordNet 3.0. In addition to the previous, the G-WordNet-Medium version contains additional information from the Princeton WordNet Gloss Corpus[11], which consist of textual definitions and usage examples for each synset, along with sense annotations (links to sense nodes) to words used in these texts. This means that selected ambiguous words from the textual definitions and examples are disambiguated by extending the graph with edges from the sentence node to the corresponding sense node. The larger version, G-WordNet-Large, contains more disambiguated

---

[9] http://www.opencypher.org/.
[10] https://neo4j.com/.
[11] http://wordnet.princeton.edu/glosstag.shtml.

sentences including all manually available corpora annotated with WordNet 3.0
senses, namely: SemCor [11] includes semantic concordances from 103 passages
of the Brown Corpus and the novel The Red Badge of Courage; OMSTI [28]
contains one million sense-tagged samples from MultiUN, SemCor, and DSO
corpus; Senseval-2 [7] is a word sense disambiguation corpus of 12 languages;
Senseval-3 task1 [27] is a corpus of words from two Wall Street Journal articles
and one excerpt from the Brown Corpus; SemEval-07 task 17 [24] includes annotated words from Wall Street Journal and the Brown Corpus; SemEval-13 task
12 [19] is a corpus of 13 articles, in 5 languages for different domains, from the
2010, 2011 and 2012 editions of the workshop on Statistical Machine Translation
(WSMT); and SemEval-15 task 13 [17] contains 4 documents from the OPUS
project, in 3 languages, for different domains (biomedical domain, maths and
computer domain, and social issues).

The availability of annotated corpora was the main reason why WordNet 3.0
was chosen instead of the latest version 3.1, for which there is not a significant
amount of annotated texts. Table 1 provides some dimensional features of the
three proposed versions.

Table 1. G-WordNet version graph features

G-WordNet version →	Small	Medium	Large
Number of nodes	514,068	658,740	1'549.290
Number of edges	1'316.101	2'588,891	4'996,181
Size/Zip compressed	164 MB/43.5 MB	335 MB/76.5 MB	981 MB/244 MB

Figure 2 shows a schema of the labels of the nodes (i.e. type of nodes) and the
relationships in G-WordNet. In that figure, nodes are represented by rounded
corners rectangles, tags represent node labels, and node attributes are listed
inside the rectangles. It is important to note that in Neo4j a node can have
several labels. That is the case of labels *words* and *lemmas*, where all words have
the label *word* (e.g. "begin", "began", "begun", "beginning") but only those in
their base form are labeled with *lemma* (e.g. "begin"). Some node attributes are
in bold face representing the uniqueness property. Unlike nodes, relationships are
constrained to have only one label. In the figure, relationships are depicted using
thick arrows. The relationships labeled as *semantic relationships* can link pairs
of synsets or pair of senses, and the label *semantic* is just a convenience label to
cover the possible semantic relationships detailed in Table 2. The attribute names
are self-explanatory or are taken from the original WordNet terminology[12].

---

[12] http://www.sparcpoint.com/Blog/Post/wordnet-the-lexical-database.

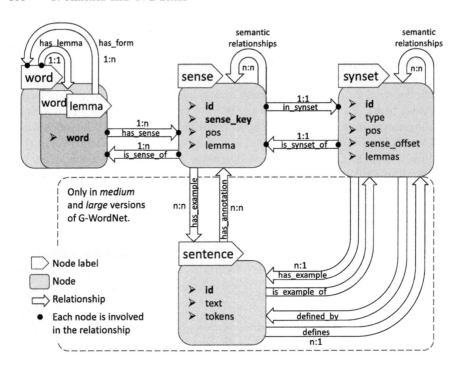

Fig. 2. G-WordNet schema

5   G-WordNet in Use

5.1   Deployment

The only prerequisite for using G-WordNet is an installation on a PC from the Neo4j Community Edition[13]. G-WordNet is distributed in the form of a ready to use compressed zip directory containing all the metadata, data and indexes. G-WordNet can be downloaded from http://gwordnet.caroycuervo.gov. co under the terms of the Creative Commons Attribution (BY) license and the licenses of all resources used in its construction[14]. For convenience, we recommend zipping the directory on My Documents/Neo4j/ directory, for Windows platforms, or on /var/lib/neo4j/data/databases/ for Linux. Once Neo4j is operational and the data is decompressed, the final step is simply to open the database by selecting the appropriate data path in the *Database Location* field in the Windows user interface. Alternatively, on Linux platforms, the name of the directory containing the data must be indicated in the line that starts with dbms.active_database=directory_name in the /etc/neo4j/neo4j.conf file. Finally, the graph can be browsed, queried and edited using any modern web browser in the URL localhost:7474.

---

[13] https://neo4j.com/download/community-edition.
[14] http://gwordnet.caroycuervo.gov.co/licence.html.

Table 2. Details of the semantic relationships in Fig. 2

Label (PoS)†[type]††	Example	Count
ANTONYM (nvar)[s]	expand↔contract, wet↔dry	7979
ALSO_SEE (va)[s]	split↔split up, sleep↔sleep in	3272
ATTRIBUTE (na)[ss]	proud→pride, dramatic↔drama	1278
CAUSE (v)[ss]	kill→[die, decease, perish]	220
DERIV_REL_FORM (nvar)[s]	respire↔respirator, pant→panting	74717
ENTAILMENT (v)[ss]	sneeze→[exhale, expire, breathe out]	408
HYPERNYM (nv)[ss]	[snooze, drowse]→[nap, catnap]→[sleep, kip]	89089
HYPONYM (nv)[ss]	[snooze, drowse]←[nap, catnap]←[sleep, kip]	89089
INSTANCE_HYPERNYM (n)[ss]	New Orleans→[city, metropolis]	8577
INSTANCE_HYPONYM (n)[ss]	New Orleans←[city, metropolis]	8577
IS_IN_DOMAIN (nvar)[ss]	[grow, rise]→[farming, agriculture]	6654
IS_THE_DOMAIN_OF (n)[ss,s]	[grow, rise]←[farming, agriculture]	6654
IS_THE_USE_FOR (n)[ss,s]	[slang, jargon]→[chuck, ditch]	1376
IS_USAGE (nvar)[ss,s]	[slang, jargon]←[chuck, ditch]	1376
IT_IS_SAID (n)[ss,s]	[Japan, Nippon]→[harakiri, harikari]	1360
USED_IN (nvar)[ss,s]	[Japan, Nippon]←[harakiri, harikari]	1360
MEMBER_HOLONYM (n)[ss]	[vegetation, flora]→[biota, biology]	12293
MEMBER_MERONYM (n)[ss]	[vegetation, flora]←[biota, biology]	12293
PARTICIPLE_OF_VERB (a)[s]	sanitize→sanitized, streaming→stream	73
PART_HOLONYM (n)[ss]	[scene, shot]→[movie, film]	9097
PART_MERONYM (n)[ss]	[scene, shot]←[movie, film]	9097
PERTANYM (r)[s]	maternal→mother	8023
SIMILAR_TO ()[ss]	[young, immature]→[adolescent, teen, teenage]	21286
SUBSTANCE_HOLONYM (n)[ss]	[pavement, paving]→[road, route]	797
SUBSTANCE_MERONYM (n)[ss]	[pavement, paving]←[road, route]	797
VERB_GROUP(v)[ss]	[collapse, fall in, give away]→[abandon, give up]	1750

† PoS (part of speech) n: noun, v: verb, a: adjective, r: adverb.
†† Type of relationship: ss: between synsets, s: between senses of lemmas.
Note: synsets are presented in the "Example" column as list of words in square brackets.

5.2   A Lexical Similarity Example

One of the essential applications of WordNet is the determination of the degree of similarity (or distance) between a pair of words. Most of the similarity measures for this purpose use the hypernym/hyponym hierarchy and some topological information that relates the two words [6]. The simplest measure is to count the number of edges connecting the two words. Although Cypher is intended to be readable by humans, to fully understand the following example, we refer the reader to a brief tutorial of the Cypher language[15].

Let's start with two English words in their base form: "car" and "train". Both lemmas are ambiguous having 5 possible senses for "car" and 17 for "train". The query for determining the possible senses of lemma is the following:

```
MATCH(:lemma{word: "train"})-[:has_sense]->(senses) RETURN senses
```

---

[15] https://neo4j.com/developer/cypher-query-language/.

This query can be read as: find the node with the label *lemma* having the property *word* equal to the string "car", look for the nodes connected to that node through edges labeled as *has_sense*, and finally, return those nodes (the sense nodes). Now, in the scenario of connecting two lemmas, the general idea of getting the shortest path on the graph is to get all the senses of both words, then consider every possible pair of senses (in practice synsets) of both words, next look for the shortest path for each pair, and finally select the path with the minimum number of edges. The following query performs such operation:

```
MATCH(:lemma{word: "car"})-[:has_sense]->()-[:in_synset]->(ss1)
MATCH(:lemma{word: "train"})-[:has_sense]->()-[:in_synset]->(ss2)
WITH ss1,ss2
MATCH path=shortestpath((ss1)-[:HYPERNYM|:HYPONYM*]->(ss2))
RETURN path ORDER BY length(path) LIMIT 1
```

In this query, the first two lines obtain the synsets associated with each word. The third line makes a Cartesian product of the two sets of synsets, which is passed to the next section of the query. The fourth line looks for the shortest path between each pair of synsets only through edges labeled as *HYPERNYM* or *HYPONYM*. Finally, the fifth line orders the paths found from shortest to longest and returns the first. The result of the query can be viewed as a spreadsheet, in JSON format or graphically as shown in Fig. 3.

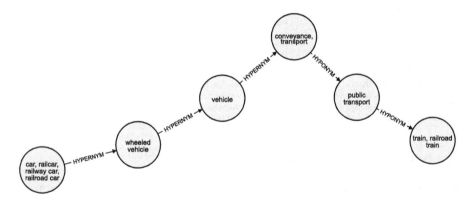

Fig. 3. Shortest path in WordNet using the hypernym/hyponym hierarchy between words "car" and "train"

This example contrasts with the one given in Subsect. 2.3. In that example, the SQL query considered (1) only paths having three edges, which is a very impractical constraint, (2) considered only *HYPERNYM* edges, (3) and started from a single known synset. The current example performs a task far complex using a considerably more readable and understandable query. In fact, expressing this task using SQL could be extremely complex, if not impossible. More examples can be found at http://www.gwordnet/caroycuervo.gov.co/examples.html.

6   Perspectives and Potential Uses of G-WordNet

6.1   Collaborative Linked Lexicography

As mentioned earlier, collaborative lexicography (e.g. Wiktionary) is an important trend, but with the current platforms, it is limited to the classical dictionary design. Since modern electronic lexicographical resources (e.g. WordNet, Babel-Net) rely on graph structures similar to those of modern on-line social communities (e.g. Linkedin, Researchgate), it seems a natural development to combine them into a collaborative platform. This means that it is possible to visualize a graph of nodes representing words and people, with edges interconnecting words by semantic relations, people by social relationships, and words-and-people by editions to the lexical information. This vision could materialize in a framework that offers updatability, scalability, reliability, and most importantly, the ability to manage large graph structures. We believe that G-WordNet is a first step towards that direction of development.

G-WordNet can also be used to conduct research in the field of lexicography. For example, G-WordNet Medium, can be used to detect cycles formed by concepts and their definitions. Previous work on that problem [22] can be improved by using sense annotations of the synsets definitions instead of the raw words.

6.2   Research Tool for Computational Linguistics

Certainly, WordNet is among the most used resources in the field of computational linguistics. As a token of this, approximately 20% of the articles in the ACL Anthology[16] –the largest collection of research papers in computational linguistics– mention the term "WordNet" (estimate obtained using Google search). However, most of the research exploit only the hypernym/hyponym hierarchy. In the same repository, the terms "hypernym/hyponym" are mentioned about 10x times more than "holonym/meronym" by the papers referring Word-Net. Perhaps this is due to the fact that most of the software tools for WordNet are focused in that hierarchy [4,21]. This limitation is not present in G-WordNet.

In addition as an added value, G-WordNet makes available to WordNet the whole set of Neo4j tools for managing graphs. As a result, research can explore new ways to use WordNet to address computational linguistics problems. In addition, because Cypher is a human-readable declarative language, researchers and practitioners from non-computer science areas could use it to explore new questions and approaches.

6.3   Off-the-shelf NLP for Applications

Some of the NLP tools are developed for research purposes using languages such as Perl, Haskel, and R, which are not common in professional software development environments. Nevertheless, other tools are available for Java and

---

[16] http://aclweb.org/anthology/.

Python, alternatives for C#, JavaScript and PHP are almost inexistent. Given the professional orientation of Neo4j, G-WordNet provides a practical source of lexical knowledge for software development.

6.4 Educational Tool

Given that no computer programming skills are needed for using G-WordNet, it becomes a practical resource for introductory courses in lexicography, linguistics, computational linguistics, and NLP. Moreover, owing to its large size and free license, G-WordNet is also a convenient resource for teaching and practicing the new paradigm of graph databases.

7   Conclusion

We proposed G-WordNet, a large and extensible lexical database for the English language based on the Princeton WordNet 3.0 and all the sense-annotated corpora available. This resource is freely available in the format of Neo4j, an increasingly popular graph database management system. This approach overcomes limitations related to availability, updatability, scalability, and ease of use of previous approaches. The proposed resource opens perspectives for research, development and education, mainly in the fields of lexicography, linguistics, NLP and databases.

References

1. Agirre, E., Diab, M., Cer, D., Gonzalez-Agirre, A.: Semeval-2012 task 6: A pilot on semantic textual similarity. In: Proceedings of the First Joint Conference on Lexical and Computational Semantics, Proceedings of the Main Conference and the Shared Task, vol. 1 and Proceedings of the Sixth International Workshop on Semantic Evaluation, vol. 2, pp. 385–393. Association for Computational Linguistics (2012)
2. Angles, R., Gutierrez, C.: Survey of graph database models. ACM Comput. Surv. **40**(1), 1 (2008)
3. Baccianella, S., Esuli, A., Sebastiani, F.: Sentiwordnet 3.0: An enhanced lexical resource for sentiment analysis and opinion mining. In: LREC, vol. 10, pp. 2200–2204 (2010)
4. Bird, S.: Nltk: the natural language toolkit. In: Proceedings of the COLING/ACL on Interactive Presentation Sessions, pp. 69–72. Association for Computational Linguistics (2006)
5. Bond, F., Foster, R.: Linking and extending an open multilingual wordnet. ACL **1**, 1352–1362 (2013)
6. Budanitsky, A., Hirst, G.: Evaluating WordNet-based measures of lexical semantic relatedness. Comput. Linguist. **32**(1), 13–47 (2006)
7. Edmonds, P., Cotton, S.: Senseval-2: overview. In: Proceedings of the Second International Workshop on Evaluating Word Sense Disambiguation Systems, pp. 1–5. Association for Computational Linguistics (2001)
8. Gonzalo, J., Verdejo, F., Chugur, I., Cigarran, J.: Indexing with WordNet synsets can improve text retrieval. arXiv preprint cmp-lg/9808002 (1998)

9. Haerder, T., Reuter, A.: Principles of transaction-oriented database recovery. ACM Comput. Surv. **15**(4), 287–317 (1983)
10. Herrera, J., Peñas, A., Verdejo, F.: Textual entailment recognition based on dependency analysis and *WordNet*. In: Quiñonero-Candela, J., Dagan, I., Magnini, B., d'Alché-Buc, F. (eds.) MLCW 2005. LNCS, vol. 3944, pp. 231–239. Springer, Heidelberg (2006). doi:10.1007/11736790_13
11. Landes, S., Leacock, C., Tengi, R.I.: WordNet: an electronic lexical database. Build. Semant. Concord. **199**(216), 199–216 (1998)
12. Liu, H., Singh, P.: Conceptneta practical commonsense reasoning tool-kit. BT Technol. J. **22**(4), 211–226 (2004)
13. Magnini, B., Negri, M., Prevete, R., Tanev, H.: A WordNet-based approach to named entities recognition. In: Proceedings of the 2002 Workshop on Building and Using Semantic Networks, vol. 11, pp. 1–7. Association for Computational Linguistics (2002)
14. Meyer, C.M., Gurevych, I.: Wiktionary: A new rival for expert-built lexicons? Exploring the possibilities of collaborative lexicography. Electronic Lexicography. Oxford University Press, Cambridge (2012)
15. Miller, G.A.: Wordnet: a lexical database for english. Commun. ACM **38**(11), 39–41 (1995)
16. Moldovan, D.I., Rus, V.: Logic form transformation of wordnet and its applicability to question answering. In: Proceedings of the 39th Annual Meeting on Association for Computational Linguistics, pp. 402–409. Association for Computational Linguistics (2001)
17. Moro, A., Navigli, R.: Semeval-2015 task 13: Multilingual all-words sense disambiguation and entity linking. In: Proceeding of SemEval-2015 (2015)
18. Navigli, R.: Word sense disambiguation: A survey. ACM Comput. Surv. **41**(2), 10 (2009)
19. Navigli, R., Jurgens, D., Vannella, D.: Semeval-2013 task 12: Multilingual word sense disambiguation. In: Second Joint Conference on Lexical and Computational Semantics (SEM), vol. 2, pp. 222–231 (2013)
20. Navigli, R., Ponzetto, S.P.: Babelnet: The automatic construction, evaluation and application of a wide-coverage multilingual semantic network. Artif. Intell. **193**, 217–250 (2012)
21. Pedersen, T., Patwardhan, S., Michelizzi, J.: Wordnet::similarity: Measuring the relatedness of concepts. In: Demonstration Papers at HLT-NAACL 2004, HLT-NAACL-Demonstrations 2004, Stroudsburg, PA, USA, pp. 38–41. Association for Computational Linguistics (2004)
22. Pichardo-Lagunas, O., Sidorov, G., Cruz-Corts, N., Gelbukh, A.: Automatic detection of semantics primitives in explicative dictionaries with bio-inspired algorithms. Onomazein **1**(29), 104–117 (2014)
23. Ponzetto, S.P., Strube, M.: Exploiting semantic role labeling, wordnet and wikipedia for coreference resolution. In: Proceedings of the Main Conference on Human Language Technology Conference of the North American Chapter of the Association of Computational Linguistics, pp. 192–199. Association for Computational Linguistics (2006)
24. Pradhan, S.S., Loper, E., Dligach, D., Palmer, M.: Semeval-2007 task 17: English lexical sample, SRL and all words. In: Proceedings of the 4th International Workshop on Semantic Evaluations, pp. 87–92. Association for Computational Linguistics (2007)
25. Quillian, M.R.: Word concepts: A theory and simulation of some basic semantic capabilities. Syst. Res. Behav. Sci. **12**(5), 410–430 (1967)

26. Silber, H.G., McCoy, K.F.: Efficiently computed lexical chains as an intermediate representation for automatic text summarization. Comput. Linguist. **28**(4), 487–496 (2002)
27. Snyder, B., Palmer, M.: The english all-words task. In: Senseval-3: Third International Workshop on the Evaluation of Systems for the Semantic Analysis of Text, pp. 41–43 (2004)
28. Taghipour, K., Ng, H.T.: One million sense-tagged instances for word sense disambiguation and induction. In: CoNLL, pp. 338–344 (2015)
29. Vicknair, C., Macias, M., Zhao, Z., Nan, X., Chen, Y., Wilkins, D.: A comparison of a graph database and a relational database: a data provenance perspective. In: Proceedings of the 48th Annual Southeast Regional Conference, p. 42, ACM (2010)
30. Webber, J.: A programmatic introduction to neo4j. In: Proceedings of the 3rd Annual Conference on Systems, Programming, and Applications: Software for Humanity, SPLASH 2012, New York, NY, USA, pp. 217–218. ACM (2012)

CREAMINKA: An Intelligent Ecosystem Based on Ontologies and Artificial Intelligence to Manage Research Processes, Knowledge Generation and Scientific Production in Higher Education

Juan P. Salgado-Guerrero[1], Jorge Galán-Mena[1,2], Daniel Pulla-Sánchez[1,2], Vladimir Robles-Bykbaev[2(✉)], and Adrián Narváez-Pacheco[3]

[1] Vicerrectorado de Investigación,
Universidad Politécnica Salesiana, Cuenca, Ecuador
{jpsalgado,jgalanm,dpulla}@ups.edu.ec
[2] Grupo de Investigación en Inteligencia Artificial y Tecnologías
de Asistencia, Universidad Politécnica Salesiana, Cuenca, Ecuador
vrobles@ups.edu.ec
[3] Departamento de Tecnologías de la Información,
Universidad Politécnica Salesiana, Cuenca, Ecuador
anarvaezp@ups.edu.ec

Abstract. According to the latest estimates of the World Bank, up to 2013 there were 2'184.419.897 scientific and technical articles published in the world. Year in and year out, a great number of these papers is produced by several education institutions, organizations and centers that carry out several research topics and processes. However, it is imperative for universities to determine guidelines and policies that efficiently enable them to manage the information that has been produced, as well as determine the impact all of these processes have on several areas, such as scientific, social and academic. Therefore, this article presents an ecosystem based on ontologies and smart tools that dynamically analyzes scientific production in a university. Our idea is capable of connecting to main scientific data bases such as SCOPUS or Science Direct and applies standards like the International Standard Classification of Education from UNESCO and the All Science Journal from SCOPUS. In order to validate our proposal, we carried out an experimental process that allowed us to supply the ontology with 1.912 individuals of papers, authors, journals and organizations. Similarly, from the 331 articles that have been processed, we have extracted information related to lines of research, keywords, scientific events and many other fields.

Keywords: Knowledge management · Scientific articles · Ontologies · Research

© Springer International Publishing AG 2017
A. Solano and H. Ordoñez (Eds.): CCC 2017, CCIS 735, pp. 115–129, 2017.
DOI: 10.1007/978-3-319-66562-7_9

1   Introduction

Currently, Higher Education Institutions (HEI) produce great amounts of information related to research processes and scientific production. According to the latest estimates of the World Bank, up to 2013 there were 2'184.419.897 scientific and technical articles published in the world [18]. The SCImago Journal & Country Rank registered 40'519.542 articles published in several journals listed in SCOPUS, worldwide [12]. This vast scientific production means it is necessary to have tools that can easily and quickly determine metadata to describe important aspects such as the orientation of the research, the social impact, the areas of knowledge, and others.

In the case of higher education institutions, scientific production usually increases year after year, so does the number of researchers or the lines or areas of research. Therefore, these institutions must be prepared and have the necessary resources in order to determine the importance of the research being conducted and place more emphasis on the research that causes a major scientific, academic or social impact.

Furthermore, the research process carried out by science groups in universities generate several types of products such as patents, prototypes, academic articles and audiovisual products. Additionally it becomes the means through which internal and external relationships and structures are created between researchers, participants and different organizations. Thus, it is very important for directors and institutions of higher education as well as institutions that carry out research processes, to have a tool that can analyze the complex relations that are produced between the different agents who are not only directly involved with the research, but all the agents who are an active part of the research in different fields of action (directly or indirectly).

In this regard, this paper suggests a complete ecosystem based on different techniques such as artificial intelligence and knowledge modeling in order to provide services that can be used by managers or people responsible for research and knowledge management in any organization engaged in these activities. The main functions of the ecosystem are:

- **Generation of improbable peers** between researchers and participants of the ecosystem. This function enables the automatic identification of areas of joint action in which researchers from different areas of science and areas of action could participate, in order to foster new synergies that cannot be established with traditional systems.
- **Dynamic analysis of the relationships** that are generated between researchers, students, external agents and between the different departments that the organization may have: research groups, coworking, etc.
- **Intelligent analysis of scientific production** in order to classify information according to internationally defined areas of knowledge such as the All Science Journal created by SCOPUS [13] or the International Standard Classification of Education (ISCED) [17].

- **Smart search of keywords, authors and organizations** in papers and scientific products. Connection with scientific repositories and data bases like SCOPUS or Science Direct.
- **Generation of reports based on nodes structures and graphical elements**, automatic generation of SPARQL Protocol and RDF Query Language [11] in order to conduct hierarchical inference processes in the information found in the ecosystem's base of triplets.

2 Related Work

Nowadays, knowledge is considered an organization's most important asset, since it is a primary resource for maintaining competitive advantage [15]. In this regard, Fend, Chen and Liou attempt to analyze the impact of a KMS in companies that adopted this type of system and where results show that they have lowered administrative costs and improved their productivity after two years of having implemented a Knowledge Management System (KMS) [3]. A KMS can be applied in different fields such as education, the industry, marketing, health, etc. For instance, Ghosh and Scott conducted a study in a hospital in order to analyze how to design and expand a clinical KMS in a nursing environment [4]. Additionally, in the field of bioscience, small and medium sized companies in Taiwan apply KMS to efficiently manage their intellectual property, this helps companies avoid conflict of interests, protect their R & D results and improve their competitive advantage [5]. It is worth mentioning that even in [2] KMS have successfully been applied to support disasters and improve the management of emergency situations through the appropriate execution of planning, creation of responses and the assignment of well-coordinated efforts during the emergency period.

Kumar and Dwivedi, S.K. (2015) presented a proposal to deal with the administration of the flow of documentation in administrative processes of different functional units in Universities. For this, they used a semantic system based on agents in order to manage knowledge that is produced in different departments. These agents carry out a communication process amongst each other, substantially reducing the flow of papers between the different departments in the organization [6].

In 2015, Séin-Echaluce et al. developed a methodology and a system of knowledge management for universities. It classifies, searches, organizes, relates and adapts learning resources by applying a semantic search system based on ontologies. Similarly, the system includes services to search for answers to questions related to different types of resources that have been created in the academic or social fields, or those directed to services [14].

Concerning the field of development of knowledge management systems, there are a great number of alternatives and methodologies that allow the different types of requirements of each organization to be addressed. For example, Delibašić and Suknović developed a methodology focused on case-based reasoning and decision-making based on multicriteria. In this paper the authors demonstrated that knowledge can be represented in the form of cases [1]. An specific application of this proposal can be found in the Building Information Modeling (BIM) module created by Motawa and Almarshad (2013). To this end, the authors used case-based reasoning, and their goal was to support professionals in decision making in the area of construction when performing corrective / preventive maintenance, learning from previously performed maintenance operations [9].

One of the most used ontologies to store and manage the context in which the research activity is carried out is the VIVO ontology (http://vivoweb.org/). As stated by Lezcano L. Jörg B., Sicilia MA in [7], there are several models and standards that have been suggested to apply semantics to research information; their study intends to contrast the use of this ontology and the CERIF standards, in addition to giving instructions so that clients can integrate data from heterogeneous sources. A clear example of using ontologies to model knowledge in research can be found in the SYNAT [19] ontology, which is a joint work carried out by institutions from Poland that describes concepts related to the scientific community and its activities; this ontology, as mentioned by the authors, presents extensions of others such as VIVO, FOAF, SIOC, among others.

Research management systems have been developed in many institutions, here are some of their proposals: [16] presents a software based on ontologies that supports the evaluation processes of research policies and decision making strategies by using a visual analysis for Higher Education Institutions (HEIs). In [10] Nonthakarn C., Wuwongse V. present a new development approach of a network of researchers called Linked OpenScholar by using Linked Open Data (LOD) technology and with metadata supported by some parts of the VIVO ontology; this software seeks to improve the visibility of researchers' information and their cooperation with other researchers from other institutions. One of the most prominent companies in research processes is Elseiver, which besides providing APIs to access information of bibliographical data bases such as SCOPUS, it is constantly developing its platform called PURE, whose aim is to facilitate the visibility and traceability of the research conducted by an institution, thus providing options to support decision making, generating evaluation exercises and cooperation networks among different institutions and researchers.

3   General System Architecture

The CREAMINKA system was developed to manage and accelerate knowledge generated in any higher education institution or organization that carries out research processes. The ecosystem is a tool that provides support for decision making regarding R+D+i (Research + Development + innovation) of an organization.

As shown in Fig. 1, the structure of the ecosystem is organized in five clearly defined layers: (i) information repositories, (ii) data collection and mapping, (iii) triplets repository, (iv) data processing and inferences and (v) data presentation.

Here is a detailed explanation of each layer and the components that make up the ecosystem:

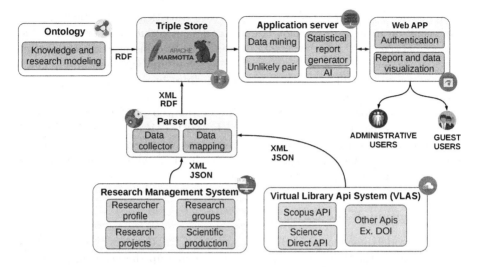

Fig. 1. General structure of the CREAMINKA ecosystem for the management of scientific information

- The academic information and scientific production repositories are the source used by the CREAMINKA system to supply the **ontology**. These repositories have two modules: (i) the university's Research Management System or SGI for its acronym in Spanish (Sistema de Gestión de Investigación) of Universidad Politécnica Salesiana (UPS) where we can find data about researchers' profile and their education, data about research groups, its members and research guidelines, data about the university's scientific production in different knowledge areas in the form of academic articles, conferences, seminars, books, etc., and data of research projects that have a scope, objectives, budget, schedule of activities, people involved, etc.; and (ii) **VLAS** (APIs system of virtual libraries), a module of virtual libraries that seeks and downloads the institution's scientific production information from APIs such as **SCOPUS** and **ScienceDirect**.
- The data collection and mapping layer (Parser tool) receives the information from the information repositories in **JSON** or **XML** format, its main goal is to map the collected information and transform it to **RDF** format so it can then be supplied in the triplets repository through **SPARQL** language.
- The ontology that models the institution's knowledge and research is stored in a triplets server like **Apache Marmotta**, whose advantages are scalability, quickness and performance. Marmotta is in charge of receiving and storing the information received from the Parser Tool. Additionally, it provides services to consult and manage the ontology and its generated instances.
- The information in the triplets server must first be processed before being presented, this will be carried out by the **Application Server layer**. First of all, this server uses reasoning mechanisms to generate inferences with the instances contained in the ontology, it also applies data mining and artificial

intelligence techniques (**IA**) in order to create statistical reports that provide information to support decision making, carry out connections or improbable peers between the different agents who are involved in the research system, encourage new research projects, create research groups with multidisciplinary teams; create, modify or eliminate research lines based on the institution's scientific production and knowledge areas, etc.

– Finally, the information is presented through a web platform that includes technologies like Javascript, JSF, Java EE and HTML5. Access is restricted essentially for two types of roles, **administrative users** who may consult information considered sensitive for the institution, while **guests** will have access to reports on general information.

3.1   Definition of the Ontology

Ontology models knowledge in different groups of stakeholders through classes that encompass the different components that make up the academic research ecosystem. These groups of stakeholders, as shown in Fig. 2, consist of a Knowledge Area, which allow us to classify the specific nature of knowledge that is acquired through different methods. We then have the Keywords, which are the most relevant words of a scientific product. Then, there is the Scientific Product which symbolizes the academic articles, the chapters of the book and other products of scientific content which are the result of the research process. Lastly, the group of stakeholders made up by the Author and the Organization.

These groups of stakeholders interact with each other through relations which are shown in Fig. 2. In the research process, both universities and foundations that belong to the Organization and the different authors within the Person are the ones in charge of carrying out the different products which are the result of the research process, such as academic articles, book chapters and prototypes,

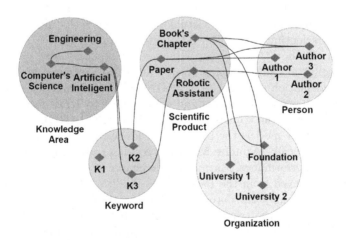

Fig. 2. Groups of stakeholders of the CREAMINKA's system ontology.

which belong to Science Product. Each one of the products that are created have keywords which are linked to different Knowledge Areas within a classification.

Each type of ontology allows an academic article to be created and it defines its components through relations with the different groups of stakeholders, this is done in order to infer and grade the most like-minded authors and create a collaborative group of workers to develop a new academic article according to several factors such as the knowledge area or the number of research groups the authors have participated in when publishing their academic articles. Figure 3 shows the partial screenshot or the relations among all the elements of the ontology using the de Protégé VOWL tool [8].

The universe of discourse **D** contains all the elements of the groups of stakeholders of the knowledge areas, production of the research groups, scientific communication and research council:

$$D = \{Clasificacion\_Science\_Direct, ASJC, CINE, Consejo\_Investigacion,$$
$$Convenio\_Institucional, Evento\_Cientifico, Formacion\_Academica, Grupo,$$
$$Keyword, Linea\_Investigacion, Medio\_Comunicacion, Organizacion, Persona,$$
$$Producto\_Comunicativo, Proyecto\_Investigacion, Rol, Lugar\}$$

The main *unary* relations defined in the ontology are the following:

- **CINE:** represents the normalized international classification of education proposed by the UNESCO.
- **Scientific Event:** National and international meetings such as congresses and symposiums.

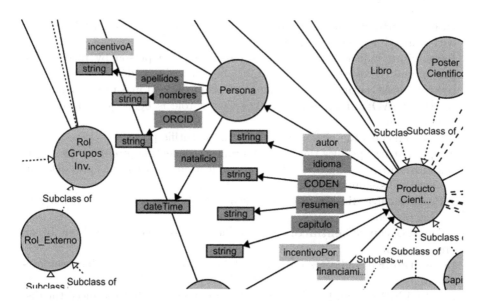

Fig. 3. Partial screenshot of CREAMINKA's ontology

- **Academic Education:** Studies undertaken by a person.
- **Research Groups:** Groups of people that get together to conduct research on a particular topic.
- **Organization:** all the organizations involved in the research.
- **Indexation Virtual Library:** represents saving a scientific product in a virtual library through indexation.
- **Person:** Agents within a research.
- **Line of Research:** The specific research topic of an area.
- **Role:** The functions carried out by a person in an organization.
- **Scientific Product:** Groups of deliverables obtained during the development of a research project.
- **Keyword:** indicates a relevant word of a scientific product.
- **ASJC:** represents the classification system used by SCOPUS for scientific categorization under knowledge areas.

The main binary relations that have been modeled are described below:

- **perteneceAArea:** specifies that each ASJC is related with a category of the three levels of the knowledge area classification CINE.
- **campoDeEstudio:** Each degree of academic education has a connection with one or more levels of the knowledge areas
- **lineaAcordeACINE:** specifies that a line of research is related to a CINE knowledge area
- **subLineaInvestigacion:** indicates that a line of research can have a sub line of research
- **clasificadoEnASJC:** specifies that a keyword can be classified in a ASJC category
- **tieneLineaInvestigacion:** indicates that a research group must be related with a matching line of research
- **formacion:** indicates the academic education of a person by relating the person and the degrees or certificates he/she has obtained
- **perteneceAGrupo:** specifies that a role is performed in a research group
- **perteneceAOrganizacion:** specifies that a role is being performed in an organization
- **autor:** indicates the person who made the scientific product
- **grupoAutor:** Specifies the research group the scientific product belongs to
- **diseminadoEn:** Indicates the communication a scientific product has through a dissemination product.
- **lePerteneceMedio:** specifies the means of communication that belongs to an organization
- **organizaEventoCientifico:** specifies the scientific event carried out by an organization
- **presentadoEn:** indicates the event where a dissemination product was presented
- **producidoPor:** specifies the means of communication that produced the dissemination product.

The set of R relations is defined as follows:

$$R = \{ perteneceAArea, campoDeEstudio, lineaAcrodeACINE,$$
$$subLineaInvestigacion, clasificacionEnASJC,$$
$$tieneLineaInvestigacion, formacion, perteneceAGrupo,$$
$$pertenceAOrganizacion, autor, grupoAutor,$$
$$diseminadoEn, lePerteneceMedio, organizaEventoCientifico \}$$

4 Experimentation Plan and Preliminary Results

In order to determine the real potential of this proposal, this section introduces the experimental process that has been carried out by employing the base of articles and publications generated by UPS in the last 3 years.

The experimentation plan to supply the CREAMINKA system is defined in 2 phases and the entire operating process of the system's different components can be observed in Fig. 4.

The aim of the first phase is to incorporate the metadata of congresses' scientific articles and journals of the digital repositories of SCOPUS and Science Direct by using Elsevier API's consumed by the system's Parser Tools in order to incorporate it to the ontology, the suggestion is also to incorporate the data

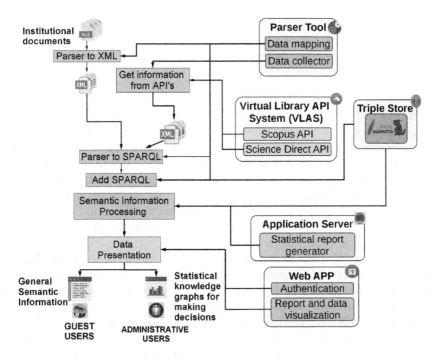

Fig. 4. Process carried out to perform an initial evaluation of CREAMINKA.

of the consolidated institutional archives of the organization's scientific production. The second phase presents the confirmation of the data migrated to the ontology through SPARQL query and the general results of the migration are presented. The CREAMINKA system provides access to the data through a web application, its functions are shown with the screenshot of the user interface.

4.1 Analysis of the Articles

In order to supply the groups of stakeholders such as the scientific articles, scientific journals, authors, organizations and indexations in virtual libraries, different consults were carried out to obtain information by using the Data Collector of the Parser Tool, these queries were done by means of the Elsevier API's that are found in the Virtual Library API System, these repositories are Scopus and Science Direct. One of the API's that were used for the query of institutional authors of different scientific products, like scientific articles and journals are shown in Table 1, where the different affiliation codes belonging to the academic organization are presented.

Table 1. SCOPUS and Science Direct API's and main classes.

Classes of interest	API
Scopus scientific articles of the academic organization	https://api.elsevier.com/content/search/scopus?query=AF-ID(XXXXX)
Science Direct scientific articles of the academic organization	https://api.elsevier.com/content/search/scidir?query=aff(XXXXX)
Internal authors of the scientific products	http://api.elsevier.com/content/search/author?query=AF-ID(XXXXX)

Other elements that are the source for supplying the ontology are the institutional archives such as spreadsheets with information of scientific production of research groups from the academic organization, which are processed through the **Data Mapping** of the Parser Tools which reads the sets of spreadsheet documents and turns them into XML metadata. Subsequently, with the use of that metadata, the Data Mapping classifies each one of its attributes as data properties and objects of ontology classes and transforms that metadata in SPARQL code, which in turn supplies the ontology through the **Triple Store** Apache Marmotta's data insertion services.

In order to verify that the supply of the ontology with the use of the **Parser Tools** is correct, SPARQL queries to the triplets repository were carried out to compare if the information in the metadata which was transformed into SPARQL code coincides with the original information of the entry metadata of the **Data Collector**. The following information shows an example of a query to Triple Store (Fig. 5), this information was compared with the original information in the metadata, the query shows the basic data of a scientific article sought by its title.

In Table 2 we can see the results obtained using the query of the Fig. 5.

```
PREFIX rdf: <http://www.w3.org/1999/02/22-rdf-syntax-ns#>
PREFIX owl: <http://www.w3.org/2002/07/owl#>
PREFIX rdfs: <http://www.w3.org/2000/01/rdf-schema#>
PREFIX xsd: <http://www.w3.org/2001/XMLSchema#>
PREFIX creaminka: <http://spelta.ec/creaminka#>
SELECT DISTINCT ?grupo ?evento ?idioma ?paginas ?volumen ?isbn ?issn ?doi ?eissn ?url
WHERE {
    ?nodeArticle rdf:type creaminka:Articulo_Cientifico;
    creaminka:titulo "A NEW APPROACH BASED ON LOCAL BINARY PATTERNS HISTOGRAM And FOURIER
    DESCRIPTORS AS SUPPORT TOOL IN PRESUMPTIVE DIAGNOSIS OF GASTRITIS.".
    Optional{?nodeArticle creaminka:ISBN ?isbn}
    Optional{?nodeArticle creaminka:ISSN ?issn}
    Optional{?nodeArticle creaminka:DOI ?doi}
    Optional{?nodeArticle creaminka:E-ISSN ?eissn}
      Optional{?nodeArticle creaminka:idioma ?idioma}
      Optional{?nodeArticle creaminka:paginas ?paginas}
    Optional{?nodeArticle creaminka:volumen ?volumen}
    Optional{?nodeArticle creaminka:diseminadoEn ?nodeIndex.
                ?nodeIndex creaminka:URL ?url.
    }
    Optional{?nodeArticle creaminka:grupoAutorPrincipal ?nodeGrupo.
                ?nodeGrupo creaminka:leyendaGrupo ?grupo.
    }
    Optional{?nodeArticle creaminka:diseminadoEn ?nodePress.
                ?nodePress creaminka:presentadoEn ?nodeEvent.
              ?nodeEvent creaminka:nombreEvento ?evento.
    }
}
```

Fig. 5. Automatically generated SPARQL query to retrieve information related with a particular scientific paper/document.

Table 2. Paper's information retrieved using an automatically SPARQL query generated by CREAMINKA.

Element	Value
Group	GIIATA
Event	VI Latin American Congress On Biomedical Engineering, Paraná-Argentina 29–31 October 2014
Language	Inglés
Pages	385–388
Volume	49
ISBN	978-3-319-13116-0
ISSN	1680-0737
DOI	10.1007/978-3-319-13117-7_99
URL	https://link.springer.com/chapter/10.1007%2F978-3-319-13117-7_99#page-1

After the implementation of the CREAMINKA system, we have reached the following number of instances in each ontology class: People = 462, Scientific Products = 331, Scientific event = 120, Means of communication = 42, Internal Role = 462, Research Group = 20, Organization = 31, City = 48, Country = 28, Scientific Journal = 49, Scientific paper = 239, Paper indexations to scientific databases = 230.

On the other hand, it is important to mention that CREAMINKA presents
the information from its triplets repository through different modules of its web
application, one of those modules is a nodes browser, which enables the display
of the knowledge information organized in nodes in a solar disposition around
an object located in the middle. This tool allows us to observe different concepts
related to an object in the repository and classify each one these objects according to the class it belongs to through different colors and descriptive captions as
shown in Fig. 6.

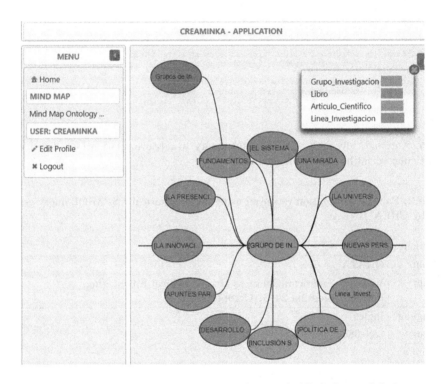

Fig. 6. Nodes of the research groups in Universidad Politécnica Salesiana

4.2   Inferring Improbable Peers

One important characteristic of CREAMINKA is the functionality to create
Improbable Peers (IP). An IP is a couple of persons that commonly have different
professions and specializations, but are working in distinct research areas that
can be overlapped due to some specific topics that they address.

For example, we have two researchers **R1** and **R2**, that are working in two
very different areas (**A1** and **A2**): mechanics and speech-language therapy based
on Information and Communication Technologies (ICTs), respectively (Fig. 7).

Researcher **R1** is applying genetic algorithms and random forest techniques
to support the fault diagnostic in spur gears, whereas researcher **R2** is using

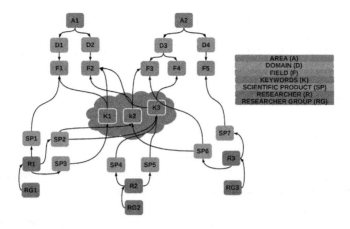

Fig. 7. Relations of the improbable peers in the ontology.

genetic algorithms to automatically create patients' profiles in a system aimed at training speech-language therapists through the study of cases of persons with communication disorders.

Based on the above, CREAMINKA can suggest researchers **R1** and **R2** to try to work together (if possible) or at least share and exchange knowledge related to genetic algorithms and its modeling in problems solving.

The creation of improbable peers has a variety of models to observe, and depending on the data that intervene in each module, its versatility, accuracy and performance may vary considerably. As shown in the figure above, the first approach that has been developed is given according to the number of connections generated by the scientific products created by different researchers in the different areas of knowledge classified by CINE. Due to the nature of the scientific products (paper, prototype, etc.), they can be linked to the knowledge areas directly through a detailed area of the CINE module, or indirectly through the use of keywords that have already been obtained and classified within a knowledge area through processes of natural language processing and artificial intelligence applied to the institution's papers. In this line, this result is inferred using Eq. 1 that considers several elements such as the number of connections that exist among scientific products and keywords, scientific products and knowledge areas, keywords and knowledge areas, among others:

$$Overlap(R1, R2) = w_1 \cdot \sum_{sp_{R1} \in |\overrightarrow{SP}_{R1}|} \sum_{sp_{R2} \in |\overrightarrow{SP}_{R2}|} \sum_{k \in K} \{NC(sp_{R1}, sp_{R2}, k)\} \tag{1}$$

where:

– $Overlap(R1, R2)$ level of overlap between researchers $R1$ and $R2$.

- $\overrightarrow{SP}_{R1}$ and $\overrightarrow{SP}_{R2}$ total of scientific products (papers) of researchers $R1$ and $R2$, respectively.
- K total of keywords related with scientific products of each researcher.
- NC represents the number of connections existing between the keyword k and each scientific product.
- w_1 weight to normalize the sum result between 0 and 1.

5 Conclusions

In this paper we have presented a complete ecosystem that dynamically analyzes the complex subjacent relations in the field of research, development, scientific production and innovation. By applying ontologies, the system is capable of adapting to the requirements of any higher education institution or organization that conducts R+D+i processes.

Based on this proposal, officials from an organization can clearly know the impact of R+D+i activities conducted in the organization on the academic, scientific and social fields. This enables the identification of opportunities and weaknesses found in the innovation process in order to redirect efforts of economic support and resources and therefore improve different indicators, both internal and external (Governmental).

In this same line, thanks to the analysis of the different products and agents involved in the process of scientific production, it is possible to understand the orientation and the areas of specialization that can be found within the organization. With this information, officials will know if the work carried out by the institution is aligned with the government's plans for development and the production matrix.

Additionally, with the initial analysis of improbable peers, it is feasible to generate new synergies that will strengthen the different processes carried out in the research groups, departments or units.

Future research lines are explained below:

- To include in Eq. 1 the professional (LinkedIn) and personal (Facebook, Twitter) profiles of researchers in order to more precisely infer the improbable peers.
- To develop a module to automatically determine the level of impact of the scientific products through social and media information.

References

1. Delibašić, B., Suknović, M.: Loan granting knowledge system. J. Dec. Syst. **15**(2–3), 309–329 (2006)
2. Dorasamy, M., Raman, M., Kaliannan, M.: Knowledge management systems in support of disasters management: a two decade review. Technol. Forecast. Soc. Chang. **80**(9), 1834–1853 (2013)

3. Feng, K., Chen, E.T., Liou, W.: Implementation of knowledge management systems and firm performance: an empirical investigation. J. Comput. Inf. Syst. **45**(2), 92–104 (2005)
4. Ghosh, B., Scott, J.E.: Effective knowledge management systems for a clinical nursing setting. Inf. Syst. Manag. **24**(1), 73–84 (2006)
5. Hsu, L.L.: The impact of industrial characteristics and organizational climate on kms and bip-taiwan bioscience industry. J. Comput. Inf. Syst. **46**(4), 8–17 (2006)
6. Kumar, A., Dwivedi, S.K.: Ontology based knowledge management for administrative processes of university. Int. J. Inf. Technol. Comput. Sci. (IJITCS) **7**(8), 51 (2015)
7. Lezcano, L., Jörg, B., Sicilia, M.-A.: Modeling the context of scientific information: mapping VIVO and CERIF. In: Bajec, M., Eder, J. (eds.) CAiSE 2012. LNBIP, vol. 112, pp. 123–129. Springer, Heidelberg (2012). doi:10.1007/978-3-642-31069-0_11
8. Lohmann, S., Negru, S., Haag, F., Ertl, T.: Visualizing ontologies with VOWL. Semant. Web **7**(4), 399–419 (2016)
9. Motawa, I., Almarshad, A.: A knowledge-based bim system for building maintenance. Autom. Construct. **29**, 173–182 (2013)
10. Nonthakarn, C., Wuwongse, V.: Linked openscholar: a researcher network using linked open data. In: Chen, H.-H., Chowdhury, G. (eds.) ICADL 2012. LNCS, vol. 7634, pp. 325–328. Springer, Heidelberg (2012). doi:10.1007/978-3-642-34752-8_41
11. Pérez, J., Arenas, M., Gutierrez, C.: Semantics and complexity of sparql. ACM Trans. Database Syst. (TODS) **34**(3), 16 (2009)
12. SCImago: Sjr scimago journal & country rank (2017). http://www.scimagojr.com/countryrank.php
13. SCOPUS: Citescore metrics faqs (2016). https://journalmetrics.scopus.com
14. Séin-Echaluce, M.L., Fidalgo Blanco, Á., J. García-Peñalvo, F., Conde, M.Á.: A knowledge management system to classify social educational resources within a subject using teamwork techniques. In: Zaphiris, P., Ioannou, A. (eds.) LCT 2015. LNCS, vol. 9192, pp. 510–519. Springer, Cham (2015). doi:10.1007/978-3-319-20609-7_48
15. Song, S.: An internet knowledge sharing system. J. Comput. Inf. Syst. **42**(3), 25–30 (2002)
16. Tsolakidis, A., Sgouropoulou, C., Papageorgiou, E., Terraz, O., Miaoulis, G.: Using visual representation for decision support in institutional research evaluation. In: Plemenos, D., Miaoulis, G. (eds.) Intelligent Computer Graphics 2012. SCI, vol. 441, pp. 41–57. Springer, Heidelberg (2013). doi:10.1007/978-3-642-31745-3_3
17. UNESCO: Clasificación internacional normalizada de la educación (2013)
18. World Bank: Scientific and technical journal articles (2017). http://data.worldbank.org/indicator/IP.JRN.ARTC.SC
19. Wróblewska, A., Podsiadly-Marczykowska, T., Bembenik, R., Rybinski, H., Protaziuk, G.: Synat system ontology: design patterns applied to modeling of scientific community, preliminary model evaluation. In: Bembenik, R., Skonieczny, L., Rybinski, H., Kryszkiewicz, M., Niezgodka, M. (eds.) Intelligent Tools for Building a Scientific Information Platform. SCI, vol. 467, pp. 323–340. Springer, Heidelberg (2013). doi:10.1007/978-3-642-35647-6_21

Process Model Proposal for Requirements Engineering in Information Mining Projects

María Florencia Pollo-Cattaneo[1,2(✉)], Patricia Pesado[3,4],
Paola Britos[5], and Ramón García-Martínez[4,6]

[1] PhD Program on Computer Science, Computer Science School,
National University of La Plata, Buenos Aires, Argentina
flo.pollo@gmail.com
[2] Information System Methodologies Research Group,
National Technological University of Buenos Aires, Buenos Aires, Argentina
[3] School of Computer Science, National University of La Plata,
Buenos Aires, Argentina
ppesado@lidi.info.unlp.edu.ar
[4] Scientific Researches Commission of Buenos Aires – CIC Bs As,
Buenos Aires, Argentina
[5] Lab R+D+I in Visualization, Information Mining Research Group,
Computer Graphics and Creative Code,
National University of Rio Negro at El Bolsón, Río Negro, Argentina
paobritos@gmail.com
[6] Information Systems Research Group, National University of Lanus,
Buenos Aires, Argentina

Abstract. Information Mining Projects provide synthesis and analysis tools which allow the available data of an organization to be transformed into useful knowledge for the decision-making process. It is for this reason that requirements of this type of project are different from requirements of traditional projects for software development. Consequently, processes associated with requirements engineering for this type of project cannot be reused in Information Mining projects. Likewise, available methodologies for these last projects leave aside activities associated with the Requirements Management of stakeholders and customers. In this context, a model giving solution to the necessities of managing project Information Mining requirements is offered.

Keywords: Information mining · Requirement management · Process · Methodology · Requirement engineering

1 Introduction

Information Mining involves applying analysis and synthesis tools so as to extract nontrivial knowledge implicitly distributed in data available from various information sources within an organization [1]. This is a previously unknown knowledge that may be useful for decision making within the organization [2]. For an expert or a person responsible for an information system, it is usually not data itself what is most relevant but the knowledge that is contained in data relationships, fluctuations, and dependencies [3].

© Springer International Publishing AG 2017
A. Solano and H. Ordoñez (Eds.): CCC 2017, CCIS 735, pp. 130–145, 2017.
DOI: 10.1007/978-3-319-66562-7_10

Whether these relationships evidence reality, for which they are valid, they bring something new and useful for decision making [4]. There are methodologies applied to project development of Information Mining among which CRISP-DM [5], P3TQ [6], and SEMMA [7] stand out. Nonetheless, though possessing maturity regarding a project development, they neglect those aspects related with both the project management and the organizational context where such project is developed, thus failing when engineering the necessary concepts during business knowledge [8].

In this context, this paper aims at proposing a Process Model for Requirements Engineering that allows to develop a proper and integral requirements management in Information Mining projects. In order to do so, the detected problem is first defined (Sect. 2); then, a solution proposal for this problem is offered (Sect. 3); and formalizing processes for requirements associated with the solution model are detailed (Sect. 4); later, influence of the proposed Process Model on project duration is shown (Sect. 5). Finally, conclusions and future work lines are presented (Sect. 6).

2 Problem Description

Information Mining projects need a proper requirements specification, consistent and traceable throughout the entire project. Such specification should allow an orderly project managing and guarantee a correct requirements understanding [9]. However, requirements for this type of projects are different from requirements for traditional software projects, since an Information Mining project does not demand the construction of a software product but the application of a process of converting available data into knowledge. Thus, requirements for this type of projects do not approach definitions of restrictions and functionalities that the software product must fulfill as in the case of Software Engineering [10].

At the beginning of an Information Mining project, its objectives describing customer's general necessities must be identified. That is, what the customer wants to obtain as final result of the project, linked to strategic and tactical business goals [11]. That is because by applying Information Mining algorithms to available data, knowledge may be generated in order to fulfill various types of objectives; as well as understanding beforehand which the organization real expectations are is necessary so as to obtain a successful final project [12].

In order to achieve a better understanding of the various aspects of the project, the parties involved must manage a common vocabulary [13]. On the other hand, once the project objectives are identified, an initial reconnaissance of available information sources in the organization is necessary. From a project objective analysis and information sources, the scope of the project can be defined and, in this way, a set of particular objectives can be obtained. These objectives may be solved by applying Information Mining processes using information mining algorithms [14]. Thus, the business problem giving rise to the project can be solved. In this context, complete methodologies originated in Software Engineering are not useful in Information Mining projects since they do not take under consideration practical aspects of the requirements specification, which is characteristic of this type of projects [15].

The available methodologies applied to developing this type of projects, such as CRISP-DM, P3TQ, and SEMMA are based on Knowledge Discovery in Databases Process (KDD) and emphasize identification of available data, while having a simplified vision of the context where the project develops [16] since activities associated with stakeholder and customer requirements are left aside [17]. From this problem, the model proposal in this paper deepens the Process Model for Information Mining projects defined in [18]. This last process model is based on the CRISP-DM methodology, incorporating principles of the COMPETISOFT methodology [19] that considers SME aspects (for its English acronym: Small and Medium Enterprise). Although the CRISP-DM methodology includes several activities spread among various phases [20], it does not specify them in detail, indicating only the techniques that must be used in any one of them. Just as in [18], work guidelines that fail to detail the requirements management can be noticed in [20]. On the other hand, the systematization of the process of requirements by putting an ontology in motion is proposed, and in [22], a Process Model for the Development of Information Exploitation Projects is proposed, leaving aside the details of processes related to the extraction of requirements in projects of this nature, thus not allowing to comprehend the existing relationships among the different activities and tools/techniques used. In the same vein, several other authors such as U. Dayal [23–25] or R. Kimball [26–28], link Business Intelligence to data warehousing or stored data, which is a set of ideas that cannot be applied directly either, as they do not belong to the nature of this project's context. As defined in [23], Data Warehousing is a set of support technologies whose aim is to assist those professionals taking part in the decision-making process - such as CEO's, executives and analysts - thereby making said activity more efficient and effective, and less time and effort consuming, whereas the proposed model focuses on a previous instance, managing the very first activities of Information Mining projects.

Therefore, this paper's proposed Process Model delves into the engineering-related activities related to the "Business Understanding" and the "Data Comprehension", thus opting out for the more technology-oriented activities performed in the next phases of said methodology, such as data preparation and modelling. Likewise, the model proposal in this paper, uses the templates defined in [13] for documenting requirements engineering, as it is noticed that a lack of techniques, methods and tools to perform an effective requirements documentation using said templates, which is why the proposed model is considered to be an evolution of the process defined in [13]. The aim of this paper is to come forward with the development of a methodological process promoting an improvement in the field of Requirements Engineering—more specifically, within the framework of the Information Mining projects— as engineering methods have proven to be able to equip development processes with objectivity, systematicity, rationality, generality and reliability, thus contributing to the advance of scientific knowledge through the usage of consistent techniques.

3 Proposed Solution Model

Due to the fact that existing methodologies for Information Exploitation projects emphasize on the identification of available data on which to apply the processes, but fail to take the activities associated to clients' and stakeholders' into consideration, a process model seeking to bring solution to the need to manage requirements in this type of project is proposed in the framework of a doctoral thesis. It is for this purpose that this proposal considers the features of Requirements Engineering and the methodologies from the Information Exploitation field, as well as our experience in requirements management in organizations belonging to different sectors.

The proposed process model is divided into five phases: (a) *Project Definition*, (b) *Business Process Engineering*, (c) *Business Process Data Engineering*, (d) *Business Conceptualization*, and (e) *Information Mining Process Specification*. A set of activities described below and a set of formalizing processes described in next section (Sect. 4) are associated with each phase. Each phase is detailed in [29].

Likewise, the results obtained applying the proposed process model to a case study, are shown in [30]. Such case study uncovers behavior patterns allowing the description of trailers used as resources in the production area of a metallurgical enterprise. These patterns will be taken under consideration for decision making when planning the assembly line of units.

3.1 Phase of Project Definition

The objective of this phase is to define the project scope, stakeholders, and objectives to reach. It is divided into three activities: (a) Identifying Project Objectives, (b) Identifying Project Stakeholders, and (c) Identifying Project Scope.

Activity of Identifying Project Objectives
For the activity of Identifying Project Objectives, the Functional Analyst coordinates, together with the Project Leader, the first meeting with project customers, so as to define their expectations and identify the people who are project representatives. Once the conceptual information gathered from the meeting is collected, this Functional Analyst coordinates the project opening meeting including all business representatives so as to compile information about business ideas and problems. As of the approved opening meeting minutes, the Functional Analyst studies the obtained information and applies part of the "Objective Identification, Success Criteria, and Project Expectations" process (defined in Sect. 4.1) so as to identify the main objectives posed for the project and fill in the "Project Objective Template" and "Requirement Objective Template".

Activity of Identifying Project Stakeholders
Once the objectives have been defined for the Identifying of Project Stakeholders, the Functional Analyst identifies the project stakeholders and sponsors, filling in the "Project Stakeholder Template". Sponsors are the organization people who have the power for decision making related to project management whereas the stakeholders are the ones who have the capacity to give necessary information regarding business processes and are repositories of data available to be used so as to develop the project.

Once the stakeholders are identified, meetings are held with them, in order to collect information regarding what expectations and success criteria will be taken under consideration so as to regard the project successful. As of that information, part of the process of "Objective Identification, Success Criteria, and Project Expectations" is applied (defined in Sect. 4.1) so as to fill in the "Project Success Criteria Template" and the "Project Expectations Template".

Activity of Identifying the Project Scope
Once the stakeholders have been identified, and success criteria defined, in the activity of Identifying the Project Scope, the Functional Analyst proceeds to define what will be included as part of the project and what will be excluded of same. This analysis will be formalized in the "Project Scope Definition Template". Likewise, the process of "Project Restriction and Assumption Identification" is applied (this is defined in Sect. 4.2). The process of "Risk Identification and Project Contingency Plans" is applied too (this is defined in Sect. 4.3); so as to define: the assumptions to take under consideration, project restrictions and risks with their respective contingency plans. The following templates are to be filled in: "Project Restrictions Template", "Project Assumptions Template", "Requirement Restrictions Template", Requirement Assumptions Template", "Project Risks Template", "Project Contingency Plans Template", "Requirement Risks Template", and "Requirement Contingency Plans Template".

3.2   Phase of Business Processes Engineering

This phase aims at identifying and surveying business processes which are significant to the project. It is structured in two activities: (a) Identifying business projects, and (b) Surveying Business Processes.

Activity of Identifying Business Processes
In the activity of Identifying Business Processes, the Functional Analyst defines the business activities that are significant to be analyzed and related to the project objectives and the requirement objectives, scope, success criteria, and project expectations posed in the previous phase. The Functional Analyst performs this identification based on the public sources given to him for consulting by the business stakeholders, e.g. procedure handbooks. After defining business activities, this Functional Analyst develops the "Business Process Diagram Template".

Activity of Surveying Business Process
In the activity of Surveying Business Process, the Functional Analyst selects among business stakeholders, the ones having the necessary knowledge for every business process which is significant for the project, and conducts interviews with them. Then, the Functional Analyst formalizes the obtained information, documenting it in the "Business Process Template". All information, forms used during the process, procedures, etc., provided by the stakeholders, are affixed to the template above mentioned.

3.3   Phase of Business Process Data Engineering

This phase objective is to identify data repositories where information of the various business processes are stored and survey the existing data there. This is structured into two activities: (a) Identifying Data Repositories, and (b) Surveying Data Repositories.

Activity of Identifying Data Repositories

In the activity of Identifying Data Repositories, based on the "Business Process Diagram Template" and the templates corresponding to every "Business Process" defined in the phase above, the Functional Analyst analyzes this documented data, searching for information used by the various business processes, determining those data repositories used or consulted by every one of the processes. These repositories can be physical files of paper documentation or entirely digital ones, for instance data bases or spreadsheets, among others. Thus, the Functional Analyst, establishes, together with the Data Specialist, the existing relationships between business processes and data repositories. Then, he formalizes the analyzed information into the "Data Repositories Template".

Activity of Surveying Data Repositories

In the following activity of Surveying Data Repositories, once repository data have been identified, the Functional Analyst studies repository structures, conducting meetings with business stakeholders. Then, the Functional Analyst, together with the Data Specialist, formalizes the information obtained, documenting it into the "Data Structure Template". All information like class diagrams, relationships with the entity diagrams, and/or examples of repository data printings provided by the stakeholders, are affixed to this template.

3.4   Phase of Business Conceptualization

This phase aims at defining business in terms of concepts used, and vocabulary employed, so as to understand the language used in business, uncovering business specific words, and the true meaning business gives to such specific words. This is structured into two activities: (a) Developing a Business Dictionary, and (b) Developing a Business Model.

Activity of Developing a Business Dictionary

In the activity of Developing a Business Dictionary, the Functional Analyst identifies business words, based on the "Business Process Diagram" template, the "Business Processes" template, the "Data Repository" template and the "Data Structure" template. Considering these templates, the most meaningful words related to both identified business processes and data repositories, are listed. Once these identified words are validated as correct by stakeholders, the "Business Dictionary" is prepared by the Functional Analyst. Likewise, part of the process of "Business Domain Formalization" (this is defined in Sect. 4.4) is applied to formulating the "Template of Abbreviations, Acronyms, and Definitions", "Graph of Relationships between Concepts", and the "Template of Attributes related to Requirements".

Activity of Developing a Business Model
In the activity of "Developing a Business Model", the Functional Analyst, together with the Data Specialist, establishes the Word-Repository relation indicating in which repository every one of the identified words is stored, and develops the "Business Model Diagram".

3.5 Phase of Information Mining Process Specification

This phase aims at identifying Information Mining Processes [28] able to be used for solving identified problems in a business process, and developing the scheduling of the remaining project activities, next. It is structured into three activities: (a) Formalizing Business Problems, (b) Identifying Information Mining Processes, and (c) Developing the Project Plan.

Activity of Formalizing Business Problems
In the activity of Formalizing Business Problems, the Functional Analyst performs an analysis of the project objectives and scope, and develops a business problem list, producing a "Business Problem Template". The language used in the problem list has to be natural, and worded according with the user's vocabulary.

Activity of Identifying Information Mining Processes
Once business problems are defined, during the activity of Identifying Information Mining Processes, the Functional Analyst selects Information Mining processes [31] applying every one of the business problems identified, so as to solve them. The Functional Analyst is to apply the same analysis procedure to every business problem. Thus, the "Information Mining Process Template" is to be developed. Before developing the project plan, the "Project Requirements Revision" process (this is defined in Sect. 4.5) is applied in parallel to both activities last mentioned, so as to both verify project objectives and consider which assumptions and limitations were taken under consideration in order to confirm if those objectives were modified after the performed analysis. Then, the column regarding the requirement objective associated with every attribute in the "Template of Attributes related to Requirements" is filled in.

Activity of Developing the Project Plan
In the activity of Developing the Project Plan, using the documents from the previous phases, and applying his Project Managing knowledge, the Project Leader is in charge of developing the project plan. Project activity duration is estimated, for developing the corresponding GANTT diagram, using the Model for Assessing Information Mining Project Feasibility, this is defined in [32]. This is an estimating method for determining the effort needed for the project. Then the "Project Plan Template" is generated. Last, the Project Leader communicates the specified plan to the business stakeholders at a formal meeting where the date for beginning the project and the following phases are agreed.

4   Requirements Formalization Processes

Five requirements formalization processes are posed in this section. They are used in the engineering process described in the previous section. Formalizing processes are employed to fill in the templates proposed in [13], which are then used to document the concepts extracted from the different phases of the extraction process. Each process applies modelling techniques from the Knowledge Engineering field [33] and is composed by a set of activities and a set of input and output products of every activity, detailed in [29]. In its annex, figures and summarizing charts associated to each one of them are included.

4.1   Process of Objective Identification, Success Criteria and Project Expectations

Activities for Identifying Project Objectives and Identifying Project Stakeholders of the Project Definition Phase (Sect. 3.1) for the proposed Engineering Process, call for this process which is applied in parallel to the tasks included in both activities. Used for preparing the documentation of the objectives, success criteria, and project expectations, from documents obtained in interviews with business stakeholders, this process is structured into three phases: *Identifying Project Objectives*; *Identifying Project Success Criteria*; and *Identifying Project Expectations*. In the phase of Identifying Project Objectives, this process aims at defining and modelling the main objectives of an information mining project. In the phase of Identifying Project Success Criteria this process aims at defining and modelling the criteria that will ensure this Information Mining success. Whereas, in the phase of Identifying Project Expectations, the customer's expectations regarding this Information Mining Project, are defined and modelled.

4.2   Process of Identifying Project Assumptions and Restrictions

The activity for Identifying Project Scope of the Project Definition Phase (Sect. 3.1) for the proposed Engineering Process, calls for this process which is developed parallelly to the tasks included in that activity. Used for preparing the documentation of the Project Assumptions and Restrictions, from minutes of interviews with business stakeholders, and models developed according to the process previously mentioned (Sect. 4.1) this process is structured in two phases: Identifying Project Assumptions, and Identifying Project Restrictions. In the phase of Identifying Project Assumptions, this process aims at defining and modelling the assumptions that will be taken into account during the project, according to the objectives previously defined. In the phase of Identifying Project Restrictions, restrictions to be taken into account during the project, are defined and modelled.

4.3   Process of Identifying Risks and Project Contingency Plans

The activity of Identifying the Project Scope of the Project Definition phase (Sect. 3.1) for the proposed Engineering Process, calls for this process which is developed simultaneously with the tasks included in that activity. Its objective is to document project risks and contingency plans associated with each of these risks. Documents obtained in interviews with business stakeholders; results of performing feasibility studies; and models resulting from the process previously detailed in Sect. 4, are used. This process is structured in two phases: *Identifying Project Risks*, and *Identifying Project Contingency Plans*. The phase of Identifying Project Risks defines and models the risks that can be present in an Information Mining project. The phase of Identifying Project Contingency Plans defines and models contingency plans that will have to be performed when the risks defined in the previous phase, occur in the course of the project.

4.4   Process of Business Domain Formalization

The phase of Business Conceptualization (Sect. 3.4) for the proposed Engineering Process, calls for this process which is performed parallelly to the activities in this phase. It is used to implement the documentation of the vocabulary used within the domain and to establish relationships among business engineered concepts. It is structured into three phases: *Identification of Domain General Terms*; *Identification of Relationships among Domain Concepts*; and *Identification of Domain Attributes*. The phase of Identification of Domain General Terms aims at defining and itemizing the vocabulary used in that business where the Information Mining project is taking place. The phase of Identification of Relationships among Domain Concepts establishes the relationships existing among concepts used within the business being study. And the phase "Identification of Domain Attributes" defines the existing relationships among concepts and their main characteristics.

4.5   Process of Project Requirements Review

The activities Formalizing Business Problems and Identifying Information Mining Processes, call for this formalizing process. The aforementioned activities correspond to the Specification of Information Mining Processes phase (Sect. 3.5) of the proposed engineering process. The formalizing process is performed parallelly to tasks included in the two activities above mentioned. As of the products made in this stage, this formalizing process is used for the verification of requirement objectives, restrictions and assumptions related to these objectives. This process is structured into four phases: *Requirement Objectives Review, Requirement Attributes Review, Requirement Assumptions Review,* and *Requirement Restrictions Review*. The phase of Requirement Objectives Review verifies if the specific objectives of the project need modifications. The phase of Requirement Attributes Review defines relationships between business problems and the specific objectives of the project and, in this way, identifies the attributes corresponding to every objective. The phase of Requirement Assumptions Review, verifies whether assumptions defined as data related to specific objectives of the project need edition. The phase of Requirement Restrictions Review verifies whither the restrictions defined as data related to specific objectives of the project need to be modified.

Representations of activities with their respective input and output products are summarized in Tables 1, 2, 3, 4 and 5, one per phase.

Table 1. Activities, input products and output products for Project Definition phase.

Activity	Input products	Process and models	Output products
Identifying Project Objectives	• Conceptual Project Definition	• Documentation Analysis • Functional Decomposition Tree	• Conceptual Minute of Meeting • Minute of Meeting of Project Start • Project Objective Template • Requirement Objective Template (completed by the process described in Sect. 4.1)
Identifying Project Stakeholders	• Minute of Meeting of Project Start	• Interviews • Workshops • "AND/OR" Graph • Knowledge Map	• Project Stakeholder Template • Project Success Criteria Template • Project Expectations Template (completed by the process described in Sect. 4.1)
Identifying Project Scope	• Project Success Criteria Template • Project Expectations Template	• Documentation Analysis • Knowledge Map • Conceptual Map • Repertory Grid	• Project Scope Definition Template • Project Restrictions Template • Project Assumptions Template • Requirement Restrictions Template • Requirement Assumptions Template (completed by the process described in Sect. 4.2) • Project Risks Template • Project Contingency Plans Template • Requirement Risks Template • Requirement Contingency Plans Template (completed by the process described in Sect. 4.3)

Table 2. Activities, input products and output products for Business Processes Engineering phase.

Activity	Input products	Process and models	Output products
Identifying Business Projects	• Project Scope Definition Template • Project Objective Template • Requirement Objective Template • Project Success Criteria Template • Project Expectations Template	• Documentation Analysis	• Business Process Diagram Template
Surveying Business Processes	• Business Process Diagram Template	• Interviews • Workshops	• Business Process Template

Table 3. Activities, input products and output products for Business Processes Data Engineering phase.

Activity	Input products	Process and models	Output products
Identifying Data Repositories	• Business Process Template • Business Process Diagram Template	• Documentation Analysis	• Data Repositories Template
Surveying Data Repositories	• Data Repositories Template	• Interviews	• Data Structure Template

Table 4. Activities, input products and output products for Business Conceptualization phase.

Activity	Input products	Process and models	Output products
Developing a Business Dictionary	• Business Process Diagram Template • Business Process Template • Data Repositories Template • Data Structure Template	• Documentation Analysis • Interviews • Concepts Dictionary • Description of Attributes • Semantic Network • Concept-Attribute-Value	• Business Dictionary • Template of Abbreviations, Acronyms, and Definitions • Graph of Relationships between Concepts • Template of Attributes related to Requirements (completed by the process described in Sect. 4.4)
Developing a Business Model	• Data Repositories Template • Data Structure Template • Business Dictionary	• Documentation Analysis	• Business Model Diagram

Table 5. Activities, input products and output products for Information Mining Process Specification phase.

Activity	Input products	Process and models	Output products
Formalizing Business Problems	• Business Model Diagram • Project Scope Definition Template • Project Objective Template • Requirement Objective Template	• Documentation Analysis	• Business Process Diagram Template • Requirement Objective Template (updated by the process described in Sect. 4.5)
Identifying Information Mining Processes	• Business Problem Template	• Documentation Analysis • Functional Decomposition Tree • Knowledge Map • Conceptual Map	• Information Mining Process Template • Requirement Restrictions Template • Requirement Assumptions Template • Template of Attributes related to Requirements (updated by the process described in Sect. 4.5)

(continued)

Table 5. (*continued*)

Activity	Input products	Process and models	Output products
Developing the Project Plan	• Project Objective Template • Requirement Objective Template • Project Stakeholder Template • Project Risks Template • Requirement Risks Template • Project Scope Definition • Information Mining Process Template	• Documentation Analysis	• Project Plan Template

5   Influence of the Proposed Process Model on Project Duration

In this section, a comparison between the average involved time for Information Mining projects and the consumed time in the case study showed in [30] is presented. In order to estimate the average involved time, information collected from 32 real Information Mining projects is considered. Projects considered have been provided by the researchers of the National University of Lanus's Productive and Technological Development Department Systems Information Research Group (GISI-DDPyT-UNLa), as well as researchers from the National Technological University of Buenos Aires's Software Engineering Methodologies Study Group (GEMIS-FRBA-UTN), and researchers from the National University of Río Negro's Applied Computer Science Laboratory's Information Mining Investigation Group. For this purpose, 15 projects of the National University of Lanus, 10 projects of the National Technological University of Buenos Aires and 7 projects of the National University of Río Negro are considered.

Results of the performed comparison are displayed in Table 6. It can be seen that in the "Business Understanding" phase more than a month's time - the average time - is employed due to a thorough requirements determination and management. In the "Data Comprehension" phase, a slight difference of time is observed, as around half a month less time is required in comparison to the average, given not only is in this phase the data collection and analysis performed, but also part of the previous phase is then validated against the first phase's stakeholder's information collected in order to ensure the reliability of the latter in the coming phases. "Data Preparation" phase shows a slight difference in time as well - around half a month more time - as data has to be formatted, cleansed and integrated. Then, "Modelling" phase highlights the very first crucial advantage to the proposed model, which is that by knowing the client's requirements and the processes worth applying, a massive amount of time in testing and re-working is saved, thus generating an estimated of six months's time saving - around a 65% less time - compared to the Project Duration Average. In the "Evaluation" phase, a nearly half a month's time saving is produced, in that by knowing the Project Success Criteria (gathered in the first phase), results evaluation is also boosted. Lastly, in the "Deployment" phase, the difference is not as huge as the others in that, in said phase, reports and presentations have to be delivered to the client. At this point, the advantage to having a better understanding towards the client and its vocabulary remains that a more effective way of delivering a presentation is thereby more likely to be arrived at.

Table 6. Average effort vs. case study effort

CRISP-DM methodology phases	Average effort (months)		Case study effort (months)		Differences (months)	
Phase 1 Business understanding	6.14	21%	7.67	36%	1.53	25.0%
Phase 2 Data comprehension	3.23	11%	2.67	13%	−0.56	−17.4%
Phase 3 Data preparation	4.63	16%	4.00	19%	−0.63	−13.6%
Phase 4 Modelling	10.20	34%	3.60	17%	−6.60	−64.7%
Phase 5 Evaluation	2.21	7%	0.80	4%	−1.41	−63.8%
Phase 6 Deployment	3.24	11%	2.40	11%	−0.84	−25.9%
Total	**29.64**	**100%**	**21.14**	**71%**	**−8.50**	**−28.7%**

Taking the final results into account, the difference is that of nearly as much as nine months less time with respect to the average times (representing a 29% of the average duration). It is due to this that the model proposed in this paper is considered to be of paramount usefulness to Information Mining Projects Management, in that by allocating more time to the first phases and properly managing the client requirements, a major time reduction in the total project duration is then granted.

6   Conclusions

The main contribution of this paper is to provide the community with elements so as to enable them to perform an integral management of requirements for developing Information Mining Projects. Thus, the paper aims at improving existing methodologies where this approach has been neglected. A five-phase process model is proposed, emphasizing on project definition, business engineering and conceptualization, and process identification of Information Mining to be used within the project. In real life business situations, the proposed Process Model is applied during the Business Understanding and Data Comprehension phases of the CRISP-DM methodology. This process was applied to case-studies covering various business problems. By applying this process, both customer requirements and project objectives related to requirements are efficiently managed.

As future lines of work, detailed structural procedures are suggested, where every document process is stated, step by step, so that techniques of these processes can be more automated. It is desirable that a software tool be developed as support for the proposed process so as to identify the condition of templates and minutes advised by the process, distinguishing the various versions of same, and reporting what every version contains, including a history record of changes, too. In this context, a thesis student is currently working on the development of said tool in order to assist the proposed process.

References

1. Schiefer, J., Jeng, J., Kapoor, S., Chowdhary, P.: Process information factory: a data management approach for enhancing business process intelligence. In: Proceedings 2004 IEEE International Conference on E-Commerce Technology, pp. 162–169 (2004)
2. Thomsen, E.: BI's promised land. Intell. Enterp. 6(4), 21–25 (2003)
3. Curtis, B., Kellner, M., Over, J.: Process modelling. Commun. ACM 35(9), 75–90 (1992)
4. Kanungo, S.: Using process theory to analyze direct and indirect value-drivers of information systems. In: Proceedings of the 38th Annual Hawaii International Conference on System Sciences, pp. 231–240 (2005)
5. Chapman, P., Clinton, J., Kerber, R., Khabaza, T., Reinartz, T., Shearer, C., Wirth, R.: CRISP-DM 1.0 step-by-step data mining guide (2000). http://tinyurl.com/crispdm. Accessed 17 May 2017
6. Pyle, D.: Business Modelling and Business Intelligence. Morgan Kaufmann Publishers, San Francisco (2003)
7. SAS: SAS Enterprise Miner: SEMMA (2008). http://tinyurl.com/semmaSAS. Accessed 17 May 2017
8. Martins, S., Pesado, P., García-Martínez, P.: Information mining projects management process. In: Proceedings 28th International Conference on Software Engineering and Knowledge Engineering, pp. 504–509 (2016). ISBN 1-891706-39-X
9. Martins, S., Rodríguez, D., García-Martínez, R.: Deriving processes of information mining based on semantic nets and frames. In: Ali, M., Pan, J.-S., Chen, S.-M., Horng, M.-F. (eds.) IEA/AIE 2014. LNCS, vol. 8482, pp. 150–159. Springer, Cham (2014). doi:10.1007/978-3-319-07467-2_16. ISSN 0302-9743
10. Wiegers, K.: Software Requirements. Microsoft Press, Redmond (2003)
11. Cao, L., Luo, D., Zhang, C.: Knowledge actionability: satisfying technical and business interestingness. Int. J. Bus. Intell. Data Min. 2(4), 496–514 (2007)
12. Gupta, G.K.: Introduction to Data Mining with Case Studies. PHI L. Pvt. Ltd. (2014)
13. Britos, P., Dieste, O., García-Martínez, R.: Requirements elicitation in data mining for business intelligence projects. In: Avison, D., Kasper, G.M., Pernici, B., Ramos, I., Roode, D. (eds.) Advances in Information Systems Research, Education and Practice. ITIFIP, vol. 274, pp. 139–150. Springer, Boston (2008). doi:10.1007/978-0-387-09682-7-9_12

14. Garcia-Martinez, R., Britos, P., Pollo-Cattaneo, F., Rodriguez, D., Pytel, P.: Information mining processes based on intelligent systems. In: Proceedings of II International Congress on Computer Science and Informatics (INFONOR–CHILE 2011), pp. 87–94 (2011). ISBN 978-956-7701-03-2
15. Rose, K.H.: A Guide to the project management body of knowledge (PMBOK® Guide) - Fifth Edition. Proj. Manag. J. **44**(3), e1 (2013)
16. Cao, L.: Actionable Knowledge Discovery and Delivery. Wiley Interdiscip. Rev. Data Min. Knowl. Disc. **2**(2), 149–163 (2012)
17. García-Martínez, R., Britos, P., Pesado, P., Bertone, R., Pollo-Cattaneo, F., Rodríguez, D., Pytel, P., Vanrell, J.: Towards an information mining engineering. In: Software Engineering, Methods, Modelling and Teaching, pp. 83–99. Editorial Universidad de Medellín (2011). ISBN 978-958-8692-32-6
18. Vanrell, J., Bertone, R., García-Martínez, R.: Un Modelo de Procesos para Proyectos de Explotación de Información. In: Proceedings Latin American Congress on Requirements Engineering and Software Testing, pp. 46–52 (2012). ISBN 978-958-46-0577-1
19. Oktaba, H., Garcia, F., Piattini, M., Ruiz, F., Pino, F.J., Alquicira, C.: Software process improvement: the COMPETISOFT project. Computer **40**(10), 21–28 (2007)
20. Marbán, O., Segovia, J., Menasalvas, E., Fernández-Baizán, C.: Toward data mining engineering: a software engineering approach. Inf. Syst. **34**(1), 87–107 (2009)
21. Neto, A., Pinto, D., Aveiro, D.: SysPRE - systematized process for requirements engineering. In: Aveiro, D., Pergl, R., Guizzardi, G., Almeida, J.P., Magalhães, R., Lekkerkerk, H. (eds.) EEWC 2017. LNBIP, vol. 284, pp. 166–180. Springer, Cham (2017). doi:10.1007/978-3-319-57955-9_13
22. Martins, S., Pesado, P., García-Martínez, R.: Intelligent systems in modeling phase of information mining development process. In: Fujita, H., Ali, M., Selamat, A., Sasaki, J., Kurematsu, M. (eds.) IEA/AIE 2016. LNCS, vol. 9799, pp. 3–15. Springer, Cham (2016). doi:10.1007/978-3-319-42007-3_1
23. Chaudhuri, S., Dayal, U.: An overview of data warehousing and OLAP technology. ACM Sigmod Rec. **26**(1), 65–74 (1997). ISSN 0163-5808
24. Dayal, U., Chen, Q., Hsu, M.: Dynamic data warehousing. In: Mohania, M., Tjoa, A.M. (eds.) DaWaK 1999. LNCS, vol. 1676, p. 132. Springer, Heidelberg (1999). doi:10.1007/3-540-48298-9_14
25. Chaudhuri, S., Dayal, U., Narasayya, V.: An overview of business intelligence technology. Commun. ACM **54**(8), 88–98 (2011)
26. Kimball, R., Margy, R.: The Data Warehouse Toolkit: The Definitive Guide to Dimensional Modelling. Wiley, Indianapolis (2013). ISBN 978-1-118-53080-1
27. Kimball, R., Margy, R.: The Kimball Group Reader. Wiley, Indianapolis (2010). ISBN 978-0-470-56310-6
28. Kimball, R., Ross, M., Thornthwaite, W., Mundy, J., Becker, B.: The Data Warehouse Lifecycle Toolkit. Wiley, Indianapolis (2008). ISBN 978-0-470-14977-5
29. Pollo-Cattaneo, M., Pesado, P., Britos, P., García-Martínez, R.: Modelo de Proceso para Elicitación de Requerimientos en Proyectos de Explotación de Información. Reporte Técnico GEMIS-TD-2017-06-RT-2017-06 (2017). http://grupogemis.com.ar/web/gemis-td-2017-06-rt-2017-06-modelo-de-proceso-para-elicitacion-de-requerimientos-en-proyectos-de-explotacion-de-informacion/. Accessed 27 June 2017
30. Pollo-Cattaneo, M., Pesado, P., Britos, P., García-Martínez, R.: Process model application for requirements engineering in metallurgical enterprise information mining project. Technical report GEMIS-TD-2016-01-RT-2016-08 (2016). http://grupogemis.com.ar/web/gemis-td-2016-01-rt-2016-08/. Accessed 17 May 2017

31. García-Martínez, R., Britos, P., Rodríguez, D.: Information mining processes based on intelligent systems. In: Ali, M., Bosse, T., Hindriks, K.V., Hoogendoorn, M., Jonker, C.M., Treur, J. (eds.) IEA/AIE 2013. LNCS, vol. 7906, pp. 402–410. Springer, Heidelberg (2013). doi:10.1007/978-3-642-38577-3_41

32. Pytel, P., Hossian, A., Britos, P., García-Martínez, R.: Feasibility and effort estimation models for medium and small size information mining projects. Inf. Syst. J. **47**, 1–14 (2015). Elsevier. ISSN 0306-4379

33. García-Martínez, R., Britos, P.: Ingeniería de Sistemas Expertos. Editorial Nueva Librería (2004). ISBN 987-1104-15-4

An Experimental Analysis of Feature Selection and Similarity Assessment for Textual Summarization

Ana Maria Schwendler Ramos, Vinicius Woloszyn, and Leandro Krug Wives[✉]

PPGC, Instituto de Informática, UFRGS, Porto Alebre, Brazil
{aschwendler,vwoloszyn,wives}@inf.ufrgs.br

Abstract. Since the access to information is increasing every day, and we can quickly acquire knowledge from many sources such as news websites, blogs, and social networks, the capacity of processing all this information becomes increasingly difficult. So, tools are needed to automatically extract the most relevant sentences, aiming to reduce the volume of text into a shorter version. One alternative to achieve this process while preserving the core information content by using a process called Automatic Text Summarization. One relevant issue in this context is the presence of typos, synonyms, and other orthographic variations since some extractive techniques are not prepared to handle them. This work presents an evaluation of different similarity approaches to minimize these problems, selecting the most appropriate sentences to represent a document in an automatically generated summary.

1 Introduction

Automatic Text Summarization (ATS) is a Natural Language Processing (NLP) task that aims to reduce a large amount of text into a shorter version while preserving the core information content [6]. This task has become important by the abundance of text available on the Web and the fact that it is hard for a person to summarize them manually. The Web, in particular, has contributed to the increasing interest on automatic summarization. Nowadays it is easy to access information by Google Trends[1] or Google News[2], which are examples of search engines specialized for news, but users are sometimes overwhelmed with this kind of information and barely have enough time to digest it in its full form. They deal with an enormous amount of information, so the demand for ATS has been massively increasing from the traditional single-document to the more recent multi-document summarization tasks.

Related work in this area relies on the Vector Space Model (VSM) [10] to represent the content and relationship of texts. Such representation implies a measure of similarity that is often based on the cosine similarity. However, the cosine similarity can be influenced and interfered by problems derived from the natural

---

[1] https://www.google.com/trends.
[2] https://www.google.com/news.

© Springer International Publishing AG 2017
A. Solano and H. Ordoñez (Eds.): CCC 2017, CCIS 735, pp. 146–155, 2017.
DOI: 10.1007/978-3-319-66562-7_11

language used inside texts, like orthographic errors, synonyms, homonyms, and other morphological variations, known as vocabulary problems. In this sense, this work evaluates different similarity approaches to be used in the process of content relationship assessment and feature selection. The main idea is that different similarity measures will select different phrases to represent the summary of the documents.

Based on this motivation, we aim to describe a method that suggests another approach to traditional automatic summarization methods. That method is based on the **degree of similarity** (gs), which is based on fuzzy logic, and has already been reported in previous works with interesting results [8, 16]. Thus, the objective of this work is to present a comparison between methods of automatic summarization, discussing the results obtained with the fuzzy similarity approach and the traditional cosine based ones.

To reach this goal, we carried out an analysis where we apply three different automatic summarization algorithms, i.e., CSTSumm (Sect. 2.1), LexRank (Sect. 2.2) and FuzzyRank (Sect. 3), to a news corpus (CSTNews [1]) and evaluate the extracts generated by those methods to a human-made extract using ROUGE [4], which is a specific method for evaluating extraction approaches.

The contributions of this work are the following: (i) a method that uses fuzzy evaluation instead of cosine similarity to automatically summarize texts, and (ii) a comparison between this approach and traditional automatic summarization methods. Then,

This document is structured as follows. Next, we describe two summarization methods that were used as the basis for the development of this work, i.e., CSTSumm and LexRank. Then we introduce our approach, namely FuzzyRank. In Sect. 3 we explain an experiment that we have performed to evaluate our approach, and in Sect. 4 we analyze their results. Finally, we present our conclusion, revisiting our contributions and discussing future work.

2   Background and Related Work

In our context, **summarization** is the process of reducing a textual document to create a summary that retains the most important points of the original document.

2.1   CSTSumm

The first algorithm considered in this study is CSTSumm, a strategy for generating multi-document summaries that represent texts as graphs. As reported by [9], the method investigated to perform multi-document automatic extractive summarization is the Segmented Bushy Path. The algorithm is organized in a few steps. Firstly, the algorithm preprocesses the source texts and computes the lexical similarity among their sentences to build a graph, where the vertices are the phrases and links have numeric values that indicate how lexically close the sentences are (using cosine measure).

Then, the algorithm divides each text into subtopics, using TextTiling, that is a technique for subdividing texts into multi-paragraph units that represent passages, or subtopics [3]. Once the texts are segmented, [9] proposes that the next step is to identify and cluster popular subtopics within and across the documents, with those clusters, the segmented bushy path is used to select the relevant information for the summary, performing the content extraction.

2.2 LexRank

The other method we selected to compare to our approach is LexRank [2], a stochastic graph-based method for computing relative importance of textual units for Natural Language Processing. As reported by [2], LexRank introduces a way for computing sentence importance based on the concept of eigenvector centrality in a graph representation of sentences. In [5] eigenvector centrality is defined by a measure of the influence of a node in a network, in this case, it calculates the importance of a node in a graph. It associates scores to all graph nodes based on those connections to high-scoring nodes add more to other nodes than equal connections to low-scoring nodes. In this model, the adjacency matrix graph representation of the sentences is represented by a connective matrix based on intra-sentence cosine similarity.

There are several ways of computing sentence centrality using the cosine similarity matrix and the corresponding graph representation. Conforming to [2], the hypothesis of LexRank is that the sentences that can better describe a text (in other words, are **similar** to the other sentences in the text) are more central (or *salient*) in the graph. To define similarity, it is used the bag-of-words model to represent each sentence as an N-dimensional vector, where N is the number of all possible words in the target language. The similarity of sentences is calculated by the cosine between two corresponding vectors:

$$idf-modified-cosine(x,y) = \frac{\sum_{w \in x,y} tf_{w,x} tf_{w,y} (idf_w)^2}{\sqrt{\sum_{x_i \in x}(tf_{x_i,x} idf_{x_i})^2} \times \sqrt{\sum_{y_i \in y}(tf_{y_i,y} idf_{y_i})^2}} \quad (1)$$

where $tf_{w,s}$ is the number of occurrences of the word w in the sentence s, and the idf_i is the *inverse document frequency* a measure used to asses the importance of the words in a sentence, that is defined by the formula [11]:

$$idf_i = \log(\frac{N}{n_i}) \quad (2)$$

2.3 Centrality

According to [2] the centrality of a sentence is often defined concerning the centrality of the words that it contains. A common way of assessing word centrality is by looking at the centroid of the cluster in a vector space. The centroid of a cluster is a pseudo-document that consists of words that have $tfxidf$ scores above a predefined threshold. In this case, tf is the frequency of a word in the cluster, and *idf* values that are typically computed over a much larger and similar dataset.

Erkan's work [2] uses cosine scores to count the degree of centrality of sentences, but different scores dramatically influence the interpretation of centrality. Too small values may mistakenly take weak similarities into consideration while too high ones may lose many of the similarity relations. After computing the centrality degree, it uses a variation of the PageRank method, where each edge is a vote to determine the overall centrality value of each node. They call this new measure the "lexical PageRank", or LexRank.

In our work, we use the fuzzy approach, present in the next section, to calculate the distance of sentences, and the PageRank method to extract the graph salience.

3   FuzzyRank

According to [13], one of the major problems of document identification and analysis is the way the features that describe and model documents are chosen. These features are not properly selected because the characteristics usually used to represent documents are the words they contain. It is clear that we cannot use all the words in a document to represent it, and a selection must be performed. The problem is that, if the choice is made based only on the number of occurrences of the words in the document, it does not accordingly represent the content of that document.

To standardize the terms used in the documents, research in the literature of the area was proposed by [13], and it was identified that the existing methods could be divided into two main groups: those that perform **statistical analysis** and those that do **natural language processing** (NLP).

Analyzing those methods, the ones from the NLP group are more complex, so the methods of statistical analysis were the most used for a time. Nevertheless, NLP techniques have been improved and minimized in terms of effort and complexity. For correct understanding, analysis and processing of texts using NLP, some support knowledge is needed, also called background knowledge, usually expressed through production rules, grammatical rules, morphological dictionaries or even using ontologies.

Using fuzzy reasoning about the cue (terms) in a document, it is possible to calculate the likelihood of a term being present in that document. Once the terms of documents are identified, we must determine the similarity among the terms of each document (or sentences). To perform this, we have chosen the following equation, which, according to [7,14], calculates the degree of similarity (gs) among two vectors (V_1,V_2) representing the terms present on two sentences being compared. This equation was already used in previous work with promising results [8,15,16].

$$gs(V_1, V_2) = \frac{\sum_{h=1}^{k} gi(a, b)}{n} \tag{3}$$

Where k is the number of concepts that sentences V_1 and V_2 have in common; n is the total number of concepts on both sentences, and gi is the degree of equality among the weighs of the hth element (a in V_1 and b in V_2), which is calculated by the following equation:

$$gi(a,b) = \frac{1}{2}\left[(a \to b) \wedge (b \to a) + (\overline{a} \to \overline{b}) \wedge (\overline{b} \to \overline{a})\right] \tag{4}$$

where $\overline{x} = 1 - x$, $a \to b = \max\{c \in [0,1] | a * c <= b\}$, and $\wedge = \min$.

In this sense, instead of calculating the average or the product between two degrees (which is performed by the traditional cosine similarity), the function determines the degree of equality between them.

The theory behind fuzzy assessment is that documents can be seen as sets of words, and words may be present at different sets at the same time with different levels of membership. In this sense, the relative frequency of each word is directly related to their importance in each document thus affecting their level of membership. Thus, in that equation, each level of membership is taken into account during the assessment, and if a word contains too different weights on two different sets, their similarity will be lowered. However, if the weights are similar, the similarity will be higher.

In this work, we use this equation in an approach to rank the phrases of a document and select the ones most appropriate to be used as the summary of this document. The process is applied to all documents of a collection. We then compare this approach to the ones described in the literature (presented in the previous section). The experiment conducted to perform this comparison, and its underlying results are presented in the next section.

4   Experiment Setup

We use CSTNews [1] as a corpus to apply the methods for the automatic summarization of texts. This corpus is composed of five groups of news articles written in Brazilian Portuguese from several sections of news such as politics, sports, world news, daily news, money, and science. Each news is collected from several mainstream online agencies (Folha de São Paulo, Estadão, O Globo, Jornal do Brasil e Gazeta do Povo). For example, an article about a hurricane in Japan is collected from many online news agencies to create a variety of sentences, about the same subject, to be explored by our summarization techniques.

We compared the three aforementioned methods: CSTSumm (Sect. 2.1), LexRank (Sect. 2.2), and our approach, FuzzyRank (Sect. 3).

We used the evaluation method ROUGE [4], which counts the number of overlapping units such as n-grams, word sequences and word pairs between the computer-generated summary to be evaluated and the ideal summaries created by humans.

4.1   Results

The size of the human-generated summaries that the corpus provides corresponds to 30% of the size of the longest article in each group of news, resulting in a compression rate of 70%. To match out summaries to the human-made extract, we decided to use the same compression rate, to make the comparison using ROUGE fair.

ROUGE calculates a score based on the set of words (e.g. n-grams that may vary from 1 to 4) in common between human- and automatically generated summaries. Then it produces the **precision** that indicates the proportion of reference n-grams in the automatic summary, the **recall** that shows the portion of reference n-grams in the automatic summary in relation to the reference summary and the **f-measure**, which is a performance measure that combines precision and recall.

For a better comprehension, the results obtained in our experiments are exposed in Table 1.

Table 1. Mean values for the FuzzyRank and the baselines

	Precision			Recall			F-score		
	FuzzyRank	LexRank	CSTSumm	FuzzyRank	LexRank	CSTSumm	FuzzyRank	LexRank	CSTSumm
Rouge-1	0.8782	0.9013	**0.9590**	**0.7743**	0.7545	0.6986	0.7898	0.7907	**0.7914**
Rouge-2	0.7578	0.7802	**0.8425**	**0.6639**	0.6451	0.6042	0.6779	0.6785	**0.6888**
Rouge-3	0.5736	0.5801	**0.6562**	**0.5015**	0.4757	0.4646	0.5113	0.5006	**0.5324**
Rouge-4	0.4642	0.4599	**0.5491**	**0.4054**	0.3746	0.3862	0.4128	0.3946	**0.4438**
Rouge-SU4	0.8262	0.8467	**0.9080**	**0.7245**	0.7035	0.6557	0.7400	0.7389	**0.7453**

Studying those results for each newsgroup, we can observe that all automatic summarization methods show very similar results in all evaluations. However, the averaged results show that precision, which evaluates the number of references in the summary itself, regarding traditional methods (i.e., LexRank, CSTSumm), obtain better results. That happens because the comparison is made based on the number of similar words, and the generated summaries have more references when compared to themselves.

Considering recall, which compares the generated summaries to the gold-standard human-made summary, we see that the proposed method (FuzzyRank) has a little advantage, since the use of fuzzy operators explores the equality of the texts, giving negative scores to terms that do not overlap. Using a Wilcoxon statistical test [12] with a significance level of 0.05, we verified that FuzzyRank recall is statistically superior, except in two cases, namely Rouge-3 and Rouge-4.

The f-score shows the method with the better average results, combining precision and recall. As we can see, CSTSumm has the best results of all three methods. However, the statistical test showed that the differences in ROUGE-1 and ROUGE-2 are not statistically significant.

Extending the evaluation results, we can make more observations of our method:

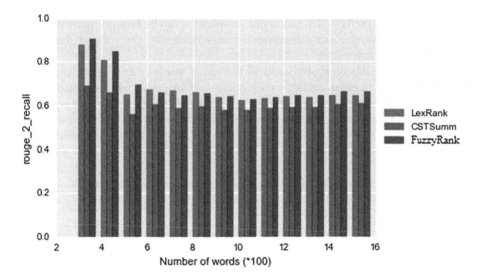

Fig. 1. ROUGE-2 recall

- The recall obtained by our approach is always higher for texts with less than 500 words, and most of the time for other sizes of documents, as it can be seen in Fig. 1.
- The FuzzyRank approach get better results when the relation type-token is higher than 3, as shown in Fig. 2. The type-token[3] relation separates types

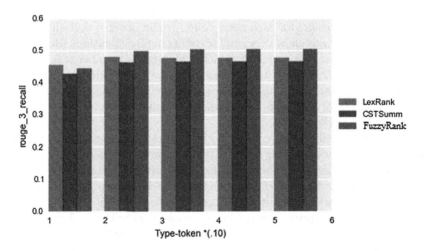

Fig. 2. ROUGE-3 recall

---

[3] http://plato.stanford.edu/entries/types-tokens/.

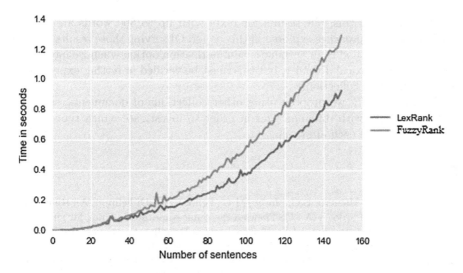

Fig. 3. Perfomance of LexRank and FuzzyRank

(representing abstract descriptive concepts) from tokens (representing objects that instantiate concepts).

- The performance of FuzzyRank and LexRank is similar. Although our method presents a higher runtime when compared to LexRank (see Fig. 3), this time may not be a problem for short texts, where the results of our approach are better.

5 Conclusion

This paper describes a method that uses the degree of similarity (gs) instead of traditional cosine based methods to help with the identification of the most relevant phrases to perform automatic text summarization. The objective was to get a summary that is more related to human-made ones. We explored the Automatic Text Summarization (ATS), a task that became important since the abundance of texts available on the internet is growing.

To validate our idea, we performed the application of some methods of automatic text summarization to a corpus that consists of a group of fifth news articles. By doing that, we conclude that our method has an advantage when the lexical diversity is high and when compared to human-made summaries. Using a Wilcoxon statistical test [12] with a significance level of 0.05, we verified that FuzzyRank's Recall is statistically superior, except in two cases, namely Rouge-3 and Rouge-4. Regarding the precision, the results achieved by our approach not outperformed the baselines. However, FuzzyRank achieves a comparable performance concerning f-score, which is the harmonic mean between precision and recall.

In addition to this, our results for texts with up to 500 words are greater than the other approaches explored in this paper. Observing those results, we can infer that our method is an automatic summarization option when we have short texts with high lexical diversity, but this must be verified in further experiments considering other collections.

For future work we propose using other collections of documents, specially containing texts with different sizes in order to investigate which type of text better works with each approach.

References

1. Cardoso, P.C., Maziero, E.G., Jorge, M.L., Seno, E.M., Di Felippo, A., Rino, L.H., Nunes, M.G., Pardo, T.A.: CSTnews-a discourse-annotated corpus for single and multi-document summarization of news texts in Brazilian Portuguese. In: Proceedings of the 3rd RST Brazilian Meeting, pp. 88–105 (2011)
2. Erkan, G., Radev, D.R.: LexRank: graph-based lexical centrality as salience in text summarization. J. Artif. Intell. Res. **42**, 457–479 (2004)
3. Hearst, M.A.: Texttiling: segmenting text into multi-paragraph subtopic passages. Comput. Linguist. **23**(1), 33–64 (1997)
4. Lin, C.Y.: Rouge: a package for automatic evaluation of summaries. In: Text Summarization Branches Out: Proceedings of the ACL-04 Workshop, Barcelona, Spain, vol. 8 (2004)
5. Murgante, B., Misra, S., Rocha, A., Torre, C., Rocha, J.G., Falcão, M.I., Taniar, D., Apduhan, B.O., Gervasi, O. (eds.): Computational Science and Its Applications - ICCSA 2014. LNCS, vol. 8583. Springer, Cham (2014). doi:10.1007/978-3-319-09156-3
6. Nenkova, A., Maskey, S., Liu, Y.: Automatic summarization. In: Proceedings Annual Meeting of the Association for Computational Linguistics, p. 3. Association for Computational Linguistics (2011)
7. Oliveira, H.M.: Seleção de entes complexos usando lógica difusa. Instituto de Informática da PUC-RS, dissertation (Masters in Computer Science) (1996)
8. Prado, H.A.D., de Oliveira, J.P.M., Ferneda, E., Wives, L.K., Silva, E.M., Loh, S.: Text mining in the context of business intelligence. In: Khosrow-Pour, M. (ed.) Encyclopedia of Information Science and Technology, 1st edn, pp. 2793–798. IGI Global, Hershey (2005)
9. Ribaldo, R., Cardoso, P.C.F., Pardo, T.A.S.: Exploring the subtopic-based relationship map strategy for multi-document summarization. Revista de Informática Teórica e Aplicada **23**(1), 183–211 (2016)
10. Salton, G., Wong, A., Yang, C.S.: A vector space model for automatic indexing. Commun. ACM **18**(11), 613–620 (1975). http://doi.acm.org/10.1145/361219.361220
11. Sparck Jones, K.: A statistical interpretation of term specificity and its application in retrieval. J. Doc. **28**(1), 11–21 (1972)
12. Wilcoxon, F., Katti, S., Wilcox, R.A.: Critical values and probability levels for the wilcoxon rank sum test and the wilcoxon signed rank test. Sel. Tables Math. Stat. **1**, 171–259 (1970)
13. Wives, L.K.: Utilizando conceitos como descritores de textos para o processo de identificação de conglomerados (clustering) de documentos. Ph.D. thesis, Universidade Federal do Rio Grande do Sul (2004)

14. Wives, L.K., Loh, S.: Recuperação de informações usando a expansão semântica e a lógica difusa. In: Congreso Internacional de Ingeniería Informática, pp. 201–211. CITA, Faculdad de Ingenieria (1998)
15. Wives, L.K., Loh, S., de Oliveira, J. P.M.: A comparative study of clustering versus classification over reuters collection. In: Proceedings of the 8th International Workshop on Pattern Recognition in Information Systems, pp. 231–236 (2009)
16. Wives, L.K., de Oliveira, J.P.M., Loh, S.: Conceptual clustering of textual documents and some insights for knowledge discovery. In: Prado, H.d., Ferneda, E. (eds.) Text Mining: Techniques and Applications, pp. 223–243. Information Science Reference, Hershey (2008)

Application of Data Mining Algorithms to Classify Biological Data: The *Coffea canephora* Genome Case

Jeferson Arango-López[1,2,6(✉)], Simon Orozco-Arias[4],
Johnny A. Salazar[3], and Romain Guyot[5]

[1] FIET, Universidad del Cauca, Calle 5 Nº 4-70, Popayán, Colombia
jal@unicauca.edu.co
[2] Facultad de Ingeniería, Universidad de Caldas,
Calle 65 Nº 26-10, Manizales, Colombia
[3] Escuela de Administración y Mercadotecnia del Quindío (EAM),
Av. Bolívar # 3-11, Armenia, Colombia
[4] Centro de Bioinformática y Biología Computacional (BIOS),
Ecoparque los Yarumos, Manizales, Colombia
[5] IRD, CIRAD, Univ. Montpellier, IPME,
BP 64501, 34394 Montpellier Cedex 5, France
[6] Departamento de lenguajes y sistemas informaticos, Universidad de Granada,
Calle Periodista Daniel Saucedo Aranda, s/n, 18071 Granada, Spain

Abstract. Bioinformatics is now one of the most important fields of modern sciences grouping different fields of research such as Biology, Genomics, Genetics and Molecular evolution. These fields generate a large amount of information via the utilization of the new generations of sequencing techniques (NGS). This amount of data requires the development of a new generation of tools able to store and analyze efficiently and rapidly the information. *Coffea canephora* also called the Robusta coffee is one of the most important tree for tropical countries. This genome has been recently sequenced. One of the characteristics of this genome is the presence of numerous repeated elements, representing more than 50% of the genome sequence. The analysis and classi-fication of such amount of repeated sequences require innovative approaches. Here, we present how data mining and machine learning can contribute to process sequencing data for the fast classification of a class of repeated sequences, called transposable elements.

Keywords: Data mining · Bioinformatics · Transposable elements · *Coffea canephora*

1 Introduction

Bioinformatics is a recent and now a major research field. Several authors have attempted to give an unambiguous *definition* for bioinformatics. From a biology per-spective, López-Gartner and coworkers define the bioinformatics as a new discipline helping with the discovery of biological information through the implementation of

A. Solano and H. Ordoñez (Eds.): CCC 2017, CCIS 735, pp. 156–170, 2017.
DOI: 10.1007/978-3-319-66562-7_12

computational techniques [1]. On the other hand, from an informatics perspective, bioinformatics is interpreted as an area of artificial intelligence applications [2] where advanced techniques and algorithms can be used to improve the bioinformatics results. In fact, bioinformatics is at the middle between different fields such as biology, informatics and mathematics with the objectives to classify and to analyze the biological data. The revolution of the new generation sequencing techniques, able to generate millions of sequences, requires new types and fast algorithms and new informatics infrastructure to store and analyze these data in a decent time.

Because Bioinformatics is the interaction between biology, informatics and mathematics, it is sometimes difficult for computer scientists to understand the need of biologists and biologists to write advanced programs and to execute them in a bash[1] console. Recently the implementation of applications with a graphic user interface like GITIRBio [3] or Galaxy [4] improved the interaction between biologists and bioinformatics tools.

On the other hand, data mining is presented like a process of examining large sets of data to search for unexpected or hidden patterns, which can give us useful information. Data mining showed a large variety of applications from the prediction of future events (such as stock prices or football scores), *the* clustering of populations into groups having similar characteristics, or estimate the likelihood of health conditions using other known variables [5]. The recent advances in data mining and machine learning algorithms allow researches in different fields such as artificial intelligence, robotics, real-time processing to organize and to classify faster big data sets.

Different tools have been developed for researchers, like Weka [6], Watson (IBM tool - https://www.ibm.com/watson/) and R language [7]. Weka, the more popular tools, is an application based on java technologies allowing the process of large quantities of structured data.

Genomics and the classification of all information from sequenced genomes are another applications of data mining. Among genome annotation, the analysis of transposable elements (TE) is an example of the successful of informatics tools in the biology field. Due to the importance of TE in eukaryotic genomes, the number of tools and projects to analyze and classify them in plant and fungus genomes are increasing such as in coffee, where LTR retrotransposons (LTR-RT), a group of TE, were used to find geographic groups [8], in fungus where the authors discovered the variability of LTR-RT [9] and in oil palm where a completed classification of LTR-RTs was presented [10].

With traditional bioinformatics tools, techniques and algorithms, the classification and identification of TE families and the relationship between transposable elements is a long and complex process. Moreover, with the revolution of the new generation sequencing (NGS) technologies, and the amount of sequenced data available, a new generation of algorithm is necessary to classify and annotate rapidly TE.

---

[1] Bash is a user interface to Unix operating system that accepts commands and generally produces text-based output [46].

Here, we tested how the data mining algorithms could be used to process genomic data to classify and annotate transposable elements in the *C. canephora* genome extracting more information than traditional techniques.

The document sections are structured as follow: Background in Sect. 2 introducing important concepts and general terms; Materials and methods in Sect. 3 details the materials used in the research process; Results, in Sect. 4 and finally the Conclusion in Sect. 5.

2   Background

2.1   *Coffea canephora* Data

The *Coffea* genus comprises 124 different species originating mainly from Africa and Madagascar. Only two *Coffea* species are cultivated, the Robusta coffee tree (*Coffea canephora*) and the Arabica coffee tree (*C. arabica*). The genome of *C. canephora* has been recently published by Denoeud et al. [11] and 80% of the 700 Mb of the *C. canephora* genome has been sequenced and released. This genome sequence represents an unevaluable tool and reference to understand the coffee genome composition, but also to help breeders to generate new varieties resistant to pest and adapted to climate changes. The diploid *Coffea canephora* genome ($2n = 2x = 22$ chromosomes) comprises 25,574 annotated protein-coding genes and a high proportion of repeated sequences, called transposable elements. They represent $\sim 50\%$ of the sequenced genome. Among these repeated sequences, 85% of them could be classified into a particular classes of transposable elements called Long Terminal Repeat (LTR) retrotransposons (LTR-RT), able to multiply their copy number in the host genome [12].

In the same line, Coffea canephora has been selected as a genomic reference for the *Coffea* genus, due to its economic importance for developing countries [13], but also because it comprises genes of interest for the improvement of the *C. arabica* species, such as resistances to pests and adaptation to the environment. So far numerous genomic data are available for *C. canephora*, such as single-pass expressed sequences (a total of 214,964 randomly picked clones from 37 cDNA libraries of *C. arabica*, *C. canephora*, *and C. racemosa*, representing specific stages of cells and plant development that after trimming resulted in 130,792, 12,381 and 10,566 sequences for each species, respectively) [14], Bacterial Artificial Clones (BAC) libraries [15, 16] BAC sequencing [13, 17], and random 454 sequencing [8].

2.2   Transposable Elements

Transposable elements (TE) are the most frequent repeated sequenced in eukaryotic genomes [9, 18]. They are mobile elements able to create mutations and to amplify their copy numbers. TEs were classified into two classes according to their replication mechanisms [12]: Class I, called retrotransposons, for TEs moving through a RNA intermediate, (also called "copy and paste" mechanisms) and Class II, or transposons, for TEs moving through a DNA intermediate (also called "Cut and Paste" mechanism) [19]. In plant genomes, Long Terminal Repeat retrotransposons (LTR-RT) are the most common Class I elements [12]. They can represent up to 80% of the genome size, such as in wheat or barley. The classification of LTR-RT is based on the presence of genes (or domains) involved in the mobility of the element. In case of the absence of some domains the elements can be classified as non-autonomous elements (see Table 1), that can be further sub-classified into TRIM [20], LARD [21], BARE-2 [22] or TR-GAG [12]. For autonomous elements, LTR are classified into two superfamilies; Gypsy and Copia [19], according to similarities and order of their coding domains (see Table 2).

Table 1. LTR-RT domains

Name	Abbreviation	Function
Reverse Transcriptase	RT	DNA synthesis using RNA as a template
RNase H	RNAseH	Degradation of the RNA template in the DNA-RNA hybrid
Intregrase	INT	Catalyze the insertion of the retrotransposon cDNA into the genome host
Aspartic Protease	AP	Processe the polyprotein into smaller protein products (domains)
Envelope	ENV	Transfer the retrovirus cell-to-cell. Hypothesis of transfer for LTR Retrotransposon
Group Specific Antigen	GAG	Structural protein for building the virus-like particles

Table 2. Autonomous LTR-RT classification [36]

Super family	Lineages for plant genomes
Copia	Bianca, Oryco, Retrofit, Sire, Tork
Gypsy	Athila, CRM, Del, Galadriel, Reina, TAT

Nowadays there are software that provide information from TE such as prediction of transposable elements (Repet TEdenovo [23], RepeatScout [24]), prediction of completed LTR-RTs (LTRharvest [25], LTR_STRUC [26], LTR-Finder [27]), identification of structural genomic variants caused by TE insertion or deletion (LoRTE [28]), annotation on the genome (Repet TEannot [23]), evolutionary analysis of LTR-RTs (LTRtype [29]), general classification of transposable elements (PASTEC [30]) and semi-automatic classification and post-processing of de novo predicted LTR-RT annotations (LTRsift [31]).

The analysis of LTR-RTs is currently done manually. Most of the studies extracted information like classification in main classes, insertion time and phylogenetic tree [32–34]. *Oryza sativa* results presented in [35], showed a very high unclassified rate (63,8%), demonstrating that current techniques are not efficient.

2.3   Bioinformatics

In the last few years, bioinformatics has impacted in a positive way researches on coffee species and more particularly on *Coffea canephora*. The release of the *C. canephora* genome allowed the development of high throughput detection of genetic polymorphisms to assess the genetic diversity of cultivated accession from Vietnam and Mexico of this species [37].

Besides, others advances include studies on drought tolerance and other important agronomic traits such as yield of a *C. canephora* conilon population, cultivated in 1175 m of altitude [38], understanding of antioxidant capacity of green coffee from different geographical origin (Brazil, Colombia, Ethiopia, Honduras, Kenya, Mexico, Peru, Uganda and Vietnam) [39] and discovering of relationship between *C. canephora* and model plant species such as *O. sativa*, Arabidopsis, *S. tuberosum*, *S. lycopersicum*, C. papaya, and V. vinifera [15].

2.4   Data Mining

Currently, there are many models and methodologies to Knowledge Discovery Process (KDP), which can be applied to multiples data sets. In our case, KDP was used to find knowledge not expressed explicitly in the file content. Some samples of these models and methodologies are: (1) KDD (Knowledge Discovery in Database) model, it is the process of discovering useful knowledge from a collection of semi-structured data; (2) SEMMA (Sample – the subset of data should be large enough to be a representative sample but not too large of a dataset to process easily, Explore – look for patterns in the data, Modify – create and transform variables, or eliminate unnecessary ones, Model – select and apply a model that best fits your situation and data, Assess – determine whether or not your results are useful and reliable) model; (3) CATALYST o P3QT. (4) CRISP-DM (Cross Industry Standard Process for Data mining), among others.

The KDD model was defined in 1996 as a knowledge discovery model to academic fields [40], and alternate proposals with different approaches have been proposed such as the models previously mentioned. Among the most notable of these proposals is CRISP-DM, initially related to the industrial field. The KDD method, more flexible, and directly related to an academic perspective has been used in our present work.

3   Materials and Methods

3.1   Bioinformatics Processes

The *Coffea canephora* genome was downloaded from the Coffee Genome Hub Project [41] [http://coffee-genome.org/], all chromosome sequences were used, including "chromosome Un" (Compilations of Unknown sequences). First, all downloaded Fasta[2] files were grouped together and the LTR_STRUC [26] was used to process the

---

[2] Fasta format is a standard for sequence files that each sequence has an identity line beginning with > character followed by its nucleotides [http://www.ncbi.nlm.nih.gov/blast/fasta.shtml].

data and to predict complete LTR-RT. The LTR_STRUC outputs were composed by 4 text files for each LTR-RT element predicted. These files were processed in order to save all information in a tabular format file, separated by ":"; LTR Identity; primer binding site (PBS); PolyPurine Tract (PPT); length; Active site; Longest Open Reading Frame (ORF); Target Site Duplication (TSD); Long Terminal Repeat (LTR) A length; LRT B length; orientation, and strand. LTR A and B sequences were extracted using Seqret and Extractseq tools from Emboss [42]. Domains were identified using blastx from NCBI-Blast using as a query the LTR Retrotransposon sequence against the domain database from The Gypsy Database Project [18]. Six Domains were searched in this study, GAG, RT, INT, RNAseH, AP and ENV (see Table 1).

Based on tabular file previously created, a first classification process of predicted elements into Gypsy, Copia and unclassified superfamilies (NON-Family) was performed using the 'RLC' and 'RLG' keywords (present into the RT, INT, and RNAseH classified domains). Gypsy and Copia superfamilies were further sub-classified into lineages using keyword subfamily (BIANCA, ORYCO, RETROFIT, SIRE, TORK, ATHILA, CRM, DEL, GALADRIEL, REINA, and TAT) present into LTR RT's domains.

The NON-Family LTR-RT elements were re-analyzed to determine if they are true LTR-RT or false positive predicted by LTR_STRUC. NON-Family sequences were blasted (BLASTN) as a query against the whole *coffea canephora* genome. Only LTR elements that appeared in the genome at least 50 times were considered as potential LTR-RT elements. Finally, NON-Family sequences were compared against classified elements using Censor [43] for doing a global alignment, to filter out Non-Family elements using elements already classified.

3.2   Informatics Process

KDD is a not trivial process to discover knowledge and useful information from different files and databases [40]. The data may be in diverse structured formats such as XML, JSON, CSV, but also in unstructured format like plain files, word, PDF documents and pictures. KDD is not an automatic process, but composed by iterative – the output of a phase could be the entry for a previous activity – and interactive – It needs an expert in the data to support the process – activities to explore big dataset to discover relationships within information [44].

A process of a knowledge discovery is used to define the data behavior, to discover patterns or tendencies, to get inferences and future predictions. It is a process composed of several phases, starting with the understanding the data domain up to results analysis and their interpretation.

For *Coffea canephora* our data is composed of predicted LTR-RTs in plain text format. This database has 1,376 instances, each one composed by 21 different attributes. We first classified the 1,376 instances into two categories: 1,019 elements classified into a lineage and 357 unclassified. The main attributes are presented in Table 3.

Table 3. Definition of main attributes in original data.

Name	Type	Description
Family	Categorical	Family or lineage classification of autonomous LTR-RT (See Table 2)
Super family	Categorical	Superfamily classification of autonomous LTR-RT (See Table 2)
Sequence length	Numerical	Length in nucleotides of the LTR-RT
Transposable element identity	Numerical	Identity percentage
Longest ORF	Numerical	Length in nucleotides for the longest Open Reading Frame (ORF) found
LTR A length	Numerical	Length in nucleotides for the Long Terminal Repeat (LTR) A section
LTR B length	Numerical	Length in nucleotides for the Long Terminal Repeat (LTR) B section

Comprise the Data Domain

In a process of knowledge discovery in a data set, is required to comprise the data nature. Which is it meaning? What do they represent? It is necessary to get a better comprehension of the obtained results, and give to researchers a good representation of them.

In this line, we applied a comprising domain through a process known as patterns identification to response the previous paragraph questions.

This process allows us to identify the main properties to predict the families that could be attributed for each LTR-RT, it was successful trough evaluation of DNA strings. In each DNA string, we found the long of each one. Another interesting feature in those data was called non-families group, this group was pairing with LTR-RT group, where each LTR-RT had an identified family.

Creating the Database

Files from bioinformatics process outputs were transformed into a CSV (comma separated values) formatted file. Twenty-one attributes for each record (in total 1,376 and 1019 with family identified, and 357 without family) were processed.

Filtering and Preprocessing the Data

This phase is the most important in the KDP process, representing up to 60% of the effort [45]. The aim of these activities is to detect empty or junk information. In our case, the process was quickly executed because the data has not problems in its structure and values. Non-numeric attributes were identified while not any null value was discovered during this process. Complete results are presented in Fig. 1.

Transforming the Data

The objective of this step is focused in reducing or increasing instances. The original data in the file are processed to know its relevance, and clean the data noise. It allows performing the data mining process easier, and reducing the computational resources needed. Finally, the dataset is segmented into subgroups to obtain independents results.

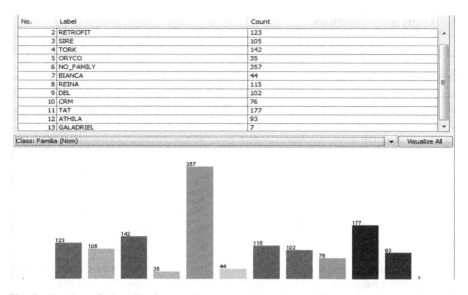

Fig. 1. Results of the filtering and preprocessing phase. There are two sections, 1. (top) Attributes values and 2. (bottom) Main properties.

In our project, the following three data segments were created: (1) The group with records that had an identified family (1,019 hits); (2) The group with records without an identified family (357 hits); (3) All the records, mixing the groups 1 and 2. Next, in each segment, several subgroups were created. Specifically, for group 2, four new segments were defined based on the InfoGain algorithm. In this process, the Ranker searcher was executed.

In the first phase the more relevant attribute was identified: INT. In the second phase, INT was omitted to discover the second most important attribute in the data set: RNAseH. Subsequently, were excluded RT and AP as most important fields in each data set. The same process was performed for files with known LTR-RT families and non-families. Each one was generated with the same attributes than the previous process.

Choosing Methods and Algorithms and Running Data Mining

To achieve the objectives, predictive and descriptive processes were applied. Predictive processes were used to find patterns in data files. It allows classifying a specific element into a family. It was accomplished through decision tree algorithms. Descriptive processes were used to group element with non-family's elements. It was performed through clustering algorithms.

4   Analysis of Results

4.1   Segment of Records Without Families

This segment is formed by records without identified families, we applied descriptive processes to find common features between them. Best results were obtained through the application of clustering algorithms and visual analytics. During the clustering process, we used the EM algorithm that discovered three main groups and their distribution, but failed to specify the common features between these groups (see Fig. 2).

```
0        32 (  9%)
1       300 ( 84%)
2        24 (  7%)
```

Fig. 2.   Group distribution with EM algorithm.

Next, the canopy algorithm was applied. Initially eight groups were found, but after filtering three groups were selected based on common features between themselves. Some groups were not considered due to their small size (see Fig. 3).

```
Cluster 0:   <0,1,3,4,5,6,7>        Clustered Instances
Cluster 1:   <0,1,3,4,6>
Cluster 2:   <2>                    0      233 ( 65%)
Cluster 3:   <0,1,3,4,5,6>          1       45 ( 12%)
Cluster 4:   <0,1,3,4,5,6>          2       25 (  8%)
Cluster 5:   <0,3,4,5,6>            3        3 (  1%)
Cluster 6:   <0,1,3,4,5,6>          4        3 (  1%)
Cluster 7:   <0,7,8>                5        9 (  2%)
Cluster 8:   <7,8>                  6        3 (  1%)
                                    7       34 (  9%)
                                    8        2 (  1%)
```

Fig. 3.   Similarity and distribution of groups with canopy algorithm.

The groups 0, 1, 2, 3, 4, 5, and 6 have similarities in their components, suggesting that they belong to the same and unique group. Another group is composed by the cluster 7 and 8. Finally, the group 2 was identified as an individual group (Fig. 3).

In the next phase, the features of the three groups presented above were analyzed using the SimpleKMeans algorithm (see Fig. 4).

The differences between the groups are evident with the sequence length and ORF length attributes. The other attributes were not relevant to separate groups.

The segmentation of records with LTRA and LTRB lengths was analyzed to predict superfamilies (RLC or Copia and RLG or Gypsy. The Fig. 5 shows the difference between LTRA and LTRB lengths according to their superfamilies. Here RLC (Copia) is the most significative.

Attribute	Full Data (357.0)	0 (57.0)
Idetificación secuencia	Coffee_8807_B3_L2_1186	Coffee_8807_B3_L2_1186
longitud de la secuencia	7511.9328	9639.8246
Identidad del elemento transponible	94.1563	94.8158
Longitud del ORF más largo	239.8123	167.0351
Longitud LTR A (IMPORTANTE)	1418.2969	3074.1754
Longitud LTR B (IMPORTANTE)	1419.2017	3076.4035
Dirección	STRAND -	STRAND -
GAG	GAG NO	GAG NO
E-value del GAG	ENO	ENO
RT	RT NO	RT NO
E-value del RT	ENO	ENO
INT	INT NO	INT NO
E-value INT	ENO	ENO
RNAseH	RNAseH NO	RNAseH NO
E-value del RNAseH	ENO	ENO
AP	AP NO	AP NO

Fig. 4. Attributes analysis with the SimpleKMeans algorithm.

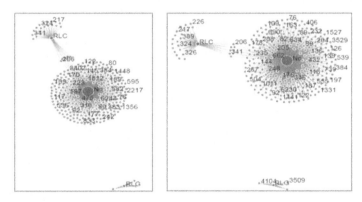

Fig. 5. The relation between LTRA and superfamilies' (left). The relation between LTRB and superfamilies (right).

4.2 Segment of Records with Families

Predictive processes were used to find tendencies in each dataset, giving the opportunity to identify families and confirm the process. Decision trees, Bayesian networks, and lazy algorithms were used, but the best results were found with decision trees algorithm (J48 algorithm). The most interesting result is related to the identification of the LTR-RT family using only LTRA and LTRB length, the longest ORF, sequence identification with a precision of 81.26% (see Fig. 6).

```
  a   b   c   d   e   f   g   h   i   j   k   <-- classified as
103   0   1   9   2   7   1   0   0   0   0 |   a = RETROFIT
  0  97   0   0   0   0   2   1   2   3   0 |   b = SIRE
  2   1 108   2   0  11   1   5  10   1   1 |   c = TORK
  5   0   1  22   0   5   1   0   0   1   0 |   d = ORYCO
  1   0   0   3  35   5   0   0   0   0   0 |   e = BIANCA
  5   0  16   2   5  83   0   0   3   1   0 |   f = REINA
  2   4   7   1   0   1  81   3   1   2   0 |   g = DEL
  1   3   9   0   0   3   1  52   7   0   0 |   h = CRM
  0   2   7   0   0   0   6   5 156   1   0 |   i = TAT
  0   2   1   0   0   0   2   1   0  87   0 |   j = ATHILA
  0   1   0   0   0   0   1   0   1   0   4 |   k = GALADRIEL
```

Fig. 6. Result of confusion matrix of J48 algorithm.

The families and their features were classified through visual analytic tools, using attributes related to LTRA, LTRB and sequence lengths. Groups with similar features were discovered confirming the relationships between the sequence length and the family type. According to these attributes the SIRE, ATHILA, TAT, DEL, and GALADRIEL families are separated from each other. However, more attributes are necessary to separate all families. The results of this analysis are detailed below in Figs. 7 and 8.

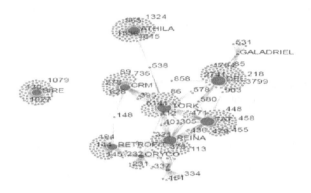

Fig. 7. Family segmentation with LTRA lengths.

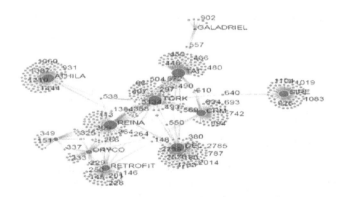

Fig. 8. Family segmentation with LTRB lengths.

5   Conclusions and Future Work

This paper presents several steps to identify characteristics in transposable elements, more particularly for LTR-RT elements that represent most of the elements in the coffee genome, using data mining algorithms collected by Weka (http://www.cs.waikato.ac.nz/ml/weka/).

Due to the high number of transposable elements annotated in the coffee genome, it is necessary to speed up the analysis of those repeat sequences to increase the compression about effects of transposable elements in the genome.

In *Coffea canephora*, 1,376 complete LTR-RTs were predicted, each one comprised 21 attributes, giving difficulties for any human to find relationships or any other extra information. Using data mining techniques, it is now possible to get more information than traditional bioinformatics processes and to extract new knowledge from biological data.

In our work, we found that the sequence lengths for each record is important to determine the LTR-RT family with a high probability. However more attributes are necessary to discover differences between families and superfamilies, such as LTRA, LTRB, sequence, the longest ORF, sequence identification and identification of each LTR-RT. In most cases, only 3 attributes are necessary to classify each LTR-RT with high probability of success. Together with the similarity between LTR-RT and known domains, the data mining may be very helpful for a fast and accurate LTR-RT classification.

For the Non-Family groups, we found 3 different subgroups that can be interpreted as Non-autonomous LTR-RT such as TRIM and LARD. However more detailed analysis and attributes are required to confirm the classification.

Interestingly, we discovered that Non-autonomous elements (LTR-RTs without coding domains) could be also classified into families, using attributes such as sequence length, longest ORF length, LTR A and LTR B lengths. This information will open new researches on the classification of non-autonomous elements in plant genomes.

Here we demonstrated that it is possible to classify coffee complete LTR-RTs using different attributes with a good probability of success. Our future work will be dedicated to create simple and fast rules to classify all LTR-RTs elements in the coffee genome and to test them in other plant genomes.

Acknowledgements. We thank the Centro de Bioinformática y Biología Computacional BIOS for using the supercomputer to process the dataset.

References

1. López-Gartner, G., Agudelo-Valencia, D., Castaño, S., Isaza, G.A., Castillo, L.F., Sánchez, M., Arango, J.: Identification of a putative ganoderic acid pathway enzyme in a *Ganoderma Australe* transcriptome by means of a Hidden Markov Model. In: Overbeek, R., Rocha, M. P., Fdez-Riverola, F., Paz, J.F. (eds.) 9th International Conference on Practical Applications of Computational Biology and Bioinformatics. AISC, vol. 375, pp. 107–115. Springer, Cham (2015). doi:10.1007/978-3-319-19776-0_12

2. Orozco, S., Jeferson, A.: Aplication of artificial intelligence in bioinformatics, advances, definitions and tools. UGCiencia **22**, 159–171 (2016)

3. Castillo, L.F., López-gartner, G., Isaza, G.A., Sánchez, M.: GITIRBio: a semantic and distributed service oriented-architecture for bioinformatics pipeline. J. Integr. Bioinform. **12**, 1–15 (2015)

4. Blankenberg, D., Von Kuster, G., Coraor, N., Ananda, G., Lazarus, R., Mangan, M., Nekrutenko, A., Taylor, J.: Galaxy: a web-based genome analysis tool for experimentalists. Curr. Protoc. Mol. Biol. 1–21 (2010)
5. Sumathi, S., Sivanandam, S.N.: Introduction to Data Mining Principles. Springer, Heidelberg (2006). doi:10.1007/978-3-540-34351-6
6. Markov, Z., Russell, I.: An introduction to the WEKA data mining system. ACM SIGCSE Bull. **38**, 367–368 (2006)
7. Jaffar, J., Michaylov, S., Stuckey, P.J., Yap, R.H.C.: The CLP(R) language and system. ACM Trans. Program. Lang. Syst. **14**, 339 (1992)
8. Guyot, R., Darré, T., Dupeyron, M., de Kochko, A., Hamon, S., Couturon, E., Crouzillat, D., Rigoreau, M., Rakotomalala, J.J., Raharimalala, N.E., Akaffou, S.D., Hamon, P.: Partial sequencing reveals the transposable element composition of *Coffea* genomes and provides evidence for distinct evolutionary stories. Mol. Genet. Genomics **291**, 1979–1990 (2016)
9. Muszewska, A., Hoffman-Sommer, M., Grynberg, M.: LTR retrotransposons in fungi. PLoS One **6** (2011)
10. Beulé, T., Agbessi, M.D., Dussert, S., Jaligot, E., Guyot, R.: Genome-wide analysis of LTR-retrotransposons in oil palm. BMC Genom. **16**, 1–14 (2015)
11. Denoeud, F., Carretero-Paulet, L., Dereeper, A., Droc, G., Guyot, R., Pietrella, M., Zheng, C., Alberti, A., Anthony, F., Aprea, G., Aury, J.-M., Bento, P., Bernard, M., Bocs, S., Campa, C., Cenci, A., Combes, M.-C., Crouzillat, D., Da Silva, C., Daddiego, L., De Bellis, F., Dussert, S., Garsmeur, O., Gayraud, T., Guignon, V., Jahn, K., Jamilloux, V., Joët, T., Labadie, K., Lan, T., Leclercq, J., Lepelley, M., Leroy, T., Li, L.-T., Librado, P., Lopez, L., Muñoz, A., Noel, B., Pallavicini, A., Perrotta, G., Poncet, V., Pot, D., Priyono, Rigoreau, M., Rouard, M., Rozas, J., Tranchant-Dubreuil, C., VanBuren, R., Zhang, Q., Andrade, A.C., Argout, X., Bertrand, B., de Kochko, A., Graziosi, G., Henry, R.J., Jayarama, Ming, R., Nagai, C., Rounsley, S., Sankoff, D., Giuliano, G., Albert, V.A., Wincker, P., Lashermes, P.: The coffee genome provides insight into the convergent evolution of caffeine biosynthesis. Science **345**, 1181–1184 (2014)
12. Chaparro, C., Gayraud, T., De Souza, R.F., Domingues, D.S., Akaffou, S., Vanzela, A.L.L., De Kochko, A., Rigoreau, M., Crouzillat, D., Hamon, S., Hamon, P., Guyot, R.: Terminal-repeat retrotransposons with gAG domain in plant genomes: a new testimony on the complex world of transposable elements. Genome Biol. Evol. **7**, 493–504 (2015)
13. Guyot, R., de la Mare, M., Viader, V., Hamon, P., Coriton, O., Bustamante-porras, J., Poncet, V., Campa, C., Hamon, S., de Kochko, A.: Microcollinearity in an ethylene receptor coding gene region of the *Coffea canephora* genome is extensively conserved with Vitis vinifera and other distant dicotyledonous sequenced genomes. BMC Plant Biol. **9**, 1–15 (2009)
14. Esteves Vieira, L.G., Andrade, A.C., Colombo, C.A., De Araújo Moraes, A.H., Metha, Â., De Oliveira, A.C., Labate, C.A., Marino, C.L., Monteiro-Vitorello, C.D.B., Monte, D.D.C., Giglioti, É., Kimura, E.T., Romano, E., Kuramae, E.E., Macedo Lemos, E.G., Pereira De Almeida, E.R., Jorge, É.C., Albuquerque, É.V.S., Da Silva, F.R., Da Vinecky, F., Sawazaki, H.E., Dorry, H.F.A., Carrer, H., Abreu, I.N., Batista, J.A.N., Teixeira, J.B., Kitajima, J.P., Xavier, K.G., De Lima, L.M., Aranha De Camargo, L.E., Protasio Pereira, L.F., Coutinho, L. L., Franco Lemos, M.V., Romano, M.R., Machado, M.A., Do Carmo Costa, M.M., Grossi De Sá, M.F., Goldman, M.H.S., Ferro, M.I.T., Penha Tinoco, M.L., Oliveira, M.C., Van Sluys, M.A., Shimizu, M.M., Maluf, M.P., Souza Da Eira, M.T., Guerreiro Filho, O., Arruda, P., Mazzafera, P., Correa Mariani, P.D.S., De Oliveira, R.L.B.C., Harakava, R., Balbao, S.F., Siu, M.T., Zingaretti Di Mauro, S.M., Santos, S.N., Siqueira, W.J., Lacerda Costa, G.G., Formighieri, E.F., Carazzolle, M.F., Guimarães Pereira, G.A.: Brazilian coffee genome project: An EST-based genomic resource. Brazilian J. Plant Physiol. **18**, 95–108 (2006)

15. Dereeper, A., Guyot, R., Tranchant-Dubreuil, C., Anthony, F., Argout, X., de Bellis, F., Combes, M.C., Gavory, F., de Kochko, A., Kudrna, D., Leroy, T., Poulain, J., Rondeau, M., Song, X., Wing, R., Lashermes, P.: BAC-end sequences analysis provides first insights into coffee (*Coffea canephora* P.) genome composition and evolution. Plant Mol. Biol. **83**, 177–189 (2013)

16. Leroy, T., Marraccini, P., Dufour, M., Montagnon, C., Lashermes, P., Sabau, X., Ferreira, L. P., Jourdan, I., Pot, D., Andrade, A.C., Glaszmann, J.C., Vieira, L.G.E., Piffanelli, P.: Construction and characterization of a *Coffea canephora* BAC library to study the organization of sucrose biosynthesis genes. Theor. Appl. Genet. **111**, 1032–1041 (2005)

17. Yu, Q., Guyot, R., De Kochko, A., Byers, A., Navajas-Pérez, R., Langston, B.J., Dubreuil-Tranchant, C., Paterson, A.H., Poncet, V., Nagai, C., Ming, R.: Micro-collinearity and genome evolution in the vicinity of an ethylene receptor gene of cultivated diploid and allotetraploid coffee species (*Coffea*). Plant J. **67**, 305–317 (2011)

18. Llorens, C., Futami, R., Covelli, L., Domínguez-Escribá, L., Viu, J.M., Tamarit, D., Aguilar-Rodríguez, J., Vicente-Ripolles, M., Fuster, G., Bernet, G.P., et al.: The Gypsy Database (GyDB) of mobile genetic elements: release 2.0. Nucleic Acids Res. (2010). doi:10.1093/nar/gkq1061

19. Wicker, T., Sabot, F., Hua-Van, A., Bennetzen, J.L., Capy, P., Chalhoub, B., Flavell, A., Leroy, P., Morgante, M., Panaud, O., Paux, E., SanMiguel, P., Schulman, A.H.: A unified classification system for eukaryotic transposable elements. Nat. Rev. Genet. **8**, 973–982 (2007)

20. Witte, C.-P., Le, Q.H., Bureau, T., Kumar, A.: Terminal-repeat retrotransposons in miniature (TRIM) are involved in restructuring plant genomes. Proc. Natl. Acad. Sci. **98**, 13778–13783 (2001)

21. Kalendar, R., Vicient, C.M., Peleg, O., Anamthawat-Jonsson, K., Bolshoy, A., Schulman, A. H.: Large retrotransposon derivatives: abundant, conserved but nonautonomous retroelements of barley and related genomes. Genetics **166**, 1437–1450 (2004)

22. Tanskanen, J.A., Sabot, F., Vicient, C., Schulman, A.H.: Life without GAG: the BARE-2 retrotransposon as a parasite's parasite. Gene **390**, 166–174 (2007)

23. Quesneville, H., Bergman, C.M., Andrieu, O., Autard, D., Nouaud, D., Ashburner, M., Anxolabehere, D.: Combined evidence annotation of transposable elements in genome sequences. PLoS Comput. Biol. **1**, 166–175 (2005)

24. Price, A.L., Jones, N.C., Pevzner, P.A.: De novo identification of repeat families in large genomes. Bioinformatics **21**, 351–358 (2005)

25. Ellinghaus, D., Kurtz, S., Willhoeft, U.: LTRharvest, an efficient and flexible software for de novo detection of LTR retrotransposons. BMC Bioinform. **9**, 18 (2008)

26. McCarthy, E.M., McDonald, J.F.: LTR_STRUC: a novel search and identification program for LTR retrotransposons. Bioinformatics **19**, 362–367 (2003)

27. Xu, Z., Wang, H.: LTR-FINDER: an efficient tool for the prediction of full-length LTR retrotransposons. Nucleic Acids Res. **35**, 265–268 (2007)

28. Disdero, E., Filée, J.: LoRTE: detecting transposon-induced genomic variants using low coverage PacBio long read sequences. Mob. DNA **8**, 5 (2017)

29. Zeng, F.-C., Zhao, Y.-J., Zhang, Q.-J., Gao, L.-Z.: LTRtype, an efficient tool to characterize structurally complex LTR retrotransposons and nested insertions on genomes. Front. Plant Sci. **8**, 1–9 (2017)

30. Hoede, C., Arnoux, S., Moisset, M., Chaumier, T., Inizan, O., Jamilloux, V., Quesneville, H.: PASTEC: an automatic transposable element classification tool. PLoS One **9**, 1–6 (2014)

31. Steinbiss, S., Kastens, S., Kurtz, S.: LTRsift: a graphical user interface for semi-automatic classification and postprocessing of de novo detected LTR retrotransposons. Mob. DNA **3**, 18 (2012)

32. Du, J., Tian, Z., Hans, C.S., Laten, H.M., Cannon, S.B., Jackson, S.A., Shoemaker, R.C., Ma, J.: Evolutionary conservation, diversity and specificity of LTR-retrotransposons in flowering plants: insights from genome-wide analysis and multi-specific comparison. Plant J. **63**, 584–598 (2010)
33. Vitte, C., Bennetzen, J.L.: Analysis of retrotransposon structural diversity uncovers properties and propensities in angiosperm genome evolution. Proc. Natl. Acad. Sci. **103**, 17638–17643 (2006)
34. Dupeyron, M., de Souza, R.F., Hamon, P., de Kochko, A., Crouzillat, D., Couturon, E., Domingues, D.S., Guyot, R.: Distribution of *Divo* in *Coffea* genomes, a poorly described family of angiosperm LTR-Retrotransposons. Mol. Genet. Genomics **292**, 741–754 (2017)
35. Zhang, Q.-J., Gao, L.-Z.: Rapid and recent evolution of LTR retrotransposons drives rice genome evolution during the speciation of AA-genome Oryza species. G3 Genes Genomes Genet. **7**, 1875–1885 (2017)
36. Llorens, C., Muñoz-Pomer, A., Bernad, L., Botella, H., Moya, A.: Network dynamics of eukaryotic LTR retroelements beyond phylogenetic trees. Biol. Direct. **4**, 41 (2009)
37. Garavito, A., Montagnon, C., Guyot, R., Bertrand, B.: Identification by the DArTseq method of the genetic origin of the *Coffea canephora* cultivated in Vietnam and Mexico. BMC Plant Biol. **16**, 242 (2016)
38. Carneiro, F.A., Rego, E., Aquino, S.O., Costa, T.S., Lima, E.A., Rocha, O.C., Rodrigues, G.C., Carvalho, M.A.F., Veiga, A.D., Guerra, A.F., et al.: Genome wide association study for drought tolerance and other agronomic traits of a# *Coffea canephora*# population (2015)
39. Babova, O., Occhipinti, A., Maffei, M.E.: Chemical partitioning and antioxidant capacity of green coffee (*Coffea arabica* and *Coffea canephora*) of different geographical origin. Phytochemistry **123**, 33–39 (2016)
40. Fayyad, U., Piatetsky-Shapiro, G., Smyth, P.: From data mining to knowledge discovery in databases. AI Mag. **17**, 37–54 (1996)
41. Denoeud, F., Carretero-Paulet, L., Dereeper, A., Droc, G., Guyot, R., Pietrella, M., Zheng, C., Alberti, A., Anthony, F., Aprea, G., et al.: The coffee genome provides insight into the convergent evolution of caffeine biosynthesis. Science **345**(6201), 1181–1184 (2014)
42. Rice, P., Longden, I., Bleasby, A.: EMBOSS: the European molecular biology open software suite. Trends Genet. **16**, 276–277 (2000)
43. Jurka, J., Klonowski, P., Dagman, V., Pelton, P.: CENSOR—a program for identification and elimination of repetitive elements from DNA sequences. Comput. Chem. **20**, 119–121 (1996)
44. Moine, J.M.: Metodologías para el descubrimiento de conocimiento en bases de datos: un estudio comparativo (2013)
45. Carreño, J.A.: Descubrimiento de conocimiento en los negocios (2008)
46. Newham, C., Rosenblatt, B.: Learning the Bash Shell: Unix Shell Programming. O'Reilly Media Inc., Sebastopol (2005)

Detection of Topics and Construction of Search Rules on Twitter

Eduardo D. Martínez[1], Juan P. Fonseca[1], Víctor M. González[1(✉)],
Guillermo Garduño[2], and Héctor H. Huipet[1]

[1] ITAM, 01080 Mexico City, Mexico
{eduardo.martinez,jfonsec1,victor.gonzalez,hector.huipet}@itam.mx
[2] Sinnia, 11560 Mexico City, Mexico
gg@sinnia.com

Abstract. This study proposes an improvement to the Insight Centre for Data Analytics algorithm, which identifies the most relevant topics in a corpus of tweets, and allows the construction of search rules for that topic or topics, in order to build a corpus of tweets for analysis. The improvement shows above 14% improvement in *Purity* and other metrics, and an execution time of 10% compared to Latent Dirichlet Allocation (LDA).

Keywords: Twitter · Topic · Detection · Clustering

1 Introduction

Twitter is an online news and social networking service on which users can share views, opinions and news through posts of 140 characters or less. In 2011, the news and social networking platform surpassed 100 million monthly active users, and as of 2016, it reached over 310 million monthly active users from around the globe. Given the broad use it has had for some time now, it is no surprise that data scientists and text miners are doing research to discover and create new and better ways to extract useful and valuable information from it.

Data mining is a field in Statistics and in Computer Science that deals with analyzing information in order to make decisions. This is a non trivial process of extracting information, relations, and useful hidden patterns from sets of data. It includes a group of techniques such as clustering,[1] and anomaly detection [1]. One sub field of data mining is text mining, which is broadly used on Twitter.

In this social networking service, every day, hundreds of millions of users send more than 500 million tweets (as of late 2013) [2]. They write not only about themselves, but also about popular topics, news, events and miscellaneous material, which makes it an abundant and valuable repository of potential information about the world [3]. Thus, its recovery and analysis is very useful in many applied fields, in services and sales, medicine and health, education, economics

---

[1] Relatively homogeneous "natural" groupings in a statistical population.

© Springer International Publishing AG 2017
A. Solano and H. Ordoñez (Eds.): CCC 2017, CCIS 735, pp. 171–183, 2017.
DOI: 10.1007/978-3-319-66562-7_13

and finance, among others [1]. Besides, it has been proved that the use of Twitter as a tool to know the public opinion is widely justified [4–6].

Many people and companies use Twitter as a primary source of news content. Because of its real-time and global nature, they seek to monitor and share the stories or events of interest that emerge from the crowd, and to find user-generated content to enrich their stories. However, it is very difficult for a single person to identify useful information on Twitter without being overwhelmed by an endless and redundant stream of tweets [7]. Due to this problem, and the interest that Sinnia (a company that provides a mining service to Twitter) has for this issue to provide its clients with a capable tool of helping them to build a specific corpus of tweets for analysis,[2] we propose here a system to detect topics and generating search rules that allow a single person focuses on a specific corpus of tweets, based on topics of his interest.

1.1 Findings and Contributions

In this study, we show in detail the development of a tool for topic detection and construction of search rules based on a corpus of tweets, based on the main ideas of the Insight Centre for Data Analytics [7] at the 2014 SNOW Data Challenge, to design a novel application for topic finding on tweets, whose main contributions are as follows:

- *Purity* and *Normalized Mutual Information* (*NMI*) [8] were used to evaluate the quality of the topics identified. These metrics were compared between our algorithm and LDA [9], it showed some improvements.
- Precision, Recall and F1 showed a considerable improvement.
- An improvement was made on the original algorithm, grouping clusters centroids instead of ngrams in the second clusterization.
- Our algorithm had a shorter execution time than LDA.
- Inclusion of a bots filter, which ignores identical tweets, where only a url is changed.
- Based on the resulting ngrams, we constructed search rules with stemming, which allows the user focusing on a subset of identified tweets, instead of only showing the tweet as a headline.

Quantitative results are detailed in Sect. 5.

2   Related Work

2.1   Tweet Cleaning

One of the most common problems is that tweets are short, have spelling mistakes, grammar mistakes, nonstandard abbreviations, combined words, multiple languages, and slang. This causes that some methods of analysis do not work

---

[2] A collection of language pieces that are selected according to explicit linguistic criteria with the purpose of being used as a language sample.

accurately. Thomas and Sindhu [3] affirm that for similar terms analysis (considering abbreviations and spelling mistakes), several statistical techniques can be used, with varying results.

Javed [10] assures that to generate a corpus of social networks, a complicated data cleaning is required. To accomplish this he proposes and implements an algorithm for the corpus-creation automation to help the social network analysis and mining. When doing text mining, especially on Twitter, it is very clear that text cleaning is one of the first important steps that must be done.

2.2 Topics Classification

One of the most common data mining techniques is Classification, which helps categorize a set in a predetermined number of classes. Classification processes usually use supervised learning, and are used for predictive models. Some algorithmic models are the following: decision trees, Support Vector Machines (SVM), neural networks, sequential minimal optimization, K Nearest Neighbors (KNN), and naïve Bayes [1, 11]. Some of these techniques are more sensible than others due to the latent curse of dimensionality.[3]

Other unsupervised methods are Clustering and Regressions. Clustering is based in identifying accumulations and grouping similar individuals in categories. Some algorithms are partition based, such as K-means, hierarchical, such as Balanced Iterative Reducing and Clustering using Hierarchies (BIRCH), and density based, such as Density-based Spatial Clustering of Applications with Noise (DBSCAN). Finally, logistic regression is used for predictive modeling [1].

Rosa et al. [12] present a study to automatically classify Twitter messages in categories, according to their topics. They proved that unsupervised clustering methods such as K-means and LDA are not as good to group tweets by topic as supervised methods that use hashtags as topic indicators. Additionally, they analyzed documents associated with the URLs of tweets that had one. However, the evaluation consistently gets worse in the latter case, contrary to intuition.

Detection events techniques can help classify by topics, since intuitively each event corresponds to a topic. Walther and Kaisser [13] describe an algorithm for geospatial events detection in Twitter. First, tweets from a specific place and time are analyzed to identify places with high occurrence of events. Then, spatial and temporal clustering together with machine learning are used to detect real world events.

Long et al. [14] propose clustering combining some event based characteristics. Events are extracted based on word frequency, occurrence of words in hashtags and word entropy. Then, a top down clustering is applied to a co-occurrence graph. A bipartite graph of maximum weight is used to create event chains. Finally, events are plotted in a timeline to merge event chain clusters.

---

[3] As the dimensions increase, data becomes sparse. Therefore, the amount of data that is needed must increase exponentially with it or there will not be enough points in the sample of more space for any type of analysis to perform.

Ozdikis et al. [15] present an event detection method based on hashtags clustering, using semantic similarities of hashtags. For this they generate vectors of the tweets. To identify the hashtags relationships, they analyze the content and apply lexical-semantic expansion, based on syntactic and semantic relations between words, through their co-occurrence vectors, before clustering agglomerative tweets.

The real problem in using the localization information in georeferenced messages is that most of the time the information is either incorrect or missing. This stands to be a big impediment when trying to use a event detection method based on geography.

There are several methods and studies to classify a set of documents by topics. These range from the more traditional methods such as SVM and KNN, to more specialized ones based on events. From these we took the most relevant ideas for our study, considering our documents are unlabeled and short, among other things. One of the algorithms we found corresponds to a participant of the SNOW 2014 Data Challenge, of which we deal with in the next subsection.

2.3   SNOW 2014 Data Challenge

The SNOW 2014 Data Challenge was a contest where participants were asked to extract topics corresponding to known events from a stream of news tweets, for a number of timeslots. Because the volume of information was very high, this task had to be done with text mining. Each topic would be in the form of a headline summarizing the topic corresponding to the news, accompanied by a set of tweets.

The best algorithm of the contest belongs to the Insight Centre for Data Analytics group of Dublin College [7]. It is explained that in order to discover and categorize events, tweets are ordered chronologically and windows are processed every 15 min (variable for different real world problems) where a "raw" amount of tweets are normalized by cleaning special characters, digits and other punctuation marks and a symbolic value is assigned (tokenize). In the next step, tweets that have more than two mentions or two hashtags and those with less than four tokens are filtered. The objective is to reduce the "noise" of the tweets, since it is understood that a tweet that has many mentions, hashtags or is very short, does not provide relevant information to any topic or news.

Aggressive filtering is the most important step because allows a fast processing in subsequent steps by reducing dimensionality. Since an ngram count of two and three words is performed, which must meet a certain threshold of repetition in the tweets both minimum and maximum. With that, a binary matrix of ngrams-tweets is constructed, where if the ngram appears in the tweet or not, is numerically reflected. This matrix again allows to filter tweets that do not meet the condition of having at least five ngrams of vocabulary. It is described as the strictest because it is the one that reduces more the set of tweets to evaluate.

Hierarchical clustering is implemented, using the cosine pair distance between tweets in the binary matrix and normalizing this distance with norm L2. This clustering was done through the fastcluster library. The idea behind this section is that the tweets belonging to a topic are grouped and so each cluster is detected topic. From the hierarchical clustering a dendrogram is generated, and from the generated dendogram, it is explained that a cut is made in the value 0.5 according to the threshold of distance and they explain that depending on where the cutting is done, the clusters can be more specific or more general.

They also provide a score to the clusters to recognize their informative importance. For this, a frequency metric is used which allows to assign weights to the terms, as well as a tool to recognize parts of the sentence, which identifies whether a word is a verb, noun, adjective, etc. Here the algorithm scores the clusters higher where nouns exist, and the cluster score is then computed and normalized with the cluster size, allowing small clusters with more nouns to qualify higher. Of the best clusters, the first tweet of each is chosen as the heading of the detected topic. In order to reduce the fragmentation of the topics, that is to say, that two different clusters have similar headings, a second grouping is realized but now only with the headings, and they are again qualified. Finally, the most recent headings are chosen and their raw tweet is presented as a heading.

This algorithm proved to be the best one in finding headlines from an event detection perspective in short texts with a time record, using clever steps like aggressive filtering and second clustering. We realized that with some modifications this could be the solution that would lead us to improve the topic detection algorithm used in Sinnia.

3   System Overview

In the previous section, we described different elements of Natural Language Processing (NLP) that would be used for the development of this project. This section depicts our solution, a tool capable of analyzing a general corpus of tweets and finding topics, as well as the most representative words or search rules describing that topic.

The baseline was build on an analysis of the corpus through LDA, this algorithm was the topic discovery solution used by Sinnia. LDA is a statistical generative method used in the field of topic discovery. The basic idea of this model is that given a set of documents there is a way to group them into hidden topics according to similar semantic characteristics. Some of its main disadvantages are processing time, resulting in a list of weighted tokens rather than clusters and their inefficiency to handle short texts [16]. We considered Ifrim et al. [7] a good approach to handle these deficiencies and construct a better solution for Sinnia.

Our purpose besides finding topics was to provide several words of what is said about a topic, so that the user could choose the most relevant words, depending on the topic of his interest; these are identified as search rules. This application tries to solve the following challenges. First of all, it reads, processes and analyzes tweets from a text file with either JSON, XML or CSV format. Secondly, it groups the tweets according to the important words that are used in them, with the aim of discovering clusters that will represent topics. Finally, for each cluster shows its most important or representative tweet, and the search rule that directs us to that cluster. In addition, a tool was created that can classify new tweets on one of the clusters or generated topics.

3.1 Modifications

Using the code published in its GitHub repository available online at https:// github.com/heerme, an implementation was made for the particular problem of this project. However, the following changes were made:

In particular, this project does not depend on very small time windows (in general), so this option is left available but the time window is the size of the distance between the most recent and the oldest, in order to process all the tweets in a single iteration.

During the integration of this solution, it became evident that the values of many of the parameters of the algorithm did not return the expected results, so they were modified to fit this problem. Values such as the threshold of tweets to accept a term composed of a given ngram, as well as the size of ngrams in the matrix had to be changed.

Also a phenomenon was observed that forced us to develop a previous filter, which are the accounts known as bots. These are accounts of fake users who are responsible for automatically speaking about something specific, in order to spread it through the trending topics of Twitter and thus try to influence the opinion of real users. So we added a module that verifies that if two tweets contain exactly the same information with minimal modification, the repeated tweets are discarded.

Finally, we had to restructure the idea of the second clustering proposed by the article, now using the centroids of each original cluster as representatives of each of them, because the results did not meet what was expected by the classification of topics. Thus, in the second cluster, each new cluster contained the original clusters.

3.2 Search Rules

In order to describe a cluster, in addition to the representative tweet, the representative ngrams of that cluster are shown. As mentioned in the beginning, the ngrams were generated of 2 and 3 words, resulting in ngrams such as: *('ganas tomar Corona', 'ganas tomar', 'tomar Corona')*, where one can recognize that the central subject is *'ganas tomar Corona'*.[4]

That is why a grouping by sets was done, where subsets are being discarded, in the end keeping only the supersets, i.e. the superset of the previous case is: 'ganas tomar Corona'. In addition to maintaining the supersets, a grouping is also performed by reducing words to their minimum expression (stemming). To achieve this we used Snowball stemmer, which does this in an algorithmic way

---

[4] The ngram 'ganas tomar Corona', refer literally to 'want drink Corona', where Corona is a beer produced in Mexico.

in Spanish [17]. This resulted in a rule-based construction of ngrams, with which one can approach tweets produced by a cluster, using a direct search to Twitter.

Original ngrams for the cluster:

('gustado video youtube', 'gustado video', 'video youtube', 'gusto video youtube', 'gusto video', 'video youtube')[5]

Search rule on Twitter using stemming:

('(gustado OR gusto) video youtube').

4   Implementation

In the previous section, the general approach of the problem was described. In the following subsections, we describe our implementation with more detail.

4.1   Tweets Preprocessing

At first, we define several parameters to be used later. The time window is defined to be such that all tweets to be classified are included in it. In other words, there is only one window.

When analyzing a set of tweets and finding their most relevant features (words or phrases), it is important to set a minimum number of allowed repetitions for them. If a feature is not repeated enough, it may not be useful or informative enough. Therefore, some frequency parameters are defined at the beginning.

Next, we define several lists and sets, of which one of them is a non-repeated tweet list that will store unique tweets. We also create a list of stop words, which are words with no meaning that are repeated a lot (such as articles, prepositions, and pronouns).

After that, the file containing the tweets is selected, and a timer starts. Then, each tweet in the file is analyzed and processed, retrieving its time, text content, handles, and hashtags. Only the text of the tweet is retained, removing also stop words. If there are less than three handles, less than three hashtags on it, and at least three features, the cleaned tweet is stored in the tweet list.

4.2   Tweets Vectorization and Distance Matrix

Once all the tweets have been analyzed, we proceed with the main algorithm. Using the sklearn class CountVectorizer (count the ngram occurrences, an alternative is to use TF-IDF), we transform the tweets into vectors of dimension n, where n is the number of bigrams and trigrams considered important enough to keep.[6] We are careful enough to not count permutations of the same ngram as different ngrams.

---

[5] The ngram 'gustado video youtube', refer literally to 'liked video youtube'.

[6] An ngram is considered important enough if it "passes" a function of our frequency parameters defined at the start. At the very least, the ngram must be repeated 5 times.

From the vectorized tweets we then construct a pairwise Euclidean distance matrix, which contains the Euclidean distance (2-norm) between all pairs of tweets. A pair of tweets that share some ngrams in common will have closer corresponding vectors than a pair of tweets which share no ngrams in common.

4.3   Clustering

Then, with the distance matrix, and with help of the fastcluster library, we do an agglomerative hierarchical clustering using the average linkage criteria [18], which is shown in Eq. 1. As it is said before, this type of clustering creates a dendogram and generates different numbers of clusters depending on the height of its cut. The higher the cut, the fewer and more general the clusters.

At this point we show the user the ngrams corresponding to each cluster, and we obtain the centroids and the number of tweets of each one. We also show some of the closest tweets to each centroid, which are displayed as the "most representative" tweets for each cluster. This information visualization is only auxiliary and helps the user know how the process evolves.

$$d(u, v) = \sum_{ij} \frac{d(u[i], v[j])}{(|u| * |v|)} \tag{1}$$

4.4   Second Clustering

Based on the centroids of the clusters, we generate a new pairwise Euclidean distance matrix. Two centroids are close together if they correspond to clusters with similar tweets. Using that matrix, and with help of the fastcluster library, we do a second agglomerative hierarchical clustering with the ward linkage criteria which uses a variance minimization algorithm [18]. Note that this is a clustering of centroids corresponding to the first obtained clusters, or a "clustering of clusters".

Near the end of our method, we assign a relevance score to each cluster. The score of each cluster is the percentage of tweets it has compared to the total number of tweets.

Finally, the clusters are shown to the user, ordered by their relevance score. Each cluster is represented with their search rules and the tweets that are closest to their respective centroids. The dendogram of the second clusterization is also shown, together with the level of the cut it made to generate the clusters shown. Additionally, search rules that help find the tweets of each cluster are shown,

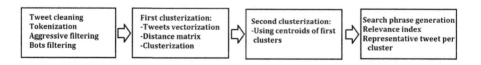

Fig. 1. Diagram of all the implementation steps.

as described in the previous section. Figure 1 shows high-level implementation steps of our solution.

5 Results

Two metrics that we used are called *Purity* and *NMI*. The first one, as suggested by its name, measures the purity in each cluster. The closer each cluster is to having elements of only one type (according to the original classification), the closer to 1 the value of *purity* will be. On the other hand, the second one measures the information the clusters share. The closer the value is to zero, the less shared information they have (resulting in better clusters).

In addition to these metrics we also include precision, recall and F1, which allow us to identify how close our unsupervised models are approaching the original classification. To achieve this relationship between non-supervised clusters against previously labeled clusters, we used the Jaccard index.

In order to generate the LDA model, we process the tweets using the same preprocessing step as in our method (stop words, stemming, tokenize). Then we construct a tweet-term matrix using *gensim*, for this we used the function *doc2bow()* to generate a bag-of-words and generate a list of vectors equal to the number of tweets. In each tweet vector is a series of tuples. The tuples are (term ID, term frequency) pairs, this vector only includes terms that actually occur, a detailed explanation can be found in [19].

We show the results of a dataset given by Sinnia, which is a separate query of three words on the Twitter API Firehose. The words are: 'Corona', 'Modelo' and 'Pan'. In these queries all tweets are in Spanish and searches were combined into a single file, providing a balanced search of approximately 30,000 tweets from each search. We process this file with our algorithm, as well as with LDA, and the results are shown in the Table 1. All the experiments were carried on a Linux server with Intel i7 3.60 GHz CPU and 8 G memory.

Improvements are shown with a plus sign, while the time is shown in absolute percentage.

Table 1. Percentage of our algorithm with respect to LDA, in a dataset provided by Sinnia.

Metric	LDA	OURS
Purity	100%	**+15%**
NMI	100%	−56%
Precision	100%	**+30%**
Recall	100%	**+15%**
F1	100%	**+17%**
Time	100%	**10%**

Tests were also performed with the TASS dataset [20–24]. This dataset is labeled by topic, so we used their classification to validate the metrics without considering the classification others. Something to mention is that the TASS dataset is multiclassification but we used only the first topic on each tweet to validate our results, which are shown in Table 2.

Table 2. Percentage of our algorithm with respect to LDA, using the TASS dataset.

Metric	LDA	OURS
Purity	100%	**+12%**
NMI	100%	−26%
Precision	100%	**+25%**
Recall	100%	**+18%**
F1	100%	**+22%**
Time	100%	**10%**

In each case the result of the average of 10 executions of the different datasets is shown, as well as the average of cuts from 0.1 to 0.9 in the dendrogram.

As one can see, the *NMI* is lower in LDA (and therefore better), but the other metrics *Purity*, Precision, Recall and F1, show a clear improvement, regardless of the level of generality of the clusters. A big improvement can also be observed in the execution *time* compared to LDA.

An improvement was made on the original algorithm, grouping clusters centroids instead of ngrams in the second clusterization. This gave a *Purity* score 1.6% better in the best cases, and 0.48% better in average.

Table 3. Topics discovered by our algorithm versus the ones discovered by LDA in the Sinnia dataset.

OURS	LDA
nuevo educativo modelo equipo marca	modelo corona super azul aunque
dulce pan cruz azul jesus	corona @corona_mx pan @mariobautista_semana
nuevo modelo comer pan comiendo	pan corona quiero queso vino
muere modelo brasileña criminal case	modelo #corona fotos marca hola
hambre hoy mañana pan lista	modelo nuevo economico via seguir
vino pan debe modelo cambiar	pan prd alianza dulce dia
veracruz oaxaca pan prd linares	corona modelo rey cerveza reina
veracruz oaxaca pan stephane suma	corona pan video modelo rico
avanzar popular permitira nuevo modelo	pan corona miss cara duro
gustado video @youtube gusto corona	modelo corona mejor hermosa @corona_futbol

Table 3 shows an example of the clusters generated by our method versus the ones generated by LDA. According to the metrics our algorithm generate purest clusters, they belong only to one topic compared to LDA where we can see a mixture of topics. There is one repeated topic 'veracruz oaxaca pan', which causes a share of information between topics and with this a high value of *NMI*.

6 Conclusion

Our goal was to create an algorithm that would allow us to obtain the search rules that define a corpus of tweets, with the goal that Sinnia's clients could improve their search of relevant information for them. For this we realized that it was necessary as a first step to detect the main topics of a corpus. Then, based on the keywords of those topics, we generated the search rules and displayed these sorted according to the number of tweets that deal with a certain topic.

Many algorithms have been tested in the search of topics based on extraction; in our search we found the algorithm of Insight Centre for Data Analytics which followed the same path as our objectives with a few differences. Adapting it to our needs and observing the behavior compared to LDA, we noticed very interesting improvements.

It is to be noted that Sinnia uses our implementation as an automatic query generator, substituting the task of manually creating queries. This makes the whole process of analyzing tweets much faster and efficient for them.

7 Future Work

We identify two perspectives for the future work, on the one hand, incorporating different algorithms of topics detection in the comparison like Non-negative Matrix Factorization (NMF), Probabilistic Latent Semantic Analysis (PLSA), biterm, adding the number of datasets and including scalability tests. On the other hand, improving the algorithm by including sentiment analysis associated with the system-generated clusters. Hence, the user could analyze the positivity or negativity that people on Twitter have towards each topic. In addition, it would be possible to include for each topic an evolution of the sentiment within a timeline. This would allow the user to analyze whether an opinion associated with some product of a brand has improved or worsened over time.

Additionally, an idea that came on the development of this project was to use active learning, i.e. using a machine learning algorithm on the topic identification together with our algorithm. Our algorithm will be used to detect new topics and on this topics the user would have the opportunity to add or remove tags according to their interests. These new tags would be used with the closest tweets to that topic to re-train the model. This approach seemed interesting because would add the ability to the system of detecting topics closer to the users interests.

Acknowledgments. This work has been supported by Asociación Mexicana de Cultura A.C. and Consejo Nacional de Ciencia y Tecnología (CONACyT).

References

1. Maksood, F.Z., Achuthan, G.: Analysis of data mining techniques and its applications. Anal. **140**(3), 0975–8887 (2016)
2. Holt, R.: Twitter in numbers (2013). http://www.telegraph.co.uk/technology/twitter/9945505/Twitter-in-numbers.html. Accessed 30 Jan 2017
3. Thomas, A., Sindhu, L.: A survey on content based semantic relations in tweets. Int. J. Comput. Appl. **132**(11), 14–18 (2015)
4. O'Connor, B., Balasubramanyan, R., Routledge, B.R., Smith, N.A.: From tweets to polls: Linking text sentiment to public opinion time series. ICWSM **11**, 1–2 (2010)
5. Adarsh, M., Ravikumar, P.: Survey: Twitter data analysis using opinion mining. Int. J. Comput. Appl. **128**(5), 34–36 (2015)
6. Anjaria, M., Reddy Guddeti, R.M.: Influence factor based opinion mining of twitter data using supervised learning. In: 2014 Sixth International Conference on Communication Systems and Networks (COMSNETS), pp. 1–8. IEEE (2014)
7. Ifrim, G., Shi, B., Brigadir, I.: Event detection in twitter using aggressive filtering and hierarchical tweet clustering. In: Second Workshop on Social News on the Web (SNOW), Seoul, Korea, p. 8. ACM (2014)
8. Manning, C., Raghavan, P.: An Introduction to Information Retrieval. Cambridge University Press, Cambridge (2008)
9. Blei, D.M., Ng, A.Y., Jordan, M.I.: Latent dirichlet allocation. J. Mach. Learn. Res. **3**, 993–1022 (2003)
10. Javed, N.: Automating corpora generation with semantic cleaning and tagging of tweets for multi-dimensional social media analytics. Int. J. Comput. Appl. **127**(12), 11–16 (2015)
11. Agarwal, V., Thakare, S., Jaiswal, A.: Survey on classification techniques for data mining. Int. J. Comput. Appl. **132**(4), 13–16 (2015)
12. Rosa, K.D., Shah, R., Lin, B., Gershman, A., Frederking, R.: Topical clustering of tweets. In: Proceedings of the ACM SIGIR: SWSM (2011)
13. Walther, M., Kaisser, M.: Geo-spatial event detection in the twitter stream. In: Serdyukov, P., Braslavski, P., Kuznetsov, S.O., Kamps, J., Rüger, S., Agichtein, E., Segalovich, I., Yilmaz, E. (eds.) ECIR 2013. LNCS, vol. 7814, pp. 356–367. Springer, Heidelberg (2013). doi:10.1007/978-3-642-36973-5_30
14. Long, R., Wang, H., Chen, Y., Jin, O., Yu, Y.: Towards effective event detection, tracking and summarization on microblog data. In: Wang, H., Li, S., Oyama, S., Hu, X., Qian, T. (eds.) WAIM 2011. LNCS, vol. 6897, pp. 652–663. Springer, Heidelberg (2011). doi:10.1007/978-3-642-23535-1_55
15. Ozdikis, O., Senkul, P., Oguztuzun, H.: Semantic expansion of tweet contents for enhanced event detection in twitter. In: Proceedings of the 2012 International Conference on Advances in Social Networks Analysis and Mining (ASONAM 2012), pp. 20–24. IEEE Computer Society (2012)
16. Hong, L., Davison, B.D.: Empirical study of topic modeling in twitter. In: Proceedings of the first workshop on social media analytics, pp. 80–88. ACM (2010)
17. Porter, M.F.: Snowball: A language for stemming algorithms (2001). http://snowball.tartarus.org/texts/introduction.html Accessed 08 Feb 2017
18. Müllner, D.: Modern hierarchical, agglomerative clustering algorithms. arXiv preprint arXiv:1109.2378 (2011)
19. Barber, J.: Latent dirichlet allocation (lda) with python (2001). https://rstudio-pubs-static.s3.amazonaws.com/79360_850b2a69980c4488b1db95987a24867a.html Accessed 21 Jun 2017]

20. García Cumbreras, M.Á., Martínez Cámara, Villena Román, J., García Morera, J.: Tass 2015-the evolution of the Spanish opinion mining systems (2016)
21. Villena Román, J., Martínez Cámara, E., García Morera, J., Jiménez Zafra, S.M.: Tass 2014-the challenge of aspect-based sentiment analysis. Procesamiento del Lenguaje Nat. **54**, 61–68 (2015)
22. Villena Román, J., García Morera, J., Lana Serrano, S., González Cristóbal, J.C.: Tass 2013-a second step in reputation analysis in Spanish (2014)
23. Villena Román, J., Lana Serrano, S., Martínez Cámara, E., González Cristóbal, J.C.: Tass-workshop on sentiment analysis at sepln (2013)
24. TASS: Taller de análisis de sentimientos en la sepln (2017). http://www.sngularmeaning.team/TASS Accessed 19 April 2017

Content In-context:
Automatic News Contextualization

Camilo Restrepo-Arango and Claudia Jiménez-Guarín[⊠] (iD)

Computing and Systems Engineering Department, School of Engineering,
Universidad de los Andes, Carrera 1 Este # 19A-40, 111711 Bogotá, Colombia
{c.restrepo235, cjimenez}@uniandes.edu.co

Abstract. News content usually refers to specific facts, people or situations. Understanding the whole relationships and context about the actual text may require the user to manually connect, search and filter other sources, with a considerable effort. This work considers the use of deep learning techniques to analyze the news content to automatically build context and ultimately to provide a valuable solution for news readers and news editors using a real dataset from the most important online newspaper. Using a news article as a seed, we relate and add valuable information to news articles, providing understanding and comprehensiveness to put information into users' perspective, based on semantic, unobvious and time changing relationships. Context is constructed by modeling news and ontological information using deep learning. Ontological information is extracted from knowledge base sources. Content In-context is a complete solution applying this approach to a Colombian real, online news dataset, produced in Spanish. Tests and results are performed considering new articles using unknown data. Results prove to be interesting compared to classical machine learning methods.

Keywords: Deep learning · Natural language processing · Neural networks

1 Introduction

News is information that affect the decision-making process every day. Reading the news, means aggregating, selecting and searching news feeds that are constantly updated. In such amount of information, it is hard to understand the context that can put news into a reader's perspective. There is a variety of tools for news aggregation and news summarization to help understand and put news into perspective, for example Flipboard, Pulse or News360. Other tools try to connect articles based on co-occurrences of named entities or try to extract relations among entities from news corpora: we distinguish three different approaches, an event tracking approach, which is focused on discovering events on news feeds and tracking them through their evolution; a search engine approach, which indexes and identify named entities to make information searchable; finally, a contextualization approach, which uses news articles as source to find relevant information related to an article. This work considers elements of all these approaches to model and enrich information from news articles.

© Springer International Publishing AG 2017
A. Solano and H. Ordoñez (Eds.): CCC 2017, CCIS 735, pp. 184–198, 2017.
DOI: 10.1007/978-3-319-66562-7_14

Searching, connecting and filtering for additional information related to a news article can be a challenging and time consuming task. A reader may need additional information when reading a news article and a journalist may need previous news or additional information to provide context for the reader to understand what he is talking about. Our solution is addressed to these two types of users.

The main contribution of this article is Content In-context, a solution that automatically generates context from news feeds to help a user understand and put news articles into perspective. Automatically generating context in an uncontrolled dataset has two main challenges. First, we must keep in mind that news feeds are published daily and each article may contain new words that have to be modeled, understood and included in the solution models. Second, there is a cost associate with the complete retraining of the solution models. Complete retraining of the solution models should be avoided because it is a time consuming and hardware intensive task.

In our solution, context is automatically constructed by modeling semantic, unobvious and time changing relationships between news, topics and named entities to provide meaningful and relevant information. It allows a reader to visualize and interact with external content while reading a news article. We evaluate the use of Deep Learning to represent news content and ontology information in a vector space model. It uses probabilistic neural language models to use semantic and syntactic features. Tests and results are performed using a Colombian political news dataset written in Spanish. The evaluation is performed using precision, recall and F1-score.

Analyzing news datasets presents a big challenge given the number of persons, locations and organizations and the context is very complex due to the nature of relationships among the different entities. The relationships in this domain have two main characteristics: they are unobvious and they are dynamic. Unobvious relationships are relationships that are not explicitly shown and are known by people. Dynamic relationships are relationships that change over time. If we model a relationship between two entities as a graph of two connected nodes by an edge, the entity represented by each node can change over time and the nature of the relationship (the edge) can also change over time. Given this, we want to automate the analysis of news content, to provide related and relevant information to a reader in the interest of automatically creating context to put information into the reader's perspective.

Our solution includes a visually attractive and interactive web application that links content in a time dimension, links content semantically, relates content geographically, relates content using people and organizations, discovers new information related to content, understands the relationships found, and provides an appropriate visualization.

The paper is organized as follows. In Sect. 2 we discuss related work related to automatically generate context in news. The basic method for automatically building context and linking news is presented in Sect. 3. The results of the method are shown in Sect. 4. Conclusions and suggestions for future work are given in Sect. 5.

2   Related Work

This section briefly reviews applications and methods that can be applied to automatically generate context in news. Although there are many ways to classify these applications and methods, we distinguish three different approaches: an event tracking approach, a search engine approach and a contextualization approach.

2.1   Event Tracking Approach

Applications that use an event tracking approach use news as a succession of events that form stories related through topics and named entities [7, 17, 19, 32]. These works focus in story identification and alignment. The relationships between different news articles are given by temporal dynamics. In this approach, a set of natural language processing tools are used to identify named entities, detect topics, summarize text and cluster the information using a time dimension and a topic dimension. The context created in this method consists in the evolution of a topic through time or in the succession of topic related events.

A drawback of all applications that use event tracking is that relationships are limited to a temporal dimension and it does not allow understanding the dynamic and unobvious relationships that can exist between named entities, events and topics. They only take into account that a topic can split or merge through time and the explanation of relations is given by topics solely.

2.2   Search Engine Approach

Approaches based on search engines use news a source to index and analyze its content in order to detect topics, named entities and make the content searchable by a user [5, 9, 18]. This approach uses a similar set of tools as the event tracking approach but use a vector space model to find similarities between events, topics and named entities and group them in order to have some meaningful relationships. The features used in the vector space model are not discussed and may vary in each implementation. In this case, the context created depends on the user's query, the similarity between news articles and the distance measure selected in the implementation to group events.

The downside of this approach is that a user must search and filter available information to satisfy its needs. Even if these applications extract more information from news articles, they do not take into account the dynamic and unobvious relationships between the elements in the news to enable the generation of context to put news articles into perspective. A user query may allow finding related content but it's the user task to build and understand the context and relationships.

2.3   Contextualization Approach

The latter approaches use the news article being read by the user to analyze and find meaning and related information. Starting from the content of the article, the applications detect named entities and topics using natural language processing tools to provide related information that can create context to put a news article into perspective.

Palmonari et al. [24] developed and application that extracts the main topic of a news article and models context using an ontology and a measure based on serendipity to quantify the relationships. A user can see the relationships but can't understand it. Hullman et al. [10] developed Contextifier, it allows to create meaningful relationships between financial news and stock prices. The main proposal of this work is similar to our solution but it is not limited to the financial domain. We propose an implementation that can manage a larger domain with dynamic and time changing relationships.

Finally, Sarmiento et al. [30] developed a system that integrates and provides uniform access to government data linked to news portals, via an automated named entity linking process, and information provided by a parliament monitoring organization. This system allows a user to understand who is a congressman but the information is generated manually and depends on its proprietary ontology.

The solution presented in this paper is analogous to this approach. Two main differences are that in our method dynamic time changing and unobvious relationships are modeled to give meaning and comprehensiveness. We propose to use Deep Learning to represent news content and ontology information in a vector space model using probabilistic neural language models to use semantic and syntactic features. These differences allow creating context and put a news article into a user's perspective.

3   Content In-context

Content In-context's main purpose is to identify the context to which belongs a textual content in Spanish to provide a user with additional related information to add value to the original content. It uses the textual content accessed by a user as a seed to collect and link information from different sources like Web pages and linked data repositories. The content is collected and cleaned so that useful and relevant information is extracted. The extracted information is analyzed to build a semantic model that links information taking into account multiple perspectives [26] (Fig. 1).

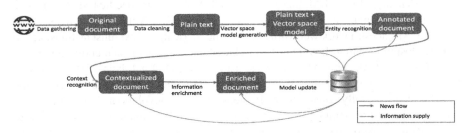

Fig. 1. Flow diagram describing the different steps of the method.

For this project, we select Colombia's political news published online by the main newspapers of the country. In fact, these news articles provide an ideal and interesting scenario from a cultural and social point of view because this topic dominate everyday life in the country. These news content refers to events, people, places and organizations that not everybody knows or has heard of and to understand the full context of a story, it is necessary to search information in multiple sources and in old news. In the next subsections, the most important steps of the method will be described.

3.1 Vector Space Model Construction

This step uses natural language processing techniques to create a news vector space model. This model captures the most important statistical features of words sequences in natural language, allowing to make predictions given the surrounding words. Vector space models allow representing words in a continuous vector space where semantically similar words are mapped to points close in the vector space. These models are based on the distributional hypothesis [8] that establishes that words that occur in similar contexts and share a semantic meaning.

This model allows having a proper representation of news content and it allows building and measuring similarities between news considering content meaning. The learnt features allow adding value to the content and finding meaningful relationships. It is important to mention that we haven't found other solutions or approaches to relate content and create context using deep learning in Spanish. Specifically, we use Word2Vec [21] to train the language model.

3.2 Named Entity Recognition

Once a vector space model is built, a named entities recognition step is executed. It is important to mention that named entities are not always found by their real, complete name. In many situations, an alias or abbreviations are used. This alias and abbreviations must be identified to relate and identify the named entities. Additionally, it is important to take into account name disambiguation. For example, Uribe may refer to a Colombian ex-president or to Santiago Uribe, his brother. This step allows correctly identifying and disambiguating named entities to avoid creating noise or misinformation over the original content.

Even if there are known entity recognition systems like Open Calais, Google NLP API or Alchemy API by IBM, these systems fall short for this specific task. On the one hand, there is language. Open Calais and Google NLP API support Spanish but Alchemy API doesn't work well with Spanish and to use it, the text must be translated to English, losing meaning. It is important to know the position of each entity in the text, Open Calais and Alchemy API return the list of entities but not their position. Finally, these APIs have a requests limit that can constraint the proposed solution functionality.

This step uses fully connected neural networks and convolutional neural networks. The named entity recognition task is modeled as a classification task where each word is classified in one of five possible classes: person, place, organization, miscellaneous and non-entity. The miscellaneous class is used for acronyms. This algorithm was chosen because neural networks can recognize complex patterns and can theoretically approximate any function [1, 2].

The proposed neural network (NN) is a three layer fully connected neural network. The network's input is a 3-gram, each word is transformed into a dense vector in the representation layer using Word2Vec [21] (Eq. 1). L is the word embedding matrix and

Table 1. Neural network hyper parameters.

Hyper parameter	Value	Hyper parameter	Value	Hyper parameter	Value
Dropout [29]	0,9	Hidden layer size (l)	100	Learning rate	0,001
Input size (k)	3	Word vector size(d)	300	Output layer size(C)	5
		Training epochs	24		

v is the vocabulary size. The second layer is modeled by Eq. 2. Finally, the output layer (Eq. 3). The loss function used is the cross-entropy error function (Eq. 4). Table 1 presents all the network's hyper parameter values.

$$x^{(t)} = [Lx_{t-1}, Lx_t, Lx_{t+1}], L \in \mathbb{R}^{|v| \times d} \tag{1}$$

$$h = \tanh\left(Wx^{(t)} + b_1\right), W \in \mathbb{R}^{3d \times l}, b_1 \in \mathbb{R}^l \tag{2}$$

$$\hat{y} = softmax(Uh + b_2), U \in \mathbb{R}^{l \times 5}, b_2 \in \mathbb{R}^5 \tag{3}$$

$$CE(y, \hat{y}) = -\sum_{c=1}^{C} y_c \log(\hat{y}_c) \tag{4}$$

Another approach is to use convolutional neural networks. This algorithm considers location invariance and local compositionality. Location invariance allows the network to understand the position of words in the phrase and local compositionality allows to represent how words are modified between them. Even if this algorithm has its origin in image processing, there have been multiple successful applications in natural language processing [12–16, 23, 28, 31, 33, 34].

Table 2. Convolutional neural network hyper parameters.

Hyper parameter	Value	Hyper parameter	Value	Hyper parameter	Value
Input size	3	Dropout [29]	0,9	Output layer size	5
Learning rate	0,001	Training epochs	24	Number of filters for each size	128
Filters sizes	1, 2, 3	Word vector size	300		

The convolutional neural network (CNN) uses a representation layer based on Word2Vec as in the NN (Eq. 5), a convolution layer, a max-pooling layer and an output layer (Eq. 6). The cross-entropy error function (Eq. 4) is used as the loss function. Table 2 presents all the network's hyper parameter values.

$$x^{(t)} = \begin{bmatrix} Lx_{t-1} \\ Lx_t \\ Lx_{t+1} \end{bmatrix}, L \in \mathbb{R}^{|v| \times d} \tag{5}$$

$$\hat{y} = Wh + b, h \in \mathbb{R}^{384}, W \in \mathbb{R}^{384 \times 5}, b \in \mathbb{R}^5 \tag{6}$$

3.3   Context Recognition

Context recognition step classifies each news document taking into account the available relationships that can exist with other news. To achieve this, a clustering algorithm using the vector space features of each document is implemented to group news according to their semantic similarity. Then a keyword generation algorithm is used to create a description of each cluster and be able to understand the semantic similarity in each cluster. This step must consider that topics or semantic similarity are not continuous over time. In fact, each topic may appear for a window of time and then reappear some time later. To solve this problem each algorithm used for context recognition is implemented using a time range and then matching the results over time using a semantic similarity measure like the cosine distance between the resulting vectors [26].

The algorithms used to semantically group news articles are Latent Dirichlet Allocation (LDA) [4], MinHash [25] and clustering [11]. For keyword generation we use Textrank [20] and RAKE [27]. The clustering algorithm uses the Word2Vec representation and each paragraph is modeled by the mean vector of its words. Then, the paragraph representations are grouped using K-means with cosine distance.

3.4   Information Enrichment

This step uses previous analyzed news and knowledge bases to add valuable infor-mation to a news article content. The knowledge bases provide information about named entities, topics and their relationships. This step allows make information readily available to users without leaving the news article being read and avoiding a manual search and filter process to understand information. All the information of other news is used to make a global picture and how the information accessed fits in that picture.

For each recognized entity, additional information is displayed to allow a user to understand the context of the news article. In addition, the user is able to explore each entity, topic and all the available information that creates context and puts news into perspective.

3.5   Data Sources

Selected news data sources are the main newspapers from Colombia that have an online version. We consider that these sources provide high quality information. The main newspapers are El Tiempo[1], El Espectador[2], Semana[3], La Silla Vacía[4] y Las Dos Orillas[5]. These pages have different points of views and address the main political events occurring in the country. It is important to mention that Colombian conflict dates

---

[1] http://www.eltiempo.com.

[2] http://www.elespectador.com/noticias.

[3] http://www.semana.com.

[4] http://lasillavacia.com.

[5] http://www.las2orillas.co.

beyond 1950, however the digital archive of news does not cover all the time since 1950 so we use the available information. We estimated 10.000 news for the past three years with respect to the amount of news published daily.

Selected knowledge base sources are DBPedia [3], Google Knowledge Graph and Wikidata. Google Knowledge Graph is the only source that provides an online access point, for the other sources the dumps are automatically processed and deployed so that Content In-context can use the information available. A global context diagram of Content In-context is presented in Fig. 2.

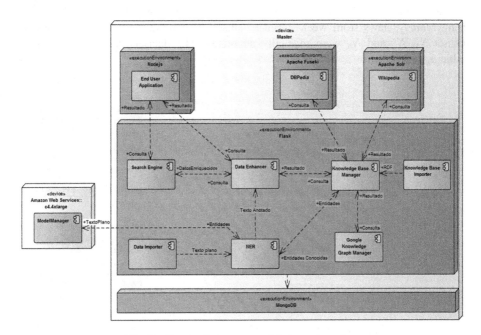

Fig. 2. Content In-context architecture overview.

The main components are Model Manager (MM), NER, Knowledge Base Manager (KBM) and Data Enhancer (DE). These components perform the operations described in 3.1 to 3.5. The other components gather and transform data to be used by the main components. MM builds a vector space model for each news article and updates a global vector space model. It interacts with KBM to save and update every model. NER uses the vector space models available to recognize the named entities in the news. It interacts with KBM to use and update the named entities. KBM responsibility is to persist and update the different news, named entities and context models generated by other components. DE uses all the data generated by MM and NER to generate and annotated and enriched news that can be consumed by a user.

4 Experiments and Results

4.1 Evaluation Method

The evaluation method (Fig. 3) is designed to simulate the publication of new articles that may contain known entities or new entities unknown to the models. The method starts at week 0 where we train a named entity recognition model with the Conll2002 dataset and evaluate its performance with news from week 1, 2 and 3. Then, we take news from week 1 and the previous model ($Model_0$) and train $Model_1$ and perform the evaluation with news from week 2 and 3. Finally, the last model ($Model_2$) is trained using $Model_1$, news from week 2 and evaluated with news from week 3. News in dataset N_1, N_2 and N_3 were manually annotated. The datasets sizes are shown in Table 3.

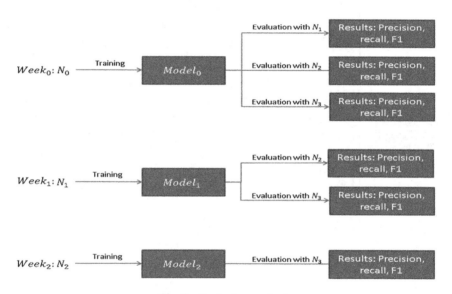

Fig. 3. Evaluation method.

Table 3. Datasets sizes.

	Training (# words)	Test (# words)
N_0	273037	54837
N_1	50901	5447
N_2	37620	6444

4.2 Results

Results are presented from three points of view: named entity recognition, context recognition and the end user application.

4.2.1   Named Entity Recognition

The named entity recognition models are evaluated against the Stanford named entity recognition software which uses Conditional Random Fields [6] using precision, recall and F1-score. The proposed models were implemented in python using Tensorflow. First, the training was done on a computer with 16 GB of ram and a 4-core processor. The training time took more than two days. Then, the training was made using an Amazon EC2 c4.4xlarge Instance with 16 cores and 30 GB of ram and the training time decreased to 6 h.

Training and Testing Steps

The results presented in this section show the accuracy and the loss function during the training step for NN model. Results for the CNN model are similar. Figures 4 and 5 show the training accuracy and loss function for Week 0. The accuracy increases rapidly and stabilizes in the first 2000 iterations. We used 24.000 iterations because these models require multiple passes over the training data to achieve a good generalization. In the same way, the loss function has a good behavior and decreases strongly in the first 2000 iterations and then stabilizes which means that the optimization of the loss function is correct.

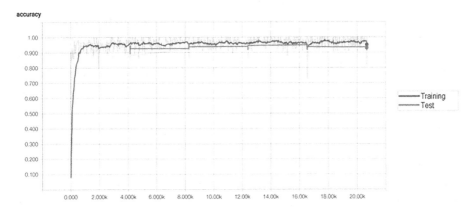

Fig. 4.   Training and test accuracy week 0.

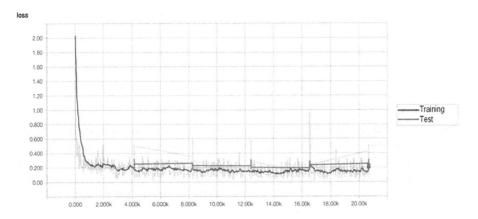

Fig. 5.   Training and test loss week 0.

As we can see in Fig. 6 the accuracy at the beginning doesn't start as low as in Fig. 4 which means that the model has a previous knowledge that allows making correct classifications. The model, at the end of training in Week 2, has accuracy over 96%. For the loss function, we can see a similar behavior. In Fig. 7 we can see that the loss function has a starting value lower than the starting value in Week 0 (Fig. 5). In addition, we can see that the accuracy in Fig. 6 has a stronger oscillation due to the amount of data used. In fact, NN model and CNN model require millions of data to be trained and display a stable behavior.

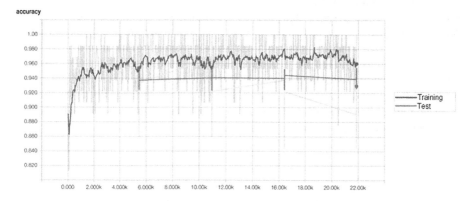

Fig. 6. Training and test accuracy week 2.

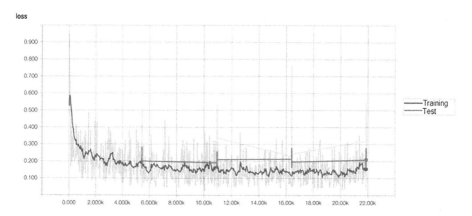

Fig. 7. Training and test loss week 2.

Validation Step

After training and testing every model we made a performance comparison (Fig. 8). As we can see in Fig. 8, at week 0 the performance of the NN model is lower than the Stanford model: NN precision (0.67), recall (0.65) and F1-score (0.65) are lower than Stanford precision (0.69), recall (0.77) and F1-score (0.71). For the CNN model, we can see a better precision (0.73) but a lower recall (0.70) and the F1-score (0.71) is close to the Stanford F1-score (0.71). At this step the best model is the Stanford model. On week 1, the overall performance of the proposed models increases. NN precision (0.81), recall (0.73) and F1-score (0.76) increased compared to Stanford precision (0.68), recall (0.74) and F1-score (0.70). The CNN model precision increase to 0.81, recall to 0.79 and F1-score to 0.80. The NN and CNN models have better performance than the Stanford model which means that these models continued to learn from the training data. The best model for Week 1 is the CNN model. On week 2, the performance of the NN and CNN models continue to increase compared to the Stanford model performance. NN model increased its precision to 0.83, recall to 0.79 and F1-score to 0.80. The Stanford model has a precision of 0.66, a recall of 0.74 and a F1-score of 0.70. The best model for this week is the CNN model with a precision of 0.83, recall of 0.84 and F1-score of 0.83.

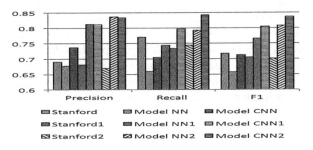

Fig. 8. Named entity recognition results.

The named entity recognition models using neural networks can continue to learn without doing a complete retrain with the data available in comparison with the traditional approach using machine learning. In fact, we consider a deep learning approach because we don't need to focus on feature engineering for named entity recognition. The model learns appropriate syntactic and semantic features and to do the classification task. Furthermore, this approach allows to classify unknown words because these models take into account the context of each word.

4.2.2   Context Recognition Results

For context recognition, we compared three algorithms [26]: LDA, MinHash and clustering using word embedding's. We used Gensim and Scikit-learn LDA implementation, for MinHash we used the Datasketch library implementation with 5-grams and 256 hash functions. Each implementation used a time window of a week. The best model was an LDA model with seven topics and coherence [22] of 0.68. The results for clustering and MinHash are not satisfactory. The MinHash implementation doesn't find any related articles and the clustering algorithm find completely unrelated news articles which means that using a mean vector for each paragraph and comparing them produces a loss in the vector features generated. The implementation of keyword extraction algorithms produced satisfactory results using the summa library TextRank implementation. The original implementation by Mihalcea [20] produced words that don't add semantic meaning like common words, even after removing stop words. The RAKE implementation [26] performs stemming and lemmatization and the results contain de prefixes and suffixes of the words which generates bad keywords.

4.2.3 End User Application

The end user application uses a Google Chrome plugin to clean and generate context automatically using a news article as seed. It allows the user to explore an annotated and enriched news article with relevant information that can add relations and useful meaning, providing understanding and comprehensiveness according to the elements of interest of the related domain. It allows understanding the news article taking into account temporal, geographic, semantic relationships and relationships between the discovered entities. He may explore each of these relationships and the application suggests other moments related with the information he is exploring.

Figure 9 shows an interactive named entity relationship graph where each node is a named entity and the size of the node represents its importance in the time window displayed in blue on top. The size of each edge represents the strength of the relationship between the entities. Additionally, the time window bar changes its color when a time window has relevant related information. A detailed description of the Web application and visualization is presented in [26].

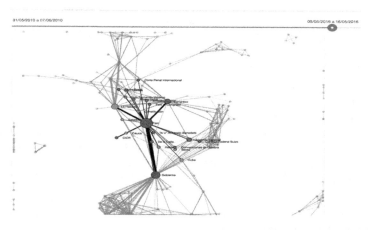

Fig. 9. End user application results.

5   Conclusions and Future Work

In this paper, we presented Context In-context a solution that automatically builds context using news articles. It relates and adds valuable information to news articles, providing understanding and comprehensiveness to put information into users' perspective, based on semantic, unobvious and time changing relationships. No user interaction or domain expert knowledge is required to generate the additional information. It uses deep learning models that don't need to be completely retrained when new articles are published. The proposed models allow to automatically recognize new entities and the relationships between them. These models use a word embedding layer to build specific syntactic and semantic Spanish features. The deep learning approach allows to perform content analysis without any journalistic knowledge.

Future work and challenges are identified from our results. First, the semantic clustering models need to be tailored using NLP techniques for the Spanish language in order to have better relationships between the news articles. Second, it is important to improve the deep learning models with more data. The amount of data used shows promising results but the available datasets in Spanish are far from being like the English datasets. Having more data enables the exploration of new models. It is also interesting to explore recurrent neural networks, more suitable for language processing but more difficult to train and need more data. For the topic modeling and semantic clustering task, the use of Deep Belief Networks may be explored.

Finally, to extend the information enrichment method, an ontology of Colombian politics can be integrated. It can enable named entity disambiguation and unification. Moreover, it can provide detailed information for entities using the Colombian context.

References

1. Bishop, C.M.: Neural Networks for Pattern Recognition. Oxford University Press, Oxford (1995)
2. Bishop, C.M.: Pattern Recognition and Machine Learning. Springer, New York (2006)
3. Bizer, C.: DBpedia - a large-scale, multilingual knowledge base extracted from wikipedia. Semant. Web J. **6**(2), 167–195 (2012)
4. Blei, D.M., et al.: Latent dirichlet allocation. J. Mach. Learn. Res. **3**, 993–1022 (2003)
5. Chasin, R., et al.: Extracting and displaying temporal entities from historical articles. Comput. J. **57**(3), 403–426 (2011)
6. Finkel, J.R., et al.: Incorporating non-local information into information extraction systems by gibbs sampling. In: Proceedings of the 43rd Annual Meeting on Association for Computational Linguistics, pp. 363–370 (2005)
7. Gruenheid, A., et al.: StoryPivot : comparing and contrasting story evolution. In: Proceedings of the 2015 ACM SIGMOD International Conference on Management of Data, pp. 1415–1420 (2015)
8. Harris, Z.S.: Distributional structure. In: Papers on Syntax, pp. 3–22 (1981)
9. Hou, L., et al.: Newsminer: multifaceted news analysis for event search. Knowl. Based Syst. **76**, 17–29 (2015)
10. Hullman, J., et al.: Contextifier : automatic generation of annotated stock visualizations. In: Proceedings of the SIGCHI Conference on Human Factors in Computing Systems, pp. 2707–2716 (2013)
11. Jannach, D., et al.: Recommender Systems: An Introduction (2011)
12. Johnson, R., Zhang, T.: Effective use of word order for text categorization with convolutional neural networks. In: NAACL 2011, pp. 103–112 (2015)
13. Johnson, R., Zhang, T.: Semi-supervised convolutional neural networks for text categorization via region embedding. In: Advances in Neural Information Processing Systems 28, pp. 919–927. Curran Associates, Inc. (2015)
14. Kalchbrenner, N., et al.: A Convolutional Neural Network for Modelling Sentences. CoRR (2014)

15. Kim, Y., et al.: Character-aware neural language models. In: Thirtieth AAAI Conference (AAAI 2016) (2016)
16. Kim, Y.: Convolutional neural networks for sentence classification. In: Proceedings of the 2014 Conference on Empirical Methods in Natural Language Processing (EMNLP 2014) (2014)
17. Krstajic, M., et al.: Story tracker: incremental visual text analytics of news story development. Inf. Vis. **12**(3–4), 308–323 (2013)
18. Leban, G., et al.: Event registry – learning about world events from news. In: Proceedings of the 23rd International Conference on World Wide Web, pp. 107–110 (2014)
19. Luo, D., et al.: EventRiver: visually exploring text collections with temporal references. IEEE Trans. Vis. Comput. Graph. **18**(1), 93–105 (2012)
20. Mihalcea, R., Tarau, P.: TextRank: bringing order into texts. In: Conference on Empirical Methods in Natural Language Processing, pp. 404–411 (2004)
21. Mikolov, T., et al.: Distributed representations of words and phrases and their compositionality. In: NIPS, pp. 1–9 (2013)
22. Mimno, D., et al.: Optimizing semantic coherence in topic models. In: Proceedings of the Conference on Empirical Methods in NLP, pp. 262–272 (2011)
23. Nguyen, T.H., Grishman, R.: Relation extraction: perspective from convolutional neural networks. In: Work. Vector Model. NLP, pp. 39–48 (2015)
24. Palmonari, M., Uboldi, G., Cremaschi, M., Ciminieri, D., Bianchi, F.: DaCENA: Serendipitous News Reading with Data Contexts. In: Gandon, F., Guéret, C., Villata, S., Breslin, J., Faron-Zucker, C., Zimmermann, A. (eds.) ESWC 2015. LNCS, vol. 9341, pp. 133–137. Springer, Cham (2015). doi:10.1007/978-3-319-25639-9_26
25. Rajaraman, A., Ullman, J.D.: Mining of Massive Datasets. Cambridge University Press, Cambridge (2011)
26. Restrepo, C.: Content In-context: enriquecimiento automático de información para contextualización de noticias. Tesis de Maestría. Universidad de los Andes (2016)
27. Rose, S., et al.: Automatic keyword extraction from individual documents. In: Text Mining: Applications and Theory. Wiley Ltd. (2010)
28. Santos, C.N., dos Gatti, M.: Deep convolutional neural networks for sentiment analysis of short texts. In: Proceedings of COLING 2014, the 25th International Conference on Computational Linguistics: Technical Papers, pp. 69–78 (2014)
29. Srivastava, N., et al.: Dropout: a simple way to prevent neural networks from overfitting. J. Mach. Learn. Res. **15**(1), 1929–1958 (2014)
30. Sarmiento Suárez, D., Jiménez-Guarín, C.: Natural language processing for linking online news and open government data. In: Indulska, M., Purao, S. (eds.) ER 2014. LNCS, vol. 8823, pp. 243–252. Springer, Cham (2014). doi:10.1007/978-3-319-12256-4_26
31. Sun, Y., et al.: Modeling mention, context and entity with neural networks for entity disambiguation. In: Proceedings of the Twenty-Fourth International Joint Conference on Artificial Intelligence (IJCAI 2015) Modeling, pp. 1333–1339 (2015)
32. Tanisha, L.F., et al.: Analyzing and visualizing news trends over time. In: 2014 IEEE International Conference on Industrial Engineering and Engineering Management (IEEM), pp. 307–311 (2014)
33. Wang, P., et al.: Semantic clustering and convolutional neural network for short text categorization. In: Proceedings of the 53rd Annual Meeting of the Association for Computational Linguistics and the 7th International Joint Conference on Natural Language Processing, pp. 352–357 (2015)
34. Zhang, Y., Wallace, B.: A Sensitivity Analysis of (and Practitioners' Guide to) Convolutional Neural Networks for Sentence Classification (2015)

Predicting the Programming Language: Extracting Knowledge from Stack Overflow Posts

Juan F. Baquero$^{(\boxtimes)}$, Jorge E. Camargo$^{(\boxtimes)}$, Felipe Restrepo-Calle$^{(\boxtimes)}$, Jairo H. Aponte$^{(\boxtimes)}$, and Fabio A. González$^{(\boxtimes)}$

Universidad Nacional de Colombia, Sede Bogotá, Colombia
{jfbaquerov,jecamargom,ferestrepoca,jhapontem,fagonzalezo}@unal.edu.co

Abstract. Stack Overflow (SO) is an important source of knowledge for developers. It provides authoritative advice as well as detailed technical information about different computer science and software engineering topics. The goal of this paper is to explore mechanisms to extract implicit knowledge, which is present in questions of SO. In particular, we want to extract information about programming languages and their relationships to such questions. The proposed approach builds a classifier model that predicts the programming language using the content (text and source code snippets) of a question. The proposed method produces word embeddings in which each term of the question is represented in a vectorial space in which it is possible to perform operations such as comparing words, sentences, and questions. The method was evaluated on a set of 18,000 questions related to 18 different programming languages. Results show that it is possible to extract interesting non-evident information from this highly unstructured data source.

Keywords: Stack Overflow · Software mining repositories · Word embedding · Knowledge extraction

1 Introduction

In the process of software building, a programmer usually faces challenges that another programmer have resolved before. It motivates an interaction between programmers through discussion platforms and dedicated social networks. In discussions platforms such as forums, a programmer creates questions to ask other developers for possible solutions of a given problem. These questions generate discussions around possible solutions that could be implemented. One of the most popular programmers communities is Stack Overflow (SO). In SO programmers help each other using a question-and-answer system (Q&A). A programmer publishes a programming related question and other programmers give possible solutions for that question. Answers are validated by the programmer who asked the question originally, and by other programmers in the programmers community. Questions are rated by its relevance, filtered by the community

© Springer International Publishing AG 2017
A. Solano and H. Ordoñez (Eds.): CCC 2017, CCIS 735, pp. 199–210, 2017.
DOI: 10.1007/978-3-319-66562-7_15

to prevent duplicated questions, and tagged by the user who asked. This process of Q&A creates a huge repository of trustable information that can be used by other programmers with similar problems.

SO gets a lot of questions and answers per day. In 2014, SO released a dataset that contains information about posts that users did in the past. One of the most interesting aspects in this dataset is that it has around 8 millions of questions and 14 millions of answers. These two types of posts show the interaction between programmers, in which they share text, source code snippets, traces of errors related with the question, and a set of user defined labels (the labels that user thinks are related with the question).

The goal of this paper is to explore mechanisms to extract knowledge from the question in SO. We use the textual and source code information available in the question's statement to find out relationships between programming languages used in the tags. We use this information and representation to visualize and extract non-evident relationships based on how the developers ask about their problems, also we are interested in exploring the contribution of text and source code features in a classification task and how they behave and relate to the tags.

We use the textual data of the question in SO to build a word embedding model using word2vec [11], and store interesting information, i.e., source code and text, into a high performance access file HDF5 [9]. The word2vec model and the HDF5 file are used to build the features of the question post. For the textual component, we use an average of the word2vec vector of each word that appears in the question post; and for the source code component, we use a n-gram representation. We build a dataset for training and test for some programming languages and use the different features to train a SVM model. After that, we use the test set to evaluate the SVM model. In addition, we use the feature representation to visualize how the programming languages are related because some questions can be solved or asked in a similar way in different programming languages.

For the experimentation, we select 18 tags of programming languages and for each tag 1,000 posts containing text and source code. In total, in this work we use 18,000 question posts to build a dataset. All the question posts selected have a unique programming language tag. With the 18,000 question posts we build two classifiers, one using textual features and other using code features. We evaluated the classifier with performance metrics, such as: f1-score, accuracy, precision, and recall. In addition, we present a visualization of the tags representation in a 2D space to show how programming languages are related to each other.

The paper is structured as follows. Section 2 presents the state of the art and related works in the field. Section 3 shows the proposed method describing step by step the proposal. Section 4 presents the conducted experiment: data set, experimental setup, and results. Finally, Sect. 5 concludes the paper.

2   Related Work

Software repositories contain large collections of data related to software projects such as source code, discussion about it, reports of bugs and execution.

These repositories are, according to [13], "data rich but information poor", because their original goal was just to be a place to store the data. This huge amount of data is interesting in terms of the information and knowledge that can be obtained through analysis.

This analysis or knowledge mining of software elements, especially the ones stored in software repositories, has been motivated by the increasing amount of data and tools to manage and extract information [5,7]. One of the main interests is to analyze aspects that are present in the process of software development. Some of these aspects are addressed in [3] like clone detection [10], defect localization [14], code optimization, among others. Knowledge mining also opens up new interesting research topics such as identifying latent relationships between developers in a social level [15], feelings analysis and their relationship with the software development process [6].

Most of the works preformed over SO have been focused on studies such as developers interest/technologies change over time [4], how programmer characteristics, such as age, influence their programming knowledge [10], and other studies based in the format of the Q&A web sites [1]. These works show the rich source of data that can be found in Stack Overflow.

Although source-code representation has not been widely studied as text representation, there are two main ways to address it: static analysis and dynamic analysis [9]. The first one uses directly the source code, and the second one uses information produced during the code execution like traces and logs of execution. Some of the typical strategies in static analysis are Natural Language Processing (NLP) techniques over the source code, clustering, tokens analysis, building the abstract syntax tree (AST: a tree representation of the syntactic structure of source code), and graph dependency analysis. In dynamic analysis some common techniques are log analysis and execution patterns.

3   Proposed Method

We want to extract information about the relationships of these programming languages. To address this task we build a classifier model that use word embeddings. This classifier allows to classify a post by tag using textual and code information (modalities).

Figure 1 shows an overall description of the method, which includes three stages: pre-processing, classification, and evaluation.

3.1   Description of Each Module/Step

Stack Overflow. Given the data of Stack Overflow we obtain a collection of posts with title, body (text, code and images), tags, score, and information of the tag creation.

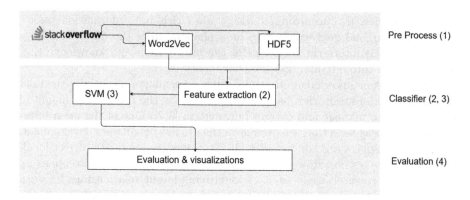

Fig. 1. Overview of the proposed method: (1) questions are pre-processed from SO; (2) an embedded word representation is generated; (3) a classification model is trained; and (4) the method is evaluated and results analyzed using visualization.

Tags Selection. To select the programming languages used in this study, we used the Github repository and extract the list of the most popular languages. We compared that list with the SO list and selected the tags that appear in more than 5,000 posts in SO.

Pre-process of Data. First, the data was changed from the original format, the new format HDF5, which is a format developed to work with big and complex collections of data, giving better performance, storage space, and access to data. This format allowed us a better mechanism in terms of time and access to information than the original XML file provided by SO.

In the process of changing the format we split the body of the post in two fields: text content and source-code content. We divided the source-code fragments (snippets) and text in columns. This was necessary to obtain a better performance in the classification tasks. The source code was selected only the fragments in the HTML tag <code>.

In the pre-processing step we used the text of the post to train several classification models using different amount of posts in training. We processed the data to generate a set of 3 millions of questions, this are used to train a new word2vec model to obtain a better performance with SO concepts. Finally, we build a dataset with posts that had the two modalities (text and code).

Text Feature Extraction. From the dataset we selected the posts that were identified as Question post. Using the text content of each post, we generate a representation of each post using the word2vec model. The word2vec model trains a neural network to embeded each word in a new vector representation space. Each post was represented as the average of the vectors of the words in the post, generating for each post a vector representation of dimension 300.

Source-Code Feature Extraction. To represent the source code we used an approach based on character n-grams. We experimented with [2–6]-grams. We generated a vector representation of the posts using the TF-IDF and the 300 most frequent n-grams.

Classification of Programming Languages. The purpose of this component was to train a classifier that is able to classify a new post in one of the 18 different classes (18 programming languages tags). We selected as a classification method a Support Vector Machine (SVM). In this stage we compared the obtained performance of the textual and source code representations.

To represent each programming language as a vector, we used the n-gram representation. We averaged the vectors of the posts that contain source code and have the same programing language tag. It is not possible for two posts having two or more programming languages.

The n-gram representation was selected because we are interested in working with different programming languages and with different syntax. Generally, a post has a small snippet of code that not necessarily is written in the language used to tag the post.

4   Experimental Evaluation

This section presents details of the experiments conducted to evaluate the proposed method.

4.1   DataSet

We started with the SO set of data published in 2014 for the MSR (Mining Software Repositories) challenge 2015. This dataset was divided into XML files, whose size is about 20 GB. We focused only on the text and source-code information of the post and its tags.

The filed "PostTypeId" was used to identify the relation between the question and answer of the post. A summary of the amount of posts for each type is presented in Table 1.

Table 1. Summary of the dataset used in this study.

Questions	Answers	Orphaned tag wiki	Tag wiki excerpt	Tag wiki	Moderator nomination
7,990,787	13,684,117	167	30,659	3,058	200

As mentioned before we worked only with posts of type Question since these posts were originally tagged, and have a good number of related posts to use.

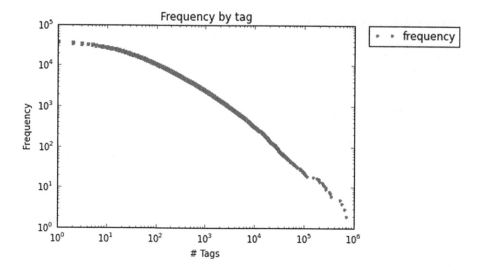

Fig. 2. Tag frequency in the dataset.

The initial set had 38,206 tags with more than 21 millions of posts. Since tags are added manually by users, some of them occur infrequently, or always occur with the same set of tags. This motivated us to do a selection of some interesting tags.

To do a better selection of elements we analyzed the tags versus its frequency. This was performed the plot presented in Fig. 2. We can see that there are some tags that rarely appear. The tags that rarely appears can be ignored, so we focused on the most frequent.

A selection of some programming languages was made using the GitHub platform as an external source of information to make a fairer selection of the final tags that were used in this study.

In the pre-processing step we stored the data in the HDF5 format. A new word2vec model was trained with a set of the SO posts to obtain a set of post/tags to be used in the classification step.

The set of tags selected were the 18 most popular programming languages used in Github, that is to say, the programming languages that occur in almost 5,000 posts. The first tag with more than 5,000 post frequency is "LUA", it is only used in 6,867 posts. This number of post gives a lower bound to doing an equitable partition in the train and test set. We show the frequency of each tag in Fig. 3.

4.2   Experimental Setup

We split the data set in training ans test sets. For training we selected 1,000 posts of each tag to train a SVM, that is to say, we selected 18,000 posts. For

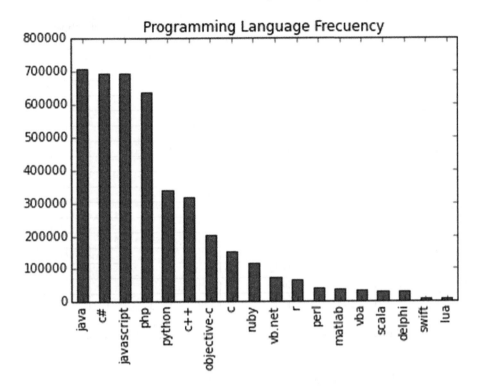

Fig. 3. Frequency of the 18 selected programming languages in this study.

the test set we also selected 100 posts for each tag. These posts were selected in such way they do not share a common programming language tag.

To evaluate the result of the classification task we use the F1 score, accuracy, precision and recall measures. These measures are commonly used to evaluate classification algorithms. We also used a set of visualizations to qualitatively measure and understand how a programming language is related each other.

We present the results in 2 parts, one part dedicated to show a visualization of the results obtained for the classification task, and the other part dedicated to visualize how programming languages are related in the feature representation space.

4.3   Results

After training and evaluating a classifier we are interested in the misclassified posts. This misclassification allows us to see the similarity between a typical problems in programming languages. Figure 4 presents a confusion matrix when the classification model is trained using text features.

To understand better the misclassification, we show in the Figs. 7 and 8 the representation of the programming languages tags in a 2D space, this to show groups and distances between different tags.

	java	python	php	c#	javascript	c++	c	objective-c	r	swift	matlab	ruby	vb.net	vba	perl	scala	lua	delphi
java	57	2	5	3	3	5	1	1	2	1	1	2	0	4	0	6	3	4
python	1	57	5	0	1	1	2	1	2	2	4	7	5	1	6	3	1	1
php	2	2	67	0	5	1	0	0	2	2	0	5	4	2	5	1	0	2
c#	4	2	3	27	5	11	6	0	0	3	4	1	16	7	0	3	2	6
javascript	1	3	1	2	82	0	0	3	1	0	0	1	1	0	4	0	0	1
c++	2	1	2	7	1	32	29	1	2	2	3	0	4	1	2	2	6	3
c	3	3	2	5	2	19	37	1	3	5	2	2	0	0	5	2	6	3
objective-c	1	1	1	1	0	2	2	68	1	14	1	2	1	0	0	2	0	3
r	1	2	2	0	1	1	1	1	80	2	7	0	0	1	0	1	0	0
swift	1	2	1	0	0	1	2	20	0	66	1	1	2	0	0	3	0	0
matlab	1	1	2	1	2	0	2	3	10	2	64	2	0	2	6	0	1	1
ruby	1	7	7	2	1	0	1	3	3	1	1	64	2	1	3	3	0	0
vb.net	5	0	3	16	5	2	0	1	1	2	1	1	50	5	1	1	0	6
vba	0	0	0	3	0	1	0	0	4	0	2	0	4	83	1	1	1	0
perl	1	1	5	1	1	2	0	1	2	1	2	2	0	1	74	3	3	0
scala	7	3	2	1	1	0	1	2	0	6	0	0	0	0	2	71	1	3
lua	0	2	7	1	4	1	5	3	2	4	4	2	1	0	2	2	59	1
delphi	7	2	3	2	1	1	4	6	2	4	3	1	1	1	1	1	2	58

Fig. 4. Confusion matrix of classification using text features.

Post Label Prediction Using Text Features. Figure 4 presents a confusion matrix for an SVM trained using text representation. This matrix shows that most of programming languages are correctly classified, although some of them were not. It is worth noting that some of the misclassified posts belong to a programming language that is considered similar according to the programming paradigm or to the language [2].

Figure 5 presents a visualization of miss-classified posts for each language with respect to other programming languages. It is interesting to see in this visualization how some programming languages share connection with other programming languages, that is to say, the model mis-classifies posts because these programming languages share common problems. For instance, objective-c and swift, C and C++, Matlab and R, etc.

When we evaluate the classifier using only textual information, we obtain a F1-score = 0.6024, accuracy = 0.6088, precision = 0.6010, and recall = 0.6088.

Post Label Prediction Using Source Code Features. Using only source code information of the question and building a n-gram feature representation, the model presents a lower performance with respect to the model based on text representation. Figure 6 shows the obtained confusion matrix for the SVM.

Table 2 shows the consolidated performance measures for the classifier for the two modalities.

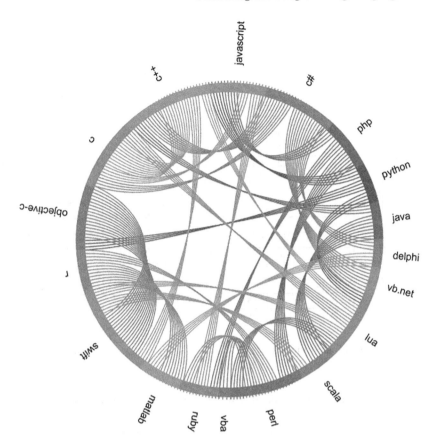

Fig. 5. Visualization of the miss-classified posts. It is worth to note how the objective-c language is confused with swift.

Language Landscape Visualization. We build a 2 dimensional visualization of the programming languages using the text and code feature representations. Figure 7 presents a 2D visualization of the feature representation of each programming language. This representation is an average of all representations of the posts sharing the same programming language. Vectors were normalized using the L1-norm. To plot each programming language vector (embedding space with word2vec) we applied the principal components analysis algorithm (PCA), which generates a set of components from which we selected the two most important to be used as coordinates to plot in a 2D coordinate system. It is expected in this visualization that similar points are projected close to each other. Figure 7 presents the obtained visualization. This visualization is very interesting because allows us to see relations between programming languages. For instance, Matlab is very close to R, which makes sense because they share many things in common, and in this case, they share similar problems in the developers community.

	java	python	php	c#	javascript	c++	c	objective-c	r	swift	matlab	ruby	vb.net	vba	perl	scala	lua	delphi
java	13	3	3	20	19	4	5	2	2	1	5	3	1	4	1	7	4	3
python	2	44	2	0	6	1	6	6	0	3	9	3	0	5	4	6	2	1
php	6	5	23	5	15	3	5	7	1	1	7	6	1	2	8	0	3	2
c#	5	3	5	26	12	1	6	8	3	4	0	2	2	7	4	3	4	5
javascript	2	1	3	0	71	2	1	6	0	3	2	0	1	1	1	2	1	3
c++	3	4	2	4	6	38	13	6	0	1	6	0	1	3	5	2	4	2
c	2	1	0	2	3	2	61	3	2	3	6	0	0	5	5	0	4	1
objective-c	0	4	3	3	4	2	4	60	1	3	3	1	0	9	0	1	0	2
r	3	4	1	0	8	0	4	2	57	0	7	2	0	3	0	2	5	2
swift	0	5	1	3	3	1	1	10	1	59	5	0	0	2	2	1	2	4
matlab	4	7	2	2	5	4	1	4	5	3	44	4	1	2	2	2	4	4
ruby	0	7	3	3	6	2	3	7	4	1	5	40	3	6	4	2	2	2
vb.net	2	1	1	5	9	1	0	5	1	1	1	4	49	7	0	4	2	7
vba	1	1	1	2	3	0	4	9	3	3	10	2	18	36	2	1	1	3
perl	2	5	10	1	8	2	4	6	1	0	7	6	0	8	33	2	4	1
scala	6	1	0	9	5	5	2	3	1	3	2	3	0	1	3	53	2	1
lua	0	2	5	5	4	10	8	5	2	2	5	2	0	2	6	0	42	0
delphi	2	4	2	4	2	1	0	5	5	5	3	2	1	7	0	2	1	54

Fig. 6. Confusion matrix of classification using code-source features.

Table 2. Performance of the classifier using text and source-code representations.

Modality	F1-score	Accuracy	Precision	Recall
Source	0.6024	0.6088	0.6010	0.6088
Code	0.4402	0.4461	0.4509	0.4461

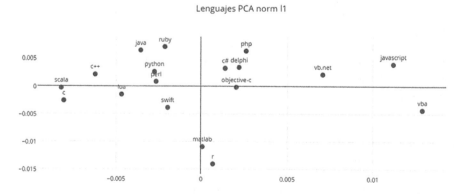

Fig. 7. Posts in a 2D space using text features.

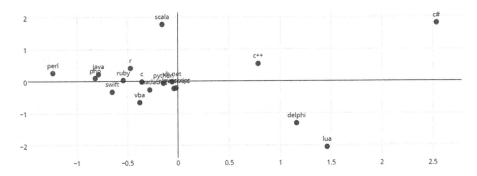

Fig. 8. Posts in a 2D space using code features.

Figure 8 presents also a 2D visualization but using the code-source embedding representation obtained with word2vec. It is worth noting that this visualization allows to see correlations between questions of programming languages but in terms of code snippets. It is important to note that the obtained relations depicted in this visualization are different to the text visualization.

5   Conclusions and Future Work

In this paper, we explore mechanisms to discover and extract information about the question post of SO. We experiment using for a question post in SO textual and code components. In the context of SO we found a short code that does not provide overwhelming information about the programing language, and using the textual information we can found better results.

The proposed method was used to visualize the relationship between 18 programming languages. We can see a cluster of some programming languages that are used in similar topics. For instance, Matlab and R are close each other and so far from another programming languages. Results show a relationship between programming languages based on how people ask about related problems.

We plan to perform experiments with other feature representations and other classifiers. We expect to find a better generic representation for the code component. Another task is try to extend the code and textual modalities using the answer post, which is used to solve the question post.

References

1. Allamanis, M., Sutton, C.: Why, when, and what: analyzing stack overflow questions by topic, type, and code. In: Proceedings of the 10th Working Conference on Mining Software Repositories, pp. 53–56. IEEE Press, May 2013
2. Allamanis, M., Sutton, C.: Mining idioms from source code. In: Proceedings of the 22nd ACM SIGSOFT International Symposium on Foundations of Software Engineering, pp. 472–483. ACM, November 2014

3. Binkley, D.: Source code analysis: a road map. In: Proceedings of FOSE, pp. 104–119 (2007). http://doi.org/10.1109/FOSE.2007.27

4. Barua, A., Thomas, S.W., Hassan, A.E.: What are developers talking about? An analysis of topics and trends in stack overflow. Empir. Softw. Eng. **19**(3), 619–654 (2014)

5. Di Penta, M., Xie, T.: Guest editorial: special section on mining software repositories. Empir. Softw. Eng. **20**(2), 291–293 (2015). http://doi.org/10.1007/s10664-015-9383-7

6. Guzman, E., Azcar, D., Li, Y.: Sentiment analysis of commit comments in GitHub: an empirical study. In: Proceedings of the 11th Working Conference on Mining Software Repositories - MSR 2014, pp. 352–355 (2014). http://doi.org/10.1145/2597073.2597118

7. Hassan, A.E.: The road ahead for mining software repositories. In: 2008 Frontiers of Software Maintenance, pp. 48–57 (2008). http://doi.org/10.1109/FOSM.2008.4659248

8. Howison, M.: Tuning HDF5 for lustre file systems. In: Workshop on Interfaces and Abstractions for Scientific Data Storage (IASDS 2010), Heraklion, Crete, Greece, 24 September 2010

9. Khatoon, S., Li, G., Mahmood, A.: Comparison and evaluation of source code mining tools and techniques: a qualitative approach. Intell. Data Anal. **17**(3), 459–484 (2013)

10. Kim, M., Notkin, D.: Using a clone genealogy extractor for understanding and supporting evolution of code clones. ACM SIGSOFT Softw. Eng. Notes **30**(4), 1 (2005). http://doi.org/10.1145/1082983.1083146

11. Mikolov, T., Chen, K., Corrado, G., Dean, J.: Efficient estimation of word representations in vector space. arXiv preprint arXiv:1301.3781 (2013)

12. Morrison, P., Murphy-Hill, E.: Is programming knowledge related to age? An exploration of stack overflow. In: 2013 10th IEEE Working Conference on Mining Software Repositories (MSR), pp. 69–72. IEEE, May 2013

13. Padhy, N., Mishra, P., Panigrahi, R.: The survey of data mining applications and feature scope. Int. J. Comput. Sci. Eng. Inf. **2**(3), 43–58 (2012). doi:10.5121/ijcseit.2012.2303

14. Rahman, M.M., Yeasmin, S., Roy, C.K.: Towards a context-aware IDE-based meta search engine for recommendation about programming errors and exceptions. In: 2014 Software Evolution Week - IEEE Conference on Software Maintenance, Reengineering, and Reverse Engineering, CSMR-WCRE 2014 - Proceedings, pp. 194–203 (2014). http://doi.org/10.1109/CSMR-WCRE.2014.6747170

15. Tang, L., Liu, H.: Relational learning via latent social dimensions. In: Proceedings of the 15th ACM International Conference on Knowledge Discovery and Data Mining, pp. 817–825 (2009). http://doi.org/10.1145/1557019

Computer Assisted Assignment of ICD Codes for Primary Admission Diagnostic in ICUs

Giovanny Quiazúa[1,2], Carlos Rojas[3], Javier Ordoñez[3], Darwin Martinez[1,2],
César Enciso-Olivera[3], and Francisco Gómez[4(✉)]

[1] Facultad de Ciencias Naturales e Ingeniería,
Universidad Jorge Tadeo Lozano, Bogotá, Colombia
[2] Department of Computer Sciences, Universidad Central, Bogotá, Colombia
[3] Intensive Care Unit, Fundación Universitaria
de Ciencias de las Salud, Bogotá, Colombia
[4] Department of Mathematics, Universidad Nacional de Colombia,
Edificio 405, Oficina 336, Bogotá, Colombia
fagomezj@unal.edu.co

Abstract. The intensive care units (ICUs) provide a constant monitoring and specialized support to patients with acute critical conditions, assuring timely interventions to rapid changes. A major determinant of the patient care in ICUs is the primary admission diagnosis. A typical diagnosis includes a nosological entity or syndrome name, with the possibility to describe the clinical condition and the patient health state. This diagnosis is the starting point to establish intervention plans and to devise epidemiological studies. In the ICU physicians are in charge to define this diagnosis. Diagnoses in ICUs are commonly described in natural language. However, a common practice is to assign a normalized code from the international classification of diseases and related health problems (ICD). Unfortunately, this codification task is time expensive and requires highly specialized medical knowledge. In this work, we introduce a text mining system to automatically recover ICD codes for diagnosis of admission in ICUs. The system is based on a novel hierarchical recovery approach which is well suited to representation used in the ICD code. The proposed approach was evaluated by using a set of 1206 codified descriptions written in Spanish language corresponding to diagnoses in an real ICU. The results suggest that this approach may account for a considerable percentage of the diagnoses codified by the expert in the ICU. In particular, the F1 measure was 0.21 ± 0.06 with a mean precision average of 0.3.

Keywords: Intensive care units · Diagnosis of admission · International classification of diseases and related health problems (ICD) · Diagnosis codification

1 Introduction

Intensive care unit (ICU) is an specialized section of a hospital that provides comprehensive and continuous care for patients who are critically ill and who

© Springer International Publishing AG 2017
A. Solano and H. Ordoñez (Eds.): CCC 2017, CCIS 735, pp. 211–223, 2017.
DOI: 10.1007/978-3-319-66562-7_16

can benefit from treatment [19]. The ICU provides a constant monitoring and support from specialist equipment and medications to assure timely interventions to the rapid changes. Principal admission diagnosis to ICUs refers to the condition established after study that is chiefly responsible for causing the patient's admission to the unit [13]. A diagnosis corresponds to a description or narrative by which an individual is assigned to a given class, or the disorder from which she/he suffers [38]. A typical diagnosis includes a description of the disease, nosological entity, syndrome or any other condition relevant to describe the patient's health state. Diagnosis are commonly described by physicians by using narratives written in natural language [38]. Primary admission diagnosis is highly valuable to determine patient condition and posterior treatment in ICU [9]. This diagnosis is also an important input for different kind of epidemiological studies, such as, relationship between morbidities and mortalities and care strategies [2,13], readmission rates [33,36] and attention costs of patients in the ICU [8,41], among others. Therefore, a precise and unambiguous determination of the principal admission diagnosis in ICU represents a paramount important task in medical informatics [2].

In order to reduce the inherent ambiguity of the narratives of diagnosis described in natural language, a widely used practice in the medical domain is the codification of these narratives by using codes taken from an standardized classification system [18]. This codification task consists in assign one or more normalized codes to the narrative of the diagnosis [18]. One of the most popular classification systems used for this codification task in ICUs is the international statistical classification of diseases and related health problems (ICD) [4,24]. The aim of this system is to provide a normalized reference set of codes for classifying different health conditions and problems, commonly found in the clinical practice [42]. This ICD codification task has been performed to study diagnosis in cardiology, psychiatry, radiology, among others medical specialties [1,39].

The task of assignation of ICD codes to narratives of primary admission diagnosis is commonly performed by medical personal [18]. In general, only highly trained experts can properly perform this task, making this codification process expensive [6]. The clinical narrative texts are usually written by health care professionals to communicate the status and history of a patient to other health care professionals or themselves. Therefore, they are commonly written in highly specific and specialized language [7]. A typical diagnosis description may include, for instance, the reason the patient was seen, progress notes documenting treatment provided, reports of consultations communicating the results of diagnostic tests, and discharge summaries recording the entire course of a hospital stay, among others [38]. This information is highly heterogeneous in their content and level of detail, resulting in an unstructured, noisy, and incomplete collection of documents. In addition, the codification task requires to choose the correct codes among thousands of available alternatives, resulting in a highly unreliable task [31]. Because of these reasons this codification task represents a major challenge even for highly trained personal [37]. These limitations are even more critical in the current electronic health systems in which thousands of diagnoses should be eventually coded [21].

Recently, natural language processing has been explored as an alternative to perform automatic coding of narratives of diagnosis obtained from electronic health records [17,27]. These approaches have been mainly proposed for specific domains different to the UCI, for instance, radiology [28,29] or psychiatry [35]. These codification systems are commonly limited to an small number of diagnosis, or they operate over descriptions defined for a narrow subset of the medical language, which are easier to process grammatically but far from the description in natural language commonly used by the physicians [28]. Other approaches require a large amount of training data in order to highly practices of coding [25]. These methods will also eventually require hospitals to rebuild their information systems to handle these new requirement. In addition, these systems are difficult to be used in post-hoc scenarios in which annotated information is not existing [15]. Other approaches based on specific constructions may also requires an specialized and time expensive modeling of the syntactical and grammatical structure specific for different kinds of diagnosis [26]. Finally, in the case of admission diagnosis for ICU in written in Spanish language there as our knowledge there is no work reported in the literature.

In this work, we introduce a text mining system to automatically recover ICD codes for diagnosis of admission in ICUs written in Spanish language. The system is based on a vectorial representation of the diagnosis and the IDC codes and a novel hierarchical recovery approach which is well suited to representation used in the ICD code. The proposed strategy was evaluated on real diagnosis of admissions, and compared with baseline methods based on flat (non-hierarchical) representations, resulting in higher performances.

2 Materials and Methods

Figure 1 illustrates the proposed approach. First, a database with narratives of primary diagnoses of admission written in Spanish was constructed, and subsequently annotated by trained physicians. Following, a preprocessing step including steaming and stop word removal was applied over the diagnostic descriptions contained in the ICD classification system and the narratives of the database of diagnoses. The ICD codes descriptions were used as a corpus to build a dictionary suitable to represent diagnosis related information. Using this dictionary a document-term vectorial representation was constructed for each ICD code and for each diagnosis. A distance between the representations of the ICD code and the diagnosis was computed. Finally, these distances were included into a hierarchical recovery strategy aimed to assign the corresponding ICD codes.

2.1 ICD Classification System

The ICD corresponds to an standardized classification system used to describe morbility and mortality in diverse applications, such as, reimbursement, administration, epidemiology, and health service research, among others [24,42]. The

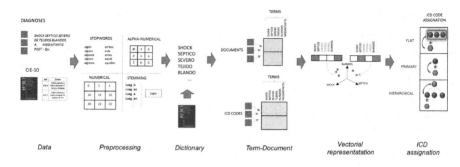

Fig. 1. Automatic assignation of ICD codes to narratives of primary admission diagnosis. First ICD codes were used to build a dictionary suitable to represent diagnostic related information. Following, the narrative of the diagnosis was represented using this corpus. A set of distances measuring the similarity between narrative of diagnosis and the narratives of the IDC codes were computed. Finally, a recovery approach that takes advantage of the natural hierarchical representation of the ICD system was used for recovery of the corresponding code.

latest version this code is the ICD-10 that contains at approximately 14.000 different codes [42]. Each code is conformed by a description in specialized language of diseases, injuries, or causes of death. These codes are organized in a hierarchically tree structure, where a secondary code represents a subdivision of its parent. For example, the category (3-digit) code A00 pertains to the condition "Cólera" and its subcategory (4-digit) code A00.0 refers to a more specific condition "Cólera debido a Vibrio cholerae 01, biotipo cholerae". Different section code A00-A09 corresponds a broader range of "Ciertas enfermedades infecciosas y parasitarias". In this work, we focused on the tasks of codification of diagnosis using the Spanish version of the ICD-10 [5]. This system contains 14.196 codes with their corresponding descriptions. The complete codification system is available to the scientific community increasing the reproducibility of the proposed method.

2.2   ICU Diagnosis Database Construction

To evaluate the proposed approach a database consisting of real diagnosis annotated by medical experts was constructed. For this, a total of 1206 diagnosis written in Spanish language were sampled from an electronic health care information system that supports ICU operations. These diagnoses corresponded to primary admission diagnosis from March to June during the 2014 from the ICU at *Hospital Infantil San Jose* in Bogotá, Colombia. For each record the information related to the descriptions of primary diagnosis was extracted. Information of patient's evolution together with the descriptions of primary diagnosis was also considered in a separated analysis. All the information related with patient identity, including, patient name and id, was removed in order to guarantee confidentiality of the patient records. Because the diagnosis information was planned not to be used for to expose patient to any intervention, according to current regulations, informed consent was not required for the patients.

In this work, we focused on the tasks of codification of narratives diagnosis using the Spanish version of the ICD-10 [5]. Previous works, have concentrated on historical records of annotated diagnoses of medical institutions previously stored in the electronic heath records. This approach may provide more data, however, it can be error-prone because of the high percentage of errors in codification reported for this kind of systems [25,34].

A specific tool was developed for the manual codification task of these codes. This tool showed each narrative of diagnosis and a tree with ICD codes (code + description), for the corresponding codification by the expert. The tool allowed the assignation of a variable number of codes for each narrative of diagnosis. The medical doctor was instructed to codify the narrative using the recommendations established by the CIE10 [42]. In addition, the coder was instructed to use the code Z99.9 "Dependencia de máquinas y dispositivos capacitantes, no clasificada en otra parte" to account for narratives of diagnosis impossible to codify [40]. The codification task was performed by an expert physician in Intensive Care Unit with at least 3 years of experience. All the assigned codes were subsequently verified by a different trained physician with at least 10 years of experience in ICD coding.

2.3 Preprocessing

Two main sources of information were considered: the ICD code description and the annotated diagnoses database. For each register in these sources a pre-processing step was performed. This preprocessing step, included, normalization of characters to non-capital, removal of non alpha-numerical symbols, stemming and stop word removal. Stemming refers to reduce inflected words to their word stem. The snow ball stemmer for Spanish language was used for this task [30]. Stop word removal refers to filter the most common words in a language [16].

2.4 Dictionary Construction

The ICD code description was used to build a dictionary to represent diagnostic information. Two different methods to build the dictionary were considered. First, the complete ICD code description information, including primary and secondary diagnoses, was used to build the dictionary. Second, the information corresponding only to the primary description of the code was used to build a dictionary. The first dictionary construction strategy aimed to consider a wide range of terms which can be present both in primary and secondary levels of the ICD. While, the second strategy aimed to model general terms that can be found in the primary levels. Subsequent experimentation was performed by considering these two dictionary construction scenarios.

2.5   Term-Document Representation

Using the dictionaries previously constructed a term-document representation was constructed for both descriptions of the ICD codes and the annotated diagnoses. This term-document provides a vectorial representation of the terms in the dictionary which are present in the narrative of the documents [3]. By using this kind of representation both narratives for diagnoses and descriptions of the ICD10 codes can be numerically represented.

2.6   ICD Code Assignation

For the codification task we mainly focused in ICD codes related to primary groups or conditions. These codes correspond to the ones with three digits. In order to determine the primary diagnosis of admission a similarity measurement between the narrative of the diagnosis and the descriptions of the ICD codes was computed. In this measurement we accounted for the hierarchical representation of the CIE10 [22,27]. For this, three different approaches were explored. The first approach (*flat*), which corresponds to a baseline, aims to determine the code for a given diagnosis by considering the narratives of a particular primary code and its secondary children as only one narrative, as follows:

$$PDC = \arg\min_{c \in D_{prim}} d(N, D_c) \qquad (1)$$

where PDC is the primary diagnostic code, N is the narrative of a particular diagnosis, D_c is text resulting from concatenating all descriptions for the primary and secondary diagnoses which included C in their ICD code, D_{prim} is the set of primary diagnosis and $d(N, D)$ is a distance measure between the two vectorial representations of N and D. In other words, $D_c = \sum_{c_j \in S_c} T_{c_j}$, where S_c is the set of ICD codes that contains the code c, T_{c_j} is a description of a ICD code, where the sum is defined as the concatenation between texts. For instance,

$$D_{I62} = T_{I62} + T_{I62.0} + T_{I62.1} + T_{I62.9} =$$
"Otras hemorragias intracraneales no traumáticas" +
"Hemorragia subdural (aguda) (no traumática)" + $\qquad (2)$
"Hemorragia extradural no traumática"+
"Hemorragia intracraneal (no traumática), no especificada".

For this code assignation strategy the dictionary corresponding to the full ICD code was used to construct the term-document representation (see Sect. 2.4).

As second approach (*primary*), which can also be considered as a baseline, consisted in the use only of the description of the primary code, i.e., D_c contained only the description of the primary diagnosis c, excluding descriptions corresponding to the secondary codes. In this case, the dictionary corresponding to the primary ICD code descriptions was used to construct the term-document representation (see Sect. 2.4).

Finally, a third approach (*hierarchical*) was proposed to take advantage of the hierarchical structure of ICD code, where a secondary child code represents a subdivision of its parent. Specifically, we use a method that assign the closest primary code by considering independently related primary and secondary codes. In particular, the PDC was defined as follows:

$$PDC = \arg \min_{c \in D_{prim}} d'(N, P_c) \tag{3}$$

where P_c corresponds to the set of diagnostic descriptions associated to codes contained in S_c, and $d'(N, T)$ is a similarity measure between the narrative of diagnosis N and a the set diagnoses P_c. The measure $d'(N, P_c)$ was defined as the minimum distance d between the vectorial representation of N and the vectorial representations of each description contained in P_c. In this case the dictionary corresponding to the full ICD code was used to construct the term-document representation (see Sect. 2.4).

3   Experimental Settings

Three proposed methods (flat, primary and hierarchical) were evaluated using the constructed database. The performance of the proposed approach was evaluated by computing precision, recall, F1-measurement and mean precision averages (MPA) [27]. The precision corresponds to the faction of documents which are relevant to the query, i.e.,

$$\text{precision} = \frac{|\text{relevant data} \cap \text{retrieved data}|}{|\text{retrieved data}|}. \tag{4}$$

where relevant data corresponds to the codes assigned by the expert, and retrieved data to the codes assigned by the system. Recall corresponds to the fraction of the documents relevant to the query that are successfully retrieved, i.e.,

$$\text{recall} = \frac{|\text{relevant data} \cap \text{retrieved data}|}{|\text{relevant data}|}. \tag{5}$$

The F-measurement combines both precision and recall in a single measurement by using the an harmonic mean between them, as follows:

$$F1 = \frac{2 \cdot \text{precision} \cdot \text{recall}}{\text{precision} + \text{recall}}. \tag{6}$$

A precision-recall curve was computed to compare the performance of the proposed methods for different query sizes. The mean average precision, i.e., the average precision for the queries was also computed to quantitatively evaluate the performance of the three code assignation methods. For the similarity computations three distance measures were explored, namely, Euclidean and cosine distance and Manhattan.

4   Results

4.1   Annotated Database Construction

A total of 1.207 narratives of diagnoses were coded by the medical experts (*male* = 645 (53.4%) and *female* = 562 (46.6%)). A total 405 narratives of diagnosis (33.5%) were assigned to the *non-existing-code* category. Posterior analyses, focused on codes properly assigned by the medical expert (802). After codification task a total of 2048 ICD codes were assigned to the set of diagnoses. Figure 2 shows the distribution the number of codes assigned for each narrative. As observed, for most of the narratives the number of ICD codes varied between two and four.

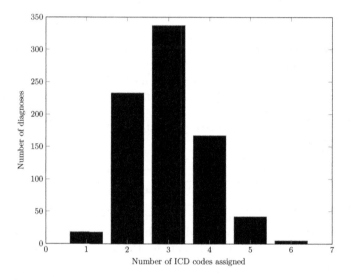

Fig. 2. Distribution of the number of ICD codes assigned for each narrative of diagnosis.

Table 1 shows some examples of the narratives of primary diagnosis and the corresponding codes assigned by the experts. As observed, in the first two examples the proposed method recovers successfully recovers the code according the occurrence of the terms. Narrative of diagnostic three is composed by acronyms and symbols that cannot be properly represented in the dictionary. While condition described in narrative of diagnostic four cannot be properly assigned to any ICD code.

4.2   ICD Codification Task

Table 1 shows some examples of the codes assigned by the system. Figure 3 shows the resulting precision-recall curve by using the narratives of the primary diagnosis for the three indexing methods, namely, *flat* (baseline), *primary* (baseline)

Table 1. Examples of narratives diagnosis. First the narrative of the diagnosis. Following, the corresponding expert and method assignations. Examples of correct (blue) and incorrect assignations (red) are shown.

Narrative of diagnosis: *Infarto agudo del miocardio, sin otra especificación*	
Expert assignation:	Method assignation:
(I21.9) Infarto agudo del miocardio, sin otra especificación	(I21.9) Infarto agudo del miocardio, sin otra especificación
(I10) Hipertension esencial (primaria).	(I23.8) Otras complicaciones presentes posteriores al infarto agudo del miocardio
(J44.9) Enfermedad pulmonar obstructiva crónica, no especificada.	(I25.2) Infarto antiguo del miocardio
Diagnosis narrative: *Arritmia cardiaca, no especificada*	
Expert assignation:	Method assignation:
(I49.9) Arritmia cardiaca, no especificada.	(I49.8) Otras arritmias cardíacas especificadas
(I50.0) Insuficiencia cardiaca.	(I51.9) Enfermedad cardíaca, no especificada
(I35.0) Estenosis (de la valvula) aortica	(I50.9) Insuficiencia cardíaca, no especificada
(I27.2) Otras hipertensiones pulmonares secundarias	
Narrative of diagnosis: *EPOC exacerbada, Neumon a adquirida en comunidad (tratada), POP TQT (03/04)*	
Expert assignation:	Method assignation:
(J44.1) Enfermedad pulmonar obstructiva crónica con exacerbación aguda, no específica	(G91.0) Hidrocéfalo comunicante
(J15.9) Neumonía bacteriana, no especificada	(T33) Congelamiento superficial
(I74.3) Embolida y trombosis de arterias de los miembros inferiores	(S10) Traumatismo superficial del cuello
(I10) Hipertensión escencial (primaria)	(T00.9) Traumatismos superficiales múltiples, no especificados
Narrative of diagnosis: *Sepsis de origen pulmonar*	
Expert assignation:	Method assignation:
(A41) Otras septicemias	(J98.4) Otros trastornos del pulmón
(—) No puede ser definido	(S27.3) Otros traumatismos del pulmón

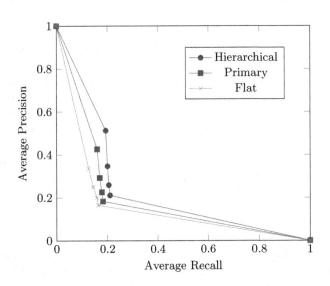

Fig. 3. Precision-recall curves for the different indexing methods.

and *hierarchical*. As observed, hierarchical representation resulted in the best performance. No differences were observed by selecting different distance measurements. The F1 measure for the three methods were 0.21 ± 0.06, 0.18 and ± 0.06 and 0.15 ± 0.05 for *hierarchical*, *primary* and *flat*, respectively. The precision averages for the three methods were 0.30, 0.28 and 0.26 for *hierarchical*, *primary* and *flat*, respectively.

When the the narratives of the primary diagnosis and the evolution field were used to recover the codes the F1 measure for the three methods were 0.21 ± 0.06, 0.16 and ± 0.05 and 0.15 ± 0.04 for *hierarchical*, *primary* and *flat*, respectively. The precision averages for the three methods were 0.30, 0.27 and 0.26 for *hierarchical*, *primary* and *flat*, respectively. As observed, hierarchical representation resulted in the best performance. Nevertheless, their performance is lower when compared to the narratives of the primary diagnosis alone.

5   Discussion

We have introduced a novel codification strategy to automatically assign ICD codes to narratives of primary admission diagnosis written in ICUs. The method is based on document-term representations and a hierarchical indexing approach adapted to the hierarchical structure of the ICD [3]. The proposed approach does not require prior datasets for training, and it is based on a publicity available source the ICD-10 description in Spanish [5]. Therefore, it is highly reproducible. The strategy was evaluated on a novel annotated database of diagnoses of admission in ICUs. The method resulted provided competitive results for the ICD codification task (see Sect. 4).

A major challenge in the ICD coding task is the language specificity. In principle, the codification of a diagnosis written in a different language may require a different recovery system [23]. In this work, this limitation was overcome by exploiting the flexibility provided by statistical text mining tools [12]. In particular, we constructed a language specific dictionary suitable to represent diagnosis information written in Spanish language by using a previously available source also written in Spanish, the ICD code system (see subsect. 2.4). By using this approach we rest the codification task on the occurrences of a specific term in the diagnosis, instead of the specific meaning of the term for a particular language [14]. The proposed approach resulted in a flexible and natural solution to this limitation. In addition, in this framework other tools used in the preprocessing, such as stopword removal and stemming, can be easily adapted to the Spanish language, resulting in a minor impact when a different language is used [16,30].

ICD diagnosis codification is a highly challenging task in medical informatics. Diagnoses may include, for instance, symbols, acronyms, and word reductions depending of the doctor [23]. For instance, diagnosis three in Table 1 includes numbers and symbols which are not included in the corpus used for representation derived from the IDC code [10,11]. Therefore, the proposed approach is limited to account for this kind of information. Future work may explore this avenue by using for instance domain knowledge to filter this information.

Recent literature suggest that IDC code may vary depending of the coder [18]. In the approach here in presented we overcome this limitation by constructing a consensus database resulting of the opinion of different experts. Nevertheless, it is important to recall that the ICD system should be considered as a reference, but no as a flawless list of diseases [20,32]. In fact, our results show that at least (33.5%) of the narratives cannot be successfully assigned to a IDC code. This result suggests that even if the ICD codes are popular a choice to codify diagnosis, this kind of system is not necessarily well suited to codify diagnosis of for particular medical domains, such as ICU.

Acknowledgment. This work was partially funded by the project *"Neuronal activity maps for low magnetic field fMRI resting state signals"* (code: 37568) from the *Convocatoria nacional de proyectos para el fortalecimiento de la investigación, creación e innovación de la Universidad Nacional de Colombia 2016–2018.*

References

1. Almeida, R.C.D., Pedroso, R.P.: Nosocomial infection in long-term care facilities. a survey in a brazilian psychiatric hospital. Rev. Inst. Med. Trop. São Paulo **41**(6), 365–370 (1999)
2. Angus, D.C., Linde-Zwirble, W.T., Lidicker, J., Clermont, G., Carcillo, J., Pinsky, M.R.: Epidemiology of severe sepsis in the united states: analysis of incidence, outcome, and associated costs of care. Crit. Care Med. **29**(7), 1303–1310 (2001)
3. Berry, M.W., Dumais, S.T., O'Brien, G.W.: Using linear algebra for intelligent information retrieval. SIAM Rev. **37**(4), 573–595 (1995)
4. Centers for Disease Control and Prevention and others: International classification of diseases, ninth revision, clinical modification (icd-9-cm) (2013). URL:http:// www.cdc.gov/nchs/about/otheract/icd9/abticd9.htm
5. Centro Venezolano de Clasificacion and Others: Clasificacion internacional de enfermedades, decima revision. Bol. Epidemiol. (Wash.) **16**(1), 14–6 (1995)
6. Chen, Y., Lu, H., Li, L.: Automatic icd-10 coding algorithm using an improved longest common subsequence based on semantic similarity. PloS one **12**(3), e0173410 (2017)
7. Demner-Fushman, D., Chapman, W.W., McDonald, C.J.: What can natural language processing do for clinical decision support? J. Biomed. Inform. **42**(5), 760–772 (2009)
8. DiGiovine, B., Chenoweth, C., Watts, C., Higgins, M.: The attributable mortality and costs of primary nosocomial bloodstream infections in the intensive care unit. Am. J. Respir. Crit. Care Med. **160**(3), 976–981 (1999)
9. Falciglia, M., Freyberg, R.W., Almenoff, P.L., D'alessio, D.A., Render, M.L.: Hyperglycemia-related mortality in critically ill patients varies with admission diagnosis. Crit. Care Med. **37**(12), 3001 (2009)
10. De Zárate, G., Catón, S., et al.: La historia clínica electrónica como herramienta de investigación (2013)
11. Guerrero, G.A.: Un punto de partida en la medicina clínica de jaén. perfil del dr. eduardo arroyo sevilla. Seminario Méd. **48**(1), 136–139 (1996)
12. Gupta, V., Lehal, G.S., et al.: A survey of text mining techniques and applications. J. Emerg. Technol. Web Intell. **1**(1), 60–76 (2009)

13. Hay, A., Bellomo, R., Pilcher, D., Jackson, G., Kaukonen, K.M., Bailey, M.: Characteristics and outcome of patients with the icu admission diagnosis of status epilepticus in australia and new zealand. J. Crit. Care **34**, 146–153 (2016)
14. Jurafsky, D., Martin, J.H.: Automatic speech recognition. an introduction to natural language processing, computational linguistics, and speech recognition, speech and language processing (2007)
15. Kukafka, R., Ancker, J.S., Chan, C., Chelico, J., Khan, S., Mortoti, S., Natarajan, K., Presley, K., Stephens, K.: Redesigning electronic health record systems to support public health. J. Biomed. Inform. **40**(4), 398–409 (2007)
16. Luhn, H.P.: Key word-in-context index for technical literature (kwic index). J. Assoc. Inf. Sci. Technol. **11**(4), 288–295 (1960)
17. Medori, J., Fairon, C.: Machine learning and features selection for semi-automatic icd-9-cm encoding. In: Proceedings of the NAACL HLT 2010 Second Louhi Workshop on Text and Data Mining of Health Documents, pp. 84–89. Association for Computational Linguistics (2010)
18. Misset, B., Nakache, D., Vesin, A., Darmon, M., Garrouste-Orgeas, M., Mourvillier, B., Adrie, C., Pease, S., de Beauregard, M.A.C., Goldgran-Toledano, D., et al.: Reliability of diagnostic coding in intensive care patients. Crit. Care **12**(4), R95 (2008)
19. Moreno, R., Singer, B., Rhodes, A.: What is an ICU. In: Flaatten, H., Moreno, R.P., Putensen, C., Rhodes, A. (eds.) Organization and management of intensive care, pp. 7–13. Medizinisch Wissenschaftliche Verlagsgesellschaft, Berlin (2010)
20. Morillo-García, Á., Aldana-Espinal, J.M., de Labry-Lima, A.O., Valencia-Martín, R., López-Márquez, R., Loscertales-Abril, M., Conde-Herrera, M.: Hospital costs associated with nosocomial infections in a pediatric intensive care unit. Gac. Sanit. **29**(4), 282–287 (2015)
21. Murdoch, T.B., Detsky, A.S.: The inevitable application of big data to health care. Jama **309**(13), 1351–1352 (2013)
22. Ning, W., Yu, M., Zhang, R.: A hierarchical method to automatically encode chinese diagnoses through semantic similarity estimation. BMC Med. Inform. Decis. Making **16**(1), 30 (2016)
23. Gallego, O.A.: Lenguaje médico 1992. Med. Clín. **99**(20), 781–783 (1992)
24. The World Health Organization, et al.: International classification of diseases (icd) (2012)
25. Pakhomov, S.V., Buntrock, J.D., Chute, C.G.: Automating the assignment of diagnosis codes to patient encounters using example-based and machine learning techniques. J. Am. Med. Inform. Assoc. **13**(5), 516–525 (2006)
26. Pérez, A., Gojenola, K., Casillas, A., Oronoz, M., de Ilarraza, A.D.: Computer aided classification of diagnostic terms in spanish. Expert Syst. Appl. **42**(6), 2949–2958 (2015)
27. Perotte, A., Pivovarov, R., Natarajan, K., Weiskopf, N., Wood, F., Elhadad, N.: Diagnosis code assignment: models and evaluation metrics. J. Am. Med. Inform. Assoc. **21**(2), 231–237 (2014)
28. Pestian, J.P., Brew, C., Matykiewicz, P., Hovermale, D.J., Johnson, N., Cohen, K.B., Duch, W.: A shared task involving multi-label classification of clinical free text. In: Proceedings of the Workshop on BioNLP 2007: Biological, Translational, and Clinical Language Processing, pp. 97–104. Association for Computational Linguistics (2007)
29. Pons, E., Braun, L.M., Hunink, M.M., Kors, J.A.: Natural language processing in radiology: a systematic review. Radiology **279**(2), 329–343 (2016)

30. Porter, M.F.: An algorithm for suffix stripping. Program **14**(3), 130–137 (1980)
31. Quan, H., Sundararajan, V., Halfon, P., Fong, A., Burnand, B., Luthi, J.C., Saunders, L.D., Beck, C.A., Feasby, T.E., Ghali, W.A.: Coding algorithms for defining comorbidities in icd-9-cm and icd-10 administrative data. Med. Care, 1130–1139 (2005)
32. Rivadeneira, A.G.: Clasificación Internacional de Enfermedades (CIE): Descifrando la CIE-10 y esperando la CIE-11. No. 7 (2015)
33. Rosenberg, A.L., Hofer, T.P., Hayward, R.A., Strachan, C., Watts, C.M.: Who bounces back? physiologic and other predictors of intensive care unit readmission. Criti. Care Med. **29**(3), 511–518 (2001)
34. Ross, M., Wei, W., Ohno-Machado, L.: "Big data" and the electronic health record. Yearb. Med. Inform. **9**(1), 97 (2014)
35. Rumshisky, A., Ghassemi, M., Naumann, T., Szolovits, P., Castro, V., McCoy, T., Perlis, R.: Predicting early psychiatric readmission with natural language processing of narrative discharge summaries. Transl. Psychiatry **6**(10), e921 (2016)
36. Santamaria, J.D., Duke, G.J., Pilcher, D.V., Cooper, D.J., Moran, J., Bellomo, R., et al.: Readmissions to intensive care: a prospective multicenter study in australia and new zealand. Crit. Care Med. **45**(2), 290–297 (2017)
37. Shedler, J., Westen, D.: The shedler-westen assessment procedure (swap): making personality diagnosis clinically meaningful. J. Pers. Assess. **89**(1), 41–55 (2007)
38. Taylor, A.: Making a diagnosis. BMJ. Br. Med. J. **327**(7413), 494 (2003)
39. Terán, C.S.R., Merino, R.G., García, M.G., Jiménez, J.V., Pérez, M.M., Huelgas, R.G., Efficiency Group of Internal Medicine, Andalusian Society of Internal Medicine (SADEMI), et al.: Analysis of 27,248 hospital discharges for heart failure: a study of an administrative database 1998–2002. Rev. Clin. Esp. 208(6), 281–287 (2008)
40. Thomas, B.S., Jafarzadeh, S.R., Warren, D.K., McCormick, S., Fraser, V.J., Marschall, J.: Temporal trends in the systemic inflammatory response syndrome, sepsis, and medical coding of sepsis. BMC Anesthesiol. **15**(1), 169 (2015)
41. Warren, D.K., Shukla, S.J., Olsen, M.A., Kollef, M.H., Hollenbeak, C.S., Cox, M.J., Cohen, M.M., Fraser, V.J.: Outcome and attributable cost of ventilator-associated pneumonia among intensive care unit patients in a suburban medical center. Crit. Care Med. **31**(5), 1312–1317 (2003)
42. World Health Organization, others: International statistical classification of diseases and related health problems (2009)

Software Engineering and IT Architectures

Architecture for a Colombian Data Cube Using Satellite Imagery for Environmental Applications

Germán Bravo[1(✉)], Harold Castro[1], Andrés Moreno[1], Christian Ariza-Porras[1],
Gustavo Galindo[2], Edersson Cabrera[2], Saralux Valbuena[2], and Pilar Lozano-Rivera[2]

[1] Systems and Computer Engineering Department, School of Engineering,
Universidad de Los Andes, Bogotá, Colombia
gbravo@uniandes.edu.co
[2] Subdirección de Ecosistemas e Información Ambiental,
Instituto de Hidrología, Meteorología y Estudios Ambientales (IDEAM), Bogotá, Colombia

Abstract. SOLAP data cubes are a main tool to help on the processing of satellite imagery. This article presents the work developed for adapting an existing SOLAP Data Cube to the current Colombian Protocol for processing satellite images to analyze deforestation. We studied different technological alternatives to support such protocol and extend the capabilities of the Australian data cube to include the whole analysis process. In this way, it is possible for different institutions to produce and consume information to/from the data cube allowing the standardization of such information. In consequence, an institution can generate new results based on previous information generated for another institution, keeping the associated metadata along the whole process. This paper introduces the defined architecture, a first implementation and the first results obtained by IDEAM, the Colombian official institution responsible for the monitoring of deforestation in the country.

Keywords: SOLAP data cubes · Deforestation · Data cubes architecture

1 Introduction

Forests have an essential role in the protection of the environment, because forested areas prevent soil erosion, landslides, avalanches and floods [12]. They also protect the water quality of rivers by filtering water from watersheds in the forests [12], and have a direct and positive impact on mitigating the effects of climate change [7] given its crucial role in the carbon cycle.

According to the "Informe del estado del Medio Ambiente y de los Recursos Naturales Renovables" report about the environment and renewable natural resources [11] and the SMBYC newsletter [16], forests have been identified as one of the most impacted natural covers in Colombia, requiring urging attention. The low management level of

This work has been developed in collaboration with the IDEAM.

© Springer International Publishing AG 2017
A. Solano and H. Ordoñez (Eds.): CCC 2017, CCIS 735, pp. 227–241, 2017.
DOI: 10.1007/978-3-319-66562-7_17

the forest as a heritage in Colombia constitutes the main cause of loss of these natural hedges, which are themselves highly productive.

The significant transformations of these coverages by factors such as colonization, infrastructure projects, the exploitation of wood for energy generation, opencast mining and non-sustainable natural forests exploitation are caused by the current model of economic development. This model should not ignore the great benefits that forest coverages offer, regardless of their category, since their disappearance and degradation aggravate the problems caused by climate change.

The hydrology, meteorology and environment national agency (Instituto de Hidrología, Meteorología y Estudios Ambientales (IDEAM)) is the Colombian entity responsible of providing environmental knowledge and information to the Environment Ministry (Ministerio de Ambiente (MADS)) and other governmental agencies in the national environment system (Sistema Nacional Ambiental (SINA)). From 2009, the implementation of the national monitoring system of forests and future potential forestlands, lead to the development of several information systems to adequately monitor forestry. Under this initiative, with the support of MADS and the Gordon and Betty Moore foundation, IDEAM developed a protocol for monitoring deforestation based on the processing of satellite imagery from remote sensors that allows IDEAM to quantify de deforestation in Colombia, and to determine the dynamics involved on earth cover changes [3, 8].

Following the paradigm of multidimensional views of information provided by OLAP cubes [6], SOLAP cubes (Spatial On Line Analytical Processing) [17] include within its dimensions and measures spatial concepts, allowing the analysts to explore data using cartographic visualization tools. In SOLAP cubes the concepts may have a spatial geometry associated, extending the functionality of the OLAP cubes. SOLAP cubes have measures to generate aggregations using the spatial geometry of concepts, and managing notions such as adjacency between regions, intersection and union of geometric entities.

The remote sensing imagery data cubes are the result of applying the SOLAP cubes concepts to remote sensor information. Hence, remote sensing images within data cubes constitute a set of raster images describing a two-dimensional area, but adding also the spectral and temporal dimensions. The adoption of the term data cube is appropriate because the different raster images cover a single geographical area over time.

The purpose of these cubes is to unify, through a single interface, the query and manipulation of remote sensing data in order to facilitate their analysis. These tools, although not using the classic approach of data management technologies, allow the efficient organization of information and facilitate the generation of remote sensing analysis products.

The goal of this article is to present the architecture defined for implementing the Colombian protocol for processing satellite images to analyze deforestation [8] using a SOLAP Data Cube. We first introduce in Sect. 2 the benefits of applying this technology for satellite image processing and the different alternatives currently available; and then we present in Sect. 3 the process followed to adapt the Australian existing solution to the Colombian context. Sections 4 and 5 present the implementation and its results. Section 6 concludes and highlights some future works.

2   Towards the Effective Use of Satellite Imagery for Environmental Applications

2.1   General Context for Remote Sensing Imagery Applications

The process for remote sensing imagery analysis implemented by IDEAM follows the stages defined in [4, 14] which are summarized in the following phases: (1) Downloading scenes: Analysts download the scenes of the land area and period object of the analysis. (2) Pre-processing: Where downloaded scenes are prepared to guarantee standardization and future comparability. (3) Processing: Processing is a two phase stage: First automatic processes generate intermediate compounds, which summarizes each valid pixel present in the downloaded images as a single reflectance value that characterizes the pixel for the period of the analysis, and then automatic detection algorithms are executed taking the compounds as inputs, giving as a result the detection of forest. (4) Adjustments and quality control: Field experts analyze these results looking for incongruences and errors. Finally, these results serve to make classification or comparisons among different periods.

This process, although useful and with relevant results, has different bottlenecks. In order to generate a report of annual deforestation, each analyst has to download many scenes and process them individually. For instance, the Landsat 7 [18] has a temporal resolution of 16 days and 64 scenes cover the continental national territory, which totals 1460 scenes per year. Since each satellite image size is approximately 535 MB, to create a coverage report for a year it is necessary to analyze approximately 781 GB of information. On the other hand, the current restrictions in infrastructure, mainly in terms of the availability of storage capacity and computational analysis tools, oblige to download and process each image individually, in desktop computers (usually one scene at a time). This implies that the analyst must repeat the same process for each image separately.

In addition to these problems, also because of storage problems, analysts must discard the intermediate results, making difficult and even impossible to replicate the process to generate the final product. Finally, due to the process complexity, data analysis services to publish results in real time is not feasible on the current infrastructure.

Another issue of dealing with remote sensing imagery is the continuous commissioning of new satellites. As new satellites appear, they increment the spectral, spatial and temporal resolutions of the images. For example, with the update from Landsat 5 to Landsat 8, the volume of daily data increased by 881%; a day of transmission of Landsat 5 takes 28.02 GB, in Landsat 8 a day of transmission occupies 247.1 GB, resulting in an annual increase from 9.9 TB to 47.33 TB [15].

In order to solve these issues, it is necessary to improve the infrastructure and build information tools able to: (1) allow the storage and management of historical collections of information coming from different sources of remote sensor imagery. (2) Handle collections of imagery whose size ranges from Terabytes to Petabytes. (3) Offer the support to create analysis products for critical processes and even the capability to generate real time reports, generating early alerts of deforestation in the country, as well as the study of dynamics of vegetal coverage.

Aware of this problem, the IDEAM acquired in 2014 a high performance computational infrastructure designed to comply with the parallelization and virtualization of processes in a scalable way. The objective is to exploit this infrastructure to support the processes of analysis of remote sensing information, not only for the purpose of deforestation analysis, but also for other purposes for which the remote sensors imagery has proven to be useful, for example to monitor changes in coverage of Earth, ecosystems, floods, weather, agriculture, among others [2, 10, 19]. Particularly for the Colombian governmental agencies, the main concerns are the system for early alerts and the system for monitoring and tracing environmental behavior [5].

By creating these tools, there should be many competitive advantages for the institutions participating in the environmental national system: (1) a coordinated management of natural resources: behavior and evolution of strategical ecosystems, forest monitoring, drainage monitoring, greenhouse effect monitoring and coastal zone monitoring. (2) Productive systems monitoring. (3) Public health and management of high-risk phenomena such as earthquakes, fires, floods and draughts.

From the information management point of view, one approach to solve these issues is the construction of an imagery data cube (explained in detail in the next section). A data cube allows not only the handling of large volumes of information from various sources, but also prevents the replication of processes and enables the implementation of specific applications that could be programmed within its structure. With the development of one of such data cubes, the idea is to promote that the various environmental entities in Colombia focus their efforts in the development of tools satisfying their specific analysis needs, instead of separate and uncoordinated processes for acquisition, preprocessing and analysis of imagery data. The data cube should stablish the technical foundations to define national projects on remote sensing imagery, leading to significant cost savings to any study requiring the observation of territorial conditions.

2.2 State of the Art

To exploit the data cube, users must create their own applications, in Python or Javascript, using a web IDE. Using the available API, users can create scripts to transform data from remote sensors, calculating the value of each pixel in the result image. The information comes from the available images collections or from pre-calculated products from these collections.

To the current authors' knowledge, there are two proposals with enough state of maturity: The Google Earth Engine and the Australian Data Science Cube (AGDC).

Google Earth Engine [9] is a computational platform for the analysis of satellite information. This platform has access to various sources of data updated automatically including the collection of Landsat imagery, and partial collections of the Sentinel and Modis projects. In addition, users are able to import their own customized images.

Australian Geoscience Data Cube - AGDC-v1
The first version of the Australian Geoscience Data Cube, available at https:// github.com/GeoscienceAustralia/agdchad had as its main objective the organization of the historical archive of Australian LANDSAT imagery for convenient storage,

processing and analysis, in order to facilitate the generation of new information from these products. This first version organizes within the cube structure more than 27 years of LANDSAT scenes. In this version, it is possible, by means of Python algorithms, to generate new compounds of processed images according to specific parameters [13].

The data cube has two main functions: the ingestion of LANDSAT scenes and the generation of analysis mosaics from these scenes.

The ingestion process divides each LANDSAT scene in tiles, being a tile a file associated with a pre-defined one degree by one degree (4000 × 4000 pixels) area and stored in GEOTIFF format. The ingestion process also indexes the images within a (PostGIS) relational database to help the data cube to determine which tiles access to answer the user queries. For the AGDC-v1, the preprocessing is specific for Australian needs and policies and it is not available in the code repository.

The mosaic generation takes the result of the user query as input. The user specifies the bands, the area, the period of time and the analysis algorithm to apply. The query is executed in two steps: the first one identifies which files are needed; once identified, the analysis algorithm is executed in parallel for each tile over the high performance computing infrastructure of the NCI (National Computational Infrastructure) generating a compound for each tile. The final mosaic results from the union of partial results of involved compounds.

Australian Geoscience Data Cube - AGDC-v2
The approach for the second implementation of the AGDC aims to mitigate the shortcomings of the management of multidimensional information present in the AGDC-v1 and to offer a modular global architecture [13]. The code for this version is available at https://github.com/data-cube/agdc-v2. At the time of this writing, it is important to clarify that this version is still a prototype aimed to demonstrate the use of a platform for large-scale multidimensional data but it is not ready to use.

The main improvement from v1 to v2 is the use of NetCDF files (Network Common Data Form), instead of GEOTIFF files to store the tiles. This format allows the storage of multiple tiles for a given time period in a single file. This improves the cube performance since queries are usually for contiguous time series over a given zone and it reduces the number of files to access in order to answer a query. This file format also allows a fast indexing of information, which is also an improvement over the previous GEOTIFF format that requires a sequential access. Another improvement is the support for metadata, which allows the tracing of the origin and the algorithms applied to each product.

Other important development on this version is the conceptualization of a general architecture to respond to requirements of large-scale remote sensing and the possibility to manage and integrate different types of remote sensors images in the analysis and generation of information products. The definition of a logical unit of storage (storage unit) for each type of product and component (Data Management and Access Module) allows the abstraction, to the same multidimensional representation, of image images of a zone, regardless of the sensor used to capture the images. A disadvantage of this approach is a greater complexity in the storage management component and that there must be a particular ingestion procedure for each of the possible storage units under consideration.

NASA Geoscience Data Cube

This version, shown in Fig. 1 is a branch of the Australian AGDC-v1 presented before-hand, with some differences:

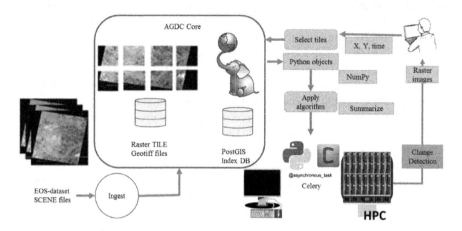

Fig. 1. NGDC architecture

The data cube allows the direct ingestion of surface reflectance LANDSAT products, contrary to the v1 version that only allowed the ingestion of Australian-style prepro-cessed images. The parallelization strategy changed: instead of executing its tasks in the NCI Infrastructure, this version uses the Celery framework, a Python platform for job execution. The configuration consists of execution nodes (usually one per processor available in the execution platform), each one with its respective task queue. Finally, Celery is highly flexible in its configuration, and it can run in high-performance computing infrastructures, or even in a desktop machine if necessary.

The work unit for this version is a tile. When two or more tiles intersect the area under study, the cube identifies them and sends each one to different execution nodes; each node executes the desired analysis algorithm and stores the result in a centralized file system; once all nodes are finished, the complete analysis for the chosen zone is the mosaic of each tile result.

The current scope of existing data cube versions (AGDC v1, v2 and NGDC), although very powerful and useful, solve only the problem of storage of scenes and their access, leaving to the analyst their preprocessing and further analysis. The analyst solves these problems by programming algorithms in Python and accessing the data via the API provided by the data cubes.

The Colombian data cube (CDCol) aims to cover the whole life cycle of imagery analysis process, as shown in following sections.

3   The Proposed Solution: CDCOL

CDCol, the Colombian Data Cube is the proposal to effectively support the generation of analysis products from remote sensor information for the purposes identified in

Sect. 1. Its requirements come from the analysis of needs of information and analysis from various disciplines and institutions participating in the national environmental system (SINA), gathered in various inter-agency workshops [5], following the general structure of remote sensor data analysis defined by [4, 14]. CDCol must support the following tasks:

1. Automatic download of satellite images
2. Image pre-processing that includes the geometric, radiometric and atmospheric correction of images
3. Data transformation, that includes clouds masking, the selection, combination and transformation for bands and the merging of data with other sources
4. Analysis, including operations like classification and comparison.

These phases are compatible with the Protocol established for deforestation monitoring and quantification in Colombia [14].

3.1   General View

The Fig. 2 shows the general process of activities that CDCol must support, including those allowed once the information is properly stored in the cube.

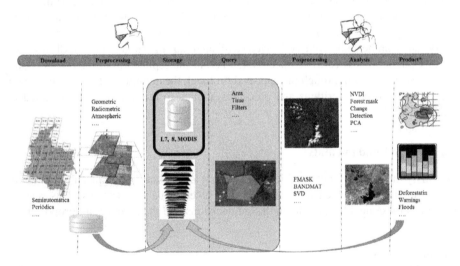

Fig. 2. CDCol general view and scope

It is important to clarify that the parameters to perform a given analysis, like the selection of area of interest and the preprocessing and analysis steps, must be specified by an expert user, who may vary the algorithm parameters and must verify their validity when each step ends. This is why it is important for the cube to provide two operation modes, one interactive and other for production. In the interactive mode, the analyst can select the area of interest and execute step by step the algorithms being part of the process, in order to validate and tune the parameters for all the algorithms involved. The production mode, aims the execution of the algorithms over the whole country. This later mode guarantees that the resulting product is uniform and standard over the whole country.

This means that CDCol must include some fundamental aspects: (1) A powerful, simple and uniform user interface addressing the whole analysis process. (2) Management of other information repositories for data and products not covered by the existing data cubes, like raw images, preprocessed scenes in various states, intermediate outcomes (e.g. median compounds for a year) and final outcomes (e.g. forest coverage mask). (3) Management of an algorithm repository, from where the user may choose the desired analysis to perform. These algorithms could include final products analysis as well as research processes. (4) Management of a workflows repository for products with complex generation processes. (5) Management of users and roles, to control the access to data and functions provided by CDCol.

CDCol addresses three user roles: the analyst who executes processes in the interactive mode, the workflows administrator who configures the workflows for the large-scale analysis using some official parameters, and the developer who is able to create, edit and delete algorithms that are part of the algorithms repository.

Having this characteristics, at the strategic level, CDCol aims to (1) Facilitate the production of information products, as well as the research activities based on the information contained in CDCol, (2) Promote the standardization of data, algorithms and processes by defining an approval protocol. Not approved (not-official) data, algorithms and workflows reflect the research activities in CDCol and are accessible only to the analysts/researchers involved. Approved (Official) data, algorithms and workflows have already public or less restricted access. (3) Avoid the replication of data, results and processes, guaranteed through the approval protocol, the definition of storage units and the trace of all the algorithms and processes applied to the information contained in CDCol.

3.2   Design Fundamentals

To satisfy the desired functionalities of CDCol, it is necessary to define a powerful and robust architecture, which must also support several quality attributes. This section illustrates these qualities, the main design decisions and the architecture proposed for CDCol.

Quality attributes
The quality attributes proposed for CDCol are:

Usability: This attribute aims the ease of user interaction with CDCol. The metrics for this attribute include the time taken by the user to develop a task, the duration of the learning curve and the user satisfaction, among others.

Performance: Due to the large volumes of information involved in CDCol, it is important to guarantee the performance of CDCol in processing tasks. Some metrics for performance are the number of geographic queries per second or the maximum size for the multidimensional array that CDCol can manage. On the other hand, the CDCol architecture must guarantee that the performance scales satisfactorily as the volume of information to be processed increases.

Flexibility and maintainability: To guarantee the ease of change and evolution, CDCol should be concerned by three issues: (1) because of the volume and diversity of analysis that CDCol should address, there will be a separation between the application layer and the services layer. (2) Because of the multiple uses of imagery information, CDCol should include all the bands of all the scenes ingested. Even if the current analysis for forest coverage monitoring does not require all of them, they could be necessary for other analysis. (3) since CDCol must support the addition of new imagery sources and the development of new analysis, it is necessary to separate the component dealing with the logic of persistence and the component dealing with the logic of the application.

Design decisions

The main design decision, with their justification are:

- CDCol architecture should comply with the AGDC-v2 architecture, because it addresses the same quality attributes aimed by CDCol, not considered in the first version (AGDC-v1 nor NGDC-v1.5).
- The images to ingest in CDCol should only have the standard preprocessing (L1T) without masking, to avoid placing limits on the quality or quantity of potential analysis over this data. While forest-monitoring analysis requires the masking of clouds and even the masking of water, other analysis may not require them. Even more, masking processes could be further improved as the spectral and spatial resolution of satellite imagery increases.
- Data storage should be distributed (e.g. distributed file system), because in this way it is possible to scale horizontally, improving the effective use of available storage, facilitating the parallel execution of tasks, allowing the data to be near to processors and then the network traffic could be minimized.
- CDCol must manage the lineage of all data contained in CDCol. Every scene, tile and product generated with CDCol should have the record of all process and analysis leading to it. This lineage assures the confidence in the generated processes, promotes the standardization of process and products and facilitates the eventual improvements of these process and products.

3.3 Proposed Architecture

According to the functional requirements, the quality attributes and the design decisions above, Fig. 3 shows the global architecture for CDCol.

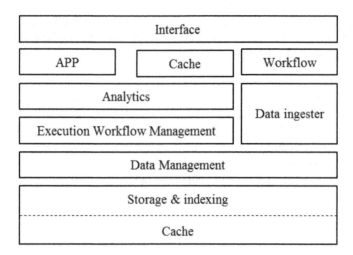

Fig. 3. CDCol global architecture

Components view

The Fig. 4 shows the components in CDCol and their relationships. Their responsibilities are as follows:

The interface is responsible for the user interaction. This includes the user administration (create, edit, authenticate, authorize), should allow a user to work interactively, to define and edit workflows, to create new algorithms and applications, to monitor the execution of current jobs and, finally, to download the results issues from these executions.

The Workflow Manager is responsible for the creation, edition, running and deletion of workflows, as well as their persistence and version management. A workflow defines an ordered execution of existing applications and services offered by the Analytics and Data Ingester components. This component also manages the concept of official workflows, used to generate official products and non-official workflows, used for research activities.

The Application Manager manages the applications using services offered by the Analytics component. Applications may be created, listed, ran, edited and deleted. This component manages also the storage and versioning of the applications. The applications defined at this level address any of the stages of analysis life cycle, taking their input from specific storage units and leaving the results on another specific storage unit. This component also manages the concept of official applications, used to generate official products and non-official applications, used for research activities.

The Application Cache allows the temporal storage of intermediate or final results of applications, in order to make them available for other applications, aiming to avoid unnecessary execution of the same applications over the same data. It also to store the results being download by users. The lifetime of these temporary files should be configurable in the system.

The Analytics component is responsible for defining and exposing analysis services useful for applications. This component provides a level of additional abstraction to the

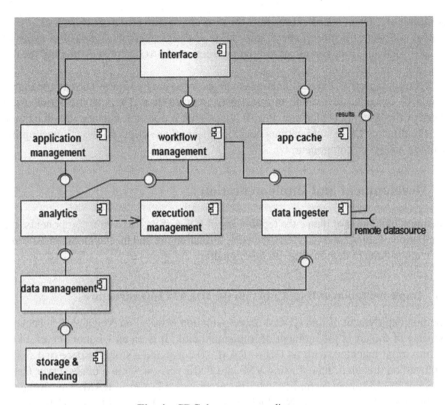

Fig. 4. CDCol components diagram

queries about data in the cube and unifies the operations that are common to several applications. The definition of these services should be independent of the implemented parallelization strategy.

The Execution Manager is responsible for the execution of processes on CDCol. It implements the parallelization strategy and allows the execution and the monitoring of processes.

The Data Ingester transforms the satellite scenes in tiles for their further analysis. It has the appropriate algorithms to deal with the different sources of remote sensing data and transform them in the standard structure of tiles.

The Data Manager allows the query of data stored on different storage units within CDCol, leaving as standard result for a query a multidimensional array. It is also responsible of take the results from an application and store them in the appropriate storage unit.

The Storage and indexing component is responsible for managing the data persistence and ensure the durability of the information in the system. It includes the management of indexes, the management of storage units and the management of distribution and replication as needed.

Mapping of CDCol architecture and the current architecture of AGDC-v2

CDCol constitutes a more general approach, since it covers the whole life cycle of imagery analysis from download to final product, while AGDC-v2 covers only the tile generation and tile query stages.

In this perspective, the modifications to propose to AGDC-v2 are: The Data Manager should be extended to include raw and preprocessed data. The analytics component overlaps the Execution Manager and Analytics, but it does not manage parallelization yet. Finally, in CDCol, applications developed as python scripts allows a low coupling with the Analytics component.

4 Development and Implementation

The implementation of data cube technology at IDEAM has two main components: the installation of software on the IDEAM HPC infrastructure and the development of some basic algorithms to demonstrate its functionality.

4.1 Implementation of Data Cubes on the IDEAM Infrastructure

The first deployment of first CDCol implementation is based on NGDC-V1.5, because the state of the art in the moment of implementation. It is on an Ubuntu Server 14.04 64-bit virtual machine, with 64 GB of RAM, 20 cores and a storage space of 1.5 TB, deployed on the environment using VMware ESXi version 5.5 in a blade server Cisco UCSB-B200-M3, Intel Xeon E5-2680 processor, and 128 GB of RAM. The storage is provisioning on VNX5500 SAN, which has access to its LUNs via fiber optics to a speed of 8 Gbps.

4.2 Algorithms Developed

To validate the implementation and test de capabilities of CDCol, several algorithms were developed, which are briefly explained below:

Best Pixel: Finds the last pixel in the time series which is not classified as NON DATA.

Median pixels composite image generation: This algorithm generates a composite image using the mean normalized reflectance value, for each pixel, from a sequence of images in a time range. The resulting images represent the status of the area in the given time range.

Forest/non forest mask: This algorithm generates a thematic classification for raster image, classifying each pixel as forest, non-forest, and no data.

The process followed by the algorithm is: Medians composite and no-data mask generation, calculate NDVI (Normalized Difference Vegetation Index) for all pixels, apply convolution matrix (box blur) with a user-defined threshold to generate the thematic raster.

Change detection (PCA): Change detection algorithm allows user to identify interest areas for analysis. This algorithm generates two temporal composited images, normalizes theirs values, generates a matrix were each row represent one pixel with the values of the interest bands for the two periods being compared, and performs a principal component analysis (PCA) to generate a new multiband image (one band for each principal component). Some bands of the PCA image represent the changes between the analyzed periods.

5   Results

CDCol was successfully deployed at IDEAM infrastructure and algorithms was validated by domain experts comparing the cube results with existent studies, which used themselves camp data and the expert knowledge about regions studied.

The ingestion process was validated using surface reflectance corrected images downloaded from USGS. The list of available images data was verified to validate the process.

Medians composite image generation was tested using one-year images for areas of 1 and 2 square degrees. Experts from IDEAM validated the results. In some areas, the experts identified quality problems, but dues to the source images.

The results for the change detection algorithm were validated for domain experts. Median composite images were generated for two periods and were compared with the

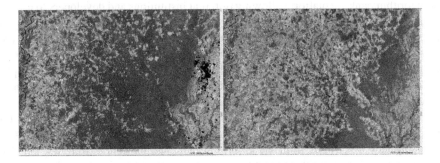

Fig. 5. Medium band 2002 with and Medium band year 2014 with 453 false-color display

Fig. 6. PCA with visualization of components using false color 537

change detection results. Figure 5 shows medians composites for years 2002 and 2014 and Fig. 6 shows the results of change algorithm between these periods.

In terms of performance, Table 1 shows the estimated time (in hours) to execute the algorithms above for one year of data for all Colombian territory (131 tiles), using one or several processors. These measures are based on their execution over one tile using one processor.

Table 1. Estimated performance to process the 131 tiles of Colombian territory (hrs)

# Processors	Best pixel	Medians	NDVI	PCA
1	5.68	14.2	14.2	56.77
5	1.17	2.93	4.68	11.7
10	0.61	1.52	2.43	6.07
20	0.31	0.76	1.22	3.04

6   Current Improvements and Further Developments

The work presented in this paper is just the beginning of a comprehensive project that must include the whole National Environmental System. In the meantime, there were some important improvements, documented in [1]. These improvements include (1) the adoption of version 2 of datacube for CDCol, the corresponding migration of the algorithms and the development of new algorithms of interest. (2) The implementation of an "algorithm bank", a platform allowing different institutions and developers to create, test and share algorithms making use of the capabilities of the datacube. We envisage a system where algorithms are ranked by their results and users can easily choose the algorithm and version they would want to apply. In this way, it is possible to generate new products with their proper lineage. (3) The design and development of a web application to facilitate the access and use of CDCol to the whole environmental community of Colombia, and also to the general public.

Further developments include, among others, (1) the design and development of a workflow manager where algorithms can be assembled to automatize processes, producing new algorithms from the algorithm bank and existent workflows. (2) The development of new algorithms to take into account national environmental particularities. (3) The improvement of performance of version 2 of datacube by defining a strategy of horizontal scalability.

References

1. Ariza-Porras, C., et al.: CDCol: a geoscience data cube that meets Colombian needs. In: Solano, A., Ordoñez, H. (eds.) CCC 2017, CCIS, vol. 735, pp. 87–99, Springer, Cham (2017)
2. Bolton, D.K.: Characterizing residual structure and forest recovery following high-severity fire in the western boreal of Canada using landsat time-series and airborne lidar data. Remote Sens. of Environ. **163**, 48–60 (2015). doi:10.1016/j.rse.2015.03.004

3. Cabrera, E.V.: Protocolo de procesamiento digital de imágenes para la cuantificación de la deforestación en Colombia, Nivel Subnacional Escala gruesa y fina. IDEAM, Bogota, D.C. (2011)
4. Campbell, J.B.: Introduction to Remote Sensing. CRC Press, Boca Raton (2002)
5. CDCol.: Memorias II Taller Inter institucional del Cubo de Datos de Colombia, Bogotá (2015)
6. Colliat, G.: OLAP, relational, and multidimensional database systems. ACM Sigmod Rec. **25**(3), 64–69 (1996)
7. Feddema, J.J.: The importance of land-cover change in simulating future climates. Science **310**, 5754 (2005)
8. Galindo, G.E.: Protocolo de procesamiento digital de imágenes para la cuantificación de la deforestación en Colombia. V 2.0. IDEAM, Bogota (2014)
9. Google Earth Engine Team: Google Earth Engine: A planetary-scale geospatial analysis platform (2015). https://earthengine.google.com
10. Guo, H.W.: Building up national Earth observing system in China. Int. J. Appl. Earth Obs. Geoinf. **6**, 167–176 (2005). doi:10.1016/j.jag.2004.10.007
11. IDEAM, IAvH, Invemar, SINCHI e IIAP: Estado de la Biodiversidad, de los ecosistemas continentales, marinos, costeros y avances en el conocimiento. Informe del Estado del Medio Ambiente y los Recursos Naturales Renovables (Vol. Tomo 2), Bogotá, D.C (2011)
12. Innes, J.L.: Forests in environmental protection. In: John, A.H., Owens, N. (eds.) Forests and Forest Plants in Encyclopedia of Life Support Systems (EOLSS). Eolss Publishers, Oxford, UK (2004)
13. Ip, A.: Generalized Data Framework Solution Architecture (Draft). Australian Goverment - Geoscience Australia (2015)
14. Khorram, S.N.: Remote Sensing. Springer, US, Boston, MA (2012)
15. Ma, Y.W.: Towards building a data-intensive index for big data computing – A case study of remote sensing data processing. Inf. Sci. **319**, 171–188 (2015). doi:10.1016/j.ins.2014.10.006
16. Andina, O.N.F.: Agosto - Septiembre, p. 15. Bosques y Cambio Climático -, Boletín Técnico N (2014)
17. Rivest, S.E.: SOLAP technology: Merging business intelligence with geospatial technology for interactive spatio-temporal exploration and analysis of data. ISPRS J. Photogramm. Remote sens. **60**(1), 17–33 (2005)
18. U.S. Geological Survey: Landsat 7 science data users handbook (1998)
19. UNESCO: Application of satellite remote sensing to support water resources management in Africa: Results from the TIGER initiative. technical documents in hydrology, 85 (2010)

FINFLEX-CM: A Conceptual Model
for Financial Analysis of Solution Architectures
Considering the Uncertainty and Flexibility

Yeimi Pena[1(✉)], Eduardo Miranda[2], and Dario Correal[3]

[1] Software Engineering Department, Universidad de Los Andes, Bogota, Colombia
yy.pena29@uniandes.edu.co
[2] Software Engineering Masters Program,
Carnegie Mellon University Pittsburgh, Pittsburgh, PA, USA
mirandae@andrew.cmu.edu
[3] Software Engineering Department, Universidad de Los Andes, Bogota, Colombia
dcorreal@uniandes.edu.co

Abstract. Financial analysis of solution architectures is essential to determine their profitability and justify their implementation. These financial analyses are supported on variables such as costs and benefits which should be standardized, clear and consistent to understand the objectives of the financial analysis, the relationship between the variables and the components of the solution architecture, and the financial indicators obtained once the financial analysis is performed. To do that, the financial analysis of solution architecture should be supported in a conceptual model that contains the concepts, relationships and explanations that support a financial analysis. However, the current models are focused on the structure of solution architectures and they are limited with respect to their financial concepts. As a result, the understanding and identification of those concepts are usually done informally, turning this process into a complicated and an error-prone task. The article presents a theoretical conceptual model, called FINFLEX-CM, that formalizes the concepts and supports the financial analysis of solution architectures, increasing understanding and promoting the standardization.

Keywords: Solution architecture · Financial analysis · Conceptual model · Design science · Uncertainty · Flexibility

1 Introduction

In recent years, organizations have increased their budget addressed to technology solutions to be competitive in the industry and respond to new technology tendencies. To guarantee the proper use of their budget, companies require having certain about technology investments and consequently achieve their business goals. Commonly, these technology investments are supported on solution architectures [6,14] that respond to enterprise architecture initiatives, business and

© Springer International Publishing AG 2017
A. Solano and H. Ordoñez (Eds.): CCC 2017, CCIS 735, pp. 242–256, 2017.
DOI: 10.1007/978-3-319-66562-7_18

operational requirements [6]. To justify the implementation of a solution architecture, technology teams have to calculate its profitability based on financial analysis [6]. In addition technology teams should consider unpredictable events (e.g., expansion of emerging markets and restructuring of business, changes on requirements, change of technologies) that can impact positively or negatively a solution [16]. These unpredictable events derive both (1) uncertainties that impact financial analysis, and (2) the need for flexibility to maintain the possibility of changing decisions over the time [7,16]. Architectural models constitute an important approach to supporting the purpose of making the complexity of the real world understandable to humans. In the case of the solution architecture field, there are several architecture models to analyze the structure of solution architectures [4,5,14]. However, the current models rarely explicitly state about financial variables, economic factors, uncertainty and flexibility concepts required on financial analyses of solution architectures [6,10]. We identified the need of standardizing and identifying the specific concepts about financial analysis related to solution and enterprise architectures in the systematic review that we performed [10]. In addition, the solution architects can face to questions such as: Are the costs defined in the documents enough for the financial analysis? How do components support the realization of the benefits? Which are the uncertainties associated with the solution? Consequently, financial analyses could be expressed in unclear and ambiguous concepts impacting the decision-making process of technology investments.

To address the previous issues, we designed FINFLEX-CM that consists of a set of standard concepts, which support the financial analysis of solution architectures considering the uncertainty and flexibility. To define FINFLEX-CM, we adopted the Design Science Research Methodology (DSR) [9]. DSR aims to build and evaluate artefacts to overcome the identified business needs [9]. This study design is valuable for multiple reasons: first, conceptual models are valid DSR artefacts [12,13]; second, there exists a body of knowledge on conceptual models addressed to solution architectures, which was used for defining our model [2,4,5,14]; third, we designed FINFLEX-CM using the methodology purposed by Lagerström et al. [5]; fourth, these kind of models have a essential contribution to solution architecture area because they standardize the concepts required to perform financial analyses and can be used to support the execution these analyses.

Following the DSR methodology [9] and the evaluation patterns in DSR purposed by Sonnenberg and J. Brocke [12], this study covers the identification of the research problem, objectives of a solution, and design of FINFLEX-CM. In Sect. 2, we define fundamental concepts used in this paper. In Sect. 3, we present a brief literature review and identify the problem and objectives. In Sect. 4, we describe the research method. Then, in Sect. 5 we introduce the design of FINFLEX-CM. We conclude, Sect. 6, describing the contributions, limitations, and future research.

2 Background About Solution Architectures, Financial Analysis, and Conceptual Models

Solution architecture seeks to plan, build and manage a particular solution to respond to business requirements, enterprise architecture initiatives, technology innovation needs, or operation requirements [6]. The definition of a solution architecture is supported in a process [6] that commonly starts with the analysis of requirements by an interdisciplinary team. The process is supported by the definitions of government institutions and practitioners [6]

Commonly, the process starts with the analysis of requirements by an interdisciplinary team. This analysis includes the analysis of the current (it includes current requirements, current technology components, stakeholders, business processes, constraints, principles, and methodologies) and objective (it includes required technology components, updates, integrations, and interfaces) situations [6]. The team designs solution architecture alternatives that represent different options to respond to the needs identified on the requirement analysis and close the gap between the current and objective situations. Then, the team defines for each alternative a set of solution components. A solution component represents a technology solution that can represent, for example, information systems, enterprise systems, data solutions, and infrastructure solutions [6].

Following the process, the team analyzes each alternative from financial and technological perspectives [6]. To perform financial analysis, it is necessary to identify, classify and analyze costs and benefits, as well as to determine the economic factors [1]. Then, the interdisciplinary team performs some financial analyses [1] to calculate the profitability of each alternative. Finally, the team, supported by the results of financial and technological analyses, selects one alternative that the company will implement.

Due to unpredictable events (e.g. expansion of emerging markets, change of technologies or new innovative solutions) the decisions can change during the solution implementation activity [16]. These events derive uncertainties that may impact decisions producing positive or adverse consequences for a company [7]. To manage the uncertainty is required to consider the flexibility to change the decisions over the time [7].

Solution architectures have two important relationships. The first relationship is between enterprise architecture (EA) and solution architecture, which is essential to support the implementation of enterprise architecture initiatives [16] and ensure the alignment of the solutions whit the EA principles [14]. The second relationship is between projects and solution architectures [7], which represents a way to fulfil the business goals through the solution architecture implementation.

Considering our theoretical model, we consider important to explain the definitions of model and conceptual model. A model is a schematic description of a theory [13] that is employed to represent a usage scenario for an explicit purpose [13]. A conceptual model enhances models with standard concepts that are commonly shared within a community in a given usage scenario to have a common understanding about a theory [2,13,14].

3   Literature Review

In this section, we describe a brief literature review of the identified models and we analyzed their scope regarding financial concepts.

The ISO/IEC/IEEE 42010 meta-model [4] captures concepts mainly relate to the technological viewpoint and architectural decisions. Some of those decisions could be related to capital expenditures, indirect costs or benefits [4]. Although some financial concepts are considered in the meta-model, they are not explicit neither complete for a financial analysis of a solution that requires the costs and benefits for technology components, economic factors, and uncertainty and flexibility variables. On the other hand, TOGAF Metamodel [14] consist of different concepts to describe architecture domains (business, data, application and technology) and the relationships between them. TOGAF has a modeling language, named Archimate [15], for describing EA components as well as solution architecture components. Although TOGAF metamodel and Archimate have been recognized for its support of EA design, it does not include specific financial concepts to support the analysis of solution architectures.

Lagerström [5] proposed a meta-model to analyze issues about system modifiability, which considers the management of costs and risks. The meta-model consists of concepts to model and estimate the costs of a software project [5]. Although this approach models the cost, it is expressly addressed to change management, and it does not consider other relevant variables for financial analysis such as benefits, uncertainty, flexibility and economic factors. Finally, Iacob et al. [2] proposed an approach to relate enterprise models to business models. This approach was directly focused on IT change processes that impact an organization's EA. The approach aims to support the quantification and justification of value of architectures and cost/benefit analysis for business, considering the costs and benefits at business strategy levels [2]. Although the approach is focused on cost/benefit analysis of EA and it describes an interesting way to relate enterprise models and business models, the approach omits some important concepts required for financial analyses such as uncertainty and flexibility.

Although previous investigations offer significant contributions, there is clear evidence the lack of a specific conceptual model focusing on financial analysis of solution architectures considering the costs, benefits, economic factors, uncertainty, and flexibility. The present paper aims at filling this gap with the definition of FINFLEX-CM addressed to the solution architecture discipline. FINFLEX-CM has the following qualitative attributes, which were selected considering the validation criteria for design specification proposed by Sonnenberg and Brocke [12]: (1) It is complete, FINFLEX-CM has a complete set of financial concepts that support financial analysis of solution architectures; (2) It is clear, FINFLEX-CM offers the definitions of the concepts, attributes, and relationships required to financial analysis of solution architectures. Although other attributes could be taking into account, we consider that selected attributes are sufficient by proving the conceptual model's foundation considering the criteria defined by Sonnenberg and Brocke [12].

We state the problem statement can thus be stated as follows: define a conceptual model such that (1) supports the identification of financial analysis concepts considering the uncertainty and flexibility of a solution architecture, (2) presents the information about the concepts, attributes, and relationships between concepts, (3) supports the identification of the relationships among solution architecture, enterprise architecture and project management, and (4) has the quality attributes listed previously.

4   Research Method for Designing FINFLEX-CM

We follow Sonnenberg and vom Brocke's framework [12] of evaluation activities in DSR (Fig. 1) to demonstrate and design FINFLEX-CM. Considering the progressive identify problem-evaluate-design-evaluate-construct-evaluate pattern, Sonnenberg and vom Brocke's framework [12] comprises four evaluation activities (EVAL1 to EVAL4). This framework considers the evaluations: ex-ante (it is used to evaluate the design of an uninstantiated artefact) [12]) and ex-post (it is used to evaluate an instantiated artefact [12]).

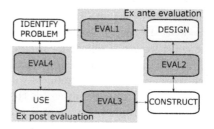

Fig. 1. Evaluation activities within a DSR process [12]

We considered ex-ante evaluation for FINFLEX-CM because it is a theoretical model and uninstantiated artefact. We performed the ex-ante evaluations EVAL1 and EVAL2. EVAL1 was focused on the identification of the problem and objectives of FINFLEX-CM, and EVAL2 was focused on the justification of the design [12].

It is important to explain that FINFLEX-CM is part of an important research that we are performing, which is addressed to the definition of a framework that supports the financial analysis of solution architectures, known as FINFLEX. The FINFLEX-CM concepts are the foundation of the FINFLEX's definitions and components. Therefore, the construction of FINFLEX's components justify the FINFLEX-CM concepts and their relationships.

4.1   Identify Problem and Objectives of FINFLEX-CM

EVAL1 focuses on justifying the research topic and research problem, as well as to support the contribution to the knowledge and demonstrate that the artefact solves the research problem [12]. We complete this activity in the introduction (Sect. 1), background (Sect. 2) and literature review (Sect. 3).

4.2   Design FINFLEX-CM

EVAL2 aims to justify the design of the artefact [12]. The design of FINFLEX-CM is not trivial considering the different concepts and their relationships, as well as the attributes required. Then, to justify the design, we apply the well-established method for creating the qualitative and quantitative parts of a meta-model by Lagerström et al. [5]. This method considers the concepts, attributes, and the relationships between concepts. We specifically followed this method to design the qualitative part of FINFLEX-CM, we do not consider quantitative perspective because FINFLEX-CM is a static model.

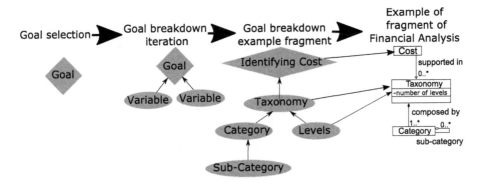

Fig. 2. The iterative process to define the conceptual model (Adapted from [5])

Following the method [5], the first step was to identify the main objective of FINFLEX-CM. In this case, the goal considered was to define a conceptual model to support the financial analysis of solution architectures considering the uncertainty and flexibility. Then, the variables associated with the main objective were identified (e.g. financial analysis, solution architecture, cost, and benefit). Next, we performed this iterative process until the variables have been broken down into the detailed variables required in financial analyses; the process to identified the variables was supported on the literature review and the needs of solution architectures.

The variables were translated to conceptual model classes, attributes, and fragments as Fig. 2 shows. The variables are directly related to the attributes, and the fragments represent a set of classes in the conceptual model that respond to the goal [5]. FINFLEX-CM consists of 5 fragments (Enterprise Architecture, Solution Architecture, Financial Analysis, Projects, Uncertainty), together, the fragments constitute the whole conceptual model (Fig. 3). Figure 3 shows FINFLEX-CM in a class diagram of the Unified Modeling Language (UML),

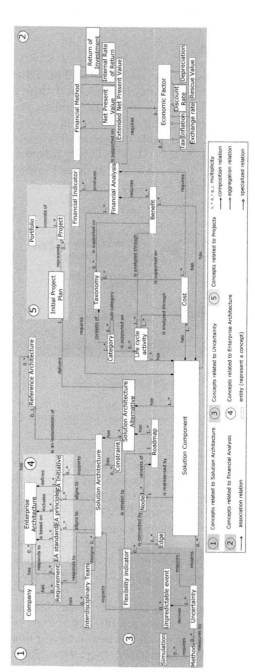

Fig. 3. FINFLEX-CM conceptual model

which symbolizes a concept represented as a class and a relationship through an association. We selected UML to present our model because it is a well-known and standardized modeling language that is widely used in solution architectures. FINFLEX-CM is explained in Sect. 5.

5   FINFLEX-CM: A Conceptual Model for Financial Analysis of Solution Architectures Considering the Uncertainty and Flexibility

This section describes FINFLEX-CM. In Subsect. 5.1, we explain the concepts of each fragment. In Subsect. 5.2, we describe the attributes of the classes related to the fragments 'Financial Analysis', 'Uncertainty' and 'Solution Architecture', which are the core of FINFLEX-CM.

5.1   Classes and Relationships

Concepts Related to Solution Architecture. The first fragment of FINFLEX-CM is associated to solution architecture concepts. *Solution Architecture* responds to a specific *Requirement* or an *EA Initiative* that could be derived from concerns of a *Company* [6]. Commonly, a *Solution Architecture* is an instantiation of a *Reference Architecture* [14], which is represented by a set of models that abstract architectural elements to maintain the standardization and unification of technologies and design/architectural decisions [14]. In the design of solution architecture, an *Interdisciplinary Team* defines *Solution Components* and *Solution Architecture Alternatives*. Each *Solution Architecture Alternative* includes a group of *Solution Components* [6], where a *Solution Component* represents an architectural design of a functionality to solve concerns and requirements [6,14].

In addition to components and alternatives, the interdisciplinary team defines a *Roadmap* that describes how the components will be implemented in a company [6,14]. To define a *Roadmap*, the interdisciplinary team considers a set of *Nodes* and *Edges*, where a *Node* represents a solution component and an *Edge* represents the connection between two nodes. As a result, the *Roadmap* has a set of connected nodes ordered over the time that represent the path to implement the solution components of a solution architecture alternative. During the solution architecture design, it is relevant to analyze the *Constraints* for its implementation. A *Constraint* is an external factor that prevents an organization from pursuing particular approaches to meet its goals.

Regarding the associations, *Solution Architecture* can have zero or more *Constraints* considering the company's environment, technology requirements and quality attributes of a solution. An *Interdisciplinary team* must design at least one *Solution Architecture Alternative*, and the *Alternative* must include at least one *Solution Component*. Finally, to implement a *Solution Architecture Alternative*, it is necessary to have one or more *Roadmaps*, where a *Roadmap* consists of minimum one *Solution Component*.

Concepts Related to Financial Analysis. The second fragment of FINFLEX-CM is associated to concepts of financial analysis. An interdisciplinary team analyzes financially solution architecture alternatives and selects the most convenient alternative for a company. A *Financial Analysis*, in this research, assesses the effectiveness of the budget addressed to an investment as well as the efficiency and profitability of a *Solution Architecture Alternative* [1]. To do that, we define the financial analysis in two levels, which are explained below. The first level represents the financial analysis of each solution component and the second level represents the financial analysis of the solution architecture alternative. We justify our decision supported on: (1) Due to the magnitude of a solution component (e.g., enterprise systems, data solutions, infrastructure solutions, among others), each component can consider different costs, benefits and economic factors. (2) Each component can have different uncertainty levels considering that different unpredictable events can impact each component. For example, a component that represents an ERP can be impacted by unpredictable events related to technology innovation, while a component that represents a data solution can be impacted by unpredictable events related to the changes in the requirements. (3) To perform the financial analysis of a solution architecture alternative, it is necessary to consider its roadmap, which organizes its solution components over the time.

Level 1. A *Financial Analysis* of a solution component receives as input *Costs*, *Benefits*, and *Economic Factors*. A *Cost* represents the purchase or rental price of a service or asset [8]. *Costs* are analyze considering the *Life Cycles Activities* of a solution component [8] to identify the life cycle of costs [8]. A Benefit is a consequence of an action to improve or promote conditions of an organization [7]. Benefits are analyzed considering the Life Cycle Activities of a solution component [8] to identify the life cycle of benefits. According to NATO, *Life Cycle Activities* include concept, development, production, utilization, support, and retirement [8]. *Economic Factors* is a set of factors that affects an investment's value (e.g. taxes). The costs and benefits are classified considering *Taxonomies* [3]. *Taxonomy* comprises a set of categories and sub-categories that classify the elements, which are selected according to each solution [3]. Financial analyses are supported on *Financial Methods* such as cost-benefit analysis [1]. An interdisciplinary team performs *Financial Methods* to obtain *Financial Indicators* [1] considering the identified and classified costs, benefits, and economic factors. *Financial Indicators* represent measures to determine the feasibility of implementing a solution component.

Regarding associations, to perform a *Financial Analysis* is required at least one *Benefit* and at least one *Cost*. Also, *Financial Analysis* could consider some *Economic Factors* considering the kind of analysis [16]. To analyze a *Cost* through the *Life cycle Activities*, a *Solution Component* can have one or more activities associated; these activities can change depend on the solution component's objective. Regarding *Costs* and *Benefits*, they can be identified since the experience of the interdisciplinary team or through a *Taxonomy*. A *Taxonomy* must have at least one category, and each category can have zero or more sub-categories [3]. It is relevant to consider that a Financial Analysis can be supported in one or more *Financial Methods*; for example, some companies prefer to consider multiple financial methods to compare the results and justify an investment [1]. *Solution Component* can have associated one or more Costs (e.g. cost of implementation, analysis, and design) [3], and each *Solution Component* can respond to one or more *Benefits* that are directly related to a *Solution Architecture Alternative*.

Level 2. A *Financial Analysis* of a solution architecture alternative is calculated considering its roadmap. As we explained in the previous section, a roadmap considers a set of nodes and edges, where a node represents a solution component and an edge represent the connection between two nodes. Once, the interdisciplinary team performs the financial analysis for each solution component, the roadmap is defined (the path to implement the solution components over the time), and the financial indicators of the roadmap are calculated (The complete definition of these financial indicators is considered for the future work of these research). These last financial indicators represent the profitability of a solution architecture alternative.

Concepts Related to Uncertainty. The third fragment of FINFLEX-CM is related to concepts of uncertainty. A company can be exposed to several change conditions (e.g. new technology, changes in costs) represented on *Unpredictable Events* [16]. An *Unpredictable Event* derives *Uncertainties* that impact the costs, benefits and economic factors of a solution component [7]. *Uncertainty* is the lack of knowledge of an event due to multiple situations that could impact positively or negatively an investment [3,7]. To manage the *Uncertainty* is required to consider the flexibility to redirect the decisions of a company toward a path to avoid negative consequences and explore new opportunities [7]. Flexibility is represented by a *Flexibility Indicator* that considers the information about the range of change options, the possibility of doing a change, and consequences of a change [7]. According to Neufville [7] and Vélez [16] the uncertainty can be measured through *Methods*. A *Method* calculates the uncertainty indicators of costs, benefits and economic factors considering attributes such as the range of values and the probability distribution (Sect. 5.2). In addition, a *Method* is supported by *Simulations* (e.g. Monte Carlo simulations) that are used to analyze the sensibility of multiple variables.

Regarding associations, an *Unpredictable Event* derives one or more *Uncertainties*, and the *Uncertainty* requires or not *Flexibility Indicators*; it depends on the impact of an unpredictable event and the need to change the solution architecture alternative. The *Uncertainty* can or cannot be measured by *Methods*; it depends on the available information to calculate the uncertainty [7]. *The method* can or not requires *Simulation* to calculate the uncertainty.

Concepts Related to Enterprise Architecture. The fourth fragment of FINFLEX-CM is related to enterprise architecture concepts. *Enterprise Archi-*

tecture (EA) responds to company's *Requirements* and it is regarded as a coherent group of *Principles, Standards*, methods and models [14]. As result of an EA, a company defines *EA initiatives* that support the achievement of business goals [14]. Solution architectures are employed to establish processes, business systems, and technical systems required to materialize the *EA initiatives*, as well as to identify their requirements, design specifications and implementation plans [6]. In addition, solution architecture incorporates *EA standards* and *Principles* to describe its structure, components, interfaces and design definitions. Regarding associations, *Enterprise Architecture* responds at least to one *Requirement* and it is based on at least one *EA standard* [14]. These *EA Standards* normally are supported in EA frameworks and adopted by the companies. An EA can have one or more *EA initiatives* [14].

Concepts Related to Projects. The fifth fragment of FINFLEX-CM is associated to concepts of Projects. Once a solution architecture alternative is selected, an *Initial Project Plan* is delivered by the interdisciplinary team to the project management office (PMO) [6]. An *Initial Project Plan* is a document that justifies a solution architecture project from financial and technology viewpoints [2]. PMO analyzes the *Initial Project Plan* to validate financial indicators and decides if the solution architecture alternative will be implemented as a *Project* of the company's *Portfolio*. A *Project* contemplates planning, scope, budget, schedule, resources, deliveries, risks and financial indicators [11] to create a unique product, service, or result [11]. Although the project management body of knowledge proposes processes, methods, and definitions for defining a project [11], the financial analysis of a solution architecture requires specific elements and definitions such as components, roadmap, uncertainty, and flexibility. *Portfolio* involves projects, programs, sub-portfolios to accomplish strategic objectives [11]. An *Initial Project Plan* can be translated to one or more *Projects* considering the scope of the plan and the PMO criteria. A *Portfolio* requires minimum one *Project* [11].

5.2   Attributes

Attributes of Financial Analysis Classes. The attributes of financial analysis classes are presented in Fig. 4. Financial Analysis includes the 'forecast of costs' $(0,...,\infty)$ and 'forecast of benefits' $(0,...,\infty)$, which are the estimated values of each variable [3]. 'Forecast of each Economic Factor' $(0,...,\infty)$ can be or not explicitly in a financial analysis. Moreover, Financial Analysis is performed in a range of dates, where the 'initial date' is the time zero, and the 'end date' represents the last period of a solution. Financial Analysis can be performed for different 'periods' (monthly, biannual or yearly), which are relevant to maintain the coherence between the rates. Financial Analysis produces financial indicators $(0,...,\infty)$ that are measured by financial methods. Finally, a financial analysis must have 'documentation' to describe the procedure, inputs and outputs of the analysis.

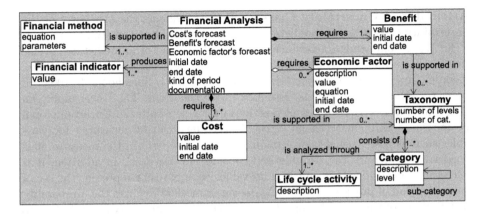

Fig. 4. Financial analysis fragment containing classes and attributes

Cost and Benefit classes have the attribute 'value' $(0,...,\infty)$ that represents the total cost or total benefit, which is calculated considering the cost or benefit of each category of a taxonomy. In addition, Cost and Benefit classes have 'initial date' and 'end date', which represent the periods when the costs and benefits are considered in the financial analysis.

Taxonomy has the attribute 'number of levels' $(0,...,\infty)$ of its categories, and the 'number of categories' $(0,...,\infty)$. The category has the attribute 'description' that includes the objective of a category, and the attribute 'level' $(0,...,\infty)$ that represents the position of a category in a taxonomy. Economic factor has the attributes 'description', 'equation', 'value' $(0,...,\infty)$, 'initial date', and 'end date' [1]. Financial Method has the attributes 'equation' and 'parameters' $(0,...,\infty)$. The values of these attributes depend on the kind of financial method (NPV, ENPV, IRR, or ROI) and the periods of time of a solution. Finally, Financial Indicator has the attribute 'value' that represents the result of the financial analysis performance.

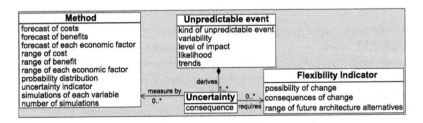

Fig. 5. Uncertainty fragment containing classes and attributes

Attributes of Uncertainty Classes. Figure 5 presents the attributes of the uncertainty classes. An Unpredictable Event must be identified [16], to do that, Vélez [16] recommends to consider the attributes: 'kind of unpredictable event' (economic, technical, regulatory), 'variability' of the event over the time (high, medium, low), 'level of impact' (high, medium, low), 'likelihood' 0,,100% to impact a solution, and 'trends' associated with the event. The Uncertainty can has 'consequences' that represent positive or adverse results [7]. Uncertainty can be measured through Methods [7,16]. Uncertainty can be measured for variables such as costs, benefits or economic factors. To perform the measure, it is necessary to identify the variable and consider its 'forecast'. In addition, it is necessary to consider the 'range' of its values $(0,...,\infty)$ that represent the set of values instead of precise values [7]. Moreover, a method requires the 'probability distribution' of the variable considering a confidence interval (CI) [7]. Before to the simulation, it is necessary to identify the 'number of simulations' $(0,...,\infty)$. As a result of performing a method, a company has a set of 'uncertainty indicators' for each variable. Flexibility Indicator includes the attribute 'consequences of change' to identify the consequences after a change [7]. In addition, Flexibility Indicator has the attributes 'possibility of change' to identify if it is possible to do a modification [7] and 'range of future solution architecture alternatives' that contemplates the possible options to change an alternative.

Attributes of Solution Architecture Classes. Figure 6 presents the attributes of the solution architecture classes; we consider only the attributes related to the financial indicators. Solution component has a set of financial indicators $(0,...,\infty)$ that are calculated by financial methods considering the variables costs, benefits, economic factors, and the uncertainty of these variables. Solution architecture alternative has a set of financial indicators $(0,...,\infty)$ that are calculated considering its roadmaps, so each roadmap can have a set of financial indicators $(0,...,\infty)$ considering its nodes and the probability to select the nodes in each edge (this calculation is part of the future work of this research).

6   Discussion and Future Work

Even if our conceptual model shares some concepts of the reviewed models, FINFLEX-CM offers a new approach to consider the financial concepts of solution architectures. We highlight the importance of the concepts related to the structure of a solution architecture, but supported in our research, we realized the importance to identify in a standard way the financial concepts to support financial analyses and decisions about technology investments. FINFLEX-CM promotes the standardization of the concepts, which favors the communication between the stakeholders and the understanding of the elements that must be considered in a financial analysis. Moreover, FINFLEX-CM can contribute in the accuracy of the financial elements and them relationships through the complete documentation of the concepts. FINFLEX-CM has some advantages such as: (1) The use of fragments supports the identification of external relations among

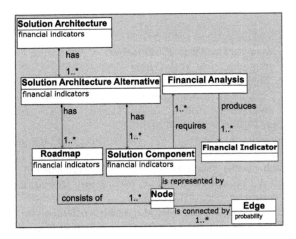

Fig. 6. Solution Architecture fragment containing classes and attributes

solution architectures, enterprise architectures, and projects; (2) FINFLEX-CM provides the concepts to identify the relationships between solution architecture, financial analysis, financial methods, and the inputs required (costs, benefits and economic factors); (3) Uncertainty concepts highlights the importance of unpredictable events that impact solution architectures as well as the flexibility required to change decisions. Considering the previous results, and the complete process to define and design our conceptual model, we consider that FINFLEX-CM is a significant contribution to the research in solution architectures. Although FINFLEX-CM is a complete model, it is necessary to take into account the solution architects judgement to consider all or some of the concepts for the financial analysis of a particular solution architecture. In addition, the financial analysis and financial methods depend on the context of a solution, the unpredictable events can vary in each solution, therefore, the uncertainty and flexibility indicators. The use of FINFLEX-CM should be a cyclical process to identify the specific concepts required.

During this research, we identified the difficulty to validate FINFLEX-CM due to the abstract level of its concepts and relationships. To solve that, we suggest as future work the following options to demonstrate its utility in the industry. First, define a framework supported on the FINFLEX-CM's concepts, which consists of components that cover the required fragments to perform the financial analysis. Second, define a domain specific language based on the FINFLEX-CM's concepts to collect the required information, design a process to identify the implicated actors as well as the activities required for the analysis, and define a component to perform financial methods and calculate the financial indicators integrating the language and process.

References

1. Brealey, R.A., Myers, S.C., Allen, F.: Principles of Corporate Finance, 10th edn. McGraw-Hill Companies, New York (2011)
2. Iacob, M.E., Meertens, L.O., Jonkers, H., Quartel, D.A.C., Nieuwenhuis, L.J.M., Sinderen, M.J.: From enterprise architecture to business models and back. Softw. Syst. Model. **13**(3), 1059–1083 (2014). http://dx.doi.org/10.1007/s10270-012-0304-6
3. Irani, Z., Ghoneim, A., Love, P.E.: Evaluating cost taxonomies for information systems management. Eur. J. Oper. Res. **173**(3), 1103–1122 (2006). http://linkinghub.elsevier.com/retrieve/pii/S0377221705004893
4. ISO/IEC/IEEE: A Conceptual Model of Architecture Description (2013). http://www.iso-architecture.org/ieee-1471/cm/
5. Lagerström, R., Johnson, P., Ekstedt, M.: Architecture analysis of enterprise systems modifiability: a metamodel for software change cost estimation. Softw. Qual. J. **18**(4), 437–468 (2010). http://link.springer.com/10.1007/s11219-010-9100-0
6. NASCIO: NASCIO EA Development Tool-Kit Solution Architecture Version 3.0. Technical report, NASCIO, Missouri, US, October 2004. http://www.nascio.org/portals/0/EAToolKit/NASCIO-AEADTool-Kitv3.pdf
7. Neufville, R.D., Scholtes, S.: Flexibility in Engineering Design. Massachusetts Institute of Technology, London (2011)
8. North Atlantic Treaty Organisation (Nato): Methods and Models for Life Cycle Costing (Méthodes et modèles d ' évaluation du coût de possession). Technical report, North Atlantic Treaty Organisation (Nato), June 2007. www.rto.nato.int
9. Peffers, K., Tuunanen, T., Rothenberger, M.A., Chatterjee, S.: A design science research methodology for information systems research. J. Manag. Inf. Syst. **24**(3), 45–78 (2007). http://dx.doi.org/10.2753/MIS0742-1222240302
10. Pena, Y., Correal, D., Miranda, E.: A review of the current situation, challenges and opportunities in the financial analysis of enterprise architectures. World Revi. Sci. Technol. Sustain. Dev. (WRSTSD) **13**(2), 145–173 (2017). http://dx.doi.org/10.1504/WRSTSD.2017.10004966
11. Project Management Institute: A Guide to the Project Management Body of Knowledge, 5th edn. Project Management Institute Inc., Pennsylvania (2013)
12. Sonnenberg, C., Brocke, J.: Evaluation patterns for design science research artefacts. In: Helfert, M., Donnellan, B. (eds.) EDSS 2011. CCIS, vol. 286, pp. 71–83. Springer, Heidelberg (2012). doi:10.1007/978-3-642-33681-2_7
13. Thalheim, B.: The science and art of conceptual modelling. In: Hameurlain, A., Küng, J., Wagner, R., Liddle, S.W., Schewe, K.-D., Zhou, X. (eds.) Transactions on Large-Scale Data-and Knowledge-Centered Systems VI. LNCS, vol. 7600, pp. 76–105. Springer, Heidelberg (2012). doi:10.1007/978-3-642-34179-3_3
14. The Open Group: TOGAF® Version 9.1. The Open Group, U.S., 9.1 edn. (2011). http://www.opengroup.org/togaf/
15. The Open Group: Archimate 2.1 Specification. Technical report, The Open Group, United Kingdom (2012). http://pubs.opengroup.org/architecture/archimate2-doc/
16. Vélez Pareja, I.: Decisiones bajo incertidumbre. In: Norma, G.E. (ed.) Decisiones Empresariales Bajo Riesgo e Incertidumbre, chap. 3, p. 48. Grupo Editorial Norma, Bogotá (2003). www.norma.com

Low-Cost Fire Alarm System Supported on the Internet of Things

Jorge Aguirre[1], Armando Ordóñez[1(✉)], and Hugo Ordóñez[2]

[1] Intelligent Management Systems Group, Fundación Universitaria de Popayán,
Popayán, Colombia
{jorgeaguirre,jaordonez}@unicauca.edu.co
[2] Research Laboratory in Development of Software Engineering,
Universidad San Buenaventura, Cali, Colombia
haordonez@usbcali.edu.co

Abstract. Most of the cities in Latin American must face the phenomenon of settlements occupied by people displaced by violence or poverty. These communities build their homes in unstable terrains or use inadequate materials (wood, cardboard). In Colombia, these settlements have suffered great tragedies due to uncontrollable wildfires. Traditionally, fire alarm systems are not oriented to solve the problems of marginalized people. This paper describes the design and implementation of a low-cost fire alarm system for two settlements in the Popayán - Colombia. The system uses Internet of things technologies and sends alarms to the fire station.

Keywords: Fire · Early warning IoT · Guidelines · Xbee · ZigBee

1 Introduction

In Latin America, most of the settlements are built in non-recommendable areas, and inadequate materials (wood, cardboard) are used. In Popayán (Colombia), theses settlements are located in areas with several risks (erosion, flood or fire) [1], among these risks, the fires are one of the most frequent. Typically, these fires are caused by candles, oil lamps or unsafe electrical connections [2].

By its part, in the Internet of Things (IoT), people and things (e.g. computers, sensors) are connected gathering and sharing data from the environment. These data from the environment are usually gathered using sensors. [3] Internet of Things may offer low-cost solutions for diverse applications [4] and involves a great variety of technologies (e.g. processors, sensors, communications networks) [5]. Furthermore, a great variety of protocols and providers exist for each IoT technology.

The decisions on the components of a particular IoT solution depend on the domain. Some constraints may low budget, low battery consumption, high security or integration with existing systems. For example, high-security constraints may require advanced encryption algorithms.

The IoT solution here described is focused on a low-cost alarm for settlements. The commune 7 of Popayán has 17 settlements with approximately 3,000 families. As

© Springer International Publishing AG 2017
A. Solano and H. Ordoñez (Eds.): CCC 2017, CCIS 735, pp. 257–266, 2017.
DOI: 10.1007/978-3-319-66562-7_19

aforementioned, the dwellings do not have the minimum requirements on structure, materials (wood and zinc), and electrical connections. Under these conditions, the fires spread quickly. During 2014 and 2015 there have been two major fires in two of these settlements. In 2015 a fire in *Juan Pablo II* settlement caused 55 houses destroyed and 150 victims among whom were children and elderly. In 2015 a fire in *Triunfemos por la Paz* settlement caused 107 houses destroyed and hundreds of victims.

Some solutions for fire control include intelligent smoke detectors with Information Processing Systems installed in buildings. These alarms alert people for evacuation and can use devices for spraying or watering [6]. However, due to the high costs, this type of solution may be prohibitive for fire control in settlements.

This paper describes the implementation of a Low-cost fire alarm system supported on the Internet of Things. The solution was designed for its implantation in two settlements. In the system, some data about temperature, CO2, gas are collected and analyzed. Once a fire has started an alarm to the fire station is sent, and a siren is activated. The design of the solution follows a set of guidelines that can be replicated in other domains. These guidelines offer help to select the hardware, protocols and software components.

Although IoT embraces a wider concept, the guidelines here described and its application in a case study allow envisage its applicability in more domains, which could cover more elements and data to reach the full potential of IoT.

The rest of this paper is organized as follows: Sect. 2 presents the state of the art. Section 3 describes the guidelines for the development of IoT Solutions. Section 4 details the implementation of the solution. Finally, the conclusions and the future work are shown in Sect. 5.

2   State of the Art

In [7] a fire alarm system supported by Geographic information systems (GIS) and IoT is presented. The system is aimed at controlling fires in buildings in China. In this system, the information from the environment (temperature, CO density, light density, etc.) is collected and sent to the monitoring center trough WSN (Wireless sensor networks). Once the fire begins, some fire-fighting systems are activated to guide the evacuation supported on GIS.

In [8] a fire control system for Natural Reserves (NR) is presented. The system monitors the activity in the NR in Real Time and notifies associated alerts to the central control. The solution is composed of sensors connected to an IoT platform, a set of Web Services that detect critical situations. For the integration of these technologies, an Enterprise Services Bus (ESB) is used.

In [9] an approach for fire control in the home is presented. In this solution, some low power communication protocols are used, and a Raspberry Pi is used as a server system, some Smartphones can be integrated. In the case of smoke, a message is sent to the smartphone including photos or video and an automatic phone call to the fire station is made. The system uses LDR (Light Dependent Resistor) sensors to detect the fire. These data pass through gateway router to the device manager. The Raspberry is used as the gateway to communicate the PCs and Smartphones. Also, a web page is provided to configure the behavior of various appliances inside the home in case of fire case.

3   Guidelines for the Design of IoT Solutions

This section describes the steps followed for the implantation of the solution.

3.1   Requirements Identification

The first step is the definition of the requirements, for this propose a set of guide questions are defined to identify the most suitable components and criteria. The initial questions below are a guide to the design.

- What variables need to be sensed? (Temperature, humidity, pressure, etc.)
- What autonomy is expected?
- What is your budget?
- What maintenance can be provided?
- How long is the solution expected to be ready?
- What is your expertise in Internet of things technologies?
- How many nodes do you need? (Number of "motes" or communication devices, sensors, processing hardware and batteries).
- What is the area to be covered?
- What data processing do you need?
- How much data are you expecting to store?
- Do you have security requirements? (Sensitive or confidential information)

3.2   Requirements Identification

The selection of components is performed using the steps described in Fig. 1. The first step is the hardware definition; the second is the configuration of this hardware. The third step is the configuration of the Wireless sensor network. The step number four is the test. Finally, the last one corresponds to the edge computing that is associated with the data processing.

Fig. 1. Design of an IoT solution

In the first step (Hardware definition), the following elements (See Fig. 2) must be analyzed: 1. Sensors, 2. Communications devices; 3. Storage devices, 4. processing devices, 5. Security devices, power supply, and cloud deployment. For the elements 1 to 5, it is desirable to have support to solve troubles and doubts during the development. Equally, a high compatibility must be guaranteed between the first 5 elements to avoid interoperability issues. It should be noted that the compatibility is not ensured by selecting the same provider, or protocol. For example, XBee Series 1 module is not compatible with the XBee Series 2. Likewise, in the elements 2, 4 and 5, it is necessary to warranty the protocol compatibility.

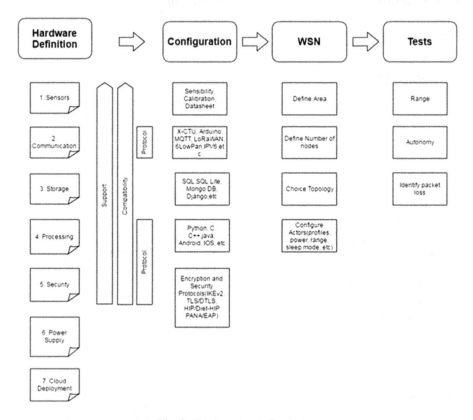

Fig. 2. Design of an IoT solution

In step 2, the hardware is configured, calibrated and documented.

Step 3 is associated with the WSN configuration. The WSN depends on the area to monitor and the number of the nodes. These elements define the topology (associated with the communication protocols), nodes configuration (coordinator, router, and end device) and nodes power requirements (transmission power).

In Step 4 some tests are performed to guarantee the quality of communications in the real deployment area.

Step 5, Edge computing, is a step where the information pre-processing is done before the data is sent to the cloud.

4   Implementation

This section describes the implementation of the solution based on the guidelines describes above.

4.1   Requirements

As a First step, the project was presented to the community, who showed great interest in the initiative. The project was also shared with the personnel of the local fire department of Popayán city, who mentioned that there were some sensors in the zone. However, the existing sensors do not provide reliable information as they are very sensible and triggers false alarms. During the initial meetings, the main risk factors were identified: material, electric cables without security, and candles among others. Moreover, the initial questions were answered with the people of two Settlements *"Villa Duran"* and *"La Fortaleza."*

From the initial questions, it was defined that the variables to be sensed were temperature, humidity, CO, smoke. The system should be of low cost, with high autonomy and low maintenance. There are no security constraints or short deadlines for the deployment.

4.2   Requirements

In steps 1 and 2, the hardware selected and configured is described below:

In addition to measuring the temperature, it is necessary to measure both the presence of gas leaks and the smoke. With this, the sensors DHT11, MQ135 and MQ7 were selected.

A development board Raspberry PI 3 was used on the server side for gathering the data obtained from the motes. The motes are conformed by sensors (temperature, humidity, CO, smoke), and an Arduino micro for data gathering. XBee PRO S2 was used for communication module. The collected data is sent to the Raspberry PI 3. The motes use a battery of LiPo at 7.4 V, regulated to 5 V for the most of the elements.

The gas sensors use a little heater inside with an electro-chemical sensor. To calibrate them it is necessary to know the type of gas and the concentration. Therefore, the selected sensors were: MQ7 (sensible to carbon monoxide CO) and the MQ135 (sensible to NH3, NOx, alcohol, benzene, smoke, CO2, etc.) [10].

The DHT11 is a low-cost device manufactured by D-Robotics UK. It measures the relative humidity among 20 and 90% with a precision of $\pm5\%$. Additionally, the temperature is measured in a range of 0 to 50 ℃, with a precision of de ±2 C., Both values are returned with a resolution of 8 bits.

The Arduino Pro mini of 5v is a little device (1.8×3.3 cm) with powerful features. This device has16 MHz, ATmega328, 16 digital input/output pins (6 can be used as PWM outputs), 6 analog inputs, a reset button, holes for mounting pin headers, an EPROM for 512 bytes programs [11, 12].

Raspberry PI 3 has: 1.2 GHz 64-bit quad-core ARMv8 CPU, 802.11n Wireless LAN, Bluetooth 4.1, Bluetooth Low Energy (BLE), 1 GB RAM, 4 USB ports, 40 GPIO pins,

Full HDMI port, Ethernet port, Combined 3.5 mm audio jack and composite video, Display interface (DSI), Micro SD card slot and has complete compatibility with Raspberry Pi 1 and 2. This device is a development card used widely for embedded projects, and projects which require very low power [13].

The XBee PRO S2B-XBP24BZ7WIT-004 is a communication module with the following specifications: Operating voltage 3.3 V, 205 mA, maximum transmission rate 250 kbps, output 63 mW (+18dBm), range 1 mile (1600 m) in line of sight; 90 m built-in antenna, certificate Fully FCC, 6 input pins of 10-bit ADC, 8 input/output pins – digitals, encryption 128-bit. Configuration local over-air, command set AT o API [14]. The configuration of this module was made with the X-CTU software (as it is the most used and with diverse available implementations).

In step 3, the wireless network is configured (See Fig. 3).

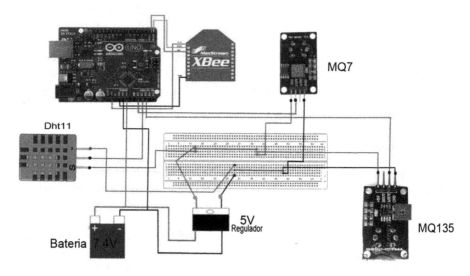

Fig. 3. Connection diagram

A Star topology is used for the network. The software X-CTU was used to configure the XBee modules "End Device" (in each mote) and "Coordinator" (RaspBerry). Depending on the covered area, the power level of each module is also configured to expand or reduce the coverage.

The system uses ZigBee as the proprietary communication protocol. This protocol defines 3 roles:

Coordinator (Network Administrator): only one administrator can exist in the network. This administrator initializes the network and allows joining devices such as Routers and endpoints. It is responsible for establishing the communication channel and the PAN ID (Network Identifier). Once the network is initialized, the coordinator performs router functions (package routing).

Router: This element is associated with the network coordinator or with other ZigBee Route. This element can act as a coordinator and performs the routing of the messages (by finding the most optimal route).

End device: Basic network element. It doesn't perform routing tasks and interacts through a parent node (coordinator or a router), that is, this element cannot send information directly to another end device. Normally the power consumption in these devices is low.

These actors work in a network topology. For ZigBee there exist the following topologies: Pair, Star, Mesh and Cluster Tree (this is a variation of mesh).

The Mesh topology was selected as it offers dynamical routing, improving communications reliability with low cost, low battery consumption, easy and cheap installation, and extensibility [15, 16].

Regarding the nodes, 3 nodes were configured as end devices (E1, E2, and E3); each node or mote can measure environmental variables: temperature and CO2, and the particles in the air generated by the smoke. Each 30 s, the information from the nodes is sent to the Coordinator node that centralizes the information

The nodes incorporate the respective sensor for measuring the variables, and the Arduino micro receives the data and transfers it to the XBee PRO S2B communication module that is in charge of sending the information and routing the messages.

The Coordinator node is implemented using Raspberry PI3. Here, the data processing and storage is carried out. This node also has an XBee PRO S2B module for receiving data from the other nodes (End Devices). This module uses a python script that works like a daemon and starts when the system boots.

Finally, a series of tests are performed on the optimum conditions of the system, evaluating the range of the network, the autonomy (battery life and possible network problems) and packet loss. Figure 4 shows the initial distribution of the nodes in the settlement.

Fig. 4. System location in "Villa Duran" settlement

Figures 5 and 6 show the lectures from sensors when they are in at rest and use. In the first test (Fig. 5), a person blows on the sensor to measure variations of CO. (The person is a non-smoker). The sensor shows variations in the range of gasses, as well as moisture and ambient temperature.

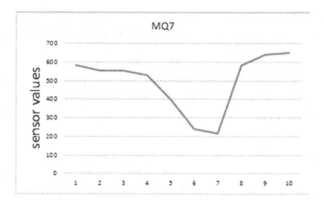

Fig. 5. Carbon monoxide measurement

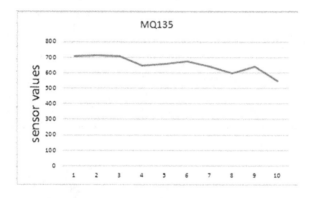

Fig. 6. Measurement of particles in the air (Smoke)

The sensor has a dual output, which comes directly from the sensor (analog) and a 5 V TTL output that comes from a comparator. The analog output varies depending on the gas concentration, where the value or parts per million will increase, depending on the concentration in the air, it can display values from 30 to 1000. The detection zone of this sensor is of about one meter.

Figure 7 shows the values of the sensors in rest mode where it can see the measurements that indicate that there is no fire. In Fig. 8 it can see the data when the sensors measure fire conditions (in controlled Environment).

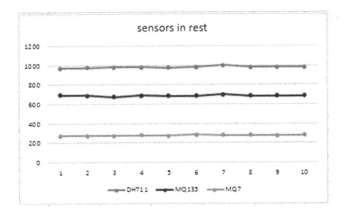

Fig. 7. Typical sensor values in rest

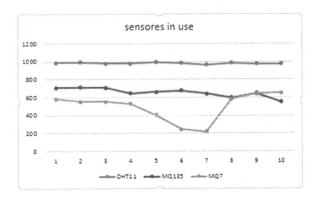

Fig. 8. Sensor values in Fire (Controlled Environment)

5   Conclusions and Future Work

Traditionally, fire alarm systems are not oriented to solve the problems of marginalized people. This paper describes the design and implementation of a low-cost fire alarm system for two settlements in the Popayán - Colombia. The system uses Internet of things technologies and sends alarms to the fire station. The design of the system is based on a set of guidelines or steps that can be used in diverse projects.

The preliminary evaluation of the system allows evidence a good performance and an excellent response from the community. The future work includes the evaluation of the system for a long time and the inclusion of new sensors. Equally these guidelines will be used in other domains.

References

1. Arango, R.A., Chilito, J.C., Cifuentes, A.: Análisis multitemporal de la expansion urbana de la ciudad de popayán, cauca entre los años 1989, 2002 y 2014, pp. 18–22 (2016)
2. Macuacé, R.A.: ¿Vive o Sobrevive la población en situación de desplazamiento en la ciudad de Popayán. Del conflicto Armado, pp. 147–173 (2008)
3. Overview of Internet of Things. https://cloud.google.com/solutions/iot-overview
4. Al-Fuqaha, A., Guizani, M., Mohammadi, M., Aledhari, M., Ayyash, M.: Internet of things: a survey on enabling technologies, protocols, and applications. IEEE Commun. Surv. Tutor. 17(4), 2347–2376 (2015). doi:10.1109/COMST.2015.2444095
5. Las 3 tecnologías clave para el internet de las cosas. https://www.xataka.com/internet-of-things/las-3-tecnologias-clave-para-el-internet-de-las-cosas
6. Liu, J., Yang, L.: Application of internet of things in the community security management. In: Proceedings of the 3rd International Conference on Computational Intelligence, Communication Systems and Networks, pp. 314–318 (2011). doi:10.1109/CICSyN.2011.72
7. Zhang, Y.C., Yu, J.: A study on the fire IOT development strategy. Proc. Eng. 52, 314–319 (2013). doi:10.1016/j.proeng.2013.02.146
8. Arjona, A., Boubeta, J., Ortiz, G.: Conservación de una Reserva Natural con un Enfoque Orientado a Servicios y Dirigido por Eventos, pp. 1–3 (2015)
9. Pavithra, D., Balakrishnan, R.: IoT based monitoring and control system for home automation. In: 2015 Global Conference on Communication Technologies (GCCT), pp. 169–173. IEEE (2015). doi:10.1109/GCCT.2015.7342646
10. Mq-135 Gas Sensor. Technical Data specification. https://www.olimex.com/Products/Components/Sensors/SNS-MQ135/resources/SNS-MQ135.pdf
11. Karumbaya, A.: IoT empowered real time environment monitoring system. Int. J. Comput. Appl. 129, 30–32 (2015). doi:10.5120/ijca2015906917
12. Perea, I., Puente, S., Candelas F.A., Torres, F.: Nueva Tarjeta de Sensorización y Control Para Robot Humanoide. In: XXXI Jornadas de Automática (2010)
13. Raspberry pi3 Technical Description. https://www.raspberrypi.org/products/raspberry-pi-3-model-b/
14. Rodríguez, E., Deco, C., Burzacca, L., Pettinari, M., Costa, S., Bender, C.: Análisis y diseño de una red sensores con tecnología inalámbrica para el monitoreo de condiciones de Higiene y Seguridad del ambiente en entornos industriales, In: Congreso Argentino Ingeniería Industrial. Facultad Regional Córdoba, pp. 1–10 (2000)
15. Fortuño, A.: Desarrollo e implementación de una red de sensores Zigbee mediante el dispositivo Xbee de Digi (2012)
16. XBee PRO S2B Configuration. http://plataformaszigbee.blogspot.com.co/2012/05/practica-1-configuracion-y-conceptos.html

Architectural Design of a Clinical Decision Support System for Clinical Triage in Emergency Departments

Analysis of Performance, Availability and Security

Felipe Tabares[1]([✉]), Jhonatan Hernandez[2], and Ivan Cabezas[3]

[1] Software Department, Cafeto Software, Cali, Colombia
ftabares@cafetosoftware.com
[2] Software Department, Axede, Cali, Colombia
jhonatan.hernandez@axede.com.co
[3] Facultad de Ingeniería, Universidad de San Buenaventura, Cali, Colombia
imcabezas@usbcali.edu.co

Abstract. Clinical triage is a key process in emergency departments because it allows clinicians to prioritize patient treatments based on their health condition. Handling this process adequately will allow those departments to operate efficiently. Most of its concerns are related to its effectiveness due to the short timeframes that clinical staff have during the process and the lack of valuable, timely and pertinent information available. In several contexts, this problem has been addressed by using clinical decision support systems. However, there is not enough information about architectural approaches dealing with key quality attributes and restrictions involved in those systems. This paper aims to analyze and discuss a feasible architectural approach to implement a clinical decision support system for clinical triage by adapting proposals from other scenarios. As main contribution, this proposal describes the architecture design process applied through a well-known standard and emphasizes tactics for performance, availability and security. For this purpose, an attribute-driven design method was followed, concluding that it is a convenient approach because it allows to iterate easily the entire system by prioritizing key elements. The achieved results are useful for architects, implementers, practitioners and researchers to extend the architecture and apply it.

Keywords: Clinical decision support systems · Software architecture design · Health care · E-health · CDSS · Clinical triage · Attribute-driven design · Performance · Availability · Security

1 Introduction

The Triage, from the French verb triar -which means to separate, classify, sift or select- arose from the exigencies of the Napoleonic wars in XVIII and was used informally in the eighteenth century [1, 2]. Clinical Triage is defined in [1] as the process of determining patients treatment priority based on their condition severity. This process is highly important because all clinical resources associated to each patient treatment

© Springer International Publishing AG 2017
A. Solano and H. Ordoñez (Eds.): CCC 2017, CCIS 735, pp. 267–281, 2017.
DOI: 10.1007/978-3-319-66562-7_20

are limited and, therefore, if triage classifications are effective and accurate, it will allow emergency departments to operate efficiently. Triage aims to prioritize, in the shortest possible time, patients who typically come to an emergency department, ensuring that the most urgent patients are treated with priority, while the rest can be continuously monitored and re-evaluated until they receive medical attention.

The main challenge facing the triage process corresponds to the lack of valuable, timely, pertinent and accessible information during the classification process made in the triage, leading to inadequate prioritization of patients and clinical resources, negatively impacting the whole service. In several scenarios [3–12], this problem has been addressed using Clinical Decision Support Systems (CDSS). CDSS are defined in [13–15] as those that provide, to physicians, staff, patients and others, the specific knowledge and information of a patient, intelligently filtered and opportunely presented, with the aim of improve health care.

From the software engineering is possible to determine what kind of CDSS implementation is feasible to be adapted and applied to clinical triage process. However, there is a lack of empirical evidence in the application of architectural methods while most of authors and software architecture practitioners are not detailing the conducted architectural design process carried on in this kind of implementations as well as there is not enough clarity about the most important architectural drivers or quality attributes involved with their advantages and cautions, as it is stated in [16].

The aim of this paper is to show the architectural design for a feasible implementation of a CDSS for clinical triage process. For this purpose, we defined the key quality attributes and designed the architecture by following the Attribute-Driven Design (ADD) method proposed in [17] as a guide, which attempts to decompose the whole system in smalls problems (called domains) to be solved from a hypothesis generate-and-test approach by applying a set of patterns and tactics based on the quality attributes. The validation of this architecture is only proposed and will be deepened in a future work.

This paper is structured as follows: Sect. 2 (Methods) deepens the problem and describes the performed architecture design process. Section 3 (Results) shows the proposed architecture, describes its key elements and shows the proposed validation to be deepened in a future work. Finally, conclusions are stated in Sect. 4.

2 Methods

2.1 Background

This paper is focused on the architecture design and main drivers for a CDSS to support the triage for patients who come to an emergency department in a healthcare center. In this scenario, an emergency is cataloged as a situation that must be solved quickly and usually has a high grade of importance or priority. As states [2], the classification of emergencies corresponds specifically to a preliminary clinical assessment that prioritizes patients given their degree of urgency before a more complex diagnostic evaluation, so that, in a healthcare service congestion or reduction of medical resources, the most urgent patients can be treated with priority, while the rest can be continuously monitored and re-evaluated. As a clinical triage has different scenarios and contexts, we began by characterizing a scenario for the aim of this paper. As result of such characterization, we performed our study over a face-to-face, simple and structured clinical triage for adults who come to an emergency department. This characterization was adapted from [1, 2, 18–20].

In [19] the sensitivity of the Hospital Triage is deeply studied, addressing a discussion generated around the use of additional information to the conventional (patient's anamnesis) as a key input to the process with the objective of achieving greater efficiency and precision. Our proposal is focused on using a CDSS to allow obtaining relevant, accurate and timely information. We think that clinical triage sensitivity will be highly positively influenced by a CDSS. CDSS has different purposes and implementations. As result of systematic mapping studies, systematic reviews and ad-hoc researching, we defined the following characteristics for a triage CDSS:

- Main function: Decision Support. Supporting clinical diagnosis and treatment plan processes; and promoting use of best practices, condition-specific guidelines, and population-based management.
- Classification: Knowledge based and Non-knowledge based.
- Type: Alerts and Reminders. Reminder systems are used to notify clinicians of important tasks that need to be done before an event occurs.

2.2 Architectural Design Process

Having the information described above as our context and scope, we conducted a systematic review [16] to determine the key quality attributes and existing architectural approaches in implementing a CDSS. To design the architecture, we followed the process described in [21]. First, we carried on a Quality Attribute Workshop (QAW) [17] to consolidate, prioritize and refine the quality attributes used to drive the design process. During this workshop, we created the following artifacts: a list of Architectural Drivers, raw scenarios, a prioritized list of raw scenarios and refined scenarios (utility tree).

An example of two refined scenarios is shown in Table 1. As result of researching and applying the QAW method, we found three key quality attributes which drove the design process: Performance, Availability and Security. At this point, we started the architecture design by using the classic attribute-driven design (ADD) method [21, 22] in conjuction with a variation proposed in [23] to design the architecture incrementally while sustainability was evaluated at the end of each iteration. According to [17], ADD is an iterative method that, at each iteration, helps the architect to choose a part of the system to design, marshal all the architecturally significant requirements (ASR), create and test a design for that part, producing a "workable" architecture early and quickly, allowing to start working on it while the software architect can still refine it. The main ADD inputs that were used to start iterating in the ADD method were:

- ASR: A list of requirements and business restrictions written at the very beginning of the process. It was provided by the selected scenarios for Triage and CDSS, our local context and legal aspects.
- Refined scenarios: Provided by applying the QAW method.

Table 1. Utility tree. Architecturally significant Triage CDSS requirements

Quality attribute	Attribute refinement	ASR	Evaluation
Performance	Transaction response time	A user requests a Hospital Emergency Classification while the system is under peak load, and the transaction completes in less than 3 min	Business value: High Architectural impact: High
Availability	No downtime	If a component fail, another instance of the same component must be initiated to continue processing pending requests	Business value: High Architectural impact: High
Security	Confidentiality	100% of cases, client requests must be completed in a secure way and data should not be viewed by unauthorized actors	Business value: High Architectural impact: Medium

- Analysis of tactics: We performed an ad-hoc research over all tactics involved with the key quality attributes. We considered tactics represented in Figs. 3, 6 and 8, respectively. Table 3 shows an example about how it was carried on a short analysis for each tactic during the ADD method process.

The main ADD outputs were a set of sketches of relevant architectural views representing elements, its interactions, checklists and recommended actions. After applying the ADD method and obtain the main outputs, we documented the architecture by applying the views and beyond approach [24] from Software Engineering Institute (SEI) [25]. A set of documented relevant views was generated following the 4 + 1 model [26]. Finally, we wrote a software architecture document (SAD) in compliance with standards ISO/IEC 42010 and IEEE 1471-2000 [27].

As final remark, we followed the standards created by SEI since they are the most influential *de-facto* standards in software engineering, which are widely used and accepted in the software industry around the globe. Previously, we found that several authors proposed software architectures related to CDSS in several domains without detailing used processes and standards, which may be due to lack of rigor. In this case, with scenarios properly defined and detailed, we can perform a future software architecture evaluation allowing other authors and practitioners to replicate our work through a clear software architecture design process.

3   Results

3.1   Architecture Overview

The main use case for this proposal is related with the classification of a hospital emergency. The top level context diagram, which defines the boundary for the entire system, is shown in Fig. 1 and is subdivided into three main use cases: applying the classification method, generating alerts and recommendations and notifying the user

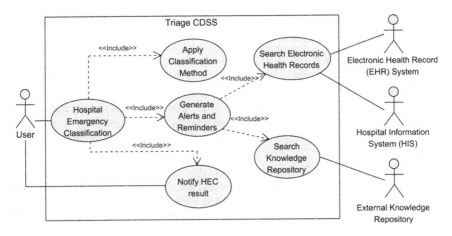

Fig. 1. Triage CDSS top level context diagram

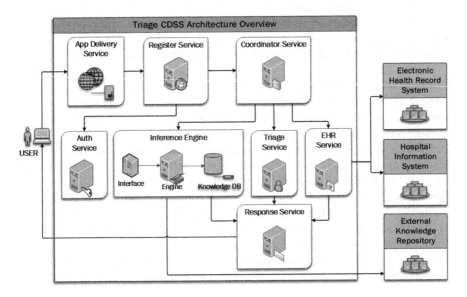

Fig. 2. Triage CDSS architecture overview

about the results of classification process. It also shows external sources or systems namely, Electronic Health Record System (EHR), Hospital Information System (HIS) and External Knowledge Repository.

Figure 2 shows an overview of a proposed architecture. It basically consists of core components such as Register service, Coordinator service, Triage engine, Electronic Health Record (EHR) service, Inference engine and Response service; and security, service delivery, monitoring and management components such as Application

Delivery and Authentication and Authorization services. We describe each proposed component below.

- Application Delivery Services: It is a set of services for delivery purposes such as load balancing, gateway and content cache as well as security and monitoring/management purposes such as attacks detection, access control, securing delivery, live or real-time activity, audit trial and alerts configuration. This component is often included in software architectures as a Third-party component to be easily implemented and transfer the risks of having high throughput, high traffic and attacks.
- Authentication and Authorization Service: It is responsible for managing users, roles, access control lists (ACL), groups and all elements involved with authentication and authorization. This component is proposed to be included in this software architecture as a Third-party service to comply with laws, standards, security and privacy policies.
- Register Service: It is responsible for receiving a request coming from a user or client (i.e. a hospital information system integrated to the CDSS for triage), validate its input information, register and dispatch it to the coordinator service for processing. This component is an inbound endpoint. It can be a web service, HTTP resource, input queue, email, among others.
- Coordinator Service: It is responsible for consulting pending requests and dispatching them in parallel to the Triage service, EHR service and Inference engine to be processed. It is based on the process coordinator pattern.
- Triage Engine: It is responsible for applying the hospital emergency classification method to pending requests previously dispatched by the coordinator. Generated results are send to the response service to notify users.
- EHR Service: It is responsible for consulting the patient electronic medical history through an external system as a main input to generate alerts and recommendations that will be send to the response service, notifying the user.
- Inference Engine: It consists of an interface component, an inference engine and internal/external knowledge repositories. Its main function is to generate alerts and recommendations based on stored knowledge. Such alerts and recommendations are send to the response service to notify users.
- Response Service: It is responsible for notifying the user about obtained results during the classification processes through the components described above.

External to the proposed architecture, we have the following components: Electronic Health Record System, Hospital Information System and External Knowledge Repository. Following, we describe relevant decisions and recommendations to implement a CDSS for Triage system based on performance, availability and security analysis.

3.2 Performance

According to [17, 21] the tactics used for performance are divided in two groups: Control resource demand and Manage resources. Figure 3 shows considered tactics for Performance.

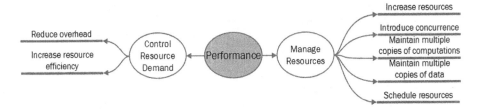

Fig. 3. Performance tactics used in architecture design

Control Resource refers to the set of tactics that for limiting the number of requests, events and/or calls that the system can process in a certain time to satisfy response times required and specified in the ASRs with available computational resources. In the proposed clinical triage scenario, the implementation of this kind of tactics is not feasible since the CDSS must deal with critical issues such as patient's health condition. Limiting the number of requests by applying one or more of the tactics described can affect patient's opportunity for care considerably, causing a negative impact on their health condition.

Based on the above, the proposed architecture considers tactics from the second group (Manage Resources), which attempts to manage and optimize the use of available computational resources to attend as most requests as possible. In this context, a request is an application to the system. We focused on three specific tactics:

- Introduce concurrency: It refers to processing several activities for the same request in parallel with the aim of reducing processing time. Using this tactic is possible because applying the triage algorithm, searching the patient's EHR and inferring alerts and recommendations from a knowledge base can be done independently. To implement this tactic, we used a process coordinator called Coordinator Service in our architecture as it is shown in Fig. 4. This component is only responsible for dispatching a same request through three main components: Triage Engine, Inference Engine and EHR Service. These components will execute the same request in parallel and will generate independent and different responses given their specialization.

- Increase resources: It consists of scale available computational resources (processors, hard disks, memory, network) during request processing. Its implementation depends on the budget allocated to the project. For example, a CDSS implementation can be supported by cloud computing models that allow access to computing resources at a low cost compared with traditional on-premise models. However, there are several restrictions, privacy and security issues to consider in this scenario. We designed independent components, communicated indirectly and asynchronously between them with separated responsibilities, allowing the implementation of the system independent of the deployment model and the underlying infrastructure.

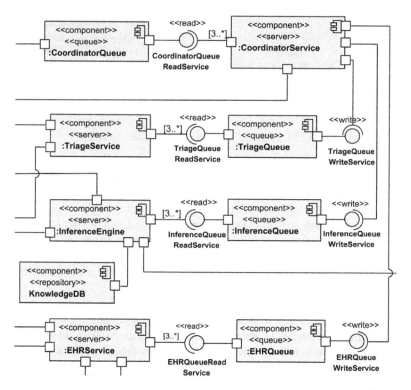

Fig. 4. Introducing concurrency through the process coordinator and message queue patterns

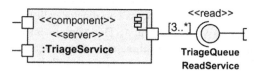

Fig. 5. Multiple instances of Triage service component

- Maintain multiple copies of computations: It consists of having multiple instances of a specific component to process multiple requests at the same time, thus reducing processing time. We recommend the use of at least three instances for each main component (Register, Coordinator, Triage, Inference, EHR and Response) as it is shown in Fig. 5. A load balancer will be used in the Register service and queues with multiple consumers in the rest of components. In this way, it would be possible to improve the system throughput, allowing to increase the number of requests served within a certain timeframe and, consequently, to increase patient's opportunity for care.

Other analyzed tactics for performance are shown in Table 2.

Table 2. Analysis of some the performance tactics considered in the architecture design

Category	Tactic	Explanation
Manage resources	Maintain multiple copies of data	In a CDSS, inferred data is one of the most valued resource but it is computationally expensive to achieve. Knowing that, the architecture considers caching key inferred data to increase performance. In this case, the system knowledge base will be cached
	Schedule resources	Resource contention is normal in all systems. For this reason, it must be defined a strategy to schedule resources given their characteristics

3.3 Availability

Availability refers to the capability to be ready to perform its tasks when required and to mask and/or repair faults such that the off-system period does not exceed the required value in a specific timeframe. There are multiple architectural styles, patterns and tactics to satisfy this attribute. According to [17, 21], tactics for availability can be divided in three groups: detect faults, recover from faults and prevent faults. Figure 6 shows considered tactics for Availability.

Monitoring by using a third-party component is a common approach as it allows to transfer this responsibility and therefore to be focused in other core components.

Recover from faults consists of strategies that allow the system to recover and return it to normal operation once a failure is presented. Redundancy is one of the most used tactics. It is divided in active (hot spare), passive (warm spare) and spare (cold spare). Each kind of redundancy offers distinct levels of availability. Its implementation depends on the budget allocated to the project. The aim of redundancy is to let another component to continue processing ongoing requests without the users being affected in the event of a failure. The proposed architecture recommends cold spare because it is possible to create and insert another instance of the same type to continue processing requests during a failure.

Another recommended tactic for recovering from faults is rollback. It allows the system to return to an earlier state before a failure, performing transaction compensation if required. The use of this tactic is possible because of the use of specialized

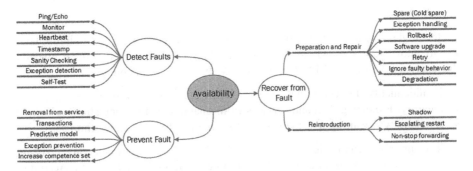

Fig. 6. Availability tactics used in architecture design

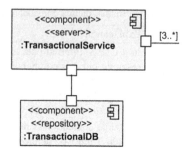

Fig. 7. Transactional service component

queues for each type of component and the request processing state handling. This is done through a component named Transactional service, which is shown in Fig. 7. The main function of this component is to determine ongoing requests. When a component suffers a fault, requests assigned again or reprocessed by another Spare with similar characteristics. That way, this architecture design ensures that all clinical triage requests received by the system are processed.

Prevent faults group consists of tactics supported in fault detection tactics. They are in charge to prevent failures in the system before presented. It consists of determining what components are not in normal operation and therefore can be possible points of failure, given a pattern. These components probably will degrade their functionality or will be removed from service (depending on the severity of the failure) and will be reintegrated when their behavior is normal again. Applying this tactic in our architecture is feasible because of the use of the coordinator service described above. The coordinator can determine, through monitoring tactics, if a key component (Triage, HER or Inference engine) is presenting failure to remove it from dispatching queue. For example, if a heartbeat or an echo test detected that our EHR service component (responsible to obtain the patient's electronic health record) is having unacceptable response times, it will be temporarily removed from the system. This way, classifications will be carried out with the other two components (Triage and Inference engine) and the system will continue providing valuable information to the process.

Other analyzed tactics for availability are shown in Table 3.

3.4   Security

It refers to the system ability to protect, from unauthorized access, data and information and to allow access to whom have the required privileges. It has three essential characteristics known by CIA (Confidentiality, Integrity, Availability):

- Confidentiality: Protecting data and services from unauthorized access.
- Integrity: Protecting data and services from unauthorized manipulation.
- Availability: Ensuring that the system will be operative for its legitim use.

The aim of security tactics is to preserve the CIA in a system by detecting, resisting, reacting or recovering from attacks through different tools and techniques. According

Table 3. Analysis of some of the availability tactics considered in the architecture design

Category	Tactic	Explanation
Recover from fault: Preparation and repair	Exception handling	It is included as part of the architecture. Handling error codes as well as using sophisticated exception handlers and researching abnormal patterns to perform corrective actions on the system
	Retry	As communications and Internet Protocols are unstable by nature, it must be included a mechanism to retry a request, event or process before declaring a permanent failure
	Ignore faulty behavior	This tactic will be used to ignore warnings that do not affect the entire system
	Degradation	Some techniques of this tactics can be used. For example, limiting resources to avoid some low-priority functionalities absorb resources from high-priority functionalities
	Escalating restart	This tactic is included in conjunction with Degradation. Each component level can be restarted separately
Recover from fault: Reintroduction	Non-stop forwarding	This tactic can be implemented partially on top on the coordinator service to allow it to "remember" paths using the analogy with a router
	Removal from service	This tactic can be implemented on main components (Triage, HER, Inference Engine) in the case of the coordinator service through a monitor detects failing
Prevent fault	Exception prevention	It should be used in conjunction with exception handling
	Increase competence set	As the CDSS for Triage architecture involves several components with different scope, each component should protect itself of faults by increasing its competence set (i.e. validating inputs, handling errors, transforming outputs)

to [17, 21], security tactics can be divided in four groups: detect attacks, resist attacks, react to attacks, and recover from attacks. Figure 8 shows considered tactics for security.

Detecting attacks is a proactive way to reduce the tech debt by identifying possible attacks related with the system and determining patterns and ways to detect them easily. To determine these patterns, we performed an attack tree where we identified attacks and analyzed their probable causes. In this architecture, we included the use of a component specialization responsible for detecting security issues. Its implementation can be done internally or by using a third-party service to reduce the risk of mitigating security issues. This component is called Application delivery services in our

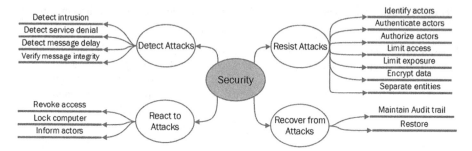

Fig. 8. Security tactics used in architecture design

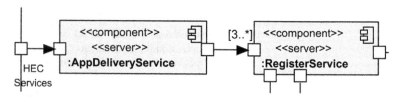

Fig. 9. Using specialized application delivery services for detecting attacks before they arrive to the register service

architecture and has functions related with security issues such as: intrusion detection, service denial detection and message delay detection. Figure 9 shows the use of the component.

Verifying message integrity is an included tactic and it will be implemented by using message or schema validation on top on the protocol used to transport messages through all the components. According to [28], schema validation is used to protect systems from maliciously formed messages. Validation of messages with schemas can protect parameters and/or fields in operation, data, and message contracts. Resisting attacks is a proactive way to protect the system before an attack is successful. There are different tactics to resist attacks. In this proposal, we considered four groups:

- Authorization and Authentication: In the proposed architecture, it is included an identity and access management service. It can be implemented by using a third-party service, which provides authentication and authorization services via tokens (i.e. JSON Web Tokens [29]), roles, permissions, ACL, Policy management, multi-factor authentication, Single sign on, and others. This component is named "Auth Service" in our architecture and it is shown in Fig. 10.
- Limiting access and exposure: This tactic is included in the underlying infrastructure by using firewalls with security groups or custom rules (for limiting access). Exposing only one component -in this case, a proxy server inside application delivery services- to the public is a key tactic for resisting attacks. Figure 10 shows how the proposed architecture only exposes one component to final users.

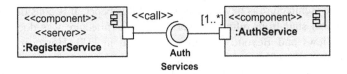

Fig. 10. Using an identity and management component (AuthService)

- Encrypting data: Encryption is included at two levels: (1) Encrypting protocol by using Secure Sockets Layer; (2) Encrypting data in some components that are using sensitive data (i.e. HER system).
- Separating entities: In the proposed architecture, it is included a physical separation between components to handle sensitive data and non-sensitive data in different servers.

Reacting to attacks is a reactive way to protect the system when a possible attack is underway. In this proposal, we considered two tactics:

- Revoke access: In the proposed architecture, we recommend the use of removal from service tactics from availability when a main component is suffering an attack. It is possible due to the use of the Coordinator service component. It can detect when the component is being attacked, then access is limited to other resources. When the attacked component is recovered - through availability tactics for repairing, it will be incorporated again for normal operation.
- Inform actors: In all cases (detecting attacks, resisting attacks and reacting to attacks), the proposed architecture considers agents informing actors about security issues so that they can make decisions on the system, all time it is in risk of an attack and most important, when it is under an attack. This will be possible by using specialized system monitoring.

Recover from attacks is a reactive way to recover the system after this was attacked. In this proposal, we recommend keeping a record of user and system actions and their effects. This is possible by using an activity log and tracking exceptions. We also recommend using availability tactics to restore the system once the attack is handled.

4   Conclusions and Future Work

In this paper, an architectural design for a Triage CDSS is addressed. It includes methods and important results. The ADD method proposed by the SEI was followed as a guide and several tactics from the same institute in conjunction with other tactics from software industry were analyzed, discussed and incorporated. The architecture design process was addressed by having performance, availability and security as key quality attributes. This paper provides a detailed design process based on software engineering standards. Other architects and implementers will have a guidance to adapt, extend or transform this architecture given their context. The methods section shows the processes and guidelines used to gather requirements, quality scenarios and quality attributes as well as the recommended tactics for each quality attribute.

Evaluating the architecture is beyond the scope of this paper. It is considered as future work which will start from refined scenarios. This architecture was documented following the Views and Beyond principles described in [17]. However, architecture documentation is not addressed in this paper.

The main contribution of this work is related with the fact that we used and detailed a clear architecture design process based on de-facto and well-known standards given the lack of rigor in this matter from other authors as we found in previous reviews. As result of this work, we build scenarios and drivers that can be reproduced easily and evaluated by other architects and implementers by using several methods. Regarding to the Triage process, our contribution relates to finding a feasible architecture design for a CDSS and stating different scenarios that allow architects and implementers to make decisions.

References

1. Iserson, K.V., Moskop, J.C.: Triage in medicine, Part I: concept, history, and types. Ann. Emerg. Med. **49**, 275–281 (2015)
2. Gomez, J.: Clasificación de pacientes en los servicios de urgencias y emergencias: Hacia un modelo de triaje estructurado de urgencias y emergencias. Emergencias **15**, 165–174 (2003)
3. Oakkar, O.: Online triage for patients: implementing a scalable and cost-effective triage platform using expert system, machine learning and natural language processing techniques (2013)
4. Halim, S., Annamalai, M., Ahmad, M.S., Ahmad, R.: A conceptualisation of an agent-oriented triage decision support system. In: Lukose, D., Ahmad, A.R., Suliman, A. (eds.) KTW 2011. CCIS, vol. 295, pp. 272–282. Springer, Heidelberg (2012). doi:10.1007/978-3-642-32826-8_28
5. Farion, K.J., Michalowski, W., Rubin, S., Wilk, S., Correll, R., Gaboury, I.: Prospective evaluation of the MET-AP system providing triage plans for acute pediatric abdominal pain. Int. J. Med. Inform. **7**, 208–218 (2007)
6. Georgopoulos, V.C., Stylios, C.D.: Introducing fuzzy cognitive maps for developing decision support system for triage at emergency room admissions for the elderly. IFAC Proc. Vol. **45**, 484–489 (2012)
7. Georgopoulos, V.C., Stylios, C.D.: Supervisory fuzzy cognitive map structure for triage assessment and decision support in the emergency department. In: Obaidat, M.S., Koziel, S., Kacprzyk, J., Leifsson, L., Ören, T. (eds.) Simulation and Modeling Methodologies, Technologies and Applications. AISC, vol. 319, pp. 255–269. Springer, Cham (2015). doi:10.1007/978-3-319-11457-6_18
8. Salman, O.H., Rasid, M.F.A., Saripan, M.I., Subramaniam, S.K.: Multi-sources data fusion framework for remote triage prioritization in telehealth. J. Med. Syst. **38**, 103 (2014)
9. Tian, Y., Zhou, T., Wang, Y., Zhang, M.: Design and development of a mobile-based system for supporting emergency triage decision making. J. Med. Syst. **38**, 65 (2014)
10. Aronsky, D., Jones, I., Raines, B., Hemphill, R., Mayberry, S.R., Luther, M.A., Slusser, T.: An integrated computerized triage system in the emergency department. AMIA Annu. Symp. Proc. 16–20 (2008)
11. Abelha, A., Pereira, E., Brandão, A., Portela, F., Santos, M.F., Machado, J., Braga, J.: Improving quality of services in maternity care triage system. Int. J. E-Health Med. Commun. **6**, 10–26 (2015)

12. Abelha, A., Pereira, E., Brandão, A., Portela, F., Santos, M., Machado, J.: Simulating a multi-level priority triage system for maternity emergency. In: Modelling and Simulation 2014 - European Simulation and Modelling Conference, ESM 2014, pp. 278–282. EUROSIS (2014)
13. Berner, E.: Clinical decision support systems: state of the art. In: Agency for Healthcare Research and Quality. AHRQ Publication No. 09-0069-EF, Rockville, Maryland (2009)
14. Centre for Health Evidence. http://www.cche.net/
15. Wyatt, J., Spiegelhalter, D.: Field trials of medical decision-aids: potential problems and solutions. Proc. Annu. Symp. Comput. Appl. Med. Care **5479**, 3–7 (1991)
16. Tabares, L., Hernandez, J., Cabezas, I.: Architectural approaches for implementing clinical decision support systems in cloud : a systematic review. In: Cloud Connected Health (CCH), Cali, Colombia, pp. 1–6 (2016)
17. Bass, L., Clements, P., Kazman, R.: Software Architecture in Practice. Addison-Wesley Longman Publishing Co., Inc., San Francisco (2012)
18. Triage Extrahospitalario | Algoritmos pediátricos | Serralco.es | Blog de salud y Enfermeria. http://serralco.es/triage-extrahospitalario-ii-algoritmos-pediatricos-y-escalas/
19. Mendoza Camargo, G., Elguero Pineda, E.: Sensibilidad del triage clínico en el Servicio de Urgencias Adultos del HRLALM del ISSSTE. Arch. Med. Urgenc. México **3**, 93–98 (2011)
20. Triage Extrahospitalario | Algoritmos Básicos y Avanzados | Serralco.es | Blog de salud y Enfermeria. http://serralco.es/triage-extrahospitalario-i-algoritmos-basicos-y-avanzados/
21. Gorton, I.: Essential Software Architecture. Springer, Heidelberg (2006). doi:10.1007/3-540-28714-0
22. Bass, L., Clements, P., Kazman, R.: Software Architecture in Practice, 3rd edn. Addison-Wesley, Reading (2012)
23. Villa, L., Cabezas, I., Lopez, M., Casas, O.: Towards a sustainable architectural design by an adaptation of the architectural driven design method. In: Gervasi, O., et al. (eds.) ICCSA 2016. LNCS, vol. 9787, pp. 71–86. Springer, Cham (2016). doi:10.1007/978-3-319-42108-7_6
24. Clements, P., Bachmann, F., Bass, L., Garlan, D., Ivers, J., Little, R., Merson, P., Nord, R., Stafford, J.: Documenting Software Architecture Views and Beyond. Addison-Wesley Longman Publishing Co., Inc., Boston (2011)
25. Software Engineering Institute. https://www.sei.cmu.edu/
26. Kruchten, P.: Architectural blueprints — the "4+1" view model of software architecture. IEEE Softw. **12**(12), 42–50 (1995)
27. Software Architecture | Tools & Methods | Documenting the Architecture | Views and Beyond: The SEI approach to architecture documentation. http://www.sei.cmu.edu/architecture/tools/document/viewsandbeyond.cfm
28. Microsoft: Message validation. https://msdn.microsoft.com/en-us/library/ff650173.aspx
29. Peyrott, E.: The JWT Handbook, Seattle, WA, United States (2016)

PISCIS: A Constraint-Based Planner for Self-adaptive Systems

Julián Cifuentes[1]([✉]), Andrés Paz[2], and Hugo Arboleda[1]

[1] Universidad Icesi, Cali, Colombia
julian.cifuentes@correo.icesi.edu.co, hfarboleda@icesi.edu.co
[2] Université du Québec, Montreal, Canada
andres.paz@me.com

Abstract. The dynamic nature of current software execution environments demands a reliable and prompt response to guarantee quality at runtime. Self-adaptive software systems contain facilities that allow for an autonomous and continuous adaptation towards such end. The facilities are, overall, structured in accordance with IBM's MAPE-K reference model. IBM's MAPE-K reference model comprises a *Monitor* and an *Analyzer* to sense and interpret context data, a *Planner* and an *Executor* to create and apply structural adaptation plans, and a *Knowledge Manager* to manage and share relevant information. The aim of this paper is to present PISCIS, our *Planner* element based on the principles of a constraint satisfaction problem (CSP) and the MAPE-K reference model. We tested PISCIS, within a controlled environment made up of a set of Eclipse plug-ins, and checked how it dynamically creates structural adaptation plans following the MAPE-K reference model. PISCIS is a constraint-based planner within the SHIFT framework, based on the MAPE-K reference model. We have verified its applicability using a running example set within an adaptation scenario.

Keywords: Self-adaptive enterprise applications · Dynamic adaptation planning · Automated reasoning · Constraint satisfaction

1 Introduction

Today's business reality is characterized by a prominent dynamicity affecting quality requirements and the levels at which enterprise applications (EAs) can satisfy them. This situation has spurred the need for strengthening the responsiveness and resiliency of EAs that support key business operations to allow them to continuously fulfill changing quality requirements regardless of their execution environments. Efficiently and effectively guaranteeing quality requirements at runtime requires an autonomic solution that provisions EAs with self-adaptation capabilities. The required infrastructure usually integrates an *autonomic manager* that is an implementation of the generic control feedback loop, from control theory, based mostly on the MAPE-K reference model [1].

© Springer International Publishing AG 2017
A. Solano and H. Ordoñez (Eds.): CCC 2017, CCIS 735, pp. 282–296, 2017.
DOI: 10.1007/978-3-319-66562-7_21

Five elements constitute the MAPE-K reference model: *Monitor, Analyzer, Planner, Executor* and *Knowledge Manager*. The *Monitor* continuously senses context conditions and the *Analyzer* interprets and compares the sensed data against the quality requirements, the *Planner* synthesizes and creates adaptation action plans when an adaptation is required. The *Planner* has the responsibility of dynamically creating a structural reconfiguration action plan from available components that when deployed can meet the new quality requirements. The resulting reconfiguration action plan needs to take into account the inherent interactions between quality requirements and their association to concrete component implementations that satisfy them. Finally, the *Executor* alters the system's behavior by modifying its structure in accordance with a given adaptation action plan delivered by the *Planner*; all the MAPE-K reference model elements share information through a *Knowledge Manager* element.

In this paper we present PISCIS, an implementation for a *Planner*, built on the principles of constraint satisfaction, targeting the adaptation of component-based EAs. Previously, in [2], the authors presented the SHIFT framework, which is based on the MAPE-K reference model and provides facilities and mechanisms for managing the whole life cycle of self-adaptive EAs. In [3], inside the frame of SHIFT, it was formulated as a Constraint Satisfaction Problem (CSP) the searching and planning for optimal components' configuration that satisfy a given set of interacting quality requirements. The authors presented a formal model, built on the principles of constraint satisfaction, and a process (respectively) to address the task of the *Planner*. In this paper we present how PISCIS implements such process using the proposed formal model to dynamically create structural adaptation plans for self-adaptive (component-based) EAs. We use an illustrative running example set within an adaptation scenario to introduce the implementation and demonstrate the applicability of the PISCIS planner.

The remainder of this paper is structured as follows. Section 2 summarizes related work. Section 3 presents the SHIFT framework together with the foundations of constraint satisfaction used for the PISCIS planner and a motivating scenario of a large-scale e-commerce application. Section 4 describes PISCIS, its implementation and its underlying formal model. Finally, Sect. 5 sets out conclusions and outlines future work.

2   Related Work

Several strategies to achieve adaptation and reconfiguration plans have been proposed. In [4] Moore *et al.* propose an approach that makes use of artificial intelligence based on hierarchical task networks. In [5] McIlraith *et al.* use artificial intelligence to create a planner. Their planner was built by adapting and extending Golog [6] a logic programming language based on the situation calculus, built on top of Prolog. SHOP2 [7] is another planner of the likes relying on hierarchical task networks based on situation calculus. None of these approaches, however, provide any support for self-adaptive infrastructures. Approaches like [8,9] implement dynamic adaptation of service compositions at the language level. These approaches can be complex and time-consuming, and with low-level implementation mechanisms for every element of the adaptation infrastructure.

The approaches proposed in [10–12] are closely related to ours. These approaches use models at runtime and implement, implicit or explicitly, the MAPE-K reference model. In [12] Alfrez *et al.* summarize good practices when implementing the MAPE-K reference model. Their approach is aimed at service re-composition at runtime. The approach is built on dynamic product line engineering practices and takes into account context- and system-sensed data. Changes to the application are realized at the service composition level by adding or removing fragments of Business Process Execution Language (WS-BPEL) code. The approach uses constraint programming at design time to verify the variability model and its possible configurations. Each possible configuration of the variability model is a reachable adaptation. No implementation details or formal specifications are provided. Furthermore, although services can be redeployed at runtime, the approach assembles and re-deploys only complete applications.

3   Preliminaries

3.1   The shift Framework

Efficiently and effectively achieving self-adaptation of enterprise applications (EAs) requires an autonomic solution. The SHIFT Framework provides a comprehensive autonomic infrastructure that enables quality awareness and automated dynamic adaptation in component-based EAs throughout their entire life cycle [2]. Figure 1 presents the high-level architectural view of the *autonomic infrastructure* level in the SHIFT Framework, which is based on the MAPE-K reference model [1]. This level contains the infrastructure that allows an EA to be adapted to unforeseen context changes in order to ensure the satisfaction of quality requirements. Comprising this infrastructure is (i) a `Monitor` that continuously senses relevant context and system control data; (ii) an `Analyzer` that interprets monitoring events reported by the `Monitor` to determine whether the quality requirements are being fulfilled; (iii) a `Planner` that creates an adaptation action plan defining the modifications required to reach the quality requirements in accordance with the current context conditions reported by the `Analyzer`; (iv) an `Executor` that realizes the optimum adaptation action plan; and (v) a `Knowledge Manager` sharing relevant information among the previous elements.

3.2   Constraint Satisfaction

Dynamically determining an adaptation action plan for a component-based EA consists in searching for an optimum configuration of components within a vast space of possible components that satisfy a given set of interacting quality requirements. In general, such a problem may be formulated as a Constraint

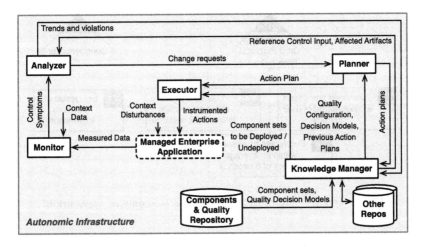

Fig. 1. High-level architectural view of the SHIFT elements

Satisfaction Problem (CSP) [3]. A CSP defines the search space as all combinations of possible values for a predefined set of variables. The elements to be searched for are particular values of such variables. Values for those elements are implicitly specified by the satisfaction of established constraints [13].

The solution of a CSP is achieved in two steps: (i) modeling the problem through logical specification, and (ii) finding its solutions through a search strategy (to the extent of this paper we carry out a basic backtracking). Modeling involves the specification of the problem variables, their domains and the constraints among them. Solving the CSP through backtracking is an attempt at trying to incrementally build resolution candidates by assigning possible values to the variables. Partial candidates that cannot become a valid solution are discarded. If all variables are bound, a resolution candidate has been found. If, after exploring all possibilities no resolution candidate has been found, then the problem does not have a solution.

Several CSP solvers exist (e.g., JaCoP [14], Choco [15]) that provide Java users with constraint programming tools. We use Choco for implementing PIS-CIS. Choco is a free and open-source Java library for describing combinatorial problems as CSPs and solving them with constraint programming techniques [16].

3.3 A Motivating Scenario

We introduce the scenario of a large-scale e-commerce application to illustrate the problem of adapting an EA at runtime when the set of quality requirements changes. We use this case as an illustrative running example throughout the remainder of this paper. The following sections give the details regarding how the PISCIS planner of the SHIFT Framework calculates possible adaptation

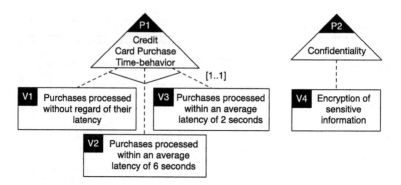

Fig. 2. Quality variability model for the e-commerce application

action plans to satisfy changing context conditions based on a set of adaptation constraints.

The e-commerce application has the need to respond to varying shopping activities, such as special offers on certain products or shopping frenzies of the likes of the *Cyber Monday*. This implies handling component compositions and adaptations driven by varying quality requirements, captured as quality scenarios, during the *monitoring* and the *analysis* steps. We use the Orthogonal Variability Model (OVM) notation [17] to represent the different quality scenarios that can be configured for the e-commerce EA. The *quality attribute, environment* and *stimuli* fields of a quality scenario [18] represent *variation points*; the *response* field represents a *variant*. Figure 2 illustrates 2 variation points (denoted by *P*) with all of their variants (denoted by *V*). In the figure, all variants are *optional*, which means that only one variant from a variation point can be selected for one configuration.

Initially, the e-commerce application is deployed fulfilling the requirement of purchase by credit card and the quality configuration corresponds to the selection of quality scenarios V2 and V4[1] from Fig. 2. The selected quality scenarios are detailed in Table 1. The *time-behavior* scenario determines an average latency of 6 s for purchases with credit card under a load of 1,000 purchases per minute, stochastically. The *confidentiality* scenario specifies all available sensitive information is encrypted to prevent unauthorized access.

Promoting a quality scenario may often require many components, thus, we refer as a *component-set* to a set of components promoting a quality scenario; an application is the deployment of *component-sets* that promotes all the required quality scenarios. For the example e-commerce application, in order to reach every possible configuration of quality scenarios (variants in Fig. 2), we have identified five *component-sets*: c_1 through c_5. We denote the composition operator as $\oplus$. Note that components marked with *prime* (′) are modified variants of the components with the same name. For instance, the components Purchase

---

[1] In the remainder of this paper we refer to every variant, *i.e.* response alternative, as one quality scenario.

Table 1. Quality scenarios for the initial deployment of the e-commerce application

Quality attribute	Performance time behavior
Environment	The application provides a set of services available to concurrent users over the Internet under normal operating conditions
Stimuli	Users initiate 1,000 purchases with credit card as payment method per minute, stochastically
Response	Every purchase is processed with an average latency of 6 s
Quality attribute	*Security Confidentiality*
Environment	The application provides a set of services that makes sensitive information available to other applications over the Internet
Stimuli	Another application intercepts data by attacking the network infrastructure in order to obtain sensitive information
Response	The architecture does not control the other application's access, but information is encrypted in order to prevent access to sensitive information

and **Purchase'** (in c_1 and c_4) are two variants of the same component aimed at satisfying **V2** and **V3**, respectively.

$$c_1 = \text{Purchase} \oplus \text{Credit Card Authorization} \oplus \\ \text{Credit Card Settlement} \oplus \text{Risk Tool} \tag{1}$$

$$c_2 = \text{Cryptography Manager} \tag{2}$$

$$c_3 = \text{Payment Processor} \tag{3}$$

$$c_4 = \text{Purchase}' \oplus \text{Credit Card Authorization}' \oplus \\ \text{Credit Card Settlement}' \tag{4}$$

$$c_5 = \text{Order Manager} \tag{5}$$

The initial component deployment for the purchase with credit card requirement involves *component-sets* c_1, c_2 and c_3 as illustrated by the component diagram in Fig. 3. The **Purchase** component manages the workflow performed for any purchase. The **Credit Card Authorization** component is in charge of performing the workflow to get the approval from the card issuing bank (or credit card association) for the transaction. A **Risk Tool** component is responsible for validating the credit card information provided by the customer and the responses sent from the issuing bank. The **Credit Card Settlement** component requests the transfer of funds from the card issuing bank into the merchant's account. A **Cryptography Manager** component processes encryption and decryption tasks when transferring information with the issuing bank. The **Payment Processor** component manages all communications to the multiple issuing banks. In the next section, we present how PISCIS support the creation of a structural adaptation plan for the e-commerce application when required quality scenarios change.

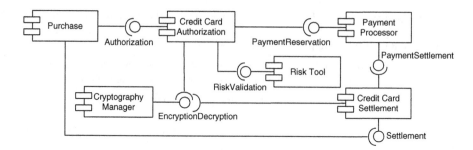

Fig. 3. Component diagram with the partial set of components for the initial deployment of the e-commerce application

4 Piscis Implementation

4.1 Adaptation Planning Overview

This section provides a summarized description of the internal behavior of PISCIS in the context of the SHIFT framework. Figure 4 presents an activity diagram depicting such a behavior. In order to illustrate it, for the e-commerce EA let us suppose that, while in operation, the *Analyzer* notices that an expected peak in system load will soon take place due to an upcoming *Cyber Monday* shopping season and requests an adaptation to the *Planner*.

The adaptation planning process starts when a change request is received from the *Analyzer*. Then, via the *Knowledge Manager*, PISCIS retrieves the *quality configuration model* (See activity 2 in Fig. 4 and Sect. 4.2) and the *decision*

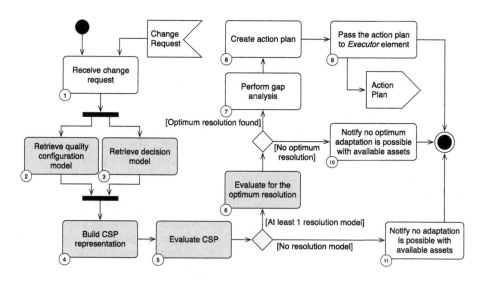

Fig. 4. Activity diagram depicting the behavior of the PISCIS planner

model (See activity 3). On the one hand, the *quality configuration model* holds the established selection of quality scenarios that must be satisfied; this has been created by software architects who know the required service level agreements for the particular context conditions related to the change request. For our e-commerce example this selection of quality scenarios correspond to those satisfying the upcoming *Cyber Monday*. On the other hand, the *decision model* describes the applicability of the available *component-sets* with respect to the different quality scenarios that can be selected; this has been also defined by software architects who know how *component-sets* composition achieve every valid configuration of quality scenarios.

Once the *quality configuration* and *decision* models have been retrieved, PISCIS uses them to build a representation in the form of a constraint satisfaction problem (CSP) (See activity 4). The CSP is the base to find, later in the process, the set of *valid solutions*, which are sets of *component-sets* that satisfy the incoming quality configuration. We have developed three constraints for the CSP in order to find valid solutions, these are: (i) a component set must be deployed satisfying the respective application relationship described in the decision model, (ii) two deployable *component-sets* must not exclude each other, and (iii) all applicable *component-set* must take into account all the quality scenarios states in the configuration.

After the CSP has been built, PISCIS evaluates it in order to find every valid solution, which are represented as *resolution models*, *i.e.* a finite set of *component-set* deployments (See activities 5 and 6). If at least one resolution model is found, PISCIS evaluates for an optimum resolution. Achieving an optimum resolution involves finding the best resolution model, within the set of possible resolution models, through the use of an optimization function over the variables that better fit to adapt the managed EA, *e.g.*, maximizing or minimizing the number of deployed *component-sets*. The current implementation of PISCIS ends at this point.

A planner must also consider that, if no optimum resolution is found, a notification must be delivered. Besides, if an optimum resolution is found, a gap analysis must be performed to compare the currently deployed components with the ones comprising the optimum resolution in order to determine the necessary, high-level actions that will achieve the target deployment. The action plan must also be created and passed to the *Executor* element for realization.

Following subsections provide the formal definitions and implementation details of the implemented activities.

4.2 Retrieving the Quality Configuration Model

In PISCIS a quality configuration model conforms to Definition 1. We have not included the variation points considered in [3], given their irrelevance within the planning process.

Definition 1. *A quality configuration Q is a finite set of variables v_i, each of which represents the selection state of a quality scenario that can be configured for the EA.*

$$Q = \{\langle v_i \rangle \mid i = 1, \ldots, n\}, \text{where } v_i = \begin{cases} 1 \text{ if } v_i \text{ is unselected} \\ 2 \text{ if } v_i \text{ is selected} \end{cases}$$

The quality configuration model matching the initial deployment for the e-commerce application example is specified in Eq. 6, where quality scenarios V2 and V4 are selected (See Sect. 3.3). The adaptation setting for *Cyber Monday* is as specified in Eq. 7, where quality scenarios V3 and V4 are selected.

$$Q_{e-commerce}^{initial} = \{v_1 = 1, v_2 = 2, v_3 = 1, v_4 = 2\} \tag{6}$$

$$Q_{e-commerce}^{cyber\ monday} = \{v_1 = 1, v_2 = 1, v_3 = 2, v_4 = 2\} \tag{7}$$

In our PISCIS implementation, a quality configuration Q is defined as a one-dimensional array of size n taking its domain in $[1..2]$. In Listing 1.1, the *Cyber Monday* quality configuration model (`qualityConfig` in line 1), delivered by the *Knowledge Manager*, is the input for building the CSP representation for the quality configuration model. Line 2 in Listing 1.1 defines an integer variable array Q. The value of each v_i corresponds to the selection state of the quality scenario in `qualityConfig` and is posted to the CSP ω as a constraint (see lines 3 and 4).

Listing 1.1. PISCIS code fragment building the CSP representation for the quality configuration model

```
1 def static void loadQualityConfiguration(List qualityConfig){
2 var IntVar[] Q = W.intVarArray("Q", n, 1, 2)
3 for (i : 0 ..< n)
4     W.arithm(Q.get(i), "=", qualityConfig.get(i)).post}
```

4.3   Retrieving the Decision Model

In PISCIS a decision model conforms to Definition 2. The decision model determines the deployment applicability of the available *component-sets* towards the selection state of the available quality scenarios. Three alternatives are possible: the deployment of the *component-set* is not constrained by the quality scenario, the deployment of the *component-set* requires the quality scenario be unselected, and the deployment of the *component-set* requires the quality scenario to be selected.

Definition 2. *A decision model D is a finite set of $m \times n$ decisions. Each decision d relates one component-set c_j with one quality scenario v_i.*

$$D = \{\langle d_j^i \rangle \mid j = 1, \ldots, m \ \wedge \ i = 1, \ldots, n\},$$

$$\text{where } d_j^i = \begin{cases} 0 \text{ if the deployment of } c_j \text{ is not constrained by } v_i \\ 1 \text{ if the deployment of } c_j \text{ requires } v_i = 1 \\ 2 \text{ if the deployment of } c_j \text{ requires } v_i = 2 \end{cases}$$

Table 2. Decision model for the e-commerce EA

Quality scenarios	Component-sets				
	c_1	c_2	c_3	c_4	c_5
v_1	✗	–	–	✗	✗
v_2	✓	–	–	✗	✗
v_3	✗	✗	–	✓	✓
v_4	–	✓	–	–	–

Table 2 presents the decision model for the e-commerce example. A ✓ indicates the deployment of the *component-set* requires the quality scenario to be selected in the configuration; on the contrary, an ✗ indicates that the deployment of the *component-set* requires the quality scenario to be unselected. A "–" indicates the deployment of the *component-set* is not constrained by the presence of the quality scenario. Equation 8 illustrates the CSP representation of the decision model presented in Table 2.

$$
\begin{aligned}
D_{e-commerce} = \{ & d_{c_1}^{v_1} = 1, d_{c_2}^{v_1} = 0, d_{c_3}^{v_1} = 0, d_{c_4}^{v_1} = 1, d_{c_5}^{v_1} = 1, \\
& d_{c_1}^{v_2} = 2, d_{c_2}^{v_2} = 0, d_{c_3}^{v_2} = 0, d_{c_4}^{v_2} = 1, d_{c_5}^{v_2} = 1, \\
& d_{c_1}^{v_3} = 1, d_{c_2}^{v_3} = 1, d_{c_3}^{v_3} = 0, d_{c_4}^{v_3} = 2, d_{c_5}^{v_3} = 2, \\
& d_{c_1}^{v_4} = 0, d_{c_2}^{v_4} = 2, d_{c_3}^{v_4} = 0, d_{c_4}^{v_4} = 0, d_{c_5}^{v_4} = 0 \}
\end{aligned}
\tag{8}
$$

In our PISCIS implementation, a decision model is a two-dimensional array of size $m \times n$ taking its domain in $[0..2]$. In Listing 1.2, the decision model for the e-commerce EA (`decisionModel` in line 1), delivered by the *Knowledge Manager*, is the input for building the CSP representation for the decision model. Line 2 defines an integer, two-dimensional array D. The value of each d_i^j corresponds to an entry in `decisionModel` and is posted to ω as a constraint (lines 3 to 5).

Listing 1.2. PISCIS code fragment building the CSP representation for the decision model

```
1 def static void loadDecisionModel(List<List> decisionModel){
2 var IntVar[][] D = W.intVarMatrix("D", m, n, 0, 2)
3 for (j : 0 ..< m)
4   for (i : 0 ..< n)
5     W.arithm(D.get(j).get(i),"=",decisionModel.get(j).get(i)).post}
```

4.4 Building the CSP Representation

Once the *Knowledge Manager* delivers the *quality configuration model* and the *decision model*, PISCIS proceeds to build the CSP that will be evaluated.

Definition 3. *Let ω be a CSP of the form (L, T, P) where L is a finite set of variables made up of the quality configuration model Q (see Definition 1), the*

decision model D (see Definition 2) and the resolution model S (see Definition 4); T is a finite set of domains for the variables in L; and P is a finite set of constraints defined on L (see Definitions 5, 6 and 7).

Once the quality configuration model and the decision model are represented in the CSP, PISCIS continues building the CSP representation by adding the *resolution model, i.e.* the solution variables (see Definition 4).

Definition 4. *A resolution model S is a finite set of component-set deployments. A deployment s_j is 0 if the component-set j should not be deployed, or 1 if the component-set j should be deployed.*

$$S = \{\langle s_j \rangle \mid j = 1, \dots, m\}, \text{where } s_j = \begin{cases} 0 \text{ if } c_j \text{ should not be deployed} \\ 1 \text{ if } c_j \text{ should be deployed} \end{cases}$$

In our PISCIS implementation, the variable that represents a possible resolution model in the CSP is an array S of size m taking its domain in $[0..1]$ (see Listing 1.3).

Listing 1.3. PISCIS code fragment building the CSP representation for the resolution model

```
1 var IntVar[] S = W.intVarArray("S", m, 0, 1)
```

PISCIS finishes building the CSP representation by adding the *core adaptation planning constraints* defined in [3]: deployment constraint (see Definition 5), non-exclusion constraint (see Definition 6) and completeness constraint (see Definition 7).

Definition 5. *Deployment constraint. Let v_i be quality variables from a quality configuration, and let d_j^i be a decision that relates the component-set c_j with the variable v_i A component-set must be deployed satisfying the respective deployment condition in the decision model.*

$$\forall j \in [1..m] \ s_j = 1 \Rightarrow \forall i \in [1..n](d_j^i = 0 \lor d_j^i = v_i)$$

In our PISCIS implementation we define three sub-constraints, namely `cons1`, `cons2` and `cons3`, before building the deployment constraint (see Listing 1.4). We use nested loops in order to include all d_j^is.

Listing 1.4. PISCIS code fragment building the CSP representation for the deployment constraint

```
1 //For all j in (0 ..< m)
2 cons1 = W.arithm(S.get(j), "=", 1)
3     //For all i in (0 ..< n)
4     cons2 = W.arithm(D.get(j).get(i), "=", 0)
5     cons3 = W.arithm(D.get(j).get(i), "=", V.get(i))
6     W.ifThen(cons1, W.or(cons2,cons3))
```

Line 6 in Listing 1.4 posts to ω the whole deployment constraint, meaning that the satisfaction of the constraint `cons1` (*i.e.* $s_j = 1$) implies that either the constraint `cons2` (*i.e.* $d_j^i = 0$) or the constraint `cons3` (*i.e.* $d_j^i = v_i$) are satisfied.

Definition 6. *Non-exclusion constraint. Two deployable component-sets belonging to S must not exclude each other.*

$$\forall j_1, j_2 \in [1..m](s_{j_1} = s_{j_2} = 1 \wedge j_1 \neq j_2) \Rightarrow$$
$$\forall i \in [1..n](d^i_{j_1} = 0 \vee d^i_{j_2} = 0 \vee d^i_{j_1} = d^i_{j_2})$$

We define in the PISCIS implementation five sub-constraints (cons1 through cons5) for each pair of *component-sets* before building and posting the non-exclusion constraint.

Listing 1.5. PISCIS code fragment building the CSP representation for the non-exclusion constraint

```
1  //For all j1, j2 in (0 ..< m), j1 != j2
2  cons1 = W.arithm(S.get(j1), "=", 1)
3  cons2 = W.arithm(S.get(j2), "=", 1)
4      //For all i in (0 ..< n)
5      cons3 = W.arithm(D.get(j1).get(i), "=", 0)
6      cons4 = W.arithm(D.get(j2).get(i), "=", 0)
7      cons5 = W.arithm(D.get(j1).get(i), "=", D.get(j2).get(i))
8      W.ifThen(model.and(cons1,cons2), model.or(cons3,cons4,cons5))
```

Line 8 in Listing 1.5 posts to ω the non-exclusion constraint, meaning that satisfaction of the constraints cons1 (*i.e.* $s_{j_1} = 1$) and cons2 (*i.e.* $s_{j_2} = 1$) implies that either constraint cons3 (*i.e.* $d^i_{j_1} = 0$), constraint cons4 (*i.e.* $d^i_{j_2} = 0$) or constraint cons5 (*i.e.* $d^i_{j_1} = d^i_{j_2}$) are satisfied.

Definition 7. *Completeness constraint. Deployable component-sets must take into account all the quality scenarios' states in the quality configuration.*

$$\forall i \in [1..n] \, \exists j \in [1..m](s_j = 1 \wedge d^i_j \neq 1)$$

We define the constraint by combining two independent constraints for each i and j. Line 4 in Listing 1.6 posts the constraint in the CSP.

Listing 1.6. PISCIS code fragment building the CSP representation for the completeness constraint

```
1  //For all i in (0 ..< n), j in (0 ..< m)
2  cons1 = W.arithm(S.get(j), "=", 1)
3  cons2 = W.arithm(D.get(j).get(i), "!=", 1)
4  W.and(cons1,cons2)
```

4.5 Evaluating the CSP and Evaluating for the Optimum Resolution

Determining an adaptation means evaluating the CSP in search for all possible resolution models.

Definition 8. *Let ω_Q^D be a CSP with input quality configuration model Q and decision model D, its solution space denoted as $sol(\omega_Q^D)$ is made up of all possible resolution models S. An adaptation can only be satisfiable if $sol(\omega_Q^D)$ is not empty.*

We used *Choco*'s default search strategy to determine the CSP's solution space. By using such a strategy, PISCIS evaluates for an optimum resolution, which is the most appropriate set of *component-sets* to satisfy the new EA's execution context. *Choco*'s search strategy can be oriented either to find one solution, all the solutions, or the optimum solution. In the first case, the solution found corresponds to the first set of values for each $s_i \in S$ such that all constraints on the CSP are satisfied. This is very time-efficient, yet the first solution that is found may not be the most appropriate one. The second alternative, finding all the solutions, is good for evaluation purposes because it determines the entire solution space but time is wasted evaluating many solutions that may turn up to be inappropriate. The third case, in turn, is a more suitable option since PISCIS evaluates for an optimum resolution. *Choco* provides native support for finding the optimum solution in the solution space through the method `findLexOptimalSolution` without the need to first calculate the entire solution space. Thus, in PISCIS we take advantage of this feature in *Choco* to implement both the *evaluate CSP* and *evaluate for the optimum resolution* steps at once. Definition 9 formally defines the optimum resolution.

Definition 9. *Let $sol(\omega_Q^D)$ be the solution space of the ω_Q^D CSP, its optimum resolution model Γ is the resolution model S' that results from applying an objective function O to every S in $sol(\omega_Q^D)$.*

$$\Gamma(sol(\omega_Q^D)) = \{S' \mid \forall S(S', S \in sol(\omega_Q^D) \wedge S' \neq S) \Rightarrow (O(S') \; \gamma \; O(S))\},$$

where γ is one of the relational operators: $>$ or $<$

For the implementation of the e-commerce scenario, the objective function O yields the number of applicable *component-sets* in the resolution model. We look to maximize the number of *component-sets*, thus we take into account the $>$ (greater than) operator. The resulting optimum resolution is the resolution model with the greater number of applicable *component-sets*. However, an adaptation analyst is the one responsible to define the objective function in terms of the variables that need to be optimized. Listing 1.7 shows the implementation of PISCIS to evaluate the CSP for the optimum resolution (an R is used in place of the Γ symbol). The `findLexOptimalSolution` method in *Choco*, takes the resolution model S that is progressively, in our case, maximized (thus, the `true` parameter).

Listing 1.7. PISCIS code fragment evaluating the CSP for the optimum resolution

```
1 var Solution R = W.solver.findLexOptimalSolution(S, true)
```

The expected optimum resolution model Γ for the *Cyber Monday* adaptation setting in our e-commerce EA is presented in Eq. 9. This resolution model indicates that the *component-sets* c_3, c_4 and c_5 should be the ones deployed in order to promote the quality scenarios for the upcoming *Cyber Monday* (see Eq. 7).

$$\Gamma_{e-commerce}^{cyber\ monday} = \{s_1 = 0, s_2 = 0, s_3 = 1, s_4 = 1, s_5 = 1\} \tag{9}$$

5   Conclusions

In this paper, we have presented PISCIS, an implementation for the planner in the MAPE-K reference model and a key element in the SHIFT framework. We developed PISCIS [19] as a kernel component of SHIFT [20], an *autonomic manager* built as a FraSCAti application. Besides, we developed a test environment made up of a set of Eclipse plug-ins in order to test its behavior. PISCIS is built on the principles of constraint satisfaction to provide it with reasoning capabilities on the set of constraints defined by reachable quality requirements and their relationships with the available components that will satisfy them. PISCIS creates a CSP representation of the quality requirements and the applicability of available *component-sets* and evaluates it for the optimum resolution. We have tested the implementation and applicability of PISCIS in the context of an e-commerce enterprise application.

As future work, we will extend the implementation of PISCIS to cover the entire process including (i) analyze the resulting optimum resolution model against the currently deployed components, (ii) create an action plan specifying the necessary high-level actions to achieve the target deployment and (iii) pass it to the *Executor* element for realization. In addition, we will explore new search strategies and objective functions in *Choco*, and the integration of other solvers such as JaCoP. Finally, we will propose and perform more extensive validations with more adaptation scenarios that involve complex interactions between quality requirements.

References

1. IBM: An architectural blueprint for autonomic computing, IBM White Paper (2006)
2. Arboleda, H., Paz, A., Jiménez, M., Tamura, G.: Development and instrumentation of a framework for the generation and management of self-adaptive enterprise applications. Ing. Univ. **20**(2), 303–333 (2016)
3. Paz, A., Arboleda, H.: A model to guide dynamic adaptation planning in self-adaptive systems. Electron. Notes Theor. Comput. Sci. **321**, 67–88 (2016)
4. Moore, C., Wang, M.X., Pahl, C.: An architecture for autonomic web service process planning. In: Binder, W., Dustdar, S. (eds.) Emerging Web Services Technology Volume III. Whitestein Series in Software Agent Technologies and Autonomic Computing, pp. 117–130. Birkhaeuser, Basel (2010)

5. McIlraith, S.A., Son, T.C.: Adapting golog for composition of semantic web services. In: Proceedings of the Eighth International Conference on Principles and Knowledge Representation and Reasoning (KR-02), Toulouse, France, pp. 482–496 (2002)
6. Levesque, H.J., Reiter, R., Lespérance, Y., Lin, F., Scherl, R.B.: GOLOG: a logic programming language for dynamic domains. J. Logic Program. **31**(1–3), 59–83 (1997). Reasoning about Action and Change
7. Kuter, U., Sirin, E., Parsia, B., Nau, D., Hendler, J.: Information gathering during planning for web service composition. Web Semantics: Sci. Serv. Agents WWW **32**(2–3), 183–205 (2005)
8. Baresi, L., Guinea, S.: Self-supervising BPEL processes. IEEE Trans. Softw. Eng. **37**(2), 247–263 (2011)
9. Narendra, N.C., Ponnalagu, K., Krishnamurthy, J., Ramkumar, R.: Run-time adaptation of non-functional properties of composite web services using aspect-oriented programming. In: Krämer, B.J., Lin, K.-J., Narasimhan, P. (eds.) ICSOC 2007. LNCS, vol. 4749, pp. 546–557. Springer, Heidelberg (2007). doi:10.1007/978-3-540-74974-5_51
10. Calinescu, R., Grunske, L., Kwiatkowska, M., Mirandola, R., Tamburrelli, G.: Dynamic QoS management and optimization in service-based systems. IEEE Trans. Softw. Eng. **37**(3), 387–409 (2011)
11. Menasce, D., Gomaa, H., Malek, S., Sousa, J.P.: SASSY: a framework for self-architecting service-oriented systems. IEEE Softw. **28**(6), 78–85 (2011)
12. Alférez, G.H., Pelechano, V., Mazo, R., Salinesi, C., Diaz, D.: Dynamic adaptation of service compositions with variability models. Syst. Softw. **91**(1), 24–47 (2014)
13. Tsang, E.: Foundations of Constraint Satisfaction. Academic Press, London (1993)
14. Jacop: Java constraint solver (jacop) (2008). http://www.jacop.eu
15. Prud'homme, C., Fages, J.-G., Lorca, X.: Choco3 documentation, Technical report, TASC, INRIA Rennes, LINA CNRS UMR 6241, COSLING S.A.S. (2014)
16. Prud'homme, C., Fages, J.-G., Lorca, X.: Choco solver documentation. Technical report, TASC, INRIA Rennes, LINA CNRS UMR 6241, COSLING S.A.S. (2016). http://www.choco-solver.org
17. Pohl, K., Böckle, G., van Der Linden, F.J.: Software Product Line Engineering: Foundations, Principles and Techniques. Springer, New York (2005)
18. Bass, L., Clements, P., Kazman, R.: Software Architecture in Practice, 3rd edn. Addison-Wesley Longman Publishing Co., Inc., Boston (2012)
19. Paz, A., Cifuentes, J., Arboleda, H.: Piscis planner project. https://github.com/unicesi/planner/releases (2016)
20. Arboleda, H., Paz, A., Jiménez, M., Tamura, G., et al.: Shift framework (2016)

Analysis of the Software Implementation Process for ERP Systems

Jennifer Erazo[1]([⊠]), Hugo Arboleda[1], and Francisco J. Pino[2]

[1] Universidad ICESI, Cali, Colombia
{jderazo,hfarboleda}@icesi.edu.co
[2] IDIS Research Group, Universidad Del Cauca, Popayán, Colombia
fjpino@unicauca.edu.co

Abstract. Software implementation is a process that aims to integrate software based services or components into the workflow of an organization. For ERP systems, which allows companies to integrate all their primary business processes, this is a critical process that becomes difficult, lengthy costly and often unsuccessful. That is why there are currently some proposals that aim to facilitate and structure ERP implementation processes through the definition of methodologies, methods, models or processes that describe the most important phases and activities of it. In this paper, the ERP implementation process is analyzed considering some methodological proposals for ERP implementation found from a systematic literature review. From this analysis five common phases that are presented in the proposals were identified (selection, project planning, design and customization, implementation and maintenance and continuous improvement) and, in addition, the main activities performed during each of these phases were defined in order to support software enterprises during the ERP implementation process.

Keywords: Enterprise Resource Planning · ERP · Implementation process · Literature analysis · Systematic review

1 Introduction

Software development process consists of different phases, among which are: requirements collection, system design, coding, testing, implementation and operation and maintenance. Software implementation is a critical phase and it consists of integrating the software services or components in business alignment with the organizational view and acceptance from the users' perspectives [1]. In the information systems area it is defined as the process that begins with the managerial decision to install computer-based organizational information system and is completed when the system is operating as an integral part of the organization's information system [2].

This paper focuses mainly on the ERP systems implementation. Enterprise Resource Systems (ERP) are information systems which allow organizations to integrate their primary business processes such as manufacturing, supply chain, sales, finance, human resources, budgeting and customer service activities, in order to improve the efficiency and maintain a competitive position [3, 4]. These systems

© Springer International Publishing AG 2017
A. Solano and H. Ordoñez (Eds.): CCC 2017, CCIS 735, pp. 297–312, 2017.
DOI: 10.1007/978-3-319-66562-7_22

provide several benefits to the organizations including the information improvement and the time and costs reduction through retooling common business functions, revamping old systems and processes, and improving integrity and availability of business data [5].

Although companies spend a large amount of money on the acquisition and implementation of ERP systems, most of them have problems particularly during the latter [6]. ERP systems are complex and for this reason many implementations become difficult, prolonged, stop before they are complete, exceed their budget, and fail to achieve their business objectives [7]. In response to some of these problems, the literature provides several proposals, which present methodologies or process models for software implementation. These proposals have the common objective of turning the implementation processes of ERP systems into successful processes, which allow the enterprises to quickly see the benefits of acquiring an ERP. However, none of the solutions has been widely accepted and tested, although they are commonly used in practice, they still remain largely unexplored and there is a lack of documentation of them in the information systems research domain [8].

Considering this, it is important to perform an analysis of the ERP implementation process in order to know how this important activity is carried out in the software industry context. In this sense, this article presents the results of a systematic literature review carried out to know about methodologies, methods, models or processes for the ERP systems implementation proposed in the literature. From these proposals, a set of phases and activities that should be considered for software implementation has been identified.

In addition to this introduction, this article describes in Sect. 2 the research methodology, in Sect. 3 the results of the systematic literature review, in Sect. 4 the analysis of the results. Finally, the conclusions and future work are outlined.

2 Research Method

The method used in this study is a systematic literature review (SLR) which is a research methodology developed in order to gather and evaluate the available evidence relevant to a particular research question or topic area [9, 10]. This study follows the guidelines for systematic literature reviews established by Kitchenham [10], the synthesis of the protocol defined for the review is presented below.

2.1 Research Question

The main research question is:

> Q1: Which are the methodologies, methods, models or processes for ERP systems implementation proposed in the literature; which of these proposals are prescriptive and which are agile?

Two secondary research questions derived from the main question were defined:

> Q1.1: Which are the proposal foundations, theoretical and/or practical?
> Q1.2: Which are the phases or stages, tasks or activities defined for ERP systems implementation?

2.2   Search String

The keywords used to answer the research questions were: *ERP, Enterprise resource planning, implementation, methodology, method, model, phases, process, strategy.* Considering these words and making combinations with logical connectors "AND" and "OR", the following search string was obtained:

("ERP" OR "enterprise resource planning") AND ("implementation") AND ("methodology" OR "method" OR "model" OR "phases" OR "process" OR "strategy").

2.3   Search Source

The database selected to make the search was Scopus [11]. The search was performed for all fields related to information technology, including title, abstract and keywords. After performing the search, 3350 studies were found.

2.4   Studies Selection

The procedure used for the selection of the studies is represented in the activity flow diagram in Fig. 1. It was adapted from [12], where the authors propose to analyze the set of primary studies found in order to generate a list of the new potential primary studies (secondary searches).

The inclusion criterion was defined as "any study whose research is relevant to the review that is being performed, in other words, a research that presents or studies a methodology, method, model, process or strategy for ERP systems implementation, or which describes the phases of these systems implementation and which allows answering the defined research questions". This based on an analysis of the title, the abstract, and the keywords from the articles obtained in the search. Only the studies published after 1 January 2000 that are in English language were included in the review. This criterion allowed us to find the articles that should be classified as relevant for the systematic review.

The exclusion criterion was "to exclude the workshops, the tutorials, the short papers, the non- indexed articles, the articles that do not clearly discuss ERP systems implementation process, that do not have as main topic the study or definition of methodologies, methods, models, processes or strategies for ERP implementation, that are not related to the software domain (e.g. medicine, biology, physics, etc.), or duplicated articles".

The quality criteria used were presented as a list of 10 questions, adapted from [10, 13–15], including: does the paper present an empirical study? Is the study context clearly described? Are the research aims clearly stated? Are the design and implementation of the solution clear and appropriate to address the research aims? Are the references to related works appropriate? Are the methods used for the validation of the research problem proposal appropriate? Is the analysis of the process validation results associated with the aims of the research, is it rigorous enough? Does the study provide value for research or practice? and finally the redaction quality, the orthography, the images, the tables, the graphics and diagrams.

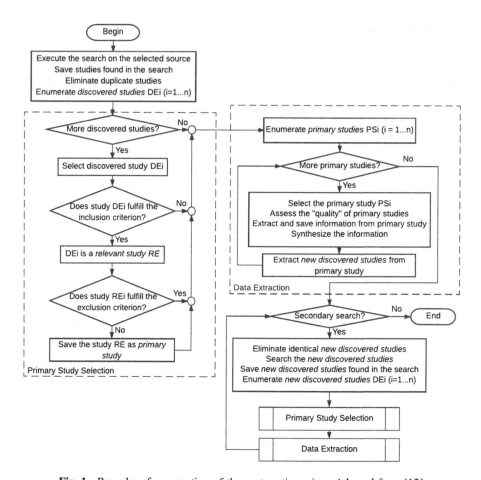

Fig. 1. Procedure for execution of the systematic review. Adapted from [12]

The studies found after the search string execution and that met the previously defined inclusion criteria are called *relevant studies*. These studies were evaluated against the exclusion criterion with the aim of finding the *primary studies* of the search. From the analysis of the primary studies a list of *new discovered studies* was generated, for these studies a secondary search was performed, and the systematic review procedure was executed. In this way, new primary studies were obtained and their information was synthesized.

After conducting the research of primary studies, applying the previously described procedure, 3350 were found, 29 of these were relevant studies and from these, 22 primary studies were obtained, including the ones found from a secondary search.

2.5   Information Extraction

After choosing the primary studies the information extraction was carried out, following the procedure shown in Fig. 1. For each study the information related to the proposal of the review and that helps to provide an answer to the defined research questions was considered. This information was stored on a chart in which for each article the following information was registered: name of the study, year of publication, authors, type of proposal (methodology, method, process, strategy, framework, etc.) and whether it is agile or not, the proposal foundations (theoretical or practical), the proposed phases or stages and tasks or activities.

3   Results

After performing the systematic literature review the defined research questions were answered as follows.

3.1   Q1: Which Are the Methodologies, Methods, Models or Processes for ERP Systems Implementation Proposed in the Literature; Which of These Proposals Are Prescriptive and Which Are Agile?

Most of the studies found propose methodologies, methods or models, most of them being models. However, many studies (9 studies) make other type of proposals, including frameworks (4 studies), taxonomy (1 study), road map (1 study), implementation steps (1 study), risk factors (1 study) and stages and obstacles in the implementation (1 study). Table 1 shows the detail of this information. It is important to keep in mind that only one of the 22 studies found presents an agile proposal [16].

Models. Eight of the studies found propose models for the implementation of ERP systems, all of them present phases and activities to structure the implementation process. Parr and Shanks [6] propose a project phase model (PPM) which synthesizes the existing ERP implementation processes and focuses in the implementation project, this model is extended and validated by Peslak et al. [18]. On the other hand, some works [17, 19] are based on the lifecycle model to identify and define relevant activities during ERP implementation. Although both studies suggest activities for the implementation, each takes a different approach, Ahituv et al. [17] suggest the stages of selection, definition, implementation and operation and define the activities that must

Table 1. Type of proposals. * = Agile proposal

Type of proposal	Number of studies	References
Model	8	[4–6, 17–21]
Methodology	4	[22–24] [16]*
Method	1	[25]
Framework	4	[26–29]
Taxonomy	1	[7]
Road map	1	[30]
Implementation steps	1	[31]
Risk factors	1	[32]
Stages and obstacles in the implementation	1	[33]

be performed in each of them, while Fu [19] identifies five fundamental components for ERP implementation (ERP software, adopting organization units, business processes, data and implementation project) and proposes an activity evolution chart for modeling state changes of the defined components.

Other studies focus on a particular aspect, for example Al-Mashari [5] presents a model oriented to the change management process, which defines a series of practices for strategic management, process improvement, ERP system deployment, project organization and organizational change management. Schniederjans and Yadav [4] propose a model that groups the factors necessary to achieve success in three constructs: technology, organization and environment and define significant aspects to improve each of these. Berchet and Habchi [20] define a five stage deployment model for ERP systems and they focus mainly on describing and identifying the risks presented in each of these phases, concluding that most of the risks occur during stabilization, progression and evolution of the ERP system.

Only one of the primary studies proposes a research model, Rajagopal [21] conducts a case study in six manufacturing firms, considering the phases proposed in the innovation – diffusion model proposed by Kwon and Zmud and managed to identify several aspects which are important in each of them and the factors that led the companies to implement ERP systems. Based on the case study, Rajagopal propose a research model to understand the implementation of ERP systems.

Methodologies. Some of the studies found [16, 22–24] propose methodologies that aim to support the ERP systems implementation process. Metaxiotis et al. [22] propose a methodology based on a planning by levels: (1) a management level focused on controllable results (milestones) throughout the project on how to organize and to achieve them and (2) a detailed level outlining the activities and responsibility for achieving these results (milestones). Leem and Kim [23] define in their methodology five components and one repository which can be customized with business scenarios and patterns according to different business environments, in the methodology roadmap the authors consider two scenarios: the first one when the enterprise develops the information system by itself and the second one when the enterprise buys, installs and runs a packaged commercial application program. On the other hand, the methodology presented by Pacheco-Comer et al. [24] has 11 phases and it focuses mainly in the selection process of the ERP system.

Only one of the studies found presents an agile methodology, this is presented by Stender [16] who propose an agile and incremental implementation methodology for enterprise systems (AI^2M) which allows users to prioritize the functionalities that should be implemented, based on the business priorities. The methodology focuses especially on the implementation of CRM systems, although it is general and it is not limited to this type of systems.

Methods. Only one of the studies found proposes a method [25]. In it, Vilpola defines a method that unifies ERP implementation process with user centered design (UCD), focusing on the requirements of both the users and the organization through the early participation of the users and the phases continue iteration. This is very important, because what makes the ERP implementation process difficult are the changes it causes in the individual's tasks.

Framework. Four of the studies found [26–29], present frameworks for the implementation of ERP systems. Chofreh et al. [26], Bhatti [27] and Markus and Tanis [28] propose conceptual or theoretical frameworks where they structure the software implementation process in different phases. For this, Chofreh et al. [26] based on the five project lifecycle phases proposed in the PMBOK (project initiation, project planning, project execution, project control and project closure) and proposed activities for the nine knowledge areas (project integration management, project scope management, project time management, project cost management, project quality management, project human resource management, project communications management, project risk management and project procurement management). On the other hand Al-Mudimigh and Al-Mashari [29] propose an integrative framework for the implementation of ERP systems that consider the essential elements that contribute to the success of ERP implementation, which should be considered throughout all implementation levels defined in the framework (strategic, tactical and operation).

Other Type of Proposals. In the remaining studies [7, 30–33] it can be found that in addition to defining the stages, phases or steps for the implementation of ERP systems, they focus on identifying the critical success factors for the implementation. In addition to this, Somers and Nelson [7] and Aloini et al. [32] establish the relevance of each of the factors during the different implementation phases.

3.2 Q2: Which Are the Proposal Foundations, Theoretical and/or Practical?

Most of the studies found (13 studies) based their proposal in theoretical foundations, only 4 of them are based just on practice and 5 are based on a mix of theoretical foundations and practice.

Theoretical Foundations. Many studies found such as the one developed by Schniederjans and Yadav [4] base their proposals on theoretical foundations, principles or known approaches. Metaxiotis et al. [22], for example, use goal directed project management principles to structure their implementation methodology and Stender [16] integrates the ideas of agile software development (mainly XP) with the incremental implementation methodology Results Driven Incrementalism (RDI) to propose an agile methodology for enterprise systems implementation. On the other hand, some works present the extension or validation of previously developed studies. These include the study by Peslak et al. [18], who propose an extension and validation of the proposal presented by Parr and Shanks, based on the critical success factors for ERP systems implementation proposed in the literature. Similarly, Markus and Tanis [28] based their framework on a process theory, designed by Soh and Markus, which explains how information technology creates business value.

Other studies are based on previously proposed methodologies or models of implementation. This is the case of Umble et al. [31] who identify the stages and critical factors of their proposal considering methodologies and studies found in the literature. Similarly, the model presented by Vilpola [25] combines the model proposed by Mäkipää, which has 8 + 2 stages, with user centered design process (UCD), which consists of four activities that are iterated until the design meets the requirements.

Ahituv et al. [17] develop their proposal based on: (i) the main models of the systems development lifecycle, (ii) systems implementation methodologies developed by software vendors, (iii) a literature search of several topics related to information systems implementation, (iv) case studies identified during the search in the literature. Al-Mashari et al. [30] base their proposal on the four stages of ERP lifecycle presented in the literature (analysis stage, planning and design stage, implementation and post-implementation stage). Some proposals are based on the combination of existing methodologies, such as the studies carried out by: Leem and Kim [23] who develop their proposal based on a comparison between three vendors methodologies: METHOD/1, IE-Expert, ASAP; Pachecho-Comer et al. [24] who mix the ERP implementation methodologies found in the literature and Parr and Shanks [6] who base their work in three models: (1) Bancroft et al. who propose the model based on the discussion of 20 practitioners and studies in three multinationals; (2) Ross and Vitale [33] and (3) Markus and Tanis [28].

Practical Foundations. There are few studies that base their proposals on observations or practical studies carried out in organizations or enterprises in which an ERP system is being implemented, among these are the works performed by: (i) Al-Mashari [5] who uses empirical based evidence drawn from a survey of many organizational practices related to ERP implementation and from many reported case studies; (ii) Chofreh et al. [26] who conduct a case study in production and service company in Iran; (iii) Berchet and Habchi [20] who base their work on the observations made to the deployment of an ERP project at the firm Alcatel, a telecommunications company, and (iv) Ross y Vitale [33] who consider the experiences of 15 manufacturing companies that have complete a significant part of the ERP implementation and that are attempting to generate a positive return on the investment made in that system.

Practical and Theoretical Foundations. There are also some primary studies based on both theoretical and practical foundations [19, 21, 27, 29], in this type of studies the authors combine a literature review with observations or studies performed in organizations that are implementing or have implemented an ERP system. Fu [19], for example, in addition to performing a literature review runs a case study in a SME in Taiwan where an ERP implementation project was carried out. The same happens with Somers and Nelson [7] who classified some critical success factors in key players an activities, based on the framework proposed by Markus and Tanis [28], on a review of the practice and on a research of the literature.

3.3   Q3: Which Are the Phases or Stages, Tasks or Activities Defined for ERP Systems Implementation

The phases proposed by each study are presented in Table 2, where it is possible to observe that the number of phases proposed by the studies varies between 3 and 11, which represents a wide difference. This is because each study presents a different approach giving more importance to either the project activities, implementation or ERP selection. The latter is the case of the study performed by Pacheco-Comer et al. [24], who present 11 phases of which the first 8 are oriented to the selection of vendor of the ERP system to be used in the company and the remaining 3 are in line with the

Table 2. Phases and stages proposed by each study

Vilpola [25]	Stender [16]	Aloini et al. [32]
UCD in evaluation stage UCD in modification stage UDC in exploitation stage	Analysis Process design and system customization System rollout	Concept Implementation Post-implementation
Ahituv et al. [17]	**Markus y Tannis [28]**	**Al-Mashari et al. [30]**
Selection Definition Implementation Operation	Project chartering Project phase Shakedown phase Onward and upward phase	Analysis Planning and designing Implementation Post-implementing
Peslak et al. [18]	**Bhatti [27]**	**Chofreh et al. [26]**
Preparation and training Transition Performance and usefulness Maintenance	Implementation planning Installation Final preparation Go live	Initiating Planning Executing Controlling Closing
Metaxiotis et al. [22]	**Berchet y Habchi [20]**	**Ross y Vitale [33]**
Marketing and presales Proposal Contract Completion Accomplishment	Selection of the vendor and software Deployment and integration of the ERP system Stabilization Progression Evolution	Design Implementation Stabilization Continuous improvement Transformation
Somers y Nelson [7]	**Rajagopal [21]**	**Leem y Kim [23]**
Initiation Adoption Adaption Acceptance Routinization	Initiation Adoption Adaption Acceptance Routinization Infusion	Planning Analysis Design Introduction Customization and running
Parr y Shanks [6]	**Pacheco-Comer et al. [24]**	
Planning Project – Set up – Re-engineering – Design – Configuration and testing – Installation Enhancement	Strategic business analysis phase Compilation of business requirements list and business readiness phase Elaboration of first candidates list and filter phase Identify and agree evaluation method phase Evaluate of short list candidates phase Elaborate evaluation matrix phase Decision make phase Negotiate contract phase Plan phase for ERP implementation phase Implementation phase Maintenance phase	

ones presented by other studies. This shows that there is not an ERP implementation standard model that integrates and presents the final phases or stages for this process, and therefore the authors of each study propose their own phases or stages.

Although most of these studies present a sequence of phases in a linear order, some of them propose iterations during certain phases, Vilpola [25], for example, presents a method to support the implementation and improvement, which combines user centered design (UCD) and ERP implementation processes describing iterations in three stages: evaluation, modification and exploitation. On the other hand, Stender [16] proposes an agile and incremental implementation methodology (AI^2M), which allows users to prioritize which functionality should be implemented first. For this, the project is divided into small release cycles dedicated to improving an agreed business goal. The methodology proposes 3 main phases within a cycle: analysis, process design and system customization and system rollout. An AI^2M iteration is limited to a fixed time. Finally, Ahituv et al. [17] propose a model that combines the components of the main systems development approaches: the information systems lifecycle model, the prototyping model and the application software package model. The proposed model is composed by four stages: (1) selection, (2) definition, (3) implementation and (4) operation. The implementation phase, considered the core of the model, is an iterative phase where the processes are redesigned to work with the ERP system, the system is implemented and user training and acceptation tests are performed.

4   Analysis

Considering the results presented in the previous section, it is observed that some proposals are based on project management principles, this because ERP systems implementation involves the execution of implementation projects that should be manage just like any other project. Although some primary studies base their proposals on project management proposals, none of them are based on the practices proposed in PMBOK guide [34], which nowadays is one of the major references for project management. The only study that refers to the PMBOK guide is the one by Chofreh et al. [26] who take into account the knowledge areas and processes groups proposed in the guide.

Similarly, although today agile methodologies are widely accepted and used for software project management, it is observed that only one of the primary studies [16] propose a methodology of this type, based on XP foundations. However, this proposal is focused on the implementation of CRM systems and not of ERP systems. This indicates that although there are studies that aim to structure and improve ERP systems implementation, the use of the principles and practices of other agile methodologies (such as scrum, Kanban, crystal, lean, among others) for ERP implementation has not yet been explored. This allows us to identify a research opportunity, since adopting the principles of agile methodologies in ERP implementation could simplify the phases, offer a better chance of success when adopting the solution, and allow the system to provide clear benefits from the beginning of the implementation. The previous analysis is limited to the scope of the systematic review performed in this study, which includes the search in the database Scopus.

On the other hand, it is noted that some primary studies based their proposal on systems development lifecycle. This is because sometimes ERP implementation involves system customization, which implies the development of additional functionalities for the system to meet the customer requirements. These are developments like any other, so they involve the common stages present in the systems development lifecycle. However, according to [35, 36] ERP systems customization should be minimized.

Another point to note is that there are few primary studies based on the practices of ERP vendors. It is interesting to consider the good practices used in the methodologies proposed by big ERP vendors, since these concentrate several years of observations and experience in implementation projects that could help to improve the software implementation process in other organizations.

In addition to the above, after observing the names of the phases presented in Table 2 and performing an analysis of the definition and activities proposed for each of them in the studies, we have found that these can be grouped in some main phases, such as those described below: (1) selection, where an analysis of the company needs is performed and the ERP system that satisfies them efficiently is searched; (2) project planning, which defines the goals, objectives and scope of the implementation project, in addition, during this phase the project manager is selected, the necessary plans are made, the project schedule is set, the necessary resources are defined and the project team is conformed and trained; (3) design and customization, where the current business process is reviewed to define whether it will be necessary to perform process reengineering or to customize the ERP system, for this a gap analysis between the selected ERP system and the organization business process is conducted, in this phase is also performed the reengineering and system customization, considering the end user participation and the construction of a prototype that aims to validate the system design and the integration of the new processes and the complementary system [17]; (4) implementation, where the ERP system is installed, the legacy system data are migrated and converted to the new system, in addition the ERP systems configuration is performed, if necessary integration with other systems is carried out, the necessary tests are performed and the new system is rolled out to support the organization operation; and (5) maintenance and continuous improvement, where systems support is provided, improvements, repairs and updates of the systems are made at the same time and the benefits of implementing the ERP system in the organization begin to be evident. Also, several studies highlight the importance of performing the end user training from initial stages of the ERP implementation and performing a correct change management in the organization, through the implementation of change management plan and a constant communication of project progress to all stakeholders.

Although the authors of some primary studies are limited only to the definition of ERP implementation phases or stages, most of them present activities or practices that are relevant during this process. When reviewing the activities proposed by each study, it is possible to determine that many of these coincide, Table 3 presents the common activities proposed in the primary studies, it is important to note that the study by Al-Mashari [5] does not proposes activities but practices related to key elements of the ERP implementation such as organizational strategic management, improvement of organizational process, system deployment, project organization and change

Table 3. Common activities classified by phases

Activities	References	Phase
Defining the benefit and impact of implementing an ERP system in the organization	[5, 21, 26, 28–30]	Selection
Performing cost-benefit analysis of the ERP system implementation	[21, 22, 26]	
Analyzing organization needs	[17, 22, 24–26, 29, 30]	
Defining user requirements	[19, 20, 24, 25, 32]	
Collecting information about ERP system vendors	[17, 24, 26]	
Selecting the appropriate ERP system	[5–7, 17, 19–21, 25, 26, 28, 29, 32]	
Defining goals, vision, and clear objectives of the project	[7, 16, 17, 20, 24–27, 29]	Project planning
Selecting the project manager	[6, 26, 28]	
Establishing a steering committee	[6, 19, 25]	
Defining project scope	[6, 16, 17, 22, 26, 27, 29, 33]	
Planning project schedule	[16, 17, 22, 25, 26, 29, 30]	
Selecting external consultants	[17, 19, 29, 33]	
Defining ERP system implementation strategy	[6, 23, 26, 27, 29]	
Defining resources, teams and supplies for the project	[6, 7, 22, 26, 30]	
Selecting and structuring project team considering the technical and business experience	[6, 17, 19, 20, 22, 24, 26, 28–30]	
Training project teams	[6, 17–19, 26, 28–31]	
Preparing implementation plan	[17–19, 24, 26–30]	
Analyzing current business processes to determine the level of business process reengineering required	[5, 6, 16, 19, 21, 25, 26, 28–31]	Design and customization
Analyzing the differences between the processes defined in the ERP system and their definition in the organization	[6, 17, 19, 20]	
Performing business process reengineering to obtain the benefits of the ERP technology	[5–7, 16, 17, 19–21, 25, 28–30, 33]	
Building prototypes to test the system design and the integration of the new processes and the system	[6, 17, 20, 25]	

(*continued*)

Table 3. (*continued*)

Activities	References	Phase
Customizing the ERP system	[7, 16, 17, 19–21, 23, 25–28]	
Installing the ERP system	[6, 17, 19, 20, 27, 31, 32]	Implementation
Integrating the systems	[20, 21, 28, 29, 32]	
Configuring ERP system	[6, 19, 24, 25, 27–29, 32]	
Performing data cleaning and conversion for the implemented ERP	[7, 17, 19, 21, 27, 28, 31, 33]	
Populating test cases with real data	[6, 16, 20]	
Performing system test, user test, acceptance test and integration test	[6, 16, 17, 19, 20, 26–28, 30–32]	
Rollout and startup of the system	[16, 19–21, 24, 28, 29, 33]	
Have the entire organization using the system. Users accept the system	[19–21, 31]	Maintenance and continuous improvement
Maintaining (repairs, improvements) and upgrading the system	[6, 17–19, 21, 23, 24, 28, 32, 33]	
Continuous business and system improvement: maximize ERP benefits	[6, 17, 19–21, 25, 28, 30–33]	
User training (from initial stages)	[6, 7, 16–21, 24, 26–31, 33]	Throughout the project
Communicating goals, scope and progress of the project	[5, 7, 22, 25, 26, 28, 29]	
Executing change management plan	[5, 7, 19, 20, 22, 28, 29]	

management, however, some of these practices coincide with the activities presented in the other studies found.

Considering the specification of each activity and its classification in the phases or stages proposed in the studies, we have grouped them in the five phases defined above (selection, project planning, design and customization, implementation and maintenance and improvement). It is also possible to observe that the activities related to user training, communication and change management are performed throughout the ERP system implementation process. In addition to the activities presented in the table, Al-Mudimigh et al. [29] and Metaxiotis et al. [22] emphasize the importance of considering risk management throughout the implementation project.

5 Conclusions and Future Work

Most of these studies structure their proposal based on theoretical foundations and few of them do so from the practice, in this way, we found studies that are based on existing proposals, principles or known approaches. Despite of this, it was found that the practices and activities established in the proposed implementation methodologies and the ones used by the most well-known ERP vendors (such as SAP and Oracle) are not considered for structuring the proposed methodologies, this could be very useful, since they have several years of experience and multiple cases of success in ERP implementation. Similarly, it was evidenced that the use of the practices and principles proposed by the agile methodologies to improve the ERP systems implementation process is an area that has not been explored in the literature, the same happens with the practices proposed by the PMBOK guide for project management. Likewise, it was found that there are many phases and activities proposed to structure the ERP system implementation. After analyzing each of these phases, considering both its name and definition, it was found that many of them coincided, so it was possible to unify them in five main phases: (1) selection, (2) project planning, (3) design and customization, (4) implementation and (5) maintenance and continuous improvement.

As future work the definition of a reference model to support the management of ERP systems implementation is being done. To structure this model, a comparison between the methodologies used by three big ERP system vendors is being performed, in order to identify the best practices and key activities of the implementation process and then unify them with the implementation phases defined in this review. In addition, the model will be based on the definition of practices that maximize the success factors in the ERP systems implementation projects, having clearly defined these practices could allow the enterprises that perform the implementation to have lower costs and shorter projects, while the organizations in which the implementation is carried out could obtain faster the benefits of the implementation of this type of systems.

References

1. Deneckere, R., Hug, C., Onderstal, J., Brinkkemper, S.: Method association approach: situational construction and evaluation of an implementation method for software products. In: Proceedings of the RCIS, pp. 274–285 (2015)
2. Zhang, Z., Lee, M.K.O., Huang, P., Zhang, L., Huang, X.: A framework of ERP systems implementation success in China: An empirical study. Int. J. Prod. Econ. 98, 56–80 (2005)
3. Ranjan, S., Jha, V.K., Pal, P.: Literature review on ERP implementation challenges. Int. J. Bus. Inf. Syst. 21, 388–402 (2016)
4. Schniederjans, D., Yadav, S.: Successful ERP implementation: An integrative model. Bus. Process Manag. J. 19, 364–398 (2013)
5. Al-Mashari, M.: A process change-oriented model for ERP application. Int. J. Hum. Comput. Interact. 16, 39–55 (2003)
6. Parr, A., Shanks, G.: A model of ERP project implementation. J. Inf. Technol. 15, 289–303 (2000)
7. Somers, T.M., Nelson, K.G.: A taxonomy of players and activities across the ERP project life cycle. Inf. Manag. 41, 257–278 (2004)

8. Kraljić, A., Kraljić, T., Poels, G., Devos, J.: ERP implementation methodologies and frameworks: a literature review. In: Proceedings of the 8th ECIME 2014, pp. 309–316. (2014)
9. Biolchini, J., Mian, P.G., Candida, A., Natali, C.: Systematic Review in Software Engineering (2005)
10. Kitchenham, B., Charters, S.: Guidelines for performing Systematic Literature reviews in Software Engineering (2007)
11. Scopus. www.scopus.com
12. Pino, F.J., García, F., Piattini, M.: Software process improvement in small and medium software enterprises: a systematic review. Softw. Qual. J. **16**, 237–261 (2008)
13. Sfetsos, P., Stamelos, I.: Empirical studies on quality in agile practices: a systematic literature review. In: Proceedings of the 7th QUATIC 2010, pp. 44–53 (2010)
14. Leedy, P.D., Ormrod, J.E.: Practical Research: Planning and Design. Prentice Hall, Upper Saddle River (2005)
15. Spencer, L., Ritchie, J., Lewis, J., Dillon, L.: Quality in qualitative evaluation: a framework for assessing research evidence a quality framework. Soc. Res. (New York) **108**, 170 (2003)
16. Stender, M.: Outline of an agile incremental implementation methodology for enterprise systems. In: AMCIS 2002 Proceedings, p. 130 (2002)
17. Ahituv, N., Neumann, S., Zviran, M.: A system development methodology for ERP systems. J. Comput. Inf. Syst. **42**, 56–67 (2002)
18. Peslak, A.R., Subramanian, G.H., Clayton, G.E.: The phases of ERP software implementation and maintenance: A model for predicting preferred ERP use. J. Comput. Inf. Syst. **48**, 25–33 (2007)
19. Fu, K.-E.: Development of a generic procedure model for the enterprise resource planning implementation in small and medium enterprises. In: Proceedings of the SICE Annual Conference, Taipei, Taiwan, pp. 3523–3528 (2010)
20. Berchet, C., Habchi, G.: The implementation and deployment of an ERP system: an industrial case study. Comput. Ind. **56**, 588–605 (2005)
21. Rajagopal, P.: An innovation - Diffusion view of implementation of enterprise resource planning (ERP) systems and development of a research model. Inf. Manag. **40**, 87–114 (2002)
22. Metaxiotis, K., Zafeiropoulos, I., Nikolinakou, K., Psarras, J.: Goal directed project management methodology for the support of ERP implementation and optimal adaptation procedure. Inf. Manag. Comput. Secur. **13**, 55–71 (2005)
23. Leem, C.S., Kim, S.: Introduction to an integrated methodology for development and implementation of enterprise information systems. J. Syst. Softw. **60**, 249–261 (2002)
24. Pacheco-Comer, A.A., González-Castolo, J.C., García-Sánchez, N.: Methodological proposal to implement enterprise resource planning systems. In: 17th AMCIS 2011, Detroit, MI, United States, pp. 1165–1174 (2011)
25. Vilpola, I.H.: A method for improving ERP implementation success by the principles and process of user-centred design. Enterp. Inf. Syst. **2**, 47–76 (2008)
26. Chofreh, A.G., Goni, F.A., Jofreh, M.G.: Enterprise Resource Planning (ERP) implementation process: project management perspective. Adv. Mater. Res. **338**, 152–155 (2011)
27. Bhatti, T.: Implementation process of enterprise resource planning (ERP): Empirical validation. In: Proceedings of the EMCIS 2006, Alicante, España (2006)
28. Markus, M.L., Tanis, C.: The Enterprise Systems Experience-From Adoption to Success. Pinnaflex Educational Resources, Cincinnati (2000)
29. Al-Mudimigh, A.S., Zairi, M., Al-Mashari, M.: ERP software implementation: an integrative framework. Eur. J. Inf. Syst. **10**, 216–226 (2001)

30. Al-Mashari, M., Zairi, M., Okazawa, K.: Enterprise Resource Planning (ERP) implementation: a useful road map. Int. J. Manag. Enterp. Dev. **3**, 169–180 (2006)
31. Umble, E.J., Haft, R.R., Umble, M.M.: Enterprise resource planning: implementation procedures and critical success factors. Eur. J. Oper. Res. **146**, 241–257 (2003)
32. Aloini, D., Dulmin, R., Mininno, V.: Risk management in ERP project introduction: review of the literature. Inf. Manag. **44**, 547–567 (2007)
33. Ross, J.W., Vitale, M.R.: The ERP revolution: surviving vs. thriving. Inf. Syst. Front. **2**, 233–241 (2000)
34. Project Management Institute: A guide to the project management body of knowledge (PMBOK ® guide). Project Management Institute, Inc. (2013)
35. Nah, F.H., Zuckweiler, K., Lau, J.L.S.: ERP implementation: chief information officers' perceptions of critical success factors. Int. J. Hum. Comput. Interact. **16**, 5–22 (2003)
36. Dezdar, S., Ainin, S.: Examining ERP implementation success from a project environment perspective. Bus. Process Manag. J. **17**, 919–939 (2011)

Architectonic Proposal for the Video Streaming Service Deployment Within the Educational Context

Pedro Luis Agudelo[1] ⓘ, Wilmar Yesid Campo[1(✉)] ⓘ, Alexandra Ruíz[1] ⓘ,
José Luis Arciniegas[2] ⓘ, and William J. Giraldo[1] ⓘ

[1] Universidad del Quindío, Armenia, Colombia
`plagudelog@uqvirtual.edu.co,`
`{wycampo,aruiz,wjgiraldo}@uniquindio.edu.co`
[2] Universidad del Cauca, Popayán, Colombia
`jlarciniegas@unicauca.edu.co`

Abstract. Video streaming is a technology that has had a great reception with internet users, and it has been integrated many platforms in different contexts like the educational one. For the video streaming distribution, the architectures use specialized protocols that manage the video transmission on the internet. In contrast, there are other alternatives proposed that allow streaming over the HyperText Transfer Protocol (HTTP). This paper proposes two streaming architectures using open source software for the distribution of Video on Demand (VoD) and live services over the HTTP. The distribution of live video is done with the Dynamic Adaptive Streaming over HTTP (DASH) standard. Through web components, video streaming is visualized from a web browser with the goal to build a virtual environment for the broadcast of educational material. These architectures are validated through a video streaming service deployment over the University of Quindío network using a case study within the educational context.

Keywords: DASH · Live Streaming · Streaming architecture · VoD streaming · Web components

1 Introduction

With the advancement of the Information and Communication Technologies, educational institutions have been able to bring knowledge to a greater number of students, overcoming limitations of time and space. These technologies include virtual platforms, which provide tools for the teacher to generate organized and structured virtual scenarios so that the student's learning process is self-directed, self-regulated, and autonomous [1].

The video content is one of the most used multimedia resources today in virtual platforms, because it stimulates the senses and positively affects the student's learning process [2]; however, its main disadvantage at the technical level is the need of bandwidths in the order of the megabits per second. Although the bandwidth offered by internet providers has been increasing over time, the demands and needs of internet users in relation to the quality of the video content have also increased. Video delivery via streaming is a technology

© Springer International Publishing AG 2017
A. Solano and H. Ordoñez (Eds.): CCC 2017, CCIS 735, pp. 313–326, 2017.
DOI: 10.1007/978-3-319-66562-7_23

created to overcome the waiting time associated with the total download of a multimedia file before it can be consumed. Therefore, the idea of video streaming is to divide the video into parts that will be transmitted and assembled in their destination and reproduced without the need to wait for all its parts as a whole. To make this possible, data must be transported over protocols designed specifically for video streaming as the real time transport protocol (RTP) [3], the real time streaming protocol (RTSP) [4], and the real time transport control protocol (RTCP) [3]. The use of these protocols requires servers to support them in such a way that the audio and video can be served to the client through specialized software to distribute the streaming. However, video streaming as a technology has evolved by taking advantage of the web, supporting new ways of transmitting its data as a source of distributed services. Thus, the video streaming service is able to support the transmission of data through the hyper text transfer protocol (HTTP), opening the possibility of integrating this service into web applications. Consequently, the service becomes much more accessible because the web browser is enough for the visualization of video streaming. When transmitting video streaming over the HTTP, it is possible to use a web server, which simplifies the architecture.

Thanks to the possibility of integrating the video streaming service as a web service over the HTTP, there have been applications that implement streaming for the playback of music, movies, and educational content, among others. For the latter, virtual education platforms have been limited to offering simple video playback components that do not provide interactivity between the user and video content or other contents. This can be a limitation for educational institutions, which in some cases depend 100 percent on this type of platforms for their teaching-learning process.

According to the described scenario, the contributions of this article focus on proposing two streaming architectures, one for the distribution of live video under the DASH standard and another for the VoD service in such a way that video streaming can be played through web components, with the aim of enriching the educational virtual platforms of teaching support. The proposed architectures are validated through the deployment of the video streaming service on the data network of the University of Quindío using a case study in the educational context. On the other hand, a set of web components are developed for the visualization of video streaming, that through a series of functionalities, offer greater interactivity for both students and teachers, and can be integrated into any web platform.

This article is organized as it follows below: section two presents the works related to streaming architectures, section three describes the proposed streaming architectures for VoD and live video transmission. In section four, a case study is described and it is exposed how interactivity is given through the development of the web components; later in section five, the obtained results are shown; and finally, section six presents the conclusions.

2   Works Related

There are several works in the literature where architectures that allow the efficient distribution of video streaming are proposed. [5] proposes a test environment for the videostreaming service support using free tools, the authors suggest that such environment can be used in the field of education.

On the other hand, [6] presents the videostreaming application Periscope which allows the transmission and live video playback from smartphones. This emerging technology is thought for global education in pathology. However, its use can also be adapted to formal education. In [7], streaming is focused as a service that can offer an opportunity for online teaching and learning since it plays an important role in the delivery of educational material to students.

[8] presents the importance of the Massive Open Online Course (MOOC) in higher education, which is based on the use of videostreaming as the main resource for delivering mass online courses.

The authors in [9], propose a model of automatic video switching used by leading videostreaming services along with a description of the communication and control protocol from the client side. From the control architecture standpoint, the automatic adaptation is achieved by two interactive control loops that have the controllers in the client and the actuators in the server; the other loop implements the switching controller between streams and aims at selecting the video level. A detailed validation of the proposed model has been carried out through experimental measurements in an emulated scenario. In [10], they start from the advantages of Content Delivery Network (CDN) and Peer-to-Peer Network (P2P) for proposing a hybrid architecture CDN-P2P for the distribution of live video, which is comprised of components responsible for the management, distribution of the video to the final user, and the P2P transfer. After the simulation, the authors identified a better performance in contrast to the one presented by the P2P or CDN architecture individually. The research was carried out in a simulated environment, so a prototype for experimentation on a real scenario is still missing.

On the other hand, in [11] they focus on the optimization of the streaming service of high demand with a cloud-based architecture. Multimedia is located on storage servers that are later distributed through proxy servers which are selected by means of optimization strategies taking into account the quality of the transmission, the maximization of the bandwidth, and the minimization of energy consumption. Although the proposal presents a streaming architecture, it does not present a way of video playback from the web.

In [12], the research is focused on video streaming compatible with web tools. They establish an architecture for bi-directional communication in real time through an architecture based on the Push technology, which is composed by a web server that creates the necessary elements for the visualization of the video and a server where the multimedia is stored that plays the content through WebSockets. While in [13], the research is centered on scalable video coding (SVC) for a transmission over HTTP under the DASH standard. This, by using different layers of SVC in different representations which are presented in the description of media presentation (Media Presentation Description MPD) which improves the performance of the IPTV service on HTTP. In the previous proposals, two important technologies for our article are put together, streaming from the HTML5 and DASH; although the inclusion of HTML5 for the ransmission on WebSockets is temporary since the process for the capture can overload the client.

It is proposed in [14] an improvement in the quality of video streaming distribution using MPEG (Moving Picture Experts Group) on wireless networks. The solution called

Intelligent Queue Management specifies the packages containing the important frames generated by the MPEG codec to protect them in case of packet loss, preserving the quality of the video reception. On the other hand, the proposal presented in [15] is based on a framework for the development of video-streaming applications for video surveillance, through the eXtensible Messaging and Presence Protocol (XMPP), the elements developed for the framework only allow to play the streaming on end-to-end connections.

Finally, [16] presents the WebRTC technology, Web Real-Time Communications, which intends to revolutionize the way web users communicate. WebRTC adds standard APIs (Application Programming Interface), capabilities, and built-in real-time audio and video codecs to the browser without a plug-in. Thanks to the benignity of video, companies such as telestax [17] or Bistri [18] emerge whose objective is providing interactive video communication solutions or videoconference platforms.

Table 1, presents a brief summary of the different researches regarding video-streaming and its use in education.

Table 1. Research carried out on streaming applied to education.

Reasearch consulted	Description	Technologies	Protocols	Application
Test environment for videostreaming support using free tools [5]	Proposes a testing environment for videostreaming service	LIVE555	RTSP	General use
		OpenRTSP	RTP	Educational
		FFMPEG	SDP	
		Hermes		
Using the periscope live video-streaming application for global pathology education: a brief introduction [6]	Presents an application for videostreaming transmission and playback from smartphones	Periscope	N/A	Education in pathology
		Android		
		iOS		
Video streaming in online learning [7]	The authors analyze streaming to integrate it in educational environments	MPEG	RTSP	Educational
		Helix server		
		Synchronized Multimedia Instruction Language		
MOOCs and Higher Education [8]	The importance of MOOCs in higher education	Learning Management System	N/A	Educational
		HTML		
WebRTC: APIs and RTCWEB Protocols of the HTML5 Real-Time Web [16]	It is a Project for the development of audio and video applications	HTML5	HTTP	General use
		JavaScript	SIP	
		VoIP	RTP	
		WebSockets	XMPP	

The works described above represent the technological foundation to reach the situation proposed, which uses video streaming technologies and web components, in order to provide tools to support teaching through platforms that use video streaming.

In addition, the importance of research in videostreaming from different perspectives and the necessity to generate architectures that allow the real deployment of this technology are evidenced. The following section covers a set of concepts related to the project described in this article.

3   Theoretical Frame

This section describes relevant concepts such as streaming, DASH, RTMP and Nginx, which are related to the development of this research.

Streaming. Streaming is a technology based on the distribution of multimedia files across the network by dividing them into parts that will be transmitted, assembling them at their destination. So they can be visualized without having to wait for all the parts. Streaming does not require a large storage capacity because a small part of the multimedia is stored temporarily by the client in a buffer as it is played, countering network problems such as fluctuating values like bandwidth, latency, jittering, packet loss rate, among other parameters [19].

DASH. The development of specific protocols has been necessary to support the streaming technology through the network. However, it is currently possible to stream through the HTTP protocol as it is with the case of DASH. This is a standard for video streaming transmission with the ability to vary the bit rate according to the network state on the client side. This is possible through a Media Presentation Descriptor (MPD) in which a structured collection of accessible data is defined, so the DASH client identifies the available content on the server [20].

RTMP. The Real Time Messaging Protocol (RTMP), initially designed for multimedia streaming between Flash players and a streaming server, is based on TCP. The streams are fragmented by default to 64 bytes for audio and 128 bytes for video and other data types. Communication between the client and the server is carried out through a handshaking, an exchange of Action Message Format (AMF) messages, and the encapsulation of the data. Due to the publication of protocol specifications, it has been possible to use it with technologies different to Flash [21].

The Nginx open source web server with a simplified BSD license, is based on threads for the management of requests. Nginx employs an asynchronous architecture based on events. It features load balancing, Flash Video (FLV) file streaming, and MP4 [22]. FLV is used for video visualization in applications developed in Flash. The MP4 container, which is part of the MPEG-4 part 14 standard, allows to transmit the video over the internet besides providing other benefits like including multiple audio tracks, subtitle support of HTTP, and HTTP2 on SSL [23].

4   Streaming Architecture Proposed

This section presents the design of two architectures in which the video is distributed through the network. The first architecture distributes the multimedia under the VoD

318 P.L. Agudelo et al.

service, and it is of the Server-less type. The second architecture proposed is for live video transmission, and it is of the Client-less type. The architectures were designed in such a way that the streaming distributed through HTTP was played through web components that took into account the applied research methodology described in [24], which allows to validate methods, techniques, and systems for which it is mandatory certain functional requirements, interaction support, or user satisfaction. The proposed architectures are described below.

4.1 Architecture for the VoD Video Streaming Service

The proposed architecture does not use any real time transfer protocol such as RTSP. Instead, it uses the HTTP protocol for multimedia transfer. Because this architecture is server-less, the specialized server is replaced by a web server that hosts services for the audio and video transmission. Due to the possibility of using a web server in the architecture to transmit video streaming, there is a significant reduction in the complexity and costs for its implementation. It has no drawbacks with firewalls since the streaming is done through the protocol and the port where it is browsed on the network. This architecture also has the possibility of being horizontally scalable.

In Fig. 1, the proposed architecture for the VoD distribution is illustrated. As it can be seen, a web server is used that manages the requests generated by the user from a web browser. The web server has a module that allows video playback under progressive

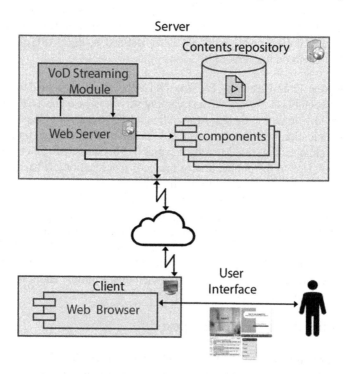

Fig. 1. Architecture of the server-less type for the VoD video streaming service.

download in MP4 format. The proposed architecture is implemented in such a way that video streaming can be played by the web components.

The modules that comprise this architecture are: (i) the web browser, which allows the user to request and interact with multimedia; (ii) the web server, which is responsible for receiving the request for visualizing the components and once the video playback starts, it sends the request to the VoD streaming module; and (iii) the VoD streaming module, which searches for the video file inside a repository and transports the video streaming over HTTP to finally be reproduced in the web components from the browser.

4.2   Architecture for the Live Video Streaming Service

The architecture proposed for the live video streaming service is of the Client-less type; that is to say, it does not have a client program that manages the visualization of the multimedia because it only requires an applet or plugin and the web browser to play the video streaming.

In Fig. 2, the architecture for the live video distribution is shown. The goal of this architecture is to perform the audio and video transmission, so it can be reproduced from

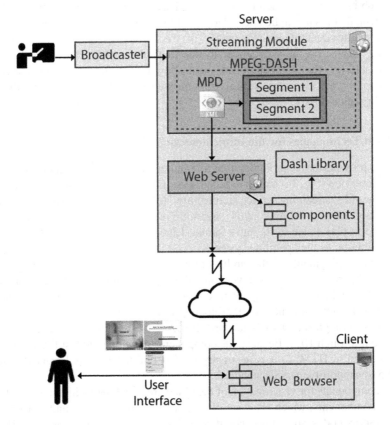

Fig. 2. Architecture of the client-less type for the live video streaming service.

a web application. Since the web browser uses the HTTP protocol for data transfer, we look for technologies that allow us to transmit video streaming over HTTP. To evaluate the proposed streaming architectures, a series of components were developed for the student to interact with video and other resources prepared by the teacher. In the context of this research, a component is defined as an element of a software that offers a specific function through a defined interface. It is mainly characterized by being standardized, independent, deployable, and documented [25].

Currently, there are several alternatives such as the HTTP Live Streaming (HLS), HTTP Dynamic Streaming (HDS), and DASH which has been standardized, features HTML5 support, and is a solution in video streaming playback before fluctuations on the network. The streaming service is enabled on the web server through a module that allows to receive audio and video to distribute them on the network through DASH.

To reproduce the live video from the web browser, it is necessary that the components be developed in a language that can be interpreted by the web browser as the HTML5 and JavaScript. Since video playback under the DASH standard is not natively implemented in HTML5, a library written in JavaScript is integrated, which allows to receive the distributed streaming through this standard.

The modules that comprise the architecture for the live video streaming service are: (i) the web browser, by which the user visualizes multimedia; (ii) a software (broadcaster), which emits the audio and video signal to the web server that is responsible for transmitting the streaming to the network; (iii) the streaming module, which enables the streaming service on the web server to distribute the multimedia using the DASH standard; and (iv) the web components that allow to visualize the emitted streaming from the server; and also, support is given to the web application so it is compatible with DASH through a library.

4.3   Used Technologies for the Implementation of the Architectures

The Fig. 3 presents the technologies used for implementing each architecture: VoD video streaming service (Fig. 3a) and Live video streaming service (Fig. 3b). For the deployment of the video streaming service architecture, VoD was used as an Apache web server in its version 2.4 plus the mod_h264_streaming module which, for testing purposes, is configured to play video in the mp4 format. Linux was used under the Ubuntu 14.04 LTS distribution as the operating system.

For the deployment of the architecture for the Live video streaming service (Fig. 3b), the Nginx web server version 1.1 plus the nginx-rtmp-module streaming module were, which is in charge of receiving the audio and video signal transmitted from a Broadcaster using the RTMP protocol. The streaming module is in charge of the distribution through the DASH standard. Besides, the module also has the ability to distribute it through HLS. Because the components developed to test the architectures are developed in HTML5, it is necessary to integrate the Dash.js library that allows HTML5 to support the DASH standard.

The components for visualization of the video are developed with the technology of the web components, which are a set of APIs that allow to encapsulate HTML, CSS, and JavaScript codes, so that it is not affected by changes in its environment. The web

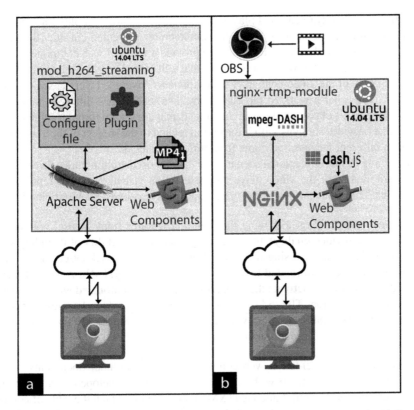

Fig. 3. Technologies used in the implementation of the (a) Architecture for the VoD video streaming service, (b) Architecture for the live video streaming service

components consist of four elements: the templates, the custom elements, the shadow DOM, and the import. Each element can be used individually or in combination, and they are described below: (i) the templates are a mechanism to maintain code that is not rendered on the client side; and thus, it can be instantiated using JavaScript; (ii) the custom elements allow the creation of customizable tags, which the service or functionality of the web component is invoked; (iii) the shadow DOM refers to the ability of the browsers to encapsulate DOM from the custom elements; this encapsulation prevents the web component to be modified or alter external elements; (iv) the import allows to include HTML5 files in other documents. Through the import it is possible to invoke the custom element in a document where it is desired to be used. To import an HTML5 document, a web server is required in order to function because the request is made through an HTTP request.

5   A Case Study Applied in the Educational Context

The architectures proposed are a response to the need for the University of Quindío in relation to providing educational video content on its virtual platform in a more interactive way than conventional players do, making it not too complex for those who use or configure the technology. Thus, the architectures presented consider the factors related to this context. For them it is posed to provide a series of web components to the virtual platform of the University of Quindío that will provide a greater interactivity for the presentation of the video content. The components developed were based on observation of the teacher's work in the classroom. The teacher has different audiovisual means to impart his class like slides or documents that are shown through a video beam. Likewise, it provides students with information related to the subject of the class, which may be in different formats and come from different sources.

According to this educational scenario for the proposed architectures, three components were identified: the video player, a presentation visualizer, and a repository of related files. The main features of the web components developed are highlighted below.

Video Player. In addition to having the common features (play, pause, volume, full screen mode, and video quality), the video player has the possibility of including subtitles in multiple languages using files with Web Video Text Track (WebVTT) format, which specifies metadata related to audio and video time in HTML. Another function included is the ability to activate the transcription that is synchronized with the video as well as the presentation. The video player has support for video playback distributed under the DASH standard, and it provides the possibility of plane-shifting (VoD service only) in case the video production has been performed with two cameras.

Presentation. The presentation web component allows to render documents in PDF format and synchronize them with any video web player developed as a component using an eXtensible Markup Language (XML) document in which the table of contents of the presentation can be configured. It also has the possibility to enable or disable syncronization with the video while playback is in progress.

Related Resources. This web component shows a list of links to resources that the teacher suggests to the student. These links are configured through an XML document where the URL, the title of the link, and the respective icon are specified according to the type of link.

6   Results

The servers used in each one of the architectures are validated through a stress test. For the Apache server, tests were performed requesting videos that were encoded at different resolutions ranging from 144 px (pixels) to 720 px. This test is performed with the ApacheBench software, a benchmarking tool used for measuring the performance of web servers. During the test, a limit of 10000 requests where the response time increases exponentially was identified. As show in Fig. 4, the tests were performed with 400 concurrent requests. The increase in the response time was greater than ten seconds for videos with resolutions varying from 144 px to 720 px. Since this waiting time is so long, the server cancels the connection. For the Nginx server, the same tests are performed with ApacheBench at the time of accessing the generated MPD file when the live video stream starts. In Fig. 5, it can be seen that the response time does not exceed 300 ms before concurrent requests that vary from 300 to 1000.

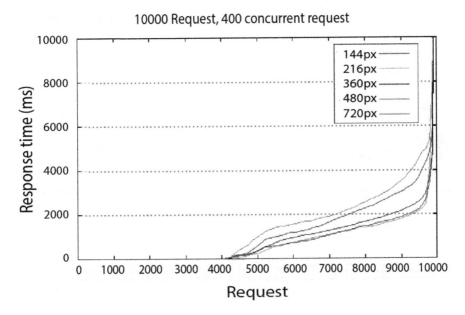

Fig. 4. Stress test to the Apache server when demanding a video with 10000 requests and 400 concurrent requests.

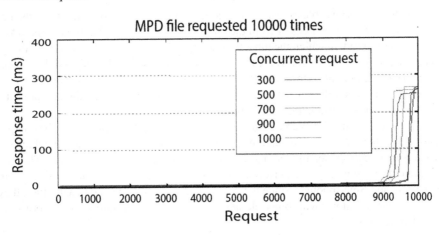

Fig. 5. Stress test to the Apache server when demanding a video with 10000 requests and 100 concurrent requests.

The Nginx server can support a larger number of requests simultaneously in comparison to the Apache server.

In Fig. 6, the web components are integrated into an HTML5 document, and they are compiled in such a way that the presentation, the video, and the transcription are synchronized. Thanks to synchronization, the user can interact with video streaming from the video player using basic functions such as pausing or starting playback from a specific point in the progress bar.

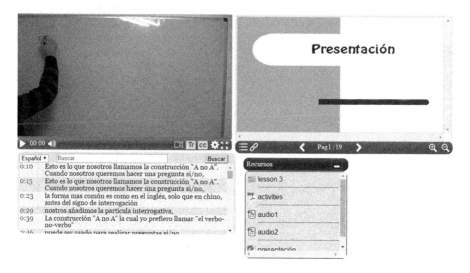

Fig. 6. Web components developed.

In addition, it is possible to search for specific content from the presentation, whether by moving between the slides or from the table of contents according to how the XML has been configured, in which the time, the corresponding page number, and the title are specified. From the transcript, where the video dialog is displayed, it is possible to identify a specific fragment of the video and start playback from that point. Thus, the user can interact in three different ways with the video streaming through the components: video player, presentation, and transcription.

It is important that the WebVTT documents and the XML are present in the components so that there is a communication between them to provide a scenario in which the dynamism increases when interacting with the transmitted audiovisual content. The web components present a good performance from the Chrome web browser for both computers and Smartphones. Since the components do not depend on each other, they can be integrated along with other elements to integrate them into web platforms for virtual education.

7   Conclusions

In this article, the proposed streaming architectures were presented, which video streaming was distributed through the VoD and live (using DASH) service by means of web servers. The architectures are validated through the transmission of educational content that is visualized from the web components developed.

In order to evaluate the capacity of the web servers used in each architecture, a stress test was performed in which it was identified that around the 10000 requests, the Apache server presented an exponential growth in the waiting time. While the Nginx server did not exceed 300 ms when making requests to the MPD document before different values of concurrent requests.

The transmission of educational content in both VoD and live on the proposed architectures was successfully achieved by reproducing the video from the Chrome web browser using the proposed components.

The web components were developed from the different audiovisual resources that a teacher uses to impart his class. The components were integrated perfectly into an HTML document in which an environment was established to provide interactivity in the video streaming visualization through a video player, a document or slide visualizer, and the transcription, which were synchronized without any inconvenience through XML and WebVTT documents.

It is proposed as future work the implementation of tests of the architectures in production that allow to obtain data from service and experience quality in educational environments. Thus, the advantages or disadvantages of the proposed architectures can be objectively compared to other alternatives.

Acknowledgement. Project 839 from the GITUQ group, funded by Vicerrectoria de investigaciones fo the Universidad del Quindío.

References

1. Aguilar, M.: Aprendizaje y Tecnologías de Información y Comunicación: Hacia nuevos escenarios educativos. Revista Latinoamericana de Ciencias Sociales, Niñez y Juventud **10**(2), 801–811 (2012)
2. Zhang, D., Zhou, L., Briggs, R.O., Nunamaker, J.F.: Instructional video in e-learning: assessing the impact of interactive video on learning effectiveness. Inf. Manag. **43**(1), 15–27 (2006)
3. Schulzrinne, H., Casner, S., Frederick, R., Jacobson, V.: RTP: a transport protocol for real-time applications, p. 19 (2003). https://tools.ietf.org/html/rfc3550
4. Schulzrinne, H., Casner, S., Frederick, R., Jacobson, V.: Real Time Streaming Protocol (RTSP) (1998). https://tools.ietf.org/html/rfc2326
5. Urbano, F.A., et al.: Entorno de pruebas para el soporte de videostreaming usando herramientas libres. Ing. Desarro **34**(2), 333–353 (2016). ISSN 0122-3461. http://dx.doi.org/10.14482/inde.33.2.6368
6. Fuller, M.Y., Mukhopadhyay, S., Gardner, J.M.: Using the periscope live video-streaming application for global pathology education: a brief introduction. Arch. Pathol. Lab. Med. **140**(11), 1273–1280 (2016). doi:10.5858/arpa.2016-0268-SA
7. Hartsell, T., Yuen, S.: Video streaming in online learning. AACE J. **14**(1), 31–43 (2006)
8. Pomerol, J.-C., Epelboin, Y., Thoury, C.: MOOCs and Higher Education MOOCs, pp. 83–100. Wiley (2015)

9. Cicco, L.D., Mascolo, S.: An adaptive video streaming control system: modeling, validation, and performance evaluation. IEEE/ACM Trans. Netw. **22**(2), 526–539 (2014). doi:10.1109/tnet.2013.2253797

10. Yin, H., Liu, X., Zhan, T., Sekar, V., Qiu, F.: Design and deployment of a hybrid CDN-P2P system for live video streaming: experiences with LiveSky. Paper Presented at the Proceedings of the 17th ACM International Conference on Multimedia, Beijing, China (2009)

11. Sebestyen, G., Hangan, A., Sebestyen, K., Vachter, R.: Self-tuning Multimedia Streaming System on Cloud Infrastructure. Procedia Comput. Sci. **18**, 1342–1351 (2013)

12. Kapetanakis, K., Panagiotakis, S., Malamos, A.: Architecture for real time communications over the web. Int. J. Web Eng. **2**, 1–8 (2013)

13. Sanchez, Y., Schierl, T., Hellge, C., Wiegand, T., Hong, D., De Vleeschauwer, D.: Efficient HTTP-based streaming using scalable video coding. Sig. Process. Image Commun. **27**(4), 329–342 (2012)

14. Haghani, E., Ansari, N., Parekh, S., Colin, D.: Traffic-aware video streaming in broadband wireless networks. Paper Presented at the 2010 IEEE Wireless Communication and Networking Conference (2010)

15. Kersten, B., van Rens, K., Mak, R.: ViFramework: a framework for networked video streaming components. In: Proceedings of the 2011 International Conference on Parallel and Distributed Processing Techniques and Applications, PDPTA 2011, pp. 286–292 (2011)

16. Johnston, A.B., Burnett, D.C.: WebRTC: APIs and RTCWEB Protocols of the HTML5 Real-Time Web: Digital Codex LLC (2012)

17. TeleStax (2017). http://www.telestax.com/. Accessed 24 June 2017

18. Bistri Communication Inside (2017). https://bistri.com/. Accessed 24 June 2017

19. Apostolopoulos, J.G., Tan, W.T., Wee, S.J.: Video streaming: concepts, algorithms, and systems. Report HPL-2002-260, HP Laboratories (2002)

20. Stockhammer, T.: Dynamic adaptive streaming over HTTP: standards and design principles. Paper Presented at the In: Proceedings of the Second Annual ACM Conference on Multimedia Systems, San Jose, CA, USA (2011)

21. Adobe's Real Time Messaging Protocol. Adobe Systems. http://www.adobe.com/devnet/rtmp.html. Accessed 20 Feb 2017

22. Nginx Admin Guide and Tutorial. http://www.nginx.com/resources/admin-guide/. Accessed 4 Jan 20174

23. Riiser, H., Halvorsen, P., Griwodz, C., Johansen, D.: Low overhead container format for adaptive streaming. Paper Presented at the Proceedings of the First Annual ACM SIGMM Conference on Multimedia Systems, Phoenix, Arizona, USA (2010)

24. Tamayo, M.: El proceso de la investigación científica: Limusa (2004)

25. Sommerville, I.: Definition of a software component and its elements. In: Sommerville, I. (ed.) Component-Based Software Engineering: Putting the Pieces Together, pp. 5–17. Addison-Wesley Professional, Boston (2001)

Requirements Elicitation Based on Inception Deck and Business Processes Models in Scrum

Manuel Pastrana[1](✉), Hugo Ordóñez[1], Armando Ordóñez[2],
and Luis Merchan[1]

[1] Research Laboratory in Development of Software Engineering,
Universidad San Buenaventura, Cali, Colombia
alexander15950@gmail.com,
{haordonez, lmerchan}@usbcali.edu.co
[2] Intelligent Management Systems, University Foundation of Popayán,
Popayán, Colombia
jaordonez@unicauca.edu.co

Abstract. Inception Deck is an elicitation technique supported by agile methodologies and frameworks like SCRUM. This paper presents an approach for requirements elicitation based on Inception Deck. In the present approach, the User Stories are replaced by Business Process Models to achieve an unambiguous vision of the requirements and high-quality software. The validation was performed with real projects and allowed evidence a positive impact of the business process modeling during the elicitation and in all the other phases of the software project.

Keywords: SCRUM · Inception deck · Business Process Model, BPM · Business Process Model Notation, BPMN

1 Introduction

Traditionally, software quality is affected by deficient and inadequate analysis of stakeholder's needs. The latter is due to the fact that a poor elicitation may involve significant changes, overcharges or even cancellation of projects [1].

The Inception deck technique [2, 3] seeks to improve the pre-analysis and analysis phases of software projects. This method is focused on creating a unified vision of the project based on the consensus of all the stakeholders (client, analysts, and developers, among others). The requirements elicitation is guided by 10 activities (not all of them are mandatory, but recommended) that include the analysis of the functionality and risks, the selection of people relevant to the project, the definition of the architecture, and the estimation of the costs. In spite of its advantages, Inception Deck may result quite costly regarding time and money since it involves all the people relevant to the project [4].

The consensus proposed by Inception Deck results in an optimization of the requirements elicitation, and an early detection of risks. However, this consensus does not prevent the ambiguity in the final product (Product Backlog in SCRUM) as the requirements information is collected using user stories in natural language. Therefore,

© Springer International Publishing AG 2017
A. Solano and H. Ordóñez (Eds.): CCC 2017, CCIS 735, pp. 327–339, 2017.
DOI: 10.1007/978-3-319-66562-7_24

it is needed a strategy to improve this elicitation. Recently, BPM (Business process model) and BPMN (Business process model notation) have emerged as a visual alternative to eliminate the ambiguity of user stories since these offer an overall and graphic view of the processes, variables, and needs [5].

In this spirit, this article describes the use of BPMN for requirements elicitation in Scrum using the Inception Deck technique. This paper is organized as follows; Sect. 2 describes the inception deck technique, Sect. 3 exposes the proposed strategy, Sect. 4 explains the use of BPM in inception deck, Sect. 5 explains the evaluation of the proposal and Sect. 6 concludes.

2   Inception Deck

Inception deck includes a set of guiding questions to unify the vision of the work team and the client about the product [4]. This exercise is carried out in a single meeting that may take between 4 to 16 h according to the size of the project. Inception deck allows sharing different points of view and identifying project risks. The questions are described below

- *Initial activity: Who is in the auditorium?*

It is necessary to start by knowing the people in the meeting and the role that they play in the project. People are grouped in pairs, and the following data are collected:

- Name
- Contact information
- What are the person likes and dislikes
- People are asked to draw an image that represents them.

The duration of this activity depends on the size of the auditorium (30 min maximum). Once the activity has finished, each person introduces himself to his partner, thus breaking the ice and gradually entering a zone of confidence. After performing this initial activity, the rules of the game are explained. Some example rules are:

- The activity has a maximum duration
- The people must be focused on the activity without distractions.
- No phones are allowed
- All participants in the meeting should give their opinion.
- All opinions are valid and will be respected.

I. *First Inception activity: Why are we here?*

This activity focuses on identifying the vision of the product. All the opinions are written on the board, later, these opinions are exchanged with the other assistants. The duration of this activity is 15 min maximum

II. *Second activity: Creating an Elevator Pitch*

This dynamic allows identifying the core of the project. An elevator pitch considers that audiences quickly lose interest if they do not know the topic, who is speaking, and what is the value offered to them. Thus a reasonable duration of this activity is 20 min. Each member of the team answers the following questions:

- Who is the solution addressed to?
- Who is identifying the need or opportunity?
- What is the name of the product?
- What is the category of the product?
- What benefits does this project bring?
- What do you dislike about the product and what alternatives do you pose?
- What is the differentiating factor of the product?

III. *Third activity: design a product box*

The auditorium is asked to imagine that the project is available in a product catalog, where the brand and the business objective must be made visible. To do this, the participants must answer these three simple topics:

- Product name
- Phrase that identifies the product
- Benefits of the product that differentiates it from others.

This step can take from 20 to 60 min. Up to this point, the questions focus on clarifying what the project is, why it should be done and its benefits

IV. *Fourth activity: create a list of "what is not"*

In this activity, the people express everything that the product "is not" delimiting technical and legal issues of the product. Thus the client and the team limit the scope of the project. Estimated duration of this activity is 20 to 40 min.

V. *Fifth activity: Meet your neighborhood*

This question identifies how the people in the auditorium interact with one another. This activity seeks to strengthen relationships to achieve the success of the project. The duration of this activity can be from 30 to 60 min. This activity allows determining the roles of the product, the needs to satisfy and the interactions of the stakeholders with the process.

VI. *Sixth activity: What keeps us up at night?*

This question focuses on identifying at an early stage the potential risks and the strategies to reduce them and minimize their impact. The estimated time for this step is 30 min to 2 h.

VII. *Seventh Activity, Show the solution*

This point is crucial as the system functionality is defined here. Some of the following techniques can be used

– *Give the app some personality*

Here the application is treated as a person, detailing how it behaves from the emotional aspect. Sometimes is complicated to apply, and it is not recommended if the emotional aspect is not relevant to the product (This exercise focuses on the usability of the application).

– *Let's make it flow*

The possible interactions between the user and the system are detailed as a workflow. This workflow offers a global view of the context and the associated elements.

– *Wireframing*

Here, the system screens and their interaction flow are depicted. Likewise, the allowed actions, the screens for each role, and other relevant aspects are detailed.

– *Stories map*

Here, the modules and user stories of the solution are described in an epic way to find a minimum viable product.

VIII. *Eighth activity: what are you going to bring?*

The objective of this question is to clarify the necessary commitments to reach the success of the project. The duration of this activity varies from 10 to 30 min

IX. *Ninth activity: how much will it cost?*

The objective of this question is to analyze the costs of the project, not only in economic but in technical terms. The duration of this step varies from 10 to 30 min.

X. *Tenth Activity, Summary*

Here, a summary of the activity is made. This summary details everything that has been done and the minimum viable product is exposed. The opinions are collected, and the activity is closed. The information is consolidated in a formal scrum document, called product backlog. Although this technique increases the probability of project success, the final result is still written in natural language, so the problem of interpretation is not resolved.

The present approach proposes a modification in the 7th activity of the inception deck (Show the solution), the change consists in modeling the information elicited using BPMN instead of user stories (an image says more than a thousand words). BPMN facilitates the communication and understanding and allows exploring different perspectives.

3   Proposal

Diverse efforts have been made to determine the key success factors for the requirements analysis in software projects. In this vein, the Standish group reports have performed comparisons between projects using agile and traditional methodologies since 1994 [1]. In the most recent report, the agile based projects show better results as they are focused on individual interactions, the collaboration with the client, the response to the change and the continuous feedback [6]. Table 1 shows the results of the most recent study.

Table 1. Successful factors (chaos report 2015 - standish group)

Size	Method	Successful	Challenged	Failed
All size	Agile	39%	52%	9%
	Waterfall	11%	60%	29%
Large size projects	Agile	18%	59%	23%
	Waterfall	3%	55%	42%
Medium size projects	Agile	27%	62%	11%
	Waterfall	7%	68%	25%
Small size projects	Agile	58%	38%	4%
	Waterfall	44%	45%	11%

The Standish group attributes the failure to two factors; the first factor is the non-involvement of users during the software development process. Even in agile methodologies that consider stakeholders through the role of the product owner, the user's involvement is not effective. In SCRUM the information elicited is consolidated in user stories and is the basis for building the product backlog. SCRUM suggests the involvement of stakeholders in the requirements elicitation and in general throughout the project. This involvement allows the product to be optimized sprint to sprint. The active participation of all stakeholders, collaborative work, and retrospective analysis tend to solve many problems that are presented in software projects, allowing verification and constant feedback on the progress of the project [7]. Accordingly, all projects should actively involve all stakeholders in the project in order to obtain the best result in the elicitation of requirements.

The second factor is related to the requirements elicitation. This elicitation is affected by the ambiguity of the resulting documentation in natural language (user stories in SCRUM, or use cases in RUP). These artifacts can be interpreted in different ways by clients, analysts or developers in later stages of the project [8]. Therefore, inadequate requirements elicitation has negative repercussions given that the client and the development team do not share the vision of the product [9].

Some techniques such as Inception Deck [3] have been proposed to address these two factors. Also, some works such as [10, 11] have combined traditional elicitation techniques (interview, questionnaires, etc.) with business process modeling (BPM). In [11] it was shown that a software analysis process could be successfully carried out if the final results are modeled using BPMN since the representation and interpretation of processes are unique and eliminate the inherent ambiguity of natural language. These results are confirmed by other works such as [10] where the process improve is exposed in detail. To ensure success in the use of BPM in the elicitation process, training in BPMN is necessary so that all participants can interpret the models resulting from the process. The time invested in the early stages of product development is compensated in the later phases since the refinement and change of the requirements is reduced [5].

The purpose of this paper is to study the advantages for SCRUM of maintaining a unified product vision through the inception deck technique and preserving this vision through an unambiguous description (BPM). For the present study, the following hypotheses are considered:

- Hypothesis 1: The number of final requirements approved by all participants in the first refinement review is greater when BPMN is used instead of user stories.
- Hypothesis 2: The appearance of new requirements decreases when BPMN is used in the elicitation process.
- Hypothesis 3: The percentage of development tasks that meet the customer acceptance is greater when BPM is used.

The inclusion of BPM seeks to maintain the unification of the vision of the product (compiled with the inception deck) through a visual representation and a unique form of interpretation that eliminates the ambiguity inherent in user stories written in natural language. In this way, it is possible to maintain the vision of the product in a Business process model, and to improve the communication of the project participants, thus contributing to a directly proportional improvement of the quality of the product to be developed.

In the present approach, each element of the user story is associated with the BPMN components. The first element of the user story is the title (which reveals the goal). The second element is the id of the user story (Version) that allows the team and the stakeholders to reference the user stories. The core of the user stories is composed of three elements [8]: Firstly, The roles are expressed as a sentence *I as a [role]* that describes who executes the action. Secondly, the characteristic/functionality is expressed in the sentence *I want to [action or functionality]* that allows identifying the name of the functionality in a clear way and recognizing the need to solve. Finally, the reason is expressed in the sentence *so that [benefit or motivation]* that denotes the reason and importance of the functionality. In addition to this structure, it is important to identify the acceptance criteria that describe the context of the project and the dependencies. These criteria allow defining the expected behavior. Table 2 shows an example of a user story.

A mapping between the components of the user stories and the BPMN elements is presented in Table 3.

Once the mapping is done the team can proceed with the construction of the process models of the project.

Table 2. User story for the smart track project

User Story ID	Statement of the User Story			
	Role	Characteristic/Functionality	Reason	Acceptance criteria
HU – Smart Track - 001	I as an [administraror]	I want to [have a login for the system]	So that [unauthorized users can't have access to the information and functionalities]	1. The screen should include a title (Agile Illusions) 2. The screen must include a field to enter the User Name. 2.1.The screen must include a field to Enter the Password 3. The password field information must be visible only with the character (•) 4. The screen must have a button to access the system, once the user presses this button the system must perform the following validations: 4.1. The User field must be filled in (Cannot be empty). In case the system is not fulfilled the following message must be generated (connection was not successful. Please enter the user) 4.2. The Password field must be filled in (Cannot be empty). In case the system is not fulfilled, the following message must be generated (connection was not successful. Please enter the password) 4.3. The User and Password must correspond to record in the DB. Otherwise, the system must generate the following message (connection was not successful, User or Password invalid) 5. The text and button fields must have the corresponding tooltips

Table 3. Comparison between user stories and BPMN elements

User stories			BPMN
Tittle	User Story Title		Process name
User Story Identification	ID for versioning		
Reference Document	Reference to a document that completes the information of the User Story. It can be a document of the process.		Attachment document that complements the process.
I as a [role]	Roles: determine the division of activities		Define the lanes of role activities.
I want to [functionality]	Task Name, example: check the taxis that have canceled services today.		Functionalities that must be performed (depends on the type of element)
So that [motivation]	Justification or Reason of the story.	Does not apply	Does not apply
Dependencies	Sub process referenced in the user story		Sub process
Acceptance criteria	Detail what is required to build the user story.		Business rules.

4 Application of the Proposal

The hypotheses were evaluated by applying the strategy in four projects: (i) Intelligent tracks: Automated taxi system for shopping centers and universities. (ii) GesDos: document management system for radiological plates. (iii) Teachers ranking: a system for classifying teachers in universities. (iv) REF, a classrooms and Resources reservation system: a mobile system to assign the resources in Universities.

For explaining purposes, the requirement elicitation process is described in the intelligent tracks project. The tracks are places where the vehicles are parked to collect the passengers who request the service. In these tracks, the dispatchers coordinate this activity. The dispatchers' job is to register the vehicle's license plate, the time and the destination address (to provide security). The project involves the development of an application that enables users to request taxis directly in a stand of the company. Also, the drivers must be notified of the service assignment. When a passenger is picked up, the driver indicates that he/she leaves the track and the state changes to "in a race" (since he/she is attending a request). Also at the end of the race, the taxi returns to the track, and the status changes and therefore new requests can be received. Finally, a Web administration module is required to manage historical data, driver penalties, and anomalies.

The inception deck technique was applied to the product owner, a technical leader of the company, and the SCRUM team to unify the vision of the product [4]. In the *"show the solution* activity," the option *"let's make it flow"* was applied. Here the interactions of the user with the application were identified, as well as the potential changes, improvements and some points that had not been detected before. The information collected was not stored in user stories, but in the business process models (BPM) using BPMN notation (BPMN). BPMN avoids the decomposition of user stories in development activities and directly identify these activities for each flow (these activities go to the scrum board).

The modeling process during the inception meeting does not require prior knowledge about BMPN; the users can diagram a basic workflow and the team in charge transcripts the resulting models to BPMN.

In the case study, three roles were identified: the user who will request a taxi, the taxi driver and the administrator. Then, the processes for each role were validated with the client (See Fig. 1). The inception deck exercise time for this project was 4 h. 2 h were dedicated to the modeling of the process.

Once the team has all the project process models, each item of the model is decomposed into development activities. These activities are placed on the scrum board for sprint planning. The latter is possible because the business process models allow visualizing the processes, interactions, roles and business rules of the system. Due to the above, the team can directly identify the activities to be carried out to build the required functionalities.

According to team perception, the business process models improved the capture of requirements and the identification of commitments for each sprint in comparison to user stories. The above was due to the ease of interpreting the elicited information; the models allowed graphically visualizing the implicit validations and the functionalities

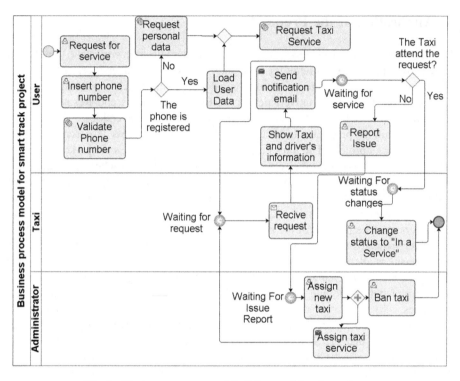

Fig. 1. Business process model of the stand for the end user

in the process flow. Business process models offered an unambiguous interpretation of information, avoiding confusion in the transfer of knowledge from the client to the team and improved communication between stakeholders.

5   Results

During the requirements analysis process of the projects above, both the user stories and the BPM models were built to compare the results. The following metrics were analyzed.

1. The number of requirements that appeared after the requirements elicitation, in the stages of analysis, specification or requirements validation [12].
2. The nonconformities or incidents (defects found by the customer or users of the product) [9].
3. The number of requirements completed by sprint iteration [12].

The summary of metrics obtained from the different projects is shown in Table 4. In this table, the total number of elicited, refined, added and completed requirements for each project is shown.

Table 4. Requirements elicited, modified, added and completed per project

Requirements	Smart tracks	GesDos	Teaching ranking	REF
Elicited	25	130	41	13
Refined	0	10	0	0
New	1	20	0	2
Total	**26**	**160**	**41**	**15**

The results of Table 4 show that the number of new requirements is low (1 for Smart track and 2 in REF project) compared with the total number of requirements. Thus hypothesis 2 is verified suggesting that the implementation of the technique allows maintaining the unified vision of the product from the inception deck.

All the requirements were completed during the projects sprints and approved by the client. This result is associated with metric 3, whose objective is to measure the number of requirements completed by iteration. The result of this metric validates the hypothesis 3 regarding the approved requirements when using BPM.

Figure 2 shows that in three of four projects, the number of refined requirements was zero. The result of this metric validates the hypothesis 1.

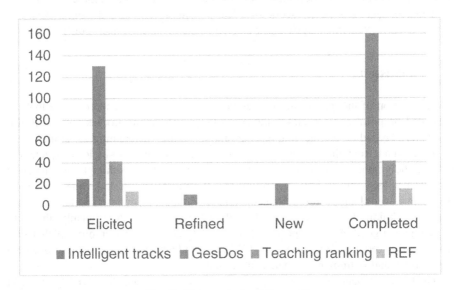

Fig. 2. Data analysis of the results

This result shows that the present approach was a success factor for the project. In GesDos new requirements were identified. However, this result appears because unlike other projects, GesDos was not built from scratch, but it was a migration project from desktop to Web platforms. The use of the inception deck technique with BPM in GesDos allowed identifying 20 new requirements and 10 requirements were refined. These refined requirements arise from the outdated process that supported the previous software application.

Regarding metric 2, Table 5 shows the nonconformities on the elicited requirements of the project. These results show the high impact of the BPMN based elicitation on product quality, not only during each of the sprints but also in the final product, allowing to fulfill the objective of providing value to the customers [6].

Table 5. Nonconformities per project

Nonconformities types	Intelligent tracks	GesDos	Teacher ranking	REF
Presentation	2	5	3	1
Functional	0	1	0	3
Blocking	0	0	0	0
Total	2	6	3	4

After analyzing the requirements, the complexity estimation was performed. Traditionally for this estimation In SCRUM, refined user stories are required, in order to measure the complexity of the activity (s) involved in the development of them. As the present approach does not have user stories, the SCRUM team once has the BPM diagrams, generates the decomposition of the models in development activities, allowing to have a complete scope of what is required to fulfill the objectives of a sprint. These development activities were estimated using the scrum poker method.

6 Conclusions

The evaluation of the metrics allows validating the hypotheses, and conclude that the presented proposal has a positive impact on the development process with SCRUM. The latter is based on the fact that business models allow maintaining the unified view of the product from the inception deck. These models offer a single interpretation, through the graphic representation of the elicited information. Although the elicitation time is increased due to BPMN training and the inception deck meeting, this effort results in fewer changes in requirements and less nonconformities. The latter implies that the technique has a direct impact on the process quality. Additionally, the technique showed good results in projects from scratch and in migration projects that start from existing requirements, in which BPM allows identifying processes improvement possibilities and optimizing outdated functionalities.

On the other hand, the SCRUM estimation was done with the POKER SCRUM method replacing the user stories by business process models. The estimation was performed using development activities for each process model.

Future work includes the study of the impact of replacing the classic story mapping technique by "wireframing" or "let's make it flow" in the 7th activity of the inception Deck ("show the solution activity" [4]). Also, it will be studied the impact of BPM based elicitation in the estimation and planning process with SCRUM, showing how the development task can be decomposed from a BMP task.

Future work also includes a study of the economic impact of an efficient elicitation process; this study may be based on the one presented in [13].

References

1. Hastie, S., Wojewoda, S.: Standish Group 2015 Chaos Report - Q&A with Jennifer Lynch (2015). http://www.infoq.com/articles/standish-chaos-2015
2. Rasmusson, J.: Agile project initiation techniques - The inception deck & boot camp. In: Proceedings - AGILE Conference, vol. 2006, pp. 337–341 (2006)
3. Rasmusson, J.: The Agile Samurai–How Agile Masters Deliver Great Software (2010)
4. Enrique Comba Riepenhausen, Inception Starting a New Project
5. Ordóñez, H., Villada, A.F.E., Vanegas, D.L.V., Cobos, C., Ordóñez, A., Segovia, R.: An impact study of business process models for requirements elicitation in XP. In: Gervasi, O., Murgante, B., Misra, S., Gavrilova, M.L., Rocha, A.M.A.C., Torre, C., Taniar, D., Apduhan, B.O. (eds.) ICCSA 2015. LNCS, vol. 9155, pp. 298–312. Springer, Cham (2015). doi:10.1007/978-3-319-21404-7_22
6. Fowler, M., Highsmith, J.: The agile manifesto. Softw. Dev. **9**, 28–35 (2001)
7. Medinilla, Á.: Retrospectives and kaizen events. In: Agile Kaizen: Managing Continuous Improvement Far Beyond Retrospectives, pp. 37–58 (2014)
8. Cohn, M.: User Stories Applied: For Agile Software Development. Addison Wesley Signature Series, vol. 1 (2004)
9. Pressman, R.S.: Ingeniería del software
10. Decreus, K., Poels, G., El Kharbili, M., Pulvermueller, E.: Policy-enabled goal-oriented requirements engineering for semantic business process management. Int. J. Intell. Syst. **25**(8), 784–812 (2010)
11. Decreus, K., El Kharbili, M., Poels, G., Pulvermueller, E.: Bridging requirements engineering and business process management. Gi-Edition. Proceedings-Lecture Notes in Informatics, p. 215 (2009)
12. Andriano, N.: Comparación del Proceso de Elicitación de Requerimientos en el desarrollo de Software a Medida y Empaquetado. Propuesta de métricas para la elicitación (2006). http://postgrado.info.unlp.edu.ar/Carreras/Magisters/Ingenieria_de_Software/Tesis/Andriano_Natalia.pdf
13. Kenett, R.S.: Implementing SCRUM using business process management and pattern analysis methodologies. Dyn. Relationships Manag. J. **2**(2), 29–48 (2013)

Educational Informatics

Onto-SPELTRA: A Robotic Assistant Based on Ontologies and Agglomerative Clustering to Support Speech-Language Therapy for Children with Disabilities

V. Robles-Bykbaev[1(✉)], M. Guamán-Heredia[1], Y. Robles-Bykbaev[2],
J. Lojano-Redrován[1], F. Pesántez-Avilés[1], D. Quisi-Peralta[1], M. López-Nores[3],
and J. Pazos-Arias[3]

[1] GI-IATa, Cátedra UNESCO Tecnologías de Apoyo para la Inclusión Educativa,
Universidad Politécnica Salesiana, Cuenca, Ecuador
{vrobles,fpesantez,dquisi}@ups.edu.ec,
{aguamanhe,jlojanor}@est.ups.edu.ec
[2] Universidad de La Coruña, Coruna, Spain
yaroslava.robles.bykbaev@udc.es
[3] Depto. Enxeñaría Telemática, AtlantTIC Research Center, Universidade de Vigo,
Vigo, Spain
{mlnores,jose}@det.uvigo.es

Abstract. According to the United Nations International Children's Emergency Fund (UNICEF), nowadays in several developing countries there is a lack of essential services for children with disabilities in important fields such as speech-language therapy, physiotherapy, and sign language instruction. Likewise, the UNICEF points that in low income countries only between 5 and 15% of children and adults who require assistive technologies have access to them. In this line, in this paper we present a system that provides three main functionalities for speech-language therapists: a decision support system for planning therapy sessions (ontologies), a robotic assistant to motivate children with disabilities to work in therapy activities, and a module to automatically create groups of patients with similar profiles and needs (agglomerative clustering). In order to validate our proposal we worked with two groups: a first one consisting on 111 youth to validate the robot's appearance and functionalities, and a second group of 70 children with communication disorders and disabilities to determine their response to therapies provided through robot. In the same way, we have used the children's profiles to populate the ontology and feed the decision support module based on clustering.

Keywords: Ontology · Children with disabilities · Agglomerative clustering · Robotic assistant · Communication disorders · Speech-language therapy

© Springer International Publishing AG 2017
A. Solano and H. Ordoñez (Eds.): CCC 2017, CCIS 735, pp. 343–357, 2017.
DOI: 10.1007/978-3-319-66562-7_25

1   Introduction

The early years of a person's life are crucial to acquire and develop different kinds of skills related with speech and language, cognition, autonomy, and in general, reach the cerebral, muscular and verbal maturity. From the birth to 3 years children experiment important changes in several areas of their development. Commonly, a baby is born with approximately 100 billion brain cells with only few connections among them. When children are 3 years old, they have hundreds of trillions of connections among cells within each of their toddlers brains [8].

However, the children which present disabilities early in life are exposed to several risk factors that can affect their development. Some of the most relevant risk factors are described below [24]:

- *Poverty*: is strongly interlkined with disabilities given that it can increase the likelihood that a person present a disability. For example, a pregnant woman living in poverty may experience poor health care services, restricted diet, etc. In the same way, children living in poverty are more likely experiencing developmental delays due they are exposed to a wide range of risks.
- *Stigma and discrimination*: the children that have disabilities are the most stigmatized and excluded in the world. Commonly, this situation is due to the limited knowledge about disabilities whiting their families, schools and communities. Some of the consequences of discrimination are the poor health and education outcomes, the low self-esteem, and the isolation of society.
- *Caregivers*: several studies point that quality of child-caregiver interaction can be compromised when a child presents a disability. The caregivers can experience poverty, lack of economic support, and have limited access to information required to provide adequate care services for the these children.
- *Institutionalization:* in several countries the children with disabilities are placed permanently in residential care institutions. A institutional environment can result damaging for children with disabilities due inadequate stimulation, lack of appropriate rehabilitation services, poor nutrition, etc.
- *Violence, abuse, exploitation and neglect:* the United Nations Study on Violence Against Children points that in some countries of the Organization for Economic Cooperation and Development (OECD) infants under one year of age are at around three times the risk of homicide than children aged one to four [16]. In this line, it is important to remark that children with disabilities are more vulnerable to sexual, physical and psychological abuse.

On the other hand, currently there are no reliable and precise estimates about the number of children with disabilities [7]. Nevertheless, the most accepted estimate points that 93 million of children (1 of each 20 children under 14 years) live with some form of moderate or severe disability [15] (other studies claim that there are 200 million of children with disabilities in the world [22]).

In developing countries this situation becomes more complex due to several difficulties such as lack of personnel, resources, structures and investment in social and health care services for children, youth, adults and elderly people with or without disabilities. For these reasons, in this paper we present a complete and open system that relies on a low-cost robotic assistant that can be easily reproduced in any institution that provides special education or health care services (especially for children). In the same way, our proposal uses knowledge model based on ontologies and support decision modules that can be adapted to any information structure used in any organization.

The rest of the paper is organized as follows. In Sect. 2 are presented some relevant researches related with the application of Information and Communication Technologies (ICTs) and intelligent systems (knowledge modelling and decision support) to Speech-Language Therapy (SLT). The general architecture of the proposed approach as well as the decision support module are described in Sect. 3. In Sect. 4 are depicted the pilot experiment carried in Cuenca city (Ecuador) and the preliminary results obtained. Finally, the Sect. 5 presents the main conclusions and some ideas for future work.

2 Related Work

During the last ten years have been developed several proposals to support different kinds of activities related with diagnosis or intervention of patients with communication disorders. However, the most of the approaches are aimed to providing support and rehabilitation services for specific communication disorders and not always deal with patients with disabilities.

In the area of robotics assistants, Pulido et al. have developed several algorithms to conduct non-contact upper-limb therapy sessions for patients with physical impairments. With these algorithms, the authors have programmed the NAO robot [21] to help and supervise patients during the execution of prescribed exercises. This proposal was evaluated with 120 children (117 healthy and 3 pediatric patients) and show excellent results in terms of enjoyment, engagement and fluency of therapy activities execution [17]. In a similar line, Malik, Yussof and Hanapiah have studied the possibility of using therapy based on social assistive robot for children with Cerebral Palsy (CP). In this contribution, the authors have analyzed three robots as potential support tools for therapy activities [11]:

- *Cosmobot:* is a 40 cm robot that has nine degrees of freedom. The interaction process with this robot is done through gestural sensors and speech recognition. This robot was exposed to 6 children with CP during 16 week. The clinical outcome of this study show that 4 of the 6 children have improved the upper extremity strength, while 3 of the 6 children have improved coordination in upper extremity [2].
- *Kinetron:* is humanoid robot that has the same height of Cosmobot and incorporates 18 servomotors to perform several and precise movements (6 in each leg and 3 in each hand). This robot was assembled from commercially available Bioloid Premium robotic kit, and was tested with 6 children with CP during two-weeks in a course of intensive neurophysiological rehabilitation. This study reports that the 6 children were motivated and participated actively in therapy activities [10].

- *Ursus:* is a 140 cm robotic assistant that is very similar to a teddy bear and has 14 degrees of freedom. Ursus is aimed on training and rehabilitation in paediatric patients with motor disorders due to Hemiplegic Cerebral Palsy and Obstetric Brachial Plexus. The main functionalities of the robot include active perception, sensor fusion, navigation, human movement capture, voice synthesis and plan execution. This robot was validated in a first stage with six children with upper-limb motor impairments. The preliminary results show that Ursus constitute an appropriate support tool (in terms of appearance and functionalities) that helps to engage children to therapy process [14].

On the other hand, some authors have studied the potential of using ontologies to model the domains of occupational therapy resources [20] and speech-language therapy. Other researchers have evaluated some aspects related with the design of materials used to carry out speech-language therapy [5]. Specifically, Martn-Ruiz et al. have developed an approach to support the children's neurodevelopment monitoring and to screening of language disorders in primary care. Their proposal was developed and validated in the following main stages [12,13,18,19]:

1. In a first stage, the authors have used 21 cases of children with language disorders with the aim of defining the structure of the ontology and a set of description logic relations. The proposed system can trigger the necessary preventive and therapeutic actions for children from birth until the age of six [19]. During the second stage, the authors worked with a sample of 60 cases of children and have included a team of seven experts from the fields of neonatology, pediatrics, neurology and language therapy. The results obtained in the second stage show that therapists have accepted proposals generated by the system in 18 cases (86% of precision) [13].
2. For the third stage the authors have conducted a deeper evaluation process on the developed tool. The number of participants were increased substantially to 146 children, 12 educators, and 1 language therapist. The results of the validation process show 83.6% (122/146) success rate in language evaluation (within the range of children from 0 to 3 years old) [18].
3. In the final stage, the authors present a modification of the proposed system with the objective of performing cooperative tasks to enhance the screening of language disorders at medical centers and schools in children under 4 years. The authors not provide reports about system precision [12].

3   General System Architecture

The robotic assistant Onto-SPELTRA is part of a complete platform that is aimed on providing services for communication disorders rehabilitation in children with or without disabilities. As can be seen in Fig. 1, both children and SLT can interact with the platform through a **interface services layer** that contains the following elements:

- A mobile application that contains information management services for the therapists and therapy activities for children. This application can be used in **smartphones and tablets.**
- A **desktop application** that allows therapists planning therapy sessions and creating children's working groups (according to their medical profile and their speech-language assessment).
- A **robotic assistant** that incorporates a touch screen with several kind of therapy activities for children aged between 2 and 7 years. This robots has a embedded mini-computer (Raspberry PI 3) and a local database that stores all collected information during therapy sessions (children, exercises scores: successes, fails, etc.). Likewise, the robot can change its appearance through several **costumes** which can represent animals (dog, lion, elephant, dinosaur, etc.) or characters.

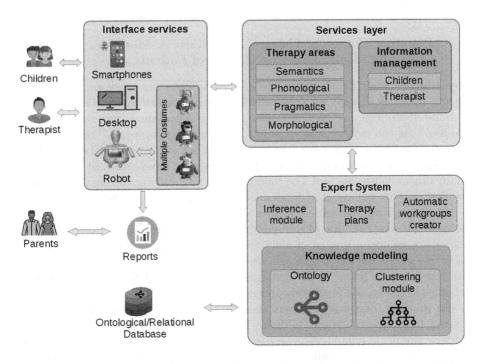

Fig. 1. General platform architecture and the different elements and services that it provides to therapists and children and their parents.

Furthermore, the services layer defines two important elements to carry out the therapies as well as manage the patients' information. These elements are described below:

- A set of educational contents and **therapy activities** focused in covering Speech-Language areas such as **semantics** (understanding and appropriate use of meaning in single words, phrases or sentences), **phonological development** (making sounds and sound patterns), **pragmatics** (social language use), and **morphological development** (*conscious awareness of the morphemic structure of words and the ability to reect on and manipulate that structure*) [3].

- A module that implements functionalities to manage **information** related with **children** (patient profiles, speech-language screening and evaluations, therapy progress, etc.) and **therapists** (user information, sessions logs, etc.).

The last layer consist on the **expert system** and a set of modules aimed in providing support for decision-making in therapy planning, and children's workgroups creation. In the next subsections are described in detail the two modules that allow expert system selecting therapy activities for children and grouping those children according to SLT's criteria (profile, communication disorder, chronological and speech-language developmental age, etc.).

3.1 Planning Common Therapy Activities: A Module to Automatically Creating Groups of Patients

According to UNICEF [7], in several developing countries there are not enough speech-language therapy services for children that present communication disorder and disabilities. For these reasons, it is very important to have a technological tool that can suggest how to group children according to SLT requirements, namely, considering different patient's features such as chronological age, medical diagnosis, communication disorder, speech-language developmental age, among many others. With this tool, the therapist can plan and organize in a better way his/her work as well as provide an adequate attention to patients.

For the above, our expert system allows therapists generating workgroups according to any criterion of combination. For example, for a therapist could be important to create groups of children considering they chronological age and their developmental language's age. For another therapist can be interesting create groups in two levels, in the first one using the medical diagnostic (disability) whereas in the second level considering the children's ages.

In this line, our expert system uses Hierarchical Agglomerative Clustering (HAC) technique to group children. The HAC has been used successfully to address problems related with decision support in medicine [1,9]. To this aim, our module to automatically create groups (Fig. 1) uses the following equation:

$$d(C_i, C_j) = w_1 \cdot lev(MD_{C_i}, MD_{C_j}) + w_2 \cdot lev(CD_{C_i}, CD_{C_j})$$
$$+ |w_3 \cdot DG_{C_i} - w_4 \cdot DG_{C_j}| \tag{1}$$

Where:

- $d(C_i, C_j)$ represents the distance between the two cases or patients' profiles (C_i and C_j) which will be compared.

- MD_{C_i} and CD_{C_i} are the medical diagnosis and communication disorder ICD 10 (International Statistical Classification of Diseases and Related Health Problems 10th Revision) string codes [23] for the case i, respectively.
- MD_{C_j} and CD_{C_j} are the medical diagnosis and communication disorder ICD 10 string codes for the case j, respectively.
- lev represents the Levenshtein distance [4] of the ICD 10 string codes of the medical diagnosis and communication disorder for the cases i and j, respectively.
- DG_{C_i} is the gap between the chronological age and developmental language age of case i.
- DG_{C_j} is the gap between the chronological age and developmental language age of case j.
- w_1, w_2, w_3, w_4 are constants used to weight each variable of the equation (according to SLTs criteria).

The Levenshtein distance is applied on the ICD-10 codes of the medical diagnosis and the communication disorder given that these codes are similar for some families of diseases. For example, if we have two patients, one with mild intellectual disability (code F70) and Specific developmental disorders of speech and language (code F80), and a second patient with moderate intellectual disability (code F71) and Specific developmental disorders of speech and language (code F80), the Levenshtein distance between them will be the following:

$$lev(C_1, C_2) = lev(\text{``F70''}, \text{``F71''}) + lev(\text{``F80''}, \text{``F80''})$$
$$= 1 + 0$$
$$= 1$$

This distance will be greater if the first patient presents Down syndrome (code Q90): $lev(\text{``Q90''}, \text{``F71''}) = 3$.

The weights are automatically adjusted according to SLTs requirements, for example, if they need to give more importance to ages, w_3 and w_4 will be greater than w_1 and w_2, and this will produce a different group of children.

3.2 Automatically Selecting Therapy Activities: A Module Based on Knowledge Modelling

Creating a therapy plan is a complex task that demands an important effort to analyze patient profile and schedule a set of activities/exercises. To this end, the expert system uses an ontology (Fig. 2) with the aim of suggesting several activities that can be part of the therapy plan.

Our ontology is made up using the FOAF (Friend of a Friend) ontology [6] and a set of classes and relations that describe the speech-language therapy elements. The main elements of the ontology are described below (the FOAF classes and relations are not mentioned):

- *Level*: represents the linguistic levels (semantic, phonological, pragmatic, and morphological).

- *Category*: are the categories to which belong the different exercises/activities designed by the therapists (phonemes, vocabulary, etc.).
- *General activity*: describes a skill that must be developed by children through the execution of *specific activities*. For example, to develop the phonological discrimination a patient must be carry out exercises related with labiodental articulation, dental articulation, etc.
- *Patient*: is a subclass of *Person* (FOAF) and can present two types of disorders. The first one is a communication *disorder*, and the second is a disability (*medical diagnosis*).

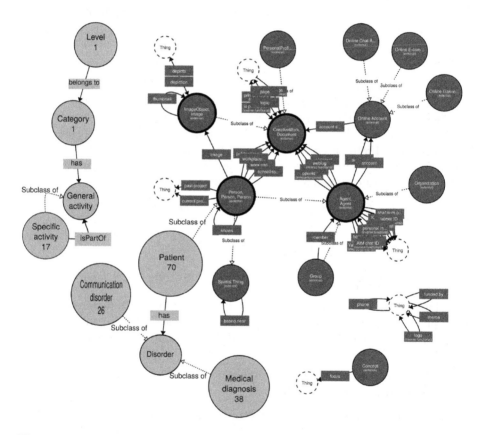

Fig. 2. The ontology that is used by the expert system to determine which exercises and therapy activities are adequate for children.

Through this ontology, the expert system is able to provide the following information to SLTs:

- Determine which exercises and therapeutic activities are adequate for a given patient according to his/her chronological age, communication disorder and medical diagnosis.

– Determine with which speech-language categories must be carried out the therapy for a given patient.
– Automatically assigning activities and exercises to a group of children provided by the clustering algorithm.
– Obtain demographic information of children according to their medical profile.

4   Experiments and Results

With the aim of evaluating the robotic assistant from a complete viewpoint, we have carried out an experiment consisting in four stages. Firstly, the robot was presented to 111 students of 11 high schools. After interacting with the robot, each student was surveyed about his/her perception about robot's functionalities and appearance.

The results of the surveys did provide us with suggestions and important ideas for improving some robot's characteristics. In the second stage a team of experts SLPs worked during with 70 children that have different kinds of disabilities and communication disorders. The objective of this stage was determining if it is possible integrating a new tool to traditional therapy sessions. In the third stage the system automatically had generated new groups of patients with the aim of providing SLPs guidelines to identify some commons needs and preparing therapy activities for more than one patient. In the last stage the system has used the ontology to select and assign therapy activities and exercises for the previously created groups. In the following sections are described the results achieved with each theses stages.

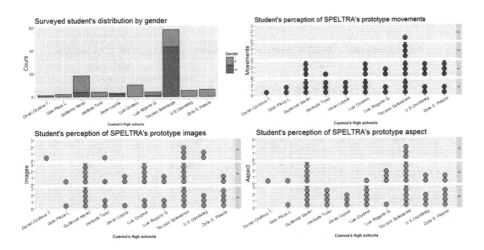

Fig. 3. High school students distribution by gender (right superior panel). The left top panel and the down panels show the perception of students about the SPELTRAs prototype, considering the educational therapy.

4.1   High Schools' Students Perceptions About SPELTRA Prototype in Educational Therapy

Figure 3 depicts surveyed students distribution. In the superior right panel we can see that "Técnico Salesianos" and "Guillermo Mensi" high schools have the highest rate male surveyed, but all the other high schools have more female surveyed students.

These phenomena can be appreciated as disturbing the understood of the prototypes perception. But in the reality, this let as to see two things. Firstly, the more surveyed high school students were from the both mentioned high schools, and second, that in the three mentioned panels regardless the surveyed high school students, the surveyed students form 10 high schools have a very high perception in the Likert scale about the aspect of the robot (prototype), also have a high perception about the movements and the images that robot can

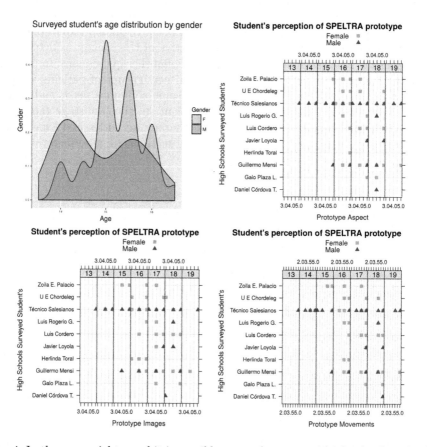

Fig. 4. In the upper right panel it is possible to see the surveyed high school student's distribution through gender. The upper left and the right and left down panels present the perception (through Likert scale) about the SPELTRA's prototype.

generate, all them relative to educational therapy application for children with disabilities.

On the other hand, as we can appreciate inf Fig. 4, the upper right panel (density histogram) shows how the survey was applied to the high school students of Cuenca city (Ecuador), thus 14 to 17 male students were prevailing.

However, surveyed male students are more regular in comparison to the female between 16 and 18 years old. The surveys were not regularly applied to female high school group, due the own characteristics of the High Schools participating in the experiment ("Técnico Salesiano" and "Guillermo Mensi" have more female students ("Técnico Salesiano" and "Guillermo Mensi" high schools did send more female students). We can see that the survey has been homogeneously applied for almost ages, except for 16 to 18 female teenagers group. In consequence, this histogram corroborates that in general terms male surveyed high school students were more regular in comparison to female surveyed students.

The second upper left panel, and the right and left down panels let us appreciate how regardless to gender and high school surveyed students, all of them -especially teenagers of 16 to 18 years- have a very high perception through Likerts scale about the aspect of SPELTRA, and also about the movements and images that this prototype can generate regarding to educational therapy. Thus, it means that in general terms the robot has a good acceptance over the teenage high school surveyed students.

Table 1. Prevalence of disabilities and communication disorders of the patients that have collaborated with the experiment.

Disability	Patients	Communication disorder	Patients
Mild intelectual disability (F70)	25	Specific developmental disorders of speech and language (F80)	46
Down syndrome (Q90)	13	Dysarthria (R47.1)	14
Cerebral palsy (G80)	11	Dysphasia (R47.0)	9
Autism spectrum disorder (F84.0)	8	Other	1
Fetal alcohol syndrome (Q86.0)	2		
Retarded development following protein-energy malnutrition (E45)	2		
Visual impairment (H54)	2		
Other	7		

4.2   Results of Therapies Carried Out with Robot and Children with Disabilities and Communication Disorders

With the aim of measuring the response to the robot by real patients, we have conducted 195 therapy activities with 70 children that present disabilities and communication disorders. These children are enrolled to three schools of special education of Cuenca, Ecuador. As we can see in Table 1, the most common disabilities are mild intellectual disability (25), Down syndrome (13), Cerebral Palsy (11), and Autism Spectrum Disorders (8). On the other hand, the most common communication disorders are Specific developmental disorders of speech and language (46), dysarthria (14), and dysphasia (9).

It is important to mention the therapists introduced robot to participants in a small ludic activity (5 min), given that the children never had seen or worked with the robot before. In Fig. 5 we can see the results reached by children during the therapy sessions. Basically, the SLTs worked in three language categories (Phonological = P, Semantics = S, Morphological = M) and two levels of difficulty (Daily Use images/pictograms = DU, and Non-Daily Use images/pictograms = NDU). The children participating in the experiment are organized in five groups according to their age: up to 5 years (initial level), up to 6 (level 1), up to 8 (level 3), up to 9 (level 4) and up to 10 (level 5). The results shown excellent scores (a general average score of 8.59/10), except for the level 1, in which the average

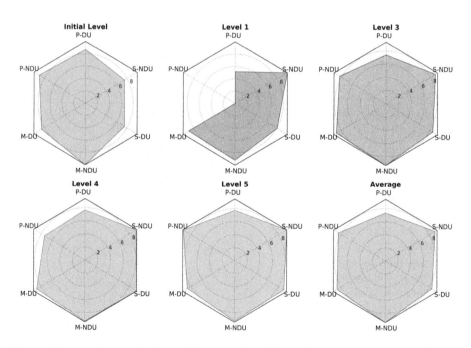

Fig. 5. The results reached by children on the different language categories with two levels of difficulties.

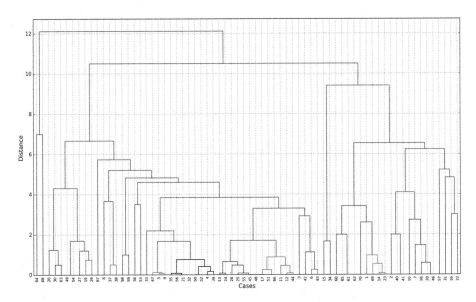

Fig. 6. The groups of patients generated by the system with the Eq. 1. The database used consists on the 70 children that have been part of the experiment.

score for phonological area (with daily use images) was 5.15 over 10 points (the children were not able to work with non-daily use images).

It is important to mention that it was not possible to work with children of level 2 due logistics issues.

4.3   Automatic Creation of Groups of Patients

The expert system is able to generate different kinds of groups adjusting the Eq. 1. In the Fig. 6 we can see a dendrogram that can be cut using a threshold of 7 units (distance) between patient's profiles. This action will produce 4 general groups of patients. The expert system provides different kinds of alternatives to create groups, weighting the variables according to SLPs needs. For example, for a SLP it could be more relevant creating groups of patients according to their chronological age and disability, whereby the system will give a higher value to weights w1, w3 and w4 of the Eq. 1.

5   Conclusions

In this paper we have presented an overview of a system to support speech-language therapy of patient that not only suffer from communication disorders, but also disabilities. Our approach can create automatically groups of patients and select the most adequate exercises to work with these patients (through ontology). The different exercises and therapy activities are delivered using the robotic assistant SPELTRA.

As could be seen in previous sections, both youth and children feel highly comfortable with the robotic assistant, and they think educational content of the robot is appropriate to carry out therapy sessions. Even though the children did not work previously with the robot, were able to understand the orders related with therapy activities and respond properly to questions presented by the robot.

As lines of future work we propose the following ones:

- To develop a module based on fuzzy logic to automatically select the cutting distance in the dendrogram.
- To develop a relevance feedback module that allows SLTs evaluating the structure quality of patients groups generated by the system.

Acknowledgments. The authors from the Universidad Politécnica Salesiana have been supported by "Sistemas Inteligentes de Soporte a la Educacin Especial (SINSAE v4)" research project. The authors from the University of Vigo have been sup-ported by the European Regional Development Fund (ERDF) and the Galician Regional Government under agreement for funding the Atlantic Research Center for Information and Communication Technologies (AtlantTIC), as well as by the Ministerio de Educación y Ciencia (Gobierno de España) research project TIN2013-42774-R (partly financed with FEDER funds).

References

1. Belhadj, S., Attia, A., Adnane, B.A., Ahmed-Foitih, Z., Ahmed, A.T.: A novel epileptic seizure detection using fast potential-based hierarchical agglomerative clustering based on emd. Int. J. Comput. Sci. Netw. Secur. (IJCSNS) **16**(5), 7 (2016)
2. Brisben, A., Safos, C., Lockerd, A., Vice, J., Lathan, C.: The cosmobot system: evaluating its usability in therapy sessions with children diagnosed with cerebral palsy. Special Issue: Rob. **12**, 14–16 (2005)
3. Carlisle, J.F., Feldman, L.: Morphological awareness and early reading achievement. In: Morphological Aspects of Language Processing, pp. 189–209 (1995)
4. Chowdhury, S.D., Bhattacharya, U., Parui, S.K.: Online handwriting recognition using levenshtein distance metric. In: 2013 12th International Conference on Document Analysis and Recognition (ICDAR), pp. 79–83. IEEE (2013)
5. Dinçer, S., Akin Şenkal, O.: Evaluation of language and speech materials for language and speech disorders: a study of meta-synthesis. Turk. Online J. Educ. Technol. **2016**, 255–260 (2016)
6. Golbeck, J., Rothstein, M.: Linking social networks on the web with FOAF: a semantic web case study. In: AAAI, vol. 8, pp. 1138–1143 (2008)
7. Groce, N., Deluca, M., Cole, E., Berman-Bieler, R., Mitra, G., Farkas, A., Sabbe, L., Burlyaeva-Norman, A., Lansdown, G.: Children and young people with disabilities: Fact sheet (UNICEF) (2013)
8. Hyson, M., Tomlinson, H.B.: The Early Years Matter: Education, Care, and the Well-Being of Children, Birth to 8. Teachers College Press, New York (2014)
9. Islam, M.A., Alizadeh, B.Z., van den Heuvel, E.R., Bruggeman, R., Cahn, W., de Haan, L., Kahn, R.S., Meijer, C., Myin-Germeys, I., van Os, J., et al.: A comparison of indices for identifying the number of clusters in hierarchical clustering: a study on cognition in schizophrenia patients. Commun. Stat. Case Stud. Data Anal. Appl. **1**(2), 98–113 (2015)

10. Kozyavkin, V., Kachmar, O., Ablikova, I.: Humanoid social robots in the rehabilitation of children with cerebral palsy. In: Proceedings of the 8th International Conference on Pervasive Computing Technologies for Healthcare, pp. 430–431. ICST (Institute for Computer Sciences, Social-Informatics and Telecommunications Engineering) (2014)
11. Malik, N.A., Yussof, H., Hanapiah, F.A.: Potential use of social assistive robot based rehabilitation for children with cerebral palsy. In: 2016 2nd IEEE International Symposium on Robotics and Manufacturing Automation (ROMA), pp. 1–6. IEEE (2016)
12. Martin-Ruiz, M.-L., Valero, M.-A., Gómez, A., Torcal, C.: A cooperative decision support system for children's neurodevelopment monitoring. In: Mandler, B., et al. (eds.) IoT360 2015. LNICST, vol. 169, pp. 461–466. Springer, Cham (2016). doi:10.1007/978-3-319-47063-4_49
13. Martín-Ruiz, M.L., Valero Duboy, M.A., Pau de la Cruz, I.: Deployment and validation of a smart system for screening of language disorders in primary care. Sensors 13(6), 7522–7545 (2013)
14. Mejas, C.S., Echevarra, C., Nuñez, P., Manso, L., Bustos, P., Leal, S., Parra, C.: Ursus: a robotic assistant for training of children with motor impairments. In: Pons, J., Torricelli, D., Pajaro, M. (eds.) Converging Clinical and Engineering Research on Neurorehabilitation. Biosystems & Biorobotics, pp. 249–253. Springer, Heidelberg (2013). doi:10.1007/978-3-642-34546-3_39
15. Organización Mundial de la Salud (OMS): Estado mundial de la infancia. niñas y niños con discapacidad. Fondo de las Naciones Unidas para la Infancia (UNICEF) (2013)
16. Pinheiro, P.S.: World report on violence against children (2006)
17. Pulido, J.C., González, J.C., Suárez-Mejías, C., Bandera, A., Bustos, P., Fernández, F.: Evaluating the child-robot interaction of the naotherapist platform in pediatric rehabilitation. Int. J. Soc. Robot., 1–16 (2017)
18. Ruiz, M.L.M., Duboy, M., Loriente, C.T., de la Cruz, I.P.: Evaluating a web-based clinical decision support system for language disorders screening in a nursery school. J. Med. Internet Res. 16(5) (2014)
19. Ruiz, M.L.M., Valero, M.A., Cruz, I.P.: Validation tool for smart screening of language disorders in pediatrics care. In: Bravo, J., Hervás, R., Rodríguez, M. (eds.) IWAAL 2012. LNCS, vol. 7657, pp. 33–40. Springer, Heidelberg (2012). doi:10.1007/978-3-642-35395-6_5
20. Sawsaa, A.F., Lu, J.: Modeling domain ontology for occupational therapy resources using natural language programming (NLP) technology to model domain ontology of occupational therapy resources. Int. J. Inf. Retriev. Res. (IJIRR) 3(4), 104–119 (2013)
21. Shamsuddin, S., Ismail, L.I., Yussof, H., Zahari, N.I., Bahari, S., Hashim, H., Jaffar, A.: Humanoid robot NAO: Review of control and motion exploration. In: 2011 IEEE International Conference on Control System, Computing and Engineering (ICCSCE), pp. 511–516. IEEE (2011)
22. UNICEF: Monitoring Child Disability in Developing Countries Results from the Multiple Indicator Cluster Surveys. United Nations Childrens Fund Division of Policy and Practice, Nueva York (2008)
23. World Health Organization: International statistical classification of diseases and related health problems 10th revision (2016)
24. World Health Organization, UNICEF: Early childhood development and disability: A discussion paper (2012)

An Extensible and Lightweight Modular Ontology for Programming Education

Christian Grévisse$^{(\boxtimes)}$, Jean Botev, and Steffen Rothkugel

University of Luxembourg, 2, avenue de l'Université,
4365 Esch-sur-Alzette, Luxembourg
{christian.grevisse,jean.botev,steffen.rothkugel}@uni.lu

Abstract. Semantic web technologies such as ontologies can foster the reusability of learning material by introducing common sets of concepts for annotation purposes. However, suggesting learning material from an open, heterogeneous corpus is a nontrivial problem. In this paper, we propose an extensible and lightweight modular ontology for programming education. Its main purpose is to integrate annotated learning material related to programming into an IDE such as Eclipse. Our ontology is based on a modular architecture, which is extensible with respect to different programming languages. Aligning language-specific concepts with user-specific tags allows us to suggest learning resources for code elements in a fine-grained and cross-curricular way. Our concrete implementation establishes relations between learning aspects in Java or C code and annotated resources such as articles on online question-and-answer sites.

Keywords: Modular ontology · Programming education · Annotations · Learning material

1 Introduction

In the context of Technology Enhanced Learning (TEL), authoring learning material is a time-intensive process, requiring the content to be reusable. However, many approaches have yielded monolithic systems with limited interoperability [11]. Semantic web technologies such as ontologies have been suggested to improve the sharing of learning resources by introducing a common set of concepts. These can be used to annotate and retrieve corresponding learning material. In addition, ontology alignment is needed to map between concepts from different sources to avoid the restrictions of local-only ontologies [17].

Integrating learning material from an open corpus constitutes another challenge. Previous approaches often rely on a closed set of documents, indexed at design time of a TEL environment [5]. Apart from taking away the possibility of dynamically adding new resources, students often feel more comfortable if learning material is not only proposed by their teachers, but also by their peers [16]. Allowing an open corpus of documents may again require the underlying ontologies to explicitly support evolvement [17].

© Springer International Publishing AG 2017
A. Solano and H. Ordoñez (Eds.): CCC 2017, CCIS 735, pp. 358–371, 2017.
DOI: 10.1007/978-3-319-66562-7_26

In this paper, we propose an extensible and lightweight modular ontology for programming education. In the context of our project, the purpose is to integrate learning material related to programming into an IDE such as Eclipse. This is realized by relating annotated resources to learning aspects in code. Our ontology comprises concepts from programming languages, which can be recognized in the abstract syntax tree of a piece of code. These language-specific modules are aligned through a language-independent core module containing abstract programming concepts in order to allow for the dynamic indexing of related learning material. Our approach is extensible with respect to different programming languages as well as user- and site-specific annotations. Through the alignment of these different modules, a cross-curricular and fine-grained integration of learning material is achieved. Our implementation comprises aligned modules with elements from the Java and C programming languages as well as tags from the Stack Overflow question-and-answer site.

The remainder of this paper is organized as follows: In Sect. 2, we present related work on ontologies for programming languages. In Sect. 3, we describe the design of our ontology, including an architectural overview and the design methodology. In Sect. 4, we discuss the resulting ontology as well as the characteristic advantages of our approach. We conclude in Sect. 5 inclusive of ideas for future work.

2 Related Work

Various ontology-based approaches for learning platforms have been proposed, however, focusing mostly on Java programming courses. Kouneli et al. proposed an ontology modeling the knowledge domain of the Java programming language, with its concepts being extracted from the formal language guide [9]. The authors used this ontology to model the learning outcomes of introductory Java courses in a distance learning context. Vesin et al. described Protus, a web-based programming tutoring system with another Java-specific ontology [19]. The hierarchy in their ontology is used to model prerequisite relations between concepts in the tutoring system. Dehors and Faron-Zucker presented QBLS [3], a semantic web based learning system with a Java-specific ontology based on Simple Knowledge Organization System (SKOS), a W3C recommendation for representing knowledge organization systems in RDF. The advantage of SKOS is that concepts can be organized in *concept schemes*, provided with a set of human-readable labels and interconnected through a set of well-defined semantic relations. Semi-automatic annotations based on formatting styles in learning resources are used to index them in QBLS to the learning aspects they contain.

Only few approaches that involve a different or more than one programming language exist, for instance for the C programming language [18] or both Java and C [14]. The former paper models the concepts to be learned by students in an introductory C course, the latter relates domain concepts to learning objects to better organize educational material. The concepts are retrieved via a glossary-based approach though. With respect to integrating Stack Overflow articles,

Ponzanelli proposed an entropy-based approach of retrieving resources related to elements in code [15]. While the user is writing code, Stack Overflow articles with similar code are provided for assistance. However, ontological metamodeling based on type abstraction may be better suited than linguistic metamodeling based on word abstraction to distinguish language-specific aspects [13]. A case study of an SKOS-based ontology design and implementation for the C programming language, including performance tests, has been presented in [12].

3   Ontology Design

The purpose was to create a modular and lightweight ontology that is extensible with respect to new, additional languages and user-specific concepts. In our implementation, the ontology comprises concepts for both the Java and C programming languages. Splitting the ontology into different modules has the advantage of organizing the concepts for different programming languages (Java, C), sources (Stack Overflow tags) and users. Allowing users to extend the ontology with custom concepts may avoid the *expert blind spot* [10]. However, it is advisable to separate these user-specific concepts from the "authoritative" set of concepts, at least until they have been curated and aligned. By using Knowledge Organization Systems (KOS), concepts can be categorized into different sets in order to disambiguate, e.g., annotations from different users by linking them to elements in the underlying KOS [1]. The complexity spectrum for ontologies is broad, however, lightweight and semi-formal ontologies might suffice for annotation purposes [1].

In our approach, we assume that classical learning materials, such as lecture notes and slides, contain metadata, e.g., annotations of concepts which are defined in our ontology. The concepts provide a human-readable label to the user to ease the annotation process. Web resources, such as Stack Overflow articles, are tagged on their respective platforms. Finally, learning aspects in a piece of code can be extracted based on the Abstract Syntax Tree (AST). Language-specific elements are commonly defined in the AST models of IDEs. Concepts used in annotations, tags on Stack Overflow and language-specific elements have to be aligned to establish the relation between learning aspects in code and corresponding learning material. The concept retrieval, alignment and overall architecture of our ontology is described hereafter.

As opposed to approaches based on learning objects, we are considering heterogeneous ad-hoc resources which can be added to our ecosystem without the need of creating a dedicated learning object based on a certain format.

3.1   Architecture

Our ontology, called ALMA (**A**daptive **L**iteracy-aware learning **M**aterial Integr**A**tion), includes the following modules:

Java Module. This module contains concepts based on the Eclipse Java Development Tools (JDT) model.

C Module. This module contains concepts based on the Eclipse C/C++ Development Tooling (CDT) model.

ALMA Core Module. This module is a language-independent KOS containing abstract programming concepts.

Stack Overflow Module. This module contains a set of selected tags from the Stack Overflow question-and-answer website.

The first two modules contain language-specific concepts based on their respective model elements. In our implementation, we are using elements from the Java and C models used in Eclipse. However, the approach would also be valid for other programming languages or IDEs, as they are usually based on a well-defined, formal specification. The structure of these modules reflects the class hierarchy of the Eclipse models. The abstract programming concepts defined in the ALMA Core module map to the language-specific concepts of the first two modules and provide human-readable labels, which are useful for the annotation user experience. Their hierarchy has been manually established according to the hierarchy of their mapped elements in the first two modules. These three modules are considered authoritative, as they provide the initial data for our KOS, avoiding the "cold start" problem [1].

The Stack Overflow module, on the other hand, contains site-specific tags without any hierarchy. As these tags are given by the users of the website, it is important to consider their frequency or curate them before adding them to the ontology. As such, the Stack Overflow module can be seen as non-authoritative. This holds also true for user-specific modules containing custom concepts, which would need to be curated before being integrated in the authoritative modules.

Similar to the approach by Dehors and Faron-Zucker [3], the architecture of our modular ontology is based on the Simple Knowledge Organization System (SKOS). SKOS is an OWL ontology by the W3C for thesauri, taxonomies and classification schemes. At its heart are *concepts*, which represent some notion or unit of thought. Concepts are regrouped in *concept schemes*. A concept can have different labels, such as the *preferred label* and *alternative labels*. Semantic relations between concepts such as *broader* or *narrower* for a hierarchy-like taxonomy or *related* for associative links are also defined in SKOS. An SKOS-based ontology shall not be considered as a formal one, and resulting taxonomies do not follow a strict inheritance-like hierarchy. Instead, such an ontology with rather soft semantics allows to keep a minimal semantic "commitment", as over-commitment may harm interoperability [6]. In addition, ontology alignment is easily feasible through semantic relations between concepts, as defined in the SKOS specification.

Each of the modules of the ALMA ontology maps to a separate concept scheme. Relations between concepts, both within and across schemes, foster the interoperability between abstract programming aspects, language-specific elements and site- or user-specific tags. There is a many-to-many mapping between concepts in the ALMA Core module and other modules. Elements from the JDT or CDT models can be related to one or more concepts in ALMA Core. Likewise, the abstract programming concepts in ALMA Core can be related to multiple concepts from different schemes. Finally, selected tags from Stack Overflow are also mapped to concepts in ALMA Core.

In Fig. 1, we show an excerpt of the ALMA ontology. The abstract programming concept `alma:ForLoop`, defined in the ALMA Core module, is related to the Java-specific concept `java:ForStatement`, the C-specific concept `c:IASTForStatement` and the Stack Overflow tag `so:for-loop`. This way, it would be possible to propose a Stack Overflow article tagged with `for-loop` on a `for`-statement in a piece of Java code. Furthermore, learning material on `for`-loops in Java could even be suggested in a piece of C code including a `for`-loop. This could help beginners in C, who already have experience in Java, to review, e.g., the concept and semantics of loops. They would also be enabled to easily compare and see the differences of this concept in both languages with the provided material. Finally, human-readable labels can be provided in different languages. In the example, an English and a Spanish label are attached to the ALMA Core concept. This can be convenient in a multilingual context to help students who feel more comfortable with concept names in their mother tongue during the learning process.

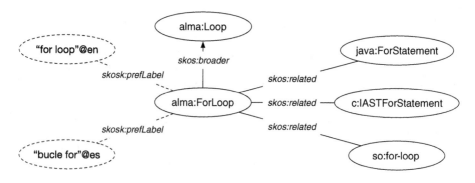

Fig. 1. Example of concepts related across different modules

The concepts in the Java (and C) module are based on classes from the Eclipse JDT (CDT) model and follow the strict inheritance hierarchy of their respective Java classes. All elements inherit from the top-level `owl:Thing` resource, which can be considered as the equivalent of the `Object` class in Java. As `owl:Thing` is of RDF-type `owl:Class`, all inheriting resources are also of that type. Therefore, the JDT elements belong to the meta-level ML1, reserved to classes. This is shown in Fig. 2.

In ALMA Core, concepts are related by a softer hierarchy based on the semantic relation `skos:broader`. Concrete concepts are of type `skos:Concept`, latter one being a class from ML1. The relation `skos:related` allows us to map concepts from ALMA Core to elements in the JDT model. However, the range and domain of the property `skos:related` expect a resource of type `skos:Concept`, which would not be the case for JDT model elements, as they are

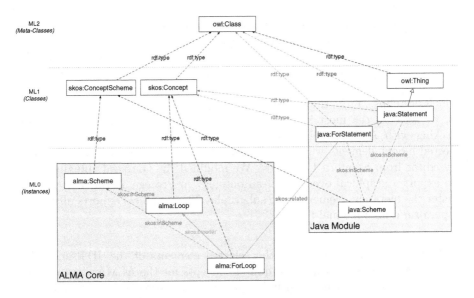

Fig. 2. Meta-level representation of the ALMA ontology

of type `owl:Class`. In fact, concrete concepts are at the instance level (ML0), while, as already mentioned, JDT elements following the strict hierarchy up to `owl:Thing`, are at class level (ML1). Fortunately, OWL-Full does not require the set of classes and instances to be disjoint, meaning that a resource may have several types, of different meta-levels. Therefore, concepts from the Java module are defined as both of type `owl:Class` (inherently given as they inherit from `owl:Thing`) and of type `skos:Concept`, which then allows us to correctly model the semantic relation. Through this resource/concept duality, we are keeping the strict inheritance defined by the JDT model while maintaining a semi-formal taxonomy in ALMA Core.

3.2   Concept Retrieval

We used a bottom-up approach for the design of the ALMA ontology, from low-level syntactical elements, retrievable from the language-specific Eclipse models, up to higher-level programming concepts. In the following, we will describe how concepts have been retrieved and organized for the different modules of our ontology.

Java and C Module. The concepts defined in the Java and C modules are based on classes from the JDT respectively CDT models defined by Eclipse. As mentioned before, ontological metamodeling based on type abstraction may be better suited than linguistic metamodeling based on word abstraction to distinguish language-specific aspects [13]. Hence, a more precise retrieval of learning material is possible due to the alignment of authoritative concepts used in annotations and the language-specific elements retrievable in the AST.

In a first step, we determined the most common elements used in the AST of Java and C programs by analysing the content of the packages of the JDT (`org.eclipse.jdt.core.dom`) and CDT (`org.eclipse.cdt.core.dom.ast.*`) models of Eclipse. From the hierarchy of classes and interfaces used in these models, we selected the most important and commonly appearing elements while checking with AST visualization tools in Eclipse. The resulting hierarchy of selected model elements was imported into Protégé[1], a free, open-source ontology editor from Stanford University. We modified the Ontograf[2] plugin, which can export a graphical overview of an ontology in Protégé, in order to visually cluster the hierarchy elements into subgraphs. The graphical exports allowed us to perform a final manual filtering.

ALMA Core Module. From the selected elements of the JDT and CDT models, we established a list of required concepts for the ALMA Core module. These concepts are not necessarily bound to a single programming language, as `for`-loops or `if`-conditions exist both in Java and C. In addition, many concepts could even be reused in further programming languages, as generics also exist in C# or Swift. We also added rather high-level topics that are not directly linked to syntax and thus to the AST elements, but which may still be used both to annotate some learning material and a piece of code. These topics were extracted from the learning material of our programming courses, the C reference book [8] and the Java Language Specification.

The ALMA Core concepts have been modeled with both a URI and a human-readable name, set as the preferred label property defined in SKOS. This way, annotation plugins in authoring tools can present the available set of concepts with easily understandable labels. We manually mapped the concepts in ALMA Core to the selected elements from the JDT and CDT models. There are concepts in ALMA Core that have related elements in both the JDT and CDT models (e.g. `for`-loops), but there are also concepts which have only a related element in a single one of these models (e.g. generics are not present in C, pointers are not present in Java).

Stack Overflow Module. To retrieve the concepts for the Stack Overflow module, we used the Stack Exchange API in order to analyze the distribution of tag frequency. The skewness of the distribution is very high: From the approximately 46500 tags retrieved, there are a little less than 500 tags with an occurrence of over 10000, whereas the remainder has a third quantile of $q_3 = 138$, which demonstrates the skewness. This confirms the findings of [7]. We then retrieved the top 500 concepts with respect to tag count, including their related tags and synonyms. These tags are representative, as tags with a reduced occurrence

---

[1] http://protege.stanford.edu.
[2] http://protegewiki.stanford.edu/wiki/OntoGraf.

might be too specific. It could be argued the other way round that frequently occurring tags might be too general. However, as articles on Stack Overflow can take up to 5 tags and are ranked by the community of users, we can retrieve relevant articles on a certain topic of interest. From this data set, we filtered tags not related to the concepts of the Java and C modules, resulting in a final set of approximately 230 Stack Overflow tags. Finally, we manually mapped these tags to ALMA Core concepts, declared them as concepts in an own, non-hierarchic concept scheme and stated the manual mappings as SKOS relations. Although tags on Stack Overflow are not hierarchically ordered, through their mapping to ALMA Core concepts (soft hierarchy) and their mapping to elements from the Java and C modules (strict hierarchy), we introduced an indirect hierarchy to the rather ill-structured set of Stack Overflow tags.

4   ALMA Ontology

The described design methodology yielded the ALMA ontology, comprising the above mentioned modules. To better illustrate their content and the relations between the contained concepts, both within and across modules, we created a visualization based on D3.js[3], a JavaScript library for data-driven documents. This visualization is shown in Fig. 3. The circular representation gives a first impression of the complexity of relations between concepts in our ontology. Each colored arc represents a different module, while concepts are preceded by the prefix of a module's namespace. The blue links represent the skos:narrower/skos:broader relations, which provide our modules a hierarchical structure. As Stack Overflow tags are not explicitly structured in a hierarchy, such blue links are not present among the concepts of the orange arc. However, as already mentioned, an implicit structure is given through their relation to concepts in ALMA Core. The skos:related relation is represented by the brown links. For the concepts in the Stack Overflow module, these relations were already given through the retrieved data set from the website, resulting in 796 links. The relations between concepts inside the other modules and across different modules were established manually. The rather limited number of concepts in a programming language made this manual mapping feasible to overcome the initial lack of connections between concepts from different languages and thus provide an alignment between them. When hovering over a concept, links to connected concepts are highlighted and an information box on the right-hand side of the screen is shown to enumerate these links. This circular representation together with its interactive features provides an intuitive yet global overview of the complex connections within our ontology.

In Table 1, we present a few numbers of our ontology. As we can see, ALMA Core has slightly more concepts than the Java and C modules. Although the overlap of syntactical features in both modules is significant, there are concepts in one language not present in the other. The hierarchical narrower/broader links in the Java and C modules are given through the class hierarchy of the

---

[3] https://d3js.org.

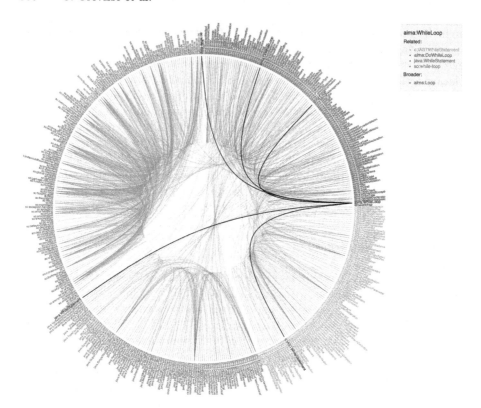

Fig. 3. Visualization of the final ALMA ontology

corresponding language models, whereas the hierarchy of the concepts in ALMA Core has been manually designed. As already mentioned, tags on Stack Overflow are not organized in a hierarchic way. For the majority of concepts in both Java and C modules, there exists a `related` link to a concept in ALMA Core. The remaining concepts might be higher-level hierarchy elements specific to the model implementation, not necessarily mappable to a concept in ALMA Core. There are also a few links within ALMA Core for related concepts (e.g. *pointers* concern *memory management*). The number of relations between Stack Overflow tags and ALMA Core concepts appears to be quite low with respect to the total number of tags, but given the fact that there exist almost 800 relations among the set of Stack Overflow tags we considered, the real number of relations between Stack Overflow tags and ALMA Core concepts is actually higher due to transitivity. In general, the number of concepts covered by relations in our ontology fosters the retrieval and suggestion of learning material even for learning aspects that are directly linked only to a very reduced set of resources.

Table 1. Statistics on the ALMA ontology

	ALMA	Java	C	Stack overflow
Concepts	115	99	91	162
`narrower`/`broader` links	103	96	88	0
`related` links to ALMA Core	24	80	72	42

4.1 Application

A possible use case of the resulting ontology is to integrate learning material related to programming topics into an IDE, as it was described in [4]. The purpose is to provide students in computer programming classes ad-hoc support to better understand syntactical and semantic features of a programming language. If a student does not understand the meaning of a certain code snippet, she can retrieve learning material related to the selected code elements directly from within the IDE. This is possible due to the language elements from the Abstract Syntax Tree being present in the Java respectively C modules of our ontology, which are linked to concepts in ALMA Core. Latter may be used to annotate learning resources. A proof-of-concept implementation of a plugin for Microsoft Word, described in [4], exemplifies this authoring step. Figure 4a shows this *Office Add-in* inside the Word iOS app, run on an iPad. Annotations, based on ALMA Core concepts, can be added to a text selection. Existing annotations are shown in a list and can be selected to highlight the corresponding text.

As concepts in ALMA Core are also related to tags in the Stack Overflow module, related articles from this question-and-answer website can also be retrieved and proposed to the student. Resources indexed for the selected concepts are retrieved and a list is proposed to the user. Figure 4b shows a proof-of-concept implementation of a plugin for the Eclipse IDE that makes use of the ALMA Ontology to (i) show the learning aspect behind the AST nodes (ii) retrieve learning material corresponding to the selected node. The view in the central part of the screen, entitled *Learning Aspects*, shows the AST hierarchy. Each node is shown by a human-readable label of the learning aspect from ALMA Core which is mapped to the corresponding language element from the Java module. Selecting some code in the editor on the left-hand side will highlight the corresponding top-most node in the AST visualization in the center view. Similarly, selecting a node in the AST will highlight the corresponding code in the editor. This behavior is similar to (formerly) existing AST views of the Eclipse Java (C) development tools. Double-clicking on an AST node will open a browser view (right-hand side), which will show a list of learning resources indexed for the corresponding learning aspect. Here, some Stack Overflow pages are shown to provide ad-hoc help on `for`-loops. At least one of the tags on these pages from the Stack Overflow module (here: `so:for-loop`) is mapped to the ALMA Core concept `alma:ForLoop`, which again is related to the Java module concept `java:ForStatement`. The AST node corresponding to the selection in the editor is indeed of type `org.eclipse.jdt.core.dom.ForStatement`.

Multiple resources can be proposed for a selected aspect. For instance, `int i = 42;` is at the same time a variable declaration but also an initialization of an integer-type variable with a number literal. All these different aspects could be related to some learning material resources. A fine-grained integration of learning material is thus given through the level of depth of the AST and the rich set of concepts in ALMA Core, fostering the divide-and-conquer approach for understanding complex expressions.

Cross-curricular relations between learning aspects in code and learning material can also be established. Having concepts in ALMA Core that are mapped to concepts in both the Java and C modules, it is possible to relate learning material from different courses on different programming languages in order to ease the cognitive links between learning aspects from one semester to the other. For instance, if loops are first introduced in a Java programming class, they can be easily learnt in a C programming class by suggesting, apart from the resources of the latter class, learning material from the former class to remind the learner about the concept of loops.

4.2 Extensibility

An advantage of the modular architecture of the ALMA ontology is its extensibility with respect to new modules. New programming languages (e.g. C#, Swift) could be added as a separate scheme with their elements being mapped to ALMA Core concepts. If necessary, already present programming languages can be expanded by new elements if, for instance, new features are introduced to a language. Other IDEs such as NetBeans or IntelliJ with different AST model elements could also be integrated in this way, fostering an IDE-independent design. Tag schemes for other platforms such as YouTube could also be introduced. As long as a mapping definition between these tags and ALMA Core exists, they get indirectly mapped to the already existing Java and C modules. ALMA Core can be regarded as a common specification the concepts from heterogeneous sources can be marshalled to. Also previous efforts by other researchers could be integrated and aligned to enhance the current set of concepts, which could foster collaboration among researchers.

In addition, new relations between already existing tags can be established. If students are given the possibility to dynamically add and index resources, e.g. a Stack Overflow article, relevant to a certain piece of code, new tags attached to the article can be correlated with the programming concepts of the selected code snippet. As these relations are ad-hoc and non-authoritative, they would need curation, either manual by a domain expert, or semi-automatic, based on the frequency of occurrence of the suggested relation: A tag attached to learning resources frequently indexed for a given programming aspect is likely to be correlated to latter.

Finally, user-specific concepts can also be added and aligned to the authoritative set of concepts. In the terminology used in [2], these *learner-based subject ontologies* are refinements of *teacher-based subject ontologies*, extending the authoritative set of concepts by student-specific ones. If a concept is frequently

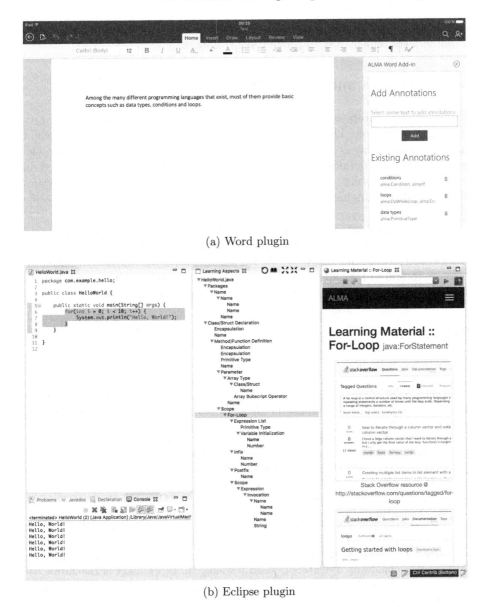

(a) Word plugin

(b) Eclipse plugin

Fig. 4. Plugins using the ALMA ontology

present in different learner-based ontologies and related to a concept in the teacher-based ontology, it could qualify for being integrated in the authoritative set. Sometimes, a different label to an already existing concept might also be sufficient, as a student might prefer a synonym or a word in a different language.

Using the *preferred* and *alternative* labels defined in the SKOS specification could be a convenient way to provide such support.

5 Conclusion and Future Work

In this paper, we propose an extensible and lightweight modular ontology for programming education. The integration of learning material in a cross-curricular and fine-grained way is possible through the alignment of language-specific elements, abstract programming concepts and user- or site-specific tags. Based on a modular architecture, the ontology is extensible with respect to new programming languages, language features and IDEs as well as user- and site-specific tags.

As future work, we intend to further develop the presented visualization tool to provide means for the curation of existing and addition of new relations as well as user- and site-specific concepts into the authoritative modules of our ontology. Also, we intend to take advantage of this ontology in order to integrate learning material in a personalized serious game we are currently developing.

References

1. Andrews, P., Zaihrayeu, I., Pane, J.: A classification of semantic annotation systems. Semant. Web **3**(3), 223–248 (2012)
2. Chung, H.S., Kim, J.M.: Ontology design for creating adaptive learning path in e-learning environment. In: Lecture Notes in Engineering and Computer Science, pp. 585–588 (2012)
3. Dehors, S., Faron-Zucker, C.: QBLS: a semantic web based learning system. In: Proceedings of EdMedia: World Conference on Educational Media and Technology 2006, pp. 2795–2802. Association for the Advancement of Computing in Education (AACE) (2006)
4. Grévisse, C., Botev, J., Rothkugel, S.: Integration of learning material into an advanced project-based learning support platform. In: Proceedings of the 11th International Technology, Education and Development Conference, INTED 2017, pp. 5711–5720 (2017)
5. Huang, Y., Yudelson, M., Han, S., He, D., Brusilovsky, P.: A framework for dynamic knowledge modeling in textbook-based learning. In: Proceedings of the 2016 Conference on User Modeling Adaptation and Personalization, UMAP 2016, pp. 141–150. ACM (2016)
6. Isaac, A.: SKOS (Simple Knowledge Organization System) - Dublin Core 2011 tutorial (2011). http://dublincore.org/resources/training/dc-2011/Tutorial_Isaac.pdf
7. Ishola, O., McCalla, G.: Tracking and reacting to the evolving knowledge needs of lifelong professional learners. In: Proceedings of the 6th Workshop on Personalization Approaches in Learning Environments (PALE 2016), pp. 68–73 (2016)
8. Kernighan, B.W., Ritchie, D.M.: The C Programming Language. Prentice Hall Englewood Cliffs, Englewood Cliffs (1988)

9. Kouneli, A., Solomou, G., Pierrakeas, C., Kameas, A.: Modeling the knowledge domain of the Java programming language as an ontology. In: Popescu, E., Li, Q., Klamma, R., Leung, H., Specht, M. (eds.) ICWL 2012. LNCS, vol. 7558, pp. 152–159. Springer, Heidelberg (2012). doi:10.1007/978-3-642-33642-3_16

10. Lohmann, S., Thalmann, S., Harrer, A., Maier, R.: Learner-generated annotation of learning resources - lessons from experiments on tagging. J. Univ. Comput. Sci. (2007)

11. Meccawy, M., Blanchfield, P., Ashman, H., Brailsford, T., Moore, A.: WHURLE 2.0: adaptive learning meets Web 2.0. In: Dillenbourg, P., Specht, M. (eds.) EC-TEL 2008. LNCS, vol. 5192, pp. 274–279. Springer, Heidelberg (2008). doi:10.1007/978-3-540-87605-2_30

12. Miranda, S., Orciuoli, F., Sampson, D.G.: A skos-based framework for subject ontologies to improve learning experiences. Comput. Hum. Behav. **61**, 609–621 (2016)

13. Pfeiffer, R.H., Wąsowski, A.: The design space of multi-language development environments. Softw. Model. **14**(1), 383–411 (2015)

14. Pierrakeas, C., Solomou, G., Kameas, A.: An ontology-based approach in learning programming languages. In: 2012 16th Panhellenic Conference on Informatics, pp. 393–398 (2012)

15. Ponzanelli, L., Bavota, G., Di Penta, M., Oliveto, R., Lanza, M.: Mining StackOverflow to turn the IDE into a self-confident programming prompter. In: Proceedings of the 11th Working Conference on Mining Software Repositories, MSR 2014, pp. 102–111 (2014)

16. Shi, L., Cristea, A.I., Stewart, C., Al Qudah, D.: Students as customers: participatory design for adaptive Web 3.0. In: The Evolution of the Internet in the Business Sector: Web 1.0 to Web 3.0, pp. 306–331 (2014)

17. Somyürek, S.: The new trends in adaptive educational hypermedia systems. Int. Rev. Res. Open Distrib. Learn. **16**(1), 221–241 (2015)

18. Sosnovsky, S., Gavrilova, T.: Development of educational ontology for C-programming. Int. J. Inf. Theor. Appl. **13**(4), 303–308 (2006)

19. Vesin, B., Ivanović, M., Klašnja-Milićević, A., Budimac, Z.: Protus 2.0: ontology-based semantic recommendation in programming tutoring system. Expert Syst. Appl. **39**(15), 12229–12246 (2012)

A Fuzzy Approach for Assessing Educational Competencies Based on Competency Maps

Diego F. Duran[1]([⊠]) [ID], Gabriel E. Chanchí[2] [ID],
and Jose L. Arciniegas[1] [ID]

[1] Universidad del Cauca, Cll. 5 #4-70, Popayan, Colombia
{dduran, jlarci}@unicauca.edu.co
[2] Institución Universitaria Colegio Mayor del Cauca,
Cra. 7 #2-34, Popayan, Colombia
gchanchi@unimayor.edu.co

Abstract. The use of linguistic terms enables teachers carry out the educational competencies assessment in a natural and significant way. However, the competency maps assessment may be an imprecise task because teachers have to consider a large amount of linguistic information, which describes relationships among elements (i.e., competencies and assessment activities), weights of such relationships and proficiency levels attained by students. In order to address this issue, this work proposes a fuzzy approach for assessing competencies based on the structure and features of the competency maps by using the 2-tuples model. In order to assess the effectiveness and the efficiency in terms of runtime of the proposal, in this work a prototype has been developed and tested using real data provided by teachers, achieving successful results. This approach intends to provide a guide to implement services for assessing educational competencies.

Keywords: Assessment · Competency maps · Education · Fuzzy logic

1 Introduction

Competencies are the various skills that students are to be taught and teachers are to be prepared to teach. Competencies are currently of great importance in the educational context because these define public criteria of the educational quality [1]. Examples of this importance are the competency-based education (developed in countries such as Colombia and Perú) and the Bologna Declaration, in which the concept of competency was selected as the basic parameter to compare higher education between the different European universities (i.e., in 29 countries such as Spain, Germany and France) [2]. In this dynamic, the competency assessment is a key task. Teachers grade Assessment Activities (AAs), assigning Proficiency Levels (PLs) depending on the student´s performance. This task can be carried out by using numerical marks in the range [0,10]; however, the use of linguistic terms (e.g., Low, High) may be more natural and significant in the assessment of some types of AAs and competencies [3], for instance if these involve observable skills and capacities of students in problem solving activities.

© Springer International Publishing AG 2017
A. Solano and H. Ordoñez (Eds.): CCC 2017, CCIS 735, pp. 372–386, 2017.
DOI: 10.1007/978-3-319-66562-7_27

Although the usage of linguistic terms is useful, the competency assessment may be a hard and imprecise process when the teacher assesses structures that relate several competencies among them, as in the case of the competency maps. These are tools used to observe the PLs attained in the curriculum of a subject, area, program or course [4]. According to the Simple Reusable Competency Map draft standard (SRCM), competency maps are composed of competencies and their relationships, which are labeled with weights (i.e., the weight indicates the importance between two competencies), and PLs assigned to each competency in the grading process. In order to address the aforementioned issue, in this paper we propose a fuzzy approach for assessing competencies based on the structure and features of the competency maps by using the linguistic 2-tuples model. The fuzzy approach is used because it allows a better representation of natural language [5]. In addition, an application of the proposal based on Java technology is presented, which computes the PLs of all the competencies of the maps by using linguistic terms, while it also shows runtimes measures.

This paper is organized as follows: Sect. 2 introduces important concepts and previous works related to this research. Section 3 describes the proposed approach, including the competency maps and student profile construction (i.e., from the computational point of view) and the PLs computing process. In Sect. 4 we present an assessment of the proposal in terms of effectiveness and runtime, by using a Java application and real data. A Conclusions and future works section is finally presented.

2 Background

2.1 Competency Maps

From the educational point of view, competency maps are tools used by teachers to observe the PLs attained by students in the curriculum of a subject, area, program or course [4]. A good approach to the structure of a competency map is given by the SRCM draft standard [6]. It defines an information model for simple, reusable competency maps to be used for describing, referencing, and exchanging data about the relationships between competencies in the educational context. In the model of SRCM, a Directed Acyclic Graph (DAG) is used to describe the maps, in which each competency is represented by a node. Since a DAG is a hierarchical collection of nodes that implies containment, a competency may be decomposed into sub-competencies, or that the sub-competences contribute to it. Figure 1 shows a fragment of a competency map based on the model of SRCM, which was provided by a math teacher that uses the Colombia's Basic Competencies Standards to stablish both the teaching and learning goals [7]. As can be seen, competency maps have the following features:

- Competencies may have sub-elements such as AAs or another competencies (note that a competency may be a sub-element or sub-competency of another competency). Hence, competency maps are composed of two or more levels.
- AAs designed by teachers (e.g., written and oral tests, problem solving, etc.) have been included as sub-elements of some competencies. In the educational practice, AAs are performed by students, then teachers carry out a grading process to assign PLs to them.

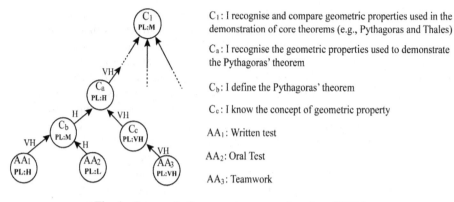

C_1: I recognise and compare geometric properties used in the demonstration of core theorems (e.g., Pythagoras and Thales)

C_a: I recognise the geometric properties used to demonstrate the Pythagoras' theorem

C_b: I define the Pythagoras' theorem

C_c: I know the concept of geometric property

AA_1: Written test

AA_2: Oral Test

AA_3: Teamwork

Fig. 1. Fragment of a competency map based on SRCM

- The structure establishes relationships between its elements, which are labeled with a weight that represents their importance.
- PLs have been assigned by teacher to all the elements of the map. Teachers usually use the PLs assigned to AAs to compute (mentally) those of all the competencies.

In the presented example, the weights and the PLs were assigned in accordance with a set of seven linguistic terms as the following:

$$S = \{\text{N: } Null, \text{VL: } Very\,Low, \text{L: } Low, \text{M: } Medium, \text{H: } High, \text{VH: } Very\,High, \text{T: } Total\} \quad (1)$$

As a final remark, although the same structure of the competency map is used for several students, each competency map belongs to each student because of it contains him/her PLs.

2.2   Issues in the Competency Assessment

According to [3], the teacher's criteria in an AA assessment process are usually determined by numerical grades from 1 to 5, or linguistic terms associated with numbers, such as in Likert Scales [8], e.g., "Very low" is associated with 1, "Low" with 2, "Medium" with 3, "High" with 4, and "Very high" with 5. When the teacher observes these possible options, his brain processes external information, and then he chooses one of these to assign a PL that describes his perception value. However, there are some aspects that may hamper this process, such as the constraints, uncertainty, and the vague knowledge of the teacher. Even, it is very difficult for teachers to ensure that the numerical criteria are equally applied when evaluating all him/her students. According to [9], these issues are specially given if the AAs involve observable skills and capacities in problem solving activities (e.g., a round table, chemical experiment, etc.) or when the assessed competencies are of a subjective nature, such as the "teamwork competency". In order to solve these issues, in works such as [3, 10, 11], the assessment is done by using linguistic terms, such as those shown in (1), which make the expert judgement more reliable and consistent. Assuming the teachers use linguistic terms to carry out the AAs assessment process, the maps assessment may be an imprecise task because a large amount of linguistic information must be considered. Consequently, PLs may be incorrectly determined, specially, in the highest levels of the maps.

2.3 Fuzzy Linguistic Approach

There are situations or activities in life in which is not appropriate the usage of a quantitative assessment. In these cases, the usage of a linguistic approach may be more convenient, in which a set of linguistic terms is used to express a perception. According to [12], a way of generating a linguistic set S involves considering all the terms distributed on a scale with a defined order. An example could be given as $S = \{s_0 : N, s_1 : VL, s_2 : L, s_3 : M, s_4 : H, s_5 : VH, s_6 : T\}$, where N represents Null, VL represents Very Low, L represents Low, M represents Medium, H represents High, VH represents Very high, and T represents Total. As can be noted, a set of indexes have been incorporated for each term in S. According to experts' criteria who participated in this research, this set is the most appropriated due to it has the terms and granularity of information (i.e., the cardinality of term set) most used in the teaching practice.

On the other hand, in this work we use triangular membership functions (see Fig. 2). According to the triangular functions, the semantic of the seven terms is the following: $N = (0, 0, 0.17), VL = (0, 0.17, 0.33), L = (0.17, 0.33, 0.5), M = (0.33, .5, 0.67), H = (0.5, 0.67, 0.83), VH = (0.67, 0.83, 1), T = (0.83, 1, 1)$. In the fuzzy linguistic approach there are computational approaches such as the based on 2-tuples and the based on extension principle, which are relevant for this research.

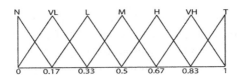

Fig. 2. A set of seven linguistic terms and their semantic

2.4 Computational Approach Based on 2-Tuples

This approach is based on the symbolic translation concept, which is defined as follows: let $S = \{s_0, \ldots, s_g\}$ be a linguistic term set, if a symbolic method aggregating linguistic information obtains a value $\beta \in [0, g]$, and $\beta \notin \{0, \ldots, g\}$ then an approximation function ($app_2(.)$) is used to express the index of the result in S. The symbolic translation of a linguistic term s_i is a numerical value assessed in $[-0.5, 0.5)$ that supports the "difference of information" between a counting of information $\beta \in [0, g]$ obtained after a symbolic aggregation operation and the closest value in $\{0, \ldots, g\}$ that indicates the index of the closest linguistic term in $S(i = round(\beta))$. The linguistic information is represented by means of 2-tuples (s_i, α_i), $s_i \in S$ and $\alpha_i \in [-0.5, 0.5)$, being s_i a representation of the linguistic label center of the information and α_i a numerical value expressing the value of the translation from the original result β to the closest index label i in the linguistic term set (s_i), i.e., the symbolic translation. A set of transformation functions between linguistic terms and 2-tuples, and between numeric values and 2-tuples are defined. The 2-tuple that expresses the equivalent information to β is obtained with the following functions:

$$\Delta : [o, g] \rightarrow Sx[-0.5.0.5] \tag{2}$$

$$\Delta(\beta) = \begin{cases} s_i, \, i = round(\beta) \\ \alpha = \beta - i, \, \alpha \in [-0.5, 0.5) \end{cases} \tag{3}$$

Where $round(.)$ is the usual round operation, s_i has the closest index label to β and α is the value of the symbolic translation. As an important remark, the conversion of a linguistic term into a linguistic 2-tuple consist of adding a value zero as symbolic translation as follows:

$$si \in S \Rightarrow (si, 0) \tag{4}$$

2.5   Computational Approach Based on Extension Principle

The extension principle has been introduced to generalize crisp mathematical operations to fuzzy sets. This approach uses linguistic aggregation operators, which act in accordance with:

$$S^n \xrightarrow{\tilde{F}} F(\mathcal{R}) \xrightarrow{app_1(.)} S \tag{5}$$

Where S^n symbolizes the n Cartesian product of S, $\tilde{F}$ is an aggregation operator based on the extension principle, $F(\mathcal{R})$ is the set of fuzzy sets over the set of real numbers $\mathcal{R}$, $app_1 : F(\mathcal{R}) \rightarrow S$ is a linguistic approximation function that returns a label from the linguistic term set S whose meaning is the closest to the obtained unlabeled fuzzy number and S is the initial term set.

2.6   Related Works

There are some works in literature focused on assessing competencies by using fuzzy linguistic approaches. In [13], a methodology for evaluating occupational competencies of students is presented. The proposal applies a fuzzy evaluation method based a on a professional competence structure, which is a tree structure composed of 3 levels with pre-defined occupational competencies. In [2], a fuzzy approach for recommending educational activities is proposed. Initially a model based on 2-tuples is defined, which enables the competency assessment by using linguistic terms on a structure composed of a set of competencies and activities. The structure defines that each competency is related to a set of activities. Then, a model of recommendation is defined by using a filter focused on the assessment results. In [14], a model for assessing occupational competencies based on fuzzy evaluation is presented. In a study case, the model is applied to a competency index system of salesman, which is a tree structure composed of 3 levels. In [15], an evaluation of enterprise core competences method is proposed. Such a method is based on the entropy and triangular fuzzy number, which enables an evaluation for enterprises objectively. It may be useful in a decision process, in which a set of enterprises is compared according to experts' criteria. In [16], a decision making method based on aggregation operators is proposed. Such method uses the model based on 2-tuples to aggregate the performances of an alternative measured by a group of evaluators. The result of the aggregation is used to take a decision from a group of alternatives.

All described related works reveal the importance of using linguistic terms in the competency and performance assessment. Several fuzzy models and approaches have been proposed to facilitate the assessment process with a high level of effectiveness. However, there is no evidence of researches based on the structure and features of the competency maps (see Sect. 2.1). In addition, although all the proposals are effective, an assessment of their viability in terms of efficiency has not been carried out.

3 Proposal

In order to compute the linguistic PLs of all the elements of a competency map, this proposal considers those attained by the students in AAs and the structure of the maps (see Sect. 2.1). From the computational point of view, next sub-sections describe how the competency map is defined and how the AAs and their corresponding PLs are included to characterize user profiles. Then, a PLs computing process based on 2-tuples is subsequently described.

3.1 Phase A: Map Structure Description

Usually, an educational curriculum is based on a group of general competencies that have been set by a government entity (e.g., the Colombia's National Ministry of Education) or by the general direction of an educational institution (e.g., School or University). These competencies must be attained or achieved by students during the schooling cycle (i.e., during a year, semester, module). In order to generate a guide about how to attain these competencies, each institution or teacher define sub-competencies from general competencies, often more easy to assess. Then, all of these are organized in a competency map, in which relationships between competencies and their respective weights are set.

In order to assess the students in function of the competencies attained by them, the teacher defines AAs which can be assessed by means of linguistic terms. From this dynamic, we can define the vectors necessary to describe the map structure:

1. Since a competency C_i is related to its k sub-elements (i.e., which may be AAs or another competencies, as the case may be), it can be defined by means of the vectors $\{C_1, C_2, \ldots, C_j \ldots, C_k\}$ or $\{AA_1, AA_2, \ldots, AA_j \ldots, AA_k\}$, as the case may be.
2. Since the weights are associated with the relationships between C_i and its sub-elements C_j or AA_j, the weights are represented by the vector $\{W_{i1}, W_{i2}, \ldots, W_{ij} \ldots, W_{ik}\}$.

At this point, the structure of the map is complete. Nevertheless, PLs have not been incorporated yet. This issue is addressed in next sub-sections.

3.2 Phase B: Initial Student Profile Construction

When a student performs an AA, the teacher grades his/her performance by assigning a linguistic PL. Thus, the student profile is composed of a set of PLs attained in each C_j or AA_j. Thus, the set of PLs of the sub-elements of C_i are represented by the vector $\{PL_1, PL_2, \ldots, PL_j, \ldots, PL_k\}$. In certain times of the schooling cycle it is necessary to know the competencies of the map achieved or acquired by the student. In order to facilitate this task, a fuzzy computing process based on the competency map structure is proposed. Such a process is explained in next sub-sections.

Example 1: Vectors definition. Figure 3 shows an example of a competency map, which is described as follows: the assessment activity AA_1 is related to the competency C_2 (AA_1 is a sub-element of C_2), AA_2 is related both to C_2 and C_3, AA_3 is related to C_3, C_2 and C_3 are sub-competencies of C_1; the weight of the relationship between AA_1 and C_2 is Medium, the weight between AA_2 and C_2 is Very High, the weight between AA_2 and C_2 is High, the weight between AA_3 and C_3 is Low, the weight between C_1 and C_2 is High, and the weight between C_1 and C_3 is Very High. Consequently, the map structure is defined by means of the vectors $C_1 = \{C_2, C_3\}$, $C_2 = \{AA_1, AA_2\}$, $C_3 = \{AA_2, AA_3\}$, $W_1 = \{H, VH\}$, $W_2 = \{M, VH\}$ and $W_3 = \{H, L\}$. Additionally, the student profile is represented by means of the vectors $NC_2 = \{L, H\}$ and $NC_3 = \{H, VH\}$.

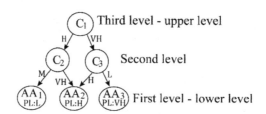

Fig. 3. An example of competency map

3.3 Phase C: Proficiency Levels Computing Process

In order to obtain the PLs of all the elements of the map, the proposed model aggregates the linguistic PLs of the student profile considering the vectors of the map. All the phases of the process, which is an adaptation of the model based on 2-tuples, are explained below.

Sub-phase C.1: Matrices construction

In this phase, the vectors of phases A and B are used to build the matrices shown in Fig. 4, which have the features required to apply fuzzy aggregation operators. This set of matrices is built for each student and level of the map. The first matrix, named Proficiency Levels Matrix (PLM), organizes the competencies in the columns and their sub-elements in the rows. The elements of PLM are the proficiency levels PL_{ij} attained by the student in the assessment activity AA_j or competency C_j (i.e., note that the matrices organize AAs or competencies in the rows, as the case may be), which are

$$
\begin{array}{c}
\textbf{Proficiency levels matrix} \\[4pt]
\begin{array}{c c c c c}
 & C_1 & C_2 & \cdots & C_n \\
AA_1\text{-}C_1 & \begin{bmatrix} PL_{11} \\ PL_{12} \\ \cdots \\ PL_{1k} \end{bmatrix} & \begin{matrix} PL_{21} \\ \cdots \\ \cdots \\ PL_{2k} \end{matrix} & \begin{matrix} \cdots \\ \cdots \\ \cdots \\ \cdots \end{matrix} & \begin{matrix} PL_{n1} \\ \cdots \\ \cdots \\ PL_{nk} \end{matrix}
\end{array}
\end{array}
\qquad
\begin{array}{c}
\textbf{Weights matrix} \\[4pt]
\begin{array}{c c c c c}
 & C_1 & C_2 & \cdots & C_n \\
AA_1\text{-}C_1 & \begin{bmatrix} W_{11} \\ W_{12} \\ \cdots \\ W_{1k} \end{bmatrix} & \begin{matrix} W_{21} \\ \cdots \\ \cdots \\ W_{2k} \end{matrix} & \begin{matrix} \cdots \\ \cdots \\ \cdots \\ \cdots \end{matrix} & \begin{matrix} W_{n1} \\ \cdots \\ \cdots \\ W_{nk} \end{matrix}
\end{array}
\end{array}
$$

Fig. 4. Proficiency levels and Weights matrices

sub-elements of C_i. The second matrix, named Weights Matrix (WM), also organizes the competencies in the columns and the AAs or competencies in the rows. However, in this case each element is the weight W_{ij} of the relationship between the assessment activity AA_j or competency C_j and the competency C_i. In both cases, if there is no relationship between certain column and row, the value for PL_{ij} or W_{ij} is zero.

On the other hand, in an aggregation process of linguistic terms, a numeric value is initially obtained as a result, which is then analyzed for the assignment of a linguistic value. In order to differentiate them, in the remainder of this paper these are named Numeric Aggregation Value (NAV) and Linguistic Aggregation Value (LAV) (LAV is the result of the computing process, and in this case, is the PL assigned to an element of the map). Since the PLs computed in certain level are used to compute those of higher levels, two possibilities of aggregation are proposed in this approach as follows:

- **P1.** The aggregation in all the levels is carried out by using the LAVs of the directly lower level. In this case, the PLM and WM are composed of linguistic terms.
- **P2.** The aggregation from the third level to the highest is carried out by using the NAVs of the directly lower level (note that in the aggregation of the second level are used the PLs of the first level, which are linguistic terms). In this case, the PLM is composed of numeric values, while the WM is composed of linguistic terms.

The use of each possibility depends on the user's criteria. However, both have implications in the model, which are addressed in next sections.

Sub-phase C.2: Conversion to 2-tuples of linguistic terms

In this sub-phase, each linguistic term of the matrices is converted to 2-tuples. In order to make symbolic translations, a zero value is added to the terms (according to (4)). Note that if the user chooses the possibility P2 shown in sub-phase C.1, the conversion is only applied on WM.

Example 2: Matrices construction. Considering Example 1, Fig. 5 shows the PLM and the WM of the second level of the competency map. Note that all the terms have been converted to 2-tuples.

Sub-phase C.3: Aggregation

Once the PLs of the AAs or competencies of a certain level of the map are known and organized in the matrices, it is necessary to compute the PLs for every element of the level directly above. For this purpose, two different aggregation processes are proposed for each one of the possibilities stablished in the sub-fase C.1.

Proficiency levels matrix

	C_2	C_3
AA₁	(L,0)	0
AA₂	(H,0)	(H,0)
AA₃	0	(VH,0)

Weights matrix

	C_2	C_3
AA₁	(M,0)	0
AA₂	(VH,0)	(H,0)
AA₃	0	(L,0)

Fig. 5. Proficiency levels and weights matrices for the example 2

1. Aggregation process for the possibility P1: the Weighted Average Operator (WAO) for 2-tuples is used, which is proposed in [12] as follows:

$$\bar{x}^e = \Delta\left(\frac{\sum_{i=1}^{n} \beta_i.w_i}{\sum_{i=1}^{n} w_i}\right) \tag{6}$$

This operator allows different values x_i have a different importance in the nature of the variable x. Hence, each value x_i has a weight associated w_i indicating its importance in the nature of the variable. In competency terms, this operator allows to aggregate different PLs attained in AAs or competencies by considering their importance for the competency of which these elements are sub-elements. An explanation of Δ function and β is presented in Sect. 2.4. The values β for all the indexes of the linguistic terms are defined in Fig. 6. For instance, the values β for L, H, and VH are 2, 4 and 5, respectively.

2. Aggregation process for the possibility P2: the WAO, defined in (6), is used with a variation of the nature of β. In this case, in order to compute the PL of certain competency, the used values β correspond to the NAVs computed for its sub-elements.

N	VL	L	M	H	VH	T
0	1	2	3	4	5	6

Fig. 6. Distribution of indexes for linguistic terms

Example 3: 2-tuples aggregation Considering Example 2, in this example we shall calculate the PL for the competencies C_2 and C_3 by adapting (6) as follows:

$$PL_{C2} = \Delta\left(\frac{2*3+4*5}{3+5}\right) = \Delta(3.25)$$

Since the NAV 3.25 is between M and H, the Δ function is used to decide which of the two options is assigned to C_2. The resulting 2-tuples are $(M, 0.25)$ and $(H, -0.75)$. Since the aggregated value is closer to M, the linguistic PL assigned to C_2 is M. Following a similar process, $PL_{C3} = \Delta(4.33)$. The resulting 2-tuples are $(H, 0.33)$ and $(VH, -0.67)$, hence the linguistic PL assigned to C_3 is H.

Proficiency levels matrix

C_1

$$C_2 \begin{bmatrix} (\text{M},0) \\ (\text{H},0) \end{bmatrix}$$
$$C_3$$

Weights matrix

C_1

$$C_2 \begin{bmatrix} (\text{H},0) \\ (\text{VH},0) \end{bmatrix}$$
$$C_3$$

Fig. 7. Proficiency levels and weights matrices for the upper level using the possibility P1

Example 4: aggregation in accordance with the two possibilities proposed in the sub-phase C.1. Considering that the competency C_1 is in the third level of the map, we can calculate the PL for C_1 by using the two possibilities mentioned in the sub-phase C.1.

1. In accordance with the possibility P1, Fig. 7 shows the matrices for the upper level of the map. The Proficiency level matrix is composed of the LAVs computed for C_2 and C_3.

   Then, the PL for C_1 is computed as follows:

$$PL_{C1} = \Delta \left(\frac{3 * 4 + 4 * 5}{4 + 5} \right) = \Delta(3.55)$$

   Hence, the PL assigned to C_1 is H.

2. In accordance with the possibility P2, Fig. 8 shows the matrices for the upper level of the map. The Proficiency level matrix is composed of the NAVs computed for C_2 and C_3.

   Then, the PL for C_1 is computing as follows:

$$PL_{C2} = \Delta \left(\frac{2 * 3 + 4 * 5}{3 + 5} \right) = \Delta(3.25)$$

   Hence, the PL assigned to C_1 is also H. As a final remark, note that the NAV is in a mid-point between M and H by using the possibility P1, while it is clearly closer to H by using the possibility P2. This is because of P2 considers the fuzzy nature of the PLs achieved by the student in all the lower levels without loss of information (i.e., it is assumed that the student has a performance both Medium and High for C_2 when computing C_1). While using P1 the calculations were carried out over the results given by the round operation (involved in Δ function), then there is a loss of information continuously (i.e., it is assumed that the student has a performance Medium for C_2 when computing C_1).

Proficiency levels matrix

C_1

$$C_2 \begin{bmatrix} 3.25 \\ 4.33 \end{bmatrix}$$
$$C_3$$

Weights matrix

C_1

$$C_2 \begin{bmatrix} (\text{H},0) \\ (\text{VH},0) \end{bmatrix}$$
$$C_3$$

Fig. 8. Proficiency levels and weights matrices for the upper level using the possibility P2

4 Assessment

This section presents a set of experiments and results carried out to assess the proposal by using real data of competency maps provided by a group of teachers.

4.1 Overview

The experiments were designed to answer the following research questions:

1. What is the effectiveness of the proposal?
2. What are the advantages provided by the proposal in terms of runtime in comparison with the model based on extension principle?

In order to answer these questions, an application based on Java technologies has been developed (see Fig. 9), which was used to carry out the experiments. The application can apply two modes to compute the PLs of the maps: Mode 1 is based on the proposal (i.e., the interface on the left) and the Mode 2 is based on the extension principle (i.e., interface on the right). The data related both to the structure of the maps and to the PLs attained by each student has been adapted to the JSON format and stored in a NoSQL MongoDB database. The application computes the PLs of the maps and shows the results by using both NAV and LAV. Additionally, the application presents the runtime measured for each map. As can be seen, the application provides the data necessary to assess the proposal.

4.2 Metrics

The metric defined in (7) was used to answer the first research question, which is defined as the percentage of PLs given by the application that are equal to those provided by the teachers. Also, it can be considered as the percentage of hits of the proposal.

$$\%Hits = \frac{N_{hits}}{T} * 100\% \tag{7}$$

Where N_{hits} is the total of hits of the application and T is the total of PLs assessed.

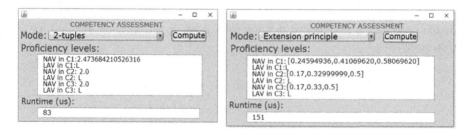

Fig. 9. Interfaces of the application

Moreover, (8) is the percentage of cases in which the proposal had problems to decide among two linguistic terms at the moment of assigning a PL for a competency. This kind of problems occurs when a numeric aggregation value is equidistant from two different membership functions (i.e., of two different linguistic terms), hence, there is a difficulty to assign one of these.

$$\%Prblms = \frac{N_{dp}}{T} * 100\% \tag{8}$$

Where N_{dp} is the decision problems count and T is the total of PLs assessed.

As regards the second research question, application runtime is a variable that depends on various factors, such as the features of the computer or its tasks performed at the moment of carry out the experiments. In order to reduce the variability of the runtime measures, we have computed an average value of time t_a of 100 measures for each experiment a as follows:

$$t_a = \frac{\sum_{i=1}^{100} t_{ia}}{100} \tag{9}$$

Where t_{ia} is the i th measure of time taken for the experiment a.

4.3 Experiments and Results

In order to asses this proposal, 75 competency maps of real educational processes were used, which are based on the Colombia's Basic Competencies Standards in Math and were provided by a group of teachers. Of these maps, there are 15 different structures (i.e., five maps per structure). The maps include the PLs attained by a group students in each AA and competency of the map. Once the information has been defined, the experiments and data collection were carried out by means of the following phases.

1. The structure of the maps was adapted to JSON format and stored in a MongoDB database. Each structure was identified by means of a unique ID.
2. The PLs achieved by the student in the AAs were introduced in the database. Each student was identified by a unique ID.
3. The PLs for all the competencies (745 in total) of the maps were computed by the application by using the proposed approach (i.e., by using the Mode 1 of the application).
4. The PLs for all the competencies were computed by using the approach based on the extension principle (i.e., by using the Mode 2 of the application).
5. In order to measure the effectiveness of the proposal, the PLs given by the application in the third and fourth phases were compared with those provided by the teachers. Then, the percentage of hits of each approach were obtained by using (7).
6. A decision problems cases count for the approaches was carried out by using (8).
7. In order to know the advantages of the proposal in terms of runtime in comparison with the model based on extension principle, all the maps were computed 100 times to measure the average runtime of each structure and approach by using (9). It is

Table 1. Number of hits and decision problems identified in experiments

Structure	Competencies per structure	T	Proposal				Approach based on extension principle			
			N_{hits}	N_{dp}	%Hits	%Prblms	N_{hits}	N_{dp}	%Hits	%Prblms
1	8	40	39	2	97.5	5	36	3	90	7.5
2	6	30	28	0	93.33	0	27	0	90	0
3	15	75	72	2	96	2.66	71	2	94.66	2.66
4	7	35	34	1	97.14	2.85	32	0	91.42	0
5	11	55	54	3	98.18	5.45	53	3	96.36	5.45
6	3	15	15	0	100	0	15	0	100	0
7	11	55	55	0	100	0	55	0	100	0
8	10	50	50	2	100	4	50	3	100	6
9	24	120	119	0	99.16	0	119	1	99.16	0.83
10	18	90	89	4	98.88	4.44	88	3	97.77	3.33
11	3	15	15	0	100	0	15	0	100	0
12	10	50	49	2	98	4	49	2	98	4
13	3	15	15	0	100	0	15	0	100	0
14	9	45	44	0	97.77	0	43	0	95.55	0
15	11	55	55	0	100	0	54	1	98.18	1.81
Total	**149**		**745**	**733**	**16**	**98.39**	**2.14**	**722**	**18**	**96.91**	**2.41**

worth mentioning that the time measures were taken for the methods of the application directly related to the processes of each approach (i.e., another methods such as those related to databases, interfaces, etc., were not included in the measures).

Table 1 shows the results achieved in the experiments of phases 5 and 6. The data is organized by assessed approach and structure of the maps. Analyzing the results, the percentages of hits are 98.39% and 96.91%, respectively, while percentages of decision problems are 2.14% and 2.41%, respectively. As a result, the effectiveness provided by the proposal can be considered as quite successful. On the other hand, the measures of average runtime for each approach and structure are shown in Fig. 10. Analyzing the

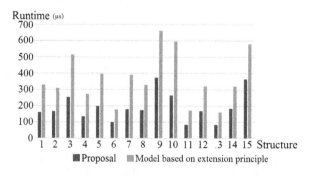

Fig. 10. Runtimes measured in experiments

results, in 40 percent of the cases, the runtimes for the approach based on the extension principle are higher between one and two times than those of the proposal, and higher more than twice in 60% of the cases.

5 Conclusions and Future Work

The evolution of computational systems involves changes in the design and assessment of the teaching and learning processes. In this case, a fuzzy approach to assess competencies based on competency maps has been described. The approach computes the PLs of all the elements of the maps by using those attained in assessment activities, allowing students and teachers to know the achieved educational goals in the curriculum of a subject, area, program or course. The approach has been implemented in a Java application and assessed with real data provided by teachers. The results indicate that the proposal is quite effective, offering a percentage of hits near to 100 percent and higher than that of the approach based on extension principle. Additionally, the proposal provides low runtime values in applications, hence, it is viable to be integrated in e-learning platforms or internet services to support real educational processes.

In future works we will study a way to incorporate the proposal to a recommender system for educational VoD (Video on Demand) contents. In order to provide user profiles, linguistic proficiency levels may be adapted to an information structure (e.g., matrices). Therefore, the filtering process could be focused on competencies not reached by the students. Additionally, we will stablish a way to relate VoD contents and competency maps by using applications profiles of metadata schemas such as TV-Anytime, Learning Object Metadata (LOM), Reusable Competency Definition (RCD) and Simple Reusable Competency Map (SRCM). The use of application profiles could help to avoid performance issues of the recommender system.

Acknowledgements. This work is supported by the National Doctorates program, call with reference number 617-2013 of Colciencias, the UsabiliTV project supported by Colciencias with ID 1103 521 2846 and the AUIP.

References

1. El Programa PISA de la OCDE. http://www.oecd.org/pisa/39730818.pdf. Accessed 21 Apr 2017. (in Spanish)
2. Serrano, J., Romero, F., Olivas, J.: Hiperion: a fuzzy approach for recommending educational activities based on the acquisition of competences. Inf. Sci. **248**, 114–129 (2013)
3. Fung, K.: A fuzzy qualitative evaluation system: a multi-granular aggregation approach using fuzzy compound linguistic variable. J. Intell. Fuzzy Syst. **24**, 61–78 (2013)
4. García, M., Gairín, J.: Los mapas de competencias: una herramienta para mejorar la calidad de la formación universitaria. Rev. Iberoamericana sobre Calid. Efic. Cambio Educ. **9**(1), 84–102 (2011). in Spanish
5. Herrera, E., López, A., Alonso, S., Moreno, J., Cabrerizo, F., Porcel, C.: A computer-supported learning system to help teachers to teach fuzzy information retrieval systems. Inf. Retrieval **12**, 179–200 (2009)

6. Simple Reusable Competency Map. http://www.ostyn.com/standardswork/competency/ReusableCompMapProp.pdf. Accessed 21 Apr 2017
7. Estándares básicos de competencias. http://www.mineducacion.gov.co/1621/articles-340021_recurso_1.pdf. Accessed 21 Apr 2017. (in Spanish)
8. Likert, R.: A technique for the measurement of attitudes. Arch. Psychol. **140**, 1–55 (1932)
9. Montero, J., Alias, F., Badía, D., Fonseca, D., Vicent, L.: A method for designing automatic assessment systems based on teachers reasoning for evaluating subjective engineering student's competences. In: 9th Iberian Conference on Information Systems and Technologies (CISTI) on Proceedings, pp. 1–9. IEEE, Barcelona (2014)
10. Zhaoa, X., Yueb, W.: A multi-subsystem fuzzy DEA model with its application in mutual funds management companies' competence evaluation. Procedia Comput. Sci. **1**, 2469–2478 (2012)
11. Massanet, S., Riera, J., Torrens, J., Herrera, E.: A new linguistic computational model based on discrete fuzzy numbers for computing with words. Inf. Sci. **248**, 277–290 (2014)
12. Herrera, F., Martínez, L.: A 2-tuple fuzzy linguistic representation model for computing with words. IEEE Trans. Fuzzy Syst. **8**(6), 746–752 (2000)
13. Pengshun, Z., Jianguo, H.: Application of fuzzy hierarchy evaluation in the occupational competency assessment of the vocational colleges. In: International Symposium on Information Technology in Medicine and Education on Proceedings, pp. 182–185. IEEE, Hokkaido (2012)
14. Zhaojun, Z., Xiao, Q., Xiaoqing, L.: Competency assessment study based on IPCA-fuzzy comprehensive evaluation. In: International Conference on Management and Service Science (MASS), pp. 1–9. IEEE, Wuhan (2010)
15. Jia, Z., Zhao, L.: Evaluation of enterprise core competence based on the entropy and triangular fuzzy number. In: International Conference on E-Business and E-Government, pp. 2045–2048. IEEE, Guangzhou (2010)
16. Zhang, H.: The multiattribute group decision making method based on aggregation operators with interval-valued 2-tuple linguistic information. Math. Comput. Model. **56**(1), 27–35 (2012)

Education Platform with Dynamic Questions Using Cloud Computing Services

Jordan A. Cortés, Jesús A. Vega, Diego C. Schotborg, and Juan C. Caicedo[✉]

Fundación Universitaria Konrad Lorenz, Bogotá, Colombia
{jordana.cortesm,jesusa.vegac,diegoc.schotborgc,
juanc.caicedor}@konradlorenz.edu.co

Abstract. We present a platform for active learning that generates dynamic questions and provides real time feedback to students. The proposed platform aims to provide alternatives to the static exercises that are found in all major learning platforms in the web, for which a fixed set of questions is defined once and then very rarely updated. We also emphasize the importance of feedback from the educational perspective, as this allows students to improve performance even when their answers are incorrect. This paper presents the learning principles that have guided the design of our platform, and discusses the various software engineering decisions that were taken to implement the platform. In particular, we describe the cloud computing technologies that allow us to serve multiple students with minimum infrastructure maintenance effort.

Keywords: Education · Cloud computing · Active learning

1 Introduction

The interest in educational technology has been steadily increasing due to the power and reach of the internet and modern computational platforms [2,8,9]. Video streaming, interactive web pages, and gamified apps are all being used to satisfy the interests of a variety of learners around the world. Similarly, massive open online courses (MOOCs) have been developed with the participation of almost all major universities, giving access to high quality contents in a variety of professional topics to a large audience with different backgrounds [11,13,15]. All these developments highlight the demand for new learning alternatives that give more autonomy to interested students.

Most educational technologies for MOOCs such as Coursera, EdX, and Khan Academy are primarily used for virtual education [14,16,18]. Despite their popularity, these systems make use of static evaluation mechanisms that are fixed and very rarely updated after they have been published. This makes the opportunity for practicing a variety of exercises very limited, which is one of the ways in which students can develop mastery in a topic. The main assumption of these platforms is that content is enough for students to learn, and the evaluation is

© Springer International Publishing AG 2017
A. Solano and H. Ordoñez (Eds.): CCC 2017, CCIS 735, pp. 387–400, 2017.
DOI: 10.1007/978-3-319-66562-7_28

required only to check if learning is happening. We have a different perspective about how platforms should support learning, where exercises are not used for evaluation but for practicing, training and improving.

In this paper, we propose a system architecture that generates dynamic questions using randomized variables. Our approach is one step towards making platforms more interactive without requiring specialized software for each different topic. We propose a general architecture that can be extended for handling question templates requiring extensions with two main responsibilities: (1) rules for completing random variables in a template, and (2) rules for grading answers proposed by students. In this way, our system encapsulates the complexity of the platform components and provides explicit mechanisms for extending the functionality to a diverse set of questions with minimal coding effort.

The proposed platform can generate a variety of questions from a bank of templates designed for a specific topic. These dynamic questions have several advantages over static evaluation forms: first, the proposed dynamic questions are used for student learning and not for student evaluation, which is equivalent to having sets of exercises to practice skills in preparation for conventional exams. Second, dynamic questions are parameterized and can be reused multiple times by students and instructors. In that way, students can practice similar exercises without the risk of memorizing their answers, because random variables will make each question unique. Third, answers to dynamic questions can be automatically checked and therefore enable a mechanism for real time feedback, which is important for learners, and difficult to provide for everyone by the instructor.

Our system has been implemented using cloud computing technologies to make it easily accessible for everyone. The proposed architecture has been implemented in the Java programming language, and deployed in a Google App Engine system [21]. The services of the system can be accessed from the Internet using web applications or mobile apps, given the decoupled client-server design. Also, we make extensive use of software design patterns to facilitate maintenance and extension of the proposed platform with new educational exercises and ever changing functionalities.

The rest of this paper presents a discussion of the previous work in Sect. 2. Section 3 discusses the learning principles that we follow to design the proposed platform. Section 4 discusses the design of the architecture and Sect. 5 its implementation. Section 6 discusses the main conclusions of this work.

2   Previous Works

Technologies for education have been explored for a long time. It has been found that just the introduction of laptops in the classroom can have a positive impact in the way students approach research problems and process information [12]. Also, the use of readily available technologies, such as blogs and social networks, can help engage students in activities and collaboration efforts [19]. During the last few years, education platforms have grown into large scale public systems that offer learning material for courses, including video lectures, homeworks and projects [11]. In our work, we do not focus in the contents of learning, but instead in the process of learning when students attempt to solve exercises.

Gamification of education is a way to stimulate engagement during the learning process [10]. There are several strategies in which serious games as well as the design of certain activities can make the learning of difficult topics more entertaining. Video games with different characters, scenes and challenges have been developed and evaluated for educational purposes [5]. However, the complexity and effort of developing such games do not necessarily justify the learning outcomes, and sometimes simpler strategies can have more impact and be more effective [6].

Feedback is particularly important for learning, and computer based approaches can improve the availability of feedback for students [20]. In this sense, tools for helping students to practice self-study with the feedback of automated quizzes have been developed [4]. Quizzes that connect social components to integrate student guidance with the help of peers and professors have been developed and evaluated [3]. More similar to our work are the systems that implement parameterized tasks with dynamic exercises that can be personalized and evaluated automatically [1, 7, 17]. We develop a similar concept based on specific learning principles, and also implement our tool in a modern cloud-based service.

3   Education Platform

The goal of the proposed platform is to support student learning by giving feedback to students when they are solving problems proposed by the professor. This is the natural way in which learning happens in classrooms, where professors design exercises for students to practice skills and to apply concepts taught in lectures. However, we identify several difficulties that classrooms face when trying to follow this natural principle:

Static set of exercises: instructors design a set of exercises that are fixed, or refer the students to exercises proposed in textbooks. This limits the number of attempts that students can practice in several ways. If the exercises are designed with increasing degree of difficulty, the student may feel early frustration when failing the easy exercises and may fall behind other students. If the exercises are designed by topic, the student may be engaged in certain type of work that gets interrupted because there are no more exercises of this type to solve, losing the opportunity to develop more expertise.

Lack of feedback: when the classroom has more than ten students, giving immediate feedback to all of them is often not possible. Then, the common practice is to collect the solutions developed by students and to assign grades that reflect their level of performance. This feedback is delayed several days, and when it arrives, the student may have lost interest and attention to the important steps to produce a successful solution. This practice has been also criticized for reducing the complex process of learning to a number or letter that does not necessarily reflect the achievements of students.

Solving these problems is a challenging task for institutions. To break the barrier of static exercises, professors would need to spend more time designing new activities and also grading them. To bridge the feedback gap and making it real time, each student would need a dedicated tutor. Fortunately, the use of information technologies can help to implement solutions for these problems that were not possible two decades ago. Here we describe a platform that implements simple solutions to these problems, but first, we describe the learning principles that guide the design of our system.

3.1 Learning Principles

Active learning: humans learn anything more efficiently by doing. This learning paradigm proposes that students should become the center of learning activities and should be in charge of the process. The proposed platform is not a content management system with a passive collection of reference materials for clarifying concepts. While important, these are already abundant in the web and textbooks. Instead, the proposed system provides active mechanisms of learning by solving problems, giving students the ability to focus on what is of interest for them.

Immediate feedback: solving problems may become a frustrating experience if the student does not receive timely feedback about the errors or misconceptions about a topic. Feedback is easier to give for physical activities such as sports or tool handling, where the activity as such is engaging. However, for more abstract topics, such as mathematics and physics, the thought process may demand attention for extended periods of time without a clue of what to do next. We propose a system that can check answers automatically, to encourage students to try even if the answer is incorrect, which helps to identify mistakes in the applied procedures.

Skills require practice: students may incorrectly think that they lack the capacity to solve these problems if they face difficulties with a few exercises. Research has shown that all what is necessary in most of the cases is more practice. Developing skills takes time and needs regular feedback to keep track of progress. Our system challenges students with new exercises and keeps track of the number of correct answers through time to encourage continued improvement.

Skills solve problems: one skill is useful in a context, in which a family of problems with similar properties can be solved with a similar strategy. If the skill has been successfully acquired, students should be able to demonstrate their ability to solve any associated problem. Also, that skill will be useful to develop other more complex skills in related areas of knowledge in the future. We propose to organize the topics of a course with a skill-oriented structure. This organization helps professors to design more effective activities that are focused on specific abilities that the student can develop with continued practice and feedback.

Problems have formulations: one problem can be found in the real world formulated in different ways while still requiring the same approach to be solved. The ability of students to recognize the problem independently of the way it is formulated is critical to apply skills in practice. The proposed system allows defining different formulations of the same problem, for stimulating associative thinking and recall of problem-solving strategies on the fly.

Problems have variables: many problems in a variety of academic areas can be formulated in terms of variables that have to be identified and processed to produce a solution. For instance, an arithmetic operation in mathematics has two variables and one result, while associating countries and capitals has one variable and one result. These variables are used frequently in textbook exercises and exams. We incorporate variables into problem formulations in our system to parameterize multiple exercises with the same structure.

3.2 Proposed Solution

We adopt the learning principles described above as requirements for the design of our system. Figure 1 presents the main relationships among the entities of the learning problem. These define the main organization and goals of the proposed platform. Knowledge in the platform is organized in a hierarchical way, starting with skills that contain problems, problems that have multiple formulations, and formulations that contain variables. This organization allows the system to provide personalization and feedback, as follows:

Exercise efficiency: the goal of the proposed platform is to bring as many different exercises to the student as possible without repetition. A trivial solution for this requirement would be to just add a large number of static exercises into a fixed database. However, this does not scale well as the effort that professors have to make to create such a database is proportional to the number of desired exercises. Instead, we propose the use of templates with variables to encode reusable problem formulations in a general way. Professors can design a problem formulation once in a machine-readable format, and let the system reuse it with different values.

Personalization: from a single template with variables, the system can generate multiple exercises by randomly sampling values from a valid domain and replace them in the template. In this way, the effort of creating new questions is reduced to incorporating more valid values into the domain of each variable. By randomizing the values in the template, we minimize the number of times that the exact same exercise is presented to the same student. This strategy stimulates learning the right concept behind an exercise instead of memorizing the right answer.

Feedback: the rules to evaluate answers for personalized exercises are incorporated in the system, and thus immediate feedback can be provided to students.

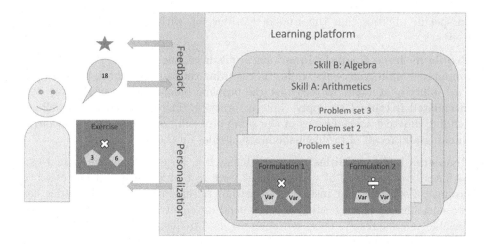

Fig. 1. Learning principles and proposed solution. Students interact with questions repeatedly to improve skills in a given topic. The system personalize these questions by replacing variables in a formulation template. These templates are designed by professors together with the rules to check answers automatically. With this, the system provides instant feedback to students and the possibility of addressing a new problem.

This is a very important property of the proposed system, as its goal is not to replace exams or formal evaluations, but instead provide a platform to train and practice for acquiring expertise.

4   Architecture

We designed a system architecture to incorporate the learning requirements presented in the previous section. The proposed design follows object oriented principles and design patterns that naturally bring entities from the real world to computer implementations that can be maintained over time. The main architecture of our system is organized in three main parts: (1) business logic components, (2) web services, and (3) user interface. We describe these three components in the following sections.

4.1   Business Logic Components

We start by modeling the basic entities of learning as classes of the system. These include `Skill`, `Problem` and `Formulation`, which have a hierarchical organization that can be modeled using composition relations in object oriented design. The main goal of these entities is to encapsulate basic information about the topics of study in a particular course curriculum. From these three, the only active entity is the `Formulation`, because this one needs to encapsulate personalization behavior, as was defined in the previous section.

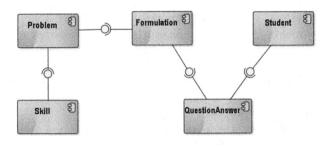

Fig. 2. Class diagram illustrating the structure of the main business logic component. The classes `Skill`, `Problem`, `Formulation` and `Student`, correspond to real world entities. The class `QuestionAnswer` has been introduced to represent a single personalized question with the correct and proposed answers.

The personalization behavior is designed to be independent of the topic of study. For instance, if the topic of study is mathematics, the way the system handles formulations should not be different as if the topic of study was geography. The main responsibilities of this component is to generate questions, identify their correct solutions, collect the proposed answer from the student, and provide feedback. The structure of this logic is presented in Fig. 2.

An example of instances of the classes in the main component of the system is illustrated in Table 1. This table presents examples of formulation templates in two different topics, and shows how they share similar structure. The table also illustrates that each subject may have different personalization rules, specifically, the variable domain and evaluation rule. To accommodate for a flexible solution, we need to design other components that can incorporate additional topics of study with minimal implementation effort. Ideally, new topics should be added with a single new class that encapsulates the domain variables and rules required to generate questions of these topics.

Table 1. Example problem formulations.

Subject	Skill	Problem	Formulation	Variable domain	Evaluation rule
Math	Arithmetic	Subtraction	We are traveling to another city that is A km away. We have traveled B km, how many are left?	A, B: positive integers [10,1000]	A − B
Geo	Political organization	Countries and Capitals	A is the capital of which country?	A: string from a list of capitals	Find the country in a parallel list of strings

We designed a subsystem that contains personalization and feedback logic in a package that we call `QuestionProcessor`. The goal of this subsystem is to provide a mechanism for extensible and flexible incorporation of new formulation rules into the system. One of the important classes in this subsystem is the QuestionAnswer entity, which represents a single personalized question to be presented to a Student for collecting the proposed answer. The personalization logic in the QuestionProcessor subsystem generates QuestionAnswer objects for Students by instantiating the correct formulation objects conditioned to the topic. The same subsystem is in charge of providing feedback by comparing the correct solution with the proposed answer.

Among the design patterns used to organize this solution are the Template Method, which is useful to define a general Formulation class that can be specialized to satisfy the requirements of topics. We also use the Facade design pattern to encapsulate the details of the subsystem in a software component that decouples the complexity of question handling (including creational processes designed as factories) with the use of a fixed interface (Fig. 3).

Fig. 3. Diagram of some classes in the QuestionProcessor subsystem. SpecialProcessor follows the Template Method design pattern, with an example class ArithmeticsProcessor. This is complemented by a Factory pattern to create questions of specific topics as needed.

4.2   Web Services

Since the proposed system will be extended in time with more subclasses of Formulation that are added to the QuestionProcessor subsystem, we resolve to separate this logic from the user interface using web services. This design imposes the non-functional requirement of creating a client-server architecture, as opposed to standalone applications in desktop computers or mobile devices. However, the design also serves the purpose of being multi-user and opens the way for multi-device interfaces. In addition, well designed web services offer a comprehensive API that serves up-to-date information with the latest business logic without having to update client components.

Web services use the exposed interface of the QuestionProcessor Facade in the core system. The QuestionProcessor subsystem interacts with the main business logic that controls Skills, Problems, Students and so on, and passes any result to the web services. This design is presented in Fig. 4 with a component diagram that shows how the server organization should be.

4.3   User Interface

The web service API can be consumed from a variety of multiple devices since the system logic is decoupled from the actual user interface. In this sense, we have

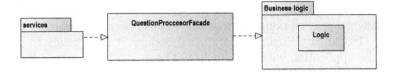

Fig. 4. Diagram of components in the server. Three main components are designed with distinct responsibilities: Main business logic, `QuestionProcessor` subsystem and web services exposed in the network.

web interfaces or mobile apps that make requests to the central application to get personalized questions, propose answers, and get feedback. The user interface for students is designed to support this basic workflow, illustrated in Fig. 1.

The business logic has mechanisms to store session information including answer timing, correct number of answers, and number of attempts, among others. These measures can be displayed in the user interface to provide additional feedback to students, and keep track of progress. Our design provides a simple web interface for students to interact with the system in an open loop that we call training session. Students can practice with as many exercises as they want, getting immediate feedback and basic aggregated measures of performance to track progress.

Another user interface needs to be used for professors that design formulation templates. We also use a simple web interface for creating, updating, and deleting all the data corresponding to skills, problems and formulations. The way teachers and instructors interact with this interface to maintain formulations is through XML templates (Fig. 5). The templates require only two types of tags to provide information about the problem type and the variables. These two tags are recognized by an XML-parser and passed to the personalization and feedback components to generate concrete question-answer pairs.

```
<question type="Arithmetics" type="Subtraction">
We are traveling to another city that is
<variable type="int" key="A" /> km away. We have traveled
<variable type="int" key="B" /> km, how many are left?
</question>
```

Fig. 5. Illustration of a formulation template with an example question. Tags in red are used to recognize the extent and type of question. Tags in blue are variables that are replaced by the personalization module. (Color figure online)

5   Implementation

We implemented the system using the Java programming language and deployed the proposed architecture in the cloud using the services provided by Google App Engine. We chose the cloud as deployment platform because it allows us to focus the development efforts on the business logic and leverage infrastructure that is ready to use. This means that we save the time of installing server software, configuring networking services and publishing applications in the web. We chose Google App Engine in particular, because it offers ready to use tools to scale the application with the number of users, and supports easy creation and configuration of web services, and datastores among others.

We created a Google App Engine project that included a datastore, the business logic, web services and user interfaces. Figure 6 illustrates these components, which are described below.

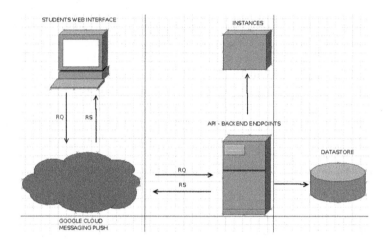

Fig. 6. Organization of the implemented components in Google App Engine. The datastore contains object information in a NoSQL database. The endpoints are the technology that supports web service publication. The instances are servers that run the business logic. The cloud messaging service links the web (or mobile) clients with the backend.

5.1   Datastore and Instances

The datastore is a service provided by Google App Engine to create NoSQL databases with atomic transactions, and high availability and scalability. The datastore provides a simple API to get, put and delete objects in tables that can be indexed and queried. Once the business logic has been defined, all we need to do to create tables is to specify which classes in our model need serialization. This can be done with the Java Persistence API (JPA) or with the low level datastore API provided by Google. We opted for JPA so the code could be reused outside the cloud if ever needed.

Instances in the App Engine ecosystem are machines that run specific versions of applications or services. In our case, instances run the business logic, including access to the datastore, as well as the execution of personalization and feedback routines. Instances can also serve web pages when the application requires, as in our case. Instances can be replicated and scaled to attend growing needs in the use of services. Replication is the ability to run more instances with the same logic with automatic load balancing, while scaling is the property of using larger hardware capacity for each instance.

5.2 Endpoints and Web Client

The endpoints are the mechanism that Google App Engine provides to publish web services. This is a simple way to provide backend methods that can be consumed by different clients, keeping a decoupled and reusable architecture. The API is published as REST methods that pass messages in the form of JSON objects with clients. The list of methods published in our current version of the API are listed in Table 2, and are divided in two different groups: one for teacher functionalities, and another for student functionalities. Notice that the methods required to serve student learning in practice are only three, giving flexibility to the type of user interfaces that can be constructed on top of the proposed service.

We connected the API components using a single page Angular.js application in a browser client. Using this technology we leverage the Model-View-Controller design pattern to create an interface that responds to the user interactions in coordination with the endpoint web services. Figure 7 illustrates the look and feel of the student web page that shows a generated question after with feedback given after the solution has been submitted. This interface also allows to accumulate the number of correct answers in the training session, as well as to interact with other functionalities for account configuration.

Fig. 7. Web and mobile interface for students. The screenshots show the feedback of the system after a math question has been presented to and answered by the student.

Table 2. Description of the methods in the API of the proposed system.

API for teacher clients	
Public Methods API Teachers	
Object Json	`insertFormulationWithProblem(long codeProblem, String nameFormulation, String descFormulation)`
	It performs the insertion of the formulation, according to an associated problem.
Object Json	`insertProblemWithSkill(long codeSkill, String nameProblem, String descProblem, String typeProblem)`
	It performs the insertion of the problem, according to an associated skill.
Object Json	`insertSkill(String nameSkill, String descSkill, String nameCourse)`
	Performs the insertion of a skill.
Array Json	`listSkillForTeacher()`
	Return list of existing skills per teacher.
Json	`updateFormulation(Formulation Formulation)`
	Updates Formulation information.
Json	`updateProblem(Problem problem)`
	Updates Problem information.
Json	`updateSkill(Skill skill)`
	Updates Skill information.

API for student clients	
Public Methods API Student	
String	`generateQuestion(long codeStudent, long idSkill)`
	Generates the dynamic question and returns it
float	`qualifyAnswer(long codeQuestion, long codeStudent, String proposedAnswer)`
	Rate the student's response and return feedback
Array Json	`listQuestion()`
	Returns list of questions and answers generated by the system.
Array Json	`listSkillForStudent()`
	Returns list of skills for the students

6   Discussions and Conclusions

We run a simple test with real student users to evaluate the performance of the application, the responsiveness of the web page and the engagement of the proposed learning scheme. The goal of this evaluation was to identify software problems rather than assess learning capabilities or prior knowledge of students. We assigned tasks using a step-by-step guide to 5 users that interacted with the system, and we measured the correctness of their answers as well as the time required to complete their task. Most importantly, we monitored potential errors thrown by the platform when users were using the system.

The tests allowed us to identify implementation problems and fix logic bugs that were encountered during the interaction of the test subjects. One part of the guide asked users to correctly complete 10 exercises in a row. This required around 2 min to be completed for a set questions in the arithmetics subject. In average, 6 out of 10 answers were correct in the first attempt, because the formulations required students to think both, the type of operation needed to solve the problem and the solution. The overall experience and feedback from this small set of users indicates that the system is a promising solution for engaging students in learning and practicing topics that they are expected to master.

We noticed that the proposed architecture provides the foundation to create gamified learning apps in the user interface, with special characters, multimedia events, levels, medals, and scores. However, we did not explore these extensions in this work. We plan to evaluate the impact of learning first in one course before considering other variations of the system.

As part of our future work we will conduct a large scale study with more students to evaluate the educational benefits of using this platform. We plan to create question templates for one course in a way that is consistent with the learning principles proposed in this work. Then, we will split student groups in control and system users. Using a final exam we aim to identify learning trends and correlate them with the use of our system using a statistical analysis. This will indicate whether our implementation supports learning in the way described in the system requirements of this paper.

References

1. Amarasinghe, A., Nawagamuwa, N., Athukorala, A., Warunika, P., Kodagoda, N.: Fully functional question and answer generating tool-quenzer (2014)
2. Bonk, C.J., Graham, C.R.: The Handbook of Blended Learning: Global Perspectives, Local Designs. Wiley, San Francisco (2012)
3. Brusilovsky, P., Hsiao, I.-H., Folajimi, Y.: QuizMap: open social student modeling and adaptive navigation support with treemaps. In: Kloos, C.D., Gillet, D., Crespo García, R.M., Wild, F., Wolpers, M. (eds.) EC-TEL 2011. LNCS, vol. 6964, pp. 71–82. Springer, Heidelberg (2011). doi:10.1007/978-3-642-23985-4_7

4. Calm, R., Ripoll, J., Masia, R., Sancho-Vinuesa, T., Olive, C., Parés, N., Pozo, F.: Wiris quizzes: an automatic and self-study tool for online mathematics: the teaching experience in engineering courses at universitat oberta de catalunya. In: 2012 International Symposium on Computers in Education (SIIE), pp. 1–6. IEEE (2012)
5. Chang, B., Chen, S.Y., Jhan, S.N.: The influences of an interactive group-based videogame: cognitive styles vs. prior ability. Comput. Educ. **88**, 399–407 (2015)
6. Dellos, R.: Kahoot! a digital game resource for learning. Instr. Technol. **12**, 53 (2015)
7. Gangur, M.: Matlab implementation of the automatic generator of the parameterized tasks
8. Garrison, D.R., Kanuka, H.: Blended learning: uncovering its transformative potential in higher education. Internet Higher Educ. **7**(2), 95–105 (2004)
9. Garrison, D.R., Vaughan, N.D.: Blended Learning in Higher Education: Framework, Principles, and Guidelines. John Wiley & Sons, New York (2008)
10. Huang, W.H.Y., Soman, D.: Gamification of education. Technical report, Research Report Series: Behavioural Economics in Action (2013)
11. Kellogg, S.: Online learning: how to make a MOOC. Nature **499**(7458), 369–371 (2013)
12. Kennedy, C., Rhoads, C., Leu, D.J.: Online research and learning in science: a one-to-one laptop comparison in two states using performance based assessments. Comput. Educ. **100**, 141–161 (2016)
13. Pappano, L.: The year of the MOOC. The New York Times **2**(12), 2012 (2012)
14. Parry, M.: 5 ways that edX could change education. Chronicle Higher Educ. **59**(6), B6–B7 (2012)
15. Pope, J.: What are MOOCs good for? MIT Technology Review December (2014)
16. Salmon, F.: Udacity and the future of online universities. Reuters Blogs-Felix Salmon (2012). http://blogs.reuters.com/felix-salmon/2012/01/23/udacity-and-the-future-of-online-universities
17. de Sande, J.C.G.: Computer-based training tool for signals and systems exercises. Int. J. Eng. Educ. **27**(5), 1150 (2011)
18. Severance, C.: Teaching the world: Daphne koller and coursera. Computer **8**, 8–9 (2012)
19. Stoyle, K.L., Morris, B.J.: Blogging mathematics: using technology to support mathematical explanations for learning fractions. Comput. Educ. **111**, 114–127 (2017)
20. Timmers, C.F., Walraven, A., Veldkamp, B.P.: The effect of regulation feedback in a computer-based formative assessment on information problem solving. Comput. Educ. **87**, 1–9 (2015)
21. Zahariev, A.: Google app engine. Helsinki University of Technology, pp. 1–5 (2009)

Student-Based Gamification Framework for Online Courses

Carlos Ricardo Calle-Archila and Olga Mariño Drews[✉]

Systems and Computing Engineering Department - School of Engineering,
Universidad de Los Andes, Bogotá, Colombia
{cr.calle,olmarino}@uniandes.edu.co

Abstract. In this document we present a research on personalized eLearning gamification and propose a framework to gamify learning environments based on a learner model in the context of online and Massive Open Online courses (MOOC). MOOCs have seen an incredible growth in the last years, covering all areas of knowledge and recruiting thousands of new students every year. Nevertheless, MOOCs are facing some issues like low rate completion, low student motivation and lack of elements to engage the students. Gamification shows promising solutions to some of these problems, but current gamification solutions are one size fit all approaches. We propose a personalized gamification framework. The framework is external to the platform and its activities are embedded seamlessly through the LTI protocol. Through editors included in the framework, both the student model and the gamification interventions can be customized. The framework was tested with the OCC emotion model on a Moodle platform.

Keywords: MOOC · Gamification · Learning · Personalization · Student model · Motivation · LTI · Learning platform

1 Introduction

This document proposes a conceptual and computational framework for using student-based gamification in blended learning courses (courses having both face to face and online components) as well as in online learning courses, either regular university small scale courses or and massive open online courses (MOOC) as a strategy to raise course completion rates and learner engagement. Gamification refers to the use of game rewards such as trophies, badges and halls of fame in a non-game environment to enhance user engagement. By student-based gamification we mean a gamification strategy based on a learner models, which can include the learners' knowledge and competencies as well as other traits such as learning styles of affective model. Gamification elements are meant not only to recognize the student effort and achievement, but also to enhance emotional levels, and thus foster student engagement and course completion.

The proposed framework enriches an Internet-based learning environment with gamification elements triggered and managed by a rule based-system is informed by a learner model. Current version of the framework works with a learner affective model but extending the model to include learner's knowledge, interests and learning styles is

© Springer International Publishing AG 2017
A. Solano and H. Ordoñez (Eds.): CCC 2017, CCIS 735, pp. 401–414, 2017.
DOI: 10.1007/978-3-319-66562-7_29

straightforward. The framework works for a Learning Management System (LMS) platform or MOOC that implements the Learning Tool Interoperability (LTI) specification for the integration of external components.

Section 2 of this paper analyses research related to both MOOCs and gamification. In Sect. 3, we present the goal of our research and methodology. Section 4 describes the architecture of the proposed framework and details the functioning of the rule-based system. The implementation and evaluation of the framework is the subject of Sect. 5. The paper ends with some conclusions and future work.

2   Gamification on MOOCs: Going a Step Further

This section presents advances and challenges both in student retention in MOOCs and on the application of gamification to MOOCs.

2.1   Massive Open Online Courses – MOOCs

Different universities around the world such as Harvard, MIT, Yale, Cambridge, Stanford and Universidad de Los Andes are offering Massive Open Online Courses (MOOC). MOOCs are online courses that can be taken simultaneously but hundreds or thousands of students from any part of the world for free (or pay a small fee to get a certificate) [1]. MOOCs are hosted on web platforms such as Coursera and edX and include different kinds of resources such as videos, audios, images, texts, links and files. Interaction between participants is mediated by tests, forums, peer review activities and file uploads. MOOC platforms support a high volume of concurrent users and use cloud infrastructure with high availability rates.

Being massive and open, MOOCs offer people from different countries and backgrounds the opportunity to interact, learn, collaborate and share interests anytime and anywhere [2]. According to Class Central [3], in 2016 58 million people signed up for 6850 MOOCs offered by more than 700 universities worldwide. This was 2500 more courses than the previous year. 16.75% of the courses were on Business and Management while science courses accounted for 11.34%, social sciences for 10.77% leading platform providers were Coursera with 24.82% of the courses, edX with 18.97%, FutureLearn with 7.01% and MiriadaX with 5.11%.

MOOC are commonly classified in two types: cMOOCs (connectivist MOOCs) and xMOOCs (Extension MOOCs); the former is less common than the latter. In xMOOCs the content is structured in a predefined sequence of modules. Each module contains information resources as well as formative or summative assessments. This type of course is content-centered and usually uses an instructivist pedagogy. The term cMOOC, proposed by Alec Couros, George Siemens, Stephen Downes, and Dave Cormier in 2008 [1] refers to courses based on the connectivist learning paradigm where the instructor is more a facilitator than a teacher. Knowledge in the course is constructed by the participants, and the content and resources are posted by the participants. In general, the learners define their own learning paths with guidance or motivation from the facilitator [1]. In addition to these types of MOOC, some authors propose the following more specialized types: POOC (Personalized Open Online Course) [4], pMOOC (project-based MOOC) [5], pMOOC (Professional MOOC) [6], aMOOC (Adaptive MOOC) [7], bMOOC (Blended MOOC) [6] and others [8].

If the types of MOOCs are varied, so are the behaviors of the enrolled students. Several studies classify MOOC students based on their interaction with the course activities [9–12]. In all these classifications, the group of students dropping out or reducing their participation amount to a vast majority (Almost always n ear to 90%) [2, 4, 13–15]. Some research relates this low completion rate and participation to a low level of engagement [14–16], some explains it because of the feeling of isolation that can experience students of large courses in which the interpersonal interaction and support is very limited [2, 17]. Still others point to the "one size fits all" underlying assumption of MOOC and underline the need to personalize the learning experience through adaptive systems [4, 14].

In the following section, we will explore a pedagogical strategy that is proposed to enhance motivation and engagement, namely the gamification of the learning experience in a MOOC learning experience. To the best of our knowledge, no research has been conducted combining MOOC gamification with personalization, which is what our framework proposes to address the problem of "one size fits all" courses for diverse learners.

2.2 Gamification in Education and MOOC Gamification

There are different definitions of gamification. Yohannis et al. [18] propose a lexical definition. They say that gamification is derived from 'gamify' with an '-ation' suffix, and the word gamify is derived from 'game' with an '-fy' suffix. The '-fy' suffix adds the sense of transforming something into a game or adding the attributes of a game to something. Then, the '-ation' suffix adds to ´gamify´ the meaning of process. Therefore, Gamification is the process of transforming something into a game or adding game attributes to something.

Lehtonen et al. [19] cite Deterding et al. to define Gamification as "the use of game design elements in non-game contexts". Borrás et al. [13] propose a similar definition, but the authors also point out that the term is based on the psychological theory of self-determination involving extrinsic and intrinsic motivations. Extrinsic motivation is the individual's willingness to do something related to money, points, or things given by the game, while intrinsic motivation is action driven by the student's internal characteristics such as autonomy, conviction or interest.

Clearly, there are different understandings of gamification. Some of them propose gamification as a way to transform a process into a game, while others describe gamification as the inclusion of game elements in non-game processes. In this paper, we will use the latter definition: applying game elements to non-game processes.

In the context of education, this means applying game-elements to learning processes. Tu, Sujo-Montes and Yen [20] state that: "Researchers have identified that integrating gaming into learning has the potential to support attitude change(Hays, 2005), behavior change (Schoech, Boyas, Black, & Elias-Lambert, 2013), enhance learning motivation (Garris, Ahlers, & Driskell, 2002), encourage collaboration (Schafer et al., 2013), induce problem-based learning, activate communication, promote active engagement (Giannetto, Chao, & Fontana, 2013; Mitchell & Savill-Smith, 2005), peer-generated user content, motivated informed action (Lee, Ceyhan, Jordan-Cooley, & Sung, 2013), particularly when engaging underserved learners (De Freitas, 2008)." [20]. Several papers have shown that gamification improves students' motivation in courses [21–24]. Moreover, Borrás et al. [13] state that gamification may be of use when reducing learning time and teaching complex subjects. Gamification could also improve the way people learn with other people and how to build communities.

Moreover, gamification might enhance the quality of students' work, by addressing some of the factor related to poor quality: lack of focus on the part of the students, lack of motivation, lack of skills, pride, learning environment and nature of the course, and finally physical, mental and emotional factors [25]. All of these points could be addressed using the right gamification elements given how gamification elements have been shown to increase participant engagement and motivation.

The application of game elements to a learning process consists on reward students' achievements with prizes such as points, badges, immediate feedback, visual/3d space/ sounds. It fosters students' engagement and performance with Leaderboards, level milestones, challenges/quests, social engagement tools, etc. It motivates students with ludic elements such as avatars, narrative context and roleplay [26]. LMS like Blackboard or Moodle provide gamification elements such as badges or completion boards, which the teachers can use in the course activities to encourage participation and achievement. Web sites such as Openbagdes.org, redcrittertracker.com, badges.webmaker.org/, Playngage.io, www.crowdrise.com, www.chorewars.com, offer libraries of gamification elements.

Despite the potential of gamification elements in education, and the affective impact these elements produce in the students, most gamification model don't take into account an affective evolving learner model; their interventions are based only on the student's' interaction with the learning platform. As explained by Hernández, Zucar and Arroyo-Figueroa [27], the student will have better outcomes in learning when an action is given according to the students' affective model. Indead, research has shown that the student emotional state or affective model influences decisions, perception, reasoning and learning [28].

This preceding literature review shows that MOOCs termination rate is very low and apparently related to lack of motivation and engagement. Also, gamification has proven useful in enhancing students' motivation and achievement. Moreover, research in education states that the learning experience offered to a student should take into account his/her particular traits, and more precisely his/her affective model.

We propose a framework to enhance online and MOOCs learning experience through the enrichment of the learning platform with gamification elements and other resources. This enrichment is based on an affective learner model. In the following section we further detail the goal of our work, the scope of the project and the methodology followed.

3   Objectives and Methodology

The goal of our research is to enrich a students' online learning experience with game elements and feedback, taking into account a learner model to customize learning content. To achieve this goal, we propose a framework through which teachers, in their MOOC, online or blended courses, can integrate gamified components capable to adapt and give feedback according to the students' user model.

One guiding principle of our research was the flexibility of the solution. The system should be completely customizable by the teacher or the person in charge of integrating the gamification elements into the platform. It should work for any learner model (affective, cognitive, etc.) as well as with any set of rewards and interventions and with any intervention strategy.

So, the main objective of this proposal is to design, to develop and to evaluate a framework to enrich online learning platforms with gamified elements using a customized learner model. To instantiate and evaluate the framework, two other specific goals were addressed:

- To define and implement a particular learner model: a learner model, or set of variables describing a learner, was chosen to test the framework. We implemented an affective model based on the OCC model [29].
- To connect the framework with LMS or MOOC platform using interoperability protocols.

The following process was carried out to fulfill the research objectives. First, the framework architecture was defined with four components: Event Manager, Rule Manager, Action Manager and Student Model Manager and with an interface to connect to the LMS or MOOC. Next, the framework were developed to provide a customized environment for teachers and activities for students. Having the framework ready, we worked on defining the student model and the gamification elements. We chose to model the students' emotions through an affective model. We then set up the whole system, tested it on a simulated context and analyzed the results of the test.

4   Framework Architecture and Operation

In this section, we explain the Student-Based Gamification Framework (SBGF), which was the framework developed to reach the aforementioned objectives. This framework can be customized by the teacher to both integrate game elements and other types of feedback in the learning platform and to hide or unblock learning contents. The main contribution of our proposal is the framework's ability to personalize the learning experience and the way in which it addresses "one size fits all" problem in online learning. It includes a learner model composed of a set of variables. Whether these variables concern the student learning styles, personality traits, competencies or knowledge is defined by the teacher when customizing the system. After defining the model, the teacher defines the behavior of the system by declaring a group of rules that consider both the student activities in the learning environments as well as the learner model.

Both of these factors determine the best action to take to enrich the learning experience. In this initial version of the system, the learner model is limited to the affective model, which is understood as a set of emotions. This model is extending to include learner knowledge and preferences.

This project works with feedback, or badges, sent to the learner when he or she has spent a particular amount of time in one or a group of activities, has attained a particular course achievement or when the level of a particular emotion in his/her learner model reaches a threshold. Main gamification elements considered for this project are:

- Feedback: It is important to give information to the user at the right time. Feedback is given when the student should receive a reinforcement.
- Levels: These are used to measure the student's emotions. When the student reaches a particular emotional state (a variable in the model reaches a threshold value), the system should generate a feedback.
- Unblock: Some of the resources received by the students are unlocked when they reach a given emotional level. Students do not need to know how they are unlocking those resources.
- Badges: Some student emotional states and achievements should give something that represents an accomplished goal to the student.
- Mechanics: The system should apply rules to the student actions to define when the system should perform an action.

4.1 SBGF Architecture

Figure 1 shows the SBGF components and the framework interaction with the student. The communication between the student and the SBGF is achieved through a LMS platform or MOOC platform. These platforms should implement a LTI protocol interface as a consumer to connect with the SBGF. LTI is a IMS Global Learning Consortium specification used to integrate an external software with an

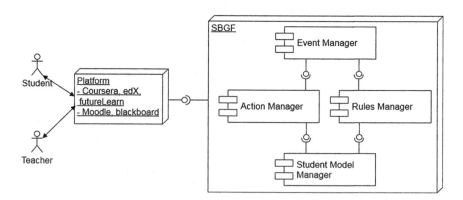

Fig. 1. Framework architecture

LMS or platform. MOOC platforms and LMS like Moodle or Blackboard implement the LTI protocol interface as consumers. Through the LTI connection, SBGF content can be embedded in the platform.

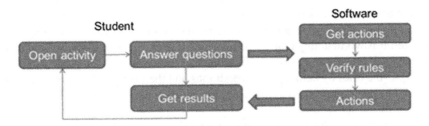

Fig. 2. Students' SBGF process

The SGBF includes the following components: Student Model Manager, Event manager, action manager, rules manager and student model manager.

The Student Model Manager allows for the definition of the student characteristics that will be used in the system. It also permits the student classification of a storage of information about the state of each student's process. These characteristics or variables could be related to emotions, personality traits, or learning styles. Each variable can take values in a predefined range. For the implementation of the framework we worked with the OCC model variables and their ranges.

The Event Manager collects information given by students when they do the SBGF activities that are embedded in the LMS, and it captures events related to both the SBGF activities and the LMS activities. The events we chose to trace follow the ones identified in [30]:

- Time: When time is less than, less than or equal to, equal to, greater than or greater than or equal to a value when the student is developing an activity.
- Activity: When an activity is initiated, finished, completed, canceled or timed out.
- Repetition: Number of times a student did an activity, number of times the student stopped and went back to the activity.
- Sequence: Activities are ordered in some sequence or activity path.
- Level: Number of completed or failed activities.
- Student model events: When a student model variable level is less than, less than or equal to, equal to, greater than or greater than or equal to a particular value.

The Event Manager implements a simple reflex agent which receives information about the environment through a sensor, applies the conditions and rules and sends the answer to the environment. Here, the data collected from the environment are the events registered. These events are sent to the Rule Manager, the entity designed for the agent actions and conditions processing.

The Rule Manager responds to the Event Manager if an action should be performed. The Rule Manager also informs the Event Manager of the action. The Event Manager in turn asks the Action Manager to perform the corresponding action.

The Rule Manager manages the sets of rules, a conjunction of one or more rules to be applied to the collected events with the responsibility of launching the actions the system must execute when the events collected meet the rules defined. A rule is defined in the SBGF as the relationship between a variable, a condition and a value taken from an event or from the student model. The Rule Manager evaluates if the events meet the rule conditions and if some actions should be selected to be performed by the Action Manager. It is worth noting that the rules are defined in a declarative way. That means that the teacher or any person configuring the gamification of a particular course "declares" the rules by defining their conditions and their actions through a rule editor provided by the framework. No code needs to be added on the LMS or on the framework to define such a set of rules.

In the same way, the Action Manager allows the teacher to define the set of actions that may be performed by the system. Some possible actions are: to send a message with a badge or a medal, to send an encouragement or advice message, or to send a message to review the topic. Messages sent to the student can be texts, images, videos or audio. One particular type of action that should be included in the list concerns the updating of the student model. Through these actions, and as a result of student achievements and interactions, the model can evolve.

4.2 SBGF Operation

Student interaction with the whole system could happen as follows: the student logs into a learning platform. We do not address the cold start problem here, thus, the learner model starts with a default configuration. During the interaction with the platform, the student opens an activity, which is actually a SBGF embedded activity. His fact is transparent to the student. The Event Manager of the SBGF then begins to collect the student's events such as the beginning or end of an activity, the answering of a question, the interaction with a content page or the time spent. At the same time, the Rule Manager is receiving all the event data and evaluating if any of its rule set may be activated.

The process for students is:

The student opens an SBGF activity, answers the SBGF questions, submits the answers, and get the results. When the student opens an SBGF activity and tries to answer the SBGF questions, the SBGF is collecting the events to send information to the student model. The student model is fed using the rule system, which collects the student SBGF activity in the learning environment and applies rules to tell the model when an emotional state update is needed.

The rule system also gets information from the student model to know when the student state is in a special range or value and identify when an intervention is needed. This student model will tell the SBGF when the student reaches a state and the SBGF will send a personalized resource (an affective or cognitive reinforcement) to encourage the student to improve the learning process. The following image shows an affective reinforcement (Fig. 3):

You should review a course section

Fig. 3. Affective reinforcement

Let us suppose that the teacher has defined the following rule sets (each set is composed of a single rule) (Fig. 4).

1. Name: time is greater than 30 seconds
2. Description: Time is greater than 30 seconds
3. Rules: Time: Time in one activity >= 30
4. Actions: Action: Decrease Joy 0.1, Action: Send encourage message to student if the level is lowest
5. Repeatable: True

1. Name: Finish activity
2. Description: Finish activity
3. Rules: State: State of activity = End, State: Grade of activity > 4.0
4. Actions: Action: Increase Joy 0.1, Action: Increase Relief 0.1
5. Repeatable: True

Fig. 4. Rule sets definition

Rule 1 in Fig. 2 states that if the time spent in the activity is greater than 30 s, then the student model should be updated (the variable joy is decreased) and a message should be sent to the student as if the variable joy is in a lower state. Rule 2 in Fig. 2 states that if the student finishes an activity, and their grade is higher than 4.0 on a 5.0 scale, then the student model should be modified, thus increasing the joy and the relief. In some cases, the SBGF updates the user model and/or sends an affective or cognitive reinforcement to the student. The first rule can apply the two actions, and the second rule just updates the user model.

The actions the Rule Manager can take are Update Student Model or Send a Resource to the Student. The actions can be parameterized as an independent element and can be used in different rules. The Fig. 5 shows the update student model action definition.

1. Name Decrease Joy 0.1
2. Description Decreases joy in 0.1
3. Value -0.1
4. Student levels Joy - Distress: [Low: [0.2, 0.4], Highest: [0.8, 1.0], Lowest: [0.0, 0.2], High: [0.6, 0.8], Medium: [0.4, 0.6]]
5. Resource Set ResourceType: Message
6. Action Type ActionType: Update user

Fig. 5. Student model action definition

4.3   SBGF Course Setup

Before launching a course, the teacher or the person in charge of adding student-based gamification should follow the following setup process:

The platforms and the SBGF communicate using the LTI protocol. To establish this communication the teacher needs to create first a course activity in the platform that can be connected to the SBGF using the LTI protocol. When he or she sets up a new course activity using the LTI protocol, a connection between the course activity and the SBGF is created. To set up the course activity with the LTI protocol, an URL, a key and a secret word are required as credentials. Once the course activity is set up, the SBGF will be embedded in the course and will look like a normal activity inside the course.

After the course activity set up, the SBGF questions, the SBGF activities and SBGF itself will look like an activity inside the course; all these components should be set up. The SBGF question setup means creating and modifying the possible questions that the students will answer. These SBGF questions are multiple choice and open text questions. They can be used in one or more SBGF activities and are always available if the same teacher is connected to different courses or activities from the same platform.

After the SBGF questions set up, the teacher attaches the questions he/she wants to use to an SBGF activity and sets up the SBGF activity parameters, like description and opening and closing dates. The activity then will be available according to its parameters, and the students will be able to do it.

When the SBGF activities are completed, the teacher tunes the SBGF itself. First, the teacher tunes the student model, that is, establishes the student's characteristics to be measured like emotions, personality traits or learning styles. Each characteristic has a valid range of values and this range is divided into classifications or qualitative measures of the characteristics. The SBGF may trigger particular actions when a characteristic of a student model attains a particular classification.

Then, the teacher set up the rule sets. Each rule set is an aggregation of rules that define one or more actions that the system should execute when all the rules in the set are met. A rule in the rule set is defined as a restriction on the value of a variable given by the name of the variable, a relational operator (greater, equal, etc.) and a value. Through a rule editor, the teacher creates all rules and rule sets of the system.

The teacher chooses the actions when defining the rule sets. There are two action types: Updating and Sending a Resource. Updating is used to modify the value of a characteristic in the student model, allowing the teacher to define whether a student's state changes by adding or subtracting the value of a characteristic, changing its state in a positive or a negative way, or modifying its level. Sending a Resource (an HTML tag that corresponds to the resource configuration) is used when the system detects that a student's variable state has reached a specific classification value and must send information to the student in order to change their emotions or motivation.

As we wanted the SBGF to be connected with different learning platforms, our solution included the implementation of the LTI interoperability protocol to connect to different platforms in a standard way.

5   Implementation

The SBGF solution was designed as an artifact to be embedded in a MOOC or LMS platform activity. As these platforms are web applications, the SBGF solution was implemented as a web component using Grails, a MVC web application framework based on Groovy programming language and Java platform.

In the first SBGF implementation, we tried to create a web component with the main purpose of embedding it into a Coursera or Moodle activity. This component was intended to work as an embedded object in a platform question or platform activity. As an embedded object, the component could catch the user actions when the student attempted a question inside the MOOC or LMS platform. To embed the component, we needed to create a connection or an iframe in the platform activities and platform questions set up and send some parameters from the platform to the component. For that, the MOOC or LMS platforms activities should have the possibility to set up an embedded object during the definition of its activities. What we found is that Coursera does not allow one to embed objects when defining an activity, and Moodle does not offer a suitable interface to embed the object, nor does it grant access to some information required to feed the event manager when embedding objects.

In the second SBGF implementation, we integrated the possibility of setting up quizzes as activities external to the platform. These quizzes may include open text questions and multiple selection questions with one answer option. The questions embed the web objects defined in the first software version as an iframe so that access to the information required to feed the Event Manager was granted. The iframe is constantly reading the user actions and sending the events to the Event Manager to obtain an answer from the SBGF when a rule is fulfilled. These SBGF activities could be used in any platform creating a new course or platform activity by connecting it as a LTI consumer to the SBGF with key and secret credentials.

The SBGF events are caught with a hidden iframe embedded in the activities and questions. This iframe has a web page with a JavaScript code in charge of sending the user events to the simple reflex agent to process the event data. When the agent sends a resource to the user, the web page alerts the parent web page and shows a modal dialog box with the resource.

To test the SBGF, the student model was defined as an affective model using the OCC model of emotions proposed by Ortony, Clore, and Collins including 22 pairs of emotions [29] as a reference. These emotions were classified in five ranges: low, medium low, medium, medium high and high. The actions considered were the student model update and the sending of resources or messages to a student. The rules included different time and activity events and the LTI activity and was set up using Moodle.

6   Results and Future Work

Several results are worth highlighting. Regarding the student model, our framework allows for the definition of the student model using any set of student variables. We used a theoretically sound but seldom implemented model, the OCC emotions model, which is integrated and available to be used by the SBGF. The SBGF also provides a subsystem for editing and parameterizing rules to update the user model and to determine the system's actions. By modifying the rules, the system can be adapted both to new learner models and to new intervention actions. Not only is the student model used to personalize the gamification, but the model itself evolves with the student experience, offering information on the accurate state of the learner at any time.

This framework is also able to trace student interaction with the activities in a far more detailed way than LMS or MOOCs do. In fact, the SBGF student activity capturing subsystem traces every action of the student in the embedded activities. We consider that the analysis of these activities could provide valuable information about the students.

Regarding the connection with the LMS and MOOC platforms, we wish to highlight that these platforms do not provide online information about user activity in real time, and the stored log is limited to activity and grade reports. To change the student's state, it was necessary to implement the activities as an external tool and to catch the student activity when the students were using the SBGF. Nevertheless, the SBGF activities look like platform embedded activities and the student does not need to leave his learning environment to carry them out. Also, the interoperability achieved by the implementation of LTI makes the tool compatible with multiple platforms.

The SGBF framework was tested on Moodle using the Moodle's External Tool Activity added to a course. This External Tool Activity allowed the teachers to perform the Teacher's Setup Process shown in Fig. 6 and allowed to different simulated students to follow the process shown in Fig. 2. The tests showed that the SBGF LTI integration with a platform was successful, therefore, the framework could be integrated straightforward on different MOOC platforms like Coursera.

Teacher

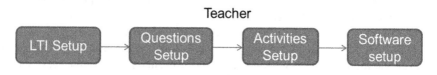

Fig. 6. Teacher's SBGF setup process

Interesting future work could include developing a more elaborated system of student model evolution, integrating other game elements and intervention actions, and offering a broader range of assessment tools.

7 Conclusions

Demotivation, isolation and lack of elements to increase the student interest in activities or in coming to the end of the course are common problems in MOOCs and online courses. Gamification elements provide alternatives to this kind of problem, and the link between gamification elements and student model state gives the opportunity to share appropriate resources to encourage students. We designed, developed and tested a system that gives personalized messages and resources and possibly game elements to blended, online and MOOC learners. The possibility to configure the rules, actions and the student model in a declarative way, without having to modify the framework code or the LMS or MOOC platform, offers the opportunity to use this tool in diverse environments and provides a research setting to test novel ideas to connect student model, intervention, gamification and personalization.

The SBGF embedded activities keep track of more student interactions than the learning platform does, which favor better learning analytics.

At a more conceptual level, learner model research can benefit from our work. Indeed, while facial recognition and voice recognition has been the trend toward analyzing student's reaction to a learning activity, we think that affective models can be a new promising approach. Most research on affective model uses Bayesian Networks to mix its elements and define how to update the user affective model. However, this research on affective models are maturing their process to achieve more general results. Our framework could be a laboratory for this research.

References

1. Tu, C.-H., Sujo-Montes, L.E.: MOOCs. In: Papa, R. (ed.) Media Rich Instruction, pp. 287–304. Springer, Cham (2015). doi:10.1007/978-3-319-00152-4_18
2. Brahimi, T., Sarirete, A.: Learning outside the classroom through MOOCs. Comput. Hum. Behav. **51**(Part B), 604–609 (2015)
3. Shah, D.: By the numbers: MOOCS in 2016 (2016)
4. EdTechReview. http://edtechreview.in/trends-insights/insights/2284-poocs-personalized-open-online-courses-not-moocs
5. Phan, T., McNeil, S.G., Robin, B.R.: Students' patterns of engagement and course performance in a Massive Open Online Course. Comput. Educ. **95**, 36–44 (2016)
6. Granow, R., Dörich, A., Steinert, F.: Strategic implementation of "professional Massive Open Online Courses" (pMOOCs) as an innovative format for transparent part-time studying. In: Wrycza, S. (ed.) SIGSAND/PLAIS 2014. LNBIP, vol. 193, pp. 12–25. Springer, Cham (2014). doi:10.1007/978-3-319-11373-9_2
7. Sonwalkar, N.: The First Adaptive MOOC: A Case Study on Pedagogy Framework and Scalable Cloud Architecture—Part I, p. 8 (2013)
8. Lisitsyna, L.S., Pershin, A.A., Kazakov, M.A.: Game mechanics used for achieving better results of massive online courses. In: Uskov, V.L., Howlett, R.J., Jain, L.C. (eds.) Smart Education and Smart e-Learning. SIST, vol. 41, pp. 183–192. Springer, Cham (2015). doi: 10.1007/978-3-319-19875-0_17
9. Futurelearn. https://partners.futurelearn.com/data/stats-dashboard/
10. Anderson, A., Huttenlocher, D., Kleinberg, J., Leskovec, J.: Engaging with massive online courses. In: Proceedings of the 23rd International Conference on World Wide Web, pp. 687–698. ACM, Seoul (2014)
11. Hill, P.: Emerging Student Patterns in MOOCs: A (Revised) Graphical View(2013)
12. Hughes, G., Dobbins, C.: The utilization of data analysis techniques in predicting student performance in massive open online courses (MOOCs). Res. Pract. Technol. Enhanced Learn. **10**, 1–18 (2015)

13. Gené, O.B., Núñez, M.M., Blanco, Á.F.: Gamification in MOOC: challenges, opportunities and proposals for advancing MOOC model. In: Proceedings of the Second International Conference on Technological Ecosystems for Enhancing Multiculturality, pp. 215–220. ACM, Salamanca (2014)

14. Bakki, A., Oubahssi, L., Cherkaoui, C., George, S.: Motivation and engagement in MOOCs: how to increase learning motivation by adapting pedagogical scenarios? In: Conole, G., Klobučar, T., Rensing, C., Konert, J., Lavoué, É. (eds.) EC-TEL 2015. LNCS, vol. 9307, pp. 556–559. Springer, Cham (2015). doi:10.1007/978-3-319-24258-3_58

15. Skonnard, A.: Edtech's Next Big Disruption Is The College Degree (2015)

16. Landry, L.: Course Completion Rates Don't Really Matter When It Comes to Open Online Learning. (2014)

17. Littlejohn, A., Hood, N., Milligan, C., Mustain, P.: Learning in MOOCs: motivations and self-regulated learning in MOOCs. Internet High. Educ. **29**, 40–48 (2016)

18. Yohannis, A.R., Prabowo, Y.D., Waworuntu, A.: Defining gamification: From lexical meaning and process viewpoint towards a gameful reality. In: 2014 International Conference on Information Technology Systems and Innovation (ICITSI), pp. 284–289

19. Lehtonen, T., Aho, T., Isohanni, E., Mikkonen, T.: On the role of gamification and localization in an open online learning environment: javala experiences. In: Proceedings of the 15th Koli Calling Conference on Computing Education Research, pp. 50–59. ACM, Koli (2015)

20. Tu, C.-H., Sujo-Montes, L.E., Yen, C.-J.: Gamification for learning. In: Papa, R. (ed.) Media Rich Instruction, pp. 203–217. Springer, Cham (2015). doi:10.1007/978-3-319-00152-4_13

21. Glover, I.: Play as you learn: gamification as a technique for motivating learners (2013)

22. Wagner, I., Minge, M.: The gods play dice together: the influence of social elements of gamification on seniors' user experience. In: Stephanidis, C. (ed.) HCI 2015. CCIS, vol. 528, pp. 334–339. Springer, Cham (2015). doi:10.1007/978-3-319-21380-4_57

23. Surendeleg, G., Tudevdagva, U., Kim, Y.S.: The contribution of gamification on user engagement in fully online course. In: Kravets, A., Shcherbakov, M., Kultsova, M., Shabalina, O. (eds.) CIT&DS 2015. CCIS, vol. 535, pp. 710–719. Springer, Cham (1991). doi: 10.1007/978-3-319-23766-4_56

24. Ebermann, C., Piccinini, E., Brauer, B., Busse, S., Kolbe, L.: The impact of gamification-induced emotions on in-car IS adoption – the difference between digital natives and digital immigrants. In: 2016 49th Hawaii International Conference on System Sciences (HICSS), pp. 1338–1347

25. Huang, W.H.-Y., Soman, D.: A Practitioner's Guide To Gamification Of Education Education (2013)

26. Nah, F.F.-H., Telaprolu, V.R., Rallapalli, S., Venkata, P.R.: Gamification of education using computer games. In: Yamamoto, S. (ed.) HIMI 2013. LNCS, vol. 8018, pp. 99–107. Springer, Heidelberg (2013). doi:10.1007/978-3-642-39226-9_12

27. Hernández, Y., Sucar, L.E., Arroyo-Figueroa, G.: Building an affective model for intelligent tutoring systems with base on teachers' expertise. In: Gelbukh, A., Morales, Eduardo F. (eds.) MICAI 2008. LNCS, vol. 5317, pp. 754–764. Springer, Heidelberg (2008). doi: 10.1007/978-3-540-88636-5_71

28. Leontidis, M., Halatsis, C.: Integrating learning styles and personality traits into an affective model to support learner's learning. In: Spaniol, M., Li, Q., Klamma, R., Lau, R.W.H. (eds.) ICWL 2009. LNCS, vol. 5686, pp. 225–234. Springer, Heidelberg (2009). doi: 10.1007/978-3-642-03426-8_29

29. Steunebrink, B.R., Dastani, M., Meyer, J.-J.C.: The OCC Model Revisited (2014)

30. Marino, O., Paquette, G.: A competency—driven advisor system for multi-actor learning environments. Procedia Comput. Sci. **1**, 2871–2876 (2010)

Strengthening Competencies for Building Software, Through a Community of Practice

Cristian Camilo Ordoñez[1(✉)], Hugo Ordoñez[2], Armando Ordoñez[1], Carlos Cobos[3], and Giovanni Hernández[4]

[1] Intelligent Management Systems, Fundación Universitaria de Popayán, Popayán, Colombia
ccoq2013@gmail.com, jaordonez@unicauca.edu.co
[2] Research Laboratory in Development of Software Engineering, Universidad San Buenaventura, Cali, Colombia
haordonez@usbcali.edu.co
[3] Information Technology Research Group (GTI), Universidad del Cauca, Popayán, Colombia
ccobos@unicauca.edu.co
[4] Grupos de investigación en Ingeniería de Sistemas (Gismar), Universidad Mariana, Pasto, Colombia
gihernandez@umariana.edu.co

Abstract. The present work describes the use of a virtual community of practice for the strengthening of capacities for software development; the study was carried out with students of informatics and related areas of higher education institutions in the southwest of Colombia. The present study was conducted in the following stages: initial approach, diagnostic, preparation, implementation, and follow-up. Results obtained allow evidence that the virtual community positively influences in the acquisition of knowledge, capabilities, and attitudes of the members of the community. The latter increases possibilities of entering the market.

Keywords: Virtual community · Programming · Internet · Competencies

1 Introduction

Information and communication technologies (ICTs) have been consolidated as an essential tool for Institutions of higher education to transform the education [1]. However, the use of ICTs in these processes requires the modification of passive and traditional educational methodologies [2, 3]. In this context, virtual communities of practice (VCoP) play a significant role in the educational innovation, firstly, by introducing a change both in the modality (face-to-face is replaced by virtual modality). Secondly, a modification of the students' training processes (autonomous and collaborative learning based on developing competencies through practice) [4].

A VCoP can be defined as a group of people who share a mutual interest in a particular domain and participate in a collective learning process [5]. In a VCoP, members (users) are like-minded, but geographically dispersed people. These members

© Springer International Publishing AG 2017
A. Solano and H. Ordoñez (Eds.): CCC 2017, CCIS 735, pp. 415–426, 2017.
DOI: 10.1007/978-3-319-66562-7_30

are not passive in the construction of the online knowledge, but also create and share their experiences, to develop competencies and attitudes in a particular subject of interest [6]. These communities of practice have multiple levels and types of participation, members can be central participants in one community, and at the same time, be peripheral participants in others. Even within a single community, members can come and go between the core and the periphery [7].

On the other hand, the ICT sector provides unique opportunities for increasing the economy and development of any country [10, 11]. Within this ICT sector, the software industry generates a significant number of well-paid sources of work. For this, workers are required to be competent in most aspects involved in software development [12]. This challenge obliges the Education Institutions to propose training alternatives for software developers. Nowadays, there is a widespread dissemination of information on the Internet, social networks and mobile devices. This information is used daily by students, and therefore, providing education through these means is a priority [9].

In this vein, this article describes a VCoP to strengthen the educational processes involved in the development of competencies in software development. Competencies are understood as a set of complex structures in the following dimensions: cognitive (Knowledge), attitudinal (Abilities) and affective-motivational (Attitudes) [13, 14]. These dimensions allow solving problems related to the software development. In this sense, the VCoP aims to cover aspects not included in the Academy, where the learning is based on imitation and decontextualized exercises.

The VCoP allows, firstly, formulating real problems, through case studies; and secondly, offering spaces that link students to share knowledge and experiences. The VCoP aims at increasing competencies in software development.

This article is organized as follows, Sect. 2 is dedicated to the related works, Sect. 3 describes the VCoP, Sect. 4 describes the appropriation of the knowledge among the members of the community, and finally, Sect. 5 concludes.

2 Related Works

Some of the most representative works on the subject of communities of practice are described below. [5, 8] propose a VCoP as an independent knowledge management system based on social networks. The VCoP use discussion forums to share the knowledge. The authors conclude that the support of social networks intensifies the exchange of knowledge between pairs. They also showed that the dialogue between friends increases the collaboration and knowledge Exchange.

On the other hand, [15, 6] describe the role of VCoP in innovation processes. The authors differentiate the types of knowledge acquired with the practice, to apply them in business innovation in a collaborative way. Regarding virtual learning, in [7] conditions for the formation of a VCoP in the field of accounting are presented, focusing on the compendium of competencies that need to be learned in the profession.

In [8] A VCoP in the health sector is described, this VCoP uses social networks, where people with different traits but a common interest are linked, The project sought to increase the social capital of the participants and create networks of trust. The results show a high impact on the members of the community. In [9] It is proposed to create effective learning groups, where the members have previous knowledge in a given domain. The study quantifies several factors, such as the diversity of the participants and the interest rate that can contribute to a successful community of practice. [16] analyzes the learning of the students of pedagogy in a VCoP. The project examines the key technological and pedagogical aspects of online learning for students. The results show that the majority of the members use the available educational resources in the VCoP.

As the studies above, the present project seeks to develop competencies in a particular area of knowledge supported on social networks and virtual learning environments. Unlike the other projects, this proposal classifies competencies in three dimensions (knowledge, competencies and aptitudes). Besides, the present study includes the planning that starts from the definition of the competencies. Subsequently, the levels of learning are defined, finally, some case studies as a learning strategy. Moreover, the resources and their use are available for the VCoP to self-manage. Likewise, in the review, it was not found a VCoP for IT students located geographically distant, that provides a virtual space to strengthen the knowledge, competencies, and attitudes in Software development through the exchange of experiences and good practices.

3 Proposed Community of Practice

This process was divided into four stages, which took place between February and November of 2015. This section details the structure, members, and roles of the community

3.1 Approach Stage

The process begins by visiting the universities with computer science or related careers in southern Colombia. These Institutions were the Mariana University, the University of Nariño and the University Institution CESMAG. A motivational talk was made to explain what a VCoP is and which is its purpose. Subsequently, students from the eighth (8th) to the tenth (10th) semester of the institutions were invited to participate in the experience, also it was established that the VCoP will be included in the elective courses related to software development in the Universities. For the formation of the VCoP, it was decided to adopt as an additional motivational and retention incentive: The members who completed the whole process would have an extra bonus on the grades.

3.2 Diagnosis Stage

At this stage, it was determined the level of competence in software development that had 300 students from the universities who voluntarily participated in the VCoP. Surveys were used to collect the perceptions and workshops were used to corroborate it. Subsequently, the information gathered was analyzed, with descriptive statistics.

According to [17], the IT professional who is dedicated to software development should have competencies in different axes that define the variables to measure to determine the degree of competencies of a professional of this area. These variables are the following: Problem Solving (PS), Programming Techniques (PT), Programming Technologies (PTs), Programming Tools (PTl), Modeling (M), Algorithm (A), Software Process (SP) and Architecture (AR). The level of performance established for the competencies was categorized as follows: Very High (VH), High (H), neither High nor Low (NH), Low (L), Very Low (VL), Do not know/No response (DK). From the data collected, an analysis of observed frequencies (OF) was performed and the equivalent to the percentage to this frequency (AF).

The variable PS is understood as a primary axis of the software development. PS relates to the ability to express a model regarding some programming language and to propose a solution. The results obtained for this variable (See Table 1) show that most of the students (57%) feel they have neither a high level nor a Low level, 36.4% of the students stated that they have a high level. As can be seen, most of the community members present difficulties in this variable.

Table 1. Results of the survey (Part I)

Var	(PS)		(PT)		(PTs)		(PTl)	
	FO	FA	FO	FA	FO	FA	FO	FA
VH	10	3%	0	0%	0	0%	0	0%
H	110	36.4	40	3%	0	0%	28	9%
NH	170	57.6	123	11%	164	55%	176	59%
L	10	3%	95	32%	122	41%	68	22%
VL	0	0%	15	45%	0	0%	0	9%
DK	0	0%	27	9%	14	4%	28	1%
Total	300	100%	300	100%	300	100%	300	100%

Very high (VH), High (H), Neither high nor low (NH), Low (L), Very Low (VL), Do not know not answer (DK)

PT variable is understood as the ability to identify strategies to write a program and define stages, tasks, metrics, tips and patterns for software development. Table 1 shows that 45% of the students present a Very Low level, followed by (32%) with Low level. These results evidence problems in the decomposition of complex requirements. Also, the study showed the difficulties in writing an algorithm based on a pattern and a skeleton.

The variable PTs is understood as the ability to handle the necessary technological elements (programming language, modeling language, among others), which allow it to express in a programming language the solution of the problem. The results presented in Table 1 show that 55% of the students have a "neither high nor Low" level, followed by 41% of students with a Low level. The latter means that members have difficulties in the use of a programming language or know it but have so far not developed a software application. Also, they do not use tools such as Java, C #, JavaScript, HTML5, and some frameworks like PrimeFaces, Dot Net.

The variable PTl is understood as the ability to use computational tools (compilers, editors, debuggers, project managers, etc.) in software development. The results presented in Table 1 show that 59% of students have a neither high nor Low level, followed by 22% of students with a Low level. The latter shows problems in the knowledge and use of software development environments. The main reason is due to the lack of experience and practice in making software out of classrooms.

The variable M (modeling) is associated with the ability to abstract the relevant information from reality and represent it through some element. The results obtained and presented in Table 2, show that the majority of students (52%), have a level neither high nor Low, and (26%) demonstrate a Low level. As can be seen, most students show difficulty in abstracting information.

Table 2. Results of the survey (Part 2)

Var.	(M)		(A)		(SP)		(Ar)	
	FO	FA	FO	FA	FO	FA	FO	FA
VH	0	0%	0	0%	0	0%	0	0%
H	55	18%	80	27%	55	18%	29	10%
NH	155	52%	96	32%	110	37%	139	46%
L	78	26%	109	36%	120	40%	120	40%
VL	0	0%	0	0%	15	5%	0	0%
DK	12	4%	15	5%	0	0%	12	4%
Total	300	100%	300	100%	300	100%	300	100%

Very high (VH), High (H), Neither high nor low (NH), Low (L), Very Low (VL), Do not know not answer (DK)

The variable A (algorithms) is an axis of programming that allows using a set of instructions to express the behavior of the abstraction of reality and solve a problem. In the results presented in Table 2, it can be seen that most of the group of participants are between the neither High nor Low (36%) and the Low (32%) levels. This result shows that most students present difficulties in designing an algorithm.

The variable SP (Software process), is an axis associated with the software quality and the possibility to estimate the effort to develop a program. On this axis, documentation and coding standards, time control, code inspection forms, and techniques for program testing were included. In the results presented in Table 2, it can be seen that 40% of the students have a Low level, followed by the neither High nor Low level (37%). The latter means that students have difficulty ensuring the quality of a software product.

The variable Ar (Architecture) makes it possible to represent the elements that constitute software in the highest level of abstraction. Table 2 shows that 46% of the students have a level neither High nor Low, followed by the low level (40%).

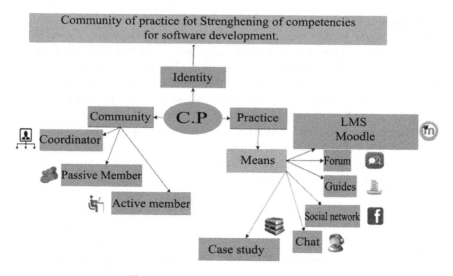

Fig. 1. Structural diagram of the VCoP

3.3   Preparation

From the results obtained in the previous stage, in this phase, the components and interactions of the community of practice were defined. In Fig. 1, the architecture (Elements and interactions) of the virtual community of practice is established taking as reference the approaches defined by [18, 19]. The first element is the Identity that is understood as the field of interest shared by the community; a collective identity is useful for motivating the members of the VCoP. In this sense, the field of interest within the community is the strengthening of competencies for software development. The second element is the Practice or activities to be carried out [18]. A fundamental aspect of the VCoP is the Resources set, in the present VCoP some case studies were used. These case studies are partially solved projects that the members of the community have to analyze, interpret, modify and put into operation [20]. Around the case studies, laboratory guides were developed. Also, a forum was created to share doubts about these guides. Likewise, a Chat and a social network were designed to enable knowledge sharing between the members. All these resources were integrated into a Learning Management system (LMS).

The third element corresponds to the Community and refers to the members who share a common interest in the community. Participants engage in joint activities in which they share knowledge and support each other [21]. In the community, some roles and interactions between were defined: (A) The Coordinator is responsible for organizing events and connecting members. This function was carried out by one of the researchers. (B) Active members attend meetings regularly and participate in forums or community activities without the level of intensity of the coordinator. This group is composed of 300 students from 8th – 10th semester (C) the peripheral members rarely participate and constitute the majority of the community. These members observe the interactions of the active members. In the VCoP this groups is formed by lower semester students.

3.4   Development

This stage was developed between June and November 2015. 4 case studies with different levels of complexity were proposed. The first case study has an average level to identify the status of the participants before entering the VCoP. Next, it is proposed to start with the first low-level case study, and from this point, the exigency will increase until reach a complex case study. After the process has been completed, the progress of the members within VCop can be observed. In addition, laboratory guides with examples have been created to assist in this process.

4   Results

To measure the impact of the VCoP the stage called Follow-up was carried out. At this stage, the progress of the members of the community was verified. For this purpose, an evaluation of the same characteristics of the diagnosis was carried out too. This evaluation was focused on identifying the number of members that strengthened the competencies. It is important to note that the members of VCoP had a bonus in the grade of their university subjects. This strategy allowed that most of the members stayed from the diagnostic stage to the follow-up stage.

Figure 2 shows the evaluation of the impact of the VCoP regarding the Problem Solving (PS) variable. 140 members (46.7%) increased their knowledge reaching a Very High level, 135 members (45%) state that they have reached a High level. As a result, 91% of the members strengthened their competencies in this variable. However, 25 members (8.3%) did not show advances in the competence, due to the lack of time or interest to participate actively in the VCoP.

Regarding the Programming Techniques (PT), Fig. 3 show that 35 members increased the level of competence reaching Very High level (11%), and 141 consider that they had achieved a High level (47%). In the VCoP, all members state that, after working collaboratively with case studies, this competence was strengthened.

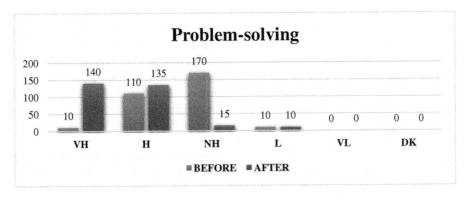

Fig. 2. Results of the problem-solving variable

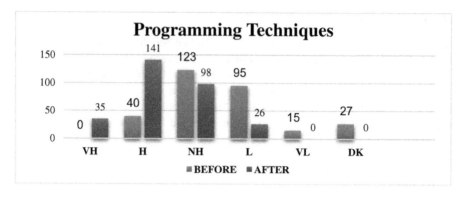

Fig. 3. Results of programming techniques

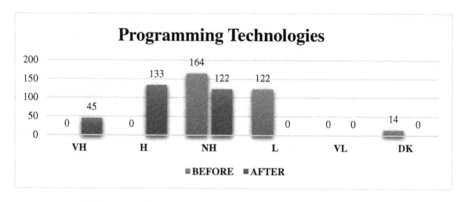

Fig. 4. results of the programming technologies PTs variable.

Figure 4 shows the results obtained for the Programming Technologies (PTs) variable. 178 members (60%) went from being neither high nor Low or Very Low to a High and Very High level. Also, the rest of the members stated that they reached a neither high nor low level. These results allow evidence that the development of the study cases increased knowledge in the used technologies: Java,.Net (Framework), PHP, HTML5, CSS, and JavaScript. None of the members stated to have a Very Low performance.

The results of the variable related to Programming Tools (PTl) are shown in Fig. 5. All members are moving towards the High and neither High nor Low levels. The members improved their knowledge and competencies in managing tools such as Dreamweaver, Sublime Text, AppArquitect, and others. Likewise, none of the members stated that they had a low or very low level.

Regarding the Modeling (M) variable, 94 members increased the level to High (32%), and 198 members went to a level neither High nor Low (66%). All members state that after working collaboratively with case studies strengthened their competencies to abstract relevant information from reality and represent it through a model (Fig. 6).

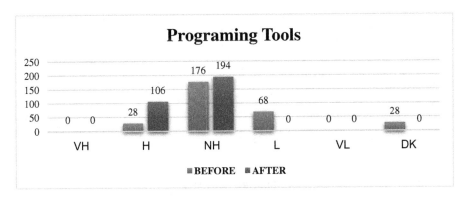

Fig. 5. Results of the programing tools variable.

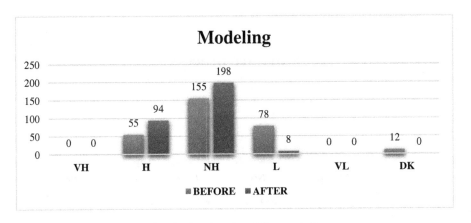

Fig. 6. Results of modeling variable

Figure 7, shows the results achieved for the Algorithm (A). In total, 140 members had a High level (47%) and 160 neither High nor Low level (53%). With the community of practice, 109 members (36%) increased the level of this competence, and none stated to have the levels Low or Very Low. This result is because the development of the case studies increased the knowledge and the ability to design algorithms.

Results of the Software Process (SP) variable are shown Fig. 8. 190 members reached the neither High nor Low level (64%) and 99 members the high level (32%). This result demonstrates that the VCoP improved the level of knowledge and competencies in quality assurance. The latter may be caused by the fact that worksheets and laboratories were used as accepted standards and used by the members of the community.

Finally, Fig. 9 shows the results obtained for the Architecture (Ar). In total 107 members (35%) of the community went from having neither High nor Low level to a High level. Also, it was possible to reduce the members with a low level to 23 (7.6%). These results demonstrate that the VCoP helped the members to identify and describe

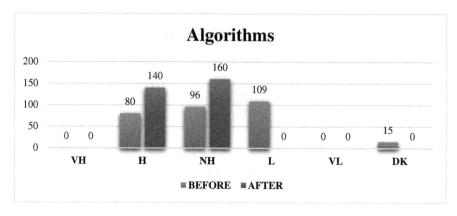

Fig. 7. Results obtained in algorithms variable

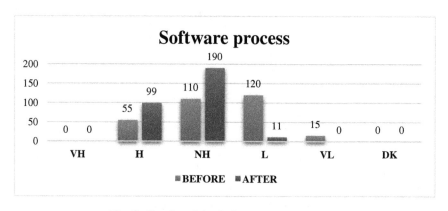

Fig. 8. Results of the Software process variable

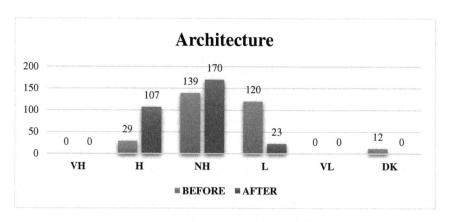

Fig. 9. Results of the architecture variable

at the highest level of abstraction the elements that constitute an application, i.e., functions, objects, Components, services, and model.

In Summary, the majority of the members strengthened the analyzed competencies. Consequently, the VCoP becomes an alternative to developing knowledge and competencies of its members, through a collaborative environment.

5 Conclusions and Future Works

The community of practice presented in this work is structured through an identity, a practice and established member roles, to be able to increase the level of knowledge, competencies, and attitudes of its members. The identity made it possible to strengthen the traditional work carried out in the Higher Education Institutions in the southwest of Colombia regarding the competencies in software development. Results of the VCoP demonstrate the impact of the VCoP on its members regarding the knowledge, competencies and attitudes for Problem Solving, Programming Techniques, Programming Technologies, Programming Tools, Modeling, Algorithms, Software Process and Architecture. It is also evidenced the positive contribution of the VCoP in strengthening the traditional work carried out in Higher Education Institutions, because, it is possible to improve the competence levels.

As a future work, it is expected to extend this community towards the development of competencies in the software development. Firstly, by incorporating new levels of complexity through case studies. Secondly, by including elements such as work teams, and new stages about requirements elicitation, design patterns and agile methodologies (such as Scrum or XP).

References

1. Kummitha, R.K.R., Majumdar, S.: Dynamic curriculum development on social entrepreneurship – a case study of TISS. Int. J. Manag. Educ. 13(3), 260–267 (2015)
2. Fernández, M., Valverde, J.: Comunidades de práctica: un modelo de intervención desde el aprendizaje colaborativo en entornos virtuales, p. 9 (2014)
3. Lupu, D., Laurenţiu, A.R.: Using new communication and information technologies in preschool education. Procedia Soc. Behav. Sci. 187, 206–210 (2015)
4. Kim, H.J., Kim, I., Lee, H.: Third-party mobile app developers' continued participation in platform-centric ecosystems: an empirical investigation of two different mechanisms. Int. J. Inf. Manage. 36(1), 44–59 (2016)
5. Pan, Y., Xu, Y.C., Wang, X., Zhang, C., Ling, H., Lin, J.: Integrating social networking support for dyadic knowledge exchange: a study in a virtual community of practice. Inf. Manag. 52(1), 61–70 (2015)
6. Rogo, F., Cricelli, L., Grimaldi, M.: Assessing the performance of open innovation practices: a case study of a community of innovation. Technol. Soc. 38, 60–80 (2014)
7. Ratzinger-Sakel, N.V.S., Gray, G.L.: Moving toward a learned profession and purposeful integration: quantifying the gap between the academic and practice communities in auditing and identifying new research opportunities. J. Account. Lit. 35, 77–103 (2015)

8. Jiménez-Zarco, A.I., González-González, I., Saigí-Rubió, F., Torrent-Sellens, J.: The co-learning process in healthcare professionals: assessing user satisfaction in virtual communities of practice. Comput. Hum. Behav. **51**, 1303–1313 (2014)
9. Dascalu, M.-I., Bodea, C.-N., Lytras, M., de Pablos, P.O., Burlacu, A.: Improving e-learning communities through optimal composition of multidisciplinary learning groups. Comput. Hum. Behav. **30**, 362–371 (2014)
10. Robertson, C.J., Gilley, K.M., Crittenden, V., Crittenden, W.F.: An analysis of the predictors of software piracy within Latin America. J. Bus. Res. **61**(6), 651–656 (2008)
11. Morueta, R.T., Carreño, Á.B., Gómez, J.I.A.: Comunidades de práctica en la red: indicadores y condiciones para su desarrollo. Tendencias Pedagógicas **28**, 22 (2009)
12. Fedesoft, Visión Estratégica Del Sector De Software Y Servicios Asociados Plan De Mercadeo Y Ventas Regionalizado Del Sector En Colombia, p. 68 (2012)
13. Tünnermann, C.: Pertinencia Y Calidad De La Educación Superior. In: Seminario Tendencias Y Desafíos De La Educación Superior, p. 33 (2009)
14. Muñoz, F.I., Bozu, Z.: Creando comunidades de práctica y conocimiento en la Universidad: una experiencia de trabajo entre las universidades de lengua catalana. Revista de Universidad y Sociedad del conocimiento, p. 10 (2010)
15. Rodríguez, D., Busco, C., Flores, R.: Information technology within society's evolution. Technol. Soc. **40**, 64–72 (2015)
16. Clarke, L.: The POD model: Using communities of practice theory to conceptualise student teachers' professional learning online. Comput. Educ. **52**(3), 521–529 (2009)
17. Villalobos, G.M.: Programación orientada a objetos con aprendizaje activo. Sci. Tech. **5**(4), 163–168 (2009)
18. Amin, A., Roberts, J.: Knowing in action: beyond communities of practice. Res. Policy **37**(2), 353–369 (2008)
19. Arbonies, Á.: Manual para crear y gestionar comunidades de práctica, vol. 1 (2012)
20. Casallas, J.V.R.: Fundamentos de Programacion : Aprendizaje Activo Basado en Casos. Prentice hall, Mexico D.F. (2007)
21. Miller, F.C., Ibert, O.: (Re-)sources of innovation: Understanding and comparing time-spatial innovation dynamics through the lens of communities of practice. Geoforum **65**, 338–350 (2015)

Method for the Integration of the Didactic Strategy Model in Virtual Learning Platforms in the University Context: A Mechanism that Takes into Account the Professor's Work

Alexandra Ruíz[1]([⊠]) , José L. Arciniegas[1,2] ,
and William J. Giraldo[2]

[1] Universidad del Quindío, Armenia, Colombia
aruiz@uniquindio.edu.co, jlarciniegas@unicauca.edu.co
[2] Universidad del Cauca, Popayán, Colombia
wjgiraldo@uniquindio.edu.co

Abstract. The Learning Management Systems (LMS) have brought great benefits and changes in the way teachers and students interact in the teaching-learning process. However, it is evidenced that the LMSs are not capturing the professor's intentions to perform his work as a teacher, but they focus on providing technology; although useful, it makes the professor's work remain in the background. Likewise, the fact that the LMSs do not supply intuitive mechanisms for the customization of the teaching-learning process considering learning styles was also identified. Having in mind these detected problems, this article pretends to contribute with a possible solution through a method that allows the inclusion of a visual model of activity sequences defined as the didactic strategy model in LMS, so that the resources offered by the LMS are exploited, and the professor can focus on his work and the students' needs. The method is implemented through a concept test in the Moodle platform.

Keywords: Didactic strategy model · e-learning · LMS · Sequence of activities

1 Introduction

Currently, one of the most used technologies both in virtual and on-site education is the Learning Management System - LMS. An LMS is a software system generally installed on a web server, which is used to create, aprove, administrate, store, distribute, and manage virtual training activities [1]. These types of systems have brought benefits and changes in the way professors and students interact in the teaching-learning process, they facilitate the synchronous or asynchronous communication, help the space and time barriers to decrease, encourage collaborative learning, among many others. However, in order to take advantage of all these benefits, professors need to know the wide range of services and variety of LMS configurations in depth. So, it can be exploited for the achievement of its learing objectives. In this way, it is perceived that the professors are the ones who must adapt to the way the LMS work, and not the other way around. When the ICTs are used for the development of educational environments,

© Springer International Publishing AG 2017
A. Solano and H. Ordoñez (Eds.): CCC 2017, CCIS 735, pp. 427–441, 2017.
DOI: 10.1007/978-3-319-66562-7_31

there is a general principle: they must be in function of the pedagogical design, not backwards. That is to say, for using a video, animation, forum, e-mail, and so on, the pedagogical need must be considered [2]. This principle, general and essential, is not being thought of in the current virtual platforms since the profesor must solve his conflicts dealing with technology first; subsequently, thinking of his duties as a teacher.

To illustrate the problem presented, let us suppose the following scenario. Planning is the primary task that a profesor performs. This is the equivalent in the LMS environment to configuring the didactic activities weekly. However, when the profesor enters the LMS to do the planning in function of the didactic activities, he only encounters technological components that do not guide him on how to do the activity unless the professor has taken an intensive course in how to use and configure them to carry out the task sucessfully. The main problem that is seen in the LMSs is that they are not capturing the professor's intentions to perform his work as a teacher; instead, they are centered on providing technology; albeit useful, they make the professor's work to remain in the background.

The second focal problem of this research is related to learning styles. People learn differently according to the senses considered most useful when receiving, processing, and responding to the information retrieved from the medium. The differences between one and the others are the ones that make each person unique regarding the way, speed, ease, and/or difficulty to learn something [3]. Taking into account this cognitive principle, it would be expected that the LMSs would have the mechanisms to make the teaching process somewhat customizable. While it is true that the LMSs have tools that allow the creation of student groups and specific activities for them, the way how a course could be designed for student groups with different learning styles and needs is not very intuitive.

There is evidence of research in the literature that has dealt with learning styles and the adaptation to the LMSs. Such is the case of the works by Castellón [4] and Leris [5], who are focused on the customization of the learning process using the conditionals proposed by the Center of Innovation for the Information Society (CICEI) for Moodle platforms. The customization is achieved from a diagnostic evaluation of the student's learning style. Once his style is recognized, a determined presentation of the course previouly designed is assigned, and it adapts gradually according to the student's process. Although these proposals work efficiently on the student's side, they have deficiencies in relation to the professor's work due to their laborious implementation.

On the other hand, initiatives within the LMSs have been created pretending to be a mechanism to design didactic strategies, but they have only offered technology. Such is the case of the "Lesson" component used by Moodle and other LMSs. This component works for proposing activities that allow evaluating the student's progress since it presents content sequentially, assessing periodically if the student achieved the objectives or needs to reinforce the subjects [6]. Despite being a useful tool for the construction of sequences of activities, it has several limitations, among them: it does not have a graphic model that guides the professor in the construction of the strategy, the construction of sequence of pages is very complex for the users, the professor focuses on building content pages and solving problems related to the management of technology instead of devoting 100 percent to the his planning work. Likewise, there is the "LAMS" (Learning Activity Management Systems) project. LAMS, in addition to being a foundation, it is a learning sequence design tool that allows to build routes graphically where students can advance in relation to their achievements [7]. Despite the LAMS versatility and advantages, it also has several disadvantages in relation to what is proposed in this research work, namely: (i) LAMS is oriented to construct sequences and not processes, reason why the notation lacks elements that guide the didactic strategy as it is conceived in reality; (ii) as in other LMSs, LAMS focus on providing technological components that do not give an indication on the type of activity to which is attached, leaving again the professor's work in the background; and (iii) although LAMS can be intergrated with some LMSs like Moodle, the technical component it offers has a different interface, which affects the mental model that the users have in relation to the platform.

There are other proposals on the side of Educational Modeling Languages (EML) that have been integrated into LMS in practical cases such as the standard IMS-LD [8], PoEML [9], E2ML [10], CoUML [8], among others. To begin with, the main purpose of IMS-LD is to allow the creation of computer didactic unit models, so the development of didactic units can be controlled and supported by ICTs. On the other hand, the perspective-oriented educational modeling language (POEML) integrates workflow and groupware aspects into educational modeling and focuses on a separation of eleven different perspectives of educational practices. Also, E2ML is a simple design language coupled with a visual notation system consisting of multiple interrelated diagrams. It was developed as a thinking tool for instructional designers and for enhancing communication within large e-learning projects. Finally, CoUML stand for "Cooperative UML", indicating that its notation system is essentially an extension of the UML used to model cooperative activities and environments. All these proposals include a diagram to create activity sequences but the way in which they have been implemented has made the professor to focus on technology again, and not on his job.

Considering the aforementioned, this article pretends to contribute with a possible solution through a method of inclusion of a didactic strategy model that can be taken to computing, and integrate it with the LMSs in such a way as to capitalize on the resources that the LMSs offer, but avoiding the professor's work to remain in the background. In order to do this, this article presents the method of inclusion of the didactic strategy model in an LMS in Sect. 2, the development of every phase of the method in the subsequent sections, and its implementation in the Moodle platform. Finally, conclusions and future work are presented in Sect. 4.

2   The Method

This section presents the method used for the inclusion of the didactic strategy model for the university context and its ensuing use in a computational environment (see Fig. 1). The didactic strategy model is a graphic representation, which is conceived as a process that is comprised of learning activities and control actions carried out by the professor. In this way, the didactic strategy model constitutes a mechanism to plan and verify the progression of the process in which the sequence of activities that comprise it can be identified. Likewise, the model pretends to be and approximation to the achievement of didactic strategies design that adapt to specific student profiles.

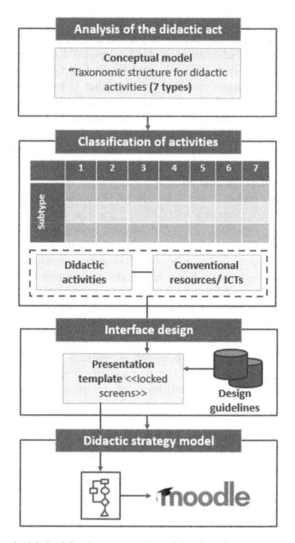

Fig. 1. Method for the construction of the didactic strategy model

In the teaching-learning process, to learn and to teach are considered didactic acts. For this reason, the method for the construction of the didactic strategy model begins with the theoretical study of the different conceptual models around the didactic act. For the purposes of this article, Marqués [11] conceptual model is presented, which shares common elements to other proposals presented by Meneses [12], Rodríguez [13] and others. Among the main elements of the didactic act are didactic activities, which according to Conole [14] are classified in seven main groups: assimilative, managerial, communicative, applicative, productive, experiential, and evaluative. In the second phase, Conole's taxonomic structure is used in order to classify the learning activities in the university teaching context, which were compiled by Marcelo [15]. Correspondingly, the activity subtypes are identified according to their nature along with the resources used by each activity, both the conventional as well as the technological-supported ones.

The classification of the resources used according to the activity constitutes the starting material for the third phase. In this phase, different interfaces are designed. They are associated to types and subtypes of didactic activities according to different combinations of resources that are supported on technology. Also, a series of design guidelines that promote the usability in the final interface are applied in this phase.

Finally, the didactic strategy model is specified in the fourth phase through the notation of the flow diagrams, and taken to the computational environment through a concept test in the Moodle platform.

In the following sections, each phase of the method for the inclusion of the didactic strategy model is developed.

3   Development of the Method Phases

This section presents the different phases that comprise the method for the inclusion of the didactic strategy.

3.1   Analysis of the Didactic Act

Teaching and learning are held as didactic acts. According to Marqués [11], the didactic act defines the performance of the teacher to facilitate the students' learning, and its nature is essentially comunicative. The didactic act is comprised by four basic elements: the teacher or tutor, the student, the contents, and the context (see Fig. 2).

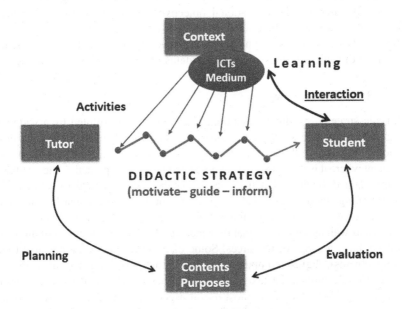

Fig. 2. Marqués didactic act

Teaching is particularized in didactic acts where the professor or tutor proposes multiple activities to the students to facilitate the desired learning. These activities are adapted to the students' characteristics, to the available resources, and to the contents to be studied. The activities must favor the comprehension of the concepts, their classification and relation, reflection, the exercising of reasoning, and transfering of knowledge. The objective of professors and students always consists in the achievement of specific educational objectives, and the key to success is the students' motivation and will to carry out the cognitive operations, interacting appropriately with the instructional media available.

The instructional media is any type of material elaborated with the intention of facilitating the teaching and learning processes. Marqués poses that the effectiveness of these media will depend to a large extent on the way the professor directs its use in the didactic strategy framework that he is using.

A strategy is, in a strict sense, an organized, formalized, and goal-oriented procedure. Its application in daily practice requires the perfection of procedures and techniques whose detailed election and design are the professor's resposibility. Therefore, the strategy is a system of planning applicable to an articulated set of actions required to attain a goal. Thus, it is not feasible to talk about the use of strategies if there is not a goal where the actions are oriented to [16]. By means of the didactic strategy as a procedure, the professor intends to facilitate the learning process in students through activities that consider their interaction with particular content. The didactic strategy must provide motivation, information, and orientation to students in order to carry out their learning process [11].

The strategy must be based on a method; but unlike it, the strategy is flexible and can be shaped around the goals needed to achieve. In its application, the strategy can use a series of techniques to attain the objectives desired. Everything must be previously planned based on the educational objectives intended. At the end, what the students achieve as well as the didactic strategy used is evaluated.

Once the basic concepts around the didactic act are presented, it is necessary to deepen in the didactic activities which the students use to achieve the desired learning.

3.2 The Didactic Activities

The didactic strategy, as already mentioned, is basically constituted by a wide set of learning activities that the students develop as it was previously planned by the professor. As Conole [14] poses it, the learning activities occur in a given context in terms of the environment where it is developed, the adopted pedagogical approaches, the institutional procedures, and difficulties that may arise, and they are designed to fulfill a set of specified learning outcomes and evaluation criteria through a series of tasks using a set of tools and resources. Thus, each learning activity proposes specific learning objectives for the students, as well as some tasks that they must do. For the development of these tasks, the students have a series of resources. Some of these resources are physical (books, laboratory objects), digital (computers, software, Internet), human (professors, assistants), etc. Conole proposes a taxonomy that defines the components that integrate a learning activity [14]. One of the most useful aspects of the taxonomy is the detailed description of the nature of the task that the students will do as part of the learning activity to achieve the desired goals. This taxonomy is enriched by Marcelo [15], which includes the "evaluation" type of activity that is not present in the original version of the taxonomy. The types of activities according to these two authors are:

- *Assimilative activities*: they intend to promote the students' comprehension about specific concepts that the professor presents via spoken, written, or visual texts.
- *Information management activities*: involve the development of data search tasks, of contrasting and/or synthesizing, of collecting and analyzing quantitative or qualitative data and of analysis of a case, text, audio, or video. They are activities that demand from students not only to look for information related to a query or problem that must be solved, but also to analyze it and understand it. They are activities that generally follow others based on assimilation.
- *Application activites*: they demand from the students to solve exercises or problems applying principles or contents previously studied in class.
- *Communicative activities*: they are those where the students are asked to present information, discuss, debate, share, inform, etc.
- *Productive activities*: through them, students have to design, elaborate, and create a device, document, or new resource.
- *Experiential activities*: they are those that try to place the students in an environment close to the future profesional practice, whether in a real or a simulated context.
- *Evaluative activities*: they are the ones whose main and only objective is the evaluation of the student, regardless of the previous activities intentions to evaluate.

3.3   Classification of Didactic Activities in Subcategories

The types of activities proposed by Conole gather a great diversity of activities that could be classified in activity subtypes. In order to arrive at this subcategorization, the research done by Marcelo et al. [15] was taken into account. They analyzed the specific components that university professors use to guide the students' learning process. And they do this through the analysis of the learning activities and tasks that they organize. One of the conclusions from this study is that there are no differences in general among professors of different fields of knowledge in function of the learning activities that they plan. Considering this conclusión, the activities can be classified in activity subtypes not discriminating the field of knowledge where it is applied to, obtaining a subclassification of general use in the universitiy context.

The process to reach the subcategorization of activities begins in the analysis of the 91 didactic activities consolidated in the study by Marcelo [15]. Having this list as an input, the activities were gathered in the types proposed Conole; and subsequently, subgroups were arranged according to the nature of the task. The consolidated activities and subactivities are presented in Table 1.

Once the types and subtypes of an activity were identified, we proceeded to specify the resources necessary to carry out each didactic activity, and how the resource could be instrumented using technology. To illustrate the process, Table 2 presents the specification of resources for assimilative activities. In the case of the assimilative-formation activity, the conventional resources used are videos, a board,

434   A. Ruíz et al.

Table 1. Types and subtypes of didactic activities

Activity type	Subtype	Examples
Assimilative	Formation	Listen to the professors' lecture
	Reading	Read materials and documents
	Observation	Visit an institution or work zone with the purpose of observing
Information management	Analysis	Analyze a document from a script
	Search	Search for information in recommended sources
Application	Training	Solve mathematical problems without the professor's presence
Communicative	Tutoring	Solve students' doubts
	Assistance	Help the student to accomplish something
	Discussion and Exchange of information	Participate in question-answer dynamics
	Presentation	Defend a work
	Agreement	Get to common grounds
	Conference	Attend a conference, congress, workshop
Productive		Write an essay or composition
Experiential		Develop practice in a real context
Evaluative	Written	Answer an evaluation instrument of previous knowledge
	Spoken	Maintain an evaluation interview with the professor
	Feedback	Provide feedback of the result of an evaluation

audiovisual aids and documents. Within the resources, the professors or presenters have been included because at the moment of bringing them to the technology, it is necessary to provide a mechanism of communication that allows the interaction between professors and students.

For this same case, the specified conventional resources could be supported on technology using a video player that is extended to support board features (the player allows navigating the video by subject or slides previously defined by the professor), a presentation or document viewer, and a file repository viewer. Communication between professor and student could be done via chat, forum, or video call.

3.4 Interface Design for Didactic Activities

Resource classification according to the type and subtype of activity where they are used are the input for the construction of the interfaces to be designed. Based on this classification, interfaces with different configurations of resources were designed according to the activity to which it is associated. For example, a professor plans an

Table 2. Resources for the assimilative activities

Resources		Assimilatives		
Conventional	Supported on ICTs	Formation	Reading	Observation
Video	Video player (live or pre-recorded)	√		√
Board	Player with board characteristics	√		
Audiovisual aids (other ais)	Presentation and/or document viewer	√	√	
Documents	Repository viewer	√	√	
Specification of the activity	Task (Moodle)			√
Resulting documents or files from the student	Task (Moodle) with attached file			
Evaluation instrument	Questionnaire			
Professor, presenter	Chat	√		
Professor, presenter	Video call	√		
Professor, presenter	Forum	√		

assimilative formation activity for the students to understand the basic concepts of databases. This activity can be done through a video explaining the concept, a written text, or the interaction of both, i.e. a video that shows an explanation, and that it is also based on other resources as a presentation or other documents.

In this way, the professor has different ways of planning the activity according to the elements available or the learning styles of student groups. Based on this assumption, a set of interfaces were designed for each activity that meet specific needs in a given context. During the design of the different variabilities of interface for each didactic activity, design guidelines that promote usability were applied. These guidelines are related to the Gestalt laws of grouping [17], Nielsen's heuristics [18], Tidwell patterns of interaction [19] and the application of different usability tests in order to capture feedback supplied by the users (professors and students). The Fig. 3 shows two examples of interface prototypes of low fidelity for the assimilative-formation activity.

3.5   Implementation of the Didactic Strategy Model

Once the interfaces for each type and subtype of activity were designed, the didactic strategy model was implemented. As it was mentioned, the didactic strategy is conceived as a process that is composed of learning activities and control actions carried out by the professor. According to this definition, the didactic strategy model must have the necessary elements that allow the modeling of a process. The literature reports a wide variety of languages for modeling processes, flow diagrams [20], (BPMN, SPEM, UML) as well as education (PoEML [9], E^{2}ML [10], CoUML [8]) among many others. Any process language could be used as a starting point for the implementation of the didactic strategy model. However, the notation language of the flowchart was chosen in order to maintain the simplicity of the model. Also, providing a greater acceptance

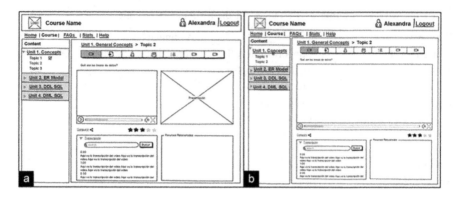

Fig. 3. Interface prototypes for the assimilative-formation activity; (a) includes the components of video player and file repository; (b) includes the components video player, presentation, and file repository

Table 3. Selected symbols of the flow diagram language for the didactic strategy model

	Symbol	Meaning
Control actions	⬭	*Start/End*: It is used to indicate the beginning and end of a didactic strategy
	◇	*Decision*: Represents the comparisons of two or more values. It has two outputs of information, true or false
	→	*Flow*: Shows the logical tracking of the diagram and the execution direction of the operations
Activity	[type] name	*Activity:* shows an action to be performed related to type of didactic activity. The type of didactic activity is shown in brackets "[]"

among the professors who know and use the flowcharts in different domains. Table 3 presents the language symbols of the selected flowcharts to implement the didactic strategy model.

For this version of the didactic strategy model, the flowchart language symbols have the same syntax but differ somewhat in their semantics, in the sense that activities are of the types and subtypes of didactic activities.

Each type of activity has interfaces associated that deploy the technological components to carry it out. Thus, a model is conceived, which taken to computation, is executed in a specified sequence, showing the student the activities to be developed in order to reach his learning objectives.

3.6   Concept Test

To validate the viability of the model on the LMS platforms, a concept test in the Moodle platform was made. To do this, a model editor was built in the Moodle

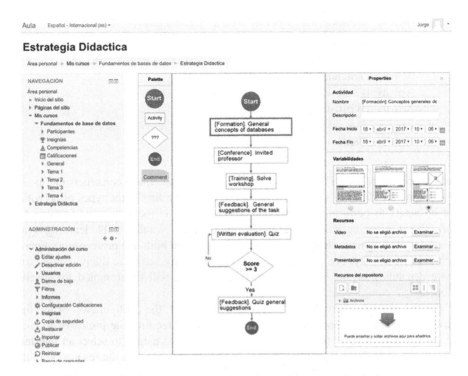

Fig. 4. Model editor of a didactic strategy in the Moodle platform

environment that allows to draw the model, select presentation interfaces for each type of activity, and execute the model following the sequence.

For the implementation of the model in the Moodle environment, a plugin that extends the internal navigation of Moodle was created, so that in any registered course in the platform has a workspace. In it, you can create, modify, visualize, and interact with the didactic strategy. In addition, this plugin allows you to extend the Moodle database to be able to consume or write the corresponding data to the didactic strategy without requiring other data sources external to the platform. For the creation of the modeling environment, the GoJS javascript library was used, which facilitates the creation of interactive editors. The models are stored in the Moodle database and then dynamically rendered to the course students within the space set for this purpose.

The process for the construction of didactic strategy models starts within the course environment. In Fig. 4, the interface of the model editor is observed, which has three sections: the palette, where the symbols of the language are; the working area, where the symbols are dragged and the model is constructed; and property zone, where the data of each activity is configured and the resources are related according to the selected interface.

To illustrate how the editor works, the sequence of activities is presented in Table 4. There, a didactic strategy model is constructed for the thematic unit "general

Table 4. Sequence of activities for the unit "General concepts of databases"

Activity: **[Formation]**. General concepts of databases
Activity: **[Conference]**. The importance of databases – Invited professor
Activity: **[Training]**. Solve workshop
Activity: **[Feedback]**. General suggestions of the task
Activity: **[Written evaluation]**. Answer quiz
Decision: If the evaluation is lower than 3, repeat. Otherwise resume
Activity: **[Feedback]**. Quiz general suggestions

concepts of databases". The professor, once in the model editor, constructs the model by dragging the different symbols to the work area according to the types of activities that he wants to perform. At this point, the professor is focused on performing his work; that is, planning according to the learning objectives and possible learning styles he has detected in his students. Once the model has been built, the professor configures each didactic activity. For this, he must select the activity and go to the properties area where depending on the type of interface selected, he will be prompted for specific resources.

For the example illustrated in Fig. 4 and in Table 4, the configuration of the first activity "*[Formation] General concepts of databases*" requires the professor to enter the general data of the activity (description, start and end dates), to select an interface type according to the resources available; and finally, to associate the resources. In the case that the teacher selects the interface that has a video player, a presentation viewer, and a file repository, the teacher will have to upload a video and its metadata, a presentation and the files that it wishes to unfold in the repository as selected files related to the activity. The interface associated to the activity that unfolds in the student's view is the one observed in Fig. 5.

If it were to set up a page similar to the one selected in the example using Moodle elements, the teacher must add each element and set it individually. This, considering the teacher knows the technology and knows how to integrate the different elements. The example above illustrates one of the advantages of the approach to be addressed in this research. The other advantages observed in the concept test are listed below:

- The model allows the teacher to focus on his planning work, so the technological aspects remain in the background
- The interfaces associated with the didactic activities are designed taking into account the specific contexts and needs of students and professors
- The configuration of the interfaces is simple
- The technological components that are arranged in the interfaces have a similar design to those that the Moodle platform deploys, so there is no breaking of the mental model that users of the platform have
- The professor can create easily different didactic strategy models according to the needs and learning styles of groups of students

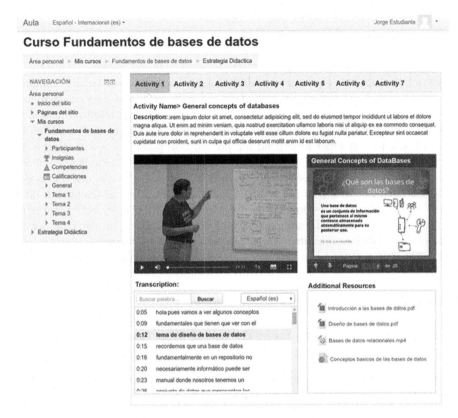

Fig. 5. Student view of the selected interface for the formation activity "General concepts of databases"

4   Conclusions and Future Works

This article presents a method for the inclusion of the didactic strategy model and its implementation in a computational environment through a concept test on the Moodle platform. The didactic strategy model is conceived from the analysis of conceptual models of the didactic act and a study on the didactic activities that the professors use in university teaching. Once the model is conceived, it is implemented in the Moodle platform, creating a model editor, which allows the creation of didactic strategies according to the needs and profiles of the students. The activities that make up the model have associated interfaces that use different configurations of the technological elements used by Moodle. The advantages offered by this method of inclusion of the didactic strategy model are varied and are emphasized in allowing the teacher to focus on the planning of didactic activities, leaving technological aspects on the background. All this can be achieved through the categorization of activities for which interfaces are designed; these consider students' and professors' specific contexts and necessities. The interface configuration is simple, and it is congruent with the mental model that

Moodle users have. Thereof, the teacher can easily create different models of didactic strategies according to his necessities and students' learning styles.

Advances in research have allowed us to identify future works in order to provide greater functionality and usability to the didactic strategy model, namely: (i) integrating new symbols that allow a greater versatility to the process flow and visually enriching the existing ones in such a way that they are expressive and easy to recognize, (ii) performing a quality assessment of the model in order to detect improvements at the usability level, (iii) creating an interface editor and generator that can be tied to the types of activities in order to expand the presentation possibilities according to the purposes of the activity and the available resources; and (iv) adopting a standard mechanism for the storage of models in such a way that didactic strategy models already created can be shared and reused. From the methodological standpoint, future works can be oriented to evaluate if the model editor in Moodle in fact improves the teacher's job regarding his traditional way of activity planning. In the same way, a comparative evaluation on other EMLs can be executed to determine if the categorization of activities improves the expressiveness and communication in the model.

References

1. Castro, S.M., Clarenc, C.A., López, C., Moreno, M.E., Tosco, N.B.: Analizamos 19 plataformas elearning- Investigación colaborativa de LMS. In: Congreso Virtual Mundial de e-Learning (2013)
2. Islas, C., Martínez, E.: El uso de las TIC como apoyo a las actividades docentes. Rev. RED (2008)
3. Uninorte. Centro de Recursos para el éxito estudiantil - ¿Porque no todo se aprende igual? (2016). http://www.uninorte.edu.co/documents/71051/2d260bbf-78d0-4f75-8de0-2b0281f914ba
4. Castelló, J., Lerís, D., Martínez, V., Sein-Echaluce, M.L.: Personalized learning on the moodle plaform using the CICEI conditionals: support course in mathematics. In: 4th International Technology, Education and Development Conference, España, pp. 277–282 (2010)
5. Lerís, D., Sein-Echaluce, M.L.: La personalización del aprendizaje: un objetivo del paradigma educativo centrado en el aprendizaje. In: ARBOR Ciencia, Pensamiento y Cultura, vol. 187 (2011)
6. Moodle.org. Modular Object-Oriented Dynamic Learning Environment – Moodle (2017). https://moodle.org/?lang=es
7. LAMSFoundation. Learning Activity Management System (2017). https://www.lamsfoundation.org/community_home.htm
8. Botturi, L., Stubbs, T.: Handbook of Visual Languages for Instructional Design: Theories and Practices: Information Science Reference - Imprint of: IGI Publishing, Hershey (2007)
9. Caeiro, M., Llamas, M., Anido, L.: Un Lenguaje Gráfico para el Modelado de Unidades Didácticas en Ingeniería. In: IEEE-RITA, vol. 2 (2007)
10. Botturi, L.: E2ML: A Visual Language for the Design of Instruction. Educ. Tech. Res. Dev. **54**, 265–293 (2006)
11. Marqués, P.: La Enseñanza Buenas Prácticas. La Motivación (2011). http://peremarques.net/
12. Meneses, G.: NTIC, Interacción y Aprendizaje en la Universidad. Doctorado, Departament de Pedagogia, Universitat Rovira I Virgili (2007)
13. Rodríguez, J.L.: Curriculum, Acto Didáctico y Teoría del Texto. Anaya Ed., España (1985)

14. Conole, G.: Describing learning activities: tools and resources to guide practice. In: Beetham, H., Sharpe, R. (eds.) Rethinking Pedagogy for a Digital Age: Designing and Delivering E-Learning. Ed: Routledge (2007)
15. Marcelo, C., Yot, C., Mayor, C., Sánchez, M., Murillo, P., Rodríguez, J.M., Pardo, A.: Las actividades de aprendizaje en la enseñanza universitaria: ¿hacia un aprendizaje autónomo de los alumnos? Rev. Educ., 363 (2014)
16. Las Estrategias y Técnicas Didácticas en el Rediseño (2005)
17. Graham, L.: Gestalt theory in interactive media design. J. Human. Soc. Sci. 2 (2008)
18. Nielsen, J.: 10 Usability Heuristics for User Interface Design (1995). https://www.nngroup.com/articles/ten-usability-heuristics/
19. Tidwell, J., Designing Interfaces: Patterns for Effective Interaction Design: O'Reilly Media, Sebastopol (2005)
20. ISO, ISO 5807: Information processing - Documentation symbols and conventions for data, program, system flowcharts, program network charts and system resources charts. Ed. ISO.org: ISO (1985)

Software Tool to Support the Improvement of the Collaborative Learning Process

Vanessa Agredo Delgado[1(✉)], Pablo H. Ruiz[1,2], Cesar A. Collazos[2],
Habib M. Fardoun[3], and Amin Y. Noaman[3]

[1] Corporación Universitaria – Unicomfacauca, Street 4 Number 8–30, Popayán, Colombia
{vagredo,pruiz}@unicomfacauca.edu.co
[2] Universidad del Cauca, Street 5 Number 4–70, Popayán, Colombia
ccollazo@unicauca.edu.co
[3] Information Systems, Faculty of Computing and Information Technology,
King Abdulaziz University, Jeddah, Saudi Arabia
{hfardoun,anoaman}@kau.edu.sa

Abstract. Computer supported collaborative learning brings together the same characteristics and qualities of traditional learning, and includes benefits at the level of interaction and collective learning, as well as the inclusion of a motivating element associated with technology, which allows monitoring more detailed, incorporate an activities record, guide, evaluate and observe the process that is executing in a collaborative activity. However, one of its main problems are caused by a lack of software tools to guarantee effective collaboration, to support the monitoring and evaluation of the process in each of its phases (Pre-Process, Process and Post-Process), and provide a compendium of mechanisms that allow the execution of a collaborative activity and increase collaboration among participants. In this paper, the MEPAC (Monitoreo y Evaluación del Proceso de Aprendizaje Colaborativo) software tool is presented to support the improvement of the collaborative learning process in each of its phases, through the integration of monitoring and evaluation. The evaluation of the MEPAC usefulness, applicability and complexity through a case study, allowed us to conclude that the development of collaborative learning activities is suitable, using monitoring and evaluation mechanisms, thus improving the collaboration between participants.

Keywords: Computer supported collaborative learning · Monitoring and evaluation mechanisms · Improve collaborative learning process · Collaborative software tool · Case study

1 Introduction

The human being by nature is a social being who needs others to achieve their survival. Taking into account this concept, investigations such as Johnson et al. [1], have shown that in education it is also necessary that there is an appropriate collaboration between people so that the learning of a particular subject is easier to understand and assimilate. Collaborative learning is defined as "a set of instructional methods for the application in small groups and mixed skills development (personal and social learning and

© Springer International Publishing AG 2017
A. Solano and H. Ordoñez (Eds.): CCC 2017, CCIS 735, pp. 442–454, 2017.
DOI: 10.1007/978-3-319-66562-7_32

development), where each of the group member is responsible for both their learning and of the group remaining members [2]", and a collaborative activity consists in "the development of a group task with a single final goal, exchanging ideas and materials, a tasks subdivision and group rewards. In summary, students working in groups who exchange ideas, ask questions, everybody listen and understand the answers, help each other before asking the tutor for help [3]". Due to in the collaborative learning process are immersed several elements that are essential for its realization and to obtain better results of collaboration and learning, is necessary to have a technological tool that allows centralizing the needs of the teacher and the student, in addition can give as result to achieve better performance. However, one of its main problems is the lack of software tools to allow guarantee an effective collaboration, that support the monitoring and evaluation of the process in each of its phases (Pre-Process, Process and Post-Process), and provide a compendium of mechanisms that will allow execute a collaborative activity and increase the collaboration between the participants, searching to provide a software tool that allows covering all the previous elements and characteristics, MEPAC is born as a tool that provides support elements for the execution of the collaborative learning process. This article is structured as follows: related works, which show some similar tools to support the collaborative learning process, MEPAC tool, which describes the tool characteristics, using MEPAC - study case, the section that shows the study case development to validate the tool, and finally the concluding section.

2   Related Works

Ramirez et al. [4] present a guide for the design of computer supported collaborative learning activities called CSCoLAD, which provides a design mechanism throughout all the collaborative learning process and defines a web tool to support the design of collaborative activities. Hernández et al. [5] present COLLAGE, a high level tool based on collaborative learning flow patterns for the design of activities, which represents the best practices that are used repeatedly in structuring the of activities flow allowing the reuse and patterns customization, in order to be effective and adapted to the needs of a particular learning situation. Chacón [6] proposes a method that allows the structuring of collaborative activities, to stimulate the incorporation of technology efficiently in the teaching and learning processes, using Web 2.0 tools to design and develop collaborative activities. Collazos et al. [7] design the tools: Chase the Cheese, MemoNet, ColorWay, CollabPet, to evaluate the process and collaboration degree, that allow to understand some of the most common problems that occur in the execution of a collaborative activity. DEGREE (Distance Learning Environment for Group Experiences) [8], supports the realization of a variety of learning tasks by small groups of students, allowing for various methods of collaboration. On the other hand, ColaboQuim [9] is a tool to support collaborative learning in chemistry, which searches to support the teaching of the chemical molecules construction, through the creation of material, execution and collaborative activities evaluation; also incorporates several positive interdependencies, and has a monitoring module. In Lovos et al. [10] present a customized environment that integrates teaching paradigms: Problem-Based Learning (PBL) and computer supported collaborative learning (CSCL). It has a collaborative learning environment in virtual teaching situations, through tools that provide synchronous and asynchronous services that are very useful in teaching - learning supported by computer. Rodríguez et al. [11] present MILLENNIUM, a prototype of a software tool that validates the integration model of the individual and collaborative environments, this prototype works under two types of environments and the users can exchange whenever they wish. Habi-Pro (Programming Habits): is a client-server application to develop good programming habits, is a collaborative learning system, synchronous, distributed in which students learn to understand and debug programs, develop good styles and also it can solve problems in a collaborative way [12]. Martinez et al. [13] define a way of evaluating interactions by capturing events and processing them, to model the interaction state, from a program that delineates the content of the interactions to store and evaluate them in computational terms in a generic way. The previous works offer tools to help the computer supported collaborative learning, but none of these provides a complete support in all phases (Pre-Process, Process and Post-Process), much less the possibility of executing a collaborative activity by the students, that is monitored and evaluated through mechanisms that help this process. Characteristics and elements that the MEPAC tool considers in its definition, being this the main contribution that the tool has respect to those previously mentioned.

3   MEPAC Tool

To check the usefulness of the conceptual model presented in [14], which considers the activities, subactivities, roles, guides, mechanisms and artifacts necessary to support the collaborative learning process in each of its phases (Pre-process, Process and Post- process), it was necessary to design and implement a software tool called MEPAC (by its initials in Spanish "Monitoreo y Evaluación del Proceso de Aprendizaje Colaborativo") tool defined by the reuse of the functionality provided by Moodle [15].

The MEPAC construction was based on the incorporation of plugins, to perform the monitoring and activities evaluation of the collaborative learning process, and embedded PHP code for the creation of forms that allowed manage the phases of the process by the teacher. MEPAC also has guides and support manuals for the teacher and the student, which allow to reach the objective of the collaborative activity and in this way, improve the process and increase the collaboration between the participants. To see the structure of MEPAC see Fig. 1.

According to the structure defined by MEPAC showed in the Fig. 1, each part of the software tool contributes to the objective of it uses in the collaborative learning process, which seeks to increase collaboration among the participants through the interaction monitoring and evaluation, each element is explained below:

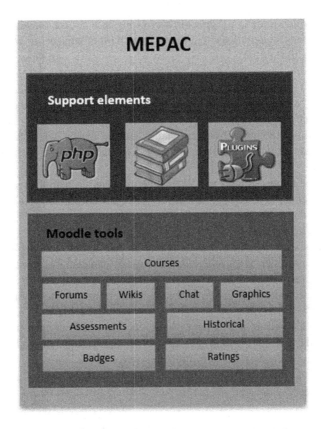

Fig. 1. MEPAC structure.

Taking into account that MEPAC reuses some elements of Moodle, which is defined as: a software designed to help teachers create high quality online courses and virtual learning environments. One of the main Moodle characteristics over other systems is that it is done on basis of the constructivist social pedagogy, where communication has a relevant space in the way of the knowledge construction, the goal being to generate an experience of enriching learning [16]. MEPAC takes Moodle tools and elements to execute a collaborative activity, elements such as:

- The courses, are pages or areas where teachers can present their resources and activities to the students, showing the necessary material and information. The courses are used to carry out collaborative activities, to upload information and for students to have spaces to upload their documents, find their grades and communicate with the teacher.
- The roles allow getting into the platform as "teacher" or "student", each having an identification with user and password. In addition to having a user profile to manage their information.

- Activities, which refer to a characteristics group in a course, usually an activity is something that a student does, that interacts with other students or with the teacher. Among the activities are:
  - Tasks: allow teachers to rate and comment on uploaded files and tasks created online and offline. They allow managing the hours and dates of delivery.
  - Election: with which the teacher creates questions and specifies a variety of multiple choice answers.
  - Exam: allows the teacher designs and assembles exams, which according to the activity can be automatically qualified or through feedback to show the correct answers.
  - Predefined survey: allows to collect student's data, to help the teachers to know their students and to analyze about the teaching. In addition to being used to gather information on teacher and student satisfaction about the software tool and the activities developed.
- Chat, allows students to have a synchronous discussion in real time, as well as involving the teacher when required. The teacher can also intervene in the talks to get the activities focus.
- Forum, created to allow students to have asynchronous discussions and request information at the teacher.
- Wikis, are a collection of web pages where any user adds or edits necessary information, used to deliver the final activities, where each student must give their contribution and build the final delivery to the teacher.
- Private messages, used by teachers and students, to send and receive private messages necessary for activities, as well as receiving notifications about tasks, forums discussions, etc.

MEPAC has functionalities that are taken from Moodle, but its contribution and difference are the following elements that are used mainly for the monitoring and evaluation of the collaborative learning process, and searching improvement it. In addition to taking into account each of the process phases (Pre-Process, Pro-cess and Post-Process):

To MEPAC also were added Moodle plugins that are not specified in the basic version, but they were installed to manage the collaborative activities:

- The grading book, each course has its own grading book, which is accessible to teachers and course's students, in addition to allowing look the progress of the activities defined by the teachers, upcoming activities and qualifying activities. This with the purpose of the teacher can verify how students work and does required movements when there is work recharge or vice versa.
- Activity ending, an action that allows the teacher to officially mark as finished, manually or automatically according to criteria specified at the beginning of the course. In addition to allowing students to see their progress during the course until it is finalized.
- Badges, are awarded manually or by using the end of activities configurations in a course and it is a way to motivate students. It is awarded at different course stages for different levels of activities progress.

- Reminder, added so that the teachers remember those activities that must qualify and of which they need to give a feedback, this in order to be in continuous contact with the students.
- Groups, allows assigning students to a group, to have a teacher management of all groups created for the collaborative activity and analyze their activities.

MEPAC also has the addition of PHP code for the creation of forms that allow the teacher to perform the three collaborative learning process phases (Pre-Process, Process, Post-Process). By means of these elements the teacher registers activities information, where at the end of the registration a PDF file is generated that must be taken for the activity monitoring and evaluation to be carried out:

- A first form for the Pre-process phase, in where fields related to the planning, management, coordination and definition of the collaborative activity are registered.
- A second form for the Process phase, where fields recorded about the collaboration activity execution as a way of achieving the teaching objectives, depending on the student's interaction with their peers and with learning resources.
- The last form referring to the Post-process phase, where information registers about the assessment individually and collective to verify the level of knowledge acquired by the students in the activity carried out, as well as information about the activity ending with feedback required.

MEPAC finally, has guides and support manuals for teachers and students, in order to facilitate the use of the elements provided by the software tool:

- Manual for the use of monitoring and evaluation mechanisms, created so that the teacher acquires knowledge of how it is the best way to use all the mechanisms proposed and obtain the benefit of necessary collaboration.
- Support material for students, guides for students to have in summary documents topics related to the activity and they can be support in the collaborative activities accomplishment.
- Process phase guide, a document generated by the teacher in the MEPAC tool, that is accessible to students, where the rules and concepts necessary for the collaborative activity execution are concentrated.

All of the elements aforementioned with their respective use, make up the structure of MEPAC and allowed to execute a process of collaborative learning, monitored and evaluated for the improvement of this.

4   Using MEPAC - Case Study

The MEPAC objective is to support the collaborative learning process phases in the classroom by means of the grouping of monitoring and evaluation mechanisms. To validate its usefulness, applicability and complexity in supporting the collaborative process improvement, it was necessary to apply the tool in a case study execution, which allowed to define the best way to use the monitoring and evaluation mechanisms, defined and presented in [17], which seek to increase collaboration in the activities carried out.

For the selection of the case study, was taken into account the case study guide defined by Runeson et al. [18], where the need to have an objective is defined; which for this project is defined as: verifying the level of usefulness, MEPAC applicability and complexity use in supporting collaborative learning through the application of monitoring and evaluation mechanisms in the undergraduate academic field. In addition, the definition of an analysis unit, which is defined for this project, as an academic environment within a process of collaborative learning. The primary information source is: the teacher who is the main person in charge of each process phases, in charge of applying the collaborative activities. According to the types of case studies defined by Benbasat et al. [19], the type for this project is holistic, due to it is considered an analysis unit with a research subject and a collaborative activity in a real case in undergraduate teaching.

The case study was developed in two undergraduate academic courses in the system engineering program, object-oriented programming of the Electronic Engineering and Telecommunications Faculty of the University of Cauca and databases modeling of the Corporación Universitaria Comfacauca – Unicomfacauca. Courses that were constituted by 16 students of the second and third semester, and 10 students of the fourth and fifth semester, respectively (See Fig. 2). For each of the previously mentioned courses, a collaborative activity was carried out, using the MEPAC tool, with the collaboration of teachers and students.

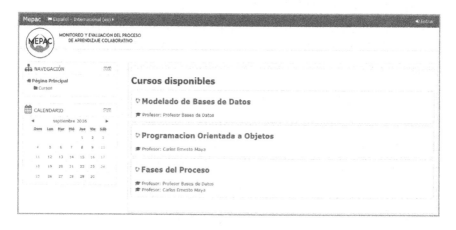

Fig. 2. Courses created for teachers and students

Guidelines for determining the MEPAC usefulness, applicability and complexity
For specifying the MEPAC tool utility, which is defined as the property by which the software tool acquires the condition of useful value to satisfy the improvement objectives proposed for the collaborative learning process, were managed as metrics: the software tool utility perception in the development of the activities by the students and by the teacher in the collaborative learning process, the students percentage who approve the developed activity, contrast the improvements made for each of the processes vs the opportunities of improvement found previously. In order to specify applicability, which is defined as the property by which MEPAC can be easily used to obtain favorable

improvement results for the collaborative learning process, metrics such as: the necessary effort by the teacher and by the student for the realization of the collaborative activity doing use of the tool. In order to specify the complexity, which is defined as the diversity of elements that compose a situation, which is interlaced and/or interconnected that contain additional information and hidden from the observer, the metrics were taken into account: the complexity perceived by the teacher to apply the monitoring and evaluation mechanisms during the collaborative activity, doing use of MEPAC, and the complexity perceived by the teacher when using it for the design, application and subsequent collaborative activity evaluation.

Taking into account the previous metrics, the guidelines that were established to calculate the utility are:

- The student's average range who consider MEPAC is a positive support for the course should be between 80% and 100%.
- The favorable responses' average range by the teacher to consider that MEPAC supports the activities of the collaborative learning process should be between 80% and 100%.
- The students' average range who pass the activity must be between 80% and 100%.
- The range of questions that have a positive impact on the improvement process obtained with MEPAC vs the improvement opportunities found previously, based on the teacher's perception, must be between level four and five (five being the degree of utility higher), and greater than or equal to 80%.

The guidelines that have been established to determine applicability are:

- The average degree of applicability of MEPAC from the teacher's perception must be between four and five (five being the highest degree of applicability), which corresponds to having a percentage greater than or equal to 80%.
- The effort to develop a collaborative activity using MEPAC, taking into account the teacher and student time (for the 3 process phases), should be on average 10 to 12 h.

The patterns that have been established to determine complexity are:

- The complexity degree average in monitoring applicability and evaluation mechanisms, using MEPAC, obtained from the teacher's perception that it is between one and five (5 being the highest degree of complexity), must be less than 70%.
- The complexity degree average of the use of MEPAC for the execution of collaborative activities based on the teacher's perception of between one and five (5 being the highest degree of complexity) must be less than 70%.

4.1 Case Study

The case study began with the Pre-process phase, in which the teachers made use of the MEPAC tool, carrying out the collaborative activity design, through a guide, which defines a compendium of activities required to complete this phase (See Fig. 3), finally generating a PDF document containing the design of said activity. In the development of the Pre-process phase teachers spent an average of 40 min.

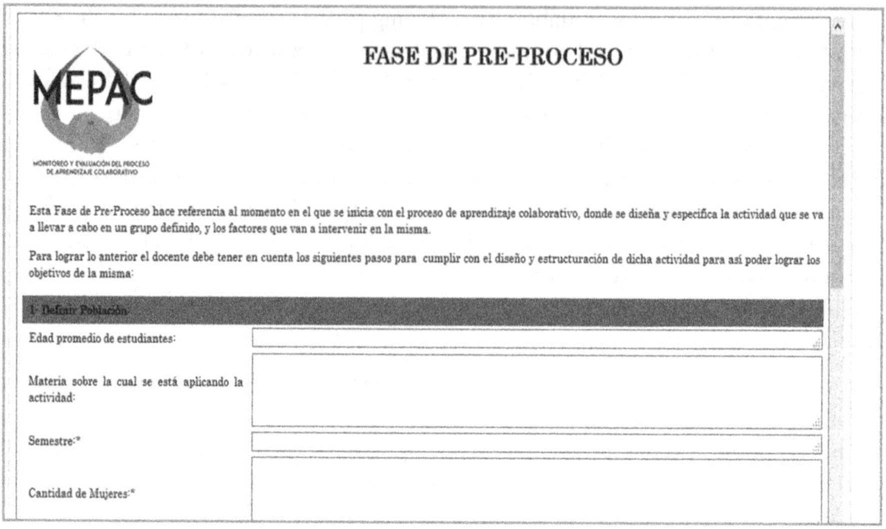

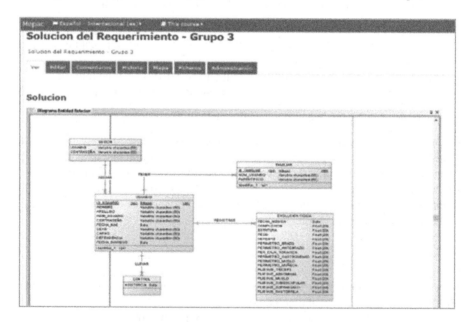

Fig. 3. Pre-process form

In the next session, the teachers were in charge of complete the form related to the phase of the Process, which takes into account defined activities for the application of the designed activity, which finally generates a new PDF file of this second phase.

Fig. 4. Wikis creation and use

Subsequently, the teachers apply the collaborative activity using MEPAC, using the guide generated in the previous phase. For the application of the collaborative activities, groups of 3 students were organized. The time of average execution of activities used by students was one and a half hours.

MEPAC, in addition to providing the monitoring and evaluation mechanisms defined in [17] of the activities carried out, which allowed the teachers to intervene at appropriate times, always seeking to increase collaboration between the groups to achieve the proposed objective, for example, the use of forums, wikis that helped in the activities execution, monitoring and evaluation, as well as it was shown in the structure of the tool and can be seen in the Fig. 4.

The additional elements that were used for the activities monitoring and evaluation were executed to increase the collaboration and to make the students learn and achieve the proposed objectives, some of the elements used can be seen in Fig. 5.

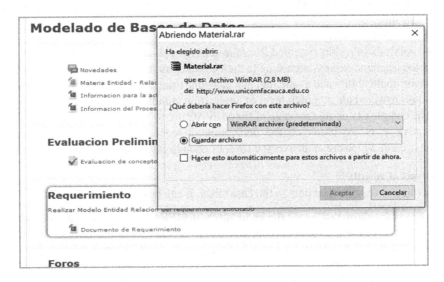

Fig. 5. Student and teacher manuals about collaborative activity

After executing the activity with the students, the teachers were in charge of completing the form for the Post-Process phase, spending in its definition half an hour, in this phase, a new PDF guide to the activities of closing and feedback of the executed activity.

Results

Taking into account the guidelines for determining the MEPAC usefulness, applicability and completeness, the following results were obtained, which were taken from both teacher and student satisfaction surveys and from MEPAC records (the values are on average, in the two courses on which the collaborative activity was applied):

• The percentage of students who defined MEPAC as positive support for the course was 88.2%.

- The 80% of the answered questions by teachers are at a high level of positive impact to consider that MEPAC supports the collaborative learning process activities.
- The student's percentage who approved the collaborative activity is 90.2%.
- The 89% of the answered questions by teachers are at a high level of positive impact on the improvement process obtained with MEPAC vs the improvement opportunities previously encountered.
- The teachers' survey allowed to determine that their perception about the applicability of MEPAC in the collaborative learning process, it is defined by 60% of the questions answered that are at a high level of ease of application.
- The effort involved in developing a collaborative activity using MEPAC (taking into account the teacher and the student time in the 3 process phases) averaged 14 h, in the different stages:
  - Training on collaborative activities, external factors involved in these activities, as well as training teachers on the correct use of monitoring and evaluation mechanisms
  - Design of material for collaborative activity.
  - Analysis of results obtained from the activity and feedback to students.
- In the teachers' survey, according to their complexity degree perception in the monitoring applicability and evaluation mechanisms, using MEPAC, the 80% of the questions answered are at a high level of application complexity.
- The complexity degree average of the MEPAC use tool for the execution of collaborative activities based on the perception of teachers is 68% of the questions answered, which are at an average level of complexity of application.

Analysis of results

According to the obtained data in the case study, it can be considered that:

- The results show that, since the application of MEPAC, the percentage of students who approve the activities is high, consolidating this tool as useful mechanisms to increase the good performance of the students in the collaborative learning process. In addition, students perceived that the tool provided to them was a support for the development of their activities and for the growth of collaboration. Also, from the teacher perspective it is possible to classify MEPAC as useful taking into account the positive impact that was generated on the process carried out from the activities carried out.
- With regard to the utility of MEPAC and the monitoring and evaluation mechanisms that are present in the tool, all the levels established in the guidelines are met, in order to conclude that it is useful for carrying out an improvement process regarding the increase of collaboration between the participants in this context and to take advantage of each one of the activities that are carried out.
- From the teachers' perceptions regarding the applicability of MEPAC in an academic collaborative learning process, the results show that the tool is not classified as easily applicable but it provides mechanisms for its application in this context. In addition to determining that to meet all stages requires a great effort in terms of time per person, from which it can be assumed that the greatest effort is necessary at the beginning (at the time that the teacher and students should appropriate concepts of the tool and

work collaboratively), an effort that can be overcome in the long term, with feasible results for teachers and students.

- The results obtained from the metric to calculate the complexity show that, from the teacher perception, to apply monitoring and evaluation mechanisms, the complexity is high, which may be due to the teacher's lack of knowledge in the development of activities of collaborative learning, and in the execution of each phases. In the case where the teacher repeats the tool use and its mechanisms, the complexity may diminish, since experience is acquired and in later uses it is not necessary to read and interpret the manuals and guides that accompany the tool and its mechanisms. And the complexity to use MEPAC, is average according to the teacher perception, since, it follows the same Moodle guidelines, for the activities in the education context.
- The results concerning the collaborative learning process improvement through the use of MEPAC were published in [20], which establishes a set of metrics to measure the improvement and cooperation implemented in collaborative activities. The results obtained in [20] allow us to compare the values before the improvement (with those case studies where monitoring and evaluation were not applied) vs the results obtained in the indicators and metrics after the improvement, from which we can conclude that the collaboration is increased through the use of MEPAC monitoring and evaluation mechanisms.

Conclusions

This article presents the MEPAC software tool that supports the collaborative learning process in each of its phases, in addition to its monitoring and evaluation, because it considers elements such as: wikis, chat, forums, manuals, guides, forms, management activities and evaluations, which are necessary and strategic to increase the collaboration between the students who carry out an activity.

According to the results obtained through the case study development it can be concluded that MEPAC is useful, applicable and moderately complex, which can facilitate its use in the collaborative activities development, providing strategies to facilitate communication and joint work between students regardless of whether of their geographical location.

References

1. Kreijns, K., Kirschner, P., Jochems, W.: Identifying the pitfalls for social interaction in computer-supported collaborative learning environments: a review of the research. Comput. Hum. Behav. 19(3), 335–353 (2003)
2. Johnson, D.W., Johnson, R.T.: Learning Together and Alone. Cooperative, Competitive, and Individualistic Learning. Allyn and Bacon, Needham Heights (1994)
3. Johnson, R.B., Onwuegbuzie, A.J.: Mixed methods research: a research paradigm whose time has come. Educ. Res. 33(7), 14–26 (2004)
4. Ramirez, D., Bolaños, J., Collazos, C.: Guía para el diseño de actividades de aprendizaje colaborativo asistida por computador (CSCoLAD). Monografía de Trabajo de Grado, Popayán, Universidad del Cauca, Colombia (2013)

5. Hernández, D., Villasclaras, E., Asensio, J., Dimitriadis, Y., Jorrín, I., Ruiz, I., Rubia, B.: COLLAGE: a collaborative learning design editor based on patterns. J. Educ. Technol. Soc. **9**(1), 58 (2006)

6. Chacón, J.: Modelo para el Diseño de Actividades Colaborativas Mediante la Utilización de Herramientas Web 2.0. (2012)

7. Collazos, C., Muñoz, J., Hernández, Y.: Aprendizaje colaborativo apoyado por computador. Lunes Científico Universidad Militar Nueva Granada, vol. 64 (2008)

8. Osuna, C., Rocha, L., Romero, M., Villa, L., Sheremetov, L., Niño, O.: Uso del modelo APRI para la evaluación de la intención en entornos de aprendizaje colaborativo. Inteligencia Artif. Revista Iberoamericana de Inteligencia Artif. **24**, 109–119 (2004)

9. Guerrero, L., Hurtado, C.: Colaboquim: Una aplicación para apoyar el aprendizaje colaborativo en química (2006)

10. Lovos, E.: El Uso de Herramientas Colaborativas en los Cursos de Introducción a la Programación, Universidad Nacional de La Plata (2012)

11. Rodríguez del Pino, J.C., Rubio Royo, E., Hernández Figueroa, Z.J.: VPL: laboratorio virtual de programación para Moodle. In: XVI Jornadas de Enseñanza Universitaria de la Informática, Universidade de Santiago de Compostela. Escola Técnica Superior d'Enxeñaría, pp. 429–435 (2010)

12. WebCT, Blackboard – Learn. http://www.blackboard.com/Platforms/Learn/Overview.aspx. Accessed 16 May 2017

13. Martínez, A., Dimitriadis, Y., Rubia, B., Gómez, E., Garrachón, I., Marcos, J.A.: Studying social aspects of computer-supported collaboration with a mixed evaluation approach. In: Proceedings of the Conference on Computer Support for Collaborative Learning: Foundations for a CSCL Community, pp. 631–632. International Society of the Learning Sciences (2002)

14. Agredo, V., Collazos, C., Paderewski, P.: Aplicación del procedimiento formal definido para evaluar, monitorear y mejorar el proceso de aprendizaje colaborativo en su etapa de Proceso mediante la creación de mecanismos, Corporación Universitaria Unicomfacauca - revista I + T +C **10**(1), 57–68 (2016)

15. Rodríguez, J.S.: Plataformas de enseñanza virtual para entornos educativos. Pixel-Bit. Revista de Medios y Educación **34**, 217–233 (2009)

16. Docs, M.: https://docs.moodle.org/all/es/Acerca_de_Moodle. Accessed 16 May 2017

17. Agredo, V., Collazos, C., Paderewski, P.: Definición de mecanismos para evaluar, monitorear y mejorar el proceso de aprendizaje colaborativo, Tecnología educativa Revista CONAIC **3**(3) (2016)

18. Runeson, P., Höst, M.: Guidelines for conducting and reporting case study research in software engineering. Empirical Softw. Eng. **14**(2), 131 (2009)

19. Benbasat, I., Goldstein, D.K., Mead, M.: The case research strategy in studies of information systems. MIS Quart. **11**(3), 369–386 (1987)

20. Agredo, V., Ruiz, P., Collazos, C., Hurtado, J.: Aplicando agile SPI – process para la construcción de mecanismos de monitoreo, evaluación y mejora del proceso de aprendizaje colaborativo, gerencia tecnología informática. GTI J. **15**(43) (2017). Universidad Industrial de Santander

Intelligent Systems and Robotics

Evolutionary Parameter Estimation of Coupled Non-linear Oscillators

Sandro-Francisco Balarezo-Gallardo
and Jesús Antonio Hernández-Riveros[⊠]

Facultad de Minas, Universidad Nacional de Colombia, Medellín, Colombia
{sfbalarezog, jahernan}@unal.edu.co

Abstract. In nature, nonlinear oscillators are observed attached to the joints of the animal's legs as they move. In this paper, a system identification method based on evolutionary computation applied to coupled nonlinear oscillators is presented. As an initial reference, is a coupled non-linear oscillator designed from a Central Pattern Generator, developed for a quadruped robot with three joints per leg, and electronically tuned. The method of identification is based on the MAGO evolutionary algorithm to minimize the error in the magnitude and in the phase shift of the signals. The procedure consists of two stages: coarse-tuning and fine-tuning. With a new parameterization of the same oscillator developed for the quadruped robot, the goodness of the identification method is revealed. The method is validated by parameterizing the Van der Pol Oscillator. The results are very satisfactory. The problem to be solved is to find a mathematical model that synthesizes the observed movement of a quadruped as it moves. From the images of the oscillations generated by the hip, knee and ankle of a horse, a system of coupled nonlinear differential equations is found that reproduce the movement of the quadruped with an approximation of more than 95%.

Keywords: Automatic learning · Neural networks · Evolutionary computation · Robotics · Systems identification · Non-linear oscillators

1 Introduction

Biological systems are a source of inspiration for solving dynamic and static problems in locomotion of articulated robots in the real world. One of the biological systems that vertebrate animals have in their spinal cord is the Central Pattern Generators (CPG). CPGs are capable of generating signals to produce voluntary rhythmic movements such as walking, flying, swimming and even involuntary movements such as heartbeat, eye blinking, etc. [1]. The coupled oscillator models can serve as models to emulate the real systems of nature, such as those mentioned above [2].

This paper shows a system identification method applied to coupled nonlinear oscillators based on evolutionary computation. As a starting point there is a CPG system developed for the displacement of a quadruped robot with three joints per leg (CPG-R4A3). The CPG-R4A3 is represented by a set of first-order coupled differential equations [3]. This system has 11 parameters that are electronically tuned and are used for an articulated quadruped robot to perform locomotion.

© Springer International Publishing AG 2017
A. Solano and H. Ordoñez (Eds.): CCC 2017, CCIS 735, pp. 457–471, 2017.
DOI: 10.1007/978-3-319-66562-7_33

On the other hand, Evolutionary Algorithms (EA) are methods of optimization and search that emulate the mechanisms of natural selection and genetic inheritance from the Neo-Darwinian theory of biological evolution [4]. To guarantee diversity and increase the exploitation of the search space, the multi-dynamics algorithm for global optimization (MAGO) uses three different population dynamics simultaneously: a uniform distribution over the search space, a conservation mechanism of the best individual, and a strategy for maintaining diversity [4]. By using the MAGO algorithm, an evolutionary parameter estimator was designed for the aforementioned CPG-R4A3 system.

The evolutionary estimator has two major processes defined as Coarse tuning and Fine-tuning. The coarse tuning is aimed at reducing the error in amplitude and frequency between the desired signal and the estimated signal. Coarse tuning has 2 stages. The objective function for the first stage is defined by the sum of the point-to-point error between the two signals. In the second stage, the correlation value between the two signals was used as the objective function. After these operations, a greater correlation value equal to 0.8 is reached and linearization can be applied by fine-tuning. The fine-tuning, also with two stages, focuses on minimizing the total amplitude and frequency error between the signals. Linearization consists of adding additive and multiplicative constants to the CPG system. In the third stage, these constants are found [5]. The fourth step is to obtain the final parameters with a point-to-point error as objective function.

The proposed method is demonstrated with a new estimate of the 11 parameters required by the CPG R4A3 system to generate locomotion signals for an articulated quadruped robot. Subsequently, it undergoes signal emulation tests to reproduce the behavior of a Van der Pol oscillator. The Van der Pol oscillator is a classical dynamic system that was originally used as a precursor to commercial radios. This oscillator has positive feedback and a non-linear resistive element [6].

Finally, based on the system of differential equations of CPG R4A3, the parameters of the coupled non-linear oscillator to reproduce the bioinspired signals in the locomotion of a quadruped (horse) are estimated. The acquisition of these locomotion signals is based on image processing, representing the time-varying angles of the hip, knee and ankle joints during locomotion in the horse's walking mode.

The theoretical foundations are presented below. In section three, the case studies. The developed method in section four, to continue in section five with the analysis of results. This paper ends with some conclusions.

2   Theoretical Foundations

2.1   Dynamic Systems and Oscillators

Dynamic System. Defined as a set of interacting elements, where the evolution of its states is given by functions of the input and output variables, which depend on the time t, such that $t \in T$. If T belongs to the integers is known as a discrete dynamic system, if T belongs to the real is a continuous dynamic system. The behavior of continuous and discrete dynamic systems is determined by a rate of change over a time interval. For the continuous case, the behavior is governed by differential equations, and for the discrete one by iterative equations.

Oscillatory Systems. It can be defined as dynamic systems whose particular behavior is determined by one or more differential equations of order n and have a solution [7]. As in Eq. (1).

$$x = [C_1 v_1\ C_2 v_2\ \dots\ C_n v_3]e^{\lambda t} \tag{1}$$

$$\text{with}\ \ \lambda = [\lambda_1\ \lambda_2\ \dots\ \lambda_m]$$

Where $\lambda_1, \lambda_2, \dots, \lambda_m$ are complex numbers. A second order linear oscillator is shown in Eq. (2).

$$ax + bx + cx = gt \tag{2}$$

The solution of this system is of the form in Eq. (3):

$$x = [C_1 v_1\ C_2 v_2]e^{\begin{bmatrix} \lambda_1 \\ \lambda_1 \end{bmatrix} t} \tag{3}$$

Linear Oscillators. Also called harmonic oscillators, have a behavior described by the second order differential equation, (2), and their solution are sinusoidal functions. The values $a, b, c, g\ (t)$ allow to have oscillators of the following type:

- Simple Harmonic (Fig. 1A), with $a > 0,\ b = 0,\ C > 0\ and\ g(t) = 0$
- Damped Harmonic (Fig. 1B), with $a > 0,\ b \neq 0,\ C > 0,\ g(t) = 0$
- Forced Harmonic (Fig. 1C), which are resonant systems with values of $a > 0,\ b \neq 0,\ C > 0,\ g(t) = Fcos(w_c t)$, [7].

Non-linear Oscillators. Have very different behavior to harmonics and are governed by non-linear differential equations. An example of this case may be electrocardiogram pulses. Nonlinear oscillators can be defined by Eq. (4) [7].

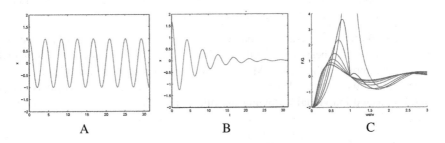

Fig. 1. (A) Simple harmonic oscillator, **(B)** Damped harmonic oscillator, and **(C)** Forced harmonic oscillator resonance

$$\ddot{x} + g(x)\dot{x} + cx = 0 \tag{4}$$

The characteristic systems for non-linear oscillators are the Van der Pol, Rayleigh, etc., oscillators.

2.2   Central Pattern Generator (CPG)

A paradigm shift in motor control emerged in the mid-1980s. Through experiments, Baev and Shimansky demonstrated that voluntary motor tasks such as reaching, grasping, releasing and rhythmic movements could be performed by deafferentation, i.e. without the inclusion of sensors. Marsden and his colleagues defined this new concept of motor control: "a set of muscular commands that are structured before a movement begins and can be sent to the muscle with the correct synchronization so that the whole sequence is carried in the absence of a feedback peripheral" [8].

Figure 2 shows the configuration and the implementation of a CPG system for locomotion in an articulated quadruped robot.

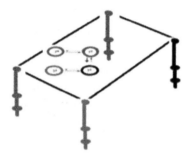

Fig. 2. Artificial CPG in an articulated quadruped robot [3].

2.3   Multi-dynamics Algorithm for Global Optimization (MAGO)

The Multidynamics Algorithm for Global Optimization (MAGO) is inspired by Estimation Distribution Algorithms, Differential Evolution and Statistical Quality Control [4]. Like most evolutionary algorithms, MAGO starts with a random initial population on the search space limited by the problem, for the following iterations new individuals are created by means of three subgroups or dynamics.

Emerging Dynamics. This subset is based on the mutation and selection of individuals who have obtained the best values in their objective function, similar to the differential evolution, but applying the Nelder-Mead method of numerical derivation [9].

A test individual is created from the selection of the best of all individuals and a randomly selected individual following the rule in Eq. (5):

$$x_T^{(j)} = x_i^{(j)} + F^{(j)} \times \left(x_B^{(j)} - x_m^{(j)} \right) \tag{5}$$

Where $x_B^{(j)}$ is the best individual of generation j and $x_m^{(j)}$ is a randomly selected individual. $F^{(j)}$ is a matrix that includes information about the covariance of the problem variables.

$$F^{(j)} = \frac{S^{(j)}}{\|S^{(j)}\|} \tag{6}$$

Where $S^{(j)}$ is the sample covariance matrix of the individual population in generation j.

Crowd Dynamics. This subgroup has the role of exploring the search space around the population mean. If the population mean and dispersion matrix for generation j are $x_M^{(j)}$ and $S^{(j)}$, then the next generation of the Crowd Dynamics is created from the uniform distribution on the hyper-rectangle $[LB^{(j)}, UB^{(j)}]$, Where Eqs. (7) and (8) are vectors with the diagonal of the population dispersion matrix of the generation j, described by Eq. (9).

$$LB^{(j)} = x_M^{(j)} - \sqrt{diag(S^{(j)})} \tag{7}$$

$$UB^{(j)} = x_M^{(j)} + \sqrt{diag(S^{(j)})} \tag{8}$$

$$S^{(j)} diag\left(S^{(j)}\right) = \left[S_{11}^{(j)} \; S_{22}^{(j)} \; \cdots \; S_m^{(j)}\right]^T \tag{9}$$

Accidental Dynamics. The two dynamics mentioned above concentrate the population around local optima, for this reason, MAGO introduces new individuals in each generation. These individuals are created by sampling a uniform distribution throughout the search space. This dynamics also maintains the numerical stability of the covariance dispersion matrix.

Cardinalities. For control tables it is assumed that if the process is outside the control limits then it is suspected that the process is out of order. The next step in MAGO is a type of variance decomposition, inspired by the well-known variance analysis (ANOVA).

Consider the population dispersion matrix of generation j, $S^{(j)}$ and its diagonal. If $Pob^{(j)}$ is the set of possible solutions in generation j, then we can define the following groups, Eqs. (10)–(12).

$$G_1 = \left\{ x \in Pob^{(j)} / x_M^{(j)} - \sqrt{diag(S^{(j)})} \le x \ge x_M^{(j)} + \sqrt{diag(S^{(j)})} \right\} \tag{10}$$

$$G_2 = \left\{ x \in Pob^{(j)} / x_M^{(j)} - 2\sqrt{diag(S^{(j)})} \le x \ge x_M^{(j)} + \sqrt{diag(S^{(j)})} \right\} \tag{11}$$

$$G_3 = \left\{ x \in Pob^{(j)} / x \leq x_M^{(j)} - 2\sqrt{diag(S^{(j)})}; \; x \geq x_M^{(j)} + 2\sqrt{diag(S^{(j)})} \right\} \quad (12)$$

The inequalities can be understood as follows: $x = (x_1, x_2, \ldots, x_n)^T$ and $y = (y_1, y_2, \ldots, y_n)^T$, then $x < y$ if and only if $x_i < y_i$ for $i = 1, 2, \ldots, n$. The same form for $\leq$, $\geq$ and $>$ (J.A. Hernández and Ospina 2010).

For groups G_1, G_2 and G_3 the cardinalities are N_1, N_2 and N_3 respectively. In Fig. 3, an example of the evolution of the MAGO algorithm can be observed to find a solution.

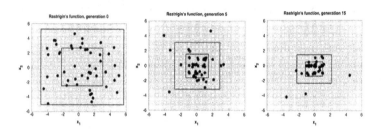

Fig. 3. (a) Generation 0, (b) Generation 5, (c) Generation 15 [4].

3   Case Studies

3.1   CPG R4A3 System

The CPG system selected for this case is the one developed in [3]. This model has four and two neurons as shown in Fig. 4.

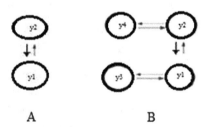

A   B

Fig. 4. (A) Two neurons CPG, (B) Four neurons CPG [3].

Equations (13)–(16) describe the network with four variables.

$$\frac{dy1}{dt} = \frac{1}{\tau 1}\left(-y1 + \frac{A(k1 - Dy2)^3}{(B + by3)^2 + (k1 - Dy2)^2}\right) \quad (13)$$

$$\frac{dy2}{dt} = \frac{1}{\tau 2}\left(-y2 + \frac{A(k2 - Dy1)^3}{(B + by4)^2 + (k2 - Dy1)^2}\right) \qquad (14)$$

$$\frac{dy3}{dt} = \frac{1}{\tau 3}\left(-y3 + Cy1^2\right) \qquad (15)$$

$$\frac{dy4}{dt} = \frac{1}{\tau 4}\left(-y4 + Cy2^2\right) \qquad (16)$$

This CPG system needs to estimate 11 parameters to obtain the desired results. These parameters are $A, B, C, D, b, \tau_1, \tau_2, \tau_3, \tau_4, k1, k2$. To find these parameters, the following procedure is currently used [3]:

- Choose random values for the parameters.
- Apply the Euler method to solve the system of equations.
- Apply a digital filter (Band Width of 10% cutoff frequency) to select the best combination of data.
- If the filter convolution is zero at all points on the curve, then return to step one.

The signals generated by this method of parameter estimation have a frequency close to the biological signals of locomotion. Some of these signals can be seen in Fig. 5.

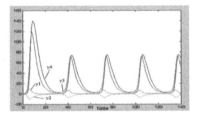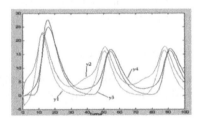

Fig. 5. Responses y1, y2, y3, y4: oscillatory movement of the recurrent neural network.

3.2 Van der Pol Oscillator

Dutch physicist and engineer Balthasar Van der Pol is known for his contributions with electrical circuits to reproduce oscillators such as the wind harp, a pneumatic hammer, the grinding of a knife on a plate, the fluttering of a flag in the wind, the buzz of a faucet, the recurrent recurrence of epidemics and economic crises. However, its most popular oscillator called the oscillator Van der Pol is born from the study of the heartbeat [6].

The Van der Pol oscillator is an oscillator with nonlinear damping and is described with the following homogeneous second order differential Eq. (17).

$$y'' - \mu(1 - y2)y' + y = 0 \qquad (17)$$

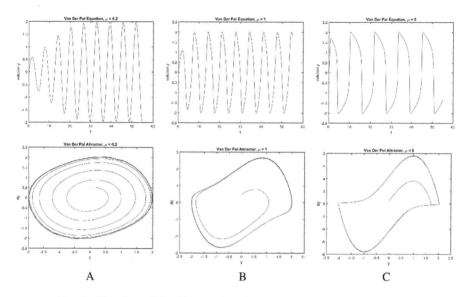

Fig. 6. Van der Pol Oscillator with: **(A)** $\mu = 0.2$, **(B)** $\mu = 1$ and **(C)** $\mu = 5$.

Where y is the dynamic variable and $\mu > 0$, data obtained by the physical characteristics of the circuit. Figure 6 shows the behavior of a Van der Pol oscillator in time,
with its respective attractor for $\mu = 0.2$, $\mu = 1$ and $\mu = 5$.

3.3   Bio Inspired Signals

The analysis of the locomotion of a horse in walking mode was made from an image
proposed by Muybridge [10]. This image has eight positions represented in Fig. 7, each
of which describes a certain angle for the joints: upper (Hip), middle (Knee) and lower
(Ankle).

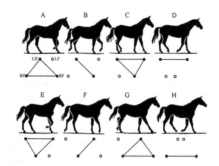

Fig. 7. Positions in locomotion of an equine.

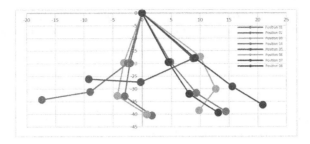

Fig. 8. Equine positions using vectors.

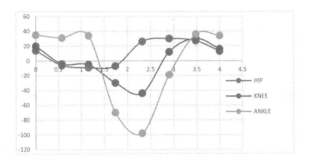

Fig. 9. Variation of angles in time.

Figure 8 shows the reproduction of the eight positions of the horse through the angles obtained and a fixed point for all positions.

Figure 9 shows the variation of the angles in time of the three joints of the horse to perform the locomotion.

4 Development

The evolutionary estimator is divided into two major processes. A coarse tuning in order to minimize the error between the desired signal and the estimated by a numerical error that affects the amplitude of the signals, together with a correlation optimization

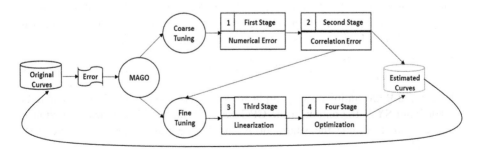

Fig. 10. Evolutionary estimation process.

that improves the frequency. A fine-tuning that minimizes the total error in amplitude and frequency between signals. In Fig. 10, the steps required to estimate the 11 parameters of the CPG system can be observed.

4.1 Coarse Tuning

First Stage. The objective functions (18), (19) and (20) have been tested to obtain a numerical error that allows an amplitude adjustment of the signals.

$$e_N = \sum y(i) - sy(i) \tag{18}$$

$$e_N = \sum (y(i) - sy(i))^2 \tag{19}$$

$$e_N = \sum |y(i) - sy(i)| \tag{20}$$

The objective function selected and with best results for this stage is defined by the calculation of a numerical error (e_N) by Eq. (21).

$$e_N = \sum |y(i) - sy(i)| \tag{21}$$

Where y is the desired signal, sy is one of the outputs of the CPG system, n is the number of points of the signals and $i = 1, 2, ..., n$.

Second Stage. The linear correlation value allows us to force the outputs of the CPG system to obtain a point-to-point linear relationship between the signals, i.e. by using the correlation the frequency of the signals can be adjusted. The function used is **corr** of the MATLAB software and the error equation used is (22).

$$e_C = 1 - (corr(y, sy))^2 \tag{22}$$

4.2 Fine-Tuning

Third Stage. When the first two stages of the evolutionary estimator (gross adjustment) are completed, a linear correlation value between the signals, equal to or greater than 0.8, is present. The two fine-tuning steps are then applied through Eq. (23) to minimize the error [5].

$$Y = A + B(SY) \tag{23}$$

Where A and B are additive and multiplicative constants. The signal Y is the one to be emulated and SY is the output of the CPG system with the 11 parameters previously estimated. To determine the values of A and B, the Eqs. (24) and (25) are used, respectively.

$$\overline{sy} = \sum sy_i$$

$$\bar{y} = \sum y_i$$

$$S_{SY}^2 = \sum sy_i^2$$

$$S_Y^2 = \sum y_i^2$$

$$S_{SYY} = \sum sy_i y_i$$

$$A = \bar{y} - B\overline{sy} \tag{24}$$

$$B = \frac{S_{SYY}}{S_{SY}^2} \tag{25}$$

Fourth Stage. At this stage, the values of the constants A and B of Eq. (23) are optimized by the objective function shown in (21). For this, the Eq. (26) is used.

$$Y = A1 + B1 * (A + B(SY))$$

$$Y = A1 + (A * B1) + (B * B1) * (SY)$$

$$Y = AT + BT(SY) \tag{26}$$

Where A1 and B1 are the new constants found by the MAGO algorithm and the original Eq. (23) has not been modified, thus maintaining the linear correlation condition.

5   Results

5.1   Evolutionary Estimation of the System CPG-R4A3

The original parameters used in the CPG system to generate four locomotion signals for an articulated quadruped robot, called (R4A3), are shown in Table 1. The result of the parameterization by the evolutionary estimation method presented in this paper and its respective output signals can be also observed [3].

With the finalization of the coarse tuning process, the eleven parameters of the CPG system are obtained and the linear correlation Eq. (26) is applied with the constants AT and BT to minimize the error between the signals. The resulting system is Eqs. (27)–(30).

$$Y1 = 0.1774 + 0.7988 * (SY1) \tag{27}$$

$$Y2 = -11.035 + 1.1183 * (SY2) \tag{28}$$

$$Y3 = -38.8613 + 1.9898 * (SY3) \qquad (29)$$

$$Y4 = -1.7573 + 2.2511 * (SY4) \qquad (30)$$

Where Y are the original CPG signals and SY are the estimated CPG signals. In Fig. 11 a comparison can be observed between: (A) normalized original CPG signal and (B) normalized estimated CPG signal.

Table 1. Original CPG signals and estimated CPG signals.

Parameters	Original CPG	Parameters	Estimated CPG
A=2.9415		A=1.9562	
B=5.3063		B=4.6021	
b=8.3242		b=9.826	
C=5.9749		C=2.7358	
D=3.3531		D=3.1845	
K1=2.9923		K1=6.5631	
K2=4.5259		K2=12.1197	
tao=4.2265		tao=2.8110	
tao2=3.5961		tao2=3.7794	
tao3=5.5832		tao3=9.3965	
tao4=7.4255		tao4=5.8328	

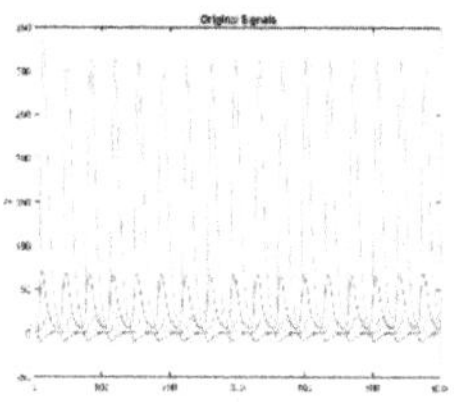

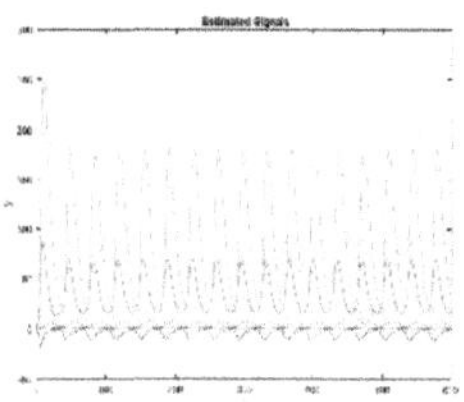

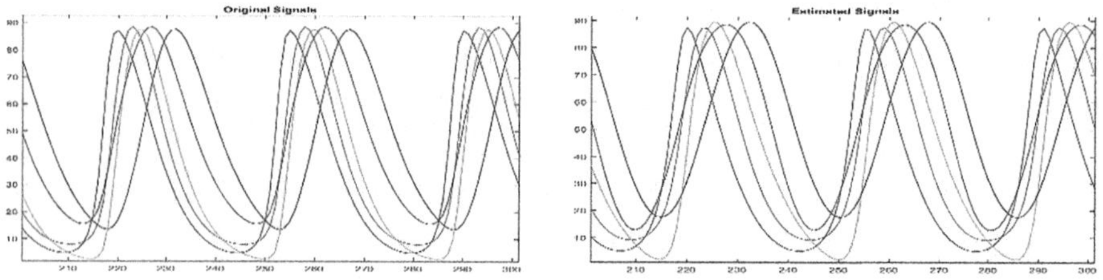

Fig. 11. (A) Normalized original CPG signal and (B) Normalized estimated CPG signal

Two types of indicators have been used to evaluate the functioning of the evolutionary estimator, the linear correlation index and an average error in amplitude. These values are shown in Table 2.

Table 2. Linear correlation index and an average error for system CPG R4A3.

Signal	Correlation index	Average error
Y1	0.9519	0.4781
Y2	0.9601	4.2645
Y3	0.9335	32.5
Y4	0.9524	0.1545

5.2   Van der Pol Oscillator

Figure 12 shows a signal of the Van der Pol oscillator with $\mu = 1$, and with an initial condition of [2; 0]; obtained by MATLAB commands.

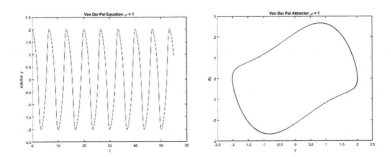

Fig. 12.   Oscillator and attractor Van der Pol with $\mu = 1$.

The evolutionary estimator is applied to generate a signal emulating the behavior of the Van der Pol oscillator and the results can be observed in Table 3. The linear correlation index and the average error are 0.9024 and 0.6065 respectively.

Table 3.   Estimated CPG to emulate oscillator Van der Pol.

Parameters	Evolutionary Estimation	Estimated Attractor
A=2.7217 B=9.4259 b=9.2975 C=3.5503 D=3.9449 K1=1.4909 K2=6.9013 tao=8.1895 tao2=4.2605 tao3=9.05 tao4=2.4054		
AT=-2.5195 BT=0.0252		

5.3   Evolutionary Identification of Bio-inspired Signals

Applying the proposed evolutionary estimator method the following results were obtained, Table 4, for the reproduction of the signals of the walking mode of a horse.

The blue color represents the bio-inspired signals in the locomotion of the horse and in green color are the outputs of the system CPG. Table 5 shows the linear correlation index and the average error in amplitude for bio-inspired signals in locomotion of a horse in walking mode.

Table 4. Evolutionary estimation of bio-inspired signals.

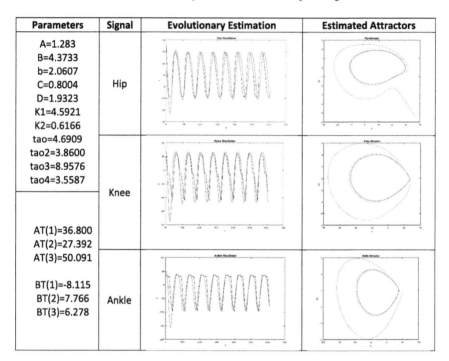

Parameters	Signal	Evolutionary Estimation	Estimated Attractors
A=1.283 B=4.3733 b=2.0607 C=0.8004 D=1.9323 K1=4.5921 K2=0.6166 tao=4.6909 tao2=3.8600 tao3=8.9576 tao4=3.5587	Hip		
	Knee		
AT(1)=36.800 AT(2)=27.392 AT(3)=50.091 BT(1)=-8.115 BT(2)=7.766 BT(3)=6.278	Ankle		

Table 5. Linear correlation index and an average error for bio-inspired signals.

Signal	Linear correlation	Average error
Hip	0.8061	6.9684
Knee	0.7985	12.9466
Ankle	0.7800	23.9836

6   Conclusion

- A method of evolutionary estimation that allows to find the best combination for the 11 parameters of the non-linear differential equations describing the articulated quadruped robotic system CPG-R4A3 was presented.
- It was verified that the course adjustment improves the difference in frequency among the signals; while fine adjustment improves the amplitude of the signals over time through the identification of constants A and B.

- The evolutionary estimator developed in this paper reproduced the behavior of a Van der Pol oscillator with a linear correlation error greater than 0.9. Confirming that the CPG-R4A3 equation system could reproduce any physical oscillator.
- It was shown that the evolutionary identification method emulates with remarkable fidelity the behavior of coupled nonlinear oscillators.
- For the coupled non-linear oscillator test cases shown herein, the differential equation system inspired in the CPG-R4A3 achieved a greater linear correlation index greater than 0.8 and an average error in amplitude less than 30.
- Future work is planned to extend the systems identification method developed in this paper for complex coupled nonlinear oscillators, such as limbs with three rotational joints.

References

1. Tran, D.T., Koo, I.M., Lee, Y.H., et al.: Central pattern generator based reflexive control of quadruped walking robots using a recurrent neural network. Robot. Auton. Syst. **62**, 1497–1516 (2014)
2. Uriostegui, U., Salvador, E., Hernández, T., et al.: Sincronización de un oscilador Van der Pol-duffing. In: XII Encuentro Participación de la Mujer en la Ciencia, pp. 1–4. León-Mexico (2015)
3. Rico, E.: Analysis and application of methods of displacement in articulated platforms based on CPG's (central pattern generator). Master thesis. Universidad Nacional de Colombia (2012)
4. Hernández, J., Ospina, J.: A multi dynamics algorithm for global optimization. Math. Comput. Model. **52**, 1271–1278 (2010)
5. Universidad Carlos III de Madrid. http://halweb.uc3m.es/esp/Personal/personas/jmmarin/esp/EDescrip/tema6.pdf. Accessed 9 Mar 2017
6. Hernández, S., Palencia, V.: El oscilador de Van Der Pol. Multidisciplina **5**, 93–102 (2011)
7. Fernández, I.: Fundamentos de sistemas dinámicos oscilatorios. In: XIX Verano de la Investigación Científica, Puebla (2009)
8. Mackay-Lyons, M.: Central pattern generation of locomotion: a review of the evidence. Phys. Ther. **82**, 69–83 (2002)
9. Kolda, G., Lewis, M., Torczon, V.: Optimization by direct search: new perspectives on some classical and modern methods. SIAM Rev. **45**, 385–482 (2003)
10. Muybridge, E.: Horses and Other Animals in Motion: 45 Classic Photographic Sequences. Courier Corporation, New York (1985)

Kernel-Based Machine Learning Models for the Prediction of Dengue and Chikungunya Morbidity in Colombia

William Caicedo-Torres[1]([✉]), Diana Montes-Grajales[2,3],
Wendy Miranda-Castro[2], Mary Fennix-Agudelo[2],
and Nicolas Agudelo-Herrera[4]

[1] Grupo de Investigación de Tecnologías Aplicadas y Sistemas de Información,
School of Engineering, Universidad Tecnológica de Bolívar,
Cartagena 130011, Colombia
wcaicedo@unitecnologica.edu.co
[2] Grupo de Investigación en Estudios Químicos y Biológicos, School of Basic
Sciences, Universidad Tecnológica de Bolívar, Cartagena 130011, Colombia
[3] Centro de Ciencias Genómicas, Universidad Nacional Autónoma de México,
565-A, Cuernavaca, Mexico
[4] School of Engineering, Universidad Tecnológica de Bolívar,
Cartagena 130011, Colombia

Abstract. Dengue and Chikungunya fever are two viral diseases of great public health concern in Colombia and other tropical countries as they are both transmitted by *Aedes* mosquitoes, which are endemic to this area. In recent years, there have been unprecedented outbreaks of these infections. Therefore, the development of computational models to forecast the number of cases based on available epidemiological data would benefit public surveillance health systems to take effective actions regarding the prevention and mitigation of these events. In this work, we present the application of machine learning algorithms to predict the morbidity dynamics of dengue and chikungunya in Colombia using time-series-forecasting methods. Available weekly incidence for dengue (2007–2016) and chikungunya (2014–2016) from the National Health Institute of Colombia was gathered and employed as input to generate and validate the models. Kernel Ridge Regression and Gaussian Processes were used at forecasting the number of cases of both diseases considering horizons of one and four weeks. In order to assess the performance of the algorithms, rolling-origin cross-validation was carried out, and the mean absolute percentage errors (MAPE), mean absolute errors (MAE), R^2 and the percentages of explained variance calculated for each model. Kernel Ridge regression with one-step ahead horizon was found to be superior to other models in forecasting both dengue and chikungunya number of cases per week. However, the power of prediction for dengue incidence was higher as there is more epidemiological data available for this disease compared to chikungunya. The results are promising and urge further research and development to achieve a tool which could be used by public health officials to manage more adequately the epidemiological dynamics of these diseases.

© Springer International Publishing AG 2017
A. Solano and H. Ordoñez (Eds.): CCC 2017, CCIS 735, pp. 472–484, 2017.
DOI: 10.1007/978-3-319-66562-7_34

Keywords: Machine learning · Forecasting · Dengue · Chikungunya · Kernel Ridge regression · Gaussian Processes

1   Introduction

Dengue and chikungunya are two infectious diseases with similar symptoms, caused by flaviviruses transmitted by the mosquitoes *Aedes aegypti* and *Aedes albopictus*, which are a public health problem in tropical and subtropical areas, affecting around 100 countries with current or potential spread [24, 26].

According to the World Health Organization (WHO), the statistics for the Americas in 2016 indicated a total of 2.38 million dengue cases, of which 103,822 were registered in Colombia; as well as 349,936 suspected and 146,914 laboratory confirmed chikungunya infections, of which Colombia reported 19,000 suspected cases [32, 33].

The predominant public health system strategy to prevent dengue and chikungunya is the vector control as an accessible and cost-effective alternative [12]. Currently, there is available a vaccine against dengue [10], and other candidates are being evaluated in medical trials [25, 28], but there are no specific therapeutics for these infections and treatments still rely in the management of the symptoms with analgesics and support therapy [15, 26, 31]. Therefore, it is an ongoing necessity to improve the outbreak alert system of these diseases to obtain reasonable estimates of the number of infected individuals in the future, to guide effective actions in reducing the number of cases per year [23, 29, 34].

Research in forecasting is generally based on space-time analysis, creating models that integrate clinical data in specific locations, such as [2], which implemented three models to forecast dengue outbreaks: a step-down linear regression, a generalized boosted regression, and a negative binomial regression to predict dengue incidence in Singapore and Bangkok; and [34] developed a prediction model for Sengalor, Malaysia, using Least Squares Support Vector Machines (LS-SVM). Regarding chikungunya, a data-driven empirical model using open-access tools and chikungunya cases data in the Americas was carried out, and results were improved as more data was made available for training [9].

Previous studies in the prediction of dengue incidence in Colombia have used geometric dynamics for national cases from 1990–2006, as a probabilistic random walk [21]; and intra and interseasonal weather-based descriptive models in Cali (Colombia) [8]. Reports for chikungunya morbidity prediction in Colombia have not been found.

Therefore, the aim of this work was to implement machine learning algorithms for the prediction the dengue and chikungunya morbidity dynamics in Colombia, as this area of artificial intelligence lead to detect complex patterns in a given dataset through the use of statistical, probabilistic and optimization techniques [7, 16, 27].

2   Materials and Methods

2.1   Dataset Construction

Epidemiological weekly data of dengue and chikungunya reported cases in Colombia from January 1, 2007–July 31, 2016, and January 1, 2014–July 31 2016, respectively, were gathered from the National Health Institute reports (http://www.ins.gov.co). A dataset was built and partitioned into training and validation subsets without preprocessing. Dengue training and rolling origin validation set includes 50% of the original data, and the remaining 50% was used on the test set. On the other hand, Chikungunya training and rolling origin validation set compromises 75% of the records, and 25% was used on test set [3].

2.2   Training and Validation

Training and validation of the models were carried out using Rolling Origin Update Cross Validation [11]. Forecasts were estimated for next week (One-Step-Ahead), and 4 weeks (Multi(h)-Step-Ahead with $h = 4$), the reason for these specific horizons being that one week is the maximum resolution in the dataset, and one month corresponds roughly to a month; with both being sensible choices for public health planning. Python 3.5 and the Scikit-learn 0.18 library [17] were used for the implementation of Kernel Ridge Regression and Gaussian Processes in the time series. Python code can be found at [1]. The measurement of models performance was carried out by mean absolute percentage error (MAPE), mean absolute error (MAE), R^2 and percentage of explained variance calculations.

2.3   Machine Learning Algorithms

In this article, we propose an autoregression model to predict the number of new cases of dengue and chikungunya to occur within a fixed time horizon in the future, using the number of cases observed in the last p time periods. This can be expressed as:

$$x_{t+h} = h(x_t, x_{t-1}, ..., x_{t-p}) \tag{1}$$

where h corresponds to our time horizon and $x_t, x_{t-1}, ..., x_{t-p}$ are the number of lags (past observations) to be used as input for the prediction model.

To find a suitable h we carry out experiments using two Machine Learning algorithms: Kernel Ridge Regression and Gaussian Processes [18,20]. A short description of these algorithms is presented in the following subsections.

Kernel Ridge Regression

Basic linear regression has been successfully adapted by penalization methods [13,14], and Ridge Regression refers to Linear Regression with a complexity penalty in its cost function in order to better approximate the out-of-sample error. The penalty term is the squared Euclidean (L2) norm of the parameter vector, which has the effect of shrinking the parameter magnitudes to reduce variance and improve prediction accuracy.

$$J(\theta) = \sum_{i=1}^{N} \left(\theta^T x_i - y_i\right)^2 + \alpha ||\theta||^2 \tag{2}$$

α is the regularization factor that controls the relative importance of the complexity penalty. Solving for optimal parameters involve finding the derivative of the cost function and causing some of this coefficient to be zero. According to this, the parameter vector that minimizes the error is:

$$\theta = \left(X^T X + \lambda I\right)^{-1} X^T y \tag{3}$$

Where

$$X$$

is the design matrix. New predictions can be calculated as follows:

$$h(x') = \theta^T x = \sum_{i=1}^{n} \theta_i x_i \tag{4}$$

Kernel Ridge regression works in a kernel induced feature space, where the original data is projected [20] without explicitly computing a possibly costly transformation [4,6]. For a lineal model, the transformation permits to adjust the data in a higher dimensional space, with regularization built-in. After algebraic manipulation, the optimal weights for Ridge Regression can be stated as

$$\theta = X^T \left(X X^T + \lambda I\right)^{-1} y \tag{5}$$

So, a prediction can be obtained by

$$h(x') = \theta^T x' = y^T \left(X X^T + \lambda I\right)^{-1} X x' \tag{6}$$

A Kernel function evaluates to a dot product of the form

$$f(x_1, x_2) = \phi(x_1) \cdot \phi(x_2) \tag{7}$$

Without explicitly computing the transform ϕ. If we define $K_{i,j} = f(x_i, x_j)$ and $k_i = f(x_i, x')$, were x_i is the i-th row of matrix X, then

$$h(x') = y^T (K + \lambda I)^{-1} k \tag{8}$$

We fitted a model in a higher dimensional space induced by ϕ without incurring in additional computational complexity. Several Kernels can be used, being popular choices the polynomial Kernel

$$k(x_1, x_2) = (\gamma x_1^T x_2 + \beta)(\delta) \tag{9}$$

Where γ and δ are a scaling coefficient and the degree of the polynomial respectively; and the Gaussian Kernel

$$k(x_1, x_2) = exp\left(-\frac{||x_1 - x_2||^2}{2\delta^2}\right) \tag{10}$$

Where δ controls the dispersion of the kernel. It is worth noting that the Gaussian Kernel induces an infinite dimension feature space [22].

Gaussian Processes

A gaussian process (GP) is a collection of random variables that have a joint Gaussian distribution, with any subset $x_1, ..., x_n$ of them also having a joint Gaussian distribution (consistency property). It can be seen as a generalization of the multivariate Gaussian probability distribution to infinite dimensions. As such, a GP can be used to describe a distribution over functions and perform inference directly in function space, using a finite set of observations. In this setting, each training target value can be considered as the mean of a Gaussian distribution which corresponds to one dimension of the GP [19].

A GP is completely characterized by a mean function $m(x) = \mathbf{E}[f(x)]$ and a covariance function $k(x, x') = \mathbf{E}[(m(x) - f(x))(m(x') - f(x'))]$. Function $k(x, x')$ controls the covariance in terms of how close to each other two examples are [30]. In this way the behavior of the functions can be specified, taking into account the data points from a training set, which in turn are used to infer the behavior of unseen data points and make predictions about them. The distribution over functions defined by the GP can then be written as

$$p(f(x), f(x')) = \mathcal{N}(\mu, \Sigma) \tag{11}$$

where

$$\mu = \begin{bmatrix} m(x) \\ m(x') \end{bmatrix} \tag{12}$$

and

$$\Sigma = \begin{bmatrix} k(x, x) & k(x, x') \\ k(x', x) & k(x', x') \end{bmatrix} \tag{13}$$

Different covariance functions can be used, being the squared exponential covariance function

$$cov(f(x), f(x')) = k(x, x') = exp(-\frac{1}{2}|x - x'|^2) \tag{14}$$

A popular choice. It can be shown that the use of a squared exponential covariance function is equivalent to Bayesian Linear Regression using a transformation $\phi(x)$ consisting of an infinite number of basis functions [5].

Using Bayes theorem, a predictive posterior distribution conditioned on the training data can be computed. Assuming the presence of noisy training data (noise is modeled as additive, independent and Gaussian distributed with variance δ_n^2), the form of the distribution is $\mathbf{f}_* | X, \mathbf{y}, X_* \sim \mathcal{N}(\bar{\mathbf{f}}_*, cov(\mathbf{f}_*))$ where

$$\bar{\mathbf{f}}_* = \mathbf{E}[\mathbf{f}_* | X, \mathbf{y}, X_*] = K(X_*, X)[K(X, X) + \delta_n^2 I]^{-1} \mathbf{y} \qquad (15)$$

and

$$cov(\mathbf{f}_*) = K(X_*, X_*) - K(X_*, X)[K(X, X) + \delta_n^2 I]^{-1} K(X, X_*) \qquad (16)$$

Here X_* represents the test inputs, f_* represents the predicted outputs for the test inputs, and $X, \mathbf{y}$ training inputs and training outputs, respectively. $K(X, X_*)$ represents the matrix of covariances evaluated at all pairs of training and test set points, with similar interpretation for the rest of appearances of K [19].

3 Results

Forecasting results for dengue in Colombia are presented in Table 1. Kernel Ridge regression was implemented with one-step ahead (Fig. 1) and four-step ahead (Fig. 2) horizons, using gamma and alpha values of 8.5×10^{-8} and 0.17 respectively. Grid search was used to find the optimal values. A one-step (Fig. 3) and 4-steps-ahead horizon Gaussian Processes models (Fig. 4) were also implemented, using the following kernels: C (Constant), RBF (Squared Exponential) and WhiteKernel (White noise).

Regarding chikungunya, time series forecasting for Colombia (Table 2) was also performed using Kernel Ridge regression and Gaussian processes, both with one-step (Figs. 5 and 6) and 4-steps-ahead (Figs. 7 and 8). Kernel Ridge Regression model used alpha = 5.0 and gamma = 1.0×10^{-15}, and GP implemented the following kernels: Matern, White noise, and Constant.

Table 1. Time series forecasting results for dengue in Colombia.

Algorithm	Horizon	Lag(s)	MAPE %	R^2	MAE	Explained variance
Kernel Ridge Regression	1-step-ahead	2	10.69	0.83	78.87	0.83
	4-step-ahead	3	18.31	0.62	132.62	0.62
Gaussian Processes	1-step-ahead	2	11.55	0.74	86.38	0.74
	4-step-ahead	2	18.55	0.61	135.01	0.61

4 Discussion

According to the time series forecasting results for dengue in Colombia, Kernel Ridge regression showed the best performance in the one-step ahead horizon prediction task (Fig. 1), as well as the lowest MAPE and MAE, and the highest R^2 and explained variance values compared to other models as shown in Table 1, fitting the tendency established by the real case data. Regarding

Table 2. Time series forecasting results for chikungunya in Colombia.

Algorithm	Horizon	Lag(s)	MAPE %	R^2	MAE	Explained Variance
Kernel Ridge Regression	1-step-ahead	3	25.96	0.49	48.34	0.52
	4-step-ahead	2	25.31	0.44	49.51	0.46
Gaussian Processes	1-step-ahead	5	27.20	0.37	51.17	0.44
	4-step-ahead	2	27.21	0.37	51.18	0.44

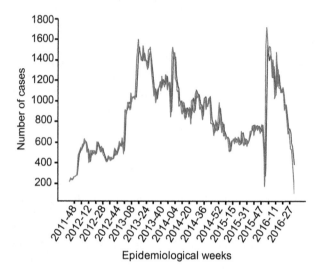

Fig. 1. Dengue test set results for Kernel Ridge Regression in Colombia, one-step-ahead (blue line) and observed results (orange line). (Color figure online)

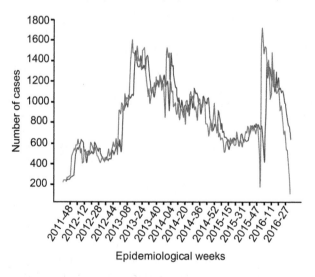

Fig. 2. Dengue test set results for Kernel Ridge Regression in Colombia, four-steps ahead (blue line) and observed results (orange line). (Color figure online)

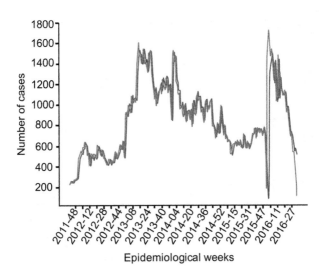

Fig. 3. Dengue test set results for Gaussian Processes in Colombia, one-step-ahead (blue line)and observed results (orange line). (Color figure online)

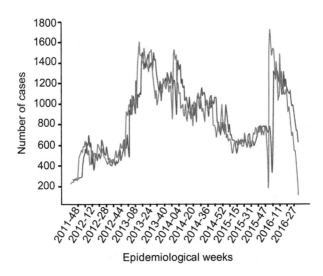

Fig. 4. Dengue test set results for Gaussian Processes in Colombia, four-steps ahead (blue line) and observed results (orange line). (Color figure online)

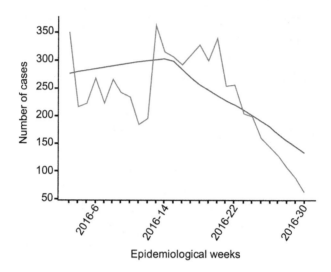

Fig. 5. Chikungunya Test set results for Kernel Ridge Regression in Colombia, one-step ahead (blue line) and observed results (orange line). (Color figure online)

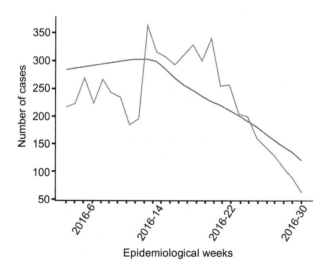

Fig. 6. Chikungunya test set results for Kernel Ridge Regression in Colombia, four-steps ahead (blue line) and observed results (orange line). (Color figure online)

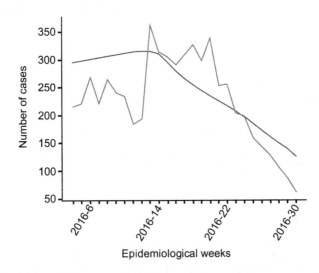

Fig. 7. Chikungunya test set results for Gaussian Processes in Colombia, one-step ahead (blue line) and observed results (orange line). (Color figure online)

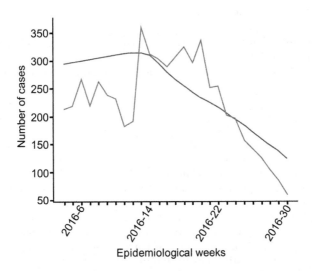

Fig. 8. Chikungunya test set results for Gaussian Processes in Colombia, four-steps ahead (blue line) and observed results (orange line). (Color figure online)

Gaussian processes, 1-step-ahead horizon model was slightly better than the 4-steps-ahead horizon (Figs. 3 and 4), which presented the highest values of MAPE and MAE, as well as the lowest R^2 and explained variance of the built models, resulting in higher gaps between weekly predictions.

On the other hand, chikungunya predictions were less accurate due to there are less epidemiological reports available compared to dengue. However, the models were able to predict the trend of the reported cases, both peaks and the current decrease of cases (Figs. 5, 6, 7 and 8); Therefore, an improvement in the power of prediction of the chikungunya models is expected when more epidemiological data are available to have a larger dataset. Similar to dengue forecasting, Kernel Ridge regression presented the best performance with one-step ahead horizon, with a MAE of 48.34, and the highest R^2 and explained variance (Table 2).

5   Conclusions

In general, Kernel Ridge regression presented the best performance with one-step ahead horizon for both dengue and chikungunya weakly morbidity predictions, the largest dataset offered the best performance and the test set results showed no evidence of overfitting. Then, more epidemiological data of chikungunya incidence is required for the improvement of the model. As we have shown, the implementation of Machine Learning algorithms to build forecasting models in the prediction of the incidence of dengue and chikungunya in Colombia results in a considerable option, since it could be useful in the development of an inexpensive application for the public health monitoring system.

Acknowledgments. The authors wish to thank the Universidad Tecnológica de Bolívar (Colombia) and Universidad Autónoma de México for their financial support (Grant: TRFCI-1P2016, D. M-G: Programa de Becas Posdoctorales en la UNAM 2016).

References

1. Morbidity prediction github repository (2017). https://github.com/williamcaicedo/morbidityPrediction. Accessed 25 Mar 2017
2. Althouse, B.M., Ng, Y.Y., Cummings, D.A.T.: Prediction of dengue incidence using search query surveillance. PLoS Negl. Trop. Dis. **5**(8), 1–7 (2011). http://dx.doi.org/10.1371
3. Caicedo-Torres, W., Payares, F.: A machine learning model for occupancy rates and demand forecasting in the hospitality industry. In: Montes-y-Gómez, M., Escalante, H.J., Segura, A., Murillo, J.D. (eds.) IBERAMIA 2016. LNCS, vol. 10022, pp. 201–211. Springer, Cham (2016). doi:10.1007/978-3-319-47955-2_17
4. Cawley, G.C., Talbot, N.L.C.: Reduced rank kernel ridge regression. Neural Process. Lett. **16**(3), 293–302 (2002). http://dx.doi.org/10.1023/A: 1021798002258
5. Chu, W., Ghahramani, Z.: Gaussian processes for ordinal regression. J. Mach. Learn. Res. **6**, 1019–1041 (2005)

6. Cortes, C., Vapnik, V.: Support-vector networks. Mach. Learn. **20**(3), 273–297 (1995). http://dx.doi.org/10.1007/BF00994018
7. Cruz, J.A., Wishart, D.S.: Applications of machine learning in cancer prediction and prognosis. Cancer Inform. **2**, 59–77 (2006). https://era.library.ualberta.ca/files/1v53jx76c/Cancer_Informatics_2_2007_59.pdf
8. Eastin, M.D., Delmelle, E., Casas, I., Wexler, J., Self, C.: Intra-and interseasonal autoregressive prediction of dengue outbreaks using local weather and regional climate for a tropical environment in colombia. Am. J. Trop. Med. Hyg. **91**(3), 598–610 (2014)
9. Escobar, L.E., Qiao, H., Peterson, A.T.: Forecasting chikungunya spread in the Americas via data-driven empirical approaches. Parasites Vectors **9**(1), 112 (2016). http://dx.doi.org/10.1186/s13071-016-1403-y
10. Flasche, S., Jit, M., Rodríguez-Barraquer, I., Coudeville, L., Recker, M., Koelle, K., Milne, G., Hladish, T.J., Perkins, T.A., Cummings, D.A., et al.: The long-term safety, public health impact, and cost-effectiveness of routine vaccination with a recombinant, live-attenuated dengue vaccine (dengvaxia): a model comparison study. PLoS Med. **13**(11), e1002181 (2016)
11. Gilliland, M., Sglavo, U., Tashman, L.: Business Forecasting: Practical Problems and Solutions. Wiley, Hoboken (2016). http://dx.doi.org/10.1002/9781119244592
12. Golding, N., Wilson, A.L., Moyes, C.L., Cano, J., Pigott, D.M., Velayudhan, R., Brooker, S.J., Smith, D.L., Hay, S.I., Lindsay, S.W.: Integrating vector control across diseases. BMC Med. **13**(1), 249 (2015). http://dx.doi.org/10.1186/s12916-015-0491-4
13. Hesterberg, T., Choi, N.H., Meier, L., Fraley, C., et al.: Least angle and 1 penalized regression: a review. Stat. Surv. **2**, 61–93 (2008)
14. Hoerl, A.E., Kennard, R.W.: Ridge regression: Biased estimation for nonorthogonal problems. Technometrics **42**(1), 80–86 (2000). http://amstat.tandfonline.com/doi/abs/10.1080/00401706.2000.10485983
15. Kucharz, E.J., Cebula-Byrska, I.: Chikungunya fever. Eur. J. Intern. Med. **23**(4), 325–329 (2012). http://www.sciencedirect.com/science/article/pii/S0953620512000337
16. Mair, C., Kadoda, G., Lefley, M., Phalp, K., Schofield, C., Shepperd, M., Webster, S.: An investigation of machine learning based prediction systems. J. Syst. Softw. **53**(1), 23–29 (2000). http://www.sciencedirect.com/science/article/pii/S0164121200000054
17. Pedregosa, F., Varoquaux, G., Gramfort, A., Michel, V., Thirion, B., Grisel, O., Blondel, M., Prettenhofer, P., Weiss, R., Dubourg, V., et al.: Scikit-learn: machine learning in python. J. Mach. Learn. Res. **12**, 2825–2830 (2011)
18. Rasmussen, C.E.: Gaussian Processes in Machine Learning, pp. 63–71. Springer, Heidelberg (2004). http://dx.doi.org/10.1007/978-3-540-28650-9_4
19. Rasmussen, C.E., Williams, C.K.: Gaussian Processes for Machine Learning. The MIT Press, Cambridge (2006). 2(3), 4
20. Robert, C.: Machine learning, a probabilistic perspective. CHANCE **27**(2), 62–63 (2014). http://dx.doi.org/10.1080/09332480.2014.914768
21. Rodríguez, J., Correa, C.: Predicción temporal de la epidemia de dengue en colombia: dinámica probabilista de la epidemia. Revista de Salud Pública **11**(3), 443–453 (2009). http://www.scielo.org.co/scielo.php?script=sci_arttext&pid=S0124-00642009000300013&nrm=iso
22. Schölkopf, B., Smola, A.J.: Learning with Kernels: Support Vector Machines, Regularization, Optimization, and Beyond. MIT press, Cambridge (2002)

23. Silawan, T., Singhasivanon, P., Kaewkungwal, J., Nimmanitya, S., Suwonkerd, W.: Temporal patterns and forecast of dengue infection in Northeastern Thailand. SE Asian J. Trop. Med. Public Health **39**(1), 90 (2008)

24. Simmons, C.P., Farrar, J.J., van Vinh Chau, N., Wills, B.: Dengue. N. Engl. J. Med. 366(15), 1423–1432 (2012). pMID: 22494122. http://dx.doi.org/10.1056/NEJMra1110265

25. Smalley, C., Erasmus, J.H., Chesson, C.B., Beasley, D.W.: Status of research and development of vaccines for chikungunya. Vaccine **34**(26), 2976–2981 (2016)

26. Solomon, T., Mallewa, M.: Dengue and other emerging flaviviruses. J. Infect. **42**(2), 104–115 (2001). http://www.sciencedirect.com/science/article/pii/S0163445301908023

27. Sutton, R.S.: Learning to predict by the methods of temporal differences. Mach. Learn. **3**(1), 9–44 (1988). http://dx.doi.org/10.1007/BF00115009

28. Vannice, K.S., Durbin, A., Hombach, J.: Status of vaccine research and development of vaccines for dengue. Vaccine **34**(26), 2934–2938 (2016)

29. Walker, T., Jeffries, C.L., Mansfield, K.L., Johnson, N.: Mosquito cell lines: history, isolation, availability and application to assess the threat of arboviral transmission in the united kingdom. Parasites Vectors **7**(1), 382 (2014). http://dx.doi.org/10.1186/1756-3305-7-382

30. Williams, C.K., Rasmussen, C.E.: Gaussian processes for regression. In: Advances in Neural Information Processing Systems, pp. 514–520 (1996)

31. World Health Organization: Dengue guidelines for diagnosis, treatment, prevention and control: new edition (2009). http://www.who.int/tdr/publications/documents/dengue-diagnosis.pdf?ua=1

32. World Health Organization: World health organization - dengue and severe dengue (2009). http://www.who.int/mediacentre/factsheets/fs117/en/. Accessed 25 March 2017

33. World Health Organization: World health organization - chikungunya (2017). http://www.who.int/mediacentre/factsheets/fs327/en/. Accessed 25 March 2017

34. Yusof, Y., Mustaffa, Z.: Dengue outbreak prediction: a least squares support vector machines approach. Int. J. Comput. Theory Eng. **3**(4), 489 (2011)

A Shallow Convolutional Neural Network Architecture for Open Domain Question Answering

Andrés Rosso-Mateus[1]([✉]), Fabio A. González[1], and Manuel Montes-y-Gómez[2]

[1] MindLab Research Group, Universidad Nacional de Colombia, Bogotá, Colombia
{aerossom,fagonzalezo}@unal.edu.co
[2] Computer Science Department, Instituto Nacional de Astrofísica,
Óptica y Electrónica, Puebla, Mexico
mmontesg@ccc.inoep.mx

Abstract. This paper addresses the problem of answering a question by choosing the best answer from a set of candidate text fragments. This task requires to identify and measure the semantical relationship between the question and the candidate answers. Unlike previous solutions to this problem based on deep neural networks with million of parameters, we present a novel convolutional neural network approach that despite having a simple architecture is able to capture the semantical relationships between terms in a generated similarity matrix. The method was systematically evaluated over two different standard data sets. The results show that our approach is competitive with state-of-the-art methods despite having a simpler and efficient architecture.

Keywords: Question answering · Information retrieval · Passage retrieval · Answer sentence selection · Answer ranking

1 Introduction

Next generation web search engines must understand user's information needs formulated in plain language, look for documents where the information resides and select an appropriate answer. The task of returning exact answers to natural language questions issued by users is a challenging task and takes an important place in the needs of user information access [4].

In general, the type of questions that users can pose define the approach that the system will use, for this reason, it is important to mention the type of questions that can be faced in question answering tasks. The following are two examples of popular question types:

– **Factoid Question:** Refers to the type of questions that drives to obtain an exact answer (fact) for a specific kind of question. For example, "Where Salma Hayek was born?", "In what month is temperature a maximum in New York?".

© Springer International Publishing AG 2017
A. Solano and H. Ordoñez (Eds.): CCC 2017, CCIS 735, pp. 485–494, 2017.
DOI: 10.1007/978-3-319-66562-7_35

– **Complex Questions:** This category corresponds to questions that can not be answered by a simple fact. This includes definitional questions, such as "Who is Bill Gates?"; entity definition questions, such as "What is RNA?"; list questions, such as "What are the bones of the human body".

Addressing the problem of automatic question answering involves different subproblems: question processing, document retrieval, passage retrieval, and answer extractions are the main ones [9]. In this paper, we address the problem of passage retrieval. This task takes as input a question the set of sentences {s1 , s2 , . . . sn}, and identify the sentence that is most related to the question.

The paper presents a novel method for passage retrieval based on neural networks. The neural network learn to predict the degree of relatedness of a question and a candidate answer pair by finding semantical relationships between question's and answer's terms. The model uses a small convolutional architecture to capture the most important correlations and return a matching probability that is used to rank the candidate answers, the simplicity of the model is represented in a low number of parameters (3,197) compared with the million of parameters of other machine learning methods for the same task [6,7].

The proposed method was validated using two standard public datasets: TrecQA Dataset [17] and WikiQA [21]. The method was compared to baseline and state-of-the-art methods using two information retrieval performance measures Mean Reciprocal Rank (MRR) and Mean Average Precision (MAP).

The paper is organized as follows. Section 2 presents the related work done in passage retrieval subtask and show some of the particularities and limitations of them. Section 3 shows the proposed architecture and the design decisions used in the approach. In Sect. 4 the experimental setup is detailed including the evaluation metrics and the dataset where the method is validated. Section 4.2 shows the results achieved by the method in the proposed datasets. Finally, we conclude our paper and discuss future work in Sect. 5.

2 Related Work

Most of the relevant methods in passage retrieval are ranked by Association for Computational Linguistics [1] using TrecQA Dataset [17]. In this rank, there are statistical models, deep learning models, pattern-based models and pure linguistic approach methods. We are going to check some of the most interesting methods and discuss its particularities.

Using the idea that questions can be generated based on correct answers, they propose a transformation model that send the question and answer to the same space and then compare how close they are [23], this method was replicated in this work and was used to compare the performance of out proposed model.

Heilman and Smith [8] represent the semantical relatedness of question-answer pairs, as a tree edit distance model and employed a tree kernel as a heuristic in a greedy search routine to extract the features from the sequences. Those sequences are then fed into a logistic regression as features to be classified as related or not.

Wang and Manning [18] proposed a probabilistic method that models tree-edit operations based on Conditional Random Fields. They treat alignments as structured latent variables that are learned as state transitions which allow incorporating a diverse set of arbitrarily overlapping features.

More recently, Yao et al. [22] based its method on Heilman and Smith's tree edit distance approach [8] but using dynamic programming to find the optimal sequences, also they take advantage of some WordNet semantic features to improve the performance.

One deep learning method was proposed by He and Lin [7] and was based on Bidirectional Long Short-Term Memory Networks that can capture the relation between sequences of terms of two sentences read in both directions (left-right and right-left). This new approach captures the interactions between terms and proposes a similarity focus layer that highlights the most relevant relations based on the weights related to each pair of terms.

Another deep learning approach was proposed by Yang et al. [20], they introduce an attention neural matching model for ranking short answer text. They adopt a value shared weighting scheme for incorporate term importance learning and in this way make the relevant terms more important than the others.

The most recent work of Rao, He and Lin [13] make use of Noise-Contrastive Estimation (NCE) modeling. Where the deep neural model should learn differentiable positive and negative samples in order to improve the ability of discriminate a good sample from its neighboring bad samples.

Nearly all of the recent works in this field make use of deep neural networks architectures, which brings an important generalization ability but with a huge number of parameters to be found. Our approach is relatively shallow compared with state of the art methods, but the performance is still competitive.

3   Model Description

The main assumption of the model presented in this paper is that the question and the answer are semantically related term by term, it means that the correlation between the question and the answer is given by the correlation between their component terms.

Figure 1 shows the overall architecture of the method. The method starts by generating a similarity matrix M, where the entry $M_{i,j}$ represents the semantic similarity of the i-th question term and the j-th answer term. The generated similarity matrix is weighted by a salience matrix that takes into account the syntactical function of terms.

A convolutional layer is applied over the weighted similarity matrix. Patterns identified by the convolutions are sub-sampled by a pooling layer. The output of the pooling layer feeds a fully-connected layer. Finally, the output of the model is generated by a sigmoid unit. This output may be interpreted as a degree of relatedness between the query and the answer.

In order to calculate the similarity matrix, we look for semantical relations term by term. We obtain the word2vec [12] vector representation for both terms (q_i, a_j) and measure their cosine similarity using the following equation.

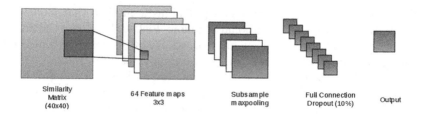

Similarity
Matrix
(40x40)

64 Feature maps
3x3

Subsample
maxpooling

Full Connection
Dropout (10%)

Output

Fig. 1. Convolutional neural network model architecture.

$$scos(q_i, a_j) = 0.5 + \frac{q_i \cdot a_j}{2 \, \|q_i\|_2 \, \|a_j\|_2} \qquad (1)$$

As not all terms are equally informative, we most weight the most salient terms in both question and answer. Based on the work done by Liu et al., and Dong et al. we give more importance to verb, noun and adjective terms [3,11].

This task is done by extracting the part-of-speech tagging information and if both terms are important the score is 1, if just one is important the score is 0.6 or 0.3 if none of them is important.

This yields the following salience function:

$$sal(q_i, a_j) = \begin{cases} 1 & if \; imp(q_i) + imp(a_j) = 2 \\ 0.6 & if \; imp(q_i) + imp(a_j) = 1 \\ 0.3 & if \; imp(q_i) + imp(a_j) = 0 \\ 0 & otherwise \end{cases} \qquad (2)$$

where $imp(t_k)$ is a indicator functions that returns 1 if the term is a verb, noun or adjective and 0 otherwise. Finally, the weighted similarity matrix is calculated as Eq. 3 shows.

$$M_{i,j} = scos(q_i, a_j) \circ sal(q_i, a_j), \qquad (3)$$

Where $\circ$ indicates the element-wise product of the matrices.

4   Experimental Evaluation

The goal of this section is to evaluate the performance of the model in two public question answering datasets. The experimental setup, as well as the results, are discussed in the following subsections.

4.1   Experimental Setup

The implementation was carried on with Keras and NLTK libraries. The code is available at Github[1].

---

[1] GitHub passage retrieval code https://github.com/andresrosso/passage_retrieval.

Test Datasets

- **TrecQA** was provided by Mengqiu Wang and collects data from the Text
  Retrieval Conference (TREC) QA track (8–13). It was first used in [19]. The
  dataset contains question and candidate answers selected from each questions
  document pool. The dataset has two partitions: TRAIN y TRAIN-ALL. In
  TRAIN partition the correctness of each answer was label manually while in
  TRAIN-ALL the correctness of candidate answer sentences was identified by
  regular expressions matching the answer. The last partition is much larger in
  a number of questions but noisier, the statistics of the referred dataset is in
  Table 1.
- **Wiki QA** is an open domain dataset released in 2015 by Microsoft research
  Group [21], that contains question-answer pairs. The Microsoft research group
  collected Bing Search Engine query logs and extract the questions the user
  submit from May of 2010 to July of 2011.
  As a quality indicator, the queries that were submitted by at least 5 users
  and that have a corresponding Wikipedia page were selected and introduced
  in the dataset.
  The answers were collected using the Wikipedia page related to the query
  and using every sentence of the summary section as candidate answer. The
  statistics of the dataset are presented in Table 2.

Table 1. TrecQA dataset

Split	#Questions	#Pairs
TRAIN ALL	1,229	53,417
TRAIN	94	4,718
DEV	82	1,148
TEST	95	1,517

Table 2. WikiQA dataset

Split	#Questions	#Pairs
TRAIN	2,118	20,358
DEV	296	2,716
TEST	633	6,156

Preprocessing. The text of both questions and answers was processed using
the following steps:

- Tokenization: Delimits the terms using the space and punctuations symbols.
- Lowercase: standardizes the terms lowercasing them. This is clearly important
  for the POS tagger which tends to tag most words that have a capital letter
  as a proper noun.
- POS tagging: NLTK pos-tagger is used to extract syntactical information [2].
- Word2vec Vector Representation: We use word2vec with the 300-dimensional
  GoogleNews trained model to represent each word [12].

It is important to mention that using stop word removal in question or answer
terms can cause the loss of important information, as for example wh-words,
verbs as "to be", etc. To avoid these extreme cases, we did not filter stop words.

Due to the variation in the sentence length, we had to limit the number of terms to calculate the similarity. The number of maximum terms was calculated adding one standard deviation (σ) to the mean (μ) of the number of terms.

$$max\_terms = \mu + \sigma \qquad (4)$$

So, for TrecQA the number of terms found was 36, and for WikiQA was 34. We use a maximum sentence length of 40 terms with zero padding.

Model Parameters. The model hyper-parameters were tunned using hyper-parameter exploration with cross-validation. The parameters chosen are listed next.

- **Convolution Parameters:** The number of convolutional filters used are 64, width 3 and length 3, the stride used is 1 without padding.
- **Convolution Activation Function:** After a convolutional layer, it is a convention to apply a nonlinear layer [5]. We choose a ReLU layer since it has been reported to have better performance in training without losing accuracy [16].
- **Pooling Layers:** For the pooling layer, we used max pooling.
- **Dropout Layer:** We add a dropout layer to help alleviate the overfitting problem [15]. The percentage of dropout was set to 10% since it produced the best results in cross-validation.

Sampling Strategy. WikiQA and TrecQA dataset are very unbalanced. Most of the question and answer pairs are not related (less than 10This may cause that the model is biased towards negative predictions. Therefore, it is essential to balance the dataset and we have alleviated the problem choosing randomly the same number of positive and negative samples in training and validation stage.

Model Training. The model training was done using rmsprop optimization algorithm with 256 samples in mini-batch. The number of maximum epochs was defined to 500, but as regularization strategy, we use early stopping with a patience value of 20 epochs, where the mean average precision (MAP) calculated over validation partition must be improved otherwise the learning is stopped.

Evaluation Metrics. We report two standard evaluation measures commonly used in IR and QA research: mean average precision (MAP) and mean reciprocal rank (MRR). All results are produced using the standard trec-eval tool. To calculate this performance measures we must define the metrics on which MAP and MRR are based on:

- **Precision:** Is calculated as the fraction of the documents retrieved, that are relevant based on the query posed.

$$P = \frac{|\{\text{relevant documents}\} \cap \{\text{retrieved documents}\}|}{|\{\text{retrieved documents}\}|} \qquad (5)$$

– **Average Precision:** This metric combine the precision and the recall metric, to give some importance to the order of retrieved documents.

$$AveP = \frac{\sum_{k=1}^{n}(P(k) \times rel(k))}{\text{number of relevant documents}} \quad (6)$$

$rel(k)$, an indicator function equaling

1, if the item at $rank_k$ is a relevant document

0, otherwise

– **Mean Average Precision:** Is the mean of the average precision scores for each query, over a set of Q querys.

$$MAP = \frac{\sum_{q=1}^{Q} AveP(q)}{Q} \quad (7)$$

– **Mean Reciprocal Rank:** Is a statistic measure for evaluating any process that produces a list of possible responses to a sample of queries, ordered by probability of correctness.

$$MRR = \frac{1}{|Q|} \sum_{i=1}^{|Q|} \frac{1}{rank_i} \quad (8)$$

$rank_i$, is the position of the first relevant document returned for the i query.

Baseline Models. We compare the performance of our method against three baselines models and some of the most remarkable methods in the state-of-the-art.

The baselines models implemented are Word Count, Weighted Word Count and a model proposed by Google Deepmind research team. The first method is based on counting the number of common non-stop-words that occur in the question and in the answer sentence, the second is a variation that re-weights the counts using semantical information [21]. The last one is a semantic parsing method that learns a distributed representation of the data [23].

Some state-of-the-art methods are also compared against our approach. Yang et al. [20] present an attention-based model that incorporates the term importance learned (aNMM). Severyn et al. [14] presents a deep convolutional method for ranking pairs of short texts, the objective is to learn an optimal representation of text pairs (CNN). He et al. presents a deep pairwise word interaction model for Semantic Similarity Measurement (Pairwise CNN) 2016 [7].

4.2   Results and Discussion

Table 3 summarizes the results for the TrecQA dataset and WikiQA dataset. In the case of TrecQA two configurations were evaluated: the TRAIN partition and the TRAIN ALL partition, which were described in Subsect. 4.1.

Table 3. Overview of results QA answer selection task datasets. We also include the results of the base line models. ('-' is Not Reported)

Method	TREC TRAIN ALL		TREC TRAIN		WikiQA	
	MAP	MRR	MAP	MRR	MAP	MRR
BaseLines						
Word count	0.6402	0.7021	0.6402	0.7021	0.4891	0.4924
Weighted word count	0.6512	0.7223	0.6512	0.7223	0.5099	0.5132
DeepMind model	0.6531	0.6885	0.6689	0.7091	0.5908	0.5951
aNMM [20]	0.7385	0.7995	0.7334	0.8020	-	-
CNN [14]	0.7459	0.8078	0.7329	0.7962	-	-
Pairwise CNN [7]	**0.7588**	**0.8219**	-	-	**0.7090**	**0.7234**
PV [10]	-	-	-	-	0.5110	0.5160
This work	0.7064	0.7947	**0.7367**	**0.8215**	0.6062	0.6171

In TrecQA the results reveal that our approach overcomes the baseline models and is very competitive with state-of-the-art methods. The proposed model performs better when the training is carried out with TRAIN partition, this could be explained because in TRAIN ALL the question-answer pairs are more noisy as was explained in Sect. 4.1.

The Mean Reciprocal Rank (MRR) score in TREC dataset is high, which is an evidence that our approach returns the correct answer in the first two positions.

In the case of the WikiQA dataset, the method with the highest score is Pairwise CNN [7], however the proposed method is still competitive with the baselines models. Compared with the rest of the state-of-the-art methods, the obtained scores are quite close to DeepMind model [23] and overcomes the result reported by Le and Mikolov [10] in distributed vector model.

The results in WikiQA dataset are not as good as in TREC dataset, the reason could be the small number of samples and the large number of negative samples in the last dataset.

The proposed model is simpler than state-of-the-art models [6,7]. In the proposed approach the number of parameters are in order of thousands while in state-of-the-art approaches are in order of millions as is reported in Table 4. A less complex computational model makes easier and faster training and evaluation stages.

Table 4. Number of parameters

Split	# of parameters
Multi-perspective CNN (2015) [6]	10.0 million
Pairwise CNN (2016) [7]	1.7 million
This work	**3,197**

5   Conclusion

This paper presents a low parametrized convolutional neural network for answer selection task, the method was tested in two of the most used question answering datasets: WikiQA and TrecQA. The method is based on a convolutional neural network to identify similarity patterns that are present in a calculated weighted cosine similarity matrix. Despite the simplicity of the architecture, the results show that our method is competitive with state-of-the-art methods. Trained with the trec 'TRAIN' partition is able to overcome the Pairwise CNN method [7], achieving the best results. The reduced number of parameters is an advantage of the proposed model which makes the training process computationally less costly.

As future work, we plan to explore the use of other linguistic features that can provide additional semantic relations between terms. The high mean reciprocal rank score obtained, reveals that the convolutional neural network is highly accurate identifying the most relevant candidate answer. This information can be used to make a re-ranking based on those relations in order to gain semantical information.

References

1. Association for Computational Linguistics — ACL: Question Answering (State of the art) (2007)
2. Bird, S.: NLTK: the natural language toolkit. In: Proceedings of the COLING/ACL on Interactive Presentation Sessions, pp. 69–72. Association for Computational Linguistics (2006)
3. Dong, L., Wei, F., Zhou, M., Xu, K.: Question answering over freebase with multi-column convolutional neural networks. In: ACL, vol. 1, pp. 260–269 (2015)
4. Etzioni, O.: Search needs a shake-up. Nature **476**(7358), 25–26 (2011)
5. Goodfellow, I., Bengio, Y., Courville, A.: Deep Learning. MIT Press, Cambridge (2016)
6. He, H., Gimpel, K., Lin, J.J.: Multi-perspective sentence similarity modeling with convolutional neural networks. In: EMNLP, pp. 1576–1586 (2015)
7. Hua, H., Lin, J.: Pairwise word interaction modeling with deep neural networks for semantic similarity measurement. In: Proceedings of NAACL-HLT, pp. 937–948 (2016)
8. Heilman, M., Smith, N.A.: Tree edit models for recognizing textual entailments, paraphrases, and answers to questions. In: Human Language Technologies, pp. 1011–1019. Association for Computational Linguistics (ACL) (2010)
9. Hirschman, L., Gaizauskas, R.: Natural language question answering: the view from here. Nat. Lang. Eng. **7**(04), 275–300 (2001)
10. Le, Q.V., Mikolov, T.: Distributed representations of sentences and documents. In: ICML, vol. 14, pp. 1188–1196 (2014)
11. Liu, F., Pennell, D., Liu, F., Liu, Y.: Unsupervised approaches for automatic keyword extraction using meeting transcripts. In: Proceedings of Human Language Technologies, pp. 620–628. Association for Computational Linguistics (ACL) (2009)

12. Mikolov, T., Chen, K., Corrado, G., Dean, J.: word2vec (2014)
13. Rao, J., He, H., Lin, J.: Noise-contrastive estimation for answer selection with deep neural networks. In: Proceedings of the 25th ACM, pp. 1913–1916. ACM (2016)
14. Severyn, A., Moschitti, A.: Learning to rank short text pairs with convolutional deep neural networks. In: Proceedings ACM SIGIR Conference, pp. 373–382. ACM (2015)
15. Srivastava, N., Hinton, G.E., Krizhevsky, A., Sutskever, I., Salakhutdinov, R.: Dropout: a simple way to prevent neural networks from overfitting. J. Mach. Learn. Res. **15**(1), 1929–1958 (2014)
16. Talathi, S.S., Vartak, A.: Improving performance of recurrent neural network with relu nonlinearity. CoRR, abs/1511.03771 (2015)
17. Wang, C., Kalyanpur, A., Boguraev, B.K.: Relation extraction and scoring in DeepQA. IBM J. Res. Dev. **56**(3), 9:1–9:12 (2012)
18. Wang, M., Manning, C.D.: Probabilistic tree-edit models with structured latent variables for textual entailment and question answering. In: ACL Proceedings, pp. 1164–1172. Association for Computational Linguistics (2010)
19. Wang, M., Smith, N.A., Mitamura, T.: What is the Jeopardy Model? A Quasi-Synchronous Grammar for QA, pp. 22–32, June 2007
20. Yang, L., Ai, Q., Guo, J., Croft, W.B.: aNNM: ranking short answer texts with attention-based neural matching model. In: Proceedings ACM, pp. 287–296. ACM (2016)
21. Yang, Y., Yih, W-T., Meek, C.: WikiQA: a challenge dataset for open-domain question answering. In: EMNLP, pp. 2013–2018. Citeseer (2015)
22. Yao, X., Van Durme, B., Callison-Burch, C., Clark, P.: Answer extraction as sequence tagging with tree edit distance. In: HLT-NAACL, pp. 858–867. Citeseer (2013)
23. Lei, Y., Hermann, K.M., Blunsom, P., Pulman, S.: Deep learning for answer sentence selection. In: NIPS Deep Learning Workshop (2014)

Analysis and Application of a Displacement CPG-Based Method on Articulated Frames

Edgar Mario Rico[1(✉)] and Jesus Antonio Hernandez[2]

[1] SENA, Medellín, Colombia
emrico@sena.edu.co
[2] Nacional University, Medellín, Colombia
jahernan@unal.edu.co

Abstract. The large evolution of robotics in the last 20 years has been developed with the great contribution of new techniques from computational intelligence, inspired in living things. They have changed the design of articulated artificial systems. The Central Pattern Generators were revealed in the 90′s as regulators of autonomous and rhythmic movements on fish, reptiles, birds and mammals. In this work, through recurrent and dynamical neural networks for the simulation and physical assembly of a quadruped robot with three joints per leg, the concept of Central Pattern Generators (CPG) is applied. A distributed autonomous control architecture based on modular and hierarchical CPG is designed and embedded in software systems. Five recurrent neural networks, organized in two layers, are simultaneously managed to generate signals, synchronize and execute the movement of each joint from each leg, and for the total movement production of different gaits. Successful autonomous decision-making results found for different gaits are shown.

Keywords: Robot motion · Legged locomotion · Neural networks · Gait recognition

1 Introduction

The robots which have been developed in the last decade mostly are designed to fulfill a specific, repetitive and predictable function. That is, they act in processes in which the control is supervised. However, there are still difficulties to perform certain characteristics and skills of living beings, and that so far it has not been possible to implement in robotics the intuitive control and voluntariness. According to Marvin Minsky this can be done through advanced techniques and procedures that are generated in artificial intelligence [1]. Thus, various investigations [2–8], have sought to work with similar systems from vertebrate beings in its physiognomy and functionality [34, 35] proposing articulated robots controlled by Central Pattern Generator (CPG). CPG are biological systems that vertebrate animals have in their spinal cord, capable of generating signals to produce voluntary rhythmic movements such as walking, flying, swimming and even involuntary movements such as heartbeat, eye blinking, etc. This approach is natural for the learning process in a robot. CPG eliminates the tedious detailed step by step programming of traditional cinematics used to train a robot for an action, mainly when

© Springer International Publishing AG 2017
A. Solano and H. Ordoñez (Eds.): CCC 2017, CCIS 735, pp. 495–510, 2017.
DOI: 10.1007/978-3-319-66562-7_36

the action is repetitive or rhythmic. A CPG could be developed for one leg and then could be replicated in the other three, reducing remarkably the effort from the analyst. Another CPG could be developed to coordinate the triggering of each leg. This is the method followed in this paper. Recurrent neural networks in continuous time (RNNCT) were used to represent the CPG. Five recurrent neural networks, organized in two layers, are simultaneously managed to generate signals, synchronizing and executing the movement of each joint from each leg, and for the total movement production. A distributed autonomous control architecture based on modular and hierarchical CPG is designed and embedded in software systems. In this work, the application of the biological method CPG with a new oscillator has been applied for quadruped loco-motion in articulated robots with 3 joints per member implementing the simulation and a physical structure to recreate a specific gait (walking).

The sections presented in this paper are ordered as follows:

- Biological processes in living organisms: Shows the different works biologists have done to determine models explaining the behavior of neurons.
- CPG models: different mathematical models used in the articulated robots are presented.
- Approaches of CPG to artificial locomotion: Presents the most relevant works of CPG in robotics in the last 10 years
- Design and implementation of CPG in a quadruped robot: the simulation results of the equation systems representing the CPG are shown.
- Control architecture with CPG: in this section, it describes the control signals used in the joint of the robot
- Construction and application of CPG in a robot: Consist in the implementation of the quadruped robotic system with three joints per leg is developed.
- Results: It presents dates about of locomotion of the walk.

2   Biological Processes in Living Beings

The central pattern generators (CPG) proposed by biologists A.H. Cohen, S. Rossignol, and S. Grillner [9], explains several motor actions that occur in animals, among which are simple reflex and involuntary movements, as the knee jerk and pupil dilation, with gradual response to a sensory stimulus classified as fixed action movements and invol-untary, such as orgasm and sneezing [10]. The studies in living beings have been focused on digestive rhythms, and movements of locomotion (land, water and air) [11–14].

3   CPG Models

The CPG in robotic systems are represented with recurrent neural networks in con-tinuous time (RNNCT) [2]. The RNNCT consist of ANN that have bidirectional connections between nodes (Fig. 1).

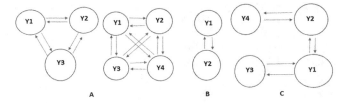

Fig. 1. (A) Structures of recurrent networks for CPG. (B) two neurons CPG. (C) four neurons CPG

The mathematical formulation of a recurrent neural network is represented by:

$$\tau_i \frac{dy}{dx} = -y_i + \sum_{j=1}^{M} w_{ji}\sigma(y_j + \theta_j) + I_i \qquad (1)$$

With i = 1...M

The state function of each neuron based on the Chiel-Beer model [15] is composed by: time constant (τ), weights of synaptic connections between neurons (w), operating point of each node (θ), transfer function of each neuron (σ), external input to the system (I). It is solved by Euler's method.

4   Approaches with CPG to Artificial Locomotion

The amphibious robot has developed using bio-inspired control models for locomotion, based in the Lamprey CPG models, developed by Ijspeert [4, 16] and which a control architecture based on CPG was implemented through a system of nonlinear oscillators [17]. Multiple studies on humanoid robot was developed using CPG in simulation and emulation based in oscillators [7, 17–19]. Biological and electrical experiments were developed by studying the CPGs [20, 28, 31]. In invertebrates such as mollusks, snails, turtles, snake among other signs of motor functions is studied and models that reproduce are presented [21–24]. Recent works is one implemented on locomotion of a fish robot by CPG with the control method of sensory feedback [29]. In quadruped robot system, the CPG on locomotion is applied for walk, trot and gallop [8, 25–27, 30].

5   Design and Implementation of CPG in a Quadruped Robot

5.1   Structure and Static Analysis of Robot

A quadruped structure is designed by CAD as in Fig. 2A. It should be noted that the robot is formed by four legs enclosed to a platform, and each leg has three joints, based on different prototypes [17, 24, 33].

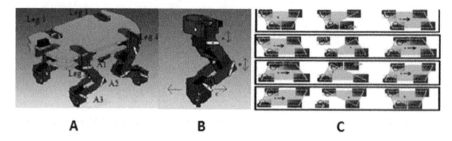

Fig. 2. (A) ObjectiÆve robotic system. (B) Displacement of joints. (C) Positions in the walk with static equilibrium for quadruped robots

If the robot is maintained in equilibrium, the projection of its center of gravity must be within the polygon formed by the supports and therefore the platform of robot [32] is stable (see Fig. 2C).

5.2   Generating Oscillating and Transient Signals

After a study of the different existing structures for the development of CPG, a model off our and two neurons was chosen (see Fig. 1B and 1C).

The network of the system of equations with 4 variables is described by Eqs. 2, 3, 4 and 5.

$$\tau_1 \frac{dy_1}{dt} = -y_1 + \frac{A(k_1 - Dy_2)^3}{(B + by_3)^2 + (k_1 - Dy_2)^2} \tag{2}$$

$$\tau_2 \frac{dy_2}{dt} = -y_2 + \frac{A(k_2 - Dy_1)^3}{(B + by_4)^2 + (k_2 - Dy_1)^2} \tag{3}$$

$$\tau_3 \frac{dy_3}{dt} = -y_3 + Cy_1^2 \tag{4}$$

$$\tau_4 \frac{dy_4}{dt} = -y_4 + Cy_2^2 \tag{5}$$

The Eqs. 6 and 7 are for the system of equations with 2 variables

$$\tau_1 \frac{dy_1}{dt} = -y_1 + \frac{A(k_1 - Dy_2)^2}{(k_1 + Dy_2)^2 + (k_1 + Dy_1)^4} \tag{6}$$

$$\tau_2 \frac{dy_2}{dt} = -y_2 + \frac{A(k_2 - Dy_1)^2}{(k_2 + Dy_1)^2 + (k_2 + Dy_2)^4} \tag{7}$$

5.3   Comparing the Model

Rayleigh Model:
Oscillator based on models of musical instruments, which is described in the Eq. 8.

$$m\ddot{x} + kx = \eta\dot{x} - \mu\dot{x}^3 \tag{8}$$

In [36] adapted the model in terms of humanoid joints, as in Eq. 9.

$$\ddot{\theta} - \varepsilon_l\left(1 - \ddot{\eta}_l\dot{\theta}_l\right)\dot{\theta}_l + \Omega_i^2(\theta_i - \theta_o) - \sum_{j=1}^{n} c_{i,j}(\theta_i - \theta_j) \tag{9}$$

$$\text{with } i = 1, 2, 3, \ldots\ldots, n, \text{ and } \varepsilon_i, \eta_i \geq 0$$

Adjusting with an analytical procedure the six parameters is an advantage of this model but a differential equation of second order requires more effort of computation than the model proposed here. The Rayleigh parameters present the form in Eqs. 10, 11, 12, 13, 14, and 15:

$$\eta_1 = \frac{4c_{1,2}(A_1 - A_2) + 4A_1\varepsilon_1 + A_3^2c_{1,3}}{12\omega^2 A_1^3\varepsilon_1} \tag{10}$$

$$\Omega_1 = 2\omega \tag{11}$$

$$\eta_2 = \frac{4c_{2,1}(A_2 - A_1) + A_2\varepsilon_2 + A_3^2c_{2,3}}{12\omega^2 A_2^3\varepsilon_2} \tag{12}$$

$$\Omega_2 = 2\omega \tag{13}$$

$$\eta_3 = \frac{4}{3\omega^2 A_3^2} \tag{14}$$

$$\Omega_3 = \omega \tag{15}$$

Matsuoka Model:
An oscillator model consisting of two conjointly neural inhibitors was proposed by Matsuoka [37]. Equations 16, 17 and 18 describe the Model.

$$\tau\dot{\mu}_{\{e,f\}i} = -\mu_{\{e,f\}i} + \omega_{fe}y_{\{f,e\}i} - \mu_0 + Feed_{\{e,f\}i} + \sum_{j=1}^{n}\omega_{ij}y_{\{e,f\}j} \tag{16}$$

$$y_{\{e,f\}i} = \max\left(\mu_{\{e,f\}i,0}\right) \tag{17}$$

$$\tau' \dot{v}_{\{ef\}i} = -v_{\{ef\}i} + y_{\{ef\}i} \tag{18}$$

The main inconvenience of this model is that it has multiple solutions to the same set of parameters (two equations with three unknowns). For its part, the model proposed here is a consistent system without dependence.

Amari-Hopfield Model:
The Amari-Hopfield model is compound by one excitatory neuron and one inhibitor neuron [38], with inhibition and excitation interconnections represented in the system of Eqs. 19 and 20:

$$\tau \dot{u} = -u + A f_\mu(u) - C f_\mu(v) + S_u(t) \tag{19}$$

$$\tau \dot{v} = -v + B f_\mu(u) - D f_\mu(v) + S_v(t) \tag{20}$$

Where f_μ is a transfer function.
The transfer function is presented in Eq. 21:

$$f_\mu(x) = \frac{1 + \tanh(\mu x)}{2} \tag{21}$$

Due to the use of trigonometric functions, this model generates a high computational cost at the time of solving the system of equations to reproduce the signals of the two neurons.

Spiking Neural Network Model:
The Spiking Neural Network (SNN) model is presented in [39, 40]. The SNN is a type of Artificial Neural Network where the timing of neural firing is the primary aspect of computation, due to the exchange of spiking events. The mathematical expression is presented in Eqs. 22, 23, 24 and 25.

$$u(t) = \sum_{t_0 \in f_0(t)} \eta(t - t_0) + \sum_i \sum_{t_i \in f_i(t)} \omega_i \epsilon(t - t_i - d_i) \tag{22}$$

$$f_0(t) = \{ t_0 | u(t_0) > \theta, t_0 < t \} \tag{23}$$

$$\eta(s) = -v \exp\left(\frac{-s}{\tau}\right) \mathcal{H}(s) \tag{24}$$

$$\epsilon(s) = \left[\exp\left(\frac{-s}{\tau_\mu}\right) - \exp\left(\frac{-s}{\tau_\sigma}\right) \right] \mathcal{H}(s) \tag{25}$$

Each neuron has two parameters. The parameters are weight and delay. The SNN uses 3 layers of neurons for locomotion of a biped robot (The input layer has ten neurons in terms of position and velocity. The hidden layer has ten neurons. The output layer has seven neurons in terms of position and angle of three joints). The SNN have 26 parameters of weights and delays with high cost of processing.

6 Control Architecture with CPG

The control system used in the robot is an open loop. It seeks to make a type of locomotion both in simulation and in real time with a flat hard surface. The architecture of distributed autonomous control based on CPG is designed in a modular and hierarchical approach. It is deployed on software for embedded systems. The operation scheme of the locomotion control (see Fig. 12) is presented below.

6.1 Stage: Advancing of Each Leg

6.1.1 Layer: Synchronization and Execution of Movement in Joints of Each Leg

For the synchronization of movements of the three joints from each leg, a four neurons recurrent neural network is applied. Each joint is controlled by a signal generated by each neuron (y2–A1, y3–A2, y4–A3), the fourth signal (y1), is employed as dead time to avoid the coincidence among a leg finishing the step and another beginning it. See Fig. 3B. As each leg will move separately, this disposition avoids a possible destabilization of the robot (See Fig. 3C). Each joint has the same system of differential equations through a microcontroller, i.e. the CPG used in each leg has the same parameters, what changes is the cyclic signal that guides each joint. To implement the coordinated movement in each leg, the differential equations system receives a command from the synchronization layer that simultaneously is received in the three joints for starting the four oscillating signals (Fig. 3A).

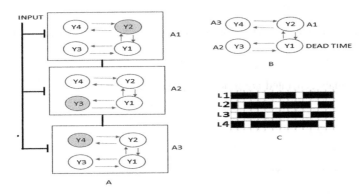

Fig. 3. (A) Representation of a leg in terms of a recurrent neural network. (B) Distribution of CPG signals in joints of a leg. (C) Diagram of support for each leg.

Each neuron generates a low frequency oscillatory signal (28 mHz, Fig. 4).

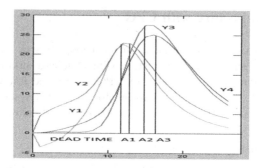

Fig. 4. Signals of control for the coordination layer, stage of advancing

6.1.2 Layer: Movement Coordination in Joints of Each Leg

The parameters of the recurrent neural network in this layer are new. Each signal (L1–y3, L2–y4, L3–y1, L4–y2, Fig. 5A) controls a leg. On the robot body, there is a controller with a cyclic recurrent neural network with parameters of different values to those defined in the coordination layer (Fig. 5B).

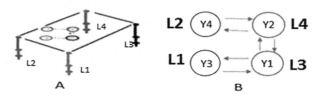

Fig. 5. (A) Distribution of signals in the coordination layer. Stage of advancing. (B) Distribution of CPG signals by leg

These signals generated are in low frequency (see Fig. 6).

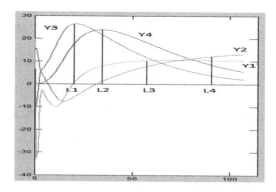

Fig. 6. Control signals of four legs

6.2   Stage: Repositioning (Returning to Initial Base Position)

Layer: synchronization

To end the cycle of the walk, the legs of the robot must be replaced in the starting position using the system of differential equations reproducing transient signals (with different parameter as above). A signal from the synchronization layer is simultaneously received by all joints to begin the execution of recurrent neural networks. This signal is an order of control for starting the returning to the initial position. In this case, the first transient signal is a dead time (y2) and the following signals correspond to the joint type A1 (signal y1) of all legs moving simultaneously, then joints type A2 (y4) moving simultaneously and finally the joints type A3 (y3) of all legs moving simultaneously (see Fig. 7).

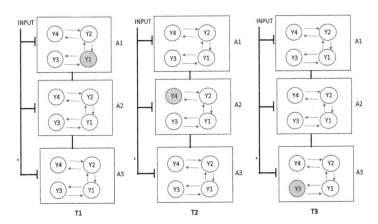

Fig. 7. Distribution of signals from the CPG in joints of the four legs.

Each neuron generates a transitory signal with stabilization time of 14 s.

These signals emulate orders of the coordination layer as typical of biological signals. In Fig. 8, the signals are intercepted by vertical lines. Each vertical line represents the response of each joint.

Layer of coordination

In order to place the robot on the starting position after the advance, a recurrent neural network of two neurons (Fig. 9B) starts to play from the last order of the recurrent neural network from the synchronization layer.

The first signal (y2) is taken as a dead time to ensure the implementation of the last leg advancing and the second signal (y1) is sent to all joints like rebooting order or excitement for running the neural networks of the coordination layer (Fig. 10) to bring the robot to the home position (Fig. 9A).

In this work, the criterion of maximum signal value is used, but could be the minimum value or the mean or the average, etc. Note that in Figs. 5, 7, 9 and 11, the signals are intercepted by vertical lines. Each vertical line represents the response of

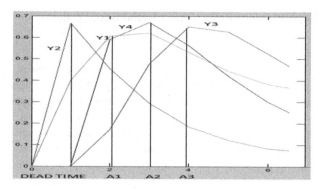

Fig. 8. Signals of control in the synchronization stage.

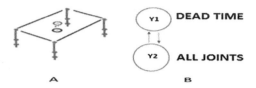

Fig. 9. (A) Order of repositioning, (B) Distribution of CPG signals for re-initiation

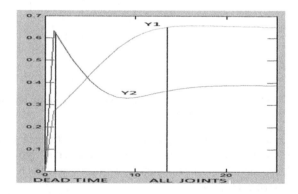

Fig. 10. Signals for repositioning; coordination layer.

each joint. Each neuron generates a transitory signal emulate orders of the coordination layer as typical of biological signals

6.3   Relation Between Order of Control and Angle of Operation of a Joint

In the timing diagrams, it can be inferred that the reproduced signals by the recurrent neural networks are a guide to determine the time of shooting or execution of the action of the joint (sweep angle with predetermined values).

7   Construction and Application of CPG in a Robot

The robot in its frame work (see Fig. 11) consists of a wooden structure, each leg has three joints, each joint has a servomotor as actuator, and a neural network embedded in a microcontroller. Additionally, there is in the body of the robot another neural network for coordination of leg.

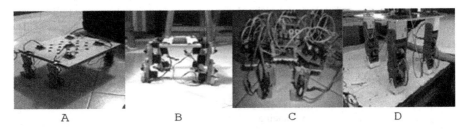

A   B   C   D

Fig. 11. Structure of the robot (A) initial release, (B) second version, (C) third version (D) final version

The application of CPG in the quadruped robot is developed by 4 recurrent neural networks (RNN) for the development of the locomotion of the walk as can be observed in Fig. 12. The coordination layer of the legs has a recurrent neural network for the advancement stage (RNN1), and a recurrent neural network for the repositioning stage (RNN2). The synchronization layer of the joints of each leg has a recurrent neural network for the advancement stage (RNN3) and a recurrent neural network for the repositioning stage (RNN4).

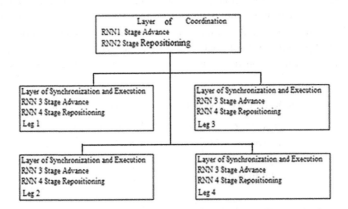

Fig. 12. General Setting of the CPG control scheme

Each joint has two recurrent neural networks (advance and repositioning) incorporated in a microcontroller and each micro-controller is connected to the microcontrollers of the joints that make up each leg, its function is the synchronization of movements and each leg is connected to a central device (Master microcontroller) responsible for the coordination of the legs using two recurrent neural networks (advance and repositioning).

8 Results

A series of data from the design and implementation of the quadruped robotic prototype (with modeled with the CPG architecture) in the type of locomotion called walking are presented on Tables 1, 2, and 3.

Table 1. Sweep angles (degrees) in joints

Stage	A1	A2	A3
Advancing	60	−60	−90
Repositioning	−60	60	90

According to biomechanics it has been proposed for each articulation of the robot a range of rotation depending on the stage in which the process of locomotion is. Note that Table 1 shows the sweep angles regarding the perpendicular to the floor surface. Therefore, it represents the set of angles used in the two stages required for locomotion of the walking mode. Note that A1 is the hip, A2 is the knee and A3 is the ankle.

The defined angles for the locomotion of the walk were previously established from simulation, also the description of the movement of locomotion presented from biomechanics and technological restrictions in the prototype of the quadruped robot.

Table 2 shows the times of a walking cycle in terms of the advancing and repositioning stages. The coordination and synchronization layers of the system control operating are in function of the behavior of the robot. The synchronization layer corresponds to the movement of the joints of each leg and the coordination layer corresponds to the movement of each leg, where the synchronization movements are immersed in the coordination movement.

Table 2. Execution time (sec) of displacement cycle

Stage/layer	Coordination	Synchronization
Advancing	6	1.5
Repositioning	2	1
Total time by cycle		8

The cycle of movement of the walking mode in the quadruped robot consists of the individual movement of each leg added to the joints movement of each leg. The total time for the execution of a cycle is 8 s corresponding to six seconds in the advancing plus two seconds in the repositioning.

Table 3 presents the travel distance in the stages of advancing and repositioning, produced by the synchronization and coordination of the legs of the robot. The forwarding movement of each leg and the movement of the body forward are combined to produce a cycle in the locomotion of the walk.

Table 3. Travel length (cm) of a displacement cycle

Stage/Layer	Coordination and synchronization
Advance	0.66
Repositioning	0.05
Total displacement cycle	0.71

The movement of the robot in the locomotion of the walk is of 0.71 cm. This is the minimum displacement distance of the robot performed in each cycle of movement. The cycle of movement is executed under the certainty of not having problems of losing balance or overturn tendency. The movements of both the body and the legs are performed in static equilibrium during the locomotion of the walk.

8.1   Discussion

A series of simulation results with the Rayleigh model as an oscillator for CPG obtained typical signals similarly the biological signals in [36]. However, no results of the locomotion of the bipedal walking as focused on the project are presented. The application approach is of prosthesis movement control.

In [37] the simulation results and a physical development with oscillators for CPG under the Matsuoka model have been applied to a quadruped robot. The type of locomotion used is the trot. The implementation of control for each joint was based on external computer systems connected to their respective actuators.

In [38] the simulation results on the Amari-Hopfield model as oscillators to assemble CPG are viable. The Amari-Hopfield model was used to generate cyclic patterns for the locomotion of the walking of a robot. However, the article does not have results of implementation about the control system in a prototype.

In [39], it was proposed the application of Spiking Neural Networks as a new option to solve robot control problems such as locomotion from a machine learning perspective. In a bipedal robot simulator, the Spiking Neural Networks technique is applied, seeking the learning of locomotion. The learning procedure uses as strategy the evolutionary algorithms. The strategy consists of multiple iterations to perfect the displacement response of the bipedal robot.

In summary, none of the publications have concrete results beyond showing the typical characteristics of biological signals of motor functions. Only [37] presents concrete results in the type of locomotion called trot. Therefore, in general terms, it is not possible to make a quantitative analysis of performance among the different works found in the literature.

In addition, the present work presents a new system of ordinary differential equations as the oscillator system. The behavior of the oscillator is like the signals of biological motor functions. The locomotion is established with predetermined angles per articulation for the specific development of the walking according to biomechanics.

9 Conclusion

The control system based on CPG is distributed, i.e. each joint has its specific task to perform and has a synchronizing element, which means that it permits multiple control devices simultaneously.

The programming code used to emulate the CPG is in blocks, meaning that it does not depend on hardware, as it is noted in the synchronization layer.

In terms of synchrony and execution of movements, in the event of changes of robot motion, with the CPG architecture only the control action must change, i.e. the PWM sent to the actuator.

When implementing a programming code based on CPG to perform a specific function, even if the robot motion is more complex, the operating frequency remains the same since the signal |processing related to the actuators is performed in parallel.

References

1. Gutiérrez, C., Castro, M.: Why do people think that computers cannot. Revista Informática y Sociedad, San José, Costa Rica, pp. 645–680 (1987). (in Spanish)
2. Fuentes, C., de la Cruz, J.: Generator of walking modes for quadruped robots based on neurophysiological principles. M.Sc. Thesis. Universidad Simón Bolívar (2006). (in Spanish)
3. Buchli, J., Ijspeert, A.J.: Distributed central pattern generator model for robotics application based on phase sensitivity analysis. In: Ijspeert, A.J., Murata, M., Wakamiya, N. (eds.) BioADIT 2004. LNCS, vol. 3141, pp. 333–349. Springer, Heidelberg (2004). doi:10.1007/978-3-540-27835-1_25
4. Crespi, A., Ijspeert, A.J.: AmphiBot II: an amphibious snake robot that crawls and swims using a central pattern generator. In: 9th International Conference on Climbing and Walking Robots, vol. 50, pp. 19–27 (2006)
5. Zhao, W., Hu, Y., Wang, L.: Construction and central pattern generator-based control of a flipper-actuated turtle-like underwater robot. Adv. Robot. **23**, 19–43 (2009)
6. Inada, H., Ishii, K.: A bipedal walk using central pattern generator (CPG). In: 1st Meeting Entitled Brain, IT, vol. 1269, pp. 185–188 (2004)
7. Huang, W., Chew, C.-M., Hong, G.-S.: Coordination in CPG and its application on bipedal walking. In: IEEE Conference on Robotics, Automation and Mechatronics, pp. 450–455 (2008)
8. Cappelletto, J., Estévez, P., Grieco, J.C., Medina-Meléndez, W., Fernández-López, G.: Gait synthesis in legged robot locomotion using a CPG-based model. In: Bio Inspiration and Robotics: Walking and Climbing Robots, Vienna, pp. 227–246 (2007)
9. Cohen, A.H., Rossignol, S., Grillner, S.: Neural Control of Rhythmic Movements in Vertebrate, p. 500. Wiley, Great Britain (1989)
10. Hooper, S.L.: Central Pattern Generators. Ohio University, Athens, Ohio, USA (2001)

11. Taylor, A.L., Goaillard, J.-M., Marder, E.: How multiple conductances determine electrophysiological properties in a multi compartment model. J. Neurosci. **29**, 5573–5586 (2009)
12. Prinz, A.A., Billimoria, C.P., Marder, E.: Alternative to hand-tuning conductance-based models: construction and analysis of databases of model neurons. J. Neurophysiol. **90**, 3998–4015 (2003)
13. Maufroy, C., Kimura, H., Takase, K.: Towards a general neural controller for 3D quadrupedal locomotion. In: SICE Annual Conference, Japan, August 2008
14. Ijspeert, A.J.: Central pattern generators for locomotion control in animals and robots: a review. Prepr. Neural Networks. **21**(4), 642–653 (2008)
15. Bower, J.M., Beeman, D.: The Book of Genesis. Springer, New York (2003). Chap. 8
16. Crespi, A., Badertscher, A., Guignard, A., Ijspeert, A.J.: AmphiBot I: an amphibious snake-like robot. Robot. Auton. Syst. **50**, 163–175 (2005)
17. Inada, H., Ishii, K.: Behavior generation of bipedal robot using central pattern generator (CPG). In: IEEE/RSJ International Conference on Intelligent Robots and Systems (IROS), vol. 4, pp. 27–31 (2003)
18. Or, J.: A control system for a flexible spine belly-dancing humanoid. Artif. Life **12**, 63–87 (2006)
19. Inada, H., Ishii, K.A.: Bipedal walk using central pattern generator (CPG). In: 1st Meeting Entitled Brain, IT, vol. 1269, pp. 185–188 (2004)
20. Vogelstein, R., Tenore, F., Etienne-Cummings, R., Lewis, M., Cohen, A.: Dynamic control of the central pattern generator for locomotion. Biol. Cybern. **95**, 555–566 (2006)
21. Huerta, R., Varona, P., Rabinovich, M., Abarbanel, H.: Topology selection by chaotic neurons of a pyloric central pattern generator. Biol. Cybern. **84**, L1–L8 (2001)
22. Vavoulis, D., Straub, V., Kemenes, I., Kemenes, G., Feng, J., Benjamin, P.: Dynamic control of a central pattern generator circuit: a computational model of the snail feeding network. Eur. J. Neurosci. **25**, 2805–2818 (2007)
23. Gonzalez-Gomez, J., Zhang, H., Boemo, E.: Locomotion principles of 1D topology pitch and pitch-yaw-connecting modular robots. In: Habib, M.K. (ed.) Bioinspiration and Robotics Walking and Climbing Robots (2007). ISBN 978-3-902613-15-8, InTech. http://www.intechopen.com/books/bioinspiration_and_robotics_walking_and_climbing_robots/locomotion_princIples_of_1d_topology_pitch_and_pitch-yaw-connecting_modular_robots
24. Matsuo, T., Ishii, K.A.: CPG control system for a modular type mobile robot. In: 3rd International Conference on Brain-Inspired Information Technology "BrainIT 2006", vol. 1301, pp. 206–209 (2006)
25. Ishii, T., Masakado, S., Ishii, K.: Locomotion of a quadruped robot using CPG. In: IEEE International Joint Conference on Neural Networks, vol. 4, pp. 25–29 (2004)
26. Fujii, A., Saito, N., Nakahira, K., Ishiguro, A., Eggenberger, P.: Generation of an adaptive controller CPG for a quadruped robot with neuromodulation mechanism. In: IEEE/RSJ International Conference on Intelligent Robots and Systems, vol. 30, pp. 619–2624 (2002)
27. Sun, L., Meng, M.Q.-H., Chen, W., Liang, H., Mei, T.: Design of quadruped robot based CPG and fuzzy neural network. In: IEEE International Conference on Automation and Logistics, pp. 2403–2408 (2007)
28. Ramírez, M., David, F.: Computational model modulating sensorimotor transformation. Ph. D. thesis in Physics. Universidad del Valle, Cali, Colombia (2006). (in Spanish)
29. Wang, M., Yu, J., Tan, M., Zhang, G.: A CPG-based sensory feedback control method for robotic fish locomotion. In: 30th Chinese Control Conference, July 2011
30. Liu, C., Chen, Q., Xu, T.: Locomotion control of quadruped robots based on central pattern generators. In: 8th World Congress on Intelligent Control and Automation, pp. 1167–1172, June 2011

31. Oliveira, M., Santos, C.P., Costa, L., Matos, V., Ferreira, M.: Multi-objective parameter CPG optimization for gait generation of a quadruped robot considering behavioral diversity. In: IEEE/RSJ International Conference on Intelligent Robots and Systems, pp. 2286–2291, September 2011
32. Katie, B., Alec, S., Sam, P., Roy, N., Tedrake, R.: Reliable dynamic motions for a stiff quadruped. tracts. Adv. Robot. **54**, 319–328 (2009)
33. Betancourt, H.J.L.: Lever mechanism design assisted by computer. Revista Ingeniería Mecánica, Habana, vol. 4, no 3, pp. 35–39 (2001). (in Spanish)
34. Pinto, C., Golubitsky, M.: Central pattern generators for bipedal locomotion. Math. Biol. **53**, 474–489 (2006)
35. Jiménez-Estrada, I.: Locomotion in vertebrates. Elementos 31, 28 (1998)
36. Nandi, G.C., Ijspeert, A.J., Chakraborty, P., Nandi, A.: Development of adaptive modular active leg (AMAL) using bipedal robotics technology. Robot. Auton. Syst. **57**, 603–616 (2009)
37. Fukuoka, Y., Kimura, H., Cohen, A.H.: Adaptive dynamic walking of a quadruped robot on irregular terrain based on biological concepts. Int. J. Robot. Res. **22**(3–4), 187–202 (2003)
38. Nakada, K., Asai, T., Amemiya, Y.: An analog current-mode CMOS implementation of central pattern generator for robot locomotion. In: Proceedings of the 2nd International Symposium on Adaptive Motion of Animals and Machines, Kyoto, Japan, March 2003
39. Wiklendt, L.: Spiking Neural Networks for Robot Locomotion Control, Ph.D. thesis, Computer Sciences, The University of Newcastle (2014)
40. Kasabov, N., et al.: NeuCube: a spiking neural network architecture for mapping, learning and understanding of spatio-temporal brain data. Neural Netw. **52**, 62–76 (2014)

Analysis of Motor Imaginary BCI Within Multi-environment Scenarios Using a Mixture of Classifiers

M. Ortega-Adarme[1], M. Moreno-Revelo[1], D.H. Peluffo-Ordoñez[2],
D. Marín Castrillon[3], A.E. Castro-Ospina[3], and M.A. Becerra[4(✉)]

[1] Universidad de Nariño, Pasto, Colombia
[2] Universidad Técnica del Norte, Ibarra, Ecuador
[3] Instituto Tecnológico Metropolitano, Medellín, Colombia
[4] Institución Universitaria Salazar y Herrera, Medellín, Colombia
mabel12-02@udenar.edu.co

Abstract. Brain-computer interface (BCI) is a system that provides communication between human beings and machines through an analysis of human brain neural activity. Several studies on BCI systems have been carried out in controlled environments, however, a functional BCI should be able to achieve an adequate performance in real environments. This paper presents a comparative study on alternative classification options to analyze motor imaginary BCI within multi-environment real scenarios based on mixtures of classifiers. The proposed methodology is as follows: The imaginary movement detection is carried out by means of feature extraction and classification, in the first stage; feature set is obtained from wavelet transform, empirical mode decomposition, entropy, variance and rates between minimum and maximum, in the second stage, where several classifier combinations are applied. The system is validated using a database, which was constructed using the Emotiv Epoc+ with 14 channels of electroencephalography (EEG) signals. These were acquired from three subject in 3 different environments with the presence and absence of disturbances. According to the different effects of the disturbances analyzed in the three environments, the performance of the mixture of classifiers presented better results when compared to the individual classifiers, making it possible to provide guidelines for choosing the appropriate classification algorithm to incorporate into a BCI system.

Keywords: Brain-computer interface · Environments · Mixture of classifiers · Signal processing

1 Introduction

BCI is a hardware and software communication system that enables humans to interact with their surroundings, without the involvement of peripheral nerves and muscles, by using control signals generated from electroencephalographic activity [1] for relaying intentions of a person to external devices such as computers, speech synthesizers, assistive appliances, and neural prostheses [2–4]. BCI systems are considered as a

© Springer International Publishing AG 2017
A. Solano and H. Ordoñez (Eds.): CCC 2017, CCIS 735, pp. 511–523, 2017.
DOI: 10.1007/978-3-319-66562-7_37

promising tool for gaming, brain-state monitoring, rehabilitation of people who are totally paralyzed or "locked in" by neurological neuromuscular disorders, and individuals with severe disabilities or neurological disorders [5, 6], which decrease cost of intensive care [1]. The typical BCI system is comprised of five main parts as shown Fig. 1, and it is explained in [7, 8].

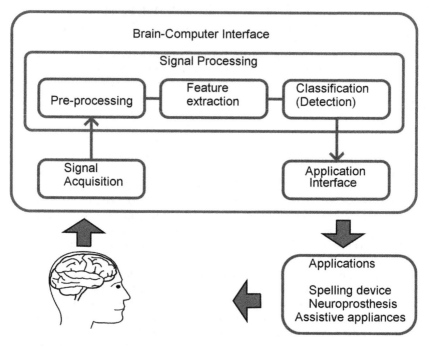

Fig. 1. Illustration of a typical BCI system [9]. This system is composed of five main parts; signal acquisition, preprocessing, feature extraction, classification and control interface.

In most existing BCI, the identification relies on a classification algorithm. Due to the rapidly growing interest for EEG-based BCI, a considerable number of published results are related to the investigation and evaluation of classification algorithms [10, 11]. Actually, the major studies of BCI systems are developed in controlled environments (CE), some of them are focused on the needs of communication and environmental interaction in order to improve the functionality with different applications showing no significant reduction respect to usability which is discussed in [12], and others are analyzed in different effects such as shown in [13], which analyze music under sound stimuli, which demonstrated positive results. However, studies of BCI in real environment are few and the results can be considered as low in term of accuracy such as discussed in [14]. Therefore, with the aim to get more advantages with the BCI development, it is recommended to take into account and to compare controlled environments and those with different disturbances that include environments that cause stress on the patients, for example, urban environments as well as peaceful situations such as rural environment (RE), because there are real conditions in which the individual interacts.

In this paper, we compare the performance of individual classifiers and several combinations of them for detecting imagination motion of right and left hand. A set of features were used as inputs for classifiers. The features were obtained from statistical measures of results of Discrete Wavelet transform (DWT) and Empirical Mode Decomposition (EMD) calculated on EEG signals. The database was constructed using the Emotiv-Epoc+ with 14 channels of EEG signals. This database recorded electroencephalography signals while the participants performed imagination motion of right and left hand. The signals were acquired from three subjects in 3 different environments with the presence and absence of disturbances as follows: Controlled, Rural, and Urban. The above allows to achieve an adequate strategy for the design of a BCI system in different real environments.

The rest of this paper is structured as follows: Sect. 2 describes the proposed methodology. Section 3 presents the proposed experimental setup. Results and discussion are gathered in Sect. 4. Finally, some concluding remarks and future works are drawn in Sect. 5.

2 Materials and Methods

2.1 Discrete Wavelet Transform

The DWT subdivides a signal into its frequency bands without temporal information loss. This time-frequency decomposition generates two sets of basic functions, i.e. wavelets and scaling functions. Mathematically, DWT can be seen as a set of wavelet transform coefficients, and computed as inner product between a wavelet basis and a finite-length sequence of the signal. These allow to analyze the spectrum of the signals as function of time [15]. Additionally, the DWT is also known as a filter bank due to the application of high-pass and low pass filters to the EEG, ECG, EMG time series and other type of signals in the decomposition process. DWT can be expressed as [16]:

$$Wf(j,k) = \sum_{N=0}^{N-1} f(n) \cdot \psi_{j,k}^*(n), \tag{1}$$

With $Wf(j,k)$ a DWT coefficient and $f(n)$ is a sequence with length N. Wavelet basis is expressed as:

$$\psi_{j,k}(n) = \frac{1}{\sqrt{s_0^j}} \psi\left(\frac{n - s_0^j \cdot k}{s_0^j}\right),$$

Where s_0^j and $s_0^j \cdot k$ refers to the discretized versions of the DWT scale and translation parameters, respectively.

2.2   EMD: Empirical Mode Decomposition

The method decomposes a signal into a sum of components, each with slowly varying amplitude and phase. Once having a signal represented in this way, the properties of each component must be analyzed using the Hilbert Transform. EMD is an adaptive method, where the produced decomposition is specific to the signal being analyzed. In theory, the outputs components should separate the phenomena that occurs on different time scales of the EMD. Each component of the EMD is called an Intrinsic Mode Function (IMF) [17]. During the implementation of EMD, high frequencies of signals are removed, repeating the process in the new signal, which is also called residue, and it is expressed as [16]:

$$x(t) = \sum_{n=1}^{N} C_n(t) + r_N(t),$$

Where N is the total number of IMFs, $C_n(t)$ for $n = 1, \ldots, N$ are each IMF, and $r_N(t)$ is known as the residual or the last IMF.

2.3   Mixture of Classifiers

BCI classification is usually performed using a single classifier [18]. However, combination strategies of classifiers are proposed to evaluate the performance of several classifiers. Particularly, the following setup is established.

- **Product combiner:** It defines the product combiner on a set of classifiers by selecting the class which yields the highest value of the product of the classifier outputs.
- **Mean combiner:** It selects the class with the mean of the outputs of the input classifiers.
- **Median combiner:** It chooses the class with the median of the outputs of the input classifiers.
- **Maximum combiner:** It selects the class that gives the maximal output of the input classifiers.
- **Minimum combiner:** It chooses the class with the minimum of the outputs of the input classifiers.
- **Voting combiner:** It selects the class with the highest vote of the base classifiers.

3   Experimental Set-up

This section outlines the proposed framework to assess the feasibility of using a mixture of classifiers, so that it is possible to identify a suitable strategy for the design of a BCI system in different real environments. Figure 2 depicts the proposed procedure for analysis of EEG signals. This system includes four stages: *(i)* Database- data acquisition, *(ii)* Pre-processing, *(iii)* Feature extraction, and *(iv)* Classification.

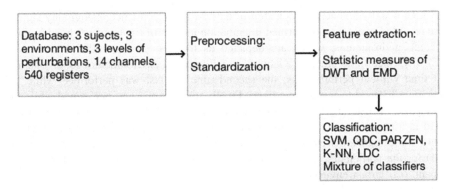

Fig. 2. Block diagram of proposed methodology for analysis of EEG signals. The aim of the comparative study on alternative classification options to analyze motor imaginary BCI within multi-environment real scenarios based on mixtures of classifiers.

3.1 Database

Signals dataset were recorded through the wireless device Emotiv Epoc+, which has 14 electrodes placed according to the international 10–20 system and sampling rate of 128 Hz. In addition, the free software BCI2000 was used to design and present the paradigm to the participants. Before starting the test, the process was explained to the participant. Then the Emotiv Epoc+ device was placed to the participant head and the quality of the connection was checked out with Test Bench application. During the test, the participant was sitting on a chair looking at screen of a computer, where a prompt appeared to indicate that the test was going to start, and it immediately began to appear twenty arrows rightward or leftward randomly to suggest the movement that the participant should imagine; each arrow was displayed for 2 s, and between them a white background was displayed during the same time to allow the participant to rest after each imagination (see Fig. 3).

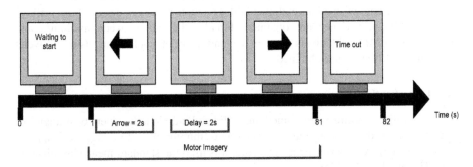

Fig. 3. Motor imagery system [16]. It represents the process to record the signals dataset through the wireless device Emotiv Epoc+ for each participant in the three different environments.

Three healthy subjects participated in the test and electroencephalography signals were recorded while they performed imagination motion of right and left hand in three different environments, which are depicted as follows: *(i)* Controlled environment (CE) was tested three times in a laboratory with normal environmental conditions, the first time without perturbations, the second time the test was performed while the participant listened to music they liked. Finally, the last one was performed while the participant was listening to music that he did not like. *(ii)* Rural environment (RE) was tested in a peaceful place with green areas and trees. Same as in the others environments, three registers were performed, one without music, one with pleasant music (PM) for the participant, and the last one with unpleasant music (UPM) for the participant. *(iii)* Urban environment (UE) was tested in a place transited by cars, motorcycles and people talking. In the same way as in the controlled an rural environment, the test was performed three times, the first without-disturbances (UD) and the other two times listening to pleasant and unpleasant music for the participant.

It should be noted that the 3 participants were men and they the day before the test slept a similar amount of hours (between 5 and 7). The participants were 23, 25 and 15 years old respectively and their body mass indexes were 20.76, 23.58 and 26.8 respectively. The 3 participants reported that they did not consume any type of hallucinogenic substances but the first one reported their habits the consumption of alcohol.

3.2   Pre-processing

Before submitting the EEG signals to the feature extraction, the signals were standardized to make sure the signals do not exceed the range $[-1\ 1]$, and thus to facilitate their analysis.

3.3   Feature Extraction

In order to represent the signals as a compact feature vector, different statistical measures were obtained from EEG signals and the results achieved by DWT and EMD applied on EEG signals. With the aim to know the most representative values of the database, area, energy, median and standard deviation measures are used, as well as, Shannon entropy, variance are obtained. Finally, the rate between minimum and maximum of EMD coefficients (2 signals) and wavelet coefficients using Wavelet Daubechies 10 (Db10) are obtained.

3.4   Classification

Six classification systems were trained and validated individually. Then, 6 strategies of combination (product, mean, median, maximum, minimum, and voting) were applied for mixing them. As a performance measure, it is used the standard mean classification error. The applied classifiers are:

- **SVM (Support Vector Machine):** This instance-based classification method takes advantage of the kernel trick to compute the most discriminative non-linear hyperplane between classes. Therefore, its performance heavily depends on the selection and tuning of the kernel type [19]. In this work, the linear kernel is used.

- **QDC (Quadratic Discriminant Classifier - Quadratic Bayes Classifier):** Bayesian classification aims at assigning to a feature vector the class it belongs to with the highest probability. The Bayes rule is used to compute the so-called a posteriori probability that a feature vector has of belonging to a given class. Bayes quadratic consists in assuming a different normal distribution of data. This leads to quadratic decision boundaries, which explains the name of the classifier [10].

- **PARZEN:** This probabilistic-based classification method requires a smoothing parameter for the Gaussian distribution computation, which is optimized.

- **k-NN (k- Nearest neighbors):** Is a nonparametric supervised classification method based on distances. This algorithm makes a posteriori estimate of the probability on the proximity of its neighbors. For the classification of a sample takes as reference the values of k nearest neighbors by means of distances, generally Euclidean [20], the value for the number of neighbors (K) is optimized by means of a leave-one-out strategy.

- **LDC (Linear Discriminant Classifier - Linear Bayes Classifier):** It is a supervised classification and prediction technique with covariance matrix shared between classes. This classifier constructs models that predict the probability of possible results.

4 Results and Discussion

To evaluate the efficiency of the proposed methodology, individual results for each participant and average error on the three participants for individual classifiers and mixture of classifiers were obtained. These averages were obtained for each environment in the three conditions: Undisturbed, pleasant music, and unpleasant music. It should be emphasized that, in the process, a certain number of iterations is repeated until a combination obtained the lowest possible error.

The next notation is used in this section and conclusions:

- Pp: Participant
- Σ: error average
- PZ: Parzen classifier
- Prod: Product combiner
- Max: Maximum combiner
- Min: Minimum combiner
- Vm: Voting combiner

Tables 1, 2, and 3 show the errors obtained with the individual classifiers and the mixture of classifiers for the environment without perturbations (CE-nonP), with pleasant music and unpleasant music, respectively.

For the participants, in the controlled environment, who were not subjected to any disturbances; individual classifiers, as in the mix, have the minimum error of 25%. However, it can be observed that with the individual classifier errors are obtained above

Table 1. Controlled environment undisturbed

P	SVM	QDC	PZ	k-NN	LDQ	Prod	Mean	Median	Max	Min	Vm
	Individual					Combination					
1	0,3	0	0,25	0,5	0,25	0	0	0,25	0	0,25	0
2	0,5	0	0,5	0,5	1	0,75	0	0,5	0	0,5	0,5
3	0,5	0,75	0,25	0,25	0,25	0,25	0,75	0,25	0,75	0	0,25
Σ	0,4	0,25	0,33	0,42	0,5	0,33	0,25	0,33	0,25	0,25	0,25

Table 2. Controlled environment with pleasant music

P	SVM	QDC	PZ	k-NN	LDQ	Prod	Mean	Median	Max	Min	Vm
	Individual					Combination					
1	0,3	0,25	0,25	0	0,25	0,25	0,25	0	0,25	0,25	0
2	0,5	0,5	0,2	0,25	0,25	0,25	0,5	0,5	0,5	0,5	0
3	0,3	0	0,75	0,75	0,25	0,25	0	0,5	0	0,5	0,25
Σ	0,3	0,25	0,4	0,33	0,25	0,25	0,25	0,33	0,25	0,42	0,08

Table 3. Controlled environment with unpleasant music

P	SVM	QDC	PZ	k-NN	LDQ	Prod	Mean	Median	Max	Min	Vm
	Individual					Combination					
1	1	0	0,75	0,5	0,75	0,5	0	0,5	0	0,75	0,75
2	0	0	0,75	0,75	0,5	0	0	0,75	0	0,75	0,25
3	0,5	0	1	0,5	0,25	0,5	0	0,75	0	1	0,25
Σ	0,5	0	0,83	0,58	0,5	0,33	0	0,67	0	0,83	0,42

40%, which is something that did not happen with the mixture of classifiers. These results are achieved in 5, 2, and 1 iterations for participants 1, 2, and 3 respectively. This can be seen in Table 1. It can also be observed that in a controlled environment undisturbed (UD), it is easier to detect the movements of participants 1 and 2 as indicated by the error rate. That is, the younger the age and the higher the body mass, the more difficult it is to detect the imaginary movements of a participant in a controlled environment undisturbed.

Table 2 shows the results obtained from controlled environment with pleasant music (CEPM), voting combiner achieved the best success rate 92%. In contrast with individual classifiers, the best success rate is 75%. Therefore, the mixture significantly reduces the average of the classification error obtained. These results were achieved in one and 7 iterations for the first and second participant, respectively. It can be observed that in the controlled environment undisturbed the classifiers and the combination present similar results for all the participants. This leads to the conclusion that in this environment features such as age and weight do not greatly influence the detection of motor imaginary.

For the case of the environment controlled with unpleasant music, individual classifiers zero errors were obtained, however, in the mixture of classifiers, two mixtures allow obtaining an error zero percent with the Mean and Max combiners for all cases. As in the previous case, similar results are presented in the error for each participant. The error depends more on the mixer or the classifier used than on the participant.

Tables 4, 5 and 6 show the errors obtained with the individual classifiers and the mixture of classifiers, for the rural environment without perturbations, with pleasant music and unpleasant music, respectively.

Table 4. Rural environment undisturbed

Individual						Combination					
P	SVM	QDC	PZ	k-NN	LDQ	Prod	Mean	Median	Max	Min	Vm
1	0,5	0,25	0,5	0	0,25	0	0,25	0,75	0,25	0,25	0,25
2	0,5	0,75	0	0,25	0,75	0,5	0,75	0	0,75	0,5	0,5
3	0,5	0	0,25	0,5	0,25	0,25	0	0,5	0	0,25	0
Σ	0,5	0,33	0,25	0,25	0,42	0,25	0,33	0,42	0,33	0,33	0,25

Table 5. Rural environment with pleasant music

Individual						Combination					
P	SVM	QDC	PZ	k-NN	LDQ	Prod	Mean	Median	Max	Min	Vm
1	0,3	0,25	0,5	0,25	0,25	0	0,25	0,25	0,25	0,5	0,25
2	0,3	0,25	0,5	0,25	0,75	0,75	0,25	0,5	0,25	0,5	0
3	0,5	0,75	0,25	0,5	0,25	0	0,75	0,5	0,75	0,25	0,5
Σ	0,3	0,42	0,42	0,33	0,42	0,25	0,42	0,42	0,42	0,42	0,25

Table 6. Rural environment with unpleasant music

Individual						Combination					
P	SVM	QDC	PZ	k-NN	LDQ	Prod	Mean	Median	Max	Min	Vm
1	0	0,25	0	0	0,25	0,25	0,25	0	0,25	0,25	0
2	0,5	0,5	0,5	0,5	0	0	0,5	0,5	0,5	0,5	0,5
3	0,5	0	0,25	0,25	0,25	0,25	0	0,25	0	0,25	0,25
Σ	0,3	0,25	0,25	0,25	0,17	0,17	0,25	0,25	0,25	0,33	0,25

When there is no disturbance in the rural environment, with the mixture, as with the individual classifiers the minimum percentage of error is 25%. However, with the mixture, the percentage error does not exceed 45%, which happens with individual classifiers (see Table 4). It can be observed that in a rural environment undisturbed, it is easier to detect the motor imaginary of a young person with a higher body mass index, features that the participant presents.

For a rural environment with pleasant music, with the individual classifiers, the minimum error rate of 30% is obtained, and with the mixture, the error is reduced to 25% with the Product and the Majority vote combiners. It is shown in Table 5.

Table 6 shows the results for the rural environment with unpleasant music. In this case, it was possible to obtain an error of 17% with the Product combiner, which is a better result than the one obtained with pleasant music and undisturbed environments.

For the rural environment with pleasant/unpleasant music it is observed that features such as the age and body mass of the people do not influence a significant way.

Tables 7, 8 and 9 show the errors obtained with the individual classifiers and the mixture of classifiers, for the urban environment without perturbations, with pleasant music and unpleasant music respectively.

Table 7. Urban environment undisturbed

Individual						Combination					
P	SVM	QDC	PZ	k-NN	LDQ	Prod	Mean	Median	Max	Min	Vm
1	0,5	0,5	0,25	0,25	0,25	0,25	0,5	0,5	0,5	0,5	0
2	0,3	0,25	0,5	0,25	0,25	0,25	0,25	0,25	0,25	0,5	0
3	0,5	0	0	0,5	0,25	0	0	0,25	0	0	0,25
Σ	0,4	0,25	0,25	0,33	0,25	0,17	0,25	0,33	0,25	0,33	0,083

Table 8. Urban environment with pleasant music

Individual						Combination					
P	SVM	QDC	PZ	k-NN	LDQ	Prod	Mean	Median	Max	Min	Vm
1	1	0,75	0,75	0,75	0,25	0	0,75	0,75	0,75	0,5	0,75
2	0,5	0,75	0	0,25	0,75	0,5	0,75	0	0,75	0,5	0,5
3	0,3	0,25	0,25	0,25	0,5	0	0,25	0,25	0,25	0,25	0,25
Σ	0,6	0,58	0,33	0,42	0,5	0,17	0,58	0,33	0,58	0,417	0,5

In Table 7, it is possible to observe that when there is no disturbance, an error rate of 8% is obtained with the majority vote combiner; the mixture improves the classification significantly, since with the individual classifiers, a 25% error was obtained.

Table 8 shows the results for the urban environment with pleasant music, where the minimum error obtained with individual classifiers was 33%; while with the mix, it was obtained a 17% error using the product combiner. As in the rural environment undisturbed, in this case it is also easier to identify the motor imaginary of the third participant.

In the case of unpleasant music in an urban environment, it becomes more difficult to classify, since with the mixture, specifically with the Median combiner, a minimum error value of 25% was obtained. But, it is worth noting that the mixture helps to reduce the error, since with the individual classifiers a minimum error of 33% is obtained, as shown in Table 9.

Table 9. Urban environment with unpleasant music

Individuals						Combination					
P	SVM	QDC	PZ	k-NN	LDQ	Prod	Mean	Median	Max	Min	Vm
1	0,5	0	0,5	0,5	0,75	0,75	0	0,25	0	0,75	0,5
2	0,5	0,25	0,25	0,5	0,25	0	0,25	0	0,25	0,5	0
3	0,5	0,75	0,25	0,25	0	0,25	0,75	0,5	0,75	0	0,5
Σ	0,5	0,33	0,333	0,42	0,33	0,33	0,33	0,25	0,33	0,42	0,33

As in rural and controlled environments, in the urban environment with pleasant/unpleasant music, the participants' age and body mass does not have a significant influence. Finally, Table 10 summarizes the results obtained in each of the environments with and without perturbations using the methodology proposed.

Table 10. Results summary

Environment	Classifier	Lowest error	Combination	Lowest error	Participant with best results
CE-UD	QDC	0,25	Mean, Max, Min y Vm	0,25	1
CE-PM	QDC, LQD	0,25	Vm	0,08	1, 2, and 3
CE-UPM	QDC	0	Mean y Max	0	1, 2, and 3
RE-UD	PZ, k-NN	0,25	Prod y Vm	0,25	3
RE-PM	SVM	0,3	Prod y Vm	0,25	1, 2, and 3
RE-UPM	LDQ	0,17	Prod	0,17	1, 2, and 3
UE-UD	QDC, PZ, LDQ	0,25	Prod	0,17	3
UE-PM	PZ	0,33	Prod	0,17	1, 2, and 3
UE-PM	QDC, PZ, LDQ	0,33	Median	0,25	1, 2, and 3

5   Conclusions and Future Work

The brain signals reflect the activities performed by humans and allow controlling the behavior of the brain or information received from other parts of the body, thus BCI provides a facility of communication between the brain and different devices such as the computer, especially for the limited people in their motor skills.

The main advantage of these strategies of combining classifiers is that they outperform individual classifiers, because the combination of classifiers minimizes the variance and hence classification error. The success rate of classifiers depends on the conditions and environments in which samples are acquired, but it should be noted that the majority vote and the product combiners allow to achieve the lowest errors in the most of the tests environments, especially in the controlled environment with pleasant music, where the majority vote combiner allows to obtain the smallest average error of the 3 participants with 0.08%. Features such as weight, height and age do not significantly influence when participants are subjected to perturbations as music. For urban and rural environments these features influence allowing to obtain better results when it comes to young people and with greater body mass. Otherwise for a controlled environment.

This study allows identifying the best combination for the detection of movement of the hands of the patients in a given environment. This is to establish the way to interact with the outside through thinking, and at the same time, to transform them into real actions in the environment. As a future work, we will extract other types of features that will help to improve the classification of the signals. These features may be the conditions in which signals are acquired, such as temperature, noise level, pressure, among others. Besides, new classifiers combinations and the performance of a stage of the feature selection can be applied with the aim to reduce the classification error. Finally, other databases to test the performance of mixtures can be considered as future work.

References

1. Nicolas, L., Gomez, J.: Brain computer interfaces, a review. Sensors **12**(2), 1211–1279 (2012)
2. Brumberg, J., Nieto, A., Kennedy, P., Guenther, F.: Brain–computer interfaces for speech communication. Speech Commun. **52**(4), 367–379 (2010)
3. Cincotti, F., Mattia, D., Aloise, F., Bufalari, S., Schalk, G., Oriolo, G., Cherubini, A., Marciani, M., Babiloni, F.: Non-invasive brain–computer interface system: towards its application as assistive technology. Brain Res. Bull. **75**(6), 796–803 (2008)
4. Dobkin, B.H.: Brain–computer interface technology as a tool to augment plasticity and outcomes for neurological rehabilitation. J. Physiol. **579**(3), 637–642 (2007)
5. Lalor, E.C., Kelly, S.P., Finucane, C., Burke, R., Smith, R., Reilly, R.B., Mcdarby, G.: Steady-state VEP-based brain-computer interface control in an immersive 3D gaming environment. EURASIP J. Appl. Sig. Process. **2005**, 3156–3164 (2005)
6. McCane, L.M., Sellers, E.W., Mcfarland, D.J., Mak, J.N., Carmack, C.S., Zeitlin, D., Vaughan, T.M.: Brain-computer interface (BCI) evaluation in people with amyotrophic lateral sclerosis. Amyotroph. Lateral Scler. Frontotemporal Degener. **15**(3–4), 207–215 (2014)
7. López, E., Tufiño L.X.: Caracterización de señales y reconocimiento de patrones para la clasificación de color obtenidos por medio del EEG analizando potenciales visuales evocados, México (2016)
8. Khalid, M.B., Rao, N.I., Rizwan-i-Haque, I., Munir, S., Tahir, F.: Towards a brain computer interface using wavelet transform with averaged and time segmented adapted wavelets. In: 2nd International Conference on Computer, Control and Communication, pp. 1–4. IEEE (2009)
9. Ulaş, Ç.: Incorporation of a language model into a brain computer interface based speller. Doctoral dissertation, Sabancı University (2013)
10. Lotte, F., Congedo, M., Lécuyer, A., Lamarche, F., Arnaldi, B.: A review of classification algorithms for EEG-based brain–computer interfaces. J. Neural Eng. **4**(2), 1–23 (2007)
11. Quitadamo, L.R., Cavrini, F., Sbernini, L., Riillo, F., Bianchi, L., Seri, S., Saggio, G.: Support vector machines to detect physiological patterns for EEG and EMG-based human–computer interaction: a review. J. Neural Eng. **14**(1), 1–27 (2017)

12. Schettini, F., Riccio, A., Simione, L., Liberati, G., Caruso, M., Frasca, V., Mattia, D.: Assistive device with conventional, alternative, and brain-computer interface inputs to enhance interaction with the environment for people with amyotrophic lateral sclerosis: a feasibility and usability study. Arch. Phys. Med. Rehabil. **96**(3), S46–S53 (2015)

13. Heo, J., Baek, H.J., Hong, S., Chang, M.H., Lee, J.S., Park, K.S.: Music and natural sounds in an auditory steady-state response based brain–computer interface to increase user acceptance. Comput. Biol. Med. **84**, 45–52 (2017)

14. Carabalona, R., Grossi, F., Tessadri, A., Castiglioni, P., Caracciolo, A., de Munari, I.: Light on! Real world evaluation of a P300-based brain–computer interface (BCI) for environment control in a smart home. Ergonomics **55**(5), 552–563 (2012)

15. Jaramillo, A., Acosta, D.F., Ochoa, J.F.: Extracción de características frecuenciales en registros EEG a partir de la transformada wavelet. Revista de investigaciones Universidad del Quindio, **27**(2) (2015)

16. Marın, D.M., Restrepo, S., Areiza, H.J., Castro, A.E., Duque, L.: Exploratory analysis of motor imagery local database for BCI systems. In: Congreso Internacional de Ciencias Básicas e Ingeniería (2016)

17. Tolwinski, S.: The Hilbert transform and empirical mode decomposition as tools for data analysis. University of Arizona, Tucson (2007)

18. Villazana, S., Montilla, G., Seijas, C., Caralli, A., Eblen, A.: Clasificación de señales electroencefalográficas utilizando entrenamiento cruzado de máquinas de vectores de soporte. Revista Ingeniería UC, **22**(2) (2015)

19. Sheather, S.J., Marron, S.J., Jones, M.C.: Density estimation. Stat. Sci. **19**(4), 588–597 (2004)

20. Campo, J.P.: Diseño de un nuevo clasificador supervisado para minera de datos. Doctoral dissertation, Master's thesis, Complutense University, Madrid (2008)

Off-line and On-line Scheduling of SAT Instances with Time Processing Constraints

Robinson Duque[1]($\boxtimes$), Alejandro Arbelaez[2], and Juan Francisco Díaz[1]

[1] Avispa Research Group, Universidad del Valle, Cali, Colombia
{robinson.duque,juanfco.diaz}@correounivalle.edu.co
[2] Riomh Research Group, Cork Institute of Technology, Cork, Ireland
alejandro.arbelaez@cit.ie

Abstract. Many combinatorial problems (e.g., SAT) are well-known NP-complete problems. Therefore, many instances cannot be solved within a reasonable time, and the runtime varies from few seconds to hours or more depending on the instance. Cloud computing offers an interesting opportunity to solve combinatorial problems in different domains. Computational time can be rented by the hour and for a given number of processors, therefore it is extremely important to find a good balance between the number of solved instances and the requested resources in the cloud.

In this work, we present two computational approaches (i.e., Off-line and On-line) that combine the use of machine learning and mixed integer programming in order to maximize the number of solved SAT instances. In the Off-line model, we assume to have all the instances before the processing phase begins. This approach attempts to maximize solved instances within a global time limit constraint. On the other hand, in the On-line model, instances with a maximum waiting time constraint have to be handled as they arrive. Thus, deciding which/when instances should be attended has a big impact in the amount of solved instances. Experimental validations with sets of SAT instances, suggest that our Off-line approach can solve up to 93% of the solvable instances within 50% of the overall execution time. Additionally, our On-line approach can solve up to 3.5x more instances than ordering policies such as FCFS and SJF.

1 Introduction

In the last decade, the interest for using cloud resources to solve large combinatorial problems has been growing and has attracted much attention of the Boolean Satisfiability (SAT) community for solving real-life problems with hundreds of thousands of variables and millions of clauses and constraints.

Indeed, SAT solvers are nowadays used in multiple domains ranging from software verification to automated planning. In this context, recently [7] used SAT technology to compute *the largest-ever mathematical proof*, a 200-terabyte proof called the Boolean Pythagorean triples problem. To solve this problem the

© Springer International Publishing AG 2017
A. Solano and H. Ordoñez (Eds.): CCC 2017, CCIS 735, pp. 524–539, 2017.
DOI: 10.1007/978-3-319-66562-7_38

authors required about 30,000 hours of CPU time to solve more than a million SAT subproblems.

Commercial cloud providers such as Amazon EC2, Microsoft Azure, and Google Cloud Platform provide users with large computing infrastructures and parallel processing. On-demand service is an increasingly popular pricing model in which users are charged on usage bases without long-term commitment. The large cloud processing power allows users to scale to an extremely large size. However, these resources come at a cost and users are often left with the tedious task of finding a good balance between the number of solved instances and requested resources in the cloud. In this document, we present two approaches to tackle Off-line and On-line combinatorial problems. Such approaches can be used to get the top performance of using cloud environments with limited budget (e.g., limited processing time). For the sake of clarity, when we refer to *Off-line Combinatorial Problems* we refer to a "batch" or bounded workload of combinatorial problems. Alternatively, when we refer to *On-line Combinatorial Problems* we refer to an unbounded number of combinatorial problems to be handled as they arrive during a period of time.

The rest of the paper is structured as follows. Section 2 introduces SAT problems and machine learning, in the context of creating models to estimate instances runtime. In Sect. 3 we describe our Off-line approach for instance processing with time limit constraints. Section 4 describes our On-line approach for instance processing with arrival and maximum waiting time constraints. Respectively, Sects. 5 and 6 present experimental results for both approaches. Finally, Sect. 7 describes related work and Sect. 8 presents our conclusions.

2   Preliminaries

Determining whether a given propositional logic formula is satisfiable or not, is one of the fundamental problems in computer science. It was the first NP-Complete problem discovered by Cook in 1971 and it is also known as the canonical NP-complete Boolean satisfiability (SAT) problem [9].

A Boolean formula is represented by a pair (X, C), where X is a set of Boolean variables and C is a set of clauses in Conjunctive Normal Form (CNF). The *Boolean variables* $\{x_1, ..., x_n\} \in X$ can be assigned truth values (true, false). A *literal* is either a variable x_i or its negation $\neg x_i$. A *clause* ω is a disjunction of literals and a CNF formula δ is a conjunction of clauses. A clause is said to be *satisfied* if at least one of its literals assumes the value of 1 and *unsatisfied* if all of its literals assume the value of 0. Consequently, a CNF formula is said to be *satisfied* if all its clauses are satisfied. Respectively, it is *unsatisfied* if at least one clause is unsatisfied.

In the literature, the satisfiability problem is typically tackled by creating *stand-alone SAT-solvers* that run sequentially or in parallel. Additionally, an increasingly studied approach consists in using a *portfolio-based algorithm selection* to solve a given problem on a case-by-case basis using existing solvers instead of developing new ones. However, state-of-the-art solvers typically display extreme runtime variations across instances and there is little theoretical understanding of this behaviour [8]. Interestingly, there have been efforts to build regression models that provide runtime estimates, using supervised machine learning.

Supervised machine learning for runtime prediction: supervised machine learning consists of inferring a model (or hypothesis) $f : \Omega \rightarrow Y$ that predicts the value of an output variable $y_i \in Y$, given the values of the example description (e.g., a vector of features, $\Omega = R^d$). The output can be numerical (i.e., regression) or categorical (i.e., classification). The idea of predicting algorithm runtime is not new and has been studied in the past using methods such as: Ridge regression [11], neural networks [14], regression trees [2], and most recently in [8], the authors use random forest and approximate Gaussian process techniques to estimate propositional satisfiability (SAT), mixed integer programming (MIP), and travelling salesperson (TSP) problems. Interestingly, random forest was the overall winner among the presented methods and tests. Mainly due to the heterogeneous datasets and also because tree-based approaches can model different parts of the data separately, in contrast to other methods.

Regression trees are typically sensitive to small changes in the data and tend to overfit. However, random forests overcome this problem by combining multiple regression trees into an ensemble. That is, a combination of tree predictors such that each tree depends on the values of a random vector sampled independently and with the same distribution for all trees in the forest [3].

SAT features: the vectors of features used for this study were extracted from the extensive literature in machine learning for runtime prediction in SAT solving. In [8], the authors provide a complete set of 138 features to describe SAT instances and divide the features into four categories according the overall complexity to collect the descriptors: trivial, cheap, moderate, and expensive. These feature categories play an important role in this study since they allow us to explore different complexity-based approaches.

3   Off-line Instance Processing with Time Limit Constraints

An off-line system assumes that all jobs are known beforehand and there are no additional arrivals once the processing phase begins [6]. These systems are ideal for *batch processing* where a group of transactions or jobs is collected over a period of time to process them as a whole. Off-line systems are also suitable for *batch job schedulers* that sort and pack the jobs together in order to minimize the total processing time [6].

An example of this batch processing approach can be observed in the annual international SAT solver competitions that provide a standardized benchmark collection for the use of researchers. Such benchmark collection typically includes instances related to three competition categories (i.e., industrial, crafted and random instances). The goal of these competitions is to determine whether a given SAT instance is satisfiable or not as quickly as possible [5, 9].

Algorithm 1. Instance execution queue based on a priority measure function

```
 1: function IEQ(Instances I, Priority function f, Instance time limit t, global time
    limit gt)
 2:     Priority queue q
 3:     for each Iᵢ in I do
 4:         mᵢ ← f(Iᵢ)
 5:         if mᵢ then
 6:             q.insert(Iᵢ, mᵢ)
 7:         end if
 8:     end for
 9:     while not q.isEmpty() and elapsed-time < gt do
10:         Iᵢ ← q.deleteMin()
11:         Solve(Iᵢ, t)
12:     end while
13: end function
```

In SAT competitions, the set of problem instances are provided one at the time and the solvers or portfolios race to solve individual instances with a given time limit per instance. Modern solvers scale surprisingly well for combinatorial problems with hundreds of variables and millions of constraints. However, many of these combinatorial problems are well-known NP-complete problems. Therefore, many instances cannot be solved within a reasonable time, and the runtime varies from few seconds to hours or more depending on the instance. For example, the lingeling SAT solver was unable to solve 93 instances in the 2014 SAT competition, which considering the 5000-second time limit in the competition, it represents about 129 hours of ineffective CPU time.

In this section, we focus our attention on off-line processing of combinatorial problems. We use supervised machine learning to determine a suitable execution order of the instances with two objectives: minimize ineffective CPU time and maximize the number of solved instances when having a global processing time limit. To sum up, we would like to highlight the following characteristics for off-line processing of combinatorial problems:

A1 The runtime of the instances is unknown.
A2 All the instances are available for processing within a global processing time limit and they have no precedence constraints.
A3 Once started, an instance must run to completion or until a cap time limit t is met. No preemption is considered.

Off-line Computational Approach

Algorithm 1 describes our *Instance Execution Queue* (IEQ) to solve unseen instances in the cloud with limited resources. The algorithm has four parameters: the target set of instances (I); the time limit per instance execution (t); the global time limit to tackle the entire set of instances (gt); and a priority function (f), this function is used to give hints of the possible instance execution hardness and it might be a continuous or discrete value. In the first part of the IEQ algorithm, instances are associated with a priority value (lines 3–8). Then, in the second part, instances are executed in the predefined order until the global execution time is met. In particular, we explored the following ordering functions:

- **SJF:** Shortest Job First, priority function where the IEQ sorts the instances in ascending order according to their execution time. We relax assumption A1 in order to use real instance runtime values as a base-line reference since the idea is to maximize the number of solved instances.
- **random:** priority function that lets the IEQ sort the SAT instances randomly.
- **numV:** priority function that lets the IEQ sort the SAT instances by the number of variables.
- **numC:** priority function that lets the IEQ sort the instances by the number of clauses in SAT instances.
- **VToC:** priority function that lets the IEQ sort the instances by the variable to clause ratio in SAT instances.
- **Regression:** priority function that lets the IEQ sort instances in ascending order by using the runtime estimations of the regression model. We differentiate between two distinct phases. A training phase and the evaluation or testing phase. The training phase involves collecting the vector of features $x_i \in X$ and the runtime $y_i \in Y$ for the instances in the training set, in order to train a regression model with X features to estimate Y. We present three ordering functions in the experiments section:

  - **R-Expensive:** regression model trained using SAT expensive features
  - **R-Cheap:** regression model trained using SAT cheap features
  - **R-Trivial:** regression model trained using SAT trivial features.

4   On-line Instance Processing with Arrival and Maximum Waiting Time Constraints

While most combinatorial problems are processed in batch until some time limit termination criterion is met, there are On-line systems that require a continuous form of processing. We assume an open On-line system where there is a stream of arriving users and each one is assumed to submit instances to the system, wait to receive a response, and then leave. Therefore, new jobs arrive independently from job completions [12].

As for NP-Complete problems, many instances cannot be solved within reasonable time and typically have a very large runtime variability. Therefore, when a solver receives a problem instance, it typically looks for an answer during a small time limit t. If the solver finds an answer, it is returned to the user. Otherwise, the user is notified that the search has timed out.

In this section, we focus our attention on on-line processing of combinatorial problems. We use supervised machine learning, Mixed Integer Programming

Algorithm 2. On-line Instance Execution Queue, based on a priority measure function or on a MIP model schedule

1: Priority queue q
2: **function** ONLINE-IEQ(Arriving Instance I_i, Priority function f)
3:     $m_i \leftarrow f(I_i)$
4:     **if** m_i **then**
5:         $q.\text{insert}(I_i, m_i)$
6:     **end if**
7: **end function**

(MIP), and a heuristic approach. The heuristic aims at processing instances and make estimations and inferences in the order in which instances will be processed in time. Additionally, we would like to highlight the following characteristics for on-line processing of combinatorial problems:

B1 The runtime of the instances is unknown.
B2 There is a stream of arriving users and each one is assumed to send an instance I_i to the system.
B3 Each user defines a maximum waiting time I_i^{ewt} for an instance I_i.
B4 An instance I_i is considered to be **attended** if:
  – its waiting time is smaller than the one defined by the user (I_i^{ewt})
  – it is assigned some processing time greater than 0
B5 An instance I_i is considered to be **solved**, only if it is attended and the system finds an answer in the assigned processing time.
B6 Once started, an instance can run using two possible execution strategies: naive execution and heuristic based execution (see Sect. 4.1 for further information).

4.1 On-line Computational Approach

In this approach we differentiate between two processes: (a) On-line Instance Execution Queue (IEQ) and Priority Functions that queue instances as they arrive; (b) Instance execution strategies that dequeue instances for processing.

(a) On-line IEQ and Priority Functions: when an instance arrives, the function *Online-IEQ* in Algorithm (2) can be triggered in order to queue the arriving instance. In the algorithm, we assume that the instance already has three attributes: I_i^a arrival time; I_i^{ewt} maximum expected waiting time; I_i^{rt} runtime estimated with the regression model. Then, each instance is queued according to one of the following functions using a priority measure:

– **FCFS:** first come first serve, lets the IEQ sort instances in ascending order by their arrival time (I_i^a).
– **SJF:** shortest job first, lets the IEQ sort the instances in ascending order by using the runtime estimations of the regression model (I_i^{rt}).

- **MIP:** mixed integer programming, lets the IEQ sort the instances in ascending order by using a mathematical model. Given that Algorithm (2) requires to queue arriving instances with an initial priority, we initially queue them with a $(I_i^a * I_i^{rt})$ priority. However, these priorities are typically irrelevant since they are constantly updated with a quick run of the MIP model every time an instance has to be selected from the queue. Therefore, initial priorities are only relevant for cases when MIP does not find a feasible schedule in the given time.

  In general, the model determines an instance execution schedule. Then, the instance start times are used as priorities. Additionally, MIP determines if an instance should be attended or not in order to maximize solved instances (see Sect. 4.2). However, there are different ways to execute this model to update queue priorities. For instance, it can be used either after a new instance arrival or when an instance has to be selected from the queue. The former execution would require to estimate the end time of the running instance in order to establish a starting time for MIP to create the execution schedule. On the other hand, the second execution would just use the system time when the machine becomes available. Thus, running MIP as instances arrive might lead to more inaccurate schedules and would require another computational node to execute the model while running instances.

(b) Instance Execution Strategies

- *The Naive Execution* presents a straight forward approach where the first instance from the queue q is taken, then it is executed to completion or until a cap time limit t is met.
- *The Heuristic Based Execution* is proposed in this paper in order to mitigate runtime missed predictions. It dequeues the first instance and runs it to completion or until a cap time limit t is met. Additionally, instance I_i can be stopped if there are 2 or more instances I_j in queue that are determined not to be attended (nor solved) if I_i continues to run. Preliminary experiments showed that 2 unsolved instances maximize the amount of solved instances using this heuristic. Equation (1) depicts how we make such decision.

  In general, we estimate the end time of the instance that is running ($I_i^{ET} = I_i^{ST} + I_i^{rt}$). That is, adding the time when the instance started to be processed and the estimated runtime. Indeed, an instance I_j from the queue won't be attended (nor solved) if its arrival plus its maximum waiting time constraint is not satisfied (i.e., $I_i^{ET} > I_j^a + I_j^{ewt}$). However, this heuristic is mostly used with estimations and the runtime of instance I_i^{rt} might be overestimated. Therefore, we decided to extend the execution of instance I_i by adding the run time I_j^{rt} of instance I_j to the constraint:

$$NotExecuted_j = \begin{cases} 1, & \text{if } I_i^{ET} > (I_j^a + I_j^{ewt} + I_j^{rt}) \\ 0, & otherwise \end{cases} \quad \forall I_j \in q$$

$$\sum_{I_j \in q} NotExecuted_j \leq 2 \tag{1}$$

4.2   Mixed Integer Programming Model

In this section we introduce a MIP model to schedule instances to maximize the amount of solved instances in a single machine using runtime estimations. Hereafter, we introduce some notation for the model:

Indices and sets:

- $\mathcal{I}$: set of instances in the queue;
- I_i, I_j: instances ($I_i, I_j \in \mathcal{I}$)

Parameters:

- I_i^a: arrival time of instance I_i;
- I_i^{rt}: runtime of instance I_i (estimation using a regression model);
- I_i^{ewt}: maximum expected waiting time of instance I_i. If the waiting time of an instance I_i is greater than this value, then it is not attended (nor solved);
- $time$: time when the system becomes available;

Decision variables:

- I_i^{ST}: start time of instance I_i;
- I_i^{ET}: end time of instance I_i;
- I_i^{WT}: waiting time of instance I_i;
- I_i^{AT}: boolean variable used to determine whether an instance I_i is attended before the maximum waiting time or not. 1, if $I_i^{WT} \leq I_i^{ewt}$. 0, otherwise;

Maximize:

$$\sum_{I_i \in I} I_i^{AT} \tag{2}$$

Subject to:

$$I_i^{ST} \geq I_i^a \wedge I_i^{ST} \geq time + 1 \quad \forall I_i \in \mathcal{I} \tag{3}$$

$$I_i^{WT} = I_i^{ST} - I_i^a \quad \forall I_i \in \mathcal{I} \tag{4}$$

$$I_i^{AT} = \begin{cases} 1, & \text{if } I_i^{WT} \leq I_i^{ewt} \\ 0, & otherwise \end{cases} \quad \forall I_i \in \mathcal{I} \tag{5}$$

$$I_i^{ET} = I_i^{ST} + (I_i^{rt} * I_i^{AT}) \quad \forall I_i \in \mathcal{I} \tag{6}$$

$$I_i^{ET} \leq I_j^{ST} - 1 \vee I_i^{ST} \geq I_j^{ET} + 1 \quad \forall I_i, I_j \in \mathcal{I}, I_i \neq I_j \tag{7}$$

$$I_i^{ST}, I_i^{ET}, I_i^{WT} \geq 0 \quad \forall I_i \in \mathcal{I} \tag{8}$$

$$I_i^{AT} \in \{0,1\} \quad \forall I_i \in \mathcal{I} \tag{9}$$

The objective of the MIP model is to compute a schedule of instances that maximizes the number of attended or solved instances. A similar approach was proposed in [10]. However, the authors attempted to create a schedule of solvers by maximizing the amount of solved instances requiring the lowest amount of time among all schedules.

Constraint (3) enforces that every instance has to start after its arrival and after the system becomes available. The values of (I_i^{ST}) are later used as instance priorities in our IEQ. Constraint (4) calculates the waiting time of each instance. It is also used to determine if an instance is attended or not in constraint (5).

Constraint (6) calculates the end time of an instance I_i. Such end time, depends mainly on its start time and on the amount of time to solve such instance. However, it can also assign an end time equals to the start time (i.e., 0 time for processing) when an instance is not marked as attended (i.e., $I_i^{ET} = I_i^{ST}$, if $I_i^{AT} = 0$). Finally, the disjunctive constraints (7) ensure that instances are not scheduled at the same time (i.e., avoid instance overlapping).

Table 1. Model evaluations and overhead to calculate features for testing the models with partition: 30% Trainig 70% Testing.

Domain	Regression models		
Features	RMSE	CC	Testing features overhead
Trivial	1.42	0.68	0 s
Cheap	0.78	0.91	26.421 s
Expensive	0.77	0.92	273.337 s

5   Off-line Experiments

We evaluate our approach using the solver MiniSAT with a time limit t of one hour. We also used the same set of instances (and algorithm runtime data) as those reported in [8]. The SAT instance set comprises 1676 industrial instances (INDU) from the annual SAT competitions and SAT races from 2002 to 2010. From the 1676 instances, MiniSAT is able to solve 1251 within one hour time limit, thus, leaving 425 unsolved instances (i.e., 425 h of ineffective CPU usage if executed naively on a cloud resource).

As indicated in Sect. 2, we use a well-known vector of features for SAT solving extracted from the literature. In particular, we use the same feature set as [8] (i,e., 138 features to characterise SAT problems) and we present results using trivial, cheap, and expensive features. In this paper, we use a random forest implementation from Weka [17] (version 3.8) with its default hyperparameters to train our regression models. A preliminary evaluation of other techniques such as Gaussian process, neural networks, and linear regression showed lower performance. We recall that this behaviour is consistent to the literature and similarly to [8], we performed a log-transformation of the runtimes to train the

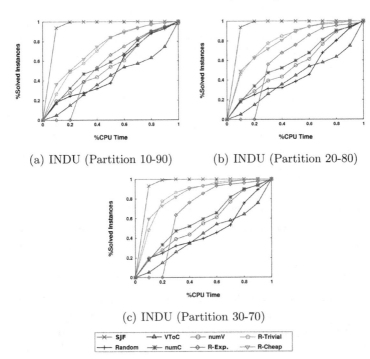

(a) INDU (Partition 10-90)   (b) INDU (Partition 20-80)

(c) INDU (Partition 30-70)

Fig. 1. Visual comparison of priority functions to create IEQs under different train-test dataset partitions for SAT-Industrial instances.

regression models. Moreover, we randomly split the instance set into 3 partitions for training-testing our regression models, namely (10%–90%, 20%–80%, 30%–70%).

We consider two measures to evaluate our regression models: root mean squared error (RMSE) and Pearson's correlation coefficient (CC). RMSE is used to measure the discrepancies between true values and the estimated ones, therefore, lower RMSE are better. The CC is a value between -1 and 1 that indicates the statistical correlation between the true value and the estimated one. In CC, 1 is a perfect correlation, 0 is no correlation, and -1 is an inverse correlation.

In Table 1, we report evaluation measures of the regression models with a 30%-70% data set partition. It also includes the CPU time required to calculate features for the testing instances. It can be observed that the regression models trained with *cheap* and *expensive* feature families, report nearly the same CC and RMSE. For instance, the correlation of the predictions is 0.91 (*cheap*) vs. 0.92 (*expensive*). Moreover, models trained with *trivial* features report a lower CC and a higher RMSE.

We observe a trade-off between the feature family and the quality of the predictions. *Trivial* features are basically free but they have an impact on the quality of the models. On the other hand, the set of *Expensive* features have a lower error and a high correlation but the computational cost to calculate the

Table 2. Experimental results varying the Train-Test sets and the global CPU time 10%, 30% and 50% of the baseline time (i.e., SJF using real runtime values). Bold numbers represent the best results per column w.r.t SJF.

Simulation	10–90			20–80			30–70		
	10%	30%	50%	10%	30%	50%	10%	30%	50%
SJF	0.94	1.00	1.00	0.94	1.00	1.00	0.93	1.00	1.00
Random	0.18	0.28	0.38	0.19	0.31	0.39	0.20	0.32	0.40
numV	0.19	0.39	0.54	0.20	0.39	0.55	0.20	0.39	0.55
numC	0.17	0.47	0.59	0.18	0.47	0.60	0.18	0.47	0.59
VtoC	0.05	0.26	0.45	0.05	0.26	0.45	0.05	0.26	0.45
R-Expensive	0.00	0.39	0.66	0.00	0.56	0.76	0.00	0.64	0.85
R-Cheap	**0.37**	**0.62**	**0.84**	**0.49**	0.72	**0.91**	**0.60**	0.82	**0.93**
R-Trivial	0.27	0.57	**0.84**	0.46	**0.77**	0.89	0.48	**0.86**	**0.93**

features is typically expensive (e.g., 75.9 h for 1174 instances). *Cheap* features unlike *trivial* and *Expensive* features, offer an interesting trade-off between prediction quality and computational cost. We want to avoid situations in which it is more expensive to compute priorities than solving the actual instances.

We now move our attention to Fig. 1. In this figure, we report the percentage of solved instances (y-axis) within certain cumulative CPU time (x-axis) using our Off-line approach with eight different ordering policies. The approach is experimented over 90%, 80%, and 70% of the instances, because a partition was used to train our regression models. We evaluated, three deterministic policies, i.e., numC, numV, VToC; three machine learning-based policies with regression, i.e., R-Trivial, R-Cheap, R-Expensive; additionally, we present a random policy (in black) in which we randomly shuffle the solving order of the instances. Moreover, we also present the best possible ordering SJF (in gray). As expected the ML-based policies perform better than the deterministic policies and are closer to the SJF policy. Additionally, the percentage of solved instances tend to be higher as we experiment using regression models trained with bigger partitions.

At the broadest level, it can be observed that the three deterministic policies and the random policy require little processing to create the IEQ. They start solving instances earlier than learning-based policies which require CPU time for feature calculation. It is worth noting the important overhead in the feature computation of using the entire feature set for industrial instances. Computing *Expensive* features represents about 20% of the overall cumulative time (the same CPU time needed for R-trivial to solve nearly 80% of the solvable instances using the 30–70 partition).

Finally, Table 2 summarizes the Off-line experiments presented in the paper. This table shows detailed information of the percentage of solved instances varying the global limit in the cumulative CPU time for three different Training-Testing partitions (10–90, 20–80, 30–70). We use the cumulative time of the SJF

Table 3. INDU (Partition 30–70) Baseline reference test with perfect predictions. Bold numbers represent the greatest amount of solved instances per test.

Test config.		Perfect estimations				
Interarrival	Waiting T.	FCFS		SJF		MIP
min-max	min-max	N	H	N	H	H
1–300	1–300	174	598	186	**624**	618
1–1000	1–500	393	646	401	**661**	655
1–300	1–600	178	629	221	**664**	651
1–300	1–1000	190	669	266	**712**	708
1–3600	1–1500	690	726	693	**731**	730
1–3600	1–3600	754	774	761	**783**	780
1–1000	1000–3000	465	763	633	**788**	786
1–500	1000–3000	252	770	602	790	**810**
1–400	1000–3000	280	763	606	785	**806**
1–300	1000–3000	186	724	630	756	**793**

policy as a baseline reference. Bold numbers represent the highest number of solved instances per cumulative time column that gets closer to SJF.

We can observe that the deterministic policies reached percentages of solved instances smaller than 59% expending up to 50% of the CPU time in the three experiment partitions, while ML-based policies get to solve up to 93% of the instances with respect to the best ordering (i.e., SJF). Notice that our IEQ with the *R-Cheap* function using 30% of the CPU time, reached 62% solved instances (with a 10–90 partition), 72% (with a 20–80 partition), and 82% (with a 30–70 partition) with respect to the maximum reported. These values highly differ from the random execution which reported 28%, 31%, 32% and represent an increment of 34%, 41%, and 50% solved instances respectively.

6   On-line Experiments

We evaluate our On-line approach using the same SAT solver and instance set from the previous section (i.e., MiniSAT for industrial SAT instances with a time limit t of one hour and algorithm runtime used and reported in [8]). We also used the same random forest models as those trained in Sect. 5 and summarized in Table 1. Additionally, as proposed in Sect. 4.1, we evaluated five combinations of three priority functions (FCFS, SJF, MIP) and our two instance execution strategies, i.e., naive and heuristic based (resp. N, H).

For MIP experiments, we run it for at most 60 s every time an instance needed to be selected from the queue. In general MIP adds low overhead and presented average solving times of 1.5 s. Moreover, we decided not to include the MIP + N execution, since preliminary experiments showed a low performance.

We also observed that MIP + H improves MIP + N performance, however, we noticed that heuristic (H) excessively affects MIP schedule. It usually stops an instance from running when MIP had already decided that such instance had to run to completion. We think that this behaviour can be improved if we only apply the heuristic H to instances that are running without being scheduled by MIP. e.g., an arriving instance when the queue is empty.

We now move our attention to Table 3, where the approach is experimented using the 30%–70% partition, i.e., 30% of the instances to build the regression model and 70% of the instances to test our On-line computational approach. For these tests, we relaxed the On-line system characteristic B1 from Sect. 4 and use true runtime values as a baseline reference. Additionally, to simulate characteristics B2 and B3 from Sect. 4 (i.e., a stream of arriving instances and waiting time constraints), we configured nine different tests using random interarrival and waiting time constraints.

Interestingly, our heuristic based execution (H) increases the amount of solved instances w.r.t the naive execution (N). It seems that our execution heuristic (H) has a bigger impact when the interarrival range is small (e.g., 1–300) and seems to decrease its impact when the interarrival range is bigger (e.g., 1–3600). For instance, in the first, second, and third tests with a random interarrival 1–300, there is an increment of (3.4x, 3.5x, 3.5x) solved instances for the FCFS priority function and (3.3x, 2.9x, 3.1x) for the SJF priority function. On the other hand, the fifth and sixth tests with a random interarrival 1–3600, present an increment of (1.05x, 1.02x) for both FCFS and SJF. We attribute this behaviour to the fact that smaller interarrivals typically conduce to have longer queues, thus stopping an instance execution has a bigger impact on the amount of queued instances.

At the broadest level, Table 3 shows that SJF + H is the best ordering policy and instance execution configuration. However, MIP + H seems to perform better than SJF + H with short interarrivals and long waiting times. Such behaviour can be observed in the last three tests. It might be because this configuration typically generate long queues and the heuristic (H) does not excessively affect MIP schedule since the waiting times are long (e.g., stop an instance from running when MIP had already decided that such instance had to run to completion).

Finally, Table 4 summarizes the On-line experiments using the regression models with *Cheap* and *Trivial* features. We omitted *Expensive* features for the computational cost that it adds to the system. We can observe that the experiments with cheap features present a similar behaviour w.r.t the baseline experiments and typically solve more instances than experiments with trivial features.

Table 4. INDU (Partition 30–70) Test results with Cheap and Trivial features. Bold numbers represent the greatest amount of solved instances per test.

Test config.		Cheap features					Trivial features				
Interarrival	Waiting T.	FCFS		SJF		MIP	FCFS		SJF		MIP
min-max	min-max	N	H	N	H	H	N	H	N	H	H
1–300	1–300	174	608	185	**619**	594	174	600	184	**611**	595
1–1000	1–500	393	655	401	**671**	658	393	655	393	**667**	654
1–300	1–600	178	645	200	**652**	651	178	636	194	**655**	653
1–300	1–1000	190	680	221	**691**	684	190	675	217	694	**696**
1–3600	1–1500	690	738	692	**742**	738	690	733	692	**735**	729
1–3600	1–3600	754	777	761	**792**	782	754	773	757	**780**	770
1–1000	1000–3000	465	777	569	763	**780**	465	**773**	566	772	772
1–500	1000–3000	252	793	481	776	**796**	252	**794**	467	777	793
1–400	1000–3000	280	766	440	755	**782**	280	753	439	759	**777**
1–300	1000–3000	186	733	422	725	**763**	186	730	418	739	**759**

7   Related Work

Cloud computing provides on-demand resources and services over a network and has brought new challenges to the construction of new architectures, workload structures, and scheduling algorithms. Many system designs give preference to short jobs applying policies like Shortest-Job-First (SJF) and to reduce fragmentation backfilling they schedule small jobs into scheduling gaps [15]. Another scheduling policy includes Preemptive-Shortest-Job-First (PSJF) where the new jobs entering the system with the smallest expected duration (size) are given preemptive priority [1].

Some scheduling policies like SJF require to know how long each job will run, which is unknown for many type of jobs, including combinatorial problems. Thus, many scheduling approaches typically assume the existence of an accurate runtime predictor. For instance, in [13] the authors assume accurate runtime predictions and propose a family of *Cloud-based, online, Hybrid scheduling policies* (CoH) in order to minimize rental cost by using on-demand and reserved instances for which the authors formulate the *resource provisioning* and *job allocation* as integer programming problems. In this paper, we propose execution schedules for typical NP-Complete problems (e.g., SAT) that present high runtime variability from instance to instance. Additionally, the best known approach to estimate runtime for these kind of problems is by using regression models which typically lead to inaccurate predictions.

In [4] the authors propose a portfolio approach to identify the most suitable parallel job scheduling policy. The authors show that selecting an appropriate policy can lead to a performance improvement from 7% to 100% when compared to the best individual policy. Contrasting with Deng et al. approach, in [16] the authors use a portfolio methodology to select robust scheduling policies in presence of system variances. Despite not using a portfolio approach, we show that naive policies SJF are badly affected by inaccurate runtime predictions and might not be able to become the best individual policies when scheduling combinatorial problems without preemption. As a result, we also show how to use a heuristic based execution to mitigate regression models missed predictions in order to improve policies performance.

8   Conclusions and Future Work

In this paper, we have presented Off-line and On-line approaches to solve SAT problems that can be extended to solve combinatorial problem in a cloud environment with budget constraints. In cloud computing, computation time can be rented by the hour and for a given number of processors. Therefore, in this paper we study the gain in the number of solved instances varying the total global CPU time in an Off-line system. Furthermore, we study ordering policies and execution heuristics to maximize the amount of solved instances in an On-line system with arrival and waiting time constraints.

To mitigate the ineffective usage of CPU time in Off-line systems, we proposed regression policies that schedule promising solvable instances first using our IEQ. We observed that with very limited global CPU time (i.e., 30% of the baseline), the ML-based methodologies solve up to 88% SAT instances. Additionally, learning-based approaches typically solve more instances than deterministic ordering approaches with considerably less time. Additionally, to get the top performance of an On-line system and maximize the amount of solved instances, we study a combination of ordering policies and execution heuristics that showed an increment of up to 3.5x solved instances, with respect to standard ordering policies such as FCFS and SJF. We also plan to extend our study in order to explore the cost/benefit of our IEQs under different cloud pricing models as the ones offer by Amazon EC2. For instance, reserving computational power and bidding for spot instances might be considerably cheaper than the on-demand approach explored in this paper.

References

1. Arpaci-Dusseau, R.H., Arpaci-Dusseau, A.C.: Chapter 7: scheduling: introduction. In: Operating Systems: Three Easy Pieces. Arpaci-Dusseau Books (2014)
2. Bartz-Beielstein, T., Markon, S.: Tuning search algorithms for real-world applications: a regression tree based approach. In: Congress on Evolutionary Computation, CEC 2004, vol. 1, pp. 1111–1118. IEEE (2004)
3. Breiman, L.: Random forests. Mach. Learn. **45**(1), 5–32 (2001)
4. Deng, K., Song, J., Ren, K., Iosup, A.: Exploring portfolio scheduling for long-term execution of scientific workloads in IaaS clouds. In: SC (2013)
5. Benchmark Descriptions: SAT COMPETITION 2014 Solver and Benchmark Descriptions (2014)

6. Feitelson, D.G., Rudolph, L.: Metrics and benchmarking for parallel job scheduling. In: Feitelson, D.G., Rudolph, L. (eds.) JSSPP 1998. LNCS, vol. 1459, pp. 1–24. Springer, Heidelberg (1998). doi:10.1007/BFb0053978

7. Heule, M.J.H., Kullmann, O., Marek, V.W.: Solving and verifying the boolean pythagorean triples problem via cube-and-conquer. In: Creignou, N., Le Berre, D. (eds.) SAT 2016. LNCS, vol. 9710, pp. 228–245. Springer, Cham (2016). doi:10.1007/978-3-319-40970-2_15

8. Hutter, F., Xu, L., Hoos, H.H., Leyton-Brown, K.: Algorithm runtime prediction: methods & evaluation. Artif. Intell. **206**, 79–111 (2014)

9. Järvisalo, M., Le Berre, D., Roussel, O., Simon, L.: The international SAT solver competitions. AI Mag. **33**(1), 89–92 (2012)

10. Kadioglu, S., Malitsky, Y., Sabharwal, A., Samulowitz, H., Sellmann, M.: Algorithm selection and scheduling. In: Lee, J. (ed.) CP 2011. LNCS, vol. 6876, pp. 454–469. Springer, Heidelberg (2011). doi:10.1007/978-3-642-23786-7_35

11. Leyton-Brown, K., Nudelman, E., Shoham, Y.: Empirical hardness models: methodology and a case study on combinatorial auctions. J. ACM (JACM) **56**(4), 22 (2009)

12. Schroeder, B., Wierman, A., Harchol-Balter, M.: Open versus closed: a cautionary tale. In: NSDI, vol. 6, p. 18 (2006)

13. Shen, S., Deng, K., Iosup, A., Epema, D.: Scheduling jobs in the cloud using on-demand and reserved instances. In: Wolf, F., Mohr, B., Mey, D. (eds.) Euro-Par 2013. LNCS, vol. 8097, pp. 242–254. Springer, Heidelberg (2013). doi:10.1007/978-3-642-40047-6_27

14. Smith-Miles, K., van Hemert, J.I.: Discovering the suitability of optimisation algorithms by learning from evolved instances. Ann. Math. Artif. Intell. **61**(2), 87 (2011)

15. Srinivasan, S., Kettimuthu, R., Subramani, V., Sadayappan, P.: Characterization of backfilling strategies for parallel job scheduling. In: ICPP Workshops, pp. 514–522 (2002)

16. Sukhija, N., Malone, B., Srivastava, S., Banicescu, I., Ciorba, F.M.: Portfolio-based selection of robust dynamic loop scheduling algorithms using machine learning. In: IPDPS Workshops (2014)

17. Witten, I.H., Frank, E., Hall, M.A.: Data Mining: Practical Machine Learning Tools and Techniques, 3rd edn. Morgan Kaufmann Publishers Inc., San Francisco (2011)

Human-Computer Interaction

Interactive System Implementation to Encourage Reading in Vulnerable Community Children

Claudia Catalina Londoño Chito$^{(\boxtimes)}$, Luis Fernando Jojoa Quintero,
and Andrés Fernando Solano Alegría

Universidad Autónoma de Occidente, Cali, Colombia
{claudia.londono,luis.jojoa,afsolano}@uao.edu.co

Abstract. This paper describes the process for the development of an interactive educational system for the children of the Siloé neighborhood of the Cali city, Colombia. Starting from the purpose of mitigating negative influences within the context of the neighborhood, this project seeks to encourage curiosity in children by reading as a core competency for their future, through a technological solution that sparks the interest of this community. In order to define the characteristics of the system, an inquiry process was carried out to identify the needs and characteristics of the target audience, as well as their preferences about technological devices and applications used by them. Once the main features were defined, the process of prototyping began based on sketches that evolved into prototypes of low and high fidelity. Then, those prototypes were evaluated with potential users, applying usability evaluation methods in order to collect information about the system and make the necessary adjustments to get an usable final product.

Keywords: Children · Technology · Reading · Prototyping · Usability · Interactive system

1 Introduction

Academic institutions are aimed at the integral education of children, instilling principles and values, strengthening further than the cognitive skills and guide them towards a better future. However, for educational institutions located in the Siloé neighborhood of the Cali city, Colombia, this target represents a greater challenge due to the conditions of the context surrounding them.

In the Siloé neighborhood, education has become an important factor for the formation of children who in the future are the reference of change. The problem is not only the level of education the children have access, but also the way in which the desire for study is inculcated to them. According to a survey conducted by the *Cali, Cómo vamos* program [1], by the year 2015 the number of children aged between 5 and 17 years old who attend public institutions has decreased by 6% compared to the year 2014 with a 62%. On the other hand, it should be noted the interest of educational institutions to develop reading skills. However, these have not had the expected results as evidenced in the Cultural Consumption Survey [2] (ECC) published by the Departamento Administrativo Nacional de Estadística (DANE) in December 2014. The survey reveals that

© Springer International Publishing AG 2017
A. Solano and H. Ordoñez (Eds.): CCC 2017, CCIS 735, pp. 543–556, 2017.
DOI: 10.1007/978-3-319-66562-7_39

51.6% of the population of 12 years and over did not read any books in 12 months and the remaining 48.4% have read just one book in the same period of time. Moreover, it was found that within the non-reading population, 55.9% does not read due to lack of interest for reading.

Based on the above, it is intended to develop a solution through an interactive system making use of resources that can have a positive impact on the child and to convert them in "curious connoisseurs" of technology and to awake in them interest in reading.

Section 2 presents the problem. Section 3 describes the target audience needs and the process for their identification. Section 4 includes the features of the proposed system, which is assessed using a usability method evaluation that is documented in the Sect. 5. Finally, Sect. 6 presents the conclusions and future work.

2   About the Problem

Currently the student drop-out rate is a relevant problem in Cali, this arises both in schools of basic education and higher education. As for dropout in universities and other higher education institutions, the reasons include the economic and academic. A significant number of students cannot afford costs and others fail to meet the academic requirements by its difficulty or poor election of academic programs, due to a weak projection at the professional level. School desertion occurs primarily in the upper grades and the main causes are: rebellion, economic limitations which entail those students need to work, in addition to the lack of vision and professional projection [3].

One of the common reasons for desertion, both in higher education and the Basic first, is the professional projection [3]. This is crucial because if a child sets its own goals and choose a career according to his preferences and skills, he can draw a path in which his training of high school will be essential, he will focus on having superior performance and he will be acting in such a way that it may be increasingly close to his target, then moving away from activities that hinder his progress.

Another barrier that prevents young people to continue with their training are SABER tests [4] that are carried out at national level at the end of the cycle of secondary education; the results of these are decisive at the time to initiate a process of admission for a professional career and even the scores allow access to scholarships and State benefits. A competition that is vital is reading comprehension [4], as this directly impacts on the performance of children in other subjects, even in those that involve numbers. Despite its importance, the level of this competition is just acceptable as evidenced by the results of the SABER test made to students in grades third, fifth and ninth, i.e. children between 8 and 14 years of public and private schools. Therefore, the educational institutions have included in their academic program a reader plan. However, the effect was not expected because according to the ECC [2] by DANE, 38% of the 12-year-old reading population read by academic demands, not on their own initiative.

Given that the community of Siloé in the city of Cali, and especially children who live in it, they are in a context demarcated by social and economic issues, they are exposed to a whole set of activities that are risky for them. The lack of opportunities, as well as other cultural factors make that crime, drugs and in some cases up to prostitution are common activities that day by day the kids of Siloé have to prove. Not intervening in the children in time can result in them a distortion of reality and because of this poor decision-making about their future. In that sense, the problem that has been identified within this community is the vulnerability of children to the choice of illicit activities as a project for their life. This is due to the high degree of influence that the neighborhood exerts on them, as well as the lack of opportunities that these children have when they finish their secondary studies by the poor orientation and of aid to continue forming them academically.

Based on the defined problem, it is intended to develop a solution for children from aged 8 to 13 years of the Siloé neighborhood, whose main characteristics are presented below.

The target public are inhabitants of the commune 20 of Cali. Most of this commune stretches over mountainous areas. Children between 8 and 13 years are enrolled between 4th and 6th grade in educational institutions in the area, mostly public, with an hourly intensity of 6 h per day. They perform extracurricular activities such as playing in the neighborhood, learning to play musical instruments, practicing soccer; somebody also help in the work of their parents. They frequently visit the Vive Digital spaces [5], for the facilities of access to technology that they do not have in their homes and to receive advice on topics of interest.

In spite of the economic limitations of the community, in this population they possess the basic technological knowledge. In most of their homes there is at least one computer and a mobile touch device (Tablet or smartphone) and they handle them without difficulty. The computer is the tool they use most to make academic consultations and to play; however, joining mobile phones and tablets it has a great use of mobile devices for leisure.

3   Target Audience Needs

After determining the problem to be addressed and defining the target audience, we proceeded to study the context and investigate the children and others involved in order to know their needs, daily activities, skills, dynamics in which they participate in the school environment, tastes and preferences regarding technology. For this, a series of interviews were first applied and after their analysis a survey was designed to collect specific data.

3.1   Interviews

The main objective of the interviews was to obtain comprehensive and detailed information on children's tastes and preferences regarding technology and the use of electronic devices. In addition to knowing the extracurricular activities in which they perform best and also know about their favorite subjects in school and the reason for this. In the interview, 11 objectives were established, which were related to 18 questions, (see Table 1).

Table 1. Interview´s objectives and questions.

Objectives		Questions associated	
1	To know the subjects of the greatest interest in children to include themes of them within the content to be developed	1	What is your favorite subject? Why?
2	To learn the practices carried out in the classroom	2	What activities are carried out in your classroom?
3	To extract good methodologies employed in class to apply them in the context of the solution	3	Which do you like? Why?
4	Establish how users may interact	4	Do you prefer to work alone or in groups?
		5	Do you compete in games?
		6	Do you like to pass the highest scores?
		7	Do you join teams or do teammates to advance or win?
5	To know what kind of technologies are familiar to children	8	Do you have in your home devices such as computer, console video games, tablet or mobile phone?
		9	What devices like these have you used?
6	To know which technology or device is easier to use for children	10	Which of these appliances do you feel most comfortable with? Why?
7	To know the most frequent activities that children make in devices that use generally	11	What do you use these electronic devices for? Do you play, do you investigate…?
8	Determine the aptitudes of children to continue working on them and ensure that these are potentiated	12	Outside the school on what else you do you consider yourself very good? Like sport, music, art, among others.
9	Determine the didactics of play that the child enjoys	13	What games do you like? Why? What are they like?
		14	Have you played in any electronic device (such as Tablet, computer or cell phone)?
		15	What of those games you like most? Why? What are they like?
10	Determine the didactics with which the child learns more easily	16	Have you ever used applications or games in order to learn?
		17	Which ones? Why did they interest you? As they are?
11	Learn the techniques of interaction that are more attractive to children	18	How do you prefer to play or use the gadgets you play with?

The interviews were carried out at the Educational Institution Eustaquio Palacios, Luis López de Mesa headquarter in the sector of Siloé. 11 children participated, 6 of them in 4th grade and the rest in 5th grade. The teachers in charge helped with the organization and choice of the children. Interviews were conducted in a directed and individual way, with an average duration of 8 min each one.

The analysis of the collected information was carried out in a qualitative way and the following results were obtained. Children enjoy technology and mathematics classes more. They argue that solving mathematical operations and problems helps them think and develop cognitive abilities, while the technology class attracts them because they have access to computers to play and search for interest information. Without leaving aside that some of them voiced great passion for art, as they can express their feelings and emotions.

About classroom activities, they enjoy being involved in the teaching of the topics, having the possibility to make meaningful contributions and exchange opinions with their classmates, so that they are recognized as active agents that help build a class more dynamic.

As for the form of work, an equitable distribution was obtained. Those who prefer to work individually argue that working with others strengthens their distraction and loss of concentration, which, given the age of this public, is a risk factor that has an impact on academic performance. On the other hand, those who defend the group work, emphasize that it promotes collaborative learning, since among them they resolve their doubts and practice what they have learned, reflecting their capacity to give and accept help towards a goal.

It was identified that all children interviewed have at least two electronic devices, mainly a computer and a smart phone or tablet. With those who feel more at ease are the tactile devices and secondly with the desktop computer. The first option because the touch screen does not require repeated actions to carry out a task. On the other hand, the desktop computer was the first device they used before using a cell phone or tablet so they dominate its handling. Another important fact is that for children it is easier to handle the mouse than the trackpad of a laptop computer.

In general, the main function that children give to the devices they use most often is oriented to the investigation of school tasks and information related to subjects seen in class that generate interest. Finally, and to a lesser extent, they use the same to play.

Among his extracurricular activities are sports and cultural practices such as soccer training, playing musical instruments, attending drawing and painting classes, in which children in his personal opinion perform well.

Board games such as parquet, staircase and chess were most prominent by children when asked about their favorites. These games entertain them and also they require that children test their mathematical and strategic skills to defeat their rivals. An important feature that was identified to a high degree is competitiveness, as the games mentioned require more than one player and the goal is to win over others.

The video games genres preferred by children are adventure, action, and racing. The characteristics in that motivate the children are the competition, the confrontation with rivals, the goal to reach first, obtain the best scores and the formation of alliances to overcome stronger rivals, denoting a strong desire to be the best one in the games.

Applications and games are a great help to children when they learn about mathematics and English, because they argue that in a didactic way they can understand subjects that are difficult for them. They also require a brief introduction to the application, which provides a quick explanation of the operation of the application and the steps to complete the interaction, so they can independently perform the proposed activities.

Finally, most stated that their preferred form of interaction is through tangible interfaces, because these are intuitive and easier to use when people interact with games and applications. Others prefer the use of physical controls arguing that each button has a unique function and therefore is easier to learn to handle and is universal for all applications.

3.2 Surveys

The execution of the interviews and their subsequent analysis allowed extracting patterns on the tastes and preferences of the children at the technological level, as well as the dynamics and mechanical interaction they prefer. Then, a survey was conducted to a set of children. With the patterns found in the interviews, 11 questions were formulated, using multiple-choice options with unique response, check boxes and Likert scale, which are listed in Table 2.

The survey was carried out to 50 children studying grade 4th and 5th in the Eustaquio Palacios School, Luis López de Mesa headquarter in the facilities of the informatics classroom. There they accessed the survey through the platform of Google Forms. It was with the accompaniment of the directors of the group and the time spent by each student to answer questions was 6 min on average.

The first two questions are oriented to know the device in which children prefer to play and how to control it. 42% of the respondents chose the computer while 28% and 26% chose tablet and cell phone, respectively. As for the way of interacting with games, 32% prefers tactile interfaces, 26% controls and 24% prefers the joining of these, therefore 56% includes tactile interfaces and 50% controls.

Regarding the game mode, only 12% play against the computer, 40% prefer to play individually and 34% and 28% involve more than one player, in multiplayer modes and teams respectively. It is evident that they enjoy playing individually but also involving other real players, since multiplayer mode and teams add up to 62%.

In terms of interaction with other users, 82% approve the exchange of gifts between players; it shows the children's interest in interacting with others and being able to help each other.

88% of respondents enjoy music and sound effects in applications, suggesting that the solution to be developed should include this as a fundamental part.

In terms of game genres, children could choose two, the favorites for them are adventure with 68% and combat with 40%, and the least approved is the genre of trivia with 10%. Therefore, the solution must have characteristics that involve exploration, solving puzzles and problems, having a narrative, interacting with characters among others.

With a Likert scale, between 1 and 5, the approval to save the process was 70%, 58% rated 5 and 12% with 4. Therefore, the need to incorporate a user account to save scores arises, as it is 60% agree to have a comparison of scores and highlight the best performances, encouraging competitiveness and motivating children to play more.

Table 2. Survey questions.

Question	Type of answer	Values
Which of these devices do you prefer to play?	Only answer	* Tablet * Cell phone * Computer * Other
How do you prefer to control the games?	Only answer	* Touch * Controls * With the body * Touch + control * Other
Which game mode do you prefer?	Check boxes (Max 2 selections)	* 1 player * Player vs. Computer * Multiplayer * Team
Would you like to be able to give and receive gifts from other players?	Only answer	* Yes * Not * Gives equal
Do you like the music and the effects of sound in a game?	Only answer	* Yes * Not * Gives equal
Choose your favorite game genres	Check boxes (maximum two selections)	* Adventure * Trivia/questions * Combat * Puzzle * Strategy * Simulation
How much you would like to have a user to save your data and progress in the game?	Likert scale	From 1 to 5
How much would you like to be able to compare your scores with other players?	Likert scale	From 1 to 5
Would you like to be finding parts throughout the game?	Only answer	* If * Not * Gives equal
How much would you the game to increase its difficulty depending on your progress like?	Likert scale	From 1 to 5
Would you like to receive rewards when you meet some task?	Only answer	* If * Not * Gives equal

On the increase of the difficulty, a Likert scale was used. 70% would like this, 54% rated 5 (maximum) and 16% rated 4. Thus, within the solution the level of difficulty must be increased progressively.

The search for parts is attractive for 94% of the respondents. Here is another way to connect children in the different activities of the solution. Finally, another important finding was that children like to receive rewards, 86% of respondents feel more excited knowing that they will be rewarded, this will also motivate them to play more often and achieve success.

3.3   User's Needs

Following interviews and surveys, important data were collected on how children behave in their daily lives, how they learn and how they use technology devices. Given the focus of the project, certain needs were determined to be met from the user's perspective and others that should characterize the type of system to be implemented. The user needs identified are as follows.

Gamification.   Children require motivation to continue with their tasks. Giving reward for good actions and good performance is a simple and effective way of doing this. Additionally, when there is competition, children want to win by being the best, so they will be motivated to frequent use of the developing solution in order to improve performance.

Collaborative work.   The post-inquiry analysis reflects the importance of third-party users or players when using an application. These generate influence against the perception and opinion that is built of the interaction, helping to create a more enriching experience. The possibility of giving and receiving help and assistance between users teaches children the value of altruism and collaborative work in order to achieve the proposed objectives.

Proactive learning.   Children are developing cognitive skills all the time and building knowledge. What they learn at this stage of their life will be critical to understanding and acquiring information later. The way in which children are taught can be crucial, thus determining whether they learn or not. Through a wide variety of applications children learn and exercise their mental capacities implicitly, this is a very productive way and changes the paradigm of traditional education methodologies. Through the solution that will be implemented, the aim is to motivate children to take part in reading through technology, so they must acquire basic knowledge and learn to use tools. However, it is important that the bases that they obtain serve to develop knowledge by themselves and that they have the ability to see the reach and all the utilities of the reading and the tools that will be shown to them.

3.4   Technical Requirements of the System

Background music.   The investigation revealed that the music is an important element of the applications and games that children use. The background music and sound effects will be implemented in the solution in order to stimulate and generate positive emotions.

Score and reward system.   The solution must include mechanics of gamification to connect users and motivate them to terminate the interaction, incentives such as scores and rewards that boost users will therefore be implemented.

Multisensory and multimodal interaction. Aiming to offer interaction with non-traditional devices and achieve a new experience, the solution should include multimodal interfaces [6] that combine two or more input modes, and stimulating several senses of the body: sight, hearing and touch.

Multi-user. In order to promote collaborative work it is necessary to have access to the solution for users, equally, it must support at least 2 users for interaction.

4   Proposed Interactive System

Taking into account inquiry made to the target audience and others involved, as well as the needs detected, an interactive system is proposed in which a story is told through the display of multimedia content, including images, sound and 2D animation; posing a conflict for the user to solve it. To do this, it is planned to establish the solution within the facilities of the Departmental Library Jorge Garcés Borrero. It is the central library in Cali, a place with a great supply of literary, cultural and artistic resources to encourage reading and research. Specifically in Maker Lab [7], a space equipped with state-of-the-art technology for exploration with the new Information and Communication Technologies. These places offer an accompaniment for those who visit these spaces, to interact with electronic equipment and devices such as: robotics kits, 3D printers, laser cutters, cameras, legos and thus to build interactive experiences, audiovisual productions, games, applications, among others, with the accompaniment of support and training staff.

The literary work chosen to shape into the system was the book "The Mystery of the Russian Ruby" [8] because it offers an interesting narrative and a conflict that gives the reader a new role of investigator to solve the mystery raised, integrating in this way game mechanics.

4.1   Interactive System Components

Desktop application. The desktop application will be developed making use of the Unity game engine, in order to take advantage of the tools that this engine provides, as the animation engine in order to perform animations needed to generate interactive and engaging content for the user, canvas to create the Head Up Display (HUD), through which the users can view their scores, collected tracks and time elapsed since the beginning of the interaction, scripts to control the actions that the user will execute and respond to them in the rendered content. In addition, media to be displayed by the user will be created with the tool suite from Adobe Illustrator, which will be designed each of the characters, scenes and objects that make up the interactive content in order to have total control over it and realize interactions defined during the experience displayed by the system.

Physical interface. The physical interface consists of a table which will represent each of the scenarios that will be deployed in virtual form in the system, in order to generate a relationship between actions that takes physical form and the feedback generated by the virtual system on the user physically. In addition, physical objects will be used that will represent elements within each of the scenarios. With these you can interact directly with the content, as they make use of RFID technology to be identified. In addition, a micro-controller (Arduino UNO) is used in order to create a communication channel between the "tagged" physical objects and the system (see Fig. 1).

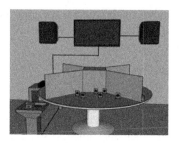

Fig. 1. 3D Model of physic interface (own source).

4.2 Visual Definition of the System

As a result of research by experts in interface design for children's sites and inquiry methods such as the *focus group*, it has been standardized that children prefer bright colors that immediately catch their attention [9], however in these studies there is no common agreement on which colors to use. Therefore, a survey was carried out on 10 children belonging to the target public, between 8 and 13 years of age, 6 children, 4 girls to know their preferences in terms of color; during the first phase they were asked to select their favorite colors (maximum 3) and they were also asked to openly mention colors that they definitely did not like, with the possibility of leaving the field empty in case they did not have a marked dislike for some color.

Significant preferences were found towards red with 60%, light green with 40% and yellow and light blue with 30% in both cases. The colors with little acceptance were the purple with 40% and with 30% the coffee, black and gray.

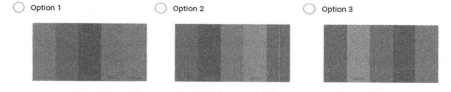

Fig. 2. Proposed color palettes (own source). (Color figure online)

Fig. 3. Color palette chosen (own source). (Color figure online)

Therefore, 5 color palettes were generated starting from the ones that the children surveyed selected as their favorites, for this the Coolors platform [10] was used, which allows to generate ideal combinations from the selection of one or several colors, applying comparisons in terms of hue, saturation and brightness, without leaving aside the concepts of complementary colors, analogues, monochromatic and color triad.

As an additional measure, 3 different pallets were generated (see Fig. 2) and were evaluated by the same respondents. The winning option was number 3 with 60% of the total votes (see Fig. 3).

4.3   Graphic User Interfaces

Application interfaces include startup, game mode selection, entry, game intro and instructions, and the set of scenes in which the player looks for clues to solve the mystery. Figure 4 presents the main interfaces.

Fig. 4. App interfaces (own source).

4.4 Potential Benefits

Multimedia content that will be displayed in the interactive system falls within the serious game category, as its ultimate goal is the implicit teaching of any specific topic without the users perceive it; for the present case the child is immersed in literature through tales and stories that are built with the help of the interventions he made in the system.

The content is created based on stories that force the user to use his reading comprehension skills. It also requires the user to make use of his memory, mental agility and collaborative work for the successful resolution of the problem that arises with such content.

The infrastructure of the system allows a quick access to the usage data, meaning this to that information which the system captures when users interact and which serve to generate statistics through which it is clear evidence the efficiency of the system. These captured data are: tracks collected by each user, total score, duration time of the interaction, user name. By storing this information, it will be able to know how many users the system used on a specific day, how many times a user interacted with the system, and system usage times.

On the other hand, the system is able to support interactive stories, each of them with different interactions and interesting stories that awaken the user's curiosity and implicitly help him develop skills or abilities. This option allows a diversity of contents that adapt to the particular tastes or preferences of each use that will interact with the system.

5   System's Preliminary Evaluation

Constructive Interaction [11] was chosen to apply as a usability evaluation method because it allows children to interact freely with the whole system while expressing their impressions and perceptions as a conversation. Thus, a previous planning was carried out in which informed consents, authorizations of use of images and permissions were designed and filled by the children's legal guardians, also the following criteria were established to evaluate:

- Buttons recognition: Measuring time between the first occurrence of the interface until the child presses the button in each case.
- Metaphors recognition: The identification of the "PLAY" button to start the game and the "X" to close, in addition to the direction arrows to go back or forward depending on the case.
- Color approval: The children's perception to interface colors.
- Reading time of instructions and alerts: Measuring the time every child required to read the game messages.
- Vocabulary: Evaluate if every used word is understandable for users.
- Time in each interface: Duration of interactions in each interface.
- Experience satisfaction: Qualitative measurement against the final comments of the users.

For the application of the evaluation, 3 pairs of children between 8 and 13 years old were organized in the Usability Laboratory of the Universidad Autonóma de Oc-cidente. Each one interacted freely with the system, with the unique condition of finishing de game receiving basic instructions.

Then, the results were grouped and averaged to obtain the following information. First of all, the buttons were immediately identified by all children, the Play button being the fastest recognition for being in the first interface, only accompanied by the Close button.

The colors were approved by the children and the majority manifested a particular pleasantness for the blue color present in some interfaces, in addition they expressed appreciation for the illustrations because for them these make history more striking. However, some presented confusion in scene 2 where there is no text orientation.

On average, the reading time of the instructions was 41 s. In children near the age of 13 the time was shorter, however it could be perceived in them eagerness to jump to the game and displeasure to read instructions. Regarding the vocabulary used, none of the children had difficulties with any word, saying that the graphs help the understanding of the elements of the interface.

The average time for all the interaction was 5 min 23 s, the less time-invested inter-faces were the initial and the input while the instructions and the scenes of the story required more time for the interaction with the physical objects.

Finally, positive comments were received about interaction in general, children were motivated to engage in solving a mystery and enjoyed the way they tell the story while they participate in it with non-traditional objects.

6 Conclusions and Future Work

Throughout the process, continuous approaches were required with the target audience as well as with stakeholders to understand the needs and context. It was fundamental to apply surveys and interviews in the process of inquiry to understand the preferences and interests of children for being such a particular audience.

It was possible to obtain a solution that mediated by the technology innovates the way of storytelling and allows to attract the attention of the children so that they interact and they are involved in a non-traditional way.

The use of technological tools in the framework of teaching in children turns out to be an alternative with great benefits. The implementation of such tools allows the construction of solutions that increase children's individual skills and abilities. In addi-tion, the creation of content based on books allows to bring the user to the reading, since through the system is provided a short version of the full story narrated in the book. With this, it is sought that the user wants to know more of the story and implicitly begin to create regular reading habits increasing their reading comprehension skills necessary in any work setting.

The use of a space such as MakerLab, equipped with high-level technological tools and located inside the facilities of a library, generating unique experiences in the users. Mainly, because this place separates spatially and temporally the user from their real context and its problems, allowing the children to know spaces that were created for self-learning, knowledge, curiosity and personal growth. On the other hand, the children will be able to participate in extracurricular activities that can be carried out during their free time and that do not generate negative impacts, otherwise these activities contribute in the personal and emotional development of the user.

The project will continue if new interactive content is created based on readings according to the ages of the target audience. In this way, new experiences can be created, so users can have a bigger offer and choose the content they prefer.

Another possibility is the incorporation of other technologies as virtual and augmented reality generating a total immersion with the content and impacting other senses, through which the user can be brought to a high satisfaction level, thanks to the feedback that the system can provide them incorporating these technologies.

Finally, due to the software architecture that the system has, there is a long-term possibility of being replicated in different libraries. This in order to create more learning spaces in which children can interact with technology in a didactic way and implicitly acquire skills and productive habits both personally and intellectually.

References

1. Cali Cómo Vamos: How are we in education. In: How are we in. Cali Cómo Vamos Portal (2014). Available via DIALOG http://www.calicomovamos.org.co/educacin. Accessed 1 Feb 2017
2. DANE: Cultural consumption survey 2014. In: Research. Departamento Administrativo Nacional de Estadísticas (2014). Available via DIALOG https://goo.gl/WKVn5W. Accessed 18 Mar 2017
3. Universidad de los Andes: Determinants of desertion 2014. In: Information systems. Ministry of Education (2014). Available via DIALOG https://goo.gl/m8WLJc. Accessed 1 Feb 2017
4. Bustamante, N.: Colombian children evidence under performance in reading comprehension. In: Archive. El Tiempo (2015). Available via DIALOG http://www.eltiempo.com/archivo/documento/CMS-15283357. Accessed 18 Mar 2017
5. Alcaldía Santiago de Cali: Maker Labs arrive at the Public Libraries Network of Cali. In: Culture. Publications (2016). Available via DIALOG https://goo.gl/4jdkGl_de_cali. Accessed 1 Feb 2017
6. Oviatt, S., Cohen, P.L. et al.: Perceptual user interfaces: multimodal interfaces that process what comes naturally. Commun. ACM (2000). Available via DIALOG https://goo.gl/AHx5aF. Accessed 17 Mar 2017
7. Alcaldía Santiago de Cali: Maker Labs arrive at the Public Libraries Network of Cali. In: Culture. Publications (2016). Available via DIALOG https://goo.gl/c8MLmj. Accessed 01 Feb 2017
8. Smyth, I.: The Mystery of the Russian Ruby: A Pop-up Whodunnit. Orchard Books, London (1994)
9. Large, A., et al.: Criteria for children's web portals: a comparison of two studies. Can. J. Inf. Libr. Sci. **28**(4), 45–72 (2004)
10. Bianchi, F.: Coolors (2016). https://coolors.co. Accessed 18 Mar 2017
11. Als, B., et al.: Comparison of think-aloud and constructive interaction in usability testing with children. In: Proceedings of the 2005 Conference on Interaction Design and Children (2005). Available via DIALOG https://goo.gl/vk1xp4. Accessed 18 Mar 2017

Roadmap for the Development of the User Interface in Interactive Systems

Maria L. Villegas[1](✉) [iD], William J. Giraldo[1] [iD], and César A. Collazos[2] [iD]

[1] Universidad del Quindío, Carrera 15 Calle 12 Norte, Armenia-Quindío, Colombia
{mlvillegas,wjgiraldo}@uniquindio.edu.co
[2] Universidad del Cauca, Calle 5 No. 4-70, Popayán-Cauca, Colombia
ccollazo@unicauca.edu.co

Abstract. In this paper we present the definition of a roadmap for the development of the user interface in interactive systems. The roadmap is supported by a set of interrelated elements to capture the information to specify and model an interactive system. Those elements are: Method, Notation and Tool. This work emphasizes only the method and the notation. We present in detail the diagrams and other artifacts that support the proposed roadmap, by defining a case study.

Keywords: Human computer interaction modeling · Roadmap for interactive systems · User interface modeling · User interface design

1 Introduction

Information systems as well as transactional interactive systems are vital part in modern organizations. During the development of this type of systems, large volumes of information are captured, generally through models. This information contains characteristics and attributes of both the organization and the interactive system.

The majority of professionals in Software Development understand that there is a division between the business side, with its requirements, and between the support being provided to address these requirements [1, 2]. But the ideal is not that there is a division, but rather traceability between Business and System levels of abstraction.

From the point of view of Software Engineering (SE), what interests is to generate software products fully functional. SE has focused on the aspect of the functionality, leaving aside some attributes inherent in interactive systems development, such as collaboration, usability, among others [2]. So, we observed that for most methodological proposals in software development, RUP [3, 4], XP [5], ICONIX [6], SCRUM [7], labor specification is the starting point towards the implementation of any software product. For this reason aspects related with the labor, activity are of great interest for this research. So, the activity is the element of cohesion, element of orchestration; the most important from the point of view of software development.

From the point of view of Human Computer Interaction (HCI), the focus is more on capturing the mental model of users and in other aspects related to cognitive psychology and the human factor [8]. We intend to capture all this information both from the

© Springer International Publishing AG 2017
A. Solano and H. Ordoñez (Eds.): CCC 2017, CCIS 735, pp. 557–571, 2017.
DOI: 10.1007/978-3-319-66562-7_40

Software Engineering as from HCI, to specify and model software products that besides being functional are also usable, secure, collaborative, etc. So, it is required mechanisms and tools that support it.

In this sense, this work continues in the line that defines the development based on frameworks as an important tool for the development of solutions to problems with specific characteristics [9], and coincides with Giraldo [10] in that this type of development must separate each element of the models both from level of business, as well as application and technology, to ensure agility and flexibility of the system models.

According to the aforementioned, this paper proposes a roadmap as a support for the development of interactive systems, specifically the user interface. This roadmap is focused on the design of task models to obtain the design of the user interface. The roadmap is supported by three essential components: Method, Notation and Tool.

In the following sections, the Proposed Roadmap Taxonomic is described. Then, the Case Study is developed. Finally, the conclusions and future work are presented.

2   Proposed Roadmap

The proposed roadmap is taken as the result of the definition of a set of uses for an Activity Taxonomy, from previous works [11–13]. The interest in these works is the modeling and execution of the activity that supports user interface design in interactive systems.

Any roadmap that supports the entire lifecycle of a software project considers three elements: proposed notation, methodology to follow and provided tools [10]. The development methodology is supported by a set of best practices and knowledge bases. This set supports the stakeholders involved in making design decisions. The notation, preferably graphic, allows communication, the planning and the description of the system being modeled. Additionally, if the notation is formalized, allows the development of editing and automation tools.

Figure 1 shows the development flow of the proposed roadmap. This roadmap is carried out at two levels of modeling. Initially, high-level business tasks and domain objects, which support them, are analyzed. Although they be technology independent, these tasks and objects, allow the understanding of the mental models of users to develop the Business User Interface (BUI) from the data being used inside of the context of each process. The objective of the BUI is to identify the forms, usually on paper, that support the entry of information to business process in a realistic and independent of technology manner. Subsequently, interactive tasks and system objects that support them are analyzed to identify the dialogue between the user and the computer. This dialog is carried out by means of a set of interfaces that are generated from an abstract specification, to a final executable specification. It is important to note that this roadmap applies the partitioning of both task models and interfaces at all levels (Fig. 1(a)). The navigation through the roadmap starts with the definition of a business process to be implemented.

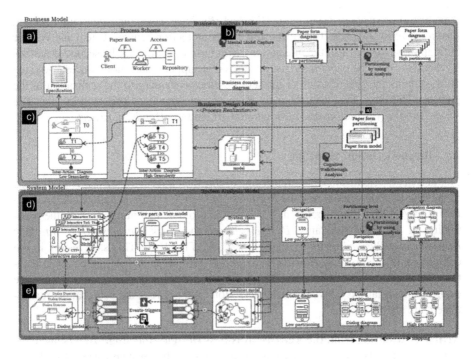

Fig. 1. Roadmap proposed. Artifacts detailed specification.

The activities that are carried out as the roadmap is executed are: Business Analysis Modeling, Business Design Modeling, System Analysis Modeling, System Design Modeling, Prototyping and Evaluation.

The following subsections describes in detail the activities and artifacts that are generated for each one of them.

2.1 Business Analysis Modeling

This activity is oriented to analyze the domain of the process to identify the client, the worker, the interaction tasks between people and the data being manipulated (Fig. 1(b)). The result of this activity is a detailed description of the process to be developed with the proposed methodology. At this level, process information is captured, in a generalized way, independent of technology. It is about understanding the context of the process and the data that are associated to that context. Techniques such as interviews, user observation, are used to capture user's mental model on how they understand the process and what data should be displayed in a business user interface, in paper and without specific widget buttons. We have named *"Business User Interface (BUI)"* to this type of interface. In this level, simplified tests of usability can be carried out. This can lead to changes in the description of the business process.

Artifacts Resulting from the Activity: Business Analysis Modeling. At this level, the following artifacts are obtained from the analysis of the Business Process

Specification: *Business Interaction Diagram, Business User Interface Diagram* and *Business Entity Diagram*. The first describes the interaction between Client and Worker through paper forms, also the interactions with business entities. The second describes a general view of the paper interface or forms that supports the whole process. And the third contains the specification of the set of entities necessary to the realization of the process. The roles that contribute to the accomplishment of this activity are: The *Processes Analyst*, the *Business Domain Expert,* and the *Database Expert.*

2.2   Business Design Modeling

This activity is oriented to realize the design of *Business Interactive Tasks*. The sequence of these tasks is described. And the *Business Interaction Diagram*, realized in the Business Analysis Modeling is retaken. It is important to note that in this activity the partitioning of the three diagrams, *Business Interactive Task, Business User Interface Diagram and Business Entity Diagram*, is done (Fig. 1(a)). This step results in the completion of the process (*Process Realization*) (Fig. 1(c)). The design of the interactions between the people involved in the process, client and worker, are realized. The design of the relations between these interactions and between the data that are manipulated, are also realized.

Artifacts Resulting from the Activity: Business Design Modeling. At this level, the following artifacts are obtained from the analysis of the Business Analysis Model: *Process Template, Business User Interface Diagram* partitioned *and Business Entity Diagram* partitioned. The Business Design Model has two levels of granularity, high and low. The low level contains 3 design artifacts: 1. *Process Template*, which in turn contains two diagrams: Business Interaction Diagram and Business Interactive Task Diagram, 2. *Business User Interface Diagram*, and 3. *Business Entity Diagram*. The high level is contained in the Business Interactive Task Diagram, where each task is broken down according to the specification of the process. The roles that contribute to the accomplishment of this activity are: *Interaction Designer, Business Domain Expert, Database Expert, User Representative,* and *Usability Evaluation Specialist.*

1. **Process Template**: The Business Interactive Task supports two abstraction levels to specify the interactive task. So, it is possible to specify tasks composed by Individual, Cooperative or Communication Tasks. A task model describes a logical and temporal ordering of the tasks that are performed by the users in the interaction with a system. A tasks model at the business level, describes both the current tasks of the users and the way in which can be done in the future. The individual elements in a task model represent the specific actions that the user can carry out [10].
2. **Business User Interface Diagram**: The number of diagrams of this type is determined by number of simple tasks specified in the *Process Template*. That is, each of these diagrams represents a partition of the interface that supports the process according to the specification of business tasks. There is a mapping relationship between the Process Template and Business User Interface Diagram. The Business User Interface is a part of the model of the user interface; is the information that the user must imagine is behind the physical screen - at the back of the system [14].

Normally this interface is drawn, in terms of user interface elements (Screens on paper) because they resemble the final screens in the computer, with graphical details and with realistic data contents. The organization of the business user interface is done by preserving the different laws of Gestalt: law of proximity, law of closure, law of good continuation and law of similarity.

3. **Business Entity Diagram**: The number of diagrams of this type is determined by the number of simple tasks specified in the Process Template. That is, each of these diagrams represents a partition of the set of entities that requires the process according to the specification of the business tasks. There is a mapping relationship between the Process Template and each Business Entity Diagram. The domain model captures the semantics of the system context and defines the requirements of information for the development of the user interface. A domain model describes the objects of an application domain. Specifies the data that people use, related with real-world entities and interactions as they are understood by the users in relation to the actions that are possible to carry out on these entities. Domain analysis is part of most development approaches, and it is not something specific to consider in the design of the user interface. Domain objects are considered as instances of classes that represent the concepts that are manipulated and totally independent of how they are displayed on the screen and how they are stored on the computer.

In Business Design Modeling, each sub-task at the Business Design level has a mapping to a user interface diagram and to a business entity diagram. In this way, the partitioning realized to the BUI from the analysis of the tasks, is reflected. As shown in Fig. 1 upper right, partitioning can result in, high, medium, or low level. The interest is to obtain a balance in such partitioning from the analysis and tests performed at the level of the Business Analysis Model.

2.3   System Analysis Modeling

In this activity the interactive design is performed. The way in which the user can interact with the system is shown (Fig. 1(d)). The cognitive walkthrough technique [8], is used for each BUI, from Business User Interface Diagrams. Then, user tasks, interactive tasks, and system tasks are identified and classified. The result is a set of Interactive Task Diagrams at the system level, where each task diagram corresponds to each interactive task defined at the high level of granularity at the level of business.

The cognitive walkthrough technique helps to define the navigation model for the process analyzed. As shown in Fig. 1, right half, the resulting navigation diagram, corresponds to the level of partitioning performed for the Business User Interfaces. Class Diagrams will have a mapping with the Business Entity Diagrams too (Fig. 1(c)).

From the interactive task diagrams and class diagrams, at the system level, gets the View Part and View Model. Each of these diagrams shows a pair between a piece of the interface and the data view corresponding to such interface.

Artifacts Resulting from the Activity: System Analysis Modeling. At this level, the artifact *Presentation Pattern* is obtained from the analysis of the Business Model. This pattern contains the set of diagrams necessary to specify, in the level of interactive system, each one of the simple tasks specified in the Process Template, at the Business Level. Each one of these tasks has traceability to the following diagrams: 1. *Interactive Task Diagram, 2. View Part Diagram, 3. View Model Diagram,* and 4. *Domain Model.* The roles that contribute to the accomplishment of this activity are: The *Interaction Designer,* and the *Database Expert.* For each of the simple tasks specified in the Process Template, you must create a *Presentation Pattern.*

1. **Interactive Task Diagram**: In this diagram the structure and relationships of the CTT notation [15] is preserved. Attributes are added to the interactive tasks for denote whether they express a task closing, an interaction with feedback or an inter-action with awareness. In addition, this diagram explicitly indicates the user performing the tasks.
2. **View Part, View Model, and Domain Model:** For the Interface View, the Data Model View and the Domain Model, the MVVM (Model-View-View Model Pattern) concept is used [16]. In this case, the View represents the structure, deploy-ment, and appearance of the concrete User Interface with its components. The Model is a representation of the data that support the specification of the concrete interface. Finally, the View Model represents the data that have a direct mapping to the concrete Interface or Vista. Basically, the Interface View is a model of the user interface that allows specifying the appearance and behavior of the user interface by means of elements that can be perceived by users [17]. Is about a specification of the user interface in terms of concrete interaction objects (CUI). A concrete inter-action object is a component of the interface that can be manipulated or perceived by the user (for example, a window, a button, a checkbox, etc.). Although the objects of concrete interface are more related to widgets, are still independent of the repre-sentation real or rendering.

2.4   System Design Modeling

In this activity the Dialog Diagrams are created, from the Interactive Task Diagrams at the system level. Detailed designs of the User Interfaces are also obtained (Fig. 1(d)). For this, rules of design and ergonomics, and usability requirements are taken into account. In the Dialog Diagrams, you define the controls that the user will need to carry out their tasks. It is also decided how to bring the actions on the interface identified in the previous step, for example, using buttons, menus, drag and drop, etc.

At this level are designed the State Diagrams that are associated with the classes of the system. These state diagrams define the life cycles of such classes. The navigation model and the state diagrams are related through a catalog of actions and a catalog of events, respectively. These catalogs define the necessary navigational functions, the navigation menu, the information and the functionality that the modeled process executes.

Artifacts Resulting from the Activity: System Design Modeling. At this level, the following artifacts are obtained from the analysis of the System Analysis Model: 1. *Dialog Diagram,* and 2. *State Diagram.* The roles that contribute to the accomplishment of this activity are: The *Interaction Designer*, the *Database Expert,* the *Implementer,* and the *Graphic Designer.*

1. **Dialog Diagram:** The Dialogue Diagram preserves the structure of the Interactive Task Diagram, specifying for each task, the type of Abstract Interaction Components (AIC) associated with the task. These interaction components represent a canonical expression of the rendering and manipulation of the concepts of the domain and the functions, in a way that is as independent as possible of the modality (aural, visual, tactile, etc.) and the computer platform [17]. Figure 2 presents the Abstract Interaction Components presented by Constantine [18].

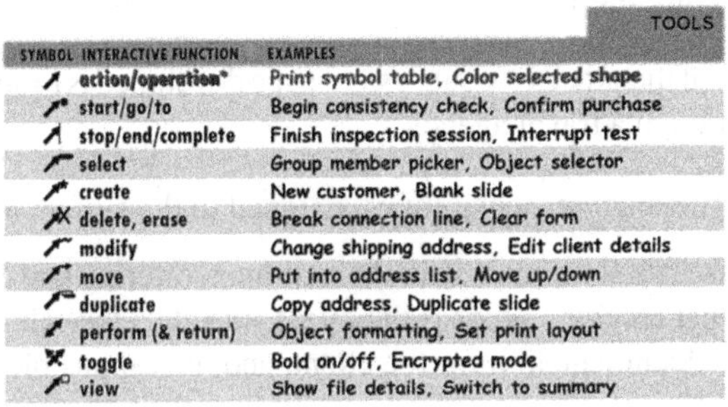

SYMBOL	INTERACTIVE FUNCTION	EXAMPLES	TOOLS
✔	action/operation*	Print symbol table, Color selected shape	
✔	start/go/to	Begin consistency check, Confirm purchase	
✔	stop/end/complete	Finish inspection session, Interrupt test	
✔	select	Group member picker, Object selector	
✔	create	New customer, Blank slide	
✔	delete, erase	Break connection line, Clear form	
✔	modify	Change shipping address, Edit client details	
✔	move	Put into address list, Move up/down	
✔	duplicate	Copy address, Duplicate slide	
✔	perform (& return)	Object formatting, Set print layout	
✘	toggle	Bold on/off, Encrypted mode	
✔	view	Show file details, Switch to summary	

Fig. 2. Canonical abstract interaction components by Constantine [18]

2. **State Diagram:** State Diagrams represent the behavior of the classes that conforms the System Model. Each class can have one or more state diagrams associated.

Navigation Diagram: The Navigation Diagram presents the interaction between patterns of presentation, through the actions that allow switching the interactive system from one task to the other interactive tasks. It serves as an orchestration element between the specifications of the mentioned models.

The Final User Interface is not specified in the roadmap because it is the user interface in operation, i.e. any user interface that runs on a computer platform, either by interpretation (for example, through a web browser) or by execution (for example, by compiling your code in an interactive development environment). The Final User Interface has two possible representations: the code that defines it and its render or its display [17].

2.5 Prototyping, Evaluation and Execution Model

Prototyping and evaluation is a stage that is executed transversally. The usability of the designed solutions is evaluated and compared with usability goals. After applying the usability tests to the prototypes, the problems are evaluated and corrected as much as possible. A heuristic evaluation to target potential problems can be performed. On the other hand, the execution model for this proposal is basically supported by two components: a real-time multitasking executive (EMTR) [19–21], and a component for the execution of UML state machines [22]. For reasons of space the execution model is not described in detail in this paper. Next in Sect. 3 is presented the case study made for this work.

3   Case Study

This section presents the application of the proposed roadmap to a case study. The case study of *"Buying a plane ticket"* is developed. This case has been chosen for being an example in which certain needs of interaction are given.

3.1   Case Study Statement

The main objective of the process or subsystem to be developed is to support the purchase of a plane ticket through a travel agency.

Process Actors. The main responsibilities assigned to the system actors are:

- *Travel agent*: takes direct contact with the customer, offering and defining a trip. This role is the one that receives, advises the client, specifies the sale of tourist services, issues the travel documentation for the client, and, is responsible for the billing and collection.
- *Customer*: requests advice regarding travel and purchase of tickets, decide the characteristics of the trip and make the payment of the tickets.

Process to Develop. *Purchase of airline tickets*: The customer requests information and advice on the trip he wants to make, to the travel agent. Travel agent provides necessary information to the customer. The customer decides the destination of the trip, the type, and the number of passengers, in accordance with such information. Then, the customer proceeds to purchase the air tickets.

3.2   Process Development Following the Proposed Roadmap

This section explains how the steps in user interface development are followed, according to the proposed roadmap.

Business Modeling. Once the process to be developed is described, the Process Template containing Business Interaction Diagrams and its Business Tasks, are defined (Fig. 3 left). Also, the Business User Interfaces Diagrams and the Business Entity Diagrams. These artifacts would be equivalent to a Case of Use Realization.

The definition of the Process Template begins with the identification of possible intentions of potential users of the future system. These intentions are defined through a division and distinction between the activities that are carried out by the user, during the execution of a business process, and actions that may be automated, e.g. the actions performed by the worker. At the level of Business Interactive Tasks, these tasks are detailed through the specification of a series of steps or business actions. These actions will be represented by mean of interactive task models at the system level. In the beginning, in the specification, it is not known whether an action will be carried out with support of technology, or will be a manual activity.

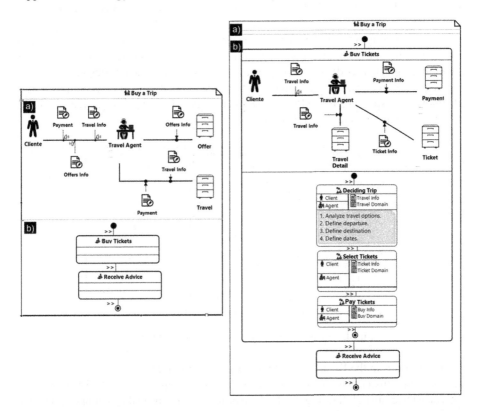

Fig. 3. Process Template for "Purchase of airline tickets", low level of granularity (left) and high level of granularity (right).

Figure 3 shows the Ticket Purchase Process Template. In this template Business Interactions are described (Fig. 3a left). These interactions are the structural part of the process. Business activities carried out by the Travel Agent and the Client to specify the dynamic of this process are described too (Fig. 3b left). The analysis of business interactive tasks gives rise to a decomposition of tasks.

The *Business Interaction Diagram* (Fig. 3a left) expresses the interaction between the customer and the worker through paper forms (*interaction*) and their interaction with the business entities (*access*). Every relationship between actors and entities represents one or more business activities.

The Process Template describes the Business Interactive Task sequence. The Process Specification gives rise to the definition of two Business Interactive Tasks: "*Buy Tickets*" and "*Receive Advise*" (Fig. 3b left). This proposal supports two granularity levels to these interactive tasks; that is to say, it is possible to specify tasks that are composed of Individual Tasks, Cooperative Tasks or Communication Tasks (Fig. 3 right). Figure 3 right shows the Process Template for this case, this time, a high level of granularity for the "Buy Tickets". It is observed that the Business Interactive Tasks Diagram contains the sequence of three Communication Tasks, "Deciding Trip", "Select Tickets", and "Pay Tickets". It is important to mention that the Business Interactive Tasks Diagram notation is based in Molina´s proposal for the CIAN Notation [23].

Every relationship between actors and entities represents one or more business activities. The entities that support the process are represented by a Business Entity Diagram (Fig. 4). This diagram contains the specification of the entities set, necessary for the process realization. The number of this type of diagrams depends on the number of simple tasks specified in the Process Template. There is a mapping between the Business Interactive Tasks and each Business Entity Diagram.

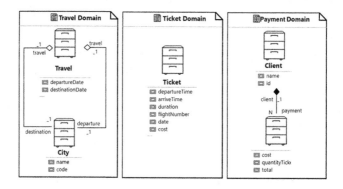

Fig. 4. Business entity diagrams for "Buy Tickets" task.

The Entities in the Business Entity represent an initial model of the context for the design of the Business User Interface. This interface is represented by a Business User Interface Diagram (BUID) (Fig. 5). This diagram is created from data being manipulated inside the context of the business processes. The BUID contains the specification of the paper interface or form, which supports the process being developed. Like Business Entity Diagrams, there is a mapping between the Business Interactive Tasks and each Business User Interface Diagram.

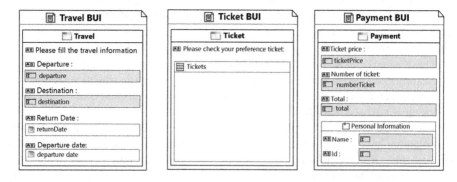

Fig. 5. Business user interface diagrams for "Buy Tickets" task.

Figure 5, presents a preliminary version of the User Interface for the Process "Purchase of Airline Tickets". A complete model of the interface has not been obtained yet, since its components must be refined with the information from tasks and from the user requirements. From this set of diagrams defined on Business Abstraction Level, it is possible to continue with the design of the process on System Abstraction Level.

System Interactive Model. Once the Process Template and its Entity and Interfaces Diagrams have been defined, it is possible to define the Presentation Pattern and the Navigation Diagram at the System Level. The Presentation Pattern contains a set of diagrams allows to define the interactions between the user and the interactive system, and their relationship with data, life cycles, navigation, dialog, and user interface. For each of the tasks specified in the Process Template, you must create a Presentation Pattern.

Below are shown in detail each diagram that forms the presentation pattern for this example and some of the mappings between them.

Figure 6a shows the interactive task diagram, which indicates the user responsible for carrying out those tasks. Typically, the tasks assigned to a Worker at the business level, are the tasks that are automated, that is, the realization of the Worker is represented by the Interactive System.

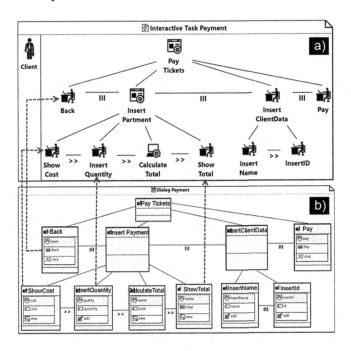

Fig. 6. Interactive tasks diagram and dialog diagram

Although the task diagram arises from the actions of Business, it is possible, to find new tasks if a cognitive walkthrough is applied (with users) from the Business User

Interfaces. The user defines the sequence of tasks that allows you to meet the goal defined by the process.

From each dialogue diagram (Fig. 6b) it is possible to define the proposal of Concrete User Interface, or View Part (Fig. 7a left). For this work, said interface is generated using the algorithm of Limbourg [17] where the hierarchical structure of tasks determines the level of grouping of the elements of the interface. The types of components that make up the View Part are determined from of the multiplicity information between the View Model elements (Fig. 7a right). Some components are associated with actions, and therefore become buttons.

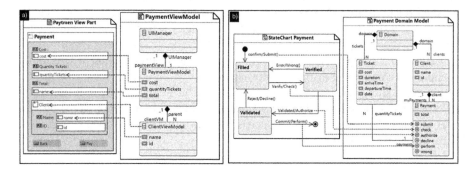

Fig. 7. Mappings between view part and view model (left), Mappings between state chart diagram and domain diagram (right)

The layout and appearance of the concrete interface is the result of a manual editing process with users, which is based on sources of knowledge both of the design of interfaces as the domain of the problem.

The State Diagrams represent the orchestration of the defined functionality for the system classes (Fig. 7b left). Each class of system can have associated more than one state diagram. In this case, Fig. 7b left shows the life cycle of the class "Payment", in which progress is made as the events specified in its life cycle occur. This way it is indicated that the development of the functionality focuses mainly in the life cycles of the system classes. In the case of the development of the user interface, the state chart diagrams are useful for the definition of the interfaces that are related to the change of state of each entity.

The Navigation diagram is the orchestration element between presentation patterns, through the actions that allow switching the interactive system from one task to the other interactive tasks (Fig. 8). Only a navigation diagram for each process to be implemented is designed.

The software tool that supports the roadmap provides a series of property views that allows mappings to be implemented between diagrams and their elements. This is the case of the connections between actions in the navigation, events in the state machines and the operations of the system classes. This view also allows you to enter the code (semantics) associated with those actions and operations that represent the functionality of the interactive system.

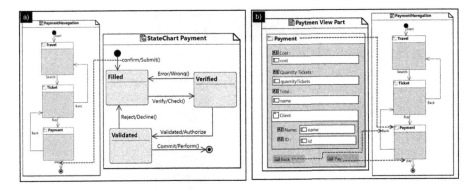

Fig. 8. Mappings between navigation diagram and state chart diagram (left), Mappings between navigation diagram and view part (right)

Figure 9 present two of the views of properties (actions and events) associated with the functionality of the task "Payment".

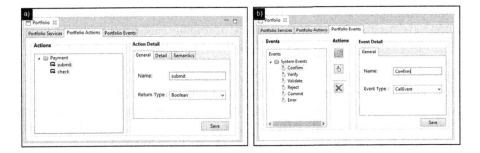

Fig. 9. View of actions and events properties in the software tool that supports the roadmap

Once a series of decisions on method and technology have been adopted which will be used, addresses the final phase of user interface development. As the final step of this process is a series of transformations. These transformations use the information that has been collected throughout the process on tasks, data, dialogues, navigation, life cycles and elements of the interface.

Figure 10 shows an example of the final interface for the "Payment of Airline Ticket" in Java and XML. In this case, the final interface is executed on the system Android operating system.

These Final Interfaces are generated from transformations from model to text that involve concrete representations in each one of the implementation technologies.

Fig. 10.   Final user interface for the task "Payment of Airline Ticket"

4   Conclusions and Future Work

In this paper, a Roadmap for the development of the User Interface on the Activity Modeling is specified. The roadmap shows the traceability between Business and System levels of abstraction, in what has to do with the specification of the Labor of the Interactive Systems. This, because HCI has focused on studying the Interaction at the level of the Computer System, but not on studying the Interaction at the level of the Organization, interaction between people. In this work the elements Role-Activity-Artifact, for each level of abstraction are specified. Highlights are the "Business User Interface Diagram", "Business Interaction Diagram", "Business Interactive Task Diagram", and "Dialog Diagram" artifacts. It stands the use of the "View-Model-View" pattern. The elements that make up the proposed roadmap make it possible to express the timing, synchronization, hierarchy, and structure, as aspects which characterize interactive systems.

As future work, it is proposed to perform the necessary test to validate the notation and consequently, the new proposed diagrams. Additionally, it is necessary to work in automatic generation of diagrams, i.e. software components that support the roadmap to automatically generate diagrams for the modeling of activity, from the level of business abstraction, to the level of system abstraction. For example, automatically generate initial versions of the interactive task diagrams, from the diagrams of business interaction, as well as dialogue diagrams from the interactive task diagrams. It would also be possible to generate diagrams of navigation from the diagrams of interactive business tasks.

Finally, it would be very useful to work in a web-based browser that facilitates navigation and learning of the roadmap. This browser must provide multiple views so that each component of the framework can be analyzed in a separate way. Additionally, through this browser, you can re-use the methods content of the roadmap for the definition of other process structures or alternative roadmaps.

References

1. Guerrero, J.: A Methodology for Developing User Interfaces to Workflow Information Systems. Université catholique de Louvain (2010)
2. Trætteberg, H.: Model-based User Interface Design. Norwegian University of Science and Technology (2002)
3. IBM_Rational: Too Navigator (Rational Unified Process) (2003)
4. Balduino, R.: Introduction to OpenUP (Open Unified Process). IBM (2007)
5. http://www.extremeprogramming.org/. Accessed 05 May 2017
6. http://www.iconixsw.com/jumpstart.html. Accessed 05 May 2017
7. http://scrummethodology.com/. Accessed 05 May 2017
8. Granollers, T.: Mpiu+A. Una Metodología que Integra la Ingeniería del Software, La Interacción Persona Ordenador y la Accesibilidad en el Contexto de Equipos de Desarrollo Multidisciplinares, Lleida (2004)
9. Ambler, S.W., Nalbone, J., Vizdos, M.: Extending the RUP with the Zachman Framework. Pearson Education, Essex (2005)
10. Giraldo, W.J.: Marco de Desarrollo de Sistemas Software Interactivos Basado en la Integración de Procesos y Notaciones. Doctoral, Universidad de Castilla-La Mancha (2010)
11. Villegas, M.L., Collázos, C.A., William, J.G.: Activity taxonomy: analysis of proposals for development of interactive systems. In: Interacción 2014 Proceedings. ACM (2014)
12. Giraldo, W.J., Villegas, M.L., Collazos, C.A.: Incorporation of HCI: Classification of activity modeling. In: 9th CCC Proceedings, pp. 150–155 (2014)
13. Villegas, M.L., Collazos, C.A., Giraldo, W.J., Gonzalez, J.M.: Activity theory as a framework for activity taxonomy in HCI. IEEE Lat. Am. Trans. **14**(2), 844–857 (2016)
14. Lauesen, S.: User Interface Design: A Software Engineering Perspective. Addison-Wesley, Redwood City (2005)
15. Paternò, F.: ConcurTaskTrees: An Engineered Notation for Task Models, pp. 483–501. Lawrence Erlbaum Associates (2004)
16. https://msdn.microsoft.com/en-us/library/hh848246.aspx. Accessed 14 Feb 2017
17. Limbourg, Q.: Multi-path Development of User Interfaces. Université catholique de Louvain (2004)
18. Constantine, L.L.: Canonical Abstract Prototypes for Abstract Visual and Interaction, pp. 1–15. Springer, Heidelberg (2003)
19. Giraldo, W.J.: Diseño de un Ejecutivo Multitarea en Tiempo Real. Universidad del Valle (2000)
20. Giraldo, W.J., Villegas, M.L., Candela, C., Castro, L.M.: Software de Automatización Industrial (SAI), Concepción y Desarrollo, Revista de Investigaciones. Universidad del Quindío, 3, pp. 112–122 (2001)
21. Giraldo, W.J., Villegas, M.L., Marín, D.F.: Diseño y construcción de un software para automatización de procesos SAI. Impactar S.A. (2004). ISBN 958-33-6548-3-L
22. Villegas, M.L., Castro, L.M., Ruiz, A.: UML Semantics v 1.1 - Implementación del Metamodelo Sobre EMTRSAI. Arte Imagen (2009). ISBN 978-958-44-5912-1
23. Molina, A.I.: Una Propuesta Metodológica Para El Desarrollo De La Interfaz De Usuario En Sistemas Groupware (CIAM). Doctoral, Universidad de Castilla-La Mancha (2006)

Accessibility Guide for the Design and Implementation of Websites According to the NTC 5854 Standard

Claudia S. Idrobo$^{(\boxtimes)}$ ⓘ, María I. Idrobo$^{(\boxtimes)}$ ⓘ,
Gabriel E. Chan-chí ⓘ, and María I. Vidal ⓘ

Institución Universitaria Colegio Mayor del Cauca,
Cra. 7 #2-34, Popayán, Colombia
{sofidrobo,gchanchi,mvidal}@unimayor.edu.co,
isabelidrobo20.ik@gmail.co

Abstract. Currently, web accessibility has gained importance because it provides mechanisms for people with different functional diversities to have the possibility of using the web under equal conditions as the rest of the people, and because it provides added benefits, like visualization of the site in different devices or better positioning in the results of web searches. At legislative level in Colombia, the norm in charge of introducing a set of guidelines for the design and implementation of accessible websites is the NTC 5854 standard. In spite of the potential advantages of the norm, its guide-lines are presented briefly, which could generate ambiguities in interpretation by developers. This article introduces an accessibility guide for the design and construction of websites stemming from the NTC 5854 standard. The objective of the guide is to provide accompaniment to software developers and designers regarding the implementation process of accessible web portals for which the guide proposed addresses and adapts in detail each of the guidelines that make up the four principles of accessibility [Perceivable, operable, Understandable, and robust] of the NTC 5854 standard. The guide proposed also intends to serve as reference for software companies around the globe that wish to involve in their software products the characteristics and advantages of accessibility.

Keywords: Accessibility · Implementation guide · Functional diversity · NTC 5854 · Web accessibility

1 Introduction

Currently, most websites and applications have accessibility barriers, which hinders their use for many people with functional diversities or other access limitations, like: visual limitation, hearing deficiencies, limited mobility, incapacity to distinguish some colors, sensitivity to changes in light intensity, dyslexia, and loss of vision with age [1]. Thus, with more software and accessible websites available on the internet, more people will be able to use the web, thus, contributing to reduce the technological divide. Accordingly, functional diversity [2] is understood as the alternative term to disability, which is being used through the initiative of individuals who have been

© Springer International Publishing AG 2017
A. Solano and H. Ordóñez (Eds.): CCC 2017, CCIS 735, pp. 572–585, 2017.
DOI: 10.1007/978-3-319-66562-7_41

labeled with the excluding term of "disability" and intends to substitute for other terms whose semantics can be considered pejorative, such as "disability" or "handicap" [2]. It is important to highlight that offering an "only-text version" in the website is not synonymous of offering web accessibility. Many web developers wrongly believe that a website is accessible when eliminating colors, images, and other visual elements. A website can be accessible and does not have to be "ugly and boring". This is a myth many people have assumed and which is false [3].

In many countries, laws have existed for years that obligate the websites of their public administrations and the certain companies to be accessible. For example, in Colombia, according to statutory law N° 1618 of 27 February 2013, all webpages of public administrations and entities must be accessible for people with limitations or functional diversities. Additionally, according to current legislation, infractions with regard to web accessibility can be sanctioned according to the internal policies of the institutions [4]. Another law associated to accessibility is statutory law 1712 of 06 March 2014, known as the law of transparency and access to public information, which concentrates as fundamental right the access all people have to public information in possession or under control of obligated parties [entities] [5].

Web accessibility refers to an accessible web design that permits people with limitations or functional diversities to perceive, understand, navigate, interact with the web, and contribute contents to it [6]. Among the limitations accessibility seeks to address, we find visual, hearing, physical, cognitive, neurological, and speaking problems along with diseases that emerge as a product of aging. Due to the afore-mentioned, it is important for people, notwithstanding their functional diversities, to access the information institutions provide.

In 2011, the Colombian Institute for technical norms and certification [ICONTEC, for the term in Spanish] published the NTC 5854 standard for web accessibility [7]. It establishes the requisites for a website to be accessible to the greatest number possible of people independent of their physical condition [visual, hearing, cognitive limitations etc.], quality of connection to the Internet, or connection device. This norm originates in the recommendations proposed by the World Wide Web Consortium [W3C], a consortium in charge of developing technical specifications and guidelines through a process designed to maximize consensus on the content of a technical report. Thus, ensuring high technical and editorial quality, as well as obtaining greater support from the W3C and from the community in general [8].

The NTC 5854 standard seeks to establish accessibility requirements that are applicable to webpages, resented in groups of three levels of conformity: A, AA, and AAA. This norm was developed by using as reference the accessibility guidelines for web contents by the W3C [WCAG 2.0] [11]. The intention of this norm is to pro-mote that web content be accessible to people with functional diversities or visual, hearing, physical, cognitive, language, learning, or neurological limitations, permit-ting them to perceive, understand, navigate, interact, and contribute to websites.

The NTC 5854 standard is intended for developers of web applications to consider it in the process of constructing accessible websites, given that generally software developed does not include a certain number of people who endure some type of special limitation [visual, hearing, cognitive limitation, etc.]. In spite of the potential advantages of the norm, it presents principles and guidelines briefly, without including graphic examples, or relating the guidelines to programming languages and technologies, which could cause ambiguities in its interpretation by readers [9]. Thereby, the principal contribution of this article is the creation of a guide that ex-plains the essential content of the NTC 5854 standard, which includes its principles, guidelines, and levels of conformity followed by the requisites associated to each level of conformity. In the guide proposed, users will see in detail the technical ex-planation of each requisite, according to this structure: textual requirements of the norm, the reason for its implementation, graphic explanation, some forms of implementation, and the glossary associated to each term. In addition, this article presents a set of web tools that were considered in the process of generating the guide. Among these tools are the five most relevant within the set of twenty-six existing tools according to the W3C, among them there are two categories namely: validation of Grammar and validation of Accessibility [10].

The guide proposed seeks to contribute to the design and implementation of ac-accessible websites to, thus, reduce limitations of access to websites, permitting developers of applications to refer to it and understand it for its correct application in the software development process. This guide will also serve students and future professionals in information technologies in the website evaluation process from the perspective of accessibility, to allow them to verify compliance with the necessary parameters for a web portal to be seen by a greater number of people without excluding them because of their limitations [12]. Thus, the guide is designed to benefit professionals in the area of software development of the production sector. Some developers ignore the magnitude and importance of the concept of web accessibility, focusing on the functionality of the site rather than on complying with accessibility requisites and impeding the use of web applications by a greater number of people independent of whether they have or do not have some type of functional diversity [10].

Finally, as a consequence of the above, with the availability of more accessible portals, development companies benefit from their income, not only because of the additional attraction of customers, but also because of the cost derived from the life cycle of The software products, where accessibility features have a presence, although no tests have been done to validate the perception in the developers, noting that this work has been consulted by students and teachers of the engineering faculty in related projects.

This article is organized in the following manner: Sect. 2 presents the conceptual framework that includes the principal concepts kept in mind to develop the article. Section 3 describes the different phases of the methodology used in this work. Section 4 presents a revision of the norm NTC5854 regarding its guidelines and conformity principles, as well as a set of tools to evaluate accessibility. Section 5 describes the format used to adapt the norm and generate the guide proposed in this work. Finally, Sect. 6 shows the conclusions and future work derived from this work.

2 Conceptual Framework

This section includes a set of concepts kept in mind to carry out this work, among which there are: accessibility, web accessibility, NTC 5854 standard.

2.1   Accessibility

According the "Real Academia Española" the concept of accessibility can refer to the degree or level in any person, beyond their physical condition or their cognitive faculties, to use something, enjoy a service, or use an infrastructure. Thus, the concept of accessibility supposes a right that grants an individual the concrete and real possibility of entering, remaining in, and wander about a place with security, com-fort, and the greatest autonomy possible [13].

2.2   Web Accessibility

Web accessibility aims to get webpages used by a greater number of people, independent of their knowledge or personal capacities, and independent of the technical characteristics of the equipment used to access the Web [14]. Currently, this is quite important, given that access to the internet from different devices, like tab-lets and mobile phones, is a trend in constant growth. Likewise, accessibility is an important aspect to improve the positioning of a website, by increasing the number of people who can access the portal without restrictions. Bearing in mind web ac-accessibility is important not only because it helps people with different limitations or functional diversities to use the web under equal conditions as the rest, but also because it provides added benefits when a website can be adequately displayed in different devices, which represents benefits in the business model of companies [3].

2.3   NTC 5854 Standard

In 2011, ICONTEC published the NTC 5854 standard [15] for web accessibility, which establishes the requisites for a website to be accessible for the greatest number possible of people, independent of their physical condition [visual, hearing, cognitive limitation, etc.]; quality of internet connection or connection device. Different government entities, academic sectors and COLNODO [an on-line communication organization], and civil society participated in creating the norm. The norm also explains essential concepts associated to accessibility, principles of accessibility [Perceivable, Operable, Understandable, and Robust], levels of conformity [A, AA, AAA], requisites of each level of conformity, and their declaration in websites. Furthermore, it explains the benefits of implementing accessible web applications, de-fining the structure of the website within organizations, when starting a project of these characteristics.

With the aforementioned in mind, the guide proposed adapts the NTC 5854 standard, presenting in detail the technical explanation of each requisite, according to this structure: textual requirements of the norm, the reason for its implementation, graphic explanation, some forms of implementation, and the glossary associated to each term. Figure 1 presents and describes briefly the four accessibility principles addressed by the NTC 5854 standard and the guide proposed.

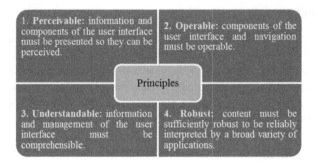

Fig. 1. Content of the norm's principles [Source: by the author]

3 Methodology

To adapt the principles and guidelines of the NTC 5854 standard in terms of an accessibility guide for websites, the methodology used contained three phases: study of the norm, adaptation of the norm, and creation of the guide [Fig. 2]. The following furnishes a description of the different phases of the methodology.

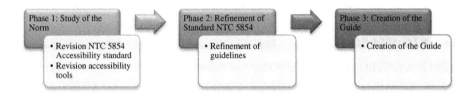

Fig. 2. Phases of the methodology. [Source: by the author]

The methodology used to create the accessibility guide from the NTC 5854 standard was divided into three phases: revision of norms and tools, adaptation of guidelines, and creation of the guide. The following describes each of the phases of the process.

Phase 1: Study of the Norm. This phase conducted a review and exhaustive study of the NTC 5854 standard to adequately understand the objective of each of the principles, guidelines, and levels of conformity of the norm, bearing in mind that several guidelines of the norm are presented briefly, which is why their interpretation by developers can lead to confusion. In addition, this phase explored the principal tools for website accessibility validation, through which it was possible to con-tribute to each of the principles and guidelines presented in the guide proposed.

Phase 2: Refinement of Standard NTC 5854. Once the analysis of the NTC 5854 standard and the accessibility tools explored, we proceeded to improve each of the accessibility guidelines and sub-guidelines, so that each one of them will be written better, achieving an improvement of them avoiding ambiguities on the part of the developer.

Phase 3: Creation of the Guide. From the guidelines written more legibly, a template was constructed to specify them in detail to include examples of use, explicative tables, fragments written in web programming language, and graphics associated to website design.

4 Review of Accessibility Guidelines and Tools

This part describes the development of phase one of the methodology used to create the guide. Thus, first, we present the generalities of the norm, as well as the guide-lines associated to each accessibility principle. Thereafter, this section shows the accessibility evaluation tools used in the conformation of the guide proposed.

4.1 Guidelines of the NTC 5854 Standard

The guidelines that make up the NTC 5854 standard contribute to the design of ac-accessible websites to, thus, reach a greater number of users, improving access conditions for individuals with physical, mental, intellectual, or sensory functional diversities. The NTC 5854 standard seeks to overcome the barriers present in the interaction with websites, which keep all users from accessing web contents under equal conditions [16]. The NTC 5854 standard is made up of 14 guidelines associated of the four basic principles [Perceivable, operable, Understandable, and robust] for accessible design. Each guideline has one or more verification points that describe how to apply said guideline to the particular characteristics of the webpages. These guidelines not only facilitate development of more accessible contents for individuals with functional diversity, but also enable the growth of the web portal's potential audience, when considering a set of recommendations mostly focused on people with hearing and visual limitations.

To clarify each of the guidelines of the NTC 5854 standard, this article introduces a guide to design accessible websites, which illustrates each guideline in detailed manner, defining a template that includes the general explanation of the guideline, detailed explanation, level of conformity associated to the guideline, and an graphic explicative example and level of programming. Table 1 shows a list of the guidelines and levels of conformity comprising each principle of the NTC 5854 standard.

The following describes briefly the principles and guidelines of the NTC 5854 standard, such as the set of values, beliefs, and norms that guide and regulate the organization. These principles are manifested in a particular order and have become a reality in the NTC 5854 standard, complying with guidelines according to need.

Principle 1 – Perceivable. The information and components of the user interface must be presented to the users in a way that they can perceive them.

Guideline 1.1. Provides textual alternatives for all non-textual content so that it can be converted to other formats people need, like larger text, braille, voice, symbols, or simpler language.

Table 1. Quantification of conformity criteria [Source: by the author]

Principle	Guideliness	Criterion of conformity
Perceivable	1	1
	2	9
	3	3
	4	9
Operable	1	3
	2	5
	3	2
	4	10
Understandable	1	6
	2	5
	3	6
Robust	1	2

Guideline 1.2. Time-dependent medium: provides alternatives for time-dependent media.

Guideline 1.3. Create content that can be presented in different forms [for example, with a simpler disposition] without losing information or structure.

Guideline 1.4. Help users see and hear the content, including the separation be-tween the first plane and the background.

Principle 2 – Operable. User interface and navigation components must be operable.

Guideline 2.1. Provides access to the whole functionality through the key-board.

Guideline 2.2. Provides users enough time to read and use the content.

Guideline 2.3. Do not design content in a manner that can provoke attacks, spasms, or convulsions.

Guideline 2.4. Provides ways to help users navigate, find content, and deter-mine where they are.

Principle 3 – Understandable. Information and management of the user interface must be Understandable.

Guideline 3.1. Make the text contents legible and Understandable.

Guideline 3.2. Make webpages appear and operate predictably.

Guideline 3.3. Help users avoid and correct errors.

Principle 4 – Robust. Components of the user interface and navigation must be operable.

Guideline 4.1. Maximize compatibility with current and future applications, including technical aids.

4.1.1 Levels of Conformity

The guidelines of the NTC 5854 standard generally describe how to implement accessible web portals without sacrificing design, i.e., without intervening in its visible appearance for the client, offering the necessary flexibility for information to be accessed under different situations and providing methods that permit its transformation into useful and clear pages [14].

Web portals can have different levels of compliance with the NTC 5854, according the number of requisites they have implemented. These levels indicate the high or low degree of accessibility and show levels of conformity. According to the norm, three possibilities exist: A, AA, and AAA [3]. Table 2 presents the levels of conformity of the NTC 5854 standard and the explanation of each.

Table 2. Levels of conformity of the NTC 5854 standard [Source: by the author]

Levels of conformity	
A	This level is basic, and the most we can do with it is to avoid the current accessibility
AA	It is now widely accepted that portals reaching this level have an acceptable degree of accessibility
AAA	With this level, we guarantee an optimal level of accessibility

4.2 Revision of Accessibility Tools

This section presents a brief description of the five accessibility tools considered for the conformation process of the guide proposed. Among the tools in mention, there are both categories [Grammar validation and Accessibility validation] and the tools that make up each group [Table 3].

The following describe each of the grammar and accessibility validation tools presented in Table 3.

Table 3. Classification of accessibility tools [Source: by the author]

Accessibility Tools			
	Type	Description	Tool
Categories	1. Grammar validation	Grammar validation tools seek to test how much pages with HTML code, like CSS, are grammatically well formed and valid	[a] W3C [X]HTML validator [b] W3C CSS validator
	1. Accessibility validation	Accessibility validation tools seek to identify automatically accessibility problems	[a] Web accessibility test [WAT] [b] W3C Link Checker [c] W3C mobile OK Checker and A Checker [Web Accessibility Checker]

4.2.1   Grammar Validation

As grammar evaluation tools, this section presents the W3C code validation tools and validation of cascade style sheets [CSS].

4.2.1.1 W3C Code Validation

Validating a page's HTML code is not a requisite, but complying with this aspect is a good practice at development level, given that it guarantees a clean, detailed, and clear code, which is a product of complying with web standards. The aforementioned permits improving maintenance, reutilization, and updating of the code by the developer or new developers [17]. The W3C permits accessing an on-line validator through http://validator.w3.org/. This validator is currently in version 1.4 and permits testing the market validity of web documents in HTML, XHTML, SMIL, MathML, etc., or finding broken links [17].

4.2.1.2 W3C Validator of Cascade Style Sheets

Most documents in the web are written by using HTML as presentation language. Although this language can be used to define the structure and design of a web portal, currently, cascade style sheets [CSS] manage aspects related to colors, text, and disposition of elements on the screen. To validate the CSS format, W3C pro-vides a service that consists of open software created to help web designers and developers to validate the CSS associated to a web portal. This service can be used on line, or downloaded and used as a java program or as a servlet java in a web server. This tool can be accessed on line at: http://jigsaw.w3.org/css-validator/ and constitutes an aid for developers to test and correct CSS according to the W3C standards [17].

4.2.2   Accessibility Validation

This section presents web accessibility test [WAT] and W3C Link Checker as accessibility evaluation tools.

4.2.2.1 Web Accessibility Test

It is a tool, conceived and developed by the Web Accessibility Unit at the CTIC foundation [Centro Tecnológico de la Información y la Comunicación] [CTIC - Jesús García Fernández, 2006] to permit automatic and manual analysis of web-site accessibility. The WAT revises integrally all the elements and pages that comprise it. At this point, it must be stressed that all tools of this type facilitate detecting accessibility problems and, hence, designing accessible websites. Nevertheless, participation from an expert in accessibility is necessary to complement the tool in areas in which a machine cannot decide, like, for example, issues related to semantics. The online version of the WAT tool analyzes accessibility guidelines according to the WCAG 2.0 standard of the W3C, from which the standard NTC 5854 is heiress.

4.2.2.2 W3C Link Checker

It is an online service to check links and hyperlinks or link to webpages or websites belonging to the W3C. The tool reads an HTML or XHTML document by extracting the list of links and checks for broken links and ensures these are not defined twice and are referenceable. Likewise, this tool warns on HTTP redirections [including the redirections directory] [AGESIC [Agency for Development, 2009]. This tool can be accessed on line at: http://validator.w3.org/checklink and it is currently in version 4.8.1 [17].

5   Adaptation of the NTC 5854 Standard

After evidencing that the NTC 5854 standard does not present clearly the different guidelines associated to the four accessibility principles, this work adapted the norm, so that each guideline was presented in more detail and by using practical examples. The adaptation proposed was embodied on a template used for each of the guidelines, which describes the guideline's objective, a detailed verbal and graphic description of the guideline, as well as implementation examples by using web-programming language [18]. The following shows the format proposed to adapt each of the guidelines of the NTC 5854 standard. First, a principle is stated, followed by the sub-guideline that will be explained related to a specific principle. Then, the lev-el of conformity is mentioned; thereafter, a literal description is made of the guideline with reference to the original version of the NTC 5854 standard, followed by the ex-planation with relation to the examples, code blocks and/or graphics. All of the is conducted for each of the 27 guidelines associated to the four principles of the NTC 5854 standard [Table 4].

Table 4. Format created for the guidelines of the NTC 5854 standard [Source: by the author]

Principle of the NTC 5854 Standard	
Guidelines	
Criterion of conformity	
Level of conformity	
Definition	
Explanation	
Examples	Example
	Code block
	Graphic

5.1   Examples of the Format

The following presents an example of the template proposed, which contains the explanation of an accessibility guideline associated to one of the four accessibility principles of the NTC 5854 standard [1. Perceivable; 2. Understandable; 3. Operable; 4. Robust]. The template intends to guide the process of designing and constructing a website according to the norm's accessibility principles.

As an example, the first principle "Perceivable" randomly chooses the "Distinguishable" guideline, which has an "AAA" level of conformity and its objective is for the web portal to have noiseless audio, avoiding echoes that can distract or confuse portal users [Table 5].

Table 5. Description of a guideline, first principle. [Source: by the author]

Principle	Perceivable
Guideline	Distinguishable
Criterion of conformity	Background sound low or absent
Level of conformity	Level AAA
Definition	For the content of only recorded audio that [1] contains talk on the first plane, [2] is not a sound CAPTCHA or an audiologue, and [3] is not a vocalization whose principal intention is to serve as musical expression [like song or rap], at least one of the following cases is fulfilled: No background sound: the audio contains no background sounds Turn off: background sounds can be switched off 20 dB: background sounds are, at least, 20 dB lower than the speech in the first plane, except for occasional sounds that last only one or two seconds Note: because of the definition of "decibel", the background sound that complies with this requisite is almost four times quieter than the principal locution
Explanation	This criterion intends to offer audio that is clean from noise, achieving that the talk does not have echoes that can distract or confuse users
Examples	To achieve a sound without noise, echoes or whispers, it is suggested to consider the tool: Adobe Audition, which is available at: www.adobe.com/products/audition.htm Au Adobe Creative Cloud Audition CC This application allows you to clean the audio and raise the volume level without damaging the contents of the original file, allowing the loading of high quality audio on the web page

¹www.adobe.com/products/audition.html.

This application permits cleaning the audio and raising the level of volume without damaging the content of the original file, permitting the upload of high-quality audio onto the webpage.

6   Conclusions and Future Work

This work presented a proposal to adapt the Colombian NTC 5854 standard with more legible terms, with regard to the examples presented in each guideline, to facilitate their comprehension by website developers and designers. The purpose was to enable the dissemination of accessibility principles and guidelines of the NTC 5854 standard two, thus, contribute to the design and implementation of accessible websites that permit broadening the number of users who access a web portal independent of their limitations or functional diversities.

This work contributed with a template to adapt the NTC 5854 standard, which ad-dresses each of the accessibility guidelines of the norm. The template proposed includes the level of conformity of each guideline, its detailed verbal and graphic ex-planation, as well as examples to implement the guideline in web portals. The objective of the template proposed is for it to serve as a guide for web developers and de-signers during the construction process of accessible websites.

- Through the guide proposed, the intention is also to promote in software development companies the importance of accessibility and its advantages, among which the following can be highlighted: having more visits to their website, accessibility makes webpage contents more Understandable and friendly for all. This guarantees that the content provided in websites easily reaches a greater number de people, including those with any visual, hearing, or cognitive limitation.
- Positioning of websites in search engines. Search engines that trace contents on a daily basis can better identify and classify the website contents when it complies with code source and content guidelines established in the NTC 5854. This in-creases the website's visibility and positioning in search engines.
- Have a multiplatform website. Implementation ensures that the website is compatible with different navigators and devices used to access the internet.
- Better usability. Being accessible implies increasing the website's usability and improves user experience when navigating in it.
- Demonstrates social responsibility. Enabling users with visual, hearing, or cognitive limitations to access and understand the website contents, shows commitment regarding the inclusion of this population, closing the existing digital divide.
- Reduction of expenses. An accessible website ensures that its structure, content, and presentation are correct. This condition facilitates changes, maintenance, or updates and diminishes learning costs, as well as delivery and implementation times.
- Compliance with legal obligations. The Ministry of Information Technology and Communications, within its on-line Government, has made it obligatory for government entities to implement the norm by levels [19].

From this work, it is possible to propose as future work the construction of a soft-ware tool that includes the principal accessibility tools studied herein, so that upon evaluating the functional modules of a web portal it can provide a general report a compliance level of the web standards and of the guidelines and principles of the NTC 5854 standard. Additionally, future work intends to create a virtual and interactive accessibility guide, which takes as reference the guide proposed in this work to propitiate in didactic manner the comprehension and application of the principles and guidelines of the NTC 5854 standard.

References

1. Colombia Discapacidad. http://discapacidadcolombia.com/Estadisticas.htm (2017). [in Spanish]
2. Romañach, J., Lobato, M.: Diversidad funcional, nuevo término para la lucha por la dignidad en la diversidad del ser humano. s.l. Foro de Vida Independiente (2005). [in Spanish]
3. Fundación Saldarriaga Concha. Norma Técnica Colombiana - NTC 5854 (2012). http://ntc5854.accesibilidadweb.co/index.php/beneficios/beneficios-de-la-norma-5854. [in Spanish]
4. Congreso de Colombia. Presidencia de la república (2013). http://wsp.presidencia.gov.co/: http://wsp.presidencia.gov.co/normativa/leyes/documents/2013/ley%201618%20del%20febrero%20de%202013.pdf. [in spanish]
5. Secretaría de transparencia. Presidencia de la República. http://www.secretariatransparencia.gov.co/Paginas/guia-implementacion-ley-transparencia.aspx (2017). [in Spanish]
6. Idrobo María Isabel e Idrobo Claudia Sofia. Guia de Accesibilidad para el diseño e implementación de sitios web teniendo en cuenta la Norma NTC 5854. Popayán, Cauca: Universidad Colegio Mayor del Cauca (2016). [in Spanish]
7. Icontec norma técnica. Accesibilidad a páginas web (2011). http://colnodo.apc.org/documento.shtml?apc=f-xx-1-&x=527. [in Spanish]
8. W3C España. Estándares (2017). http://www.w3c.es/estandares/. [in Spanish]
9. Mascaeaque, E.S.: Accesibilidad Web para discapacitados visuales. [Departamento de Ciencias de la Computación] Universidad de Alcalá (2008). [in Spanish]
10. COCENFE. Observatorio de la Accesibilidad. Observatorio de la Accesibilidad (2015). http://www.observatoriodelaaccesibilidad.es/. [in Spanish]
11. Henry, S.L.: Understanding web accessibility. In: Constructing Accessible Web Sites. Glasshaus. Understanding Web Accessibility (2012). http://www.macromedia.com/macromedia/accessibility/pub/acc_sites_chap01.pdf. Glasshaus: ISBN: 1904151000
12. García, C.E.: Información sobre discapacidad. Información sobre discapacidad (2009). http://usuarios.discapnet.es/disweb200/PautaWAI/WCAG10.htm. [in spanish]
13. Real Academia Española. Real Academia Española. con colaboración de IBM (2017). http://www.rae.es/. [in Spanish]
14. Norma Técnica Colombiana 5854/ Razones para implementar (2012). http://ntc5854.accesibilidadweb.co/index.php/beneficios/beneficios-de-la-norma-5854. [in Spanish]
15. Instituto Colombiano de Normas Técnicas y Certificación. Colnodo y Programa Gobierno en línea (2011). http://colnodo.apc.org/documento.shtml?apc=f-xx-1-&x=527. [in Spanish]
16. Delgado, A.: WCAG 2.0 Pautas de Accesibilidad al Contenido Web 2.0. Discapacidad motora Ceguera Baja visión Baja audición Sordera Problemas cognitivos Personas (2011). http://servidorti.uib.es/adelaida/accesibilidad/WCAG20.ppt. [in Spanish]
17. W3C Servicio de Validación de mercado (2013). http://validator.w3.org/. [in Spanish]
18. Nielsen, J. Beyond Accessibility: Treating People with Disabilities as People. Beyond Accessibility: Treating People with Disabilities as People. Alertbox (2011). http://www.useit.com/alertbox/20011111.html. [in Spanish]

19. Fundación Saldarriaga Concha, Discapacidad E Inclusión Social En Colombia (2017). http://www.saldarriagaconcha.org/es/
20. Fung, K.K.: A Fuzzy Qualitative Evaluation System: a multi-granular aggregation approach using fuzzy compound linguistic variable. J. Intell. Fuzzy Syst. **24**, 61–78 (2013). [in Spanish]
21. Likert, R.: A technique for the measurement of attitudes. Arch. Psychol. **140**, 1–55 (1932)
22. Zhaoa, X., Yueb, W.: A multi-subsystem fuzzy DEA model with its application in mutual funds management companies' competence evaluation. Procedia Comput. Sci. **1**, 2469–2478 (2012)
23. Massanet, S., et al.: A new linguistic computational model based on discrete fuzzy numbers for computing with words. Inf. Sci. **248**, 277–290 (2014)
24. Montero, J., et al.: A method for designing automatic assessment systems based on teachers reasoning for evaluating subjective engineering student's competences. In: 9th Iberian Conference on Information Systems and Technologies [CISTI] (2014)
25. García, M.J., Gairín, J.: Los Mapas de Competencias: una Herramienta para mejorar la Calidad de la Formación Universitaria. Revista Iberoamericana sobre Calidad, Eficacia y Cambio en Educación **9**, 84–102. [in Spanish]
26. Ostyn.Consulting.Simple.Reusable.Competency.Map   (2006).   http://www.ostyn.com/standardswork/competency/ReusableCompMapProp.pdf
27. Herrera, F., Martínez, L.: A 2-tuple fuzzy linguistic representation model for computing with words. IEEE Trans. Fuzzy Syst. **8**(6), 746–752 (2000)
28. Zhang, P., Hu, J.: Application of fuzzy hierarchy evaluation in the occupational competency assessment of the vocational colleges. In: International Symposium on Information Technology in Medicine and Education, pp. 182–185 (2012)
29. Serrano, J., Romero, F., Olivas, J.: Hiperion: a fuzzy approach for recommending educational activities based on the acquisition of competences. Inf. Sci. **248**, 114–129 (2013)
30. Zhang, Z., Qin, X., Li, X.: Competency assessment study based on IPCA-fuzzy comprehensive evaluation. In: International Conference on Management and Service Science [MASS], pp. 1–9 (2010)
31. Zhang, H.: The multiattribute group decision making method based on aggregation operators with interval-valued 2-tuple linguistic information. Math. Comput. Model. **56**, 27–35 (2012)
32. Herrera, E., et al.: Inf. Retriev. **12**, 179–200 (2009)
33. Ministerio de Educación de Colombia. Estándares básicos de competencias (2006). http://www.mineducacion.gov.co/1621/articles340021_recurso_1.pdf. [in Spanish]
34. OCDE.El Programa PISA de la OCDE (2006). http://www.oecd.org/pisa/39730818.pdf

Mixing Art and Technology: An Interactive Radio for a Museum Exhibition

Diego F. Loaiza[1], Edmond C. Prakash[2], Isidro Moreno[3],
and Andrés A. Navarro-Newball[4(⊠)]

[1] Universidad Santiago de Cali, Cali, Colombia
diego.loaiza02@usc.edu.co
[2] University of Westminster, London, UK
e.prakash@westminster.ac.uk
[3] Universidad Complutense de Madrid, Madrid, Spain
ims@ucm.es
[4] Pontificia Universidad Javeriana, Cali, Colombia
anavarro@javerianacali.edu.co

Abstract. Technology can inspire art. Art explores the context of technology. Combined, they empower artists to create innovative ways to captivate their audiences. Technology can enhance the ability of artists to express themselves. Such enhancement was required for one temporary art exhibit, where a recording had to be played when there was a visitor close to an interactive radio. To support it, we implemented motion sensing of exhibit visitors to allow contextual sound playback based on the visitor's location. This allowed the artist to add an audible dialogue experience to the art exhibit. We interacted with a local artist and understood the artist vision to define and agree on technical requirements. A preliminary validation at the exhibit showed general acceptance of the system, positive feedback on the experience and areas for future improvement. In general, we believe that more research is required in terms of the artist-visitor relationship mediated by technology.

Keywords: Museum · Interactive · Art · Technology · Radio · Motion detection

1 Introduction

Technology can benefit art and art can challenge technological advances; when put together, they can capture audiences and empower artists in innovative ways. Uchiyama et al. [1] describe a system to display Japan's nature and culture of each season relying on Augmented Reality (AR) techniques. The system displays from flying insects to Japanese poetry. Konieczny and Meyer [2] explain a computerised airbrush with a 3D interface to replicate the process of real airbrushing while they suggest that their system could yield to possible additions into existing artwork interfaces. This idea is similar to the immersive 3D painting system proposed earlier by Keefe et al. [3]. Pucihar et al. [4] introduce a system

© Springer International Publishing AG 2017
A. Solano and H. Ordoñez (Eds.): CCC 2017, CCIS 735, pp. 586–594, 2017.
DOI: 10.1007/978-3-319-66562-7_42

to engage young visitors in art museums using games and AR, allowing them to create unique personalised versions of the displayed artwork. Carbonell [5] introduce AR based documental narration developing a system where the spectator plays with the concept of reading using 3D elements. Coulton et al. [6] use mobile AR to present the views of the artist to the visitors allowing the latter to curate their own AR art exhibitions in their homes. Novak [7] explores the idea that a musical network interconnects different locations using AR. Yoshida et al. [8] create an installation where a painter can feel the attributes of digital colours. Haute's [9] experiment with synthetic doubles using avatars. Aaron and Blackwell [10] explore new forms of music notations using functional languages. Meanwhile, Minuto et al. [11] develop smart material interfaces to aid new forms of art. In this project, 15 fine arts students have learnt to program the smart materials and created interesting artefacts.

On the other hand, Sengers and Csikszentmihlyi [12] already explored the difficulties of human computer interaction and arts convergence and more recently Kang [13] observed the role of users in art and design using a breakable wall that is destroyed when hit by the user. Nowadays, technology such as drones [14] are also used in arts, however, challenges related to automatic navigation still exists and developers are able to put in place programming based solutions. Indeed, most projects described in this section required abstract modelling and programming, structured interdisciplinary design [6] and mathematical formulas. Thus, the role of technology development in art is clear: it provides artist with novel ways for expressing ideas. Still, artists can be immersed navigating the known path of traditional art or proven technology. As an example, artists can be trained to obtain professional certifications in well known tools using expensive computational resources (e.g. certifications for media edition and creation by Adobe, Apple and Avid). However, in such situations, artists' creative process is limited to what these technologies allow them to do while they miss the joy of different trends, platforms and interdisciplinary work that could take their creativity even further.

Our work does not relate to the ones described in terms of the technologies used or the art creations obtained. It reinforces the idea of how artists can benefit from technological development. Many of these art creations constitute proof of concepts with great potential. However, they require further study, particularly, in terms of how they promote the artist-visitor relationship. To achieve this, as further work, we are developing an Emerging Media Space (EMS) to enable and study art and technological development in an interdisciplinary cross platform manner. Next, we present a case of collaboration for a temporary exhibition at the archaeological museum, Museo Arqueolgico La Merced (MUSA) in Cali Colombia. We present a preliminary evaluation of this relationship.

1.1   The Entramados Exhibition

One local artist wanted an exhibition to allow the visitor to explore the relationship between humans and objects. He wanted the exhibition to show how the pre-Columbian inhabitants created their elements in a similar manner that people do these days. The final touch the artist wanted in the exhibition was an interactive radio capable of starting a speech about how, when we are gone, we leave many objects behind and become objects ourselves. Figure 1A shows the exhibition's layout. There are ceramic objects all around the room. For the central display the artist took advantage of a mirror in order to suggest a relationship between ancient and modern objects. The radio was hidden behind the wall at the end of the exhibition producing a crackling noise to capture user's attention. Figure 1B shows the interactive radio. The four-month long exhibition opened at the MUSA on November the 6th, 2014 and closed on March 1st, 2015. Our technical requirements included: the solution must adjust to limited funds; the visible interface must be and old radio (all technological gadgets must be hidden); in idle state, the radio produces white noise; once a visitor is detected, the radio must synthesize and play a speech; use a simple motion detection technique (the algorithm must perform well in a low capacity computer).

A)

B)

Central display

Fig. 1. (A) Entramados exhibition. (B) Interactive radio

2 Development

2.1 Setup

The main artifact within the interactive radio is a recording that invites the visitor to reflect on his or her relationship with everyday objects and to establish a parallel with that held by the former pre-Columbian settlers with their own objects. From the initial design, we had to simulate a recording coming out from some radio or recorder. This recording had to be played only when there was a visitor close to the radio. We decided to implement motion detection using a low cost webcam, a notebook PC with 4 GB of RAM running the Windows operating system. With these resources, we used Processing 2 to generate a Java executable that was able to control motion detection and audio playback. Both the webcam and the small notebook were properly installed, hidden out of sight under the radio. A monaural speaker connected to the notebook was used and camouflaged in the radio shell.

2.2   Motion Detection

The motion detection algorithm was based on the one proposed by Daniel Shiffman [15]. The detection in this algorithm is based on the calculation of the difference between the pixels of two consecutive grayscale frames (the current and the previous one): it traverses the pixels of the two frames and calculates the intensity difference pixel by pixel. If the difference is greater than a threshold (threshold parameter), that pixel is considered to correspond to a motion pixel. The number of moving pixels (movingPixels parameter) is counted in order to parameterize the area of the image that corresponds to the object that was moving, thus discarding the movement of small elements. Since the objective was simply to detect if there was a movement or not, the algorithm used, fulfilled its purpose, after adjusting the parameters threshold and movingPixels: A threshold of 50 and a value of movingPixels of 1000, for an image resolution of 640 * 480, gave satisfactory results. The main steps of the algorithm are:

1. Load pixels from new video frame.
2. Load pixels from previous frame.
3. BEGIN LOOP: walk through every pixel.
   (a) Get current pixel location.
   (b) Get current pixel colour.
   (c) Get previous pixel colour.
   (d) Compare colours (previous vs. current).
   (e) Measure how different colours are.
   (f) If colour at the current pixel has changed, then there is motion at that pixel.
   (g) If motion play speech, if not, play white noise.

2.3   State Machine

The detection algorithm was incorporated into the main processing loop, and capture and detection was performed in the draw method, which was executed for each video frame. The state machine determines the behaviour of audio in the presence or absence of a visitor (Fig. 2). Initially, when no motion has been detected, an audio similar to that of static of a detuned radio or white noise is played. Once motion is detected, the main audio is played in loop until it ends, in which case it returns to the idle state of inactive, getting ready to start the process from the beginning.

not motionDetected / playWhiteNoiseAudio, detectMotion

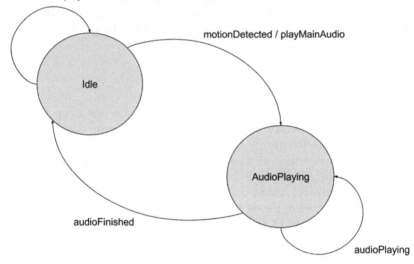

motionDetected / playMainAudio

Idle

AudioPlaying

audioFinished

audioPlaying

Fig. 2. State machine for the playback of the audio of the exhibit

3   Results

For four months, the interactive radio served as a complementary expressive element to the artist's exhibition for both adults and children. Figure 3A shows some adults listening to the radio's speech. Figure 3B shows a child whose attention was captured by the detuned radio noise produced. Figure 3C shows the museum's guide using the radio to illustrate to a number of primary school children. In order to keep order, when a larger group of children arrived at the exhibition it was better to have them sit around the radio.

While the exhibition was running, we performed a preliminary summative empiric user experience validation [16] to be able to evaluate a smaller number of adult user participants and observed children's behaviour at the exhibition. Ethical approval was received for the experiment. The goal of the validation was to find out how easy the interactive radio was discovered, how easy it was for them to realise the radio changed the detuned radio noise for the speech and how the discourse was received. We used a Likert scale from 0 "I do not agree at all" to 5 "I totally agree" to rate affirmations shown in Table 1. We applied the instrument to 20 adult users. Most interviewed visitors (14) confirmed that they did not find the radio until someone showed them the way to it, but 6 of them arrived at the radio because of the detuned radio sound. That explains why "the radio is located in the right place" was the item with lower rating. One of the 6 visitors who arrived at the radio without any help stated that "it was like magic". All of them agreed that the radio made them reflect about life. In general the radio was found to be coherent and useful for the exhibition

Fig. 3. (A) A group of adults listening to the radio's speech. (B) A child filming the radio with his mobile phone. (C) The guide, the teachers and the primary school children sitting around the radio. We blurred the images to protect identities of the visitors.

Table 1. Radio's preliminary validation.

Affirmation	Average rating
The radio's speech is clear	5
The volume is adequate	5
Interaction with the radio is natural	4.3
The moment interaction starts is clear	4.8
Interaction occurs on time	4.3
The radio helps in making us understand our relationship with objects	4.5
The exhibition helps in making us understand our relationship with objects	5
The radio maintains coherence with the rest of the exhibition	4.5
The radio gives context to the exhibition	5
The radio is located in the right place	3.5
I liked the interactive radio	5
The sound of the radio interferes with the exhibition	1.8
Average	**4.4**

(it helps to understand the human-objects relationship). Finally, when the primary school children arrived we were able to observe some interesting behaviours:

1. Teachers in charge of the children tried to turn down the radio's volume.
2. In one rare situation, the motion sensor technology used, started when it detected motion from a far distance. Even though the radio was behind a wall to avoid this problem, there is some probability that the sensor detected motion through a hole on the wall.
3. The mirror was the part of the exhibition which captured more attention from the visitors.
4. Sometimes children went past the radio without listening to the speech. However, the most curious children stayed interacting (Fig. 3B).
5. The group of 30 children were seated around the radio by the museum guide (Fig. 3C).
6. 16 out of 30 children came back to explore the radio with their teachers because they found it fun.

4   Discussion

Technology can benefit art and art can challenge technological advances. When put together, they can capture audiences and empower artists in innovative ways. However, the pieces of art produced need to be tested with real visitors in order to study people's behaviours and technology limitations. Our interactive radio was quite successful, however, for several visitors (including children who just passed it) it was not located at the right place within the exhibition. Limitations of the technology used, impeded the placement of the radio at the other side of the wall. Possible solutions could have been:

1. Using stickers or arrows on the floor to guide visitors to the radio.
2. Refining the motion recognition algorithms.
3. Using different visitor detection techniques.
4 Using different way to capture visitors' attention.

None of the options were implemented because of the short period available to implement the whole exhibition. User tests occurred after the exhibition opened impeding us to refine it. Nevertheless, the radio was well received overall.

5   Conclusions and Further Work

An algorithm using a simple calculation, the pixel intensity difference between two frames, and a low resolution image, made fast motion detection possible in a low end laptop. Within a four months period, it was reported to "fail" only in one situation detecting motion from a far distance. Here, the problem was not the algorithm itself, which responded to motion in the environment, but possibly a hole on one of the walls in the exhibit which let motion information pass to the camera. This fact evidences that the artist and the developer need to agree on and test art setup issues beforehand. However, some of these issues may be unpredictable before the piece of art or exhibit is shown to the public.

An art exhibition setup aided by technology requires not only summative validation, which we performed, but also formative user experience validation. If we have had more time to test the experience, the interactive radio could have been easier to find by visitors. The preliminary summative validation showed that most of the visitors could not find the radio. However, once the radio was found by the visitors, it made sense. Indeed, the speech played by the radio made visitors reflect about life and objects, fulfilling the artist vision and helping in promoting the artist-visitor relationship mediated through technology. Overall (1), the radio was likeable, interesting, easy to interact with, aided the exhibition and helped the artist send a message to the visitors.

Regarding the Entramados exhibition, there is nothing else to be done. However, the kind of interaction proposed, an old radio playing a speech or sound as people come close, can be explored further in terms of its use in other contexts or other pieces of art. Additional kinds of outputs (e.g. a light turning on as a visitor comes closer) or devices (e.g. an interactive TV) could be explored, as well.

Finally, our further work will include further research about art and technology, particularly, in terms of how they promote the artist-visitor relationship. Our idea is to propose an experimentation space or EMS were both, artist and developers (computer scientists, engineers) nurture their creativity together.

Acknowledgments. Authors would like to thank the Museo Arqueolgico La Merced (MUSA) in Cali - Colombia and artist Oscar Sanabria.

References

1. Uchiyama, H., Sato, A., Takai, M., Shibasaki, M., Ookura, M., Imai, M., Hara, T., Takeda, Y., Tanaka, M., Komatsubara, S.: SHI KI BAKO "Box of Four Seasons". In: Proceedings of the International Conference on Advances in Computer Entertainment Technology (ACE 2009), p. 450. ACM, New York (2009). doi:10.1145/1690388.1690498
2. Konieczny, J., Meyer, G.: Airbrush simulation for artwork and computer modeling. In: Spencer, S.N. (ed.) Proceedings of the 7th International Symposium on Non-photorealistic Animation and Rendering (NPAR 2009), pp. 61–69. ACM, New York (2009). doi:10.1145/1572614.1572625
3. Keefe, D.F., Feliz, D.A., Moscovich, T., Laidlaw, D.H., LaViola, J.J.: CavePainting: a fully immersive 3D artistic medium and interactive experience. In: Proceedings of the 2001 Symposium on Interactive 3D Graphics (I3D 2001), pp. 85–93. ACM, New York (2001). doi:10.1145/364338.364370
4. Pucihar, K.C., Kljun, M., Coulton, P.: Playing with the artworks: engaging with art through an augmented reality game. In: Proceedings of the 2016 CHI Conference Extended Abstracts on Human Factors in Computing Systems (CHI EA 2016), pp. 1842–1848. ACM, New York (2016). doi:10.1145/2851581.2892322

5. Carbonell, M.M., Martnez, F.G., Andrs, J.M.: Notbook AR. In: Proceedings of the 2005 ACM SIGCHI International Conference on Advances in Computer Entertainment Technology (ACE 2005), pp. 356–357. ACM, New York (2005). doi:10.1145/1178477.1178546

6. Coulton, P., Smith, R., Murphy, E., Pucihar, K.C., Lochrie, M.: Designing mobile augmented reality art applications: addressing the views of the galleries and the artists. In: Proceedings of the 18th International Academic MindTrek Conference: Media Business. Management, Content & Services (AcademicMindTrek 2014), pp. 177–182. ACM, New York (2014). doi:10.1145/2676467.2676490

7. Novak, S.: Site weave: revealing interconnections through music. In: Do, E.Y.-L., Dow, S., Ox, J., Smith, S., Nishimoto, K., Tan, C.T. (eds.) Proceedings of the 9th ACM Conference on Creativity & Cognition (C&C 2013), pp. 418–419. ACM, New York (2013). doi:10.1145/2466627.2481215

8. Yoshida, S., Kurumisawa, J., Noma, H., Tetsutani, N., Hosaka, K.: Sumi-nagashi: creation of new style media art with haptic digital colors. In: Proceedings of the 12th Annual ACM International Conference on Multimedia (MULTIMEDIA 2004), pp. 636–643. ACM, New York (2004). doi:10.1145/1027527.1027675

9. Haute, L.: The touch of the avatar, artistic research and performance with synthetic doubles. In: Proceedings of the 2014 Virtual Reality International Conference (VRIC 2014) Article 17, 6 p. ACM, New York (2014). doi:10.1145/2617841.2620705

10. Aaron, S., Blackwell, A.F.: From sonic Pi to overtone: creative musical experiences with domain-specific and functional languages. In: Proceedings of the First ACM SIGPLAN Workshop on Functional Art, Music, Modeling & Design (FARM 2013), pp. 35–46. ACM, New York (2013). doi:10.1145/2505341.2505346

11. Minuto, A., Pittarello, F., Nijholt, A.: New materials = new expressive powers: smart material interfaces and arts, an interactive experience made possible thanks to smart materials. In: Proceedings of the 2014 International Working Conference on Advanced Visual Interfaces (AVI 2014), pp. 141–144. ACM, New York (2014). doi:10.1145/2598153.2598198

12. Sengers, P., Csikszentmihlyi, C.: HCI and the arts: a conflicted convergence? In: CHI 2003 Extended Abstracts on Human Factors in Computing Systems (CHI EA 2003), pp. 876–877. ACM, New York (2003). doi:10.1145/765891.766044

13. Kang, L.: Breaking AndyWall: transgressive and playful exploration on the dynamic role of users in art and design. In: Proceedings of the 2016 CHI Conference Extended Abstracts on Human Factors in Computing Systems (CHI EA 2016), pp. 3855–3858. ACM, New York (2016). doi:10.1145/2851581.2891100

14. Fleureau, J., Galvane, Q., Tariolle, F.L., Guillotel, P.: POSTER: generic drone control platform for autonomous capture of cinema scenes submission. In: Proceedings of the 14th Annual International Conference on Mobile Systems, Applications, and Services Companion (MobiSys 2016 Companion), p. 133. ACM, New York (2016). doi:10.1145/2938559.2953925

15. Shiffman, D.: A simple motion detection in Processing (2017). http://learningprocessing.com/examples/chp.16/example-16-13-MotionPixels

16. Hartson, R., Pyla, P.S.: The UX Book. Process and Guidelines for Ensuring a Quality User Experience. Elsevier, Amsterdam (2012)

Analysis of Mouse Movement and Body Response in Distance Learning Environments

Oscar Yair Ortegón-Romero, Kael Vieira de Oliveira Fraga,
Luciana Porcher Nedel, and Leandro Krug Wives[(✉)]

PPGC, Instituto de Informática, UFRGS, Porto Alegre, Brazil
{oscarortegon.romero,nedel,wives}@inf.ufrgs.br, kaelfraga@hotmail.com

Abstract. Virtual lessons are often used as a teaching strategy to promote dynamic learning processes. The objective of the present study was to investigate the relationship between the mouse use allied to users' corporal responses and engagement feeling during virtual lessons. Ten participants were recruited and submitted to two activities: one video lesson and a slideshow, as well as questionnaires related to the contents and quality aspects of the lessons. The data was collected using a smartphone accelerometer and a mouse tracker (developed from a Google Chrome browser extension). A correlation between the mouse tracker and the user's experience questionnaires was observed a correlation between the number of mouse movements as well as the number of clicks with the items obstructive/conductor. In addition, a correlation was found between the number of clicks and the item easy/difficult. No significant differences were found between the lessons; finally, we concluded that the use of the mouse movements could be an engagement indicator during a virtual lesson between men and women. However, is it important to state that the proposed experiment script and its resources need to be reviewed and restructured for guaranteeing higher data accuracy.

1 Introduction

The advance of new technologies and the demand for more high-quality information have proposed a gradual evolution of educational systems. Consequently, on-line systems with educational focus have increased. For instance, Khan Academy[1], contain lessons with diverse topics such as mathematics, computing, arts, and economics. Moodle[2] is also a virtual platform used by many educational institutions to perform distance learning.

The teaching environments virtualization process and the possibility of sharing educational contents through the Web have promoted a growing concern among educators and content producers on how to develop attractive, efficient and engaging material. Parameters such us engagement trough the mouse movements were not evaluated in an environment close to the reality. Thus, the present

---

[1] http://www.khanacademy.org/.
[2] http://moodle.org/.

A. Solano and H. Ordoñez (Eds.): CCC 2017, CCIS 735, pp. 595–607, 2017.
DOI: 10.1007/978-3-319-66562-7_43

work describes an experiment with users exposed to distance learning activities with the aim of assessing corporeal reactions and their association with the engagement feeling or disinterest of users during virtual lessons.

Considering the user's interaction with the environment during a virtual lesson, variables concerning the use of the mouse and body movements were collected to confirm the following assumptions:

- The movement of the mouse through the display can be used to measure the loss of engagement during the lessons;
- The frequency of changing browser tabs can be used to identify the user's engagement loss;
- Body movements can be used to measure the user's engagement loss during lessons.

To evaluate such assumptions, an application was developed and an experiment was conducted. In this sense, this paper is structured as the following. Background concepts and related works are presented in the next Sect. 2. Then, Materials and Methods are described (Sect. 3). Section 4 presents the results of the study. Finally, in the conclusions, results are discussed and further research questions are mentioned.

2   Background and Related Work

Virtual teaching has evolved as one of the solutions for the global access of learning. In fact, one of the main technological requirements for the student is to have internet access, allowing diverse study spaces [1]. Nevertheless, these spaces could be generating a significant number of stimuli that could also divert students' attention. Facing this situation, we ask whether users are losing their attention due to possible negative emotions generated by an application or by the environment that surrounds them and, whether the performance can be affected by these factors.

Alberts et al. [1]argue that learning in education programs is so efficient due to the flexibility provided to the students in terms of time, place and rhythm. However, its process can be negatively influenced by inappropriate learning strategies such as the kind of fostering. Thus, the author concludes that learning evolution is inevitable, nevertheless, it is necessary to create structures and limits for the students.

Seeing the need to create a follow-up to the learning process is the ALAS-KA platform [8] that shows how this process evaluates in an e-learning platform such as Khan Academy, providing guidelines and examples to help teachers to Make decisions based on the data from students who used the platform.

Continuing with the follow-up to the learning process, Gallego et al. [3] present a global virtual platform (OPENET4VE) that can monitor and record the interaction between students and teachers through the events recorded by them. With this record and using data mining algorithms, the actual learning flow of the course is automatically extracted, so that teachers can add changes to the learning flow that were proposed at the beginning.

However, such studies still indicate the lack of strategies to solve the negative impact that the multiple stimuli generated for students by the environment during their learning process.

Human motor responses can be indicators of negative emotions under stressful or less motivating situations. Neurological studies suggest that negative emotions have a particular and direct connection with cerebral structures responsible for motor response, including arms and hands movements [5]. In this sense, Coelho et al. [2] showed the relationship between negative emotions and the use of the mouse, and that the feelings generated by Web environment can be expressed by an increase in the use of the mouse. Moreover, they suggest that negative emotions can interfere with memory processes and task performances.

3   Materials and Methods

To confirm assumptions one and two, a Google Chrome extension [7] was developed to register mouse activities, including the number of clicks and the coordinates of the mouse cursor on the screen. The application is also able to record the number of browser tabs changes as an indicator of the activities performed in the user interface (shown in Figs. 1 and 2). This data was collected using an extension and recorded in a JavaScript Object Notation (JSON) file.

To evaluate the body movement during the lessons, as mentioned in assumption 3, a mobile application for Android called Accelerometer Analyzer [9] was used (Fig. 3). This application was able to register the movement of the user

Fig. 1. Bitcoin video lesson with mouse tracker extension (Source: [4])

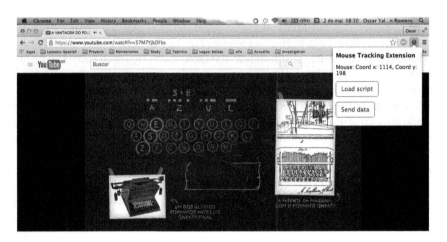

Fig. 2. Nerdologia video lesson with mouse tracker extension (Source: [6])

in three axes (X, Y, and Z), and the time interval (in milliseconds) between each capture. During each lesson, the measurements were performed using a smartphone, located in the user's left pocket. All data were stored in a MySQL database, and a reporting generation interface in PHP was implemented [10].

3.1   Volunteers and Resources

A total of 12 volunteers (six women and six men), between 17 and 50 years old were recruited for the experiment. Educational information was collected and, the volunteers were also asked about medical conditions associated with anxiety disorders and attention deficits. Furthermore, users' perception about these aspects were inquired using the following questions: "How anxious are you?" and "What is your ability to keep the attention during an activity?". All the information was recorded in the questionnaire 1 - Google Forms to the volunteer characterization[3].

For running the mobile application and monitoring the accelerometer sensor, two different smartphones were used: an Asus Zenfone 27 and an ARGIM plus LG G Pro Lite 8. The mouse tracking extension was developed on Google Chrome platform version 51.0.2704.103.

For the evaluations, two lessons were chosen. The first lesson was a YouTube video called "Nerdologia" [6], regarding human thumbs and typing. The second lesson was a slideshow about Bitcoin [4]. After each lesson, a specific content questionnaire was applied: questionnaire 4 to the video lesson[4] and questionnaire 5 to the slideshow lesson[5]. The User's Experience Questionnaire (UEQ)[6]

---

[3] http://goo.gl/forms/5WH36OgYGeqvCHZv2.

[4] http://goo.gl/forms/RpfVtiqlG28xL7SB3.

[5] http://goo.gl/forms/PeTBv5tchG8Ut1A93.

[6] http://www.ueq-online.org/ueq-download/.

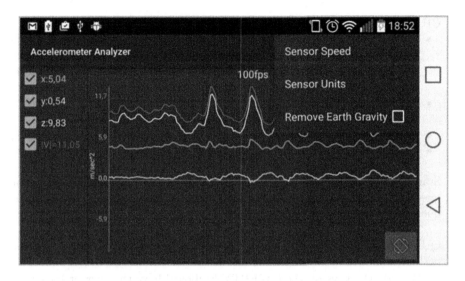

Fig. 3. Accelerometer's interface (Source: [9])

measures the user's experience of the user during the interaction with web environments through the expression of feelings, impressions, and attitudes. The scales of the questionnaire develop aspects in terms of usability like efficiency, perspicuity, dependability and user experience with originality and stimulation.

3.2 Experimental Procedures

In this section, we describe how the experiment was conducted, using the resources and volunteers available. The space used was an enclosed room with a table, a chair, and a desktop computer. Researchers were present to give needed assistance, but they did not interfere with the results. The experiment started with the researchers explaining the objective of the study, the need for keeping the smartphone in the left pocket (for getting body movement data), the tests that should be applied, and what users must not perform (e.g., closing the browser tab containing the video lessons would stop the tracking extension). The information about the movements tracking of the mouse was omitted to the users, so as not compromise the results of the research.

The script for performing the experiment was the following:

1. Accommodate the user in a chair in front of the desktop computer available for the experiment;
2. Start the application on the smartphone and put it in the left pocket of the user;
3. Ask the user to answer the characterization questionnaire that was composed for the questions and answers as follow:

CHARACTERIZATION QUESTIONNAIRE
- Which hand do you prefer to use for activities: Writing, Closing, Using scissors, Brushing teeth, Cutting with knives, Handling a spoon, Using the computer mouse. options: (Left always, usually left, no preference, usually right)
- Do you have any weakness or medical condition associated with anxiety problems? If yes, please describe.
- From 1 to 5, how much do you consider yourself anxious?
- From 1 to 5, how much do you consider your ability to pay attention to an activity?

4. Start the first activity (Video-lesson) and subsequently the application of the questionnaire based on the content of this lesson, that was composed for the questions and answers as follow:

QUESTIONNAIRE 4 FOR VIDEO-LESSON. The correct answer is marked with (*)
- Why do the keys on the QWERTY keyboard have the current layout?
  - For users to type more slowly because old typewriters were fragile.
  - Because of the most commonly used combinations of letters in the English language.
  - Because it facilitated the typing of the telegraph operators, who had to transcribe messages in Morse code. (*)
  - Because the inventor of the keyboard was Russian and in Russia, the alphabetical order is organized in this way.
- Why is the KALQ keyboard, designed to speed up typing on touch devices, not currently used?
  - Because it is better to enter using a QWERTY keyboard.
  - Because most users are already accustomed to the QWERTY model. (*)
  - Because it does not respect the alphabetical order of the most spoken languages in the world.
  - Because the cost to manufacture KALQ keyboards is greater than the cost of QWERTY keyboards.
- Among the advantages that the human being developed by owning an opposing thumb, is NOT one of them:
  - Climbing trees (*)
  - Precision footprint
  - Handling Tools
  - Force footprint
- Which of these is a unique muscle of the human, related to the thumb?
  - Superficial flexor of Fingers
  - Long flexor of the thumb (*)
  - Descending Trapezoid
  - Short abdurer of the thumb
- What following activity is only possible by human dexterity with the opposing thumb?

- Play video game
- Distribute the force of a punch without breaking the joints
- To type
- All alternatives are correct (*)

5. Apply the qualitative questionnaire about the lesson viewed;
6. Start the second activity (slideshow) and, the respective questionnaire, that composed for the questions and answers as follow:

   QUESTIONNAIRE 5 FOR SLIDESHOW. The correct answer is marked with (*)

   - Among the options below, which one is NOT part of the Bitcoin concept?
     - Currency,
     - Payment System,
     - Virtual Credits (*)
     - Contracts Network
   - According to the slideshow which territory is the most used Bitcoins?
     - Eastern North America
     - Northern Europe (*)
     - Southern South America
     - Eastern Asia
   - Month and year in which Bitcoin reached a value of 1
     - February 2011 *
     - May 2010
     - November 2008
     - January 2009
   - How did Stefan Molyneux make money using Bitcoins?
     - Through the sale and resale of bitcoins
     - Through donations from your viewers (*)
     - Through the monetization of youtube
     - Through the subscription systems of your podcast
   - How are the shipments and receipts of Bitcoins made?
     - Via sms messages
     - Through printed coupons
     - Through bank transactions
     - Through QR codes generated in a virtual wallet (*)

7. Apply the qualitative questionnaire about the second lesson.

Volunteers were explained to use the Web freely to search additional information during the lesson, to answer the questions related to the lesson conducted. So, they could search and return to the questionnaire as much as were required, allowing capture more data from the tracking applications. To access the activities, public links from the Web were used, in order to visualize the lessons were randomized. Once the user finished the questionnaires, the examiner was informed and the mouse tracking results were submitted to the data storage server. Also, accelerometer's data were recorded. After data collection, data normality distribution was confirmed by Shapiro-Wilk test. To determine differences between the virtual lesson 1 and virtual lesson two the student's t-test was conducted. One-way ANOVA was used in order to evaluate differences between women and men. Benchmark analysis was used to the UEQ data. To establish the correlation between the UEQ and data obtained during the visualization of the lesson (accelerometer and movement of the mouse), the Pearson correlation coefficient was used. P-values $<= 0.05$ were considered significant.

4   Results

In this section, we present the results obtained in the analysis of quantitative and qualitative data, as provided by the applied questionnaires and collected by the Chrome extension and the Android application. Two volunteers were eliminated from the analysis due to a problem in submitting the mouse data during the virtual lesson. Thus, data of 10 users were analyzed.

In this section, we present the results obtained in the analysis of quantitative and qualitative data, as provided by the applied questionnaires and collected by the Chrome extension and the Android application. Two volunteers were excluded from the analysis due to a problem in submitting the mouse data during the virtual lesson. Thus, for the statistical analysis, the data of 10 users were analyzed.

According to the characterization of the volunteers, 40% of the users were men, and 60% were women. The mean of age was 30 years old, and 50% of the users had completed the elementary school (Fig. 4a). The self-evaluation of anxiety and self-evaluation of attention levels showed that most of the volunteers (58.3%) were moderately anxious and had a good ability to pay attention during an activity, as indicated in Figs. 4b and c, respectively. 60% of the volunteers visualized the video lesson Nerdologia first and the other users the slide show Bitcoin. The Table 1 shows the score results obtained in the lessons showing a better response in the video lesson with an effectiveness of 80% against 72% obtained by the users during the slideshow lesson. The paired-sample t-test did not reveal significant differences between the first and the second lesson and the questionnaires 4 and 5 Respectively ($T = 0.885$, $P > 0.05$). The corporal responses perceived by the accelerometer from the beginning of the experiment to the start of the first activity were taken as baseline values, and are presented in Table 2. Taking into account the data of the accelerometer for each axis during the two lessons, the paired-sample t-test did not reveal significant differences between the body movements of the users when comparing the first and the second lesson ($P > 0.05$). However, considering the sex of the volunteers and the difference between the baseline data and the lesson 2 data, one-way ANOVA showed that women increased the number of movements in the Y axis when compared with men ($F_{(1,9)} = 5.926, p = 0.041$), as it can be seen in Fig. 5a. No significant differences were observed in lesson 1 or the other axes of lesson 2 ($P > 0.05$).

Concerning data obtained using the mouse tracking application, the outcomes regarding the number of tab exchanges (NTE), mouse movements (NMM),

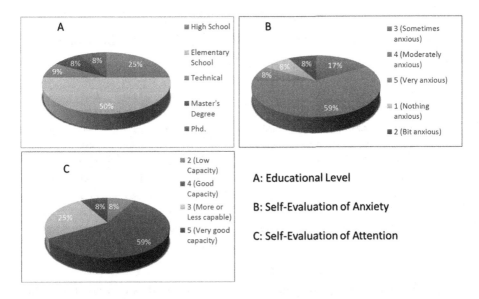

Fig. 4. Characterization of the users

mouse clicks (NMC), and correct answers to the questionnaire (NCA) are presented in Table 3. The t-student test did not show a significant difference when comparing lessons 1 and 2 for such variables. However, when the sex of the users was considered, the women exhibited a greater number of total mouse's movement during the lesson 2 when compared with the men $(F(1;9) = 6.668;$ $p = 0.032)$ as shown in Fig. 5b.

Regarding the results obtained with the UEQ test, significant differences were observed between the lessons $(P < 0.01)$, and we have found that the video lesson was better qualified than the slideshow. Through the benchmark analysis pro-

Table 1. User's score

User	Video Lesson	Slideshow
1	100%	100%
2	80%	100%
3	80%	100%
4	60%	60%
5	100%	60%
6	80%	60%
7	80%	80%
8	40%	60%
9	80%	40%
10	100%	60%
Mean	**80%**	**72%**

Table 2. Accelerometer's data

User	Baseline			Lesson 1: Nerdology			Lesson 2: Bitcoin		
	X	Y	Z	X	Y	Z	X	Y	Z
1	-1,202	-14,022	2,397	-1,197	-14,029	2,384	-1,526	-14,056	3,279
2	2,427	2,676	4,968	1,419	5,239	2,703	-2,384	1,139	9,108
3	-1,262	-2,081	10,386	1,657	-2,230	10,510	-2,085	-2,548	10,191
4	1,341	-4,287	5,799	1,258	-2,716	10,728	-1,294	-2,447	10,641
5	2,750	5,752	-4,884	3,679	5,207	-7,518	3,603	5,487	-7,346
6	-3,124	-1,179	-2,991	-86,092	-3,950	1,286	-9,400	-1,323	1,664
7	-3,043	1,638	9,244	-3,011	1,600	9,254	-2,971	1,767	9,232
8	5,344	3,716	-9,638	1,967	2,166	-9,394	3,503	1,123	-9,169
9	-3,550	1,815	9,731	-3,768	1,456	8,979	-3,734	-1,245	9,094
10	-4,554	-1,758	-3,406	-6,023	-1,812	-7,300	-6,223	-1,675	-7,171

vided by the UEQ, the Nerdologia video lesson was rated as very good regarding attractiveness, clarity, efficiency, confidence, stimulus, and creativity, while the lesson slideshow got a bad rating. Figures 6a and b show the benchmark graphs of the slideshow Bitcoin and the video lesson Nerdologia respectively. Considering the data obtained by the accelerometer, the mouse tracking and the UEQ, a correlation was found between the number of mouse movements as well as the number of clicks with the item Dependability (obstructive /supportive) with ($R = -0.508$, $p = 0.022$ and $R = -0.0498$, $p = 0.026$, respectively) and Perspicuity (easy/complicate) with ($R = -0.512$, $p = 0.021$ and $R = -0.523$, $p = 0.018$),

Table 3. Data obtained by Chrome extension and Questionnaires

USER	Lesson 1: "Nerdologia"				Lesson 2: "Bitcoin"			
	number of tab exchanges	number of mouse movements	number of mouse clicks	number of correct answers to the questionnaire	number of tab exchanges	number of mouse movements	number of mouse clicks	number of correct answers to the questionnaire
	(NTE)	(NMM)	(NMC)	(NCA)	(NTE)	(NMM)	(NMC)	(NCA)
1	0	243	5	5	0	443	3	3
2	1	176	2	4	0	53	2	4
3	0	8	0	2	0	233	3	3
4	0	4	0	4	0	232	1	2
5	0	66	3	4	0	6187	143	5
6	3	2762	111	5	4	2176	49	5
7	0	54	3	5	1	6596	193	3
8	1	2946	17	4	0	159	29	5
9	1	974	33	4	0	78	35	3
10	0	1265	16	3	0	223	7	3
MEAN	0,6	849,8	19	4	0,5	1638	46,5	3,6

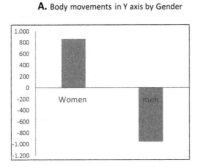

A. Body movements in Y axis by Gender

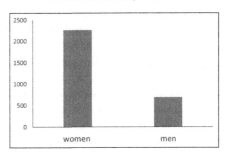

B. Mouse movements by Gender

Fig. 5. Accelerometer and Mouse-tracking data during the slide-show.

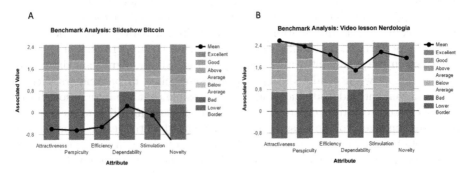

Fig. 6. Qualitative results for video-lesson and slide-show.

both items of the Use quality Dimension. Also, a correlation was found between the number of clicks and the item Dependability (easy/difficult) of the Use Quality Dimension, learning of the UEQ (R = 0.451, p = 0.046). No correlation was found with the accelerometer data.

5   Conclusion

We observed that the mouse tracking have an association with the mouse movement and to aspects related to the engagement during the lesson, being possible to confirm our assumption 1: "The movement of the mouse through the display can be used to measure the loss of engagement during the lessons". Thus, the use of the mouse can be used like an indicator for measure the engagement level and to have a relation such the learning process. No significant differences were observed in the number of changes between the tabs, as proposed in Assumption 2: "The frequency of changing browser tabs can be used to identify the user's engagement loss", which could be caused by some technical problems observed while the experiment was conducted. One hypothesis for this failure was that being the application Chrome browser extension, the tests were subject to errors from the platform as well as the sites that published the lessons. For instance, the platform used for the slideshow refreshed the page after the last slide of the presentation, which resulted in the loss of the data collected by the application. Another observed issue was that Chrome closed the section during the test of one user, also causing the data loss. Future research should be conducted in a more controlled environment to avoid external interference to reduce the examiners' intervention during data send and the sequence of the lesson.

There were no significant differences between the baseline body movements and the data recorded during the lessons using the accelerometer. Also, we did not find a correlation between the body movement and the user's experience not being possible to confirm the assumption 3: "Body movements can be used to measure the user's engagement loss during lessons". During the lessons, the researchers observed that the users make more movements in the upper body, which implies that, the fact that the smartphone located in the user's pocket did not capture this information with the desired accuracy. Thus, new tests should be performed, positioning the smartphone in the upper member as above the waist, in the dominant arm or the back. Interestingly, significant differences were found between gender during the slideshow class in parameters such as mouse movement and body movement. It is possible that the interaction during internet lessons could be different according to the sex (in which women appear to be less engaged to the class lesson) evidencing that the lesson type used or the emotional characteristics, can also be a relevant factor in a future study.

In summary, the mouse-tracking application and the accelerometer instrument could be useful tools to determine the grade of engagement of students during an internet lesson. However, methodological aspects should be improved to obtain more clear, accurate and efficient data. Besides, increasing the number of participants as well as the kind of lessons, are important aspects to consider in this research field.

References

1. Alberts, P.P., Murray, L.A., Griffin, D.K., Stephenson, J.E.: Blended learning: beyond web page design for the delivery of content. In: Workshop on Blended Learning, pp. 61–71 (2007)
2. Coelho, C.M., Lipp, O., Marinovic, W., Wallis, G., Riek, S.: Increased corticospinal excitability induced by unpleasant visual stimuli. Neurosci. Lett. **481**(3), 135–138 (2010)
3. Fernández-Gallego, B., Lama, M., Vidal, J.C., Mucientes, M.: Learning analytics framework for educational virtual worlds. In: 2013 International Conference on Virtual and Augmented Reality in Education, pp. 443–447 (2013)
4. Geyer, P.: Bitcoin (2015). http://pt.slideshare.net/paulogeyer/bitcoin-45347265. Accessed Jun 2016
5. Hibbeln, M.T., Jenkins, J.L., Schneider, C., Valacich, J., Weinmann, M.: Inferring negative emotion from mouse cursor movements. MIS Q. (Forthcoming) (2016). https://ssrn.com/abstract=2708108. Accessed Feb 2017

6. Iamarino, A., Tucano, R., Machado, F., Haeckeliano, B.: A vantagem do polegar opositor—nerdologia 33 (2014). https://www.youtube.com/watch?v=57M7YjkDFbs. Accessed Jun 2016
7. Mehta, P.: Creating Google Chrome Extensions, vol. 1. Apress (2016)
8. Ruipérez, J.A., Muñoz, P.J., Derick, L., Delgado, C.: Alas-ka: a learning analytics extension for better understanding the learning process in the khan academy platform. Comput. Hum. Behav. **47**, 139–148 (2015)
9. Tools, M.: Accelerometer analyzer (2016). https://play.google.com/store/apps/details?id=com.lul.accelerometer. Accessed Jun 2016
10. Yank, K.: Build Your Own Database Driven Website Using PHP & MySQL, vol. 4. SitePoint Pty. Ltd., Victoria (2009)

Distributed Systems and Large-Scale Architectures

Reliable Control Architecture with PLEXIL and ROS for Autonomous Wheeled Robots

Héctor Cadavid[1], Alexander Pérez[1], and Camilo Rocha[2(✉)]

[1] Escuela Colombiana de Ingeniería Julio Garavito,
AK 45 No 205-59, Bogotá, D.C., Colombia
{hector.cadavid,alexander.perez}@escuelaing.edu.co
[2] Pontificia Universidad Javeriana, Calle 18 No 118-250, Santiago de Cali, Colombia
camilo.rocha@javerianacali.edu.co

Abstract. Today's autonomous robots are being used for complex tasks, including space exploration, military applications, and precision agriculture. As the complexity of control architectures increases, reliability of autonomous robots becomes more challenging to guarantee. This paper presents a hybrid control architecture, based on the *Plan Execution Interchange Language* (PLEXIL), for autonomy of wheeled robots running the *Robot Operating System* (ROS). PLEXIL is a synchronous reactive language developed by NASA for mission critical robotic systems, while ROS is one of the most popular frameworks for robotic middleware development. Given the safety-critical nature of spacecraft operations, PLEXIL operational semantics has been mathematically defined, and formal techniques and tools have been developed to automatically analyze plans written in this language. The hybrid control architecture proposed in this paper is showcased in a path tracking scenario using the Husky robot platform via a Gazebo simulation. Thanks to the architecture presented in this paper, all formal analysis techniques and tools currently available to PLEXIL are now available to build reliable plans for ROS-enabled wheeled robots.

Keywords: Robot autonomy · Plan Execution Interchange Language (PLEXIL) · Robot Operating System (ROS) · Control architectures · Formal verification · Rewriting logic · Automatic reachability analysis

1 Introduction

Wheeled robots are popular because of the simplicity and versatility of their components. Nowadays, autonomous wheeled robots are being used for complex tasks, including space exploration, mission-critical military applications, and precision agriculture. The integration of a vast amount of sensors and their interaction with the environment, make these robots highly concurrent. This

Camilo Rocha—The first two authors have been supported in part by grant DII/C008/2016 funded by Escuela Colombiana de Ingeniería.

© Springer International Publishing AG 2017
A. Solano and H. Ordoñez (Eds.): CCC 2017, CCIS 735, pp. 611–626, 2017.
DOI: 10.1007/978-3-319-66562-7_44

scenario poses a significant challenge for guaranteeing correct behavior such as safe navigation, precise goal tracking, and fault tolerance [2]. Moreover, because of the high value of some of the components and the costs associated to malfunction (e.g., money investment, human lives, or crop production), autonomous robots are expected to be highly reliable [13].

The robotics community has developed near-real simulation environments to test control architectures in operation conditions that can help in designtesting a robot development before its deployment. Nevertheless, due to the intrinsic limitations of simulation-based testing, these environments are far from answering the important question of, up to a high degree of confidence, how reliable control architectures really are. The inherent non-deterministic nature of robot autonomy, and the divide between the mathematical properties and the operational semantics of the language used to program the robot, can make this situation more dramatic. For example, an extensive test-guided validation in the design phase of a robot development could suggest absence of deadlocks in a control architecture. However, deadlocks may be present in the resulting implementation because of semantic issues with synchronization structures in the programming language.

Today's formal methods are scaling up to meet the challenges in the development of mission-critical software and hardware. The notion of software/hardware verification via automatic reachability analysis or model checking has evolved to become an accepted technology in development processes. Moreover, new symbolic techniques based, e.g., on the satisfiability modulo theories (SMT) approach are being readied for industrial use as a solution to the state-explosion problem, commonly faced in the algorithmic verification of concurrent systems. Nowadays, formal methods are being used in the development, e.g., of unmanned aircraft systems [15] and have had big impact in the design of policies for unmanned aircraft systems [25]. A key benefit of the formal methods approach is that it provides techniques, tools, and insights highly valuable in a mission-critical development.

This paper presents a hybrid control architecture, based on the *Plan Execution Interchange Language* [6] (PLEXIL), for autonomy of wheeled robots running the *Robot Operating System* [8] (ROS). PLEXIL is a synchronous reactive language created by NASA for mission-critical robotic systems. ROS is one of the most popular frameworks for robotics middle-ware development. The proposed hybrid architecture is given in a deliberative/reactive/driver layered setting. PLEXIL is used in the reactive layer to implement behavior in a mission plan with a hierarchical composition of nodes, where the ones at the top represent high-level behavior and the ones at the bottom basic actions (e.g., primitive robot commands and variable assignment). On the other hand, ROS (and its drivers) is used to represent components specific to wheeled robots as a hardware abstraction at the level of the robot's sensors. The deliberative layer, where mission plans are generated according to some given goals, is not directly addressed in this paper. The technical contribution of this paper can now be better explained. The integration between PLEXIL and ROS is a bi-directional software adapter between the reactive and driver layers. This adapter enables: (i) the execution of PLEXIL low-level commands in a wheeled robot running ROS, and (ii) the interaction of PLEXIL with the external environment via events triggered by sensors under the control of ROS in the driver layer. This approach is showcased in a path tracking scenario using the Husky robot platform via a Gazebo simulation.

The integration of PLEXIL and ROS presented in this paper has the additional benefit of making available to ROS-enabled robots all the formal analysis and verification tools already developed for PLEXIL. These tools include a rewriting logic semantics in Maude [5], an interactive environment for automatic reachability analysis and LTL model checking [22], and automatic symbolic reachability analysis based on rewriting modulo SMT [23]. This integration opens the door of formal verification to a wide class of ROS modules, thus making autonomous planning more reliable. Furthermore, new plans can now be developed following a more rigorous formal methods-oriented approach.

The rest of the paper is organized as follows. Section 2 reviews some related work. Sections 3 and 4 present, respectively, a high-level description of PLEXIL and ROS. Section 5 proposes the layered architecture based on the PLEXIL-ROS integration and Sect. 6 exhibits a proof of concept. Section 7 concludes the paper.

2   Related Work

There is a vast amount of research in the field of control architecture for autonomous robots. Control architectures can be classified in several categories: by the type of interaction between control modules (e.g., hierarchical or centralized architectures), by the type of functionality assigned to each module (e.g., general or specific purpose), and by the way modules interact with the external environment (e.g., event-based or procedural behavior). The latter category, which is closest to the proposal in this paper, can be further classified as deliberative, reactive, or hybrid. In a *deliberative* control architecture, a plan is generated based on a goal and a static model of the environment targeted after successful operation. In a *reactive* control architecture, control commands are generated during operation based on interaction with the environment. In a *hybrid* control architecture, a deliberative agent statically generates plans that will be executed by reacting to the external environment during operation. Fairly complete surveys of works in each category and subcategory are [13,17,27].

There are significant efforts to have reliable and modular hybrid control architectures for autonomy in robotic systems. On the one hand, the main focus is on using languages with mathematically proven properties, e.g., PLEXIL as the intermediate layer for plan representation and execution. On the other hand, the main focus is on defining control structures on top of ROS-enabled systems. Muñoz et al. [16] propose a control architecture for the Ptinto robot, a hexapod robot for exploration in difficult terrains. They use PLEXIL as the intermediate plan specification language and reactive layer for SGPlan (a deliberative planner that automatically partitions large planing problems into subproblems with specific goals). However, in their work, the hardware abstraction layer is proprietary and therefore the architecture is tied to the specific target robot. Jenson et al. [10], propose a control architecture for AMIGO and other ROS-enabled robots to perform tasks in human environments. Their system uses a *hierarchical ordered planner*, a special type of deliberative system in which a predefined set of actions is hierarchically arranged once a goal is set for the autonomous robot. Benjamin et al. [1] propose ROSoClingo, a control architecture with a reactive layer for ROS-enabled robots. Their approach uses *answer set programming* (ASP), a declarative programming paradigm intended to solve NP-hard combinatorial search problems. The proposed architecture encodes adaptive behaviors directly in a declarative knowledge formalism, which requires the addition of reactive capabilities not necessarily available from the target robot.

It is fair to say that the main difference between the above-mentioned works and the proposal in this paper, is that the latter aims at combining the best elements of both worlds: a robust, mathematically verifiable high-level language such as PLEXIL for the reactive layer, and ROS, the actual de-facto standard for robotic middle-ware. This unique combination brings an important advantage to future projects in robotics. Namely, the possibility of having verified – and eventually certified – control architecture software for autonomous robots that use conventional and affordable hardware.

3 The Plan Execution Interchange Language

The Plan Execution Interchange Language [6] (PLEXIL) is a synchronous reactive language developed by NASA to support autonomous spacecraft operations. It has been used on applications such as robotic rovers, a prototype of a Mars drill, and to demonstrate automation capabilities for potential future use on the International Space Station. Programs in PLEXIL, called plans, specify actions to be executed by an autonomous system as part of normal spacecraft operations or as reactions to changes in the environment. The computer system on board the spacecraft that executes plans is called the Universal Executive [26].

3.1 PLEXIL in a Nutshell

A PLEXIL plan consists of a set of nodes representing a hierarchical decomposition of tasks. A leaf node in the tree represents a primitive task such as variable assignment or a command execution, whereas an intermediate node defines the control structure of its descendants such as sequential or concurrent execution. Each node is equipped with a set of conditions that trigger its execution, e.g., a start condition and an end condition. At any time, each node offers information about its execution state: *inactive, waiting, executing, iterationended, failing, finishing*, or *finished*. There is also information about the termination status of a task: *success, skipped*, or *failure*.

When events are reported by interaction with the external environment (e.g., by sensors or timers), the nodes triggered by such events are executed concurrently, updating e.g., local variables, until quiescence. The internal execution of each node, in turn, can trigger the execution of other nodes. Although more than one event can become enabled simultaneously, all parallel operations in PLEXIL are synchronized and will not arbitrarily interleave. This is because PLEXIL semantics is designed under the synchronous hypothesis [18]. One important feature of PLEXIL semantics is that it guarantees determinism (in the absence of external events), which is a convenient property for autonomous programming because it helps in having a clean mathematical semantics.

As an example, consider the simple PLEXIL plan in Fig. 1. It consists of a tree with three nodes: the root node `SamplePlan`, and the leaf nodes `ActionOne` and `ActionTwo`. In this plan, there are two integer variables, namely, x and y, which are accessible from any node in the plan. The run-to-completion semantics of the leaf nodes depends on the value of the variable `sensorOne`, which is under control of the external environment. For instance, if the value of `sensorOne` becomes 201, then both leaf nodes will execute in parallel. In an asynchronous setting, such an execution would result in an unpredictable outcome because of the race condition in the assignment of x and y. However, thanks to its synchronous semantics, PLEXIL guarantees a consistent variable swap in this case so that x is assigned the value 20 and y is assigned the value 10, without any race condition.

```
SamplePlan:{
  Concurrence{
    Integer x=10,y=20;
    ActionOne{
      start Lookup (sensorOne>100)
      x=y;
    }
    ActionTwo{
      start Lookup(sensorOne>200)
      y=x;
    }
  }
}
```

Fig. 1. A very simple PLEXIL plan.

3.2   Rewriting Logic-Based Automatic Analysis

PLEXIL has been designed with verification and validation in mind, and has motivated the development of an important amount of research and tools in the rewriting logic community. Rewriting logic [14] is a semantic framework that unifies a wide range of models of concurrency. Specifications in rewriting logic are called rewrite theories and can be executed in the rewriting logic implementation Maude [4]. By being executable, they benefit from a set of formal analysis tools available to Maude, such as state-space exploration and automata-based LTL model checking. A *rewrite theory* is a tuple $\mathcal{R} = (\Sigma, E \uplus B, R)$ with: (i) $(\Sigma, E \uplus B)$ an order-sorted equational theory with signature Σ, E a set of equations over the set T_Σ of Σ-terms, and B a set of structural axioms – disjoint from the set of equations E – over T_Σ for which there exists a finitary matching algorithm (e.g., associativity, commutativity, and identity, or combinations of them); and (ii) R a finite set of rewrite rules over T_Σ. Intuitively, $\mathcal{R}$ specifies a concurrent system whose states are elements of the set $T_{\Sigma/E \uplus B}$ of Σ-terms modulo $E \uplus B$ and whose concurrent transitions are axiomatized by the rewrite rules R. In particular, for $t, t' \in T_\Sigma$ representing states of the concurrent system described by $\mathcal{R}$, a transition from t to t' is captured by a formula of the form $[t]_{E \uplus B} \rightarrow_\mathcal{R} [t']_{E \uplus B}$; the symbol $\rightarrow_\mathcal{R}$ denotes the binary rewrite relation induced by R over $T_{\Sigma/E \uplus B}$.

The *ground* rewriting logic semantics of PLEXIL [5] is a rewrite theory $\mathcal{R}_{\text{PLEXIL}}$ with *topsort* $\mathfrak{s}$, meaning that concurrent transitions in the system are mathematically captured by $\rightarrow_{\mathcal{R}_{\text{PLEXIL}}}$ and are over the set $T_{\Sigma,\mathfrak{s}}$ of Σ-terms of sort $\mathfrak{s}$. The *symbolic* rewriting logic semantics of PLEXIL [21,23], based on the rewriting modulo SMT technique, is a rewrite theory $\mathcal{S}_{\text{PLEXIL}}$ with topsort $\mathfrak{s} \times \Gamma$, meaning that symbolic concurrent transitions in the system are mathematically captured by $\rightarrow_{\mathcal{S}_{\text{PLEXIL}}}$ and are over state pairs of the form $(t \,;\varphi)$ with $t \in T_\Sigma(X)_\mathfrak{s}$ and $\varphi(X)$ a quantifier-free first-order logic formula under the control of the SMT solver. Intuitively, a symbolic state $(t \,;\varphi)$ in $\mathcal{S}_{\text{PLEXIL}}$ can represent infinitely many concrete states, namely, those states $t\sigma$ for each ground substitution σ satisfying φ. The constraint φ in a symbolic state is used to model the behavior of variables under control of the external environment. Techniques and tools for reachability analysis and LTL model checking with $\rightarrow_{\mathcal{R}_{\text{PLEXIL}}}$ and $\rightarrow_{\mathcal{S}_{\text{PLEXIL}}}$ have been developed. They have been used for detecting the violation of safety properties such as invariants, race conditions, and deadlock freedom. For details, the reader is referred to [22,24].

4   The Robot Operating System

The creation and development of robots involves the interaction and collaboration of several areas of knowledge such as mechanics, electronics, and computer science. For example, once a robotic device has been mechanically designed and its electronic components able to read data from the environment, software artifacts may be developed to pursue autonomy. In general, a large-span robotics project can require a vast amount of collaborative effort – both in time and money. Thus, it would be highly convenient to reuse as many artifacts as possible across similar projects.

An open source initiative promoted by Willow Garage has emerged and, as a result, the Open Source Robotic Foundation (OSRF) has been established recently. The *Robot Operating System* (ROS) has been created by the OSRF with the goal of increasing the reusability of the software components specifically developed for robots. The adoption of ROS can also dramatically decrease the time and money needed to deploy robot applications. During the past few years, ROS has gradually become the de-facto standard in robot development. For example, the paper [19] introducing ROS has been cited 3350+ times since 2009. ROS has not only gained a distinguished position in the research community, but it has also become an important player in the robot manufacturing industry: the ROS Industrial Consortium has the support of 42 of the most prestigious robot manufacturers in the world.

The Robot Operating System is defined in [8] as follows:

> ROS is a meta-operating system for your robot. It provides the services you would expect from an operating system, including hardware abstraction, low-level device control, implementation of commonly-used functionality, message-passing between processes, and package management. It also provides tools and libraries for obtaining, building, writing, and running code across multiple computers.

ROS has been designed to be modular at a fine-grained scale, where the basic unit is a *node* representing a process. For example, one node can control a laser range-finder, or the wheel motors, or perform localization. A robot application in ROS can be specified as a computation graph representing the peer-to-peer network resulting from node interaction: an edge in this graph denotes message-passing communication between two processes. Figure 2 depicts a graph corresponding to a ROS program.

Tools are provided by ROS to analyze and visualize data, simulate robots and environments, and to store large amounts of data generated by sensors and processes. For instance, RViz [9] and Gazebo [7] are useful tools to visualize and analyze the data captured by sensors and kinematics. RViz has been designed to visually interact with almost all processes running in a ROS graph. Gazebo, on the other hand, is an open source 3D dynamic simulator [11], which will be included by the OSFR in modern distributions of ROS.

Figure 3 depicts the interaction between the Gazebo simulation environment and a Husky robot deployed in an environment with obstacles. On the left, a computer simulation of the environment can be seen. On the right, a RViz application is shown with the information retrieved by several sensors. For example, data captured from the camera and laser mounted on the Husky has been interpreted and drawn by RViz.

One key effort in ROS has been the standardization of message-passing and the abstraction of the format they use. Messages are important in ROS because they are at the heart of interaction infrastructure. Each message in ROS is a data structure comprising different types of fields such as integers, floating point values, Booleans, and arrays of primitive types. For example, the Twist message format is part of the geometry package in ROS, and is used to communicate linear and angular velocities of a body:

```
Vector3  linear
Vector3  angular
```

The message standardization in ROS makes it possible to create a *clean* hardware abstraction layer (HAL) between hardware and software. In particular,

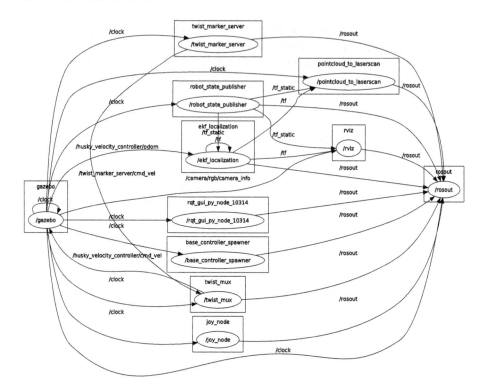

Fig. 2. An example of a ROS program. It is a graph where a node is a process providing or obtaining data from other processes. Related processes are linked by edges and denote interaction based on message passing.

it makes it possible to define a common communication channel between software components that control the behavior of the robot and the hardware components actually enforcing such a behavior. In this sense, ROS reduces the effort of tailoring software components to each particular kind of robot. For example, in ROS, any robot can be commanded to move by using the Twist message by indicating the linear and angular velocities. ROS assumes that each robot will execute this command accordingly to its own "anatomy". In the case of wheeled robots, only linear velocity has an important meaning since the angular velocity in the axis of movement is perpendicular to the floor. In the case of aerial vehicles, they can be commanded to change position by using three linear and three angular velocities, without any kinematic restriction.

5   Layered Architecture for the Integration

This section presents the main contribution of this paper. The key idea is to use PLEXIL as reactive layer and thus, by taking advantage of all automatic formal analysis techniques and tools available to it, enable the development of autonomous control modules for ROS with high degrees of reliability.

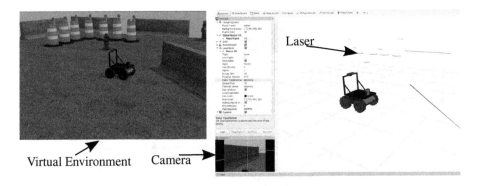

Fig. 3. Example of interaction between the Gazebo simulation environment and a Husky robot deployed in an environment with obstacles.

The proposed architecture is depicted in Fig. 4. It is based on the hybrid deliberative/reactive paradigm (see Sect. 2) and has the following elements:

The top layer (or deliberative layer): a software component that uses a global "environment model" (e.g., it contains terrain features and obstacles) and on a set of goals or problem description. It ultimately generates a mission plan composed of subtasks required to accomplish the goals in the given world model.

The deliberative/reactive binding layer: a software component responsible for providing compatibility between the format of the mission plan generated by the planner in the deliberative layer and the language used to describe the hierarchy of action nodes in the reactive layer.

The reactive layer: a hierarchical composition of nodes in which nodes at the top represent high-level behavior in the mission plan and the ones at the bottom represent basic actions in the plan (e.g., primitive robot commands and variable assignment).

The driver layer: a software component using ROS and the ROS drivers required for the specific robot components. This layer represents the hardware abstraction for the robot at the level of sensor actions and their access.

In particular, the control architecture resides in the reactive layer. On the one hand, this layer handles information from the environment such as changes on Yaw or position coordinates, which are updated based on data received via the driver layer from ROS drivers. On the other hand, the hierarchical composition of nodes in this layer has, at the top level, goal-oriented nodes such as driving straight for a distance or following a sequence of points. Such nodes will decompose in lower-level action nodes that, for instance, can perform tracking strategies such as follow-the-carrot or pure-pursuit [12] by calculating the required speed and steering settings.

As a proof of concept, a general purpose PLEXIL-ROS adapter has been developed by the authors, following the ideas proposed as future work in [3]. Conceptually, this adapter transforms ROS events triggered by the environment into

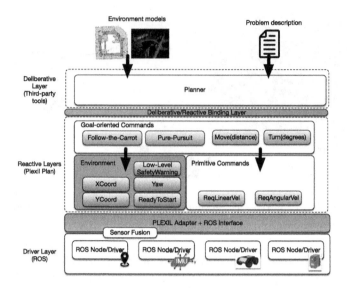

Fig. 4. Proposed ROS and PLEXIL layered architecture.

variables that PLEXIL plans can handle, and PLEXIL commands into requests to ROS driver nodes. Figure 5 depicts how the PLEXIL-ROS adapter integrates PLEXIL plans and ROS nodes, transforming the data that flows from the layers when necessary:

1. The PLEXIL Universal Executive executes the plan defined for the reactive layer of the architecture using a PLEXIL adapter.
2. The adapter defines the low-level operations and environment variables for such a plan.
3. The adapter uses an interface that is subscribed to relevant events in ROS.
4. The adapter transforms the generated events by updating environment variables and handles command invocation by publishing ROS events.
5. The message-oriented middle-ware of ROS (ROSCORE) enables the indirect communication with a real or simulated robot.

As a technical detail, it is important to note that in order to ensure that the PLEXIL plan in the reactive layer is able to check that the environment information has been initialized – preventing the initialization of the plan with inconsistent data –, a special variable called 'Ready' is assigned true when ROS reports the status of the robot for the first time. The current implementation of the adapter, for testing purposes, is based on the Husky platform [20].

6   Proof of Concept

This section presents a proof of concept of the implementation of the PLEXIL-ROS adapter proposed in Sect. 5. The Husky robot platform – via a Gazebo

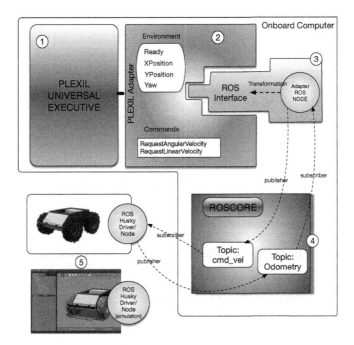

Fig. 5. Proposed PLEXIL-ROS integration architecture.

simulation – and a basic path tracking scenario were chosen for the experiment. The goal of the experiment is to demonstrate how a PLEXIL plan in the reactive layer can command a ROS-enabled robot whose drivers are in the hardware-abstraction layer. Note that for the purpose of this paper, the plan has been developed manually and without the help of a deliberative layer software.

The experiment is the following: make a Husky follow a fixed-size square-shaped path specified by a PLEXIL plan. Figure 6 depicts the logical description of the plan as a tree of tasks and Listing 1.1 presents the code of the plan. Intuitively, the PLEXIL plan consists of:

- Two high-level nodes: move forward for a given distance and turn a given amount of degrees.
- The plan performs four consecutive iterations of the sequence: move N meters, stop, and turn 90 degrees.
- The Move node is defined as a sequence of two nodes: OdometryUpdate and MoveUntilDistanceReached. The first one performs a lookup of the current position and the second one performs a LinearVelocityRequest until the repeat condition is not met (i.e., until the distance from the starting point to the current position is less than the expected distance).
- Angular velocity is continuously requested by Stop.
- Node Turn re-calculates the angular displacement every time a new Yaw is reported. Once the angular displacement is approximately close to the

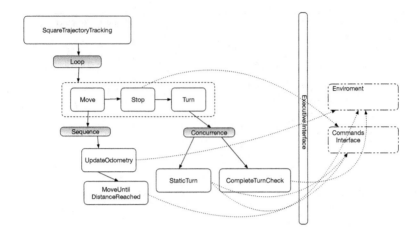

Fig. 6. PLEXIL plan tree for the proof of concept.

expected one, `CompleteTurnCheck` makes `StaticTurn` reach the final (i.e., FINISHED) state in the plan.

Listing 1.1. PLEXIL plan for the proof of concept.

```
Command RequestLinearVelocity(Real);
Command RequestAngularVelocity(Real);
Command pprint(...);
SquareTrajectoryTracking:{
  Boolean completeTurn=false, goal=false;
  Real PI=3.1416, initialYaw=0, WIDTH=5;
  Start Lookup(Ready);
  initialYaw=Lookup(Yaw);
  //four times: move forward, turn 90deg
  for (Integer i = 1; i <= 4; i + 1) {
    //Move until distance from starting position (aprox)== WIDTH
    Move:{
      Real currXPos,currYPos;
      Sequence{
        UpdateOdom:{
          currXPos=Lookup(XPosition);
          currYPos=Lookup(YPosition);
        }
        MoveUntilDistanceReached:{
          Start
            sqrt((currXPos−Lookup(XPosition))*(currXPos−Lookup(XPosition))+
              (currYPos−Lookup(YPosition))*(currYPos−Lookup(YPosition))) <
                WIDTH;
          Repeat
            sqrt((currXPos−Lookup(XPosition))*(currXPos−Lookup(XPosition))+
              (currYPos−Lookup(YPosition))*(currYPos−Lookup(YPosition))) <
                WIDTH;
            RequestLinearVelocity(1);
```

```
            }
          }
        }
        Stop:{
            RequestAngularVelocity(0);
        }
        //turn until a PI/2 rotation is achieved
        Turn:{
            initialYaw=Lookup(Yaw);
            completeTurn=false;
            Concurrence{
                StaticTurn:{
                    Repeat completeTurn==false;
                    RequestAngularVelocity(0.1);
                }
                CompleteTurnCheck:{
                    Start   (abs(initialYaw−Lookup(Yaw)) <= PI &&
                            abs(initialYaw−Lookup(Yaw))>=PI/2) ||
                            (abs(initialYaw−Lookup(Yaw)) > PI &&
                            (2*PI−abs(initialYaw−Lookup(Yaw))))>=PI/2);
                    completeTurn=true;
                }
            }
        }
    }
```

Finally, Fig. 7 shows a superposition of screenshots of the simulation executed in Gazebo.

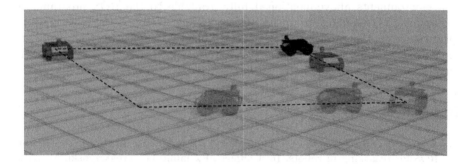

Fig. 7. Gazebo simulation.

7   Concluding Remarks

Designing and developing control software for an autonomous robot is a challenging and complex task, specially considering that – with cyber-physical systems – the costs of failure or unexpected behaviors can be dramatic. Unfortunately, formal verification methods, a powerful set of techniques and tools aimed at ensuring software correctness and reliability are not easily accessible to most robot developers. Although ROS has simplified the development of robotic solutions with its low level control layer commanding a robot to perform desired movements, moving the actuators (e.g., servo-motors), and process data provided by sensors, the problem of identifying control flaws is far from solved. Common flaws include deadlocks, violation of conformance to temporal, spatial, or timed constraints, which are key to mission-critical applications.

This paper has presented a software architecture and implementation for integrating PLEXIL and ROS. The main idea is to use PLEXIL, a synchronous reactive language created by NASA for mission critical robotic systems, in the reactive layer in a hybrid architecture to command ROS-enabled robots. PLEXIL has been proved to be mathematically reliable and robust by the scientific community. Given the fact that during the past 10 years ROS has become a de-facto standard in robotics, both in research and in industry, the PLEXIL-ROS integration can have positive impact in the development of mission-critical plans for autonomy in rovers. For example, it offers automatic verification techniques and tools already available for PLEXIL to ROS programmers. The proposed architecture has been validated and illustrated with an example consisting of an autonomous plan written in PLEXIL for a wheeled ROS-enabled robot.

Future work will integrate PLEXIL-compatible modules in the deliberative layer, which will be tested with specific tasks. They can include strategic areas in Colombia where reliable automation is needed. These include, for instance, precision agriculture. On the other hand, it will be ideal to deploy an official PLEXIL-ROS package to make the integration of components and the validation environments above-mentioned fully available to the ROS programming community. The feedback from the ROS community will be a valuable input for future stages of this project. Finally, specific-purpose verification techniques and tools need to be developed for the PLEXIL-ROS integration depending on the area of use.

References

1. Andres, B., Rajaratnam, D., Sabuncu, O., Schaub, T.: Integrating ASP into ROS for reasoning in robots. In: Calimeri, F., Ianni, G., Truszczynski, M. (eds.) LPNMR 2015. LNCS, vol. 9345, pp. 69–82. Springer, Cham (2015). doi:10.1007/978-3-319-23264-5_7
2. Broenink, J., Brodskiy, Y., Dresscher, D., Stramigioli, S.: Robustness inembedded software for autonomous robots. Mikroniek **54**, 38–45 (2014)
3. Cadavid, H.F., Chaparro, J.A.: Hardware and software architecture for plexil-based, simulation supported, robot automation. In: IEEE Colombian Conference on Robotics and Automation (CCRA), pp. 1–6. IEEE (2016)
4. Clavel, M., Durán, F., Eker, S., Lincoln, P., Martí-Oliet, N., Meseguer, J., Talcott, C.: All About Maude - A High-Performance Logical Framework: How to Specify, Program and Verify Systems in Rewriting Logic. LNCS, vol. 4350. Springer, Heidelberg (2007)

5. Dowek, G., Muñoz, C., Rocha, C.: Rewriting logic semantics of a plan execution language. Electron. Proc. Theoret. Comput. Sci. **18**, 77–91 (2010)
6. Estlin, T., Jonsson, A., Pasareanu, C., Simmons, R., Tso, K., Verma, V.: Plan Execution Interchange Language (PLEXIL). Technical report TM-2006-213483, NASA, April 2006
7. O. S. R. Foundation. GAZEBO: A 3D dynamic simulator. http://gazebosim.org. Accessed 19 May 2017
8. O. S. R. Foundation. ROS: Robot operating system. http://wiki.ros.org. Accessed 19 May 2017
9. O. S. R. Foundation. RViz: 3D visualization tool for ROS. http://wiki.ros.org/rviz. Accessed 19 May 2017
10. Janssen, R., van Meijl, E., Di Marco, D., van de Molengraft, R., Steinbuch, M.: Integrating planning and execution for ros enabled service robots using hierarchical action representations. In: 2013 16th International Conference on Advanced Robotics (ICAR), pp. 1–7. IEEE (2013)
11. Koenig, N., Howard, A.: Design and use paradigms for gazebo, an open-source multi-robot simulator. In: IEEE/RSJ International Conference on Intelligent Robots and Systems, Sendai, Japan, pp. 2149–2154, September 2004
12. Lundgren, M.: Path tracking for a miniature robot. Department of Computer Science, University of Umea, Masters (2003)
13. Medeiros, A.A.: A survey of control architectures for autonomous mobile robots. J. Braz. Comput. Soc. **4**(3) (1998)
14. Meseguer, J.: Conditional rewriting logic as a unified model of concurrency. Theoret. Comput. Sci. **96**(1), 73–155 (1992)
15. Muñoz, C.A., Dutle, A., Narkawicz, A., Upchurch, J.: Unmanned aircraft systems in the national airspace system: a formal methods perspective. SIGLOG News **3**(3), 67–76 (2016)
16. Muñoz, P., R-Moreno, M.D., Castaño, B.: Integrating a PDDL-based planner and a PLEXIL-executor into the ptinto robot. In: García-Pedrajas, N., Herrera, F., Fyfe, C., Benítez, J.M., Ali, M. (eds.) IEA/AIE 2010. LNCS, vol. 6096, pp. 72–81. Springer, Heidelberg (2010). doi:10.1007/978-3-642-13022-9_8
17. Nakhaeinia, D., Tang, S.H., Noor, S.M., Motlagh, O.: A review of control architectures for autonomous navigation of mobile robots. Int. J. Phys. Sci. **6**(2), 169–174 (2011)
18. Potop-Butucaru, D., de Simone, R., Talpin, J.-P.: The synchronous hypothesis and synchronous languages. In: The Embedded Systems Handbook, pp. 1–21 (2005)
19. Quigley, M., Conley, K., Gerkey, B., Faust, J., Foote, T., Leibs, J., Wheeler, R., Ng, A.Y.: Ros: an open-source robot operating system. In: ICRA Workshop on Open Source Software, vol. 3, p. 5 (2009)
20. Robotics, C.: Husky-unmanned ground vehicle. Technical Specifications, Clearpath Robotics, Kitcener, Ontario, Canada (2013)
21. Rocha, C.: Symbolic Reachability Analysis for Rewrite Theories. Ph.D. thesis, University of Illinois, December 2012
22. Rocha, C., Cadavid, H., Muñoz, C., Siminiceanu, R.: A formal interactive verification environment for the plan execution interchange language. In: Derrick, J., Gnesi, S., Latella, D., Treharne, H. (eds.) IFM 2012. LNCS, vol. 7321, pp. 343–357. Springer, Heidelberg (2012). doi:10.1007/978-3-642-30729-4_24
23. Rocha, C., Meseguer, J., Muñoz, C.: Rewriting modulo SMT and open system analysis. J. Logic. Algebr. Methods Program. **86**(1), 269–297 (2017)

24. Rocha, C., Muñoz, C., Cadavid, H.: A graphical environment for the semantic validation of a plan execution language. In: Third IEEE International Conference on Space Mission Challenges for Information Technology (SMC-IT 2009), pp. 201–207. IEEE, July 2009
25. Rozier, K.Y.: Specification: the biggest bottleneck in formal methods and autonomy. In: Blazy, S., Chechik, M. (eds.) VSTTE 2016. LNCS, vol. 9971, pp. 8–26. Springer, Cham (2016). doi:10.1007/978-3-319-48869-1_2
26. Verma, V., Jonsson, A., Pasareanu, C., Iatauro, M.: Universal-executive and PLEXIL: engine and language for robust spacecraft control and operations. In: American Institute of Aeronautics and Astronautics SPACE Forum (Space 2006). American Institute of Aeronautics and Astronautics, September 2006
27. Zheltoukhov, A.A., Stankevich, L.A.: A survey of control architectures for autonomous mobile robots. In: 2017 IEEE Conference of Russian Young Researchers in Electrical and Electronic Engineering (EIConRus), pp. 1094–1099. IEEE (2017)

Parallel Programming in Biological Sciences, Taking Advantage of Supercomputing in Genomics

Simon Orozco-Arias[1]([✉]), Reinel Tabares-Soto[1,3], Diego Ceballos[1], and Romain Guyot[2]

[1] Centro de Bioinformática y Biología Computacional BIOS,
Manizales, Colombia
simon.orozco.arias@gmail.com
[2] IRD, CIRAD, University Montpellier, IPME,
BP 64501, 34394 Montpellier Cedex 5, France
[3] Universidad Autónoma de Manizales, Manizales, Colombia

Abstract. New sequencing technologies has been increasing the size of current genomes rapidly reducing its cost at the same time, those data need to be processed with efficient and innovated tools using high performance computing (HPC), but for taking advantage of nowadays supercomputers, parallel programming techniques and strategies have to be used. Plant genomes are full of Long Terminal Repeat Retrotransposons (LTR-RT), which are the most frequent repeated sequences; very important agronomical commodity such as Robusta Coffee and Maize have genomes that are composed by $\sim 50\%$ and $\sim 85\%$ respectively of this class of mobile elements, new parallel bioinformatics pipelines are making possible to use whole genomes like those in research projects, generating a lot of new information and impacting in many ways the knowledge that researchers have about them. Here we presented the utility of multi-core architectures and parallel programming for analyzing and classifying massive quantity of genomic information up to 16 times faster.

Keywords: HPC · Bioinformatics · Transposable elements · Parallel programming · MPI

1 Introduction

Thanks to advances in sequencing technologies, biological researchers have generated fast and huge genomic information. At the end of 2009, 1,052 genomes representing 720 individual species (636 bacteria, 61 archaea, and 23 eukaryotes) were completely sequenced, deposited in the public nucleotide sequence databases (GenBank\EMBL\ DDBJ) and made freely available over the internet [1]. In June 2015, NCBI Genome collection contained more than 35,000 genome sequence assemblies from almost 13,000 different organisms (species) [2]. These advances have improved research in many topics such as autism disorders [3], sarcomeric cardiomyopathies [4], cancer research using single-cell sequencing technologies [5], among others, reducing its costs and time duration.

© Springer International Publishing AG 2017
A. Solano and H. Ordoñez (Eds.): CCC 2017, CCIS 735, pp. 627–643, 2017.
DOI: 10.1007/978-3-319-66562-7_45

Bioinformatics tools have impacted many investigations because of its ability to analyze data in biological field through computational and statistical approaches [6], improving the reliability of the results, reducing times and costs and discovering new information. Nevertheless, traditional techniques are inadequate when researchers try to analyze massive genomes like pine tree (*Pinus taeda*) with 22 billons of base pairs approximately 7 times the human genome) [7] or Maize (*Zea mays*) [8] with 2.3 Gb. To resolve the analysis of massive data, one is to take advantage of current super-computers and its architectures like many-cores, multi-cores or a mixed of them, known as heterogeneous platforms [9], through parallel programming [10]. In this way is possible to speed up the execution, reducing runtimes and making possible to use massive data produced in research such as in current genomics.

Coffea canephora and *Zea mays* have a large and complex genome, composed respectively of ∼50% and ∼85% of transposable elements (TE), which are the most common repeated sequences in plant genomes [11]. TEs are divided in two classes (Class I and II), according to their replication mode. Class I known as retrotransposons, which use a RNA intermediate, via a mechanism called "copy and paste" and Class II, also named transposons, using DNA intermediate via a mechanism called "cut and paste" [12]. Class I and especially Long Terminal Repeat retrotransposons (LTR-RT) are the most common TEs in plant genomes [12]. LTR-RT are classified as autonomous (see Table 2) or non-autonomous elements based on the presence or the absence, respectively, of both the POL and GAG coding domains (see Table 1) that are required for transposition [13]. LTR-RT can be further sub-classified into two superfamilies;

Table 1. LTR-RT domains

Domain complete name	Domain short name	Function
Reverse Transciptase	RT	Responsible for DNA synthesis using RNA as a template
RNase H	RNAseH	Responsible for the degradation of the RNA template in the DNA-RNA hybrid
Intregrase	INT	Responsible for catalysis insertion of the retrotransposon cDNA into de genome of a host cell
Aspartic protease	AP	Responsible for processing the large transposon transcripts into smaller protein products
Envelope	ENV	Responsible for transferring retroviruses cell-to-cell
Group Specific Antigen	GAG	Structural protein for virus-like particles

Table 2. Autonomous LTR-RT classification

Super Family	Lineages for plant genomes
Copia	Bianca, Oryco, Retrofit, Sire, Tork
Gypsy	Athila, CRM, Del, Galadriel, Reina, TAT

Gypsy and Copia [14] for autonomous and into TRIM [15], LARD [16], BARE-2 [17] or TR-GAG [11] for non-autonomous elements.

2 Problem Statement

In 1995 the first whole-sequenced genome of a cellular-life form was presented by Fleischmann et al. [18], with a size of 1.8 Mb. Due to dramatically advances in sequencing technologies, current sequenced genomes have bigger sizes such as Robusta Coffee (*Coffea canephora*, 568.6 Mb) [19], Maize (*Zea mays*, 2.3 Gb) [8] and Rice (*Oryza sativa*, 389 Mb) [20]. Because of the increasing genome size of current sequencing projects, traditional computational techniques are creating delays in sequence analyses. In contrast, new parallel algorithms are able to use different numbers of processor for doing analysis depending of the size of the input data, improving runtimes, decreasing delays and doing the possibility to use whole information in each experiment in supercomputers, which is very important for researchers.

Thanks to new supercomputing approaches, it is possible to develop scalable algorithms running on multiple processors and taking advantage of multi-core architectures like Message Passing Interface (MPI) [21]. The principal problem is divided into sub-problems and each one is executed at the same time in different cores, which is very useful in biological fields, especially when researchers have to analyze a huge amount of sequences in short time or many times.

In this article, we demonstrated the advantage of using high performance computing (HPC), particularly parallel programming on multi-core technologies using a parallel pipeline developed by the authors for analyzing LTR-RTs in plant genomes with various sizes, showing the relationship between performance and number of cores used in each case.

3 Materials and Methods

3.1 Genomic Data

Four plant genomes were used in this research. *Arabidopsis thaliana*, rice (*Oryza sativa*) and maize (*Zea mays*) were downloaded from Ensembl genomes project [22], Robusta coffee (*Coffea canephora*) was downloaded from Coffee Genome Hub Project [23] (see Table 3).

Table 3. Genomic data used in the research.

Genome	Size (Mb)	URL
Arabidopsis thaliana	117	http://plants.ensembl.org/Arabidopsis_thaliana/Info/Index
Oryza sativa	412	http://plants.ensembl.org/Oryza_sativa/Info/Index
Coffea canephora	553	http://coffee-genome.org/
Zea mays	2048	http://plants.ensembl.org/Zea_mays/Info/Index

3.2   Initial Step

Firstly for each genome, all downloaded files were intermingled in one. LTR_STRUC [24] was used to identify complete LTR Retrotransposon sequences (LTR-RT) (see Table 4). Four text files composed its output for each predicted LTR-RT. At the end of this part, 4 different directories were created, each one containing the LTR_STRUC output from each genome.

Table 4.   LTR-RT elements predicted by LTR_STRUC.

Genome	Number
Arabidopsis thaliana	198
Oryza sativa	683
Coffea canephora	1766
Zea mays	6625

3.3   Serial Bioinformatics Pipeline

The principal objective of this pipeline is the phylogenetic analysis and classification of complete LTR-RTs predicted by LTR_STRUC as well as their insertion time analysis. The pipeline developed in bash was subdivided into the next sections:

Preprocessing
The objective here was to group together all information from the LTR_STRUC output into one tabular text file, to organize the information. We used two LTR_STRUC files: (i) in report file we got features such as LTR Identity, primer binding site (PBS), PolyPurine Tract (PPT), length, Active size, Longest Open Reading Frame (ORF), Target Site Duplication (TSD), Long Terminal Repeat (LTR) A length, LTR B length, and strand; (ii) in another file, we used Fasta file to extract important sequences like LTR A and B using Seqret and Extractseq tools from Emboss [25] and the sequence of the full element. Using BLASTx with the full sequence as a query against cores database from The Gypsy Database Project [26], we extracted the best conserved domain and its e-value. Six domains were searched in this study, GAG, RT, INT, RNAseH, AP and ENV (see Table 1). Result file from this step was a tabular file with ":" as field separator.

Classification process
Using the result file from previous process a classification was performed as follow: (i) if the element carried at least one principal domain (RT, INT, and RNAseH) with keywords RLC or RLG, the LTR-RT was classified as complete-family element (Copia or Gypsy); (ii) if the element didn't carry any domain, it was classified as non-autonomous element; (iii) if the element had only a GAG domain or GAG and AP domains, the element was classified as TR-GAG elements. We used complete-family elements for doing a new classification into sub-families; counting how many times keyword subfamily (BIANCA, ORYCO, RETROFIT, SIRE, TORK, ATHILA, CRM, DEL, GALADRIEL, REINA, and TAT) appeared in LTR RT's domains. In addition we created an extra text file, which contained all LTR-RTs than was not in any

classification, and named no-class elements. Finally we extracted the complete sequence of each LTR-RT of each classification, including no-class.

Reverse-Transcriptase domain extraction
In this part of the process, we were interested into the extraction of RT domain sequences from each complete-family element, because this domain is the most conserved and appropriated for phylogenetic analysis. At the beginning BLASTx was executed using Fasta file of all complete-family elements as query and RT domain database from The Gypsy Database Project [26] as database. Then the BLASTx output (tabular format) was processed line by line, extracting the sequence that matched with the database from complete-family file using Seqret, fetching the RT sequence from database and translating the RT domain found in LTR-RT into protein using Genewise [27] with the option –pep. Only translated sequences larger 200 amino acids were conserved for further analysis. Lastly all RTs from database were intermingled into a final Fasta file.

Analyzing LTR insertion times
The insertion times of full-length copies, as defined by a minimum of 80% of nucleotide identity over 100% of the reference element length, were dated [11]. Timing of insertion was based on the divergence of the $5'$ and $3'$ LTR sequences of each copy. The two LTRs were aligned using stretcher (EMBOSS), and the divergence was calculated using the Kimura 2-parameter method implemented in distmat (EMBOSS). The insertion dates were estimated using an average base substitution rate of 1.3 E-8 [28].

Phylogenetic tree creation
Using final Fasta file from **Reverse-Transcriptase domain extraction** section, a multiple alignment was done using Muscle [29] with parameter –msf to indicate that output will be write in GCG MSF format. Then phylogenetic tree was created with Clustalw [30] using the follwing parameters: -OUTPUTTREE = nj -BOOTSTRAP = 100 -BOOTLABELS = node.

Cleaning
This final step deleted all temporal files from all sections of this pipeline.

3.4 Parallel Bioinformatics Pipeline

Previous shown pipeline was parallelized with MPI; Analysis of insertion time and phylogenetic tree creation sections were not used in this process because of its non-parallelizable features, the others parts of the pipeline were kept. Each module needed a splitter part before executed it, which create one subject file per MPI-process, thanks to this division it was possible to run multiple pipeline at the same time, each one using one processor and a smaller file than the original. Master process (with identification zero) managed the execution of each module and joined all partial result in one final file; others executed the serial corresponding process (Fig. 1).

MPI standard uses messages for sharing data between independent processes. We chosen as parallelization strategy division of input information per MPI-process (see Algorithm 1).

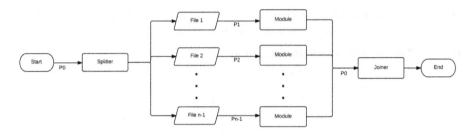

Fig. 1. General process parallelization diagram.

```
If id_process = 0 then {master process}
    Execute splitter with input data
    For n from 1 to number_MPI_processes
        Send initial signal to process n
    End-for
    For n from 1 to number_MPI_processes
        Receive done signal from process n
    End-for
    Execute joiner process with all partial results
Else {slave process}
    Receive initial signal from master process
    Execute module with partial data
    Send done signal to master process
End-If
```

Algorithm 1. MPI communication between independent processes

Splitter process
Two kinds of splitters were developed, one for tabular files and another one for Fasta files, both in bash. This process was executed in one processor before all modules and its purpose was to create files with the number of LTR-RT calculated by:

$$num\_elem\_per\_proc = total\_num\_ele \, / \, (num\_MPI\_proc - 1) \qquad (1)$$

Pre-processing module
First all element names were split in many files as number of MPI-processes minus one, each one with quantity of elements calculated in (1). Then were launched many serial pre-processing as number of MPI-processes minus one at the same time, using as data input, the file created previously in this step. This module created one tabular file.

Classification module
Through the duk program (included in bash), the final result file from pre-processing module was divided by tabular splitter process, and many serial classification processes

were executed as quantity of MPI-processes minus one at the same time. This process created 5 tabular files (one per classification) and 5 corresponding Fasta files.

Reverse-Transcriptase domain extraction module
The Fasta splitter process was run here to separate the complete-family classification file using Seqret (Emboss). Then were launched many serial RT domain extraction processes as quantity of MPI-processes minus one at the same time. The output was one Fasta file with all RT domain found in the input.

3.5 Computational Architecture and Software Used

All experiments were done using a server with 32 cores Xeon E5-2670 (with HT enabled), 256 GB of memory RAM and operative system Centos 6.7, managed by Slurm [31]. All software used in this study (Table 5) were installed in a non-standard directory and were loaded using Environmental Modules [32]. Source code of parallel pipeline can be found in http://bios.co/Portals/0/HPC/Software/Parallan/Latest/parallan.zip, under GNU GPLv3 license.

Table 5. Software used in pipeline.

Software	Version
NCBI-Blast	2.5.0
Emboss	6.6.0
Wise2	2.4.0
OpenMPI	1.8.8
Muscle	3.8.31
ClustalW	2.1

4 Results

The experiments carried out in this research have the following characteristics: (i) implementation of algorithms using sequential and parallel strategy, (ii) for each genome the algorithm was executed using a sequential strategy (1 core) and times for each step (Break-Down) and the total time were measured, (iii) for each genome the algorithm was executed using a parallel strategy increasing the number of cores as follows: 4, 8, 16 and 32 cores and the times for each parallel step (Break-Down) and the total time of parallel pipeline were measured, (iiii) each of the above experiments was repeated 10 times in order to give reliability of the results, (vi) the standard deviation, average runtime consumed per step, total average runtime and the average percentage of runtime consumed per step compared to total time were calculated, (v) all results were expressed in seconds and the analysis of results and conclusions was done with the average runtimes of the 10 replicates for each experiment.

Tables 6, 7, 8 and 9 show average times for each step, total average time, standard deviation and percentage of average time of each step applied to a sequential strategy (1 Core), and a parallel strategy (4, 8, 16 and 32 Cores). This was done for each of the genomes used in this study.

Table 6. *Arabidopsis thaliana* results.

Arabidopsis thaliana

Number of cores	Step	Average runtime in seconds (10 Repetitions)	Standard deviation in seconds	Percentage (Break-Down)
Sequential (1 Core)	Pre-Processing and Extraction of information	557,88	34,39	90,58
	Classification	9,84	1,79	1,60
	Extraction of interested region	47,53	3,27	7,72
	Cleaner	0,65	0,80	0,11
	Total Time	615,90	37,75	100,00
4	Pre-Processing and Extraction of information	232,83	16,15	91,57
	Classification	4,44	0,77	1,75
	Extraction of interested region	16,54	2,35	6,51
	Cleaner	0,44	0,12	0,17
	Total Time	254,26	16,43	100,00
8	Pre-Processing and Extraction of information	121,87	11,15	90,77
	Classification	3,09	0,77	2,30
	Extraction of interested region	8,89	0,58	6,62
	Cleaner	0,41	0,07	0,30
	Total Time	134,26	11,91	100,00
16	Pre-Processing and Extraction of information	240,63	8,81	85,25
	Classification	18,69	1,81	6,62
	Extraction of interested region	15,27	1,21	5,41
	Cleaner	7,68	1,63	2,72
	Total Time	282,27	8,94	100,00
32	Pre-Processing and Extraction of information	241,07	14,58	83,71
	Classification	23,44	5,20	8,14
	Extraction of interested region	15,07	6,06	5,23
	Cleaner	8,39	2,79	2,91
	Total Time	287,98	11,01	100,00

Table 7. *Oryza sativa* results.

Oryza sativa				
Number of cores	Step	Average runtime in seconds (10 Repetitions)	Standard deviation in seconds	Percentage (Break-Down)
Sequential (1 Core)	Pre-Processing and Extraction of information	2060,28	32,05	89,82
	Classification	46,78	3,60	2,04
	Extraction of interested region	185,72	4,66	8,10
	Cleaner	1,05	0,11	0,05
	Total Time	2293,83	32,84	100,00
4	Pre-Processing and Extraction of information	797,39	19,80	90,34
	Classification	18,95	3,39	2,15
	Extraction of interested region	65,15	5,18	7,38
	Cleaner	1,16	0,22	0,13
	Total Time	882,65	17,90	100,00
8	Pre-Processing and Extraction of information	500,82	34,87	92,89
	Classification	8,02	1,69	1,49
	Extraction of interested region	29,22	3,29	5,42
	Cleaner	1,12	0,10	0,21
	Total Time	539,18	37,23	100,00
16	Pre-Processing and Extraction of information	303,32	6,94	92,20
	Classification	8,55	0,15	2,60
	Extraction of interested region	15,62	0,21	4,75
	Cleaner	1,50	0,07	0,46
	Total Time	328,99	6,90	100,00
32	Pre-Processing and Extraction of information	259,50	3,45	90,11
	Classification	13,77	1,09	4,78
	Extraction of interested region	12,99	0,61	4,51
	Cleaner	1,71	0,10	0,59
	Total Time	287,97	4,30	100,00

Table 8. *Coffea canephora* results.

Coffea canephora				
Number of cores	Step	Average runtime in seconds (10 Repetitions)	Standard deviation in seconds	Percentage (Break-Down)
Sequential (1 Core)	Pre-Processing and Extraction of information	11992,19	594,35	87,69
	Classification	496,25	156,81	3,63
	Extraction of interested region	1143,22	113,51	8,36
	Cleaner	44,66	8,12	0,33
	Total Time	13676,32	782,74	100,00
4	Pre-Processing and Extraction of information	2259,70	206,40	90,19
	Classification	45,87	23,86	1,83
	Extraction of interested region	192,43	54,73	7,68
	Cleaner	7,59	10,54	0,30
	Total Time	2505,60	257,04	100,00
8	Pre-Processing and Extraction of information	1219,95	143,27	88,25
	Classification	35,95	9,12	2,60
	Extraction of interested region	110,19	64,94	7,97
	Cleaner	16,25	21,12	1,18
	Total Time	1382,33	170,13	100,00
16	Pre-Processing and Extraction of information	859,28	25,20	91,70
	Classification	21,59	7,20	2,30
	Extraction of interested region	45,53	8,36	4,86
	Cleaner	10,70	14,80	1,14
	Total Time	937,11	40,24	100,00
32	Pre-Processing and Extraction of information	684,25	73,80	82,55
	Classification	58,60	44,50	7,07
	Extraction of interested region	58,90	32,46	7,11
	Cleaner	27,12	36,19	3,27
	Total Time	828,87	108,02	100,00

Table 9. *Zea mays* results.

Zea mays				
Number of cores	Step	Average runtime in seconds (10 Repetitions)	Standard deviation in seconds	Percentage (Break-Down)
Sequential (1 Core)	Pre-Processing and Extraction of information	29360,32	215,90	84,40
	Classification	904,65	34,60	2,60
	Extraction of interested region	4508,87	12,73	12,96
	Cleaner	13,40	0,68	0,04
	Total Time	34787,24	190,12	100,00
4	Pre-Processing and Extraction of information	10117,28	324,90	87,61
	Classification	140,67	28,39	1,22
	Extraction of interested region	1273,25	121,11	11,03
	Cleaner	17,13	1,69	0,15
	Total Time	11548,32	412,97	100,00
8	Pre-Processing and Extraction of information	5169,38	236,08	90,01
	Classification	65,69	2,62	1,14
	Extraction of interested region	493,31	6,23	8,59
	Cleaner	14,96	1,07	0,26
	Total Time	5743,34	244,12	100,00
16	Pre-Processing and Extraction of information	3529,71	40,36	90,76
	Classification	89,71	2,16	2,31
	Extraction of interested region	250,48	5,01	6,44
	Cleaner	19,18	0,45	0,49
	Total Time	3889,09	40,17	100,00
32	Pre-Processing and Extraction of information	2829,73	56,83	89,60
	Classification	116,88	15,54	3,70
	Extraction of interested region	192,31	5,17	6,09
	Cleaner	19,42	1,18	0,61
	Total Time	3158,35	52,78	100,00

Table 10. Speed-Up obtained from different species depending on the number of cores.

Specie	Sequential (1 core) runtime	Parallel runtime	Number of cores	Speed-up
Arabidopsis thaliana	615,90	254,26	4	**2,4**
		134,26	8	**4,6**
		282,27	16	**2,2**
		287,98	32	**2,1**
Oryza sativa	2293,83	882,65	4	**2,6**
		539,18	8	**4,3**
		328,99	16	**7,0**
		287,97	32	**8,0**
Coffea canephora	13676,32	2505,60	4	**5,5**
		1382,33	8	**9,9**
		937,11	16	**14,6**
		828,87	32	**16,5**
Zea mays	34787,24	11548,32	4	**3,0**
		5743,34	8	**6,1**
		3889,09	16	**8,9**
		3158,35	32	**11,0**

The Table 10 shows the accelerations obtained for the 4 species studied in this research. The way in which these accelerations were calculated consists of dividing the runtime obtained by using a parallel strategy for the different numbers of cores, over the runtime obtained using a sequential strategy. The construction of this table is made with reference to the data obtained in Tables 6, 7, 8 and 9.

The Figure 2 shows the average times of each step as a function of the number of cores for specie *Coffea canephora*.

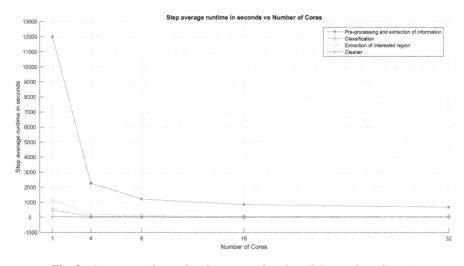

Fig. 2. Average runtimes of each step as a function of the number of cores.

The Fig. 3 shows the percentages of the average times of each step (Break-Down) compared to the total time using 1 and 32 cores for specie *Coffea canephora.*

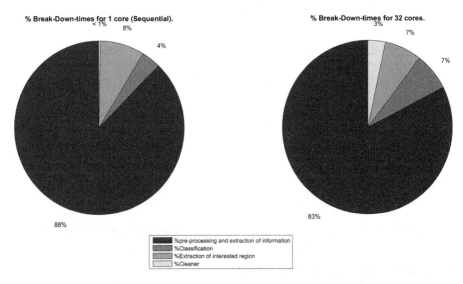

Fig. 3. Percentage of Break-Down times for specie *Coffea canephora.*

The Fig. 4 shows average runtimes of each step for all species as a function of the number of cores.

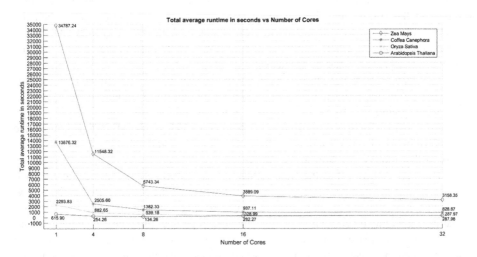

Fig. 4. Average runtime of each species as a function of the number of cores.

The Fig. 5 shows the average Speed-Up of each species, comparing the average executed time of parallel strategy and run time taken for sequential strategy as a function of the number of cores.

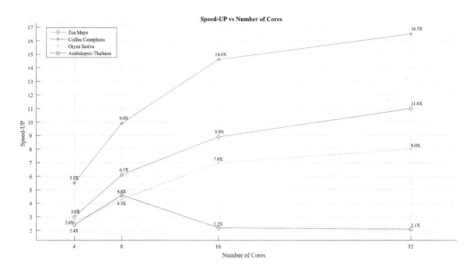

Fig. 5. Average Speed-Up of each species as a function of the number of cores.

5 Conclusions and Future Work

For large genomes such as *Coffea canephora*, *Zea mays* and *Oryza sativa* the Speed-Up
increase when more quantity of cores were used until 16.5X, 11X and 8X respectively.
At the opposite, for smaller genome such as *Arabidopsis thaliana*, it was not possible
to improve the Speed-Up using a parallel strategy, because each step took a very short
time and the splitter and the communication processes added more time when the
number of cores used increased. So, for small genomes ($\sim$100 Mb), it appears
important to find the efficient number of cores that will be used in the parallel pipeline
to avoid a decrease in the performance.

The Parallel strategy implemented in this research showed direct relationships
between the increase of the data size to process and the improvement of the Speed-Up
(*Coffea canephora* - 16.5X - 553 MB). However a limit was found for very large
genomes and so the Speed-up decreased (*Zea mays* - 11X -2048 MB). This limit is due
to overflowing in each module, generating saturation and queuing processes, suggesting that more processors are required (>32).

The Fig. 4 shows that the time reduction is approximately exponential for each
module when the number of cores is increased, whatever the genome used in this study,
demonstrating that the parallel strategy generated successful results. The Fig. 2 shows
that the time reduction for all steps implemented in parallel pipeline, when the quantity
of cores used increase. The Pre-processing module demonstrated the best performance
improvement because it required the most computational demanding process taking the
83% of total parallel pipeline runtime for the *Coffea canephora* case (see Fig. 3).

In addition, Thanks to MPI standard, it is possible to find the maximum number of
cores to process the data according to the input data size, adding scalability to this
parallel strategy. So this pipeline is both able to process genomes greater than 2 GB

(*Zea mays*), using more processors if they are available and to process genomes smaller than 117 MB (*Arabidopsis thaliana*).

As a future work we will implement the Phylogenetic tree creation and insertion time analysis steps with parallel strategy showed in this research to improve the performance of this current serial process. In addition, we will process larger genome size, with more processors to look for the efficient relationship between genome size and quantity of CPUs used.

Acknowledgements. We thank the Centro de Bioinformática y Biología Computacional BIOS for using the supercomputer.

Founding. This work was supported by the Royalties Project "Caldas Bioregión, fortalecimiento de CTeI en biotecnología para el departamento de Caldas apoyado por infraestructura computacional avanzada y trabajo colaborativo".

References

1. Galperin, M.Y., Koonin, E.V.: From complete genome sequence to "complete" understanding? Trends Biotechnol. **28**, 398–406 (2010)
2. Tatusova, T.: Update on genomic databases and resources at the national center for biotechnology information. In: Carugo, O., Eisenhaber, F. (eds.) Data Mining Techniques for the Life Sciences. MMB, vol. 1415, pp. 3–30. Springer, New York (2016). doi:10.1007/978-1-4939-3572-7_1
3. Sener, E.F., Canatan, H., Ozkul, Y.: Recent advances in autism spectrum disorders: applications of whole exome sequencing technology. Psychiatry Investig. **13**, 255–264 (2016)
4. Ho, C.Y., Charron, P., Richard, P., Girolami, F., Van Spaendonck-Zwarts, K.Y., Pinto, Y.: Genetic advances in sarcomeric cardiomyopathies: state of the art. Cardiovasc. Res. **105**, 397–408 (2015)
5. Wang, Y., Navin, N.E.: Advances and applications of single-cell sequencing technologies. Mol. Cell **58**, 598–609 (2015)
6. Orozco, S., Jeferson, A.: Aplicación de la inteligencia artificial en la bioinformática, avances, definiciones y herramientas* Aplication of Artificial Intelligence in Bioinformatics, advances, definitions and tools. UGCiencia, pp. 159–171 (2016)
7. Neale, D.B., Wegrzyn, J.L., Stevens, K.A., Zimin, A.V., Puiu, D., Crepeau, M.W., Cardeno, C., Koriabine, M., Holtz-Morris, A.E., Liechty, J.D.: Decoding the massive genome of loblolly pine using haploid DNA and novel assembly strategies. Genome Biol. **15**, 59 (2014)
8. Schnable, P.S., Ware, D., Fulton, R.S., Stein, J.C., Wei, F., Pasternak, S., et al.: The B73 maize genome: complexity, diversity, and dynamics. Science **80**(326), 1112–1115 (2009)
9. Monsalve, M., Castrillon, N.: Indexing GPU acceleration for solutions approximation of the Laplace equation. In: 2015 10th (10CCC), pp. 568–574 (2015)
10. Tabares Soto, R.: Programación paralela sobre arquitecturas heterogéneas 80 (2016)
11. Chaparro, C., Gayraud, T., De Souza, R.F., Domingues, D.S., Akaffou, S., Vanzela, A.L.L., De Kochko, A., Rigoreau, M., Crouzillat, D., Hamon, S., Hamon, P., Guyot, R.: Terminal-repeat retrotransposons with gAG domain in plant genomes: a new testimony on the complex world of transposable elements. Genome Biol. Evol. **7**, 493–504 (2015)

12. Guyot, R., Darré, T., Dupeyron, M., de Kochko, A., Hamon, S., Couturon, E., Crouzillat, D., Rigoreau, M., Rakotomalala, J.J., Raharimalala, N.E., Akaffou, S.D., Hamon, P.: Partial sequencing reveals the transposable element composition of Coffea genomes and provides evidence for distinct evolutionary stories. Mol. Genet. Genomics **291**, 1979–1990 (2016)

13. Beulé, T., Agbessi, M.D., Dussert, S., Jaligot, E., Guyot, R.: Genome-wide analysis of LTR-retrotransposons in oil palm. BMC Genom. **16**, 1–14 (2015)

14. Wicker, T., Sabot, F., Hua-Van, A., Bennetzen, J.L., Capy, P., Chalhoub, B., et al.: A unified classification system for eukaryotic transposable elements. Nat. Rev. Genet. **8**, 973–982 (2007)

15. Witte, C.-P., Le, Q.H., Bureau, T., Kumar, A.: Terminal-repeat retrotransposons in miniature (TRIM) are involved in restructuring plant genomes. Proc. Natl. Acad. Sci. **98**, 13778–13783 (2001)

16. Kalendar, R., Vicient, C.M., Peleg, O., Anamthawat-Jonsson, K., Bolshoy, A., Schulman, A.H.: Large retrotransposon derivatives: abundant, conserved but nonautonomous retroelements of barley and related genomes. Genetics **166**, 1437–1450 (2004)

17. Tanskanen, J.A., Sabot, F., Vicient, C., Schulman, A.H.: Life without GAG: the BARE-2 retrotransposon as a parasite's parasite. Gene **390**, 166–174 (2007)

18. Fleischmann, R.D., Adams, M.D., White, O., Clayton, R.A., et al.: Whole-genome random sequencing and assembly of Haemophilus-Influenzae Rd. Science **80**(269), 496–512 (1995)

19. Denoeud, F., Carretero-Paulet, L., Dereeper, A., Droc, G., Guyot, R., Pietrella, M., Zheng, C., Alberti, A., Anthony, F., et al.: The coffee genome provides insight into the convergent evolution of caffeine biosynthesis. Science **345**, 1181–1184 (2014)

20. Yu, J., Hu, S., Wang, J., Wong, G.K., Li, S., Liu, B., Deng, Y., Dai, L., Zhou, Y., Zhang, X., Cao, M., Liu, J., et al.: T HE R ICE G ENOME a draft sequence of the rice genome (Oryza sativa L. ssp.). Science **80**(296), 79–92 (2002)

21. Gropp, W., Lusk, E., Skjellum, A.: Message passing interface, 1–11 (2004)

22. Kersey, P.J., Allen, J.E., Armean, I., Boddu, S., Bolt, B.J., Carvalho-Silva, D., Christensen, M., Davis, P., Falin, L.J., et al.: Ensembl Genomes 2016: more genomes, more complexity. Nucleic Acids Res. **44**, D574–D580 (2016)

23. Dereeper, A., Bocs, S., Rouard, M., Guignon, V., Ravel, S., Tranchant-Dubreuil, C., Poncet, V., Garsmeur, O., Lashermes, P., Droc, G.: The coffee genome hub: a resource for coffee genomes. Nucleic Acids Res. **43**, D1028–D1035 (2015)

24. McCarthy, E.M., McDonald, J.F.: LTR_STRUC: a novel search and identification program for LTR retrotransposons. Bioinformatics **19**, 362–367 (2003)

25. Rice, P., Longden, I., Bleasby, A.: EMBOSS: the European molecular biology open software suite (2000)

26. Llorens, C., Futami, R., Covelli, L., Domínguez-Escribá, L., Viu, J.M., Tamarit, D., Aguilar-Rodríguez, J., Vicente-Ripolles, M., Fuster, G., Bernet, G.P., et al.: The Gypsy Database (GyDB) of mobile genetic elements: release 2.0. Nucleic Acids Res. gkq1061 (2010)

27. Birney, E., Durbin, R.: Using GeneWise in the Drosophila annotation experiment. Genome Res. **10**, 547–548 (2000)

28. Ma, J., Bennetzen, J.L.: Rapid recent growth and divergence of rice nuclear genomes. Proc. Natl. Acad. Sci. U. S. A. **101**, 12404–12410 (2004)

29. Edgar, R.C.: MUSCLE: Multiple sequence alignment with high accuracy and high throughput. Nucleic Acids Res. **32**, 1792–1797 (2004)

30. Larkin, M.A., Blackshields, G., Brown, N.P., Chenna, R., Mcgettigan, P.A., McWilliam, H., Valentin, F., Wallace, I.M., Wilm, A., Lopez, R., Thompson, J.D., Gibson, T.J., Higgins, D. G.: Clustal W and Clustal X version 2.0. Bioinformatics **23**, 2947–2948 (2007)

31. Yoo, A.B., Jette, M.A., Grondona, M.: Slurm: Simple Linux utility for resource management. In: Workshop on Job Scheduling Strategies for Parallel Processing, pp. 44–60 (2003)
32. Furlani, J.L., Osel, P.W.: Abstract yourself with modules. In: Proceedings of the 10th USENIX Conference on System Administration, pp. 193–204. USENIX Association, Berkeley, CA, USA (1996)

A General Purpose Architecture
for IoT Data Acquisition

Diego Acosta-Ortiz[✉], Raúl Ramos-Pollán, and Gabriel Pedraza

Universidad Industrial Santander, Bucaramanga, Colombia
dacosta@radiogis.uis.edu.co, {rramosp,gpedraza}@uis.edu.co

Abstract. This paper presents a description of a data acquisition IoT platform architecture which has been designed to provide two additional extensible mechanisms at server and device levels. From the device perspective we support implementations for two data acquisition modes: near real time and batch. From the server side we allow data analytics processes to be seamlessly configured and launched over the data acquired. Our approach pursues to reduce the efforts and cost of integration of new hardware devices. Along with the architecture description we provide an API definition, a platform reference implementation and its performance evaluation. Our main purpose is to guarantee integration, modularity, flexibility and extensibility to cover a wide range of applications and use cases.

Keywords: Internet of Things (IoT) · Software architecture · API · Data acquisition · Embedded systems

1 Introduction

Traditional research was based in observation and experimentation, and since decades ago this process has been improved by the technology itself. In modern research, technology drives and influences virtually all fields in different ways, from simulation to modeling, to large scale data analytics, to data acquisition, etc. In many cases, science and industry exploit differently the technological advances while in others the motivations and needs are similar and, thus, cooperation and synergies emerge naturally. This is the case of technologies under the notion of Internet of Things(IoT) where, from a general perspective, physical systems are endowed with computing capabilities and ubiquitous connectivity to conform data acquisition networks, large scale control systems, etc. This includes, vehicles, buildings, devices, wearables, etc. and spans a large variety of industry and research fields (automotion, smart cities, medicine, sports, climate, manufacturing, etc.) [1–3].

In particular, *single board computers* (SBC) [4] have played a key role in the development and proliferation of IoT devices facilitating the design, programming and assembly of embedded systems and devices in general. SBCs reduce the cost-effort required to design, assemble and test IoT devices, providing a

© Springer International Publishing AG 2017
A. Solano and H. Ordoñez (Eds.): CCC 2017, CCIS 735, pp. 644–658, 2017.
DOI: 10.1007/978-3-319-66562-7_46

platform whose programmability is akin to a large number of engineers, and able to integrate a wide variety of sensors, connectivity protocols and widgets. The Raspberry PI, Intel's Edison or ODROID are just a few of the platforms available in this sense. In fact, many makers' communities have emerged gathering together interests and spreading knowledge on these technologies. See for instances Intel's Makers [5].

Still, with this potentially large distributed set of data acquisition devices we were continuously facing the need to define a data collection, transmission and storage architecture for each different project we participated, both in industry and academy. This includes developing modules or drivers to be running on the devices themselves, a central storage to gather data and appropriate communications protocols. Although there exist platforms to partly address these needs (see Sect. 2 below) we always found ourselves facing the same kinds of tasks in each particular scenario: implementing near real time and batch data transmission scenarios, assembling device drivers for specific sensors to run on the SBC, configuring server side platforms to gather and store data, etc.

This work therefore describes the architecture we devised to rationalize and streamline the development of SBC IoT data acquisition networks for real time and batch data transmission scenarios. This architecture includes (1) a set of components targeted for SBC for enabling easy integration of device drivers (for sensors, etc.), (2) a set of APIs for lightweight SBC to server communication and (3) a server architecture based on NoSQL for large scale data storage.

The rest of this paper is organized as follows. Section 2 describes related work. Section 3 explains the architecture proposed and the concepts upon which it relies. Section 4 describes the communications API devices for data transmission and Sect. 5 describes the proof of concept evaluation performed. Finally Sect. 6 draws our conclusions.

2   Related Work

Several architectures have been proposed in the IoT field and the number is growing constantly. Each one of those proposals is based on different perspectives of IoT, resulting in architectural solutions with different focus and designs. The lack of one standard [6] or reference architecture [7] complicates decisions about platforms' architectures. However as requirements and focus are different among applications and use cases, one unique reference architecture is a hard moving target.

Two approaches for IoT architecture definitions have been taken. First, there are IoT architectures for vertical solutions targeting a specific application domain (health, transportation, smart home). Then, there are generalistic solutions targeted to a range of application domains. In addition, architectures are based in two different perspectives: service or user centric. The former perspective focuses on how services interacts and benefits from the architecture, the later allows users interact with the system and data.

In the health domain, the Home Health-IoT platform [8] provides an implementation allowing the collection of data about health and medicines intake by older people at home. Then, this data is transferred to centers with doctors assigned to a set of patients to offer medical services. This approach is service-centric. In the smart cities domain, the City Hub platform [9] offers the possibility of integrating different types of data of interest within a city. Data is then sorted into real time data (i.e. traffic flow) and static data (i.e. list of bridges). The platform has focused on how to build and scale a cloud-based IoT middleware that can be used across a broad range of Smart City Hubs. This is also a service centric approach. In addition, the work in [10] is concerned with integration of several data sources and proposed added value services on based upon data processing. Besides those, [11] also provides a IoT architecture for smart cities, but it offers resources to users as private networks, where they can then manage, consume and share data on their networks. This is a user centric approach.

For generalistic solutions, the approach proposed in [12] is based on a context-aware GNS (Global Sensor Networks) elements. On the other hand, [13] addresses security as core in its architecture. Besides, [14] is concerned with scalability rather than other properties. It uses SCADA as reference architecture to improve scalability. All those three solutions take a service centric approach, but each one focuses in different properties.

The review on [15] describes 26 popular platforms existing in the market. These platforms are categorized under different application domains where our proposal falls into the "cloud service" category. It also summarizes a list of different technical challenges associated with current state of art of IoT platforms. In contrast, our proposal aims at covering the general lack of support for the following issues:

- Integrating devices: adding new devices to the platform is mostly handled through interacting with an API, but nothing is said about device embedded software architectures. The more constrained approach only offers supports for a predetermined set of device types.
- Combining types of data: data can be produced at any time. Sometimes near real time (NRT) modes are required where data is delivered as it is acquired. In other cases data can be consumed in a batch way, with larger delivery delays. Most of platforms are focusing in one type of data, few of them support both.
- Open to extension: extension of service centric platforms is based in addition of new services to the platform. On the other hand, user centric platforms are extended mainly by the addition of device's networks to the platform.

3   Architecture

The architecture proposal introduced here establishes a set of interoperational software components that use interfaces among them. In order to provide a more formal description, in the following subsection we describe key concepts and then the API described in next section.

3.1 Key Concepts

Platform. The platform can be understood as the whole set of components, this has been divided in two main components: devices and servers. Networks of devices acquire data and send it to an array of servers.

Device. A Device is a hardware component that can be seen as an embedded system with processing and networking capabilities. On top of a device resides the software which manages each sensor attached to it and collects data from them. This component provides a way to send the gathered data to a remote server through the network.

Sensor. A sensor could be a small piece of hardware providing optionally computational capabilities. Its main feature is to measure a magnitude from the real world and returns it as data. One of the key challenges is to add new sensors to any device to enhance its features.

Server. A remote computer with large storing and processing capabilities. All incoming data from the devices is received through the network interface for later processing and storing.

Profile. In order to provide a way to check the integrity of the incoming data, devices follow predefined profiles, establishing which labels and data integrity conditions for mandatory and optional values (sensors) devices must follow when contributing with acquired data to the platform.

Operation Mode. The proposed platform considers two kinds of operation modes for the devices it manages.

- **NRT, Near Real Time.** On this mode the device captures measures from sensors and immediately it sends those to the remote server which is listening to new data streaming. This operation mode is desirable for problems that require to visualize data and take decisions as data is made available. We take no commitment for transmission and availability times and thus the term *near* real time. Data acquired while communication is broken is discarded.
- **Batch.** This mode allows the device to gather and consolidate data before than send it to the remote platform, which is done upon sensor defined conditions (at regular intervals, when data reaches a fixed size, etc.). This mode allows more independence of operation to devices and does not require a continuous connection.

3.2 Architectural Design

The platform is divided in two main components, Fig. 1 summarizes the side that corresponds to the device and Fig. 2 shows the server side. Both sides communicate through a communication protocol.

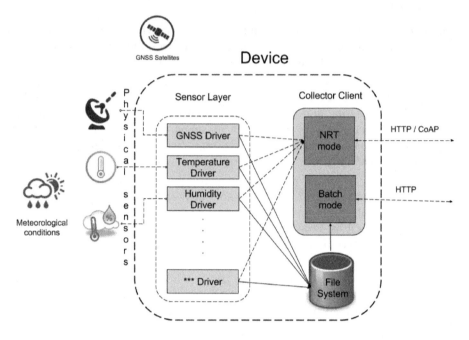

Fig. 1. Device components.

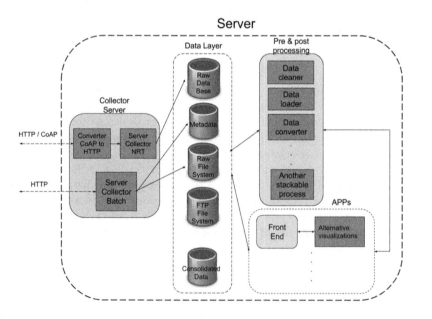

Fig. 2. Server components.

Device Components

- **File System.** When a sensor operates in batch mode, the data is stored temporarily in a file system before being sent to the remote server. Besides this, it also serves as a way to provide persistence to the device for storing its operating system, software components, sensor drivers, etc.
- **Collector Client.** This software component is the one that gathers all the data that was streamed from each sensor and sends it to the remote server through a communication protocol. Also this component adds labels and metadata before being sent.
- **Sensor Layer.** This software layer provides a set of logical drivers for each sensor that is physically connected to the device. An API regulates how new drivers provide acquired data to the collector client and, thus, allowing the extensibility of devices with new sensors.

Server Components

- **Collector server.** The collector server functions as an intermediary between the data layer and the network interface where the data arrives from the devices. This network interface is designed to support different protocols such as REST over HTTP, CoAP, etc. When receiving data from NRT devices the collector feeds an NoSQL database accordingly tagging the data per application and sensor type. Batch data is received as files which are stored in the file system and metadata on them is added to the NoSQL database.
- **Data layer.** This layer corresponds to the NoSQL database where data and metadata is stored and the file system where batch data is persisted.
- **Pre/post Processing layer.** Analytics on data is generally performed querying the NoSQL database and accessing the batch files. There may be several levels of processing for cleaning up and simple aggregations of data. The results of this preprocessing are also stored in the data layer available for further applications.
- **Applications.** The platform can hold applications consuming contents of the data layer. This will typically be visualizations and more elaborated analytics. These applications components are to be typically deployed on containers to distribute the requirements on processing resources.

3.3   Architecture Extensibility

Similarly to most of the existing IoT platforms, the extension of the architecture is based on new devices following a set of APIs. However, in our approach the platform architecture has been designed to provide several extensibility mechanisms at the server and device levels.

Server Level Architecture Extension. The main goal of the target IoT platform is data acquisition for further analytics on them. Extensibility in this sense is assured by the possibility of adding data analytical scripts in the pre & post-processing layer of the server component. Interaction among analytical scripts and the collector is made through the data layer for raw data from NRT sensors, raw files from batch collected data and finally a metadata to store description of the collected data. The metadata repository plays a central role allowing developers know how data is structured, where it was acquired and its compliance to specific profiles. In order to maintain clear concerns separation at the server side we distinguish three developers roles:

- **Server Base Developer** responsible for base components development, API specification and enforcement.
- **Data Processing Developers** responsible for adding new processing scripts to the platform. These developers are users of the extension mechanism at server level.
- **Service and application developers** responsible for adding new services or application to the platform. Although is not the main purpose of the platform, service and application development on top of collected data is possible and the interaction with the rest of the platform is also made through data repositories.

Device Level Architecture Extension. Our device level extension mechanism goes beyond of simply adding new devices to the platform, considering devices black-boxes, and enforcing them to follow the defined API. Our approach goes deep into the device to specify an internal software architecture, and offers an extension mechanism allowing developers to easily create new ready-to-use devices to be added to the platform. This device level mechanism was designed having in mind the high heterogeneity in terms of hardware, software and communication technologies of sensors associated to devices. In that perspective, base components requesting data from sensors, sending it to the server side or storing it into the device (for batch mode) are provided by the platform. Extenders must provide logical sensor drivers and deploy them in the corresponding layer in the device internal architecture. Here, we refer to those components as logical drivers in contrast with physical drivers provided to OS level. In order to assure integration between new logical drivers and the collector component, drivers must conformed with a platform interface for all sensors drivers. The API of this interface will be described in next section. Finally, we can also made a differentiation between two developers roles:

- **Device developer** responsible for development of the platform base components assuring collecting data from sensors, send it to the server and storing it in the device.
- **Logical driver developer** responsible for implementing logical drivers following the proposed API and hiding device OS complexities to the platform.

4   API Description

The API pursues to provide flexibility and modularity within software components looking to keep the generality and platform extensibility, making it easier to add new devices to the platform and new sensors to the devices. This description includes the definition of some subroutines such as the sensor drivers and the functions or methods that those have to provide, along with some architectural elements.

4.1   Device Side

Logical Sensor Drivers. Starting by the sensor drivers, each driver can be built by the logical driver developer as an independent module which corresponds to a class that creates an abstraction of the sensor functioning and hides OS level complexity.

On the NRT mode these classes possess two methods described as follows:

- **Constructor(init-parameters):** This constructor will be use to build the instances. It will be fed by a set of parameters as required by the sensor driver, for example the sensor port, the baud rate, the measure frequency and so on.
- **Read():** This method is used to retrieve data from the sensor. It requires no parameters and returns a dictionary with the measures.

On the batch mode the class possess four methods described as follows:

- **Constructor(init-parameters):** As the NRT mode, in the batch mode the constructor of each driver class will be fed by a set of parameters for its operation.
- **Start():** This method will launch a subprocess that reads the data from the sensor and stores it on the file system for a later use by the corresponding platform component (device collector) in charge of delivering it to the platform server.
- **Stop():** This will stop the subroutine associated with the measuring if it is required.
- **is-Alive():** This method checks if the reading subroutine is in fact still running.

Configuration File. To control both operation modes, we define a configuration file holding a set of variables necessary for the operation of the device. This configuration file can be structured in subsections as follows:

- Device
- Sensor1
- Sensor2
- ...
- SensorN

Where the device section provides all the general configurations such as the remote port and ip of the server, the mac address, the device name, the sending frequency, the number of connected sensors and so on. Then, each sensor section provides 3 variables:

- **Model:** This identifies the sensor, for example the sensor name can be the name could be used by the driver developer to identify it.
- **Mode:** This references the operation mode for the sensor: NRT or batch.
- **Init-param:** This is a dictionary of parameters which are required by the constructor of each driver class and it is sensor specific.

FileSystem (Device). On the architecture section this component was described as the place where the data persist. On the API the persistence FileSystem can be divided into three directories. First, the "incoming" directory is where the files are being consolidated during a data acquisition campaign. Then, after a file is considered consolidated it will be moved to a second directory named "send-queue" holding the data that is waiting to be send to the server by the platform device collector module. Finally, all the sent data will be moved to a third directory called "sent", where it will persist for backup purposes and will be removed when a certain capacity is reached on a first-in first-out log rotation basis.

Collector (Device). The collector module of the device is an application that sends the gathered data from the device to a remote server. In batch mode it launches a set of subprocess of sensor drivers and a subprocess that checks periodically if there is new consolidated data in the filesystem to send.

4.2   Server Side

Collector (Server). As data arrives, the collector decides what to do with it according to the originating device operation mode. If the data arrives as a batch file, the collector stores the file inside of the filesystem and adds the corresponding metadata in the NoSQL database. Otherwise, in the nrt mode, streaming data is stored directly in the database.

Database. Sent data is stored in the databases for later use, along with the filesystem hierarchy where batch files are organized into directories.

APPs. Any modern platform pursues to integrate new modules that improve the services provided by the platform. For example, final users could visualize data or download it by using FTP.

5 Evaluation

In order to evaluate the architecture and API proposal a reference implementation was constructed which was also used to evaluate the feasibility of our platform.

5.1 Reference Implementation

The reference implementation uses Python as main programming language. This language has been chosen because it has a support to a wide range of libraries, and allows developers to create quick implementations without investing long time dealing with low level details. On the server side the framework Django was used for serving APIs (through the DjangoRestFramework and MongoDB as NoSQL database along with PyMongo) to perform the basic CRUD operations.

On the device side the pycurl library was used to send the messages through HTTP/REST. For the sensor drivers two libraries supported by intel have been used: the libmraa (Low Level Skeleton Library for Communication on GNU/Linux platforms)[16] and the upm (Useful Packages and Modules)[17] library. These libraries are used to allow control of low level communication protocol by high level languages.

Following the API criteria, inside of the directory where the collector resides there is a directory called "sensors", gathering all the logical sensor drivers. Each of those has its own directory named by its model. In Python a directory is used as a module by adding an empty file called `__init__.py`. So when a new sensor is connected to the device, the new logical sensor directory is added in the "sensors" directory and the platform automatically detects it. Finally in the configuration file we list the new logical sensor along with its mode of operation, the directory and the parameters needed by the constructor of the class.

5.2 Experimental Setup

Initially the architecture was settled to provide generic way to integrate sensors and devices to the platform. The experimental setup and validation were devised in the context of a project that pursues to develop a platform for ionospheric gradients detection using single frequency GNSS receivers. This provides a use case for both NRT and batch operation modes. Data analysis process starts from data acquisition which in later phases of the process must be cleaned and consolidated before being analyzed. For testing purposes we focused on the data acquisition process. Nowadays embedded systems have popularized as viable option to perform computing tasks but a critical issue that the hardware has processing constraints that can't be ignored, then we will evaluate the resources consumption.

Two devices were disposed, both devices were intended to measure GNSS signals along with atmospheric measures although there are slight differences between them. The following Table 1 summarizes them:

Table 1. Device description

	Device 1	Device 2
Embedded system	Intel®Edison	Intel®Edison
Sensors	Meteorological (BME280) GNSS/NMEA (ublox neo-m8n)	Meteorological (BME280) GNSS/RAW (NV08C-CSM)
Operation mode	NRT	Batch
Profile	Test 1	Test 2
Gather frequency	3 s	1 h
Send frequency	3 s	1 h

For Device 1, a data acquisition campaign was set during 6 h, sensor frequency was set to 3 s and sending frequency was set to 3 s as well. During the test the device was disposed inside of car that was moving during some part of the test. For Device 2 the campaign lasted 24 h, batch data consolidation was set to 1 h and sending frequency was set to 1 h as well.

In order to validate the data received on the server, two profiles were set:

Profile 1: This profile defines a device which is collecting data from a atmospheric sensors along with the device's position from the GNSS receiver, both sensors are in NRT mode. The fields defined by the profile are:

– Device id, Prof id, Dev time, Latitude, Longitude, Altitude, Temperature, Pressure, Humidity

Profile 2: This profile defines a device with its two sensors functioning under batch mode it has to send information of the following fields:

– Device id, Prof id, Dev time, Filename, File Checksum

5.3   Results

For the device 1, the experiment shows that the resource consumption was constant. Also we can notice that in terms of cpu and ram, the reference implementation consumed less than the 5% of the embedded systems' resources (Figs. 3 and 4).

For the device 2 some peaks can be noticed, these represent the moments when data is being sent from the device to the server but this consumption is less than 50% of the device cpu resources (Figs. 5 and 6).

Figure 7 shows the map of Bucaramanga and the data received from the GNSS receiver of Device 1. This figure demonstrate a coherent trajectory through the city but also we can notice that in some parts the line is not continuous. This can be due to the lost of connection of the device to internet or the lost of track of satellital signals. On the server we used the verification of data conformity in order to check whenever if a measure is valid or not, the rate of measures with valid conformity was 95%.

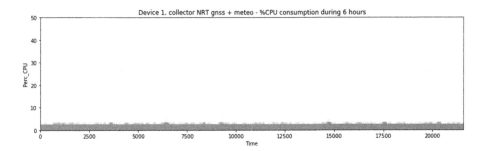

Fig. 3. Device 1 - CPU consumption during 6 h

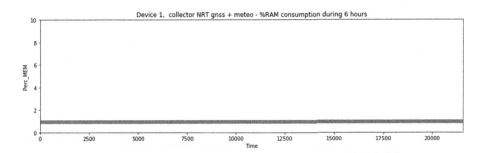

Fig. 4. Device 1 - RAM consumption during 6 h

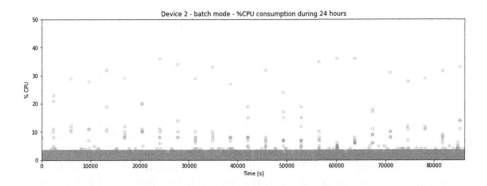

Fig. 5. Device 2 - CPU consumption during 24 h

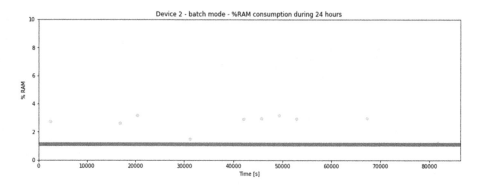

Fig. 6. Device 2 - RAM consumption during 24 h

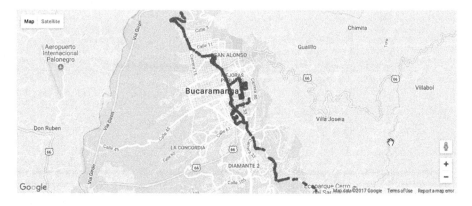

Fig. 7. Data visualization from Device 1

6   Conclusions

One of the most valuable advantages that provides this platform is that allows control over the whole data process. This gives autonomy and confidence to the researchers on their own work and reduce the dependency on third party data sources or cloud computing platforms.

The architecture was settled as solid base for future extension because the centric approach pursues to add new devices to the platform along with new data processing software valuable for developers, researches and final users. In future work new applications will be displayed on the server side to process data and provide further functionality to end users, such as elaborate visualizations.

Devices in both operation modes performed their tasks as expected. The reference implementation in Python displayed acceptable performance because the resources consumption on the target embedded system (Intel Edison) were under reasonable levels. In future works we expect to integrate more sensors on a single device along with several devices on the platform.

Despite that an implementation in Python code is not a full optimized option (such as a native C/C++ implementation), Python has been a reasonable compromise providing very acceptable performance and rapid prototyping, reduced cost maintenance and low learning curves for new developers joining the team.

One are of further work is on communication between devices (peer to peer), but and we may foresee the possibility of enabling communication between devices in same geographical area through a corresponding API to reduce cost-efforts of device developers.

Acknowledgment. We thank the Vicerrectoría de Investigación y Extensión at Universidad Industrial de Santander who funded this work under project number 1905.

References

1. Jayavardhana, G., Rajkumar, B., Slaven, M., Marimuthu, P.: Internet of things (IoT): a vision, architectural elements, and future directions. Future Gener. Comput. Syst. **29**(7), 1645–1660 (2013)
2. Al-Fuqaha, A., Guizani, M., Mohammadi, M., Aledhari, M., Ayyash, M.: Internet of things: a survey on enabling technologies, protocols, and applications. IEEE Commun. Surv. Tutor. **17**(4), 2347–2376 (2015)
3. Stankovic, J.A.: Research directions for the internet of things. IEEE Internet Things J. **1**(1), 3–9 (2014)
4. Rosch, W.L.: Hardware Bible, pp. 50–51. QUE, Indianapolis (1999)
5. Intel®: The maker movement powered by Intel: what will you make? May 2017. http://www.intel.com/content/www/us/en/do-it-yourself/maker.html
6. Al-Qaseemi, S.A., Almulhim, H.A., Almulhim, M.F., Chaudhry, S.R.: IoT architecture challenges and issues: lack of standardization. In: 2016 Future Technologies Conference (FTC), pp. 731–738, December 2016
7. Cavalcante, E., Alves, M.P., Batista, T., Delicato, F.C., Pires, P.F.: An analysis of reference architectures for the internet of things. In: Proceedings of the 1st International Workshop on Exploring Component-Based Techniques for Constructing Reference Architectures, CobRA 2015, pp. 13–16. ACM, New York (2015)
8. Yang, G., Xie, L., Mäntysalo, M., Zhou, X., Pang, Z., Xu, L.D., Kao-Walter, S., Chen, Q., Zheng, L.R.: A health-IoT platform based on the integration of intelligent packaging, unobtrusive bio-sensor, and intelligent medicine box. IEEE Trans. Ind. Inform. **10**(4), 2180–2191 (2014)
9. Lea, R., Blackstock, M.: City hub: a cloud-based IoT platform for smart cities. In: 2014 IEEE 6th International Conference on Cloud Computing Technology and Science, pp. 799–804, December 2014
10. Jalali, R., El-khatib, K., McGregor, C.: Smart City architecture for community level services through the internet of things. In: 2015 18th International Conference on Intelligence in Next Generation Networks, pp. 108–113, February 2015
11. Shaikh, T., Ismail, S., Stevens, J.D.: Aura Minora: a user centric IoT architecture for Smart City. In: Proceedings of the International Conference on Big Data and Advanced Wireless Technologies, BDAW 2016, pp. 59:1–59:5. ACM, New York (2016)

12. Ha, T., Lee, S., Kim, N.: Development of a user-oriented iot middleware architecture based on users' context data. In: Streitz, N., Markopoulos, P. (eds.) DAPI 2015. LNCS, vol. 9189, pp. 287–295. Springer, Cham (2015). doi:10.1007/978-3-319-20804-6_26

13. Jerald, A.V., Rabara, S.A., Bai, D.P.: Secure IoT architecture for integrated smart services environment. In: 2016 3rd International Conference on Computing for Sustainable Global Development (INDIACom), pp. 800–805, March 2016

14. Liang, F., Guo, H., Yi, S., Ma, S.: A scalable data acquisition architecture in web-based IOT. In: Qu, X., Yang, Y. (eds.) IBI 2011. CCIS, vol. 267, pp. 102–108. Springer, Heidelberg (2012). doi:10.1007/978-3-642-29084-8_16

15. Ray, P.P.: A survey on internet of things architectures. J. King Saud Univ. Comput. Inf. Sci., 9–23 (2016)

16. Intel® IoT Developer Kit: libmraa - low level skeleton library for communication on GNU/Linux platforms, April 2017. https://github.com/intel-iot-devkit/mraa

17. Intel® IoT Developer Kit: UPM (useful packages and modules) sensor/actuator repository for MRAA, April 2017. https://github.com/intel-iot-devkit/upm

A Distributed Connection Admission Control Strategy for Wireless Multimedia Sensor Networks

Luis Cobo[1]([⊠]), Harold Castro[2], and Camilo Mejía[1]

[1] Universidad EAN, Bogotá, Colombia
lacobo@universidadean.edu.co
[2] Universidad de Los Andes, Bogotá, Colombia

Abstract. Wireless Multimedia Sensor Networks (WMSN) is an evolution of typical Wireless sensor networks, where in addition to scalar data, devices in the network are able to retrieve video, audio streams, and still images, from the environment. Providing QoS guarantees for the multimedia traffic in WMSNs, requires sophisticated traffic management and admission control procedures. In this paper, taking multiple parameters into account, we propose a novel connection admission control scheme for this multimedia traffic. The proposed scheme is able to determine if a new flow can be admitted in the network considering the current link states and the energy of the nodes. The decision about accepting is made in a distributed way, without trusting a central entity to take this decision. In addition, our scheme works like a plug-in, being easily adaptable to any routing and MAC protocols. Our simulation results show the effectiveness of our approach to satisfy QoS requirements of flows and achieve fair bandwidth utilization and low jitter.

1 Introduction

Wireless Sensor Networks (WSNs) have attracted attention from both academia and the industry over the last few years, mainly due to the various applications that can be built on them. A WSN consists of spatially distributed sensor nodes. In such a WSN, each sensor node is capable to independently perform certain processing tasks and they are able to gather information from the environment. Most of this sensed information is scalar (such as pressure, temperature, light intensity or location of objects). Furthermore, sensor nodes communicate with each other via radio in order to forward their detected information to a central base station or perform some collaborative tasks such as data fusion with other nodes in the network. In general, most of the applications currently deployed on a WSN have low bandwidth demands in order to allow the transmission of scalar data, and they are usually delay and packet-loss tolerant [1].

More recently, the accelerated advance experienced in the sensor hardware field, micro-electro-mechanical systems (MEMS) and embedded computing, coupled with the availability of new and inexpensive CMOS (Complementary Metal

© Springer International Publishing AG 2017
A. Solano and H. Ordoñez (Eds.): CCC 2017, CCIS 735, pp. 659–679, 2017.
DOI: 10.1007/978-3-319-66562-7_47

Oxide Semiconductor) cameras and microphones that are capable of collecting multimedia based data (image, video or sound) from the environment, generated the emergence of so called Wireless Multimedia Sensor Networks (WMSNs). A WMSN is a network of wirelessly interconnected sensor nodes equipped with multimedia devices, such as cameras and microphones, and these nodes can retrieve video and audio streams, still images, as well as scalar sensor data [2]. Over time, WMSNs will become increasingly popular and consequently these networks will give rise to a greater range of applications in both civilian and military areas which require visual and audio information such as multimedia surveillance sensor networks, traffic avoidance systems, enforcement and control systems, advanced health care delivery, automated assistance to elderly and family monitors, environmental monitoring and industrial process control.

The aforementioned applications require that WMSNs provide mechanisms to deliver multimedia content with a certain level of Quality of Service (QoS). These requirements are a consequence of the nature of real time multimedia data such as high bandwidth demand, real-time delivery, tolerable end-to-end delay, and proper jitter and frame loss rates. Moreover, in WMSNs, many different resource constraints exist, related to energy consumption, bandwidth, data rate, memory, buffer size and processing capability due to the physically small size of the sensors and the nature of the multimedia application which typically produces a huge quantity of data [3]. Therefore, meeting QoS requirements and using the scarce resources of the network in a suitable and efficient manner pose a number of challenges. In addition, guaranteeing QoS in a WMSN is a distributed task by nature, because of the use of error-prone wireless channels to communicate as well as its ever changing dynamic and infrastructure lacking topology. As a result, it is difficult for a central entity to achieve an exact map of the network state and make various decisions such as route selections, for instance.

Much effort has been invested in protocols that provide QoS in WSNs [4], but most of them do not take an important factor into account when providing QoS to application flows in the network: dynamic Connection Admission Control (CAC). CAC is an essential mechanism designed to accept or reject a new flow based on determined constraints requested by the application and the available resources in the network. Without an adequate admission control mechanism, the network can admit traffic flows that will generate saturated and overloaded communication links causing unbearable performance degradation to the already admitted flows. In this paper, we propose a framework for an end-to-end Connection Admission control mechanism that considers multiple QoS requirements simultaneously. Our framework:

- takes important QoS parameters into account which are required by most applications executed on a WMSN. These parameters include bandwidth, packet-error rate, delay and jitter.
- is implemented as a separate scheme on top of routing protocols such as AODV. This independence of the underlying routing protocol will allow our CAC to work as a plug-in for any protocol that needs an admission control

scheme. Nevertheless, In order to reduce overhead and improve response time, our framework will use information concerning link and node states gathered by the routing and MAC protocols.

- guarantees the global end-to-end QoS requirements by way of joint local decisions of the participating nodes. This operation is based on the concept of *Hop-by-Hop QoS contracts* introduced in [5].
- also makes it possible for the new flow to reserve of the required resources, so that when the routing protocol begins to transmit packets, the network conditions for the new flow do not differ from those of the found framework.

The remainder of the paper is organized as follows: Sect. 2 addresses related work. Section 3 presents our scheme for end-to-end call admission control. Section 4 describes simulations and results. Finally, Sect. 5 draws the main conclusions.

2   Related Work

Solutions have been proposed in the literature to provide QoS support in Wireless Ad-Hoc Networks or Wireless Sensor Networks. Lee et al. [6] propose INSIGNIA, a CAC framework that is independent of the routing protocol and is implemented on top of it. The framework is based on an in-band signaling and soft-state resource management approach that is well suited to support mobility and end-to-end QoS in highly dynamic environments where the network topology, node connectivity, and end-to-end QoS vary in time. However, this framework collects bandwidth information by itself (without taking into account the underlying routing and MAC information), generating high overhead, slow response time and overall inefficiency.

The Contention-aware Admission Control Protocol (CACP) presented by Yang and Kravets [7] aims to determine whether the resources available in the system can meet the bandwidth requirements of a new flow, while maintaining bandwidth levels for existing flows. CACP is governed by three main characteristics: (a) Prediction of available bandwidth; (b) Contacting relevant neighborhoods and (c) Forecasting of bandwidth consumption by the flow. However, CACP has significant overhead since high power packet transmission affects the ongoing transmission significantly, making the use of this framework unlikely due the pertinence of the energy has in these kind of networks. Perceptive Admission Control (PAC), proposed by Chakeres et al. [8] is yet another CAC protocol that enables high QoS by limiting the network flows. PAC monitors the wireless channel and dynamically adapts admission control decisions (increasing or decreasing the carrier sensing range) to enable high network usage while preventing congestion. Although that can be an acceptable solution for a ad-hoc network, in a WSN, the extension of the sensing range will decrease spatial reuse, causing some incorrect flow rejection decisions.

Zhu and Chlamtac [9] introduce another framework which is compatible with existing AODV routing protocol. It achieves bandwidth estimations, QoS routing and admission decisions by way of a cross layer cooperation between an IEEE 802.11 MAC and AODV-QoS routing protocol. Unfortunately, this solution is closely tied to the MAC protocol, making it difficult to implement the solution hard to implement if one wishes to use other link protocols. Furthermore, this framework does not consider significant QoS measures such as jitter or end-to-end delay when making flow admission decision.

With respect to WSNs or WMSNs, the literature provides few solutions to address this issue. However, the following two: Yin et al. [10] model an admission control algorithm for real-time traffic in a WSN, taking into account both delay and reliability. Moreover, their algorithm provides a fairness-aware rate control for non-real-time control traffic. The scheme works in a cross-layer way, using information provided by the MAC layer. Although the reliability and delay are important factors for the transmission of multimedia data, this protocol ignores other important elements such as jitter or bandwidth usage. Aside from that, the flow admission decisions are solely based on local information, omitting to query the neighbors regarding their capacity when a new flow is admitted. Finally, Melodia and Akyildiz in [5], present an excellent mechanism for admission control in WMSNs. Their algorithm is based on the concept of *Hop-by-Hop QoS contracts*, where end-to-end QoS requirements for a new flow, are guaranteed by establishing local contracts. Each single device that participates in the communication is responsible for guaranteeing the new flow performance objectives locally. The global, end-to-end objective is thus achieved by a joint local decision of the participating devices. Nevertheless, the scheme is strongly tied to a UWB (Ultra Wide Band) radio technology and geographic routing. These technologies cannot be found in many types of devices deployed in WMSN nowadays.

Another interesting solution is presented in [19]. The authors of this work present an original schema for the admission of new packets in a WSN. The proposed mechanism is called "cross-layer admission control" or CLAC. This new mechanism tries to enhace the network performance and, at the same time, improves the energy efficiency. All these objectives are reached by avoiding the transmission of useless packets. In order to know if a packet is or not useless, CLAC uses an estimation technique that allows to preview packets end-to-end delay (EED). Only these packets that the protocol expect to meet the EED deadline such as it is defined by the application, are admited into the network. In the otherwise, the packets are dropped. According to the authors, the results obtained show an enhacement in the packet delivery ration in high network loads and an improvement in the energy efficiency in every network load. But, they only consider the delay as parameter to decide if a packet is admitted or not. Besides that, the mechanism do packet admission, and it is unable to do a complete flow admission. The decission is made packet by packet, and that is inconvenient if we have, for example, multimedia packet transmission. Also, it is worth to mention [18]. This work presents a vision for control admission from the perspective of security. The objectivtenere is to detect malicious packets before they enter into the network. The schema does not take into consideration very important parameters like the network load or energy eficiency. It only concentrates in the security. In spite of its importance, the security must be one the parameters to consider. In a WSN, there are a lot of elements that must be kept in mind in an admission control process.

Up to now, none of the previously proposed solutions consider the problem of satisfying multiple QoS constraints at the moment a new flow admission control is carried out. Besides, these solutions do not have the capacity to be plugged into a routing protocol supporting the task of flow admission neither they are not capable of interacting in a cross-layer way with the MAC layer in order to get the necessary information to accomplish such task.

3   Admission Control Strategy

According to [13], the purpose of an admission control (AC) mechanism is to restrict the access to the network based on resource availability in order to prevent network congestion, service degradation, connection failures, etc. for a new data flow. A new request is accepted only if there are enough resources to meet the QoS requirements without violating the QoS of already accepted requests.

Our AC mechanism is implemented by using the concept of *Hop-by-Hop QoS Contracts*. In this case, in order to determine if a route fulfills the end-to-end levels of QoS required by a new data flow, each node that is part of the route is responsible to guarantee given local performance objectives, namely its *contract*. The global, end-to-end objective is thus achieved by the joint local decisions of the participating nodes. In other words, each node and each hop in the route have a QoS responsibility (a *contract*) derived from the end-to-end QoS requirements of the new flow. If each node in the route has sufficient resources to accomplish its local contract, the global needs of the new flow can be satisfied and, as result, the new flow can be admitted.

3.1   Metrics to Specify QoS Requirements

Before we explain our algorithms for admission control in WMSNs, we present a sample of the metrics used by applications to specify their QoS requirements to the routing protocol. An application's QoS requirements are usually derived from its traffic specification. The requirements can typically be expressed using one or more of the following metrics [14]:

- Minimum Required Bandwidth or Channel Capacity (in bps);
- Maximum End-to-End Packet Delay (in seconds): the accumulation of the queuing and MAC delays at each node plus the propagation delay in the route between the source and the sink;
- Maximum Variation in End-to-End Jitter Delay: according to [17], this term can be defined as the difference between the upper bound on end-to-end delay and the absolute minimum delay;
- Maximum Packet Loss Ratio (PLR): the acceptable percentage of total packets sent, which are lost en-route. The packet losses could be due to buffer overflow when congestion occurs, due to the retransmission limit being exceeded

during periods of poor channel quality or after the energy of a node is depleted, or owing to timeout while waiting for a new route to be discovered.

- Minimum Battery Charge: the tolerable level of energy at each node in the route. That is an important parameter in a WMSN due to the utilization of battery to provide energy to the node and the impossibility to get recharging facilities for those batteries.

3.2   Network Model

In this work, a multimedia sensor network is represented as a graph $G(V, E)$, where $V = \{v_1, v_2, \cdots, v_N\}$ is a finite set of nodes in a determined finite-dimension terrain, where $N = |V|$, the number of network nodes, and E identifies the set of links between nodes, in other words, $e_{ij} \in E$ iff nodes v_i and v_j are within each other's transmission range. Node v_N represents the network sink. Each link e_{ij} holds knowledge regarding its available bandwidth β_{ij} and the energy spent in the transmission of a bit, which are dependent on the distance d_{ij} between nodes v_i and v_j (that we called i and j in the rest of the paper for the sake of simplicity).

3.3   Operation of Our CAC Approach

Our CAC mechanism works in the following manner: given a requested new flow $\Phi(\delta, \beta, \chi, \rho)$, with a maximum end-to-end delay δ, a minimum guaranteed bandwidth β, a maximum end-to-end packet error rate χ and a maximum end-to-end jitter ρ, generated at a node i that requires a connection with the sink, our algorithm will return an "ACCEPT" message , if at least one multi-hop path exists from i to the sink that can provide and guarantee all the new flow requirements. Otherwise, a "REJECT" message is generated and the new flow will not be accepted.

3.4   Assumptions

Our CAC scheme will operate as a plug-in for the routing protocol of each network node. The admission control mechanism is placed between the routing module and the MAC layer (see Fig. 1), and it operates in a cross-layer fashion, obtaining information from both the MAC layer and the routing protocol, and accepting or rejecting a new connection for a flow of data the application layer wants to establish with the sink. We suppose that both the MAC and the routing layers are able to provide the required information to the CAC module. This information includes:

- *MAC Layer:* link states and statistic data such as average number of packets sent, the node's neighborhood, the energy used to transmit a packet, the packet error rate, etc.
- *Routing Layer:* paths to the sink from a determined node, routing layer packet error rate, queue delays, jitter, node identification, etc.

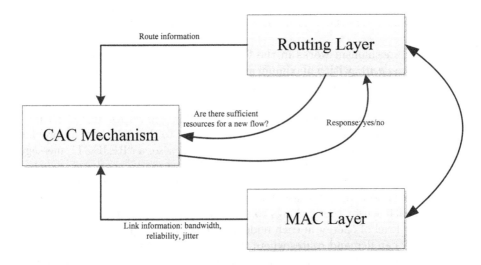

Fig. 1. CAC Modeling

This first assumption actually implies that the MAC and routing protocols used by our AC mechanism are QoS-aware protocols. Typically, that kind of protocol maintains and deals with this information, as described by Bhuyan et al. [4]. It can also be deduced here that the routing protocol knows at least one route from node i to the sink before performing admission control. Knowing the paths between any flow source node and the sink is an important requirement for our AC mechanism.

In order to get a correct operation, our AC scheme also assumes that each node in the network has enough memory to store the needed information to determine if a new flow can be admitted or not. The sensor are also assumed to have an enough computing power to process such information.

We also suppose that nodes can estimate their available link bandwidth at any time (for example, using the method presented by Alzate et al. [11] or in [20]) in a simple way. Likewise, an application can provide the bandwidth information required by each data flow.

In the current state of art about the WSN, these assumptions are valid and realistic. Such as it is presented in the articles, nodes are able to store analytical information about the packets that arrive to the sensor. In the same way, these nodes can estimate, without any difficulty, the bandwidth of each link, using simple mechanisms that do not consume a lot of quantities of energy. An example of that can be read in

Description of the AC Mechanism. As mentioned above, the goal of a AC scheme consists of providing decisions regarding the admission of a new flow admission while considering certain QoS needs. In cases where a route cannot be found to provide the needed end-to-end QoS requirements for the new flow, it can be admitted in the network and the application can start transmitting its packets.

Our AC mechanism works in the following manner: given a requested new flow $\Phi_i(\delta, \beta, \chi, \rho, \eta)$, with a maximum end-to-end delay δ, a minimum guaranteed bandwidth β, a maximum end-to-end packet error rate χ, a maximum end-to-end jitter ρ, and a minimum energy level at each node η, generated at a node i that requires a connection to the sink, our algorithm will return an "ACCEPT" message , if at least one multi-hop path exists from i to the sink that can provide and guarantee all the new flow requirements. Otherwise, a "REJECT" message is generated and the new flow will not be accepted.

The energy (η parameter) is a flow "node-requirement", that is, it is a condition on each node in the route. The new flow can demand a minimum level of energy in each sensor that belongs to the found route. In addition to requiring a minimum level of energy in each node, new flows that require an admission to the network can demand routes where the energy level of the nodes is above the average energy of all nodes in the network. In that way we obtain a fair energy consumption at the different nodes of the network, increasing the lifetime of the nodes and allowing the admission of a greater number of flows to the network. In order to get this, once a route to the sink has been successfully gotten, the sink initiates a "periodically path probing" in the route to the source. This path probing works in both ways: to the sink and from the sink. When the packets travel from the sink, they store the average energy in the nodes that belong to the route. Each node that receive this packet will update the state of the path with this energy level. When the packet goes to the sink, each node stores its own energy level in the packet, and in that way, when the packet is received by the sink, it can calculate an average energy level in the network with the received information from the packet and it (the sink) can begin a new "path probing" energy update packet with that new information.

We name the parameters $\delta, \beta, \chi, \rho$ as flow "hop-requirements", because they are conditions on each link in the route between the source node i and the sink.

Now, the hop requirements can be obtained by uniformly partitioning these end-to-end requirements at all hops in a route. As previously pointed out, if the hop requirement can be achieved at each hop, the end-to-end QoS requirements can also be met. A node can satisfy the hop requirement by selecting the next hop nodes based on the conditions of the link.

Now we are going to establish how to satisfy each flow parameter. Let's begin with the bandwidth (β). Clearly, the required bandwidth β needs to be provided at each hop. That is, for a given path p,

$$\beta \leq \beta_{ij} \tag{1}$$

where β_{ij} represents the available bandwidth of links (i, j) on path p. With regard to the delay parameter, and taking into account its additive nature over the whole path, we are going to establish the following contract for the maximum delay (δ_{ij}) at each link (i, j) en route to the sink.

$$\sum_{}^{n} \delta_{ij} \leq \frac{n \cdot \delta}{\hat{N}_{ij}} \tag{2}$$

where n is the number of links analyzed so far in the process of admission control and $\hat{N}_{ij}$ denotes the number of hops of the longest route from any node to the sink in the networks. The value of $\hat{N}_{ij}$ must be calculated and provided by the routing layer at each network node. This contract specifies that it is necessary to take the accumulation of delays into account in each link of the route being discovered and analyzed. Thus we have a reliable measure of the channel capacity for the route found.

A similar concept can be applied to the jitter ρ_{ij}, that is:

$$\sum_{}^{n} \rho_{ij} = \frac{n \cdot \rho}{\hat{N}_{ij}}. \tag{3}$$

On the other hand, the packet error rate is multiplicative. Consequently, the contract is somewhat different, yet the same concept of proportionality is maintained. That is,

$$1 - (1 - \chi_{ij})^{\hat{N}_{ij}} \leq \chi, \tag{4}$$

which leads to

$$\chi_{ij} \leq 1 - \sqrt[\hat{N}_{ij}]{(1 - \chi)}. \tag{5}$$

In this way, we obtain the four contracts each hop must achieve in order to admit a new flow. These values are computed by the source node i once, before the CAC operation begins, and they are used by each node to select the next hop en route towards the sink. Obviously, the contracts are based on information collected by the routing and MAC layers. Our CAC mechanism uses such information only for the task where it decides whether a new flow should be admitted.

Admission of new flows is regulated by a *connection admission control protocol*, which works as follows. When receiving a new flow connection request from its application layer, node i checks whether it has sufficient resources to accommodate this new flow while satisfying its QoS requirements. If so, it broadcasts a CONTRACT_REQUEST packet, with the required characteristics of the contract for the new flow being generated at i. If a node j, which is i's neighbor, has a route to the sink and is able to provide the requested service with the necessary QoS (that is, node j has at least one link with another node on its route to the sink –other than i– that satisfies all the aforementioned contracts), it replies with a CONTRACT_ACCEPTED control packet, which also includes the available battery power. Hence, node i receives a CONTRACT_ACCEPTED packet from all neighbors that are able to satisfy the contract for the new flow. Among these, the best node j^* (the one with the most battery power) is selected. The node source will then send an ADMISSION_REQUEST control packet to the selected node. This process is depicted in the pseudo code presented in the Algorithms 1 and 2.

When a node lacks s resources to satisfy the required contract, i.e., β_{ij}, δ_{ij}, ρ_{ij}, χ_{ij} for the new flow, it immediately sends a CONTRACT_REJECTED packet

---

ALGORITHM 1. Beginning of CAC at source node i

Input: A connection admission request for flow $\Phi(\delta, \beta, \chi, \rho)$

1 **if not** *enough resources* **then**
2 | Reject connection request for Φ ;
3 | **return**
4 **end**
5 Calculate Contract δ_{ij}, β_{ij}, χ_{ij}, ρ_{ij} ;
6 Broadcast packet CONTRACT_REQ with Contract ;
7 **while not** TIMEOUT **do**
8 | Receive packet from a neighbor h;
9 | **if** *received packet* is CONTRACT_ACCEPT **then**
10 | | Store h info ;
11 | **end**
12 **end**
13 **if** *a neighbor accepted* Contract **then**
      | // Best node = max energy
14 | $j^* \leftarrow$ Best neighbor among info received;
      | // Initialize path to sink
15 | Path $\leftarrow [i]$;
16 | Send packet { ADMISSION_REQ, Contract, Path } to node j^* ;
17 **else**
18 | Reject connection request
19 **end**

ALGORITHM 2. Behavior of a intermediate node when it receives a CONTRACT_REQUEST

Input: A packet CONTRACT_REQ has arrived from node i

1 **if** *Request has not been received before* **then**
2 | **if** Contract *can be satisfied* **and** *there is a route to sink* **then**
3 | | Reply with CONTRACT_ACCEPT battery_level to node i ;
4 | **else**
5 | | Reply with CONTRACT_REJECT to node i ;
6 | **end**
7 **end**

---

to the previous node. If a CONTRACT_ACCEPTED packet is not received, the CAC procedure is aborted for that node, and an ADMISSION_DENIED packet is sent to the upstream node, which will put the downstream node on a blacklist in order to avoid contacting it again, and the CAC procedure will continue with the next best node. If is no more neighbor nodes are left, the node will also send an ADMISSION_DENIED control packet to the upstream node. When the flow originator node receives ADMISSION_DENIED packets from all its neighbors, it will notify the routing layer that the new flow cannot be admitted. The Algorithms 3 and 4 present this process at any node in the network.

ALGORITHM 3. An intermediate node receives an ADMISSION_REQ packet

---

Input: A packet { ADMISSION_REQ, Contract, Path } has arrived from node i

1 Broadcast packet CONTRACT_REQ with Contract ;
2 **while not** TIMEOUT **do**
3   Receive packet from a neighbor h;
4   **if** *received packet* **is** CONTRACT_ACCEPT **then**
5   Store h info ;
6   **end**
7 **end**
8 **if** *a neighbor accepted* Contract **then**
    // Best node = max energy
9      $j^* \leftarrow$ Best neighbor among info received;
10   Add myself to Path ;
11   Send packet { ADMISSION_REQ, Contract, Path } to node j^*;
12 **else**
13   Send packet ADMISSION_DENIED to node i
14 **end**

ALGORITHM 4. Behavior when an ADMISSION_DENIED packet arrives

---

Input: An {ADMISSION_DENIED, Path } packet has arrived from node j

    // Add node j to a blacklist
1 Blacklist j ;
    // Choose the next best node
2 **if** *there is more neighbors* **then**
3      $j^* \leftarrow$ next best neighbor $\neq j$;
4   Send packet { ADMISSION_REQ, Contract, Path } to node j^*;
5 **else**
6   Remove myself from Path ;
7   **if** *I am the flow originator* **then**
8   Reject new flow ;
9   **else**
10        $i \leftarrow$ last node in Path ;
11   Send { ADMISSION_DENIED, Path } packet to i ;
12   **end**
13 **end**

When a ADMISSION_REQUEST packet arrives at the sink, the latter will issue the CONNECTION_ADMITTED control packet to the corresponding source node, taking the same route in the opposite way. After receiving the CONNECTION_ADMITTED packet, the source node will inform the routing layer that the new flow has been admitted, that there is a route that satisfies the new flow

---

ALGORITHM 5. A sink received an ADMISSION_REQUEST packet

Input: An { ADMISSION_REQ, Contract, Path } packet has been received

1 $j \leftarrow$ Last node in Path ;
2 Send {CONNECTION_ADMITTED, Path } to node j;

ALGORITHM 6. An intermediate node received an ADMISSION_REQUEST packet

---

Input: An { CONNECTION_ADMITTED, Path } packet has been received

1 **if** *I am the originator of the new flow* **then**
2 | Accept the new flow ;
3 **else**
4 | $j \leftarrow$ previous node of me in Path ;
5 | Send { CONNECTION_ADMITTED, Path } to node j ;
6 **end**

---

requirements and that it can send the packets stored in its buffer for the flow to the sink. This process is shown by the Algorithms 5 and 6.

4   Experimental Results

In order to assess the performance of this new CAC mechanism, several simulations were conducted on the NS2 network simulator version 2.34 [12]. Various tests were carried out with diverse network topologies and conditions. For these experiments, the protocol AODV was modified to use the route found by the CAC algorithm after the flow is admitted for packet transmission. In addition, before the CAC starts to work, all routes between all nodes and the sink are found, using the normal AODV route finding mechanism.

In our first experiment, we show that our CAC scheme is able to get routes that satisfy the requirements of a new flow entering the network. For this simulation, we considered a scenario consisting of a 1000 m × 1000 m terrain with 49 nodes deployed in a grid structure. The sink is located at the center of the terrain. Each node has a transmission range of 50 m. The IEEE 802.11 MAC protocol and the AODV routing protocol are employed. We assume that the channel capacity is 1 Mbps.

The this first scenario comprises three flows, each one generating traffic with a bandwidth requirement of 320 kbps, maximum end-to-end packet delivery delay of 20 ms, packet error rate of 0% and maximum jitter of 10 ms. Each flow generates CBR traffic at a rate of 80 packets per second with a packet size of 512 bytes. The second flow is started 10 s after the first flow, and the third flow, 10 s after the second. Figure 2 shows the throughput of each of the three flows while Fig. 3 shows the average end-to-end packet delay for all three flows. The graphs confirm the advantages of the new CAC scheme. For instance, a stable throughput for

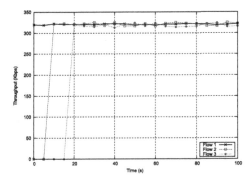

Fig. 2. Throughput for flows with admission control

each flow is guaranteed once it is accepted. Furthermore, the requirements are fulfilled throughout the simulations. Delays are also maintained throughout the duration of the transmission with reduced fluctuations (low jitter). The found routes are adequate for the flows and their requirements.

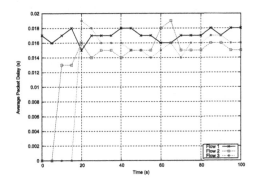

Fig. 3. Packet delay for flows with admission control

In a second scenario, flows with admission control are compared with flows without admission control in order to assess the advantages of using CAC when transmitting multimedia information and bypassing AODV data transmission when admission control is not used. This scenario is also deployed over a 1000 m × 1000 m terrain and 49 nodes are deployed in a grid structure with the sink located in the center of the terrain. The network involves 20 nodes (randomly chosen) that transmit CBR information to the sink. Ten of these data flows require 200 kbps bandwidth, 100 ms end-to-end delay and 0% packet error rate. The other ten flows need a bandwidth of 500 kbps, 100 ms end-to-end delay and up to 10% for the packet error rate. Figures 4 and 5 indicate the differences between flow data transmission with and without CAC. Figure 4 shows the average throughput of both groups of flows where there is no QoS support in AODV.

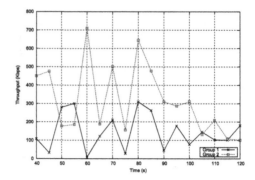

Fig. 4. Throughput of flows without admission control

This illustration reveals that in spite of all the admitted flows, the throughput of each flow varies dramatically, the channel becomes congested and, consequently, there is a significant level of instability in the throughput of all flows. Figure 6 presents the average end-to-end delay for both groups of flows when CAC is not used. As expected, we find that with all flows transmitting data, there are large packet delay, with tremendous variations (big jitter). Such alterations fail to satisfy flow demands and they are unsuitable for multimedia data transmission.

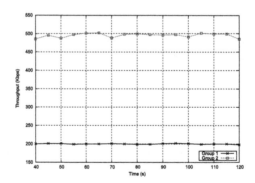

Fig. 5. Throughput of flows with admission control

In contrast with the poor performance of the scenario without QoS, the use of CAC achieve enhanced stability for the admitted flows, thus providing much better service. However, despite the fact that only 8 flows are admitted (5 flows of the first group and only 3 flows of the second group), these admitted flows can achieve their requirements for the entire duration of the transmission. When comparing Fig. 4 with Fig. 5, we notice that the traffic throughput for each group of flows is nearly constant. Flows in Group 1 have an average throughput of almost 200 kbps, while flows in Group 2 depict an average throughput of approximately

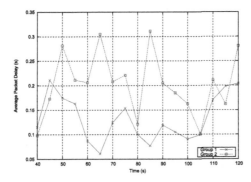

Fig. 6. Packet delay of flows without admission control

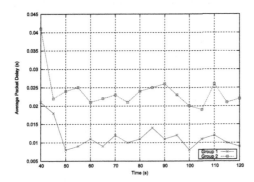

Fig. 7. Packet delay of flows with admission control

490 kbps while the requirements are fulfilled. As shown in Fig. 7, delays are minimal when CAC is used. The average end-to-end delays of the admitted flows of both groups remain below the required admission values. These short delays, along with an adequate level of throughput that is achieved demonstrate that our CAC mechanism can be used to sustain multimedia traffic, such as audio or video.

Next, we want to evaluate the energy consumption in the network by using our AC mechanism. We used the results from the second scenario to depict the network lifetime in both cases: with and without our AC. Figures 8 and 9 shows the number of nodes that are alive during different simulation times and the average residual energy in the nodes respectively. We noticed that while using our AC mechanism more nodes remain alive leading to an increased network lifetime. Concerning energy consumption, it can be noted that at the beginning of the network operation, the utilization of the AC mechanism leads to a higher energy consumption, causing a lower residual energy in the network nodes. Subsequently, because of the inferior number of flows admitted in the network by the AC mechanism, we can get a greater amount of energy in the different network nodes for a longer time allowing a better operation of the network.

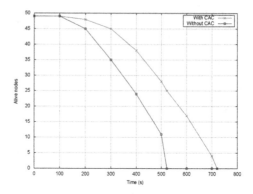

Fig. 8. Alive nodes in the network

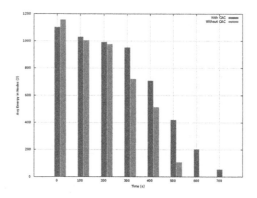

Fig. 9. Energy consumption

Energy consumption is one of the most important aspects in the design of a communication protocol for a WMSN. Figure 10 shows the comparison between our AC and the Melodia AC scheme [5]. In this experience, a number of 50 connections requested admission at moment 1 of the simulation time, and 50 flows more at moment 2. All flows have an energy requirement of 100 J. In our AC mechanism, only 75% of the flows obtained the admission to the network. In the Melodia schema, all flows were admitted. For this latter schema, the energy is not an important factor when deciding the admission of a new flow into the network. In our schema the energy is considered vital in considering a new flow admission, and in Fig. 10 we can see that although not all were admitted flows, the largest number of existing connections in the Melodia AC schema shows where the average energy of our nodes is sharply reduced. Our AC schema is able to maintain a higher level of energy in the nodes and a higher network lifetime.

In the following experiment we will work with flows that require a minimum level of energy of 1 J (i.e., the node is running). The aim is to compare our AC

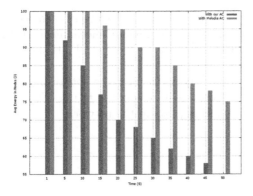

Fig. 10. Energy consumption comparison

against the Melodia AC in order to determine the influence of the energy in the admission of new flows. Every second, 10 new flows are requested for admission to the network with a minimum energy level of 1 J (i.e. the node is working). Figure 11 shows that the number of flows supported by our AC exceeds the number of supported flows by the AC of Melodia by 40%. The reason of that is the fact that our algorithm finds routes that allow an equitable distribution of power between the nodes of the network. Those node have more primarily used energy in their batteries than other nodes with limited energy. Melody AC ignores energy while finding routes to the sink. That is the reason why after a while, there are nodes with little energy on their batteries, preventing the admission of new flows to the network.

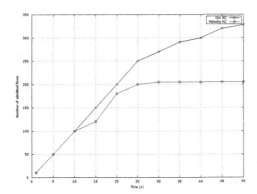

Fig. 11. Energy consumption comparison

An important feature of our AC mechanism is the ability to find alternative routes that have nodes with more energy to improve the network lifetime. Our AC mechanism also achieves a larger number of admitted flows. Figure 12 shows the standard deviation of the amount of energy in each sensor node, a comparison to our AC mechanism versus Melody mechanism. In that figure, we can see in the Melody AC mechanism that more admitted flows and more energy difference in the nodes. The Melody mechanism only searches a route that meets the requirements of a flow trying to enter the network. Our mechanism seeks a route that meets the energy requirements of the new flow and allows a better distribution of energy consumption in the network.

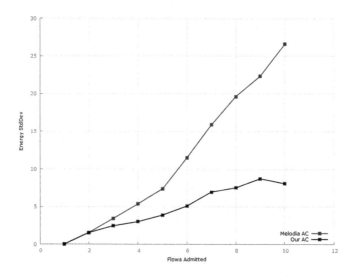

Fig. 12. Energy distribution in the network

Another interesting aspect to evaluate with respect to the quality of an admission control mechanism is related with the FRR (False Rejection Ratio). According to [15], this ratio can be defined as "the number of false rejections normalized by the number of admitted sessions or admission requests". That is, the ratio of false positives which occur in the admission control process. Sessions that should be admitted, but that the algorithm rejects although the network does have enough resources to support them. If this ratio is too high, the admission control mechanism is too restricted and useless to the purposes of the network and the application. Figure 13 shows a comparison between our admission control mechanism and the mechanism proposed by [5]. For this simulation, a number between 1 and 20 sessions will request for admission to the network while trying to connect different nodes to the sink. Each session requires 20ms latency, and network nodes can support this requirement for all sessions. However, the latency distribution between the various nodes is not equally distributed among the different nodes. There are nodes in the network with a large latency and other with a low latency. As can be observed, the mechanism proposed by [5] has a much higher FRR than our AC mechanism and a lot of sessions are rejected, albeit the network has enough resources for them. The way the mechanism works is the reason of the difference in the results. This mechanism does not take into account the additive nature of delay and jitter, and demands that all links have similar values for these parameters. Our mechanism is best suited to networks where QoS parameters, such as delay, are not the same for the different nodes in the network.

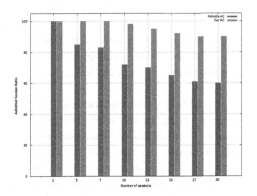

Fig. 13. FRR comparison

Finally, a simulation is conducted using the same characteristics of the second scenario. In this case, the new AC is compared with the admission control scheme implemented by AODV-QoS [16]. AODV-QoS is a modification of the popular protocol AODV, yet it supports "route finding" while considering bandwidth and time as QoS parameters. Table 1 illustrates the comparison among both admission control schemes. A total of 20 flows are trying to connect with the sink. Both, AODV-QoS and our scheme, use a distributed way to admit flow, and any node can make the decision. The number of admitted flows is similar in both schemes. The number of packets indicates how many network packets are needed to admit a flow, in average. In this case, the results are very similar for both mechanisms. The lifetime, i.e. the time required to totally drain the battery of a node, is better with our mechanism as we consider node energy at the moment routes are found. Energy level is secondary for AODV-QoS protocol, but when a node is chosen to ask to admit a flow, that node becomes the most appropriate, as it is endowed with greater energy levels compared to the others.

Table 1. Comparison among admission control schemes

Protocol	Admitted flows	Packets	Lifetime
Our CAC	11	10	411 s
AODV-QoS	12	11	304 s

5   Conclusions

In this paper, a framework for Admission Control (AC) to provide QoS in Wireless Multimedia Sensor Networks was presented. This new AC scheme is capable of discovering a route that satisfies multiple requirements (such as bandwidth, delay, packet error rate and jitter) and, on this basis, determines whether a flow can be admitted. This scheme is distributed (no central entity takes the admission decisions) and adaptive to the link stated at the moment the new flow requests admission. Performance evaluations show that the proposed scheme is effective in supporting multimedia data transmissions with QoS guarantees. In particular, delays are minimal, jitter remains low, and throughput is quite constant over time.

The protocol for admission control can be improved in a very gamma of ways. In future works we are going to consider another parameters, like security or specific elements lied to multimedia data transmission (quality of the sound or perceived quality of an image). In that way, a flow can only be admitted if it will offer a secure transmission of packets or if the new packets will not affect the perceived quality of the transmitted images or sounds. We can inspect a new way to admit flows using technique of artificial intelligence or fuzzy logic, for example.

References

1. Akyildiz, I., Su, W., Sankarasubramaniam, Y., Cayirci, E.: Wireless sensor networks: a survey. Comput. Netw. **38**, 393–422 (2002)
2. Akyildiz, I., Melodia, T., Chowdhury, K.: A survey on wireless multimedia sensor networks. Comput. Netw. **51**, 921–960 (2007)
3. Almalkawi, I.T., Guerrero Zapata, M., Al-Karaki, J.N., Morillo-Pozo, J.: Wireless multimedia sensor networks: current trends and future directions. Sensors **10**, 6662–6717 (2010)
4. Bhuyan, B., Sarma, S.H.K.D., Sarma, N., Kar, A., Rall, R.: Quality of Service (QoS) provisions in wireless sensor networks and related challenges. Wirel. Sens. Netw. **2**, 861–868 (2010)
5. Melodia, T., Akyildiz, I.: Cross-layer QoS-aware communication for ultra wide band wireless multimedia sensor networks. IEEE J. Sel. Areas Commun. **28**, 653–663 (2010)
6. Lee, S.-B., Ahn, G.-S., Zhang, X., Campbell, A.T.: INSIGNIA: an IP-based quality of service framework for mobile ad hoc networks. J. Parallel Distrib. Comput. **60**, 374–406 (2000)
7. Yang, Y., Kravets, R.: Contention-aware admission control for ad hoc networks. IEEE Trans. Mob. Comput. **4**, 363–377 (2005)
8. Chakeres, I.D., Belding-Royer, E.M., MackerC, J.P.: Perceptive admission control for wireless network quality of service. Ad Hoc Netw. **5**, 1129–1148 (2007)
9. Zhu, H., Chlamtac, I.: Admission control and bandwidth reservation in multi-hop ad hoc networks. Comput. Netw. **50**, 1653–1674 (2006)
10. Yin, X., Zhou, X., Pan, M., Li, S.: Admission control with multi-constrained QoS providing in wireless sensor networks. In: Proceedings of the International Networking, Sensing and Control (ICNSC) Conference, pp. 524–529

11. Alzate, M., Pagan, J.-C., Pena, N., Labrador, M.: End-to-end bandwidth and available bandwidth estimation in multi-hop IEEE 802.11b ad hoc networks. In: 42nd Annual Conference on Information Sciences and Systems, pp. 659–664. IEEE (2008)
12. ns, The Network Simulator NS-2 (2010). http://www.isi.edu/nsnam/ns/
13. Vijaya Kumar, B.P., Dilip Kumar, S.M.: EAAC: energy-aware admission control scheme for ad hoc networks. World Acad. Sci. Eng. Technol. 27, 934–943 (2009)
14. Hanzo-II, L., Tafazolli, R.: A survey of QoS routing solutions for mobile ad hoc networks. IEEE Commun. Surv. Tutorials 9(2), 50–70 (2007)
15. Hanzo, L., Tafazolli, R.: Admission control schemes for 802.11-based multi-hop mobile ad hoc networks: a survey. IEEE Commun. Surv. Tutorials 11(4), 78–108 (2009)
16. Perkins, C.E., Belding-Royer, E.M.: Quality of Service for Ad hoc On-Demand Distance Vector Routing. Internet Draft, draft-perkins-manet-aodvqos-02.txt (2003)
17. Bashandy, A.R., Chong, E.K.P., Ghafoor, A.: Generalized quality-of-service routing with resource allocation. IEEE J. Sel. Areas Commun. 23(2), 450–463 (2005)
18. Oliveira, L.M.L., Rodrigues, J.J.P.C., de Sousa, A.F., Denisov, V.M.: Network admission control solution for 6LoWPAN networks based on symmetric key mechanisms. IEEE Trans. Ind. Inf. 12(6), 2186–2195 (2016)
19. Pinto, P., Pinto, A., Ricardo, M.: Cross-layer admission control to enhance the support of real-time applications in WSN. IEEE Sens. J. 15(12), 6945–6953 (2015)
20. Zhou, Y., Huang, C., Jiang, T., Cui, S.: Wireless sensor networks and the internet of things: optimal estimation with nonuniform quantization and bandwidth allocation. IEEE Sens. J. 13(10), 3568–3574 (2013)

Development of a SOA Platform to Support the Integration of Software Components Based on Mobile Devices for a Smart Campus

Fabián E. Capote[1], Leandro Flórez Aristizábal[1](✉) ⓘ, Ana M. Rojas Calero[1],
Carlos A. Bolaños[1], Sandra Cano[2], and César A. Collazos[3]

[1] GRINTIC Group, Inst. Univ. Antonio José Camacho, Av. 6N #28N102, Cali, Colombia
fabianesteban1991@gmail.com,
{learistizabal,amrojas,cabo}@admon.uniajc.edu.co
[2] LIDIS Group, University of San Buenaventura, Av. 10 de Mayo, La Umbria, Cali, Colombia
sandra.cano@gmail.com
[3] IDIS Group, University of Cauca, Calle 5 #4-70, Popayán, Colombia
ccollazo@unicauca.edu.co

Abstract. This study is part of a larger project called Smart Campus Ecosystem (SCE), which is being developed at Institución Universitaria Antonio José Camacho (UNIAJC). The SCE aims to tackle problems in different areas of the university, such as slow and obsolete academic and administrative processes, infrastructure, environmental impacts and bad use of resources (natural and technological). As a contribution to the SCE, in this study, we present the development of a platform to support services through computers and mobile devices that will be consumed by all community that is part of the university. The platform is based on the use of the principles provided by SOA (Service Oriented Architecture), as a framework in the design and development of information systems for the university towards to become a Smart Campus. The results of the development of a practical case are presented, implementing the standards and the philosophy that this architecture provides and how it works through the development of two mobile client apps for Android devices.

Keywords: Smart Campus · Service-Oriented Architecture · Android · Web service · Database · Academusoft

1 Introduction

The UNIAJC is a public institution that provides educational services to the community of Valle del Cauca, Colombia. The UNIAJC experienced a growth of 506% in the number of students in 10 years (2005–2015). To attend this situation, the university has developed an infrastructure that allows to offer its services in the north and south of the city and this has also increased the number of employees and processes carried out by all dependencies. Unfortunately, the UNIAJC still experiences problems at an organizational level and it is reflected in some services, such as delays in some academic and administrative processes, desertion of students, lack of technological resources among

© Springer International Publishing AG 2017
A. Solano and H. Ordoñez (Eds.): CCC 2017, CCIS 735, pp. 680–692, 2017.
DOI: 10.1007/978-3-319-66562-7_48

others. This is why, the university started a research project that aims to design and develop a platform to provide services based on ICT, towards the transformation of the university in its academic and administrative processes in order to make them more efficient.

This study, focuses on the development of the UNIAJC Apps Platform (UAP), a platform based on SOA principles that will support the services that will be provided through the development of software-based applications. The idea is to have a centralized service for all applications independent of the kind of device they will be running (PCs, mobile devices) or operating system (Android, iOS, Windows, Linux). Two mobile apps were also developed in this study to test the platform, one of them is the authentication app that will grant access to the rest of the applications of the SCE and also to some services provided by the UAP. The second app will allow students to have access to their grades of the current semester as well as the historical grades of previous semesters. This is achieved thanks to a service provided by the UAP where it accesses information from Academusoft which is the current platform where all academic services and data are hosted for teachers and students.

This paper is structured as follows: Sect. 2 presents an overview of Smart Campus and the Service-Oriented Architecture (SOA) as well. Section 3 presents the current structure of developments at UNIAJC. The design and development of the proposed platform and mobile clients are described in Sect. 4. In Sect. 5, the results after implementing the platform are presented. Future work and recommendations are given in Sect. 6. Finally, Sect. 7 includes a set of conclusions.

2 Background

2.1 Smart Campus

Information technology (IT) is being developed and enhanced rapidly, thus, an upgrade of the existing IT architecture in higher education is necessary [1] and establishing a smart campus has emerged as an important issue in universities worldwide [2] where they rely on technology, mainly on connectivity to Internet and the ability to use computing resources from anywhere in the world [3]. Some examples of universities that have adopted a model to become a Smart Campus are: The University of Glasgow which through a supporting program of research and teaching, the University and its partners will build a world-class physical environment designed to embed the use of smart technology into the daily life of the campus and integrate an enhanced research program within the new campus focused on new materials, advanced design, sensors, urban informatics, as well as health, transport, energy and environmental management [4]. In South Korea, Yonsei University has developed a Smart Campus based on services that are mainly delivered through smartphones. All cultural, art, academic activities will be notified to students via mobile calendar, students can be part of lectures given by teachers with no need to be inside the classroom and they can even enter libraries and check for location of the shuttle bus on campus and whether the cafeterias are packed with students or not [5]. Finally, the University Alicante in Spain created the project Smart University where they will develop a university model that will improve quality of life of all people involved in the university by making intensive, efficient and sustainable use of IT resources and thus linking people and services offered by the university. Their focus encompasses main areas of a Smart City, such as Smart Economy, Smart Mobility, Smart Environment, Smart People, Smart Living and Smart Government [6].

2.2 Service-Oriented Architecture (SOA)

SOA establishes an architectural model whose purpose is to enhance the efficiency, agility, and productivity of an organization [7] by modularizing information systems into services [8]. One of the principles of the SOA philosophy is reuse and the benefits of this feature are the improvement of agility of solutions by allowing to assemble new processes from existing services, reduction of cost by avoiding duplication of code and finally the reduction of risks by reusing previously tested code [9]. SOA also emphasizes in the concept of standardization, because it makes publishing, discovering and invoking services possible across the organization [10] and it is very important that all the parties involved in the development process speak the same language and implement the solutions under the same structure of work.

SOA seeks to optimally align the goals of an organization with the support of IT solutions, seen as a set of functionalities that are transversal to all areas and departments in the company.

3   Current State of Developments for Business Processes at UNIAJC

All academic services at UNIAJC are managed by a platform called Academusoft®. This platform integrates applications developed for specific functions of business processes for academic and financial management among others [11]. Nowadays, the UNIAJC has developed or keep using applications for different purposes and areas of the university which supports a particular process and each one of these applications works with its own functionalities, data repositories, authentication methods and are

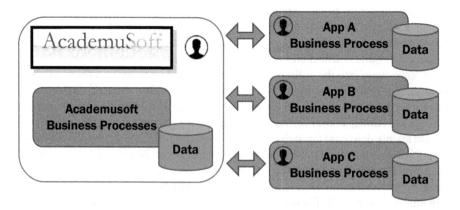

Fig. 1. Graphical representation of the current state of development structure at UNIAJC

running on their own platform where there is no integration between them or with *Academusoft*. The problem with this situation is that it is getting more difficult to manage all these services separately and it is becoming a waste of resources and time. Figure 1 shows the current state of the development and implementation structure at UNIAJC.

4   Design and Development of the Platform

Based on the information collected, we propose a SOA approach for all software services at UNIAJC. In this approach, there is an intermediate layer between *Academusoft* and processes from different dependencies of the university, acting as a bridge where all existing and future business processes converge. This proposed architecture will also help to unify repetitive processes such as email notifications, data storage or authentication, the latter avoiding the creation of multiple credentials for users. Figure 2 shows the proposed solution.

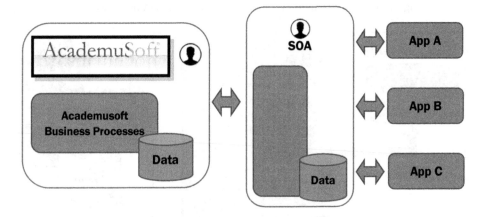

Fig. 2. Graphical representation of the proposed structure for UNIAJC

Building functionalities with high cohesion and low coupling is vital for the long-term development based on this architectural model. This will help to enrich the growth of the platform to respond to the multiple needs demanded by the different areas of the university.

The proposed architecture is based on a three-abstraction-layer model that describes the SOA approach as can be seen in Fig. 3.

The first layer is the *Business Process*es which is where lies all processes supported by the university. In these processes, we can find the people that interact to achieve the goals of the organization (students, staff, visitors) as well as rules and business logic. Once all the business processes were identified, an abstraction of them was made in order to transform them into services supported by an information system. At UNIAJC, different kinds of processes are found such as: financial, academic, logistic or administrative. In this project, we focused on the academic field and the department in charge of providing this kind of services to students and teachers is *Academic Registry*. This department manages all academic information such as grades, student and teacher records, academic policies and regulations, examination arrangements, student graduation ceremonies.

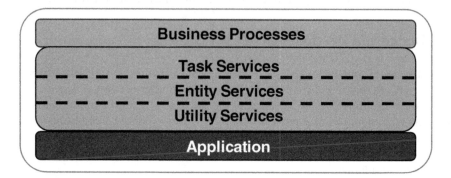

Fig. 3. Three-abstraction-layer model to describe the SOA implementation

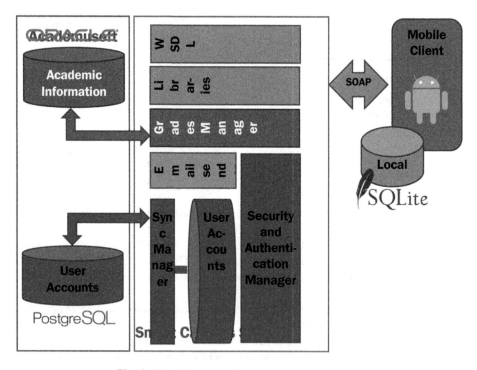

Fig. 4. Block diagram of the implemented platform

The second layer is *Services* which is considered a bridge between the other two layers and is characterized by a set of services that carry out individual business functions. *Services* can be divided into three sub-layers: *Task service* layer, *entity service* layer and *utility service* layer. *Task service* layer is seen as a functional unit directly associated with a specific business task or process. As mentioned before, we focused on *Academic Registry* processes, in this case, we developed a software-based service to allow students to have access to the information related to their grades during the current semester and the grades of previous semesters. This information is managed by the *Academusoft* platform along with the necessary logic to store it and assign the different percentages to each grade. The *Entity service* layer represents a business-centric service that bases its functional boundary and context on one or more related business entities. Due to it is agnostic to most parent business processes, it is considered a highly reusable service and a single entity service can be leveraged to automate multiple parent business processes. The developed component to register and authenticate users in this study has the capability to be reused by other services. The information needed to log in a user comes from the *Academusoft* platform and with it, apps that consume such service can access to its functionalities. The *Utility service* layer is seen as a functional unit capable of performing general activities that are transversal to the work done by most of the components involved in an information system. This kind of service must be flexible and highly parametrical. The service to send emails is used in this study as a utility service since its functionality is general and usable by any process of the university, in this case, it is used to send emails to users with a random password to log in for the first time and also to recover the password when the user has forgotten it.

The third layer of the architecture is *Application*. In this layer we can find all IT resources that support the platform and make possible the functionalities of the developed software-based components. For this study, the developed platform consists of a Windows server where the web services reside. In this server, we needed the Java Environment, Apache Tomcat as applications publisher and Postgres SQL Engine to store in parallel form the information of users that comes from a VORTAL server of *Academusoft* which uses the same engine. The synchronization of this information is done by a software-based component developed on the *Academusoft's* datacenter side. An ORACLE database engine is also involved in this layer due to all the information of UNIAJC in *Academusoft* is stored in this database manager.

Figure 4 shows the block diagram of the implemented platform for UNIAJC where the Smart Campus Server (SCS) includes all the necessary components to work properly.

4.1 Development of the Sync Manager

A module was developed to mirror the information of all user accounts that are stored in the *Academusoft* platform into a parallel server (SCS) to manage the security and authentication processes. The module was developed to be executed through a graphical interface (see Fig. 5) where all necessary parameters can be set in order to get access to the repositories of *Academusoft*. It can be used manually by an administrative user or automatically by another subsystem that can automate tasks like Windows' task scheduler or Linux's Cron. The automated feature was implemented so the system can update the information periodically with no human intervention.

4.2   Development of the Security/Authentication Manager and Grades Manager

The module to authenticate and manage the security of user accounts uses the information of accounts that are stored in the *Academusoft* Platform but this information is also kept in another repository that is part of the SCS. The service provided by this module accesses the information, validates the user and assigns a token if the user wants to keep the session active. It is also in charge of providing an auto-generated password for a new user and manages password changes made by the user. Finally, it is also in charge of making a global Log out in case the user wants to close all sessions in different devices. The Security/Authentication Manager (SAM) is the module that will allow all software

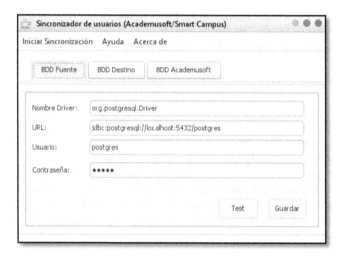

Fig. 5. Graphical interface of the Sync Manager module

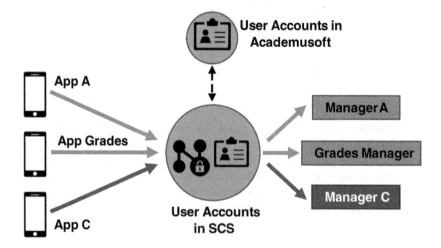

Fig. 6. Security/Authentication Manager and Grades Manager structure

applications to access resources from Academusoft and other platforms of UNIAJC. In this study, a mobile app was developed to show students their grades stored in *Academusoft* which are visible only through a web page that is not responsive and its design is appropriate only for desktop computers. To get access to this information, the SAM validates the credentials given by the user through the user interface (UI) of the app and if login action is successful, then the Grades Manager (GM) module gets permission to get the information from the *Academusoft's* database. Figure 6 shows how these modules work and how future applications will work in the same way.

4.3 Communication Protocol

The protocol used for the communication of the platform and the mobile client was SOAP (Simple Object Access Protocol). We decided to implement SOAP because it is an industry standard with a well-defined protocol, besides, the set of rules to be implemented are well-established and add the security needed for this project. SOAP is an XML-based protocol consisting of three parts: an envelope, a set of encoding rules and a convention for representing procedure calls and responses. The use of JSON (JavaScript Object Notation) format is more suitable to work with mobile devices, thus, in order to make the communication process with the mobile client possible, we made use of two libraries that make it easy to implement.

GSON. It is an open-source library for the Java Programming Language to allow serialization/deserialization of Java Objects into JSON and back.

KSOAP2. Another open-source library that allows the interchange of data based on the SOAP protocol. It has a de/serializer responsible for mapping the object representation to the xml representation and back again. It also contains an XML parser and a transport layer.

4.4 Development of the Mobile Clients

To test the implemented platform, two mobile apps for Android devices were developed. The first one will manage the authentication process to the platform and the second one will show the information of grades in current and previous semesters to students. A native development was done using the official IDE Android Studio and following Material Design guidelines for the design of the UI. The app can run on devices with Android OS with an API 14 or higher. The SQLite database of Android devices was used to store all the information of grades in order to have access to it while offline. The SharedPreferences class was also used to store the Token assigned by the platform to keep the session active.

To understand how the app works, Fig. 7 shows the activity diagram of it.

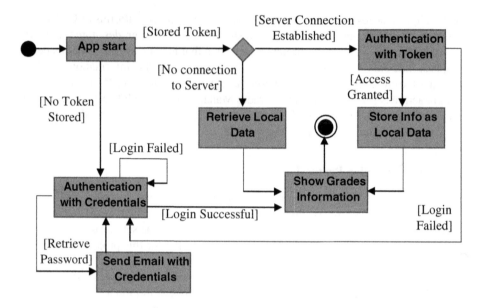

Fig. 7. Activity diagram of mobile app

Design of User Interface. In Android, a single Screen with the user interface is known as an Activity. This mobile app contains the following Activities:

Login and Register Activity. This activity is the first screen the user interacts with. The Login Fragment of the activity requests the username and password to log in. The first time the user wants to use the service s/he does not have a password. The passwords stored in *Academusoft* are not accessible for security reasons, that's why the platform has a service that syncs and stores the information of usernames from *Academusoft* and their passwords are randomly generated, so the user will use the same username from *Academusoft* and it is up to him/her to create the same password for our platform or a different one. To get the new password, the user must navigate to the Register Fragment of the activity and use his/her username which will be used by the system to look for the email saved in Academusoft and send an email with the auto-generated password which will be used to log in the first time and the user is encouraged to create a new one. The Login Fragment has the option to keep the session active so the user does not have to use the credentials every time the app is opened. When this option is checked, the system will return a token that will be stored in a Shared Preference and it will be used to log in automatically every time the app is run. Figures 8a and b show these interfaces.

Grades Activity. Once the user is Logged in, s/he has access to the current grades of the semester in the Grades Activity. This activity was designed using CardViews to list every course of the semester. Each of these cards shows the overall progress of the course

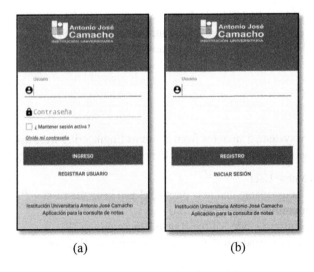

(a)   (b)

Fig. 8. Activity to log in and register to the service

and we made them expandable, so the user can see the details of every grade of a particular course without the need to navigate to another activity. Figure 9 shows the design of this UI.

Fig. 9. Grades information deployed in CardViews (Color figure online)

The colors used in the UI to represent the overall performance of the course change according to the grades obtained so far in it, for instance, if the student has obtained low grades, the bar will turn RED or ORANGE, while great grades make the bar turn

YELLOW, GREEN or BLUE in the best case scenario. BLUE was chosen as the color for the highest grades since it is the institutional color of UNIAJC. An emoticon was added to this view in order to give an emotional representation of the current state of the course.

5   Tests

To test the entire system, 5 students from Systems Engineering were asked to install the app on their own smartphones. The tasks they had to do while using the app were:

- Register as a new User
- Log in with its username and new password and keep the session "Active"
- Change your auto-generated password
- Look for the current grades of the course Programming IV
- Search for the final grade of the course Programming II (2 semesters ago)
- Log out

One person from the research group was next to each student taking notes about the use of the app during the tasks. Every notetaker had a form with the tasks and the steps required for the user to finish each task successfully. Notekers were not allowed to give hints to students while using the apps, fortunately, it was not necessary due to the simplicity of both applications.

The system was tested using real IDs of students who received their first random password via email and all participants logged in with no problem. Two of the students were running the app with a slow Internet connection, which made evident that there is a delay before the app shows the Login Activity.

For the second app, the students changed their auto-generated password easily and navigated through the app reviewing their current and previous grades according to the tasks. The offline cache of the app allowed students to keep the data without the need of an Internet connection. During the test, students reported a lag when expanding the views to see the summary of the grades from courses of the current semester.

6   Results

After the test, the algorithms used for the expandable card views to show the grades had to be changed because it gave the user the feeling of bad performance due to the slow or sudden transitions. The final result after modifying the algorithm, gives smooth transitions to the card views from collapsed to expanded with no delays.

The first app to authenticate the user worked as expected. The UI of both apps proved to be usable, since there were no problems using the different features of the applications.

The system proved to work perfectly with both apps. The integration of the components developed and *Academusoft* was correct, preserving the current security of the platforms and giving the students the possibility to do a very common activity such as checking their grades in their smartphones.

7   Conclusions and Future Work

A platform based on the SOA philosophy was implemented at UNIAJC along with two mobile apps to test the functionality and reliability of the system. Regarding the communication, well-defined protocols were used which will allow flexibility and ease to implement future developments independent of the platform or programming language used.

The maintainability of the development structure at UNIAJC was enhanced by centralizing resources and developed modules, since they all share the same basis and philosophy which means order and ease of response to changes or problem solving. Besides, a reduction of time is perceived for future changes or improvements due to the modularity of the implemented architecture.

The implemented platform is ready to receive more services to automate and make processes of UNIAJC accessible from multiple platforms. Currently, three more apps are being developed to offer services for the Smart Campus Ecosystem. One of them is an app focused also in other *Academic Registry* processes, in this case the app will allow students to request digital certificates through their mobile devices, avoiding to go personally to the *Academic Registry* office to request it and to receive it. Another app aims to provide a communication channel between teachers and students without sharing personal information such as phone numbers or personal email addresses. This app will allow both, students and teachers, to share documents, send notifications, create comments and chat in real time. The third app will offer academic tests uploaded by the teachers to students to evaluate their knowledge in different areas of their careers. The app will also allow students to take a quiz using their mobile devices in real time during the class and managed by the teacher through a web service.

Future developments must take into account previously developed components so they can re-use it and thus avoiding multiple implementations of the same service. When developing new components for the implemented architecture, designers and developers should considerer building it in a way that can be easily coupled with current and future developments and platforms. Finally, business logic or rules of the university should be implemented on web services and not in client applications, this way changes in the rules or logic of the processes will not affect the client applications and re-design of UIs in clients will not impact the business model of the University.

Final results of the platform synthesize the use of trendy and current technologies for the development of the system by implementing a service-oriented architecture and based on modular components which will guarantee quality attributes for future developments and that all Smart Campus applications will share a common architecture and authentication method. This architecture will also allow to have a global vision of processes and the systems that support them.

References

1. Shaoyong, C., Yirong, T., Zhefu, L.: UNITA: a reference model of university IT architecture. In: Proceedings of the 2016 International Conference on Communication and Information Systems, ICCIS 2016, pp. 73–77 (2016)

2. Rha, J.-Y., Lee, J.-M., Li, H.-Y., Jo, E.-B.: From a literature review to a conceptual framework, issues and challenges for Smart Campus. J. Digit. Converg. **14**, 19–31 (2016)
3. Abuelyaman, E.: Making a Smart Campus in Saudi Arabia. Educause Q. **31**, 10–12 (2008)
4. University of Glasgow: Smart Campus. http://www.gla.ac.uk/about/campus/overview/smartcampus/
5. Yonsei University: World's Best Smart Campus: The future of the world begins at YONSEI. http://www.yonsei.ac.kr/en_sc/campus/scampus.jsp
6. Maciá Pérez, F., Berná Martinez, J.V., Sánchez Bernabéu, J.M., Lorenzo Fonseca, I., Fuster Guilló, A.: Smart University. Hacia una Universidad más Abierta. Marcombo (2016)
7. Erl, T.: SOA Principles of Service Design. Prentice Hall, New York (2008)
8. Brown, P.C.: Implementing SOA: Total Architecture in Practice. Addison-Wesley Professional, Reading (2008)
9. Dan, A., Johnson, R.D., Carrato, T.: SOA service reuse by design. In: Proceedings of the 2nd International Workshop on Systems Development in SOA Environments, SDSOA 2008, p. 4 (2008)
10. Lyons, K., Oh, C.: SOA4DM applying an SOA paradigm to coordination in humanitarian disaster response. In: 2015 IEEE/ACM 37th IEEE International Conference on Software Engineering, pp. 519–522 (2015)
11. Universidad de Pamplona: Implantación de Academusoft®: Campus Colaborativo, Campus Académico, Campus Administrativo, Campus Servicios, Campus Virtual y SNIES (2009)

Image Processing, Computer Vision and Multimedia

Automatic Speech-to-Text Transcription in an Ecuadorian Radio Broadcast Context

Erik Sigcha[1], José Medina[2], Francisco Vega[3], Víctor Saquicela[3],
and Mauricio Espinoza[3(✉)]

[1] School of Systems Engineering, University of Cuenca, Cuenca, Ecuador
erik.sigchaq@ucuenca.ec
[2] Department of Electrical, Electronic Engineering and Telecommunications,
University of Cuenca, Cuenca, Ecuador
jose.medina@ucuenca.edu.ec
[3] Computer Science Department, University of Cuenca, Cuenca, Ecuador
{francisco.vegaz,victor.saquicela,mauricio.espinoza}@ucuenca.edu.ec

Abstract. A key element to enable the analysis and accessing to radio broadcast content is the development of automatic speech-to-text systems. The building of these systems has been possible given the current available of different speech resources, models, and open source services designed mainly for English language. However, the most of these tools have been migrated to other languages like Spanish for avoiding the creation of these systems from scratch.

Despite existing efforts there is no clear evidence of the tools that can be used to convert audio to text in other dialects of Spanish. Also, the most of these systems are trained to consider a specific context, therefore, audio transcription systems personalized for a language and a specific context are needed. This article describes the implementation of an architecture oriented to automatic speech-to-text transcription applied on Ecuadorian radio broadcasters, using available free tools for performing audio segmentation and transcription. The selected tools were evaluated measuring their performance and facilities for adjusting to the defined architecture. At the end, a Web application was developed and its final performance was compared with IBM Watson speech to text service; the results show that the proposed system improves the accuracy and achieves a Word Error Rate around 10%. The obtained results allow to suggest the use of a free tools set in order to train models oriented to specific speech-to-text transcription scenarios.

Keywords: Automatic speech recognition · Automatic audio segmentation · Python · Speech to text · Audio content analysis

1 Introduction

A solution that has received a lot of attention in the last years and that can serve as the basis for an advanced automatic classification and indexing of radio broadcast content is the design and implementation of speech-to-text transcription systems. These systems work by converting speech signals that take place

© Springer International Publishing AG 2017
A. Solano and H. Ordoñez (Eds.): CCC 2017, CCIS 735, pp. 695–709, 2017.
DOI: 10.1007/978-3-319-66562-7_49

on radio (or other audio visual media) into text. Once converted, the text can be analyzed and categorized by different topics of interest. Much of the recent development in speech-to-text transcription has been oriented towards the transcription of broadcast data, of telephone conversations, and more recently, multi-person meetings [14].

Radio broadcast content has some peculiarities that differ from other media, such as the presence of non-homogeneous data in the transmission, for instance a variety of talkers or segments with various acoustic natures. To support these specific features, a typical audio transcription system relies on two main elements: a robust audio segmentation component and an automatic speech recognition component. Audio segmentation techniques are used in order to divide the input audio stream into acoustically homogeneous segments such as speech, music, or speech mixed with music. On the other hand, automatic speech recognition techniques allow to convert a speech signal to a sequence of words (i.e., spoken words to text) by means of an algorithm implemented as a computer program [2].

Both techniques are well supported by a number of commercial and open-source systems such as CMUSphinx[1], Kaldi[2], SmartAction[3], or Vocapia[4]. However, most of approaches have received more attention in the case of the English language, proposing a large amount of text data needed for training language models and acoustic data along with their transcriptions for training acoustic models. This situation has allowed to transfer these models and resources to other languages like Spanish in order to avoid to create speech-to-text systems from scratch. Nevertheless, there are very few references about the applicability of these tools on other dialects of Spanish language. In addition to the language problem, the most of audio transcription systems are trained to consider a specific context, for instance, systems trained for telephone conversation cannot be applied to radio broadcast data with the same accuracy. Therefore, personalized audio transcription systems for a language and a specific context are needed.

This paper describes the implementation of an architecture oriented to automatic speech-to-text transcription applied on Ecuadorian radio broadcasters, using available open-source tools for supporting audio segmentation and speech to text conversion. The main contributions of this paper are: (i) the analysis and selection of different training techniques that can be used in automatic audio segmentation, (ii) the analysis and selection of tools that support the automatic speech transcription, and (iii) the description and evaluation of different models that are generated by the selected tools. The main objective is to decide the most efficient models for the context of Ecuadorian radio broadcast data transcription. The obtained results with the trained models allow to suggest these same resources for other Spanish-language dialects.

---

[1] https://cmusphinx.github.io/.

[2] http://kaldi-asr.org/doc/about.html.

[3] https://www.smartaction.com.

[4] http://www.vocapia.com/.

The rest of the paper is organized as follows. Section 2 reviews the work related to audio segmentation and speech to text transcription. The architecture of the audio segmentation and transcription services and the components that comprise it are described in Sect. 3. Section 4 describes the process used for the implementation of these services. Section 5 describes the evaluation of the audio segmentation and transcription services. The conclusions and future lines of research are presented in Sect. 6.

2   Related Works

This section describes some related works to the process of creation or application of audio segmentation and automatic speech recognition tools, which are the fundamental components of a speech-to-text system.

2.1   Automatic Audio Segmentation

The automatic audio segmentation is the process of dividing a digital audio signal into segments, which can contain audio information of any specific type such as people dialogues, music, animal vocalizations, ambient sounds, or noises [28]. Several approaches can be distinguished according to the applicability of segmentation. In [13] the segmentation is applied in order to obtain the structural components of songs by means of the identification of vocal segments, nonvocal segments, and silences. In [4] the authors present two segmentation experiments, the first one identifies sections that contain events such as door, sofa, or key noises; and the second one verifies the occurrence of musical notes. On the other hand, in [3] aims to separate the sections containing voice, sections containing silences, or breathing noises of a speech signal.

Architecture is another aspect that differentiates segmentation systems. In [5,19] a post-processing is applied to the results to refine the segmentation response. In addition to the post-processing step, [19] proposes a step-by-step segmentation such as: classify, segment, and refine the results. Another architecture approach as described in [32] considers a similar process without the need to use post-processing. Despite the interest in the development of segmentation systems, the availability of open source tools remains yet as a necessity. In fact, the most authors do not offer details about the applied software and, usually, they focus on presenting only theoretical aspects of their systems. Giannakopoulos [7] is one of the few works that present programming tools to build audio segmentation systems. This author offers a python library called PyAudioAnalysis[5] with several functionalities for audio analysis along with the possibility of applying two segmentation approaches whose algorithms are based on Support Vector Machines (SVM), K-Nearest Neighbor (KNN) and Hidden Markov Models (HMM).

---

[5] https://github.com/tyiannak/pyAudioAnalysis.

2.2   Automatic Speech Recognition

Automatic Speech Recognition or ASR, as it is known in short, is the technology that allows convert speech from a recorded audio signal to text [15]. The
applicability of ASR technology is varied. In [11,24] these tools are applied for
automatic subtitling. The author in [27] focuses on automatically transcribing
speeches from the European Parliament. The approach described in [8] proposes
to use ASR technology for the identification of topics addressed in videos. In [23]
the aim is to create a system that helps in taking class notes. The work described
in [25] proposes a system that allows to make recommendations of video scenes
in social networks by means of the selection of quotes or phrases mentioned in
sections of the video, which are transcribed applying ASR.

A fundamental aspect to consider in the ASR systems, is the language to
recognize. In [18,30], speech recognition systems are built for the Spanish language, however, these works use techniques that have not been validated by the
scientific community. In addition, most of the approaches for Latin American
dialects are based on the corpora built in [9,20], however, the few proposals
that implement systems with these resources, recognize the need of expanding
these corpora with phrases or words used in the context. Taking as a starting
point, the tools described in [1,6] is possible to expand a corpus of the language
and build a solid ASR tool applied to the context of Spanish-language in Latin
America.

3   General System Architecture

A process of extracting and analyzing the contents from audio signals can be
performed through the modules described in Fig. 1.

As an initial step, the reception of TV or Radio signals is processed by an
audio extraction module, which is responsible of obtaining only the audio signal
from the transmissions, then, this signal is sent to a *module of speech extraction
and transformation to text*, which obtain the texts of the speech transcripts. As
the final step, these transcripts are sent to a *content analysis module*, which can
be used in the content classification into categories or the automatic organization

Fig. 1. General architecture for audio content analysis

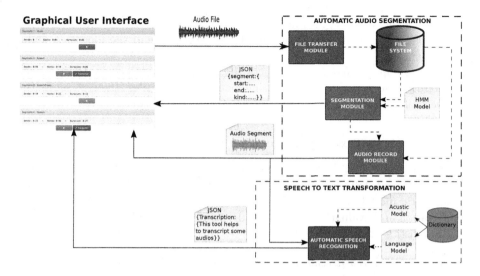

Fig. 2. Architecture of the audio segmentation and transcription service

of audio content in large databases. The approach described in this paper focuses only in the design and implementation of the central module shown in Fig. 1.

Figure 2 shows the high-level architecture of the process for extracting speech from an audio signal and converting it to text, using technologies such as automatic audio segmentation and automatic speech recognition. The tools and models used in the services that involve the architecture were evaluated prior to implementation. The methodology used for the selection of tools and training of the models, and the results obtained in the evaluation process are presented in Sects. 4 and 5, respectively. The functionalities of the modules that support the proposed architecture are described in this section.

3.1   Automatic Audio Segmentation Component

This component focuses on identifying three types of audio segments: music, speech, and speech mixed with music. The reason for adopting this classification is because these three types of audio are very frequent in any radio broadcasting. This component receives as input an audio signal usually in an uncompressed format (e.g. WAV format), which is analyzed to identify its audio segments. The execution of this component depends on the three modules described below:

- *File Transfer Module:* It allows to transfer the user-provided audio files to a local file system so that they can be processed by the other modules of the system.
- *Audio Segmentation Module:* It aims is to separate the audio file parts that are music, speech, or speech with music. This module requires a test data set for

training the audio segmentation process. The result is a JSON file describing the positions of the collection, in which begin and end the identified audio segments.

- *Audio Clipping Module:* It extracts the segments identified by the previous module, and separates them as independent audio files, then, it sends the speech fragments to the speech-to-text transcription component.

3.2   Speech to Text Transformation Component

This component applies ASR technology to transcribe an audio file containing voice. A typical ASR system is developed with major components that include an acoustic model, a language model, and a dictionary [2]. The procedure for the creation and evaluation of these models is presented in Sect. 4. The technical characteristics of the module that executes this service are described below:

- *Automatic Speech Recognition Module.* For this use case, it module receives an audio segment containing speech and using the trained acoustic and language models provides the speech transcription. The modularity of the audio sample is important in the implementation of this module because according to the trained language model the audio could be small and contain simple words or sentences, or be large and contain complete dialogues. In order to enable real-time recognition, a client-server model based on Web Sockets is used. This configuration also offers partial transcripts for each incoming audio fragment.

3.3   Graphical User Interface (GUI)

The GUI aims to show the different activities performed, giving to the user the results obtained in each part of the process. Although for the present work a Web interface is used, this component can be replaced by a standalone application that allows to the user to input the audio streaming and to show the results of the audio segmentation and transcription processes.

4   Implementation

This section describes the process used for the implementation of the components defined previously: audio segmentation and speech to text transformation. The implementation of both components was performed in two phases: (i) the analysis and selection of available open source tools that allow to be configured according to the needs of this work, and (ii) the application of different training techniques on the models required by each tool, using a test data set. The subsequent sections provide a brief description of this process.

4.1 Audio Segmentation

The tasks performed for the implementation of this component were:

Tool Selection. Even though, there are currently a large number of available libraries that can be used for automatic audio segmentation, this work focus on compare techniques for segmentation, for that reason, our expertize and the analysis of works described in [16,28] allowed to chose PyAudioAnalysis [7] as the most appropriate tool for this purpose. This library provides in our opinion the most complete range of audio analysis functionalities. This tool can be used to extract audio features, train and apply audio classifiers, segment an audio stream using supervised or unsupervised methodologies and visualize content relationships [7]. The library works with two segmentation approaches. The first one is a segmentation and classification approach, whereby an audio is arbitrarily segmented and each segment is classified separately. On the other hand, the second approach is called segmentation by classification, which first identifies audio features to determine the duration of a segment. These two approaches use two segmentation techniques: Based on fixed size and Hidden Markov Model (HMM) models. The two techniques support a supervised audio segmentation, obtaining the models used to segment a set of test data.

Model Training. Given the two segmentation techniques provided by the tool, it is necessary to develop a training process for every functionality:

– *Segmentation based on fixed size.* This technique is used for the segmentation and classification approach, and requires the use of a classifier. Two types of classifiers could be used: Support Vector Machine (SVM) and K-Nearest Neighbors (KNN) algorithms. For the creation of these models is necessary to group the audio files, depending on the acoustic type (music, speech, and speech mixed with music). The result of this process is a set of files containing the values of the trained classifier models.
– *HMM-based segmentation.* It is used for the segmentation by classification approach. In order to train an HMM model, manually tagged audio files are used. For this, audio files with data containing the starting point, the end point, and the label of each audio segment must be provided. The resulting file contains the transition values and matrices that define an HMM audio segmentation model.

In both cases, the main parameter to consider is the frame size of each segment. The smaller the frame the more features can be extracted, which can help to improve the classification of an audio segment; but if the number of features is high the segmentation will not be uniform and may have very small audio segments.

4.2 Transformation from Speech to Text

The implementation of the speech-to-text transformation component also consists of the steps described in the previous section.

Selection of Tools. For this task, several proposals [6,12,17,29] comparing open source ASR technologies were analyzed, focusing mainly on those works that show results for Spanish dialects. After this analysis, three tools of high diffusion in the community, easy access, and simple use were selected:

- *HTK.* It is a set of tools to build and manipulate HMM models. HTK is mainly used in areas such as: speech recognition, speech synthesis and character recognition [31].
- *CMU Sphinx-4.* It is a modular framework written in Java, used for the development of automatic speech recognition systems based on HMM models [10].
- *Kaldi.* It is a set of tools developed in C++ for speech recognition. Its main feature is that it is based on Finite State Transducers (FST) [22].

Model Training. The automatic speech recognition system requires to train two models (acoustic and language) together with a dictionary. This process is described in the following:

- *Acoustic Model.* The acoustic model is a representation of all sounds or acoustic units of the language that can be recognized. In a general way, the training of an acoustic model involves the following phases:
  - *Features Extraction:* It consists of taking audio frames and transform them into a set of feature vectors.
  - *Context independent training:* It is the first stage of the training called monophoneme. For each audio, it decomposes the transcriptions into phonemes. The decomposition into phonemes together with the feature vectors are used to initialize and train HMM models for each phoneme (called monophoneme models). Also, additional models representing silences and any other non-vocal expressions are added at this stage.
  - *Training Alignment:* It uses the monophoneme models to make a first recognition of the training data. The idea is to align the words of the original transcripts with the recognition vectors in each audio file.
  - *Context-dependent training:* The transcripts at the phoneme level of the previous phase are converted into transcriptions at the level of triphonemes, which generates a list of all triphonemes that appear in the training set (called triphoneme models).
- *Language Model.* The language model specifies all word combinations with semantic meaning that can be formed and their probability of occurrence. The language model was created using the SRLIM tool[6], using a text file containing all the sentences that compose the data set or corpus. The format to be used in the model is ARPA 3-GRAM [26].

  The most used corpora in the Latin American Spanish language are the DIMEX100 [20] and CIEMPIESS [9]. However, in this work, data related to the context of radio stations were added to improve the accuracy of the

---

[6] http://www.speech.sri.com/projects/srilm/download.html.

language model. Also, in order to analyze the incidence of the corpus in the recognition process, the next section shows the results of using an incomplete model with the generic corpora and a complete model that integrates a corpus of the context to be studied.

– *Dictionary:* Acoustic and language models need a dictionary in order to integrate phonemes and transcriptions of different pronunciations for a word. A dictionary is characterized by its level of granularity for transcription in phonemes. The level of granularity refers to the number of phonemes that compose the alphabet applied in the decomposition of words. The evaluation described by [20] shown that there is not an impact in the results when applying one level of granularity or another. Thus, this work uses a phonetic alphabet of 17 consonants and 5 vowels of the Mexican Spanish language. Also, taking advantage of the study done in [20], the approach uses the dictionary DIMEX100, which contains a total of 11477 words.

5   Evaluation

This section describes the processes carried out to determine the accuracy of the selected tools and the variation in the response of the trained models for supporting the audio segmentation and transcription services.

5.1   Audio Segmentation

The evaluation focuses on comparing the different techniques used for the training of the models and deciding what technique has most accurate.

Data Set. The data set contains Ecuadorian audio media streaming. The selected files contain radio programming of 4 stations, with a duration of 33 h, which were sampled at 44.1 KHz on 2 audio channels. The radio programing includes the contents of locutions, advertising, and music. Of the three types of content to be evaluated the data set consists of 70% of music, 15% of narration and 15% of narrative mixed with music. From the total of data, approximately 25 h were separated for training (70%) and 7 h and 30 min for testing (30%).

Evaluation of Results. The evaluation includes the execution of the implemented audio segmentation service using the data set separated for the tests and applying the models trained in the previous phase. The metric for the evaluation is the average percentage of accuracy in the segmentation of each test audio. The Eq. 1 is used to calculate the accuracy.

$$Accuracy = \frac{\text{Time of the audio correctly segmented}}{\text{duration of total audio time}} \tag{1}$$

Table 1 shows the average accuracy of the segmentation service. In the table, it can be observed that the segmentation algorithm based on HMM model offers

Table 1. Average segmentation accuracy using the KNN, SVM, and HMM models

Segmentation model	Average accuracy
KNN model	85,7%
SVM model	85,4%
HMM model	89,9%

Table 2. Accuracy varing window size and shifting size over HMM model

Window size [seconds]	Shifting size 100%	Shifting size 50%
2	85.2	84.5
1.5	89.0	88.5
1	89.9	89.1
0.5	86.0	85.5
0.1	79.6	79.8

better precision results than the others segmentation models. For this reason, the audio segmentation based on HMM models was used for the implementation of this component.

At this point, it is also necessary to perform an evaluation considering the size frame used for the training of the model, which directly affects the accuracy. It is known that each frame has an overlap which makes that two contiguous frames can have a correlation, this helps to group contiguous frames or discriminate them according to their type. Five frame sizes 2, 1.5, 1, 0.5 and 0.1 s and a 50% and 100% overlap were used. The results are shown in Table 2 where a frame size of 1 s and a 100% offset for contiguous frames is the better combination.

5.2   Speech to Text Transformation

The evaluation of this component involved the comparison of the selected tools (identified in Sect. 4.2), in order to implement a speech-to-text service using the tool with better accuracy and compare it with a service of general purpose, such as the IBM Speech to Text[7].

Data Set. The data set used to train the acoustic and language models contains the DIMEX100 corpus, the CIEMPIESS corpus and a corpus called Radios Ecuador, which was created manually from some narrative segments of the data set used in the segmentation. Table 3 shows some characteristics of the corpora used.

The total duration of the data set used is about 25 h with 40 min distributed in more than 20000 audio files. From this data set a part is defined as training

---

[7] https://www.ibm.com/watson/developercloud/speech-to-text.html.

Table 3. Features of the three corpora used as data set

Corpus:	Dimex100	CIEMPIESS	Radios ecuador
Language:	Latin American Spanish	Latin American Spanish	Latin American Spanish
Country:	Mexico	Mexico	Ecuador
Recording type:	Studio recording	Recordings obtained from a Podcast	Files obtained from radio recordings
Audio duration (approximate):	6 h 10 min (6000 audios)	18 h	1 h 30 min
Sampling frequency:	44.1 kHz	16 kHz	44.1 kHz
Audio format:	WAV	SPH (PCM)	WAV
Recording environment:	Noise free	Radial transmission	Radial transmission
Characteristics of the speakers:	Mexican speakers between 16 and 36 years old	78 % female speakers, 22 % female speakers	Several radio narrators

set (70%) and another as tests set (30%). For this reason, each corpus is divided separately:

- DIMEX100: Approximately 4 h with 50 min for training and 1 h with 15 min for testing.
- CIEMPIESS: In [9], the creators define within the corpus a test set and a training set.
- Radios Ecuador: Approximately 1 h for training and 20 min for tests.

Evaluation of Results. Two measures were proposed to evaluate the speech-to-text transformation component, which was executed in a computer with basic resources (macOS Sierra version 10.12, Intel Core i5 2,9 GHz and 16 GB DDR3). Word Error Rate (WER) is applied to measure the accuracy of the selected speech recognition tools. WER can be computed using Eq. 2 as given in [2].

$$WER = \frac{S + D + I}{N} \tag{2}$$

Where:

S is the number of words substituted in the transcription.
D is the number of words deleted or omitted.
I is the number of words inserted that do not belong to the transcription.
N is the number of words in the reference ($N = S + D + C$).

The second metric corresponds to the Real-Time Factor (RTF), which measures the speed at which the recognition is performed comparing it with the duration of the recognized speech signal [21]. To measure the RTF, the Eq. 3 is used.

$$RTF = \frac{\text{Decoding audio time}}{\text{Audio duration time}} \tag{3}$$

Table 4 shows the results of the evaluation performed to determine the accuracy of the three tools, CMU Sphinx-4, Kaldi, and HTK. In order to determine the incidence of corpus size in the final results two separated models were trained. The incomplete model formed by the DIMEX100 and CIEMPIESS corpora, reach a maximum value of WER of 29.13%. The complete model is generated by adding a corpus related to Ecuadorian radio broadcast, where it is possible to see the great improvement of the WER. For instance, CMU Sphinx-4 shown a reduction around 20% reaching a WER value of 18.8%.

In the comparison of these models it is possible seen as Kaldi not only has better results in the WER, but also improves the average RTF, reaching a factor of 0.10, allowing to monitor up to 10 streams of audio in real time. Also, Table 4 includes two more indicators that generate an idea of the computer resources that spend every tool. It is evident that there is no reasonable differences between amount of memory and CPU use, because tests were performed over samples whose average length is 3.85 s. If the ASR system requires to work with samples that could spent more resources, CMU Sphinx could be a good option due to it has the optimal configuration for low memory-need (around 34% less that both Kaldi and HTK).

Table 5 presents the results of comparing the two services on the same data set. Underprivileged IBM account does not provide a measure of time or another performance indicator. Furthermore, IBM recognizer is a Cloud service and its configuration is not comparable with Kaldy system that was evaluated in a computer with basic resources (Intel Core i5 2,9 GHz and 16 GB DDR3). However,

Table 4. Comparison among CMU Sphinx, Kaldi and HTK

Speech recognition tool		CMU Sphinx-4	Kaldi	HTK
WER	Language model incomplete	38.99%	29.13%	30.27%
	Language model complete	18.80%	13.58%	14.76%
Average RTF		0.28	0.1079	0.425
Average memory per file (MB)		36.25	55.13	53.60
Average % CPU		99.63	99.24	99.83

Table 5. WER comparison between proposed system and IBM recognition service

	Proposed recognition service	Speech to text IBM service
WER	10.83%	16.49%

an overall evaluation could be made by comparing the WER between these two tools. It can be observed that the service implemented in this work reach a lower WER, although both services offer an acceptable precision. It should be mentioned that the IBM recognizer shows several complex aspects such as the generation of the required training models, and does not give access to a customization in the service configuration, making it difficult to perform tasks such as inclusion of words from context to vocabulary of the recognizer. In addition, the IBM language model was not trained with the actual transcriptions data set used to evaluate the recognizers, it can be deduced that there must be words outside the vocabulary of the IBM recognizer, which influences in a less precision.

6   Conclusions and Future Work

This article presents an architecture for the execution of a process of extracting information from audio signals through the application of audio segmentation technologies and ASR. The evaluation results of the segmentation algorithms allowed to know that, the approach of segmentation by classification applying models HMM offers a greater precision in its results than the approach of segmentation and classification based on distances. However, it should be noted that the level of precision obtained in [7] could not be reached, presumably because the audios were divided into three types unlike [7] where only two are considered.

The evaluation of the tools shows the influence of the size of the corpus on the accuracy of the system. It is to be expected that as language corpus is mixed the system will have a greater capacity to transcribe sentences since they will be present in the trained models. But this same size of the corpus can be analyzed taking into account its effect in the RTF that if it rises too much can affect the transcription of audios in real time, which is essential in scenarios like media monitoring. Within the implementation of the transcription component, the comparison of the two systems leads us to deduce that the key for that a system to respond properly has to do with the context to be used. While IBM has trained models in English that reaches high accuracy, for Latin American Spanish they are still not precise. The proposed system to improve these levels of precision because it considers corpus related to the context of Ecuadorian broadcasters.

As future lines of research, we see the need to refine the results of audio segmentation by applying some of the hybrid architectures as proposed in [28]. Another aspect is the implementation of a more extensive corpus that not only consider narratives, but also music or mixtures of these two, focusing the results to make an evaluation of how the size of the corpus influences the speed of response of the algorithms.

Acknowledgments. This work is part of the project "Use of semantic technologies to analyze multimedia content broadcasted by digital television" supported by the Research Direction of the University of Cuenca.

References

1. Alumäe, T.: Full-duplex speech-to-text system for Estonian. In: Baltic HLT, pp. 3–10 (2014)
2. Anusuya, M.A., Katti, S.K.: Speech recognition by machine, A review. IJCSIS **2**, 181–205 (2010)
3. Bachu, R., Kopparthi, S., Adapa, B., Barkana, B.: Separation of voiced and unvoiced using zero crossing rate and energy of the speech signal. In: American Society for Engineering Education (ASEE) Zone Conference Proceedings, pp. 1–7 (2008)
4. Bietti, A., Bach, F., Cont, A.: An online EM algorithm in hidden (semi-) markov models for audio segmentation and clustering. In: International Conference on Acoustics, Speech and Signal Processing, pp. 1881–1885. IEEE (2015)
5. Castán, D., Ortega, A., Miguel, A., Lleida, E.: Audio segmentation-by-classification approach based on factor analysis in broadcast news domain. EURASIP J. Audio Speech Music Process. **2014**(1), 1–13 (2014)
6. Gaida, C., Lange, P., Petrick, R., Proba, P., Malatawy, A., Suendermann-Oeft, D.: Comparing open-source speech recognition toolkits. In: NLPCS 2014 (2014)
7. Giannakopoulos, T.: pyAudioAnalysis: an open-source python library for audio signal analysis. PloS one **10**(12), e0144610 (2015)
8. Guinaudeau, C., Gravier, G., Sébillot, P., et al.: Improving ASR-based topic segmentation of TV programs with confidence measures and semantic relations. In: INTERSPEECH, pp. 1365–1368 (2010)
9. Hernández-Mena, C.D., Herrera-Camacho, J.: CIEMPIESS: a new open-sourced Mexican Spanish radio corpus. In: LREC, vol. 14, pp. 371–375 (2014)
10. Huggins-Daines, D., Kumar, M., Chan, A., Black, A.W., Ravishankar, M., Rudnicky, A.I.: Pocketsphinx: a free, real-time continuous speech recognition system for hand-held devices. In: International Conference on Acoustics, Speech and Signal Processing, vol. 1. IEEE (2006)
11. Imai, T., Kobayashi, A., Sato, S., Homma, S., Onoe, K., Kobayakawa, T.: Speech recognition for subtitling Japanese live broadcasts. In: Proceedings of ICA, pp. 165–168 (2004)
12. Këpuska, V., Bohouta, G.: Comparing speech recognition systems (Microsoft API, Google API and CMU Sphinx). Int. J. Eng. Res. Appl. **7**, 20–24 (2017)
13. Kulkarni, A., Iyer, D., Sridharan, S.R.: Audio segmentation. In: IEEE International Conference on Data Mining, ICDM, pp. 105–110 (2001)
14. Lamel, L., Gauvain, J., Adda, G., Adda-Decker, M., Canseco-Rodriguez, L., Chen, L., Galibert, O., Messaoudi, A., Schwenk, H.: Speech transcription in multiple languages. In: IEEE International Conference on Acoustics, Speech, and Signal Processing, ICASSP, pp. 757–760 (2004)
15. Li, J., Deng, L., Haeb-Umbach, R., Gong, Y.: Chapter 2 – fundamentals of speech recognition. In: Li, J., Deng, L., Haeb-Umbach, R., Gong, Y. (eds.) Robust Automatic Speech Recognition, pp. 9–40. Academic Press, Waltham (2016)
16. Moffat, D., Ronan, D., Reiss, J.D.: An evaluation of audio feature extraction toolboxes. In: Proceedings of 18th International Conference on Digital Audio Effects (2015)
17. NeoSpeech: Top 5 open source speech recognition toolkits (2016). http://blog.neospeech.com/top-5-open-source-speech-recognition-toolkits
18. Niculescu, A., de Jong, F.: Development of a speech recognition system for Spanish broadcast news. Technical report, Centre for Telematics and Information Technology, University of Twente (2008)

19. Pikrakis, A., Giannakopoulos, T., Theodoridis, S.: A speech/music discriminator of radio recordings based on dynamic programming and bayesian networks. IEEE Trans. Multimedia **10**(5), 846–857 (2008)
20. Pineda, L.A., Pineda, L.V., Cuétara, J., Castellanos, H., López, I.: DIMEx100: a new phonetic and speech corpus for Mexican Spanish. In: Lemaître, C., Reyes, C.A., González, J.A. (eds.) IBERAMIA 2004. LNCS, vol. 3315, pp. 974–983. Springer, Heidelberg (2004). doi:10.1007/978-3-540-30498-2_97
21. Plátek, O., Jurcıcek, F.: Free on-line speech recogniser based on Kaldi ASR toolkit producing word posterior lattices. In: Proceedings of the 15th Annual Meeting of the Special Interest Group on Discourse and Dialogue (SIGDIAL), pp. 108–112 (2014)
22. Povey, D., Ghoshal, A., Boulianne, G., Burget, L., Glembek, O., Goel, N., Hannemann, M., Motlicek, P., Qian, Y., Schwarz, P., et al.: The Kaldi speech recognition toolkit. In: IEEE 2011 Workshop on Automatic Speech Recognition and Understanding. IEEE Signal Processing Society (2011)
23. Ranchal, R., Taber-Doughty, T., Guo, Y., Bain, K., Martin, H., Robinson, J.P., Duerstock, B.S.: Using speech recognition for real-time captioning and lecture transcription in the classroom. IEEE Trans. Learn. Technol. **6**(4), 299–311 (2013)
24. Robert-Ribes, J.: On the use of automatic speech recognition for TV captioning. In: ICSLP (1998)
25. Schneider, D., Tschöpel, S., Schwenninger, J.: Social recommendation using speech recognition: sharing TV scenes in social networks. In: WIAMIS, pp. 1–4 (2012)
26. Stolcke, A., et al.: SRILM-an extensible language modeling toolkit. In: Interspeech (2002)
27. Stüker, S., Fügen, C., Kraft, F., Wölfel, M.: The ISL 2007 English speech transcription system for European parliament speeches. In: INTERSPEECH, pp. 2609–2612 (2007)
28. Theodorou, T., Mporas, I., Fakotakis, N.: An overview of automatic audio segmentation. Int. J. Inf. Technol. Comput. Sci. (IJITCS) **6**(11), 1 (2014)
29. Thompson, C.: Open source toolkits for speech recognition. Looking at CMU Sphinx, Kaldi, HTK, Julius, and ISIP (2017). https://svds.com/open-source-toolkits-speech-recognition
30. Varela, A., Cuayáhuitl, H., Nolazco-Flores, J.A.: Creating a Mexican Spanish version of the CMU Sphinx-III speech recognition system. In: Sanfeliu, A., Ruiz-Shulcloper, J. (eds.) CIARP 2003. LNCS, vol. 2905, pp. 251–258. Springer, Heidelberg (2003). doi:10.1007/978-3-540-24586-5_30
31. Young, S., Evermann, G., Gales, M., Hain, T., Kershaw, D., Liu, X., Moore, G., Odell, J., Ollason, D., Povey, D., et al.: The HTK Book (v3. 4). Cambridge University, Cambridge (2006)
32. Zahid, S., Hussain, F., Rashid, M., Yousaf, M.H., Habib, H.A.: Optimized audio classification and segmentation algorithm by using ensemble methods. Math. Probl. Eng. **2015**, 11 (2015)

Automatic Computation of Poetic Creativity in Parallel Corpora

Daniel F. Zuñiga[2], Teresa Amido[3], and Jorge E. Camargo[1(✉)]

[1] Laboratory for Advanced Computational Science and Engineering Research,
Universidad Antonio Nariño, Bogotá, Colombia
jorgecamargo@uan.edu.co
[2] Universidad Nacional de Colombia, Sede Bogotá, Colombia
dfzunigah@unal.edu.co
[3] Universitat des Saarlandes, Saarbrücken, Germany
t.amido@mx.uni-saarland.de

Abstract. Text representation has been broadly studied in information retrieval and natural language processing. The process of building a good representation is an aspect to consider because it captures the most important aspects of the text in order to support other tasks such as classification, sentiment analysis, and automatic translation. The most common techniques used to represent text are based on the hand-crafted features paradigm: the bag of words model, n-grams analysis, and recently, the learned-features paradigm: the word-to-vec model and other deep learning techniques. However, both of them need of a large corpus to extract general structure to represent each document. In this paper we present a method to represent small poetry parallel corpora, in which a set of features are extracted from the poem to build a vector representation of the poem. We use this representation to compute poetic creativity. We evaluated the proposed method in a bilingual corpus English → Spanish, being the source language English and the target one Spanish. Up to best of our knowledge, this is the first attempt to automatically measure poetic creativity in parallel corpora.

Keywords: Poetic creativity · Poem representation · Automatic translation

1 Introduction

Creativity can be seen as a feature of originality, flexibility and thought-fluidity. In the framework of translation studies, especially in poetry, the notion of creativity is considered as an inherent feature of the translation process [4]. A poet uses its creativity to transcreate the text in the target language, taking into account both verbal and non-verbal content [7].

Spite of the marked tradition of creativity translation, mainly related to literary texts [3,5,6], there is not a wide variety of studies which focus on how to measure it. The few that exist made some attempts to deal with the problem

© Springer International Publishing AG 2017
A. Solano and H. Ordoñez (Eds.): CCC 2017, CCIS 735, pp. 710–720, 2017.
DOI: 10.1007/978-3-319-66562-7_50

but it does not exist a specific process model to describe it [2]. In this field of research some measuring manual methods have been proposed to measure how measurable creativity is, being the creativity test the most remarkable one (ibid).

Measuring creativity becomes a difficult task mainly due to the subjectivity of the concept itself which may increase when trying to measure it in poetry translation. How to identify how much of the original poem was preserved in the target language after the translation process or find out exactly how much of the original text has been adapted linguistically and culturally to the target audience are tasks that have already been dealt with in a manual and philosophical way. However we think it may be interesting to find out an automatic method to measure creativity in such a kind of translation.

In this work we propose an automatic method to measure poetic creativity. The proposed method is based on information retrieval techniques (this approach was already used in other works [9] which were used as start point for this investigation), in which a set of poems (original and translated) are processed to extract features that are used to measure how much of poem elements are preserved in the target language. We evaluated the proposed method in a set of original and translated poems.

Up to the best of our knowledge this is an attempt to use computer science to automatically measure poetic creativity. We are working with a bilingual corpus (EN>ES) of poems and their translation. In this first attempt the poems to analyze are part of the work Leaves of Grass of the north-american poet Walt Whitman and its translation into Spanish, *Hojas de hierba* - done by the argentinian poet and translator *Jorge Luis Borges*, who also theorized about the creativity in the translation of poetry. In this first attempt, we focused on the possible automatic methods to apply, trying to find out solutions which may give us a finally method to measure creativity. However linguistic aspects such as phonetic differences among languages have not been taken in consideration up the date. This will be dealt with in future experiments.

The rest of the paper is organized as follows. Section 2 describes the proposed method, Sect. 3 presents the experimental setup, Sect. 4 presents the obtained results, and finally, Sect. 4 concludes the paper.

2 Proposed Method

In this section the proposed method is presented, which is composed of three stages: feature extraction stage, feature vector representation, creativity computation, and analysis. Figure 1 shows an illustration of these stages.

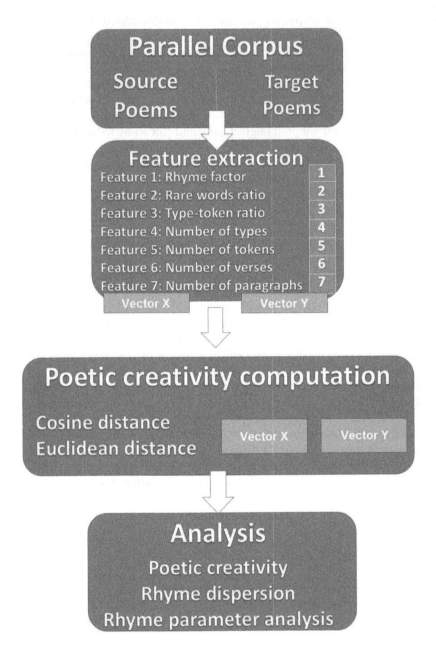

Fig. 1. Overview of the proposed method to calculate poetic creativity in a parallel corpus. In the first step a set of features are extracted from the original and translated poems. In the second step poetic creativity is calculated using the obtained vectors. In the last step, creativity and rhyme are analyzed to evaluate the poetic creativity of the poet.

2.1 Feature Extraction Process

Each poem is analyzed to automatically extract a set of features using the textual content of the poem. A set of seven features were extracted as it is described in next sections.

Rhyme Factor. After erasing punctuation marks, we use a Rhyme-Length Parameter to identify rhyme in the poem. Rhyme is represented as a boolean vector where 1 indicates the existence of rhyme and 0 absence of rhyme. These values are then computed as follows to obtain the rhyme factor:

$$Rhyme\ Factor = \frac{1}{N} \sum_{i=1}^{N} V_i, \tag{1}$$

where V is a verse than rhymes with other verse, and N is the number of verses of the poem.

Number of Types. This feature measures the number of words (tokens) used only once in the poem. This is a particular case of the rare words ratio.

Number of Tokens. The total number of words used in the poem.

Rare Words Ratio. This features is an indicator of the vocabulary richness of the poem. It is computed as the number of rare words.

$$VR = \frac{1}{Number\ of\ types} \sum_{i=1}^{N} Hapax \sum_{i=1}^{N} Bis \sum_{i=1}^{N} Tris \qquad VR \in [0,1], \tag{2}$$

where N is the number of verses of the poem, *Hapax* are words repeated only once, *Bis* are those repeated twice and *Tris* the ones repeated three times.

Type-Token Ratio. This feature is other indicator of the vocabulary richness of the poem. It is calculated as follows,

$$VR = \frac{Number\ of\ types}{Number\ of\ tokens} * 100 \qquad VR \in [0,100]. \tag{3}$$

Number of Paragraphs. Using a simple computational method, the number of paragraphs are equal to the summation of the number of double line breaks in the poem.

$$Number\ of\ paragraphs = \sum_{i=1}^{N} P_i, \tag{4}$$

where P_i is a double line break and N is the number of verses of the poem.

Number of Verses. Are calculated by the summation of all lines minus the number of paragraphs plus one,

$$Number\ of\ verses = \sum_{i=1}^{N} V_i + (1 - Number\ of\ paragraphs), \quad (5)$$

where V_i is a verse of the poem and N is the total number of verses of the poem.

2.2   Feature Vector Representation

The before mentioned set of features are used to build a vector representation of the poem, that is, each component of the vector x corresponds to each feature as follows,

$$x = [feature_1, feature_2, feature_3, ..., feature_N], \quad (6)$$

where N is 7 to this set of features, but it can be extended to other features.

The resulting vector x is normalized using the L_1 norm as follows,

$$||x||_{L_1} = \frac{x_i}{\sum x_i} \quad (7)$$

where x_i is the i-th feature.

It is worth noting that these set of features are independent of the language. That is to say, they are not dependent of characteristics such as grammar, length and layout of the poem, etc. The representation of a poem in a origin language (source) can be compared to the translated version in other language (target). Therefore, we can use this vector representation to compare a poem in any source language to any target language.

2.3   Poetic Creativity Computation

We propose two ways of calculating poetic creativity. The first one is based on the cosine function, and the second one is based on the euclidean distance, both using the vector representation of the poems.

Creativity Measure Based on the Cosine Function. Being x the poem on the original language and y the translated poem, creativity can be computed by the cosine distance as follows,

$$C_{cosine}(x, y) = 1 - \frac{x \cdot y}{||x|| \cdot ||y||} \quad C \in [0, 1], \quad (8)$$

where x is the vector representation of the origin poem, and y is the vector representation of the target (translated) poem.

Creativity Measure Based on the Euclidean Distance. Being x the poem on the original language and y the translated poem, creativity can be computed by the euclidean distance as follows,

$$C_{euclidean}(x,y) = \sqrt{\sum_{i=1}^{n}(x_i - y_i)^2} \quad C \in [0,1], \tag{9}$$

where x is the vector representation of the origin poem, and y is the vector representation of the target (translated) poem.

It is worth noting that poetic creativity C measures how much a poet preserved important aspects of the poem after the translation process. A value close to 0 indicates that the poet does not preserve much relevant features of the original poem, and on the other hand, a value close to 1 indicates that the poem preserved most of the poem features after the translation.

3   Experimental Setup

To evaluated the proposed method we used a set of poems that are part of the work *Leaves of Grass* of the north-american poet *Walt Whitman*, which were published in 1855 and its translation into Spanish, *Hojas de hierba* - done by the argentinian poet and translator *Jorge Luis Borges*.

The dataset is composed of 67 poems originally written in English and its corresponding translations. The English versions were extracted from e-book publicly available on the web[1], and the translated versions were extracted from the PDF e-book published on *Biblioteca Virtual Universal*[2].

We developed a set of algorithms in Python to implement the proposed method. These algorithms were executed in a Core i5 machine with 8 Gb of RAM.

4   Results

This section presents the obtained results. In the first part we present results for poetic creativity and in the second part an analysis focused on the poem rhyme.

4.1   Poetic Creativity Results

Tables 1 and 2 present the obtained poetic creativity for the 67 poems. The poem 9 "To You" obtained the highest poetic creativity, 0.17 and 0.01 in terms of cosine and euclidean distance, respectively. On the contrary, the lowest poetic creativity value is obtained in the poem 57 "To a Western Boy", with 0.0001 and 0.016, in terms of cosine and euclidean distance, respectively.

---

[1] http://www.gutenberg.org/ebooks/1322.
[2] www.biblioteca.org.ar/libros/157154.pdf.

Cosine distance was implemented due to its wide implementation as an indicator of cohesion of clusters of texts. Euclidean distance has some disadvantages as dissimilarity metric because of its sensitivity to high values, so after being normalized it was used as a reference to compare.

4.2   Rhyme Analysis

One of the most interesting features extracted from the poem is the rhyme. Preserve the rhyme in the translation process is very difficult because the poet has to find out words in the target language that preserve the source words meaning and, at the same time, these words have to rhyme. In Fig. 2 we plot the complete set of poems using its rhyme factor.

Poems close to the diagonal indicate that they poet preserve as much as possible the rhyme in the translation version of the poem. For instance, poems 26, 28, 63, 64 and 66 are the poems with maximum similarity in terms of rhyme.

On the contrary, poems far from the diagonal indicate that they do not preserve the original poem rhyme of the source language. For instance, in poems 20 and 47 the poet create rhymes that did not exist in the original versions of the poems.

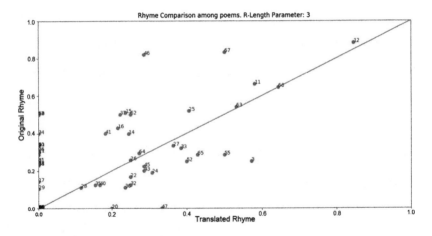

Fig. 2. Rhyme dispersion of the complete set of poems. Poems close to the diagonal indicate that the poet preserve in a high level the rhyme after the translation process.

In Fig. 3 the rhyme factor was analyzed when the parameter of the number of characters at the end of the last word of a verse is increased from 1 to 10. This rhyme factor was computed to all the poems in the source and target languages. It is worth noting that the rhyme factor is higher in the source language than in the target language. This result is not surprising since as it was said, it is very difficult to preserve the rhyme after the translation process.

Table 1. Poetic creativity results for the 67 poems (part 1).

Poem name	C_{cosine}	$C_{euclidean}$
1. One's Self I Sing	0.0043	0.0930
2. To Foreign Lands	0.0003	0.0269
3. Eidolons	0.0026	0.0728
4. Beginning My Studies	0.0023	0.0684
5. To the States	0.0074	0.1219
6. Still Though the One I Sing	0.0009	0.0439
7. Shut Not Your Doors	0.0033	0.0814
8. Poets to Come	0.0004	0.0300
9. **To You**	**0.0146**	**0.1713**
10. Thou Reader	0.0010	0.0450
11. Starting from Paumanok	0.0009	0.0444
12. Song of Myself	0.0010	0.0453
13. To the Garden the World	0.0006	0.0351
14. From Pent-Up Aching Rivers	0.0008	0.0419
15. A Woman Waits for Me	0.0006	0.0347
16. Spontaneous Me	0.0005	0.0319
17. One Hour to Madness and Joy	0.0023	0.0685
18. O Hymen! O Hymenee!	0.0031	0.0789
19. I Am He That Aches with Love	0.0073	0.1210
20. Native Moments	0.0006	0.0370
21. Once I Pass'd Through a Populous City	0.0031	0.0794
22. Facing West from California's Shores	0.0024	0.0706
23. As Adam Early in the Morning	0.0003	0.0271
24. In Paths Untrodden	0.0007	0.0398
25. Scented Herbage of My Breast	0.0008	0.0420
26. Whoever You Are Holding Me Now in Hand	0.0014	0.0542
27. For You, O Democracy	0.0017	0.0590
28. These I Singing in Spring	0.0004	0.0313
29. Not Heaving from My Ribb'd Breast Only	0.0002	0.0228
30. Of the Terrible Doubt of Appearances	0.0012	0.0501
31. The Base of All Metaphysics	0.0018	0.0602
32. Recorders Ages Hence	0.0002	0.02376
33. When I Heard at the Close of the day	0.0011	0.04891
34. Are You the New Person Drawn Toward Me	0.0047	0.09770

Table 2. Poetic creativity results for the 67 poems (part 2).

Poem name	C_{cosine}	$C_{euclidean}$
35. Roots and Leaves Themselves Alone	0.0005	0.0329
36. Not Heat Flames Up and Consumes	0.0023	0.0684
37. Trickle Drops	0.0013	0.0520
38. City of Orgies	0.0006	0.0351
39. Behold This Swarthy Face	0.0067	0.1164
40. I Saw in Louisiana a Live-Oak Growing	0.0024	0.0703
41. To a Stranger	0.0033	0.0817
42. This Moment Yearning and Thoughtful	0.0021	0.0655
43. I Hear It Was Charged Against Me	0.0007	0.0395
44. The Prairie-Grass Dividing	0.0022	0.0666
45. When I Persue the Conquer'd Fame	0.0013	0.0527
46. We Two Boys Together Clinging	0.0096	0.1389
47. A Promise to California	0.0029	0.0772
48. Here the Frailest Leaves of Me	0.0009	0.0442
49. No Labor-Saving Machine	0.0053	0.1032
50. A Glimpse	0.0043	0.0934
51. A Leaf for Hand in Hand	0.0023	0.0678
52. Earth, My Likeness	0.0015	0.0548
53. I Dream'd in a Dream	0.0021	0.0650
54. What Think You I Take My Pen in Hand	0.0023	0.0683
55. To the East and to the West	0.0014	0.0534
56. Sometimes with One I Love	0.0064	0.1137
57. **To a Western Boy**	**0.0001**	**0.0163**
58. Fast Anchor'd Eternal O Love!	0.0019	0.0624
59. Among the Multitude	0.0024	0.0696
60. O You Whom I Often and Silently Come	0.0007	0.0398
61. That Shadow My Likeness	0.0010	0.0456
62. Full of Life Now	0.0008	0.0401
63. Salut au Monde!	0.0009	0.0439
64. Europe[The 72d and 73d Years of These States]	0.0008	0.0401
65. Gods	0.0026	0.0726
66. When Lilacs Last in the Dooryard Bloom'd	0.0005	0.0327
67. O Captain! My Captain!	0.0011	0.0470

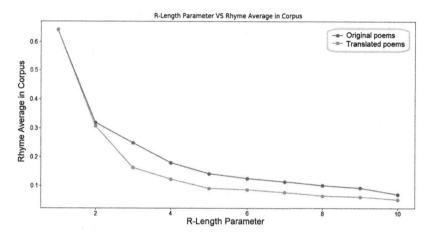

Fig. 3. Analysis of poem rhyme varying the amount of characters of the last word of a verse used to calculate rhyme.

5   Conclusions and Future Work

This paper presented a method to compute poetic creativity in parallel corpora. The method was evaluated in a set of 67 poems written in English and its translated versions in Spanish. The main contributions of the paper is twofold. First, we propose a vector representation of the poems that is language independent, which can be applied to poems written in any language. Second, we propose a method to compute poetic creativity, which tries to measure how much creativity a poet uses to translate a poem preserving as much as possible the characteristics of the poem.

As it was argued in the introduction section of this paper, recent directions of text representation are focused on methods that learn the representation from large volume of data. However, parallel corpora is generally small and very difficult to acquire. Therefore, the proposed method, although is based on handcrafted features, is more feasible in this context.

Although the results, the current method analyzes few characteristics, additional features may lead to a more accurate analysis so as future work we want to extract more features that allows to get additional information of the poem. We will also want to include phonetic features that allow to address linguistic aspects such as phonetic differences among languages. This aspect is very important in the process of compute the rhyme factor of a poem. We also want to experiment the proposed method using other parallel corpora.

References

1. Bayer-Hohenwarter, G.: Die Entwicklung translatorischer Kreativitt. TransComp, Universitt Graz, Austria (cfr. supra 1.1, infra 2.1.6.3.) (2011)
2. Bayer-Hohenwarter, G.: Comparing translational creativity scores of students and professionals: flexible problem-solving and/or fluent routine behaviour? In: Gpferich, S., Alves, F., Mees, I.M. (eds.) New Approaches in Translation Process Research. Copenhagen Studies in Language, vol. 39, pp. 83–111. Samfundslitteratur, Copenhagen (2010)
3. Jones, F.: Unlocking the black box: researching poetry translation processes. In: Perteghella, M., Loffredi, E. (eds.) Translation and Creativity. Perspectives on Creative Writing and Translation Studies, London, New York, pp. 59–74. Continuum (2006)
4. Kumaul, P.: Types of creative translating. In: Chesterman, A., San Salvador, N.G., Gambier, Y. (eds.) Translation in Context. Selected Papers from the EST Congress, Granada 1998, Benjamins, Amsterdam (Benjamins translation library 39), pp. 117–126 (2000)
5. Pendlebury, D.: Creative Translation. Antony Rowe, Eastbourne (2005)
6. Perteghella, M., Loffredi, E. (eds.): Translation and Creativity. Perspectives on Creative Writing and Translation Studies. Continuum, London, New York (2006)
7. Rike, S.: Transcreation - a service to be provided by translators and an area of research for translation studies? In: EST Newsletter, vol. 44, pp. 8–9 (2014)
8. Thom, S.: Creativity in Translation. An Interdisciplinary Approach (doctoral dissertation). Univ. of Salzburg, Department of Anglistics, Salzburg (2003)
9. Delmonte, R.: Computing Poetry. Venezia Ca' Foscari University, Department of Language Studies (2013)

Data Fusion Applied to Biometric Identification – A Review

J.C. Zapata[1], C.M. Duque[1], Y. Rojas-Idarraga[1], M.E. Gonzalez[1],
J.A. Guzmán[2], and M.A. Becerra Botero[1,2(✉)]

[1] Institución Universitaria Salazar y Herrera, Medellín, Colombia
migb2b@gmail.com
[2] Universidad Nacional de Colombia, Medellín, Colombia

Abstract. There is a growing interest in data fusion oriented to identification and authentication from biometric traits and physiological signals, because of its capacity for combining multiple sources and multimodal analysis allows improving the performance of these systems. Thus, we considered necessary make an analytical review on this domain. This paper summarizes the state of the art of the data fusion oriented to biometric authentication and identification, exploring its techniques, benefits, advantages, disadvantages, and challenges.

Keywords: Biometric · Data fusion · Multimodal systems · Physiological signals · Signal processing

1 Introduction

The biometrics systems are used for access control and identification of human beings, and they are based on different physiological measures such as physical traits (PT), physiological signals, Deoxyribonucleic acid (DNA), among others. This type of identity recognition is very attractive since each person possesses different physical features that cannot be copied easily [5]. Nowadays, it is applied widely to assure computers, smartphones, communication systems, buildings, and confidential information, among others. However, the multiple techniques of individual identification had become vulnerable to falsification such as the identification system based on digital fingerprint [1, 2], which has been used for several years, but it can be falsified with different methods [4], putting at risk the legal and financial integrity of an individual.

Although some physical features are hard to imitate/duplicate, it is not impossible. Therefore, different researchers have proposed the fusion or combination of multiple physiological signals (PS) and traits with the goal of providing major sturdiness to the system [6–34]. However, the biometric is an open research area focused on the type and quantity of the data, algorithms, and functionality modes and they are classified by 3 categories of biometric modalities as follows: *(i)* biological, it is based on the analysis of data obtained from DNA; *(ii)* behavioral, this is based on the analysis of the behavior of the individual; and *(iii)* morphology data, they are based on specific physical features that are permanent and unique to every individual (e.g. face or fingerprints) [1].

© Springer International Publishing AG 2017
A. Solano and H. Ordoñez (Eds.): CCC 2017, CCIS 735, pp. 721–733, 2017.
DOI: 10.1007/978-3-319-66562-7_51

In this paper, we discuss PS and traits applied to biometry authentication together with different combinations among them (i.e. multiple signals and multiple traits) using data fusion techniques. The review was carried out on Scopus and Web of Sciences database based on these search criteria: *(i)* (biometric) and ("physiological signals"); and *(ii)* (("data fusion") or ("information fusion") and (biometric)) or ("physiological signals"). The selected papers were reported between years 2008 and 2017 in journals of quartile 1 and quartile 2 principally.

2 Physiological Signals and Traits Applied in Biometrics Systems

Nowadays, the use of PS has gone from being used only by medical diagnostics, to convert into a very important tool for security demonstrating the capability to provide characteristics that allow identified an individual with high precision.

The PS must comply with a series of criteria that is apt in biometric. The criteria are the following: *(i)* the signal must be able to be recollected in any person; *(ii)* singularity, the signal must able to distinguish different individuals; *(iii)* permanence, the signal must not be abruptly altered in the time; *(iv)* sturdiness against attacks, it must not be imitated easily [35].

Figure 1 shows a summarized taxonomy of the traits and PS reported for biometric authentication and/or identification.

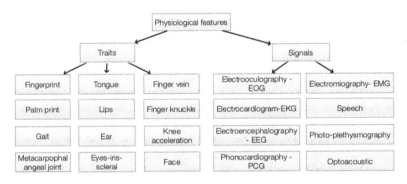

Fig. 1. Taxonomy of physiological signals and physiological traits applied in biometric.

Table 1 presents the results of the review regarding the use of the signals and traits including the type of modality. 56 biometric studies based on unimodal and multimodal modalities (i.e unimodal is the application only one signal or trait and multimodal is the application of two or more signals and PT). Multiple signals and traits have been studied independently (monomodal authentication or identification) such as: Electroencephalogram-EEG, Electrocardiogram-EKG, phonocardiography-PCG, electrooculography-EOG, Electromyogram-EMG, photo-plethysmography-PPG, fingerprint, palmprint, periocular, Laser Doppler Vibrometry-LDV, Speech, Finger Knuckle Print-FKP, finger vein, tongue, Iris, face, ear, lips, eyes, gait, and Knee

Table 1. Monomodal and multimodal biometric studies

Multimodal	References	Monomodal	References
EEG - EOG	[1]	EEG	[2–6]
EKG - EMG	[8]	EKG	[9–16]
EKG - PCG	[17]	FKP	[18, 19]
EKG, face, fingerprint	[20]	Iris	[21–23]
PCG and EKG	[24]	Face	[25–28]
EKG and physical activity	[29]	PCG	[30]
EEG and face	[31]	Palmprint	[32, 33]
Face and palmprint	[34]	Periocular	[35]
Face and iris	[36–39]	Fingerprint	[40–42]
Face and ear	[43]	Tongue	[44]
Face and lips	[45]	Gait	[46]
EKG and LDV	[47]	Scleral	[48]
Fingerprint and palmprint	[49]	KnA	[50]
		Ear	[51]
		Eyes	[52]
		LDV	[53]
		Finger vein	[54]
		Speech	[55]
		PPG	[56]

Acceleration-knA. Other studies are based on combination or fusion of multiples signals together with multiple traits (multimodal authentication or identification) are evidenced.

2.1 Physiological Signals Applied in Biometrics

The EKG and PCG are noninvasive measures and they take heart information, particularly the EKG takes information about heart electrical activity. This signal is acquired situating electrodes in the thoracic zone, with the purpose to collect the signals produced by myocardium, while the PCG signals are based on the analysis of the features of the frequency of the cardiac sounds, these sounds are presented in systole (S1) and diastole (S2) [30, 31]. The condition of the atria, ventricles and heart valves among other, each of these characteristics mentioned are different for each individual when both characteristics are used at the same time we get a lot of information from the heart. In [31] is fused both types of signals obtaining a lower error rate in comparison to the error obtained with the individual signals.

The EEG signals are noninvasive too, and they are usually recorded from the surface of scalp [5]. These signals are split into five frequency bands as follows: Delta (δ) 0.5–4 Hz, Theta (θ) 4–8 Hz, Alpha (α) 8–14 Hz, Beta (β) 14–30 Hz y Gamma (γ) more of 30 Hz [6]. EEG signals can be a great option for biometric identification due to that the brain electrical activity is unique in each individual and besides closely related with the visual, mood, auditory stimuli and in general any stimulus experienced by the person. Therefore is necessary to consider that the cerebral response to any of these stimuli is different for each individual causing that EEG signals are difficult of supplant and get, therefore this signals are practical in biometrics.

Others signals have been less reported in the biometric area such as EOG signals, which consists in the registration of potential difference existing between cornea and retina for ocular movements detecting [55, 56]. Although it is possible to get relevant information about an individual, it is very difficult to implement because it is uncomfortable for the participant since the electrodes located on both sides of the eyes, above and below of these collect the potentials generated from the movement of eyeballs [56]. The EKG, EEG, EOG and PCG have very important characteristics for their use in biometrics since they are not easily accessible and also provide reliable information of the individual.

2.2 Physiological Trait Applied to Biometrics

Figure 2 shows images of the physiological traits reported in the literature, even so, have characteristics quite promising in the recognition of people. These images correspond from left to right to Finger knuckle [17], finger vein [46], lips [44], tongue [47], metacarpophalangeal [57], and gait recognition [48] respectively. The more popular trait nowadays is the fingerprint. It is highly used in personal authentication by the well-known fact that each individual has a unique fingerprint and its acquisition highly easy and cheap [58]. Fingerprint refers to the patterns located on the fingertips. On the other hand, the hands have a lot amount of folds in the knuckles which are used in recognition, this method is named finger knuckle (FKP) and it is based on capture of image around surface of phalangeal joint of the finger [18, 59], whereas, the identification based on patterns in the Metacarpophalangeal joint (MPJs), consists in the obtaining of patterns of the rear surface of the hand, given that this zone presents many lines and folds that allow discriminating a person of other. The MJP recognition offers a promising and robust alternative for authentication of identity [57], although the advantage of these methods is the high quantity of information available, such as lines, forms, and patterns, which are different for each individual, a difficulty in FKP and MJP recognition are the false rejects due to the variation of finger knuckle position on the take of the image [17].

Fig. 2. Physiological traits applied in biometrics

In [46] was proposed a verification system using the finger vein as a biometric feature in response to high vulnerability registered in biometric systems based on the fingerprint. Finger vein recognition consists of locating a beam in the finger, which makes visible the veins in this zone. The patterns of the veins are considered an interesting trait, given that this patterns not easily affordable and different for each person. Blood's temperature and volume, and the incorrect positioning of the surface to analyze affect this feature.

Recently, the gait recognition has been studied in biometric, it is based on gait biomechanics to extract own features of each person. One of its advantages more marked is the possibility of getting hundreds of samples of the cycle of gait in few minutes. This feature is significant given that the success of the design and validation of a pattern recognition system depend to a large degree of the sample size, but also has some challenges such as the clothes of the subject, sensibility to environment variations, angle camera capture and distance between the subject and the camera, which makes the gait recognition systems a difficult task to carry out in the real environment [48–50].

Another biometric trait is the lips, given that is an important feature of the human face. The lips features are geometric simple features based on the contour of these, they are can interpret as multiple spatial thickness and height from of mass center [44]. To be a trait captured by images it presents the same difficulty than previous features, as the incorrect positioning of the area of interest. Also, comes the question of whether it is possible to get a good rate of recognition when the lips are in movement.

The tongue is a trait, which has been very little studied but has features very interesting in biometric identification; it has used dynamic and static features obtained from the tongue. Within of the dynamic features are the texture, geometry, thickness and cracks. All obtained from the image but as is well known all system is exposed to attacks and eventually the system could not be able to differentiate image of a living person and a dead. Therefore, the researchers have raised the need for performing the detection of vitality with the last purpose of securing that the input patterns are not coming from an inanimate object. The dynamic features refer to obtaining of patterns related continuous movement and involuntary of the tongue, is an excellent dynamic firm for biometric. Thanks to all these features, the tongue is used as a physiological trait in biometric [47]. Finally, we had summarized the advantages and disadvantages of PS and traits applied to biometric in Table 2.

Table 2. Traits and physiological signals advantages and disadvantages

Signal/Trait	Advantages	Disadvantages
EKG	Highly reliable source. -It provides too precise features about of electrical activity and physiological of an individual. -The research performed of this signal report high performance. -Difficulty to reproduce EKG signals artificially [9]. -It can easily fuse with others signal [20]	One of the great difficulties encountered in the literature is the lack of acceptance by the user since it is quite uncomfortable its implementation at the physical level [16]. -Few studies on cardiac signals with any medical condition [57]. -Body posture affects cardiac signals [13]

(continued)

Table 2. (*continued*)

Signal/Trait	Advantages	Disadvantages
Fingerprint	Ease in acquiring the signal. -High user acceptance. -It is the most widely used biometric trait today [58]	-Susceptible to external factors [41] -Fingerprints can be replaced using fingerprints generated artificially [40, 49]
EEG	It is very difficult to imitate signal. Brain electrical activity varies from one person to another. -The capacity of register the neuron electrical activity since the scalp [2]. EEG shows greater security because they are less likely to be generated artificially [1]	They are complex and irregular signals, which are easily contaminated by external interference [4, 6]. -Difficulty in retrieving the sources of neuronal activity, due to its low spatial resolution [2]. -Published studies on biometrics based on this signal used medical equipment of high cost [59]. -Participants reported discomfort since it is necessary to apply on scalp neck gel to improve conduction between electrodes [59]
PCG	They have individual characteristics that can be considered for use in biometrics [30]	For the acquisition of these signals are susceptible to noise [60]
EOG	This signals are low cost and aren't invasive [61]	The electrodes used for the acquirement of the signals can present instability to eye flicker [62]. -The signals are highly affected by noises on the environment [61]
Finger vein	Low computational complexity. -The pattern of the finger vein it is not exposed to another equipment or people in ordinary situations. -The size of the device that acquires the image is small	It requires a full finger image for getting a template
Lips	Easy acquisition and obtainment of lips characteristics. -It is possible to extract the outline when the person has beard or mustache	The image of lips can not be acquired when the lip is moving
MPJs	Easy acquisition and lots of information from a single image	The trait is very exposed by which can be easily falsified
Tongue	It is an excellent dynamic firm for biometric. Thanks to all these features [44]	The system would not be able to identify the image of a living person and a dead one [44]
FKP	The area of the knuckle has many lines and folds difficult to falsify [63]	The acquisition device is very big and hand must always be in the same position [18, 19]
Gait recognition	The gait is not easily imitable and it is unique to every person [46]	In the recognition, the light affects the results another disadvantage is that the clothing may affect the results [46]

3   Multimodal Systems

The human interaction is considered a natural multimodal process and contains deep physiological and psychological expressions. A multimodal biometric system combines two or more signals or traits [65], during years the authentication has been based on monomodal biometric systems, which compare only one characteristic, however, the performance of these systems vary depending on the presence of external factors, such as noise, computational cost, and the quality devices of signal acquisitions. Therefore, in the ultimate years has been introduced the multimodal biometric system with the purpose to overcome the weaknesses of the monomodal biometric system.

3.1   Architecture of Multimodal Processing Systems

In [66] is presented a description of the architecture of the multimodal system (see Fig. 3) Once has been determined the different biometric sources, the next step to follow is the selection of the architecture of the system. In general, there are two mine type of design of multimodal system, serial and parallel

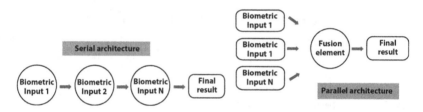

Fig. 3. Multimodal system architecture [66]

(i) serial: Into the serial architecture, also called as cascade architecture, the signal processing is performed in sequence. Therefore the out of first biometric feature influence the transmission second feature; *(ii)* parallel: Into the parallel architecture, the processing of several biometric inputs are independent of one another. Once both signals are processed separately, the results are combined.

4   Data Fusion Systems

Data fusion has notion rather fuzzy that take various interpretations with the applications and specific purposes [67]. However, in this paper the definition adopted in [68] as a set methodologies and technology that possibility the combination synergistic of heterogeneous data of several sources together with new data, content more information than the sum of each source. Through several terms have been reported in the literature such as: decision fusion [69], data combination [70], data aggregation [71] multisensor integration [72], multisensor data fusion [73], and information fusion [74]. In spite that these terms describe the same task, with some variations in terms of application and the type of data that can be difficult to differentiate, which is discussed by [75], Those who used interchangeably term data fusion and information fusion.

Data fusion is considered a very challenging task for several reasons: *(i)* the complexity of data; *(ii)* the processes depend on n variables without being all measurable; *(iii)* in heterogeneous data sets is hard to exploit the advantages of each set and discard the disadvantages [67]. For data fusion are used different techniques such as, the probabilistic, soft-computing, algorithm optimization, among others, whose use (characterization, estimation, aggregation, classification, compression among others) It depends on the type of application and also is necessary consider the advantages and disadvantages of techniques for a proper selection in order to get an effective performance. The Fig. 3, presents the taxonomy of the methodologies of data fusion from which can be categorized data fusion algorithms and are widely discussed in [76].

Particularly in the case of biometrics, the data fusion is highly used a level of signals fusion, level characteristics fusion and level classifiers fusion allowing to improve the performance the identification systems using several PS as reported in [77–79].

Table 3 shows the biometric signals and their respective techniques which got characterization and subsequent classification.

Table 3. Fusion methods used in biometrics

Signals	Data fusion techniques	Ref
EEG-EOG	-Score level fusion: Product, sum, minimum, maximum rules -Bayes decision rule -CCA feature fusion	[1]
EKG-PCG	Feature level fusion	[17]
EKG fingerprint	Weighted sum rule, Computing weights on the equal error rate Computing weights on match scores distributions	[20]
Otoacoustic	MaxScore, SumScore, MulScore, SumRank, MulRank, SumWtRank (classification fusion)	[66]
EKG-physical activity	Feature level fusión, score level fusion	[29]
Palmprint	Feature level fusion: Proposed method (feature fusion)	[32]
Periocular	Score level fusión: Sum rule, weighted sum rule (feature fusion)	[35]
Fingerprint	Transformation-based score fusion: sum rule, mean rule, product rule, max rule, and min rule, Random Subspace of SVM (RSVM), Dempster–Shafer (DS), Dynamic Score Selection (DYN) (feature fusion)	[40]
Face-palmprint	Feature level fusion	[34]
Face	Score level fusion: sum and product rule Decision level fusion - rule OR (logical OR) (classification fusion)	[26]
Face and Iris	Score fusion - product and sum rule Score level fusion - Weighted Sum Rule	[36]
Face and ear	The maximum vote	[43]
Face-iris	Score level fusion: sum rule, Weighted Sum Rule	[37]

(continued)

Table 3. (*continued*)

Signals	Data fusion techniques	Ref
Face and Lips	Feature level fusion Score level fusión: based on the likelihood function	[45]
LDV	Data fusion: This method models the intersession variability by the variance (as the log-normal model) Information fusion: train single session based models and separately extract model-dependent informative components. (feature fusion)	[53]
Face	Information fusión: the sum of the scores, AND, OR of the decisions (feature fusion)	[71]
Tongue	Sum rule, product rule, median rule (feature fusion)	[44]
Ear	Score level fusion: weighted sum rule (classification fusion)	[51]
Finger-palmprint	Feature level fusion	[49]
Palm-print	Weighted sum rule, Neyman –Pearson rule, heuristic rule, proposed heuristic rule. (feature fusion)	[33]
EEG-gyroscope	Score level fusion: Mean, product, maximum and minimum rules Decision level fusión: Logical AND method, Logical OR method	[73]
Scleral	Score level fusion - sum rule, min rule, max rule (feature fusion)	[48]
FKP	Sum rule, min rule (feature fusion)	[19]
Face-Iris	Decision level fusion - weighted sum rule, sum rule	[39]
Face-Iris	Feature level fusion Score level fusión: weighted sum rule	[38]
Eyes	Weights mean fusion (Feature fusion)	[52]

5 Conclusion

This review described advantages, disadvantages, and shortcomings of PS and traits oriented to biometric, when they are mixed the identification error rate can be reduced. Until now, an ideal biometric signal that meets criteria of high security, easy acquisition, low computational cost and that the user feels comfortable during the process has been not achieved yet.

In general, the unimodal systems compared to the multimodal systems, these last report less percentage of error. EEG, EOG, PCG, and EKG, among others, they are considered highly promising in the biometric for different authors since they have a fairly small mistake and it ensures the identified subject this alive. Nevertheless, the accessibility to them is very restricted, but in turn involves high-tech equipment due to the complex acquisition, and eventually generating discomfort to the user. In addition, some problems must be solved how analysis of signals with pathologies, noise ratio of the signals, improving the acquisition devices in together with the development of sensors with special characteristics.

Other physiological biometric parameter or of behavior can be fused to do the authentication more dependable [9]. Although the present work shows that there is great potential in the used of PS to the biometric recognition, is important that the future analysis is performed with a grouping largest set of signals. Respect tot he PT, these have the nowadays challenges of the images recognition such as angle of capture of the image. Besides some recognized methods don't detect if the subject is live. Therefore, studies on areas of the body in movement are necessary. Finally, We pose as challenges the study of other biometric techniques such identification bio-inspired and data fusion architectures for PS and traits processing oriented to biometric authentication.

Acknowledgments. This work was supported by the Doctoral thesis "Data fusion model oriented to information quality" at the "Universidad Nacional of Colombia".

References

1. Abo-Zahhad, M., Ahmed, S.M., Abbas, S.N.: A new multi-level approach to EEG based human authentication using eye blinking. Pattern Recognit. Lett., 1–10 (2015)
2. Ferdowsi, S., Abolghasemi, V., Sanei, S.: A new informed tensor factorization approach to EEG–fMRI fusion. J. Neurosci. Methods **254**, 27–35 (2015)
3. Yeom, S.-K., Suk, H.-I., Lee, S.-W.: Person authentication from neural activity of face-specific visual self-representation. Pattern Recognit. **46**(4), 1159–1169 (2013)
4. Molla, M.K.I., Rabiul Islam, M., Tanaka, T., Rutkowski, T.M.: Artifact suppression from EEG signals using data adaptive time domain filtering. Neurocomputing **97**, 297–308 (2012)
5. Campisi, P., La Rocca, D.: Brain waves for automatic biometric-based user recognition. IEEE Trans. Inf. Forensics Secur. **9**(5), 782–800 (2014)
6. O'Regan, S., Marnane, W.: Multimodal detection of head-movement artefacts in EEG. J. Neurosci. Methods **218**(1), 110–120 (2013)
7. Al-Hudhud, G., Abdulaziz Alzamel, M., Alattas, E., Alwabil, A.: Using brain signals patterns for biometric identity verification systems. Comput. Human Behav. **31**, 224–229 (2014)
8. Belgacem, N., Fournier, R., Nait-Ali, A., Bereksi-Reguig, F.: A novel biometric authentication approach using ECG and EMG signals. J. Med. Eng. Technol. **39**(4), 226–238 (2015)
9. Pal, S., Mitra, M.: Increasing the accuracy of ECG based biometric analysis by data modelling. Meas. J. Int. Meas. Confed. **45**(7), 1927–1932 (2012)
10. Tseng, K.K., Luo, J., Hegarty, R., Wang, W., Haiting, D.: Sparse matrix for ECG identification with two-lead features. Sci. World J. **2015** (2015)
11. Luz, E.J.D.S., Menotti, D., Schwartz, W.R.: Evaluating the use of ECG signal in low frequencies as a biometry. Expert Syst. Appl. **41**(5), 2309–2315 (2014)
12. Jekova, I., Bortolan, G.: Personal Verification/Identification via Analysis of the Peripheral ECG Leads: Influence of the Personal Health Status on the Accuracy, vol. 2015 (2015)
13. Wahabi, S., Member, S., Pouryayevali, S., Member, S.: On evaluating ECG biometric systems: session-dependence and body posture **9**(11), 2002–2013 (2014)
14. Gargiulo, F., Fratini, A., Sansone, M., Sansone, C.: Subject identification via ECG fiducial-based systems: Influence of the type of QT interval correction. Comput. Methods Programs Biomed. **121**(3), 127–136 (2015)
15. Singh, Y.N.: Human recognition using fisher's discriminant analysis of heartbeat interval features and ECG morphology. Neurocomputing **167**, 322–335 (2015)
16. Lourenço, A., Silva, H., Fred, A.: Unveiling the biometric potential of finger-based ECG signals. Comput. Intell. Neurosci. **2011**, 1–8 (2011)

17. Bugdol, M.D., Mitas, A.W.: Multimodal biometric system combining ECG and sound signals. Pattern Recognit. Lett. **38**(1), 107–112 (2014)
18. Gao, G., Zhang, L., Yang, J., Zhang, L., Zhang, D.: Reconstruction based finger-knuckle-print. IEEE Trans. Image Process. **22**(12), 5050–5062 (2013)
19. Zhang, L., Zhang, L., Zhang, D., Zhu, H.: Online finger-knuckle-print verification for personal authentication. Pattern Recognit. **43**(7), 2560–2571 (2010)
20. Singh, Y.N., Singh, S.K., Gupta, P.: Fusion of electrocardiogram with unobtrusive biometrics: An efficient individual authentication system. Pattern Recognit. Lett. **33**(14), 1932–1941 (2012)
21. de Mira, J., Neto, H.V., Neves, E.B., Schneider, F.K.: Biometric-oriented iris identification based on mathematical morphology. J. Signal Process. Syst. **80**(2), 181–195 (2015)
22. Alvarez-Betancourt, Y., Garcia-Silvente, M.: A keypoints-based feature extraction method for iris recognition under variable image quality conditions. Knowledge-Based Syst. **92**, 169–182 (2016)
23. Wang, Q., Zhang, X., Li, M., Dong, X., Zhou, Q., Yin, Y.: Adaboost and multi-orientation 2D Gabor-based noisy iris recognition. Pattern Recognit. Lett. **33**(8), 978–983 (2012)
24. Abo-Zahhad, M., Ahmed, S.M., Abbas, S.N.: Biometric authentication based on PCG and ECG signals: present status and future directions. Signal, Image Video Process. **8**(4), 739–751 (2014)
25. Poursaberi, A., Noubari, H., Gavrilova, M., Yanushkevich, S.N.: Gauss–Laguerre wavelet textural feature fusion with geometrical information for facial expression identification. EURASIP J. Image Video Process. **2012**(1), 17 (2012)
26. Travieso, C.M., Del Pozo-Banos, M., Alonso, J.B.: Fused intra-bimodal face verification approach based on Scale-Invariant Feature Transform and a vocabulary tree. Pattern Recognit. Lett. **36**(1), 254–260 (2014)
27. Li, A., Shan, S., Chen, X., Gao, W.: Cross-pose face recognition based on partial least squares. Pattern Recognit. Lett. **32**(15), 1948–1955 (2011)
28. Raghavendra, R., Dorizzi, B., Rao, A., Hemantha Kumar, G.: Particle swarm optimization based fusion of near infrared and visible images for improved face verification. Pattern Recognit. **44**(2), 401–411 (2011)
29. Li, M., et al.: Multimodal physical activity recognition by fusing temporal and cepstral information. IEEE Trans. Neural Syst. Rehabil. Eng. **18**(4), 369–380 (2010)
30. Beritelli, F., Serrano, S.: Biometric identification based on frequency analysis of cardiac sounds. IEEE Trans. Inf. Forensics Secur. **2**(3), 596–604 (2007)
31. Klonovs, J., Petersen, C., Olesen, H., Hammershoj, A.: ID proof on the go: development of a mobile EEG-based biometric authentication system. IEEE Veh. Technol. Mag. **8**(1), 81–89 (2013)
32. Xu, Y., Fan, Z., Qiu, M., Zhang, D., Yang, J.Y.: A sparse representation method of bimodal biometrics and palmprint recognition experiments. Neurocomputing **103**, 164–171 (2013)
33. Dai, J., Zhou, J., Member, S.: Multifeature-based high-resolution palmprint recognition **33**(5), 945–957 (2011)
34. Bhavsar, A.A., Kshirsagar, V.: Face and palmprint multi-modal biometric recognition based on feature level fusion abstract **3**(2), 368–372 (2014)
35. Park, U., Jillela, R.R., Ross, A., Jain, A.K.: Periocular biometrics in the visible spectrum. IEEE Trans. Inf. Forensics Secur. **6**(1), 96–106 (2011)
36. Eskandari, M., Toygar, Ö., Demirel, H.: Feature extractor selection for face-iris multimodal recognition. Signal Image Video Process. **8**(6), 1189–1198 (2014)
37. Liau, H.F., Isa, D.: Feature selection for support vector machine-based face-iris multimodal biometric system. Expert Syst. Appl. **38**(9), 11105–11111 (2011)

732 J.C. Zapata et al.

38. Eskandari, M., Toygar, Ö.: Selection of optimized features and weights on face-iris fusion using distance images. Comput. Vis. Image Underst. **137**, 63–75 (2014)
39. Benaliouche, H., Touahria, M.: Comparative study of multimodal biometric recognition by fusion of iris and fingerprint. Sci. World J. **2014** (2014)
40. Nanni, L., Lumini, A., Ferrara, M., Cappelli, R.: Combining biometric matchers by means of machine learning and statistical approaches. Neurocomputing **149**(PB), 526–535 (2015)
41. Murillo-Escobar, M.A., Cruz-Hernández, C., Abundiz-Pérez, F., López-Gutiérrez, R.M.: A robust embedded biometric authentication system based on fingerprint and chaotic encryption. Expert Syst. Appl. **42**(21), 8198–8211 (2015)
42. Martinez-Diaz, M., Fierrez, J., Galbally, J., Ortega-Garcia, J.: An evaluation of indirect attacks and countermeasures in fingerprint verification systems. Pattern Recognit. Lett. **32**(12), 1643–1651 (2011)
43. Ahmadian, K., Gavrilova, M.: A multi-modal approach for high-dimensional feature recognition. User Model. User-Adapt. Interact. **29**(2), 123–130 (2013)
44. Zhang, D., Liu, Z., Yan, J.: Dynamic tongueprint: a novel biometric identifier. Pattern Recognit. **43**(3), 1071–1082 (2010)
45. Travieso, C.M., Zhang, J., Miller, P., Alonso, J.B., Ferrer, M.A.: Bimodal biometric verification based on face and lips. Neurocomputing **74**(14–15), 2407–2410 (2011)
46. Xue, Z., Ming, D., Song, W., Wan, B., Jin, S.: Infrared gait recognition based on wavelet transform and support vector machine. Pattern Recognit. **43**(8), 2904–2910 (2010)
47. Odinaka, I., O'Sullivan, J.A., Sirevaag, E.J., Rohrbaugh, J.W.: Cardiovascular biometrics: Combining mechanical and electrical signals. IEEE Trans. Inf. Forensics Secur. **10**(1), 16–27 (2015)
48. Crihalmeanu, S., Ross, A.: Multispectral scleral patterns for ocular biometric recognition. Pattern Recognit. Lett. **33**(14), 1860–1869 (2012)
49. Chin, Y.J., Ong, T.S., Teoh, A.B.J., Goh, K.O.M.: Integrated biometrics template protection technique based on fingerprint and palmprint feature-level fusion. Inf. Fusion **18**(1), 161–174 (2014)
50. Hang, L.W., Hong, C.Y., Yen, C.W., Chang, D.J., Nagurka, M.L.: Gait verification using knee acceleration signals. Expert Syst. Appl. **38**(12), 14550–14554 (2011)
51. Yuan, L., Mu, Z.C.: Ear recognition based on local information fusion. Pattern Recognit. Lett. **33**(2), 182–190 (2012)
52. Rigas, I., Abdulin, E., Komogortsev, O.: Towards a multi-source fusion approach for eye movement-driven recognition. Inf. Fusion, 1–13 (2015)
53. Chen, M., et al.: Laser doppler vibrometry measures of physiological function: Evaluation of biometric capabilities. IEEE Trans. Inf. Forensics Secur. **5**(3), 449–460 (2010)
54. Song, W., Kim, T., Kim, H.C., Choi, J.H., Kong, H.-J., Lee, S.-R.: A finger-vein verification system using mean curvature. Pattern Recognit. Lett. **32**(11), 1541–1547 (2011)
55. Wang, J.-C., Wang, C.-Y., Chin, Y.-H., Liu, Y.-T., Chen, E.-T., Chang, P.-C.: Spectral-temporal receptive fields and MFCC balanced feature extraction for robust speaker recognition. Multimed. Tools Appl. **76**(3), 4055–4068 (2017)
56. Lee, A., Kim, Y.: Photoplethysmography as a form of biometric authentication. In: 2015 IEEE SENSORS, pp. 1–2 (2015)
57. Sidek, K.A., Khalil, I., Jelinek, H.F.: ECG biometric with abnormal cardiac conditions in remote monitoring system. IEEE Trans. Syst. Man Cybern. **44**(11), 1498–1509 (2014)
58. Sengottuvelan, P.: Analysis of living and dead finger impression identification for biometric applications. Comput. Intell. (c), 471–475 (2007)
59. Su, F., Xia, L., Cai, A., Ma, J.: A dual-biometric-modality identification system based on fingerprint and EEG. In: IEEE 4th International Conference on Biometrics Theory, Applications and Systems, BTAS 2010, pp. 3–8 (2010)

60. Kumar, S.B.B.: Analysis of phonocardiogram signal for biometric identification system (c), 2–5 (2015)
61. Sanjeeva Reddy, M., Narasimha, B., Suresh, E., Subba Rao, K.: Analysis of EOG signals using wavelet transform for detecting eye blinks. In: 2010 International Conference on Wireless Communications & Signal Processing, WCSP 2010, pp. 1–3 (2010)
62. Punsawad, Y., Wongsawat, Y., Parnichkun, M.: Hybrid EEG-EOG brain-computer interface system for practical machine control. In: 2010 Annual International Conference of the IEEE Engineering in Medicine Biology Society, EMBC 2010, pp. 1360–1363 (2010)
63. Woodard, D.L., Flynn, P.J.: Finger surface as a biometric identifier. Comput. Vis. Image Underst. 100(3), 357–384 (2005)
64. Belgacem, N., Fournier, R., Nait-Ali, A., Bereksi-Reguig, F.: A novel biometric authentication approach using ECG and EMG signals. J. Med. Eng. Technol. 39(4), 226–238 (2015)
65. Polikar, R., et al.: An ensemble based data fusion approach for early diagnosis of Alzheimer's disease. Inf. Fusion 9(1), 83–95 (2008)
66. Liu, Y., Hatzinakos, D., Member, S.: Earprint : transient evoked otoacoustic emission for biometrics 9(12), 2291–2301 (2014)
67. Zhao, Z., Yang, L.: ECG identification based on Matching Pursuit. In: 2011 4th International Conference on Biomedical Engineering and Informatics, pp. 721–724 (2011)
68. Annapurani, K., Sadiq, M.A.K., Malathy, C.: Fusion of shape of the ear and tragus – a unique feature extraction method for ear authentication system. Expert Syst. Appl. 42(1), 649–656 (2015)
69. Wübbeler, G., Stavridis, M., Kreiseler, D., Bousseljot, R.D., Elster, C.: Verification of humans using the electrocardiogram. Pattern Recognit. Lett. 28, 1172–1175 (2007)
70. Fridman, L., et al.: Multi-modal decision fusion for continuous authentication. Comput. Electr. Eng. 41(C), 142–156 (2015)
71. Tao, Q., Veldhuis, R.: Biometric authentication system on mobile personal devices. IEEE Trans. Instrum. Meas. 59(4), 763–773 (2010)
72. Ozkaya, N.: Metacarpophalangeal joint patterns based personal identification system. Appl. Soft Comput. 37, 288–295 (2015)
73. O'Regan, S., Marnane, W.: Multimodal detection of head-movement artefacts in EEG. J. Neurosci. Methods 218(1), 110–120 (2013)

Presenting Two Tumor' Edge Analyzing Strategies to Assert Lobularity Quantification on Digital Breast Tomosythesis Images

Fernando Yepes-Calderon[1](✉), Camila Ospina[2], Flor Marina[2], and Jose Abella[2]

[1] Division of Neurosurgery, Children's Hospital Los Angeles, Los Angeles, CA, USA
fyepes@chla.usc.edu
[2] Fundación Valle del Lili, Cali, Colombia

Abstract. Tumor grading is as important as difficult to assert, and there is a growing interest in making this possible from the medical images. Very often radiologist deal with the lack of consensus regarding tumor classification and grading. Despite there is an apparently comprehensive guide to qualify the masses, the qualitative nature of the classification directives guides the specialists to different appreciations. Then, the histology dissolves any hesitation at the expense of time and patient discomfort. Having a reliable quantifying strategy would not only assist the radiologist in their verdicts, but it will also speed up the diagnosing processes and may avoid the need for invasive and uncomfortable procedures such as the biopsy. In this manuscript, we present two algorithms that extract numbers in a slice by slice fashion using the tumor edging irregularities. As a proof of concetp, clinical breast tomosythesis images are treated under the mentioned methods and their outcomes are presented next to the extracted numerical insights.

Keywords: Tumor grading · Cancer · Tumor characterization · Medical image analysis

1 Introduction

With the advent of medical technology that allows in vivo visualization of tissue, the radiology departments have a new set of tools to track abnormalities. The case of malignant masses can be explored with different imaging methods, being the most used the Magnetic Resonance Imaging (MRI) and the Computer Tomography (CT) [1,2]. The medical images have gained an outstanding resolution, and although, cell level is still invisible, the macro manifestations of a disordered cell growing can be appreciated since very early stages.

However, the image is a representation that provides qualitative insights and very often, the interpretations do not find convergence among the specialists [3]. There is then a necessity of quantifying the findings in the images with the constraints that the mechanisms utilized to obtain the desired numbers, must be accurate and repeatable.

© Springer International Publishing AG 2017
A. Solano and H. Ordoñez (Eds.): CCC 2017, CCIS 735, pp. 734–745, 2017.
DOI: 10.1007/978-3-319-66562-7_52

Some quantifying approaches target cancer in specific parts of the body [4,5], some other focus on particular kinds of cancer [6,7]. In the cited research contributions, the authors' goal is to differentiate between malign and benign masses, which is a good first step in the automation of the diagnosis pipeline but still lacks the needed generalization and robustness to be included in the standard of care procedures. Recall that besides malign or benign characterization, tumor grading is ultimately the index that defines the treatment and it is in this aim where most of the inter-observer discrepancies arise. The biopsy is the gold standard that destroys any discordance in the verdicts involving treatment costs increases, patient discomfort and, according to [8,9] this procedure may increase morbidity.

A general feature manifested in all cancer affections is the disordered cell proliferation [10,11] which creates lobulated forms with irregular margins in the images. The edge irregularity is common to all types of malign masses regardless of the organ affected.

This paper presents two strategies that quantize edge spiculation of the masses in a slice by slice basis. The methods have been thoroughly tested in digitally created phantoms and digital breast tomosynthesis (DBT) images.

2 Materials and Methods

The following statements refers to the functional blocks in the flow diagram presented in Fig. 1.

2.1 Algorithms' Common Root

The tumor masks are extracted from the images and then, isometric bounding Boxes (BS) are used in every slice to enclosed the tumor masks *(Block II)*. The dimensions of the biggest bounding box (BBS) in the study or in the population is saved as reference *(Block I)*. Next, all other masks are scaled to the size of the BBS, *Block III*. To this end, the slices are isometrically adjusted until one point on the mask's edge touches the limits of the BBS. Adaptive super-sampling [12,13] is used to scale every slice to the size of the object enclosed by the BBS without smoothing their edges. The bounding-boxes in *Blocks I-III* have the property of being square. They also frame the object under study in a way that ensures that the mask is always centered, both horizontally and vertically, that is, all of the phantom's slices share a common center point located at $x = y = (BBS/2)$. From this moment on, all the tumor shapes contain similar amount of points in their edges, the differences should be due to inhomogeneities in the boundaries, a factor of utmost importance for the subsequent steps and the pursued quantification.

Once this sizing standardization process is done, the masks' edges are detected automatically using a Canny edge detector [14], *Block IV*. Although, the edging points appear graphically in the field of view (FOV), it is necessary to extract their coordinates as a prerequisite for the posterior computations.

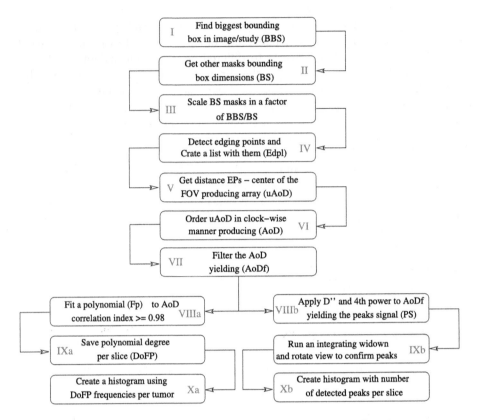

Fig. 1. Edge analysis algorithms. The proposed algorithms have a common root where dimensional standardization is reached. Then, the two branches present different automatic procedures to extract numbers which are descriptive of tumor spiculation.

Initially, the edging point coordinates are read by saving the pixels that yield a value different from background in a row by row swept, creating the list of edging points (Edpl). See Eq. 1.

$$Edpl[m] = \begin{cases} [x_n, y_n] & \text{if } FOV(x_n, y_n) = 1 \\ \text{Do nothing} & \text{Otherwise} \end{cases} \quad \forall (x_n, y_n) \in FOV \quad (1)$$

where FOV refers to the artificial FOV created in previous steps. Recall that index m is only incremented when the condition in Eq. 1 is met.

Next, the algorithm computes the distance of each edging point to the center of the artificially created FOV *Block V* creating and unordered array of distances (uAoD), as in Eq. 2.

$$uAoD[m] = \sqrt{(x_m - \frac{BBS}{2})^2 + (y_n - \frac{BBS}{2})^2} \quad \forall p_n(x_n, y_n) \in E \quad (2)$$

If follows ordering the $uAoD$ by iterating in counter clock-wise manner through its contents. For this procedure, we start at point $p_1 = [BBS/2, y_e]$, and ended at the edge point approaching from the left, which appear at a distance of $sqrt(2)$ to p_1 *Block VI*. In all cases, y_e is the first edging point found when searching from top to bottom along the line described by $f(x) = BBS/2$. Additionally, the ending condition makes sense if considering the tumor-slice residing in a FOV which dimensions are in discrete units, such as the one used in this implementation.

$\forall$ $p_m = (x_m, y_m) \in uAoD$, let the vector p_{m-1}, p_m have magnitude, k, and direction θ. p_{m+1} will be the first coordinate in Eq. 3, where $p_m \in FOV$ and $i = 2, 5, 4, 3, 1, 0$:

$$P_{m+1} = (x_m, y_m) + (\frac{\sqrt{2}}{2k}(1 + (-1)^{i+1}) + \frac{k}{2}(1 + (-1)^i))(cos(\theta + 90 - 45i), sin(\theta + 90 - 45i)) \quad (3)$$

By following the given sequence of i, Eq. 3 checks for the existence of an edge point in the direction we are moving first - following the gradient-, if a edging point is not found there, the sequence in i, will force Eq. 3 to search for the point at $-135°$, then $-90°, -45°, 45°$, and $90°$, all these rotations having as reference, the initial gradient direction. This algorithm works in a first-in, first-served fashion; thus, if the point is found in a searched position, the i sequence is broken, the found point is set as a seed and the searching process starts again in the new position. In the case the searching position already exists in the AoD, the current point will be ignored. The Eq. 3 generalizes the searching sequence and the moving angle explicitly, it also defines automatically the magnitude of the displacement per coordinate and, therefore, the gradient direction. The process defined in Eq. 3, yields the (AoD), a collection of clock-wise ordered distances. The AoD not only contains the edge shape information, it also contains a high frequency component due to the unavoidable step-like shape stemming from the pixels in the mask. This undesirable effect is filtered out in the Fourier domain by cutting out the highest frequencies until the spectral power reaches 80% of its original value *Block VII*. This frequency-cutting value is presented by [15], as the passing-power spectrum window where the important content of the signal is held. In the filtered version of the array of distances (AoDf), the intensities are slightly modified while the positions are unaffected.

Until this point, the referred steps provides the computation with size standardization and a common measuring referencing. The distances to the center of the synthetically created FOV captures not only size of the tumor, but also spiculation; and both, size and spiculation are of relevance in the characterization of masses as malign or benign.

2.2 Branch A. Tumor Characterization by Polynomial Fitting

The AoDf signal undergoes a polynomial fitting until the function described by the obtained polynomial reaches a correlation index of 95% with the model signal. See *Block VIIIa*. The degree of the fitted polynomial (DoFP) from every slice is saved for subsequent analysis *Block IXa*. The tumor is then described by the histogram signature of the DoFPs, where the number of bins is selected by the user depending on the desired precision, *Block Xa*.

The fitted polynomial will have the form shown in Eq. 4

$$F_p = a_0 + a_1 x + a_2 x^2 + a_3 x^3 + ... + a_n x^n + \epsilon \tag{4}$$

The index n of the polynomial is increase until the expression in Eq. 5, reaches the value 0.95. Recall that the correlation operator, by definition, yields a number in the range $[-1,1]$. A value of -1 means that the two operating signals are antagonistic, meanwhile a value of 1 means that the two operating signals are perfectly equal. Since all the shapes are treated in the same manner, the degree of the fitted polynomial is a good representation of the heterogeneity found at the edge of each tumor slice.

$$Corr(AoD_f, F_p) = \frac{1}{\sqrt{(E(AoD_f)E(F_p))}} \sum_{m=1}^{m=t} (AoD_f[m])(F_p[m]) \tag{5}$$

where t is length of the $AoDf$ and the energy E of a signal (s) is obtained by $\sum_{m=1}^{m=t} s(m)^2$ in Eq. 5.

The A branch of the Fig. 1 depicts the procedures described above, while partial graphical results of the process are presented in Fig. 2.

2.3   Branch B. Tumor Characterization by Peak Detection

In this branch, the AoDf is filtered and a five point differentiation is applied to find the regions of rapid change; next, a second five point differentiation is executed to recover the inflections points. These group of operations are generalized to each point in AoDf as shown in Eq. 6.

$$p'_n = \frac{(d_n - d_{n-2}) + (d_n - d_{n-1}) + (d_{n+1} - d_n) + (d_{n+2} - d_n)}{4} \tag{6}$$

The second derivative – p'' obtained with a second pass of Eq. 6 – is where peaks are detected. To exaggerate the strongest changes and diminish the weaker, each point is raised to the 4th power. Then, a moving-averaging window of length N enfold the regions where the signals present rapid changes. The results of the moving windows is an area calculated for each step s. This moving window procedure, is generalized by the Eq. 7. Assume points $p(s) = (s, d)$ to be enfolded by the moving windows; therefore the area A for the current step s is:

$$A(s) = \sum_{i=\frac{N}{2}}^{\frac{N}{2}} p[(\frac{sN}{2}) - (\frac{N}{2} + i)] \tag{7}$$

Some graphical insights of the presented strategy's branch B, is shown in Fig. 3.

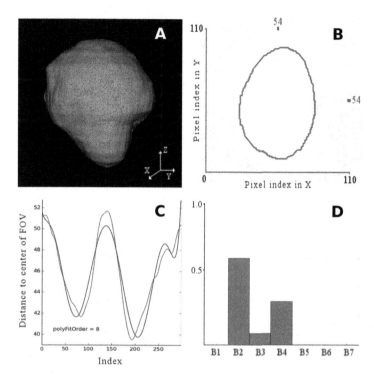

Fig. 2. Edge analysis by polynomial fitting. Panel A shows a 3D reconstruction of a tumor. Panel B presents the results of the edge detection algorithm, block IV in the common root of Fig. 1. In panel C, the filtered array of distances and its fitted polynomial. Panel D shows the histogram signature of the tumor. Here the bins collect the frequencies of the polynomial order obtained in each slice.

2.4   Datasets

Synthetically Created Data. The synthetically created data consists of two toy volumes that present extreme spiculation cases and one more volume located in between those extremes. The first volume was created as a perfect sphere (lowRef), the other extreme is an extrapolation of a sinusoidal affected with noise which used to create the edge of a single slice. Then, the area of each slice in the perfectly spheric sample, is emulated for creating each slice in the extremely spiculated toy (highRef). This procedure creates two 3D objects that have different surfaces but theoretically, the same volume. For the sample in between the extremes (BtwRef), the procedure is the same but the modulating sinusoidal are kept in the low frequency and low amplitude regime.

Clinical Data. The testing dataset consists of eight volumetric samples of digital breast tomosythesis (DBT). In this novel modality for clinical use, X-ray low dose tubes move around the sample acquiring and image every two degrees,

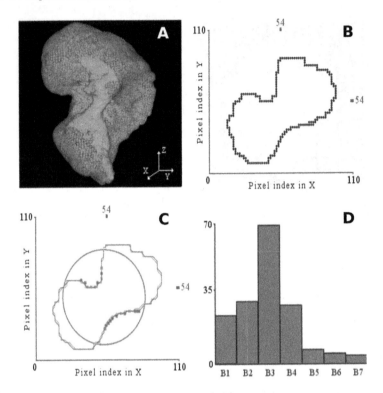

Fig. 3. Edge analysis by peak detection. Panel A holds a 3D reconstruction of a randomly selected tumor. In panel B, it is shown the results of the edging point detection step in one of the slices of the tumor in A. Panel C shows the peak detection dynamics and how the sliding windows electively collects the points that are farther away from a perfect circle that has the same area as the mask being analyzed. Panel D is the histogram created with the frequencies of the amount of points collected per each slice.

which yields between 60 to 90 slices depending of the size of the breast and more importantly, give deepness capacity in opposition to the conventional mammography where the structures appear overlapped in the FOV. The images were acquired with a Siemens Mammomat unit and the local IRB at the Fundación Valle del Lili approved the use of this retrospective data for the purposes of the study presented in this manuscript.

3   Results

3.1   Test on Synthetic Data

In the Fig. 4 the histogram responses are of easy interpretation. Highly spiculated tumors tend to fill the most right bins, while masses with smooth boundaries fill the bins on the left preferably. In between these extremes, the bins are filled

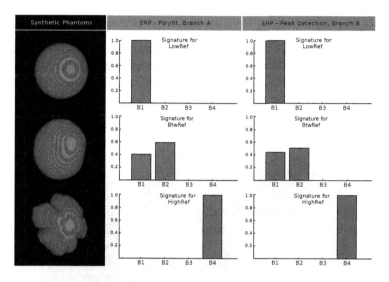

Fig. 4. Phantoms' edge characterization. In the left column from top to bottom, synthetically created images for a non spiculated mass (LowRef), a mildly spiculated mass (BtwRef) and a highly spiculated mass (HigRef). Middle column and right column are the outcomes yield by the used algorithms.

according to the intermediate edge spiculation of the sample under study. This statement holds true for both branches of the implemented algorithm.

The Table 1 presents commonly used indexes for volume analysis. To note, the fact that these indexes are not able to capture the huge differences induced in the phantoms. The volume, the sphericity and all other indexes refer to general characteristics that hinder the abrupt events that may occur in the surface of the masses.

Table 1. List with some of the common criteria for shape analysis and their values for each of the objects shown in Fig. 4. These values were obtained with imageJ [16].

Index	lowRef	BtwRef	highRef
Volume	235965	235956	235944
Volume of bounding box	440896	445440	445440
Volume of box ratio	0.53	0.53	0.53
Sphericity	0.66	0.66	0.66
Volume of ellipsoid	235974	237205	242666
Compactness	0.99	0.99	0.99
Ellipsoid elongation	1.00	1.11	1.04

3.2   Edge Quantification in Tomosythesis Datasets

The Fig. 5 shows some critical steps of taking the analysis from the tomosythesis images to the quantization stage. As it can be seen in Fig. 6, both presented algorithm perform equally good with clinical data as they did with the synthetic data; therefore, the interpretation is the same: highly spiculated masses contribute to the right-most bins in the histogram signature.

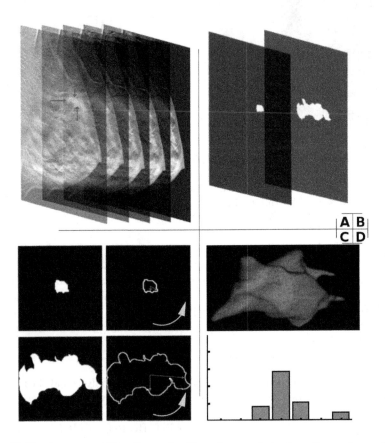

Fig. 5. Full edge quantification pipeline. In panel A, few slices of a real DBT volume. Red arrows point to an apparent tumor lesion. In panel B, the lesion has been segmented. Panel C shows the standard directionality of edging points reading that yields the organized array of distances (AoD) for two slices in the study of panel A. On top of panel D, a 3D digital reconstruction of the segmented mass, and on the bottom, the edge quantifying signature using the peak detection branch. (Color figure online)

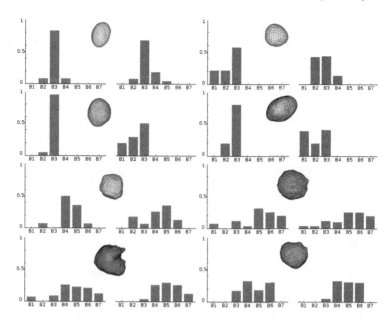

Fig. 6. Full edge quantification pipeline. Histogram signatures for the eight DBT datasets under both presented algorithms; polynomial fitting in the left and peak detection in the right side of each tumor

4   Discussion

In the Fig. 4 of the results section, there is a relation between the degree of lobularity of the created objects and the histogram yield by the both presented quantifying strategies; more relevant is the fact, that the mentioned relation is repeatable and coherent with the pragmatic idea of homogeneity that one can infer from visualizing the synthetic objects. This strong correlation between what is observed and the analytical result is often difficult to find with other indexes.

The results on clinical data follow the ones obtained within the phantoms' tests and, since the code supporting this development has been written in python, it is attachable to the existing software devices inside the radiology units, which may fasten its implementation in real environments. Moreover, the methods presented here, work equally good in images presented as stacks of 2D slices, such as MRI and CT, often use clinically to screen and treat cancer in several other organs different from the breast.

The reader may see the histograms as another qualitative representation of tumor spiculation. Recall that the bar plots are created out of the frequencies presented in the phenomena used to describe the edge lobularity. In the case of the polynomial fitting, the bins hold the number of polynomials describing the tumor with a degree in the domain of the particular bin. In the case of the peak detection, the bins hold the number of detected points. Regardless of the method implemented, the histograms are numbers and the flexibility in the number of beans to be used that can even be asymmetrical is of outstanding relevance in the generation of features. Recall that each frequency in the histogram can be seen as an independent feature which can be feed to any modern artificial intelligence tool, so leaving the quantifying stage to jump into the automatic diagnosis is feasible.

Previous attempts to generate numbers out of the images either require the input of a human operator [17,18] re-creating the operator-dependent issue that we are willing to eliminate or, despite fully automatic, are specific of a type of cancer such as in [19,20] by segmenting the region of interest. Direct comparison between the cited methods and the ones proposed here is not feasible since the outcome formats are different. However, the wider scope of our methods present an advantage with respect to other proposals.

5   Conclusions

Cancer is one of the most devastating affections that humans can suffer. The early detection and an accurate diagnosis have a big impact in the survival rate. The qualitative nature of the tools that drive the specialist to a verdict is the main source of the lack of consensus. Quantifying tools such as the ones presented in this manuscript are high demand in clinical oncology units. The further actions include the use of the repeatable numbers yield by the presented quantifying strategies to feed artificial intelligence devices where in the light to the unlimited and growing amount of data produced by hospitals, the methods gain in accuracy and soon a reliable assisting tool is launched to improve the diagnosing accuracy and documented follow up.

References

1. Arakeri, M.P., Reddy, R.M.: A novel CBIR approach to differential diagnosis of liver tumor on computed tomography images. Procedia Eng. **38**, 528–536 (2012)
2. Chaudhry, H.S., Davenport, M.S., Nieman, C.M., Ho, L.M., Neville, A.M.: Histogram analysis of small solid renal masses: differentiating minimal fat angiomyolipoma from renal cell carcinoma. Genitourin. Imaging **1**, 1–3 (2011)
3. Halpin, S.F.S.: Medico-legal claims against english radiologists: 1995–2006. Br. J. Radiol. **82**(984), 982–988 (2009). PMID: 19470570
4. Fütterer, J., Heijmink, S., Scheenen, T., Veltman, J., Huisman, H.J.: Prostate cancer localization with dynamic contrast-enhanced MR imaging and proton MR spectroscopic imaging. RSNA Radiol. **241**(2), 449–458 (2006)
5. Oto, A., Kayhan, A., Jiang, Y., Tretiakova, M., Yang, C., Antic, T.: Prostate cancer: differentiation of central gland cancer from benign prostatic hyperplasia by using diffusion-weighted and dynamic contrast-enhanced MR imaging. RSNA Radiol. **257**(3), 715–723 (2010)
6. Mendez, A., Tahoces, P., Lado, M., Souto, M., Correa, J., Vidal, J.: Automatic detection of breast border and nipple in digital mammograms. Comput. Methods Progr. Biomed. **49**(3), 253–262 (1996)
7. Doyle, S., Rodriguez, C.: Detecting prostatic adenocarcinoma from digitized histology using a multi-scale hierarchical classification approach. In: EMB-IEEE (2006)

8. Bedossa, P.: Liver biopsy. Grastroenterol. Clin. Bio. **32**, 4–7 (2008)
9. Stigliano, R., Marelli, L., Yu, D., Davies, N., Patch, D., Burroughs, A.K.: Seeding following percutaneous diagnostic and therapeutic approaches for hepatocellular carcinoma. what is the risk and the outcome? seeding risk for percutaneous approach of hcc. Cancer Treat. Rev. **33**(5), 437–47 (2007)
10. Brown, J.M., Giaccia, A.J.: The unique physiology of solid tumors: opportunities (and problems) for cancer therapy. Cancer Res. **7**, 1408–1416 (1998)
11. Ambrosi, D., Mollica, F.: On the mechanics of a growing tumor. Int. J. Eng. Sci. **40**, 1297–1316 (2002)
12. Whitted, T.: An improved illumination model for shaded display. Commun. ACM **13**(2), 343–349 (1980)
13. Rigau, J., FEixas, M., Sbert, M.: New contrast measurements for pixel supersampling. In: Proceedings of CGI 2002 (2002)
14. Canny, J.: A computational approach to edge detection. PAMI **8**, 679–698 (1986)
15. Shannon, C.E.: A mathematical theory of communication. Bell Syst. Tech. J. **27**, 379–423, 623–656 (1948)
16. Abramoff, M., Magalhaes, P., Ram, S.: Image processing with imagej. Biophotonics Int. **11**(7), 36–42 (2004)
17. Schulz, J., Skrøvseth, S.O., Tømmerås, V.K., Marienhagen, K., Godtliebsen, F.: A semiautomatic tool for prostate segmentation in radiotherapy treatment planning. BMC Med. Imaging **12**(1), 1 (2014)
18. dos Santos, D.P., Kloeckner, R., Wunder, K., Bornemann, L., Düber, C., Mildenberger, P.: Effect of kernels used for the reconstruction of MDCT datasets on the semi-automated segmentation and volumetry of liver lesions. Tech. Med. Phys. **19**, 780–784 (2013)
19. Guo, Y., Feng, Y., Sun, J., Zhang, N., Lin, W., Sa, Y., Wang, P.: Automatic lung tumor segmentation on pet/ct images using fuzzy markov random field model. Comput. Math. Methods Med. **2014**, 8–10 (2014)
20. Zhang, J., Barboriak, D.P., Hobbs, H., Mazurowski, M.A.: A fully automatic extraction of magnetic resonance image features in glioblastoma patients. Med. Phys. **41**, 1–13 (2014)

Security of the Information

Towards Guidelines for Management and Custody of Electronic Health Records in Colombia

Laura Martinez[1], Andres Soto[1], Luis Eraso[1,2],
Armando Ordóñez[1,2(✉)], and Hugo Ordoñez[1,2]

[1] Intelligent Management Systems Group,
Fundación Universitaria de Popayán, Popayán, Colombia
{lauramarz20,andres.sottol}@fup.edu.co
[2] Research Laboratory in Development of Software Engineering,
Universidad San Buenaventura, Cali, Colombia
{luise,jaordonez}@unicauca.edu.co,
haordonez@usbcali.edu.co

Abstract. Many countries among them Colombia are in the process of implementing Electronic Health record. However, there are currently no guidelines for providing security and confidentiality to the records. This article presents an analysis of the existing gaps in the Colombian regulations regarding security of health records. Based on this analysis, a set of guidelines for the proper management and custody of electronic health records is proposed. These guidelines are based on international standards and regulations in this area. Finally, an evaluation of compliance with the proposed guidelines of two software platforms is presented.

Keywords: Electronic Health Record (EHR) · Security · Privacy · Guidelines

1 Introduction

An Electronic Health Record (EHR) is a digital repository containing information on people health [1]. This information is collected and managed in EHR Systems (EHR-S) [2]. This information can be shared among different institutions to make health processes more efficient. EHR may become one of the major sources of information for epidemiological and population studies, and besides important legal and probative evidence. Due to the sensitivity of the EHR information, it must be protected by security and privacy rules.

Information security implies diverse elements such as privacy, availability, integrity among others. Privacy is the right to limit access to personal information, that is, people preferences on the use of medical information must be guaranteed. The World Health Organization (WHO) has been focusing its efforts recently on studying the legal and ethical aspects of EHR privacy in different countries [2]. The health data belong to the patients, and the institutions are in charge of the custody of these data [4]. In this field, some guidelines have been defined for the management and custody of the physical information. However, these same processes do not exist for digital information [5].

© Springer International Publishing AG 2017
A. Solano and H. Ordoñez (Eds.): CCC 2017, CCIS 735, pp. 749–758, 2017.
DOI: 10.1007/978-3-319-66562-7_53

The process of systematizing the medical records in many countries is still at an early stage; therefore many shortcomings exist in the management of this information. In particular, security guidelines in accordance with existing regulations do not exist. Also, the electronic mechanisms to detect and prevent inappropriate use of data are also unclear.

Given this need, this article presents the following contributions

- An analysis of the existing gaps in the Colombian regulations and the weakness in some of the health-care institutions
- A set of guidelines for the proper management and custody of EHR is proposed. These guidelines are consistent with existing international models and regulations on the subject.
- An evaluation of the compliance with the proposed guidelines of two EHRs (deployed in a Hospital in Colombia).

The rest of the paper is organized as follows; Sect. 2 presents the conceptual and legal background. Section 3 describes the proposed guidelines. Section 4 exposes the evaluation two EHR-S in the light of the guidelines the guidelines. Finally, Sect. 5 concludes and presents the future work.

2 Background

2.1 Conceptual Background

Security model: A security model includes three general aspects: integrity, confidentiality, and availability. The compliance of a system with these aspects can be achieved by providing diverse services, such as encryption, user identification, firewalls, etc. Although these services are part of different system layers, together, they help to ensure the confidentiality of the information. Likewise, other functionalities such as replicated databases, and backups, help to ensure the integrity of the information. Finally, clustering and load balancers help to ensure the availability. The security of an EHR-S is the implementation of a set of services that provide these aspects, and the information security is the result of applying the safety guidelines.

Integrity is the guarantee of the accuracy of the information and its processing. The information must be safe and without modifications. Availability is the assurance that the authorized users have access to the information when required. Access to data by authorized persons must be granted correctly and in real time (24 h a day, 7 days a week). Confidentiality is the assurance that information is accessible only to authorized users. It is important to highlight the difference between Privacy and Confidentiality. Meanwhile privacy means that no one (unauthorized) can access the health information, confidentiality implies that the data stored or in transit are protected (e.g. using encryption) and thus these data are not visible to anyone until made available to the authorized personel.

Digital Identity: Characteristics through which something is recognizable and differentiated [7]. The concept of access control is comprised of three elements: identification, authentication, and authorization. Identification is the means by which a system identifies a user (e.g. an username or an ID card). Authentication is the process that verifies the identity of the user (e.g. passwords or speech recognition). Authorization occurs after authentication and identification and defines the resources that can be accessed. The integration of these three aspects creates a "digital identity."

2.2   Colombian Legal Framework

Resolution 3374 of 2000 refers to the Individual record of Health Services Delivery (RIPS in Spanish), which is the set of minimum and basic data that health providers must collect and send periodically. These data are required by the General System of Social Security for the direction, regulation, and control of health services. RIPS structure is unified and standardized for all entities. On the other hand, law 1581 of 2012 is related to the protection of data, so that all the measures (technical and legal) must be taken to ensure that the information is free of unauthorized access. Equally, Law 1438 of 2011 establishes that the Single Electronic Clinical History will be mandatory from December 31 of the year 2013. Finally, Resolution 1995 of 1999 promotes the development and use of computer medical records.

Despite the advances in the regulation of the management and custody of the EHR, no guidelines or detailed guidelines exist on the security of health information.

3   Proposed Guidelines

The guidelines seek to ensure that an EHR-S provides information security (integrity, confidentiality, and availability). As the Colombian regulations on the subject are very basic, a search was conducted for standards and regulations around the world. From this review, some general requirements were identified. These requirements are mainly based on the United States standard "Health Insurance Portability and Accountability Act (HIPAA)" [8]. HIPAA defines in detail the access and security control requirements that an EHR-S must fulfill. Besides, the standard defines a role-based access control. For the definition of the privacy guidelines, the European data protection Directive 95/46/EC [7] and the statutory law 1581 of 2012 [9] (handling and custody of sensitive information) were considered.

3.1   Access Control Guidelines (ACG)

These guidelines are based on the HIPAA standard. The guidelines are ACG1: Single user, ACG2: Emergency Access, ACG3: Automatic logout, ACG4. Encryption and decryption.

ACG1. Single user: "Assign a unique name or identification number to each user and carry out the tracking of his identity." [8] in item §164.312(a)(2)(i). The identification of a particular user in an information system is usually made using a name and/or number. A unique identifier allows tracking the user's activity. This guideline does not define an identification format. Therefore this can be determined by the organizations. Some organizations may use, for example, a variation of the name (e.g. jdoe for John Doe).

ACG2. Emergency Access: "Establish and implement the procedures for the management of the information during an emergency" [8] in item §164.312(a)(2)(ii). For example, in the case of a natural disaster or a power failure.

ACG3. Automatic logout "Implement electronic procedures to expire an electronic session after a predefined period of inactivity" [8] in item §164.312(a)(2)(iii). This guideline is useful when workers that do not remember to close the session and prevents unauthorized users from accessing the EHR-S.

ACG4. Encryption and decryption: "Implement a mechanism to encrypt and decrypt the health information." [8] in item §164.312(a)(2)(iv). Encryption converts an original text message into encoded text using an algorithm. If the information is encrypted, it would have a little probability that any other receiving party will be able to decipher the text.

3.2 Security Guidelines (SG)

For defining these guidelines, the Role Based Access Control standard developed by the National Institute of Standards and Technology (NIST) was considered [6]. The RBAC was chosen due to the detailed information available, its popularity in traditional systems and the low complexity of implementation that reduces the errors in the administration. The guidelines defined are SG1: Roles and permissions, SG2: Separation of tasks and SG3: Hierarchy of Roles.

SG1. Roles and permissions: this mechanism protects the information from unauthorized access. A role is a job or function in the context of the organization. Permission is an approval to perform an operation on a particular resource. The purpose of any access control mechanism is to protect system resources (these can be data). Each user has a role, and each role has multiple functions assigned to them [6]. Users are assigned to roles, and also the permissions are assigned to roles. A user can be a human being, machine, network, etc.

SG2. Separation of tasks: RBAC proposes the separation of tasks or responsibilities using static or dynamic methods. The static method forms a set of roles that a particular user can possess. On the other hand, the dynamic method allows a user to have multiple functions that may have conflicts, but the user is not allowed to execute conflicting actions simultaneously [6]. The separation of tasks is a security mechanism to prevent fraud because it requires the participation of several users to carry out one fraud.

SG3. Roles hierarchy: A role hierarchy allows roles to inherit permissions from other roles [6]. This guideline is based on the RBAC NIST standard.

3.3 Privacy Guidelines (PG)

Colombian law asks health agencies to ensure the management and custody of sensitive information such as EHR [9]. Likewise, the French Law establishes measures for the protection of data based on the European Directive on data protection 95/46/EC [7]. From these laws some guidelines are defined: PG1: Confidentiality and handling of information, PG2: Data processing, PG2.1: Within the Institution, PG2.2: Outside the Institution.

PG1. Information confidentiality and management: Health providers are required to inspect the use of the personal data stored in their information systems and to define policies for the management of this information. These policies should respond to the principles of data management and privacy rights.

PG2. Data processing: The processing of personal data refers to any operation on the medical data, (e.g. modification, extraction, consultation, use, dissemination) [9]. Organizations responsible for the information should take all necessary precautions to protect the data. Altering the information is extremely sensitive. Two sub-guidelines are defined for this guideline:

PG2.1 Inside the institution: The information system must guarantee the privacy of the data, and that only allowed users have access to this information, it must also prevent misuse of the information, for example, modifications in medical records should not be allowed, as errors in the treatment may affect the patient health. Also, in systems with various modules other than EHR, a user with access to other areas (e.g. accounting) should not have access to EHRs.

PG2.2 Outside the institution: Some control or government entities may require reports based on EHR information, for example, the copy of the medical history to support a payment. It is important to have control over what is sent outside the entity.

4 Evaluation

The verification of the proposed guidelines was carried out in two EHR-S. The EHR-S are currently deployed in the Susana López Hospital located in Popayán, Colombia. The evaluated platforms are OpenMRS (Open source) and Management Dynamics (Licensed). It is fair to say that Open MRS was implemented as a demo within the Hospital, while Dynamics General is currently in production. The verification was done through the revision of compliance with the proposed guidelines.

Management Dynamics (MD): This software is composed of modules that integrate all the areas that make up the health care institutions in Colombia. MD is centered on the *medical act* that affects the other functional units including the administrative area. The *Clinical Histories module* is the tool for consultation and registration of the clinical history of patients. MD integrates a model of diagnosis, follow-up, and decision-making, MD minimizes the manual tasks as all areas of attention are integrated [10].

OpenMRS: Is an application that allows managing medical records system without any programming knowledge (although medical and systems analysis knowledge is required). OpenMRS is a framework on which medical informatics efforts in developing countries can be integrated. OpenMRS has a community of people behind focused on solving problems in resource-limited contexts [11].

4.1 Evaluation Methodology

The criteria to be evaluated for each guideline are listed below
Access Control Guidelines (ACG)

ACG1. Single User

UU.   Each member of the organization has a unique user identifier
IF.   A format is defined for the unique user identification
AT.   The system allows tracking the activity of the user using the identifier

ACG2. Emergency Access

EA.   It allows defining who has access to the EHR in case of an emergency
EP.   Incorporates procedures to grant access in emergency situations

ACG3. Automatic logout

AL.   The software has automatic logout functionality
GL.   This feature can be enabled on all workstations

ACG4. Encryption and decryption

CD.   The software incorporates encryption and decryption mechanisms

Security Guidelines (SG)

SG1. Roles and permissions

RC.   The software supports the creation and configuration of roles
GR.   Roles apply to all users on all the workstations with access to EHRs

LS2. Separation of tasks

TS.   The software incorporates the functionality of separation of tasks

LS3. Roles hierarchy

RH.   The software includes roles hierarchy
GH.   This role setting can be made for all users

Privacy guidelines (PG)

PG1. Confidentiality and information management

IP.   The software has information privacy mechanisms
DP.   The software allows defining the purpose for which the data is created

PG2. Data processing

DP.   The SW has some procedure or restriction for data processing

PG2.1. Within the institution

PP.   The SW has some procedure or restriction for data processing

PG2.2. Outside the institution

OI.   The SW allows controlling the information sent outside the entity.

4.2 Results Evaluation

Table 1 shows the evaluation of the access control guidelines. The MD system allows configuring the format of the unique identifier, and the organization uses as an identifier the citizenship card and the Foreign ID. However, MD does not record the modifications to the data, and therefore the organization currently does not comply with this criterion. OpenMRS supports 100% of compliance, while DG only 2 of 3 conditions (66% approx.).

Table 1. Access control guidelines (CR: Criteria, C: comply)

Management dynamics			Open MRS	
CR	C	Observations	C	Observations
ACG1. Single user				
UU	Y	Access granted by human resources division	Y	
IF	Y	Any nomenclature is supported	Y	Any format is supported
AT	N	The user who makes the data entry is recorded	Y	The user who makes the data entry and modification is recorded
ACG 2. Emergency access				
EA	N	The organization has no procedure	N	The organization has no procedure
EP	N	The organization has no procedure	N	The organization has no procedure
ACG 3. Automatic logout				
AL	N	Desktop application	Y	Configurable in the server
GL	N	Desktop application	Y	Configurable in the server
ACG 4. Encryption and decryption				
CD	Y	the user's password is encrypted	N	This criterion is not supported

In the case of Emergency Access, the organization does not define this procedure, nor do the platforms provide a temporary emergency procedure (0% of compliance).

Regarding automatic logout (AL), Management Dynamics does not support it (0% of compliance). On the other hand, OpenMRS is a Web application that allows configuring the session timeout (100%).

Table 1 in the encryption and decryption criterion, Management Dynamics complies with this guideline by default (100% compliance) whereas OpenMRS does not support it (0% compliance).

Table 2 shows a summary of compliance with the security guidelines. Regarding roles and permissions both applications includes this functionality (100% compliance). This functionality makes it possible to assign permissions when the organization is large and also provides more security and restriction.

Table 2. Security guidelines

Management dynamics			Open MRS	
Cr	C	Observations	C	Observations
SG1. Roles and permissions				
RC	Y	Creation and modification	Y	Creation and modification
GR	Y	Basic configuration	Y	
SG2. Separation of tasks				
TS	N	Non-configurable	Y	Separation of tasks
SG3. Roles hierarchy				
RH	N	Roles hierarchy	Y	Changes apply automatically
GH	N	Basic configuration	Y	Flexible configuration

In the security guideline separation of tasks, MD does not have this function (0%) unlike OpenMRS (100%).

In the hierarchy of roles criterion, MD does not have this functionality (0% compliance), unlike OpenMRS that provides greater flexibility in its regard (100%).

In the privacy, confidentiality and information management criteria both applications comply since they allow configuring roles and purpose of the information (100%).

Finally, Table 3 shows the compliance with the access control guidelines. In the treatment of privacy data treatment, both applications lack this configuration since they do not provide any procedure to control how the information is handled inside and outside the institution. This criterion must be implemented by the organization (0% compliance).

Table 3. Privacy guidelines

Management			Open MRS	
C	C	Observations	C	Observations
PG1. Confidentiality and handling of information				
IP	Y	Roles and permissions	Y	This software has its model based on international standards
DP	Y	Patient follow-up, billing	Y	Patient follow-up
PG2. Data processing				
DP	N	This SW doesn't control who access or modify the information	N	This SW doesn't control who modify the information but controls the access to the info.
PG2.1 inside				
PP	N	Control of who creates the EHR, and it is configurable by the Institution	N	Control of who creates and modifies the HER
PG2.2 outside				
OI	N	This SW doesn't support this criterion	N	This SW doesn't support this criterion

A comparison between the two systems (see Table 4) shows that both meet the basic guidelines. However, OpenMRS has a higher percentage of compliance. Besides, Open MRS is open source and guided by international standards. For its part, DG is licensed and closed so any modification can generate additional costs.

Table 4. Summary of guidelines implementation

Guideline	MD	Open MRS
ACG1. Single user	66%	100%
ACG 2. Emergency access	0%	0%
ACG 3. Automatic logout	0%	100%
ACG 4. Encryption and decryption	100%	0%
SG1. Roles and permissions	100%	100%
SG 2. Separation of tasks	0%	100%
SG 3. Roles hierarchy	0%	100%
PG1. Confidentiality	100%	100%
PG 2. Data processing	0%	0%
PG 2.1 inside the organization	0%	0%
PG 2.2 outside the organization	0%	0%

Finally, regarding compliance with the guidelines by the organization, it can be observed that the issue of access in case of emergency and the treatment of data inside and outside the organization are entirely unexplored. Also, although DG supports tools such as information tracking and role management, they are not being used correctly.

5 Conclusions and Future Work

This article presents a set of guidelines for the proper management and custody of Electronic Health Records (EHR) and evaluates the level of implementation of the guidelines defined in two EHR-S in a hospital in Colombia. The two systems comply with most of the criteria. However, OpenMRS complies with more guidelines. It is concluded that the health entities have a computer support to secure patients information and that these entities can use the guidelines described here to implement their policies. Likewise, these guidelines serve as the basis for the development of new software systems. As future work, a more detailed verification of the implementation of the proposed guidelines is planned including an analysis based on security assessment tools in systems. Equally, a validation based on the interaction with medical and hospital administrative personnel will be performed.

References

1. International Standards Organization: ISO/TR 20514:2005-Health informatics - Electronic health record - Definition, scope and context. https://www.iso.org/standard/39525.html
2. The Health Information Technology for Economic and Clinical Health (HITECH). https://www.fpc.gov/health-information-technology-for-economic-and-clinical-health-act-of-2009-hitech/
3. World Health Organization and WHO Global Observatory for eHealth: Legal frameworks for eHealth. http://whqlibdoc.who.int/publications/2012/9789241503143_eng.pdf
4. Ministerio de Salud: República de Colombia. Resolución 1995, 8 julio 1999. http://www.disanejercito.mil.co/index.php?idcategoria=27101
5. Congreso de Colombia República de Colombia: Ley 1438, 19 Enero 2011. https://www.minsalud.gov.co/Paginas/ReformaalasaludLey1438de2011.aspx
6. Ferraiolo, D.F., Sandhu, R., Gavrila, S., Kuhn, D.R., Chandramouli, R.: Proposed NIST standard for role-based access control. ACM Trans. Inf. Syst. Secur. **4**, 224–274 (2001)
7. Directive, E.U.: 95/46/EC-The Data Protection Directive. Official Journal of European Communities (1995). http://ec.europa.eu/justice/policies/privacy/docs/95-46-ce/dir1995-46_part1_en.pdf
8. Centers for Medicare & Medicaid Services: The health insurance portability and accountability act of 1996 (HIPAA) (1996). http://www.cms.hhs.gov/hipaa
9. Alcaldía de Bogotá: Ley estatutaria 1581 de 2012. http://www.alcaldiabogota.gov.co/sisjur/normas/Norma1.jsp
10. Dinámica Gerencial. http://www.syac.net.co
11. OpenMRS: http://openmrs.org

Leveraging 1-wire Communication Bus System for Secure Home Automation

Luz A. Magre Colorado and Juan C. Martíinez-Santos[✉]

Faculty of Engineering, Universidad Tecnológica de Bolívar, Cartagena, Colombia
juanc.martinez.santos@gmail.com

Abstract. Home automation is a rising technology that is available to anyone thanks to the reduce cost of the embedded systems. Since the appearance of different products to create your own domotic system, and the recent popularity around the Internet of Things (IoT) technology, the domotics industry has changed. The ability to control devices through the Internet creates numerous vulnerabilities to the system, allowing an attacker to control or see everything. In this work, we present a domotic system which uses a leveraged 1-wire as its communication channel. The original system lacks of any kind of security. Our objective is to implement information security through the encryption of the system's commands, so we can assure the CIA triad (Confidentiality, Integrity and Availability). The results show that we achieve a secure communication without affecting the user experience due to the low overhead our approach provides.

Keywords: Home automation · Secure communication · 1-wire

1 Introduction

There are a lot of definitions for home automation. Some define it as "the capability to automate and control multiple systems" [1,2]. Others, like Goodwin [3], define it as anything the home does to make people's lives more productive or comfortable. Jima [4] claims domotics is a set of systems that allow control and automation of a household and is made by a master that controls and manages the activities of all the elements in the system. Although we have different ways to define what a domotic system is, we can agree in the fact that the system needs to automate devices to make people's lives easier.

Domotics allows users to have a variety of commodities that makes their lives a little bit easier. From simple things like turning on and off the lights of the household with one remote control, to others much more complex like choosing what do you want to hear in your sound system, or even having your living room turned into a home cinema with the touch of button. Even knowing the temperature of certain rooms and how much electricity are you spending [5]. There is an infinity of uses and applications for domotics, this is why we can see an increasing number of smart homes every year. Just in 2016, there were

© Springer International Publishing AG 2017
A. Solano and H. Ordoñez (Eds.): CCC 2017, CCIS 735, pp. 759–771, 2017.
DOI: 10.1007/978-3-319-66562-7_54

around 7.37 million existing smart homes in the United States alone, and this number is expected to grow by 2020 to 24.45 million smart homes, according to Statista [6]. With this number permanently increasing, we can't take security for granted.

1-wire is a device communications bus system designed by Dallas Semiconductor Corp. that provides low-speed data, signaling, and power over a single conductor. 1-Wire is similar in concept to I^2C, but with lower data rates and longer range [7]. 1-Wire devices are often used in domotics and sensor networks for home automation by taking advantage of their use in a contact environment and that is the most economical way to add functionality to devices with no previous electronic functions [8,9].

Communication also allows the users to connect the system to the Internet, so they can control their houses remotely. This feature is very useful, but it comes with a price, the system can be attacked if there is no secure communication. An attacker could control a household remotely or simply see what is the routine of the people living there [10]. This could easily become a direct physical attack to the user, since the intruder could open the door remotely, or control the devices in a way that can hurt the people living in the house [11–13].

The objective of this work is to identify and validate a cryptographic technique capable of defend the system against the most common attacks (ciphertext-only attack, known plaintext attack, chosen plaintext attack), and also fulfills the security requirements such as confidentiality, integrity and availability. The chosen technique needs to be adjusted to the system constraints of the 1-wire system applied to domotics such as velocity (9600 baud), sending one command at a time and no flexibility in the commands protocol. At the same time, we need to maintain the performance of the system to the end-user.

The article is organized as follows. In Sect. 2, we show the approach of other authors in this topic. In Sect. 3, we present the approach taken in this work, and how we are developing it. In Sect. 4, we show the results of our work in terms of execution time and how it affects the response time of the system. Finally, Sect. 5 draws our conclusions and future work.

2   Related Work

The 1-wire protocol was created by Dallas Semiconductor, now known as Maxim Integrated [7] and is widely used in sensor networks, digital interfaces of sensors and domotic systems [14–18]. The protocol follows a strict master-slave scheme, as depicted in Fig. 1.

1-wire has no information security implemented itself. The devices using the 1-wire technology often are embedded with a SHA-1 MAC (message authentication code) to provide this security. An example of this is a device named iButton, also developed by Maxim Integrated [20], that is used as an authentication token. The objective of this device is to replace smartcards, magnetic stripe cards, barcodes, and radio-frequency proximity cards (RFID) for use in access control, cashless transactions, PKI, authentication, identification, Internet

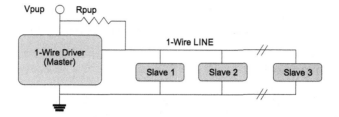

Fig. 1. Basic scheme of 1-wire system bus. All slaves share the 1-wire communication line and have the same reference node. Each slave has its own power supplied (hiding in this scheme). Based on [19].

commerce and many other solutions that require portability and security [21]. The authors claim that this device is tamper resistant and has a cryptographic engine that uses SHA-1 (Secure Hash Algorithm 1) to hide the valuable information that stores.

Although this device seems to be secure, different types of attacks managed to break the iButton, such as a dictionary attack made by Kingpin [22], where they proved that the false response to a false password is not random, but calculated based on the input password and a constant block of data stored within the device. So they pre-computed the 48-byte return value expected for an incorrect password and checked if the returned value matches or not, if it doesn't, that must be the correct password and subkey data.

Oswald [23], on the other hand, uses a non-invasive side-channel analysis to extract the 64-bit secret key out of the device. Brandt et al. [24] show how to break the iButton as well, but using a differential fault attack and implementation attack and managed to get the secret key in less than ten minutes, including target preparation. This research shows that there is still a lot to do to make this device secure enough to be used a smart-card to make payments.

We can see that although there is previous work trying to accomplish a security implementation for 1-wire, they have been unsuccessful. Furthermore, notice that there is no security implementation for a domotic system that uses this kind of communication protocol.

There are a lot of ciphers that could accomplish basic security requirements (Confidentiality, Integrity and Availability) for high constrained devices and systems. These ciphers are in a new category of security called *Lightweight Cryptography*. This type of ciphers appeared along with the new arising of the Internet of Things (IoT) paradigm, where a new necessity in security came along: To provide information security to highly constrained devices in all aspects that have to do with memory space, energy, and others. In this new field of security, we can find several ciphers such as KLEIN [25], KATAN [26], HIGHT [27], TEA [28], PRESENT [29], Hummingbird [30], Curupira [31], DESL [32], Simon and Speck [33] among others [34,35]. The majority of these are block ciphers. This type of ciphers are sensitive to linear and differential cryptanalysis, depending on the amount and complexity of their rounds [36]. For this work, we chose the families of algorithms Simon and Speck [33], because of their good performance in 8-bit microcontrollers and low memory usage compared to the others.

3   Our Approach

The approach that we took to provide security for this system required a previous definition of the scenario that we are working on. Then, we proceed to select a cryptographic algorithm that suits the system. After that, we make the proper implementation of the selected algorithm to the system through a cryptographic module.

3.1   Scenario

In the particular domotic system that is being studied, there is no inherent security implemented, there is no encryption or key management at all. An attacker can connect a master in the same bus and start controlling the system. By observing the different commands, anyone can guess which command is used to turn on/off the lights, the music, among other devices that are connected to the bus.

In Fig. 2, we can see the original scenario managed over a LAN (Local Area Network). The desired scenario for this domotic system is to be controlled in a WAN (Wide Area Network) through a public IP. Taking into account that the system is completely exposed to attacks, this is not an option until we can secure the information of the system.

One strategy to add security is to add a cryptographic module to the system, given that remaking the whole system would elevate greatly the costs of the security implementation. The encryption would be done in these low layers as a

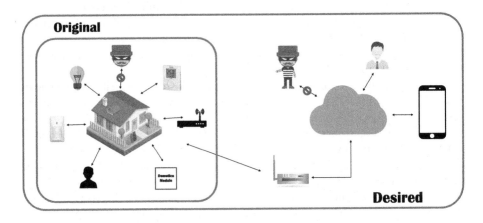

Fig. 2. General scenario of the system.

way of preventing an attack, when the intruder has the opportunity to connect physically to the system to gain access. This adds another level of security for the system besides TLS/SSL when the control is made through Internet connection.

3.2 Cryptographic Algorithm

The first step is to select a cryptographic algorithm that meets the performance and security requirements for the system. We have to keep in mind that the final user's perception of the system needs to remain the same. The extra encryption/decryption process that we'll be adding increases the communication time between commands. We need to minimize this time as much as we can, so the user won't notice the change on the execution of the commands. This is to avoid the user get annoyed by an increasing response time from the system.

Simon and Speck [33] are families of lightweight block ciphers publicly released by the National Security Agency (NSA) in June 2013. These two families were made to work in both hardware and software, but it was shown that Simon works better for hardware implementations and Speck for software implementations. These families of block ciphers were made to be used in no specific application. Given that they offer a range of block and key sizes, it's easier to adapt the algorithm to your own application providing more flexibility to the developer. These ciphers ensure an exceptional performance in 8-bit microcontrollers with minimal flash and SRAM usage. The authors claim that these algorithms outperform the best comparable software algorithms (in terms of code size and memory usage). We will use these ciphers to encrypt and decrypt the different commands that are sent to the domotic system to perform a specific action in the domotic system.

The ciphers Simon and Speck, as mentioned before, are families of block ciphers with different block and key sizes. This allows both algorithms to have more flexibility depending on the application. Each algorithm inside Simon's family is denoted Simon$2n/mn$ representing a $2n$-bit block and a mn-bit key [33]. The notation for Speck can be taken just as the one for Simon, being denoted as Speck$2n/mn$. Table 1 shows the different Simon and Speck versions according to their block size.

Table 1. Block and key sizes for Simon and Speck. Sizes are in bits.

Block size ($2n$)	Key size (mn)
32	64
48	72, 96
64	96, 128
96	96, 144
128	128, 192, 256

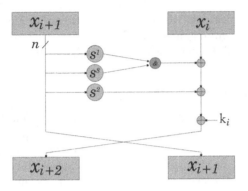

Fig. 3. One round of Simon. Based on Beaulieu et al. [33]

Simon Algorithm. Simon follows a Feistel network structure. As shown in Fig. 3, each round requires three main operations:

- Bitwise XOR, $\oplus$
- Bitwise AND, &
- Left circular shift, S^j, by j bits.

One round of Simon is defined by Eq. 1:

$$R_k(x,y) = (y \oplus f(x) \oplus k, x) \tag{1}$$

Where $f(x) = (Sx \& S^8x) \oplus S^2x)$, and k is the round key [33].

For the decryption of the message, we use the inverse of the previous operation, defined by Eq. 2:

$$R^-1_k(x,y) = (y, x \oplus f(y) \oplus k) \tag{2}$$

Simon includes no plaintext and ciphertext whitening steps, because it would affect the size of the circuit. The first and last rounds do nothing cryptographically, they just bring in the first and last round keys [33].

The Simon key schedules use a sequence of 1-bit round constants eliminate any circular shift symmetries due to the fact that all rounds in Simon are exactly the same apart from the round key. There are five different sequences $(Z_0, ..., Z_4)$ defined to differentiate Simon version with the same block size.

Speck Algorithm. For a round of SPECK, as shown in Fig. 4, the following operations are needed:

- Bitwise XOR, $\oplus$
- Addition modulo 2^n, $+$ &
- Left and right circular shifts, S^j, S^-j, by j bits.

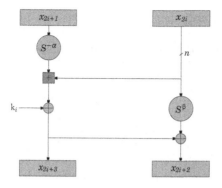

Fig. 4. One round of Speck. Based on Beaulieu et al. [33]

One round of Speck is defined by Eq. 3:

$$R_k(x,y) = ((S^{-\alpha}x + y) \oplus k, S^\beta y \oplus (S^{-\alpha}x + y) \oplus k) \qquad (3)$$

Where α and β represent the rotation amounts for each round. If $n = 16$ then the values are $\alpha = 7$ and $\beta = 2$. And the same values will be $\alpha = 8$ and $\beta = 3$ for the rest of the values of n.

The inverse function used for decryption is depicted in Eq. 4:

$$R_k^{-1}(x,y) = ((S^\alpha((x \oplus k) - S^{-\beta}(x \oplus y)), S^{-\beta}(x \oplus y)) \qquad (4)$$

The key schedule of the Speck generates round keys k_i by using the round function. The Key K used is defined by a sequence of values k_i and l_i as $K = (l_{m-2}, ..., l_0, k_0)$. The sequence l_{i+m-1} is defined as $l_{i+m-1} = (k_i + S^{-\alpha}l_i) \oplus i$. The sequence k_i is defined as $k_{i+1} = S^\beta k_i \oplus l_{i+m-1}$.

3.3 Implementation

For our implementation, we used a Raspberry Pi 3 and an Arduino Uno. The Raspberry Pi 3 was included to the system to help us control the system remotely through a web application. We chose to use a Raspberry Pi 3 given that it fulfills the requirements needed for this work at a reasonable price along with a bigger community than other SBC (Single Board Computer) boards. This Raspberry Pi 3 becomes a master of the system capable of sending commands on its own and monitoring what's being send through the whole system.

We are using as the cryptographic module an Arduino UNO as shown in the left-hand side of Fig. 5, where we also added an interface that allows to go from the Arduino's serial port (Tx and Rx pins, also known as UART) to 1-wire. The Arduino is in charge of encrypting and sending as well as receiving and decrypting the incoming commands from the system's masters. When we move on from the prototyping process, the intention is to minimize the use of physical space of the Arduino inside each domotic module by using an integrated chip that will do the previously mentioned functions in a much smaller space. This will also help to avoid attacks to the system when sending the command to the encryption module. The Raspberry Pi, that was implemented as a master, does not need to have one of these cryptographic modules, given that it can encrypt and send, and receive and decrypt on its own.

In terms of the cryptographic algorithm, we made a software implementation based on the python algorithm by Calvin McCoy [37]. However, given that the size of the commands vary depending on what action we want to execute, we take the received command and divide it into 32 bits chunks and encrypt each of them. After encrypting each part of the command, we join them and this way is ready to send. The same happens when we want decrypt the command, we take the encrypted message and divide it in the same 32 bits chunks and after decrypting we join them again. This way, we can have very large commands coming from the system, and we are still capable to encrypt and decrypt them successfully. We used the Simon32/64 and the Speck 32/64 for the encryption and decryption and compared them to finally choose which of them would suit better for our application.

4 Results

We have implemented the Arduino Uno to the system as shown in Fig. 5. The communication between the devices has been successfully made. The Arduino Uno is capable of receiving commands and send them to the system. In addition, we have tested with commands of different lengths to determine the execution time of the encryption and decryption process using Simon and Speck algorithms. Based on these times, we can approximate what is the latency that the system will have and analyze the impact on the users that will use the system.

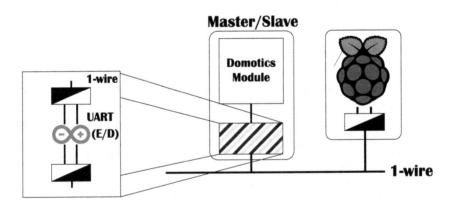

Fig. 5. Current implementation. The cryptographic module is implemented with an Arduino Uno (on the left), and the Raspberry Pi 3 acts as a master module (on the right).

4.1   Execution Time

The execution time indicates how long will it take to encrypt a string coming from the domotic system. In these particular ciphers, the decryption process is the inverse of the encryption. Then, we can assume that the encryption and decryption times are very similar.

For the execution time in both software implementations, we used a mixed factorial design to see if the length of the plaintext and the algorithm used (Simon and Speck) affect the encryption and decryption time of a given command. Both implementations were executed in a Raspberry Pi 3 model B with the parameters described in Table 2.

We also tested different lengths of plaintext (32, 48, 64, 96, 128, 160 and 192 bits). Given that we won't get the same execution time every time we run the program, we need to make several runs of it and take the average time of execution for that platform and length of plaintext. To take the data, we ran the program 10,000 times with one replicate to make sure that our average execution time is statistically significant. In Table 3, we can see the measured execution time and its replicate for both Speck and Simon algorithm.

In Fig. 6, we can observe the differences in the execution time when using the Simon and Speck algorithm in different lengths of the command sent. We can notice that the execution time for Speck algorithm does not have a great

Table 2. Paramenters of the Raspberry Pi 3 used for testing.

Parameter	Value
CPU Model	64-bit quad-core ARMv8
Frequency	1.2 GHz
RAM	1 GB
Operating System	Raspbian Jessie

Table 3. Execution time data. We ran the program 10.000 times twice for each algorithm. The left result is the average of the first running and the one in the right is the average of the second.

Length	Algorithm			
	Speck [ms]		Simon [ms]	
32 bits	0.5411137	0.5409502	0.8170261	0.8228535
48 bits	0.8173872	0.8144342	1.452703	1.453392
64 bits	0.813048	0.8173257	1.453032	1.457409
96 bits	1.099465	1.093212	2.10735	2.10833
128 bits	1.381253	1.376364	2.719511	2.721607
160 bits	1.639491	1.624422	3.356103	3.382519
192 bits	1.932254	1.915469	3.980706	3.986703

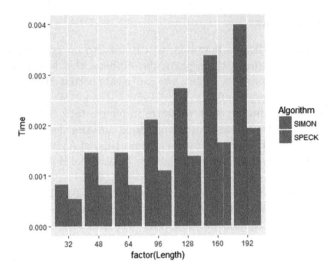

Fig. 6. Comparison of execution times between Simon and Speck algorithms. The time is in seconds and the length is in bits.

increase of this time when encrypting different lengths of a command. Instead, with the Simon algorithm, the execution time for a command length of 192 bits is much greater than the one for 32 bits in length. With these results, we can say that the best option would be to use Speck as the selected cryptographic algorithm to secure the system. Nevertheless, we need to make sure that these times, in both algorithms would not affect the response time of the system.

4.2 Latency of the System

As we said previously, we need to add this cryptographic module without affecting the performance of the system. We need to make sure that the added time the encryption and decryption would take it's not noticeable for the end-user.

The baud rate of the domotic system is set to be 9600 baud, at this moment is not possible to increase this value, given that the hardware of this particular domotic system is not prepared for a higher baud rate yet. Because of this, we made all tests with only this value of 9600 baud. We know that $bittime = \frac{1}{9600}$, so we have that the system takes 104 μs to send one bit. For 32 bits, this gives us 3.328 ms. For the largest command tested (192 bits), we got an execution time of 19.968 ms. In Fig. 7, we can see the process that the command sent will go through. The command transmitted is received by the cryptographic module, then the encrypted message will be transmitted again and received by the destination's cryptographic module and decrypt the command. After this, the decrypted command is finally sent to destination.

Taking a look at Table 3, we notice that it takes approximately 3.9 and 1.9 ms to encrypt/decrypt the largest command with Simon and Speck respectively.

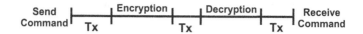

Fig. 7. Process to send a command.

If we have an ideal system, with no overhead, the command that sends 192 bits would take approximately 67.704 ms with Simon and 63.704 ms with Speck to send, encrypt and decrypt the command. With this result, we can say that the time that it takes to send and encrypt/decrypt is too small for the users to notice, given that according to Miller [38] a response time of 100ms is perceived as instantaneous. So there would be no changes in the performance of the system from the user's point of view. If this is the result when a command of 192 bits is being sent, the longest command that the system has, we can say that the other commands with less bits would take less time to go through the whole encryption/decryption process. Then, the latency of the system can be up to 67.704 ms. Although the response times obtained in both algorithms are below 100 ms, it is important to reduce this time as much as we can to improve even more the user's experience.

5   Conclusions and Future Work

In this work, we have shown that the scenario of the studied system is vulnerable. We used an embedded system to provide a custom solution for a domotic system that uses 1-wire as communication protocol. The use of a Raspberry Pi allows the system to be connected and controlled over the Internet. In our approach, we have established a secure communication between the modules of the system. We show that by using the Simon and Speck algorithms we can still send and receive commands with all the encryption and decryption process with no apparent alteration of the user's perception over the system's performance.

This cryptographic application can be implemented not only on systems or sensor networks that use 1-wire as communication protocol. The work presented here can be used by wired networks and systems where a serial communication can be established so we are able to use embedded systems to encrypt and decrypt messages, data or commands. Some examples are the CAN Bus [39], the I2C Bus [40], SDI-12 [41], SCADA [42], among others. All these communication protocols are used for different applications, but what they have in common is that the information travels plain through the whole transmission in a wired arrangement.

As far as we know, there is no other security implementation for 1-wire applied to domotics systems or any other system that uses a wired communication protocol.

For future work, we want to minimize the communication overhead to optimize the response time due to the encryption/decryption process so we can assure a good performance. In addition, we need to validate with different attacks that the system is indeed secure.

References

1. Brush, A., Lee, B., Mahajan, R., Agarwal, S., Saroiu, S., Dixon, C.: Home automation in the wild: challenges and opportunities. In: Proceedings of the SIGCHI Conference on Human Factors in Computing Systems, pp. 2115–2124. ACM (2011)
2. Lucero, S., Burden, K.: Home automation and control. ABI Research (2010)
3. Goodwin, S.: Smart home automation with Linux and Raspberry Pi. Apress (2013)
4. Jima Masache, M.E., Zambrano Espinosa, J.H.: Diseño e implementación de un prototipo de sistema domótico para permitir el control centralizado de dispositivos dentro del hogar controlado por FPGA utilizando el protocolo X10. Ph.D. thesis, EPN, Quito (2015)
5. Sabalza, M.M., Santos, J.C.M., et al.: Design and construction of a power meter to optimize usage of the electric power. In: 2014 III International Congress of Engineering Mechatronics and Automation (CIIMA), pp. 1–5. IEEE (2014)
6. Statista.com: Digital market outlook: smart home (2015)
7. Maxim Integrated: Dallas semiconductor (2016)
8. Hagras, H., Callaghan, V., Colley, M., Clarke, G., Pounds-Cornish, A., Duman, H.: Creating an ambient-intelligence environment using embedded agents. IEEE Intell. Syst. 19(6), 12–20 (2004)
9. Debono, C.J., Abela, K.: Implementation of a home automation system through a central FPGA controller. In: 2012 16th IEEE Mediterranean Electrotechnical Conference (MELECON), pp. 641–644. IEEE (2012)
10. Hill, K.: When 'smart homes' get hacked: I haunted a complete stranger's house via the internet (2013)
11. Oluwafemi, T., Kohno, T., Gupta, S., Patel, S.: Experimental security analyses of non-networked compact fluorescent lamps: a case study of home automation security. In: Proceedings of the LASER 2013 (LASER 2013), pp. 13–24 (2013)
12. Moore, N.C.: Hacking into homes: 'smart home' security flaws found in popular system, May 2016
13. Higgins, K.J.: Popular home automation system backdoored via unpatched flaw, April 2015
14. Maceková, L.: 1-wire-the technology for sensor networks. Acta Electrotechnica et Informatica 12(4), 52 (2012)
15. Jayakody, J., Wijesundara, M.: An automated monitoring and alert system for a typical server room (2014)
16. Anoprienko, A., Varzar, R., Anoprienko, A.Y., Varzar, R.L., Anoprnko, O.Y.: Intelligent supersensory computer network for measurement and analysis of environmental hazards (2012)
17. Wu, Q., Zhang, G., Yan, L.: Temperature and humidity sensor research based on monobus technology (2016)
18. Akpan, V.A., Osakwe, R.A.: Real-time embedded system for online temperature and pressure measurements for automated fluid flow monitoring and control (2015)
19. Maxim Integrated: Determining the recovery time for multiple-slave 1-wire networks, June 2006
20. Maxim Integrated: iButton RTC (2013)
21. Dallas Semiconductor iButton: A practical introduction to the Dallas semiconductor iButton (2002)
22. Grand, J.: Ds1991 multikey iButton dictionary attack vulnerability (2001)
23. Oswald, D.: Side-channel attacks on SHA-1-based product authentication ICs. In: Homma, N., Medwed, M. (eds.) CARDIS 2015. LNCS, vol. 9514, pp. 3–14. Springer, Cham (2016). doi:10.1007/978-3-319-31271-2_1

24. Brandt, C., Kasper, M.: Don't push it: breaking iButton security. In: Danger, J.-L., Debbabi, M., Marion, J.-Y., Garcia-Alfaro, J., Zincir Heywood, N. (eds.) FPS 2013. LNCS, vol. 8352, pp. 369–387. Springer, Cham (2014). doi:10.1007/978-3-319-05302-8_23
25. Gong, Z., Nikova, S., Law, Y.W.: KLEIN: a new family of lightweight block ciphers. In: Juels, A., Paar, C. (eds.) RFIDSec 2011. LNCS, vol. 7055, pp. 1–18. Springer, Heidelberg (2012). doi:10.1007/978-3-642-25286-0_1
26. Cannière, C., Dunkelman, O., Knežević, M.: KATAN and KTANTAN — a family of small and efficient hardware-oriented block ciphers. In: Clavier, C., Gaj, K. (eds.) CHES 2009. LNCS, vol. 5747, pp. 272–288. Springer, Heidelberg (2009). doi:10.1007/978-3-642-04138-9_20
27. Hong, D., et al.: HIGHT: a new block cipher suitable for low-resource device. In: Goubin, L., Matsui, M. (eds.) CHES 2006. LNCS, vol. 4249, pp. 46–59. Springer, Heidelberg (2006). doi:10.1007/11894063_4
28. Wheeler, D.J., Needham, R.M.: TEA, a tiny encryption algorithm. In: Preneel, B. (ed.) FSE 1994. LNCS, vol. 1008, pp. 363–366. Springer, Heidelberg (1995). doi:10.1007/3-540-60590-8_29
29. Bogdanov, A., Knudsen, L.R., Leander, G., Paar, C., Poschmann, A., Robshaw, M.J.B., Seurin, Y., Vikkelsoe, C.: PRESENT: an ultra-lightweight block cipher. In: Paillier, P., Verbauwhede, I. (eds.) CHES 2007. LNCS, vol. 4727, pp. 450–466. Springer, Heidelberg (2007). doi:10.1007/978-3-540-74735-2_31
30. Engels, D., Fan, X., Gong, G., Hu, H., Smith, E.M.: Hummingbird: ultra-lightweight cryptography for resource-constrained devices. In: Sion, R., Curtmola, R., Dietrich, S., Kiayias, A., Miret, J.M., Sako, K., Sebé, F. (eds.) FC 2010. LNCS, vol. 6054, pp. 3–18. Springer, Heidelberg (2010). doi:10.1007/978-3-642-14992-4_2
31. Barreto, P., Simplicio, M.: CURUPIRA, a block cipher for constrained platforms. Simpósio Brasileiro de Redes de Computadores e Sistemas Distribuídos-SBRC 2007 (2007)
32. Poschmann, A., Leander, G., Schramm, K., Paar, C.: New light-weight crypto algorithms for RFID. In: IEEE International Symposium on Circuits and Systems, pp. 1843–1846. IEEE (2007)
33. Beaulieu, R., Shors, D., Smith, J., Treatman-Clark, S., Weeks, B., Wingers, L.: The Simon and Speck lightweight block ciphers. In: Proceedings of the 52nd Annual Design Automation Conference, p. 175. ACM (2015)
34. Panasenko, S., Smagin, S.: Lightweight cryptography: underlying principles and approaches. Int. J. Comput. Theor. Eng. 3(4), 516 (2011)
35. Alizadeh, M., Salleh, M., Zamani, M., Shayan, J., Karamizadeh, S.: Security and performance evaluation of lightweight cryptographic algorithms in RFID, Kos Island, Greece (2012)
36. Stamp, M.: Information Security: Principles and Practice. Wiley, Hoboken (2011)
37. McCoy, C.: Implementations of the Simon and Speck block ciphers, March 2015
38. Miller, R.B.: Response time in man-computer conversational transactions. In: Proceedings of the Fall Joint Computer Conference, Part I, pp. 267–277. ACM, 9–11 December 1968
39. Voss, W.: A Comprehensible Guide to Controller Area Network. Copperhill Media, New York (2008)
40. Mankar, J., Darode, C., Trivedi, K., Kanoje, M., Shahare, P.: Review of I2C protocol. Int. J. 2(1), 474–479 (2014)
41. Group, S.S: SDI-12 support group-serial digital interface at 1200 baud (1988)
42. Boyer, S.A.: SCADA: supervisory control and data acquisition. International Society of Automation (2009)

Formal Methods, Computational Logic
and Theory of Computation

Axiomatic Set Theory à la Dijkstra and Scholten

Ernesto Acosta[1], Bernarda Aldana[1], Jaime Bohórquez[1], and Camilo Rocha[2]($\boxtimes$)

[1] Escuela Colombiana de Ingeniería Julio Garavito, Bogotá, Colombia
[2] Pontificia Universidad Javeriana, Cali, Colombia
camilo.rocha@javerianacali.edu.co

Abstract. The algebraic approach by E.W. Dijkstra and C.S. Scholten to formal logic is a proof calculus, where the notion of proof is a sequence of equivalences proved – mainly – by using substitution of 'equals for equals'. This paper presents Set, a first-order logic axiomatization for set theory using the approach of Dijkstra and Scholten. What is novel about the approach presented in this paper is that symbolic manipulation of formulas is an effective tool for teaching an axiomatic set theory course to sophomore-year undergraduate students in mathematics. This paper contains many examples on how argumentative proofs can be easily expressed in Set and points out how the rigorous approach of Set can enrich the learning experience of students. The results presented in this paper are part of a larger effort to formally study and mechanize topics in mathematics and computer science with the algebraic approach of Dijkstra and Scholten.

Keywords: Axiomatic set theory · Dijkstra-Scholten logic · Derivation · Formal system · Zermelo-Fraenkel (ZF) · Symbolic manipulation · Undergraduate-level course

1 Introduction

Axiomatic set theory is the branch of mathematics that studies collections of objects from the viewpoint of mathematical logic. In general, axiomatic set theory focuses on the properties of the membership relation '$\in$' given the existence of some basic sets (e.g., the empty set). Unlike 'naive' set theory – where definitions are given in natural language, and Venn diagrams and Boolean algebra are used to support reasoning about collections – the axiomatic study of sets begins with a set of axioms and then associates axiomatic rules to suitably defined sets and constructive relations. Beyond its own right as a branch of mathematics, set theory plays an important role as foundational system of any other theory in mathematics (e.g., number theory, topology).

An axiomatic theory for sets is usually given as a first-order logic theory, i.e., in a formal system that uses universally and existentially quantified variables over

E. Acosta et al.—Supported in part by grant DII/C004/2015 funded by Escuela Colombiana de Ingeniería.

© Springer International Publishing AG 2017
A. Solano and H. Ordoñez (Eds.): CCC 2017, CCIS 735, pp. 775–791, 2017.
DOI: 10.1007/978-3-319-66562-7_55

non-logical objects, and formulas that can contain variables, function symbols, and predicate symbols. In this case, variables range over collections, function symbols include the empty set, projections, and cardinality, and predicate symbols include membership and equality. The Zermelo-Fraenkel (ZF) is the most common axiomatic set theory [7], sometimes including the axiom of choice (ZFC), and it is intended to formalize the notion of *pure set* or *hereditary well-founded set* so that all entities in the universe of discourse are such collections.

This paper presents an axiomatization for set theory using the *calculational* approach developed by E.W. Dijkstra and C.S. Scholten to formal logic [1]. More precisely, the main contribution of this paper is a first-order theory for sets having as its main feature the symbolic manipulation of formulas under the principle known as Leibniz's rule: the substitution of 'equals for equals'. While there are many deductive systems for first-order logic which are both sound (i.e., all provable statements are true in all models) and complete (i.e., all statements which are true in all models are provable), the notion of proof in the Dijkstra-Scholten logic favors the use of logical equivalence over implication. In general, the Dijkstra-Scholten logic can be seen as a correct choice of connectives, axioms, and inference rules, allowing for proofs of logical formulas by symbol manipulation and without the need for introducing unnecessary assumptions.

The algebraic approach by E.W. Dijkstra and C.S. Scholten to formal logic, in general, is a *proof calculus* [8]. In the case of the axiomatic theory of sets presented in this paper, Dijkstra-Scholten refers to the logical system resulting from the combination of first-order logic and their proof style. The notion of 'proof' in the Dijkstra-Scholten system is actually a *derivation* [10], i.e., a sequence of equivalences proved, mainly, by using Leibniz principle: if two formulas are provably equivalent, then substituting one for the other in a formula does not alter the meaning of such a formula. In a nutshell, a derivation can come in different flavors and it can always be translated into a formal proof [10] (e.g., in a Hilbert-like system). For an axiomatic theory of sets, derivations result in rigorous and elegant counterparts to argumentative proofs, commonly found in textbooks, and can help students in proving theorems succinctly.

The results presented in this paper are a partial report on a two-term seminar experience to symbolically rewrite all proofs and solve all exercises, using the Dijkstra-Scholten approach, in Sects. 1, 2, and 9 of Chap. 1 in [6]. The metamathematical aspects of set theory such as those of semantics, completeness, and axiom independence were not considered since the main interest was to realize how to teach formal thinking to novice undergraduates. After the seminar experience, a sophomore-year course with this approach has been already successfully taught twice.

This work is also a part of a larger effort to formally study and mechanize topics in mathematics and computer science with the algebraic approach of E.W. Dijkstra and C.S. Scholten. In particular, the set theory axiomatization of ZF in first-order logic presented in this paper is the first step towards a mechanization in rewriting logic [9], a logic in which concurrent rewriting coincides with logical deduction. What is appealing about mechanizing theories à la Dijkstra-Scholten is that they are written in a relatively strict format that can be easily accessed by humans (which is seldom the case with most tools). In the case of rewriting logic, the notion of substitution of 'equals for equals' is a natural part of deduction because it is a more general case of equational logic.

To sum up, the main contributions of this paper are:

- a set theory axiomatization of ZF in first-order logic using the calculational style of E.W. Dijkstra and C.S. Scholten;
- examples of some proofs obtained by using derivations, compared to their argumentative versions found in textbooks; and
- a discussion on how student experience has improved in a sophomore-year undergraduate-level axiomatic set theory course taught à la Dijkstra and Scholten.

The rest of the paper is organized as follows. Section 2 presents the first-order Dijkstra-Scholten system. Section 3 presents the axiomatic set theory à la Dijkstra-Scholten and Sect. 4 presents some examples of proofs in this theory obtained by using derivations. Section 5 presents a discussion explaining how the use of the approach presented in this paper has helped in teaching an undergraduate-level course on axiomatic set theory. Finally, Sect. 6 presents some related work and concluding remarks.

2   The Formal System of Dijkstra and Scholten

This section presents an overview of the Dijkstra and Scholten first-order formal system, and it is a summary of Sects. 2–5 in [10].

A formal system uses an alphabet to construct a formal language from a collection of axioms through inferential rules of formation. More precisely, a formal system [3] consists of: a (possibly infinite) collection of symbols or alphabet; a grammar defining how well-formed formulas are constructed out of the symbols in the alphabet; a collection of axioms; and a collection of inference rules. The collections of formulas of the formal systems presented in this paper all have a decidable membership problem.

Definition 1. *Let* F *be a formal system,* Γ *a collection of* F*-formulas, and* φ_n *a* F*-formula. A* proof *of* φ_n *from* Γ *in* F *is a sequence of* F*-formulas* $\varphi_0, \varphi_1, \ldots, \varphi_n$ *such that for any* $0 \leq i \leq n$: *(i)* φ_i *is an axiom, (ii)* $\varphi_i \in \Gamma$, *or (iii)* φ_i *is the conclusion of an inference rule with premises appearing in* $\varphi_0, \ldots, \varphi_{i-1}$. *An* F*-formula* φ *is a* theorem *from* Γ *in* F, *written* $\Gamma \vdash_\mathsf{F} \varphi$, *if and only if there is a proof of* φ *from* Γ *in* F; *in the case when* $\Gamma = \varnothing$, φ *is called a* theorem of F *and it is written* $\vdash_\mathsf{F} \varphi$.

The first-order system of E.W. Dijkstra and C.S. Scholten (with equality) is presented as the formal system $\mathsf{DS}(\mathcal{L})$, which is parametric on a first-order language $\mathcal{L}$.

Definition 2. *The symbols of* DS($\mathcal{L}$) *are:*

- *An infinite collection $\mathcal{X}$ of* variables $x_0, x_1, x_2, \ldots$.
- *A collection $\mathcal{F}$ of* function symbols.
- *A collection $\mathcal{P}$ of* predicate symbols, *which includes infinitely many* constants $P_0, P_1, P_2, \ldots$.
- *An arity function* $ar : \mathcal{F} \cup \mathcal{P} \to \mathbb{N}$ *for function and predicate symbols.*
- *Left parenthesis* '(', *right parenthesis* ')', *and comma* ','.
- *The* logical connectives *$true, false, \neg, \equiv, \not\equiv, \vee, \wedge, \to, \leftarrow, \forall, \exists$.*

The infinitely many constant predicate symbols assumed to be in $\mathcal{P}$ are key for formula manipulation in the formal system. The logical connectives of DS($\mathcal{L}$) include the Boolean constants *true* and *false*, negation '$\neg$', equivalence '$\equiv$', discrepancy '$\not\equiv$', disjunction '$\vee$', conjunction '$\wedge$', implication '$\to$', consequence '$\leftarrow$', and '$\forall$' for universal quantification and '$\exists$' for existential quantification.

Terms and formulas in DS($\mathcal{L}$) are built in the usual way. A term is built from variables and the application of a function symbol to a sequence of terms. A formula is built from the Boolean constants, term equality, and Boolean combination of formulas, with the application of a predicate symbol to a sequence of terms and universal/existential quantified formulas. The *atomic formulas* of DS($\mathcal{L}$) are the Boolean constants *true* and *false*, equality of terms, and the formulas obtained by applying a predicate symbol to zero or more terms. Definition 3 formally introduces the terms and formulas of DS($\mathcal{L}$).

Definition 3. *The collection of* terms *and the collection of* formulas *of the formal system* DS($\mathcal{L}$) *are given by the following BNF definitions, where $x \in \mathcal{X}$, $c \in \mathcal{F}$ with $ar(c) = 0$, $f \in \mathcal{F}$ with $ar = m > 0$, $P \in \mathcal{P}$ with $ar(P) = 0$, $Q \in \mathcal{P}$ with $ar(Q) = n > 0$, t is a term, and φ is a formula:*

$$t ::= x \mid c \mid f(t, \ldots, t)$$
$$\varphi ::= true \mid false \mid t = t \mid P \mid Q(t, \ldots, t) \mid (\neg\varphi) \mid (\varphi \equiv \varphi) \mid (\varphi \not\equiv \varphi) \mid (\varphi \vee \varphi)$$
$$\mid (\varphi \wedge \varphi) \mid (\varphi \to \varphi) \mid (\varphi \leftarrow \varphi) \mid (\forall x\, \varphi) \mid (\exists x\, \varphi).$$

The expressions $\mathcal{T}(\mathcal{X}, \mathcal{F})$ and $\mathcal{T}(\mathcal{X}, \mathcal{F}, \mathcal{P})$ denote, respectively, the collection of terms *and the collection of* formulas *over $\mathcal{X}$, $\mathcal{F}$, and $\mathcal{P}$.*

In the Dijkstra-Scholten first-order logic, the textual substitution operator $\_[\_ := \_]$ is overloaded both for replacing variables for terms and for replacing constant predicate symbols for formulas. The concept of a free occurrence of a variable in a formula in the Dijkstra-Scholten logic is the traditional one, i.e., an occurrence of a variable x in a formula φ is *free* iff such an occurrence of x is not under the scope of a $\forall x$ or $\exists x$. Similarly, a term t is *free* for x in a formula φ iff every free occurrence of x in φ is such that if it is under the scope of a $\forall y$ or $\exists y$, then y is not a variable in t.

Definition 4. *Let $x \in \mathcal{X}$, $t \in \mathcal{T}(\mathcal{X}, \mathcal{F})$, and $\varphi, \psi \in \mathcal{T}(\mathcal{X}, \mathcal{F}, \mathcal{P})$. The collection* of axioms of DS($\mathcal{L}$) *is given by the following axiom schemata:*

$(Ax1)$ $((\varphi \equiv (\psi \equiv \tau)) \equiv ((\varphi \equiv \psi) \equiv \tau))$.
$(Ax2)$ $((\varphi \equiv \psi) \equiv (\psi \equiv \varphi))$.
$(Ax3)$ $((\varphi \equiv true) \equiv \varphi)$.
$(Ax4)$ $((\varphi \vee (\psi \vee \tau)) \equiv ((\varphi \vee \psi) \vee \tau))$.
$(Ax5)$ $((\varphi \vee \psi) \equiv (\psi \vee \varphi))$.
$(Ax6)$ $((\varphi \vee false) \equiv \varphi)$.
$(Ax7)$ $((\varphi \vee \varphi) \equiv \varphi)$.
$(Ax8)$ $((\varphi \vee (\psi \equiv \tau)) \equiv ((\varphi \vee \psi) \equiv (\varphi \vee \tau)))$.
$(Ax9)$ $((\neg\varphi) \equiv (\varphi \equiv false))$.
$(Ax10)$ $((\varphi \not\equiv \psi) \equiv ((\neg\varphi) \equiv \psi))$.
$(Ax11)$ $((\varphi \wedge \psi) \equiv (\varphi \equiv (\psi \equiv (\varphi \vee \psi))))$.
$(Ax12)$ $((\varphi \rightarrow \psi) \equiv ((\varphi \vee \psi) \equiv \psi))$.
$(Ax13)$ $((\varphi \leftarrow \psi) \equiv (\psi \rightarrow \varphi))$.
$(Bx1)$ $((\forall x\, \varphi) \equiv \varphi)$, *if x is not free in φ.*
$(Bx2)$ $((\varphi \vee (\forall x\, \psi)) \equiv (\forall x\, (\varphi \vee \psi)))$, *if x is not free in φ.*
$(Bx3)$ $(((\forall x\, \varphi) \wedge (\forall x\, \psi)) \equiv (\forall x\, (\varphi \wedge \psi)))$.
$(Bx4)$ $((\forall x\, \varphi) \rightarrow \varphi[x := t])$, *if t is free for x in φ.*
$(Bx5)$ $((\exists x\, \varphi) \equiv (\neg\, (\forall x\, (\neg\varphi))))$.
$(Bx6)$ $(x = x)$.
$(Bx7)$ $((x = t) \rightarrow (\varphi \equiv \varphi[x := t]))$, *if t is free for x in φ.*

The axioms of $\mathsf{DS}(\mathcal{L})$ can be divided into two groups, namely, $(Ax1)$–$(Ax13)$ and $(Bx1)$–$(Bx7)$. Axioms $(Ax1)$, $(Ax2)$, and $(Ax3)$ define, respectively, that equivalence is associative, commutative, and has identity element *true*. Similarly, axioms $(Ax4)$, $(Ax5)$, and $(Ax6)$ define, respectively, that disjunction is associative, commutative, and has identity element *false*. Disjunction is idempotent by Axiom $(Ax7)$ and distributes over equivalence by Axiom $(Ax8)$. The remaining axioms $(Ax9)$–$(Ax13)$ present axiomatic definitions for the connectives in the propositional fragment of $\mathsf{DS}(\mathcal{L})$. Axiom $(Bx1)$ states that a universal quantifier on variable x can be omitted whenever the formula it quantifies has no free occurrences of x. Axiom $(Bx2)$ states that disjunction distributes over universal quantification whenever there is no variable capture, while Axiom $(Bx3)$ states that conjunction and universal quantification commute. By Axiom $(Bx4)$, it is possible to particularize any universal quantification with a term t whenever the variables in t are not captured by the substitution. Finally, Axiom $(Bx5)$ is an axiomatic definition for existential quantification.

Note that by having $\{P_0, P_1, \ldots\} \subseteq \mathcal{P}$ in Definition 2, propositions over propositional variables $\{p_0, p_1, \ldots\}$ can be represented as atomic formulas in $\mathcal{T}(\varnothing, \varnothing, \mathcal{P})$ via the mapping $p_i \mapsto P_i$. With this embedding, axioms $(Ax1)$–$(Ax13)$ characterize $\{true, false, \equiv, \vee\}$ as a complete collection of connectives for the propositional fragment of $\mathsf{DS}(\mathcal{L})$. Likewise, $\{true, false, \equiv, \vee, \forall\}$ is a complete collection of connectives for $\mathsf{DS}(\mathcal{L})$.

Definition 5. *Let $x \in \mathcal{X}$, $P \in \mathcal{P}$ with $ar(P) = 0$, and $\varphi, \psi, \tau \in \mathcal{T}(\mathcal{X}, \mathcal{F}, \mathcal{P})$. The inference rules of $\mathsf{DS}(\mathcal{L})$ are:*

$$\frac{\psi \qquad (\psi \equiv \varphi)}{\varphi} \text{ Equanimity} \quad \frac{(\psi \equiv \tau)}{(\varphi[P := \psi] \equiv \varphi[P := \tau])} \text{ Leibniz} \quad \frac{\varphi}{(\forall x\, \varphi)} \text{ Generalization.}$$

Rules EQUANIMITY and LEIBNIZ allow for symbolic manipulation based on equality by substitution of 'equals for equals'. Rule GENERALIZATION is the usual first-order rule stating that universally quantifying any theorem results in a theorem. The assumption about the *infinite* collection of constant predicate symbols in $\mathsf{DS}(\mathcal{L})$ is key for the Rule LEIBNIZ to work when substituting formulas in any given formula. Other important fact regarding Rule LEIBNIZ is that from it some interesting meta-properties can be proved with almost no effort: (i) any substitution instance of a tautology (i.e., of a theorem in the propositional fragment of $\mathsf{DS}(\mathcal{L})$) is a theorem of $\mathsf{DS}(\mathcal{L})$ and (ii) the collection of theorems of $\mathsf{DS}(\mathcal{L})$ is closed under formula substitution.

'Proofs' in the Dijkstra-Scholten calculational style are not proofs in the strict sense of a formal system. Instead, they are sequences of formulas related, mainly, by equivalence. This approach takes advantage of the transitive properties of these connectives to obtain compact proof calculations.

Definition 6. *Let Γ be a collection of formulas of $\mathsf{DS}(\mathcal{L})$. A derivation from Γ in $\mathsf{DS}(\mathcal{L})$ is a non-empty finite sequence of formulas $\varphi_0, \varphi_1, \ldots, \varphi_n$ of $\mathsf{DS}(\mathcal{L})$ satisfying, for any $0 < k \le n$, $\Gamma \vdash_{\mathsf{DS}(\mathcal{L})} (\varphi_{k-1} \equiv \varphi_k)$.*

The connection between a derivation and a proof is made precise in Proposition 1.

Proposition 1. [10] *Let Γ be a collection of formulas of $\mathsf{DS}(\mathcal{L})$ and $\varphi_0, \varphi_1, \ldots, \varphi_n$ be a derivation in $\mathsf{DS}(\mathcal{L})$ from Γ. It holds that $\Gamma \vdash_{\mathsf{DS}(\mathcal{L})} (\varphi_0 \equiv \varphi_n)$.*

It is important to note that any proof in the formal system $\mathsf{DS}(\mathcal{L})$ is a derivation in $\mathsf{DS}(\mathcal{L})$ but a derivation is *not* necessarily a proof. Consider, for instance, the sequence "*false, false*" which is a derivation because Boolean equivalence is reflexive, but this sequence is not a proof because *false* is not a theorem. The key fact about proofs in a formal system is that every formula in a proof is a theorem, while this is not necessarily the case in a derivation. There are other types of derivations where implication or consequence can be combined with equivalence (see [10] for details).

In practice, derivations are not written directly as a sequence of formulas but instead as a bi-dimensional arrangement of formulas and text explaining each derivation step.

Remark 1. A derivation $\varphi_0, \varphi_1, \ldots, \varphi_n$ from Γ in $\mathsf{DS}(\mathcal{L})$ is usually written as:

$$\varphi_0$$
$$\equiv \quad \langle \text{ ``explanation}_0\text{'' } \rangle$$
$$\varphi_1$$
$$\vdots \quad \langle \ldots \rangle$$
$$\varphi_{n-1}$$
$$\equiv \quad \langle \text{ ``explanation}_{n-1}\text{'' } \rangle$$
$$\varphi_n$$

in which "explanation$_i$" is a text describing why $\Gamma \vdash_{\mathsf{DS}} (\varphi_i \equiv \varphi_{i+1})$.

Finally, the Dijkstra-Scholten logic proposes an alternative notation for writing quantified formulas. The main idea is that proof verification and derivation in such a syntax becomes simpler thanks to the resemblance between, for example, the notation of a (finite) quantification and the operational semantics of repetitive constructs in an imperative programming language.

Remark 2. Let $x \in \mathcal{X}$ and φ, ψ be formulas of $\mathsf{DS}(\mathcal{L})$.

– The expression $(\forall x \mid \psi : \varphi)$ is syntactic sugar for $(\forall x \, (\psi \to \varphi))$; in particular, $(\forall x \mid true : \varphi)$ can be written as $(\forall x \mid: \varphi)$.
– The expression $(\exists x \mid \psi : \varphi)$ is syntactic sugar for $(\exists x \, (\psi \wedge \varphi))$; in particular, $(\exists x \mid true : \varphi)$ can be written as $(\exists x \mid: \varphi)$.

In the formulas $(\forall x \mid \psi : \varphi)$ and $(\exists x \mid \psi : \varphi)$, ψ is called the *range* and φ the *subject* of the quantification.

3   An Axiomatic Set Theory

This section presents Set, a Zermelo-Franekel first-order system in the language $\mathcal{L}_{\mathsf{Set}} = (\mathcal{X}, \mathcal{F}, \mathcal{P})$, that results from extending $\mathsf{DS}(\mathcal{L}_{\mathsf{Set}})$ with axioms for sets. In $\mathcal{L}_{\mathsf{Set}}$, the infinitely many variables $\mathcal{X}$ range over elements in the domain of discourse, $\mathcal{F}$ contains the constant $\varnothing$ and the unary symbols $\bigcup, \mathbb{P}$, and the only predicate symbol in $\mathcal{P}$ is the binary symbol $\in$. Intuitively, the function symbols represent the empty set, generalized union, and the power set; the predicate symbol $\in$ represents membership. The axioms of Set in Definition 7 include axiomatic definitions for all symbols in $\mathcal{F}$, meaning that $\in$ is a complete connective for Set (i.e., the entire language of set theory can be built from the membership predicate symbol). Symbols not in $\mathcal{L}_{\mathsf{Set}}$ such as the binary function symbols $\cup$ and $\cap$ denoting union and intersection, respectively, and the binary predicate symbol $\subseteq$ denoting inclusion can be added by means of the usual axiomatic definitions. Some examples on this regard will be given at the end of the section.

Note that there is no mention in $\mathcal{L}_{\mathsf{Set}}$ of the common 'curly braces' notation $\{ \_ \mid \_ \}$ used for identifying collections. The reason is that this notation can also be seen as an abbreviation just like $\varnothing$ or $\subseteq$. Technically, $\{ \_ \mid \_ \}$ is a binary meta-symbol used as a term-forming operator that can be defined with the *definite description* operator ι, for any variable $x \in \mathcal{X}$ and formula $\varphi \in \mathcal{T}(\mathcal{X}, \mathcal{F}, \mathcal{P})$, as follows:

$$\{ x \mid \varphi(x) \} \equiv (\iota y \mid: (\forall x \mid: x \in y \equiv \varphi(x))).$$

It can be shown, although it is beyond the scope of this paper, that $\{ x \mid \varphi \}$ identifies a unique element. Therefore, Set allows the 'curly braces' notation to be used as an abbreviation for a unique element in the domain of discourse. The reader is referred to [13, p. 126] for details on the definite description operator and its properties.

The notion of univalent formula is needed before introducing the axioms of Set. A formula $\varphi \in \mathcal{T}(\mathcal{X}, \mathcal{F}, \mathcal{P})$ is *univalent* iff $(\forall x, y, z \mid \varphi \wedge (x, z)\varphi(y, z) : x = y)$. Intuitively, if φ is univalent and $\varphi(x, z)$ is true, then x is the only element that makes $\varphi(\_, z)$ true.

Definition 7. *Let* $\varphi, \psi \in \mathcal{T}(\mathcal{X}, \mathcal{F}, \mathcal{P})$ *be such that* φ *has exactly one free variable and* ψ *is univalent. The axioms of* Set *are given by the following axiom schemata:*

$(C x1)$ $(\forall x \mid: x = \varnothing \equiv (\forall y \mid: \neg y \in x)).$
$(C x2)$ $(\forall x, y \mid: x = y \equiv (\forall u \mid: u \in x \equiv u \in y)).$
$(C x3)$ $(\forall x, y, z \mid: x = \{y, z\} \equiv (\forall u \mid: (u \in x \equiv u = y \vee u = z))).$
$(C x4)$ $(\forall x, y \mid: y = \{u \in x \mid \varphi(u)\} \equiv (\forall u \mid: u \in y \equiv u \in x \wedge \varphi(u))).$
$(C x5)$ $(\forall x, y \mid: y = \bigcup x \equiv (\forall u \mid: u \in y \equiv (\exists z \mid z \in x : u \in z))).$
$(C x6)$ $(\forall x, y \mid: y = \mathbb{P}x \equiv (\forall u \mid: u \in y \equiv (\forall z \mid z \in u : z \in x))).$
$(C x7)$ $(\forall x, y \mid: y = \psi[x] \equiv (\forall u \mid: u \in y \equiv (\exists z \mid z \in x : \psi(u, z)))).$
$(C x8)$ $(\exists x \mid \varnothing \in x : (\forall y \mid y \in x : y \cup \{y\} \in x)).$

The *axiom of existence* $(C x1)$ serves two purposes: on the one hand, it states the existence of an unique set without elements, namely, the empty set; on the other hand, it is a 'definitional extension' for function symbol $\varnothing$, which is the name assigned to the empty set. Note that, by identifying 'the' set without elements with $\varnothing$, there is the need to prove that such a set is unique (this proof is left to the reader as a routine exercise after covering this section). The *axiom of extensionality* $(C x2)$ characterizes equality: two elements are equal whenever they have the same elements. The *axiom of pairing* $(C x3)$ states the existence of an element having two given elements. The *axiom schema of separation* $(C x4)$, which represents as many axioms as formulas φ with exactly one variable are, states how an element can be obtained from other element by selecting exactly those elements that satisfy a given formula. The *axiom of union* $(C x5)$ and the *axiom of power* $(C x6)$, respectively, define generalized union and the power element construction. The *axiom schema of replacement* $(C x7)$ uses an univalent formula to define an element $\psi[x]$ comprising precisely those elements witnessing the satisfaction of $\psi(\_, z)$, for each $z \in x$. Finally, the *axiom of infinity* $(C x8)$ introduces the existence of (at least) one *inductive set*: (i) $\varnothing$ belongs to this set; and (ii) if x belongs to this set, then $x \cup \{x\}$ (i.e., its *successor set*) is also one of its members. It is easy to see that such sets must necessarily have infinitely many elements starting from $\varnothing$, the successor of $\varnothing$, and so on. Also note that in Definition 7 the only axiom schemata are $(C x4)$ and $(C x7)$ because they are parametric on given formulas.

In general, these axioms are similar to the ones usually studied in graduate-level axiomatic set theory courses. In this sense, a contribution of Set is a rewrite of the axioms in the notation of Dijkstra-Scholten. However, as illustrated in Sect. 4 with examples, the main contribution of Set is that it enables an under-graduate proof-based course on set theory using simple algebraic manipulation.

One important cornerstone of any axiomatic set theory, including Set, is the distinction between elements that are 'well-behaved' and those that are not. More precisely, an important feature of axiomatic set theory is distinguishing those elements that can be called a *set* from many others that are not, namely, the broader concept of a *class*. Technically, a class is any collection, but a set is a more refined version of a class: a set is a collection that can be *identified* by only using the axioms in Definition 7. For instance, $\varnothing$ and $\{\varnothing\}$ are sets because of axioms $(Cx1)$ and $(Cx8)$. Theorem 1 presents a fundamental theorem of Set, with a proof à la Dijkstra-Scholten, and identifies a class that is not a set: the collection of all sets.

Theorem 1. *There exists no universal set.*

Proof. Towards a contradiction, assume such a set V exists. Thus, $\vdash_{\mathsf{Set}}$ $(\forall x \mid: x \in V)$. Consider the set $S = \{x \in V \mid x \notin x\}$, in which $x \notin x$ abbreviates $\neg x \in x$:

$$S \in S$$
$$\equiv \quad \langle \text{ definition of } S \rangle$$
$$S \in \{x \in V \mid x \notin x\}$$
$$\equiv \quad \langle \text{ axiom of separation } (Cx4) \rangle$$
$$S \in V \wedge S \notin S$$
$$\equiv \quad \langle V \text{ is a universal set } \rangle$$
$$true \wedge S \notin S$$
$$\equiv \quad \langle \text{ propositional logic } \rangle$$
$$S \notin S.$$

That is, $\vdash_{\mathsf{Set}} S \in S \equiv S \notin S$, which is a contradiction. Therefore, V cannot exist. □

As mentioned at the beginning of this section, other usual function and predicate symbols can be added to Set by means of definitional extensions. Some of these symbols are included in Definition 8.

Definition 8. *The following axioms define pairing, binary union and intersection, difference, and inclusion:*

$(Cx10)$ $(\forall x, y, z \mid: x = (y, z) \equiv (\forall u \mid: u \in x \equiv u = \{y\} \vee u = \{y, z\}))$.
$(Cx11)$ $(\forall x, y, z \mid: x = y \cup z \equiv (\forall u \mid: u \in x \equiv u \in y \vee u \in z))$.
$(Cx12)$ $(\forall x, y, z \mid: x = y \cap z \equiv (\forall u \mid: u \in x \equiv u \in y \wedge u \in z))$.
$(Cx13)$ $(\forall x, y, z \mid: x = y \setminus z \equiv (\forall u \mid: u \in x \equiv u \in y \wedge u \notin z))$.
$(Cx14)$ $(\forall x, y, z \mid: x = y \times z \equiv (\forall u \mid: u \in x \equiv (\exists v, w \mid v \in y \wedge w \in z : u = (v, w))))$.
$(Cx15)$ $(\forall x, y \mid: x \subseteq y \equiv (\forall u \mid u \in x : u \in y))$.

Other operations such as the generalized Cartesian product and generalized intersections, and even the axiom of choice can be defined similarly in the syntax of Set.

4   Calculational Proofs for the Classroom

This section presents some notorious features of Set that have been identified, mainly, by teaching a 16-weeks undergraduate set theory course. It is important to note that most of the students in such a course are in their sophomore year and have had very little exposure to mathematical logic. First, as it is often the case in set theory, computation of operations between sets depends heavily on the axiom of extensionality ($Cx2$). Since Set is based mainly on Boolean equivalence, algebraic manipulations are simple to grasp and can help a student in discovering proofs. Second, the precise language required for writing formulas exposes their logical structure, thus making it possible in a proof to transform one formula into another in a clean way. Furthermore, in the Dijkstra-Scholten style a student can deal symbolically with the parts of a proof argument that have to do exclusively with propositional logic, usually hidden in a rhetorical argument. Finally, Set helps in identifying the logical structure of a theorem text in order to anticipate relevant lemmas for its proof.

4.1   Algebraic Exploration

One of the advantages of Set is that it facilitates the computation of operations between elements in the domain of discourse. The axiom of extensionality ($Cx2$) is key in situations when the goal is to transform a formula $x \in A$ to another formula $x \in B$. In this setting, A is a set whose definition is known, while B is a set to be found.

Example 1. The goal is to simplify $\bigcup\{\varnothing, \{\varnothing\}\}$:

$$x \in \cup\{\varnothing, \{\varnothing\}\}$$
$\equiv$ ⟨ axiom of union ($Cx5$) ⟩
$$(\exists y \mid y \in \{\varnothing, \{\varnothing\}\} : x \in y)$$
$\equiv$ ⟨ axiom of pair ($Cx3$) ⟩
$$(\exists y \mid y = \varnothing \vee y = \{\varnothing\} : x \in y)$$
$\equiv$ ⟨ syntactic sugar for existential quantification; propositional logic ⟩
$$(\exists y \mid: (y = \varnothing \wedge x \in y) \vee (y = \{\varnothing\} \wedge x \in y))$$
$\equiv$ ⟨ axiom of empty set ($Cx1$) : no element belongs in the empty set ⟩
$$(\exists y \mid: \textit{false} \vee (y = \{\varnothing\} \wedge x \in y))$$

$\equiv$ ⟨ syntactic sugar for existential quantification; propositional logic ⟩
$$(\exists y \mid y = \{\varnothing\} : x \in y)$$
$\equiv$ ⟨ exactly one element satisfies the range ⟩
$$x \in \{\varnothing\}.$$

Thus, $\bigcup\{\varnothing, \{\varnothing\}\} = \{\varnothing\}$.   □

Another illustrative example is reasoning with function composition. If f and g are two functions, then $g \circ f$ is defined by:

$$(\forall x, y \mid: (x, y) \in g \circ f \equiv (\exists z \mid: (x, z) \in f \wedge (z, y) \in g)) \,.$$

In [4], the expression $\langle f_i \mid i \in I \rangle$ denotes the function f with domain I. For example, the function $f(x) = x^2$ with domain $[0, 1]$ can be represented as

$\langle x^2 \mid x \in [0,1] \rangle$. The formula $(u,v) \in \langle x^2 \mid x \in [0,1] \rangle$ means that $v = u^2$ and that $u \in [0,1]$. One illustrative example in [4] is to calculate $\langle \sqrt{x} \mid x > 0 \rangle \circ \langle x^2 + 1 \mid x \in \mathbb{R} \rangle$. For that purpose, the authors of the text book use a previous theorem to first determine the domain of the composition and then proceed to compute it. As presented by Example 2, it is not required to use the preliminary theorem because the domain of the composition can obtained simultaneously with the proof.

Example 2. The goal is to compute $\langle \sqrt{x} \mid x > 0 \rangle \circ \langle x^2 - 1 \mid x \in \mathbb{R} \rangle$:

$$(u,v) \in \langle \sqrt{x} \mid x > 0 \rangle \circ \langle x^2 - 1 \mid x \in \mathbb{R} \rangle$$
$\equiv$ $\langle$ definition of function composition $\rangle$
$$\left(\exists z \mid : (u,z) \in \langle x^2 - 1 \mid x \in \mathbb{R} \rangle \wedge (z,v) \in \langle \sqrt{x} \mid x > 0 \rangle \right)$$
$\equiv$ $\langle$ syntactic sugar ; $\langle \_ \mid \_ \rangle$ notation $\rangle$
$$\left(\exists z \mid : z = u^2 - 1 \wedge u \in \mathbb{R} \wedge v = \sqrt{z} \wedge z > 0 \right)$$
$\equiv$ $\langle$ Axiom $(Bx3)$; Axiom $(Bx1)$ $\rangle$
$$u \in \mathbb{R} \wedge \left(\exists z \mid : z = u^2 - 1 \wedge v = \sqrt{z} \wedge z > 0 \right)$$
$\equiv$ $\langle$ only one element satisfies the range $\rangle$
$$u \in \mathbb{R} \wedge v = \sqrt{u^2 - 1} \wedge u^2 - 1 > 0$$
$\equiv$ $\langle$ syntactic sugar ; $\langle \_ \mid \_ \rangle$ notation $\rangle$
$$(u,v) \in \left\langle \sqrt{x^2 - 1} \mid x^2 - 1 > 0 \right\rangle .$$

Therefore, $\langle \sqrt{x} \mid x > 0 \rangle \circ \langle x^2 - 1 \mid x \in \mathbb{R} \rangle = \langle \sqrt{x^2 - 1} \mid x^2 > 1 \rangle$. $\qquad \square$

4.2 Discovery of Logical Structure

The calculative style requires writing the propositions in a very precise language that, in the end, reveals their logical structure. This makes it possible to carry out the required transformations from one proposition to another in a proof more transparently than when using a language that has not been designed for such a purpose. In an axiomatic theory, arguments in a proof are expected to be very precise, leaving aside – as far as possible, colloquial ones. For example, without much difficulty, it can be proved that the Cartesian product of two sets is empty iff one of its factors is empty. Of course, nobody doubts this fact but, in order to proceed formally, it requires a proof.

Example 3. Prove $\vdash_{\mathsf{Set}} (\forall x, y \mid: x \times y = \varnothing \equiv (x = \varnothing \vee y = \varnothing))$.

$$x \times y = \varnothing$$

$\equiv$ ⟨ axiom of empty set $(Cx1)$ ⟩

$$(\forall u, v \mid: \neg(u, v) \in x \times y)$$

$\equiv$ ⟨ axiom of Cartesian product $(Cx14)$ ⟩

$$(\forall u, v \mid: \neg(u \in x \wedge v \in y))$$

$\equiv$ ⟨ propositional logic: De Morgan's law ⟩

$$(\forall u, v \mid: u \notin x \vee v \notin y)$$

$\equiv$ ⟨ first-order logic ⟩

$$(\forall u \mid: u \notin x) \vee (\forall v \mid: v \notin y)$$

$\equiv$ ⟨ axiom of empty set $(Cx1)$ ⟩

$$x = \varnothing \vee y = \varnothing.$$

Therefore, $(\forall x, y \mid: x \times y = \varnothing \equiv (x = \varnothing \vee y = \varnothing))$ is a theorem of Set.   □

One of the objectives of teaching a set theory course is to develop the ability to properly write a proof in natural language, involving all necessary arguments. This task is a complex one for students, specially when the arguments are related with Boolean reasoning. This is because such a reasoning is used implicitly in proofs, leaving the bitter feeling that the argument is correct but it is not clear why. In argumentative proofs, in general, the reasoning rests more on aesthetic matters rather than on logical ones. Within the Set formal system all arguments are made explicit, which helps in improving the clarity and forcefulness of the proofs without resorting to the elegance and skill in the use of the natural language. In Example 4, it is proved that a function is invertible iff it is one to one. This is a case of use of appropriate language when searching for a proof. The predicate $\mathrm{fun}(f)$ stands for "f is a function", $\mathrm{inv}(f)$ for "f is invertible", and $\mathrm{oto}(f)$ for "f is one to one". Symbolically,

$$(\forall f \mid: \mathrm{fun}(f) \equiv (\forall x, y, z \mid (x, y) \in f \wedge (x, z) \in f : y = z)).$$
$$(\forall f \mid: \mathrm{inv}(f) \equiv \mathrm{fun}(f^{-1})).$$
$$(\forall f \mid: \mathrm{oto}(f) \equiv (\forall x, y, z \mid (x, z) \in f \wedge (y, z) \in f : x = y)).$$

Example 4. Prove $\vdash_{\mathsf{Set}} (\forall x \mid: \mathrm{inv}(f) \equiv \mathrm{oto}(f))$.

$$\mathrm{inv}(f)$$

$\equiv$ ⟨ definition of invertible function ⟩

$$\mathrm{fun}(f^{-1})$$

$\equiv$ ⟨ definition of function ⟩

$$(\forall x, y, z \mid (x, y) \in f^{-1} \wedge (x, z) \in f^{-1} : y = z)$$

$\equiv$ ⟨ definition of inverse relation ⟩

$$(\forall x, y, z \mid (y, x) \in f \wedge (z, x) \in f : y = z)$$

$\equiv$ ⟨ definition of one to one function ⟩

$$\mathrm{oto}(f).$$

□

Example 5 presents a proof in Set that natural numbers with the usual order $<$ are a well-ordered set. The set $\mathbb{N}$ of natural numbers is the smallest inductive set and membership is a strictly linear relation in it. Well-ordering of $\mathbb{N}$ means that all non-empty subsets of $\mathbb{N}$ have a first (or $<$-minimal) element. Consider the set of least numbers x_{min} of a given set $x \subseteq \mathbb{N}$:

$$(\forall x \mid x \subseteq \mathbb{N} : x_{min} = \{y \in x \mid (\forall z \mid z \in x : z \leq y)\}).$$

Of course, if x_{min} is not empty, then it is unitary. Next consider the unary predicate $wo_<$ defined as follows:

$$(\forall x \mid x \subseteq \mathbb{N} : wo_<(x) \equiv (\forall y \mid y \subseteq x : y \neq \varnothing \to y_{min} \neq \varnothing)).$$

Note that $wo_<(\mathbb{N})$ means that the set of natural numbers is well-ordered. The definition of well-order can be equivalently written, thanks to $\vdash_{DS(\mathcal{L})} (\varphi \to \psi) \equiv (\neg\psi \to \neg\varphi)$:

$$(\forall x \mid x \subseteq \mathbb{N} : wo_<(x) \equiv (\forall y \mid y \subseteq x : y_{min} = \varnothing \to y = \varnothing)).$$

In addition, Example 5 uses a form of derivation in which logical implication is allowed to relate a deduction step. Such a sequence is called *relaxed derivation* and the reader is referred to [10] for its definition and properties.

Example 5. Prove $\vdash_{Set} (\forall x \mid x \subseteq \mathbb{N} : x_{min} = \varnothing \to x = \varnothing)$.

$$x_{min} = \varnothing$$
$$\equiv \quad \langle \text{ axiom of empty set } (Cx1) \rangle$$
$$(\forall n \mid: n \notin x_{min})$$
$$\equiv \quad \langle \text{ definition of } x_{min} \rangle$$
$$(\forall n \mid: n \notin x \vee (\exists k \mid k \in x : k < n))$$
$$\equiv \quad \langle \text{ first-order logic } \rangle$$
$$(\forall n \mid: (\forall k \mid k < n : k \notin x) \to n \notin x)$$
$$\to \quad \langle \text{ induction principle for natural numbers } \rangle$$
$$(\forall n \mid: n \notin x)$$
$$\equiv \quad \langle \text{ axiom of empty set } (Cx1) \rangle$$
$$x = \varnothing.$$

$\square$

4.3   Proof Structure and Organization

The calculative style can be used to anticipate auxiliary lemmas. Indeed, this is the case in some induction theorems, such as the proof of commutativity of natural number addition. Addition of natural numbers is as a function $+ : \mathbb{N} \times \mathbb{N} \longrightarrow \mathbb{N}$ defined à la Peano by:

$$(\forall m \mid m \in \mathbb{N} : +(0, m) = m),$$
$$(\forall m, n \mid m \in \mathbb{N} \wedge n \in \mathbb{N} : +(m, +(n, 1)) = +(+(m, n), 1)).$$

The goal is to prove that natural number addition is commutative, i.e., that

$$(\forall m, n \mid m \in \mathbb{N} \wedge n \in \mathbb{N} : +(m,n) = +(n,m)) .$$

In [4, Theorem 4.4, p. 53], the proof of this fact is hard to follow because there is an auxiliary induction proof inside the main induction proof:

> We prove that every $n \in \mathbb{N}$ commutes, by induction on n. To show that 0 commutes, it suffices to show that $0 + m = m$ for all m. .... Clearly $0 + 0 = 0$, and if $0 + m = m$, then $0 + (m + 1) = (0 + m) + 1 = m + 1$. So the claim follows by induction (on m). Let us assume that n commutes, an let us show that $n + 1$ commutes. We prove, by induction on m, that $m + (n + 1) = (n + 1) + m$ for all $n \in \mathbb{N}$. ...(proof follows)...

In [2, Sect. 13, p. 50], the following is the proof of the same property:

> The proof that addition is commutative ... is a little tricky; a straightforward attack might fail. The trick is to prove, by induction on n, that (i) $0 + n = n$ and (ii) $m^+ + n = (m + n)^+$ and then to prove the desire commutativity equation by induction on m, via (i) y (ii).

It will be better for a student to identify beforehand some lemmas needed for the proof.

Example 6. Note that the theorem statement has the form $(\forall n \mid n \in \mathbb{N} : q(n))$, where

$$q(n) \equiv (\forall m \mid m \in \mathbb{N} : p(m,n)) .$$

Some lemmas can be found from this formulation:

$$(\forall n \mid n \in \mathbb{N} : q(n))$$
$$\leftarrow \quad \langle \text{ induction principle } \rangle$$
$$q(0) \wedge (\forall n \mid q(n) : q(n + 1)) .$$

Therefore, the goal now is to first prove $(\forall m \mid m \in \mathbb{N} : p(m,0))$ and then, under hypothesis $(\forall m \mid m \in \mathbb{N} : p(m,n))$, prove $(\forall m \mid m \in \mathbb{N} : p(m,n + 1))$.

5   Classroom Experience

With the calculational style there is an opportunity to read differently theorem statements and to rethink theorem formulations in the teaching of mathematics. Sometimes the logical complexity of the statements exceeds the capacity of the students and the complexity of informal speech can blur the simplicity of logical structure. It is gratifying to have a language to explore the meaning of the statements by cleansing them from literary linguistic figures. The style of Dijkstra and Scholten can do precisely that. Reading and writing proofs in the style of Dijkstra and Scholten reveals structural propositions that are hidden in the nooks and crannies of literary languages.

Sophomore students in the axiomatic set theory class, in which Set is taught, are familiarized quickly with the formal system $DS(\mathcal{L})$ before beginning the study of set theory. Without being logic experts and after learning these logic rudiments, they develop an ability to translate the statements of the theorems and proofs contained in a textbook such as [4]. Students are bound by their teacher to do the inverse process of reading and writing in literary language what they have written symbolically.

Later on, students in the class begin to propose their own proofs, aside from those found in the textbook. At a later stage, they see the need to introduce new symbols to the language (e.g., a predicate symbol) in the quest to incorporate what is said of objects as part of the symbolic discourse. The teachers are very strict in requiring students to write sentences in symbolic language and precise spelling is enforced. Finally, students have no difficulty in accepting the need to introduce new sets to the theory in order to 'package' information and to be able to argue on a more abstract level: 'set-set' rather than 'set-element' (e.g., instead of referring to the minimum of a set x, they need to refer to the subset x_{min} of x).

6   Concluding Remarks

Most textbooks on set theory avoid dealing with formal logic directly. They include not only the introductory ones such as [2], but also graduate-level ones such as [4,6,7]. It is strongly believed among the mathematical community that detailed formal proof involves a large amount of trivial details that would make a standard hundred-page mathematical book run for many thousands of pages. However, this is hardly the case with the approach of Dijkstra and Scholten, as shown with Set. First-order logic systems such as natural deduction or sequent calculus are suitable for mechanical reasoning but not for human reasoning. It is fair to say that the substitution of 'equals for equals' is ultimately the reason why the calculational approach is practical for human reasoning. Important meta-mathematical aspects of $DS(\mathcal{L})$ that have been omitted in this paper, such as the deduction, soundness, and completeness results can be found in [10,12]. Moreover, a sequent-like formalization of $DS(\mathcal{L})$ can be found in [12], as well as an explanation about the relationship between the propositional fragment of $DS(\mathcal{L})$ and the celebrated rewrite-based decision procedure for Boolean rings of J. Hsiang [5].

Perhaps, the only textbook that takes a self-contained approach to set theory, in the sense that includes all tools needed from mathematical logic, is the one of Tourlakis [13]. His work is situated between two opposite poles: on the one hand, it works within the theory, that is, uses the tools and the axioms for the sole purpose of proving theorems. On the other hand, it takes the entire theory as an object of study and "from the outside" answers questions about its power and reliability. Although in his work the use of formal reasoning as a tool to calculate proofs is recommended, not many proofs in the book are obtained in this way. Furthermore, he states that "we do not have to be that formal always, nor can we

afford to be so when our arguments get more involved. We will frequently relax
the proof style to shorten proofs. This relaxing will invariably use shorthand tools
such as English text, class terms, and a judicious omission of (proof) details." Its
level of exposition is designed to fit a spectrum of mathematical sophistication,
well beyond the reach of most inexperienced undergraduate students. With Set,
there is a strong case in favor of using formal proofs when teaching set theory
at undergraduate level.

The results presented in this paper are part of a larger effort to formally study
and mechanize topics in mathematics and computer science with the algebraic
approach of E.W. Dijkstra and C.S. Scholten. The next step is to mechanize
Set in rewriting logic [9]. There is already experience by some of the authors in
mechanizing logical systems in rewriting logic, e.g., [11,12]. Finally, there is also
interest in exploring the formalization and use of the Dijkstra-Scholten style in
other branches of mathematics and computer science such as topology, number
theory, and finite model theory.

References

1. Dijkstra, E.W., Scholten, C.S.: Predicate Calculus and Program Semantics. Texts
   and Monographs in Computer Science. Springer, New York (1990)
2. Halmos, P.R.: Naive Set Theory. Undergraduate Texts in Mathematics. Springer,
   New York (1974)
3. Hodel, R.E.: An Introduction to Mathematical Logic. Dover Publications Inc., New
   York (2013)
4. Hrbacek, K., Jech, T.J.: Introduction to Set Theory. Monographs and Textbooks
   in Pure and Applied Mathematics, vol. 220, 3rd edn. M. Dekker, New York (1999).
   Rev. and expanded edition
5. Hsiang, J.: Refutational theorem proving using term-rewriting systems. Artif.
   Intell. **25**(3), 255–300 (1985)
6. Jech, T.J.: Set Theory. Pure and Applied Mathematics, a Series of Monographs
   and Textbooks, vol. 79. Academic Press, New York (1978)
7. Kunen, K.: Set Theory. Studies in Logic, vol. 34. College Publications, London
   (2013). Revised edition
8. Meseguer, J.: General logics. In: Logic Colloquium 1987: Proceedings. Studies in
   Logic and the Foundations of Mathematics, 1st edn., vol. 129, pp. 275–330. Elsevier,
   Granada, August 1989
9. Meseguer, J.: Conditional rewriting logic as a unified model of concurrency. Theor.
   Comput. Sci. **96**(1), 73–155 (1992)
10. Rocha, C.: The formal system of Dijkstra and Scholten. In: Martí-Oliet, N.,
    Ölveczky, P.C., Talcott, C. (eds.) Logic, Rewriting, and Concurrency. LNCS, vol.
    9200, pp. 580–597. Springer, Cham (2015). doi:10.1007/978-3-319-23165-5_27
11. Rocha, C., Meseguer, J.: A rewriting decision procedure for Dijkstra-Scholten's
    syllogistic logic with complements. Revista Colombiana de Computación **8**(2), 101–
    130 (2007)

12. Rocha, C., Meseguer, J.: Theorem proving modulo based on boolean equational procedures. In: Berghammer, R., Möller, B., Struth, G. (eds.) RelMiCS 2008. LNCS, vol. 4988, pp. 337–351. Springer, Heidelberg (2008). doi:10.1007/978-3-540-78913-0_25

13. Tourlakis, G.J.: Lectures in Logic and Set Theory. Cambridge Studies in Advanced Mathematics, vol. 82–83. Cambridge University Press, Cambridge (2003)

Two Novel Clustering Performance Measures Based on Coherence and Relative Assignments of Clusters

H.J. Areiza-Laverde[1], A.E. Castro-Ospina[1(✉)], P. Rosero-Montalvo[2],
D.H. Peluffo-Ordóñez[2], J.L. Rodríguez-Sotelo[3], and M.A. Becerra-Botero[4]

[1] Instituto Tecnológico Metropolitano - ITM, Medellín, Colombia
andrescastro@itm.edu.co
[2] Universidad Técnica del Norte, Ibarra, Ecuador
[3] Universidad Autónoma de Manizales, Manizales, Colombia
[4] Institución Universitaria Salazar y Herrera, Medellín, Colombia

Abstract. This work proposes two novel alternatives for dealing with the highly important issue of the clustering performance estimation. One of the measures is the cluster coherence aimed to quantifying the normalized ratio of cuts within a graph-partitioning framework, and therefore it uses a graph-driven approach to explore the nature of data regarding the cluster assignment. The another one is the probability-based-performance quantifier, which calculates a probability value for each cluster through relative frequencies. Proposed measures are tested on some clustering representative techniques applied to real and artificial data sets. Experimental results probe the readability and robustness to noisy labels of our measures.

Keywords: Cluster coherence · Clustering · Graph-partitioning · Probabilities · Relative frequencies

1 Introduction

Clustering encompasses all the pattern recognition approaches aimed at grouping similar objects into subsets by following discriminative, unsupervised criteria. Some of its remarkable applications to be mentioned are human motion analysis and people identification [1,2], image segmentation [3–5] and video analysis [6,7], among others. In broad terms, clustering approaches have shown to be a powerful technique for grouping and/or rank data as well as a proper alternative for unlabeled problems. Due to its versatility, applicability and feasibility, it has been preferred in many approaches. Nevertheless, despite several clustering techniques having been introduced, the selection and design of a grouping system is not a trivial task. Often, it is mandatory to analyze in detail the structure of data and the specific initial conditions of the problem in order to group the homogenous data points. Besides, it must be done in such a way that an accurate

© Springer International Publishing AG 2017
A. Solano and H. Ordoñez (Eds.): CCC 2017, CCIS 735, pp. 792–804, 2017.
DOI: 10.1007/978-3-319-66562-7_56

cluster recognition is accomplished. Therefore, the proper quantification of clustering performance is a crucial aspect to fairly comparing clustering techniques. Nonetheless, given its unlabeled nature, the diversity of available grouping criteria, and the variability of the structure of data, defining a proper clustering criterion is a non-trivial and very challenging task.

In this work, we propose two novel alternatives for estimating the clustering performance followed from two criteria: The first measure -here so-called cluster coherence- quantifies the normalized ratio of cuts within a graph-partitioning framework. The second one is the probability-based-performance quantifier, which calculates a probability value for each cluster through relative frequencies. Proposed measures are tested on some clustering representative techniques (k-means, fuzzy c-means and Ng-Jordan-Weiss (NJW) spectral clustering) applied to real and artificial data sets. Results show the readability of our measures, even in noisy-label scenarios.

The remaining of this paper is structured as follows: Sects. 2 and 3 describe respectively the proposed cluster coherence and PPQ measures. Sections 4 and 5 present describe and discuss the experimental setup and obtained results, respectively. Finally, in Sect. 6, the concluding remarks are drawn.

2   Cluster Coherence

As demonstrated in some studies [8,9], the clustering quality can be assessed through a spectral graph partitioning criterion, when a good clustering desires both tight connections within partitions and loose connections between partitions. In terms of graph theory, the variable $\mathbb{V} = \{1, \cdots, N\}$ represents a collection of indexes of the data set to be grouped. Then, the aim of spectral clustering is to group the N data points from $\mathbb{V}$ into K disjoint subsets, so that $\mathbb{V} = \cup_{l=1}^{K} \mathbb{V}_l$ and $\mathbb{V}_l \cap \mathbb{V}_m = \emptyset, \forall l \neq m$. Commonly, this decomposition is done by using spectral information and orthonormal transformations. Let us analyze two special linkratios: The first one is linkratio$(\mathbb{V}_k, \mathbb{V}_k)$, which measures the ratio of links staying within $\mathbb{V}_k$ itself [10]. The second one is linkratio$(\mathbb{V}_k, \mathbb{V}_k \backslash \mathbb{V})$, which measures the ratio of links escaping from $\mathbb{V}_k$, being a complement of the first one. According to this, a suitable clustering is then achieved when both maximizing connections within partitions and minimizing connections between partitions. These two goals can be expressed as the k–way–normalized associations (knassoc) and normalized cut criteria (kncuts), which are respectively as follows:

$$\text{knassoc}(\Gamma_{\mathbb{V}}^K) = \frac{1}{K} \sum_{k=1}^{K} \text{linkratio}(\mathbb{V}_k, \mathbb{V}_k) \tag{1}$$

and

$$\text{kncuts}(\Gamma_{\mathbb{V}}^K) = \frac{1}{K} \sum_{k=1}^{K} \text{linkratio}(\mathbb{V}_k, \mathbb{V}_k \backslash \mathbb{V}), \tag{2}$$

being $\Gamma_{\mathbb{V}}^K = \{\mathbb{V}_1, \cdots, \mathbb{V}_K\}$ the set containing all partitions.

Also, because a normalization term is applied, we can easily verify that

$$\text{knassoc}(\Gamma_{\mathbb{V}}^K) + \text{kncuts}(\Gamma_{\mathbb{V}}^K) = 1. \tag{3}$$

From Eq. (3), we can infer that maximizing the associations and minimizing the cuts are achieved simultaneously. Therefore, the objective function to be maximized for clustering purposes is in the form:

$$\varepsilon(\Gamma_{\mathbb{V}}^K) = \text{knassoc}(\Gamma_{\mathbb{V}}^K). \tag{4}$$

Alternatively, the partition set $\Gamma_{\mathbb{V}}^K$ is to be represented by a cluster binary indicator matrix $\boldsymbol{M} \in \{0,1\}^{N \times K}$ such that $\boldsymbol{M} = [\boldsymbol{M}_1, \ldots, \boldsymbol{M}_K]$. Matrix $\boldsymbol{M}$ holds the membership of each data point regarding a certain cluster, in such a way that m_{ik} is the membership value of the data point i with respect to cluster k, so:

$$m_{ik} = \lfloor i \in \mathbb{V}_k \rfloor, \quad i \in \mathbb{V}, \quad k \in [K], \tag{5}$$

where $[K]$ denotes the set of entire numbers ranged into the interval $[1, K]$, m_{ik} is the ik entry of matrix $\boldsymbol{M}$, $\lfloor \cdot \rfloor$ is a binary indicator: it becomes 1 if the argument its true and 0 otherwise. Beside, since each node can only belong to one cluster, the condition $\boldsymbol{M}\boldsymbol{1}_K = \boldsymbol{1}_N$ must be guaranteed, where $\boldsymbol{1}_d$ is a d-dimensional all ones vector. Let $\boldsymbol{D} \in \mathbb{R}^{N \times N}$ be the degree matrix for the similarity matrix defined as:

$$\boldsymbol{D} = \text{Diag}(\boldsymbol{\Omega}\boldsymbol{1}_N), \tag{6}$$

where $\text{Diag}(\cdot)$ denotes a diagonal matrix formed by the argument vector. Then, in matrix, degree and links measures can be also written as:

$$\text{links}(\mathbb{V}_k, \mathbb{V}_k) = \boldsymbol{M}_k^{\mathsf{T}} \boldsymbol{\Omega} \boldsymbol{M}_k \tag{7}$$

and

$$\text{degree}(\mathbb{V}_k) = \boldsymbol{M}_k^{\mathsf{T}} \boldsymbol{D} \boldsymbol{M}_k. \tag{8}$$

According to the above, the multi-cluster partitioning criterion can be expressed as:

$$\max \ \varepsilon(\boldsymbol{M}) = \frac{1}{K} \sum_{k=1}^{K} \frac{\boldsymbol{M}_k^{\mathsf{T}} \boldsymbol{\Omega} \boldsymbol{M}_k}{\boldsymbol{M}_k^{\mathsf{T}} \boldsymbol{D} \boldsymbol{M}_k} \tag{9}$$

$$\text{s. t. } \boldsymbol{M} \in \{0,1\}^{N \times K}, \quad \boldsymbol{M}\boldsymbol{1}_K = \boldsymbol{1}_N. \tag{10}$$

Thus, the cluster coherence is calculated as follows:

$$\epsilon_M = \frac{1}{K} \sum_{l=1}^{K} \frac{\boldsymbol{M}_l^{\mathsf{T}} \boldsymbol{\Omega} \boldsymbol{M}_l}{\boldsymbol{M}_l^{\mathsf{T}} \boldsymbol{D} \boldsymbol{M}_l},$$

where $\boldsymbol{M}$ is the matrix formed by the membership values of all elements to each cluster: $m_{ij} = m(\boldsymbol{q}_j / \boldsymbol{x}_i)$, $\boldsymbol{M}_l$ denotes a membership submatrix associated to the cluster l, $\boldsymbol{\Omega}$ is the assumed similarity matrix and $\boldsymbol{D}$ is the degree of matrix $\boldsymbol{\Omega}$. Due to the normalization with respect to the similarity matrix, the maximum value of ϵ_M is 1, therefore, it indicates a good clustering if its value is near 1. Furthermore, because of the nature of the function, a large set of groups is penalized.

3   Probability-Based-Performance Quantifier

Here, we propose a novel supervised measurement that takes advantages of the original labels. This measurement, named probability-based performance quantification and denoted as PPQ, returns a number between 0 and 1 per cluster being 1 when all data points are rightly clustered in accordance to the original labels. Let $\boldsymbol{c} \in \mathbb{R}^N$ be a vector containing the original labels in such a manner $c_i \in [K]$ and $N_1 + \ldots + N_K = N$, where N_k is the number of data points assigned to cluster k. In a similar way as a Bayes' rule, PPQ related to cluster k is calculated as:

$$PPQ(k) = \frac{\sum\limits_{\ell=1}^{K} p(\mathbb{V}_k == \ell | \mathbb{V}) p(k | \mathbb{V}_\ell)}{p((\boldsymbol{c} == k) | \mathbb{V})}, \tag{11}$$

where

$$p(\mathbb{V}_k == \mathbb{V}_\ell | \mathbb{V}) = \frac{n_e(\mathbb{V}_k == \mathbb{V}_\ell)}{N}$$

is the probability that data points labeled with k to be grouped into cluster ℓ,

$$p(k | \mathbb{V}_\ell) = \frac{n_e(\mathbb{V}_k == \mathbb{V}_\ell)}{N_\ell}$$

is the relative probability that data points labeled with k are grouped as ℓ regarding its own cluster,

$$p(k | \mathbb{V}) = n_e(\boldsymbol{c} == k)/N$$

is the total probability that a data point can be grouped as k-labeled and $n_e(\cdot)$ denotes the number of nodes satisfying its argument condition. As can be observed, term $p(k | \mathbb{V}_\ell)$ works as a penalty factor avoiding that measurement becomes one in all cases, since it ceases being 1 in case of wrongly assignments, i.e., when there are label-mixed clusters.

Let us consider the example given in Fig. 1.

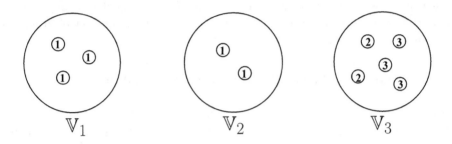

Fig. 1. Supervised measurement

According to the example, we have:

$$PPQ(1) = \frac{P(\mathbb{V}_1 == 1|\mathbb{V})P(\mathbb{V}_1|\mathbb{V}_1) + P(\mathbb{V}_1 == 2|\mathbb{V})P(\mathbb{V}_1|\mathbb{V}_2) + P(\mathbb{V}_1 == 3|\mathbb{V})P(\mathbb{V}_1|\mathbb{V}_3)}{P(\mathbb{V}_1|\mathbb{V})}$$

$$= \frac{0.3 * 1 + 0.2 * 1 + 0 * 0}{0.5} = 1$$

$$PPQ(2) = \frac{P(\mathbb{V}_2 == 1|\mathbb{V})P(\mathbb{V}_2|\mathbb{V}_1) + P(\mathbb{V}_2 == 2|\mathbb{V})P(\mathbb{V}_2|\mathbb{V}_2) + P(\mathbb{V}_2 == 3|\mathbb{V})P(\mathbb{V}_2|\mathbb{V}_3)}{P(\mathbb{V}_2|\mathbb{V})}$$

$$PPQ(2) = \frac{0 * 0 + 0 * 0 + 0.4 * 0.2}{0.2} = 0.4$$

$$PPQ(3) = \frac{P(\mathbb{V}_3 == 1|\mathbb{V})P(\mathbb{V}_3|\mathbb{V}_1) + P(\mathbb{V}_3 == 2|\mathbb{V})P(\mathbb{V}_3|\mathbb{V}_2) + P(\mathbb{V}_3 == 3|\mathbb{V})P(\mathbb{V}_3|\mathbb{V}_3)}{P(\mathbb{V}_3|\mathbb{V})}$$

$$PPQ(3) = \frac{0 * 0 + 0 * 0 + 0.6 * 0.3}{0.3} = 0.6$$

4   Experimental Setup

4.1   Databases

To assess the ability of quantifying the clustering performance of the proposed measures, real data is used, which is described in Table 1. Real data is used with the aim of compute quantitative result performances which allow to compare against different clustering measures found on the state of the art. A detailed analysis could be performed on the partitions made by several clustering techniques to identify the similarity between comparison and proposed clustering measures in order to highlight the advantages of the proposed ones.

Furthermore, some synthetic data bases are used as well, with the purpose of being able to evaluate the proposed measures performance under a controlled environment which also allows to make a visual analysis of obtained results for both clustering technique as clustering performance measure.

Table 1. Real databases information

Database	Instances	Features	Number of classes
Iris	150	4	3
Breast	699	9	2
Wine	178	13	3
Sonar	208	60	2
Biomed	194	5	2
Diabetes	768	8	2
x80	45	8	3
Ecoli	336	7	8
Glass	214	9	4
Heart	297	13	2
Imox	192	8	4
Ionosphere	351	34	2
Liver	345	6	2
Twonorm	7400	20	2
Ringnorm	7400	20	2

4.2 Clustering Techniques

Three well known clustering techniques are taken into account, namely, k-means [11], fuzzy c-means [12] and the Ng-Jordan-Weiss (NJW) spectral clustering [13]. For each data set the number of clusters is set as the true value. For fuzzy c-means the exponent of the membership matrix is set as default equal to 2 and a maximum number of 100 iterations. Finally, Local Scaling approach [14] was used for the affinity matrix construction, required to perform NJW spectral clustering.

4.3 Clustering Indexes

Both external and internal criteria [15] was used to compare clustering performance against proposed performance measures. Namely, Fisher, silhouette, purity, normalized mutual information (NMI), adjusted rand index (ARI) [16–18]. Such clustering criteria are used to measure the performance of each resulting partition, given the three considered clustering techniques as well as to compare results against our proposed measures, as it is shown in Sect. 5.

4.4 Labels Contamination Process

As an additional experimental step and with the purpose of testing the proposed clustering performance measures in a controlled fashion, a procedure is designed to contaminate with wrong data the original labels of the synthetic data sets.

Contamination was added in a balanced way taking into account the real number of classes for each data set. Clustering performance was worsened by altering a determined percentage of the original data labels corresponding to each class, namely 0%, 10%, 20%, 30%, 40% and 50%. Such modifications should be reflected on the whole set of computed performance measures (including the proposed measures) by lowering its values as the percentage of contamination increases.

5   Results

Achieved clustering results for real data sets are shown in Tables 2, 3 and 4, using fuzzy c-means, k-means and spectral clustering techniques, respectively. It can be seen how the proposed PPQ criteria behaves as other measures, for the three selected clustering techniques. Moreover, PPQ has the advantage of provide a separate evaluation for each one of the clusters in the data set, allowing to focus on the performance of a particular cluster.

Three synthetic data sets are used to depicts how the proposed clustering performance measures behaves both in numerical and visual manner, which leads to highlight the properties of PPQ and Coherence measures as shown in Fig. 2. Where it can be seen how for the *happy* dataset in Fig. 2(a), when the partition is not correct, i.e. Fig. 2(d) and (g), PPQ measure is low for the clusters, in this case, given the error on identifying the "smile" on data. For *hm2* dataset in Fig. 2(b), it can be visually inspected how three results are not correct, which is clearly quantified by the proposed measures, however, for k-means the half moon at bottom, has fewer mistakes, which is captured by PPQ. Lastly, for the complex *Tar* dataset in Fig. 2(c), which has four outlier groups, one at each corner, the proposed measures are higher when the central group is correctly identify by spectral clustering technique as seen in Fig. 2(1).

Aiming to assess the proposed clustering performance measures against other found in the state of the art, a procedure is designed to contaminate with wrong labels the ground truth of toy data previously presented. Such contamination was added in a balanced way, taking into account the number of clusters in every data set. Different percentages of contamination are used, namely: 0%, 10%, 20%, 30%, 40% and 50%. For the new labels vectors obtained by the contamination procedure each of the clustering performance measures is computed. It is expected for the proposed measures and the comparison ones to decrease as the simulated clustering results become more contaminated.

In Fig. 3 is shown how, as expected, each of the perfomance measures tested decreases as the contamination percentage of the original labels is increased. For the seven data sets used, such inverse behavior is similar. Since the proposed PPQ returns a performance measure for every cluster in the data set and all the classes are contaminated with the same proportion, the mean value is used to depicts a single performance curve.

Achieved results demonstrates how both PPQ and Coherence measures meet the expected behavior, reaching its lowest value when the contamination is high. Comparison measures attain a similar response, except Fisher value, which not

Table 2. Clustering results for real data sets using fuzzy c-means

Database	Fisher	Silhouette $\mu \pm \sigma$	Purity	NMI	ARI	PPQ		Coherence
Iris	1.069	0.647 ± 0.231	0.840	0.666	0.630	k = 1	1.000	0.901
						k = 2	0.635	
						k = 3	0.635	
Breast	0.523	0.725 ± 0.316	0.948	0.692	0.802	k = 1	0.925	0.938
						k = 2	0.858	
Wine	0.277	0.451 ± 0.208	0.966	0.876	0.897	k = 1	0.952	0.766
						k = 2	0.920	
						k = 3	0.941	
Sonar	0.074	0.219 ± 0.126	0.562	0.012	0.011	k = 1	0.541	0.644
						k = 2	0.475	
Biomed	0.185	0.477 ± 0.473	0.871	0.420	0.546	k = 1	0.683	0.877
						k = 2	0.833	
Diabetes	0.095	0.282 ± 0.245	0.714	0.135	0.181	k = 1	0.463	0.798
						k = 2	0.712	
x80	0.155	0.245 ± 0.265	0.889	0.687	0.691	k = 1	0.722	0.571
						k = 2	0.938	
						k = 3	0.768	
Ecoli	0.116	0.209 ± 0.391	0.548	0.558	0.368	k = 1	0.878	0.642
						k = 2	0.024	
						k = 3	0.665	
						k = 4	0.024	
						k = 5	0.505	
						k = 6	0.681	
						k = 7	0.063	
						k = 8	0.668	
Glass	0.208	0.311 ± 0.256	0.519	0.202	0.113	k = 1	0.384	0.779
						k = 2	0.431	
						k = 3	0.100	
						k = 4	0.622	
Heart	0.101	0.276 ± 0.178	0.801	0.279	0.361	k = 1	0.705	0.691
						k = 2	0.656	
Imox	0.206	0.317 ± 0.318	0.818	0.699	0.645	k = 1	0.571	0.714
						k = 2	0.921	
						k = 3	0.921	
						k = 4	0.544	
Ionosphere	0.132	0.371 ± 0.344	0.701	0.120	0.159	k = 1	0.697	0.848
						k = 2	0.459	
Liver	0.152	0.471 ± 0.417	0.704	0.008	-0.006	k = 1	0.426	0.794
						k = 2	0.584	
Twonorm	0.102	0.279 ± 0.106	0.978	0.849	0.915	k = 1	0.957	0.714
						k = 2	0.957	
Ringnorm	0.020	0.112 ± 0.249	0.705	0.127	0.168	k = 1	0.581	0.582
						k = 2	0.589	

Table 3. Clustering results for real data sets using k-means

Database	Fisher	Silhouette $\mu \pm \sigma$	Purity	NMI	ARI	PPQ		Coherence
Iris	0.862	0.654 ± 0.221	0.853	0.590	0.429	k = 1	0.935	0.926
						k = 2	0.455	
						k = 3	0.521	
Breast	0.518	0.720 ± 0.334	0.957	0.729	0.834	k = 1	0.937	0.951
						k = 2	0.881	
Wine	0.277	0.451 ± 0.208	0.966	0.876	0.897	k = 1	0.952	0.766
						k = 2	0.920	
						k = 3	0.941	
Sonar	0.076	0.313 ± 0.320	0.659	0.012	0.004	k = 1	0.541	0.642
						k = 2	0.475	
Biomed	0.203	0.577 ± 0.405	0.887	0.500	0.587	k = 1	0.714	0.862
						k = 2	0.849	
Diabetes	0.098	0.279 ± 0.163	0.667	0.062	0.106	k = 1	0.403	0.772
						k = 2	0.680	
x80	0.158	0.312 ± 0.246	0.800	0.562	0.524	k = 1	0.528	0.555
						k = 2	0.750	
						k = 3	0.778	
Ecoli	0.159	0.393 ± 0.258	0.696	0.607	0.577	k = 1	0.866	0.734
						k = 2	0.200	
						k = 3	0.672	
						k = 4	0.023	
						k = 5	0.516	
						k = 6	0.771	
						k = 7	0.500	
						k = 8	0.675	
Glass	0.175	0.365 ± 0.355	0.607	0.227	0.138	k = 1	0.388	0.769
						k = 2	0.424	
						k = 3	0.099	
						k = 4	0.681	
Heart	0.108	0.299 ± 0.154	0.832	0.359	0.438	k = 1	0.743	0.694
						k = 2	0.700	
Imox	0.210	0.254 ± 0.171	0.641	0.414	0.275	k = 1	0.421	0.633
						k = 2	0.801	
						k = 3	0.422	
						k = 4	0.323	
Ionosphere	0.132	0.374 ± 0.343	0.707	0.125	0.168	k = 1	0.700	0.852
						k = 2	0.464	
Liver	0.257	0.667 ± 0.257	0.867	0.002	-0.007	k = 1	0.421	0.819
						k = 2	0.580	
Twonorm	0.102	0.279 ± 0.106	0.979	0.850	0.916	k = 1	0.958	0.714
						k = 2	0.958	
Ringnorm	0.025	0.221 ± 0.277	0.765	0.281	0.280	k = 1	0.659	0.614
						k = 2	0.666	

Table 4. Clustering results for real data sets using Spectral Clustering

Database	Fisher	Silhouette $\mu \pm \sigma$	Purity	NMI	ARI	PPQ		Coherence
Iris	1.074	0.651 ± 0.259	0.867	0.655	0.445	k = 1	1.000	0.934
						k = 2	0.500	
						k = 3	0.500	
Breast	0.128	-0.171 ± 0.722	0.815	0.160	-0.037	k = 1	0.696	1.000
						k = 2	0.423	
Wine	0.280	0.450 ± 0.226	0.978	0.909	0.931	k = 1	0.967	0.768
						k = 2	0.946	
						k = 3	0.960	
Sonar	0.074	0.160 ± 0.381	0.577	0.016	0.019	k = 1	0.544	0.653
						k = 2	0.478	
Biomed	0.171	0.404 ± 0.517	0.830	0.351	0.432	k = 1	0.627	0.889
						k = 2	0.803	
Diabetes	0.247	0.517 ± 0.125	0.951	0.002	0.008	k = 1	0.350	0.889
						k = 2	0.651	
x80	0.147	0.200 ± 0.338	0.867	0.647	0.634	k = 1	0.719	0.595
						k = 2	0.775	
						k = 3	0.833	
Ecoli	0.164	0.318 ± 0.332	0.560	0.576	0.368	k = 1	0.855	0.745
						k = 2	0.200	
						k = 3	0.661	
						k = 4	0.016	
						k = 5	0.500	
						k = 6	0.733	
						k = 7	0.500	
						k = 8	0.632	
Glass	0.214	0.250 ± 0.593	0.481	0.254	0.127	k = 1	0.371	0.843
						k = 2	0.438	
						k = 3	0.099	
						k = 4	0.659	
Heart	0.098	0.250 ± 0.224	0.778	0.249	0.306	k = 1	0.686	0.695
						k = 2	0.634	
Imox	0.284	0.293 ± 0.366	0.875	0.757	0.676	k = 1	0.557	0.757
						k = 2	0.980	
						k = 3	0.959	
						k = 4	0.553	
Ionosphere	0.101	0.256 ± 0.519	0.732	0.223	0.213	k = 1	0.737	0.888
						k = 2	0.531	
Liver	0.124	0.429 ± 0.485	0.655	0.004	-0.005	k = 1	0.423	0.815
						k = 2	0.582	
Twonorm	0.102	0.279 ± 0.106	0.978	0.850	0.915	k = 1	0.958	0.714
						k = 2	0.958	
Ringnorm	0.011	0.144 ± 0.487	0.982	0.871	0.928	k = 1	0.964	0.683
						k = 2	0.964	

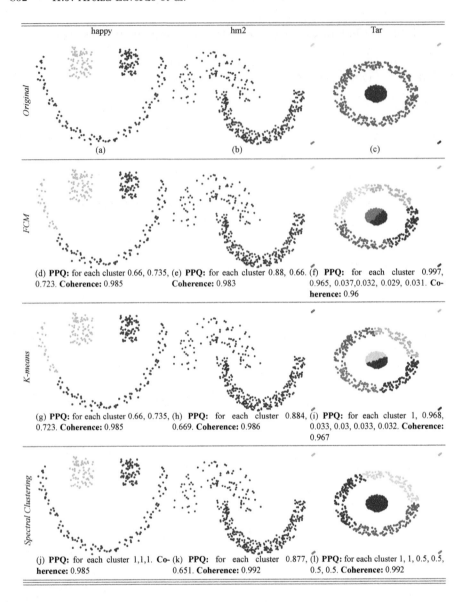

Fig. 2. Clustering results for the proposed measures over synthetic data sets

only has a low value slope but also presents a opposite behavior to the expected on the *dc3* data set, i.e. increasing its value as the label contamination gets bigger.

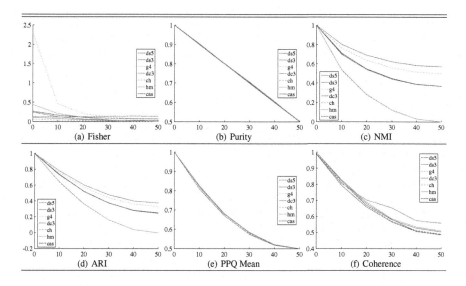

Fig. 3. Performance measures against contaminated labels

6 Conclusions and Future Work

This work introduces two measures of evaluation for grouping algorithms called cluster coherence and PPQ. Both measures have a significan degree of novelty and validity. On one hand, cluster coherence takes advantage of graph spectral grouping criterion to measure the performance of the clustering algorithm. Specifically, a normalized cuts criterion is employed. On the other hand, PPQ allows for obtaining an individual rating for each cluster and therefore provides a more detailed analysis of the clustering performance. Experimentally, we prove the readability of our measures, even when dealing with noisy-label databases.

As a future work, we are aimed at exploring more versatile and generalized criteria to quantifying the clustering performance so that a fair comparison/selection of techniques can be performed. As well, other ways to incorporate information on the structure of data within the measuring performance are to be designed.

References

1. Agarwal, A., Triggs, B.: Monocular human motion capture with a mixture of regressors. In: IEEE Computer Society Conference on Computer Vision and Pattern Recognition-Workshops, 2005, CVPR Workshops, p. 72. IEEE (2005)
2. Truong Cong, D., Khoudour, L., Achard, C., Meurie, C., Lezoray, O.: People re-identification by spectral classification of silhouettes. Signal Process. **90**(8), 2362–2374 (2010)

3. You, L., Zhou, S., Gao, G., Leng, M.: Scalable spectral clustering combined with adjacencies merging for image segmentation. In: Wu, Y. (ed.) Advances in Computer, Communication, Control and Automation. LNEE, vol. 121. Springer, Heidelberg (2012)

4. Wang, L., Dong, M.: Multi-level low-rank approximation-based spectral clustering for image segmentation. Pattern Recogn. Lett. **33**(16), 2206–2215 (2012)

5. Molina-Giraldo, S., Álvarez-Meza, A., Peluffo-Ordoñez, D., Castellanos-Domínguez, G.: Image segmentation based on multi-kernel learning and feature relevance analysis. In: Advances in Artificial Intelligence-IBERAMIA 2012, pp. 501–510 (2012)

6. Ekin, A., Pankanti, S., Hampapur, A.: Initialization-independent spectral clustering with applications to automatic video analysis. In: IEEE International Conference on Acoustics, Speech, and Signal Processing, 2004, Proceedings ICASSP 2004, vol. 3, pp. 3–641. IEEE (2004)

7. Zhang, D., Lin, C., Chang, S., Smith, J.: Semantic video clustering across sources using bipartite spectral clustering. In: 2004 IEEE International Conference on Multimedia and Expo, ICME 2004, vol. 1, pp. 117–120. IEEE (2004)

8. Stella, X.Y., Shi, J.: Multiclass spectral clustering. In: ICCV, pp. 313–319 (2003)

9. Wolf, L., Shashua, A.: Feature selection for unsupervised and supervised inference: the emergence of sparsity in a weight-based approach. J. Mach. Learn. **6**, 1855–1887 (2005)

10. Stella, X.Y., Jianbo, S.: Multiclass spectral clustering. In: ICCV 2003: Proceedings of the Ninth IEEE International Conference on Computer Vision, p. 313. IEEE Computer Society, Washington (2003)

11. MacQueen, J., et al.: Some methods for classification and analysis of multivariate observations. In: Proceedings of the Fifth Berkeley Symposium on Mathematical Statistics and Probability, vol. 1, Oakland, CA, USA, pp. 281–297 (1967)

12. Bezdek, J.C., Ehrlich, R., Full, W.: Fcm: The fuzzy c-means clustering algorithm. Comput. Geosci. **10**(2–3), 191–203 (1984)

13. Ng, A.Y., Jordan, M.I., Weiss, Y., et al.: On spectral clustering: analysis and an algorithm. In: NIPS, vol. 14, pp. 849–856 (2001)

14. Zelnik-Manor, L., Perona, P.: Self-tuning spectral clustering. In: NIPS, vol. 17, p. 16 (2004)

15. Halkidi, M., Batistakis, Y., Vazirgiannis, M.: Cluster validity methods: part i. ACM Sigmod Rec. **31**(2), 40–45 (2002)

16. Amigó, E., Gonzalo, J., Artiles, J., Verdejo, F.: A comparison of extrinsic clustering evaluation metrics based on formal constraints. Inf. Retrieval **12**(4), 461–486 (2009)

17. Beauchemin, M.: A density-based similarity matrix construction for spectral clustering. Neurocomputing **151**, 835–844 (2015)

18. Chen, G., Jaradat, S.A., Banerjee, N., Tanaka, T.S., Ko, M.S., Zhang, M.Q.: Evaluation and comparison of clustering algorithms in analyzing es cell gene expression data. Statistica Sinica **12**, 241–262 (2002). http://www.jstor.org/stable/24307044?seq=1#page_scan_tab_contents

Author Index

Printed in the United States
By Bookmasters